For Deb,

with love + thanks,

Sarah

CHILDREN AND THE LAW

DOCTRINE, POLICY AND PRACTICE

By

Douglas E. Abrams
Associate Professor of Law
University of Missouri-Columbia

Sarah H. Ramsey
Professor of Law
Syracuse University College of Law

AMERICAN CASEBOOK SERIES®

WEST
GROUP

ST. PAUL, MINN., 2000

 *TEXT IS PRINTED ON 10% POST CONSUMER RECYCLED PAPER*

Preface

This book is about child advocacy. It provides the core materials for Children and the Law, Juvenile Law and similar upperclass electives which examine the status, rights and obligations of children throughout the American legal system. Because students will shortly embark on professional journeys along divergent paths, the casebook has three missions:

1. *The casebook seeks to prepare students for careers in child advocacy.* Many students elect the Children and the Law course because they aspire to careers in juvenile or family court, social services agencies, or public interest organizations, or as practitioners representing children. In today's sometimes turbulent times, few other areas of law provide such rewarding opportunities for combining a legal career with unstinting service to the nation, the community and persons in need.

2. *The casebook seeks to prepare students who will periodically confront child advocacy issues in their general practices.* Children's issues frequently arise in general law practices that do not emphasize juvenile court or family court representation. Business and commercial clients, for example, commonly seek advice about matters such as federal and state child labor laws, common and statutory law regulating juveniles' capacity to contract, and the child abuse registry statutes' practical effects on employers' hiring practices. In the criminal arena, prosecutors regularly invoke criminal abuse and neglect statutes. General practitioners also frequently represent parties in abuse, neglect, custody, adoption or delinquency proceedings.

3. *The casebook seeks to prepare students for service in government or on bar association committees, law revision commissions and similar bodies that seek to improve children's welfare in the public interest.* Many of our Children and the Law students are keenly interested in children's issues, but wish to specialize in other areas of law. These students can pursue their interest through public service in the legislative or executive branches of national, state or local government, or service on private and public bodies dedicated to scrutinizing and reforming laws relating to children.

We are convinced that the Children and the Law course best fulfills these missions when doctrine, policy and practice complement one another throughout the learning process. The casebook illuminates doctrine, policy and practice by developing three themes: (1) the interrelationship of rights and responsibilities among the child, parents and government, (2) perceptions of children's competence as a basis for government regulation, and (3) the role of the child's lawyer. We have emphasized recent cases to encourage students to grapple with current child advocacy issues. We hope students will inquire not only about what the law is, but also about what it should be. Because of the importance of statutory analysis, we also stress statutes that lawyers are likely to encounter in their representation of children's interests. To help students actively apply their learning rather than proceed as passive recipients, practical problems inviting cooperative classroom resolution are available throughout the casebook.

Child advocacy necessarily depends on lawyers' healthy collaboration with professionals trained in disciplines whose insights complement and enrich our own. Lawyers might wish they held ready expertise in psychology, sociology, medicine, education, criminology and a wide variety of other disciplines that affect children's lives and legal interests. For most of us, however, the wish remains an idle aspiration. Child advocates should strive for a general understanding of these disciplines but must remain sufficiently humble, whenever the need and opportunity arise, to seek out trained professionals who know more about them than we do. The casebook contains interdisciplinary materials designed to explore essentially nonlegal issues central to the efforts of child advocates. Rather than seek to provide expertise, however, these materials serve as an invitation to seek professional collaboration.

Like law itself, books about law thrive on persistent reexamination and refinement. To help students and faculty remain current in this vibrant field, we plan annual updates and periodic supplements and new editions. We invite comments from professors and students who use this book because you are truly indispensable collaborators in our efforts. As your recommendations and advice help the book achieve its three missions, children and the legal system will be the ultimate beneficiaries.

Writing a book, like teaching in the classroom, is a team effort that depends on the talents of others. The casebook is already enriched by passages from writers who have graciously consented to reproduction of their thoughtful work. A number of colleagues provided valuable advice and professional insight as we wrote this casebook. We thank Judge Leonard Edwards and Dr. Frank I. Clark and Professors Peter A. Bell, Leslie Bender, James R. Devine, Linda D. Elrod, Carl H. Esbeck, Katherine Hunt Federle, William B. Fisch, David Fischer, Chris Guthrie, Timothy J. Heinsz, Joan Heifetz Hollinger, Robert F. Kelly, Lisa Key, Mary Kay Kisthardt, Susan V. Mangold, Robert J. Rabin, Jennifer L. Rosato, Suellyn Scarnecchia, Merril Sobie, and Steven Wechsler. We also thank Melody Daily for her editorial assistance and librarian Steven Lambson. We are grateful to Lynn M. Oatman, Senior Secretary, for her patient work on permission requests and multiple drafts. We also thank our student research assistants from Missouri: Greta Bassett, Russell Boyd, Reggie Breshears, Joshua Bullock, Arthur "Chip" Gentry, John Serafine, and Elena Vega; and from Syracuse: Melanie Cuevas, Gina C.R. Fiss, Kelly A. Olsen, Pamela R. Strassberg and Liane V. Watkins. We thank our Deans,

Timothy J. Heinsz and Daan Braveman, for their encouragement and support.

Finally a special thank you to all the law students we have taught throughout our careers. Law students provided valuable "focus groups" for these materials as we fashioned the final product over the past few years. Further, as we watch our students proceed in their professional lives, they serve as constant reminders that the rewards of teaching are too great to be put into words.

DOUGLAS E. ABRAMS
SARAH H. RAMSEY

January, 2000

Authors' Note: Footnotes and textual citations of courts and commentators have been omitted without so specifying. Numbered footnotes are from the original materials and retain the original numbering. Lettered footnotes are the authors'.

*

Acknowledgments

American Academy of Pediatrics Committee on Community Health Services, *Health Needs of Homeless Children and Families*, 98 Pediatrics 789 (1996). © American Academy of Pediatrics. Used with permission of the American Academy of Pediatrics.

American Academy of Pediatrics Committee on Environmental Health, *The Hazards of Child Labor*, 95 Pediatrics 311 (Feb. 1995). © American Academy of Pediatrics. Used with permission of the American Academy of Pediatrics.

American Bar Association Working Group on the Unmet Legal Needs of Children and Their Families, America's Children at Risk: A National Agenda for Legal Action 3-8 (1993). © American Bar Association. Reprinted by permission.

Askowitz, Lisa R.and Graham, Michael H., *The Reliability of Expert Psychological Testimony in Child Sexual Abuse Prosecutions*, 15 Cardozo L. Rev. 2027, 2033-34 (1994). © 1994 Yeshiva University; Lisa R. Askowitz; Michael H. Graham. Reprinted by permission.

Bartlett, Katherine T., *Rethinking Parenthood as an Exclusive Status: The Need for Legal Alternatives When the Premise of the Nuclear Family Has Failed*, 70 Va. L. Rev. 879, 879-83 (1984). © 1984 by the Virginia Law Review Association; Katherine T. Bartlett;. Reprinted by permission.

Bartholet, Elizabeth, *International Adoption: Propriety, Prospects and Pragmatics* 13 J. Am. Acad. Matrim. Law. 181 (1996). © 1996 American Academy of Matrimonial Lawyers; Elizabeth Bartholet. Reprinted with permission.

Besharov, Douglas, J., *Child Abuse and Neglect Reporting and Investigation: Policy Guidelines for Decision Making*, 22 Family Law Quarterly 1, 14-15 (1988). © 1988 American Bar Association. Reprinted with permission.

Bross, Donald C., *Terminating the Parent-Child Relationship as a Response to Child Sexual Abuse*, 26 Loy. U. Chi. L.J. 287, 239-96 (1995). © 1995 by Loyola University Chicago School of Law; Donald C. Bross. Reprinted by permission.

Carnegie Council on Adolescent Development, Carnegie Corporation of New York, Starting Points: Meeting the Needs of Our Youngest Children, vii-viii, xiii-xiv (1994). © Carnegie Corporation of New York. Reprinted by permission of Carnegie Corporation of New York.

Carnegie Council on Adolescent Development, Carnegie Corporation of New York, Great Transitions: Preparing Adolescents for a New Century 9-10 (1995). © Carnegie Corporation of New York . Reprinted by permission of Carnegie Corporation of New York.

Edwards, Leonard P., *A Comprehensive Approach to the Representation of Children : the Child Advocacy Coordinating Council*, 27 Fam. L.Q. 417-20 (1993). © 1993 American Bar Association. Reprinted with permission.

Edwards, Leonard P., Inger, Sagatun, J., *Who Speaks for the Child?* 2 U. Chi. L. Sch. Roundtable 67, 67-68 (1995). © 1995 University of Chicago Law School Roundtable; Leonard P. Edwards; Inger J. Sagatun. Reprinted by permission.

Eisenburg, Howard B., *A "Modest Proposal": State Licensing of Parents*, 26 Connecticut Law Review 1415, 1416-17, 1452 (1994). © 1994 by the Connecticut Law Review; Howard B. Eisenburg. Reprinted by permission.

Elrod, Linda Henry, *The Federalization of Child Support Guidelines*, 6 J. Am. Acad. Matrim. Law. 103, 109-115 (1990). © 1990 American Academy of Matrimonial Lawyers; Linda Henry Elrod. Reprinted by permission.

Diana J. English, *The Extent and Consequences of Child Maltreatment*, 8 The Future of Children 39, 45-47 (Spring 1998). The Future of Children is a publication of the Center for the Future of Children, The David and Lucille Packard Foundation. Permission not required.

Federle, Katherine Hunt, *Children, Curfews, and the Constitution* 73 Wash. U.L.Q. 1315 (1995). © Washington University Law Quarterly; Katherine Hunt Federle. Reprinted by permission.

Feld, Barry C., Abolish the Juvenile Court: Youthfulness, Criminal Responsibility, and Sentencing Policy, 88 Journal of Law & Criminology 68, 91-97, 133-34 (1997). © Journal of Criminal Law and Criminology. Reprinted by special permission of Northwestern University School of Law, *Journal of Criminal Law and Criminology*.

Greene, Bob, *Supreme Injustice for a Little Boy*, Chicago Tribune, Sunday, June 19, 1994. © Tribune Media Services, Inc. All Rights Reserved. Reprinted with permission.

Hafen, Bruce C., *Children's Liberation and the New Egalitarianism: Some Reservations about Abandoning Youth to Their "Rights,"* 1976 BYU L. Rev. 605, 613, 644, 646-48, 650. © Brigham Young University Law Review. Reprinted by permission of the author and Brigham Young University Law Review.

Hardin, Mark, *Child Protection Cases in a Unified Family Court*, 32 Family Law Quarterly 147, 153-60 (1998). © 1998 American Bar Association. Reprinted by permission.

Howe, Ruth Arlene W., *Transracial Adoption (TRA): Old Prejudices and Discrimination Float Under a New Halo*, 6 B.U. Pub. Int.L.J. 409, 417-20, 440-41, 466, 470-72 (1997). © Ruth Arlene W. Howe. Reprinted by permission.

Jackson, David and Cornelia Grumman, *States Put Kids Lives on the Block: How Troubled Youth Become Big Business*, Chicago Tribune, September 26, 1999 at 1. Reprinted with permission of Knight/Ridder/Tribune Information Services.

Kennedy, Randall, *Orphans of Separatism: The Painful Politics of Trans-Racial Adoption*, The American Prospect 38 (Spring, 1994). © The American Prospect. Reprinted with permission from *The American Prospect*.

Knepper, Kathleen, *Withholding Medical Treatment from Infants: When Is It Child Neglect?*, 33 U. Louisville J. Fam. L. 1, 12-26 (1995). © University of Louisville; Kathleen Knepper (assigned to Aspen Publishers, Inc). Reprinted by permission.

Legler, Paul K., *The Coming Revolution in Child Support Policy: Implications of the 1996 Welfare Act*, 30 Family Law Quarterly 519, 527-38, 538-57 (1996) © 1996 by the American Bar Association; Paul K. Legler. Reprinted by permission.

Mlyniec, Wallace J., *A Judge's Ethical Dilemma: Assessing a Child's Capacity to Choose*, 64 Fordham Law Review 1873, 1878-85 (1996). © 1996 by Fordham L.Rev; Wallace J. Mlyniec. Reprinted by permission.

Mnookin, Robert H., In the Interests of Children 78-79, 92-93 (1985). © Robert H. Mnookin. Reprinted by permission.

Mosteller, Robert P., *Child Abuse Reporting Laws and Attorney-Client Confidences: The Reality and the Specter of Lawyer as Informant*, 42 Duke L.J. 203 (1992). © 1992 by the Duke Law Journal; Robert P. Mosteller. Reprinted by permission.

Mosteller, Robert P., *Remaking Confrontation Clause and Hearsay Doctrine Under the Challenge of Child Sexual Abuse Prosecutions*, 1993 U. Ill. L. Rev. 691, 691-94. © 1993 The Board of Trustees of the University of Illinois; Robert P. Mosteller. Reprinted by permission.

Myers, John E.B., et al., *Expert Testimony in Child Sexual Abuse Litigation*, 68 Neb. L. Rev. 1, 3-4, 32-144 (1989). Copyright 1989 by the University of Nebraska; John B. Myers, Jan Bays, Judith Becker, Lucy Berliner, David L. Corwin, and Karen J. Saywitz. Reprinted by permission.

Perry, Nancy W., and Teply, Larry, L., *Interviewing Counseling, and In-Court Examination of Children: Practical Approaches*, 18 Creighton L. Rev. 1369, 1375-80 (1985). © 1985 by Creighton University; Nancy W. Perry and Larry L. Teply; Reprinted by permission.

Posner, Richard A., *The Regulation of the Market in Adoptions*. Volume 67:1, Boston University Law Review 59, 64-71 (1987). © Richard A. Posner; 1987 Trustees of Boston University. Forum of original publication. Reprinted with permission

Redding, Richard E., *Juveniles Transferred to Criminal Court: Legal Reform proposals based on Social Science Research*, 1997 Utah L. Rev. 709, 711-14, 716-20. © 1997 Utah Law Review Society; Richard E. Redding. Reprinted by permission.

Rosenberg, Irene Merker, *Leaving Bad Enough Alone: A Response to the Juvenile Court Abolitionists*, 1993 Wis. L. Rev. 163, 165-69, 171-75, 178-80, 182-85. Copyright 1993 by The Board of Regents of the University of Wisconsin System; Irene Merker Rosenberg. Reprinted by permission of the Wisconsin Law Review and the author.

Rosenthal, Michael P., *The Minimum Drinking Age for Young People: an Observation*, 92 Dickinson Law Review 649, 649-55 (1988). © Michael P. Rosenthal; Dickinson School of Law. Reprinted by permission of Dickinson School of Law.

Schneider, Carl E., *Moral Discourse and the Transformation of American Family Law,* 83 Mich. L. Rev. 1803, 1835-39 (1985). © 1986 Michigan Law Review Association; Carl E. Schneider. Reprinted by permission.

Schneider, Carl E., *On the Duties and Rights of Parents*, 81 Va. L. Rev. 2477, 2484-88 (1995). © 1995 by Virginia Law Review Association; Carl E. Schneider. Reprinted by permission.

Schwartz, Meryl, *Reinventing Guardianship: Subsidized Guardianship, Foster Care, and Child Welfare*, 22 New York University Review of Law and Social Change 441, 446-47, 456-58, 474 (1996). © by New York University Review of Law and Social Change; Meryl Schwartz. Reprinted by permission.

Scott, Elizabeth S. and Robert E. Scott, *Parents as Fiduciaries*, 81 Va. L. Rev. 2401, 2405-15 (1995). © 1995 Virginia Law Review Association; Elizabeth S. Scott; Robert E. Scott. Reprinted by permission.

Singer, Jana B., *The Privatization of Family Law*, 1992 Wisconsin L. Rev. 1443, 1444, 1478-86. © 1992 by The Board of Regents of the University of Wisconsin System; Jana B. Singer. Reprinted by permission of the Wisconsin Law Review and the author.

Wald, Michael S., *Children's Rights: A Framework for Analysis,* 12 U.C. Davis L. Rev. 255, 258-60 (1979). This work was originally published in 12 U.C. Davis L. Rev. 255 (1979). © Michael S. Wald; Copyright 1979 by The Regents of the University of California. Reprinted by permission.

Waldfogel, Jane, *Rethinking the Paradigm for Child Protection*, 8 The Future of Children 104, 106 (1998). The Future of Children is a publication of the Center for the Future of Children, The David and Lucille Packard Foundation. Permission not required.

Winslade, William, et al., *Castrating Pedophiles Convicted of Sex Offenses Against Children: New Treatment or Old Punishment?* 51 SMU L. Rev. 349, 357-60 (1998). Copyright © 1998 Southern Methodist University; William Winslade, T. Howard Stone, Michele Smith-Bell, Denise M. Webb. Originally appearing in Vol. 51, No. 2 of the *SMU Law Review*. Reprinted with permission from the *SMU Law Review* and the Southern Methodist University School of Law and William Winslade.

Wilson, John J. and James C. Howell, *Serious and Violent Juvenile Crime: A Comprehensive Strategy*, 45 Juvenile and Family Court Journal

3, 9-11 (No. 2 1994). © Juvenile and Family Court Journal. Reprinted by permission.

Woodhouse, Barbara Bennett, *Who Owns the Child?:* Meyer *and* Pierce *and the Child as Property,* 33 William & Mary L. Rev. 995, 1059-68 (1992). © Barbara Bennett Woodhouse; William and Mary Law Review. Reprinted by permission.

Woodhouse, Barbara Bennett, *Hatching the Egg: A Child-Centered Perspective on Parents' Rights,* 14 Cardozo L. Rev. 1747, 1756,1814-17, 1838-39, 1840-41 (1993). © Barbara Bennett Woodhouse; Cardozo Law Review. This article appeared in 14 Cardozo L. Rev. 1747 (May 1993). Reprinted by permission.

Zainaldin, Jamil S., *The Emergence of a Modern American Family Law: Child Custody, Adoption, and the Courts, 1796-1851,* 73 Nw. U. L. Rev. 1038, 1041-45 (1979). © 1979 Northwestern University School of Law, Northwestern University; Jamil S. Zainaldin. Reprinted by permission of the author and special permission of Northwestern University School of Law, *Law Review.*

*

Summary of Contents

Table of Contents

*

Table of Cases

The principal cases are in bold type. Cases cited or discussed in the text are roman type. References are to pages. Cases cited in principal cases and within other quoted materials are not included.

*

CHILDREN AND THE LAW

DOCTRINE, POLICY AND PRACTICE

*

Chapter 1

THE STATUS, RIGHTS AND OBLIGATIONS OF CHILDREN

By exploring the status, rights and obligations of children in contemporary America, this chapter introduces the book's three major themes: (1) the delicate interrelationship of rights and responsibilities among children, parents and government, (2) perceptions of children's competence as a basis for government regulation, and (3) the role of the child's lawyer. As the chapter proceeds, consider how children, parents and government are portrayed and how increasing or diminishing children's rights may affect the child-parent-government interrelationship. Consider also how differing views of this relationship and of the child's status influence the lawyer's role and the law's assessment of the child's competence.

SECTION 1. CHILDHOOD IN AMERICA

A. *Contemporary Conditions and Needs*

CARNEGIE COUNCIL ON ADOLESCENT DEVELOPMENT, CARNEGIE CORPORATION OF NEW YORK

STARTING POINTS: MEETING THE NEEDS OF OUR YOUNGEST CHILDREN vii-viii, xiii-xiv

(1994).

In the United States today—probably the most technologically advanced, affluent, and democratic society the world has ever known—the crucially formative years of early childhood have become a time of peril and loss for millions of children and their families. Now, however, there

1

is an opportunity to prevent much of this damage. A remarkable degree of consensus is emerging on the essential requirements that positively influence a child's early growth and development as well as on the ways that parents and others can provide our youngest children with a healthy start.

The human being experiences a prolonged period of immaturity and vulnerability—the longest of any known species. During the first three years of life, much has to be acquired, much mastered, much tried and found wanting, much discovered and put to use. Ideally, this learning time is spent in close relationship with adults who offer nurturing love, protection, guidance, stimulation, and support. For the caregivers, it is an enduring, long-term, highly challenging commitment. Rearing by a few caring, responsive, dependable adults leads to strong attachments and provides a secure base from which the infant can explore the larger social and physical world. Such secure early attachments are essential for human development.

Historically, several requirements have been valuable for healthy child development:

- An intact, cohesive, nuclear family, dependable under stress
- A relationship with at least one parent who is consistently nurturing, loving, enjoying, teaching, and coping
- Easy access to supportive extended family members
- A supportive community, whether it be a neighborhood, religious, ethnic, or political group
- Parents exposed to childrearing during the years of their own growth and development through explicit and implicit education for parenthood
- A perception of opportunity during childhood with a tangible basis for hope of an attractive future
- Predictability about the adult environment that enables a child to take advantage of opportunities in the environment

The ancient and fundamental desire of parents to do well by their children has not changed, but the setting is now quite different. Economic, social, and demographic pressures affect American families powerfully. In the past three decades—a moment in human history—the change in regular patterns of contact between American children and their adult relatives is remarkable. Not only are their mothers home much less, but there is little if any evidence that fathers spend more time with their children, and grandparents, too, are largely absent from the daily life of most children. Nor is quality child care sufficiently available to fill the gap. Powerful institutions of society such as business and government have done little to strengthen families in the rapidly changing circumstances of the late 20th century. * * *

Our nation's infants and toddlers and their families are in trouble. Compared with most other industrialized countries, the United States has a higher infant mortality rate, a higher proportion of low-birth-weight babies, a smaller proportion of babies immunized against childhood diseases, and a much higher rate of babies born to adolescent mothers. Of the twelve million children under the age of three in the United States today, a staggering number are affected by one or more risk factors that undermine healthy development. One in four lives in poverty. One in four lives in a single-parent family. One in three victims of physical abuse is a baby under the age of one.

These numbers reflect a pattern of neglect that must be reversed. It has long been known that the first years of life are crucial for later development, and recent scientific findings provide a basis for these observations. We can now say, with greater confidence than ever before, that the quality of young children's environment and social experience has a decisive, long-lasting impact on their well-being and ability to learn.

The risks are clearer than ever before: an adverse environment can compromise a young child's brain function and overall development, placing him or her at greater risk of developing a variety of cognitive, behavioral, and physical difficulties. In some cases these effects may be irreversible. But the opportunities are equally dramatic: adequate pre- and postnatal care, dependable caregivers, and strong community support can prevent damage and provide a child with a decent start in life.

Researchers have thoroughly documented the importance of the pre- and postnatal months and the first three years, but a wide gap remains between scientific knowledge and social policy. Today, changes in the American economy and family, combined with the lack of affordable health and child care and the crumbling of other family supports, make it increasingly difficult for parents to provide the essential requirements for their young children's healthy development.

More than half of mothers of children under the age of three work outside the home. This is a matter of concern because minimal parental leave is available at the time of birth, and child care for infants and toddlers is often hard to find and of poor quality. Most parents feel overwhelmed by the dual demands of work and family, have less time to spend with their children, and worry about the unreliable and substandard child care in which many infants and toddlers spend long hours. These problems affect all families, but for families living in poverty, the lack of prenatal and child health care, human services, and social support in increasingly violent neighborhoods further stacks the deck against their children.

These facts add up to a crisis that jeopardizes our children's healthy development, undermines school readiness, and ultimately threatens our nation's economic strength. Once a world leader and innovator in education, the United States today is making insufficient investments in its future workforce—our youngest children. In contrast to all the other leading industrialized nations, the United States fails to give parents time to be with their newborns, fails to ensure pre-and postnatal health care for mothers and infants, and fails to provide adequate child care.

The crisis among our youngest children and their families is a quiet crisis. After all, babies seldom make the news. Their parents—often young people struggling to balance their home and work responsibilities—tend to have little economic clout and little say in community affairs. Moreover, children's early experience is associated with the home—a private realm into which many policymakers have been reluctant to intrude.

* * *

CARNEGIE COUNCIL ON ADOLESCENT DEVELOPMENT, CARNEGIE CORPORATION OF NEW YORK

GREAT TRANSITIONS: PREPARING ADOLESCENTS FOR A NEW CENTURY 9–10
(1995).

Adolescence is one of the most fascinating and complex transitions in the life span: a time of accelerated growth and change second only to infancy; a time of expanding horizons, self-discovery, and emerging independence; a time of metamorphosis from childhood to adulthood. Its beginning is associated with biological, physical, behavioral, and social transformations that roughly correspond with the move from elementary school to middle or junior high school. The events of this crucially formative phase can shape an individual's life course and thus the future of the whole society.

Early adolescence, encompassing the sexual awakenings of puberty as well as new social and educational demands, is an age of particular vulnerability. Barely out of childhood, young people ages ten to fourteen are today experiencing more freedom, autonomy, and choice than ever at a time when they still need special nurturing, protection, and guidance. Without the sustained involvement of parents and other adults in safeguarding their welfare, young adolescents are at risk of harming themselves and others.

Many adolescents manage to negotiate their way through this critical transition with relative success. With caring families, good schools, and supportive community institutions, they grow up reasonably well educated, committed to families and friends, and prepared for the workplace and for the responsibilities of citizenship. Even under less-than-optimal conditions for growth and development—the absence of supportive and caring adults, poverty, unsafe schools, and distressed communities—adolescents can become contributing members of society. Some achieve this status despite facing threats to their well-being, such as AIDS and easy access to lethal weapons and drugs, that were all but unknown to their parents and grandparents.

For many others, however, the obstacles in their path can impair their physical and emotional health, destroy their motivation and ability to succeed in school and jobs, and damage their personal relationships. Many reach adulthood ill-equipped to participate responsibly in our democratic society. * * *

Across America today, adolescents are confronting pressures to use alcohol, cigarettes, or other drugs and to have sex at earlier ages. Many are depressed: About a third of adolescents report they have contemplated suicide. Others are growing up lacking the competence to handle interpersonal conflict without resorting to violence. By age seventeen, about a quarter of all adolescents have engaged in behaviors that are harmful or dangerous to themselves and others: getting pregnant, using drugs, taking part in antisocial activity, and failing in school. Altogether, nearly half of American adolescents are at high or moderate risk of seriously damaging their life chances. The damage may be near term and vivid, or it may be delayed, like a time bomb set in youth.

The social and technological changes of this century, and especially of recent decades, have provided many young people with remarkable material benefits and opportunities to master technical skills; they have also introduced new stresses and risks into the adolescent experience. Today, with high divorce rates, increases in both parents working, and the growth of single-parent families, slightly more than half of all American children will spend at least part of their childhood or adolescence living with only one parent. In this situation, exacerbated by the erosion of neighborhood networks and other traditional social support systems, children now spend significantly less time in the company of adults than a few decades ago; more of their time is spent in front of the television set or with their peers in age-segregated, unsupervised environments.

Such conditions occur among families of all income levels and backgrounds and in cities, suburbs, and rural areas. But they are especially severe in neighborhoods of concentrated poverty, where young adolescents are more likely to lack two crucial prerequisites for their healthy growth and development: a close relationship with a dependable adult and the perception of meaningful opportunities in mainstream society.

For today's adolescents, particularly those who do not intend to go beyond high school, there is much less chance to earn a decent living wage, support a family, and participate actively in the life of the community and nation than there was a few decades ago. Many adolescents feel adult-like pressures without experiencing the rewards of belonging and of being useful in the valued settings of adult life. Especially in low-income neighborhoods where good education and jobs are scarce, young people can grow up with a bleak sense of the future.

* * *

Notes

1. *Children as a percentage of the population.* In 1998, children comprised 26% of the United States population, down from a peak of 36% in 1964, the end of the "baby boom." Children have been decreasing as a proportion of the population since the mid–1960s, but children will remain a fairly stable percentage of the population in the near future. Children are projected to comprise 24% of the population in 2020. See Federal Interagency Forum on Child and Family Statistics, America's Children: Key National Indicators of Well–Being 4 (1999) ("Key National Indicators 1999").

2. *Racial and ethnic composition.* In 1998, 65% of children in the United States were white, non-Hispanic; 15% were black, non-Hispanic; 15% were Hispanic; 4% were Asian or Pacific Islander; and 1% were American Indian or Alaskan Native. From 1980 to 1998, the percentage of white, non-Hispanic children decreased from 74% to 65%; the percentages of black, American Indian and Alaskan Native children remained fairly stable; the percentage of Hispanic children increased more rapidly than that of any other racial or ethnic group, from 9% to 15%; and the percentage of Asian or Pacific Islander children doubled from 2% to 4%. It is projected that by 2020, one in five children in the United States will be Hispanic. See Key National Indicators 1999, supra at 5.

3. *Life expectancy.* In 1996, the life expectancy of white children born in the United States was 73.8 years for males and 79.6 years for females. For black children, life expectancy was 66.1 years for males and 74.2 years for females. U.S. Bureau of the Census, Statistical Abstract of the United States 1998, at 94, tbl. 128.

4. *Poverty.* In 1997, 19% of American children lived in families with cash incomes below the federal poverty line (that is, below $16,400 for a family of four). See Key National Indicators 1999, at 12. Nearly half these poor children (47%) lived in "deep poverty." A family lives in deep poverty if its income is 50% or more below the poverty line. In nine states and the District of Columbia, a quarter or more of all children were poor in 1996. The states are Kentucky (25%), New York (25%), Texas (25%), West Virginia (25%), Arizona (26%), California (26%), Mississippi (30%), New Mexico (30%) and Louisiana (32%). The District's child poverty rate was 40%. See Annie E. Casey Foundation, Kids Count Data Book 1999, at 39 (1999) ("Kids Count Data Book 1999").

The 19% U.S. child poverty rate is the highest by far of any nation in the developed world. In 1992, for example, the U.S. rate dwarfed the rates of Canada (9.3%), Australia (9%), Britain (7.4%), France (4.6%), Holland (3.8%), Germany (2.8%) and Sweden (1.6%). See Urie Bronfenbrenner et al., The State of Americans: This Generation and the Next 148 (1996).

The 19% child poverty rate is higher than the poverty rate for other segments of the U.S. population. In 1997, only 9.9% of prime-aged adults (age 18 to 64) and 10.2% of the elderly (age 65 and over) lived in poverty. See Nat'l Center for Children in Poverty, Young Children in Poverty: A Statistical Update 2, fig. 2 (June 1999). Most poor children are white and non-Hispanic, but minority children are overrepresented. In 1997, only 11% of white, non-Hispanic children lived in poverty, but 37% of black and 36% of

Hispanic children lived in poverty. See Key National Indicators 1999, supra at 12.

Many observers associate child poverty with life in the inner cities. In both 1980 and 1990, however, poor rural children accounted for about 29% of all poor children in the United States. In 1990, the percentage of rural children living in poverty (20%) exceeded the percentage of urban children living in poverty (16%). Rural child poverty rates were highest in the south and southwest, where sixteen states had rural child poverty rates higher than the national rate. See U.S. Gen. Accounting Office, Rural Children: Increasing Poverty Rates Pose Educational Challenges 5, 6 (Jan. 1994).

It is also sometimes thought that most poor children have parents who are unemployed and receiving public assistance. In 1990, however, 57% of poor infants and toddlers lived in families with at least one working parent, and over 90% of near-poor infants and toddlers lived with at least one working parent. See U.S. Gen. Accounting Office, Infants and Toddlers: Dramatic Increases in Numbers Living in Poverty 25 (Apr. 1994). Throughout the 1990s, the number of children in working-poor families (where at least one parent worked 26 or more weeks, but family income remained below the federal poverty line) increased significantly, from 4.3 million in 1989 to 5.6 million in 1997. See Kids Count Data Book 1999, supra at 23 (1999).

"[G]rowth in the ranks of poor children over the past few decades has not been due to an increase in the number of welfare-dependent families, but rather it is because the ranks of the working-poor have been growing. Between 1976 and 1997, the number of poor children increased by approximately 3.3 million. Roughly two-thirds of the increase occurred among children in families who had income from earnings, but no income from welfare. The number of children living in poor families totally dependent on welfare actually fell slightly over the past few decades." Id. at 24.

The 19% U.S. child poverty rate may underestimate the percentage of children in dire financial straits because the federal poverty line has been called "unrealistically low." Id. According to the Carnegie Council, "the official poverty line is drawn far below what most Americans actually believe constitutes poverty. Since 1946, in Gallup and Roper polls Americans have been asked what they consider the smallest amount of money a family of four in their community needs to get along, the figure below which a family could be considered 'poor.' Year after year their answer has been not the poverty line but rather a figure approximating half the median income for such a family." Kenneth Keniston and the Carnegie Council on Children, All Our Children: The American Family Under Pressure 27 (1977). In 1996, a family of four with an annual income below $16,400 was below the federal poverty line; the median income for a family of four was $51,405. See Key National Indicators 1999, supra at 12; Statistical Abstract of the United States 1998, at 469, tbl. 740.

5. *Divorce.* "Today's children are the first generation in the country's history who think divorce and separation are a normal part of family life." Alvin P. Sanoff and Jeannye Thornton, Our Neglected Kids, U.S. News & World Rep., Aug. 9, 1982, at 54 (quoting sociologist Andrew J. Cherlin). Nearly half of all marriages in the United States end in divorce, the highest

rate in the industrialized world. The median age of divorcing parents is in the low to mid thirties, the median length of marriages ending in divorce is about seven years, and each year more than a million children experience their parents' divorce. See Statistical Abstract of the United States 1998, at 112, tbl. 160. Sixty-five percent of divorcing couples have minor children. See Andrew Schepard, Parental Conflict Prevention Programs and the Unified Family Court: A Public Health Perspective, 32 Fam. L.Q. 95, 100 (1998).

Sociologist Andrew J. Cherlin recently analyzed the available research concerning the impact of divorce on children. He found that researchers have identified a crisis period that occurs the first year or two after divorce for the custodial parent and the children. The custodial parent (usually the mother) is less able to parent because of her own anger, depression and, frequently, financial distress. "[A]lmost all children experience an initial period of intense emotional upset" from the loss of the other parent, ongoing parental conflict, and other transitions, such as the decline in available income, sale of the family home, and a move to a new school system. Cherlin noted, however, that the conflicts that harm children often occur well before divorce. In a study that compared the records of thousands of children of divorce with children whose parents stayed married, researchers found that children whose parents would eventually divorce showed more school and behavior problems than those whose parents stayed married. Andrew J. Cherlin, Public and Private Families: An Introduction 389–93 (2d ed. 1999).

After the crisis period, most children of divorce resume normal development without serious problems. One study, however, found that five years after disruption, 15% to 20% more adolescents whose parents had divorced displayed serious behavior problems than children who were living with both parents. E. Mavis Hetherington and W. Glenn Clingempeel, Coping with Marital Transitions, 57 Monographs of the Society for Research in Child Development, nos. 2–3 (1992).

"[A] minority of children experience some long-term psychological problems as a result of the breakup that may persist into adulthood. From the glass-half-empty perspective, we can conclude that divorce may cause a substantial percentage increase in the number of individuals who may need the help of a mental health professional or who may not obtain as much education as they should or may be unemployed more often than they should. * * * From the glass-half-full perspective, however, it seems that most individuals do not suffer serious long-term harm as a result of their parents' divorce." Andrew J. Cherlin. Public and Private Families: An Introduction 393–94 (2d ed. 1999)

6. *Adolescent death rate.* In 1997, nearly 28,000 children between the ages of one and nineteen died in the United States. Since 1979, however, death rates have declined 45% for children one to four years old, 41% for children five to nine, 27% for children ten to fourteen, and 26% for children fifteen to nineteen. See Bernard Guyer et al., Annual Summary of Vital Statistics— 1997, 102 Pediatrics 1333, tbl. 12 (1998).

The American Academy of Pediatrics tempered news of evident improvement with the observation that "a large proportion of childhood deaths continue to occur as a result of preventable injuries." Id. at 1333. In 1997, unintentional injury remained the leading cause of death among children of all age groups, accounting for 36% of all deaths of children between one and four, 42% of all deaths of children between five and nine, 41% of all deaths of children between ten and fourteen, and 46% of all deaths of teens between fifteen and nineteen. For younger children, the most common types of unintentional injuries resulting in death were ones related to motor vehicles, followed by fires and burns, drowning, choking, falls and firearm injuries. For older children, motor vehicle accidents accounted for nearly a quarter of deaths, with drowning, fires and burns, and firearm injuries also occurring in high numbers. Since 1979, child death rates from unintentional injury have declined significantly, thanks partly to accident prevention measures such as mandatory car seat statutes, and to smoke alarms and sprinkler systems in homes and schools. Id.

7. *Childhood homicide, suicide, and firearm-related death rates.* In 1996, the U.S. Centers for Disease Control and Prevention (CDC) reported both good news and bad news. On the one hand, the overall annual death rate for children under fifteen declined substantially from 1950 to 1993, primarily from decreases in deaths associated with unintentional injuries, pneumonia, influenza, cancer, and congenital anomalies. During the same period, however, child homicide rates tripled and child suicide rates quadrupled. In 1994, homicide was the fourth leading cause of death among children between one and four; homicide was the third leading cause of death and suicide was the sixth among children between five and fourteen. See U.S. Centers for Disease Control and Prevention, Rates of Homicide, Suicide, and Firearm–Related Death Among Children—26 Industrialized Countries, 46 Morbidity and Mortality Weekly Rep. 101 (Feb. 7, 1997).

The CDC found that among twenty-six leading industrialized countries, the United States has the highest rates of child homicide, suicide, and firearm-related death. Id. The homicide rate for children in the United States is five times higher than the rates for children in the other twenty-five countries combined; the suicide rate for children in the United States is twice as high as the rates in the other twenty-five countries combined; and the overall firearm-related death rate among United States children under fifteen is nearly twelve times higher than the rates among such children in the other twenty-five countries combined. The United States firearm-related homicide rate is nearly sixteen times higher than the rates in all the other countries combined; the firearm-related suicide rate is nearly eleven times higher; and the unintentional firearm-related death rate is nine times higher. Id. at 102–03.

The child suicide rate remains a cause for concern. For every child suicide completed, an estimated fifty to 200 are attempted. See Joe M. Sanders, Jr. et al., Suicide and Suicide Attempts in Adolescents and Young Adults, 81 Pediatrics 322 (1988). Conservative estimates suggest that more than 250,000 American youths attempt suicide each year. See Susan E. Swedo, Can Adolescent Suicide Attempters Be Distinguished From At–Risk Adolescents?, 88 Pediatrics 620 (1991). Indeed the published child suicide rates may be underestimates because many medical experts believe that numerous adolescent deaths reported as ''accidental'' are actually suicides. See Leon Eisenberg, The Epidemiology of Suicide in Adolescents, 13 Pediatr. Ann. 47 (1984). Boys are more likely to complete suicide because they tend to use more lethal methods that frequently do not permit rescue, such as firearms or hanging. Girls are more likely to attempt suicide by taking pills, which frequently permits medical intervention. Sanders, supra.

B. *The Lawyer's Role*

Most of this book's readers will begin practicing law within two years, whether specializing in child advocacy or in another field. Children may appear in juvenile court with retained counsel. Because children needing legal assistance are frequently from poor or near-poor families, however, most private practitioners do not find it remunerative to emphasize representation of children in proceedings involving such matters as abuse and neglect, foster care, access to quality health care, and delinquency. Sometimes children's counsel are private practitioners who appear pro bono or are compensated at rates set for court appointment; public defenders, legal services lawyers, or social services agency lawyers also represent children.

In most places, child advocates are in short supply. Throughout this book, consider the impact of lawyers who represent children. The following report urged lawyers to devote at least a portion of their professional time to meeting children's needs as retained counsel, or by pro bono service in the best traditions of the profession.

AMERICAN BAR ASSOCIATION WORKING GROUP ON THE UNMET LEGAL NEEDS OF CHILDREN AND THEIR FAMILIES

AMERICA'S CHILDREN AT RISK: A NATIONAL AGENDA FOR LEGAL ACTION 3–8

(1993).

* * *

Lawyers must view the nation's children, as a group and as individuals, as their clients in the broadest sense. Attorneys should advocate on behalf of children long before problems develop that place a child before a court. Whether their clients are individuals seeking advice from small town general practitioners or large corporations served by major law firms, good attorneys often help their clients to solve problems and resolve disputes *before* they escalate enough to land the client in court. America's children need the same kind of help.

* * *

[M]any federal, state and local laws, programs and policies to benefit children are already in place. But these laws and programs do not reach every eligible child who needs services because families do not know their rights or how to get help, or because programs are not funded at levels that would provide services to all who qualify under law. Lawyers can help. Lawyers know how to identify resources, cut through red tape and work out inter-agency jurisdictional conflicts. We do it for adult and corporate clients every day. Individual children need the same sort of representation.

Children, simply by virtue of being children, are denied legal rights that adults take for granted. Many children routinely appear in court without benefit of legal counsel in situations where any adult who had the resources or know-how would retain a lawyer. Many children involved in legal proceedings concerning child abuse and neglect, custody, visitation disputes, status offenses, delinquency and other important matters are unrepresented from the beginning to the end of their cases. The lack of legal counsel is particularly devastating to children, who often cannot express their own views and may not fully understand the choices they are making.

* * *

We hope that all sorts of attorneys will commit themselves to represent children: major law firms, law departments in major corporations, existing public interest and pro bono projects, law school faculty and students in clinical training programs, small practitioners, government attorneys, and even those who are not actively engaged in practicing law, whether because they have entered a related field or are retired.* * *

Volunteers should not limit their services to high profile cases brought in order to change policy, but should also represent individual children in routine legal matters. Representation should be available to children who need services and those involved in cases concerning, among other things, abuse and neglect, education, disabilities, housing and homelessness, adoption, public benefits, institutionalization, status offenses, juvenile delinquency, custody and visitation, and other issues with a critical and direct impact on their lives.

* * *

Let us be clear: pro bono efforts are no substitute for paid representation where children are entitled under law to representation. Such representation should be more readily available and compensated at levels that generally prevail for private attorneys in each community. As part of this challenge, our nation must also improve the quality of representation for children * * * and ensure meaningful access to high quality representation where the law promises counsel to children.

* * *

Children's cases are often "processed," not advocated, and too frequently children's interests are poorly represented. In the past decades, courts have been increasingly inundated with cases concerning family matters; rarely have resources for competent representation or services grown to meet the expanded needs. Many jurisdictions offer representation for low-income children and families only at certain stages in proceedings, or at the discretion of the court. Others provide representation through public defender organizations, assigned counsel panels, and so forth. As a result, many children are represented—when they are represented at all—by underpaid lawyers with overwhelming caseloads, minimal training and little supervision. Even the most dedicated and competent lawyers find it an uphill battle to provide adequate representation under such circumstances.

Meaningful protection of children's rights requires that children be represented by highly skilled counsel at critical stages of critical proceedings. Competent professional representation in proceedings that involve children is vital in a system where decisions about children's rights and liberties and those of their parents are decided.

* * *

Notes

1. *A look toward the future.* "[D]omestic relations cases frequently involve children whose future is in the hands of the court through no fault of their own." Catherine J. Ross, The Failure of Fragmentation: The Promise of a System of Unified Family Courts, 32 Fam. L.Q. 3, 4 (1998). Demographic trends suggest that the need for counsel to represent children will continue to grow in the foreseeable future. There were 69.9 million children in the United States in 1998; the number is projected to increase to 77.6 million in 2020. Forum on Child and Family Statistics, America's Children: Key National Indicators of Well–Being 3 (1999). "Alone, this population growth will lead to an increased number of juvenile victims of abuse and neglect, more juvenile offenders, and increased case flow into the juvenile justice system." Howard N. Snyder and Melissa Sickmund, Juvenile Offenders and Victims: A National Report 2 (OJJDP 1995). Chapter 3 explores issues in the representation of children.

2. *The juvenile court system.* Each state has a trial court devoted to proceedings relating to children, called the "juvenile court" in most states. In some states, the juvenile court is a distinct trial court; in some states, the general jurisdiction trial court has juvenile jurisdiction; in other states, the juvenile court is a separate division of the general-jurisdiction trial court, such as "the juvenile division of the probate court" or "of the superior court."

Juvenile courts typically have exclusive original jurisdiction over four major categories of proceedings:

a. abuse and neglect (Chapter 4). Civil abuse and neglect proceedings determine the state's claims that a parent or custodian (1) has physically, sexually or emotionally abused the child, or (2) has failed to provide the child a minimal level of support, education, nutrition, or medical or other care necessary for the child's well-being. (Criminal abuse or neglect charges against the parent or custodian are heard in criminal court rather than juvenile court.). An abuse or neglect proceeding determines the child's condition, not the parent's guilt or liability. This arm of juvenile court jurisdiction generally confers jurisdiction to decide termination-of-parental-rights petitions filed by the state seeking to permanently sever the parent-child relationship because of gross abuse or gross neglect.

b. adoption (Chapter 7). Adoption terminates the parent-child relationship between the child and the natural parents, and creates a new parent-child relationship between the child and the adoptive parents. A child may be adopted only if the parental rights of both natural parents have been terminated by consent or court order, and if the juvenile court approves the adoption as being in the best interests of the child. In some states, adoption jurisdiction is in the probate or surrogate's court.

c. status offenses (Chapter 10). A status offense alleges conduct sanctionable only where the person committing it is a minor. Prime examples are ungovernability (that the minor habitually resists reasonable discipline from his or her parents and is beyond their control), truancy, runaway behavior, and curfew violations.

d. delinquency (Chapter 11). A delinquency proceeding alleges that the juvenile has committed an act that would be a crime if committed by an adult.

In some states, the juvenile court may also hear and decide various other matters, such as juvenile traffic offenses, guardianship proceedings, commitment proceedings for mentally ill or seriously disabled children, proceedings for consent to an abortion or underage marriage, and paternity and child support proceedings. State appellate codes provide for appeals of juvenile court decisions.

3. *Unified family courts.* Several jurisdictions have replaced the juvenile court with a unified family court. Family courts enable one judge, working with social service workers and other support personnel, to resolve all matters typically associated with distressed families. The family court's subject matter jurisdiction includes not only matters within the four major categories of juvenile court jurisdiction, but also an array of matters traditionally heard in general jurisdiction courts. This array typically includes divorce proceedings, paternity suits, criminal prosecutions charging abuse or neglect or domestic violence, emancipation proceedings, and proceedings for protective orders under child abuse and adult abuse statutes. See Symposium on Unified Family Courts, 32 Fam. L.Q. 3 (1998).

Proponents assert that unified family courts can produce consistency and efficiency that serve the best interests of children, families and courts. Families and the judicial system save time, effort and resources when one decisionmaker remains abreast of the family's circumstances and resolves all family-related matters. Family members are spared the ordeal of appearing in multiple courts that determine frequently interrelated factual and legal issues. Children are spared the discomfort of testifying in multiple proceedings. Consider, for example, the plight of a young child allegedly molested by her father. In a jurisdiction without a unified family court, the child may be forced to testify about the same or similar events in multiple proceedings if the mother files for divorce after learning of the sexual assault, if child protective authorities file a civil abuse proceeding to remove the child from the home, and if the prosecutor files criminal charges. See John E.B. Myers, Adjudication of Child Sexual Abuse Cases, in 4 The Future of Children 84, 96 (Summer/Fall 1994).

Proponents argue that the one-judge-one-family approach enables the family court to treat family dysfunction efficiently while minimizing the risk of inconsistent judgments or of multiple initiatives that each overlook a basic need. A generation ago, a Presidential Commission urged creation of unified family courts, which "by dealing with all intrafamily matters including those now generally handled by juvenile courts, would provide one means of achieving the consistency and continuity of treatment now too often undercut by fragmented jurisdiction." President's Commission on Law Enforcement and Administration of Justice: The Challenge of Crime in a Free Society 85 (1967). In 1994, the ABA reaffirmed its commitment to unified family courts. See American Bar Association Policy on Unified Family Courts, 32 Fam. L.Q. 1 (1998) (adopted Aug. 1994).

Can you think of reasons why only about twenty states have created unified family courts so far?

See, e.g., Herbert H. Lou, Juvenile Courts in the United States 203–12 (1927); Lindsay G. Arthur, A Family Court—Why Not?, 51 Minn. L. Rev. 233 (1966); Barbara A. Babb, Fashioning an Interdisciplinary Framework for Court Reform in Family Law: A Blueprint to Construct a Unified Family Court, 71 S. Cal. L. Rev. 469 (1998); Sanford N. Katz & Jeffrey A. Kuhn, Recommendations for a Model Family Court: A Report From the National Family Court Symposium (1991); Catherine J. Ross, Unified Family Courts: Good Sense, Good Justice, 35 Trial 30 (Jan. 1999); Andrew Schepard, Law and Children: Introduction to Unified Family Courts, N.Y.L.J., Apr. 16, 1997, at 3; Robert E. Shepherd, The Unified Family Court: An Idea Whose Time Has Come, 8 Crim. Just. 37 (1993).

SECTION 2.   THE LAW'S EVOLVING CONCEPTION OF CHILDREN'S STATUS, RIGHTS AND OBLIGATIONS

A.   *The Status of Childhood: An Introduction*

When does the law classify a person as a "child"? For most purposes, the status of childhood lasts until a person reaches the general age of majority, which is now eighteen in nearly all states. Throughout most of the nation's history, the age was twenty-one, the age at which feudal English common law determined that a boy became an adult because he could handle the weight of a full suit of armor. See T. E. James, The Age of Majority, 4 Am. J. Legal Hist. 22 (1960). Most states lowered the age to eighteen in the early 1970s, shortly after the Twenty–Sixth Amendment to the federal Constitution established eighteen as the minimum voting age in federal and state elections. The lowering of the general age of majority occurred in all states except Alaska, Nebraska and Wyoming; in these three states, the age is nineteen. The Supreme Court has held that equal protection requires that the general age of majority be the same for boys and girls. See Stanton v. Stanton, 421 U.S. 7 (1975).

Statutes continue to define some circumstances in which persons first assume adult rights and obligations at an age higher or lower than eighteen. Chapter 10, for example, discusses the alcoholic beverage control laws, which set the minimum drinking age at twenty-one in all states. Many states terminate delinquency jurisdiction at an age lower than eighteen (see Chapter 11). Statutes also frequently permit persons under eighteen to make medical treatment decisions for some diseases, such as sexually transmitted diseases (see Chapter 8).

The general age of majority, and statutes departing from that age, apply to all persons, regardless of whether an individual is sufficiently mature to exercise a particular right or assume a particular obligation sooner. These blanket statutes have the advantage of being easy to administer, but the disadvantage of ignoring individual differences.

In some circumstances, adult status is conferred by individualized determination, rather than by blanket rule. If a court finds a pregnant girl to be mature, for example, she may make an abortion decision without parental consent to the procedure (see Bellotti v. Baird, below). Before reaching the age of majority, a child may also gain most adult rights and obligations through "emancipation," which is discussed in Chapter 2. A statute may provide for emancipation when a particular event occurs (such as when the child marries or enters military service), or by court order on a showing that the child has left home with parental consent and can be economically self-sufficient. Courts making individualized determinations must carefully weigh the concept of maturity and the means of assessing it.

The status of childhood is a complex concept indeed, and a person may be a child for some purposes and an adult for others. Children are viewed as vulnerable, incapable and needing protection in some circumstances and as individuals with rights, decisionmaking capacity and personal responsibility in others. A fourteen-year-old, for example, may not sign a binding contract but may be tried as an adult and sentenced to life in prison for a crime.

B.   The Parens Patriae Doctrine, Parental Prerogatives, and the Child's Obligation to Obey

1.   Common Law Background

III BLACKSTONE, COMMENTARIES ON
THE LAWS OF ENGLAND 47
(W.D. Lewis ed. 1902).

The King's chancellor "is the general guardian of all infants, idiots, and lunatics; and has the general superintendance of all charitable uses in the kingdom."

GEORGE B. CURTIS, THE CHECKERED CAREER OF
PARENS PATRIAE:
THE STATE AS PARENT OR TYRANT?
25 DePaul L. Rev. 895, 897–902 (1976).

* * * Initially, *parens patriae* established the king as a protector or supreme guardian of those classes threatened by forces beyond their control. * * *

* * *

However, the extension of royal protection to all the children of the realm was an impossible task. In practice, the *parens patriae* theory was applied in cases of wardships of the children of the landed gentry—those children with estates profitable to the realm and subject to the concupiscence of their relatives. Wardship of his tenants' infant heirs assured the king income; sale of the wardship could produce needed revenues.* * * [T]he profit motive was clearly at the forefront of the king's decision to offer his protection. This application of *parens patriae* to lucrative wardships served to narrow the ultimate limits of the concept.

While the actual origins of the term *parens patriae* remain unclear, both commentators and judges have agreed that it was founded in the *Prerogative Regis* and applied essentially to three groups: children, mental incompetents, and charities. Practical forces such as pecuniary interests served to focus the king's interest on these three classes. Unlike its modern American counterpart, the English common law forbade the sovereign or his chancery court to intrude into distinctly political areas or to claim jurisdiction over criminal matters. Although other areas of the king's prerogative might justify such intrusions, *parens patriae* was limited to a parental concern for dependent classes.

In their headlong rush to embrace the doctrine of *parens patriae* as the justification for the juvenile court movement, reformers both of the nineteenth and twentieth centuries overlooked two fundamental aspects of the chancery court's *parens patriae* jurisdiction. They failed to perceive the economic interests which underlay much of the king's activity as public protector. More significantly, the reformers seemed to miss completely the subtle, yet crucial, fact that the doctrine embraced the *dependent* and not the *delinquent* child.

English children who received royal protection had not violated the norms of society; rather, they had summoned the care of the realm because of their dependent and propertied status. The motivating reason to apply the *parens patriae* theory was the need to support and to care for children, not to reform or rehabilitate them. The chancery courts, in applying and developing the theory, did not have to grapple with the problems of deviant conduct. The theory was conceived to aid the child who stood as a source of hope for the kingdom, not as a threat to its stability.* * *

Despite certain theoretical inconsistencies, *parens patriae* has evidenced remarkable staying power. It formed the basic rationale for the operation of the juvenile court system and, to a limited extent, still functions in that role today. Its popularity in juvenile reform largely stems from its parental nexus in which the state as parent is viewed as capable of achieving only good.

* * *

Notes

1. *The boundaries of parens patriae.* Following the American Revolution, states assumed parens patriae authority earlier held by the English Crown.

The Supreme Court's early parens patriae decisions concerned the government's authority to regulate charities, but children also attracted the law's attention. See, e.g., Joseph Story, Commentaries on Equity Jurisprudence § 1341 (3d ed. 1843) ("[P]arents are intrusted with the custody of the persons, and the education, of their children; yet this is done upon the natural presumption, that the children will be properly taken care of * * *; and that they will be treated with kindness and affection. But, whenever * * * a father * * * acts in a manner injurious to the morals or interests of his children; in every such case, the Court of Chancery will interfere."). In Mormon Church v. United States, 136 U.S. 1, 57 (1890), the Court held that the parens patriae doctrine is "inherent in the supreme power of every State * * *, a most beneficent function, and often necessary to be exercised in the interests of humanity, and for the prevention of injury to those who cannot protect themselves."

Today the parens patriae doctrine is central to much federal and state regulation of children's welfare in abuse, neglect, delinquency and other areas covered by this casebook. Once this chapter sets the conceptual framework, the remaining chapters test the doctrine's limits by inviting consideration of four fundamental questions:

- Should the government have a voice in determining how parents raise and care for their children?

- In a particular circumstance, how much of a voice should the government have when parents or the child, or both, oppose the government's position?

- What procedural and substantive safeguards should constrain the government's exercise of parens patriae authority?

- What rights, if any, should parents and children have to state assistance?

2. *The police power.* In addition to parens patriae authority, states may regulate children and the family under their general police powers. Parens patriae is "the state's limited paternalistic power to protect or promote the welfare of certain individuals, like young children * * * who lack the capacity to act in their own best interests." The police power is "the state's inherent plenary power both to prevent its citizens from harming one another and to promote all aspects of the public welfare." Developments in the Law—The Constitution and the Family, 93 Harv. L. Rev. 1156, 1198–99 (1980). "Acting under its parens patriae power, the state may pursue ends that would be impermissible under the police power because they are unrelated to any harm to third parties or to the public welfare. At the same time, however, when the state acts as parens patriae, it should advance only the best interests of the incompetent individual and not attempt to further other objectives, deriving from its police power, that may conflict with the individual's welfare. * * * [T]he state should seek, if possible, to make its decisions in the same way that the individual would were he fully competent." Id. at 1199 & n.14.

3. *The nonintervention tradition.* The parens patriae doctrine's practical application is sometimes affected by the law's reluctance to intervene in family affairs. This reluctance may lead authorities and courts to avoid

determinations relating to conduct within the family, including some parental conduct affecting children. Professor Carl E. Schneider explains that the
tradition "rests in large measure on the practical difficulties of enforcing
family law and the practical consequences of trying to do so":

> Enforcement difficulties arise first because much of what family law
> seeks to regulate—from child and spouse abuse to fornication—occurs in
> private. The distastefulness of investigating private life is sharp enough
> to have been used to justify the doctrine of constitutional privacy and to
> have contributed to the rise of no-fault divorce. Family privacy is often
> hard to breach because the parties all participated in the violation of
> law, because they wish to protect those who did participate, or because
> they are ashamed to have people know about the incident in which the
> state is interested. Families may also seek to maintain their privacy
> because they disagree with the law's definition of immoral behavior
> * * *, because they dislike the law's meddling in family affairs, or
> because they feel the common urge of a family to unite against outside
> criticism.
>
> Family law's second enforcement problem is that the person en-
> forced against is often specially able to injure the very person the law
> intervened to protect. The spouse who wishes to resist divorce, the
> abused child or spouse, the pregnant woman, and her fetus are all
> vulnerable in this way. Legal intervention in these situations thus may
> be fruitless, or, worse, might provoke the person enforced against to
> retaliate against the person the law wants to protect. Because the
> person to be protected often depends on the person enforced against,
> even legal punishment itself can injure the person to be protected by
> depriving him or her of the presence or affection of the other.
>
> The third enforcement difficulty arises from the fact that, in many
> critical areas of family law, the people the law wishes to regulate live in
> emotional settings and under psychological pressures which make them
> little susceptible to the law's persuasion or even coercion. None of us is
> immune "from the frailties of nature," and we are all "sometimes
> moved by the mysteries of passion," but many of those whom family law
> most wants to reach lead lives so distressful they can hardly control
> themselves or their circumstances. * * *
>
> The tradition of noninterference persists not only because we fear
> the state's power, but also because we doubt the state's efficacy. The
> state's retreat from direct regulation of some areas of family life has
> reinforced the popular belief that "you can't enforce morality." And that
> retreat has encouraged people to believe that family law's ultimate goals
> of permitting, inspiring, and sustaining decent relations between hus-
> bands and wives and parents and children can be secured—if society can
> secure them—only through comprehensive and costly social services and
> social reform. But the programs such people advocate are so comprehen-
> sive and so costly that they are politically absurd. Furthermore, there is
> now a sense that even comprehensive social reform has proved unsuc-
> cessful, and a sense that social science lacks the predictive and analytic
> power to reverse that failure.

Carl E. Schneider, Moral Discourse and the Transformation of American Family Law, 83 Mich. L. Rev. 1803, 1835–39 (1985).

4. *The child's role.* At common law, children were expected to obey their parents and heed the Biblical command to "honor thy father and mother." In colonial New England, a 1641 law provided that "[i]f any child, or children, above sixteen years old, and of sufficient understanding shall CURSE or SMITE their natural FATHER or MOTHER, he or she shall be putt to death, unless it can be sufficiently testifyed that the Parents have been very unchristianly negligent in the education of such children: so provoked them by extreme and cruel correction, that they have been forced thereunto, to preserve themselves from death or maiming." Joseph M. Hawes, The Children's Rights Movement 4 (1991). Professor Hawes also reports that "[t]o ensure that children understood their place," the Rev. Cotton Mather "recommended threatening children with eternal damnation to make them conform. 'Disobedient Children! my heart aches for you,' Mather wrote, for I have seen the judgments of God making such as you the most astonishing monuments of his indignation." Id. Although not stated as dramatically, the expectation that children will obey their parents' wishes about education and religion is implicit in *Meyer* and *Pierce* below, the Supreme Court's early decisions protecting parents against state coercion.

5. *References.* Judith Areen, Intervention Between Parent and Child: A Reappraisal of the State's Role in Child Neglect and Abuse Cases, 63 Geo. L.J. 887, 894–917 (1975); Neil Cogan, Juvenile Law, Before and After the Entrance of "Parens Patriae," 22 S.C. L. Rev. 147 (1970); Lawrence B. Custer, The Origins of the Doctrine of *Parens Patriae*, 27 Emory L.J. 195, 195 (1978); Alexander W. Pisciotta, Saving the Children: The Promise and Practice of *Parens Patriae*, 1838–98, 28 Crime & Delinq. 410 (1982); Douglas R. Rendleman, Parens Patriae: From Chancery to the Juvenile Court, 23 S.C. L. Rev. 205, 256 (1971).

PROBLEM 1–1

The National Environmental Policy Act requires federal agencies to prepare Environmental Impact Statements analyzing the likely environmental effects of their activities. Judge Charles D. Gill has urged Congress and state legislatures to require child impact statements before enacting legislation. "[W]e do it for the spotted owl. We do it for bugs and beasts and birds, but not for babies." Charles D. Gill, Children of the 21st Century: Chattel or Constitutionally Protected Citizens, 2 Quinnipiac Health L.J. 97, 101 (1998). In 1995, Senator Paul Wellstone (D–Minn.) proposed a Sense of the Congress Resolution to require a child impact statement before Congress enacts new legislation. 141 Cong. Rec. S707, S720. As a member of Congress or a state legislator, would you vote for this bill?:

> With the exception of appropriation bills, every bill shall, before being acted upon, be submitted to the appropriate committee for preparation of a child impact statement. The committee staff shall prepare the child impact statement, which shall determine whether the proposed legislation would affect children's emotional, physical,

intellectual and financial needs and access to resources; would affect specific groups of children more than others; or would have an impact on parents and caregivers in their ability to ensure children's emotional, physical, intellectual and financial well-being.

2.   *The American Conception*

a.   *The Traditional Roles of Parents and the Government*

Throughout most of the nation's early history, the law viewed children as incompetent until they reached the general age of majority. See, e.g., Morrissey v. Perry, 137 U.S. 157, 159 (1890). The law remained generally unconcerned with affairs within the family, recognized almost absolute parental authority over children, and perceived children almost as the property of their parents, particularly of the father. The property analogy was not altogether inapt because children frequently had economic value to their parents before enactment of child labor and compulsory education laws. The analogy, however, was not perfect because the law permitted parents, for example, to kill or destroy their property but not to kill their children. The property analogy nonetheless helps explain why children were effectively voiceless in controversies with state authorities.

By the early twentieth century, psychological thought had begun to question the prevailing perception of children merely as "little adults." Creation of the nation's first juvenile court in 1899 culminated decades of efforts by reformers who argued that children have distinct physical and emotional needs worthy of the law's recognition. The next two decisions are landmarks, not only because they gave parental rights constitutional status in disputes with governmental authority, but also because they provided a foundation for ongoing reevaluation of the status, rights and obligations of children.

MEYER v. NEBRASKA

Supreme Court of the United States, 1923.
262 U.S. 390.

Mr. Justice McReynolds delivered the opinion of the Court.

Plaintiff in error was tried and convicted in the District Court for Hamilton County, Nebraska, under an information which charged that on May 25, 1920, while an instructor in Zion Parochial School he unlawfully taught the subject of reading in the German language to Raymond Parpart, a child of ten years, who had not attained and successfully passed the eighth grade. The information is based upon "An act relating to the teaching of foreign languages in the state of Nebraska," approved April 9, 1919, which follows:

"Section 1.   No person, individually or as a teacher, shall, in any private, denominational, parochial or public school, teach any subject to any person in any language other than the English language.

"Sec. 2. Languages, other than the English language, may be taught as languages only after a pupil shall have attained and successfully passed the eighth grade as evidenced by a certificate of graduation issued by the county superintendent of the county in which the child resides."

* * *

The Supreme Court of the State affirmed the judgment of conviction. * * *

The problem for our determination is whether the statute as construed and applied unreasonably infringes the liberty guaranteed to the plaintiff in error by the Fourteenth Amendment: "No state shall * * * deprive any person of life, liberty or property without due process of law."

While this Court has not attempted to define with exactness the liberty thus guaranteed, the term has received much consideration and some of the included things have been definitely stated. Without doubt, it denotes not merely freedom from bodily restraint but also the right of the individual to contract, to engage in any of the common occupations of life, to acquire useful knowledge, to marry, establish a home and bring up children, to worship God according to the dictates of his own conscience, and generally to enjoy those privileges long recognized at common law as essential to the orderly pursuit of happiness by free men. The established doctrine is that this liberty may not be interfered with, under the guise of protecting the public interest, by legislative action which is arbitrary or without reasonable relation to some purpose within the competency of the state to effect. Determination by the Legislature of what constitutes proper exercise of police power is not final or conclusive but is subject to supervision by the courts.

* * * Corresponding to the right of control, it is the natural duty of the parent to give his children education suitable to their station in life; and nearly all the states, including Nebraska, enforce this obligation by compulsory laws.

Practically, education of the young is only possible in schools conducted by especially qualified persons who devote themselves thereto. The calling always has been regarded as useful and honorable, essential, indeed, to the public welfare. Mere knowledge of the German language cannot reasonably be regarded as harmful. Heretofore it has been commonly looked upon as helpful and desirable. Plaintiff in error taught this language in school as part of his occupation. His right thus to teach and the right of parents to engage him so to instruct their children, we think, are within the liberty of the Amendment.

* * *

It is said the purpose of the legislation was to promote civic development by inhibiting training and education of the immature in foreign tongues and ideals before they could learn English and acquire

American ideals, and "that the English language should be and become the mother tongue of all children reared in this state." It is also affirmed that the foreign born population is very large, that certain communities commonly use foreign words, follow foreign leaders, move in a foreign atmosphere, and that the children are thereby hindered from becoming citizens of the most useful type and the public safety is imperiled.

That the state may do much, go very far, indeed, in order to improve the quality of its citizens, physically, mentally and morally, is clear; but the individual has certain fundamental rights which must be respected. The protection of the Constitution extends to all, to those who speak other languages as well as to those born with English on the tongue. Perhaps it would be highly advantageous if all had ready understanding of our ordinary speech, but this cannot be coerced by methods which conflict with the Constitution—a desirable end cannot be promoted by prohibited means.

For the welfare of his Ideal Commonwealth, Plato suggested a law which should provide: "That the wives of our guardians are to be common, and their children are to be common, and no parent is to know his own child, nor any child his parent. * * * The proper officers will take the offspring of the good parents to the pen or fold, and there they will deposit them with certain nurses who dwell in a separate quarter; but the offspring of the inferior, or of the better when they chance to be deformed, will be put away in some mysterious, unknown place, as they should be." In order to submerge the individual and develop ideal citizens, Sparta assembled the males at seven into barracks and intrusted their subsequent education and training to official guardians. Although such measures have been deliberately approved by men of great genius their ideas touching the relation between individual and state were wholly different from those upon which our institutions rest; and it hardly will be affirmed that any Legislature could impose such restrictions upon the people of a state without doing violence to both letter and spirit of the Constitution.

The desire of the Legislature to foster a homogeneous people with American ideals prepared readily to understand current discussions of civic matters is easy to appreciate. Unfortunate experiences during the late war and aversion toward every characteristic of truculent adversaries were certainly enough to quicken that aspiration. But the means adopted, we think, exceed the limitations upon the power of the state and conflict with rights assured to plaintiff in error. The interference is plain enough and no adequate reason therefor in time of peace and domestic tranquility has been shown.

The power of the State to compel attendance at some school and to make reasonable regulations for all schools, including a requirement that they shall give instructions in English, is not questioned. Nor has challenge been made of the State's power to prescribe a curriculum for institutions which it supports. Those matters are not within the present controversy. Our concern is with the prohibition approved by the [state]

Supreme Court. * * * No emergency has arisen which renders knowledge by a child of some language other than English so clearly harmful as to justify its inhibition with the consequent infringement of rights long freely enjoyed. We are constrained to conclude that the statute as applied is arbitrary and without reasonable relation to any end within the competency of the state.

As the statute undertakes to interfere only with teaching which involves a modern language, leaving complete freedom as to other matters, there seems no adequate foundation for the suggestion that the purpose was to protect the child's health by limiting his mental activities. It is well known that proficiency in a foreign language seldom comes to one not instructed at an early age, and experience shows that this is not injurious to the health, morals or understanding of the ordinary child.

* * *

Reversed.

[Mr. Justice Holmes and Mr. Justice Sutherland dissented.]

PIERCE v. SOCIETY OF SISTERS

Supreme Court of the United States, 1925.
268 U.S. 510.

Mr. Justice McReynolds delivered the opinion of the Court.

* * *

* * * The challenged act [adopted by Oregon voters under the state constitution's initiative provision], effective September 1, 1926, requires every parent, guardian, or other person having control or charge or custody of a child between 8 and 16 years to send him "to a public school for the period of time a public school shall be held during the current year" in the district where the child resides; and failure so to do is declared a misdemeanor. There are exemptions—not specially important here—for children who are not normal, or who have completed the eighth grade, or whose parents or private teachers reside at considerable distances from any public school, or who hold special permits from the county superintendent. The manifest purpose is to compel general attendance at public schools by normal children, between 8 and 16, who have not completed the eighth grade. And without doubt enforcement of the statute would seriously impair, perhaps destroy, the profitable features of appellees' business and greatly diminish the value of their property.

Appellee the Society of Sisters is an Oregon corporation, organized in 1880, with power to care for orphans, educate and instruct the youth, establish and maintain academies or schools, and acquire necessary real and personal property. It has long devoted its property and effort to the secular and religious education and care of children, and has acquired the valuable good will of many parents and guardians. * * * In its primary schools many children between those ages are taught the subjects usually pursued in Oregon public schools during the first eight years. Systematic religious instruction and moral training according to the tenets of the Roman Catholic Church are also regularly provided. All courses of study, both temporal and religious, contemplate continuity of training under appellee's charge; the primary schools are essential to the system and the most profitable. It owns valuable buildings, especially constructed and equipped for school purposes. The business is remunerative—the annual income from primary schools exceeds $30,000—and the successful conduct of this requires long time contracts with teachers and parents. The Compulsory Education Act of 1922 has already caused the withdrawal from its schools of children who would otherwise continue, and their income has steadily declined. The appellants, public officers, have proclaimed their purpose strictly to enforce the statute.

After setting out the above facts, the Society's bill alleges that the enactment conflicts with the right of parents to choose schools where their children will receive appropriate mental and religious training, the right of the child to influence the parents' choice of a school, the right of schools and teachers therein to engage in a useful business or profession, and is accordingly repugnant to the Constitution and void. And, further, that unless enforcement of the measure is enjoined the corporation's business and property will suffer irreparable injury.

[The Court then described appellee Hill Military Academy, a private military school for boys, and its claims of constitutional deprivation. The lower court granted the requested injunctions.].

* * *

No question is raised concerning the power of the state reasonably to regulate all schools, to inspect, supervise and examine them, their teachers and pupils; to require that all children of proper age attend some school, that teachers shall be of good moral character and patriotic disposition, that certain studies plainly essential to good citizenship must be taught, and that nothing be taught which is manifestly inimical to the public welfare.

The inevitable practical result of enforcing the act under consideration would be destruction of appellees' primary schools, and perhaps all other private primary schools for normal children within the state of Oregon. Appellees are engaged in a kind of undertaking not inherently harmful, but long regarded as useful and meritorious. Certainly there is nothing in the present records to indicate that they have failed to discharge their obligations to patrons, students, or the state. And there are no peculiar circumstances or present emergencies which demand extraordinary measures relative to primary education.

Under the doctrine of *Meyer* v. *Nebraska*, we think it entirely plain that the Act of 1922 unreasonably interferes with the liberty of parents and guardians to direct the upbringing and education of children under their control. As often heretofore pointed out, rights guaranteed by the

Constitution may not be abridged by legislation which has no reasonable relation to some purpose within the competency of the state. The fundamental theory of liberty upon which all governments in this Union repose excludes any general power of the state to standardize its children by forcing them to accept instruction from public teachers only. The child is not the mere creature of the state; those who nurture him and direct his destiny have the right, coupled with the high duty, to recognize and prepare him for additional obligations.

* * *

The decrees below are affirmed.

Notes and Questions

1. *Weighing the interests in* Meyer *and* Pierce. (a) In these two decisions, how much weight did the Court give the government's parens patriae interest?,

(b) How much weight did the Court give the parents' interest? What interests of the parents did the Court vindicate?,

(c) How can we tell that the parents' interest received considerable weight?,

(d) What, if anything, did the decisions say about the children's interests?

2. *The lasting legacy of* Meyer *and* Pierce. *Meyer* and *Pierce* have stimulated ongoing scholarly inquiry, fueled largely by a seeming paradox. On the one hand, the two venerable decisions striking at anti-German sentiment and religious intolerance have become enduring "liberal icons" that "stand for the values of pluralism, family autonomy, and the right 'to heed the music of different drummers'." Barbara Bennett Woodhouse, Who Owns the Child?: *Meyer* and *Pierce* and the Child as Property, 33 Wm. & Mary L. Rev. 995, 997 (1992). On the other hand, both decisions were written by the archconservative Justice James C. McReynolds, "the most bigoted, vitriolic, and intolerant individual ever to have sat on the Supreme Court." Id. at 1081. The "liberal" Justice Oliver Wendell Holmes, Jr. dissented in *Meyer*.

Federal and state courts still cite *Meyer* and *Pierce* in dozens of juvenile and family law decisions each year, and Professor Woodhouse is surely right that Justice McReynolds would "turn over in his grave" if he knew many of the uses to which later courts have put his words. Id. at 1110. For example, Chapter 7 presents Stanley v. Illinois, 405 U.S. 645, 651 (1972), which cited *Meyer* to support the proposition that following the natural mother's death, due process and equal protection guarantee an unwed father a fitness hearing before the state may deny him custody of his children born out of wedlock.

Professor Woodhouse argues that the liberal family law doctrine of *Meyer* and *Pierce* has outlasted the decisions' grounding in the conservative (and now-discredited) economic substantive due process prevalent in the early years of the twentieth century. *Meyer* and *Pierce* surely protected academic inquiry and religious liberty, she argues, but they also "constitutionalized a narrow, tradition-bound vision of the child as essentially private property," and "announced a dangerous form of liberty, the right to control another human being. Stamped on the reverse side of the coinage of family privacy and parental rights are the child's voicelessness, objectification, and isolation from the community." Id. at 997, 1001.

Professor Stephen L. Carter rejects Professor Woodhouse's argument, and suggests that the decisions' role as bulwarks of diversity should not have been entirely unexpected: "[The Court] referred to children 'under their control,' suggesting perhaps a hierarchy but at best a temporary one: today the parents 'control' their children, but those children are, tomorrow, adults. When they are adults, what values will they hold? Nothing in the Court's analysis suggests any clear predictability, except for one tantalizing and often overlooked line: the State lacks the authority 'to standardize its children by forcing them to accept instruction from public teachers only.' This language suggests a normative claim that the state should not try to ensure that all citizens have a common view of the world * * *." Stephen L. Carter, Parents, Religion, and Schools: Reflections on *Pierce*, 70 Years Later, 27 Seton Hall L. Rev. 1194, 1203 (1997).

Other writings about *Meyer* and *Pierce* include Clement E. Vose, Constitutional Change: Amendment Politics and Supreme Court Litigation Since 1900, ch. 6 (1972); Jay S. Bybee, Substantive Due Process and the Free Exercise of Religion: *Meyer, Pierce* and the Origins of *Wisconsin v. Yoder*, 25 Cap. U. L. Rev. 887 (1996); William G. Ross, A Judicial Janus: *Meyer v. Nebraska* in Historical Perspective, 57 U. Cin. L. Rev. 125 (1988).

3. *The structure of public elementary and secondary education. Pierce* concerned state compulsory education statutes, which require children to attend school until they reach their mid-teen years, usually sixteen. Parents have three basic choices when determining the education their children will receive. Children may attend public schools, ordinarily pursuant to a right to free public education granted in the state constitution. *Pierce* guarantees the right of parents to place their children in sectarian or nonsectarian private schools. Parents may also opt for home schooling, where children are taught at home by their parents or other adults under guidelines established by state statute and administrative regulations.

In recent years, growing numbers of parents have chosen home schooling. Some parents use this alternative to provide their children a religious-based education; others wish to provide more specialized education that public schools may not be able to provide, or to avoid violence, drugs and other such influences in public schools. See, e.g., Steve Stecklow, Class Revolution—The Rebellion Against Public Schools, Wall St. J., May 10, 1994, at 1; Barbara Kantrowitz and Debra Rosenberg, In a Class of Their Own, Newsweek, Jan. 10, 1994, at 58.

b. The Movement Toward "Children's Rights"

After *Meyer* and *Pierce*, American jurisprudence gradually began to recognize that children hold constitutional rights. As you read this section's decisions, identify what rights of children the Supreme Court recognizes and consider how these rights differ from the rights of adults. Consider too whether the Court's recognition of children's rights imposes concomitant responsibilities on their parents or the government.

PRINCE v. MASSACHUSETTS

Supreme Court of the United States, 1944.
321 U.S. 158.

MR. JUSTICE RUTLEDGE delivered the opinion of the Court.

The case brings for review another episode in the conflict between Jehovah's Witnesses and state authority. This time Sarah Prince appeals from convictions for violating Massachusetts' child labor laws, by acts said to be a rightful exercise of her religious convictions.

When the offenses were committed she was the aunt and custodian of Betty M. Simmons, a girl nine years of age. [The state Supreme Judicial Court affirmed the aunt's conviction for violating the state child labor law. The question before the Supreme Court is whether that law, "as applied, contravene[d] the Fourteenth Amendment by denying or abridging appellant's freedom of religion and by denying to her the equal protection of the laws."].

Sections 80 and 81 form parts of Massachusetts' comprehensive child labor law. They provide methods for enforcing the prohibitions of Section 69, which is as follows:

"No boy under twelve and no girl under eighteen shall sell, expose or offer for sale any newspapers, magazines, periodicals or any other articles of merchandise of any description, or exercise the trade of bootblack or scavenger, or any other trade, in any street or public place."

Section 80 and 81, so far as pertinent, read:

"Whoever furnishes or sells to any minor any article of any description with the knowledge that the minor intends to sell such article in violation of any provision of sections sixty-nine to seventy-three, inclusive, or after having received written notice to this effect from any officer charged with the enforcement thereof, or knowingly procures or encourages any minor to violate any provisions of said sections, shall be punished by a fine of not less than ten nor more than two hundred dollars or by imprisonment for not more than two months, or both."

"Any parent, guardian or custodian having a minor under his control who compels or permits such minor to work in violation of any provision of sections sixty to seventy-four, inclusive, * * * shall for a first offence be punished by a fine of not less than two nor more than ten dollars or by imprisonment for not more than five days, or both; * * *."

* * * Mrs. Prince, living in Brockton, is the mother of two young sons. She also has legal custody of Betty Simmons who lives with them. The children too are Jehovah's Witnesses and both Mrs. Prince and Betty testified they were ordained ministers. The former was accustomed to go each week on the streets of Brockton to distribute "Watchtower" and "Consolation," according to the usual plan. She had permitted the children to engage in this activity previously, and had been warned

against doing so by the school attendance officer, Mr. Perkins. But, until December 18, 1941, she generally did not take them with her at night.

That evening, as Mrs. Prince was preparing to leave her home, the children asked to go. She at first refused. Childlike, they resorted to tears and, motherlike, she yielded. Arriving downtown, Mrs. Prince permitted the children "to engage in the preaching work with her upon the sidewalks." That is, with specific reference to Betty, she and Mrs. Prince took positions about twenty feet apart near a street intersection. Betty held up in her hand, for passersby to see, copies of "Watch Tower" and "Consolation." From her shoulder hung the usual canvas magazine bag, on which was printed "Watchtower and Consolation 5 cents per copy." No one accepted a copy from Betty that evening and she received no money. Nor did her aunt. But on other occasions, Betty had received funds and given out copies.

Mrs. Prince and Betty remained until 8:45 p.m. A few minutes before this Mr. Perkins approached Mrs. Prince. A discussion ensued. He inquired and she refused to give Betty's name. However, she stated the child attended the Shaw School. Mr. Perkins referred to his previous warnings and said he would allow five minutes for them to get off the street. Mrs. Prince admitted she supplied Betty with the magazines and said, "(N)either you nor anybody else can stop me * * *. This child is exercising her God-given right and her constitutional right to preach the gospel, and no creature has a right to interfere with God's commands." However, Mrs. Prince and Betty departed. She remarked as she went, "I'm not going through this any more. We've been through it time and time again. I'm going home and put the little girl to bed." It may be added that testimony, by Betty, her aunt and others, was offered at the trials, and was excluded, to show that Betty believed it was her religious duty to perform this work and failure would bring condemnation "to everlasting destruction at Armageddon."

* * *

Appellant * * * rests squarely on freedom of religion under the First Amendment, applied by the Fourteenth to the states. She buttresses this foundation, however, with a claim of parental right as secured by the due process clause of the latter Amendment. *Cf. Meyer* v. *Nebraska.* These guaranties, she thinks, guard alike herself and the child in what they have done. Thus, two claimed liberties are at stake. One is the parent's, to bring up the child in the way he should go, which for appellant means to teach him the tenets and the practices of their faith. The other freedom is the child's, to observe these; and among them is "to preach the gospel * * * by public distribution" of "Watchtower" and "Consolation," in conformity with the scripture: "A little child shall lead them."

* * *

To make accommodation between these freedoms and an exercise of state authority always is delicate. It hardly could be more so than in such a clash as this case presents. On one side is the obviously earnest claim for freedom of conscience and religious practice. With it is allied the parent's claim to authority in her own household and in the rearing of her children. The parent's conflict with the state over control of the child and his training is serious enough when only secular matters are concerned. It becomes the more so when an element of religious conviction enters. Against these sacred private interests, basic in a democracy, stand the interests of society to protect the welfare of children, and the state's assertion of authority to that end, made here in a manner conceded valid if only secular things were involved. The last is no mere corporate concern of official authority. It is the interest of youth itself, and of the whole community, that children be both safeguarded from abuses and given opportunities for growth into free and independent well-developed men and citizens. Between contrary pulls of such weight, the safest and most objective recourse is to the lines already marked out, not precisely but for guides, in narrowing the no man's land where this battle has gone on.

The rights of children to exercise their religion, and of parents to give them religious training and to encourage them in the practice of religious belief, as against preponderant sentiment and assertion of state power voicing it, have had recognition here, most recently in *West Virginia State Board of Education* v. *Barnette*. Previously in *Pierce* v. *Society of Sisters*, this Court had sustained the parent's authority to provide religious with secular schooling, and the child's right to receive it, as against the state's requirement of attendance at public schools. And in *Meyer* v. *Nebraska*, children's rights to receive teaching in languages other than the nation's common tongue were guarded against the state's encroachment. It is cardinal with us that the custody, care and nurture of the child reside first in the parents, whose primary function and freedom include preparation for obligations the state can neither supply nor hinder. *Pierce* v. *Society of Sisters*. And it is in recognition of this that these decisions have respected the private realm of family life which the state cannot enter.

But the family itself is not beyond regulation in the public interest, as against a claim of religious liberty. And neither rights of religion nor rights of parenthood are beyond limitation. Acting to guard the general interest in youth's well being, the state as *parens patriae* may restrict the parent's control by requiring school attendance, regulating or prohibiting the child's labor, and in many other ways. Its authority is not nullified merely because the parent grounds his claim to control the child's course of conduct on religion or conscience. Thus, he cannot claim freedom from compulsory vaccination for the child more than for himself on religious grounds. The right to practice religion freely does not include liberty to expose the community or the child to communicable disease or the latter to ill health or death. The catalogue need not be lengthened. It is sufficient to show what indeed appellant hardly disputes, that the state has a wide range of power for limiting parental freedom and authority in things affecting the child's welfare; and that this includes, to some extent, matters of conscience and religious conviction.

* * *

Concededly a statute or ordinance identical in terms with Section 69, except that it is applicable to adults or all persons generally, would be invalid. But the mere fact a state could not wholly prohibit this form of adult activity, whether characterized locally as a "sale" or otherwise, does not mean it cannot do so for children. Such a conclusion granted would mean that a state could impose no greater limitation upon child labor than upon adult labor. Or, if an adult were free to enter dance halls, saloons, and disreputable places generally, in order to discharge his conceived religious duty to admonish or dissuade persons from frequenting such places, so would be a child with similar convictions and objectives, if not alone then in the parent's company, against the state's command.

The state's authority over children's activities is broader than over like actions of adults. This is peculiarly true of public activities and in matters of employment. A democratic society rests, for its continuance, upon the healthy, well-rounded growth of young people into full maturity as citizens, with all that implies. It may secure this against impeding restraints and dangers, within a broad range of selection. Among evils most appropriate for such action are the crippling effects of child employment, more especially in public places, and the possible harms arising from other activities subject to all the diverse influences of the street. It is too late now to doubt that legislation appropriately designed to reach such evils is within the state's police power, whether against the parents claim to control of the child or one that religious scruples dictate contrary action.

It is true children have rights, in common with older people, in the primary use of highways. But even in such use streets afford dangers for them not affecting adults. And in other uses, whether in work or in other things, this difference may be magnified. This is so not only when children are unaccompanied but certainly to some extent when they are with their parents. What may be wholly permissible for adults therefore may not be so for children, either with or without their parents' presence.

Street preaching, whether oral or by handing out literature, is not the primary use of the highway, even for adults. While for them it cannot be wholly prohibited, it can be regulated within reasonable limits in accommodation to the primary and other incidental uses. But, for obvious reasons, notwithstanding appellant's contrary view, the validity of such a prohibition applied to children not accompanied by an older person hardly would seem open to question. The case reduces itself therefore to the question whether the presence of the child's guardian puts a limit to the state's power. That fact may lessen the likelihood that some evils the legislation seeks to avert will occur. But it cannot forestall all of them. The zealous though lawful exercise of the right to engage in propagandizing the community, whether in religious, political or other matters, may and at times does create situations difficult enough for adults to cope with and wholly inappropriate for children, especially of tender years, to face. Other harmful possibilities could be stated, of emotional excitement and psychological or physical injury. Parents may be free to become martyrs themselves. But it does not follow they are free, in identical circumstances, to make martyrs of their children before they have reached the age of full and legal discretion when they can make that choice for themselves. Massachusetts has determined that an absolute prohibition, though one limited to streets and public places and to the incidental uses proscribed, is necessary to accomplish its legitimate objectives. Its power to attain them is broad enough to reach these peripheral instances in which the parent's supervision may reduce but cannot eliminate entirely the ill effects of the prohibited conduct. We think that with reference to the public proclaiming of religion, upon the streets and in other similar public places, the power of the state to control the conduct of children reaches beyond the scope of its authority over adults, as is true in the case of other freedoms, and the rightful boundary of its power has not been crossed in this case.

In so ruling we dispose also of appellant's argument founded upon denial of equal protection. It falls with that based on denial of religious freedom, since in this instance the one is but another phrasing of the other. Shortly, the contention is that the street, for Jehovah's Witnesses and their children, is their church, since their conviction makes it so; and to deny them access to it for religious purposes as was done here has the same effect as excluding altar boys, youthful choristers, and other children from the edifices in which they practice their religious beliefs and worship. The argument hardly needs more than statement, after what has been said, to refute it. However Jehovah's Witnesses may conceive them, the public highways have not become their religious property merely by their assertion. And there is no denial of equal protection in excluding their children from doing there what no other children may do.

Our ruling does not extend beyond the facts the case presents. We neither lay the foundation "for any [that is, every] state intervention in the indoctrination and participation of children in religion" which may be done "in the name of their health and welfare" nor give warrant for "every limitation on their religious training and activities." The religious training and indoctrination of children may be accomplished in many ways, some of which, as we have noted, have received constitutional protection through decisions of this Court. These and all others except the public proclaiming of religion on the streets, if this may be taken as either training or indoctrination of the proclaimer, remain unaffected by the decision.

The judgment is affirmed.

[The opinions of Justices Jackson, Roberts, Frankfurter and Murphy are omitted.]

Notes and Questions

1. *Weighing the interests (again).* (a) What weight did *Prince* give the respective interests of the government, parents and children?,

(b) Why did the government fare better in *Prince* than in *Meyer* or *Pierce*?,

(c) If a parent wishes to allow his or her child to sell newspapers or magazines on the street corner after dark, why should the state have authority to forbid this behavior?

2. Meyer *and* Pierce *redux. Prince* states that in *Meyer,* "children's rights to receive teaching in languages other than the nation's common tongue were guarded against the state's encroachment." *Prince* further states that *Pierce* "sustained the parent's authority to provide religious with secular schooling, *and the child's right to receive it,* as against the state's requirement of attendance at public schools" (emphasis added). Did *Meyer* or *Pierce* articulate any such constitutional rights of the child?

3. *Prince's legacy.* Does *Prince* explicitly state that children hold rights under the federal Constitution? What rights do children hold in disputes with the government? Does *Prince* give children rights in disputes with their parents? Does the decision impose new responsibilities on parents?

Neither the Constitution nor the Bill of Rights speaks explicitly about children's rights, and nothing in the proceedings of the Constitutional Convention or the ensuing ratification debates indicates that the Founders or the states ever considered such rights. Silence is interesting because several colonial charters and bills of rights did address children's legal capacity, their standing in civil and criminal proceedings, their inheritance rights, their treatment by parents, and their education. The debates that produced the Civil War Amendments similarly yield no evidence that children's interests received any attention. See Homer H. Clark, Jr., Children and the Constitution, 1992 U. Ill. L. Rev. 1, 1–2.

Professor Clark advances two reasons why children received no explicit attention when the federal Constitution was drafted. "The most obvious is that it never occurred to the Framers that children, as distinguished from adults, needed constitutional status. The assumption may well have been that common-law parental power and authority over children, reinforced by parental affection and concern, were sufficient to protect the children's interests." He also suggests that federal constitutional silence about children stemmed from the doctrine that "states, rather than the federal government, should regulate the relationship of parent and child." Id. at 2.

After *Prince* the Supreme Court has never again questioned the core proposition that children, like parents and the government, have rights and interests entitled to consideration in matters concerning their welfare. The central issues now are the weight the child's interest receives in a particular circumstance, whether children may articulate their interest personally or through a parent or non-parent committed to representing the child, and whether children's claims may prevail over parental opposition. Does *Prince* yield any clues about the answers to these questions?

4. Prince's *antecedents*. Historians have chronicled World War II's profound effect on the evolution of civil rights in our nation. *Prince* numbered children among the nation's rightsholders.

Prince cited West Virginia State Bd. of Educ. v. Barnette, 319 U.S. 624 (1943). On a finding that "national unity is the basis of national security" barely a month after the Japanese attack on Pearl Harbor, the state board of education ordered all public school teachers and pupils to salute the flag and recite the Pledge of Allegiance each day. Students who refused to participate were subject to expulsion, delinquency proceedings and confinement in "reformatories maintained for criminally inclined juveniles"; their parents were subject to fine and imprisonment for causing delinquency. Id. at 629–30. *Barnette* held that the state order violated the First and Fourteenth amendments. The Court took the unusual step of overruling an 8–1 decision it had handed down only four years earlier, Minersville Sch. Dist. v. Gobitis, 310 U.S. 586 (1939).

Barnette was a suit by parents on behalf of themselves and their children. The challenged state order had already resulted in imposition of sanctions against parents and children alike. The Court was keenly aware that children were involved: "Neither our domestic tranquility nor our martial effort in war," wrote concurring Justices Black and Douglas, "depend on compelling little children to participate in a ceremony which ends in nothing for them but a fear of spiritual condemnation." 319 U.S. at 644. The majority opinion, however, failed to specify whether the constitutional rights vindicated were held by the children themselves, by their parents, or both.

Prince, *Gobitis* and *Barnette* were appeals by members of the Jehovah's Witnesses, an unpopular religious minority often before the Court during the period. See, e.g., Merlin Newton, Armed With the Constitution: Jehovah's Witnesses in Alabama and the U.S. Supreme Court, 1939–1946 (1995); John T. Noonan, Jr., The Lustre of Our Country: The American Experience of Religious Freedom 241–44 (1998).

5. Prince, *child labor laws and other state constitutional guarantees*. *Prince* remains the Supreme Court's leading decision upholding state authority under the federal Constitution to enact child labor legislation. *Prince* did not close the door, however, to suits alleging that state child labor laws violate state constitutional guarantees. Courts have rejected various challenges to state child labor legislation under the federal and state constitutions. See, e.g., City of Portland v. Thornton, 149 P.2d 972 (Or.1944) (five months after *Prince*, affirming conviction of Jehovah's Witness for permitting her ten-year-old daughter to accompany her and sell the group's magazines on a public street in violation of the state child labor act; holding that application of the child labor act did not violate the state constitution's religious freedom guarantees).

PROBLEM 1–2

You are a young lawyer in a medium-sized law firm. Toward the end of a busy day, Daniel and Mary Peters walk in and ask to speak with someone in the firm. They explain that they fear they are in danger of losing custody of their child Donald, who suffers from leukemia. The child has been a patient at a local hospital, which has just reported to the state Department of Family Services that he may be a victim of neglect. The hospital reported after the parents refused to consent to chemotherapy for Donald. A neglect petition has been filed in juvenile court. If the court finds the child neglected, it may order protective remedies. These remedies may include ordering medical treatment, or even removing Donald from the parents' custody temporarily or permanently.

You quickly peruse the state statutes. "Neglect" means "the failure to provide, by those responsible for the care, custody, and control of the child, the proper or necessary * * * medical, surgical, or any other care necessary for the child's well-being." You sense that this definition vests considerable discretion in the court. Using the materials presented in this chapter thus far, formulate answers to the following questions:

1) Whose interests should the court weigh in reaching its decision? What is the nature of each interest, and why is each one entitled to consideration?

2) What weight should the court give to each interest?

3) What arguments would you raise on the parents' behalf? What arguments would you make if you represented Donald? What arguments would you anticipate from the Department of Family Services?

4) To help formulate your answers, what further facts would you seek to elicit from the Peters'?

A NOTE ABOUT BROWN v. BOARD OF EDUCATION (1954) AND IN RE GAULT (1967)

A decade after *Prince*, Brown v. Board of Educ., 347 U.S. 483 (1954), unanimously held that racial segregation in the public schools denies equal protection guaranteed by the Fourteenth Amendment. The named plaintiffs were the school children themselves, suing through their legal representatives. Id. at 486 n.1. The Court decided the consolidated cases on the premise that the rights vindicated were held by the children, and not by their parents: "[S]egregation of children in public schools solely on the basis of race, even though the physical facilities and other 'tangible' factors may be equal, deprive[s] the children of the minority group of equal educational opportunities." Id. at 493.

Four years later, Cooper v. Aaron, 358 U.S. 1 (1958), reiterated that *Brown* had squarely vindicated the rights of the children themselves. *Cooper* rejected efforts by Arkansas' governor and legislature to delay implementation of *Brown* amid violence that led President Eisenhower to send federal troops and then federalize the National Guard to assure safe admission of black students to the previously segregated public high school. In an opinion signed by the entire Court, *Cooper* stated that "delay in any guise in order to deny the constitutional rights of Negro children could not be countenanced," and that "law and order are not here to be preserved by depriving the Negro children of their constitutional rights." Id. at 7, 16.

Thirteen years after *Brown*, the Court decided In re Gault, 387 U.S. 1 (1967) [infra p. 1125], its most celebrated juvenile law decision. The juvenile court had adjudicated fifteen-year-old Gerald Gault delinquent for making lewd telephone calls to a neighbor and had committed him to the state industrial school until the age of twenty-one. The Supreme Court reversed on the ground that the trial court's adjudicatory procedures did not comport with due process.

Writing for *Gault's* majority, Justice Abe Fortas stated explicitly that "neither the Fourteenth Amendment nor the Bill of Rights is for adults alone." Id. at 13. By thus holding that children are persons under the Fourteenth Amendment, the Court expressly overcame the Constitution's failure to explicitly mention children. *Gault* mandated specified due process rights during the adjudicatory phase of any delinquency proceeding which might result in secure detention. The Court held (1) that alleged delinquents and their parents must be given particularized notice of the proceedings sufficiently in advance to permit them reasonable opportunity to prepare, (2) that alleged delinquents and their parents must be notified of the child's right to be represented by retained counsel or, if they are unable to afford counsel, by counsel appointed to represent the child, (3) that the alleged delinquents enjoy the privilege against compulsory self-incrimination, and (4) that absent a valid confession, an order committing a delinquent to a state institution must be based on sworn testimony subject to the opportunity for cross-examination.

Gault undermined the state's parens patriae authority to exercise informal discretion virtually free of procedural guarantees available to adults charged with criminal conduct. Concluding that parens patriae had been "a great help to those who sought to rationalize the exclusion of juveniles from the constitutional scheme," *Gault* imposed due process constraints because "unbridled discretion, however benevolently motivated, is frequently a poor substitute for principle and procedure." Id. at 16, 18.

Brown and *Gault* were watershed decisions for reasons that transcend their precise holdings. *Meyer* and *Pierce* had perceived the underlying disputes as pitting the government against the parents; *Prince* had signaled a new direction; *Brown* and *Gault* explicitly framed the disputes as pitting the government against the child and then vindicated the child's position. *Brown* vindicated children's substantive constitutional rights, and *Gault* vindicated their procedural constitutional rights. *Brown* and *Gault* together established that children hold constitutional rights in disputes with the government. In Planned Parenthood v. Danforth, 428 U.S. 52, 74 (1976), for example, the Court spoke unequivocally: "Constitutional rights do not mature and come into being magically only when one attains the state-defined age of majority. Minors, as well as adults, are protected by the Constitution and possess constitutional rights."

To decide that children hold constitutional rights is not necessarily to decide that the rights are coextensive with the constitutional rights held by adults. *Danforth* made the point: "The Court * * * long has recognized that the State has somewhat broader authority to regulate the activities of children than of adults." Id. The next several decisions continue to refine the status, rights and obligations of children.

TINKER v. DES MOINES INDEPENDENT COMMUNITY SCHOOL DISTRICT

Supreme Court of the United States, 1969.
393 U.S. 503.

Mr. Justice Fortas delivered the opinion of the Court.

Petitioner John F. Tinker, 15 years old, and petitioner Christopher Eckhardt, 16 years old, attended high schools in Des Moines, Iowa. Petitioner Mary Beth Tinker, John's sister, was a 13–year-old student in junior high school.

In December 1965, a group of adults and students in Des Moines held a meeting at the Eckhardt home. The group determined to publicize their objections to the hostilities in Vietnam and their support for a truce by wearing black armbands during the holiday season and by fasting on December 16 and New Year's Eve. Petitioners and their parents had previously engaged in similar activities, and they decided to participate in the program.

The principals of the Des Moines schools became aware of the plan to wear armbands. On December 14, 1965, they met and adopted a policy that any student wearing an armband to school would be asked to remove it, and if he refused he would be suspended until he returned without the armband. Petitioners were aware of the regulation that the school authorities adopted.

On December 16, Mary Beth and Christopher wore black armbands to their schools. John Tinker wore his armband the next day. They were all sent home and suspended from school until they would come back without their armbands. They did not return to school until after the planned period for wearing armbands had expired—that is, until after New Year's Day.

[The district court dismissed the complaint for an injunction enjoining the school officials and the school district from disciplining the children. The Eighth Circuit en banc affirmed by an equally divided court.]. We granted certiorari.

I.

The District Court recognized that the wearing of an armband for the purpose of expressing certain views is the type of symbolic act that is within the Free Speech Clause of the First Amendment. As we shall discuss, the wearing of armbands in the circumstances of this case was entirely divorced from actually or potentially disruptive conduct by those participating in it. It was closely akin to "pure speech" which, we have repeatedly held, is entitled to comprehensive protection under the First Amendment.

First Amendment rights, applied in light of the special characteristics of the school environment, are available to teachers and students. It can hardly be argued that either students or teachers shed their constitutional rights to freedom of speech or expression at the schoolhouse gate. This has been the unmistakable holding of this Court for almost 50 years. In *Meyer* v. *Nebraska* * * *, this Court * * * held that the Due Process Clause of the Fourteenth Amendment prevents States from forbidding the teaching of a foreign language to young students. Statutes to this effect, the Court held, unconstitutionally interfere with the liberty of teacher, student, and parent. See also *Pierce* v. *Society of Sisters*.

* * *

On the other hand, the Court has repeatedly emphasized the need for affirming the comprehensive authority of the States and of school officials, consistent with fundamental constitutional safeguards, to prescribe and control conduct in the schools. Our problem lies in the area where students in the exercise of First Amendment rights collide with the rules of the school authorities.

II.

The problem posed by the present case does not relate to regulation of the length of skirts or the type of clothing, to hair style, or deportment. It does not concern aggressive, disruptive action or even group demonstrations. Our problem involves direct, primary First Amendment rights akin to "pure speech."

The school officials banned and sought to punish petitioners for a silent, passive expression of opinion, unaccompanied by any disorder or disturbance on the part of petitioners. There is here no evidence whatever of petitioners' interference, actual or nascent, with the schools' work or of collision with the rights of other students to be secure and to be let alone. Accordingly, this case does not concern speech or action that intrudes upon the work of the schools or the rights of other students.

Only a few of the 18,000 students in the school system wore the black armbands. Only five students were suspended for wearing them. There is no indication that the work of the schools or any class was disrupted. Outside the classrooms, a few students made hostile remarks to the children wearing armbands, but there were no threats or acts of violence on school premises.

The District Court concluded that the action of the school authorities was reasonable because it was based upon their fear of disturbance from the wearing of the armbands. But, in our system, undifferentiated fear or apprehension of disturbance is not enough to overcome the right to freedom of expression. Any departure from absolute regimentation may cause trouble. Any variation from the majority's opinion may inspire fear. Any word spoken, in class, in the lunchroom, or on the campus, that deviates from the views of another person may start an argument or cause a disturbance. But our Constitution says we must take this risk; and our history says that it is this sort of hazardous freedom—this kind of openness—that is the basis of our national strength and of the independence and vigor of Americans who grow up and live in this relatively permissive, often disputatious, society.

In order for the State in the person of school officials to justify prohibition of a particular expression of opinion, it must be able to show that its action was caused by something more than a mere desire to avoid the discomfort and unpleasantness that always accompany an unpopular viewpoint. Certainly where there is no finding and no showing that engaging in the forbidden conduct would "materially and substantially interfere with the requirements of appropriate discipline in the operation of the school," the prohibition cannot be sustained.

In the present case, the District Court made no such finding, and our independent examination of the record fails to yield evidence that the school authorities had reason to anticipate that the wearing of the armbands would substantially interfere with the work of the school or impinge upon the rights of other students. Even an official memorandum prepared after the suspension that listed the reasons for the ban on wearing the armbands made no reference to the anticipation of such disruption.

On the contrary, the action of the school authorities appears to have been based upon an urgent wish to avoid the controversy which might result from the expression, even by the silent symbol of armbands, of opposition to this Nation's part in the conflagration in Vietnam. * * *

It is also relevant that the school authorities did not purport to prohibit the wearing of all symbols of political or controversial significance. The record shows that students in some of the schools wore buttons relating to national political campaigns, and some even wore the Iron Cross, traditionally a symbol of Nazism. The order prohibiting the wearing of armbands did not extend to these. Instead, a particular symbol—black armbands worn to exhibit opposition to this Nation's involvement in Vietnam—was singled out for prohibition. Clearly, the prohibition of expression of one particular opinion, at least without evidence that it is necessary to avoid material and substantial interference with schoolwork or discipline, is not constitutionally permissible.

In our system, state-operated schools may not be enclaves of totalitarianism. School officials do not possess absolute authority over their students. Students in school as well as out of school are "persons" under our Constitution. They are possessed of fundamental rights which the State must respect, just as they themselves must respect their obligations to the State. In our system, students may not be regarded as closed-circuit recipients of only that which the State chooses to communicate. They may not be confined to the expression of those sentiments that are officially approved. In the absence of a specific showing of constitutionally valid reasons to regulate their speech, students are entitled to freedom of expression of their views. * * *

In *Meyer* v. *Nebraska*, Mr. Justice McReynolds expressed this Nation's repudiation of the principle that a State might so conduct its schools as to "foster a homogeneous people." * * * In *Keyishian* v. *Board of Regents* [in 1967], MR. JUSTICE BRENNAN, speaking for the Court, said:

> " 'The vigilant protection of constitutional freedoms is nowhere more vital than in the community of American schools.' * * * The classroom is peculiarly the 'marketplace of ideas.' The Nation's future depends upon leaders trained through wide exposure to that robust exchange of ideas which discovers truth 'out of a multitude of tongues, [rather] than through any kind of authoritative selection."

The principle of these cases is not confined to the supervised and ordained discussion which takes place in the classroom. The principal use to which the schools are dedicated is to accommodate students during prescribed hours for the purpose of certain types of activities. Among those activities is personal intercommunication among the students. This is not only an inevitable part of the process of attending school; it is also an important part of the educational process. A student's rights, therefore, do not embrace merely the classroom hours. When he is in the cafeteria, or on the playing field, or on the campus during the authorized hours, he may express his opinions, even on controversial subjects like the conflict in Vietnam, if he does so without "materially and substantially interfer[ing] with the requirements of appropriate discipline in the operation of the school" and without colliding with the rights of others. But conduct by the student, in class or out of it, which for any reason—whether it stems from time, place, or type of behavior—materially disrupts classwork or involves substantial disorder or invasion of the rights of others is, of course, not immunized by the constitutional guarantee of freedom of speech.

Under our Constitution, free speech is not a right that is given only to be so circumscribed that it exists in principle but not in fact. Freedom of expression would not truly exist if the right could be exercised only in an area that a benevolent government has provided as a safe haven for crackpots. The Constitution says that Congress (and the States) may not abridge the right to free speech. This provision means what it says. We properly read it to permit reasonable regulation of speech-connected activities in carefully restricted circumstances. But we do not confine the permissible exercise of First Amendment rights to a telephone booth or the four corners of a pamphlet, or to supervised and ordained discussion in a school classroom.

If a regulation were adopted by school officials forbidding discussion of the Vietnam conflict, or the expression by any student of opposition to it anywhere on school property except as part of a prescribed classroom exercise, it would be obvious that the regulation would violate the constitutional rights of students, at least if it could not be justified by a showing that the students' activities would materially and substantially disrupt the work and discipline of the school. In the circumstances of the present case, the prohibition of the silent, passive 'witness of the armbands,' as one of the children called it, is no less offensive to the constitution's guarantees.

As we have discussed, the record does not demonstrate any facts which might reasonably have led school authorities to forecast substantial disruption of or material interference with school activities, and no disturbances or disorders on the school premises in fact occurred. These petitioners merely went about their ordained rounds in school. Their deviation consisted only in wearing on their sleeve a band of black cloth, not more than two inches wide. They wore it to exhibit their disapproval of the Vietnam hostilities and their advocacy of a truce, to make their views known, and, by their example, to influence others to adopt them. They neither interrupted school activities nor sought to intrude in the school affairs or the lives of others. They caused discussion outside of the classrooms, but no interference with work and no disorder. In the circumstances, our Constitution does not permit officials of the State to deny their form of expression.

* * *

Reversed and remanded.

[Mr. Justice Stewart's and Mr. Justice White's concurring opinions are omitted.]

MR. JUSTICE BLACK, dissenting.

The Court's holding in this case ushers in what I deem to be an entirely new era in which the power to control pupils by the elected "officials of state supported public schools * * *" in the United States is in ultimate effect transferred to the Supreme Court. The Court brought this particular case here on a petition for certiorari urging that the First and Fourteenth Amendments protect the right of school pupils to express their political views all the way "from kindergarten through high school." Here the constitutional right to "political expression" asserted was a right to wear black armbands during school hours and at classes in order to demonstrate to the other students that the petitioners were mourning because of the death of United States soldiers in Vietnam and to protest that war which they were against. Ordered to refrain from wearing the armbands in school by the elected school officials and the teachers vested with state authority to do so, apparently only seven out of the school system's 18,000 pupils deliberately refused to obey the order. One defying pupil was Paul Tinker, 8 years old, who was in the second grade; another, Hope Tinker, was 11 years old and in the fifth grade; a third member of the Tinker family was 13, in the eighth grade; and a fourth member of the same family was John Tinker, 15 years old, an 11th grade high school pupil. Their father, a Methodist minister without a church, is paid a salary by the American Friends Service Committee. Another student who defied the school order and insisted on wearing an armband in school was Christopher Eckhardt, an 11th grade pupil and a petitioner in this case. His mother is an official in the Women's International League for Peace and Freedom.

* * *

Assuming that the Court is correct in holding that the conduct of wearing armbands for the purpose of conveying political ideas is protected by the First Amendment, the crucial remaining questions are whether students and teachers may use the schools at their whim as a platform for the exercise of free speech—"symbolic" or "pure"—and whether the courts will allocate to themselves the function of deciding how the pupils' school day will be spent. While I have always believed that under the First and Fourteenth Amendments neither the State nor the Federal Government has any authority to regulate or censor the content of speech, I have never believed that any person has a right to give speeches or engage in demonstrations where he pleased and when he pleases. * * *

* * *

While the record does not show that any of these armband students shouted, used profane language, or were violent in any manner, detailed testimony by some of them shows their armbands caused comments, warnings by other students, the poking of fun at them, and a warning by an older football player that other, nonprotesting students had better let them alone. There is also evidence that a teacher of mathematics had his lesson period practically "wrecked" chiefly by disputes with Mary Beth Tinker, who wore her armband for her "demonstration." Even a casual reading of the record shows that this armband did divert students' minds from their regular lessons, and that talk, comments, etc., made John Tinker "self-conscious" in attending school with his armband. While the absence of obscene remarks or boisterous and loud disorder perhaps justifies the Court's statement that the few armband students did not actually "disrupt" the classwork, I think the record overwhelmingly shows that the armbands did exactly what the elected school officials and principals foresaw they would, that is, took the students' minds off their classwork and diverted them to thoughts about the highly emotional subject of the Vietnam war. And I repeat that if the time has come when pupils of state-supported schools, kindergartens, grammar schools, or high schools, can defy and flout orders of school officials to keep their minds on their own schoolwork, it is the beginning of a new revolutionary era of permissiveness in this country fostered by the judiciary. * * *

I deny, therefore, that it has been the "unmistakable holding of this Court for almost 50 years" that "students" and "teachers" take with them into the "schoolhouse gate" constitutional rights to "freedom of speech or expression." Even *Meyer* did not hold that. * * * In fact, I think the majority's reason for invalidating the Nebraska law was that it did not like it * * *.

* * *

In my view, teachers in state-controlled public schools are hired to teach there. Although Mr. Justice McReynolds may have intimated to the contrary in *Meyer* v. *Nebraska*, certainly a teacher is not paid to go into school and teach subjects the State does not hire him to teach as a part of its selected curriculum. Nor are public school students sent to the schools at public expense to broadcast political or any other views to educate and inform the public. The original idea of schools, which I do not believe is yet abandoned as worthless or out of date, was that children had not yet reached the point of experience and wisdom which enabled them to teach all of their elders. It may be that the Nation has outworn the old-fashioned slogan that "children are to be seen not heard,'" but one may, I hope, be permitted to harbor the thought that taxpayers send children to school on the premise that at their age they need to learn, not teach.

* * *

Change has been said to be truly the law of life but sometimes the old and the tried and true are worth holding. The schools of this Nation have undoubtedly contributed to giving us tranquility and to making us a more law-abiding people. Uncontrolled and uncontrollable liberty is an enemy to domestic peace. We cannot close our eyes to the fact that some of the country's greatest problems are crimes committed by the youth, too many of school age. School discipline, like parental discipline, is an integral and important part of training our children to be good citizens— to be better citizens. Here a very small number of students have crisply and summarily refused to obey a school order designed to give pupils who want to learn the opportunity to do so. One does not need to be a prophet or the son of a prophet to know that after the Court's holding today some students in Iowa schools and indeed in all schools will be ready, able, and willing to defy their teachers on practically all orders. This is the more unfortunate for the schools since groups of students all over the land are already running loose, conducting break-ins, sit-ins, lie-ins, and smash-ins. Many of these student groups, as is all too familiar to all who read the newspapers and watch the television news programs, have already engaged in rioting, property seizures, and destruction. They have picketed schools to force students not to cross their picket lines and have too often violently attacked earnest but frightened students who wanted an education that the pickets did not want them to get. Students engaged in such activities are apparently confident that they know far more about how to operate public school systems than do their parents, teachers, and elected school officials. It is no answer to say that the particular students here have not yet reached such high points in their demands to attend classes in order to exercise their political pressures. Turned loose with lawsuits for damages and injunctions against their teachers as they are here, it is nothing but wishful thinking to imagine that young, immature students will not soon believe it is their right to control the schools rather than the right of the States that collect the taxes to hire the teachers for the benefit of the pupils. This case, therefore, wholly without constitutional reasons in my judgment, subjects all the public schools in the country to the whims and caprices of their loudest-mouthed, but maybe not their brightest, students. I, for one, am not fully persuaded that school pupils are wise enough, even with this Court's expert help from Washington, to run the 23,390 public school systems in our 50 States. I wish, therefore, wholly to disclaim any purpose on my part to hold that the Federal Constitution compels the teachers, parents, and elected school officials to surrender control of the American public school system to public school students. I dissent.

MR. JUSTICE HARLAN, dissenting.

I certainly agree that state public school authorities in the discharge of their responsibilities are not wholly exempt from the requirements of the Fourteenth Amendment respecting the freedoms of expression and association. At the same time I am reluctant to believe that there is any disagreement between the majority and myself on the proposition that school officials should be accorded the widest authority in maintaining discipline and good order in their institutions. To translate that proposition into a workable constitutional rule, I would, in cases like this, cast upon those complaining the burden of showing that a particular school measure was motivated by other than legitimate school concerns—for example, a desire to prohibit the expression of an unpopular point of view, while permitting expression of the dominant opinion.

Finding nothing in this record which impugns the good faith of respondents in promulgating the armband regulation, I would affirm the judgment below.

Notes and Questions

1. *Weighing the interests (again).* Citing *Meyer* and *Pierce,* Justice Fortas states unequivocally: "It can hardly be argued that either students or teachers shed their constitutional rights to freedom of speech or expression at the schoolhouse gate. This has been the unmistakable holding of this Court for almost 50 years." Did *Meyer* or *Pierce* announce any such "unmistakable" holding?

2. *Questions about* Tinker. (a) What is *Tinker's* holding?,

   (b) Compare *Tinker's* holding with the majority opinion. Does the opinion contain much broad language (including dictum) unnecessary to the decision of the case at hand?,

   (c) Assume you are a school official who wishes to respect students' rights but also to maintain discipline and assure a safe learning environment. Does *Tinker's* majority opinion enable you to distinguish lawful measures from the unlawful? Does the opinion provide useful guidelines when student misconduct may involve drug or weapons possession on school grounds?,

(d) What insights do *Tinker's* language and rationale provide about the relative strength of children's rights in disputes with the state?,

(e) What, if anything, does *Tinker* suggest about the strength of the state's parens patriae interest in protecting children?

3. *Aftermath*. According to one historian, "[t]he three students who assumed the role of the named plaintiffs [John and Mary Beth Tinker and Christopher Eckhardt] * * * were well-scrubbed, thoughtful kids attending public schools in Des Moines, Iowa–hardly a hotbed of protest activity in the 1960s. Before the events * * * took place, none of their teachers or school officials would have characterized the three teenagers as troublemakers." John W. Johnson, The Struggle for Student Rights: *Tinker v. Des Moines* and the 1960s ix-x (1997). John Tinker, for example, played the sousaphone in the school band and the violin in the orchestra and had a paper route. Christopher Eckhardt was a Boy Scout, a student council president in his elementary and junior high schools, a student government representative in high school, a member of the school track team, and a youth leader at church. Id. at 10, 12.

The children's parents, Leonard and Lorena Jeanne Tinker and William and Margaret Eckhardt, were committed to the civil rights and antiwar movements, a commitment that outlasted the Vietnam War. In early 1991, 69–year-old Lorena Jeanne Tinker was charged with first-degree trespass for protesting the Persian Gulf War by sitting in and refusing to leave a Marine recruiting office in Columbia, Missouri. After deliberating less than an hour, the jury found her guilty but recommended a fine without imprisonment. R. Paul Holst, Jr., Activist Pays for Peace, Columbia Missourian, Oct. 18, 1991.

For other accounts of *Tinker's* background, see Peter Irons, The Courage of Their Convictions 231–52 (1988), and Doreen Rappaport, Tinker v. Des Moines (1993).

4. *Were the children's free-expression rights at stake in* Tinker? Professor Robert A. Burt intimated that "the children's armbands reflected more their parents' convictions than theirs." Robert A. Burt, Developing Constitutional Rights Of, In and For Children, 39 Law & Contemp. Probs. 118, 124 (1975). Professor Burt argued that *Tinker* "ignored the possibility that school officials might exclude parental political views from school in order to free children to think through these questions for themselves." He suggested that the outcome should have been different if the defendant school district had argued that "they were acting not to impose their political views on students, but rather on behalf of the root values of the first amendment— tolerance, diversity of thought, individual autonomy—against parental impositions on children." Id.

If the school district had indeed made this argument, would the courts have unduly intruded on family autonomy if they had speculated or taken testimony about the motives of the parents and their children? Should courts seek to protect children from their parents' ideas? If the school district had instead disciplined the children for wearing a symbol *supporting* United

States policy in Vietnam, would parental influence have been relevant in determining the children's First Amendment rights? The record indicated that Des Moines school children wore crosses and other religious symbols to school in December of 1965; should school administrators have requested the children to remove these religious symbols "to free children to think through these questions for themselves"?

5. *Justice Black.* A biographer reported that the other members of the Court were "in various stages of shock" when Justice Black read his stinging *Tinker* dissent from the bench. See Roger K. Newman, Hugo Black: A Biography 592 (2d ed. 1997). The case hit close to home while Justice Black was writing it. After oral argument, his grandson was suspended from high school for producing an underground newspaper that called the school administration " 'brutal, vicious' and 'finkos.' " Black wrote the boy's mother that "the school has done exactly right * * *. The time has come in this country when it must be known that children cannot run the school which they attend at government expense." Id.

Justice Black "had become increasingly crotchety in his eighties and had lost his patience with the younger generation." Peter Irons, The Courage of Their Convictions 241 (1988). Sitting as a Circuit Justice shortly before his death in 1971, he denied a motion to vacate a stay of a district court order that had enjoined public school authorities from enforcing rules regarding the length of schoolboys' hair. "There can, of course, be honest differences of opinion as to whether any government, state or federal, should as a matter of public policy regulate the length of haircuts, but it would be difficult to prove by reason, logic, or common sense that the federal judiciary is more competent to deal with hair length than are the local school authorities and state legislatures of all our 50 States." Karr v. Schmidt, 401 U.S. 1201, 1203 (1971).

6. *Hair length, dress codes and school uniforms. Tinker* and its progeny have figured prominently in decisions concerning the constitutional rights of public school students in a variety of circumstances, including these:

Hair length regulations. Most of the earliest decisions concerned grooming and attire standards, particularly hair length regulations in an era when boys wore longer hair than they generally wear nowadays. Students challenging hair length regulations have invoked a variety of constitutional guarantees, most notably the First Amendment right to "symbolic speech" and the Fourteenth Amendment substantive due process interest in determining one's own appearance. The First Amendment challenges raise two questions. First, does the student's hair length constitute symbolic speech at all? If so, may school officials nonetheless enforce hair length regulations because students enjoy only diminished First Amendment protections when faced with efforts to maintain order in the schools and enhance the educational environment?

The Supreme Court has held that nonverbal conduct warrants First Amendment protection as symbolic speech where a person "intend[s] to convey a particularized message" and a great likelihood exists that "the message would be understood by those who viewed it." Spence v. Washington, 418 U.S. 405, 410–11 (1974). Government regulation affecting symbolic speech is justified only where the regulation furthers "an important or substantial governmental interest" unrelated to suppression of free expression, and where the incidental restriction on First Amendment freedoms is "no greater than is essential" to further that interest. United States v. O'Brien, 391 U.S. 367, 377 (1968).

Challenges to hair-length regulations have sharply divided the courts. A number of decisions have held that such challenges are not cognizable in the federal courts because "the federal court system is ill-equipped to make value judgments on hair lengths in terms of the Constitution" and because "the wisdom and experience of school authorities must be deemed superior and preferable to the federal judiciary's." Zeller v. Donegal Sch. Dist., 517 F.2d 600, 606–07 (3d Cir.1975) (en banc). See also, e.g., Barber v. Colorado Indep. Sch. Dist., 901 S.W.2d 447 (Tex.1995). A number of decisions have upheld the constitutionality of hair length requirements, generally rejecting efforts to invoke *Tinker* to strike down the assailed regulations for violating symbolic-speech rights. See, e.g., Kraus v. Board of Educ., 492 S.W.2d 783 (Mo.1973).

On the other hand, several decisions have struck down hair length regulations as violating students' constitutional rights. See, e.g., Holsapple v. Woods, 500 F.2d 49, 50, 52 (7th Cir. 1974) (First and Fourteenth Amendments); Massie v. Henry, 455 F.2d 779, 783 (4th Cir. 1972) (Fourteenth Amendment substantive due process interest in determining one's own appearance).

Dress codes and uniforms. In recent years, many public school districts have instituted dress codes, and a growing number have begun mandating that students wear uniforms. At least half the states have enacted legislation authorizing local school boards to adopt school dress codes or uniform policies. See, e.g., Ohio Rev. Code § 3313.665. By 1997, so many of the nation's school districts had adopted uniform policies that in many areas, uniforms "are no longer the exception, but the rule." Tamar Lewin, More Public School Pupils Now Don Uniforms, N.Y. Times, Sept. 25, 1997, at 1.

School officials defend dress code and student uniform requirements as helpful in maintaining discipline, instilling a sense of school and personal pride, weakening gangs by prohibiting children from wearing gang colors and gang insignias, and promoting a sense of safety by avoiding violence against children who wear jewelry or designer and other expensive clothing or who inadvertently wear gang colors. Dress codes and uniform requirements are also said to enable school officials to prohibit baggy pants and other clothing that might conceal weapons, to prohibit vulgar and obscene messages on clothing that detract from the educational environment, to boost the self-esteem of children whose parents cannot afford expensive clothing, and to make trespassers easier to identify on the school campus.

For their part, critics charge that the effectiveness of dress codes and uniforms is unproved, that they often operate in a racially biased fashion by banning clothing associated with minority gangs but not necessarily that associated with other gangs such as white supremacist groups, that they stifle efforts to teach students self expression, that they are often adopted in districts without widespread gang and violence problems, and that they enable politicians to embrace cost-free measures that give the appearance of action but in fact divert attention from societal and cultural causes for the distressed state of public education. Positions pro and con are discussed in Keith A. King, Should School Uniforms Be Mandated in Elementary Schools?, 68 J. Sch. Health 32 (Jan. 1998).

Courts have not determined the constitutionality of school uniform requirements, and court challenges have been blunted because many districts provide free uniforms for children of poor families and allow parents to opt out of the requirements on their children's behalf. Courts have also upheld dress code regulations prohibiting students from wearing apparel determined by school officials to be gang-related; courts find such regulations, in the words of *Tinker*, "necessary to avoid material and substantial interference with schoolwork or discipline." See, e.g., Bivens v. Albuquerque Pub. Sch., 899 F.Supp. 556 (D.N.M.1995) (upholding dress code provision prohibiting baggy pants); Jeglin v. San Jacinto Unified Sch. Dist., 827 F.Supp. 1459 (C.D.Cal.1993) (upholding high school dress code provision prohibiting apparel with collegiate or professional sport teams' insignias (said to indicate gang membership), but striking down provision in middle and elementary schools because school officials did not establish gang problem at those levels).

7. *Due process rights of public school students.* Since *Tinker*, the Court has continued to speak about the constitutional rights of schoolchildren. This note and the next two survey major decisions before the next principal case, Vernonia Sch. Dist. 47J v. Acton (1995).

Where a public school student faces suspension for misconduct, the student's procedural due process rights are "exceedingly limited." C.B. v. Driscoll, 82 F.3d 383, 385 (11th Cir.1996). In Goss v. Lopez, 419 U.S. 565 (1975), the Court held that where a state provides an entitlement to a free public education, public school students have a Fourteenth Amendment property interest in that entitlement and a liberty interest in not having their reputations sullied by suspension for less than good cause. The Court also recognized, however, that "[j]udicial interposition in the operation of the public school system * * * raises problems requiring care and restraint." 419 U.S. at 578.

When a student faces suspension for less than ten days, *Goss* requires only "an informal give-and-take between student and disciplinarian." The student must receive "oral or written notice of the charges against him and, if he denies them, an explanation of the evidence the authorities have and an opportunity to present his side of the story." "[A]s a general rule notice and hearing should precede removal of the student from school." Removal may occur before the rudimentary hearing, however, where the student's presence poses "a continuing danger to persons or property or an ongoing threat of disrupting the academic process." 419 U.S. at 581–84. The parents may present the child's side of the story. See, e.g., Meyer v. Austin Indep. Sch. Dist., 161 F.3d 271, 275 (5th Cir. 1998), cert. denied, 119 S.Ct. 1806 (1999). Discussion of the *Goss* litigation appears in Franklin E. Zimring and Rayman L. Solomon, *Goss v. Lopez*: The Principle of the Thing, in In the Interest of Children 449 (Robert H. Mnookin ed., 1985).

8. *Do children have a First Amendment "right to receive information"?* In Board of Educ. v. Pico, 457 U.S. 853 (1982) (plurality opinion), the sharply divided Court grappled with the question whether the First Amendment

limits a school board's authority to remove books from high school and junior high school libraries. Several students sued after the defendant board removed books which it characterized as "anti-American, anti-Christian, anti-Semitic, and just plain filthy." The board explained that "[i]t is our duty, our moral obligation, to protect the children in our schools from this moral danger as surely as from physical and medical dangers." Id. at 857.

Pico produced seven opinions with widely divergent views. Justice Brennan's plurality opinion (for himself and Justices Marshall and Stevens) concluded that a school board's removal of library books implicates students' First Amendment right to "receive information and ideas." Id. at 867. The plurality acknowledged that students' First Amendment rights must be construed "in light of the special characteristics of the school environment," but concluded that the board denies these rights when it acts with intent to deny students access to ideas with which the board disagrees. Id. at 871. Justice Blackmun similarly would have held that "school officials may not remove books for the *purpose* of restricting access to the political ideas or social perspectives discussed in them, when that action is motivated simply by the officials' disapproval of the ideas involved." Id. at 879–80 (Blackmun, J., concurring) (emphasis in original).

The dissenters defined the competing constitutional principles differently. To Chief Justice Burger (dissenting for himself and Justices Rehnquist, Powell and O'Connor), the case turned on "whether local schools are to be administered by elected school boards, or by federal judges and teenage pupils; and * * * whether the values of morality, good taste, and relevance to education are valid reasons for school board decisions concerning the contents of a school library." Id. at 885. "[A]s a matter of *educational policy* students should have wide access to information and ideas. But the people elect school boards, who in turn select administrators, who select the teachers, and these are the individuals best able to determine the substance of that policy." Id. at 891 (emphasis in original). Justice Rehnquist (dissenting for himself and Chief Justice Burger and Justice Powell) would also have deferred to local school boards. Id. at 914.

9. *Search and seizure.* In New Jersey v. T.L.O., 469 U.S. 325, 338 (1985), the Court signaled that the constitutional rights of children in public schools are more restricted than those of adults. *T.L.O.* held that the constitutionality of a search of a student by a school official depends on the search's reasonableness under all the circumstances, and not on probable cause. *T.L.O.* is a main case in Chapter 11, Delinquency.

10. *Distinguishing* Tinker. Once the Warren Court era passed, the Court grew uneasy with *Tinker's* broad articulation of children's rights. *Pico* highlighted the unease, with the plurality and concurrence stressing the earlier decision and the dissenters acknowledging *Tinker* but distancing themselves from it. *Tinker* was distinguished in two other decisions that held for the school authorities, Bethel School Dist. v. Fraser, 478 U.S. 675 (1986), and Hazelwood School Dist. v. Kuhlmeier, 484 U.S. 260 (1988).

a. *Fraser* upheld the three-day suspension of a high school student for making a speech laced with "pervasive sexual innuendo" during an assembly attended by 600 students. 478 U.S. at 683. The Court found a "marked distinction between the political 'message' of the armbands in *Tinker* and the sexual content" of the assembly speech. Id. at 680. *Fraser* emphasized that "the constitutional rights of students in public school are not automatically coextensive with the rights of adults in other settings": "The First Amendment guarantees wide freedom in matters of adult public discourse. * * * It does not follow, however, that simply because the use of an offensive form of expression may not be prohibited to adults making what the speaker considers a political point, the same latitude must be permitted to children in a public school." Id. at 682. "Surely it is a highly appropriate function of public school education to prohibit the use of vulgar and offensive terms in public discourse," and "[t]he determination of what manner of speech in the classroom or in school assembly is inappropriate properly rests with the school board." Id. at 683. To show how far the Court had moved from *Tinker*, *Fraser* found the penultimate sentence of Justice Black's stinging *Tinker* dissent "especially relevant" and quoted it. Id. at 686. Do courts undermine school officials' disciplinary authority by requiring the school district to litigate for three years to vindicate its suspension of a student for three days for making an assembly speech deemed vulgar and offensive, or are students' First Amendment rights sufficiently important to encourage their assertion?

Fraser has loomed large in decisions resolving constitutional challenges to suspensions of public school students for wearing T-shirts and other clothing featuring messages deemed obscene or otherwise inappropriate. A central issue has been whether the court deemed the message political (as in *Tinker*), or vulgar or obscene (as in *Fraser*). Compare, e.g., Chandler v. McMinnville Sch. Dist., 978 F.2d 524 (9th Cir. 1992) (applying *Tinker* to overturn suspensions of students for wearing buttons reading "Do Scabs Bleed?" and "I'm Not Listening Scab" to support a teachers strike), with Broussard v. School Bd., 801 F.Supp. 1526 (E.D.Va.1992) (applying *Fraser* to uphold action sending child home for wearing T-shirt reading "Drugs Suck").

b. *Kuhlmeier* upheld the defendant school district's authority to exercise editorial control over the contents of a high school newspaper produced as part of the journalism curriculum. The student staff members' suit contended that school officials had violated their First Amendment rights by deleting two articles from an issue of the paper. One article described three students' experiences with pregnancy; the second discussed the impact of divorce on students.

Beginning with the core proposition that "the First Amendment rights of students in the public schools 'are not automatically coextensive with the rights of adults in other settings' " and "must be 'applied in light of the special characteristics of the school environment,' " 484 U.S. at 266, the five-Justice *Kuhlmeier* majority reaffirmed *Tinker* but distinguished it: "The question whether the First Amendment requires a school to tolerate particular student speech—the question that we addressed in *Tinker*—is different from the question whether the First Amendment requires a school affirmatively to promote particular student speech. The former question addresses educators' ability to silence a student's personal expression that happens to occur on the school premises. The latter question concerns educators' authority over school-sponsored publications, theatrical productions, and other expressive activities that students, parents, and members of the public might reasonably perceive to bear the imprimatur of the school. These activities may fairly be characterized as part of the school curriculum, whether or not they occur in a traditional classroom setting, so long as they are supervised by faculty members and designed to impart particular knowledge or skills to student participants and audiences." Id. at 271.

Kuhlmeier held that "educators do not offend the First Amendment by exercising editorial control over the style and content of student speech in school-sponsored expressive activities so long as their actions are reasonably related to legitimate pedagogical concerns." Id. at 272. According to the Court, "the education of the Nation's youth is primarily the responsibility of parents, teachers, and state and local school officials, and not of federal judges. It is only when the decision to censor a school-sponsored publication, theatrical production, or other vehicle of student expression has no valid educational purpose that the First Amendment is so 'directly and sharply implicate[d],' as to require judicial intervention to protect students' constitutional rights." Id. at 273.

What insights do *Fraser* and *Kuhlmeier* provide about the relative strength of children's rights in disputes with the government? What continued vitality does *Tinker* have after the two decisions? Do you agree with Justice Brennan's *Kuhlmeier* dissent, which accused the majority of "abandoning *Tinker*"?

11. *School disruption.* As *Tinker's* majority viewed the record, the decision "d[id] not concern speech or action that intrudes upon the work of the schools or the rights of other students" because there was "no indication" that the student demonstration caused any disruption of the school's ordinary functioning. Since *Tinker*, lower courts have frequently read that decision as not protecting students' expressive activity where actual or potential disruption could be shown.

Some decisions have distinguished *Tinker* on the ground that school officials reasonably foresaw the likelihood of disruption or violence. "School authorities * * * are not required to wait until disorder or invasion occurs." Phillips v. Anderson County Sch. Dist. Five, 987 F.Supp. 488, 490, 492 (D.S.C.1997) (holding that school officials had reasonable basis for determining that the middle school student's Confederate flag jacket would result in substantial disruption of the educational process, and that they appropriately suspended the student for refusing to comply with the request that he remove the jacket).

If school officials may act when they reasonably foresee the likelihood of disruption, how reasonable must their foresight be? May school officials act merely because a few students might notice the silent political demonstration and pass remarks, or must some threat of violence or serious interruption of school functioning appear likely? If a low threshold of reasonableness suffices, would the exceptions swallow the *Tinker* rule?

12. *The Black and Harlan* Tinker *dissents.* Finding that "[p]arents of diverse social and economic backgrounds—white and black, wealthy and middle class—are removing their children from public schools due to concerns about order and safety," Professor Anne Proffitt Dupre believes that *Tinker* and its progeny are a major reason for the "defiance, disrespect and disorder [that are] daily occurrences in many of our public schools." Anne

Proffitt Dupre, Should Students Have Constitutional Rights? Keeping Order in the Public Schools, 65 Geo. Wash. L. Rev. 49, 50–51 (1996):

> Constitutional doctrine has made it more difficult for the public schools to reclaim the order and discipline necessary to educate students. Although the deterioration of other institutions that are important to the child—family, religion, and community—has certainly played a part in this tragedy, the Supreme Court must also accept responsibility for intervening in the day-to-day running of our nation's public schools. Researchers have inferred, not surprisingly, that the "adversarial and legalistic character of urban public schools"—qualities attributable to the Court's school jurisprudence of recent years—and the corresponding unwillingness of teachers to maintain order have affected educational quality. As other institutions were crumbling, the Court, instead of shoring up the public school as an institution, cleared the way for its decline. The Court's analysis in the school power cases has exacerbated the loss of respect, deference, and trust in the public school as an institution and has wrongly insinuated that these qualities are incompatible with liberty. Indeed, order in the schools increasingly has become "what will stand up in court."

* * *

> The chaos that has overtaken many of our public schools did not happen overnight. Serious discipline problems usually do not arise spontaneously in a school. They creep in as children realize that schools are unwilling or unable to take disciplinary action for lesser conduct. Each time that misconduct by an individual student went unquestioned because the teacher or principal was afraid that it did not meet the "substantial disruption" standard set forth by the Supreme Court [in *Tinker*], we took one more step toward the turmoil that exists in the public school community today. * * *

Id. at 50–52. Professor Dupre concludes that the ever-present threat of litigation breeds timidity that often encourages school officials to avoid imposing discipline: "The prospect of a lawsuit, with its resulting publicity, expense, and unpleasantness is hardly one that will be relished by either teacher or school administrator, even if the school and teacher are ultimately vindicated. Indeed, a threat by a student or parent, even if it is based on a groundless claim and falls short of a formal lawsuit, is an extremely disagreeable experience that most teachers and school administrators will attempt to avoid if at all possible." Id. at 94–95. Consider whether she is right that *Acton*, the next principal decision, is "a step in the right direction" because it views public schools as custodians and guardians of students. Id. at 53. Professor Dupre believes recognition of the custodian-guardian relationship will "enhance the ability of the public school to provide each student with a serious education" by "allow[ing] school officials to predict with more certainty the extent to which specific efforts to keep order are permissible." Id. at 53.

Is Professor Dupre correct that the threat of student litigation undermines efforts to maintain school discipline? What balance should be struck between school officials' interest in preserving discipline and safety, and students' interests in exercising constitutional rights? Does

Justice Black strike an appropriate balance? Under the test Justice Harlan articulated in his dissent, would school officials have greater authority to maintain discipline without sacrificing students' constitutional rights?

* * *

The scene now shifts. *Tinker* and its progeny generally explored children's First Amendment rights, while the next decision explores their Fourth Amendment rights. Focus on any hints *Acton* provides about the relative weight the Court will accord children's rights in disputes with government. Consider also whether *Acton* indeed suggests a new approach to public school students' claims of constitutional deprivation.

VERNONIA SCHOOL DISTRICT 47J v. ACTON

Supreme Court of the United States, 1995.
515 U.S. 646.

JUSTICE SCALIA delivered the opinion of the Court.

The Student Athlete Drug Policy adopted by School District 47J in the town of Vernonia, Oregon, authorizes random urinalysis drug testing of students who participate in the District's school athletics programs. We granted certiorari to decide whether this violates the Fourth and Fourteenth Amendments to the United States Constitution.

I

A

Petitioner Vernonia School District 47J (District) operates one high school and three grade schools in the logging community of Vernonia, Oregon. As elsewhere in small-town America, school sports play a prominent role in the town's life, and student athletes are admired in their schools and in the community.

Drugs had not been a major problem in Vernonia schools. In the mid-to-late 1980's, however, teachers and administrators observed a sharp increase in drug use. Students began to speak out about their attraction to the drug culture, and to boast that there was nothing the school could do about it. Along with more drugs came more disciplinary problems. Between 1988 and 1989 the number of disciplinary referrals in Vernonia schools rose to more than twice the number reported in the early 1980's, and several students were suspended. Students became increasingly rude during class; outbursts of profane language became common.

Not only were student athletes included among the drug users but, as the District Court found, athletes were the leaders of the drug culture. This caused the District's administrators particular concern, since drug use increases the risk of sports-related injury. Expert testimony at the trial confirmed the deleterious effects of drugs on motivation, memory, judgment, reaction, coordination, and performance. The high school football and wrestling coach witnessed a severe sternum injury suffered by a wrestler, and various omissions of safety procedures and misexecutions by football players, all attributable in his belief to the effects of drug use.

Initially, the District responded to the drug problem by offering special classes, speakers, and presentations designed to deter drug use. It even brought in a specially trained dog to detect drugs, but the drug problem persisted. According to the District Court:

> "[T]he administration was at its wits end and . . . a large segment of the student body, particularly those involved in interscholastic athletics, was in a state of rebellion. Disciplinary problems had reached 'epidemic proportions.' The coincidence of an almost three-fold increase in classroom disruptions and disciplinary reports along with the staff's direct observations of students using drugs or glamorizing drug and alcohol use led the administration to the inescapable conclusion that the rebellion was being fueled by alcohol and drug abuse as well as the student's misperceptions about the drug culture."

At that point, District officials began considering a drug-testing program. They held a parent "input night" to discuss the proposed Student Athlete Drug Policy (Policy), and the parents in attendance gave their unanimous approval. The school board approved the Policy for implementation in the fall of 1989. Its expressed purpose is to prevent student athletes from using drugs, to protect their health and safety, and to provide drug users with assistance programs.

B

The Policy applies to all students participating in interscholastic athletics. Students wishing to play sports must sign a form consenting to the testing and must obtain the written consent of their parents. Athletes are tested at the beginning of the season for their sport. In addition, once each week of the season the names of the athletes are placed in a "pool" from which a student, with the supervision of two adults, blindly draws the names of 10% of the athletes for random testing. Those selected are notified and tested that same day, if possible.

The student to be tested completes a specimen control form which bears an assigned number. Prescription medications that the student is taking must be identified by providing a copy of the prescription or a doctor's authorization. The student then enters an empty locker room accompanied by an adult monitor of the same sex. Each boy selected produces a sample at a urinal, remaining fully clothed with his back to the monitor, who stands approximately 12 to 15 feet behind the student. Monitors may (though do not always) watch the student while he produces the sample, and they listen for normal sounds of urination. Girls produce samples in an enclosed bathroom stall, so that they can be heard but not observed. After the sample is produced, it is given to the monitor, who checks it for temperature and tampering and then transfers it to a vial.

The samples are sent to an independent laboratory, which routinely tests them for amphetamines, cocaine, and marijuana. Other drugs, such as LSD, may be screened at the request of the District, but the identity of a particular student does not determine which drugs will be tested. The laboratory's procedures are 99.94% accurate. The District follows strict procedures regarding the chain of custody and access to test results. The laboratory does not know the identity of the students whose samples it tests. It is authorized to mail written test reports only to the superintendent and to provide test results to District personnel by telephone only after the requesting official recites a code confirming his authority. Only the superintendent, principals, vice-principals, and athletic directors have access to test results, and the results are not kept for more than one year.

If a sample tests positive, a second test is administered as soon as possible to confirm the result. If the second test is negative, no further action is taken. If the second test is positive, the athlete's parents are notified, and the school principal convenes a meeting with the student and his parents, at which the student is given the option of (1) participating for six weeks in an assistance program that includes weekly urinalysis, or (2) suffering suspension from athletics for the remainder of the current season and the next athletic season. The student is then retested prior to the start of the next athletic season for which he or she is eligible. The Policy states that a second offense results in automatic imposition of option (2); a third offense in suspension for the remainder of the current season and the next two athletic seasons.

C

In the fall of 1991, respondent James Acton, then a seventh-grader, signed up to play football at one of the District's grade schools. He was denied participation, however, because he and his parents refused to sign the testing consent forms. The Actons filed suit, seeking declaratory and injunctive relief from enforcement of the Policy on the grounds that it violated the Fourth and Fourteenth Amendments to the United States Constitution and Article I, § 9, of the Oregon Constitution. After a bench trial, the District Court entered an order denying the claims on the merits and dismissing the action. The United States Court of Appeals for the Ninth Circuit reversed, holding that the Policy violated both the Fourth and Fourteenth Amendments and Article I, § 9, of the Oregon Constitution. We granted certiorari.

II

The Fourth Amendment to the United States Constitution provides that the Federal Government shall not violate "[t]he right of the people to be secure in their persons, houses, papers, and effects, against unreasonable searches and seizures, ..." We have held that the Fourteenth Amendment extends this constitutional guarantee to searches and seizures by state officers, including public school officials. In *Skinner* v. *Railway Labor Executives' Assn.* (1989), we held that state-compelled collection and testing of urine, such as that required by the Student Athlete Drug Policy, constitutes a "search" subject to the demands of the Fourth Amendment.

As the text of the Fourth Amendment indicates, the ultimate measure of the constitutionality of a governmental search is "reasonableness." At least in a case such as this, where there was no clear practice, either approving or disapproving the type of search at issue, at the time the constitutional provision was enacted, whether a particular search meets the reasonableness standard " 'is judged by balancing its intrusion on the individual's Fourth Amendment interests against its promotion of legitimate governmental interests.' "Where a search is undertaken by law enforcement officials to discover evidence of criminal wrongdoing, this Court has said that reasonableness generally requires the obtaining of a judicial warrant. Warrants cannot be issued, of course, without the showing of probable cause required by the Warrant Clause. But a warrant is not required to establish the reasonableness of all government searches; and when a warrant is not required (and the Warrant Clause therefore not applicable), probable cause is not invariably required either. A search unsupported by probable cause can be constitutional, we have said, "when special needs, beyond the normal need for law enforcement, make the warrant and probable-cause requirement impracticable."

We have found such "special needs" to exist in the public school context. There, the warrant requirement "would unduly interfere with the maintenance of the swift and informal disciplinary procedures [that are] needed," and "strict adherence to the requirement that searches be based upon probable cause" would undercut "the substantial need of teachers and administrators for freedom to maintain order in the schools." The school search we approved in [*New Jersey* v.] *T.L.O.* (1985) [infra. p.], while not based on probable cause, *was* based on individualized suspicion of wrongdoing. As we explicitly acknowledged, however, " 'the Fourth Amendment imposes no irreducible requirement of such suspicion.' "We have upheld suspicionless searches and seizures to conduct drug testing of railroad personnel involved in train accidents; to conduct random drug testing of federal customs officers who carry arms or are involved in drug interdiction; and to maintain automobile checkpoints looking for illegal immigrants and contraband and drunk drivers.

III

The first factor to be considered is the nature of the privacy interest upon which the search here at issue intrudes. The Fourth Amendment does not protect all subjective expectations of privacy, but only those that society recognizes as "legitimate." * * * [T]he legitimacy of certain privacy expectations vis-a-vis the State may depend upon the individual's legal relationship with the State. * * * Central, in our view, to the present case is the fact that the subjects of the Policy are (1) children, who (2) have been committed to the temporary custody of the State as schoolmaster.

Traditionally at common law, and still today, unemancipated minors lack some of the most fundamental rights of self-determination—including even the right of liberty in its narrow sense, *i.e.*, the right to come and go at will. They are subject, even as to their physical freedom, to the control of their parents or guardians. When parents place minor children in private schools for their education, the teachers and administrators of those schools stand *in loco parentis* over the children entrusted to them. In fact, the tutor or schoolmaster is the very prototype of that status. * * *

In *T.L.O.* we rejected the notion that public schools, like private schools, exercise only parental power over their students, which of course is not subject to constitutional constraints. Such a view of things, we said, "is not entirely 'consonant with compulsory education laws,' "and is inconsistent with our prior decisions treating school officials as state actors for purposes of the Due Process and Free Speech Clauses. But while denying that the State's power over schoolchildren is formally no more than the delegated power of their parents, *T.L.O.* did not deny, but indeed emphasized, that the nature of that power is custodial and tutelary, permitting a degree of supervision and control that could not be exercised over free adults. "[A] proper educational environment requires close supervision of schoolchildren, as well as the enforcement of rules against conduct that would be perfectly permissible if undertaken by an adult." While we do not, of course, suggest that public schools as a general matter have such a degree of control over children as to give rise to a constitutional "duty to protect," see *DeShaney* v. *Winnebago County Dept. of Social Servs.* (1989) [infra p. 374], we have acknowledged that for many purposes "school authorities ac[t] in loco parentis," with the power and indeed the duty to "inculcate the habits and manners of civility." Thus, while children assuredly do not "shed their constitutional rights ... at the schoolhouse gate," *Tinker* v. *Des Moines Independent Community School Dist.*, the nature of those rights is what is appropriate for children in school.

Fourth Amendment rights, no less than First and Fourteenth Amendment rights, are different in public schools than elsewhere; the "reasonableness" inquiry cannot disregard the schools' custodial and tutelary responsibility for children. For their own good and that of their classmates, public school children are routinely required to submit to various physical examinations, and to be vaccinated against various diseases. * * * Particularly with regard to medical examinations and procedures, therefore, "students within the school environment have a lesser expectation of privacy than members of the population generally."

Legitimate privacy expectations are even less with regard to student athletes. School sports are not for the bashful. They require "suiting up" before each practice or event, and showering and changing afterwards. Public school locker rooms, the usual sites for these activities, are not notable for the privacy they afford. The locker rooms in Vernonia are typical: no individual dressing rooms are provided; shower heads are lined up along a wall, unseparated by any sort of partition or curtain;

not even all the toilet stalls have doors. As the United States Court of Appeals for the Seventh Circuit has noted, there is "an element of 'communal undress' inherent in athletic participation."

There is an additional respect in which school athletes have a reduced expectation of privacy. By choosing to "go out for the team," they voluntarily subject themselves to a degree of regulation even higher than that imposed on students generally. In Vernonia's public schools, they must submit to a preseason physical exam (James testified that his included the giving of a urine sample), they must acquire adequate insurance coverage or sign an insurance waiver, maintain a minimum grade point average, and comply with any "rules of conduct, dress, training hours and related matters as may be established for each sport by the head coach and athletic director with the principal's approval." Somewhat like adults who choose to participate in a "closely regulated industry," students who voluntarily participate in school athletics have reason to expect intrusions upon normal rights and privileges, including privacy.

IV

Having considered the scope of the legitimate expectation of privacy at issue here, we turn next to the character of the intrusion that is complained of. We recognized in *Skinner* that collecting the samples for urinalysis intrudes upon "an excretory function traditionally shielded by great privacy." We noted, however, that the degree of intrusion depends upon the manner in which production of the urine sample is monitored. Under the District's Policy, male students produce samples at a urinal along a wall. They remain fully clothed and are only observed from behind, if at all. Female students produce samples in an enclosed stall, with a female monitor standing outside listening only for sounds of tampering. These conditions are nearly identical to those typically encountered in public restrooms, which men, women, and especially school children use daily. Under such conditions, the privacy interests compromised by the process of obtaining the urine sample are in our view negligible.

The other privacy-invasive aspect of urinalysis is, of course, the information it discloses concerning the state of the subject's body, and the materials he has ingested. In this regard it is significant that the tests at issue here look only for drugs, and not for whether the student is, for example, epileptic, pregnant, or diabetic. Moreover, the drugs for which the samples are screened are standard, and do not vary according to the identity of the student. And finally, the results of the tests are disclosed only to a limited class of school personnel who have a need to know; and they are not turned over to law enforcement authorities or used for any internal disciplinary function.

Respondents argue, however, that the District's Policy is in fact more intrusive than this suggests, because it requires the students, if they are to avoid sanctions for a falsely positive test, to identify *in* *advance* prescription medications they are taking. We agree that this raises some cause for concern. * * *

* * * It may well be that, if and when James was selected for random testing at a time that he was taking medication, the School District would have permitted him to provide the requested information in a confidential manner—for example, in a sealed envelope delivered to the testing lab. Nothing in the Policy contradicts that, and when respondents choose, in effect, to challenge the Policy on its face, we will not assume the worst. Accordingly, * * * the invasion of privacy was not significant.

V

Finally, we turn to consider the nature and immediacy of the governmental concern at issue here, and the efficacy of this means for meeting it. * * * [T]he District Court held that because the District's program also called for drug testing in the absence of individualized suspicion, the District "must demonstrate a 'compelling need' for the program." The Court of Appeals appears to have agreed with this view. It is a mistake, however, to think that the phrase "compelling state interest," in the Fourth Amendment context, describes a fixed, minimum quantum of governmental concern, so that one can dispose of a case by answering in isolation the question: Is there a compelling state interest here? Rather, the phrase describes an interest that appears *important enough* to justify the particular search at hand, in light of other factors that show the search to be relatively intrusive upon a genuine expectation of privacy. Whether that relatively high degree of government concern is necessary in this case or not, we think it is met.

That the nature of the concern is important—indeed, perhaps compelling—can hardly be doubted. * * * School years are the time when the physical, psychological, and addictive effects of drugs are most severe. "Maturing nervous systems are more critically impaired by intoxicants than mature ones are; childhood losses in learning are lifelong and profound"; "children grow chemically dependent more quickly than adults, and their record of recovery is depressingly poor." And of course the effects of a drug-infested school are visited not just upon the users, but upon the entire student body and faculty, as the educational process is disrupted. In the present case, moreover, the necessity for the State to act is magnified by the fact that this evil is being visited not just upon individuals at large, but upon children for whom it has undertaken a special responsibility of care and direction. Finally, it must not be lost sight of that this program is directed more narrowly to drug use by school athletes, where the risk of immediate physical harm to the drug user or those with whom he is playing his sport is particularly high. Apart from psychological effects, which include impairment of judgment, slow reaction time, and a lessening of the perception of pain, the particular drugs screened by the District's Policy

have been demonstrated to pose substantial physical risks to athletes.
* * *

* * *

As to the efficacy of this means for addressing the problem: It seems
to us self-evident that a drug problem largely fueled by the "role model"
effect of athletes' drug use, and of particular danger to athletes, is
effectively addressed by making sure that athletes do not use drugs.
Respondents argue that a "less intrusive means to the same end" was
available, namely, "drug testing on suspicion of drug use." We have
repeatedly refused to declare that only the "least intrusive" search
practicable can be reasonable under the Fourth Amendment. Respondents' alternative entails substantial difficulties—if it is indeed practicable at all. It may be impracticable, for one thing, simply because the
parents who are willing to accept random drug testing for athletes are
not willing to accept accusatory drug testing for all students, which
transforms the process into a badge of shame. Respondents' proposal
brings the risk that teachers will impose testing arbitrarily upon troublesome but not drug-likely students. It generates the expense of defending
lawsuits that charge such arbitrary imposition, or that simply demand
greater process before accusatory drug testing is imposed. And not least
of all, it adds to the ever-expanding diversionary duties of schoolteachers
the new function of spotting and bringing to account drug abuse, a task
for which they are ill prepared, and which is not readily compatible with
their vocation. * * * In many respects, we think, testing based on
"suspicion" of drug use would not be better, but worse.

VI

Taking into account all the factors we have considered above—the
decreased expectation of privacy, the relative unobtrusiveness of the
search, and the severity of the need met by the search—we conclude
Vernonia's Policy is reasonable and hence constitutional.

We caution against the assumption that suspicionless drug testing
will readily pass constitutional muster in other contexts. The most
significant element in this case is the first we discussed: that the Policy
was undertaken in furtherance of the government's responsibilities,
under a public school system, as guardian and tutor of children entrusted to its care. * * * [W]hen the government acts as guardian and tutor
the relevant question is whether the search is one that a reasonable
guardian and tutor might undertake. Given the findings of need made by
the District Court, we conclude that in the present case it is.

We may note that the primary guardians of Vernonia's schoolchildren appear to agree. The record shows no objection to this districtwide
program by any parents other than the couple before us here—even
though, as we have described, a public meeting was held to obtain
parents' views. We find insufficient basis to contradict the judgment of

Vernonia's parents, its school board, and the District Court, as to what was reasonably in the interest of these children under the circumstances.

* * *

JUSTICE GINSBURG, concurring.

The Court constantly observes that the School District's drug-testing policy applies only to students who voluntarily participate in interscholastic athletics. Correspondingly, the most severe sanction allowed under the District's policy is suspension from extracurricular athletic programs. I comprehend the Court's opinion as reserving the question whether the District, on no more than the showing made here, constitutionally could impose routine drug testing not only on those seeking to engage with others in team sports, but on all students required to attend school.

[Justice O'Connor's dissenting opinion, joined by Justices Stevens and Souter, appears in Chapter 11, Delinquency.].

Notes and Questions

1. *Aftermath.* James Acton continued to refuse to participate in the school's drug testing program, and he began playing on an independent soccer team that did not require such testing. He left Vernonia High School after his junior year; his parents began home schooling him and he attended classes at a local community college. See Rachel Bachman, After Winning, Schools Lax on Test, Portland Oregonian, Feb. 12, 1997, at B1; Tanya Bricking, High School Drug–Testing Debate Rages On, USA Today, Nov. 14, 1995, at 1C.

2. *Questions about* Acton. (a) After *Acton,* what is left of *Tinker's* view of children's rights in disputes with public school authorities?

(b) What insights do *Acton's* rationale and holding provide about the strength of children's rights in disputes with the government generally? What, if anything, do the rationale and holding suggest about the strength of the government's parens patriae interest?

(c) If parents do not wish to allow their child to submit to random public school drug testing, why should the government have any authority to require such testing as a condition for participating in interscholastic athletics?

3. *Probing* Acton's *reach.* Justice Ginsburg seeks to limit the decision to students who "voluntarily participate in interscholastic athletics." This note probes whether the decision can be so limited.

(a) The Court says interscholastic athletes are "role models" for their fellow students. In this respect, are athletes any different from the student body president, the stars of the student musical, or the prom king or queen? Should students be subject to random suspicionless drug testing whenever they assume a perceived leadership role? Should an adolescent's constitutional rights depend on whether someone might view the adolescent as a "role model"?

(b) *Acton* says that in interscholastic athletics, "the risk of immediate physical harm to the drug user or those with whom he is playing his sport is particularly high." Are most of the risks the Court cites appreciably different for athletes than for driver education students on the public highways, students who mix toxic chemicals in the chemistry lab, students who use power tools in vocational education class, or students with permission to drive off school grounds for lunch? What about students who take physical education classes required for graduation, namely the entire student body? Don't physical education students face "risk of immediate physical harm" from athletic participation similar to risk faced by interscholastic athletes (and arguably even greater because required physical education classes contain many students with limited skills in sports that emphasize risk-taking and physical contact)?

(c) *Acton* says student-athletes have only a diminished expectation of privacy because "[s]chool sports are not for the bashful" and public school locker rooms "are not notable for the privacy they afford." Does this rationale suggest that the school district could require drug tests of all physical education students?

(d) *Acton* says student-athletes have only a diminished expectation of privacy because "[b]y choosing to 'go out for the team,' they voluntarily subject themselves to a degree of regulation even higher than that imposed on students generally." Should a higher degree of regulation also apply to students who voluntarily enroll in all extracurricular activities, from the marching band to the Young Republicans? See Trinidad Sch. Dist. No. 1 v. Lopez, 963 P.2d 1095, 1097 (Colo.1998) (school district's suspicionless drug testing policy violated Fourth Amendment with respect to students in the marching band).

(e) In the final analysis, does the Court's decision turn on the fact that James Acton was a student, or does it turn on the fact that he was a student-athlete?

4.   Acton *and adult drug testing.* (a) If random suspicionless drug tests are appropriate because student-athletes are "role models," should the Vernonia School District also impose such tests on its adult role models, such as the school superintendent, principals, teachers and coaches? When the adults walk into the school, for example, do they have a greater expectation of privacy than students because they are adults and the students are children? Would random suspicionless drug testing of the adults pass constitutional muster? See Knox County Educ. Ass'n v. Knox County Bd. of Educ., 158 F.3d 361 (6th Cir. 1998) (rejecting Fourth Amendment challenge to random suspicionless drug testing of principals, assistant principals, teachers, traveling teachers, teacher aides, substitute teachers, school secretaries and school bus drivers; and to suspicion-based drug testing of other school personnel); Aubrey v. School Bd., 148 F.3d 559 (5th Cir. 1998) (rejecting elementary school custodian's Fourth Amendment challenge to random suspicionless drug testing).

(b) *Acton* says student-athletes have diminished Fourth Amendment privacy expectations because of the "element of 'communal undress' inherent in athletic participation." The Court describes, for example, the open shower facilities common in student locker rooms. Are student locker rooms any different in this regard from locker rooms frequented by adults in community recreation centers and similar public athletic facilities? Would the adults also have diminished privacy expectations because they "suit up" before hitting the golf course or squash courts and hit the showers afterwards?

(c) *Acton* cites decisions upholding random suspicionless drug testing of adults in particularly sensitive occupations. A number of federal courts of appeals have also upheld such drug testing of adults employed in fields in which substance abuse would risk significant danger to the public. These fields include airline pilots, air traffic controllers, commercial truck drivers, and police officers. Do *Acton's* young athletes pose similar danger? In Chandler v. Miller, 520 U.S. 305, 309 (1997), the Court struck down a Georgia statute that required all candidates for state public office to pass a drug test. The Court held that the requirement did not "fit within the closely guarded category of constitutionally permissible suspicionless searches." *Chandler* explained *Acton's* contrary outcome by reiterating that " 'students within the school environment have a lesser expectation of privacy than members of the population generally.' " 520 U.S. at 1302.

5. *The in loco parentis doctrine.* Under the common law in loco parentis doctrine ("in the place of a parent"), a person who assumes parental obligations is treated as a parent for some purposes. As discussed in Chapter 2, the person may hold both parental rights and parental obligations. The doctrine is also relevant to the exercise of parental authority by schools and other institutions with children in their care. How does *Acton* limit the doctrine's application to public schools?

6. *Public sentiment.* The Court says the record contained no indication that any family other than the Actons had objected to the school district's drug testing program. Is it fair to infer approval from silence when students ultimately need recommendations and other faculty support on their college or employment applications and thus may not wish to be branded as litigious troublemakers? Is the inference fair when students may be unable to play a particular sport except in the interscholastic league? Is it fair when civil litigation may be fraught with anxiety even when an advocacy group may cover fees and costs? From a broader perspective, should the question whether a Bill of Rights provision protects a child (or anyone else, for that matter) depend on how many other people also happen to object?

In a 1997 poll conducted by Columbia University's National Center on Addiction and Substance Abuse, 30% of teenagers "strongly favored" drug testing of all students, and 22% "somewhat favored" such testing. Such testing was "strongly favored" by 25% of parents and "somewhat favored" by 17%. See U.S. Dep't of Justice, Bureau of Justice Statistics, Sourcebook of Criminal Justice Statistics 1997, tbl. 2.12, at 104 (1998). In the same poll, 50% of teenagers "strongly favored" drug testing of all student-athletes, and 23% "somewhat favored" such testing. Such testing was "strongly favored" by 53% of parents and "somewhat favored" by 26%. Id.

7. *Post-Acton decisions.* Since *Acton,* a number of public school districts have flirted with mandating random suspicionless drug testing for athletes and other students. Some districts have mandated such testing, while others

have declined to do so because they fear saddling taxpayers with the expense of litigating against federal and state constitutional challenges. A school district's insurance policy may not cover litigation costs. A few districts have reportedly considered testing students' hair rather than urine to detect drugs. See Christopher S. Wren, Hair Testing by Schools Intensifies Drug Debate, N.Y. Times, June 14, 1999, at A14.

The Seventh Circuit has grappled with public school drug testing programs with mixed results. In Todd v. Rush County Schools, 133 F.3d 984 (7th Cir.), cert. denied, 525 U.S. 824 (1998), the court of appeals upheld a program prohibiting high school students from participating in any extracurricular activities or driving to and from school unless the student and the parent or guardian consented to random, unannounced urinalysis tests for drugs, alcohol or tobacco. The drug testing policy covered participation not only on athletic teams, but also in other extracurricular activities such as student council, foreign language clubs, Fellowship of Christian Athletes, Future Farmers of America officers and the Library Club. The panel cited *Acton* because "successful extracurricular activities require healthy students." 133 F.3d at 986. Two judges dissented from denial of the petition for en banc rehearing, asserting that the panel decision had "sanction[ed] by implication, the use of a urine sample as the price of admission to the public schools in this circuit." 139 F.3d at 571. See also Miller v. Wilkes, 172 F.3d 574 (8th Cir. 1999) (upholding public school district's random suspicionless drug and alcohol testing policy for students in all extracurricular activities).

On the other hand, in Willis v. Anderson Community Sch. Corp., 158 F.3d 415 (7th Cir.1998), cert. denied, 119 S.Ct. 1254 (1999), the court of appeals struck down a school district policy mandating a drug and alcohol test for any student suspended for three or more days for fighting. The court held that statistical data and professional literature concerning a causal connection between student use of illicit substances and violent behavior were insufficient to establish reasonable suspicion that the plaintiff suspended for fighting was using such substances. The panel also found the policy unjustified by special needs. The panel distinguished *Acton* on the grounds that student-athletes have a lesser privacy expectation than the general student population because of the "element of 'communal undress' inherent in athletic participation," and that student-athletes voluntarily choose to try out for the sports team. 158 F.3d at 421–22.

C.   May Children Articulate Their Own Interests?

Where a child is a party to a lawsuit, the child is provided representatives. But should children also have a right to be heard in other controversies whose resolution may affect their interests? When should the legislature confer such a right? In the absence of statute, should courts recognize a constitutional or common law right? Should any such right to be heard depend on the child's ability to state a reasoned preference? What factors should the court examine to determine whether the child has this ability?

1. The General Question

WISCONSIN v. YODER

Supreme Court of the United States, 1972.
406 U.S. 205.

Mr. Chief Justice Burger delivered the opinion of the Court.

[The respondents, three Amish parents, were convicted and fined $5 each under the state compulsory school attendance statute, which required them to cause their children to attend public or private school until the age of sixteen. The parents agreed that their children would attend school until the end of the eighth grade, but declined to send their 14- and 15-year-old children to school afterwards.

The majority concluded that the convictions violated the parents' rights under the First Amendment free exercise clause. The Court stressed that "[t]he history and culture of Western civilization reflect a strong tradition of parental concern for the nurture and upbringing of their children." On the strength of uncontradicted expert testimony concerning the Amish record of "three centuries as an identifiable religious sect and a long history as a successful and self-sufficient segment of American society," the Court held that the parents' interest outweighed the state interest in regulating the duration of basic education. The Court found that the parents "believed * * * that their children's attendance at high school, public or private, was contrary to the Amish religion and way of life. They believed that by sending their children to high school, they would not only expose themselves to the danger of the censure of the church community, but * * * also endanger their own salvation and that of their children." The Court held that in this circumstance, enforcement of the compulsory education statute "would gravely endanger if not destroy the free exercise of respondents' religious beliefs."

The Court rejected the state's contention that "a decision exempting Amish children from the State's requirement fails to recognize the substantive right of the Amish child to a secondary education, and fails to give due regard to the power of the State as *parens patriae* to extend the benefit of secondary education to children regardless of the wishes of their parents":]

Contrary to the suggestion of the dissenting opinion of Mr. Justice Douglas, our holding today in no degree depends on the assertion of the religious interest of the child as contrasted with that of the parents. It is the parents who are subject to prosecution here for failing to cause their children to attend school, and it is their right of free exercise, not that of their children, that must determine Wisconsin's power to impose criminal penalties on the parent. The dissent argues that a child who expresses a desire to attend public high school in conflict with the wishes of his parents should not be prevented from doing so. There is no reason for the Court to consider that point since it is not an issue in the case.

The children are not parties to this litigation. The State has at no point tried this case on the theory that respondents were preventing their children from attending school against their expressed desires, and indeed the record is to the contrary.[21] The State's position from the outset has been that it is empowered to apply its compulsory-attendance law to Amish parents in the same manner as to other parents—that is, without regard to the wishes of the child. That is the claim we reject today.

Our holding in no way determines the proper resolution of possible competing interests of parents, children, and the State in an appropriate state court proceeding in which the power of the State is asserted on the theory that Amish parents are preventing their minor children from attending high school despite their expressed desires to the contrary. Recognition of the claim of the State in such a proceeding would, of course, call into question traditional concepts of parental control over the religious upbringing and education of their minor children recognized in this Court's past decisions. It is clear that such an intrusion by a State into family decisions in the area of religious training would give rise to grave questions of religious freedom comparable to those raised here and those presented in *Pierce* v. *Society of Sisters*. On this record we neither reach nor decide those issues.

* * *

[The concurring opinions are omitted.]

MR. JUSTICE DOUGLAS, dissenting in part.

I

I agree with the Court that the religious scruples of the Amish are opposed to the education of their children beyond the grade schools, yet I disagree with the Court's conclusion that the matter is within the dispensation of parents alone. The Court's analysis assumes that the only interests at stake in the case are those of the Amish parents on the one hand, and those of the State on the other. The difficulty with this approach is that, despite the Court's claim, the parents are seeking to vindicate not only their own free exercise claims, but also those of their high-school-age children. * * *

* * * If the parents in this case are allowed a religious exemption, the inevitable effect is to impose the parents' notions of religious duty upon their children. Where the child is mature enough to express potentially conflicting desires, it would be an invasion of the child's rights to permit such an imposition without canvassing his views. * * * As the child has no other effective forum, it is in this litigation that his rights should be considered. And, if an Amish child desires to attend

---

21. The only relevant testimony in the record is to the effect that the wishes of the one child who testified corresponded with those of her parents. Testimony of Frieda Yoder, to the effect that her personal reli-gious beliefs guided her decision to discontinue school attendance after the eighth grade. The other children were not called by either side.

high school, and is mature enough to have that desire respected, the State may well be able to override the parents' religiously motivated objections.

Religion is an individual experience. It is not necessary, nor even appropriate, for every Amish child to express his views on the subject in a prosecution of a single adult. Crucial, however, are the views of the child whose parent is the subject of the suit. Frieda Yoder has in fact testified that her own religious views are opposed to high-school education. I therefore join the judgment of the Court as to respondent Jonas Yoder. But Frieda Yoder's views may not be those of Vernon Yutzy or Barbara Miller. I must dissent, therefore, as to respondents Adin Yutzy and Wallace Miller as their motion to dismiss also raised the question of their children's religious liberty.

II

This issue has never been squarely presented before today. Our opinions are full of talk about the power of the parents over the child's education. See *Pierce* v. *Society of Sisters*; *Meyer* v. *Nebraska*. And we have in the past analyzed similar conflicts between parent and State with little regard for the views of the child. *Prince* v. *Massachusetts*. Recent cases, however, have clearly held that the children themselves have constitutionally protectible interests.

These children are "persons" within the meaning of the Bill of Rights. We have so held over and over again. * * *

* * *

On this important and vital matter of education, I think the children should be entitled to be heard. While the parents, absent dissent, normally speak for the entire family, the education of the child is a matter on which the child will often have decided views. He may want to be a pianist or an astronaut or an oceanographer. To do so he will have to break from the Amish tradition.

It is the future of the student, not the future of the parents, that is imperiled by today's decision. If a parent keeps his child out of school beyond the grade school, then the child will be forever barred from entry into the new and amazing world of diversity that we have today. The child may decide that that is the preferred course, or he may rebel. It is the student's judgment, not his parents', that is essential if we are to give full meaning to what we have said about the Bill of Rights and of the right of students to be masters of their own destiny. If he is harnessed to the Amish way of life by those in authority over him and if his education is truncated, his entire life may be stunted and deformed. The child, therefore, should be given an opportunity to be heard before the State gives the exemption which we honor today.

* * *

Notes and Questions

1. *Questions about* Yoder. (a) By holding that the parents could prevent their children from attending school and by not even seeking the children's views about whether they wished to attend, was *Yoder* consistent with the exposition of children's rights enunciated in such decisions as *Brown* and *Tinker*?,

(b) What was the source of the right Justice Douglas sought to recognize?,

(c) Suppose that Justice Douglas' view had prevailed, and that on remand one of the Yoder children testified she wanted to finish high school so she could pursue higher education and become a brain surgeon. What weight would Justice Douglas have the trial court give this testimony? Would the testimony have permitted or required the court to reject the parents' position?

2. *Statutory rights to be heard.* Questions concerning a child's constitutional right to be heard do not arise in some categories of disputes because statutes grant children rights to articulate their positions in open court or in in camera proceedings.

An express statutory right to be heard frequently exists, for example, in adoption, custody and guardianship proceedings. See, e.g., Mass. Ann. Laws ch. 210, § 2 ("A decree of adoption shall not be made * * * without the written consent of the child to be adopted, if above the age of twelve * * *. "); Ky. Rev. Stat. § 403.270 (2) (b) (in determining custody, "the court shall consider all relevant factors including: * * * The wishes of the child as to his custodian * * *."). Should the weight the court gives the child's wishes depend on the child's age and maturity? By recognizing the maturity of many older minors and by instructing courts to consider their views, these statutes introduce the next topic, the mature-minor doctrine.

3. *Matters of principle.* Yoder is worth remembering for a reason transcending its holding. The Amish parents were each fined only five dollars for violating the compulsory education act. You may periodically have clients who wish to vindicate principles they deem important even though they may have suffered only apparently minuscule sanction. With congested dockets, your opponents may find a receptive judicial ear when they assert that the case is "a waste of the court's time." You should remind court and counsel that even the Supreme Court hears cases in which principles far outweigh the magnitude of the sanction.

2. *The Mature–Minor Doctrine*

In recent years, the "mature minor" doctrine has sometimes enabled courts to consider the wishes of a child who appears capable of articulating a reasoned preference on matters important to the child's welfare. *Bellotti* stakes out a relatively narrow constitutional zone of privacy for children. *Lori M* demonstrates the willingness of some courts to broaden this zone. Finally, *E.G.,* discussed in note 1 after *Lori M,* finds a common law basis for autonomy by mature children.

BELLOTTI v. BAIRD

Supreme Court of the United States, 1979.
443 U.S. 622.

MR. JUSTICE POWELL announced the judgment of the Court and delivered an opinion, in which THE CHIEF JUSTICE, MR. JUSTICE STEWART, and MR. JUSTICE REHNQUIST joined.

These appeals present a challenge to the constitutionality of a state statute regulating the access of minors to abortions. * * *

I

A

On August 2, 1974, the Legislature of the Commonwealth of Massachusetts passed, over the Governor's veto, an Act pertaining to abortions performed within the State. * * *

Section 12S provides in part:

> "If the mother is less than eighteen years of age and has not married, the consent of both the mother and her parents [to an abortion to be performed on the mother] is required. If one or both of the mother's parents refuse such consent, consent may be obtained by order of a judge of the superior court for good cause shown, after such hearing as he deems necessary. Such a hearing will not require the appointment of a guardian for the mother. If one of the parents has died or has deserted his or her family, consent by the remaining parent is sufficient. If both parents have died or have deserted their family, consent of the mother's guardian or other person having duties similar to a guardian, or any person who had assumed the care and custody of the mother is sufficient. * * *"

* * *

II

A child, merely on account of his minority, is not beyond the protection of the Constitution. As the Court said in *In re Gault,* "whatever may be their precise impact, neither the Fourteenth Amendment nor the Bill of Rights is for adults alone." This observation, of course, is but the beginning of the analysis. The Court long has recognized that the status of minors under the law is unique in many respects. As Mr. Justice Frankfurter aptly put it: "[C]hildren have a very special place in life which law should reflect. Legal theories and their phrasing in other cases readily lead to fallacious reasoning if uncritically transferred to determination of a State's duty towards children." The unique role in our society of the family, the institution by which "we inculcate and pass down many of our most cherished values, moral and cultural," requires that constitutional principles be applied with sensitivity and flexibility to the special needs of parents and children. We have recognized three reasons justifying the conclusion that the constitutional rights of children cannot be equated with those of adults: the peculiar vulnerability of children; their inability to make critical decisions in an informed, mature manner; and the importance of the parental role in child rearing.

A

The Court's concern for the vulnerability of children is demonstrated in its decisions dealing with minors' claims to constitutional protection against deprivations of liberty or property interests by the State. With respect to many of these claims, we have concluded that the child's right is virtually coextensive with that of an adult. For example, the Court has held that the Fourteenth Amendment's guarantee against the deprivation of liberty without due process of law is applicable to children in juvenile delinquency proceedings. *In re Gault, supra.* In particular, minors involved in such proceedings are entitled to adequate notice, the assistance of counsel, and the opportunity to confront their accusers. They can be found guilty only upon proof beyond a reasonable doubt, and they may assert the privilege against compulsory self-incrimination. *In re Winship* [infra p. 1148]; *In re Gault.* * * *

* * *

These rulings have not been made on the uncritical assumption that the constitutional rights of children are indistinguishable from those of adults. Indeed, our acceptance of juvenile courts distinct from the adult criminal justice system assumes that juvenile offenders constitutionally may be treated differently from adults. * * * Viewed together, our cases show that although children generally are protected by the same constitutional guarantees against governmental deprivations as are adults, the State is entitled to adjust its legal system to account for children's vulnerability and their needs for "concern, ... sympathy, and ... paternal attention."

B

Second, the Court has held that the States validly may limit the freedom of children to choose for themselves in the making of important, affirmative choices with potentially serious consequences. These rulings have been grounded in the recognition that, during the formative years of childhood and adolescence, minors often lack the experience, perspective, and judgment to recognize and avoid choices that could be detrimental to them.

* * *

C

Third, the guiding role of parents in the upbringing of their children justifies limitations on the freedoms of minors. The State commonly protects its youth from adverse governmental action and from their own immaturity by requiring parental consent to or involvement in important decisions by minors. But an additional and more important justification for state deference to parental control over children is that "[t]he child is not the mere creature of the state; those who nurture him and direct his destiny have the right, coupled with the high duty, to recognize and prepare him for additional obligations." *Pierce* v. *Society of Sisters*. "The duty to prepare the child for 'additional obligations' ... must be read to include the inculcation of moral standards, religious beliefs, and elements of good citizenship." *Wisconsin* v. *Yoder*. This affirmative process of teaching, guiding, and inspiring by precept and example is essential to the growth of young people into mature, socially responsible citizens.

We have believed in this country that this process, in large part, is beyond the competence of impersonal political institutions. Indeed, affirmative sponsorship of particular ethical, religious, or political beliefs is something we expect the State *not* to attempt in a society constitutionally committed to the ideal of individual liberty and freedom of choice. Thus, "[i]t is cardinal with us that the custody, care and nurture of the child reside first in the parents, whose primary function and freedom include *preparation for obligations the state can neither supply nor hinder*." *Prince* v. *Massachusetts* (emphasis added).

Unquestionably, there are many competing theories about the most effective way for parents to fulfill their central role in assisting their children on the way to responsible adulthood. While we do not pretend any special wisdom on this subject, we cannot ignore that central to many of these theories, and deeply rooted in our Nation's history and tradition, is the belief that the parental role implies a substantial measure of authority over one's children. Indeed, "constitutional interpretation has consistently recognized that the parents' claim to authority in their own household to direct the rearing of their children is basic in the structure of our society."

Properly understood, then, the tradition of parental authority is not inconsistent with our tradition of individual liberty; rather, the former is one of the basic presuppositions of the latter. Legal restrictions on minors, especially those supportive of the parental role, may be important to the child's chances for the full growth and maturity that make eventual participation in a free society meaningful and rewarding. Under the Constitution, the State can "properly conclude that parents and others, teachers for example, who have [the] primary responsibility for children's well-being are entitled to the support of laws designed to aid discharge of that responsibility."[18]

III

* * * The question before us * * * is whether § 12S, as authoritatively interpreted by the Supreme Judicial Court, provides for parental

---

18. The Court's opinions discussed in the text above—*Pierce, Yoder, Prince,* and *Ginsberg* [infra p. 625]—all have contributed to a line of decisions suggesting the existence of a constitutional parental right against undue, adverse interference by the State.

notice and consent in a manner that does not unduly burden the right to seek an abortion.

* * * As stated in Part II above, * * * parental notice and consent are qualifications that typically may be imposed by the State on a minor's right to make important decisions. As immature minors often lack the ability to make fully informed choices that take account of both immediate and long-range consequences, a State reasonably may determine that parental consultation often is desirable and in the best interest of the minor. It may further determine, as a general proposition, that such consultation is particularly desirable with respect to the abortion decision—one that for some people raises profound moral and religious concerns. * * *

* * * The abortion decision differs in important ways from other decisions that may be made during minority. The need to preserve the constitutional right and the unique nature of the abortion decision, especially when made by a minor, require a State to act with particular sensitivity when it legislates to foster parental involvement in this matter.

A

The pregnant minor's options are much different from those facing a minor in other situations, such as deciding whether to marry. A minor not permitted to marry before the age of majority is required simply to postpone her decision. She and her intended spouse may preserve the opportunity for later marriage should they continue to desire it. A pregnant adolescent, however, cannot preserve for long the possibility of aborting, which effectively expires in a matter of weeks from the onset of pregnancy.

Moreover, the potentially severe detriment facing a pregnant woman, is not mitigated by her minority. Indeed, considering her probable education, employment skills, financial resources, and emotional maturity, unwanted motherhood may be exceptionally burdensome for a minor. In addition, the fact of having a child brings with it adult legal responsibility, for parenthood, like attainment of the age of majority, is one of the traditional criteria for the termination of the legal disabilities of minority. In sum, there are few situations in which denying a minor the right to make an important decision will have consequences so grave and indelible.

Yet, an abortion may not be the best choice for the minor. The circumstances in which this issue arises will vary widely. In a given case, alternatives to abortion, such as marriage to the father of the child, arranging for its adoption, or assuming the responsibilities of motherhood with the assured support of family, may be feasible and relevant to the minor's best interests. Nonetheless, the abortion decision is one that simply cannot be postponed, or it will be made by default with far-reaching consequences.

For these reasons, as we held in *Planned Parenthood of Central Missouri* v. *Danforth*, "the State may not impose a blanket provision . . . requiring the consent of a parent or person *in loco parentis* as a condition for abortion of an unmarried minor during the first 12 weeks of her pregnancy." Although * * * such deference to parents may be permissible with respect to other choices facing a minor, the unique nature and consequences of the abortion decision make it inappropriate "to give a third party an absolute, and possibly arbitrary, veto over the decision of the physician and his patient to terminate the patient's pregnancy, regardless of the reason for withholding the consent." We therefore conclude that if the State decides to require a pregnant minor to obtain one or both parents' consent to an abortion, it also must provide an alternative procedure whereby authorization for the abortion can be obtained.

A pregnant minor is entitled in such a proceeding to show either: (1) that she is mature enough and well enough informed to make her abortion decision, in consultation with her physician, independently of her parents' wishes;[23] or (2) that even if she is not able to make this decision independently, the desired abortion would be in her best interests. * * *

B

* * *

(1)

* * *

We conclude * * * that under state regulation such as that undertaken by Massachusetts, every minor must have the opportunity—if she so desires—to go directly to a court without first consulting or notifying her parents. If she satisfies the court that she is mature and well enough informed to make intelligently the abortion decision on her own, the court must authorize her to act without parental consultation or consent. If she fails to satisfy the court that she is competent to make this decision independently, she must be permitted to show that an abortion nevertheless would be in her best interests. If the court is persuaded that it is, the court must authorize the abortion. If, however, the court is not persuaded by the minor that she is mature or that the abortion would be in her best interests, it may decline to sanction the operation.

---

23. The nature of both the State's interest in fostering parental authority and the problem of determining "maturity" makes clear why the State generally may resort to objective, though inevitably arbitrary, criteria such as age limits, marital status, or membership in the Armed Forces for lifting some or all of the legal disabilities of minority. Not only is it difficult to define, let alone determine, maturity, but also the fact that a minor may be very much an adult in some respects does not mean that his or her need and opportunity for growth under parental guidance and discipline have ended. As discussed in the text, however, the peculiar nature of the abortion decision requires the opportunity for case-by-case evaluations of the maturity of pregnant minors.

There is, however, an important state interest in encouraging a family rather than a judicial resolution of a minor's abortion decision. Also, as we have observed above, parents naturally take an interest in the welfare of their children—an interest that is particularly strong where a normal family relationship exists and where the child is living with one or both parents. These factors properly may be taken into account by a court called upon to determine whether an abortion in fact is in a minor's best interests. If, all things considered, the court determines that an abortion is in the minor's best interests, she is entitled to court authorization without any parental involvement. On the other hand, the court may deny the abortion request of an immature minor in the absence of parental consultation if it concludes that her best interests would be served thereby, or the court may in such a case defer decision until there is parental consultation in which the court may participate. But this is the full extent to which parental involvement may be required. For the reasons stated above, the constitutional right to seek an abortion may not be unduly burdened by state-imposed conditions upon initial access to court.

* * *

(3)

Another of the questions certified by the District Court to the Supreme Judicial Court was the following: "If the superior court finds that the minor is capable [of making], and has, in fact, made and adhered to, an informed and reasonable decision to have an abortion, may the court refuse its consent based on a finding that a parent's, or its own, contrary decision is a better one?" To this the state court answered:

"[W]e do not view the judge's role as limited to a determination that the minor is capable of making, and has made, an informed and reasonable decision to have an abortion. * * * [I]n circumstances where he determines that the best interests of the minor will not be served by an abortion, the judge's determination should prevail, assuming that his conclusion is supported by the evidence and adequate findings of fact."

The Supreme Judicial Court's statement reflects the general rule that a State may require a minor to wait until the age of majority before being permitted to exercise legal rights independently. But we are concerned here with the exercise of a constitutional right of unique character. As stated above, if the minor satisfies a court that she has attained sufficient maturity to make a fully informed decision, she then is entitled to make her abortion decision independently. We therefore agree with the District Court that § 12S cannot constitutionally permit judicial disregard of the abortion decision of a minor who has been determined to be mature and fully competent to assess the implications of the choice she has made.

IV

Although it satisfies constitutional standards in large part, § 12S falls short of them in two respects: First, it permits judicial authorization for an abortion to be withheld from a minor who is found by the superior court to be mature and fully competent to make this decision independently. Second, it requires parental consultation or notification in every instance, without affording the pregnant minor an opportunity to receive an independent judicial determination that she is mature enough to consent or that an abortion would be in her best interests. Accordingly, we affirm the judgment of the District Court insofar as it invalidates this statute and enjoins its enforcement.

Affirmed.

[The concurring and dissenting Justices did not take issue with Part II of the plurality opinion, which articulates factors that justify treating children's constitutional rights as less weighty that adults', and proceeds to discuss maturity.].

Notes and Questions

1.   *Questions about* Bellotti. (a) Where the court solicits the child's views, what factors should it consider when determining whether a minor "has attained sufficient maturity to make an informed decision"?,

> (b) If an unmarried child becomes pregnant, she is likely a statutory rape victim. Statutory rape statutes conclusively presume that an underage victim is incapable of giving consent. If the victim, as a matter of law, is too immature to give consent, why should the court consider whether she is mature enough to request an abortion?,

> (c) If abortion is a woman's constitutional right, why should a pregnant minor sometimes have to secure a parent's consent before the procedure may be performed?,

> (d) If a girl under eighteen is mature enough to decide whether to keep and raise the child she delivers, why must a court investigate whether she is mature enough to decide whether to have an abortion?,

> (e) What, if anything, does *Bellotti's* plurality suggest about the strength of the state's parens patriae interest?

2.   *What limits on the mature-minor doctrine?* Does *Bellotti* provide criteria enabling courts to determine whether to extend the mature-minor doctrine beyond the abortion context? In Parham v. J.R., 442 U.S. 584, 602–03 (1979), the Court suggested that invocation of the doctrine should be the exception rather than the rule: "The law's concept of family rests on a presumption that parents possess what a child lacks in maturity, experience, and capacity for judgment required for making life's difficult decisions. * * * Most children, even in adolescence, simply are not able to make sound judgments concerning many decisions, including their need for medical care or treatment. Parents can and must make those judgments."

Relying on psychological literature, some writers would accord the mature-minor doctrine a considerably broader role on the ground that adolescents have decisionmaking capacity. Professor Robert Batey, for example, argues that "parents should not be allowed to make decisions for their competent adolescent children." He believes that "the law should accord the considered choices of competent adolescents the same treatment it accords similar choices of adults," and thus that where "the state would defer to the desires of an adult, the state can refuse to defer to the considered choices of an adolescent only upon a showing that the adolescent is not competent to make the decision." Robert Batey, The Rights of Adolescents, 23 Wm. & Mary L. Rev. 363, 364, 373 (1982).

Professor Gary B. Melton concludes that "for most purposes, there is no basis for differentiation of adolescents from adults on the ground of competence alone"; he further concludes that "even elementary school children, when given decision making authority, are likely to behave in ways that create little risk of harm." Gary B. Melton, Developmental Psychology and the Law: The State of the Art, 22 J. Fam. L. 445, 463 (1984). He then advances reasons why the law might treat competent adolescents differently from adults: "First, there may be reason to support parental autonomy, especially where parents bear financial liability for their children's decisions. Second, recognition of liberty and autonomy need not be accompanied by full moral and legal responsibility. A benevolent society might choose to show solicitude toward its younger members (a sort of "second chance" theory). Third, that children have the *capacity* to perform competently and responsibly does not mean that they will exercise such maturity of judgment, particularly when the decision is made under circumstances of great stress or when social norms elicit undesirable behavior." Id. at 465–66.

Legislatures may mandate a voice for mature minors, for example in adoption, custody and guardianship statutes. Conversely courts may not invoke the mature-minor doctrine where a statute precludes its invocation. For example, a seventeen-year-old charged with consuming alcohol may not avoid liability by establishing that he can drink in a mature fashion; the alcohol control laws establish a minimum drinking age of twenty-one with no ifs, ands or buts.

3. *Tension with the age of majority.* The mature-minor doctrine necessarily creates tension with the general age of majority. Professor Wendy Anton Fitzgerald has noted that the age is "more arbitrary than empirically or logically justified," for example because "[a]n uninformed and politically indifferent adult may vote, * * * while a child prodigy well-versed in the salient issues may not." Wendy Anton Fitzgerald, Maturity, Difference, and Mystery: Children's Perspectives and the Law, 36 Ariz. L. Rev. 11 (1994). Other commentators have argued that the law must tolerate such arbitrariness (and the incongruity or harshness that might sometimes result in particular cases) because "the relevant factor of maturity lacks operational criteria":

> Although a test or an administrative process can accurately determine whether a driver is mechanically competent, how could we evaluate the maturity and judgment necessary to be a safe driver? If there is more to driving a car than mechanical competence, the inability to test individuals for the maturity factor leaves society in a dilemma. Either we license anyone who has mechanical competence and thus abandon our concern for maturity, or we use a specific age as a fallible proxy for

maturity. Because our society is unwilling to give a driver's license to every person who is able to pass the existing tests, it has chosen the latter course. One consequence is that some licensed adults are too immature to be safe drivers, but that outcome is implied in the nature of the test.

John E. Coons et al., Puzzling Over Children's Rights, 1991 BYU L. Rev. 307, 342. Moreover, "even if maturity could be determined on an individual basis, making the necessary judgments for the various functions would be enormously expensive to administer" and would "require many wise, seasoned, and well-paid decision makers." Professor Coons explains that "[h]earings might be necessary, followed by appeals for the unsuccessful. Perhaps legal counsel would participate. The process would also be repetitive because individual 'maturity' may change in a matter of months. If this is what is necessary to liberate from the state, would we not prefer to let a precocious child bear the temporary burdens of an arbitrary age line?" Id. See also, e.g., Jane Rutherford, One Child, One Vote: Proxies for Parents, 82 Minn. L. Rev. 1463, 1490 (1998) ("It is nearly impossible to determine which adolescents are good decision makers at which times because no clear standard of maturity exists.").

4. *Related privacy issues.* The Supreme Court has not decided whether a state law requiring mere parental notice (rather than consent) about a child's abortion decision must include a judicial bypass. Legislatures and lower courts, however, have assumed that a *Bellotti*-type bypass is constitutionally required. See, e.g., Wicklund v. Salvagni, 93 F.3d 567 (9th Cir. 1996), cert. granted and judgment reversed, 520 U.S. 292 (1997), on remand sub nom. Wicklund v. Lambert, 979 F.Supp. 1285 (D.Mont.1997) (upholding state law that provided a judicial bypass procedure for parental notice as well as parental consent). The Supreme Court has recognized a minor's privacy right to obtain contraceptives. See Carey v. Population Servs. Int'l, 431 U.S. 678 (1977).

IN THE MATTER OF LORI M

Family Court, Richmond County, 1985.
496 N.Y.S.2d 940.

DANIEL D. LEDDY, JR., JUDGE:

The petitioner in this proceeding alleges that her daughter is a person in need of supervision (PINS). For the purpose of this proceeding, Family Court Act § 712(a) defines such a person as one who is "incorrigible, ungovernable or habitually disobedient and beyond the lawful control of parent."

The petitioner mother alleges that her daughter, Lori, is associating with a 21-year-old lesbian named Ellen. This petition was filed when Lori absconded from home in defiance of her mother's directive that she have no contact or communication whatsoever with her older friend. Since that date, the respondent has been living with her maternal aunt, to whom she confided that she was bi-sexual. Neither the respondent's mother nor her aunt have had any other disciplinary problems with the child. She is obedient, respectful, and regularly adheres to her curfew. Lori attends a parochial high school on Staten Island where she receives excellent grades. The petitioner conceded that her complaint is based on the fact that the relationship is lesbian in nature and not the fact that Ellen is 21. The mother admitted that she would not be so upset if Lori was with a 21 year old male.

The child testified on her own behalf at the hearing and the Court was most impressed with her maturity. She stated very clearly that there had been no coercion involved and that it was her own decision to enter into this relationship. She stated that she has also had relationships with boys and that she has not made a final choice as to her sexual preference but that for now she is in love with Ellen, enjoys being with her, and wants to continue the relationship. Lori testified that she is very comfortable with her sexual feelings and does not believe that there is any need for counseling. She stated that her classmates at school are not aware of her feelings or her relationship with Ellen. And while she would prefer for things to remain that way, she is determined to persevere in this relationship regardless of what reaction that may evoke from her classmates, friends, or the general public. * * *

* * *

In the situation before this Court, the respondent invokes her right of privacy to decide and pursue her own sexual orientation. Homosexuality is no longer considered a psychiatric illness, and the Court does not presume to make a moral judgment regarding the respondent's choice. * * * [T]he Supreme Court has held that a mature child's right to make her own decision regarding abortion and contraception is constitutionally protected from parental or state interference. Where a child demonstrates sufficient maturity, her sexual orientation and choices in pursuit thereof must be held to be similarly protected.

Concededly, the constitutional rights of children cannot be completely equated with those of adults [citing *Prince* and *Bellotti*]. And it is clear that parents have not only the right but the obligation to direct the upbringing of children under their control. This parental right is of constitutional dimension and is, itself, entitled to protection. *Pierce v. Society of Sisters.* And where a child habitually disobeys the reasonable commands of his or her parents, state intervention by the parent may be had under Family Court Act article 7. However, not every parental direction may be enforced by state action. * * * [W]here a parental edict affects a substantial right of the child and is opposed by the child, resolution of the matter depends upon the nature of the right asserted by the child and the child's maturity.

* * *

[T]he New York courts have held that by age 14, a child is generally mature enough to have his choice of a religion respected, even if it conflicts with the views of his parents.

This 15–year-old respondent in this case impressed the Court with her maturity. It is clear that she has given a great deal of thought to her decision and its possible ramifications. And, since the right being asserted by her falls within the constitutionally protected zone of privacy, her mother may not invoke the power of the state to intervene. When the respondent left her home, she went to live with her aunt where she was well behaved and regularly attended school. The Court cannot adjudicate the respondent a person in need of supervision because of action on her part that was reasonably calculated to protect her constitutional rights.

Although the respondent is free to choose her sexual orientation without interference from this court, she is not free to act entirely as she wishes. Penal Law § 130.40 provides, *inter alia*, that it is a Class E felony for someone 21 years of age or older to engage in deviate sexual intercourse with a person less than 17 years of age. Notwithstanding the level of maturity reached by Lori, the Legislature has undertaken to proscribe such conduct in absolute terms insofar as children under seventeen are concerned. Accordingly, Lori is admonished in the strongest terms to avoid engaging in any conduct violative of the Penal Law of this State. * * *

For the reasons set forth herein, the petition is dismissed.

Notes and Questions

1. *Questions about* Lori M. (a) What constitutional right was Lori M. asserting?,

(b) Why did the court dismiss the PINS petition filed by Lori's mother?,

(c) What effect does the decision have on parents' ability to regulate the social activities of their mature children?,

(d) The court found that Lori was an obedient, respectful girl who adhered to her curfew and received excellent grades in school. Would the court have found her sufficiently mature if all this remained true but she was living with a friend or lover, or on the street, rather than with her aunt?

2. *The common law mature-minor doctrine.* In cases involving medical decisionmaking, courts frequently consider the wishes of mature minors. In In re E.G., 549 N.E.2d 322 (Ill. 1989), for example, a seventeen-year-old leukemia victim and her mother refused on religious grounds to consent to blood transfusions needed to treat the disease. The state filed a neglect petition and sought appointment of a guardian to consent to transfusions on the child's behalf. Holding that "a mature minor may exercise a common law right to consent or refuse medical care," the state supreme court expunged the order that found the victim neglected. *E.G.* appears as a principal case in Chapter 8, Medical Decision-making.

3. *Child vs. parent.* For all we can tell, the children in *Meyer, Pierce* and *Prince* wanted the same results as their parents; *Tinker* makes clear that the parents and children were united in support of the children's protest and the ensuing litigation; and parents served as their children's guardians ad litem in that case and the later decisions. Because the parents and children spoke without discordant voices, none of these decisions raises questions suggested

by Justice Douglas' *Yoder* dissent and squarely presented by *Bellotti* and many other mature-minor decisions: How should the court decide when the case pits the child against the parent, the child and the government against the parent, or the child against the parent and the government?

Most parent-child disputes are resolved within the family without court intervention. But if the dispute reaches the courtroom, when (if at all) may the child prevail? As a springboard for discussion, consider these passages from Parham v. J.R., 442 U.S. 584, 602–04 (1979):

> Our jurisprudence historically has reflected Western civilization concepts of the family as a unit with broad parental authority over minor children. * * * The law's concept of the family rests on a presumption that parents possess what a child lacks in maturity, experience, and capacity for judgment required for making life's difficult decisions. More important, historically it has recognized that natural bonds of affection lead parents to act in the best interests of their children.

> As with so many other legal presumptions, experience and reality may rebut what the law accepts as a starting point; the incidence of child neglect and abuse cases attests to this. That some parents "may at times be acting against the interests of their children" * * * creates a basis for caution, but is hardly a reason to discard wholesale those pages of human experience that teach that parents generally do act in the child's best interests. * * *

> Nonetheless, we have recognized that a state is not without constitutional control over parental discretion in dealing with children when their physical or mental health is jeopardized. See *Wisconsin* v. *Yoder*; *Prince* v. *Massachusetts*. * * *

> * * * Simply because the decision of a parent is not agreeable to a child or because it involves risks does not automatically transfer the power to make that decision from the parents to some agency or officer of the state. * * * Most children, even in adolescence, simply are not able to make sound judgments concerning many decisions, including their need for medical care or treatment. Parents can and must make those judgments. * * * We cannot assume that the result in *Meyer* v. *Nebraska* and *Pierce* v. *Society of Sisters* would have been different if the children there had announced a preference to learn only English or a preference to go to a public, rather than a church, school. The fact that a child may balk at hospitalization or complain about a parental refusal to provide cosmetic surgery does not diminish the parents' authority to decide what is best for the child. Neither state officials nor federal courts are equipped to review such parental decisions.

Parham determined the process due a child whose parents seek to voluntarily commit him to a state mental hospital, and specifically whether due process requires a precommitment hearing. The Court found a primary parental role: "[O]ur precedents permit the parents to retain a substantial, if not the dominant, role in the decision, absent a finding of neglect or abuse, and * * * the traditional presumption that the parents act in the best interests of their child should apply. * * * [But] the child's rights and the nature of the commitment decision are such that parents cannot always have absolute and unreviewable discretion to decide whether to have a child institutionalized." 442 U.S. at 604. *Parham* appears as a principal case in Chapter 8, Medical Decision-making.

Does the child's ability to overcome the parent depend in part on the importance of the disputed issue to the child's health or welfare? Does *Bellotti* stand for the proposition that some issues are so important to the child that a mature child must be heard? Should the law consider that the family structure may be irreparably harmed if the child prevails against the parent in litigation? What impact on family structure might *Lori M.* have? Because "the custody, care and nurture of the child reside first in the parents" (*Prince*), should the law defer to parents who appear serious about doing what they believe is best for the child, regardless of the child's age?

PROBLEM 1–3

Students at W. T. Clarke High School must complete fifty hours of community service during grades nine through twelve as a condition for graduation. The program has no opt-out provision for students who object to performing community service. Students must perform the required community service after school, on weekends or holidays, or during summer vacations. The high school's community service coordinator maintains a list of approved agencies and organizations the students may serve. The list is extensive and includes agencies and organizations with significantly different purposes and philosophies.

Students may not satisfy the service requirement with activities that provide monetary compensation. Credit may not be received for serving a for-profit organization unless the service provides a benefit otherwise unavailable to the organization's clients. Credit is not provided for service that promotes political parties or individual candidates. Students must establish their own work schedule and provide their own transportation to and from the service location. When students arrive to perform their service, they must sign in with the organization and a contact person with the organization must document the hours the student works. Students must return time sheets to Dr. Arnold Wallace, Clarke's respected veteran assistant principal. After completing the fifty hours of required service, students must submit a one-to-two-page paper discussing their experience.

A group of students and their parents file suit alleging that the school's public service requirement violates the students' rights to personal liberty and the parents' rights to direct their children's upbringing and education. Based on the decisions presented in this chapter so far, what arguments would you make to the court as counsel for the school district? As counsel for the parents? As counsel for the students? In each role, what arguments would you make if the parents sued to prevent the children's participation in the community service program but the children wished to participate?

D. *Statutory Influence*

Thus far this chapter has demonstrated that children's status, rights and obligations have frequently been shaped through constitutional litigation. Recent decades have also seen what Judge Guido Calabresi has called the "statutorification" of American law. Guido Calabresi, A Common Law for the Age of Statutes 1 (1982). As statutes (and their attendant administrative regulations) have come to play a more dominant role in American life, statutes have profoundly affected the lives of children. By examining two major statutes, this section sets the stage for the book's discussion of a wide range of social and economic legislation that influences the place of children in American society.

1. *The Individuals with Disabilities Education Act*

CEDAR RAPIDS COMMUNITY SCHOOL DISTRICT v. GARRET F.

Supreme Court of the United States, 1999.
526 U.S. 66.

JUSTICE STEVENS delivered the opinion of the Court.

The Individuals with Disabilities Education Act (IDEA), as amended, was enacted, in part, "to assure that all children with disabilities have available to them . . . a free appropriate public education which emphasizes special education and related services designed to meet their unique needs." Consistent with this purpose, the IDEA authorizes federal financial assistance to States that agree to provide disabled children with special education and "related services." The question presented in this case is whether the definition of "related services" in [20 U.S.C.] § 1401(a)(17)[1] requires a public school district in a participating State to provide a ventilator-dependent student with certain nursing services during school hours.

I

Respondent Garret F. is a friendly, creative, and intelligent young man. When Garret was four years old, his spinal column was severed in a motorcycle accident. Though paralyzed from the neck down, his mental capacities were unaffected. He is able to speak, to control his motorized wheelchair through use of a puff and suck straw, and to operate a computer with a device that responds to head movements. Garret is currently a student in the Cedar Rapids Community School District (District), he attends regular classes in a typical school program, and his

---

1. "The term 'related services' means transportation, and such developmental, corrective, and other supportive services (including speech pathology and audiology, psychological services, physical and occupational therapy, recreation, including therapeutic recreation, social work services, counseling services, including rehabilitation counseling, and medical services, except that such medical services shall be for diagnostic and evaluation purposes only) as may be required to assist a child with a disability to benefit from special education, and includes the early identification and assessment of disabling conditions in children."

academic performance has been a success. Garret is, however, ventilator dependent,[2] and therefore requires a responsible individual nearby to attend to certain physical needs while he is in school.[3]

During Garret's early years at school his family provided for his physical care during the school day. When he was in kindergarten, his 18–year-old aunt attended him; in the next four years, his family used settlement proceeds they received after the accident, their insurance, and other resources to employ a licensed practical nurse. In 1993, Garret's mother requested the District to accept financial responsibility for the health care services that Garret requires during the school day. The District denied the request, believing that it was not legally obligated to provide continuous one-on-one nursing services.

Relying on both the IDEA and Iowa law, Garret's mother requested a hearing before the Iowa Department of Education. An Administrative Law Judge (ALJ) received extensive evidence concerning Garret's special needs, the District's treatment of other disabled students, and the assistance provided to other ventilator-dependent children in other parts of the country. In his 47–page report, the ALJ found that the District has about 17,500 students, of whom approximately 2,200 need some form of special education or special services. Although Garret is the only ventilator-dependent student in the District, most of the health care services that he needs are already provided for some other students. "The primary difference between Garret's situation and that of other students is his dependency on his ventilator for life support." The ALJ noted that the parties disagreed over the training or licensure required for the care and supervision of such students, and that those providing such care in other parts of the country ranged from nonlicensed personnel to registered nurses. However, the District did not contend that only a licensed physician could provide the services in question.

The ALJ explained that federal law requires that children with a variety of health impairments be provided with "special education and related services" when their disabilities adversely affect their academic performance, and that such children should be educated to the maximum

---

2. In his report in this case, the Administrative Law Judge explained that "[b]eing ventilator dependent means that [Garret] breathes only with external aids, usually an electric ventilator, and occasionally by someone else's manual pumping of an air bag attached to his tracheotomy tube when the ventilator is being maintained. This later procedure is called ambu bagging."

3. "He needs assistance with urinary bladder catheterization once a day, the suctioning of his tracheotomy tube as needed, but at least once every six hours, with food and drink at lunchtime, in getting into a reclining position for five minutes of each hour, and ambu bagging occasionally as needed when the ventilator is checked for proper functioning. He also needs assistance from someone familiar with his venti-

lator in the event there is a malfunction or electrical problem, and someone who can perform emergency procedures in the event he experiences autonomic hyperreflexia. Autonomic hyperreflexia is an uncontrolled visceral reaction to anxiety or a full bladder. Blood pressure increases, heart rate increases, and flushing and sweating may occur. Garret has not experienced autonomic hyperreflexia frequently in recent years, and it has usually been alleviated by catheterization. He has not ever experienced autonomic hyperreflexia at school. Garret is capable of communicating his needs orally or in another fashion so long as he has not been rendered unable to do so by an extended lack of oxygen."

extent appropriate with children who are not disabled. In addition, the ALJ explained that applicable federal regulations distinguish between "school health services," which are provided by a "qualified school nurse or other qualified person," and "medical services," which are provided by a licensed physician. The District must provide the former, but need not provide the latter (except, of course, those "medical services" that are for diagnostic or evaluation purposes). According to the ALJ, the distinction in the regulations does not just depend on "the title of the person providing the service"; instead, the "medical services" exclusion is limited to services that are "in the special training, knowledge, and judgment of a physician to carry out." The ALJ thus concluded that the IDEA required the District to bear financial responsibility for all of the services in dispute, including continuous nursing services.

The District challenged the ALJ's decision in Federal District Court, but that Court approved the ALJ's IDEA ruling and granted summary judgment against the District. The Court of Appeals affirmed. * * *

II

The District contends that § 1401(a)(17) does not require it to provide Garret with "continuous one-on-one nursing services" during the school day, even though Garret cannot remain in school without such care. However, the IDEA's definition of "related services," our decision in *Irving Independent School Dist.* v. *Tatro* (1984), and the overall statutory scheme all support the decision of the Court of Appeals.

The text of the "related services" definition, see n. 1, *supra*, broadly encompasses those supportive services that "may be required to assist a child with a disability to benefit from special education." * * * As a general matter, services that enable a disabled child to remain in school during the day provide the student with "the meaningful access to education that Congress envisioned."

This general definition of "related services" is illuminated by a parenthetical phrase listing examples of particular services that are included within the statute's coverage. "Medical services" are enumerated in this list, but such services are limited to those that are "for diagnostic and evaluation purposes." The statute does not contain a more specific definition of the "medical services" that are excepted from the coverage of § 1401(a)(17).

The scope of the "medical services" exclusion is not a matter of first impression in this Court. In *Tatro* we concluded that the Secretary of Education had reasonably determined that the term "medical services" referred only to services that must be performed by a physician, and not to school health services. Accordingly, we held that a specific form of health care (clean intermittent catherization) that is often, though not always, performed by a nurse is not an excluded medical service. We referenced the likely cost of the services and the competence of school staff as justifications for drawing a line between physician and other services, but our endorsement of that line was unmistakable. It is thus settled that the phrase "medical services" in § 1401(a)(17) does not embrace all forms of care that might loosely be described as "medical" in other contexts, such as a claim for an income tax deduction.

The District does not ask us to define the term so broadly. Indeed, the District does not argue that any of the items of care that Garret needs, considered individually, could be excluded from the scope of § 1401(a)(17). It could not make such an argument, considering that one of the services Garret needs (catheterization) was at issue in *Tatro*, and the others may be provided competently by a school nurse or other trained personnel. As the ALJ concluded, most of the requested services are already provided by the District to other students, and the in-school care necessitated by Garret's ventilator dependency does not demand the training, knowledge, and judgment of a licensed physician. While more extensive, the in-school services Garret needs are no more "medical" than was the care sought in *Tatro*.

Instead, the District points to the combined and continuous character of the required care, and proposes a test under which the outcome in any particular case would "depend upon a series of factors, such as [1] whether the care is continuous or intermittent, [2] whether existing school health personnel can provide the service, [3] the cost of the service, and [4] the potential consequences if the service is not properly performed."

The District's multi-factor test is not supported by any recognized source of legal authority. * * *

Finally, the District raises broader concerns about the financial burden that it must bear to provide the services that Garret needs to stay in school. The problem for the District in providing these services is not that its staff cannot be trained to deliver them; the problem, the District contends, is that the existing school health staff cannot meet all of their responsibilities and provide for Garret at the same time. Through its multi-factor test, the District seeks to establish a kind of undue-burden exemption primarily based on the cost of the requested services. The first two factors can be seen as examples of cost-based distinctions: intermittent care is often less expensive than continuous care, and the use of existing personnel is cheaper than hiring additional employees. The third factor—the cost of the service—would then encompass the first two. The relevance of the fourth factor is likewise related to cost because extra care may be necessary if potential consequences are especially serious.

The District may have legitimate financial concerns, but our role in this dispute is to interpret existing law. Defining "related services" in a manner that *accommodates* the cost concerns Congress may have had is altogether different from using cost *itself* as the definition. Given that § 1401(a)(17) does not employ cost in its definition of "related services" or excluded "medical services," accepting the District's cost-based standard as the sole test for determining the scope of the provision would require us to engage in judicial lawmaking without any guidance from

Congress. It would also create some tension with the purposes of the IDEA. The statute may not require public schools to maximize the potential of disabled students commensurate with the opportunities provided to other children; and the potential financial burdens imposed on participating States may be relevant to arriving at a sensible construction of the IDEA. But Congress intended "to open the door of public education" to all qualified children and "require[d] participating States to educate handicapped children with nonhandicapped children whenever possible."

This case is about whether meaningful access to the public schools will be assured, not the level of education that a school must finance once access is attained. It is undisputed that the services at issue must be provided if Garret is to remain in school. Under the statute, our precedent, and the purposes of the IDEA, the District must fund such "related services" in order to help guarantee that students like Garret are integrated into the public schools.

The judgment of the Court of Appeals is accordingly

Affirmed.

JUSTICE THOMAS, with whom JUSTICE KENNEDY joins, dissenting.

* * *

Unlike clean intermittent catheterization [the care at issue in *Tatro*], * * * a school nurse cannot provide the services that respondent requires and continue to perform her normal duties. To the contrary, because respondent requires continuous, one-on-one care throughout the entire school day, all agree that the district must hire an additional employee to attend solely to respondent. This will cost a minimum of $18,000 per year. Although the majority recognizes this fact, it nonetheless concludes that the "more extensive" nature of the services that respondent needs is irrelevant to the question whether those services fall under the medical services exclusion. This approach * * * blindsides unwary States with fiscal obligations that they could not have anticipated.

* * *

Notes and Questions

1. *The IDEA in perspective.* Congress first addressed the matter of educating children with disabilities in 1966, when it amended the Elementary and Secondary Education Act of 1965 to establish a grant program to "assist[] the states in the initiation, expansion, and improvement of programs and projects * * * for the education of handicapped children." Pub. L. 89–750 § 161, 80 Stat. 1204. In 1970 the Education of the Handicapped Act, Pub. L. 91–230, 84 Stat. 175, repealed the grant program and established a similar grant program. Neither the 1966 nor the 1970 legislation established guidelines to regulate state use of the grant funding, but merely sought to stimulate states to educate disabled children. Most states did not respond meaningfully to the stimulation. "[S]ome states had passed laws to improve

the educational services afforded handicapped children, but many of these children were excluded completely from any form of public education or were left to fend for themselves in classrooms designed for education of their nonhandicapped peers." Board of Educ. v. Rowley, 458 U.S. 176, 191 (1982).

With states moving only sluggishly, Congress in 1974 enacted interim funding legislation that required states for the first time to adopt "a goal of providing full educational opportunities to all handicapped children." Pub. L. 93–380, 88 Stat. 579, 583. The following year, Congress enacted the Education of All Handicapped Children Act, which conferred on disabled students an enforceable substantive right to public education in participating states, and conditioned federal funding on a state's compliance with the Act's intricate substantive and procedural requirements. The Act's drafters were influenced by settlement agreements reached in class actions challenging the constitutionality of public education provided to children with disabilities. See Pennsylvania Assoc. for Retarded Children v. Pennsylvania, 334 F.Supp. 1257 (E.D.Pa.1971), 343 F.Supp. 279 (E.D.Pa.1972); Mills v. Board of Educ., 348 F.Supp. 866 (D.D.C.1972). Congress renamed the Act the Individuals with Disabilities Education Act (IDEA) in 1990 and enacted comprehensive amendments to the IDEA in 1997. All states now participate in the IDEA's joint federal-state initiative.

The landmark 1975 Act came twenty-one years after the Supreme Court had called education "perhaps the most important function of state and local governments." Brown v. Board of Educ., 347 U.S. 483, 493 (1954). States had provided some public instruction to children with disabilities, but the haphazard programs depended on official discretion rather than legal entitlement.

Until the mid–1970s, most states authorized localities to decline to enroll children found "ineducable." Many courts remained inhospitable to the children's claims of constitutional or statutory right. For example, in Pierce v. Society of Sisters [supra p. 23] the Supreme Court expressed no difficulty with a statute that exempted from the public schools "children who are not normal." See also, e.g., Department of Pub. Welfare v. Haas, 154 N.E.2d 265, 270 (Ill. 1958) (state constitution did not guarantee free public education to the "feeble minded or mentally deficient" who could not "receive a good common school education"); State ex rel. Beattie v. Board of Educ., 172 N.W. 153, 154 (Wis. 1919) (approving exclusion of "a crippled and defective child" who had "a depressing and nauseating effect upon the teachers and school children," which "distract[ed] the attention of other pupils, and interfere[d] generally with the school's discipline and progress"). But see, e.g., In re Downey, 340 N.Y.S.2d 687, 690 (Fam. Ct. 1973) (awarding father $6,496 tuition for his disabled child's education; "while at first blush this may seem like a substantial outlay of funds for one child, when compared with the dollar cost of maintaining a child in an institution all his life or on public assistance the cost is minimal; not to speak of the incalculable cost to society of losing a potentially productive adult").

By the mid–1970s, congressional studies had demonstrated that more than half the nation's eight million children with disabilities still "were either totally excluded from schools or sitting idly in regular classrooms awaiting the time when they were old enough to 'drop out.'" H.R. Rep. No.

94–332, at 2 (1975). Congressional statistics revealed that in 1974, the educational needs of 82% of emotionally disturbed children went unmet. See S. Rep. No. 94–168, at 8 (1975).

One commentator has called the IDEA "[t]he third revolution in American education," following the creation of compulsory education and the *Brown* desegregation decision. Seymour B. Sarason, Parental Involvement and the Political Principle 35 (1995). To be sure, the third revolution came with a price because the IDEA has been "among the most costly and heavily litigated statutes passed by Congress in the last two decades." 2 Donald T. Kramer, Legal Rights of Children § 26–10, at 631 (2d ed. 1994). By some estimates, services for students with disabilities now account for as much as 12% of public school expenditures nationwide. See Thomas B. Parrish and Jay G. Chambers, Financing Special Education, in 6 The Future of Children 121, 121 (1996).

The IDEA provides federal grants to participating states to educate disabled children, but the costs to states and local school districts of fulfilling the Act's mandates considerably exceed the federal contribution. Federal IDEA grants provide only about eight percent of the total cost nationwide for special education and related services, while states and localities shoulder 56% and 36% of the cost respectively. See Parrish and Chambers, supra at 122.

Financial burdens may divide school districts and parents. Districts may seek to contain the seemingly high cost of providing special services to a relatively small number of students ($18,000 per year for Garret F. alone, according to Justice Thomas' dissent). Parents of disabled children, and the children themselves, seek enrichment and opportunities made available by free public education, a right guaranteed to all children by state constitution and statute.

2. *"Children with disabilities."* The IDEA defines "child with a disability" to mean a child who needs special education and related services because of "mental retardation, hearing impairments (including deafness), speech or language impairments, visual impairments (including blindness), serious emotional disturbance * * *, orthopedic impairments, autism, traumatic brain injury, other health impairments, or specific learning disabilities." 20 U.S.C. § 1401(3)(A).

About 11% of public school students receive some form of special education under the IDEA, and the number is expected to continue rising because of demographic trends and social factors, such as the rising number of babies born with positive drug toxicologies in recent years. See Donna L. Terman et al., Special Education for Students with Disabilities: Analysis and Recommendations, in 6 The Future of Children 4 (1996). In 1992–93, 51% of elementary and secondary students served by the IDEA had learning disabilities as their primary disability; 22% had language or speech impairments; 11% had mental retardation; 9% had serious emotional disturbance; and 7% had hearing or visual impairments, orthopedic impairments, autism, traumatic brain injury, or multiple disabilities. Id. at 7.

The IDEA does not wait until a disabled child becomes eligible to enroll in the public school system. A participating state may also provide special education and related services to infants and toddlers and children between three and nine who qualify. 20 U.S.C. § 1401(3)(B).

3. *"Free appropriate public education."* To receive federal grants, a state must have in effect policies and procedures to ensure that with limited exceptions, "[a] free appropriate public education is available to all children with disabilities in the State between the ages of 3 and 21, inclusive, including children with disabilities who have been suspended or expelled from school." 20 U.S.C. § 1412(a)(1).

In Board of Educ. v. Rowley, 458 U.S. 176, 192 (1982), the Supreme Court held that the IDEA's purpose was "more to open the door of public education to handicapped children on appropriate terms than to guarantee any particular level of education once inside." The free-appropriate-public-education mandate requires only that the state offer a disabled child "meaningful" access to "specialized instruction and related services which are individually designed to provide educational benefit." Id. at 192, 201. *Rowley* rejected the contention that the state must provide "strict equality of opportunity or services," or "every special service necessary to maximize each handicapped child's potential * * * commensurate with the opportunity provided nonhandicapped children." Id. at 198–200.

Since *Rowley*, courts of appeals have required states to provide disabled children educational programs that confer "more than a trivial or de minimis educational benefit." See Polk v. Central Susquehanna Intermediate Unit 16, 853 F.2d 171, 180–85 (3d Cir.1988). A free appropriate public education is one that is "likely to produce progress, not regression." Cypress–Fairbanks Indep. Sch. Dist. v. Michael F., 118 F.3d 245, 248 (5th Cir.1997), cert. denied, 522 U.S. 1047 (1998). The District of Columbia Circuit, however, has stated that because public "resources are not infinite," the IDEA "does not secure the best education money can buy." Lunceford v. District of Columbia Bd. of Educ., 745 F.2d 1577, 1583 (D.C.Cir.1984) (Ruth Bader Ginsburg, J.).

State law may provide disabled children greater rights than the IDEA. Massachusetts, for example, requires the state Department of Education to administer programs that "assure the maximum possible development of a child with special needs." See, e.g., Stock v. Massachusetts Hosp. Sch., 467 N.E.2d 448, 453 (Mass.1984).

Where a school district fails to provide a disabled child a free appropriate public education for some period, a court may require the district to provide educational services past the child's twenty-first birthday. See, e.g., M.C. v. Central Regional Sch. Dist., 81 F.3d 389, 395 (3d Cir.1996). Many decisions awarding such "compensatory education" involve egregious or flagrant failure by the state to comply with IDEA. See, e.g., Carlisle Area Sch. Dist. v. Scott P., 62 F.3d 520, 536–37 (3d Cir.1995). *M.C.* held, however, that a compensatory education award is proper whenever the district knows or should know that it is not providing an appropriate education, even where the district does not act in bad faith. 81 F.3d at 396.

4. *The "individualized education program."* The primary vehicle for implementing the IDEA's goals is the "individualized education program" (IEP), which the school must have in place for the disabled child at the beginning of each school year. 20 U.S.C. § 1414(d)(2)(A). The IEP is a detailed written

statement that summarizes the particular child's abilities, outlines the goals for the child's education and specifies the services the child will receive. See 20 U.S.C. § 1414(d)(1)(A).

The IDEA seeks to empower parents in the process that determines their disabled child's education. The student's IEP is developed by a team consisting of the parents, the child's regular and special education teachers, a school district representative, and, where appropriate, the child. 20 U.S.C. § 1414(d)(1)(B). A non-custodial parent after a divorce may participate in formulating the IEP, even where the custodial parent has sole legal custody. See, e.g., Doe v. Anrig, 651 F.Supp. 424, 428 (D.Mass.1987). The IEP must be reviewed "periodically, but not less than annually to determine whether the annual goals for the child are being achieved," and must be revised as appropriate. 20 U.S.C. § 1414(d)(4)(A). Parents may challenge the IEP in administrative proceedings subject to judicial review; such a challenge reached the Supreme Court in *Garret F.*

5. *An "undue burden" defense?* The defendant Cedar Rapids school district argued that in determining its IDEA obligations to Garret F., the court should weigh the cost of providing the requested daily one-on-one care. The Americans with Disabilities Act contains an undue-burden defense, but the IDEA does not. Shortly before the Supreme Court decided *Garret F.*, the Seventh Circuit suggested that the defense might be "implicit in the statutory concepts of an 'appropriate' education and 'related' services. Perhaps at some point the expense of keeping a disabled child alive during the school day is so disproportionate to any plausible educational objective for the child that the expense should not be considered a component of an appropriate education for a severely disabled child or a service reasonably related to such an education." Morton Community Unit Sch. Dist. v. J.M., 152 F.3d 583, 586 (7th Cir.1998).

Garret F. rebuffed the school district's effort to raise an "undue burden" defense, stating that the case concerned "whether meaningful access to the public schools will be assured, not the level of education that a school must finance once access is attained." Because "the services at issue must be provided if Garret is to remain in school," the Court held that the IDEA required the school district to provide the requested services. Would *Garret F.* require the school district to bear the cost if a court finds that a particular disabled child could benefit from a free appropriate public education only if the school built a bubble chamber for him and staffed it every day with a team of technicians and registered nurses but not a licensed physician?

6. *Mainstreaming.* The IDEA requires participating states to ensure (1) that "[t]o the maximum extent appropriate, children with disabilities * * * are educated with children who are not disabled," and (2) that "special classes, separate schooling, or other removal of children with disabilities from the regular educational environment occurs only when the nature or severity of the disability of a child is such that education in regular classes with the use of supplementary aids and services cannot be achieved satisfactorily." 20 U.S.C. § 1412(a)(5)(A). This "mainstreaming" requirement enunciates a "strong congressional preference for integrating children with disabilities in regular classrooms." Oberti v. Board of Educ., 995 F.2d 1204, 1214 (3d Cir.1993). The preference's strength is demonstrated by the re-

quirement, added by the comprehensive 1997 amendments to the IDEA, that each IEP include an "explanation of the extent, if any, to which the child will not participate with nondisabled children in the regular class." 20 U.S.C. § 1414(d)(1)(A)(iv). Indeed the Senate Report stated that the 1997 amendments contain not merely a strong preference, but "a presumption that children with disabilities are to be educated in regular classes." Sen. Comm. Rept. on P.L. 105–17, at 26 (1997). Several circuits have specified that mainstreaming's benefits may inure not only to disabled students who benefit from associating with nondisabled peers, but also to nondisabled youngsters who learn to work and communicate with the disabled. See, e.g., Oberti, supra, 995 F.2d at 1216 n.24.

The mainstreaming preference (or presumption) is not an inflexible mandate. In close cases, mainstreaming's social benefits may be at logger-heads with the need for specialized educational services and perhaps with the need to maintain an orderly educational environment. In DeVries v. Fairfax County Sch. Bd., 882 F.2d 876, 879 (4th Cir.1989), for example, the court held that mainstreaming is not required (1) where the disabled child would not receive an educational benefit from participation in a regular class, (2) where any marginal benefit from mainstreaming would be significantly outweighed by benefits the disabled child could receive only in a separate instructional setting, or (3) where the disabled child is a disruptive force in a regular classroom setting.

Congress addressed mainstreaming because disabled children, frequently over their parents' protests, had often been "warehoused" in special classes and segregated programs beyond the sight and sound of nondisabled students. Dispute may also arise, however, when the school district seeks to mainstream a disabled child and the child's parents request the district to provide and fund segregated special education. In the latter event, the court affirms the district's decision where it finds mainstreaming appropriate to the child's educational needs. See, e.g., Jonathan G. v. Lower Merion Sch. Dist., 955 F.Supp. 413 (E.D.Pa.1997).

Mainstreaming has had a significant effect on education of children with disabilities. Before the IDEA, an estimated 70% of these children were instructed in separate classes or separate buildings. Now most children with disabilities are served in non-segregated settings. Today 34.9% of children diagnosed as disabled are served in regular classes, 36.3% in part-time resource room programs, 23.5% in separate classes within regular school buildings, 3.9% in separate schools, 0.9% in residential facilities and 0.5% in homebound or hospital programs. See Michael A. Rebell and Robert L. Hughes, Special Educational Inclusion and the Courts: A Proposal for a New Remedial Approach, 25 J. L. & Educ. 523, 524 (1996).

7. *Unilateral parental action.* In School Comm. v. Department of Educ., 471 U.S. 359 (1985), the Court held that a court may order school authorities to reimburse parents for their expenditures on private special education for their child if the court ultimately determines that such placement, rather than a proposed IEP, is proper under the IDEA. In Florence County Sch. Dist. Four v. Carter, 510 U.S. 7, 11–13 (1993), the Court held that a court may order reimbursement even where the parents' placement did not meet the statutory definition of a "free appropriate public education." A parent

taking unilateral action, of course, runs the risk that money spent today will never be reimbursed because the school authorities' proposed plan is found sufficient under the Act.

8. *Providing services in sectarian schools.* In Zobrest v. Catalina Foothills Sch. Dist., 509 U.S. 1 (1993), the Court held, 5–4, that the First Amendment Establishment Clause did not prevent the defendant school district under the IDEA from furnishing a sign-language interpreter to a deaf student on the premises of the Catholic high school he attended. *Zobrest* drew on the so-called "child benefit" theory, reasoning that the IDEA "creates a neutral government program dispensing aid not to schools but to individual handicapped children." Id. at 13.

Zobrest concerned the question whether the Establishment Clause *permits* school districts to pay for services provided to disabled students on the premises of the sectarian schools they attend. Once the permission question is resolved, the IDEA itself determines whether the district is *required* to pay for such services. The IDEA answers the "requirement" question by distinguishing between students placed in private schools by the school district itself, and students voluntarily placed in private schools by their parents without the school district's consent or referral. Children placed in private schools by the school district "are provided special education and related services, in accordance with an individualized educational program, at no cost to their parents." 20 U.S.C. § 1412(a)(10)(B)(i). The 1997 IDEA amendments, however, specify that the Act "does not require a local educational agency to pay for the cost of education, including special education and related services, of a child with a disability at a private school or facility if that agency made a free appropriate public education available to the child and the parents elected to place the child in such private school or facility." 20 U.S.C. § 1412(a)(10)(C)(i).

9. *Suspending or expelling disabled students.* Like other students, students with disabilities may engage in disruptive, violent or criminal behavior in school. Case law consistently interpreted the IDEA to prohibit unilateral suspensions for more than ten days and unilateral expulsions for behavior relating to the student's disability. A longer suspension or expulsion constituted a change in placement, which could occur only with the consent of both the school and the parents. The comprehensive 1997 IDEA amendments reaffirmed existing law but created two public safety exceptions to "make sure that no child who is dangerous is forced on the other children in the classroom." 143 Cong. Rec. S4358 (daily ed. May 13, 1997) (statement of Sen. Jeffords).

Under the IDEA's "stay-put" provision, parents who disagree with a school district's decision to remove a disabled child from the present educational setting may request an administrative hearing, subject to judicial review. The provision states that "unless the State or local educational agency and the parents otherwise agree, the child shall remain in the then-current educational placement" during the pendency of any administrative proceeding or judicial appeal challenging a removal order. 20 U.S.C. § 1415(j). The provision applies to efforts to suspend or expel a disabled child, which would work a removal.

The two new exceptions, however, enable school personnel (1) to unilaterally suspend the disabled child or move him to an alternative educational setting for not more than ten days, and (2) to unilaterally move the disabled child to an alternative educational setting for not more than 45 days if the child carries a weapon to school or to a school function, or if the child knowingly possesses or uses illegal drugs or sells or solicits the sale of a controlled substance while at school or a school function. In either event, the disabled child may be removed only to the extent a nondisabled child would be subject to removal for the same conduct.

The IDEA requires participating states, with minor exceptions, to ensure that "[a] free appropriate public education is available to all children with disabilities residing in the State between the ages of 3 and 21, inclusive, including children with disabilities who have been suspended or expelled from school." 20 U.S.C. § 1412(a)(1)(A). The school district thus may suspend or expel a disabled student regardless of whether the student's underlying conduct was related to the disability, but then must provide the suspended or expelled student alternative educational services.

The alternative education requirement applies whether or not the suspension or expulsion resulted from conduct related to the student's disability. The requirement also applies even in states in which nondisabled students would not be entitled to free public alternative education after suspension or expulsion. Because the IDEA requires alternative education for disabled students who are suspended or expelled, could a state as a practical matter deny such an education to nondisabled students who suffer such sanctions?

Two other disciplinary matters deserve mention. First, the IDEA now expressly authorizes school officials to contact law enforcement officers if a disabled child is suspected of committing a crime; the school may provide the law enforcement agency with the student's special education and disciplinary records. See 20 U.S.C. § 1415(k)(9)(B). The IDEA does not prevent prosecution of the child under state or federal law. See 20 U.S.C. § 1415(k)(9).

Second, the 1997 IDEA amendments clarify that where a student violates the school district code of conduct, the parents may invoke the Act on the child's behalf only where the district had knowledge of the student's disability. The district had knowledge if (1) the parents expressed concern in writing that their child may require special education, (2) the child's behavior indicated he or she needed special education, (3) the parents requested an evaluation, or (4) the child's teacher expressed concern about the child's performance or behavior to school personnel. See 20 U.S.C. § 1415(k)(8)(B). If the school district did not have knowledge, the student may be disciplined as a nondisabled student would be disciplined.

10. *Other potential statutory remedies.* (a) *The Rehabilitation Act of 1973 and the Americans with Disabilities Act of 1990 (ADA).* The Rehabilitation Act of 1973, 29 U.S.C. § 701 et seq., prohibits discrimination based on disability in federally funded programs. To establish a violation of § 504 of the Rehabilitation Act, the plaintiff must prove (1) that he is "disabled" as defined by the Act, (2) that he is "otherwise qualified" to participate in school activities, (3) that the school or the board of education receives federal financial assistance, and (4) that he was excluded from participation in,

denied the benefits of, or subject to discrimination at, the school because of his disability. See, e.g., W.B. v. Matula, 67 F.3d 484, 492 (3d Cir.1995). The plaintiff must also demonstrate that the defendant knew or should be reasonably expected to have known of his disability; most courts hold, however that the plaintiff need not prove that the defendants' discrimination was intentional. Id.

Congress enacted the ADA to create "a comprehensive national mandate for the elimination of discrimination against individuals with disabilities." 42 U.S.C. § 12010(b)(1), (2). The ADA prohibits discrimination against persons with disabilities in the private and public sectors alike. The ADA extends section 504's protections to programs, activities, and services that do not receive federal funds and thus lie outside section 504.

There are few differences between the IDEA's affirmative duty and the negative prohibition of § 504 of the Rehabilitation Act; indeed regulations implementing § 504 require that a school district "provide a free appropriate education to each qualified handicapped person in [the] jurisdiction." Matula, supra, 67 F.3d at 492–93. Nonetheless, § 504 or the ADA would provide a remedy for some important matters beyond the IDEA's scope. For example, a student who has a disability (such as HIV) but does not require special education would be entitled to reasonable accommodations under section 504 and the ADA. The Rehabilitation Act and the ADA also reach some educational matters not reached by the IDEA, such as a disabled student's right to participate in interscholastic athletics and other extracurricular activities. See, e.g., Sandison v. Michigan High Sch. Athletic Ass'n, 64 F.3d 1026, 1030–37 (6th Cir. 1995) (defendants did not violate Rehabilitation Act or ADA by refusing to allow plaintiffs, students with learning disabilities, to participate in track and cross-country pursuant to regulation declaring 19–year-olds ineligible to participate in any high school sport); Bingham v. Oregon Sch. Activities Ass'n, 37 F. Supp.2d 1189, 1205 (D.Or.1999) (waiver of rule prohibiting fifth-year seniors from competing in interscholastic sports was a reasonable accommodation to accommodate the plaintiff student's learning disability).

b. *42 U.S.C. § 1983.* This statute creates a private right of action against a person who, acting under color of state law, deprives a person of any right "secured by the Constitution and laws." Because school officials act under the color of state law, the section would permit suit for their conduct which would have the effect of depriving a student with disabilities of rights secured by a federal act such as the IDEA.

2. *The Indian Child Welfare Act*

As part of an assimilation policy, the U.S. Bureau of Indian Affairs historically facilitated removal of large numbers of Native American children from their homes for placement with non-Indian parents. The Indian Child Welfare Act of 1978, 25 U.S.C. § 1901 et seq. (ICWA), limits the removal of Native American children from their tribes. Section 1902 of the Act recites congressional policy to "protect the best interests of Indian children and to promote the stability and security of Indian tribes and families by the establishment of minimum Federal standards for the removal of Indian children from their families and the placement of such children in foster or adoptive homes which will reflect the unique values of Indian culture, and by providing for assistance to Indian tribes in the operation of child and family service programs."

In 1978, one tribal chief testified before a House subcommittee about the deleterious effects of removing Indian children from their homes and placing them with non-Indians:

> Culturally, the chances of Indian survival are significantly reduced if our children, the only real means for the transmission of the tribal heritage, are to be raised in non-Indian homes and denied exposure to the ways of their People. Furthermore, these practices seriously undercut the tribes' ability to continue as self-governing communities. Probably in no area is it more important that tribal sovereignty be respected than in an area as socially and culturally determinative as family relationships.

* * *

> One of the most serious failings of the present system is that Indian children are removed from the custody of their natural parents by nontribal government authorities who have no basis for intelligently evaluating the cultural and social premises underlying Indian home life and childrearing. Many of the individuals who decide the fate of our children are at best ignorant of our cultural values, and at worst contemptful of the Indian way and convinced that removal, usually to a non-Indian household or institution, can only benefit an Indian child.

Mississippi Band of Choctaw Indians v. Holyfield, 490 U.S. 30, 34–35 (1989). The ICWA establishes "a Federal policy that, wherever possible, an indian child should remain in the Indian community," and ensures that Indian child welfare determinations are not made on "a white, middle-class standard which, in many cases, forecloses placement with [an] Indian family." H.R. Rep. No. 95–1386, at 23–24.

The ICWA requires that placement decisions for Indian children be made using different standards than those used for other children. As Professor Jennifer Carleton explains:

> ICWA embodies implicit assumptions about what is in the "best interests" of an Indian child. When it enacted ICWA, Congress recognized that the best interests of Indian children are of tantamount importance, that the best interests of an Indian child are served by ensuring tribal participation in placement and adoption proceedings, and that tribal participation in proceedings involving Indian children is necessary because "the States, exercising their recognized jurisdiction over Indian child custody proceedings throught administrative and judicial bodies, have often failed to recognize the essential tribal relations of Indian people and the cultural and social standards prevailing in Indian communities and families." The underlying premise of ICWA is that Indian tribes, as sovereign governments, have a vital interest in any decision as to

whether Indian children should be separated from their families. To that end, ICWA applies a "best interests of the tribe" standard, in addition to the best interests of the child and the parent.

Jennifer Nutt Carleton, The Indian Child Welfare Act: A Study in the Codification of the Ethnic Best Interests of the Child, 81 Marq.L. Rev. 21 (1997).

The ICWA applies in state court "child custody proceedings" concerning an Indian child and, under the federal Constitution's Supremacy Clause, preempts state law inconsistent with it. These proceedings are ones involving foster care placement, termination of parental rights, pre-adoptive placement, and adoptive placement; the Act expressly excludes delinquency placements, custody awards to a parent in divorce actions, and state intervention in Indian families that does not contemplate removing the child. 25 U.S.C. § 1903(1). An "Indian child" is any unmarried person under eighteen who (1) is either a member of an Indian tribe or is eligible for membership in an Indian tribe and (2) is the biological child of a member of an Indian tribe. 25 U.S.C. § 1903(4).

The Act provides that "[i]n any adoptive placement of an Indian child under State law, a preference shall be given, in the absence of good cause to the contrary, to a placement with (1) a member of the child's extended family; (2) other members of the Indian child's tribe; or (3) other Indian families. 25 U.S.C. § 1915(a). In the absence of good cause to the contrary, foster care placement of an Indian child must be made with (1) a member of the child's extended family, (2) a foster home licensed, approved or specified by the child's tribe, (3) an Indian foster home licensed or approved by a non-Indian licensing authority, or (4) an institution for children approved by an Indian tribe or operated by an Indian organization which has a program suitable to meet the child's needs." 25 U.S.C. § 1915(b). These placement preferences are considered the "real bite" of the ICWA, and they apply to both state and tribal agencies. Carleton, supra, at 26. Placement agencies "must adhere to 'prevailing social and cultural standards of the Indian community in which the parent or extended family resides.'" 25 U.S.C. § 1915(d).

The Act includes stringent standards for removing children from the home and for and terminating parental rights:

(e) No foster care placement may be ordered * * * in the absence of a determination, supported by clear and convincing evidence, including testimony of qualified expert witnesses, that the continued custody of the child by the parent or Indian custodian is likely to result in serious emotional or physical damage to the child.

(f) No termination of parental rights may be ordered * * * in the absence of a determination, supported by evidence beyond a reasonable doubt, including testimony of qualified expert witnesses, that the continued custody of the child by the parent or Indian custodian is likely to result in serious emotional or physical damage to the child.

25 U.S.C. § 1912. *Holyfield* reversed a judgment that would have allowed state court jurisdiction to supplant tribal jurisdiction in many ICWA cases. The Court did not address the ICWA's constitutionality, but lower courts have found or assumed the Act constitutional. For example, in Angus v. Joseph, 655 P.2d 208, 213 (Or.App.1982), the court of appeals found "protection of the integrity of Indian families" a permissible goal rationally tied to the fulfillment of "Congress' unique guardianship obligation toward Indians."

Courts remain split on whether to recognize the judicially-created "existing Indian family" doctrine, which precludes application of the ICWA when the Indian child's parent or parents have not maintained a significant social, cultural or political relationship with the tribe. Courts applying the doctrine view it as effectuating the ICWA's policy of maintaining tribal heritage; courts rejecting the doctrine view it as contrary to the Act's plain language. See, e.g., State in the Interest of D.A.C., 933 P.2d 993, 997 & n. 6 (Utah App.1997) (citing decisions).

Further discussion of ICWA appears in Chapter 7, Adoption.

E. An International–Law Basis for Children's Rights?

The United Nations Convention on the Rights of the Child, adopted by the U.N. General Assembly in 1989 and now ratified by virtually every nation, is the most widely ratified human rights treaty in history. The Convention continues along the path blazed by the Geneva Declaration of the Rights of the Child, which the Assembly of the League of Nations accepted in 1924, and the U.N. Declaration of the Rights of the Child, which the U.N. General Assembly adopted in 1959. The two brief declarations are nonbinding, but they express general principles that still guide national aspirations.

The first legally binding provisions protecting children's rights appeared in two covenants the U.N. adopted in 1966. The first, the International Covenant on Civil and Political Rights, provides that "[e]very child shall have, without any discrimination as to race, colour, sex, language, religion, national or social origin, property or birth, the right to such measures of protection as are required by his status as a minor, on the part of his family, society and the State." 999 U.N.T.S. 171 (entered into force Mar. 23, 1976). The second, the International Covenant on Economic, Social and Cultural Rights, provides that "[s]pecial measures of protection and assistance should be taken on behalf of all children and young persons without any discrimination for reasons of parentage or other conditions." 993 U.N.T.S. 3 (entered into force Jan. 3, 1976). The United States has signed both covenants, but has ratified only the first.

Several dozen other international instruments also carry provisions relating to children. The Convention on the Rights of the Child, however, is the first international instrument to comprehensively cover children's civil, political, economic, social and cultural rights. The Commission on Human Rights began deliberating and drafting the Convention in 1979, the International Year of the Child. The U.N. General Assembly unanimously adopted the Convention on November 20, 1989, and it was opened for signature on January 26, 1990. Sixty-one nations signed it on the first day, a greater first-day response than any other international human rights treaty had ever received. The Convention entered into force when the twentieth nation ratified it only seven months later, more swiftly than any other human rights convention.

By early 1999, the Convention had been ratified by 191 of the 193 nations recognized by the United Nations. Somalia (which does not have a recognized government capable of ratifying a treaty) and the United States are the only holdouts. After considerable delay, the United States on February 23,1995 became the 177th nation to sign the Convention, but the Senate has not considered it for ratification because of strong conservative opposition.

Opponents have argued that the Convention would clash with important aspects of domestic law, would produce unwarranted and unprecedented federal interference with state law, would impose costly unfunded mandates on the states, and would interfere with parents' rights to raise their children as they see fit. Phyllis Schlafly has assailed the Convention as "a dagger pointed at our American Bill of Rights, our concept of federalism, and our national sovereignty" because it "would authorize a UN bureaucracy to supervise the relationship between parents and children under the excuse of protecting the rights of the child." The UN's 50th Anniversary (1995), available at <http://www.eagleforum.org/column> (visited Nov. 15, 1999). The Family Research Council says the Convention "has the potential to destroy all that is best in Christian civilization, replacing it with a profoundly chaotic, harmful and ultimately evil empire." Charles Francis, The Wrongs of the United Nations' Rights of the Child, available at <http://www.frc.org/insight> (Family Research Council website, visited Nov. 15, 1999).

Supporters have argued that the Convention would guide policymakers who wish to assure the health and well-being of America's children, and would be "a useful vehicle for throwing the spotlight on horrible abuses of children around the world." A Convention Worth Attending To, Cleveland Plain Dealer, Feb. 28, 1995, at 8B (editorial quoting Sen. Richard Lugar). Supporters assert that the United States must lead world efforts to implement the Convention and to improve the lot of impoverished children, but that the nation lacks authority while it remains the only functioning government in the world to spurn ratification.

The Convention reaches all persons under eighteen "unless, under the law applicable to the child, majority is attained earlier." Article 1. Commentators have described the covered rights as the three P's: participation of children in society and in decisions affecting their own future; protection of children against discrimination, neglect and exploitation; and provision of assistance for children's basic needs. See The United Nations Convention on the Rights of the Child: A Guide to the

Travaux Preparatories (Sharon Detrick ed., 1992); <http://www.tufts.edu/fletcher/multi/texts/BH953.txt> (visited Nov. 15, 1999)(text of the Convention). The following provisions relate to matters treated throughout this casebook.

UNITED NATIONS CONVENTION ON THE RIGHTS OF THE CHILD
28 I.L.M. 1448, 1457–76 (1989).

* * *

Article 2

1. States Parties shall respect and ensure the rights set forth in the present Convention to each child within their jurisdiction without discrimination of any kind, irrespective of the child's or his or her parent's or legal guardian's race, colour, sex, language, religion, political or other opinion, national, ethnic or social origin, property, disability, birth or other status.

* * *

Article 3

1. In all actions concerning children, whether undertaken by public or private social welfare institutions, courts of law, administrative authorities or legislative bodies, the best interests of the child shall be a primary consideration.

2. States Parties undertake to ensure the child such protection and care as is necessary for his or her well-being, taking into account the rights and duties of his or her parents, legal guardians, or other individuals legally responsible for him or her * * *.

3. States Parties shall ensure that the institutions, services and facilities responsible for the care or protection of children shall conform with the standards established by competent authorities, particularly in the areas of safety, health, in the number and suitability of their staff, as well as competent supervision. * * *

* * *

Article 5

States Parties shall respect the responsibilities, rights and duties of parents or, where applicable, the members of the extended family or community as provided for by local custom, legal guardians or other persons legally responsible for the child, to provide, in a manner consistent with the evolving capacities of the child, appropriate direction and guidance in the exercise by the child of the rights recognized in the present Convention.

Article 6

1. States Parties recognize that every child has the inherent right to life. * * *

* * *

Article 7

1. The child * * * shall have * * *, as far as possible, the right to know and be cared for by his or her parents.

* * *

Article 9

1. States Parties shall ensure that a child shall not be separated from his or her parents against their will, except when competent authorities subject to judicial review determine, in accordance with applicable law and procedures, that such separation is necessary for the best interests of the child. * * *

* * *

3. States Parties shall respect the right of the child who is separated from one or both parents to maintain personal relations and direct contact with both parents on a regular basis, except if it is contrary to the child's best interests.

* * *

Article 12

1. States Parties shall assure to the child who is capable of forming his or her own views the right to express those views freely in all matters affecting the child, the views of the child being given due weight in accordance with the age and maturity of the child.

2. For this purpose, the child shall in particular be provided the opportunity to be heard in any judicial and administrative proceedings affecting the child, either directly, or through a representative or an appropriate body, in a manner consistent with the procedural rules of national law.

Article 13

1. The child shall have the right to freedom of expression; this right shall include freedom to seek, receive and impart information and ideas of all kinds, regardless of frontiers, either orally, in writing or in print, in the form of art, or through any other media of the child's choice.

2. The exercise of this right may be subject to certain restrictions, but these shall only be such as are provided by law and are necessary:

    (a) For respect of the rights or reputations of others; or

(b) For the protection of national security or of public order (*ordre public*), or of public health or morals.

Article 14

1. States Parties shall respect the right of the child to freedom of thought, conscience and religion.

2. States Parties shall respect the rights and duties of the parents and, when applicable, legal guardians, to provide direction to the child in the exercise of his or her right in a manner consistent with the evolving capacities of the child.

3. Freedom to manifest one's religion or beliefs may be subject only to such limitations as are prescribed by law and are necessary to protect public safety, order, health or morals, or the fundamental rights and freedoms of others.

Article 15

1. States Parties recognize the rights of the child to freedom of association and to freedom of peaceful assembly.

2. No restrictions may be placed on the exercise of these rights other than those imposed in conformity with the law and which are necessary in a democratic society in the interests of national security or public safety, public order (*ordre public*), the protection of public health or morals or the protection of the rights and freedoms of others.

* * *

Article 18

1. States Parties shall use their best efforts to ensure recognition of the principle that both parents have common responsibilities for the up-bringing and development of the child. Parents or, as the case may be, legal guardians, have the primary responsibility for the upbringing and development of the child. The best interests of the child will be their basic concern.

2. For the purpose of guaranteeing and promoting the rights set forth in the present Convention, States Parties shall render appropriate assistance to parents and legal guardians in the performance of their child-rearing responsibilities and shall ensure the development of institutions, facilities and services for the care of children.

3. States Parties shall take all appropriate measures to ensure that children of working parents have the right to benefit from child-care services and facilities for which they are eligible.

Article 19

1. States Parties shall take all appropriate legislative, administrative, social and educational measures to protect the child from all forms of physical or mental violence, injury or abuse, neglect or negligent treatment, maltreatment or exploitation, including sexual abuse, while in the

care of parent(s), legal guardian(s) or any other person who has the care of the child.

2. Such protective measures should, as appropriate, include effective procedures for the establishment of social programmes to provide necessary support for the child and for those who have the care of the child, as well as for other forms of prevention and for identification, reporting, referral, investigation, treatment and follow-up of instances of child maltreatment described heretofore, and, as appropriate, for judicial involvement.

Article 20

1. A child temporarily or permanently deprived of his or her family environment, or in whose own best interests cannot be allowed to remain in that environment, shall be entitled to special protection and assistance provided by the State [such as by foster placement, adoption or institutional placement].

* * *

Article 23

1. States Parties recognize that a mentally or physically disabled child should enjoy a full and decent life, in conditions which ensure dignity, promote self-reliance and facilitate the child's active participation in the community.

2. States Parties recognize the right of the disabled child to special care and shall encourage and ensure the extension, subject to available resources, to the eligible child and those responsible for his or her care, of assistance for which application is made and which is appropriate to the child's condition and to the circumstances of the parents or others caring for the child.

* * *

Article 24

1. States Parties recognize the right of the child to the enjoyment of the highest attainable standard of health and to facilities for the treatment of illness and rehabilitation of health. * * *

* * *

Article 27

1. States Parties recognize the right of every child to a standard of living adequate for the child's physical, mental, spiritual, moral and social development.

2. The parent(s) or others responsible for the child have the primary responsibility to secure, within their abilities and financial capacities, the conditions of living necessary for the child's development.

3. States Parties, in accordance with national conditions and within their means, shall take appropriate measures to assist parents and others responsible for the child to implement this right and shall in case of need provide material assistance and support programmes, particularly with regard to nutrition, clothing and housing.

* * *

Article 28

1. States Parties recognize the right of the child to education * * *.

* * *

Article 32

1. States Parties recognize the right of the child to be protected from economic exploitation and from performing any work that is likely to be hazardous or to interfere with the child's education, or to be harmful to the child's health or physical, mental, spiritual, moral or social development.

* * *

Article 37

States Parties shall ensure that:

(a) No child shall be subjected to torture or other cruel, inhuman or degrading treatment or punishment. Neither capital punishment nor life imprisonment without possibility of release shall be imposed for offences committed by persons below eighteen years of age;

(b) No child shall be deprived of his or her liberty unlawfully or arbitrarily. The arrest, detention or imprisonment of a child shall be in conformity with the law and shall be used only as a measure of last resort and for the shortest appropriate period of time;

(c) * * * [E]very child deprived of liberty shall be separated from adults unless it is considered in the child's best interest not to do so and shall have the right to maintain contact with his or her family through correspondence and visits, save in exceptional circumstances;

(d) Every child deprived of his or her liberty shall have the right to prompt access to legal and other appropriate assistance, as well as the right to challenge the legality of the deprivation of his or her liberty before a court or other competent, independent and impartial authority, and to a prompt decision on any such action.

* * *

Article 40

1. States Parties recognize the right of every child alleged as, accused of, or recognized as having infringed the penal law to be treated in a manner consistent with the promotion of the child's sense of dignity and

worth, which reinforces the child's respect for the human rights and fundamental freedoms of others and which takes into account the child's age and the desirability of promoting the child's reintegration and the child's assuming a constructive role in society.

2.   To this end, and having regard to the relevant provisions of international instruments, States Parties shall, in particular, ensure that:

* * *

(b) Every child alleged as or accused of having infringed the penal law has at least the following guarantees:

(i) To be presumed innocent until proven guilty according to law;

(ii) To be informed promptly and directly of the charges against him or her, and, if appropriate, through his or her parents or legal guardians, and to have legal or other appropriate assistance in the preparation and presentation of his or her defence;

(iii) To have the matter determined without delay by a competent, independent and impartial authority or judicial body in a fair hearing according to law, in the presence of legal or other appropriate assistance and, unless it is considered not to be in the best interest of the child, in particular, taking into account his or her age or situation, his or her parents or legal guardians;

(iv) Not to be compelled to give testimony or to confess guilt; to examine or have examined adverse witnesses and to obtain the participation and examination of witnesses on his or her behalf under conditions of equality;

(v) If considered to have infringed the penal law, to have this decision and any measures imposed in consequence thereof reviewed by a higher competent, independent and impartial authority or judicial body according to law;

(vi) To have the free assistance of an interpreter if the child cannot understand or speak the language used;

(vii) To have his or her privacy fully respected at all stages of the proceedings.

* * *

Notes and Questions

1. *Background.* The evolution of children's international human rights from the 1924 Geneva Declaration to the Convention provides parallels to the evolution of children's rights in the United States. The 1924 Declaration (much like the Supreme Court in *Meyer* and *Pierce* during the same period) saw children as beneficiaries of adult welfare rather than as independent rightsholders; by contrast, the Convention enumerates a number of rights held by children. Contrast the Convention's language with the language of the Declaration, whose five articles provided in full as follows:

I.   The child must be given the means requisite for its normal development, both materially and spiritually.

II.   The child that is hungry must be fed; the child that is sick must be nursed; the child that is backward must be helped; the delinquent child must be reclaimed; and the orphan and the waif must be sheltered and succored.

III.   The child must be the first to receive relief in times of distress.

IV.   The child must be put in a position to earn a livelihood and must be protected against every form of exploitation.

V.   The child must be brought up in the consciousness that its talents must be devoted to the service of its fellowmen.

Lawrence J. LeBlanc, The Convention on the Rights of the Child, Appendix A (1995).

2. *Legal effect.* Under the federal Constitution's Supremacy Clause, a ratified treaty becomes the "supreme law of the land," with authority equal to a federal statute. The treaty would thus override inconsistent state and local law as well as prior federal law. See, e.g., Edye v. Robertson, 112 U.S. 580 (1884). The Convention's potential effect would be greatest on state and local jurisdictions because most of its articles concern matters regulated by state rather than federal law. The United States might blunt or avoid this effect by ratifying the Convention with reservations, understandings or declarations that particular articles or provisions would not create rights in criminal proceedings or claims or defenses in federal or state civil litigation. (To avoid effects on domestic law, the Senate has attached "RUDs" to a number of other human rights treaties it has ratified.).

A number of nations have already ratified the Convention with reservations, but the right to do so has limits. Article 51(2) provides that "[a] reservation incompatible with the object and purpose of the present Convention shall not be permitted." This Article aside, would United States ratification with a bevy of RUDs diminish the nation's capacity to participate meaningfully in world efforts to implement the Convention's central goals? What would such conditional ratification say about child welfare initiatives in the United States? Would it say anything different than the nation's refusal to ratify the Convention at all?

In the absence of RUD's, questions about the Convention's potential effect on domestic law are not merely academic. Consider, for example, whether Article 12 would grant children the right to be heard in circumstances such those presented in Wisconsin v. Yoder. Would Articles 19, 24 and 27 obligate federal and state governments to provide adequate child protective services, and health and welfare benefits, even at a cost of millions or billions of dollars to the taxpayers? If the answer is "yes" and the United States ratifies without attaching appropriate RUDs, persons claiming violation in a domestic court might assert that the noncomplying state or federal government is in violation of international law.

3. *Customary international law.* International law has two basic sources, international agreements ("conventional law") and customary law. The Convention is an international agreement, which creates law for the nations that ratify it, subject to any valid RUD's. Customary international law

"results from a general and consistent practice of states followed by them from a sense of legal obligation," and binds nations that have not dissented from the rule while it was developing. Restatement (Third) Foreign Relations Law of the United States § 102 & cmt. d.

The United States is not bound by the Convention, which the nation has not ratified. The question would remain, however, whether any of the Convention's articles would hold the status of customary international law binding on a nonratifying nation. The Supreme Court long ago held that customary law is "part of our law, and must be ascertained and administered by the courts of justice of appropriate jurisdiction, as often as questions of right depending upon it are duly presented for their determination." The Paquete Habana, 175 U.S. 677, 700 (1900). Under the Supremacy Clause, customary international law would supersede inconsistent state law or policy. Restatement, supra § 115 cmt. e.

The juvenile death penalty, discussed in Chapter 11, has directly implicated the need to ascertain customary international law. See Article 37 of the Convention. In Stanford v. Kentucky, 492 U.S. 361 (1989), the Court held that executing a defendant who was sixteen or seventeen at the time of the crime does not constitute cruel and unusual punishment in violation of the Eighth Amendment. The majority concluded that such executions do not violate "evolving standards of decency" because a majority of the American states permitting capital punishment authorize it for crimes committed at age sixteen or older. 492 U.S. at 371. The Court firmly rejected a role for customary international law: "We emphasize that it is American conceptions of decency that are dispositive, rejecting the contention * * * that the sentencing practices of other countries are relevant." 492 U.S. at 369 n.1.

4. *Enforcement.* The Convention itself creates no authority to compel nations to comply with its terms and imposes no sanctions for noncompliance. The Convention only creates a Committee on the Rights of the Child, whose members the ratifying nations elect. The Committee's only interchange is with the ratifying nations themselves, each of which must file with the Committee a detailed report about its compliance within two years after ratification or accession and every five years thereafter. Based on these reports, the Committee monitors compliance with the Convention and engages in a dialog with ratifying nations concerning their progress toward realizing the rights guaranteed by the Convention. The Committee may not act like a court and may not entertain complaints by individuals or groups who charge that a ratifying nation has violated their human rights.

5. Should the United States ratify the Convention on the Rights of the Child? (As you proceed through this casebook and gain a greater understanding of juvenile law, you should periodically return to this question, which is likely to be publicly debated in future years.).

6. *References.* Rachel Hodgkin and Peter Newell, Implementation Handbook for the Convention on the Rights of the Child (1998); Cynthia Price Cohen, An Introduction to the Developing Jurisprudence of the Rights of the Child, 3 ILSA J. Int'l & Comp. L. 659 (1997); Paula Donnolo & Kim K. Azzarelli, Ignoring the Human Rights of Children: A Perspective on America's Failure to Ratify the United Nations Convention on the Rights of the Child, 5 J.L. & Pol'y 203 (1996); Sanford J. Fox, Beyond the American Legal

System For the Protection of Children's Rights, 31 Fam. L.Q. 237 (1997); Bruce C. Hafen & Jonathan O. Hafen, Abandoning Children to Their Autonomy: The United Nations Convention on the Rights of the Child, 37 Harv. Int'l L.J. 449 (1996); Symposium: Implementation of the United Nations Convention on the Rights of the Child, 6 Transnat'l L. & Contemp. Probs. (1996); Symposium, The United Nations Convention on the Rights of the Child: Benefits to American Children, Effects on American Law, 5 Geo. J. on Fighting Poverty (1998).

Section 3.   Perspectives on Children's Rights

As questions concerning children's status, rights and obligations have attracted growing attention from scholars and practitioners since *Brown* and *Gault,* children's advocates have staked out a number of disparate positions. This chapter closes with entries that provide a sense of the ongoing debate which continues in legal and popular media, legislative halls and courtrooms alike.

MICHAEL S. WALD, CHILDREN'S RIGHTS: A FRAMEWORK FOR ANALYSIS

12 U.C. Davis L. Rev. 255, 258–60, 282 (1979).

* * * To date, neither legislatures nor courts have developed a coherent philosophy or approach when addressing questions relating to children's rights. Different courts and legislatures have been willing to give some new rights to children, while denying them others, without explaining the difference in outcome.

The absence of a coherent theory is not surprising. The status of children in society raises extremely perplexing issues. The demand for children's rights calls into question basic beliefs of our society. Implementation of many of the rights being claimed for children could involve substantially altering the role of the state towards parents and children and the role or parents towards children. Most legal and social policy is based on the beliefs that children lack the capacity to make decisions on their own and that parental control of children is needed to support a stable family system, which is crucial to the well-being of society. These views are widely held and, at least for young children, seem intuitively correct. On the other hand, our society is unwilling to treat children merely as the property of adults. Given our commitment to individual liberty, there needs to be substantial reason for treating any class of individuals in a special way. Therefore, it is necessary to examine closely the claims of children's rights advocates in order to see whether the existing legal structure should be altered.

* * * In order to assess the need for further extension of children's rights, it is first necessary to separate the various type of claims being made on behalf of children. By lumping a wide range of claims under the heading "children's rights," proponents of expanded rights broaden their appeal while masking significant differences in the desirability or undesirability of granting specific rights to children. In addition, assuming that children should have some additional rights, the means of achieving and enforcing various rights depends on the type of "right" being advocated. * * *

There are four different types of claims under the general rubric of children's rights. While there is some overlap among the categories, each has special characteristics relevant to analyzing whether children should be given such rights. The categories are: (A) generalized claims against the world, e.g., the right of freedom from discrimination and poverty; (B) the right to greater protection from abuse, neglect or exploitation by adults; (C) the right to be treated in the same manner as an adult, with the same constitutional protections, in relationship to state actions; (D) the right to act independently of parental control and/or guidance.

* * *

* * * The analysis assumes that the capacity of children for decision-making and the impact of autonomy on family structures are relevant to deciding whether children should have more rights. These assumptions need not be accepted. Other commentators have approached the subject as a moral issue. They believe children should have autonomy because they are independent individuals. Giving parents control of children can be viewed as treating children as property. As one commentator concluded "in the final analysis the * * * justification * * * for * * * honoring children's rights is that it is right and fair." One must wonder, however, whether such an approach is, in effect, a case of abandoning children to their rights.

BRUCE C. HAFEN, CHILDREN'S LIBERATION AND THE NEW EGALITARIANISM: SOME RESERVATIONS ABOUT ABANDONING YOUTH TO THEIR "RIGHTS"

1976 BYU L. Rev. 605, 613, 629–30, 644, 646–48, 650–2, 657.

* * *

The law has long assumed the necessity of capacity. The assumption is reflected in restrictions on the freedom of children to vote, hold office, marry, drive automobiles, shoot firearms, gamble, enter into contracts, consent to sexual acts, and to make many other binding decisions about their own lives. The presumption of minors' incapacity has been so strong that the growth of democratic ideals in American society, rather than encouraging the "liberation" of children from limitations upon their liberty, has encouraged even greater discrimination on the basis of age—to protect children from the excesses of their immature faculties and to promote the development of their ability ultimately to assume responsibility. * * *

* * *

The family tradition has developed its own balance between the rights of parents and the rights of children; its purpose is to support the family as an institution and at the same time provide state protection for children where parental authority is abused. * * *

* * *

When children are involved, a significant distinction can be drawn between legal rights that protect one from undue interference by the state or from the harmful acts of others and legal rights that permit persons to make affirmative choices of binding consequence, such as voting, marrying, exercising religious preferences, and choosing whether to seek education. For purposes of this discussion, the first category will be referred to as rights of protection; the second, rights of choice.

Rights of protection include the right not to be imprisoned without due process, rights to property, and rights to physical protection. * * *

The statutes creating juvenile court jurisdiction over parents are also in the "protection" category, being designed to protect children against harmful abuse, neglect, or abandonment by their parents. Moreover, the entire juvenile justice system is based upon the premise that children who are yet in the developmental stages of becoming mature adults should be protected against the long term implications of their own decisions made at the time when they lack sufficient capacity and experience to be held as responsible as an adult would be fore the same decision. Thus, legal limitations on the effect of minors' choices are in fact "rights" designed for minors' protection. * * *

* * *

The presumptions arising from the limited capacities of minors account in large part for the general limitation on their exercise of rights that are in the "choice" category, because the law assumes * * * that a basic capacity to make responsible choices is a prerequisite to the meaningful exercise of choice rights. * * *

The serious question about the capacity limitation is where to draw the age line above which a given right or activity may be permitted. Children develop from incapacity toward capacity. That incontrovertible natural pattern is consistent with the presumption that capacity does not exist for children as a class until the general weight of evidence shows that a given level of capacity does in fact exist. To presume, to the contrary, that rational and judgmental capacities exist until the evidence demonstrates otherwise is to defy both logic and experience, because the evidence already demonstrates from the outset that such capacities among infants are negligible. Thus, the presumption if incapacity to make certain choices is compelled by nature.

* * *

The term "choice rights" as it has been used here applies to minors' decisions having serious long term consequences that have traditionally required either legal or parental approval (or both) in order to be enforceable. To suggest that legal rights of this special character should not be given premature approval is, however, not to argue for increased state-supported parental interference with the vast variety of less solemn choices that arise daily in the lives of children. Indeed, the availability of gradually increasing freedom to live with the consequences of one's own decisions is a critical element in the development of mature judgmental capacities. Still, the development of the capacity for responsible choice selection is an educational process in which growth can be smothered and stunted if unlimited freedom and unlimited responsibility are thrust too soon upon the young. Moreover, the lifelong effects of binding, childish choices can create permanent deprivations far more detrimental than the temporary limitations upon freedom inherent in the discipline of educational processes.

The development of the capacity to function as a mature, independent member of society is essential to the meaningful exercise of the full range of choice rights characteristic of the individual tradition. Precisely because of their lack of capacity, minors should enjoy legally protected rights to special treatment (including some protection against their own immaturity) that will optimize their opportunities for the development of mature capabilities that are in their best interest. Children will outgrow their restricted state, but the more important question is whether they will outgrow it with maximized capacities. An assumption that rational and moral capacity exists, when in fact it does not exist, may lead to an abandonment of the protections, processes, and opportunities that can develop these very capacities. In this sense, the concept of restricting certain choice rights is in fact an important form of protecting rights. For these reasons, some distinction between rights of protection and rights of choice must be preserved. * * *

* * *

The influences of some parental authority and responsibility are inevitable in view of the natural dependence of children. Rather than inhibiting optimal child development, however, this element of the parent-child relationship may be the child's most valuable source of developmental sustenance. * * * Children have many special needs that must be met in their quest for maturity and independence. The most critical of these needs is a satisfactory and permanent psychological relationship with their parents. * * *

* * *

This thesis suggests that parental authority must be regarded as a sovereign right if the psychological needs of children are in fact to be met. If there is insecurity or lack of commitment in the relationship, either because of governmental intrusion or because a parent has substantial doubts about the extent of his or her personal authority, serious psychological deficiencies are more likely to exist in the relationship. * * *

* * *

Family life, rather than subjecting the young to the permanent disadvantages caused by certain unfair discriminations against other classes, has served to nurture children's readiness for responsible participation in the individual tradition. * * *

* * *

KATHERINE HUNT FEDERLE, CHILDREN, CURFEWS AND THE CONSTITUTION
73 Wash. U. L.Q. 1315, 1367 (1995).

* * *

Children clearly have been disadvantaged by a rights theory premised upon capacity. In the context of juvenile curfew laws, the incapacities of children and their concomitant need to be protected from themselves and others permit the state to restrict the activities of children in ways that are impermissible in the case of adults. Furthermore, these incompetencies suggest that the rights children do have are somehow different, less fundamental, and more easily overridden by paternalistic concerns for their safety and well-being. Consequently, the courts have authorized significant restrictions on the constitutional interests of children as legitimate protective measures. Nevertheless, curfew laws may subject children, and even some adults, to selective and discriminatory law enforcement practices with concomitantly greater restrictions on their liberty than those originally envisioned.

An empowerment rights perspective offers a more coherent account of the rights of children. It is, in the first instance, a political theory grounded in a conception of power as an organizing force in our interactions with one another. From an empowerment perspective, children would have rights because they are powerless and would be able to make claims that must be treated seriously. Furthermore, empowerment rights prohibit others from defining the class of rights holders and the nature and extent of the rights held; they would require that the rights holder be treated nonpaternalistically. Capacity would be irrelevant.

How children would actually make such claims still poses a problem even if we do not tie having a right to the present ability to exercise that right. It is difficult to assess the true extent of children's capabilities in a society that presumes their incompetence. Certainly, children recognize the limitations imposed upon them, and it is conceivable that their failure to assert their capacities is simply a recognition of its futility. I do think, however, that most children, given the opportunity in a society that truly respects them, can and will assert their rights if we are willing to listen and take them seriously. As for the youngest children, those who simply cannot communicate, some other must assert the rights claim. Again, I think this must be a very different kind of intervention than one premised upon paternalistic considerations.

Interestingly, the claims of parents as they are currently structured would not survive. Parental rights based on control and dominance would no longer be acceptable. Challenges based on the state's failure to respect the rights of children by controlling their activities would have continued legitimacy. Moreover, it is conceivable that such claims may be even more successful because they would not involve power struggles between parents and the state over children. In this sense, children's and parents' interests would truly be commensurate.

* * *

BARBARA BENNETT WOODHOUSE, HATCHING THE EGG: A CHILD–CENTERED PERSPECTIVE ON PARENTS' RIGHTS

14 Cardozo L. Rev. 1747, 1756, 1814–17, 1837, 1838–39, 1840–41 (1993).

* * *

I propose a new perspective on generational justice that recognizes that meeting the needs of children is the primary concern of family law, and justice towards the next generation its motivating force. Justice across generations, or generism, calls for a metaphor of dynamic stewardship, in which power over children is conferred by the community, with children's interests and their emerging capacities the foremost consideration. Stewardship must be earned through actual care giving, and lost if not exercised with responsibility. Generism would place children, not adults, firmly at the center and take as its central values not adult individualism, possession, and autonomy, as embodied in parental rights, nor even the dyadic intimacy of parent/child relationships. It would value most highly concrete service to the needs of the next generation, in public and private spheres, and encourage adult partnership and mutuality in the work of family, as well as collective community responsibility for the well-being of children.

* * *

Realism compels a consciously child-centered evaluation of power over children as a necessary antidote to children's own powerlessness. In an ideal world, generational relations might perhaps begin from a firm base of adult concern for children that warranted a reciprocal concern for adults. We are too far from that ideal to make fairness to adults and adults' interests a co-equal point of reference with concern for children. * * *

Fairness also compels a child-centered perspective. Adults enter into relationships of power with children at a time when children have no say in the matter. In order to be legitimate and not constitute a form of bondage, adult power over children should not be predicated on "right," but rather it should be earned through demonstrated responsibility. This conclusion flows from the recognition that children are humans deserving of respect and are not to be objectified—a principle that has a long history in descriptions of just relations between people and generations.

* * *

Generists must do more than listen to children. They must apply adult intelligence to examine children's status in law and move children from the margin to the center of formal legal analysis. Adults must begin to ask "the child question"—how have children's experiences and values been left out of the law? How does the mismatch between children's experiences and law's assumptions and imposed structures serve the interests of those who hold power over children? In an ideal world, what would the life situation of children look like and how could law play a role in bringing this ideal world about?

Law adopts and advances views of children's nature that tend to justify adult dominion and silence children. Thus, children are not denied the right to testify by inhospitable rules of evidence, they are simply characterized as incompetent or unreliable witnesses. Children are not denied due process in foster care, custody, or commitment proceedings. Their interests are simply subsumed in the unity of family life and are presumptively one with those of their parents. Research has shown children to be remarkably distinct individuals even in infancy. However, children are often conceptualized by law as empty vessels for adults to fill and reempty at will, as if they have no religious, moral, or spiritual lives outside those of their parents. Anyone who takes children seriously (parents as well as professionals) is aware of the integrity, power, and individuality of children's spiritual lives, and the strength of their wills.

* * *

Asking the child question, listening to children's authentic voices, and employing child-centered practical reasoning are not the same as allowing children to decide. They are strategies to insure that children's authentic voices are heard and acknowledged by adults who make decisions. The hard choices—whether to remove a child from a care giver who is mentally ill or provide family preservation services; or whether to place an African–American child with an African–American family or leave him with the white foster parents he knows as "Mommy" and "Daddy"—call for hard listening to children's needs and experiences.

* * *

I have consciously avoided couching my argument in terms of "children's rights" because a child-centered perspective calls for a rhetoric that speaks less about competing rights and more about adult responsibility and children's needs.

* * *

MARTHA MINOW, WHAT EVER HAPPENED TO CHILDREN'S RIGHTS?

80 Minn. L. Rev. 267, 294–95 (1995).

* * *

I have no plan or even hope for mobilizing public support for children, especially poor children, at this point in American history. Each of the four rhetorics—child protection, children's liberation, children's rights as potential adults, and redistribution—have failed to find a strong constituency. Instead, political figures win strong support by invoking conventional authority structures, family privacy, and self-reliance, and by attacking a social welfare state. It is tempting to look at other Western industrialized countries and to wonder why state-subsidized health care, day care, child allowances, and other programs are so well-established elsewhere but so politically infeasible here. The failure of the varied rhetorics for children, however, can be only a symptom of and not an explanation for the failure of initiatives for children here.

What, then, might explain the failure of children's initiatives? History suggests four. First, children do not vote, and no other lobby has appeared on their behalf. Second, we have seen cycles of reform and disillusionment, epitomized by changes in juvenile court. The reforms of one generation become the problems to be reformed by a later generation; the earlier reforms and subsequent problems then caution against further reform. Third, children's needs are connected to larger, intractable issues, such as the economy's failure to provide good jobs for many people, the presence of women in the paid labor force without reallocation of some of child care from mothers to fathers and others, negative views of poor parents, misallocated health care expenditures, failures of public education, and divisive conflicts over abortion and crime control. Finally, our culture and ideology produce great resistance to state intervention in families; a resistance articulated both by the political left and the right. Conceptions of personal responsibility and privacy, government bungling and individual freedom, and cultural diversity and mutual distrust fuel this resistance. The cultural resistance to rights for children thus reflects a fear that such public rights would disrupt private traditions and fail to meet children's needs compared with reliance on private families. As a result, we treat other people's children as beyond public concern. Perhaps because of our troubled heterogeneity, with historic racism and intergroup distrust, we do not view other people's children as *ours* in many important ways.

* * *

Notes and Questions

1. *"Children's liberation."* In addition to the views of Professors Hafen, Federle and Woodhouse, consider the "children's liberationists," who have argued that children should hold the same rights as adults. Among the rights

Richard Farson, for example, would grant children are (1) the right to avoid their parents' "daily influence" because "parents are not all that necessary or beneficial for children," (2) the right not to be "incarcerated against their will" in school, (3) the right not to be subjected to corporal punishment, a "weapon[] used against children to force their compliance and submission to authority," (4) the same right as adults to receive pornography, "an important source" of sex information, (5) the right to "conduct their own sexual lives with no more restrictions than adults," including the right to engage in (or refuse to engage in) "sexual experimentation" with adults and other children, (6) the right to "economic power," including the right "[t]o work at any job, to work as an alternative to school, to work alongside adults," (7) the right to sue without a parent or other adult acting as a guardian ad litem, and (8) the right to vote "at any age" and to hold public office. Richard Farson, Birthrights 43, 96, 121, 135, 152–54, 163, 165, 177, 185 (1974). Farson concludes that "[u]ntil society's views as to what a child might be undergo radical change, the child is trapped, a prisoner of childhood." Id. at 214. See also, e.g., Children's Liberation (David Gottlieb ed., 1972); John Holt, Escape From Childhood (1974).

2. *Attempting synthesis.* As you endeavor to make sense of the decisions and viewpoints presented in this chapter, you should realize the difficulty of neat synthesis. Professor Wald is not the only commentator to point out the lack of a coherent legislative or judicial approach to determining the status, rights and obligations of children. See also, e.g., John Gibeaut, Who's Raising the Kids?, 83 A.B.A. J. 62, 64 (Aug. 1997) ("Given mixed guidance from above, individual lower court decisions in cases involving children's rights form an unsurprising crazy quilt. They leave succeeding courts to play a judicial game of spin the bottle to see which precedent points in the desired direction.").

Professor Mnookin suggests that the Supreme Court's children's rights decisions evince three themes "constantly in conflict": "First, that parents have primary responsibility to raise children. Second, that the state has special responsibilities to children, to intervene and protect them. And third, that children as people have rights of their own and have rights as individuals in relation to the family and in relation to the state." See Glenn Collins, Debate Over Rights of Children is Intensifying, N.Y. Times, July 21, 1981, at A1 (quoting Prof. Mnookin). These themes may "make sense individually, but no clear lines demark which view should prevail in a given case." Martha Minow, What Ever Happened to Children's Rights?, 80 Minn. L. Rev. 267, 287 (1995).

3. *Questions about the various writers.* (a) What views of children, childhood, parenthood and families are posited by Professors Hafen, Federle and Woodhouse? How do each writer's views differ from the others'?, (b) Which writer(s) views best serve the interests of children?, (c) Which writer(s) views best preserve parental prerogatives over their children's upbringing?, (d) Which writer(s) views best comport with the law of parent-child-government relations enunciated by the Supreme Court decisions presented in this chapter?, (e) Do you share Professor Minow's pessimism?

4. *Should children hold the right to vote?* Some commentators believe the answer is yes because government entitlement programs have dramatically

improved senior citizens' economic position in recent years while reductions in children's programs have left child poverty rates uncomfortably high. These commentators attribute the situation largely to the fact that the elderly vote in high numbers while children cannot vote and thus are "barred from the political process of interest group bargaining that takes place in a democracy." Jane Rutherford, One Child, One Vote: Proxies for Parents, 82 Minn. L. Rev. 1463, 1464 (1998). Even if voting patterns were uniform, children remain "dramatically underrepresented in the political process": "Parents and the children who live with them comprise over two-thirds of the people within an average congressional district but control just over half the votes. In contrast, adults not living with children comprise less than one-third of the people but control nearly half the votes." Id. at 1466.

Professor Rutherford proposes that parents be granted the right to vote as proxies for their children who reside with them. Where a child lives with both parents, each parent would get a proxy worth one-half vote for each child. Where the parents live apart, the parent with whom the child primarily resides would get a proxy worth one vote for each child. Professor Rutherford recognizes that many parents would not necessarily vote in their children's best interests, but concludes that "[w]e vest parents with power not because we believe parents are perfect, but because we prefer family decisions to institutional or governmental ones." Id. at 1509. See also, e.g., J. Lawrence Aber, Let Children Make Their Votes Count, Newsday, Nov. 18, 1996, at A31 (proposing that parents or guardians be given an additional vote to use for each of their children under fifteen, and that children fifteen and older be allowed to apply for a voter's permit enabling them to vote in the presence of a parent or guardian).

5. *References.* Children's Rights and the Law (Philip Alston, Stephen Parker, & John Seymour eds.,1992); Henry H. Foster, A "Bill of Rights" For Children (1974); Sanford N. Katz, The Legal Rights of Children (1974); James G. Dwyer, Parents' Religion and Children's Welfare: Debunking the Doctrine of Parental Rights, 82 Cal. L. Rev. 1371 (1994); Theresa Glennon and Robert G. Schwartz, Foreword: Looking Back, Looking Ahead: The Evolution of Children's Rights, 68 Temp. L. Rev. 1557 (1995); Francis Barry McCarthy, The Confused Constitutional Status and Meaning of Parental Rights, 22 Ga. L. Rev. 975 (1988); Janet Leach Richards, Redefining Parenthood: Parental Rights Versus Child Rights, 40 Wayne L. Rev. 1227 (1994); Sharon Elizabeth Rush, The Warren and Burger Courts on State, Parent, and Child Conflict Resolution: A Comparative Analysis and Proposed Methodology, 36 Hast. L.J. 461 (1985); Special Symposium Issue on the Rights of Children, 27 Fam. L.Q. 301 (1993).

PROBLEM 1–4

By a margin of 58% to 42%, Colorado voters in 1996 rejected a proposed state constitutional amendment that would have guaranteed parents the "natural, essential and inalienable right[] * * * to direct and control the upbringing, education, values, and discipline of their children." Similar "parental rights" amendments and statutes were pending in more than half the states and in Congress. See, e.g., Parental Rights and Responsibilities Act of 1995, H.R. 1946, 104th Cong., 1st Sess. (1995); S. 984, 104th Cong, 1st Sess. (1995). The measures, which were silent about any rights held by children, have not been enacted.

The proposed Colorado amendment produced a long, and sometimes bitter, election campaign waged in public forums and the media. Supporters stated that parents, and not government or its agencies, should be responsible for raising their children and instilling basic values. They asserted that the government frequently intruded on parental prerogatives in areas ranging from requiring children's attendance in public school sex education classes to advising children about condom distribution to monitoring spanking and other parental discipline. They argued that the amendment was based on rights already guaranteed under the *Meyer-Pierce* line of Supreme Court decisions. Some suggested that the measure was necessary to forestall any effect of the yet-to-be-ratified United Nations Convention on the Rights of the Child.

According to Webster's New Collegiate Dictionary, "inalienable" means "incapable of being alienated, surrendered, or transferred." Opponents charged that unlike the *Meyer-Pierce* line (which balances parents' rights with state interests and children's rights), the proposed amendment sought to grant parents absolute rights. Opponents raised a number of questions, including these: Would the proposed amendment enable parents to ignore compulsory education statutes and to challenge routine public school curricular decisions? Would the amendment grant parents a defense to abuse and neglect proceedings? Would the amendment provide parents a defense to enforcement of protective legislation such as child labor laws and mandatory immunization statutes? Currently courts decide custody, adoption, abuse and neglect proceedings under the "best interests of the child" standard; would the amendment substitute a "best interests of the parent" standard? Would the amendment make adoption impossible by granting natural parents an inalienable right to recover the child afterwards? Would the amendment grant natural parents the right to continually challenge unfavorable custody decisions following separation or divorce? Would the amendment prevent courts from ordering life-saving medical treatment for children after their parents withheld medical care? See generally Gene Nichol, Which Way on Parental Rights? Best Interests of Children in Jeopardy, Denver Post, Oct. 6, 1996, at D–1.

The proposed federal legislation is extensively critiqued in Barbara Bennett Woodhouse, A Public Role in the Private Family: The Parental Rights and Responsibilities Act and the Politics of Child Protection and Education, 57 Ohio St. L.J. 393 (1996), and Emily Buss, Parents' Rights and Parents Wronged, id. at 431.

Would you vote in favor of a parental responsibility amendment such as the one proposed in Colorado? Do you believe the Colorado amendment struck an appropriate balance in disputes among the child, parents and government? Would you vote for an amendment with different language?

Chapter 2

DEFINING THE CHILD–PARENT RELATIONSHIP

By exploring the status, rights and obligations of children, Chapter 1 necessarily also treated the rights and obligations of parents. This chapter refines that analysis by exploring the complex questions sometimes involved in determining who may hold the status of a child's "parent," and what rights and responsibilities that status will include. The Chapter begins with a brief historical review of American law concerning children born to unmarried parents, and then describes modern problems related to establishing paternity and maternity. Next the Chapter addresses decisions involving claims by adults who want parental status, but face legal barriers prohibiting them from being "parents." As you read this Chapter, consider what concept of parenthood best serves children's interests.

Section 1.   Establishing Paternity and Maternity

A.   *The Importance of Marriage*

Historically children born to unmarried parents were labeled "bastards" or "illegitimate," and had fewer rights and opportunities than children born to married parents. By constitutional and statutory mandate, however, American law has now removed most distinctions based on parentage. This section begins with historical materials and then examines contemporary law.

1.   *Historical Background on Children Born to Unmarried Parents*

I WILLIAM BLACKSTONE, COMMENTARIES ON THE LAWS OF ENGLAND *459

* * * I proceed next to the rights and incapacities which appertain to a bastard. The rights are very few, being only such as he can *acquire*;

for he can *inherit* nothing, being looked upon as the son of nobody; and sometimes called *filius nullius*, sometimes *filius populi* [child of no one, or child of the people]. Yet he may gain a surname by reputation, though he has none by inheritance. All other children have their primary settlement in their father's parish; but a bastard in the parish where born, for he hath no father. However, in case of fraud, as if a woman be sent either by order of justices, or comes to beg as a vagrant, to a parish where she does not belong to, and drops her bastard there, the bastard shall, in the first case, be settled in the parish from whence she was illegally removed; or, in the latter case, in the mother's own parish, if the mother be apprehended for her vagrancy. Bastards also born in any licensed hospital for pregnant women, are settled in the parishes to which the mothers belong. The incapacity of a bastard consists principally in this, that he cannot be heir to any one, neither can he have heirs, but of his own body; for, being *nullius filius*, he is therefore of kin to nobody, and has no ancestor from whom any inheritable blood can be derived. A bastard was also, in strictness, incapable of holy orders; and, though that were dispensed with, yet he was utterly disqualified from holding any dignity in the church: but this doctrine seems now obsolete; and, in all other respects, there is no distinction between a bastard and another man. And really any other distinction, but that of not inheriting, which civil policy renders necessary, would, with regard to the innocent offspring of his parents' crimes, be odious, unjust, and cruel to the last degree: and yet the civil law, so boasted of for its equitable decisions, made bastards, in some cases, incapable even of a gift from their parents. A bastard may, lastly, be made legitimate, and capable of inheriting, by the transcendent power of an act of parliament, and not otherwise: as was done in the case of John of Gaunt's bastard children, by a statute of Richard the Second.

II KENT, COMMENTARIES ON AMERICAN LAW 258–267
(O.W. Holmes, Jr. ed., 12th ed. 1873).

I proceed next to examine the situation of illegitimate children, or bastards, being persons who are begotten and born out of lawful wedlock.

These unhappy fruits of illicit connection were, by the civil and canon laws, made capable of being legitimated by the subsequent marriage of their parents; * * * [b]ut this principle has never been introduced into the English law; and Sir William Blackstone has zealously maintained, in this respect, the superior policy of the common law. * * *

But not only children born before marriage, but those who are born so long after the death of the husband as to destroy all presumption of their being his; and also all children born during the long and continued absence of the husband, so that no access to the mother can be presumed, are reputed bastards. * * * The rule is, that where it clearly appears that the husband could not have been the father of the child, it is a bastard, though born, or begotten and born, during marriage.* * *

A bastard being in the eye of the law *nullius filius* [child of no one], * * * he has no inheritable blood, and is incapable of inheriting as heir, either to his putative father, or his mother, or to any one else, nor can he have heirs but of his own body. This rule of the common law, so far at least as it excludes him from inheriting as heir to his mother, is supposed to be founded partly in policy, to discourage illicit commerce between the sexes.* * * [In twelve states], bastards can inherit from, and transmit to their mothers, real and personal estate, under some modifications * * *; and in New York, the estate of an illegitimate intestate descends to the mother, and the relatives on the part of the mother. In North Carolina, the legislature enabled bastards to be legitimated, on the intermarriage of the putative father with the mother, or, if she be dead, or reside out of the state, or married to another, on his petition, so far as to enable the child to inherit, as if he was lawfully born, the real and personal estate of the father.* * *

This relaxation in the laws of so many of the states, of the severity of the common law, rests upon the principle that the relation of parent and child, which exists in this unhappy case, in all its native and binding force, ought to produce the ordinary legal consequences of that consanguinity.* * * We have, in this respect, followed the spirit of the laws of some of the ancient nations, who denied to bastards an equal share of their father's estate (for that would be giving too much countenance to the indulgence of criminal desire), but admitted them to a certain portion, and would not suffer them to be cast naked and destitute upon the world.

The mother, or reputed father, is generally in this country chargeable by law with the maintenance of the bastard child;* * * and the goods, chattels, and real estate of the parents are seizable for the support of such children, if the parents have absconded. The reputed father is liable to arrest and imprisonment until he give security to indemnify the town chargeable with the maintenance of the child. These provisions are intended for the public indemnity, and were borrowed from the several English statutes on the subject; and similar regulations to coerce the putative father to maintain the child, and indemnify the town or parish, have been adopted in the several states.

The father of a bastard child is liable upon his implied contract for its necessary maintenance, without any compulsory order being made upon him, provided he has adopted the child as his own, and acquiesced in any particular disposition of it. The adoption must be voluntary, and with the consent of the mother, for the putative father has no legal right to the custody of a bastard child, in opposition to the claim of the mother; and except the cases of the intervention of the town officers, under the statute of provisions, or under the implied contract founded on the adoption of the child, the mother has no power to compel the putative father to support the child. She has a right to the custody bound to maintain it as its natural guardian; though perhaps the putative father might assert a right to the custody of the child as against a stranger.

There are cases in which the courts of equity have regarded bastards as having strong claims to equitable protection, and have decreed a specific performance of voluntary settlements made by the father in favor of the mother of her natural child. On the other hand, there are cases in which the courts of equity have withheld from the illegitimate child every favorable intendment which the lawful heir would have been entitled to as of course.* * * [T]he language of Lord Ch. J. King * * * is certainly much more conformable to justice and humanity. "If a man," says he, "does mislead an innocent woman, it is both reason and justice that he should make her reparation. The case is stronger in respect to the innocent child, whom the father has occasioned to be brought into the world in this shameful manner, and for whom, in justice, he ought to provide."* * *

Note

1. The harsh common law view of out-of-wedlock births, evident in Blackstone's and Kent's Commentaries, persisted well into this century in the United States. Consider this 1927 observation by a prominent proponent of the new juvenile court: "[I]llegitimate children contribute largely to the classes of dependent and neglected children, and contribute more than their share to the number of juveniles who come in conflict with the law or who are wayward and difficult to control. This is partly because of the fact that mentally defective persons, especially feeble-minded girls and women, are probably more likely to have illegitimate children than the mentally normal * * *." Herbert H. Lou, Juvenile Courts in the United States 61 (1927).

2. Surnames

By custom and law, children born to married parents have been given their fathers' surnames. "The recognition * * * of a preference for paternal surnames is supported by Western custom and law spanning more than six centuries. The practice of children assuming the father's surname is traceable to the English medieval property system in which the husband controlled all marital property. That preference continued in America, reflecting not only the long-standing English tradition but also the societal distinctions in the status of men and women. Until the latter part of this century, the assumption that children would bear their father's surnames was a matter of common understanding and the preference for paternal surnames was rarely challenged." Gubernat v. Deremer, 657 A.2d 856 (N.J. 1995).

Petitions to change the marital child's surname from the father's have usually been denied if the father objects. Even though the test for a name change may be the child's "best interests," the court may "recite the time honored interest of the father to have his progeny bear his name." Lisa Kelly, Divining the Deep and Inscrutable: Toward a Gender–Neutral, Child–Centered Approach to Child Name Change Proceedings, 99 W. Va. L. Rev. 1, 33 (1996).

At common law, a child born to unmarried parents was considered the child of no one and had no surname at birth. As Blackstone notes, the child's surname was acquired later in life based on reputation rather than lineage. As the law began to give non-marital children a right to inherit from their mothers and to give mothers custody and support obligations, these children began to receive their mothers' surnames as well. This practice gradually moved from custom to law:

> The fact that the law sanctioned, and indeed, at times strictly enforced the custom of giving the mother's surname at birth to the child born outside of marriage is reflected in past and some present-day statutes governing the completion of birth certificates. Today, some state statutes reflect the presumption that the child born outside of marriage will be named if not after the mother, at least by her. Some states explicitly give the mother the right to name the child. Others explicitly accord her the exclusive right to amend the given name of the child on the birth certificate. Still others assume that the child born out of wedlock bears the surname of the mother which would be changed to the father's should the parents marry or, if the mother consents, after the adjudication of paternity.

Kelly, supra at 19.

Fathers' petitions to change the names of their nonmarital children from the mothers' name to their own have usually been denied. Some courts have held that maintaining the status quo, the mother's surname, was in the child's bests interests; other courts have favored the mother's surname because she was the custodial parent; and some have used "gender-neutral, child-centered" factors. Kelly, supra, at 53.

In *Gubernat*, the Supreme Court of New Jersey adopted a rule, intended to be gender-neutral, to apply to name changes for all children without regard to the parents' marital status:

> * * * [T]he historical justifications that once supported a tradition in the law for children to bear paternal surnames have been overtaken by society's recognition of full legal equality for women, an equality that is incompatible with continued recognition of a presumption that children must bear their father's surname. * * * We hold * * * that in contested cases the surname selected by the custodial parent—the parent primarily charged with making custodial decisions in the child's best interest—shall be presumed to be consistent with that child's best interests, a presumption rebuttable by evidence that a different surname would better serve those interests.

Gubernat at 857–858.

Gubernat involved a three-year-old, out of-wedlock boy who had his mother's surname. The court denied the father's petition to change the boy's surname to his. Tragically, three days after the decision was announced, the father killed himself and his son. Merle H. Weiner, "We are Family": Valuing Associationalism in Disputes over Children's Surnames, 75 N.C.L. Rev. 1625 (1997)(Professor Weiner provides an extensive feminist analysis of surname rules, including a critique of the *Gubernat* decision).

What role should the child's preference play in the choice of a surname? At common law a person may adopt a new name without any legal proceeding, provided the name change has no fraudulent purpose or effect. The common law rule also applies to minors, without the "ordinary disabilities attendant upon minority." Hall v. Hall, 351 A.2d 917 (Md. Ct. Spec. App. 1976). In fact, however, a father's objection to a child's name change frequently controls. Kelly, supra at 32. Professor Kelly proposes a new approach that would give increasing deference to the child's wishes as the child grows older:

> * * * For children below the age of six, the custodial deference standard articulated in *Gubernat* should apply. Specifically, a presumption should exist in favor of the custodial parent's choice of name for the child. This presumption can only be overcome by the noncustodial parent's showing by a preponderance of the evidence that the name chosen by the custodial parent is not in the child's best interest. However, in determining whether the noncustodial parent has met his or her burden of proof the court must look for evidence using a set of child-centered, gender-neutral factors. These factors should include: 1) the length of time that the child has used his or her current name; 2) the name by which the child has customarily been called; 3) whether a name change will cause insecurity or identity confusion; 4) the potential impact of the requested name change on the child's relationship with each parent; 5) the motivations of the parties in seeking a name change; 6) the identification of the child with a particular family unit, giving proper weight to step-parents, step-siblings and half-siblings who comprise that unit; 7) any embarrassment, discomfort, or inconvenience that may result if the child's surname differs from that of the custodial parent; and 8) the degree of community respect associated with the present and proposed surnames.

> For the child between the ages of six and fourteen, the court should make a determination concerning the child's ability to state a preference and should hear such preferences in chambers, on the record, and outside the presence of the parents. The court should then consider the child's preference along with the above enumerated factors in determining whether to change the child's name.

> The wishes of the mature child should always be respected on a matter so basic as his or her name. Therefore, for the child over fourteen, the child's preference should control and no petition for name change should be allowed without the consent of the child.

Kelly, supra at 79–80.

Do you favor adopting Professor Kelly's proposal? As you formulate your answer, review the Chapter 1 materials on the mature-minor doctrine.

3. Unmarried Parents: The Contemporary Context

a. "Illegitimacy"

The term "illegitimate children" has been central to our language for generations. Kent reflects the common law's harshness, calling these children "unhappy fruits of illicit connection" and justifying legal disability in an effort "to discourage illicit commerce between the sexes" and to avoid "giving too much continence to the indulgence of criminal desire." We still frequently hear the term, perhaps without pondering whether it unfairly imposes enduring stigma on innocent children for behavior over which they obviously had no control, namely their parents' behavior at conception. As we examine contemporary constitutional and statutory law, it might be useful to recall a statement in a judicial decision a generation ago: "[T]here are no illegitimate children, only illegitimate parents." Estate of Woodward, 40 Cal.Rptr. 781, 784 (Cal. App.1964).

The harsh traditional label has not entirely disappeared from the statute books. In 1997, for example, the Washington Supreme Court struck down a statute which permitted a father to recover for the wrongful death of his child born out of wedlock only if he had contributed regularly to the child's financial support before death. The basis of decision was the state constitution's equal protection guarantee because the statute imposed no similar requirement on mothers. The concurring opinion chided the legislature for retaining the term "illegitimate child" in the statute: "Certainly 'illegitimate' is a better word than 'bastard,' a word common in earlier statutes and decisions * * * We have made great strides in amending statutes to remove age-old terms which are offensive in our present-day society. The legislative process can use words which convey the same meaning, but are less demeaning to children." Guard v. Jackson, 940 P.2d 642, 646 (Wash.1997) (Smith, J., concurring).

b. Constitutional and Statutory Reform

In Levy v. Louisiana, 391 U.S. 68 (1968), the Supreme Court held for the first time that children born to unmarried parents are "persons" within the meaning of the Fourteenth Amendment's Equal Protection clause. Levy held that the clause prohibits states from denying these children the right to recover for the wrongful death of their mother on whom they were dependent. The Court rejected the lower court's determination that "[d]enying illegitimate children the right to recover * * * [was] based on morals and general welfare because it discourages bringing children into the world out of wedlock." 192 So.2d 193, 195 (La.Ct. App.1966).

In the years since *Levy*, the Court's equal protection jurisprudence has outlawed most discrimination against nonmarital children. The Court summarized its rationale in Weber v. Aetna Casualty & Surety, 406 U.S. 164, 175–76 (1972), which struck down a state workers' compensation statute that denied equal recovery rights, following the natural father's death, to the decedent's dependent, unacknowledged, nonmarital children. "The status of illegitimacy has expressed through the ages society's condemnation of irresponsible liaisons beyond the bonds of marriage. But visiting this condemnation on the head of an infant is illogical and unjust. Moreover, imposing disabilities on the illegitimate child is contrary to the basic concept of our system that legal burdens should bear some relationship to individual responsibility or wrongdoing. Obviously, no child is responsible for his birth and penalizing the illegitimate child is an ineffectual—as well as an unjust—way of deterring the parent."

Legislative reform has also been important in changing the status of children born to unmarried parents. In 1973, the Uniform Law Commissioners promulgated the Uniform Parentage Act, which seeks to "provid[e] substantive legal equality for all children regardless of the marital status of their parents." As of 1997, the Act had been adopted wholly or in part by eighteen states.

The Uniform Act's first two sections seek to achieve legal equality: Section 2 mandates that "[t]he parent and child relationship extends equally to every child and to every parent, regardless of the marital status of the parents." Section 3 defines "parent and child relationship" as "the legal relationship existing between a child and his natural or adoptive parents incident to which the law confers or imposes rights, privileges, duties, and obligations. It includes the mother and child relationship and the father and child relationship."

The Act's remaining sections concern the important matter of determining the identity of the child's parents so that attendant rights, privileges, duties and obligations may take effect. Where the child is born to unmarried parents, the focus of attention is usually on the father's identity because the mother's identity is normally not in doubt. The Act sets out elaborate provisions governing paternity suits.

In states that have not enacted the Uniform Act, the Supreme Court's equal protection decisions nonetheless enforce general legal equality between children born in and out of wedlock. Intestate succession provides a significant exception to this general rule.

c. *Intestate Succession*

In Trimble v. Gordon, 430 U.S. 762 (1977), the Court struck down an Illinois Probate Act provision that ameliorated the harsh common law, but only a bit. As Kent's Commentaries stated, a child born out of wedlock could inherit from neither parent at common law. The Probate Act provision allowed such children to inherit by intestate succession only from their mothers, whereas children born in wedlock could inherit by intestate succession from both their mothers and their fathers. The provision further provided that a child born to unmarried parents could inherit from the father if the father and mother intermarried and the father acknowledged the child as his.

Pursuant to the statutory command, the Illinois probate court denied the Trimble child's claim despite the fact that in a paternity proceeding before the decedent's death, a state court had found the decedent to be her father and had ordered him to pay child support. The father thereafter paid support and openly acknowledged the child as his daughter.

As an initial matter, *Trimble* refused to find illegitimacy to be a suspect classification, a finding that would have triggered strict scrutiny and would have required the state to advance a compelling state interest to support the statute's discrimination. The Court instead embraced an intermediate standard, noting that *Levy* and its progeny had established that the scrutiny of discrimination against non-marital children "is not a toothless one." Id. at 767.

Illinois advanced two interests in the effort to defeat the equal protection challenge to the probate act provision. First the state argued that the provision helped promote legitimate family relationships. The Court gave short shrift to this argument, calling it "the mere incantation of a proper state purpose." Id. at 769. "No one disputes the appropriateness of Illinois' concern with the family unit, perhaps the most fundamental social institution of our society," Justice Powell wrote for the majority, but "a state may [not] attempt to influence the actions of men and women by imposing sanctions on the children born of their illegitimate relationships." Id.

Second the state advanced an interest in maintaining an accurate, efficient method of property distribution that avoided the difficulties of proving paternity and the related danger of spurious claims. The Court found this interest "proper" and "more substantial." Id. at 770. The majority acknowledged that "[t]he more serious problems of proving paternity might justify a more demanding standard for illegitimate children claiming under their fathers' estates than that required either for illegitimate children claiming under their mothers' estates or for legitimate children generally." Id. The Court struck down the Illinois statute, however, because its blanket prohibition failed to recognize that "[f]or at least some significant categories of illegitimate children of intestate men, inheritance rights can be recognized without jeopardizing the orderly settlement of estates or the dependability of titles to property passing under intestacy laws." Id. at 771. Because a state court during the decedent's lifetime had determined him to be the daughter's father, "the State's interest in the accurate and efficient disposition of property at death would not be compromised in any way by allowing [the child's] claim in these circumstances." Id. at 772.

The Court distinguished *Trimble* in Lalli v. Lalli, 439 U.S. 259 (1978). *Lalli* concerned a New York statute that required nonmarital children who would inherit from their fathers by intestate succession to prove that a court had entered a filiation order during the father's lifetime. The state of New York had not sought to justify the statute as a means of promoting "legitimate" families. The plurality concluded that the requirement was "substantially related to the important state interests the statute is intended to promote," namely the need "to provide for the just and orderly disposition of property at death." Id. at 268, 275–76. The plurality stressed "peculiar problems of proof" that attend paternal inheritance: "Establishing maternity is seldom difficult. * * * '[T]he birth of the child is a recorded or registered event usually taking place in the presence of others. In most cases the child remains with the mother and for a time is necessarily reared by her. * * *' Proof of paternity, by contrast, frequently is difficult when the father is not part of a formal family unit. 'The putative father often goes his way unconscious of the birth of a child. Even if conscious, he is very often totally unconcerned because of the absence of any ties to the mother. Indeed the mother may not know who is responsible for her pregnancy.' " Id. at 268–69.

Lalli held that the state used appropriate means to vindicate its substantial interests: "The administration of an estate will be facilitated, and the possibility of delay and uncertainty minimized, where the entitlement of an illegitimate child to notice and participation is a matter of judicial record before the administration commences. Fraudulent assertions of paternity will be much less likely to succeed, or even to arise, where the proof is put before a court of law at a time when the putative father is available to respond, rather than first brought to light when the distribution of the assets of an estate is in the offing." Id. at 271–72.

Notes and Questions

1. *Questions about Trimble and Lalli.* (a) In light of *Trimble* and *Lalli,* when does Equal Protection permit a state to distinguish between rights accorded to children born to unmarried parents and rights accorded to other children? Could a dependent child's social security benefits depend on the decedent wage earner's acknowledgement of paternity during his lifetime? (b) After you have read about scientific advances in establishing paternity described in part B, infra at 129, consider whether the New York statute discussed in *Lalli* should be amended and if so, how?

2. *The Uniform Putative and Unknown Fathers Act.* The Uniform Putative and Unknown Fathers Act, approved in 1988 by the National Conference of Commissioners on Uniform State Laws, was intended to codify Supreme Court decisions on unwed fathers' claims and to provide guidance in areas that are still unclear, such as the extent of notice these fathers must be given in adoption or termination of parental rights proceedings. The Act does not apply to divorce or custody modifications and was intended to supplement, not replace, the Uniform Parentage Act. According to the Prefatory Note the Act's fundamental objective is to protect the best interest of the child. "The child's interest includes support, inheritance, and emotional relationships with both parents, whether identified or unidentified. At the same time, this Act seeks to protect (1) the efficiency and security of the

adoption process, (2) the mother from harassment by the father, and (3) the legitimate interests of the father who wants to maintain or establish and develop a parental relationship with his child. This Act seeks to accommodate that objective and those protections with the various state and federal constitutional requirements.''

3.   *Teen parents*. In 1997, teenage childbearing in the United States fell for the sixth consecutive year to 52.9 births per 1000 females 15 to 19 years old, 3% lower than the 1996 rate of 54.5 and 15% lower than the 1991 rate of 62.1. Id., tbl. 3. The United States adolescent birth rate nonetheless remains the highest of all developed countries, and 72% of births to U.S. adolescents were outside marriage in 1993. For every 1000 females 15 to 19 years old in 1992, four gave birth in Japan, eight in The Netherlands, 33 in the United Kingdom and 41 in Canada. See Am. Acad. Pediatrics, Adolescent Pregnancy–Current Trends and Issues: 1998, 103 Pediatrics 516 (1999). The reasons for the disparities are unclear, but the American Academy of Pediatrics reports that "[w]elfare benefits tend to be more generous in Europe than in the United States; thus, it is unlikely that the present welfare system motivates American teenagers to have children." Id.

4.   *Single–parent households*. Together with a divorce rate that nearly tripled from 1960 to 1990, the out-of-wedlock birthrate has greatly increased the number of children who live in single-parent households. In 1998, only 68% of American children lived with two parents, down from 77% in 1980. Federal Interagency Forum on Child and Family Statistics, America's Children: Key National Indicators of Well–Being 7 (1999). Children living in single-parent households have been called "half orphans." Robert F. Drinan, Saving Our Children: Focusing the World's Attention on the Abuse of Children, 26 Loyola U. Chi. L.J. 137, 143 (1995)

The increase in single-parent households has occurred in both white and black families. The percentage of white families with children under eighteen and both parents living at home fell from 90% in 1970 to 77% in 1990. For black families, the decline was from 64% in 1970 to 39% in 1990. Despite the lower percentage of white single-parent families in 1990, most single-parent families were white because whites comprise a greater percentage of the general population. See Howard N. Snyder and Melissa Sicmund, Juvenile Offenders and Victims: A National Report, Office of Juvenile Justice and Delinquency Prevention 10 (1995).

Children living in single-parent families are more likely to be in poverty than children living in two-parent families. In 1997, 49% of children in female-householder families were living in poverty, compared with only 10% of children in two-parent families. See Key National Indicators 1999, supra at 12.

Is child poverty due to the increase in single-parent families? Consider the following:

> The principal remedy that conservatives and liberals would apply to the problems of children is to restore the two-parent family by reducing out-of-wedlock births, increasing the presence of fathers, and encouraging couples who are having marital difficulties to avoid divorce for the sake of their children. Feminists, on the other hand, are skeptical that

illegitimacy, father absence, or divorce are the principal culprits they are made out to be. * * *

* * * Rather than attempt to force families back into the traditional mold, feminists note that divorce, lone-mother families, and women's employment are on the rise in every industrialized nation. But other countries have not seen the same devastating decline in child well-being, teen pregnancy, suicides and violent death, school failure, and a rising population of children in poverty. The other countries have four key elements of social and family policy which protect all children and their mothers: (1) work guarantees and other economic supports; (2) child care; (3) health care; (4) housing subsidies.

Janet Z. Giele, Decline of the Family: Conservative, Liberal and Feminist Views in Promises to Keep: Decline and Renewal of Marriage in America (Popenow, Elshtain, and Blanenhorn, eds. 1996); reprinted in Margaret Brinig, Carl E. Schneider, and Lee E. Teitelbaum, Family Law in Action, 19, 28–29 (1999). See also Deborah Jones Merritt, Ending Poverty by Cutting Teenage Births: Promise, Failure, and Paths to the Future, 57 Ohio St. L. J. 441 (1996).

5.   *The worldwide context.* "While much has been made of the fact that 30% of births in the United States are to unmarried parents, this is not inconsistent with the experience of other Western countries: It is 29% in Canada, 33% in France, 46% in Denmark and 50% in Sweden." Robert Scheer, All Children Deserve a Chance, Los Angeles Times, Sept. 26, 1995, at 9B.

6.   *If unmarried parenthood is a problem, is shame the answer?* From 1980 to 1997, the annual percentage of American children born out of wedlock increased from 18.4% to 32.4%. The increase was from 11.0% to 25.8% for white births, and from 55.5% to 69.1% for black births. See B. Guyer et. al., Annual Summary of Vital Statistics—1997, 102 Pediatrics 1333, tbl. 5 (Dec. 1998).

With nearly a third of all American children born to unmarried parents, some social commentators have warned that this rate is the root cause of a variety of social ills. Charles Murray, for example, has written that "illegitimacy is the single most important problem of our time—more important than crime, drugs, poverty, illiteracy, welfare or homelessness because it drives everything else." The Coming White Underclass, Wall St. J., Oct. 29, 1993, at A14.

Arguing that "[t]he child deserves society's support [but] [t]he parent does not," Murray would "end all economic support for single mothers." He predicts that without public welfare assistance, poor single mothers would be forced to seek support from friends, relatives and other private sources. Where such help is forthcoming, mature adults would then become involved in the upbringing of some children. "Many young women who shouldn't be mothers [would] place their babies for adoption." Seeing the unavailability of public assistance, still other women would "take steps not to get pregnant." If a woman cannot support a child she nonetheless wishes to keep, neglect statutes would serve as a prelude to adoption in appropriate cases. Murray hopes for a return of the stigma that has traditionally surrounded out-of-wedlock births: "The pressure on relatives and communities to pay for the folly of their children will make an illegitimate birth the socially horrific act it used to be, and getting a girl pregnant something boys do at the risk of facing a shotgun. Stigma and shotgun marriages may or may not be good for those on the receiving end, but their deterrent effect on others is wonderful—and indispensable." Id.

Richard Lamm, former governor of Colorado also connects illegitimacy to a multitude of social ills and recommends this societal response: "If society expresses its disapproval—that is, restigmatizes illegitimacy—at least it will start to make a statement that this life style is causing chaos in America." Richard Lamm, Why We Must Restigmatize the Institution of Illegitimacy, 57 The Humanist 35, March 13, 1997.

Would "shotgun" marriages provide increased financial support for a mother and child? If marriage is an appropriate punishment for adults who produce children out of marriage, should the same punishment apply to minors? In 1995 approximately 31% of nonmarital births were to women under 20. U.S. Dep't of Health and Human Services, Office of the Assistant Secretary for Planning and Evaluation, Trends in the Well–Being of America's Children & Youth (1998). Another punitive approach that focuses on teen pregnancy is to prosecute under statutory rape laws adult men who impregnate young girls, an issue discussed in Chapter 6, Criminal Abuse and Neglect.

Many commentators feel that shame is inappropriate, ineffective or counterproductive. One writer notes that "dozens of research studies show that the most effective deterrent to early childbearing is a teen's access to other sources of satisfaction and hope for the future. Good schools and jobs are the best methods of birth control and escape from welfare that anyone has yet devised." Stephanie Coontz, The American Family and the Nostalgia Trap: Attributing Americans, Social Problems to The Breakdown of the Traditional Family, Phi Delta Kappan (March, 1995, at K1).

Consider also the thoughts of this letter writer: "It takes two to make a baby, but only one will be left holding the bag of shame. Why is it that women and shame seem to go together? * * * Using shame as a tool for behavior modification can have unintended results. Not long ago * * * a teenage couple * * * hid their newborn in a trash can rather than face their parents' shame." Tampa Tribune, Mar. 30, 1997, at 3 (letter to the editor).

B. Who Is a "Father"?

In response to concerns that welfare costs were rising dramatically because so many single mothers were not receiving child support, the federal government began to assume an active role in paternity establishment and child support enforcement in the mid–1970's. In 1975 Congress passed Title IV–D of the Social Security Act. Title IV–D established the Office of Child Support Enforcement as a cooperative federal agency to assist the states in paternity establishment and child support establishment and collection. Paternity and child support programs thus are frequently referred to as IV–D programs. Because domestic relations law is traditionally under state, not federal, control, the federal government implemented the new legislation by providing federal funds only to states that amended their laws to meet the Act's requirements.

Additional amendments to Title IV–D and new laws have increasingly added federal requirements to paternity and child support rules. Child support is discussed in Chapter 9. The following article describes recent major changes in paternity establishment.

PAUL K. LEGLER, THE COMING REVOLUTION IN CHILD SUPPORT POLICY: IMPLICATIONS OF THE 1996 WELFARE ACT

30 Fam. L.Q. 519, 527–38(1996).

* * *

A.   Background Leading to Changes

The changes in paternity establishment law mandated by PRWORA [Personal Responsibility and Work Opportunity Reconciliation Act of 1996] are the result of three developments that have occurred over the past decade: a change in social perspective, in-hospital paternity establishment, and advancement in genetic testing.

Perhaps the major catalyst for change in paternity law has been the change in social perspective on the importance of paternity establishment. As policymakers began to pay attention to the mushrooming number of out-of-wedlock births during the 1980s, there was a growing focus on the poverty often associated with single parenthood. Establishing paternity was seen as a way to alleviate some of the poverty because it opened the door to the possible receipt of child support. A rising body of evidence showed that, contrary to the opinion of many observers, most unwed fathers could pay some financial support for their children. Even in cases of out-of-wedlock births for teen mothers, most of the fathers were not teen fathers. A large percentage were older males with some income. Most importantly, even when fathers had low incomes at the time of the birth of the child, their incomes tended to rise relatively rapidly after that, increasing their ability to pay support. Furthermore, evidence showed that paternity establishment was cost effective, even for welfare cases.

Single parenthood was also linked to a number of negative social consequences faced by children in single parent homes. The magnitude and causality of the link can be debated, but an increasing body of research, and a number of social scientists, supports the view that there is some link, even if only modest. Establishing paternity was seen as a way to help alleviate some of the problems associated with single parenthood and to begin to make an emotional, as well as financial, link to fathers.

The second catalyst for the change in paternity establishment law and procedure came out of the social sciences. Esther Wattenburg published a study in 1991 focusing on the relationship of young fathers and mothers at the time of out-of-wedlock births. The findings indicated that such births were often the result of established relationships, not casual ones, and that the mothers almost always knew who the father was and where he could be found. Significantly, Wattenburg found that two-thirds of fathers went to the hospital at the time of the out-of-wedlock birth and some 80 percent of young unmarried fathers took care of the baby in some way in the year following the birth. This research pointed to the time of the birth at the hospital as a critical time to establish paternity. While ties are close, many fathers show a clear desire to acknowledge their connection to the child. But as time passes, contact falls off rapidly, interest often fades, and the chances for successful paternity establishment decline rapidly.

Almost simultaneously with the release of the Wattenburg study, the State of Washington issued a report on a successful, innovative program it had started to obtain voluntary paternity acknowledgments at the time of the birth at the hospital. This information persuaded the Clinton Administration to include a provision in the Omnibus Budget Reconciliation Act of 1993 [OBRA] requiring all states to adopt in-hospital paternity establishment programs. Initial results have shown remarkable success.

The third catalyst for the change in the paternity establishment process was the advancement made in scientific testing for paternity, especially the use of DNA testing. DNA testing made the identification of fathers a near certainty and suggests the possibility that fathers could be readily and confidently identified, particularly if the legal processes were to be changed to make it easier to obtain genetic tests.

B. Changes in Voluntary Acknowledgment of Paternity Under PRWORA

PRWORA compels changes in state laws and procedures in the area of child support enforcement through mandates imposed on states. The Act imposes a number of requirements to expand the scope of existing in-hospital paternity establishment programs and make them more uniform. First, the legal status of a signed voluntary acknowledgment of paternity is clarified. States are required to provide that a signed voluntary acknowledgment of paternity is considered a legal finding of paternity subject to rescission within the earlier of sixty days or the date of an administrative or judicial proceeding in which the signatory is a party. After the sixty-day period the acknowledgment may only be challenged under limited circumstances. Judicial or administrative proceedings are not required or permitted to ratify an unchallenged acknowledgment of paternity, and voluntary acknowledgments are entitled to full faith and credit in other states. The combined effect of these changes is that signing an acknowledgment of paternity will have definite, tangible consequences—it establishes paternity without any further legal action (absent a challenge).

In recognition of the added significance of signing an acknowledgment of paternity, the Act provides that both the mother and the man acknowledging paternity must be given notice, orally and in writing, of the legal consequences and rights and responsibilities that arise from signing the acknowledgment. Data elements of a model affidavit will be developed by the Secretary, and state affidavits must include the minimum requirements established by the Secretary.

Another requirement of the Act pertaining to voluntary paternity establishment is that the name of the father can be included on the record of birth only if the mother and father have signed a voluntary acknowledgment. This requirement was included as an inducement for fathers and mothers to sign acknowledgments of paternity and to provide uniform legal consequences arising from having the father's name on the birth certificate.

C.   Changes in the Paternity Establishment Process

The Act requires states to take a number of steps to streamline their processes for paternity establishment. The key to these streamlined processes is "up-front" genetic testing—obtaining the genetic test as quickly as possible. Once the test is completed, the paternity issue is essentially resolved because the results will either exclude the father or result in a very high probability (in most cases, above 99 percent) of paternity. Most fathers typically admit paternity when faced with such test results, so the vast majority of cases can then be resolved by obtaining a signed acknowledgment.

This procedure precludes the necessity of first filing an action in court or having a court hearing. Under up-front genetic testing, all of the initial steps can be performed directly by the child support agency: ordering that the putative father submit to a genetic test, scheduling the test, and obtaining signed acknowledgments. The child support agency then simply files the matter with the court and registers the voluntary acknowledgment with the vital records agency.

In order to create this simplified process, the Act imposes a number of state mandates. First, states must provide authority for the state child support agency to order genetic tests "without the necessity of obtaining an order from any judicial or administrative tribunal." Put simply, the child support agency must be able to administratively order a genetic test. States must have procedures which require parties in contested paternity proceedings to submit to a genetic test (subject to good cause exceptions or unless otherwise barred by state law), if the request is supported by a sworn statement setting forth facts establishing a reasonable possibility of the requisite sexual contact between the parties. The Act also requires the state agency to pay costs of genetic tests, (subject to recoupment, if the state so elects, from the alleged father if paternity is established) and to obtain additional testing if an original test result is contested, upon advance payment by the contestant.

For those cases where the alleged father still seeks to contest the matter after a genetic test, the process is further streamlined and the incentive for delay is removed. Evidentiary rules are simplified by providing that the results of any genetic test are admissible if the test is of a type generally acknowledged to be reliable by accreditation bodies designated by the Secretary and performed by a laboratory approved by such an accreditation body. Bills for pregnancy, childbirth, and genetic tests are admissible without third-party foundation. In addition, states must have procedures for entering temporary orders for support if there is clear and convincing evidence of paternity (on the basis of a genetic test or otherwise). Finally, jury trials for paternity cases are eliminated.

These changes complement legislative changes made in OBRA 1993. Those changes required that: (1) states must have procedures which create either a rebuttable or conclusive presumption of paternity upon genetic test results showing a threshold probability of paternity; (2) any objections to such test results must be made in writing within a specified period after obtaining the results; and (3) the results are admissible without foundation unless an objection is made.

The implications of the combined changes in PRWORA and under OBRA are immense. In virtually every IV–D paternity case a genetic test can be obtained up-front. If the alleged father is not excluded, the results create a presumption of paternity. The vast majority of fathers should voluntarily acknowledge paternity at this point because such a presumption would be virtually impossible to overcome, and the ability and incentive to delay is removed. As a result, the vast majority of routine IV–D cases will be processed and an order of paternity entered through administrative steps by the child support agency, without the necessity of any significant court involvement. Of course, there will still be some cases that turn on unique fact situations, and there will still be occasional trials; but such cases will not pose a significant problem for the system because the vast majority of routine cases will have been resolved quickly and simply.

D.   Changes in the Cooperation Determination

Another area of paternity establishment process that is changed under PRWORA is in the area of required paternity cooperation. It has been a requirement since the inception of the program that recipients of AFDC [Aid to Families with Dependent Children] assign their right to support and "cooperate" in establishing paternity and securing support. During the development of the new legislation, there was a spirited debate about whether this cooperation requirement is sufficient to ensure that fathers are identified. One viewpoint was that the existing requirements were adequate and that mothers generally did cooperate with paternity establishment efforts. Another viewpoint was that cooperation was a significant problem. This latter viewpoint was bolstered by the release of a study by Kathryn Edin in 1994 which showed that many mothers engaged in "covert noncompliance," whereby they pretend to cooperate, but in fact hide identifying information from the authorities.

Various solutions to the perceived problem of noncooperation were considered. Proposals were introduced in Congress that would have required that paternity actually be legally established before someone could get any cash welfare benefits or full benefits. These proposals were opposed by the Clinton Administration on the basis that it would be unfair to reduce or deny benefits in cases where the mother had fully cooperated but the state had not determined paternity for some other reason. Instead, in July 1996, preceding the enactment of PRWORA, the Clinton Administration published a proposed rule which would require a stricter definition of cooperation and require the cooperation determination be made at the time of the welfare application.

The PRWORA addressed the whole cooperation issue by resorting to state flexibility. States were given broad flexibility to define what constitutes "cooperation," to define "good cause" for noncooperation, to determine the penalty for noncooperation (but not less than 25 percent of the family grant), and to determine which agency (welfare or child support) makes the "good cause" determination.

It remains to be seen whether such a broad grant of discretion raises a new set of problems. Although most states are likely to adopt reasonable policies similar to those under existing law or as proposed in the Work and Responsibility Act, some states could use this authority to adopt punitive state requirements that result in large numbers of women being determined ineligible in an attempt to save welfare dollars. States could also use this flexibility to remove the difficult cases from their welfare rolls in order to meet paternity establishment standards. In addition, stricter cooperation requirements are likely to increase the number of good cause claims for domestic violence.

* * *

PROBLEM 2–1

Matilda, an unmarried mother, brings a paternity action against George, her child's father. George, an attorney, pays her $15,000 in return for her signing a covenant not to sue and dismissing her pending paternity action with prejudice. Should the child, Ann, be able to bring an independent paternity action in her own name? How might the interests of the child and mother differ? Would the child have a claim based in constitutional law?

MICHAEL H. v. GERALD D.
Supreme Court of the United States, 1989.
491 U.S. 110.

JUSTICE SCALIA announced the judgment of the Court and delivered an opinion, in which THE CHIEF JUSTICE joins, and in all but footnote 6ᵃ of which JUSTICE O'CONNOR and JUSTICE KENNEDY join.

Under California law, a child born to a married woman living with her husband is presumed to be a child of the marriage. The presumption

a. Footnote 6 discusses the appropriateness of the methodology Justice Scalia used to justify finding that the father, Michael, had no due process liberty interest in his relationship with Victoria, the child.

of legitimacy may be rebutted only by the husband or wife, and then only in limited circumstances. The instant appeal presents the claim that this presumption infringes upon the due process rights of a man who wishes to establish his paternity of a child born to the wife of another man, and the claim that it infringes upon the constitutional right of the child to maintain a relationship with her natural father.

I

The facts of this case are, we must hope, extraordinary. On May 9, 1976, in Las Vegas, Nevada, Carole D., an international model, and Gerald D., a top executive in a French oil company, were married. The couple established a home in Playa del Rey, California, in which they resided as husband and wife when one or the other was not out of the country on business. In the summer of 1978, Carole became involved in an adulterous affair with a neighbor, Michael H. In September 1980, she conceived a child, Victoria D., who was born on May 11, 1981. Gerald was listed as father on the birth certificate and has always held Victoria out to the world as his daughter. Soon after delivery of the child, however, Carole informed Michael that she believed he might be the father.

In the first three years of her life, Victoria remained always with Carole, but found herself within a variety of quasi-family units. In October 1981, Gerald moved to New York City to pursue his business interests, but Carole chose to remain in California. At the end of that month, Carole and Michael had blood tests of themselves and Victoria, which showed a 98.07% probability that Michael was Victoria's father. In January 1982, Carole visited Michael in St. Thomas, where his primary business interests were based. There Michael held Victoria out as his child. In March, however, Carole left Michael and returned to California, where she took up residence with yet another man, Scott K. Later that spring, and again in the summer, Carole and Victoria spent time with Gerald in New York City, as well as on vacation in Europe. In the fall, they returned to Scott in California.

In November 1982, rebuffed in his attempts to visit Victoria, Michael filed a filiation action in California Superior Court to establish his paternity and right to visitation. In March 1983, the court appointed an attorney and guardian ad litem to represent Victoria's interests. Victoria then filed a cross-complaint asserting that if she had more than one psychological or *de facto* father, she was entitled to maintain her filial relationship, with all of the attendant rights, duties, and obligations, with both. In May 1983, Carole filed a motion for summary judgment. During this period, from March through July 1983, Carole was again living with Gerald in New York. In August, however, she returned to California, became involved once again with Michael, and instructed her attorneys to remove the summary judgment motion from the calendar.

For the ensuing eight months, when Michael was not in St. Thomas he lived with Carole and Victoria in Carole's apartment in Los Angeles and held Victoria out as his daughter. In April 1984, Carole and Michael signed a stipulation that Michael was Victoria's natural father. Carole left Michael the next month, however, and instructed her attorneys not to file the stipulation. In June 1984, Carole reconciled with Gerald and joined him in New York, where they now live with Victoria and two other children since born into the marriage.

In May 1984, Michael and Victoria, through her guardian ad litem, sought visitation rights for Michael *pendente lite*. To assist in determining whether visitation would be in Victoria's best interests, the Superior Court appointed a psychologist to evaluate Victoria, Gerald, Michael, and Carole. The psychologist recommended that Carole retain sole custody, but that Michael be allowed continued contact with Victoria pursuant to a restricted visitation schedule. The court concurred and ordered that Michael be provided with limited visitation privileges *pendente lite*.

On October 19, 1984, Gerald, who had intervened in the action, moved for summary judgment on the ground that under Cal.Evid.Code § 621 there were no triable issues of fact as to Victoria's paternity. This law provides that "the issue of a wife cohabiting with her husband, who is not impotent or sterile, is conclusively presumed to be a child of the marriage." The presumption may be rebutted by blood tests, but only if a motion for such tests is made, within two years from the date of the child's birth, either by the husband or, if the natural father has filed an affidavit acknowledging paternity, by the wife.

On January 28, 1985, having found that affidavits submitted by Carole and Gerald sufficed to demonstrate that the two were cohabiting at conception and birth and that Gerald was neither sterile nor impotent, the Superior Court granted Gerald's motion for summary judgment, rejecting Michael's and Victoria's challenges to the constitutionality of § 621. The court also denied their motions for continued visitation pending the appeal under Cal.Civ.Code § 4601, which provides that a court may, in its discretion, grant "reasonable visitation rights ... to any ... person having an interest in the welfare of the child." It found that allowing such visitation would "violat[e] the intention of the Legislature by impugning the integrity of the family unit."

On appeal, Michael asserted, *inter alia*, that the Superior Court's application of § 621 had violated his procedural and substantive due process rights. Victoria also raised a due process challenge to the statute, seeking to preserve her *de facto* relationship with Michael as well as with Gerald. She contended, in addition, that as § 621 allows the husband and, at least to a limited extent, the mother, but not the child, to rebut the presumption of legitimacy, it violates the child's right to equal protection. Finally, she asserted a right to continued visitation with Michael under § 4601. After submission of briefs and a hearing, the California Court of Appeal affirmed the judgment of the Superior Court and upheld the constitutionality of the statute. It interpreted that judgment, moreover, as having denied permanent visitation rights under § 4601 * * *.

* * * Michael and Victoria both raise equal protection and due process challenges. We do not reach Michael's equal protection claim, however, as it was neither raised nor passed upon below.

* * *

III

We address first the claims of Michael. At the outset, it is necessary to clarify what he sought and what he was denied. California law, like nature itself, makes no provision for dual fatherhood. Michael was seeking to be declared *the* father of Victoria. The immediate benefit he evidently sought to obtain from that status was visitation rights. See Cal.Civ.Code Ann. § 4601 (West 1983) (parent has statutory right to visitation "unless it is shown that such visitation would be detrimental to the best interests of the child"). But if Michael were successful in being declared the father, other rights would follow—most importantly, the right to be considered as the parent who should have custody, a status which "embrace[s] the sum of parental rights with respect to the rearing of a child, including the child's care; the right to the child's services and earnings; the right to direct the child's activities; the right to make decisions regarding the control, education, and health of the child; and the right, as well as the duty, to prepare the child for additional obligations, which includes the teaching of moral standards, religious beliefs, and elements of good citizenship." All parental rights, including visitation, were automatically denied by denying Michael status as the father. While Cal.Civ.Code Ann. § 4601 places it within the discretionary power of a court to award visitation rights to a nonparent, the Superior Court here, affirmed by the Court of Appeal, held that California law denies visitation, against the wishes of the mother, to a putative father who has been prevented by § 621 from establishing his paternity.

Michael raises two related challenges to the constitutionality of § 621. First, he asserts that requirements of procedural due process prevent the State from terminating his liberty interest in his relationship with his child without affording him an opportunity to demonstrate his paternity in an evidentiary hearing. We believe this claim derives from a fundamental misconception of the nature of the California statute. While § 621 is phrased in terms of a presumption, that rule of evidence is the implementation of a substantive rule of law. California declares it to be, except in limited circumstances, *irrelevant* for paternity purposes whether a child conceived during, and born into, an existing marriage was begotten by someone other than the husband and had a prior relationship with him.* * * [T]he conclusive presumption not only expresses the State's substantive policy but also furthers it, excluding inquiries into the child's paternity that would be destructive of family integrity and privacy.

* * * We therefore reject Michael's procedural due process challenge and proceed to his substantive claim.

Michael contends as a matter of substantive due process that, because he has established a parental relationship with Victoria, protection of Gerald's and Carole's marital union is an insufficient state interest to support termination of that relationship. This argument is, of course, predicated on the assertion that Michael has a constitutionally protected liberty interest in his relationship with Victoria.

It is an established part of our constitutional jurisprudence that the term "liberty" in the Due Process Clause extends beyond freedom from physical restraint. * * * In an attempt to limit and guide interpretation of the Clause, we have insisted not merely that the interest denominated as a "liberty" be "fundamental" (a concept that, in isolation, is hard to objectify), but also that it be an interest traditionally protected by our society.

* * *

Thus, the legal issue in the present case reduces to whether the relationship between persons in the situation of Michael and Victoria has been treated as a protected family unit under the historic practices of our society, or whether on any other basis it has been accorded special protection. We think it impossible to find that it has. In fact, quite to the contrary, our traditions have protected the marital family (Gerald, Carole, and the child they acknowledge to be theirs) against the sort of claim Michael asserts.

The presumption of legitimacy was a fundamental principle of the common law. Traditionally, that presumption could be rebutted only by proof that a husband was incapable of procreation or had had no access to his wife during the relevant period. As explained by Blackstone, nonaccess could only be proved "if the husband be out of the kingdom of England (or, as the law somewhat loosely phrases it, *extra quatuor maria* [beyond the four seas]) for above nine months....". And, under the common law both in England and here, "neither husband nor wife [could] be a witness to prove access or nonaccess." The primary policy rationale underlying the common law's severe restrictions on rebuttal of the presumption appears to have been an aversion to declaring children illegitimate, thereby depriving them of rights of inheritance and succession, and likely making them wards of the state. A secondary policy concern was the interest in promoting the "peace and tranquillity of States and families," a goal that is obviously impaired by facilitating suits against husband and wife asserting that their children are illegitimate. Even though, as bastardy laws became less harsh, "[j]udges in both [England and the United States] gradually widened the acceptable range of evidence that could be offered by spouses, and placed restraints on the 'four seas rule' ... [,] the law retained a strong bias against ruling the children of married women illegitimate." * * *

We have found nothing in the older sources, nor in the older cases, addressing specifically the power of the natural father to assert parental rights over a child born into a woman's existing marriage with another man. Since it is Michael's burden to establish that such a power (at least where the natural father has established a relationship with the child) is so deeply imbedded within our traditions as to be a fundamental right, the lack of evidence alone might defeat his case. But the evidence shows that even in modern times—when, as we have noted, the rigid protection of the marital family has in other respects been relaxed—the ability of a person in Michael's position to claim paternity has not been generally acknowledged. * * *

* * *

* * * Here, to *provide* protection to an adulterous natural father is to *deny* protection to a marital father, and vice versa. If Michael has a "freedom not to conform" (whatever that means), Gerald must equivalently have a "freedom to conform." One of them will pay a price for asserting that "freedom"—Michael by being unable to act as father of the child he has adulterously begotten, or Gerald by being unable to preserve the integrity of the traditional family unit he and Victoria have established. Our disposition does not choose between these two "freedoms," but leaves that to the people of California. * * *

IV

We have never had occasion to decide whether a child has a liberty interest, symmetrical with that of her parent, in maintaining her filial relationship. We need not do so here because, even assuming that such a right exists, Victoria's claim must fail. Victoria's due process challenge is, if anything, weaker than Michael's. Her basic claim is not that California has erred in preventing her from establishing that Michael, not Gerald, should stand as her legal father. Rather, she claims a due process right to maintain filial relationships with both Michael and Gerald. This assertion merits little discussion, for, whatever the merits of the guardian ad litem's belief that such an arrangement can be of great psychological benefit to a child, the claim that a State must recognize multiple fatherhood has no support in the history or traditions of this country. Moreover, even if we were to construe Victoria's argument as forwarding the lesser proposition that, whatever her status vis-a-vis Gerald, she has a liberty interest in maintaining a filial relationship with her natural father, Michael, we find that, at best, her claim is the obverse of Michael's and fails for the same reasons.

Victoria claims in addition that her equal protection rights have been violated because, unlike her mother and presumed father, she had no opportunity to rebut the presumption of her legitimacy. We find this argument wholly without merit. We reject, at the outset, Victoria's suggestion that her equal protection challenge must be assessed under a standard of strict scrutiny because, in denying her the right to maintain a filial relationship with Michael, the State is discriminating against her on the basis of her illegitimacy. Illegitimacy is a legal construct, not a natural trait. Under California law, Victoria is not illegitimate, and she is treated in the same manner as all other legitimate children: she is entitled to maintain a filial relationship with her legal parents.

We apply, therefore, the ordinary "rational relationship" test to Victoria's equal protection challenge. The primary rationale underlying § 621's limitation on those who may rebut the presumption of legitimacy is a concern that allowing persons other than the husband or wife to do so may undermine the integrity of the marital union. When the husband or wife contests the legitimacy of their child, the stability of the marriage has already been shaken. In contrast, allowing a claim of illegitimacy to be pressed by the child—or, more accurately, by a court-appointed guardian ad litem—may well disrupt an otherwise peaceful union. Since it pursues a legitimate end by rational means, California's decision to treat Victoria differently from her parents is not a denial of equal protection.

The judgment of the California Court of Appeal is affirmed.

[The concurring opinions of Justices O'Connor, Kennedy, and Stevens are discussed in the chapter on Adoption.]

JUSTICE BRENNAN, with whom JUSTICE MARSHALL and JUSTICE BLACKMUN join, dissenting.

In a case that has yielded so many opinions as has this one, it is fruitful to begin by emphasizing the common ground shared by a majority of this Court. Five Members of the Court refuse to foreclose "the possibility that a natural father might ever have a constitutionally protected interest in his relationship with a child whose mother was married to, and cohabiting with, another man at the time of the child's conception and birth." Five Justices agree that the flaw inhering in a conclusive presumption that terminates a constitutionally protected interest without any hearing whatsoever is a procedural one. Four Members of the Court agree that Michael H. has a liberty interest in his relationship with Victoria, and one assumes for purposes of this case that he does.

* * *

Make no mistake: to say that the State must provide Michael with a hearing to prove his paternity is not to express any opinion of the ultimate state of affairs between Michael and Victoria and Carole and Gerald. In order to change the current situation among these people, Michael first must convince a court that he is Victoria's father, and even if he is able to do this, he will be denied visitation rights if that would be in Victoria's best interests. It is elementary that a determination that a State must afford procedures before it terminates a given right is not a prediction about the end result of those procedures.[12]

---

12. The plurality's failure to see this point causes it to misstate Michael's claim in the following way: "Michael contends as a matter of substantive due process that, because he has established a parental relationship with Victoria, protection of Gerald's and Carole's marital union is an insufficient state interest to support termination of that relationship." Michael does not claim that the State may not, under any circumstance, terminate his relationship with Victoria; instead, he simply claims that the State may not do so without affording him a hearing on the issue—paternity—that it deems vital to the question whether their relationship may be discontinued. The

IV

The atmosphere surrounding today's decision is one of make-believe. Beginning with the suggestion that the situation confronting us here does not repeat itself every day in every corner of the country, moving on to the claim that it is tradition alone that supplies the details of the liberty that the Constitution protects, and passing finally to the notion that the Court always has recognized a cramped vision of "the family," today's decision lets stand California's pronouncement that Michael—whom blood tests show to a 98 percent probability to be Victoria's father—is not Victoria's father. When and if the Court awakes to reality, it will find a world very different from the one it expects.

JUSTICE WHITE, with whom JUSTICE BRENNAN joins, dissenting.

California law, as the plurality describes it, tells us that, except in limited circumstances, California declares it to be "*irrelevant* for paternity purposes whether a child conceived during, and born into, an existing marriage was begotten by someone other than the husband" (emphasis in original). This I do not accept, for the fact that Michael H. is the biological father of Victoria is to me highly relevant to whether he has rights, as a father or otherwise, with respect to the child. Because I believe that Michael H. has a liberty interest that cannot be denied without due process of the law, I must dissent.

* * *

As the Court has said: "The significance of the biological connection is that it offers the natural father an opportunity that no other male possesses to develop a relationship with his offspring. If he grasps that opportunity and accepts some measure of responsibility for the child's future, he may enjoy the blessings of the parent-child relationship and make uniquely valuable contributions to the child's development." Lehr, 463 U.S., at 262. It is as if this passage was addressed to Michael. Yet the plurality today recants. Michael eagerly grasped the opportunity to have a relationship with his daughter (he lived with her; he declared her to be his child; he provided financial support for her) and still, with today's opinion, his opportunity has vanished. He has been rendered a stranger to his child.

Because Cal.Evid.Code Ann. § 621, as applied, should be held unconstitutional under the Due Process Clause of the Fourteenth Amendment, I respectfully dissent.

Notes and Questions

1. *Questions about* Michael H. (a) According to *Michael H.*, what characteristics make a man a child's "father"? (b) Does the statutory presumption

plurality makes Michael's claim easier to knock down by turning it into such a big target.

The plurality's misunderstanding of Michael's claim also leads to its assertion that "to *provide* protection to an adulterous nat-

ural father is to *deny* protection to a marital father." To allow Michael a chance to prove his paternity, however, in no way guarantees that Gerald's relationship with Victoria will be changed.

that decided this case make sense now that paternity can be established with virtual certainty? What public policies underlie the legislative decision to prevent a man in Michael's position from establishing paternity? (c) What does Victoria want and what is the basis for her claims? (d) Under California law, when may the court grant a non-parent visitation? When may the court deny a parent visitation? (e) What rights would Michael have if he were allowed to establish his paternity?

2. *Later amendment.* The California statute was amended after *Michael H.* to allow a "presumed father" to petition for a blood test within two years of the child's birth, even though the mother was married to another man. California Family Code § 7611. "Presumed fathers" include men who meet any of the following conditions:

(a) He and the child's natural mother are or have been married to each other and the child is born during the marriage, or within 300 days after the marriage is terminated by death, annulment, declaration of invalidity, or divorce, or after a judgment of separation is entered by a court.

(b) Before the child's birth, he and the child's natural mother have attempted to marry each other by a marriage solemnized in apparent compliance with law * * *

(c) After the child's birth, he and the child's natural mother have married, or attempted to marry, each other by a marriage solemnized in apparent compliance with law.* * *

(d) He receives the child into his home and openly holds out the child as his natural child. * * *

Would this amendment have changed the result in *Michael H.?*

3. *Standing and best interests.* Either by statute or judicial decision, approximately two-thirds of the states now give putative fathers a right to rebut the presumption that a child born in wedlock is a child of the marriage. Should a putative father hold this right in all circumstances, or is this more selective analysis preferable?

* * * Ordinarily, a person establishes standing merely by alleging that he has been injured or that he possesses "arguably" protected interests. In actions that call into question the paternity of a child born in wedlock, however, this minimal threshold is inappropriate. Such a standard "could become a blanket license for any person to disrupt long-fostered family relationships by claiming to be the parent of a child." A putative father, therefore, must demonstrate something more before he can acquire standing to rebut the presumption of legitimacy of a child born in wedlock.

Courts * * * that have considered this issue have taken two approaches. Under the first approach, * * * the * * * trial court focuses primarily on the child and the child's best interests in determining whether to allow the action to proceed. * * *

Under the second approach, * * * the court must focus primarily on the putative father and whether he has developed a "substantial parent-child relationship" with the child. * * *

We recognize that each of these tests reflects a judicial attempt to strike a careful balance between the significant, and sometimes competing, interests of the child, the child's family and the putative father. We are mindful, for example, of the strong interests that remain even today in preserving the legitimacy of the child. Similarly, we acknowledge the importance of preserving the integrity of the family unit and the right of privacy of both the child and other family members. Further, we are respectful of the biological father's right to have contact with his child.

Nevertheless, we are reluctant to adopt either of these approaches to the exclusion of the other, or to attempt to formulate our own definitive list of the elements that will establish legal standing in such a case. Every paternity action revolves around its own unique set of facts and personal relationships, and a trial court must have flexibility to weigh the multiplicity of competing interests that may hang in the balance. This is particularly true in paternity actions that call into question the paternity of a child who was born in wedlock. Such sensitive and personal affairs are no place for an immutable legal standard that is bordered by bright lines. Indeed, we have recognized that it is preferable to leave "the delicate and difficult process of factfinding in family matters to flexible, individualized adjudication of the particular facts of each case without the constraint of objective guidelines." Whether a putative father has a special interest sufficient to enable him to bring a paternity action "is, in its nature, a fact-based question." "Not all putative fathers and not all families are similarly situated; thus their ... interests cannot be protected by a blanket [rule of law] that treats all putative fathers alike."

Accordingly, we conclude that a man's mere assertion that he is the biological father, without more, is insufficient to confer standing to challenge the paternity of a child born in wedlock. Rather, we hold that a putative father of such a child must offer proof, at a preliminary evidentiary hearing devoted to standing, that he is entitled to set in motion the judicial machinery to determine whether he is the biological father of the child. In deciding whether the putative father has standing, the trial court, on the basis of all the evidence before it, must determine whether the putative father has established that his interests and the best interests of the child outweigh those of the marital family unit.

Weidenbacher v. Duclos, 661 A.2d 988 (Conn.1995).

4. *Due process protections for unwilling fathers.* Should the state be required to prove paternity by clear and convincing evidence, given the responsibilities paternity entails? A preponderance of the evidence satisfies due process according to Rivera v. Minnich, 483 U.S. 574 (1987). Should the state be required to pay for paternity testing for indigent fathers? Yes, according to Little v. Streater, 452 U.S. 1 (1981).

5. *References.* For a comprehensive discussion of *Michael H.*, see Mary Kay Kisthardt, Of Fatherhood, Families and Fantasy: The Legacy of Michael H. v. Gerald D., 65 Tul L. Rev. 585 (1991). The issue of dual parenthood has arisen in a number of difficult adoption cases. For additional discussion, see Chapter 7, Adoption.

C. Who Is a "Mother?"

In contrast to the difficulties that may attend identification of a child's father, identification of the mother is not usually disputed. New reproductive technology, however, has resulted in complex issues related to determining "mother."

JOHNSON v. CALVERT

Supreme Court of California, 1993.
851 P.2d 776.

PANELLI, JUSTICE.

In this case we address several of the legal questions raised by recent advances in reproductive technology. When, pursuant to a surrogacy agreement, a zygote[1] formed of the gametes[2] of a husband and wife is implanted in the uterus of another woman, who carries the resulting fetus to term and gives birth to a child not genetically related to her, who is the child's "natural mother" under California law? Does a determination that the wife is the child's natural mother work a deprivation of the gestating woman's constitutional rights? And is such an agreement barred by any public policy of this state?

* * *

FACTS

Mark and Crispina Calvert are a married couple who desired to have a child. Crispina was forced to undergo a hysterectomy in 1984. Her ovaries remained capable of producing eggs, however, and the couple eventually considered surrogacy. In 1989 Anna Johnson heard about Crispina's plight from a coworker and offered to serve as a surrogate for the Calverts.

On January 15, 1990, Mark, Crispina, and Anna signed a contract providing that an embryo created by the sperm of Mark and the egg of Crispina would be implanted in Anna and the child born would be taken into Mark and Crispina's home "as their child." Anna agreed she would relinquish "all parental rights" to the child in favor of Mark and Crispina. In return, Mark and Crispina would pay Anna $10,000 in a series of installments, the last to be paid six weeks after the child's birth. Mark and Crispina were also to pay for a $200,000 life insurance policy on Anna's life.[4]

The zygote was implanted on January 19, 1990. Less than a month later, an ultrasound test confirmed Anna was pregnant.

---

1. An organism produced by the union of two gametes.

2. A cell that participates in fertilization and development of a new organism, also known as a germ cell or sex cell.

4. At the time of the agreement, Anna already had a daughter, Erica, born in 1987.

Unfortunately, relations deteriorated between the two sides. Mark learned that Anna had not disclosed she had suffered several stillbirths and miscarriages. Anna felt Mark and Crispina did not do enough to obtain the required insurance policy. She also felt abandoned during an onset of premature labor in June.

In July 1990, Anna sent Mark and Crispina a letter demanding the balance of the payments due her or else she would refuse to give up the child. The following month, Mark and Crispina responded with a lawsuit, seeking a declaration they were the legal parents of the unborn child. Anna filed her own action to be declared the mother of the child, and the two cases were eventually consolidated. The parties agreed to an independent guardian ad litem for the purposes of the suit.

The child was born on September 19, 1990, and blood samples were obtained from both Anna and the child for analysis. The blood test results excluded Anna as the genetic mother. The parties agreed to a court order providing that the child would remain with Mark and Crispina on a temporary basis with visits by Anna.

At trial in October 1990, the parties stipulated that Mark and Crispina were the child's genetic parents. After hearing evidence and arguments, the trial court ruled that Mark and Crispina were the child's "genetic, biological and natural" father and mother, that Anna had no "parental" rights to the child, and that the surrogacy contract was legal and enforceable against Anna's claims. The court also terminated the order allowing visitation. * * *

DISCUSSION

Determining Maternity Under the Uniform Parentage Act

The Uniform Parentage Act (the Act) was part of a package of legislation introduced in 1975 * * *. The legislation's purpose was to eliminate the legal distinction between legitimate and illegitimate children. The Act followed in the wake of certain United States Supreme Court decisions mandating equal treatment of legitimate and illegitimate children. * * *

* * *

[The Uniform Parentage Act] replace[ed] the distinction between legitimate and illegitimate children with the concept of the "parent and child relationship." The "parent and child relationship" means "the legal relationship existing between a child and his natural or adoptive parents incident to which the law confers or imposes rights, privileges, duties, and obligations. It includes the mother and child relationship and the father and child relationship." "The parent and child relationship extends equally to every child and to every parent, regardless of the marital status of the parents." The "parent and child relationship" is thus a legal relationship encompassing two kinds of parents, "natural" and "adoptive."

Passage of the Act clearly was not motivated by the need to resolve surrogacy disputes, which were virtually unknown in 1975. Yet it facially applies to any parentage determination, including the rare case in which a child's maternity is in issue. * * * [T]he Act offers a mechanism to resolve this dispute, albeit one not specifically tooled for it. We therefore proceed to analyze the parties' contentions within the Act's framework.

* * *

* * *[W]e are left with the undisputed evidence that Anna, not Crispina, gave birth to the child and that Crispina, not Anna, is genetically related to him. Both women thus have adduced evidence of a mother and child relationship as contemplated by the Act. Yet for any child California law recognizes only one natural mother, despite advances in reproductive technology rendering a different outcome biologically possible.[8]

* * *

Because two women each have presented acceptable proof of maternity, we do not believe this case can be decided without inquiring into the parties' intentions as manifested in the surrogacy agreement. Mark and Crispina are a couple who desired to have a child of their own genetic stock but are physically unable to do so without the help of reproductive technology. They affirmatively intended the birth of the child, and took the steps necessary to effect in vitro fertilization. But for their acted-on intention, the child would not exist. Anna agreed to facilitate the procreation of Mark's and Crispina's child. The parties' aim was to bring Mark's and Crispina's child into the world, not for Mark and Crispina to donate a zygote to Anna. Crispina from the outset intended to be the child's mother. Although the gestative function Anna performed was necessary to bring about the child's birth, it is safe to say that Anna would not have been given the opportunity to gestate or deliver the child had she, prior to implantation of the zygote, manifested her own intent to be the child's mother. No reason appears why Anna's later change of heart should vitiate the determination that Crispina is the child's natural mother.

We conclude that although the Act recognizes both genetic consanguinity and giving birth as means of establishing a mother and child relationship, when the two means do not coincide in one woman, she who intended to procreate the child—that is, she who intended to bring about the birth of a child that she intended to raise as her own—is the natural mother under California law.[10]

8. We decline to accept the contention of amicus curiae the American Civil Liberties Union (ACLU) that we should find the child has two mothers. Even though rising divorce rates have made multiple parent arrangements common in our society, we see no compelling reason to recognize such a situation here. The Calverts are the genetic and intending parents of their son and have provided him, by all accounts, with a stable, intact, and nurturing home. To recognize parental rights in a third party with whom the Calvert family has had little contact since shortly after the child's birth would diminish Crispina's role as mother.

10. Thus, under our analysis, in a true "egg donation" situation, where a woman gestates and gives birth to a child formed

Our conclusion finds support in the writings of several legal commentators. Professor Hill,[b] arguing that the genetic relationship *per se* should not be accorded priority in the determination of the parent-child relationship in the surrogacy context, notes that "while all of the players in the procreative arrangement are necessary in bringing a child into the world, the child would not have been born but for the efforts of the intended parents.... [T]he intended parents are the first cause, or the prime movers, of the procreative relationship."

Similarly, Professor Shultz[c] observes that recent developments in the field of reproductive technology "dramatically extend affirmative intentionality.... Steps can be taken to bring into being a child who would not otherwise have existed." "Within the context of artificial reproductive techniques," Professor Shultz argues, "intentions that are voluntarily chosen, deliberate, express and bargained-for ought presumptively to determine legal parenthood."

* * *

Moreover, as Professor Shultz recognizes, the interests of children, particularly at the outset of their lives, are "[un]likely to run contrary to those of adults who choose to bring them into being." Thus, "[h]onoring the plans and expectations of adults who will be responsible for a child's welfare is likely to correlate significantly with positive outcomes for parents and children alike." Under Anna's interpretation of the Act, by contrast, a woman who agreed to gestate a fetus genetically related to the intending parents would, contrary to her expectations, be held to be the child's natural mother, with all the responsibilities that ruling would entail, if the intending mother declined to accept the child after its birth. In what we must hope will be the extremely rare situation in which neither the gestator nor the woman who provided the ovum for fertilization is willing to assume custody of the child after birth, a rule recogniz-

from the egg of another woman with the intent to raise the child as her own, the birth mother is the natural mother under California law.

The dissent would decide parentage based on the best interests of the child. Such an approach raises the repugnant specter of governmental interference in matters implicating our most fundamental notions of privacy, and confuses concepts of parentage and custody. Logically, the determination of parentage must precede, and should not be dictated by, eventual custody decisions. The implicit assumption of the dissent is that a recognition of the genetic intending mother as the natural mother may sometimes harm the child. This assumption overlooks California's dependency laws, which are designed to protect all children irrespective of the manner of birth or conception. More-

over, the best interests standard poorly serves the child in the present situation: it fosters instability during litigation and, if applied to recognize the gestator as the natural mother, results in a split of custody between the natural father and the gestator, an outcome not likely to benefit the child. Further, it may be argued that, by voluntarily contracting away any rights to the child, the gestator has, in effect, conceded the best interests of the child are not with her.

b. John Lawrence Hill, What Does It Mean to Be a "Parent"? The Claims of Biology As the Basis for Parental Rights, 66 N.Y.U.L.Rev. 353 (1991).

c. Marjorie Maguire Shultz, Reproductive Technology and Intent–Based Parenthood: An Opportunity for Gender Neutrality 1990 Wis.L.Rev. 297 (1990).

ing the intending parents as the child's legal, natural parents should best promote certainty and stability for the child.

In deciding the issue of maternity under the Act we have felt free to take into account the parties' intentions, as expressed in the surrogacy contract, because in our view the agreement is not, on its face, inconsistent with public policy.

* * *

We are unpersuaded that gestational surrogacy arrangements are so likely to cause * * * untoward results * * * as to demand their invalidation on public policy grounds. Although common sense suggests that women of lesser means serve as surrogate mothers more often than do wealthy women, there has been no proof that surrogacy contracts exploit poor women to any greater degree than economic necessity in general exploits them by inducing them to accept lower-paid or otherwise undesirable employment. We are likewise unpersuaded by the claim that surrogacy will foster the attitude that children are mere commodities; no evidence is offered to support it. The limited data available seem to reflect an absence of significant adverse effects of surrogacy on all participants.

The argument that a woman cannot knowingly and intelligently agree to gestate and deliver a baby for intending parents carries overtones of the reasoning that for centuries prevented women from attaining equal economic rights and professional status under the law. To resurrect this view is both to foreclose a personal and economic choice on the part of the surrogate mother, and to deny intending parents what may be their only means of procreating a child of their own genetic stock. Certainly in the present case it cannot seriously be argued that Anna, a licensed vocational nurse who had done well in school and who had previously borne a child, lacked the intellectual wherewithal or life experience necessary to make an informed decision to enter into the surrogacy contract.

Constitutionality of the Determination That Anna Johnson Is Not the Natural Mother

Anna argues at length that her right to the continued companionship of the child is protected under the federal Constitution.

First, we note the constitutional rights that are *not* implicated here.

There is no issue of procedural due process: although Anna broadly contends that the procedures prescribed for adoptions should be followed in the situation of a gestational surrogate's relinquishment to the genetic parents of the child she has carried and delivered, she cites no specific deficiency in the notice or hearing this matter received.

* * *

Anna relies mainly on theories of substantive due process, privacy, and procreative freedom, citing a number of decisions recognizing the fundamental liberty interest of natural parents in the custody and care of their children.* * *

* * *

Anna's argument depends on a prior determination that she is indeed the child's mother. Since Crispina is the child's mother under California law because she, not Anna, provided the ovum for the in vitro fertilization procedure, intending to raise the child as her own, it follows that any constitutional interests Anna possesses in this situation are something less than those of a mother. As counsel for the minor points out, the issue in this case is not whether Anna's asserted rights as a natural mother were unconstitutionally violated, but rather whether the determination that she is not the legal natural mother at all is constitutional.

Anna relies principally on the decision of the United States Supreme Court in Michael H. v. Gerald D. to support her claim to a constitutionally protected liberty interest in the companionship of the child, based on her status as "birth mother." In that case, a plurality of the court held that a state may constitutionally deny a man parental rights with respect to a child he fathered during a liaison with the wife of another man, since it is the marital family that traditionally has been accorded a protected liberty interest, as reflected in the historic presumption of legitimacy of a child born into such a family. The reasoning of the plurality in Michael H. does not assist Anna. Society has not traditionally protected the right of a woman who gestates and delivers a baby pursuant to an agreement with a couple who supply the zygote from which the baby develops and who intend to raise the child as their own; such arrangements are of too recent an origin to claim the protection of tradition. To the extent that tradition has a bearing on the present case, we believe it supports the claim of the couple who exercise their right to procreate in order to form a family of their own, albeit through novel medical procedures.

* * *

KENNARD, JUSTICE, dissenting.

* * *

[I]n California the existing statutory law applicable to this case is the Uniform Parentage Act, which was never designed to govern the new reproductive technology of gestational surrogacy. Under the UPA, both the genetic mother and the gestational mother have an equal right to be the child's natural mother. But the UPA allows one natural mother for each child, and thus this court is required to make a choice. To break this "tie" between the genetic mother and the gestational mother, the majority uses the legal concept of intent. In so doing, the majority has articulated a rationale for using the concept of intent that is grounded in principles of tort, intellectual property and commercial contract law.

But, as I have pointed out, we are not deciding a case involving the commission of a tort, the ownership of intellectual property, or the delivery of goods under a commercial contract; we are deciding the fate of a child. In the absence of legislation that is designed to address the unique problems of gestational surrogacy, this court should look not to tort, property or contract law, but to family law, as the governing paradigm and source of a rule of decision.

The allocation of parental rights and responsibilities necessarily impacts the welfare of a minor child. And in issues of child welfare, the standard that courts frequently apply is the best interests of the child. Indeed, it is highly significant that the UPA itself looks to a child's best interests in deciding another question of parental rights. This "best interests" standard serves to assure that in the judicial resolution of disputes affecting a child's well-being, protection of the minor child is the foremost consideration. Consequently, I would apply "the best interests of the child" standard to determine who can best assume the social and legal responsibilities of motherhood for a child born of a gestational surrogacy arrangement.

* * *

Notes and Questions

1. *Questions about* Calvert. (a) What is the basis for the determination that Crispina is the child's mother? (b) Why does the majority reject a "best interests of the child" standard for deciding the case? (c) Did the majority pay sufficient attention to the issues of exploitation of low income women and the commodification of children? How would evidence on these issues be relevant? (d) Would you favor a determination that the child has two mothers?

2. Do children have a right to know their genetic origins? See Michael Freeman, The New Birth Right? Identity and the Child of the Reproduction Revolution, 4 Int'l J. of Children's Rts. 273, 291 (1996)(the right to identity is the "right not to be deceived about ones' true origins.").

3. *Dual maternity*. Could both Anna and Crispina have had a role in the child's life? For a proposal that they could, see Randy Frances Kandel, Which Came First: The Mother or the Egg? A Kinship Solution to Gestational Surrogacy, 47 Rutgers L. Rev. 165 (1994)(the article "uses anthropological theory and cross-cultural materials to explain the persistence of the one mother/nuclear family construct and proposes a unique approach to the custody of gestational surrogacy children. This approach, * * * 'contractual kinship,' recognizes the maternity of both the genetic mother and the gestational mother and involves them both in the child's social rearing. Rather than privileging the one mother/nuclear family model as the standard to which gestational surrogacy families must conform or compare,* * * [the approach takes] a broader view of the family as a kinship group.") What would be the practical effects of recognizing dual maternity?

4. *Surrogacy contracts.* Should the law enforce a woman's contract to become pregnant through artificial insemination with the semen of another woman's husband, to carry the child to term and surrender the infant at birth to the husband and his wife? If the contract is not enforced, should the husband have primary custody, because he and his wife were the couple who had wanted the child initially? For a lengthy discussion of surrogacy contracts, see In re Baby M., 537 A.2d 1227 (N.J.1988), a highly publicized case which held that such contracts were invalid because they were in conflict with New Jersey statutes and public policy. The court granted custody to the biological father based on the best interests of the child, but voided the termination of the biological (surrogate) mother's parental rights and the adoption of the child by the father's wife. The case was remanded to determine the visitation rights of the biological mother (the surrogate mother). For a thoughtful discussion of surrogacy contracts and a listing of state surrogacy statutes, see R.R. v. M.H., 689 N.E.2d 790 (Mass.1998) (surrogacy agreement before the court was unenforceable, but surrogacy agreements which met conditions specified might be enforceable).

5. *The Uniform Status of Children of Assisted Conception Act.* The Uniform Status of Children of Assisted Conception Act, drafted by the National Conference of Commissioners on Uniform State Laws in 1988, provides two alternatives for states to consider. One alternative would allow surrogacy arrangements, and the other would declare them void. In a jurisdiction that did not allow surrogacy arrangements, Anna would have been considered the mother under the Act.

6. *Additional references*: A vigorous and on-going debate continues about new reproductive technologies and surrogate motherhood. For a comprehensive summary of issues and positions, see Janet L. Dolgin, Defining the Family: Law, Technology, and Reproduction in an Uneasy Age (1997). The National Conference of Commissioners on Uniform State Laws is revising the Uniform Parentage Act, the Uniform Putative and Unknown Fathers Act, and the Uniform Status of Children of Assisted Conception Act and consolidating them; for a draft of the new proposed Act, see <http:\\www.nccusl.org>.

Section 2.   Questioning the Definition of "Parent"

As the *Meyer* and *Pierce* decisions in Chapter 1 demonstrate, constitutional protections for parents are not easily overcome. Usually a person's status as a child's parent, with all the rights and responsibilities of parenthood, is not disputed. Difficult questions may arise, however, when someone who has fulfilled a parental role (such as a stepparent), or who has a biological claim (such as Michael H.), wants at least some of the legal rights of a parent, but is classified by law as a non-parent. Attempts to define "parent" lead to questions about the value of children's rights over parents' rights and about the role of parents in their children's lives. As the cases and articles that follow show, no consensus about how these questions should be answered has emerged.

A. Applying the Law

IN RE ALISON D. v. VIRGINIA M.

Court of Appeals of New York, 1991.
572 N.E.2d 27.

PER CURIAM.

At issue in this case is whether petitioner, a biological stranger to a child who is properly in the custody of his biological mother, has standing to seek visitation with the child under Domestic Relations Law § 70. Petitioner relies on both her established relationship with the child and her alleged agreement with the biological mother to support her claim that she has standing. We agree with the Appellate Division, that, although petitioner apparently nurtured a close and loving relationship with the child, she is not a parent within the meaning of Domestic Relations Law § 70. Accordingly, we affirm.

I

Petitioner Alison D. and respondent Virginia M. established a relationship in September 1977 and began living together in March 1978. In March 1980, they decided to have a child and agreed that respondent would be artificially inseminated. Together, they planned for the conception and birth of the child and agreed to share jointly all rights and responsibilities of child-rearing. In July 1981, respondent gave birth to a baby boy, A.D.M., who was given petitioner's last name as his middle name and respondent's last name became his last name. Petitioner shared in all birthing expenses and, after A.D.M.'s birth, continued to provide for his support. During A.D.M.'s first two years, petitioner and respondent jointly cared for and made decisions regarding the child.

In November 1983, when the child was 2 years and 4 months old, petitioner and respondent terminated their relationship and petitioner moved out of the home they jointly owned. Petitioner and respondent agreed to a visitation schedule whereby petitioner continued to see the child a few times a week. Petitioner also agreed to continue to pay one half of the mortgage and major household expenses. By this time, the child had referred to both respondent and petitioner as "mommy". Petitioner's visitation with the child continued until 1986, at which time respondent bought out petitioner's interest in the house and then began to restrict petitioner's visitation with the child. In 1987 petitioner moved to Ireland to pursue career opportunities, but continued her attempts to communicate with the child. Thereafter, respondent terminated all contact between petitioner and the child, returning all of petitioner's gifts and letters. No dispute exists that respondent is a fit parent. Petitioner commenced this proceeding seeking visitation rights pursuant to Domestic Relations Law § 70.

* * *

II

Pursuant to Domestic Relations Law § 70 "either parent may apply to the supreme court for a writ of habeas corpus to have such minor child brought before such court; and [the court] may award the natural guardianship, charge and custody of such child to either parent * * * as the case may require". Although the Court is mindful of petitioner's understandable concern for and interest in the child and of her expectation and desire that her contact with the child would continue, she has no right under Domestic Relations Law § 70 to seek visitation and, thereby, limit or diminish the right of the concededly fit biological parent to choose with whom her child associates. She is not a "parent" within the meaning of section 70.

Petitioner concedes that she is not the child's "parent"; that is, she is not the biological mother of the child nor is she a legal parent by virtue of an adoption. Rather she claims to have acted as a *"de facto"* parent or that she should be viewed as a parent "by estoppel". Therefore, she claims she has standing to seek visitation rights. These claims, however, are insufficient under section 70. Traditionally, in this State it is the child's mother and father who, assuming fitness, have the right to the care and custody of their child, even in situations where the nonparent has exercised some control over the child with the parents' consent. "It has long been recognized that, as between a parent and a third person, parental custody of a child may not be displaced absent grievous cause or necessity." To allow the courts to award visitation—a limited form of custody—to a third person would necessarily impair the parents' right to custody and control. Petitioner concedes that respondent is a fit parent. Therefore she has no right to petition the court to displace the choice made by this fit parent in deciding what is in the child's best interests.

Section 70 gives *parents* the right to bring proceedings to ensure their proper exercise of their care, custody and control. Where the Legislature deemed it appropriate, it gave other categories of persons standing to seek visitation and it gave the courts the power to determine whether an award of visitation would be in the child's best interests (*see, e.g.*, Domestic Relations Law § 71 [special proceeding or habeas corpus to obtain visitation rights for siblings]; § 72 [special proceeding or habeas corpus to obtain visitation rights for grandparents]* * *). We decline petitioner's invitation to read the term parent in section 70 to include categories of nonparents who have developed a relationship with a child or who have had prior relationships with a child's parents and who wish to continue visitation with the child. While one may dispute in an individual case whether it would be beneficial to a child to have continued contact with a nonparent, the Legislature did not in section 70 give such nonparent the opportunity to compel a fit parent to allow them to do so (* * * *compare*, Oregon Rev.Stat.Ann. § 109.119[1] [giving "(a)ny person including but not limited to a foster parent, stepparent, grandparent * * * who has established emotional ties creating a child-parent relationship with a child" the right to seek visitation or other right of custody]).

* * *

KAYE, JUDGE (dissenting).

The Court's decision, fixing biology[1] as the key to visitation rights, has impact far beyond this particular controversy, one that may affect a wide spectrum of relationships—including those of longtime heterosexual stepparents, "common-law" and nonheterosexual partners such as involved here, and even participants in scientific reproduction procedures. Estimates that more than 15.5 million children do not live with two biological parents, and that as many as 8 to 10 million children are born into families with a gay or lesbian parent, suggest just how widespread the impact may be.

But the impact of today's decision falls hardest on the children of those relationships, limiting their opportunity to maintain bonds that may be crucial to their development. The majority's retreat from the courts' proper role—its tightening of rules that should in visitation petitions, above all, retain the capacity to take the children's interests into account—compels this dissent.

In focusing the difference, it is perhaps helpful to begin with what is *not* at issue. This is not a custody case, but solely a visitation petition. The issue on this appeal is not whether petitioner should actually have visitation rights. Nor is the issue the relationship between Alison D. and Virginia M. Rather, the sole issue is the relationship between Alison D. and A.D.M., in particular whether Alison D.'s petition for visitation should even be considered on its merits. I would conclude that the trial court had jurisdiction to hear the merits of this petition.

The relevant facts are amply described in the Court's opinion. Most significantly, Virginia M. agrees that, after long cohabitation with Alison D. and before A.D.M.'s conception, it was "explicitly planned that the child would be theirs to raise together." It is also uncontested that the two shared "financial and emotional preparations" for the birth, and that for several years Alison D. actually filled the role of coparent to A.D.M., both tangibly and intangibly. In all, a parent-child relationship—encouraged or at least condoned by Virginia M.—apparently existed between A.D.M. and Alison D. during the first six years of the child's life.

While acknowledging that relationship, the Court nonetheless proclaims powerlessness to consider the child's interest at all, because the word "parent" in the statute imposes an absolute barrier to Alison D.'s petition for visitation. That same conclusion would follow, as the Appellate Division dissenter noted, were the coparenting relationship one of 10

---

1. While the opinion speaks of biological and legal parenthood, this Court has not yet passed on the legality of adoption by a second mother. [In an opinion authored by Chief Judge Kaye, the Court of Appeals subsequently ruled that a lesbian partner did have standing to adopt. In the Matter of Jacob, 660 N.E. 2d 397 (1995).]

or more years, and irrespective of how close or deep the emotional ties might be between petitioner and child, or how devastating isolation might be to the child. I cannot agree that such a result is mandated by section 70, or any other law.

Domestic Relations Law § 70 provides a mechanism for "either parent" to bring a habeas corpus proceeding to determine a child's custody. Other State Legislatures, in comparable statutes, have defined "parent" specifically and that definition has of course bound the courts. Significantly, the Domestic Relations Law contains no such limitation. Indeed, it does not define the term "parent" at all. That remains for the courts to do, as often happens when statutory terms are undefined.

The majority insists, however, that, the word "parent" in this case can only be read to mean biological parent; the response "one fit parent" now forecloses all inquiry into the child's best interest, even in visitation proceedings. We have not previously taken such a hard line in these matters, but in the absence of express legislative direction have attempted to read otherwise undefined words of the statute so as to effectuate the legislative purposes. The Legislature has made plain an objective in section 70 to promote "the best interest of the child" and the child's "welfare and happiness." Those words should not be ignored by us in defining standing for visitation purposes—they have not been in prior case law.

* * *

Of course there must be some limitation on who can petition for visitation. Domestic Relations Law § 70 specifies that the person must be the child's "parent," and the law additionally recognizes certain rights of biological and legal parents. Arguments that every dedicated caretaker could sue for visitation if the term "parent" were broadened, or that such action would necessarily effect sweeping change throughout the law, overlook and misportray the Court's role in defining otherwise undefined statutory terms to effect particular statutory purposes, and to do so narrowly, for those purposes only.

* * *

It is not my intention to spell out a definition but only to point out that it is surely within our competence to do so. It is indeed regrettable that we decline to exercise that authority in this visitation matter, given the explicit statutory objectives, the courts' power, and the fact that all consideration of the child's interest is, for the future, otherwise absolutely foreclosed.

I would remand the case to Supreme Court for an exercise of its discretion in determining whether Alison D. stands in loco parentis to A.D.M. and, if so, whether it is in the child's best interest to allow her the visitation rights she claims.

Notes and Questions

1. *Questions about* Alison D. (a) What weight does the court give to the child's interest in maintaining a relationship with Alison D., whom he calls "Mommy"?, (b) What right is Alison D. asserting and what is her argument for entitlement to that right? What right is Virginia M. asserting and what is the basis for her entitlement argument?, (c) If Alison D. had succeeded in getting visitation, would she have been considered a parent for other purposes, such as making decisions about the child's medical care and education?

2. *Functional definition of "parent."* In *Alison D.* an interdisciplinary group of academics filed an amici brief arguing that child development research supported the concept of functional parent and urging the court to adopt a functional definition of parent. Amici's definition required a showing, among other things, that "the child has in fact looked to the person as a parent" and that "the biological parent had consented to the assumption of a parental role by this person." Amici stated that these limits were needed to "separate out persons who have lived with a child, an aunt or a live-in babysitter, but have never been identified by the child as 'parent' and are less likely to have served as a central attachment figure in the child's life. It is also a desirable limit in order to protect the legitimate interests of biologic parents: that is, in circumstances in which the person seeking visitation has lived with the child together with a biologic parent, the biologic parent can later be required to permit visitation only in circumstances in which the biologic parent himself or herself has encouraged the child to look to the person as a 'parent'. Such a restriction adequately protects the legitimate (and constitutionally protected) interests of biologic parents in guiding the lives of their children." Brief for *Amici Curiae*, Eleven Concerned Academics (on the brief: David Chambers and Martha Minow).

What are the advantages and disadvantages of a functional definition of "parent"? For further discussion see Martha Minow, Redefining Families: Who's In and Who's Out?, 62 U. Colo. L. Rev. 269 (1991)(The disadvantages of a functional definition include its unpredictability and potential for manipulation by the parties and abuse by government, but because the definition recommended by *amici* focused on the interests of the child, it better serves children's needs than does the approach taken by the *Alison D.* majority; "From the child's point of view, the marital status, biological or nonbiological connection, and also the sexual orientation of such adults is irrelevant. Children form strong attachments without asking about such things. . . .")

3. *Same-sex parents.* Should heterosexuality and homosexuality be relevant in defining "parent"? For opposing views, see Nancy D. Polikoff, This Child Does Have Two Mothers: Redefining Parenthood To Meet the Needs of Children in Lesbian–Mother and Other Nontraditional Families, 78 Geo. L. J. 459 (1990)(arguing that rules developed for nontraditional heterosexual families should apply to lesbian-mother families) and Lynn D. Wardle, The Potential Impact of Homosexual Parenting on Children, 1997 U. Ill. L. R. 833 (1997) (arguing that states should adopt a rebuttable presumption that on-going homosexual relations by an adult seeking or exercising parental rights are not in the best interests of the child).

IN RE A.R.A.

Supreme Court of Montana, 1996.
919 P.2d 388.

ERDMANN, JUSTICE.

* * *

Tracy Erger and William (Bill) Askren were married in 1983. A.R.A. was born to them in 1987. Tracy and Bill divorced in 1989 when A.R.A. was nineteen months old. In the divorce decree, Tracy was awarded custody of A.R.A. and Bill was given reasonable rights of visitation. Bill was ordered to pay child support in the amount of $200 per month but became delinquent on those payments. Bill moved out of state and was not able to exercise his visitation rights to their full extent. He did, however, keep in touch by telephone and saw A.R.A. approximately once a year for extended periods.

Bill remarried in 1989 to Colleen. They had a daughter in 1990 and were expecting another child at the time of trial. Colleen's daughter from a previous marriage also lives with them. Colleen works as a secretary for the Salt Lake County Sheriff's Department and Bill, while not employed, attends a junior college and is studying to become a paralegal.

Tracy married Patrick in 1990 and they had a son, Joshua, in February 1992. In September 1992, Patrick was transferred to Billings and Tracy, A.R.A., and Joshua moved shortly thereafter. Tracy was killed in an airplane crash on December 18, 1992. In her will, Tracy had named Patrick as A.R.A.'s guardian.

Bill, as the surviving natural parent, came to Billings to pick up A.R.A. Patrick refused to relinquish physical custody of A.R.A. to Bill and petitioned the court for custody * * * . The District Court held a hearing on the matter and ordered that Patrick was the appropriate individual to have custody under the best interest of the child test even though he was not the natural father. From that order, Bill appeals.

ISSUE 1

Did the District Court err in awarding custody of the child to a stepparent over a natural parent based on the best interest of the child test?

Patrick requested a custody hearing pursuant to § 40–4–221, MCA. That section provides:

(1) Upon the death of a parent granted custody of a child, custody shall pass to the noncustodial parent unless one or more parties named in subsection (2) request a custody hearing. The noncustodial parent shall be a party in any proceeding brought under this section.

(2) Upon the death of a parent granted custody of a child, any of the following parties may request a custody hearing and seek custody of the child:

. . .

(b) the surviving spouse of the deceased custodial parent;

(c) a person nominated by the will of the deceased custodial parent;

. . .

(3) The hearing and determination of custody shall be governed by this part.

According to part 2 of Title 40, Chapter 4, Montana Code Annotated, a court shall determine custody pursuant to the best interest of the child. Section 40–4–212, MCA. The factors relevant to the child's best interest include the following:

(a) the wishes of the child's parent or parents as to custody;

(b) the wishes of the child as to a custodian;

(c) the interaction and interrelationship of the child with the child's parent or parents and siblings and with any other person who may significantly affect the child's best interest;

(d) the child's adjustment to home, school, and community;

(e) the mental and physical health of all individuals involved;

(f) physical abuse or threat of physical abuse by one parent against the other parent or the child; and

(g) chemical dependency * * * or chemical abuse on the part of either parent.

. . .

(4) The following are rebuttable presumptions:

(a) A knowing failure to pay birth-related costs that the person is able to pay is not in the best interest of the child.

(b) Failure to pay child support that the person is able to pay is not in the best interest of a child in need of the child support.

The District Court found that there was a close relationship between Patrick and A.R.A.; that A.R.A. was attached to her brother Joshua; that Patrick's parenting skills are superior to those possessed by Bill; that A.R.A. would be adversely affected by changing schools, therapists, and her primary residence; and that it was in her best interest that she remain in Billings in the family unit to which she had grown accustomed. Based on these findings, the court determined that A.R.A.'s best interest warranted the award of her custody to Patrick.

Bill contends that the court's use of the best interest of the child test in awarding custody to a stepparent abrogates his constitutional right to parent his child. Patrick concedes that Bill has a constitutional right to parent his child but argues that A.R.A.'s fundamental liberty interest and right to privacy in the association with her family is also constitutionally protected. Patrick maintains that the District Court properly balanced the rights of both Bill and A.R.A. in using the best interest of the child test as directed by § 40–4–221, MCA.

* * *

The District Court interpreted § 40–4–221, MCA, as giving the court the authority to award custody to a stepparent rather than a surviving natural parent using the best interest of the child test. A statute is to be construed according to the plain meaning of its language. However, it is paramount that we give such construction to the statute as will preserve the constitutional rights of the parties.

* * *

[T]he state's ability to intrude upon the parent/child relationship must be guarded. For that reason, "[a] finding of abuse, neglect, or dependency is the jurisdictional prerequisite for any court-ordered transfer of custody from a natural parent to a third party." Therefore, where a surviving parent does not voluntarily relinquish custody, the best interest of the child test can be used only after a showing of dependency or abuse and neglect by the natural parent.

* * *

While we recognize that § 40–4–221, MCA, gives a nonparent standing to request a custody hearing, that section does not give the district court authority to deprive a natural parent of his or her constitutionally protected rights absent a finding of abuse and neglect or dependency. Accordingly, we hold that the District Court erred in awarding custody of A.R.A. to Patrick based on the best interest of the child test in view of the fact there were no allegations of abuse and neglect or dependency on the part of Bill. We therefore reverse the District Court and award custody of A.R.A. to Bill, the natural father.

* * *

Notes and Questions

1. *Questions about* A.R.A. (a) What right does the stepfather assert in this case? How does it differ from the right Alison D.'s asserted? (b) What standard does the trial court use to decide between A.R.A.'s stepfather and her biological father? What standard does the appellate court use? Would the result be different if the stepfather had wanted visitation, rather than custody? (c) What, if any, rights does A.R.A. have in this dispute? Would your answer change if she was a mature 15-year-old and wanted to stay with the stepfather? Does the mature minor doctrine enunciated in Bellotti v. Baird (in Chapter 1) give the child any rights?, (d) Tracy, A.R.A.'s mother, had named her husband Patrick as A.R.A.'s guardian in her will. Why did her will not settle the custody question?

2. Under the holding of this case, could a stepparent (or other "nonparent") ever get custody absent a finding that the biological parent is unfit? Some states apply a more liberal standard. See, e.g., Stanley D. v. Deborah D., 467 A.2d 249 (N.H. 1983) (upon divorce of mother and stepfather, using a

best interests of the child standard, the court awarded the parties joint legal custody and the stepfather sole physical custody). If stepparents are required to support their stepchildren during marriage, would they have a stronger claim to custody or visitation when the marriage ends? See Bodwell v. Brooks, 686 A.2d 1179 (N.H.1996)(noting that a stepparent is required to support a stepchild under New Hampshire law).

3. *"Parent" and context.* A stepparent might be classified as a "parent" for some purposes, depending on the context. In Ynocencio v. Fesko, 338 N.W.2d 461, 463–64 (Wis.1983), for example, a stepmother who signed as a sponsor for her minor stepson's driver's license application was a "parent" liable for damages caused by the minor's negligent operation of a motor vehicle. The court noted that "[t]he word 'parent' is frequently used in everyday conversation more broadly to include a stepmother or stepfather, who is in de facto charge of the child concerned and has established what one might call a parental relationship with the child."

KATHARINE T. BARTLETT, RETHINKING PARENTHOOD AS AN EXCLUSIVE STATUS: THE NEED FOR LEGAL ALTERNATIVES WHEN THE PREMISE OF THE NUCLEAR FAMILY HAS FAILED

70 Va. L. Rev. 879, 879–83 (1984).

Parenthood, with few exceptions, is an exclusive status. The law recognizes only one set of parents for a child at any one time, and these parents are autonomous, possessing comprehensive privileges and duties that they share with no one else.

A fundamental premise of the law of exclusive parenthood is that parents raise their own children in nuclear families. The nuclear family, which is the preferred social unit in our society, is itself an exclusive unit, its membership reserved to a married couple and their dependent children. Exclusivity gives the family much of its moral power over the lives of its members, for it forges in them a sense of common destiny and mutual commitment. Parental or family autonomy builds upon this commitment, encouraging parents to raise their children in the best way that they can by making them secure in the knowledge that neither the state nor outside individuals may ordinarily intervene.

Although the premise of the nuclear family underlies the legal norm of parental autonomy, an increasing number of children do not live in traditional nuclear families. * * * One authority estimates that by 1990 this figure will grow to forty percent. The reasons for this phenomenon are familiar. More and more parents obtain divorces, resulting in single parent families or, as divorced parents remarry, step-families. An increasing number of parents never marry. Some parents abandon their children; others give their children to temporary caretakers; and still others are judged unfit to raise their children, who are then placed in foster homes.

Children—affected by these circumstances often form attachments to adults outside the conjugal nuclear family—to stepparents, foster parents, and other caretakers. Current law provides virtually no satisfactory means of accommodating such extra-parental attachments, however, because the presumption of exclusive parenthood requires that these relationships compete with others for legal recognition. According to traditional parental rights doctrine, applied still in many states, the state will not recognize relationships formed by adults other than the child's legal parents unless the legal parents are unfit or have abandoned the child. Thus, psychological relationships are often subordinated to those based on biological ties. Under tests applied in other states, which focus on the welfare (or 'best interests') of the child instead of parental unfitness, biological relationships may be sacrificed to those that are psychological. Both approaches, however, share the premise that parenthood is exclusive. Competing relationships are important not as potential objects of the law's protection but as evidence in determining an individual's legal right to exclusive parenthood. Thus, for example, a stepfather and a natural father cannot simultaneously have a legal parenting relationship with a child; one must have all parental rights and duties and the other may have none.

This paper challenges the law's adherence to the exclusive view of parenthood when the premise of the nuclear family has failed. In such a situation, the child's need for continuity in intimate relationships demands that the state provide the opportunity to maintain important familial relationships with more than one parent or set of parents. Modern experts defend exclusive parenthood on the grounds that children need one parent (or set of parents) who have unequivocal and undivided parental authority over them. Although persuasive enough to warrant the concentration of parental authority in natural parents at a child's birth, this argument fails to consider the situation of children who form child-parent relationships with adults outside of nuclear families. Current research demonstrates that even if nuclear families are best for children, when children form parental relationships outside of the nuclear family they often lose more from the law's enforcement of exclusive parental relationships than they gain.

This article is concerned not with how children form parenting relationships outside the nuclear family, but with how the law should regard those relationships that do form. In doing so, it urges that states develop options that do not presume the exclusivity of parenthood. This approach does not compel a uniform solution of all conflicts over children. Indeed, nonexclusive parenting alternatives for example, those developed in the context of divorce may reflect a variety of positions states have taken on such matters as the weight of the custodial preference given to the child's primary caretaker, or the conditions, if any, under which a court should order joint custody. However these issues are resolved, the wider availability of nonexclusive parenthood alternatives will better enable the law to recognize familial relationships that children have developed. Such recognition will allow children to experience the continuity of familial relationships that they need in the growing range of circumstances in which these relationships are formed outside the nuclear family.

* * *

Notes and Questions

1. If *A.R.A.* had used Professor Bartlett's concept of nonexclusive parenthood, what would the result have been?

2. *De facto parents.* The American Law Institute is currently developing a restatement of the law relating to custody and other family law matters, with Professor Bartlett as reporter for the custody section. Her ideas about emphasizing parental responsibility and connection rather than rights, and about non-exclusive parenthood have influenced the current draft. The draft proposes that in custody disputes courts allocate "custodial responsibility" and "decision-making responsibility." The draft uses the *de facto parent* concept. A *de facto parent* is:

> a person other than a legal parent or parent by estoppel who, for a significant period of time not less than two years
>
> > (i) has resided with the child, and
> >
> > (ii) for reasons primarily other than financial compensation, and with the consent of a legal parent to the formation of a de facto parent relationship or as a result of a complete failure or inability of any legal parent to perform caretaking functions,
> >
> > > (A) regularly performed a majority of the caretaking functions for the child, or
> > >
> > > (B) regularly performed a share of caretaking functions at least as great as that of the parent with whom the child primarily lived.

American Law Institute, Principles of the Law of Family Dissolution: Analysis and Recommendations, Council Draft No. 5, § 2.03 (Oct. 6, 1998).

Comment *b* to section 2.03 emphasizes that "[t]o avoid unnecessary and inappropriate intrusion into the relationships between legal parents and their children, the definition of a de facto parent is a narrow one that few individuals who are not legal parents will be able to satisfy." Stepparents, live-in relatives, and a parent's partner who has served as a co-parent are the most likely persons to meet the de facto parent definition. (Section 2.21, Comment *b*.) The de facto parent status is inferior to that of the legal parent in the allocation of parental responsibility, as Section 2.21 explains:

> The court should allocate responsibility to a de facto parent * * *, except that
>
> > it should allocate primary custodial responsibility to a de facto parent over the objection of a legal parent who is fit and willing to assume primary custodial responsibility only if
> >
> > > the legal parent has not been performing a reasonable share of parenting functions, * * * or
> > >
> > > the alternative would be harmful to the child; and

it should limit or deny an allocation otherwise to be made if, in light of the number of other adults to be allocated responsibility, the allocation would be impractical * * *.

American Law Institute, Principles of the Law of Family Dissolution: Analysis and Recommendations, Tentative Draft Number 3, § 2.21(1) (1998).

3. *The in loco parentis doctrine.* Whether an in loco parentis relationship exists is determined on a case by case basis. Where a person claims in loco parentis status, the court examines the person's conduct and statements to determine whether the person intentionally assumed parental responsibilities. A person in loco parentis may be considered a parent for some purposes, but not others. In her comprehensive treatise on stepfamily law, Professor Margaret Mahoney notes that "stepparents who stand in loco parentis to their stepchildren have frequently been accorded the same treatment as biologic parents in the areas of workers' compensation and parental-child tort immunity. Conversely, the courts have rejected the in loco parentis doctrine as a basis for stepfamily claims in many other important fields, including inheritance and wrongful death." Margaret M. Mahoney, Stepfamilies and the Law 7 (1994).

Unlike a biological parental relationship, the in loco parentis relationship can be terminated at will. Hence the doctrine has been used more to sort out past obligations, such as whether a stepparent who has supported a stepchild is entitled to reimbursement, than to impose future obligations, such as an ongoing support obligation. Courts have sometimes invoked the doctrine to justify prospective "parental" claims, however, such as giving a stepparent visitation rights after divorce from the custodial, biological parent based on the stepparent's in loco parentis status. Carter v. Brodrick, 644 P.2d 850 (Alaska 1982).

PROBLEM 2–2

You are a member of the Montana legislature and have received a number of complaints from your constituents about the *A.R.A.* result. They feel that Patrick, the stepfather, should have retained custody of the child. Would you propose amending Montana law to follow § 2.03 of the draft ALI restatement? How would *A.R.A.* have been decided under the A.L.I. draft?

IN RE MARRIAGE OF GALLAGHER

Supreme Court of Iowa, 1995.
539 N.W.2d 479.

HARRIS, JUSTICE.

A few weeks before trial of this dissolution of marriage proceeding it was revealed that the husband was not the natural father of a child who is the subject of this custody dispute. In Petition of Ash, 507 N.W.2d 400, 403 (Iowa 1993),[d] we rejected the equitable parent doctrine. The husband

d. James Ash lived with the child's mother prior to the birth of the child, was at the hospital when the child was born, and may have signed an affidavit of paterni-

in the present case, pursuing parental rights regarding a child born during the marriage and whom he had considered his own, asks that we reconsider the rejection announced in Ash. In the alternative, he asks that the mother be equitably estopped from denying he is the father of the child. We conclude that Ash is not controlling under the circumstances here. We therefore reverse and remand.

John and Amy Gallagher were married in 1988. In 1991, while the parties were residing together as husband and wife, a child, Riley, was conceived and born. John was listed on the official birth certificate as the child's natural father. Understandably, John considered the child to be his own, and the two developed a father/daughter relationship. Sometime during 1992 John and Amy started to experience marital problems, and in 1993 John filed a dissolution of marriage petition. Before trial the district court placed joint custody of Riley in both John and Amy.

John and Amy agreed to have a home study performed for the purposes of recommending child placement. The home study concluded John would be the appropriate parent for custody of Riley. Subsequently, only three weeks prior to trial, Amy for the first time informed John he was not Riley's natural father. Blood tests confirmed this and the parties so stipulated.

On Amy's application for adjudication of law points the trial court held that John, as neither biological nor adoptive father, had no parental rights. The court also expressly rejected the theory of equitable estoppel and granted summary judgment against John. We granted John permission to bring this interlocutory appeal from that ruling. Other issues in the dissolution proceeding remain pending in district court.

* * *

In prior cases we have rejected the equitable parent doctrine. In doing so under the facts in Ash, we pointed out that Ash

> is a stranger to the child. He is an interested third party. He is not the child's biological father. He is not her adoptive father. He is not her stepfather. He is not her foster parent. He never married the child's mother. He is merely a man who lived with—and cared for— her mother, and who, understandably, became smitten with fatherhood after the child's birth.

We also said that no common law or statutory authority for the doctrine existed under those circumstances. We explained:

> Straining to legitimize such an action under current law would foster a superfluity of claims by parties who shared a special

ty . He may also have had "a strong suspicion" that the child was not his, however. Although the mother left James a year after the child was born, he continued to visit and support the child and provided occa-sional financial help to the mother. When the child was five the mother, who had married, cut off his visitation and told the child that James was not her father.

relationship with children based neither upon affinity nor consanguinity.

* * *

The facts assumed in the adjudication here are far different. Here the biological fact of nonpaternity appeared unexpectedly in contradiction of an existing family relationship. In every way, Riley was received by both John and Amy as their daughter, and the family relationship developed accordingly. John was no stranger, or even a mere stepfather. The facts here demonstrate how different it is when a child is born into a marriage, even though (unknown to the father) it is conceived outside it.

The relationship between the husband and child in such a situation is highly likely to be much closer than those between a child and a man whose relationship is derived only as an adjunct to that man's relationship with the child's mother. Where both the child and the husband reasonably believe they share a biological relationship, the bonding should—and can be expected to—develop to such a stage that its rupture might be devastating to both. Devastation to the child is of course the first and paramount concern because the best interest of the child is the dominating consideration in all child custody disputes.

Ash furnished no factual basis for adoption of the equitable parent doctrine in Iowa. Applying general equitable principles, however, we believe equitable parenthood may be established in a proper case by a father who establishes all the following: (1) he was married to the mother when the child is conceived and born; (2) he reasonably believes he is the child's father; (3) he establishes a parental relationship with the child; and (4) shows that judicial recognition of the relationship is in the child's best interest.

* * * Focusing on the best interest of the child, we expressed great concern with the lack of any obligation on the part of a stepparent claimant to pay child support. Of course, willingness to support the child, though an important one, is only one factor in the determination of a child's best interest. But we think it is significant that John has supported Riley from her birth and is struggling by this action to become obligated to continue doing so. Willingness to support the child, though an incomplete test of a child's best interest, is surely a crucial consideration in the determination. * * *

To apply the equitable parent doctrine under these facts is entirely consistent with the principles underlying equitable estoppel. Issues of paternity, child custody, and child support are determined by a court of equity. * * * One such equitable principle is the doctrine of estoppel. Estoppel was long available in certain situations converse to the one appearing here; more than a century ago we held that one who marries a woman known by him to be enceinte is regarded by the law as adopting the child into his family at its birth, and he becomes liable for its support as a parent, and an action against the natural father for its support will not lie. We reasoned that such a child

> is received into the family of the husband, who stands as to it in loco parentis. This being the law, [the child] enters into the marriage contract between the mother and the husband. When this relationship is established, the law raises a conclusive presumption the husband is the father of the wife's ... child.

We need not hold that any such presumption exists today. But we do note that a number of jurisdictions have estopped the husband from denying paternity in divorce proceedings. * * *

Equitable estoppel is a doctrine based on fair dealing, good faith, and justice. The elements of equitable estoppel are as follows:

1. A false representation or concealment of a material fact;

2. A lack of knowledge of the true facts on the part of the actor;

3. The intention that the representation or concealment be acted upon; and

4. Reliance thereon by the party to whom it is made, to his or her prejudice and injury.

These four elements clearly appear here. So long as it served her purposes Amy concealed from John that Riley was not his natural daughter. Indeed her every indication would lead John to think Riley was a child of their marriage. John was listed as father on the birth certificate. As late as when the home study was made in this proceeding, Amy did not hint John was not the biological father and it was because of Amy's concealment that John was unaware of the truth. Amy's intent that John act on her concealment can easily be inferred. She was afraid John would divorce her for having an affair. When dissolution proceedings were undertaken she continued her concealment in the hope of custody and support. She was prompted to reveal the truth only when the home placement study favored John as Riley's custodian. Without doubt John relied on the concealment to his detriment. He developed emotional ties with Riley and acknowledged her to the world as his daughter.

A number of reasons exist for adopting the equitable parent doctrine in dissolution cases such as this one, where paternity is an issue. These are essentially the same considerations that underlie any application of estoppel. Several other jurisdictions have followed this rationale and estopped a wife from challenging paternity in dissolution related proceedings subsequent to dissolution.

III. As between himself and Amy, John clearly can establish the elements of equitable parenthood. The record is however incomplete. The case must be remanded for further proceedings in which John must show that the adjudication he seeks is in Riley's best interest. We note that any adjudication on the present record would not bind Riley or her biological father. Natural parents have fundamental rights that must be addressed. The rights of natural parents of course are not unlimited and can be waived by abandonment. Indeed we recently pointed out that:

> A parent who fails to develop a relationship with his or her child while that child is establishing a family relationship with [someone else] must recognize the child thereby puts down roots that are of critical importance. Courts must carefully deal with those roots in determining the child's best interests.

IV. Because the parties did not raise the issue, we have not considered the effect of a recent statutory amendment. A year after our decision in Ash, the Iowa legislature enacted Iowa Code section 600B.41A. 1994 Iowa Acts, ch. 1171, § 48. This section states in pertinent part:

> 1. Paternity which is legally established may be overcome as provided in this section if subsequent blood or genetic testing indicates that the previously established father of a child is not the biological father of the child * * * [and].
>
> > g. The court finds that it is in the best interests of the child to overcome the establishment of paternity. In determining the best interests of the child, the court shall consider all of the following:
> >
> > > (1) The age of the child.
> > >
> > > (2) The length of time since the establishment of paternity.
> > >
> > > (3) The previous relationship between the child and the established father, including but not limited to the duration and frequency of any time periods during which the child and established father resided in the same household or engaged in a parent-child relationship as defined in section 600A.2.
> > >
> > > (4) The possibility that the child could benefit by establishing the child's actual paternity.
> > >
> > > (5) Additional factors which the court determines are relevant to the individual situation.

Although this section was not argued here, it may control future cases presenting similar issues.

[Reversed and remanded].

TERNUS, JUSTICE (dissenting).

I respectfully dissent. The majority has tried to bandage a broken relationship; the result feels right, but its legal basis does not withstand close scrutiny.

* * *

III. Policy Demands a Rejection of Equitable Fatherhood.

* * *

B. *Equitable fatherhood is inconsistent with custody principles.* We should consider the relationship between the doctrine adopted by the majority and our long-standing rule that a biological parent has a right to custody over third parties unless the biological parent is unsuitable. * * * By virtue of our decision today, however, we have set the stage for an entirely suitable "real" parent to lose custody if the elements of equitable parenthood are met. The court-created fiction that John is now a "parent" does not alter the fact that our traditional rule giving priority to the biological or adoptive parent is severely undermined.

* * *

IV. *Ramifications of Adopting Equitable Fatherhood.*

Even if our statutes regulating child visitation, adoption and termination of parental rights are not seen as a barrier to our recognition of equitable parenthood, we should be very slow to venture into an area that is so fraught with unsolvable problems. The majority conveniently remands the case to the trial court "for further proceedings in conformance with this opinion." It fails to consider the complex consequences of its decision.

Perhaps we should take a moment to think about the task facing the trial court. If the biological father appears, will his assertion of custody or visitation rights prevent the assertion of similar rights by John? If not, do John and the biological father have the parental rights of a father? Are the expectations of a third party or the actions of the child's mother a constitutionally-sufficient basis to require the biological father to share his precious parental rights with another man? If the biological father is reasonably unaware of the present proceedings, may he later overturn a finding of equitable parenthood in order to preserve his rights as a father for himself alone? Are the rights of the biological father superior to those of the equitable father, or do the superior rights belong to the "father" most bonded to the child? If the "father" with the strongest emotional ties to the child has the superior rights, does he lose those rights if the child's emotional ties to the other "father" become predominant? With whom does the child spend father's day? As one court has commented in considering whether to bestow parental rights on a person who is neither the biological nor adoptive parent, "It would be virtually impossible to ensure *equity* to all parties and protect the best interests of the child under such a scenario."

The collateral problems that the courts will be asked to resolve are nearly endless. Can the child inherit from both fathers? If the child dies, do the two fathers share the inheritance to which the biological father would normally be entitled? Can a child bring a wrongful death claim for her equitable father's death? Does the tortfeasor negligently causing the death of a child owe loss of consortium damages to both natural parents and the equitable father? Iowa Code chapter 232 governs juvenile delinquency, termination of parental rights and child-in-need-of-assistance proceedings. It defines a "parent" as "a biological or adoptive mother or father of a child". Will John as an equitable parent have any rights or responsibilities under this statute? Will all parents—biological, adoptive and equitable—have the same rights and responsibilities, or are we establishing degrees of parenthood?

V.   *Equitable Fatherhood Adopted: Result Over Reason.*

What the majority does today is a profound departure from the philosophy of our prior cases and the statutes enacted by the Iowa legislature. Both the judicial branch and the legislative branch have placed paramount importance on the relationship between the biological or adoptive parents and the child. Today we run roughshod over that relationship because we are offended by the biological mother's conduct and sympathize with the third party's emotional plight. Given the complex practical, social and constitutional ramifications of the equitable parent doctrine, we should have a much more solid basis upon which to rest our decision than our general sense that equity requires this result.

I would affirm the ruling of the district court that John Gallagher, who is neither the biological father nor the adoptive father of Riley, has no parental rights to the child.

McGiverin, C.J., and Carter and Lavorato, JJ., join this dissent.

Notes and Questions

1.   *Questions about* Gallagher. (a) How would John Gallagher's status as an equitable parent differ from the status of Gerald D., the husband in Michael H. v. Gerald D. (in Section 1.B of this Chapter)? (b) If you represented John Gallagher on remand, what evidence would you present to demonstrate that equitable parenthood was in the child's best interests? How would you respond to an argument that it was important for the child to know her biological origins? (c) Under the amended statute discussed in the last paragraph of the majority opinion, would John Gallagher or the biological father be more likely to prevail?

2.   *Parent by estoppel.* The recent American Law Institute draft proposes that a *parent by estoppel* have the same privileges and responsibilities as a legal parent. A *parent by estoppel* is:

a person who is liable for child support * * *

a man who lived with the child for a significant period of time not less than two years and

> over that period had a reasonable good faith belief that he was the child's biological father based on his marriage to the mother or the actions or representations of the mother, and fully accepted parental responsibilities consistent with that belief, and

> after that period continued to make reasonable, good faith efforts to accept responsibilities as the child's father, even if that belief no longer existed; * * *

American Law Institute, Principles of the Law of Family Dissolution: Analysis and Recommendations, Council Draft No. 5 § 2.03(1)(b)(1998). A later draft will add a section on parental status created by agreement.

6. Equitable adoption is discussed in the Chapter 7, Adoption.

SMITH v. COLE

Supreme Court of Louisiana, 1989.
553 So.2d 847.

COLE, JUSTICE

The issue is whether a biological father is obligated to provide support for his child notwithstanding the child was conceived or born during the mother's marriage to another person and thus the legitimate child of that other person. In this instance, the mother asserts a filiation and support action against the alleged biological father. * * * The trial court * * * dismissed the action, invoking La.Civil Code article 184 which provides: "The husband of the mother is presumed to be the father of all children born or conceived during the marriage." The court of appeal, applying the concept of dual paternity, held a biological father has an obligation to support his child. It thus reversed and remanded for further proceedings. We affirm.

FACTUAL AND PROCEDURAL HISTORY

Plaintiff, Ledora McCathen Smith, married Henry Smith on March 28, 1970. They had two sons, Henry and Derrick. During the fall of 1974, the Smiths physically separated, never reconciling. Thereafter, plaintiff began her five year cohabitation with defendant, Playville Cole. The child who is the subject of this action, Donel Patrice Smith, was born on December 25, 1975, approximately a year after plaintiff and defendant began living together. The birth certificate names Smith as Donel's father. The Smiths were not divorced until April 5, 1978.

The affidavit of Henry Smith, now a resident of California, avers he is not the biological father of Donel and affirms he never petitioned to disavow her paternity. Smith swears that Cole acknowledged to him his paternity of Donel; and, during late 1976, plaintiff and Cole attempted to influence him into executing certain documents which would allow Cole to change Donel's surname from Smith to Cole, "but that he refused to cooperate with them out of anger and the matter was dropped."

Plaintiff's divorce from Henry Smith was uncontested. * * * The divorce petition declared only that "of this marriage, two children were born: Henry Smith, born September 29, 1970 and Derrick Smith, born June 13, 1974." Accordingly, the divorce judgment granted plaintiff "permanent custody of the minor children born of the marriage, namely, Henry and Derrick Smith." The divorce judgment did not mention Donel Patrice Smith.

Plaintiff and Cole ceased their cohabitation in February of 1980. On May 18, 1988 plaintiff brought this action against Cole, in forma pauperis, to prove paternity and obtain child support. The petition claimed that 1) plaintiff and Cole are the natural parents of Donel Patrice Smith, born December 25, 1975 and 2) Cole has acknowledged he is the father of this child by his acts and admissions.

* * * [Cole] claimed that as the Smiths were married when Donel was born and as Henry Smith did not disavow paternity, he is Donel's presumed father. * * * Cole asserted that because Donel has a legitimate father, her mother should not be allowed to bastardize her just to obtain money. In response, plaintiff filed only the previously described affidavit of Henry Smith.

* * *

DUAL PATERNITY IN LOUISIANA

Promotion and protection of the family unit were the principal reasons behind Louisiana's historically harsh treatment of illegitimate children. * * *

With the social and legal stigmas which attached to illegitimacy, it is not surprising that the courts rigorously applied the presumption of LSA–C.C. art. 184, that "the law considers the husband of the mother as the father of all children conceived during the marriage." The policy was to protect innocent children against attacks upon their paternity and the presumption was the strongest known in law. * * *

The Article 184 presumption was not without flaws. While it promoted the policy against bastardizing children, it often failed to conform with reality. A husband, who could not possibly be or who clearly was not the biological father, was nonetheless conclusively presumed to be so. Consequently, in an attempt to moderate the prevailing statutory and jurisprudential rules, on the recommendation of the Louisiana State Law Institute, the Legislature amended the Civil Code articles on paternity by Act 430 of 1976. These codal amendments made the "irrebuttable" presumption of Article 184 rebuttable. But the amendments did not alter the rule that only the husband or his heir may disavow paternity.

* * *

EFFECTS OF DUAL PATERNITY

Recognition of actual paternity, through filiation actions brought by the legitimate child, the biological father or the state, does not affect the child's statutory classification of legitimacy.

Consequently, this paternity and support action will not alter Donel Smith's status as the legitimate offspring of her mother's former husband, Henry Smith.

Through the presumption of Article 184, which extends to all children born or conceived during the marriage, and the expiration of the peremptive period of Civil Code art. 189, Donel is conclusively presumed to be Smith's legitimate offspring. The disavowal action was personal to Smith and only he or his heirs had the right to disavow Donel's paternity. His failure to do so timely established Donel as his legal and legitimate child. The legal tie of paternity will not be affected by subsequent proof of the child's actual biological tie. Legitimate children cannot be bastardized by succeeding proof of actual parentage.

The Article 184 presumption will not be extended beyond its useful sphere. The presumption was intended to protect innocent children from the stigma attached to illegitimacy and to prevent case-by-case determinations of paternity. It was not intended to shield biological fathers from their support obligations. The presumed father's acceptance of paternal responsibilities, either by intent or default, does not enure to the benefit of the biological father. It is the fact of biological paternity or maternity which obliges parents to nourish their children. The biological father does not escape his support obligations merely because others may share with him the responsibility. Biological fathers are civilly obligated for the support of their offspring. They are also criminally responsible for their support.

Moreover, because of his actual relationship with Donel, developed when he and plaintiff lived together as a family unit, defendant may have parental rights which are constitutionally protected. Since Henry Smith's failure to disavow paternity would not preclude defendant from bringing an avowal action, it would be unjust to construe the presumption so as to provide defendant with a safe harbor from child support obligations. Articles 208 and 209 give the child or the child's mother, the right to bring a filiation proceeding. Further, as the child is in necessitous circumstances, it appears to be in her best interest to recognize the biological tie. Such recognition results in defendant being obligated to provide his biological child with support.

In summary, Louisiana law may provide the presumption that the husband of the mother is the legal father of her child while it recognizes a biological father's actual paternity. When the presumptive father does not timely disavow paternity, he becomes the legal father. A filiation action brought on behalf of the child, then, merely establishes the biological fact of paternity. The filiation action does not bastardize the child or otherwise affect the child's legitimacy status. The result here is that the biological father and the mother share the support obligations of the child.

The question of whether the "legal" father in this case also shares the support obligation is not before the court. We decline for now to hold the legal father will, in all factual contexts, be made to share the support obligations with the biological father and the mother.

* * *

Questions

Questions about Cole. (a) What is Donal's legal relationship to Henry Smith? What rights and responsibilities should Smith have? (b) How does the court justify ordering Playville Cole to support Donal? What rights and responsibilities should Cole have? (c) Why was dual paternity accepted in *Cole* but rejected in *Michael H.*?

PROBLEM 2–3

Mary and Tom, both age 26, had dated since graduating from college. Mary ended their relationship and shortly thereafter married Fred. Unfortunately, the marriage lasted only a few months and Mary was left pregnant and alone. She moved in with Tom and had the baby, whom she named Andy. Although Fred was the biological father, Tom and Mary planned to marry, but never did. Tom treated the baby as his own and was the primary caretaker from the time the child was two years old.

After seven years, Mary and Tom split up. At the same time, Mary decided to finally get her divorce from Fred. Fred has had no contact with Andy and has not paid child support; on the other hand, Mary never asked him for support and friends of hers told him that she did not want him to have any contact with her or Andy.

Fred now wants to get to know Andy and would like to have liberal visitation. He has volunteered to pay support.

Tom wants custody. He is willing to let Fred and Mary both have liberal visitation.

Mary wants custody and does not want Tom or Fred to have visitation.

Andy wants to stay with Tom, but see Mary often and get to know Fred.

What arguments would Mary, Tom, Andy and Fred make to get what they want? Explain how you would resolve this case and what parental rights and responsibilities would belong to the claimants under your resolution of the dispute.

B.   *Evaluating Claims to Parenthood*

ELIZABETH S. SCOTT AND ROBERT E. SCOTT, PARENTS AS FIDUCIARIES

81 Va. L. Rev. 2401, 2405–415 (1995).

* * *

Legal deference to the claims of biological parents recently has come under attack in the courts, in the academic literature, and in the popular media. Cases such as the highly publicized dispute between the DeBoers and Daniel Schmidt over the custody of "Baby Jessica"[8] contribute to a view that the law, frozen in ancient doctrine, accords unwarranted legal

---

8.   See DeBoer v. Schmidt (In re Baby Girl Clausen, 502 N.W.2d 649 (Mich.1993)) In re B.G.C., 496 N.W.2d 239 (Iowa 1992). "Baby Jessica" was given up for adoption by her mother only hours after birth, without the knowledge of her biological father, Daniel Schmidt, and placed in temporary custody with the DeBoers. A few weeks later, upon learning that he was the father of the child, Schmidt initiated legal efforts to gain custody, on the grounds that he had not consented to the termination of his parental rights. During the pendency of the legal battle, Jessica remained in the home

protection to biological parents in ways that are both directly harmful and symbolically corrosive to the interests of their children. For example, recognition of the rights of non-custodial biological parents can undermine a relationship between the child and a more suitable social parent. Further, the latitude given to parents in rearing their children is seen as excessive, allowing some parents to inflict unmonitored and unsanctioned harm on their children. More indirectly, to the extent that the law emphasizes parental rights, it encourages parents' inclination to put their own interests before those of their children, both in the intact family and on divorce or dissolution.

However controversial this issue may be today, the tradition of legal protection of parental rights has deep historical roots. Before the twentieth century, the combined status of biological parenthood and marriage signified a legal authority of almost limitless scope. Until the social reform movement at the beginning of this century, the state took little interest in family governance. Parents, particularly fathers as heads of household, had extensive legal authority over the lives of their children. Parental rights were understood to be grounded in natural law and were not dependent on behavior that promoted the child's interest. Parents' interest under traditional law was property-like in many respects. A parent's right to the custody of his children so approximated property ownership that it could be transferred by contract, and lost only by abandonment or unfitness. In the 1920s, the United States Supreme Court elevated parental rights to constitutional stature, restricting the extent to which the state can override parental authority. Although modern courts vigorously reject the characterization of children as the property of their parents, many argue that this legacy continues to cast a shadow.

In fact, the situation is even more complex than the critics recognize. Although many assume that outcomes such as that reached in the DeBoers–Schmidt dispute result from the failure to reform archaic legal doctrine, the extension of parental rights to unmarried biological fathers is actually a relatively recent development. Historically, unmarried fathers were invisible parents, presumed by courts and legislatures to have no legal interest in their children. * * *Today, the rhetoric of parental rights extends to this group of parents, and consent of the unmarried father to the adoption of his child (either by strangers or by a stepparent) has become a factor of much greater importance. The outcome in the DeBoers case, vindicating the paternal rights of Daniel Schmidt, fits into this legal framework.

Outside of the adoption context, non-custodial biological parents often win custody contests with stepparents and other third parties who

of the DeBoers, who resisted Schmidt's efforts to reclaim his daughter. Despite testimony from experts who warned that return to her father's custody would be emotionally traumatic for Jessica, the Iowa Supreme Court ruled that Schmidt was legally entitled to custody of his daughter. Although a subsequent determination by a Michigan court concluded that transferring custody was not in Jessica's best interests, the Michigan Supreme Court deferred to the jurisdiction of the Iowa courts, enforcing the order to return Jessica to her biological parents.

have functioned in a parental role. To the consternation of critics, traditional law gives little legal protection to the relationship between the faithful stepparent and the child if the biological parent is fit. Similarly poignant are cases in which a grandparent or other relative has assumed the care of a child who is neglected or informally abandoned by his parent. Months or even years later, the wayward parent who mends her ways may assert her parental rights and often successfully reclaim custody.

Critics of parental rights also decry the legal response to seriously deficient parental conduct. State agents are constrained from directly monitoring the quality of parental care by policies that support parental authority and family privacy. Many critics view these policies as leaving children vulnerable and without adequate protection from their parents' neglectful or abusive behavior. Even when children are in state custody, the spectre of parental rights casts a shadow. Foster care placement tends to extend indefinitely for a large percentage of these children, who are neither returned to their parents' custody nor available for adoption because parental rights are not terminated.* * *

* * *

Although the critics whose concerns we have articulated concur that beneficial family law reforms would deemphasize parental entitlement, there is no consensus about how best to promote children's welfare. One alternative is to enhance the state's role as parens patriae within the traditional paradigm, which purports to balance parental rights against the interest of the state in promoting the welfare of children. This approach would demand a larger state presence in the family, with increased supervision of parental care and greater readiness to terminate parental rights. While this perspective does not focus directly on the parent-child relationship, its effect is to discount the interests of parents and to reduce parental authority and rights. This is because the interest-balancing approach pits the welfare of children against the interest of parents and presumes that the latter will be diminished if the former is enhanced.

Simply shifting the focus of legal regulation toward greater protection of the needs of children is unhelpful, in our view. This is so not because such a perspective misunderstands the social goals that drive the regulation of parent-child relationships, but rather because a child-centered approach, standing alone, will not lead reliably to legal rules that effect those objectives. Presumably, the social goal at stake in the regulation of the parent-child relationship is to ensure children the care necessary for their development into healthy, productive adults. This goal is more likely to be achieved if the law focuses principally on the relationship between parent and child, rather than on the child's needs per se. Parents are not fungible child rearers. The link between parent and child has substantial and intrinsic value to the child; the substitution of another parent and/or termination of the relationship is accomplished only at considerable cost to the child. Moreover, as a general matter, the state is not well suited to substitute for parents in the job of rearing children. If the calculus used to determine the optimal state role focuses on the child's interest discounted by the (now less weighty) parental interest, the presumption that these interests are inherently in tension persists and the central importance of the relationship is likely to be obscured. Moreover, assuming that we are correct that parents presumptively are the "first best" child-rearers, an interest-balancing approach offers no grounding for a regulatory regime that promotes optimal parental performance.

* * *

[The Scotts recommend using a "relational" model of parents as fiduciaries to evaluate the legal regulation of parent-child relationships.]

CARL E. SCHNEIDER, ON THE DUTIES AND RIGHTS OF PARENTS

81 Va. L. Rev. 2477, 2484–488 (1995).

* * *

I quite agree with the Scotts that the parental-rights doctrine may be conceived of as a rule intended to serve children's interests. And I believe the Scotts perform an estimable service in reminding us of this fundamental assumption. Parents' rights have commonly been assumed to protect children exactly because people have thought that, as a rule, parents and children have a community of interest and that parents thus have a duty and ability to speak for their children, children who are presumptively unable to speak for themselves.

If the parents' rights principle is substantially based on the child's interests, as the Scotts and I contend, why is it presently criticized as inimical to children's interests? Let me suggest two among the several possible causes. The first has to do with the nature of American rights discourse. As the Scotts note, the rhetoric of rights has a force of its own both in legal and popular culture, a force which can drive parents, officials, and judges to an enthusiasm for parents' rights that quite outstrips the rationale for them. In addition, our rights language sadly lacks an adequate vocabulary for expressing countervailing interests. In technical terms, constitutional rights-analysis has generally scanted the state interests that may conflict with the parent's right. Thus the prudential origins of parental rights are all too easily forgotten. To put the point somewhat differently, parents' rights can be so unyielding that the only thing powerful enough to blast them loose is a countervailing right, like children's rights.

A second cause of the present discontent has to do, I think, with the fact that any legal regime governing the relations of parent and child will inevitably produce some deplorable cases. Any such regime must rely on some combination of rules and discretion, and both rules and discretion regularly fail. Discretion may be abused, and the people to whom discretion is confided will sometimes err. Rules are a kind of generalization, and all generalizations are false. Error is thus inevitable. Unhappily, we too easily respond to error by assuming that our grant of discretion was improvident or that our rule is unwise. Our rule has been parents' rights, and it has produced its errors. We now seek to prevent such errors from arising in the future by instituting a new rule—children's rights. Yet this rule will ineluctably cause errors (possibly more numerous and more distressing) of its own.

Ultimately, I doubt there really is much disagreement about the broad goal of legal policy regarding children. At base, rather, there is a consensus about the centrality of children's well-being, at least within the rather narrow ambit of the law's capacity. The question is just how you reach that goal. I am not even sure how much genuine difference there is among the controversialists. Indeed, as I have been implying, the presumably conflicting tests tend to collapse into each other. The Scotts, for instance, say that the law should focus "principally on the relationship between parent and child, rather than on the child's needs per se." But an important part of what the child needs is a good relationship with its parents, and that relationship partly depends on the child's needs being met. Parents' rights take children's claims into account. Children's interests depend on good relations with their parents.

The Scotts recognize how interrelated the contending rules are. Indeed, their article could be taken as an effort to show how readily those rules can be reconciled. However, the Scotts continue to feel that the choice among the rules matters. And this brings me to my last point. As I have argued, the debate to which the Scotts have so ably contributed is largely about what rule we need to write to produce good results. I have suggested that there is rough social agreement about what a good result is. There is, however, real disagreement about how to produce it. To resolve that disagreement, we need to ask the right questions: How do courts and agencies interpret the various possible rules? How would the rules thus interpreted actually affect the behavior of courts and of agencies? And what effect would that behavior have on the short-and long-term well-being of children and their parents?

These crucial questions cannot be answered by doctrinal analysis, however acute, nor by theoretical argument, however keen. They are questions that demand empirical investigation. To be sure, such empirical work must be informed by other kinds of scholarship. To be sure, such empirical work will rely on normative assumptions and have normative consequences. But everything depends on that empirical work.

* * *

KATHARINE T. BARTLETT, RE–EXPRESSING PARENTHOOD

98 Yale L.J. 293, 295 (1988).

I argue that the law currently applied to one particular set of child custody disputes expresses a view of parenthood which is undesirable. This view is grounded in notions of exchange and individual rights, and implicitly encourages parental possessiveness and self-centeredness. I suggest how we might proceed to reshape the law to express a better view of parenthood. This alternative view is based upon notions of benevolence and responsibility, and is intended to reinforce parental dispositions toward generosity and other-directedness. I focus on custody disputes in which one biological parent seeks to deny parental status to the other. These include claims by unmarried women seeking 'nonmarital motherhood-by-choice,' claims by single women seeking to place their newborn children for adoption over the objection of the biological father, and claims by 'surrogate' mothers who, after agreeing to bear a child for another, change their minds and seek to retain custody. These cases, which raise fundamental questions about the meaning of parenthood, provide a rich landscape for examining the law's expressive functions.

* * *

I propose that we attempt to re-direct the law applicable to disputes over parental status toward a view of parenthood based on responsibility and connection. The law should force parents to state their claims, and courts to evaluate such claims, not from the competing, individuated perspectives of either parent or even of the child, but from the perspective of each parent-child relationship. And in evaluating (and thereby giving meaning to) that relationship, the law should focus on parental responsibility rather than reciprocal "rights," and express a view of parenthood based upon the cycle of gift rather than the cycle of exchange.

* * *

Notes and Questions

1. Based on these articles, what circumstances or factors define "parent" under present law? What changes do the authors advocate? In what circumstances would these changes make a difference?

2. *Additional references.* James B. Boskey, The Swamps of Home: A Reconstruction of the Parent–Child Relationship, 26 U. Tol. L. Rev. 805 (1995)(arguing that the law should recognize multiple parent-child relationships between adults and children in appropriate circumstances based on the interests of children); Karen Czapanskiy, Interdependencies, Families, and Children, 39 Santa Clara L. Rev. (1999) (legal intervention should be assessed in relation to impact on the caregiver's ability to care for the child); Leslie Joan Harris, Reconsidering the Criteria for Legal Fatherhood, 1996 Utah Law Review 461 (1996) (recommending that functional parenthood

become more accepted in law and pointing out that "emphasis on biology minimizes and devalues acts of caretaking and assumption of responsibility by adults not biologically related to children"); Gilbert A. Holmes, The Tie that Binds: The Constitutional Right of Children to Maintain Relationships with Parent-like Individuals, 53 Md. L. Rev. 358 (1994)(arguing that the law should recognize a child's independent liberty interest in relationships with "nonlegal" parents); Carolyn Wilkes Kaas, Breaking Up a Family or Putting It Back Together Again: Refining the Preference in Favor of the Parent in Third–Party Custody Disputes, 37 Wm. & Mary Law Review 1045 (1996) (proposing a system for determining decisional standards for third-party custody disputes and recommending that in disputes between third-parties and parents, courts should give preference to parents in most cases); Janet Leach Richards, Redefining Parenthood: Parental Rights Versus Child Rights, 40 Wayne L. Rev. 1227 (1994) (arguing that the definition of "parent" should be expanded or limited based on the best interests of the child).

The preceding article excerpts focused primarily on ways of considering and weighing children's and parents' interests. The next article examines a different issue, namely qualifications for being a "parent."

HOWARD B. EISENBERG, A "MODEST PROPOSAL": STATE LICENSING OF PARENTS

26 Conn. L. Rev. 1415, 1416–17, 1452 (1994).

We have created a generation of children, many of whom, by age ten or twelve, have already been lost. By that early age the stage has been set for a life of emotional hardship; low paying jobs; exclusion from mainstream society; poor health and limited access to health care; poverty; perhaps prison; and, all-too-often, premature death. These problems are by no means limited to low-income persons. Today in suburbia we are raising children who show the same signs of parental neglect, abuse, violence, and the lack of a home environment calculated to result in responsible and caring members of society. In fact, easy access to money allows children from affluent backgrounds more direct and immediate access to drugs, alcohol, weapons, and destructive life styles than their less well off counterparts in urban and rural America.

* * *

It is time to say aloud what many people are saying privately: society must be much more proactive in assuring that only people who can properly raise children are allowed to become and remain parents. Moreover, society has an obligation to assure that adequate moral, sex, and health education; birth control information; prenatal care; parenting classes; daycare; respite care; counseling; and educational programs (for both parent and child) are available to assure that those persons who desire children can properly raise and support those children. * * *

* * *

[Professor Eisenberg goes on to propose that no person be allowed to have custody of a child without a parenting license issued by the state and provides details about how the licensing plan would be enforced. He acknowledges that his proposal is not politically realistic, but he suggests that "we must fundamentally rethink government's involvement in issues of family and children." He states that:]

The state can, and should, mold the development of parents to assure that they are not bearing children they cannot afford and that they possess the skills to raise, educate, discipline, and keep children safe and healthy. A comprehensive overhaul of the child welfare system is necessary to shift the emphasis from responding to the needs of "at risk" children and families, to assuring that the number of such children and families decreases. Comprehensive family education, understanding certain basic concepts, and acceptance of responsibility for one's actions are important principles that the state must reinforce through its policies.

* * *

Notes and Questions

1. Do you think increased state intervention would produce the benefits Professor Eisenberg desires? How would you implement his proposals? Would state licensing of parents be constitutional?

2. For additional commentary on licensing parents, see C.P. Mangel, Licensing Parents: How Feasible?, 22 Fam. L.Q. 17 (1988), and Michael J. Sandmire & Michael S. Wald, Licensing Parents—A Response to Claudia Mangel's Proposal, 24 Fam. L. Q. 53 (1990)(opposing parental licensing and pointing out the methodological flaws in predictive screening).

SECTION 3. GUARDIANSHIP

A. Contested Guardianship

GUARDIANSHIP OF PHILLIP B.

Court of Appeal, First District, Division 1, California, 1983.
188 Cal.Rptr. 781.

RACANELLI, PRESIDING JUSTICE.

Few human experiences evoke the poignancy of a filial relationship and the pathos attendant upon its disruption in society's effort to afford every child a meaningful chance to live life to its fullest promise. This appeal, posing a sensitive confrontation between the fundamental right of parental custody and the well being of a retarded child, reflects the deeply ingrained concern that the needs of the child remain paramount in the judicial monitoring of custody. In reaching our decision to affirm, we neither suggest nor imply that appellants' subjectively motivated custodial objectives affront conventional norms of parental fitness; rather, we determine only that on the unusual factual record before us, the challenged order of guardianship must be upheld in order to avert potential harm to the minor ward likely to result from appellants' continuing custody and to subserve his best interests.

Procedural Background

Preliminarily, we trace the sequence of procedural events leading to our review.

On February 23, 1981, respondents Herbert and Patsy H. filed a petition for appointment as guardians of the person and estate of Phillip B., then 14 years of age. Phillip's parents, appellants Warren and Patricia B., appeared in opposition to the petition.

On August 7, 1981, following a 12–day trial, the trial court filed a lengthy memorandum of decision ordering—*inter alia*—1) the issuance of letters of guardianship to respondents with authority to permit a heart catheterization to be performed on Phillip, and 2) the immediate delivery (by appellants) of Phillip to the Sheriff and Juvenile Authority of Santa Clara County. That same day appellants filed a notice of appeal from both orders followed by a petition to this court for a writ of supersedeas which we summarily denied.

* * *

I

Sufficiency of the Evidence

* * *

Phillip B. was born on October 16, 1966, with Down's Syndrome, a chromosomal anomaly—usually the presence of an extra chromosome attached to the number 21 pair—resulting in varying degrees of mental retardation and a number of abnormal physical characteristics. Down's Syndrome reportedly occurs in approximately 1/10 of 1 percent of live births.

Appellants, deeply distraught over Phillip's disability, decided upon institutionalization, a course of action recommended by a state social worker and approved by appellants' pediatrician. A few days later, Phillip was transferred from the hospital to a licensed board and care facility for disabled youngsters. Although the facility was clean, it offered no structured educational or developmental programs and required that all the children (up to 8 years of age) sleep in cribs. Appellants initially visited Phillip frequently; but soon their visits became less frequent and they became more detached from him.

When Phillip was three years old a pediatrician informed appellants that Phillip had a congenital heart defect, a condition afflicting half of Down's Syndrome children. Open heart surgery was suggested when Phillip attained age six. However, appellants took no action to investigate or remedy the suspected medical problem.

After the board and care facility had been sold during the summer of 1971, appellants discovered that the condition of the facility had seriously deteriorated under the new management; it had become dirty and cluttered with soiled clothing, and smelled strongly of urine. Phillip was very thin and listless and was being fed watery oatmeal from a bottle. At appellants' request, a state social worker arranged for Phillip's transfer in January, 1972, to We Care, a licensed residential facility for developmentally disabled children located in San Jose, where he remained up to the time of trial.

At that time, the facility—which cared for about 20 children more severely handicapped than Phillip—operated under very limited conditions: it had no programs of education or therapy; the children were not enrolled in outside programs; the facility lacked an outdoor play area; the building was in poor repair; and the kitchen had only a two-burner hot plate used to cook pureed food.

In April 1972, We Care employed Jeanne Haight (later to become program director and assistant administrator of the facility) to organize a volunteer program. Mrs. Haight quickly noticed Phillip's debilitated condition. She found him unusually small and thin for his age (five); he was not toilet trained and wore diapers, still slept in a crib, walked like a toddler, and crawled down stairs only inches high. His speech was limited and mostly unintelligible; his teeth were in poor condition.

Mrs. Haight, who undertook a recruitment program for volunteers, soon recruited respondent Patsy H., who had helped to found a school for children with learning disabilities where Mrs. Haight had once been vice-principal. Mrs. H. began working at We Care on a daily basis. Her husband, respondent Herbert H., and their children, soon joined in the volunteer activities.

Mrs. H., initially assigned to work with Phillip and another child, assisted Phillip in experimenting with basic sensory experiences, improving body coordination, and in overcoming his fear of steps. Mr. H. and one of the H. children helped fence the yard area, put in a lawn, a sandbox, and install some climbing equipment.

Mrs. Haight promptly initiated efforts to enroll Phillip in a preschool program for the fall of 1972, which required parental consent.[4] She contacted Mr. B. who agreed to permit Phillip to participate provided learning aptitude could be demonstrated. Mrs. H. used vocabulary cards to teach Phillip 25 to 50 new words and to comprehend word association. Although Mr. B. failed to appear at the appointed time in order to observe what Phillip had learned, he eventually gave his parental consent enabling Phillip to attend Hope Preschool in October, 1972.

4. Apparently, Phillip had received no formal preschool education for the retarded even though such training programs were available in the community. Expert testimony established that early introduction to preschool training is of vital importance in preparing a retarded child for entry level public education.

Respondents continued working with Phillip coordinating their efforts with his classroom lessons. Among other things, they concentrated on development of feeding skills and toilet training and Mr. H. and the two eldest children gradually became more involved in the volunteer program.

Phillip subsequently attended a school for the trainable mentally retarded (TMR) where the children are taught basic survival words. They are capable of learning to feed and dress themselves appropriately, doing basic community activities such as shopping, and engaging in recreational activities. There is no attempt to teach them academics, and they are expected to live in sheltered settings as adults. In contrast, children capable of attending classes for the educable mentally retarded (EMR) are taught reading, writing, and simple computation, with the objective of developing independent living skills as adults.

A pattern of physical and emotional detachment from their son was developed by appellants over the next several years. In contrast, during the same period, respondents established a close and caring relationship with Phillip. Beginning in December, 1972, Phillip became a frequent visitor at respondents' home; with appellants' consent, Phillip was permitted to spend weekends with respondents, a practice which continued regularly and often included weekday evenings. At the same time, respondents maintained frequent contact with Phillip at We Care as regular volunteer visitors. Meanwhile, appellants visited Phillip at the facility only a few times a year; however, no overnight home visits occurred until after the underlying litigation ensued.

Respondents played an active role in Phillip's behavioral development and educational training. They consistently supplemented basic skills training given Phillip at We Care.[5]

Phillip was openly accepted as a member of the H. family whom he came to love and trust. He eventually had his own bedroom; he was included in sharing household chores. Mr. H. set up a workbench for Phillip and helped him make simple wooden toys; they attended special Boy Scout meetings together. And Phillip regularly participated in family outings. Phillip referred to the H. residence as "my house." When Phillip began to refer to the H. as "Mom" and "Dad," they initially discouraged the familar reference, eventually succeeding in persuading Phillip to use the discriminate references "Mama Pat" and "Dada Bert" and "Mama B." and "Daddy B."[6] Both Mrs. Haight and Phillip's teacher observed significant improvements in Phillip's development and behavior. Phillip had developed, in Mrs. Haight's opinion, "true love and strong [emotional] feelings" for respondents.

---

5. In addition to their efforts to improve Phillip's communication and reading skills through basic sign language and word association exercises, respondents toilet-trained Phillip and taught him to use eating utensils and to sleep in a regular bed (the latter frequently monitored during the night).

6. At respondents' suggestion, Mrs. Haight requested a photograph of appellants to show Phillip who his parents were; but appellants failed to provide one.

Meanwhile, appellants continued to remain physically and emotionally detached from Phillip. The natural parents intellectualized their decision to treat Phillip differently from their other children. Appellants testified that Phillip, whom they felt would always require institutionalization, should not be permitted to form close emotional attachments which—upon inevitable disruption—would traumatize the youngster.

In matters of Phillip's health care needs, appellants manifested a reluctant—if not neglectful—concern. When Dr. Gathman, a pediatric cardiologist, diagnosed a ventricular septal defect [7] in Phillip's heart in early 1973 and recommended catheterization (a medically accepted pre-surgery procedure to measure pressure and to examine the interior of the heart), appellants refused their consent.

In the spring of 1977, Dr. Gathman again recommended heart catheterization in connection with the anticipated use of general anesthesia during Phillip's major dental surgery. Appellants consented to the pre-operative procedure which revealed that the heart defect was surgically correctible with a maximum risk factor of 5 percent. At a conference attended by appellants and Mrs. Haight in June, 1977, Dr. Gathman recommended corrective surgery in order to avoid a progressively deteriorating condition resulting in a "bed-to-chair existence" and the probability of death before the age of 30. Although Dr. Gathman—as requested by Mrs. B.—supplied the name of a parent of Down's Syndrome children with similar heart disease, no contact was ever made. Later that summer, appellants decided—without obtaining an independent medical consultation—against surgery. Appellants' stated reason was that Dr. Gathman had "painted" an inaccurate picture of the situation. They felt that surgery would be merely life-prolonging rather than life-saving, presenting the possibility that they would be unable to care for Phillip during his later years. A few months later, in early 1978, appellants' decision was challenged in a juvenile dependency proceeding initiated by the district attorney on the ground that the withholding of surgery constituted neglect within the meaning of Welfare and Institutions Code section 300, subdivision (b); the juvenile court's dismissal of the action on the basis of inconclusive evidence was ultimately sustained on appeal (In re Phillip B. (1979) 156 Cal.Rptr. 48, cert. den. sub nom. Bothman v. Warren B. (1980) 445 U.S. 949).

In September, 1978, upon hearing from a staff member of We Care that Phillip had been regularly spending weekends at respondents' home, Mr. B. promptly forbade Phillip's removal from the facility (except for medical purposes and school attendance) and requested that respondents be denied personal visits with Phillip at We Care. Although respondents continued to visit Phillip daily at the facility, the abrupt cessation of home visits produced regressive changes in Phillip's behavior: he began acting out violently when respondents prepared to leave,

---

7. The disease, found in a large number of Down's Syndrome children , consists of an opening or "hole" between the heart chambers resulting in elevated blood pressure and impairment of vascular functions. The disease can become a progressive, and ultimately fatal, disorder.

begging to be taken "home"; he resorted to profanity; he became sullen and withdrawn when respondents were gone; bed-wetting regularly occurred, a recognized symptom of emotional disturbance in children. He began to blame himself for the apparent rejection by respondents; he began playing with matches and on one occasion he set his clothes afire; on another, he rode his tricycle to respondents' residence a few blocks away proclaiming on arrival that he was "home." He continuously pleaded to return home with respondents. Many of the behavioral changes continued to the time of trial. [10]

Appellants unsuccessfully pressed to remove Phillip from We Care notwithstanding the excellent care he was receiving. However, in January, 1981, the regional center monitoring public assistance for residential care and training of the handicapped, consented to Phillip's removal to a suitable alternate facility. Despite an extended search, none could be found which met Phillip's individualized needs. Meanwhile, Phillip continued living at We Care, periodically visiting at appellants' home. But throughout, the strong emotional attachment between Phillip and respondents remained intact.

Evidence established that Phillip, with a recently tested I.Q. score of 57,[11] is a highly functioning Down's Syndrome child capable of learning sufficient basic and employable skills to live independently or semi-independently in a non-institutional setting.

Courts generally may appoint a guardian over the person or estate of a minor "if it appears necessary or convenient." But the right of parents to retain custody of a child is fundamental and may be disturbed " '. . . only in extreme cases of persons acting in a fashion incompatible with parenthood.' " Accordingly, the Legislature has imposed the stringent requirement that before a court may make an order awarding custody of a child to a nonparent without consent of the parents, "it shall make a finding that an award of custody to a parent would be detrimental to the child and the award to a nonparent is required to serve the best interests of the child." That requirement is equally applicable to guardianship proceedings * * * . The legislative shift in emphasis from parental unfitness to detriment to the child did not, however, signal a retreat from the judicial practice granting custodial preference to nonparents "only in unusual or extreme cases."

The trial court expressly found that an award of custody to appellants would be harmful to Phillip in light of the psychological or "de

---

10. During a pretrial psychological evaluation, Phillip suddenly recoiled in his chair, hiding his face, in response to the examiner's question how he felt about being unable to visit respondents' home. In the examiner's opinion, such reaction manifested continuing emotional pain in light of the earlier trauma and regressive behavior following termination of home visits. Contrary to appellants' argument, they were not entitled to be present at the pretrial psychological examination. The need for an

accurate report, itself subservient to the interest of an effective examination through a free and open communication exchange, is adequately safeguarded through discovery, cross-examination and production of other expert testimony.

11. A retarded child within an I.Q. range of 55–70 is generally considered as mildly retarded and classified as educable under California school standards.

facto" parental relationship established between him and respondents. Such relationships have long been recognized in the fields of law and psychology. * * * Persons who assume such responsibility have been characterized by some interested professional observers as "psychological parents": "Whether any adult becomes the psychological parent of a child is based . . . on day-to-day interaction, companionship, and shared experiences. The role can be fulfilled either by a biological parent or by an adoptive parent or by any other caring adult—but never by an absent, inactive adult, whatever his biological or legal relationship to the child may be."[e]

Appellants vigorously challenge the evidence and finding that respondents have become Phillip's de facto or psychological parents since he did not reside with them full-time, as underscored in previous California decisions which have recognized de facto parenthood. They argue that the subjective concept of psychological parenthood, relying on such nebulous factors as "love and affection" is susceptible to abuse and requires the countervailing element of objectivity provided by a showing of the child's long-term residency in the home of the claimed psychological parent.

We disagree. Adoption of the proposed standard would require this court to endorse a novel doctrine of child psychology unsupported either by a demonstrated general acceptance in the field of psychology or by the record before us. Although psychological parenthood is said to result from "day-to-day attention to [the child's] needs for physical care, nourishment, comfort, affection, and stimulation" (Goldstein, supra, p. 17), appellants fail to point to any authority or body of professional opinion that equates daily attention with full-time residency. To the contrary, the record contains uncontradicted expert testimony that while psychological parenthood usually will require residency on a "24–hour basis," it is not an absolute requirement; further, that the frequency and quality of Phillip's weekend visits with respondents, together with the regular weekday visits at We Care, provided an adequate foundation to establish the crucial parent-child relationship.

Nor are we persuaded by appellants' suggested policy considerations concerning the arguably subjective inquiry involved in determining psychological parenthood. Trial fact-finders commonly grapple with elusive subjective legal concepts without aid of "countervailing" objective criteria. * * *

Appellants also challenge the sufficiency of the evidence to support the finding that their retention of custody would have been detrimental to Phillip. In making the critical finding, the trial court correctly applied the "clear and convincing" standard of proof necessary to protect the fundamental rights of parents in all cases involving a nonparent's bid for custody. This court must, as noted, review the whole record in the light

---

e. Joseph Goldstein, Anna Freud, & Albert Solnit, Beyond the Best Interests of   the Child 19 (1973).

most favorable to the award of guardianship to determine whether there was substantial evidence that parental custody would have been detrimental to Phillip based on clear and convincing evidence.

The record contains abundant evidence that appellants' retention of custody would cause Phillip profound emotional harm. Notwithstanding Phillip's strong emotional ties with respondents, appellants abruptly foreclosed home visits and set out to end all contact between them. When Phillip's home visits terminated in 1978, he displayed many signs of severe emotional trauma: he appeared depressed and withdrawn and became visibly distressed at being unable to return to "my house," a request he steadily voiced up until trial. He became enuretic, which a psychologist, Dr. Edward Becking, testified indicates emotional stress in children. Dr. Becking testified to other signs of emotional disturbance which were present nearly three years after the termination of home visits.

Our law recognizes that children generally will sustain serious emotional harm when deprived of the emotional benefits flowing from a true parent-child relationship.

There was uncontroverted expert testimony that Phillip would sustain further emotional trauma in the event of total separation from respondents: the testimony indicated that, as with all children, Phillip needs love and affection, and he would be profoundly hurt if he were deprived of the existing psychological parental relationship with respondents in favor of maintaining unity with his biological parents.

Phillip's conduct unmistakably demonstrated that he derived none of the emotional benefits attending a close parental relationship largely as a result of appellants' individualized decision to abandon that traditional supporting role. Dr. Becking testified that no "bonding or attachment" has occurred between Phillip and his biological parents, a result palpably consistent with appellants' view that Phillip had none of the emotional needs uniquely filled by natural parents. We conclude that such substantial evidence adequately supports the finding that parental custody would have resulted in harmful deprivation of these human needs contrary to Phillip's best interests.

Finally, there was also evidence that Phillip would experience educational and developmental injury if parental custody remains unchanged. At Phillip's functioning level of disability, he can normally be expected to live at least semi-independently as an adult in a supervised residential setting and be suitably trained to work in a sheltered workshop or even a competitive environment (e.g., performing assembly duties or custodial tasks in a fast-food restaurant). Active involvement of a parent figure during the formative stages of education and habilitation is of immeasurable aid in reaching his full potential. Unfortunately, appellants' deliberate abdication of that central role would effectively deny Phillip any meaningful opportunity to develop whatever skills he may be capable of achieving. Indeed, Dr. Becking testified that further separation from respondents would not only impair Phillip's ability to form new relationships but would "for a long while" seriously impair Phillip's development of necessary prevocational and independent-living skills for his future life.

Nor can we overlook evidence of potential physical harm to Phillip due to appellants' passive neglect in response to Phillip's medical condition. Although it appears probable that the congenital heart defect is no longer correctible by surgery, the trial court could have reasonably concluded that appellants' past conduct reflected a dangerously passive approach to Phillip's future medical needs.

It is a clearly stated legislative policy that persons with developmental disabilities shall enjoy—*inter alia*—the right to treatment and rehabilitation services, the right to publicly supported education, the right to social interaction, and the right to prompt medical care and treatment. Moreover, the legislative purpose underlying Civil Code section 4600 is to protect the needs of children generally " '. . . to be raised with love, emotional security and physical safety.' " When a trial court is called upon to determine the custody of a developmentally disabled or handicapped child, as here, it must be guided by such overriding policies rather than by the personal beliefs or attitudes of the contesting parties, since it is the child's interest which remains paramount. Clearly, the trial court faithfully complied with such legislative mandate in exercising its sound discretion based upon the evidence presented. We find no abuse as contended by appellants.

We strongly emphasize, as the trial court correctly concluded, that the fact of detriment cannot be proved solely by evidence that the biological parent has elected to institutionalize a handicapped child, or that nonparents are able and willing to offer the child the advantages of their home in lieu of institutional placement. Sound reasons may exist justifying institutionalization of a handicapped child. But the totality of the evidence under review permits of no rational conclusion other than that the detriment caused Phillip, and its possible recurrence, was due not to appellants' choice to institutionalize but their calculated decision to remain emotionally and physically detached—abdicating the conventional role of competent decision-maker in times of demonstrated need—thus effectively depriving him of any of the substantial benefits of a true parental relationship. It is the emotional abandonment of Phillip, not his institutionalization, which inevitably has created the unusual circumstances which led to the award of limited custody to respondents. We do not question the sincerity of appellants' belief that their approach to Phillip's welfare was in their combined best interests. But the record is replete with substantial and credible evidence supporting the trial court's determination, tested by the standard of clear and convincing proof, that appellants' retention of custody has caused and will continue to cause serious detriment to Phillip and that his best interests will be served through the guardianship award of custody to respondents. In light of such compelling circumstances, no legal basis is shown to disturb that carefully considered determination.

* * *

Notes and Questions

1. *Questions about* Phillip B. (a) What finding must the trial court have to make before Mr. and Mrs. H. (the Heaths) can be made guardians without the consent of Phillip's parents? (b) Are other parents who commit a child to an institution likely to lose custody as a result of the *Phillip B.* decision? (c) What is a psychological parent ?

2. *A judge's courage.* Professor Robert Mnookin, who assisted the plaintiffs, provides a moving account of the trial court proceedings in *Phillip B:*

* * *

On August 7, 1981, [trial court] Judge William Fernandez summoned the parties and their lawyers to the courtroom, which was filled with reporters and well-wishers. When the judge began reading his opinion, [the plaintiffs' lawyers] had no idea what the result would be because during the trial, the judge had done nothing to tip his hand. Judge Fernandez wrote:

California does not provide a method by which a mentally retarded child may state a preference. Other states have used a substituted judgment procedure to allow the court to state such a preference for the incompetent. This doctrine requires the court to ascertain as nearly as possible the incompetent person's "actual interests and preferences." . . . .

In our case the use of the substituted judgment method to arrive at Phillip's preference may best be stated in the form of a platonic dialogue with the court posing the choices to Phillip and Phillip's preference being ascertained from the more logical choice. The dialogue begins:

The Court: "Phillip . . . [your] first choice will lead you to a room in an institution where you will live. You will be fed, housed, and clothed but you will not receive any life prolonging medical care. . . . You will not be given an opportunity to add to your basic skills or to your motor skills and . . . will be treated as if you are . . . incapable of learning and not fit to enter into society. You will not be allowed to become attached to any person, in fact efforts will be made to prevent any such attachments. Your biological parents will visit you occasionally, but their love and caring for you will at best be ambivalent. . . . "

Your second choice Phillip will lead you to a private home where you will be bathed in the love and affection of your psychological parents. . . . You will be given private tutoring and one on one training. . . . Your psychological parents believe that you are educable and will do all in their power to help you receive the education you may need to care for yourself and to secure work when you are an adult. You will have a chance for life prolonging surgery as well as receiving all the medical care that you need. Even if life prolonging surgery cannot be performed, your psychological parents will always be there to comfort you and care for you in the dark times of your final illness. Best of all, your psychological parents will do all in their power to involve your biological parents in your habilitation and to unite both families together in ensuring for you a life that is worth living.

In my view, the dialogue would end with Phillip choosing to live with the Heaths.

* * *

* * *He concluded by reading:

[T]his is not a hearing to determine surgery for Phillip. That must wait another time and a sound parenting decision. This is a hearing for the purpose of giving Phillip Becker another parenting choice. It is a hearing responsive to Phillip's need for habilitation, and responsive to his desire for a chance to secure a life worth living. I will give him that chance.''

When Judge Fernandez finished, the court personnel, the reporters in the courtroom, the Heaths, and their attorneys were in tears, not only because of the joyous result, but also because of this extraordinary demonstration of humanity by a courageous judge.

That day the judge signed the guardianship papers, appointing the Heaths guardians. He also authorized a heart catheterization to be done to determine whether surgery was still possible. A court order also authorized the Heaths to take Phillip home for reasonable visitation, and later for custody.

Robert H. Mnookin, The Guardianship of Philip B: Jay Spears' Achievement, 40 Stan. L. Rev. 841, 849–40 (1988).

2. *Aftermath*. In 1983 Phillip had the heart surgery he needed and became an active participant in the Special Olympics. In February 1985, after he had turned 18, the Heaths, his guardians, adopted Phillip without objection from the Beckers, his biological parents. The efforts of the young lawyer, Jay Spears, who took the case on a pro bono basis, were complete. He devoted over 2000 hours to the case, and his firm contributed over 3000 hours, which if billed would have amounted to over $400,000. Robert H. Mnookin, supra. Tragically, Jay Spears, a 1976 Stanford Law School graduate, died from AIDS in December, 1986. In Memory of Jay M. Spears, 40 Stan. L. Rev. 839 (1988).

3. *Beyond the Best Interests. Phillip B.* refers to the well-known work by Joseph Goldstein, Anna Freud, and Albert Solnit, Beyond the Best Interests of the Child 98–99 (1973). The book promoted the concepts of "wanted child," "psychological parent" and "least detrimental available alternative" and defined these concepts as follows:

A wanted child is one who receives affection and nourishment on a continuing basis from at least one adult and who feels that he or she is and continues to be valued by those who take care of him or her.

A psychological parent is one who, on a continuing day-to-day basis, through interaction, companionship, interplay, and mutuality, fulfills the child's psychological needs for a parent, as well as the child's physical needs. The psychological parent may be a biological, adoptive, foster, or common-law parent, or any other person. There is no presumption in favor of any of these after the initial assignment at birth.

A common-law parent-child relationship is a psychological parent-wanted child relationship which is developed outside of adoption, assignment by custody in separation or divorce proceedings, or the initial assignment at birth of a child to his or her biological parents.

The least detrimental available alternative is that child placement and procedure for child placement which maximizes, in accord with the child's sense of time, the child's opportunity for being wanted and for maintaining on a continuous, unconditional, and permanent basis a relationship with at least one adult who is or will become the child's psychological parent.

The book has been extensively criticized for the methodology of the authors' research and inattention to the value of multiple caretakers for a child. See, e.g. Richard E. Crouch, An Essay on the Critical and Judicial Perception of Beyond the Best Interests of the Child, 13 Fam. L.Q. 49 (1979). The concept of psychological parent also arises in termination of parental rights cases, which raise issues similar to *Phillip B.* For additional discussion see note 6, infra at 450.

B. *The Guardian's Role*

MERYL SCHWARTZ, REINVENTING GUARDIANSHIP: SUBSIDIZED GUARDIANSHIP, FOSTER CARE, AND CHILD WELFARE

22 N.Y.U. Rev. L. & Soc. Change 441, 474–478 (1996).

* * *

The legal relationship of guardian to ward developed to protect the interests of children with property. Because infancy itself is a legal disability, a child under the age of majority cannot enter into a binding agreement. Children with assets, therefore, cannot manage their own property; they must rely on guardians to do so for them.

At common law, until this century, a father was the natural guardian of his child and had the power to manage the child's estate as well as make decisions about his or her upbringing. Upon the death or incapacity of a child's father, an ecclesiastical court would often appoint a guardian to look after the child's interests. The law of guardianship was not concerned with the unpropertied child who would not inherit.

Modern day probate law emerges from this history. While it has abandoned its male privileges, modern probate law retains its historical emphasis on the appointment, powers, and duties of guardians over the property of a minor. Modern probate law also typically provides for the appointment of a guardian over the person of a minor.

Today, both parents—rather than fathers—are the natural guardians of their children and are free to rear them as they see fit so long as they do not abandon, abuse or neglect them. When these natural guardians are unable to carry out their responsibilities, a third party may attempt to gain custody and control of the children, but may not legally act on the child's behalf until a court has invested them with formal authority. Appointment of a probate guardian over the person of a minor confers the legal authority necessary for a third party to act like a parent.

Probate courts generally appoint guardians over the person of a minor child upon the death of both parents or when a child is otherwise in need of parental authority. In addition, probate courts in some states continue to appoint guardians when parents are deemed by the court to be unfit. However, in states following the Uniform Probate Code, the probate court is typically without jurisdiction to appoint a guardian on the grounds of parental unfitness. The Uniform Probate Code restricts the power of probate courts to appoint guardians over the person of a minor with living parents to situations where parental rights of custody have been terminated or suspended by circumstances or prior court order. In effect, the Code requires that non-probate courts take primary responsibility for determining parental fitness.

In the majority of states, the probate court can appoint a guardian over the objection of the natural guardians. Where the parents oppose the appointment, the court will hold a hearing to decide the issue. Many states express a strong preference for custody and control remaining with a parent who is fit, so those courts give parents priority in custody disputes. A contested guardianship proceeding is essentially a custody dispute, so parental preference will likely be applied, and, if the parents are fit, a court will usually uphold natural guardianship rights. If the court finds the parents unfit, it will award guardianship to a third person over the objection of the parents. Even in these contested cases, appointment of a guardian does not terminate all parental rights. Absent the parent's voluntary surrender of those rights or a judicial termination of parental rights, parents retain the duty to support, the right to visitation, and the power to consent to adoption.

Guardians owe a fiduciary duty to their wards, including an obligation to care and protect. A guardian is responsible for providing for the child's health, education and maintenance. To carry out these duties, the guardian is given the power to make decisions a parent would otherwise make. It is said that a guardian stands in loco parentis to a child and is entitled to decide where and with whom the child should live. Probate guardians can make decisions on medical or professional treatment or care, approve of marriage, consent to enlistment in the armed forces, and make educational decisions. The choice of the child's religion is usually left to the parents. The most significant power remaining with the parents is the power to consent to adoption, although where the biological parent's rights have been terminated, a guardian may be authorized to give or withhold such consent.

Although a guardian will ordinarily have physical custody of the child, the court could award physical custody to another party if to do so would be in the best interest of the child. For example, a grandparent might be made guardian over the person, responsible for making all important decisions for the child, but the court might direct that the child live with an aunt who would have the power to make ordinary decisions.

* * *

Guardians generally do not have a fiduciary duty to support their wards. Unless parental rights have been terminated, a child's parents remain liable for child support. If the child has an estate and there is no parental support, a guardian of the property can petition the court to use the child's assets. Guardians for children without property do not have to use their own funds to care for the child. If otherwise eligible, the child can receive public assistance.

* * *

Following the appointment, probate courts retain jurisdiction over the guardians, but there is little supervision by the court. In contrast to guardians over the estate of a minor, who are required to file an annual accounting with the court and to seek the court's guidance when certain transactions are contemplated, guardians over the person of the child are rarely required to inform the court of their actions or to regularly file reports.

The guardianship is automatically terminated when the ward marries, reaches the age of majority, or dies. It also terminates, if the court removes the guardian, if the court permits the guardian to resign, or if the guardian dies.

Any interested person can ask the court to review the suitability of the appointment at any time and to revoke the letters in the best interest of the child. In states where parental rights are not terminated before the appointment of a guardian, a parent can ask for the guardian to be removed.

* * *

Notes and Questions

1. Does a guardianship enable a child to have two sets of "parents," or do the guardians replace the biological parents replaced by the guardians?

2. Phillip B. How did *Phillip B.* differ from the usual guardianship case? Note that the state had brought a medical neglect action against Phillip's biological parents, but had lost. Strategically, the guardianship petition was the Heaths' last chance to take control of Phillip away from his parents and assume control themselves.

Who is responsible for supporting Phillip—his parents or his guardians? After the *Phillip B.* decision, the Heaths and the Beckers agreed to a settlement that provided that the Heaths would assume full responsibility for Phillip's care and would indemnify the Beckers against liability for costs of the care. Robert H. Mnookin, The Guardianship of Philip B: Jay Spears' Achievement, 40 Stan. L. Rev. 841, 852 (1988).

3. *Testamentary and stand-by guardians.* Parents may name a guardian for their minor children in a will, and the named guardian is appointed upon the parents' death if the probate court approves. The AIDS epidemic, however, focused attention on the problem of planning for the care of children when a single parent is terminally ill. These parents need someone to be legally capable of assuming the care and custody of their children when they can no longer do so themselves. Because the parent wants to retain custody and control for as long as possible, the guardianship procedure described in the Schwartz article is not appropriate.

In response to this problem, states have begun to enact standby guardian statutes that allow a parent to designate a guardian who will become active when the parent is incapacitated. The parent retains custody and control, including authority to revoke the standby guardianship, until the parent becomes incapacitated or dies. The states differ with regard to a noncustodial parent's rights, but typically that parent is entitled at least to notice and an opportunity to object. Guardians are not obligated to support their wards, but if the child has no property or income from a trust or benefit plan, such as social security, the guardian may have difficulty finding financial resources for the child. The child might be eligible for a welfare program that would provide some support, or for foster care money if the guardian became a foster parent. These options could entail a relatively high level of state intervention for a small amount of money, however. For discussion of standby guardianship statutes, see Joyce McConnell, Standby Guardianship: Sharing the Legal Responsibility For Children, 7 Md. J. Contemp. Legal Iss. 249 (1995–96). Lenore M. Molee, The Ultimate Demonstration of Love for a Child: Choosing a Standby Guardian, 22 Seton Hall Legis.J. 475 (1998); Deborah Weimer, Implementation of Standby Guardianship: Respect for Family Autonomy, 100 Dick.L.Rev. 65 (1995).

4. *Children with property.* Although the guardian-ward relationship was developed to protect children with property, it is now viewed as being more useful as a mechanism for conferring other parental rights and responsibilities on a non-parent. Using court appointed guardians or conservators for property management is cumbersome and expensive. Trusts or gifts made under a Uniform Transfer to Minors Act are now preferred. Children and Property are discussed in Chapter 9, Financial Responsibility and Control.

PROBLEM 2–4

Mrs. Howard is the mother of a 5–year-old girl. Her husband, the child's father, was killed in an auto accident. Mrs. Howard has been diagnosed with a heart condition and must soon be hospitalized for surgery. Her best friend lives in the same town as Mrs. Howard and will care for her daughter while she is in the hospital. Mrs. Howard has never made a will. What advice would you give Mrs. Howard about providing for her daughter?

Section 4.   Emancipation: The Hastening of Adulthood

IN RE THOMAS C.

Superior Court of Connecticut, Juvenile Matters, 1996.
691 A.2d 1140.

DYER, JUDGE.

This is an action concerning the emancipation of Thomas C., a minor whose date of birth is May 29, 1979. The petitioners are Jeffrey and Maureen C., his parents. * * *

Thomas is sixteen years of age and will turn seventeen on May 29, 1996. He is the eldest of four boys born to Jeffrey and Maureen C. Thomas resides in the family home with his parents and three brothers. He dropped out of Goodwin [Technical School] a week prior to his sixteenth birthday, but had disciplinary problems there for approximately one year prior to quitting school. He has not participated in any educational program since then, and refuses to do so. He is unemployed and refuses to look for work. He is dependent on his parents for food and shelter.

Thomas suffers from a learning disability known as attention deficit disorder. He was "main streamed" into regular classes at Goodwin, but received supportive services for his learning disability from the school's resource room and psychologist. Thomas is very intelligent, but displayed very little motivation academically. He had difficulty attending to his academic tasks, and appeared frustrated at times. There was some academic improvement when Thomas was prescribed Ritalin for his learning disability. This was short-lived however, and Greenfield [a special education teacher and department head at the E.C. Goodwin Technical School] articulated the suspicion that Thomas "didn't always take" the medicine. According to Greenfield, Thomas had problems with self esteem, and gravitated toward other students with social and emotional problems. Although he could interact appropriately with teachers and peers "when he wanted to," he was, on other occasions, "troubled and difficult." He began to display an escalating pattern of rules violations, particularly infractions related to being in unassigned areas of the school. These disciplinary problems resulted in a number of suspensions. Thomas was resistant to the rules and structure which Goodwin attempted to impose, and angrily blamed teachers and staff there for the problems he was experiencing. The school recommended counseling, a suggestion which was accepted by the parents but rejected by Thomas.

Thomas's behavior at home has been even more problematic. He is frequently verbally abusive to his parents, calling them obscene names. He has been physically and verbally abusive to his younger brothers, particularly his twelve year old brother, whom Thomas cruelly taunts about his weight and physical appearance. Thomas was arrested and charged with breach of the peace as the result of a domestic dispute with his father. This charge was later nolled. Thomas's antagonistic attitude toward his parents and brothers results in great tension within the home. Family members "walk on egg shells" to avoid confrontations with Thomas.

Thomas resided away from the family home for approximately six months during 1995. Around June of that year, he began living in the home of his maternal uncle and maternal grandmother. His behavior there was good. According to the uncle, Timothy D., Thomas obeyed household rules and did not display violent or aggressive behavior. He remained with his uncle and grandmother throughout the summer. One day, shortly after the start of the academic year in September, Thomas went to school one morning but did not return to his relatives' home that afternoon. The uncle subsequently discovered that Thomas had begun living with someone in New Britain. The uncle was unclear as to the cause of Thomas's departure, and said that his nephew was welcome to stay with the grandmother and him. Thomas remained in the New Britain residence until around November, 1995, when he returned to live with his parents. He has lived with his parents and siblings in the family home since then.

During trial, the father, Jeffrey C., testified that he did not intend to seek Thomas's immediate removal from the home if the court granted the emancipation petition. He said that he intends to use the decree as a "lever," hoping that the legal ability to deny Thomas shelter and support would compel him to become more respectful and compliant at home. The father stated that he was "looking to hold this [an emancipation order] over his head."

Boyer, the court services officer, indicated in her report to the court that the parents expressed concern about their vicarious financial liability for civil or criminal wrongdoing by Thomas, and their feeling that they do not have any control over their son's behavior. She also indicated that Thomas and his parents "stated that they would like to improve communication and develop closer relationships with one another." Boyer adds: "However, it appears that both Thomas and his parents do not know how to resolve the current difficulties they are having." Boyer did not offer a recommendation as to whether the court should grant emancipation. She did express the opinion that the "family could benefit from family therapy to address communication and conflict resolution, if all parties agreed to attend."

* * * General Statutes § 46b–150b * * * specifies four separate grounds for granting a decree of emancipation. The petitioners have stipulated that only the fourth ground, delineated in subsection four of the statute, applies in the present case. Section 46b–150b(4) states that the court may grant an order emancipating a minor if the court finds that "for good cause shown, it is in the best interest of the minor, any child of the minor, or the parents or guardian of the minor...."[d]

---

d. Subsections (1)–(3) authorize the court to enter an emancipation order where: "(1) The minor has entered into a valid marriage, whether or not that marriage has been terminated by dissolution; or (2) the minor is on active duty with any of

* * * General Statutes § 46b–150d sets forth the effects of an emancipation order and provides in relevant part that: "(a) The minor may consent to medical, dental or psychiatric care, without parental consent, knowledge or liability; (b) the minor may enter into a binding contract; (c) the minor may sue and be sued in his own name; (d) the minor shall be entitled to his own earnings and shall be free of control by his parents or guardian; (e) the minor may establish his own residence; (f) the minor may buy and sell real and personal property; (g) the minor may not thereafter be the subject of a petition * * * as an abused, dependent, neglected or uncared for child or youth; (h) the minor may enroll in any school or college, without parental consent; (i) the minor shall be deemed to be over eighteen years of age for purposes of securing [a motor vehicle] operator's license * * * and a marriage license * * * without parental consent; (j) the minor shall be deemed to be over eighteen years of age for purposes of registering a motor vehicle * * * ; (k) the parents of the minor shall no longer be guardians of the minor * * * ; (*l*) the parents of a minor shall be relieved of any obligations respecting his school attendance * * * ; (m) the parents shall be relieved of all obligation to support the minor; (n) the minor shall be emancipated for the purposes of parental liability for his acts * * * ; (*o*) the minor may execute releases in his own name * * * ; and (p) the minor may enlist in the armed forces of the United States without parental consent."

This is an unfortunate and problematic case. Thomas's defiance of parental, school and legal authority causes great problems, both for himself, and for his family. The court is empathetic with the plight of his parents and siblings, who must endure the fallout of his unmotivated lifestyle and abusive behavior. The present case is another example of the inability of parents, schools, courts and social service agencies to deal effectively with the so-called "gray area" cases. Such cases involve sixteen and seventeen year old minors, who cannot be legally compelled to attend school or to obey the household rules, but whose parents are legally obligated to support and to shelter them. The parents believe that a decree of emancipation would somehow serve as a legal wake-up call to Thomas—with the threat of removal from the home and withdrawal of parental support transforming him into an obedient and motivated young man. While the court wishes that it could prompt such a response, the legal remedy requested by the petitioners is not likely to do so, and the court, in the exercise of its discretion, finds that it is not appropriate to grant emancipation, based on the facts of the present case.

The evidence and testimony adduced at trial prove that emancipation would be extremely detrimental to the best interests of Thomas. He lives with his parents, is totally dependent on them for food, shelter and necessities, and lacks the educational, emotional and financial wherewithal and stability to live independently. This fact is tacitly acknowl-

the armed forces of the United States of America; or (3) the minor willingly lives separate and apart from his parents or guardian, with or without the consent of the parents or guardian, and that the minor is managing his own financial affairs, regardless of the source of any lawful income * * *."

edged by the father, who testified that he intended to support and to shelter Thomas, if possible, after an emancipation decree entered. It is also clear that there is no real plan for Thomas should he ultimately be required to vacate the parental home and to fend for himself. Setting this learning disabled and obviously immature youth totally adrift without some realistic planning for his future needs would be courting a head-on collision with disaster. The court also notes parenthetically that it is highly unlikely that a decree freeing Thomas from parental controls will somehow make him more responsive to his parents' guidance or direction. It would also be improvident to confer unsupervised adult rights like the ability to contract, to register a motor vehicle, to sign releases, to buy and sell property and to obtain a driver's license on an impulsive teenager who has frequently displayed a proclivity for inappropriate behavior.

The rights of parents to raise and to nurture their children are among the most fundamental and basic of human rights. * * * From that premise flows the corollary that parental obligations and responsibilities cannot be lightly shed or abrogated by a child's parent or guardian. Although unfortunate, it is one of the realities of life that parents must shoulder burdensome responsibilities for children who misbehave, or become physically or emotionally ill. A decree legally excusing parents from the obligations and duties of parenthood should not be granted without a substantial reason. Although the petitioners' stated reasons for seeking emancipation are understandable, the court finds that they do not meet the burden of a good cause showing that it would be in the best interest of the child, or his parents, to emancipate Thomas.

For all of the aforementioned reasons, the petition for emancipation is hereby denied.

Notes and Questions

1. *Questions about* Thomas C. What policies does the court seek to advance? What practical difficulties might arise if courts routinely granted emancipation petitions brought by parents in circumstances such as those presented in this case? Should courts employ the emancipation doctrine to assist parents' efforts to discipline children?

2. *Becoming emancipated.* Emancipation is the process by which minors attain legal adulthood before reaching the age of majority. Carol Sanger and Eleanor Willemsen, Minor Changes: Emancipating Children in Modern Times, 25 U. Mich. J. L. Ref. 239, 240 (1992). The emancipated child thus assumes most adult rights and obligations. Connecticut is typical of nearly twenty states that provide for statutory emancipation, that is, for emancipation pursuant to statutes that prescribe not only discrete grounds (such as marriage or active military service), but also a broad best-interests ground that vests considerable discretion in the court. In states without emancipation statutes, the propriety of judicial emancipation depends on the attendant circumstances.

"Emancipation is an extraordinary grant of authority to minors in a legal system where even older children are permitted to decide very little for themselves." Id. at 244. The best-interests standard recognizes that emancipation results not only in a measure of freedom for the child, but also in a loss of protections ordinarily afforded children. On the one hand, emancipated children may secure employment otherwise unavailable because of the child labor laws, or may purchase, sell or rent property free from the constraints of the capacity-to-contract doctrine. The child is no longer bound to obey the parent. On the other hand, emancipated children lose the protections these laws provide and the right to financial support from their parents. Parents are no longer responsible for the child's debts and expenses, including medical expenses. Because emancipated minors hold capacity to sue and be sued, they lose the protection of statutes that toll limitations periods during minority. Emancipated minors are not covered under abuse and neglect laws, status offense jurisdiction relating to runaways, or by most other general protective legislation.

In their 1992 empirical study of California's emancipation statute and its application, Professors Sanger and Willemsen reached conclusions that bear on application of such statutes generally. For one thing, they found that while the legislature intended the emancipation statute to assist mature minors seeking recognition of their de facto independence, many emancipation petitions resulted from the suggestion and effort of parents seeking to resolve family strife or to end their liability or support obligations; the statute thus sometimes facilitated "an abdication by parents of caretaking responsibilities" without due regard for the child's needs. Id. at 247. The authors also found that while the statute required the court to determine the child's best interests, emancipation hearings were perfunctory, often taking only five or ten minutes. Id. at 315–17.

From their study, the authors evaluated emancipation's advantages and disadvantages to parents and their children. Among the advantages the authors found that (1) parents achieve an end to their support obligation and a limit of their vicarious liability for the child's conduct, neither of which may be achieved by other out-of-home placements or by having the child run away; (2) minors and parents may agree to seek emancipation without intervention by child welfare agencies or other government agencies; (3) unlike running away or invoking the court's delinquency or status offense jurisdiction, emancipation is relatively stigma-free because it is grounded in the minor's maturity; and (4) emancipation is almost always permanent. Among the disadvantages, the authors found that judges frequently did not closely scrutinize the child's best interests because the proceeding was nonadversarial when parents and child moved jointly; instead courts tended to take the parents' statements supporting emancipation as satisfying the best interests inquiry. Id. at 317.

2. *Is emancipation reversible?* What if a court adjudges a 16–year-old child to be emancipated, but the child falls on unexpected hard times the next year? May the child secure a court order reimposing the parental support obligation until that obligation would otherwise end? Courts generally answer in the affirmative. See, e.g., Wulff v. Wulff, 500 N.W.2d 845, 849 (Neb.1993). What policy considerations underlie these decisions?

PROBLEM 2–5

The defendant has been indicted for using a minor for obscene purposes. The victim, who allegedly posed or modeled for the defendant's obscene film, was a sixteen year-old female who was married and had a child. The criminal statute provides that the term "minor" means "any person who has not reached the age of eighteen years." The defense is that the victim's marriage resulted in her emancipation as a matter of law, and thus that the defendant committed no crime. Assume that under state law, marriage indeed produces emancipation as a matter of law. Has the defendant committed the crime charged?

Chapter 3

REPRESENTING CHILDREN

SECTION 1. INTRODUCTION

Child advocacy is a controversial subject. There is a surprising amount of disagreement about when children should be represented, who should represent them, and what the representative's role should be. The triangle of tensions among the rights and obligations of children, parents and government discussed in Chapter 1 fuels the controversy because these tensions produce conflicting views about when a child should have an independent voice. Different views of how children's competence should be defined and measured in legal decision-making add to the controversy.

This chapter provides an overview to help you develop a framework for analyzing the representative's role in particular types of proceedings studied in depth in later chapters. This chapter focuses on representation of children by attorneys, rather than looking more broadly at other representatives, such as parents, social workers, or trained volunteers.

LEONARD P. EDWARDS AND INGER J. SAGATUN, WHO SPEAKS FOR THE CHILD?

2 U. Chi. L. Sch. Roundtable 67, 67–68 (1995).

Child advocacy is a recent phenomenon. Fifty years ago there was little concern about who would speak for children in legal proceedings that affected them. Not until the 1967 decision in *In re Gault* were children guaranteed the right to an attorney in delinquency proceedings. A few years later, Congress passed the Child Abuse Prevention and Treatment Act (CAPTA), which, in part, provided federal financial assistance to state child protective services agencies so long as the state enacted legislation ensuring that every child involved in a child welfare proceeding had a court-appointed guardian ad litem. While neither *Gault* nor CAPTA has resulted in representation for all children in juvenile delinquency or dependency cases, they at least established the goal of full representation for all jurisdictions to follow. In other legal settings the law has been even slower to provide for the representation of children.

The dramatic rise in child abuse and neglect reports over the past twenty years has led many persons within the legal system to examine how best to represent children. A growing consensus has rejected the traditional assumption that persons involved in legal proceedings will look out for the interests of the child. Even when a child's interests are at stake, the other participants in the proceeding cannot be counted on to speak for the child. Parents and those who represent them have their own perspectives to present, while the court, with all of its other legal responsibilities, cannot be expected to focus upon the needs of the child. Moreover, child advocacy is needed both within and outside of the courtroom. Many now recognize that the legal system was not designed for children and that a child may be traumatized by the very system designed to provide protection.

* * *

All children should have someone who speaks for them in any legal proceeding in which their significant interests are at stake. This means that children should have access to a primary knowledgeable, caring person whose responsibility is to guide the child through the investigative and court processes, to look out for the child's emotional well-being and best interests, to protect the child's legal rights, and to identify other advocacy and support services for the child. * * *

* * *

LEONARD P. EDWARDS, A COMPREHENSIVE APPROACH TO THE REPRESENTATION OF CHILDREN: THE CHILD ADVOCACY COORDINATING COUNCIL

27 Fam. L.Q. 417, 417–20 (1993).

Children's interests are regularly litigated in our legal system. Children appear as parties or witnesses in every type of legal action, including domestic relations, custody and support disputes, child welfare/juvenile dependency proceedings, mental health actions, probate guardianships, paternity actions, termination of parental rights cases, emancipation matters, domestic violence cases, adoptions and juvenile delinquency matters, as well as in other criminal and civil cases. When children have a significant interest in these legal proceedings, they should have effective and independent representation to address their legal and nonlegal needs, both inside and outside the courtroom. But budgetary constraints, legal norms, and prevailing attitudes have conspired to inhibit the development of a comprehensive and coordinated system of representation for children.

* * *

Trained attorneys are critical to an effective child advocacy system, but children's attorneys often have the least experience, the lowest status, and receive the lowest compensation within the legal community. In part, this may be attributable to our failure to develop and effectuate comprehensive provisions for the representation of children. * * *

Second, inadequate resources are allocated to the representation of children. In many jurisdictions where representation is provided, caseloads are so high that attorneys have insufficient time to investigate, consult, and prepare for cases. Such a context simply does not allow for meaningful or effective advocacy. Moreover, in many communities the funding for this type of representation is perceived as unnecessary. Politicians are often reluctant to devote any public funds to provide for representation because they assume others in the legal system will speak for the child. In the competition for scarce dollars, advocacy for children often loses to more powerful political forces.

Third, those offices and organizations that do represent the interests of children often have other responsibilities and, in the competition for high-quality attorneys, children's needs usually come last. Particularly in public law offices, assignments involving the representation of children have the least status and are the least desirable. Attorneys in these offices view any work with children in juvenile court as less important than the "real work" of the office, such as representing felony defendants. Assignment policies reflect the widespread belief that juvenile court and child representation is merely a form of training to be completed before a felony trial assignment, and a senior lawyer who is assigned to work with children's issues is often perceived as being punished. In addition, career ladders for attorneys working with children are much more limited.

In jurisdictions that utilize a court-appointed panel system for the representation of children, the results are similar. Representing children is the first and most basic assignment given to new attorneys. The pay and status are lower, the experience level necessary for appointment is less, and the training requirements are less substantial than those for criminal attorneys. As a result, attorneys conclude that representing children demands less skill and care, deserves less time and energy, and should be phased out of their law practice as soon as higher-paying opportunities arise. Such an attitude necessarily reduces the quality of legal services provided to children.

The quality of representation in any field of law is directly related to the interest, ability, and length of time a particular attorney has practiced in that area. When there is rapid turnover, when attorneys remain in an assignment for only a few months, or when attorneys regard the assignment as a stepping stone to more important work, their work will inevitably be of lower quality.

Change is possible, but change depends on commitment and leadership within the legal community at the national, state, and local levels. * * *

* * *

Notes and Questions

1. *The nature of juvenile and family court practice.* As Judge Edwards states, lawyers for children do not ordinarily enjoy the status or financial rewards enjoyed by lawyers in other practice areas. The legal profession is not alone in this predicament. Consider Nancy Gibbs, Shameful Bequests to The Next Generation, Time, Oct. 8, 1990, at 42:

> Across the board, people who deal with children are more ill paid, unregulated and less respected than other professionals. Among physicians, pediatricians' income ranks near the bottom. In Michigan pre-school teachers with five years' experience earn $12,000, and prison guards with the same amount of seniority earn almost $30,000. U.S. airline pilots are vigilantly trained, screened and monitored; schoolbus drivers are not. "My hairdresser needs 1,500 hours of schooling, takes a written and practical test and is relicensed every year," says Flora Patterson, a foster parent in San Gabriel, Calif. "For foster parents in Los Angeles County there is no mandated training, yet we are dealing with life and death." The typical foster parent there earns about 80 cents an hour.

2. *Caseload pressures.* In a 1995 report focusing on delinquency cases, an ABA group found that among public defenders and appointed counsel alike, high caseloads were "the single most important barrier to effective representation." A Call for Justice: An Assessment of Access to Counsel and Quality of Representation in Delinquency Proceedings 8 (1995). The report explained that "[a]ttorneys with heavy caseload burdens find it difficult to meet their young clients to explain the proceedings before they appear at their detention hearings, conduct thorough investigations of the circumstances of the alleged offenses, learn about youths' ties to their families and to their communities, research and write individualized pretrial motions, keep informed on community-based alternatives to secure detention, develop dispositional plan that may be preferable to institutional confinement, follow up with clients during dispositional reviews, or monitor placement problems that may arise regarding needed services or conditions of confinement." Id. The report also called attention to the "debilitating impact" of high caseloads on devoted child advocates: "Burnout, job dissatisfaction, and anxiety over never having enough time to do a complete job are serious problems for many caring juvenile defense attorneys." Id.

Professionals in the field have been recommended that a lawyer providing legal services to indigent juveniles maintain a caseload of no more than 200 cases per year. See National Legal Aid and Defender Assn., Guidelines for Negotiating and Awarding Indigent Legal Defense Contracts, Guideline III–5 (1983 draft); National Advisory Commn. on Criminal Justice Standards and Goals, Task Force on Court Standards 13.12 (1973). In a 1989 telephone survey of urban public defender offices throughout the nation, Professor Janet E. Ainsworth did not find a single office that met the 200–case guideline. Caseloads per attorney ranged from a low of 250 cases to a staggering high of 550. Professor Ainsworth suggested the situation might be "even more desperate" in rural areas, noting that one rural Washington county assigned 912 juvenile cases to one lawyer. See Janet E. Ainsworth,

Re–Imagining and Reconstructing the Legal Order: The Case for Abolishing the Juvenile Court, 69 N.C. L. Rev. 1083, 1128 n. 305 (1991).

As Judge Edwards reports, caseload pressures inevitably take their toll. In a 1982 survey of juvenile counsel, 16.7% of the sample reported spending an hour or less preparing each case, 44.4% reported spending one to two hours preparing, 27.7% reported spending three to four hours preparing. Only 11.1% reported spending five or more hours preparing. Appointed counsel were 88.9% of the sample. See Richard A. Lawrence, The Role of Legal Counsel in Juveniles' Understanding of Their Rights, 34 Juv. & Fam. Ct. J. 49, 54 tbl. 4 (Winter 1983–84).

3. *Extraordinary effort.* Representation of children can be personally rewarding work as the attorney for *Philip B.* (Chapter 2) discovered. After the *Philip B.* trial, he knew "why he'd gone to law school and why he had become a trial lawyer." Robert H. Mnookin, The Guardianship of Philip B.: Jay Spears' Achievement, 40 Stan.L.Rev. 841 (1988). *Philip B.* demanded extraordinary effort. The multiple proceedings, concluding with Philip's adoption, took five years and produced 11 volumes of pleadings and 12 boxes of files. Philip's attorney spent over 2000 hours on the case and his firm contributed 3025 hours which would have cost $419,082 if the firm had charged for its work. Id.

4. *Multidisciplinary practice.* The child's lawyer frequently needs to collaborate with persons in other disciplines such as social work, education, psychology, and medicine. Misunderstandings about role, ethics and expertise can cause needless conflicts and delays harmful to the child. For information about the perspectives of other disciplines, see Interdisciplinary Perspectives in Child Abuse and Neglect (Faye F. Ulntalan and Crystal S. Mills, eds. 1992); Paul Johnson and Katharine Cahn, Improving Child Welfare Practice Through Improvements in Attorney–Social Worker Relationships, 54 U.Pitt.L.Rev 229 (1992); Jean Koh Peters, Concrete Strategies For Managing Ethically–Based Conflicts Between Children's Lawyers and Consulting Social Workers Who Serve the Same Client, 10 Children's Leg. Rts. J. 15 (1989). For an analysis of client confidentiality issues, see Gerald F. Glynn, Multidisciplinary Representation of Children: Conflicts over Disclosures of Client Communications, 27 John Marshall L. Rev. 617 (1994); Lisa A. Stranger, Note, Conflicts Between Attorneys and Social Workers Representing Children in Delinquency Proceedings, 65 Fordham L. Rev. 1123 (1996).

5. *Additional References.* For comprehensive texts on representing children, see Donald N. Duquette, Advocating for the Child in Protection Proceedings: A Handbook for Lawyers and Court Appointed Special Advocates (1990); Ann M. Haralambie, The Child's Attorney: A Guide to Representing Children in Custody, Adoption and Protection Cases (1993); Jean Koh Peters, Representing Children in Protection Proceedings: Ethical and Practical Dimensions (1997); Randy Hertz et al., Trial Manual for Defense Attorneys in Juvenile Court, (A.L.I.-A.B.A., 1991); Mark Soler et al., Representing the Child Client (1991); and the special issue of the Fordham Law Review on Proceedings of the Conference on Ethical Issues in the Legal Representation of Children, 64 Fordham L.Rev. 1281–2074 (1996). Annotated biographies include: National Center for Child Advocacy and Protection,

Annotated Bibliography of Guardian ad Litem Law Review Articles (1980) and Nancy Levit, Representing Children: An Annotated Bibliography, 1989–94, 13 J. Am. Acad. Matrim. Law. 137 (1995).

SECTION 2. CHILDREN'S ABILITIES AND DISABILITIES

Children's abilities and legal disabilities are important issues in representation. They are at the heart of much of the debate about the role of the child's attorney and are important in determining the child's rights and reception by others. This section examines children's abilities in several contexts. It begins with a survey of child development research which has tried to measure children's actual abilities, and ends with a case illustrating a legal disability, the prohibition on children's suing in their own names.

A. *Child Development Research*

Child development research can help attorneys understand and communicate with their child clients. The following survey provides an introduction to child development concepts.

WALLACE J. MLYNIEC, A JUDGE'S ETHICAL DILEMMA: ASSESSING A CHILD'S CAPACITY TO CHOOSE
64 Fordham L. Rev. 1873, 1878–1885 (1996).

* * *

In the past, societies deduced distinctions between adults and children from human experience and observation. In modern times, the research of child development theorists has validated such distinctions, despite the fact that many theories of child development have gained and lost prominence over the years. Stage theory, social learning theory, Freudian psychology, behavioralism, humanism, and ecological theory all have added to a modern understanding of the differences and similarities between the cognitive abilities of adults and children. Researchers subscribing to these theories have added to our understanding of how children learn and how their capabilities develop.[16] R. Murray Thomas has synthesized the various theories and offers four principles that guide modern thinking about children's development. According to Thomas:

> (1) genetic endowment defines a range of potential intellectual ability within which environmental influences can operate to produce the actual intellectual skills people display in their lives, (2) such genetic endowment can differ from one person to another, so that one individual's potential will differ from another's, (3) the flowering of genetic potential evolves gradually over the first two decades of life, and (4) the maturation of this flowering can differ from one person to another.

---

16. See generally R. Murray Thomas, Comparing Theories of Child Development (3d ed. 1992) (providing a comparative analysis of various child development theories).

Modern thinking about child development has evolved over time. The following subpart reviews the development theory of Piaget and considers, in particular, how he viewed children's decision-making capacity in light of cognitive function, behavior, and learning.

1.   Piagetian Cognitive Development Theory

Jean Piaget has emerged as perhaps the most influential researcher in the area of child development. Working over a period of many years, Piaget observed children and developed the theory that knowledge develops continually from a state of lesser knowledge to one that is more complete and effective.[18] Calling his system stage theory or cognitive theory, Piaget believed that all people possess certain internal motivation points (the stages) at which learning occurs. Piaget further theorized that physically experiencing an object (self learning) and social transmission (education) influence these motivation points.

Piaget posited four basic levels of development. Level One, called the sensory motor period, occurs from birth to two years old. During this period, children move from reflexive and adaptive actions through experimentation, and begin to demonstrate some mentally inventive acts of intelligence. At the end of this stage, children can mentally plan simple physical tasks using objects in view. David Elkind describes the main task of children at this level as the "conquest of the object."[22] Level Two, called the preoperational thought period, occurs between two and seven years of age. Passing through two substages, at this level children gain a facility for language and move from simple problem solving, based on what they hear and see directly, to incipient logical thought. Nonetheless, direct perception, rather than logical thought and governing principles, primarily influence this intuitive thinking. Thus, according to Piaget, children under the age of seven cannot engage in truly intellectual activity. Elkind describes the main task of children at this level as the "conquest of the symbol." Level Three, called the concrete operations period, occurs between seven and eleven years of age. During this period, children begin to understand causation, gain a more objective view of the universe, and attain a better understanding of others' perceptions. During this period, children begin to understand why physical events occur. Elkind describes the main task of children at this level as the "mastering [of] classes, relations, and quantities." Level Four, the formal operations period, occurs between eleven and fifteen years of age. During this period, children can imagine the past, present, and future conditions of a problem and create hypotheses about what might logically occur under different conditions. They can engage in pure thought independent of actions they see or perform. They can hypothesize and draw deductions, understand theories, and combine them to solve prob-

18. Jean Piaget, Psychology and Epistemology 5–7 (Arnold Rosin trans., 1971). Piaget wrote many books in his lifetime. Throughout this section, this Article will be drawing on the synthesis of Piaget's work found in Thomas. See Thomas, supra note 16, at 273–318.

22. David Elkind, Egocentrism in Adolescence, 38 Child Dev. 1025, 1026 (1967).

lems. Elkind describes the main task of children at this level as "the conquest of thought." In Piagetian theory, by the age of fifteen, a child's thinking has evolved into a mature state and adult thought exists within the child's repertoire of mental functions.

2. Piaget's Successors: Followers and Detractors, Recent Child Development Theorists

Piaget's influence on child development theory cannot be overstated. Subsequent theorists have often reworked, as well as reacted to, stage theory. The following subpart describes recent developments in the field and the varied perspectives on children's competence for decision making.

Theorists have criticized Piagetian Cognitive Development Theory for a number of reasons.[29] For example, Piaget studied only the average child and paid little attention to the effect the behavior of other people might have on an individual.[30] Further, he studied concepts like space, number, and time that are not likely to be "contextually dynamic."[31] Moreover, Piaget's stages present somewhat inflexible conceptual categories, and do not account for the interaction between each child's unique environmental experiences and a person's particular genetic structure. Thus, his theory does not easily account for differences among children in terms of acquired skills or in terms of when the skills could be acquired. Some theorists have discounted stage theory altogether. Gardner, Scherer, and Tester, for example, believe that adolescent development does not occur in stages, and that skills in different task domains develop at different times.[34]

On the other hand, some researchers have developed theories compatible with those of Piaget. For example, the ecological theory, as developed by Urie Bronfenbrenner, explains to some extent an individual child's deviance from Piaget's predictions and has elucidated how social and physical settings affect development.[35] Notwithstanding these and other criticisms and refinements, Piaget's theories remain an important guide to children's thinking processes and, when modified by the conclusions of later cognitive theorists, provide a framework to understand how children think. Perhaps, as Gary Melton says, "if research contradicts

---

29. See, e.g., Recent Advances in Cognitive–Developmental Theory: Progress in Cognitive Development Research (Charles J. Brainerd ed., 1983) (surveying events in the area of cognitive development theory, including broad empirical and theoretical advances); Elizabeth S. Scott et al., Evaluating Adolescent Decision Making in Legal Contexts, 19 Law & Hum. Behav. 221, 224–26 (1995) * * *.

30. Barry J. Zimmerman, Social Learning Theory: A Contextualist Account of Cognitive Functioning, in Recent Advances in Cognitive–Developmental Theory: Progress in Cognitive Development Research 1, 4 (Charles J. Brainerd ed., 1983); see also

Thomas, supra note 16, at 316 (stating that Piaget "did not offer any careful analysis of how different factors or agents in the social setting influence the attainment of the wide variety of differences in cognitive functions that children exhibit").

31. Zimmerman, supra note 30, at 4.

34. William Gardner et al., Asserting Scientific Authority: Cognitive Development and Adolescent Legal Rights, 44 Am. Psychologist 895, 898 (1989).

35. Urie Bronfenbrenner, The Ecology of Human Development: Experiments by Nature and Design 9–10, 1642 (1979).

the Piagetian hypotheses at all, it generally is in the direction of competence of even younger minors to make personal decisions."[37]

Many experiments, aside from those conducted by Piaget himself, have confirmed his theories. In general, research suggests significant differences between the cognitive abilities of children and adolescents and little or no difference between the cognitive abilities of later adolescents and adults. For example, Weithorn and Campbell studied developmental differences between children and adults when making medical and psychiatric treatment decisions.[38] In considering evidence of choice, reasonable outcome, rational reasons, and understanding as measures of competency, this research team found that the decision making of fourteen-year-olds did not differ from that of adults, but that nine-year-olds demonstrated less competent decision making. Another group of researchers, Nakajima and Hotta, studied how individuals searched for information in decision making.[40] They found that children age twelve and under did not consider more information than adults, but that children age fifteen and older pursued more systematic methods of selection strategies. Yet another researcher, Catherine Lewis, studied five areas of adolescents' decision making: "risk awareness; future orientation; sources of advice for decisions; recognition of 'vested interests'; and revisions of attitudes about adults in light of new information."[42] She found that older adolescents considered risk and future consequences more frequently than younger adolescents; better recognized vested interest on the part of information providers; and more frequently consulted outside experts. Denise Davidson, studying developmental differences in decision making, found that the ability to focus selectively on relevant information and to systematically compare information about alternatives improves between the ages of ten and thirteen.[44] Grisso and Belter concluded that nine-year-olds had difficulty recognizing or protecting their rights, while youths between the ages of fifteen and twenty-one fared better than the nine-year olds, but performed equally with each other in this regard.[45] Catherine Lewis com-

37. Gary B. Melton, Taking *Gault* Seriously: Toward a New Juvenile Court, 68 Neb. L. Rev. 146, 153 (1989).

38. Lois A. Weithorn & Susan B. Campbell, The Competency of Children and Adolescents to Make Informed Treatment Decisions, 53 Child Dev. 1589, 1590—91 (1982).

40. Yoshiaki Nakajima & Miho Hotta, A Developmental Study of Cognitive Processes in Decision Making: Information Searching as a Function of Task Complexity, 64 Psychol. Rep. 67 (1989). Denise Davidson also studied information searching techniques and found that preschool children used incomplete and unsystematic strategies. Denise Davidson, Children's Decision-Making Examined with an Information–Board Procedure, 6 Cognitive Dev. 77, 79 (1991).

42. Catherine C. Lewis, How Adolescents Approach Decisions: Changes over Grades Seven to Twelve and Policy Implications, 52 Child Dev. 538 (1981).

44. Denise Davidson, Developmental Differences in Children's Search of Predecisional Information, 52 J. Experimental Child Psychol. 239, 241 (1991).

45. Ronald W. Belter & Thomas Grisso, Children's Recognition of Rights Violations in Counseling, 15 Prof. Psychol. Res. & Prac. 899, 907–08 (1984); see also Thomas Grisso, Juveniles' Capacities to Waive Miranda Rights: An Empirical Analysis, 68 Cal. L. Rev. 1134, 1143 (1980) (stating that juveniles under fifteen years of age do not "understand the rights of silence and of counsel").

pared decisions by adults and minors concerning pregnancy,[46] and found little difference between adults' and children's knowledge of the law or in their reasoning processes. Finally, Ambuel and Rappaport also studied adolescents' competency in relation to pregnancy decisions.[48] They found that, by middle adolescence, minors can "reason abstractly about hypothetical situations, reason about multiple alternatives and consequences, consider multiple variables, combine variables in more complex ways, and use information systematically." Further they found no difference in legal competency between older minors and adults.

These and other studies consistently demonstrate the general validity of Piagetian theory as reinterpreted by modern stage theorists. The research indicates that children who have yet to enter early adolescence and Piaget's formal operations stage process information differently from both adults and older adolescents. These studies further show that, as a matter of cognitive functioning, adolescents possess a capacity equal to adults for making decisions about significant life events. Piaget believed that adolescents acquired such skills around age fifteen. The research has also revealed that most children (who are not subject to neurological or environmental deficiencies) probably acquire such skills even earlier.

Some critics have questioned the conclusions drawn from these studies. Elizabeth Scott correctly points out that only limited and perhaps tentative empirical data supports the capability of adolescents to make decisions as well as adults.[55] She also questions whether the research findings can be generalized across persons, settings, and times. Notwithstanding these valid observations, observers cannot ignore the consistency reported to date in the research on decision making as it relates to cognitive functioning. Similarly, as the next subpart describes, the research examining adolescent behavior has also added to the debate regarding children's decision-making competence.

3. Adolescent Behavior and Decision–Making Competence

Scott, and her colleagues Reppucci and Woolard, pose another challenge to those who would alter paternalistic policies that deprive children of personal and legal autonomy.[57] They believe that focusing on cognitive functioning directs attention away from other historical bases for paternalistic policies. Using what they term the judgment model, they propose to add adolescent behaviors, which appear to be stage related (i.e., exist in adolescents but disappear as a person grows older), to cognitive functioning in the decision-making equation. These behav-

46. Catherine C. Lewis, A Comparison of Minors' and Adults' Pregnancy Decisions, 50 Am. J. Orthopsychiatry 446 (1980).

48. Bruce Ambuel & Julian Rappaport, Developmental Trends in Adolescents' Psychological and Legal Competence to Consent to Abortion, 16 Law & Hum. Behav. 129 (1992).

55. Elizabeth S. Scott, Judgment and Reasoning in Adolescent Decisionmaking, 37 Vill. L. Rev. 1607, 1632 (1992).

57. Scott, Evaluating Adolescent Decision Making, [19 Law & Hum. Behav. 221], 222–23 (1995).

iors include: (1) susceptibility to peer influence; (2) a tendency to focus on immediate rather than long term consequences; and (3) an inclination to make riskier choices than adults.

Although all adults "intuitively" recognize these adolescent traits, some research suggests that this intuition may be verifiable. Research has demonstrated the effects of peer and parental influence on social comparison and conformity. Berndt's work, however, shows that peer conformity in antisocial and neutral behaviors peaks around the ninth grade.[62] Other research also demonstrates that such influence depends on the context and perhaps on the quality of the relationship. Some research also reveals that adolescents have different perceptions of risk than do adults, but whether attitudes towards risk remain constant across different decision-making contexts is unclear. Other researchers, however, found little difference in the assessment of risk by adults and adolescents since both believe that accidents happen to other people.[66] Research also indicates differences between adolescents and adults regarding temporal perspective. These studies demonstrate that adolescents generally place greater value on short-term consequences while adults place a greater value on longer term consequences. On the other hand, Nurmi found that older adolescents do orient towards the future when they consider issues such as education, occupation, and family.[69] As Scott and her colleagues note, research concerning these concepts require further investigation. Nonetheless, this research brings to the debate on competency a recognition of the environmental and psychosocial influences that affect youths as they pass through adolescence. Piaget's cool calculating fifteen-year-old appears to be subject to some very hot influences during adolescence. Such experiences must be taken into account in a judge's assessment.

4.   Learning and Decision–Making Competence

Cognitive functioning and influence of common adolescent behavioral traits upon it, however, do not present the only issues to consider when assessing decision-making competency. Decision making and judgment, like most other activities in life, constitute learned skills. As Piaget and others have noted, learning involves a dynamic process. Human beings process information by adding new information to their cognitive structures and then reformulating the cognitive structures to account for new, different, and more complex information. Knowledge develops through contextual interactions and increases when an individ-

62. Thomas J. Berndt, Developmental Changes in Conformity to Peers And Parents, 15 Developmental Psychol. 608, 615 (1979). Berndt also found that the quality of the parent-child relationship influenced conformity. See id. at 615–16.

66. Marilyn Jacobs Quadrel et al., Adolescent (In)vulnerability, 48 Am. Psychologist 102, 104–05 (1993). They also found

that adults and teens rely on similar psychological processes when estimating risk. Id. at 112.

69. Jari–Erik Nurmi, How Do Adolescents See Their Future?: A Review of the Development of Future Orientation and Planning, 11 Developmental Rev. 1, 28 (1991).

ual tests it against a set of circumstances, reformulates it in relation to the current experience, and stores it for further use. Each iteration of the testing process refines the knowledge or skill and serves to improve performance if it is used again. Not surprisingly, most people, subject to hereditary limits, improve a skill each time they use it. Improvement of skills upon repeated use applies to making judgments or decisions as well. Decision making involves, after all, a process of making choices among competing courses of action. The decision maker identifies possible options, considers the possible consequences that follow from each option, evaluates the desirability of each, ascertains the likelihood of each consequence, and assesses all of these considerations against some decisional rule, such as maximizing well-being or enjoyment. One would expect that people who have increased their knowledge base through multiple reformulations and refinements acquired through repeated encounters with the information should make better decisions. Early attempts at decision making may produce errors in judgment and bad decisions; but improvement occurs over time and with repeated efforts. Thus, as the sages remind us, experience is a good teacher. Professor Frank Zimring has viewed adolescence as a learner's permit for adulthood, stating that: "If the exercise of independent choice is an essential element of maturity, part of the process of becoming mature is learning to make independent decisions."[79] Improving one's ability to make good decisions requires practice. Thus, the experience of making judgements in context presents as important a factor as cognitive development and the influence of normal adolescent behavior traits in developing good decision-making skills.

* * *

Notes and Questions

1. Based on what you know about children, how accurate do you think Piaget's four levels of development are? How would you assess a child client's ability to understand, communicate, and make decisions? How might social and economic status affect a child's development?

2. *References.* For more comprehensive resources on child development, see William Crain, Theories of Development (3rd ed. 1992) and R. Murray Thomas, Comparing Theories of Child Development (3d ed. 1992). For a review of socio-cognitive literature ("developmental literature that considers how children's understanding of and participation in relationships change as they grow") and critiques of proposed models of child client-lawyer relationships, see Emily Buss, Confronting Developmental Barriers to Empowerment of Child Clients, 84 Cornell L. Rev. 895 (1999). For consideration of children's competence in various legal contexts, see Children's Competence to Consent (Gary B. Melton, Gerald P. Koocher and Michael J. Saks, eds., 1983).

79. [Franklin E. Zimring, The Changing   Legal World of Adolescence at 91 (1982).]

B. Interviewing Children

Nancy W. Perry and Larry L. Teply, Interviewing,
Counseling, and In–Court Examination of
Children: Practical Approaches

18 Creighton L. Rev. 1369, 1375–80 (1985).

* * *

In any interview situation, a variety of circumstances and factors
will promote effective communication; at the same time, others may
hinder it. The lawyer's principal communication tasks in an interview
are to minimize or avoid these situations that block, mislead, and
discourage communication and to utilize or stress those skills that
facilitate, encourage, and motivate. In this regard, lawyers must take
special care in interviews with children. First, children ordinarily are not
the initiators of the interview or the attorney-client relationship; thus,
they are more likely to be involuntary participants. Second, they may
have fundamental misconceptions about the purpose of the interview
and the role of the attorney in the legal process. Third, they may fail to
understand a lawyer's questions because their cognitive and conceptual
skills are not fully developed. Fourth, for the same reasons, they may be
unable to express themselves clearly or interpret facts properly. Fifth,
because of their relative immaturity and inexperience, they may be less
able to deal with emotional blocks or social pressures. Failure to be
sensitive to these considerations and to adjust an interview to take them
into account can cause a child to decide that, on balance, it is not
worthwhile to communicate; further, it can lead to inaccuracies or
distortions in the information or opinions elicited; and ultimately it can
cause inappropriate advice and unfortunate legal determinations.

A. OPENING THE INTERVIEW, DEALING WITH MISCONCEPTIONS, AND ESTABLISHING A
GOOD WORKING RELATIONSHIP

It often is said that it is important "to get off on the right foot."
This cliché summarizes a significant aspect of an interview with a child
in legal setting. Often the beginning not only will affect the entire course
of the interview, but also it will be one of the key elements in setting the
long-term relationship between the attorney and the child. As in any
interview, the goal at the outset of the interview is to put the interviewee at ease and to establish a good working relationship. To do so requires
an awareness of the differences between children and adults as interviewees and an effort to modify the interview to take into account those
differences.

One important difference is the lack of "common ground" between
the attorney and the child. Attorneys often engage in "small talk" at the
outset of an interview, which has the laudable effect of helping the
interviewee to relax and become used to talking with the attorney.
Concurrently, it aids in building rapport. Generally speaking, it is easy
for attorneys to engage in such conversations with other adults because

the topics arise naturally—the weather, sports, family, job, etc. But special care must be taken in selecting the topic for such conversations with children, because, as Rich suggests, "[i]f an adult's concept of the child's world is determined mainly by the points at which that world impinges on the adult world, [the interviewer] is liable to bring up the wrong topics."[a] For example, many adults unwittingly begin conversations with children by asking how they are doing at school. Another common variant is how they like school. Rich suggests that most children do not want to talk about school and that it is better to open the conversation with questions about their leisure activities or hobbies. In this regard, it is useful for the attorney to find out some information about the child's leisure activities before the interview so that the attorney can direct the opening discussion to these activities. By listening carefully to what the child says, the attorney helps to build the child's self-confidence and shows that the attorney is interested in what the child has to say.

Freeman and Weihofen[b] also suggest that the attorney should not be unduly friendly with children at the outset of the interview because it may be disconcerting, especially when it is unexpected. Also it is best to avoid conduct which children might view as disrespectful, such as addressing them by a nickname without asking them what they like to be called.

In the beginning stage of the interview, a structural guide should be given that suggests in broad terms how the lawyer sees the interview progressing. For example, the lawyer might explain that the lawyer would like the child to describe certain events. Then the child will be asked some questions by the lawyer; after that, (if it is relevant) they will discuss how they can arrive at some solutions or the interview will be over. In addition, the child should be given a chance to give input, which may be accomplished by the attorney asking, "Is that okay?" or the like. It also provides an early opportunity to deal with any apparent hostility.

Another important difference between interviewing children and adults is the child's limited knowledge of the law, the legal process, and the role of an attorney within that process. Through experience, common knowledge, and a mature cognitive system, adults ordinarily realize the "representative" function of an attorney: someone is the attorney's client, to whom the attorney owes undivided loyalty and who the attorney is obligated to represent zealously. In contrast, children may have only a vague understanding of the lawyer's position in the legal system. They have no "scorecard" to help them understand the intertwining roles of private attorney, policeman, prosecutor and judge. It is even more confusing to them to attempt to comprehend the lawyer's multiple roles as defender, facilitator, negotiator, and counselor. Thus, if

a. J. Rich, Interviewing Children and Adolescents (1968).

b. H. Freeman and J. Weihofen, Clinical Law Training (1972).

they are the accused, they will not fully comprehend the meaning and significance of the advocate on their behalf in the legal system.

It is, therefore, useful to explain in concrete terms, early in the interview, what the relationship of the attorney is to the child and why the interview is being conducted.* * *

This general approach has several benefits. First, it performs a socially valuable educational function. Second, it helps to build rapport to the extent that it conveys that the attorney is on "their side" (if that is the case). Third, by making it clear what the general purpose of the interview is, such as finding out information, learning their opinion, etc., it may help relieve some anxiety, at least that which is based upon fear of the unknown. Fourth, it may clear up some misconceptions or counteract misinformation given to the child, assuming the child believes the attorney. Finally, it will facilitate a better understanding of what the attorney can do for the child or why the attorney needs the child's help, which thus offers some degree of motivation to cooperate.

In the course of this explanation, the attorney may include an assurance of confidentiality—if the child is the client. This assurance may encourage children to speak more freely, especially if they have some reason to be apprehensive (which usually is the case when they are accused of some wrongdoing). It probably should be omitted, however, when they have no reason to be apprehensive or, of course, when confidentiality obligations do not apply (e.g., when they are witnesses).

Another important issue in interviewing children as opposed to adults is the general difficulty children have in assuming an active "client" role. Instead, they are likely to remain in the natural "child" role. To compound the problem, attorneys also have a natural tendency to assume the "parent" role rather than that of "counselor." In this skewed relationship, the "parent" (attorney) assesses, decides, judges, directs and manipulates. The "child" (client), on the other hand, is passive, submissive, and docile. As in school, children are expected to listen and obey rather than retaining their independence, viewing the attorney as one who works for them, and considering themselves as "equals," as would an adult.

For most legal interviewing and counseling purposes, a parent-child relationship will be unproductive. It supplies only a low level of motivation to cooperate. Furthermore, "decisions" reached without a collaborative effort are judgments that reflect the attorney's values, which are not necessarily the same as the child's. Such decisions also are less likely to be ones that the child will be satisfied with or that the child will follow in the long-run.

In this regard, it is important to remember that the success of the interview may depend upon the manner in which attorneys verbally approach children. When speaking with children, adults have a tendency to change their facial expressions (opening the eyes wide and raising the eyebrows), their voices (elevating pitch and lowering volume), and the content of their messages (sometimes even using "baby-talk"). A much more successful and less demeaning approach is to maintain an adult manner while simplifying the language and content of the verbal message.

* * *

Notes and Questions

1. How would the child's age affect the way you structure an interview? Imagine that you were appointed to represent two–year–old Victoria in Michael H. v. Gerald D. (Chapter 2 at 134) or sixteen–year–old Thomas C. in In re Thomas C. (Chapter 2 at 195). What information would you want to elicit from them and how would you do it?

2. *Race, ethnicity, culture and class.* In addition to the communication barriers described in the article, race, ethnicity, culture and class can cause substantial communication problems as well. The attorney needs to be aware of these differences and develop a "facility in managing conversations" across these barriers. Michael L. Lindsay, Ethical Issues in Interviewing, Counseling, and the Use of Psychological Data with Child and Adolescent Clients, 64 Fordham L. Rev. 2035, 2038 (1996).

3. *References.* Anne Graffam Walker, Handbook on Questioning Children: A Linguistic Perspective (1994); John Rich, Interviewing Children and Adolescents (1968). For a videotape of a lawyer interviewing a child client in a protective proceeding, see Sarah H. Ramsey, Richard E. Ellison, and Kirk Hazen, Child Abuse and Neglect: The Attorney's Role (1990).

C. Children as Witnesses

Representatives for children may need to consider their clients' role as witnesses in proceedings. Will the children be found competent to testify? Are children more or less truthful or accurate than adults? This section provides an overview of these issues. (Additional material about children as witnesses, including the problem of the trauma of testifying, appears in Chapter 6, Criminal Abuse and Neglect.)

1. Competency To Testify

LUCY S. MCGOUGH, CHILD WITNESSES: FRAGILE VOICES IN THE AMERICAN LEGAL SYSTEM 97–99 (1994)

* * *

DETERMINING THE COMPETENCY OF THE CHILD WITNESS

English common law disqualified some persons from giving testimony: infants, witnesses with a pecuniary interest in the outcome of the case, and the spouse of a party. Today in all American jurisdictions except Massachusetts courts can permit any person to provide evidence. The task of any witness in a legal proceeding is to give an accurate account of an accurate perception of a past event. A commitment to tell the truth is meaningless unless the witness could originally form an accurate perception of the observed event and then faithfully reports that perception. So, too, perceptual and memorial accuracy are meaningless unless the witness also agrees to speak truthfully when summoned to the stand. Historically, the law has used the voir dire, or preliminary examination, as a screening device to test both the cognitive skills and the truthfulness of a witness. Once that hurdle is crossed, the law then depends primarily upon rigorous cross-examination to dislodge any misperception or deceit.

Determination of a witness's "competency" have historically been made according to what social scientists call a "dichotomous variable"–that is, either a witness possesses a full complement of relevant cognitive and social skills or the witness lacks one or more of them altogether. Competency determinations are similar to sanity assessments in criminal trials, which ask: Is the accused sane (and thus fully accountable for the offense) or is he or she insane (and hence excused from criminal sanction)? Following such an all-or-nothing policy, the rules of evidence for the federal court and the courts of all states have now abandoned the requirement of any threshold showing of competency for *adult* trial witnesses. This means that any adult witness can give testimony, although the opposing party may, in rebuttal, challenge the witness's credibility or reliability. As a result, the adult witness's testimony can be weakened or discounted altogether by the finder of fact.

The Federal Rules of Evidence draw no distinction between adult and child witnesses, and thus, any child witness may testify without a preliminary showing of competence. However, in spite of the substantial regularizing influence of the Federal Rules of Evidence, only slightly more than a third of the states have followed the "no competency inquiry" of the federal rules's model insofar as child witnesses are concerned. Thirty-six American jurisdictions retain either an "oath understanding" or a "full inquiry" preliminary examination when a child is offered as a witness. Thus, whether children should be singled out for such a special showing of testimonial capability remains a lively topic of legal debate.

In most states that retain the competency voir dire for children, the counsel who offers the child as a witness conducts the examination, eliciting relevant information by posing questions to the child. The skills thought relevant were formulated by Wigmore: the witness must demonstrate a capacity for observation, for recollection, and for communication. Communication capacity, in turn, is composed of two elements: an ability to understand and respond intelligently to questions, and a sense of "moral responsibility," defined as a "consciousness of the duty to speak the truth" (2 Wigmore 1979, § 506, 713). The child is then subject to cross-examination by counsel for the adverse party.

In these states, the trial judge plays a limited role as the arbiter of any objections arising out of the child's examination and as the decision-maker on the ultimate issue of the child's competency to testify in the trial. This voir dire always takes place outside the presence of any jury, since its purpose is to decide whether the child possesses the ability to provide truthful, accurate information or might instead provide misleading information. In all jurisdictions, the court may also pose questions to the child, but the exploration of competency is usually left to the adversarial process of examination and cross examination.

At least in criminal prosecutions, constitutional problems would arise if the responsibility for conducting the voir dire were to be shifted from trial lawyers to the court. In *Kentucky v. Stincer* (1987), the trial court conducted its own competency examinations of two child witnesses in an in-chambers hearing from which the defendant had been excluded, though his lawyer was present. The U.S. Supreme Court held that an accused must be afforded the right to conduct a full and complete cross-examination of a witness's competency in order to effectuate the commands of the Confrontation Clause of the Sixth Amendment and the Due Process Clause of the Fourteenth Amendment. *Stincer* does not require that a competency voir dire be conducted; these constitutional guarantees may be satisfied by postponed cross-examination on competency issues at trial. However, because according to *Stincer*, the due process clause is implicated by competency determinations, the competency screening function can probably be fulfilled only by extending the opportunity for cross-examination in both civil and criminal cases.

* * *

PEOPLE v. MITCHELL

Illinois Court of Appeals, 1991.
576 N.E.2d 78.

* * *

Prior to trial, the court held a competency hearing for R.J.M. [who was about four at the time of the alleged assault].* * * During the competency hearing, R.J.M. testified that he was five years of age and lived in a brown house on Chicago Road with Keith, his mom and younger brother, two-year-old J.R.M. R.J.M. also testified that he had a sister named J.S.M. When the judge asked R.J.M., "Do you promise . . . to tell the truth, and nothing but the truth, so help you God?" he responded, "[y]eah, I do."

When asked what it means to tell the truth, R.J.M. indicated that it meant not to tell a lie. R.J.M. testified that the assistant State's Attorney was wearing a brown jacket and that it would be a lie to call it red. R.J.M. further demonstrated his understanding of the difference between the truth and a lie when asked about the color of a book. R.J.M. testified that the fact that the book was green was a truth and it would be a lie to say that it was red, yellow or pink. R.J.M. further testified that although he had met with the assistant State's Attorney on numerous occasions, he was never told by the prosecutor or his mother to say certain things. R.J.M. testified that both his mother and the assistant

State's Attorney told him to tell the judge the truth. R.J.M. counted to 19 and recited his alphabet through the letter p. R.J.M. also demonstrated his understanding of shapes by drawing a square, triangle, rectangle and a circle. The prosecutor questioned R.J.M. regarding the events of the day of the alleged assault and R.J.M. demonstrated that he recalled the events leading up to the assault. At the conclusion of the hearing, the trial court found R.J.M. competent to testify.

The criteria for determining whether a child is competent to testify in court are whether the witness is sufficiently mature (1) to receive correct impressions by his senses; (2) to recollect these impressions; (3) to understand questions and narrate answers intelligently; and (4) to appreciate the moral duty to tell the truth. Further, it is not necessary for the child to give perfect answers to questions asked during the competency determination or at trial to be deemed a competent witness. Once the court has determined that the minor is competent to testify, any confusion or contradiction in later testimony only goes to credibility as a witness, not competency to testify.

Defendant argues that R.J.M. made many illogical and unresponsive statements in response to simple questions and that therefore he was incompetent to testify. While R.J.M. did make some unresponsive remarks to questions posed, he also demonstrated the typical impatience of a five-year-old by asking when the questioning was going to be over, stating that he was hungry, asking when the restaurant would be open and asking at one point to be excused so that he could go to the bathroom. However, despite these digressions during questioning, R.J.M. demonstrated in a variety of ways that he knew the difference between the truth and a lie. R.J.M. testified that to tell the truth meant not to tell a lie. In addition, R.J.M. demonstrated the ability to receive correct impressions from his senses and recall these impressions when he described the color of a book and the prosecutor's coat jacket as well as when he counted the number of pencils in the prosecutor's pocket. In addition, R.J.M. recited his alphabet and drew various geometric shapes. In sum, R.J.M. adequately demonstrated that he was competent to testify. We therefore conclude that the trial court did not err in ruling that R.J.M. was competent to testify in this matter.

* * *

Notes and Questions

1. Do you think that R.J.M. was competent to testify? Do you think he understood the oath?

2. *A child's general competency.* States traditionally determined by age a child's competency to testify. Older children (usually above the age of about twelve) were presumptively competent; particularly young children (usually below the age of about seven) were incompetent; children in the middle age range were presumptively incompetent. What does child development research indicate about children's capacities in these age groups? Where the child is of an age that renders him presumptively incompetent under the

statute, the court may hold a competency hearing to make a particularized determination.

In the past two decades, a number of states have enacted statutes making even the youngest children at least presumptively competent to testify in sex abuse prosecutions, provided the child can communicate. A number of statutes now go a step further, conferring competency as a matter of law on any child sex abuse victim, no matter how young. Connecticut's competency statute, for example, provides that "any child who is a victim of assault, sexual assault or abuse shall be competent to testify without prior qualification. The weight to be given the evidence and the credibility of the witness shall be for the determination of the trier of fact." Conn. Gen. Stat. § 5486h.

With children's competency not specifically regulated by the Federal Rules of Evidence, Congress in 1990 enacted 18 U.S.C. § 3509(c), which governs federal court testimony of children who are victims of physical, emotional or sexual abuse; children who are victims of child exploitation (child pornography or child prostitution), or children who witness a crime against another person. The statute presumes that children are competent, and authorizes competency hearings only for a compelling reason other than age; any such hearing must be outside the jury's presence, with a guardian ad litem appearing for the child if necessary.

3. *Understanding the oath.* Some courts inquire about the child's understanding of the oath or affirmation that the child gives for sworn testimony. Professor McGough found that "[w]hen using the oath understanding test, most courts seek to determine if the child appreciates the difference between a true and a false statement and if he or she realizes that lying brings on punishment of some sort, even if only of the earthly variety. A child witness's response is deemed sufficient if he or she indicates that lying means not going to heaven or 'I be bad'; that 'It's good to tell the truth'; or that 'I'd get a whipping.' " Child Witnesses, supra at 101.

4. *Unsworn testimony.* Unsworn testimony may also be allowed. Section 60.20 of New York's criminal procedure law, for example, provides:

Every witness more than twelve years old may testify only under oath unless the court is satisfied that such witness cannot, as a result of mental disease or defect, understand the nature of an oath. A child less than twelve years old may not testify under oath unless the court is satisfied that he understands the nature of an oath. If the court is not so satisfied, such child or such witness over twelve years old who cannot, as a result of mental disease or defect, understand the nature of an oath may nevertheless be permitted to give unsworn evidence if the court is satisfied that the witness possess sufficient intelligence and capacity to justify the reception thereof. N.Y.C.P.L.R. Sec 60.20(1)(2).

2. *Accuracy*

To determine how competent children are as witnesses, Professor McGough reviewed social science studies of children and adults related to cognitive capability, the effect of confabulation and trauma, memory, susceptibility and conscious deception. She found that children's performance is similar to adults' in many areas, but that children under six are less able to describe past events accurately without cues and are more susceptible to suggestion. To reduce the effect of these problems, she recommends that interviews with children be videotaped and further, that interviews be conducted by a trained, neutral interviewer soon after the event at issue.

A significant source of inaccurate testimony from children comes from suggestive interviews. For a comprehensive review of social science research on interviewing children with recommendations for more accurate interviewing, see Stephen J. Ceci and Maggie Bruck, Jeopardy in the Courtroom: A Scientific Analysis of Children's Testimony (1995); Debra A. Poole and Michael E. Lamb, Investigative Interviews of Children (1998). For a critique of research that suggests that children are likely to make false allegations of sexual abuse, see Thomas D. Lyon, The New Wave in Children's Suggestibility Research: A Critique, 84 Cornell L. Rev. 1004 (1999).

D. The Child's Right to Bring Suit

Because minors are not considered capable of bringing or defending a lawsuit in their own names, they must have adults represent them. Traditionally a next friend, or prochein ami, was appointed to represent the minor plaintiff and a guardian ad litem was appointed to represent a minor defendant. The distinction between these terms frequently has not been maintained, however, and their meaning, particularly of the term "guardian ad litem", has become ambiguous. "Guardian ad litem" can refer to the child's attornet or to a non-attorney representative. The term also refers to an attorney serving both as the representative and attorney for the child without regard to whether the child is a plaintiff, a defendant, or the subject of an action such as an abuse and neglect proceeding. The next case made headlines and was characterized as a child trying to "divorce" his parents, in part because he tried to sue in his own name, rather than through a representative.

KINGSLEY v. KINGSLEY

District Court of Appeal of Florida, 1993.
623 So.2d 780.

DIAMANTIS, JUDGE.

Rachel Kingsley, the natural mother of Gregory, a minor child, appeals the trial court's final orders terminating her parental rights based upon findings of abandonment and neglect, and granting the petition for adoption filed by Gregory's foster parents, George and Elizabeth Russ.[1] * * *

On June 25, 1992, Gregory, then 11 years of age, filed in the juvenile division of the circuit court a petition for termination of the parental

---

1. Because all interested parties have voluntarily appeared in the public arena and made their names known, and because the trial court proceedings were televised, the names of the parties have become part of the public domain and are used in this opinion.

rights of his natural parents. He separately filed, in the civil division of the circuit court, a complaint for declaration of rights and adoption by his foster parents. This adoption was later transferred to the juvenile division by court order. On July 21, 1992, the trial court ruled that Gregory, as a natural person who had knowledge of the facts alleged, had standing to initiate the action for termination of parental rights. In that order, the trial court implicitly accorded Gregory capacity to file the petition although he was an unemancipated minor. Prior to entering this order, the trial court, noting that there was a distinction between the roles of guardian ad litem and attorney ad litem, appointed one of Gregory's attorneys, Jerri A. Blair, as his attorney ad litem.[2] The trial court made no ruling concerning Gregory's standing to file the adoption petition; however, Gregory's foster parents filed a petition for adoption on September 3, 1992, with the written consent of Gregory and Gregory's natural father.[3] Between August 11, 1992, and September 11, 1992, four additional petitions for termination of parental rights were filed on behalf of Gregory: the August 11, 1992, petition by George Russ, the foster father; the August 25, 1992, petition by Catherine A. Tucker, Gregory's guardian ad litem; the September 10, 1992, petition by the Department of Health and Rehabilitative Services (HRS); and the September 11, 1992, petition by Elizabeth Russ, the foster mother. On September 17, 1992, Gregory filed an amended petition for termination of parental rights, and on September 18, 1992, Gregory's foster family filed a notice that its members were joining in, and adopting, Gregory's amended petition for termination of parental rights.

* * *

1. CAPACITY

Rachel contends that the trial court erred in holding that Gregory has the capacity to bring a termination of parental rights proceeding in his own right. Specifically, Rachel argues that the disability of nonage prevents a minor from initiating or maintaining an action for termination of parental rights. We agree.

Capacity to sue means the absence of a legal disability which would deprive a party of the right to come into court.

In Earls v. King, 785 S.W.2d 741 (Mo.Ct.App.1990), the court succinctly set forth the legal effect of the concept of capacity to sue:

Capacity to sue is the right to come into court which exists if one is free of general disability, such as infancy or insanity. Nearly all adults have capacity to sue.

Courts historically have recognized that unemancipated minors do not have the legal capacity to initiate legal proceedings in their own

---

2. Gregory's foster father, George Russ, later became an additional attorney of record for Gregory. Because the order appointing an attorney ad litem is not challenged on appeal, we do not decide the issue of the propriety of such appointment in a termination of parental rights proceeding.

3. Gregory's natural father died during the pendency of this appeal.

names. This historic concept is incorporated into Florida Rule of Civil Procedure 1.210(b), which provides as follows:

* * *

(b) Infants or Incompetent Persons. When an infant or incompetent person has a representative, such as a guardian or other like fiduciary, the representative may sue or defend on behalf of the infant or incompetent person. An infant or incompetent person who does not have a duly appointed representative may sue by next friend or by a guardian ad litem. The court shall appoint a guardian ad litem for an infant or incompetent person not otherwise represented in an action or shall make such other order as it deems proper for the protection of the infant or incompetent person.

* * *

This disability of nonage has been described as procedural, rather than jurisdictional, in character because if a minor mistakenly brings an action in his own name such defect can be cured by the subsequent appointment of a next friend or guardian ad litem. Thus, the concept of capacity determines the procedure which a minor must invoke in order to pursue a cause of action.

* * *

As a general rule, states "may require a minor to wait until the age of majority before being permitted to exercise legal rights independently." Bellotti v. Baird (1979). Objective criteria, such as age limits, although inevitably arbitrary, are not unconstitutional unless they unduly burden the minor's pursuit of a fundamental right. Gregory's lack of capacity due to nonage is a procedural, not substantive, impediment which minimally restricts his right to participate as a party in proceedings brought to terminate the parental rights of his natural parents; therefore, we conclude that this procedural requirement does not unduly burden a child's fundamental liberty interest to be "free of physical and emotional violence at the hands of his . . . most trusted caretaker."

Although we conclude that the trial court erred in allowing Gregory to file the petition in his own name because Gregory lacked the requisite legal capacity, this error was rendered harmless by the fact that separate petitions for termination of parental rights were filed on behalf of Gregory by the foster father, the guardian ad litem, HRS, and the foster mother.

* * *

Notes and Questions

1. *Questions about* Kingsley. (a) Why did the trial court appoint an "attorney ad litem" when Gregory already had a guardian ad litem? In footnote four, the court stated, "[I]nexplicably, Jerri A. Blair, Gregory's attorney and attorney ad litem, did not file a petition on behalf of Gregory." If you were

Gregory K.'s attorney, would you have filed a petition for termination of parental rights on his behalf? (b) What was the basis for the appellate court's decision that Gregory did not have capacity to file a termination of parental rights petition? If Gregory were 13 or 15 would the court have reached a different result? (c) If you were appointed to represent an 11–year–old in Gregory's situation, what assumptions would you have made about his capacity based on child development research? What concerns would you have about your initial interview with him? (d) Whose authority is protected by the rule that children may not initiate legal proceedings in their own names?

2. *Aftermath.* Three years after Gregory K. filed his petition, his foster parents adopted him. His story, complete with excerpts from his testimony at the hearing to terminate his mother's parental rights, is in a videorecording, The Boy Who Divorced his Parents: The Parental Rights Case of Gregory K., Courtroom Television Network, 1992.

In another highly publicized case, a Florida court did allow a child to sue in her own name. The plaintiff was Kimberly Mays, who was switched at birth in the hospital and reared by a couple who were not biologically related to her. She sued to end all contact with her biological parents. Twigg v. Mays, 1993 WL 330624 (Fla.Cir.Ct.1993).

3. *Federal Rules of Civil Procedure.* Rule 17(c) of the Federal Rules of Civil Procedure is substantially the same as the Florida Rule of Civil Procedure 1.210(b) quoted in *Kingsley.* A number of decisions interpreting Rule 17(c) have emphasized the importance of protecting the child's interests. See, e.g., M.K. v. Harter, 716 F.Supp. 1333 (E.D.Cal.1989) ("[T]he court is under a legal duty to inquire into the circumstances to determine if the minor is adequately represented."); Geddes v. Cessna Aircraft Co., 881 F.Supp. 94 (E.D.N.Y.1995)(guardian ad litem needed because of conflict of interest between parent and child in wrongful death action, even though appointment of guardian ad litem might cause family disharmony and guardian ad litem's fees would diminish the amount of the award).

4. *Service of process on children.* Service of process on a child in a federal judicial district shall be made in accordance with the law of the state in which service is made. Fed. R. Civ. P. 4(g). State procedural laws typically require service on the child's parent, guardian or guardian ad litem. Service on the child may or may not also be required. See, e.g., Fla. Stat.Ann. § 48.041; Ga. Code Ann. § 9–11–4. A minor is not permitted to waive service of process under the waiver procedure established in 1993. Fed. R. Civ. P. 4(d)(2).

5. *Default.* Under Fed. R. Civ. P. 55(b)(1), the clerk of the federal court may not enter a default judgment for any monetary relief against a minor who has failed to appear in the action. Under Fed. R. Civ. P. 55 (b)(2), a court may enter a default judgment against a child if the child's representative has appeared in the action. What purposes do these rules seek to achieve?

6. *Domicile.* Domicile is the place of a person's true, fixed, and permanent home. The domicile concept helps define not only judicial jurisdiction, but also substantive rights and obligations.

Because an unemancipated child lacks capacity to acquire a domicile of choice, a child's domicile is usually the domicile of one or both parents. See, e.g., Mississippi Band of Choctaw Indians v. Holyfield, 490 U.S. 30 (1989). Section 22 of the Restatement (Second) of Conflicts of Laws, summarizes a number of principles concerning children's domiciles, including these:

(a) A child born in wedlock is assigned the father's domicile when the child lives with the father in the same home. At birth, the child takes the father's domicile; if the father's domicile changes, the child takes the father's new domicile. Id. comment a.

The child takes the mother's domicile, however, if the child is born out of wedlock, or born after the father's death without appointment of a guardian of the child's person; the child's domicile would then follow the mother's, regardless of whether the child lives with the mother. Holyfield, supra, 490 U.S. at 48.

(b) After parents separate or divorce, the child's domicile is the domicile of the parent with lawful custody. If custody has not been fixed, the child's domicile is the domicile of the parent with whom the child lives or (if the child lives with neither parent) the domicile of the living father. On the death of the parent with lawful custody or the parent with whom the child has been living, the child's domicile shifts to that of the other parent. Restatement, supra comment d.

(c) If a father but not the mother abandons the child, the child takes the mother's domicile. If the mother but not the father abandons the child, the child takes the father's domicile. A child abandoned by both parents generally retains the domicile of the latter abandoning parent; a child abandoned by both parents simultaneously retains the father's domicile at the time of abandonment. Id. comment e.

(d) Because adoption extinguishes the natural parent-child relationship and creates a parent-child relationship with the adoptive parents, an adopted child assumes the adoptive parents' domicile at the moment of adoption. The child's domicile thereafter follows the adoptive parents' and is determined according to the rules for determining the domicile of a child born in wedlock. Id. comment g.

These principles do not apply to emancipated children, who have capacity to establish a domicile. The parent has no power to control an emancipated child's domicile, and the emancipated child's domicile is not changed merely because the parent's domicile changes. Id. comment f. See generally Eugene F. Scoles and Peter Hay, Conflict of Laws §§ 4.37–4.44 (2d ed. 1992).

SECTION 3. THE ROLE OF THE CHILD'S COUNSEL

When should children have legal counsel and what is counsel's role? The answers to these questions are disputed, evolving, and complex. Access to counsel and understanding of role vary by the type of case, the jurisdiction, and the preferences and predilections of judges and attorneys.

A. *Children's Ability to Advise Counsel*

How should lawyers for children relate to their clients? Some lawyers pay little or no attention to their child client, and others feel the child should be treated like an adult client as much as possible. Some lawyers feel that they should represent what they think is best for the child client, and others feel they should represent what the client wants. Some believe the type of proceeding or the age of the child determines the role. Underlying this uncertainty is concern about the child client's capacity, frequently coupled with confusion about the purpose of representation in a particular case.

These questions are not resolved by the major professional codes, the American Bar Association Model Rules of Professional Conduct, and its predecessor, the Model Code of Professional Responsibility (which is still the basis for a number of state ethics codes). The Model Rules, for example, provide that "when a client's ability to make adequately considered decisions in connection with the representation is impaired, whether because of minority, mental disability, or for some other reason, the lawyer shall, as far as reasonably possible, maintain a normal client-lawyer relationship with the client." Rule 1.14(a). The Rules are silent, however, about what standard should be used to judge the client's decision-making ability.

Although there is no consensus about what approach the child's lawyer should take, particularly in abuse and neglect cases, the variety of opinions provides a window for examining our views about children and children's rights. The following article excerpts are but a sampling of the diverse views on this issue. One author recommends that the lawyer for the young child should enforce the child's legal rights, without extensive involvement of the client. Another argues that the purpose of representation should be empowerment of the child client. The third recommends that the attorney represent what the child wants when the child is capable of making a considered decision and recommends that capacity be assessed in relation to the issue being considered. The fourth believes all child clients can contribute something to their representation.

MARTIN GUGGENHEIM, A PARADIGM FOR DETERMINING THE ROLE OF COUNSEL FOR CHILDREN

64 Fordham L. Rev. 1399, 1420–21, 1432–33 (1996).

* * *

A common error commentators make in divining the purpose of counsel is unduly concentrating on the rule that lawyers for adults must allow their clients to set the objectives of representation. Although this rule is certainly important, what is even more important is its underlying policy. As we have seen, the reason an adult's lawyer must let the adult set the objectives has little to do with an inherent aspect of lawyering. Instead, it has everything to do with the legal rights and powers adults possess.

A lawyer's first role is to enforce and advance her clients' legal rights. Everything else is secondary to this. When clients such as unimpaired adults or pregnant minors have autonomy rights to control their own destiny, lawyers are obliged to let them set the objectives of the case. Moreover, in such circumstances, lawyers are not only permitted, but required, to forcefully advocate for the results chosen by their clients. In dramatic contrast, however, when clients do not have autonomy rights (such as young children in most, but not all situations), lawyers should not allow their clients to set the objectives.

For these reasons, when determining the role of counsel for children it is essential to engage in a careful study of the legal rights and powers children enjoy in the particular subject matter implicated by the proceeding. The role of counsel for young children necessarily will vary across a variety of legal matters. This is because the role of counsel is not developed in a vacuum. What a lawyer for a young child must or may do will depend directly on the rights of the young child in the particular matter involved. Because lawyers, above all else, are the enforcers of their client's rights, the principal task when determining counsel's role for young children is to examine the relevant legislation and case law in the particular subject area. Once those rights have been identified, the only remaining inquiry is to determine the most effective way to enforce them.

* * *

* * * I argue that counsel's principal objective should be to become the child client's law enforcer (that is, the precise, uniform service counsel performs when she carries out the instructions of a client authorized by law to set objectives for a matter). The law enforcer role is not furthered, however, when lawyers empower children to set the objectives for a case when the relevant substantive law has disempowered them.

In those cases in which lawyers are not constrained by law, this Article argues that the principle of being law enforcer is better served by assisting the judge to decide the case correctly with a minimum of involvement by the child. The only way to accomplish this and perform a consistent role is for the lawyer to uncover relevant facts that place the judge in the best position to decide the case and to protect the child from harm that may result from the litigation itself. When lawyers perform this role, the danger that the case will be contaminated by the lawyer's values are minimized. At the same time, the lawyer will have performed a role that is most likely to increase the prospects that a child's rights will be advanced.

* * *

KATHERINE HUNT FEDERLE, THE ETHICS OF EMPOWERMENT: RETHINKING THE ROLE OF LAWYERS IN INTERVIEWING AND COUNSELING THE CHILD CLIENT

64 Fordham L. Rev. 1655, 1656, 1693–96 (1996).

* * *

This emphasis on capacity has structured much of our discussion about children's rights and ethical issues in interviewing and counseling child clients. The dominant lawyering paradigms, for example, center on issues of client autonomy and lawyer independence, on who gets to make decisions about the case. These models implicitly reflect rights constructs that, ultimately, inform the lawyer about what she may or may not do for the client. Moreover, rights theories themselves rest on some under-lying notion about capacity as a prerequisite to having and exercising rights. But because children are not seen as capable, autonomous beings, much of our rights talk, and our lawyering, cannot accommodate chil-dren. What is needed is a new way of thinking about rights and lawyering that will account for children as rights holders.

* * *

I think that a coherent account of rights must be premised upon notions of power. Power structures the interactions between and among individuals and the state. It is power that permits an individual to assert a claim against another and power that permits the enforcement of that claim. It is through the exercise of that power that individuals are recognized by others as worthy and their objectives as having value. Moreover, power creates access by claiming the attention and respect of others.

* * *

By moving our rights talk away from notions of capacity and towards conceptions of power, we may find it easier to reconceptualize a paradigm of lawyering. From within a coherent account of rights, it is the powerlessness of the individual, rather than her capacity to make an intelligent or reasoned decision, that is determinative of her status as a rights holder. Moreover, the rights of the powerless do not promote their dependent status. Consequently, lawyering paradigms that turn on the competency of the decision maker cannot adequately account for those individuals who may lack the requisite capabilities. But if rights flow to the powerless, then a lawyering paradigm that facilitates the recognition of the rights of the marginalized has coherence.

From this perspective, client empowerment is the central value of a lawyering model. The lawyer must recognize that existing legal struc-tures, as well as the attorney-client relationship itself, may disempower the client. By freeing the client from subordinating lawyering practices, the attorney enhances the client's participation in the lawyer-client relationship. The attorney has an ethical obligation to ensure that the client has the power to make decisions about her case and to determine the true objectives of her representation. Moreover, client empowerment encourages a more meaningful expression of the client's goals and may foster a true collaboration with the lawyer.

This approach to lawyering also permits the attorney to challenge dominant visions of her client's abilities. For example, claims by powerful elites that an individual lacks rights holder status because of her incompetencies should be viewed skeptically. By seeing relationships in terms of dominance and subordination, however, a coherent account of rights may reveal the ways in which powerful elites oppress and marginalize. Rights, therefore, have value because they allow challenges to these hierarchies and force these elites to hear the claims of those without power. The advantage of seeing rights in this way is to recognize the rights claims of all those, including children, who have been oppressed.

The lawyer for the child, therefore, must be aware of the ways in which she, as an adult, may dominate her child client. Because children are powerless, they do not expect adults to treat them with respect or to listen to their opinions. They are treated as passive and subordinate beings who must follow the instructions of an older and wiser adult. The lawyer, therefore, must be cognizant of the effect she may have on her client and must take steps to facilitate the client's empowerment in the relationship. By acknowledging that the association between attorney and child is an unequal power relationship, the lawyer begins the process of client empowerment.

Interviewing and counseling are effective mechanisms for facilitating the child client's full participation in both the legal system and the attorney-client relationship. From this perspective, the lawyer has an ethical obligation to meet with the client and discover information about the client's situation. The lawyer also has an obligation to foster communication between the lawyer and the child and to utilize whatever techniques may be necessary to accommodate the child client. While some of these methods may account for the child's variable linguistic and cognitive capacities, they nevertheless serve to free the child from potential domination by the adult lawyer. Moreover, by empowering the child in the attorney-client relationship, the lawyer also enhances the child's ability to participate in the legal system.

Counseling methodologies also need to be sensitive to the disempowering effects of the attorney-client relationship. Manipulative and deceptive practices subordinate the client and have no place in a lawyering model which promotes client empowerment. The lawyer should be particularly careful to avoid the imposition of her own views as to what she thinks is best for the client and to empower the client to make her own decisions. This sort of counseling is premised upon a deep respect for the client as a rights holder and the ethics of promoting the client's status in the face of domination. Additionally, because the goal of counseling is to facilitate the client's decision making, it is focussed not on the correctness of the decision made but on the process by which the client reaches her decision.

To put it another way, the point of client empowerment is not to make sure that the child client has made a good decision or the best choice; nor is it to ensure that the way in which she reached her decision is a reasoned one. Rather, by empowering the client, the lawyer ensures that the child, and no other, has truly made her own choice. Of course, this may mean that some decisions will be made by the child that the lawyer believes are wrong or ill-conceived, but then, all clients, not just those of a certain age, are capable of making and have made bad choices. Nevertheless there is value in allowing a client to speak in her own voice and to determine her own goals. This is the essence of empowerment and of ethical lawyering.

* * *

SARAH H. RAMSEY, REPRESENTATION OF THE CHILD IN PROTECTION PROCEEDINGS: THE DETERMINATION OF DECISION–MAKING CAPACITY

17 Fam. L. Q. 287, 305–07, 309, 319–20 (1983).

* * *

Since the professional codes do not provide a standard for assessing a client's competence and the standards used by lawyers in practice are far from uniform, we are left with the question of what standard should be used. It seems clear that the answer to this question turns on the purpose of representation. Defining capacity in the abstract is not useful; the question of capability should be considered in relation to achieving particular goals.

If the primary and overriding purpose of representation is to give the child a voice, then the measure of capability could be simply the child's ability to express a preference related to the question at issue. Thus, if the child could state his wishes, the lawyer would be directed by them. On the other hand, if the primary purpose of representation is to protect the child's interests, then the standard at its most stringent might require the child to make a "right" decision, a decision which is beneficial to him. Competency would be determined by the quality of the decision.

Both of these standards seem seriously flawed. The first places the highest value on having a person's choice presented, but seems meaningless without *some* consideration of the individual's capacity to understand the significance of the choice he is making. Although this article supports having a lawyer represent the child's wishes, it does not suggest that the lawyer ignore the client's decision-making capacity. Expecting a person to make a decision which he is not capable of making is not supportive of an individual's rights, even of an adult's. The ideal of autonomy depends upon the individual's being capable of shaping his life through his own choices. Although the use of this standard would minimize the chance that a capable person would be overlooked, it should be rejected because the ability to express a preference is not a sufficient test of capacity.

The second standard errs in the opposite direction, placing too little importance on autonomy. Even if the assessment of the quality of the child's decision were meant to be in relation to the child's own values, it seems inevitable that an absolute measure of what was "right" would be used.* * * A standard which assesses children's competence by the quality of their decision would virtually rule out representation of a child's wishes which were not substantially the same as the lawyer's view of the child's best interest. This standard is very appealing to lawyer's in practice, however, because many are uncomfortable with advocating for an outcome for a child which they do not feel is "right."

A standard which represents a compromise between these two extremes of (1)being able to express a preference and (2) being able to make the right decision, is the standard which should be used. If the child has the mental and emotional abilities needed to make a decision which has a reasonable possibility of accuracy, the child should be considered capable.

* * *

[T]he components of decision-making must be identified. Major components needed are an ability to understand, to reason, and to communicate. Being able to use information received in life experiences and from others is necessary so relevant information can be used in evaluating events and understanding proposed alternatives. The decision-maker needs to be able to communicate requests for information and a decision once it is made. The ability to reason is needed to consider and judge alternatives based on values and possible outcomes. Another necessary component of decision making is a sense of values, or a sense of what the individual perceives as desirable for himself, which has some internal consistency. This sense of "good" is needed so that the individual can consider alternatives in relation to his view of what is beneficial or detrimental and so that he has a basis for adhering to a decision he has made.

* * *

[I]n this context capacity is basically a legal question. Additionally, it is a question which should be answered in relation to the decision to be made. Capacity is not an absolute but a relative concept. A child's ability to make a particular decision would depend on the child's ability to incorporate information about the legal options available and to communicate his desires to the lawyer so the lawyer will know how to proceed. Ideally the client's decision making and the lawyer's assessment of it would be part of an ongoing dialogue, an exchange of information, between lawyer and client.

* * *

JEAN KOH PETERS, THE ROLES AND CONTENT OF BEST INTERESTS IN CLIENT–DIRECTED LAWYERING FOR CHILDREN IN CHILD PROTECTIVE PROCEEDINGS
64 Fordham L. Rev. 1505, 1509–11 (1996).

* * *

* * * I firmly believe * * * that *lawyers can and must individualize every representation, in a way that allows the maximum possible participation of the client so that the representation reflects the uniqueness of each child client.*

The conceptual change that I am suggesting may be understood in the following way. Posit a spectrum in which a fully competent, involved, adult client contributes 100% to his representation—by providing information, listening to counseling, providing direction for the representation, and expressing opinions about substantive and procedural choices to be made. Traditional thinking about lawyering for anything but this fully competent client suggests that competency is a light switch—on or off: if the client cannot contribute 100%, the client should not be expected to contribute at all. At that point, the lawyer is free to determine the goals and methods of representation with total discretion.

I believe, however, that every client can contribute some amount to his lawyer's representation. Even the newborn child evinces a personality, a level of health, physical characteristics, a gestational and birth history, and a family context and history that distinguishes her from the next newborn client. While this uniqueness may provide, perhaps, only eighteen or twenty-six percent of what the lawyer requires to determine how to represent the child, *the lawyer's representation must reflect this contribution, and remain true to its individuality.* Competency, in this context, is a dimmer switch: the client can shed light on some aspects of the representation, even though she cannot participate in all of it. The lawyer must strive to incorporate every percentage of the client's contribution into the representation. Thus, I would suggest that a lawyer whose client can contribute thirty percent to the representation, but who assumes that the client can only contribute fifteen percent, is failing to represent her client to a significant degree.

* * *

To double check the lawyer's actions and their harmony with Rule 1.14 [of the Model Rules of Professional Conduct, quoted on page 226, supra] * * * the following seven questions [are set forth] to keep lawyers for children honest:

(1) In making decisions about the representation, am I seeing the case, as much as I can, from my client's point of view, rather than from an adult's point of view?

(2) Does the child understand as much as I can explain about what is happening in his case?

(3) If my client were an adult, would I be taking the same actions, making the same decisions and treating her in the same way?

(4) If I decide to treat my client differently from the way I would treat an adult in a similar situation, in what ways will my client concretely benefit from that deviation? Is that benefit one which I can explain to my client?

(5) Is it possible that I am making decisions in the case for the gratification of the adults in the case, and not for the child?

(6) Is it possible that I am making decisions in the case for my own gratification, and not for that of my client?

(7) Does the representation, seen as a whole, reflect what is unique and idiosyncratically characteristic of this child?

These questions memorialize my concern that, when lawyers are asked to exercise broad discretion over their client's lives, filling in, for example, the seventy percent that the infant client cannot provide to the representation, adult concerns and the lawyer's own needs will tend to fill the vacuum. Representation of very young and nonverbal clients can and ought to resemble the child's perspective and not those of the adults around him.

* * *

Questions

1. What are your initial reactions to these authors? Which position do you identify with most and why?

B. The Traditional Role

GRUNEWALD v. TECHNIBILT CORPORATION

Court of Appeals of Texas, Dallas.
931 S.W.2d 593 (1996).

STEWART, JUSTICE (Retired).

Gary and Jane Grunewald, as natural parents and next friends of minor Rachael Grunewald, appeal from the trial court's approval of a settlement recommended by the guardian ad litem. The guardian ad litem urges that the parents have no standing to challenge the trial court's approval of his settlement recommendation. * * *

STATEMENT OF FACTS

On April 20, 1992, the parents filed suit against appellees claiming damages arising out of the partial amputation of the child's finger when a shopping cart turned over at E.B. Mott's Grocery store ("Mott"). The parents alleged that Mott negligently failed to maintain the cart, failed to equip the cart with a seatbelt, failed to warn of the condition, and committed other acts of negligence. The parents also alleged that Technibilt Corporation, Gleason Corporation, and Whittaker Corporation ("the Technibilt defendants") negligently designed, manufactured, and marketed the shopping cart as an unreasonably dangerous product. The parents sought damages individually and as next friends of their minor daughter.

In an agreed motion, the parties sought appointment of a guardian ad litem based on the adverse interests existing between the child and her parents, who sought damages for their individual claims. On December 6, 1993, * * * the trial court appointed Leon Russell as guardian ad litem to represent the child in this action.

On June 13, 1994, the day set for a trial of the matter, the parents and the guardian ad litem announced that the parties had reached a settlement of the parents' individual claims and the child's claims against Mott.[3] The guardian ad litem advised the trial court that he recommended settlement of the child's claim against Mott, and the trial court approved that settlement. The parties advised the trial court that settlement negotiations were continuing between the guardian ad litem and the Technibilt defendants for settlement of the child's remaining claims. During the course of the day, the guardian ad litem recommended three settlement proposals to the trial court. The parents' counsel objected to each of these settlement recommendations and requested the trial court proceed with a trial against the Technibilt defendants on all claims, theirs and the child's. The parents' counsel based his objections on his opinion that a jury would give the child more money than that offered in any of the settlement proposals. The trial court refused to approve either of the first two settlement proposals submitted by the guardian ad litem, but did approve his third recommendation for settlement of the child's claims against the Technibilt defendants.

The guardian ad litem stated on the record that he based his recommendation for settlement on various factors, including: (1) his experience handling amputation and products cases; (2) his review of jury verdicts from Dallas and North Texas; (3) his review of the file, attendance at some of the depositions, and review of other deposition testimony; and (4) his concern about proving liability against the Technibilt defendants. The parents' counsel objected to the settlement approval and again requested the trial court go forward with a trial of all claims against the Technibilt defendants, including the child's. Instead, the trial court instructed the parties to return the following day for a trial of the parents' individual claims against the Technibilt defendants. The trial court stated that because it had approved the settlement of all the child's

3. The parents do not appeal the Mott settlement.

claims, the guardian ad litem need not appear at the trial on the parents' claims.

On June 14, 1994, the parents announced to the trial court that they had also reached a settlement agreement with the Technibilt defendants for their individual claims. The parents testified that they objected to the trial court's approval of the settlement of the child's claims against the Technibilt defendants and renewed their request that the trial court go forward with a trial of those claims. * * *

On September 16, 1994, the trial court entered a final judgment disposing of the child's claims against all defendants. The judgment recited that the guardian ad litem recommended settlement approval after conducting an investigation and determining that the settlement offer was fair and just, and in the child's best interests. The trial court did not discharge the guardian ad litem.

* * *

STANDING

Applicable Law

Under the Texas Rules of Civil Procedure, a guardian ad litem can be appointed only when a minor is represented by a next friend or guardian who appears to the courts to have an interest adverse to the minor. Once appointed, the guardian ad litem displaces the next friend and becomes the personal representative of the individual who is subject to a legal disability.

A guardian ad litem's representation is limited to matters related to the suit for which he or she is appointed. A guardian ad litem may be useful in all stages of a case, not just the trial.

The guardian ad litem participates in the case to the extent necessary to adequately protect the minor's interests and has considerable latitude in determining what activities are necessary to that effort. A guardian ad litem can: (1) prosecute an appeal from the trial court in which the guardian was appointed; (2) remove, under the proper circumstances, a suit to federal court from state court; and (3) initiate an extraordinary proceeding, such as a writ of mandamus or prohibition, on behalf of a minor whom the guardian ad litem was appointed to represent.

The service of the guardian ad litem burdens the parties to a case, but such a burden is necessary when the ward's rights cannot legally be served by a parent, next friend, or guardian with conflicting interests. Consequently, the appointment of a guardian ad litem and a settlement hearing are often necessary in comprising any suit involving a minor. Because a guardian ad litem displaces the next friend, the trial court should exercise great caution in appointing an ad litem.

Application of the Law to the Facts

The guardian ad litem argues that the parents, as next friends, have no standing to bring this appeal. The guardian ad litem asserts that the very nature of this appeal demonstrates the probable conflict between the parents and the child has not been removed, but continues to exist on appeal. He contends that as guardian ad litem, he displaced the parents as next friends, and became the child's personal representative. The guardian ad litem also contends that the parents, as next friends, may not represent the child concurrently with an appointed guardian ad litem while a conflict exists. Finally, he argues that the next friend has no right to bring an appeal once a guardian ad litem has been appointed.

We agree with the guardian ad litem that the parents have no standing to challenge the trial court's approval of the guardian ad litem's settlement recommendation in this case. Rule 173 of the Texas Rules of Civil Procedure provides that the trial court shall appoint a guardian ad litem where "a minor . . . is a party to a suit . . . and is represented by a next friend or a guardian who appears to the court to have an interest adverse to such minor." The trial court properly appointed a guardian ad litem to represent the child's interests in this suit because a conflict existed between the child and her parents, who had filed their own individual claims against the Technibilt defendants. We conclude that at the time the trial court appointed the guardian ad litem, the guardian ad litem displaced the parents as the child's representative for purposes of this suit.

* * *

As stated above, the judgment in this case is based on the settlement agreement negotiated and recommended to the trial court by the guardian ad litem. After the trial court approved the settlement agreement and entered its judgment incorporating and implementing its terms, the settlement agreement became forever binding and conclusive on the child. The trial court's judgment in this case is a final resolution of the child's interests as represented by the guardian ad litem. Thus, because the child cannot appeal, the next friends have no standing to appeal.
* * *

* * *

* * * [T]he parents and guardian ad litem here do not coexist and complement each other as the child's legal representatives in the lawsuit because the parents' interests conflicted with the child's interests. The record fails to reveal the removal of that conflict prior to the time the trial court approved the settlement recommendation and entered its judgment. The parents' actions during the pendency of the lawsuit support this conclusion. While the conflict existed, the parents opposed and objected to the guardian ad litem's actions in the following respects: (1) objecting to the guardian ad litem's settlement recommendation of the child's claims and requesting the trial court to proceed with a trial on the child's claims against the Technibilt defendants; (2) objecting to the trial court's approval of the guardian ad litem's settlement recommendation at the time they announced settlement of their own claims against the Technibilt defendants; (3) filing a written pleading objecting to entry of submission of settlement documents and to entry of final settlement judgment and release of the child's claims against the Technibilt defendants; and (4) continuing to object to the trial court's approval of the settlement recommendation by bringing this appeal.

Our holding that the parents, as next friends, have no standing to appeal the trial court's judgment in this case does not leave the child without a remedy. A guardian ad litem must act as a fiduciary with respect to the child's interests. As a fiduciary, the guardian ad litem's duty to the child is one of integrity, loyalty, and the utmost good faith. In this case, the guardian ad litem owed the child a fiduciary duty with respect to the settlement of her claims. Thus, the guardian ad litem remains accountable to the child, who may properly assert liability in a civil action for damages resulting from any alleged breach of his duties as her personal representative in this action.

* * *

Dismissed.

Notes and Questions

1. *Questions about* Grunewald. (a) Why did the trial court appoint a guardian ad litem for the child? What control did the parents' have over their child's lawsuit after the guardian ad litem was appointed? (b) If Rachel Grunewald were ten rather than a toddler, should the guardian ad litem have consulted with her about the settlement or should he have decided based on his own expertise?

2. *Parents' rights*. What rights should parents have to decide about their child's tort litigation when there is no initial conflict of interest between parent and child and the parents are thus the child's representatives? Should parents be able to reject a settlement offer that a judge thinks is fair, or would this be contrary to the child's best interests? In Ott v. Little Co. of Mary Hosp., 652 N.E.2d 1051 (Ill. App. Ct. 1995), parents sued as the child's representatives in an obstetrical malpractice action for injuries the child received at birth. The court appointed a guardian ad litem to review a settlement offer that the judge thought was fair, but that the parents had rejected. The guardian ad litem decided that the settlement was in the child's best interests, and it was approved by the court. The parents continued to represent the child for other purposes and therefore had no right to a hearing on the court's appointment of the guardian ad litem because they had not been removed as the child's representatives.

3. *Pro se proceedings*. Should a parent be able to represent a child in court or must an attorney be employed? An attorney should be employed so that the child has trained legal counsel and her rights are fully protected. See, e.g., Osei–Afriyie v. Medical College of Pennsylvania, 937 F.2d 876 (3d Cir.1991). Parents do not have the right to act as counsel for their children in actions brought under the Individuals with Disabilities Education Act (IDEA) either. See, e.g., Collinsgru v. Palmyra Bd. of Educ., 161 F.3d 225 (3d

Cir.1998); Devine v. Indian River County Sch. Bd., 121 F.3d 576 (11th Cir.1997).

4. *Attorneys' Fees.* If a parent retains counsel for a child, is the fee arrangement binding on the child? No, according to one court, because the court has the responsibility to protect minor in litigation and should determine whether the attorney's fee is reasonable. Leonard C. Arnold, Ltd. v. Northern Trust Co., 506 N.E.2d 1279(Ill. 1987); see also Hoffert v. General Motors, 656 F.2d 161 (5th Cir. 1981)(court has broad authority to review matters related to amount minor would receive). Both decisions concerned contingency fees.

5. *The guardian ad litem's liability. Gruenwald* notes that the child could bring a damage action against the guardian for a breach of duty, if any. However, if the guardian ad litem is considered an officer of the court expected to assist the tribunal in determining the reasonableness of a proposed settlement, the guardian may be entitled to absolute immunity. See Collins v. Tabet, 806 P.2d 40 (N.M. 1991)(guardian ad litem entitled to absolute immunity if assisting the court, but not if he is zealously advocating for a settlement in his ward's best interests.)

PROBLEM 3–1

Fifteen–year–old Fred was severely injured in a bike accident caused by his best friend, John. Fred's parents want to file suit on Fred's behalf and have asked you to represent them. Must you have Fred's consent before you file a complaint against John?

C. Counsel's Role in Abuse, Neglect and Adoption Cases

IN RE JAMIE TT

Supreme Court, Appellate Division, 1993.
599 N.Y.S.2d 892.

LEVINE, JUSTICE.

* * *

In December 1991, a child abuse petition was filed in the Family Court by petitioner alleging that Jamie "TT", a female child then 13 years old, had been sexually molested by respondent, her adoptive father and the husband of her biological mother. Annexed to the petition was the affidavit of petitioner's investigating caseworker. The affidavit related that Jamie had first disclosed to a school social worker and her guidance counselor in early December 1991 that respondent had fondled her breasts and vagina, that his sexual advances had begun over a year earlier when respondent had asked her to show her breasts to him, and that it had become progressively more intrusive and ultimately intolerable. Both educators spoke well of Jamie as an above average student of good character and reputation.

Respondent denied the allegations of the petition and the matter proceeded to a factfinding hearing, in which petitioner was represented by the County Attorney's office and a Law Guardian[c] appeared on Jamie's behalf. The only witness called by petitioner was Jamie, who testified in detail concerning a history of sexual touching by respondent for more than a year, occurring most often on weekday afternoons after school during the one hour period between respondent's return from work and the mother's return from work. Respondent testified on his own behalf, categorically denying engaging in any sexual abuse of Jamie. At the conclusion of the testimony, Family Court rendered a bench decision stating that it was unable, subjectively, to resolve whether Jamie or respondent was telling the truth. The court therefore ruled that petitioner had failed in meeting the statutory burden of proving the allegations of the petition by a preponderance of the evidence, and the petition was dismissed. By consent of both parties, temporary custody of Jamie was continued with her grandparents. Petitioner and the Law Guardian appeal.

* * *

* * * [T]he Law Guardian urges that there should be a reversal and a remittal for a new trial because Jamie was denied the effective assistance of counsel at the factfinding hearing. The threshold issue on this contention is whether Jamie, as the subject of the child abuse petition brought under Family Court Act article 10, had a legally cognizable right to the effective assistance of counsel throughout the proceeding. We conclude that she did. First, New York statutory law guarantees a child, allegedly abused or neglected by a parent, independent legal representation in a Family Court Act article 10 proceeding based upon a legislative finding that "counsel [for minors in Family Court proceedings] is often indispensable to a practical realization of due process of law and may be helpful in making reasoned determinations of fact and proper orders of disposition."

We are also of the view, however, that the Due Process Clauses of the Federal and State Constitutions mandate that there be *some form* of legal representation of Jamie's interests in the proceedings on the petition. Jamie's liberty interest was clearly at stake. The effect of Family Court's exoneration of respondent was to restore to him the primary right to custody of Jamie.[3] Upon the dismissal of the child abuse petition, decisional law made respondent's right to custody of Jamie superior to third persons, including her grandparents, which could only be overcome by proof of extraordinary circumstances. Thus, custody and control of Jamie by the person she claimed had sexually molested her while in his prior custody were inextricably involved in the proceedings on the abuse petition. Moreover, once custody of her was restored to respondent, he had the right to invoke State sanctions against her in a

---

c. "Law guardian" is the term used in New York for the representative of children in abuse and neglect, status offense and delinquency cases. The law guardian must bean attorney. The law guardian who represented Jamie at the fact-finding hearing was replaced by another law guardian who represented her on appeal.

3. Throughout the proceeding, Jamie's mother supported respondent's claim of innocence of the allegations of sexual abuse and she continued to reside with him.

person in need of supervision proceeding if Jamie challenged his authority by "ungovernab[le]" behavior or running away. We would be callously ignoring the realities of Jamie's plight during the pendency of this abuse proceeding if we failed to accord her a liberty interest in the outcome of that proceeding, entitling her to the protection of procedural due process.

Applying the threefold analysis of Mathews v. Eldridge [424 U.S. 319(1976)], we have no hesitancy in concluding that the process due Jamie included effective legal representation of her interests during the child abuse proceedings against respondent. Notably, Jamie had a strong interest in obtaining State intervention to protect her from further abuse and to provide social and psychological services for the eventual rehabilitation of the family unit in an environment safe for her. Furthermore, Jamie's interest in procedural protection was heightened because of the irreconcilably conflicting positions of her and her parents in this litigation The governmental interest in this child abuse proceeding coincided with that of Jamie. * * * "[T]he interest in protecting children from the infliction of serious physical harm or sexual molestation by a parent is the apotheosis of the State's *parens patriae* role". The appearance of a lawyer to protect Jamie's interests seems clearly necessary to avoid an erroneous outcome unfavorable to Jamie in the proceeding. A factfinding hearing under Family Court Act article 10 on a sexual abuse charge is a completely adversarial trial with few deviations from the procedures applied in civil and criminal trials. A respondent parent in such a proceeding is afforded the full right to counsel, including assignment of an attorney if indigent. And, as previously noted, the risk of an erroneous factual determination rejecting Jamie's claim of sexual abuse would be restoration of the custodial rights of the person accused of molesting her, a result * * * "approach[ing] the level of absolute abhorrence" and the Court of Appeals characterized as "disastrous."

Thus, Jamie had a constitutional as well as a statutory right to legal representation of her interests in the proceedings on the abuse petition. Her constitutional and statutory rights to be represented by counsel were not satisfied merely by the State's supplying a lawyer's physical presence in the courtroom; Jamie was entitled to "adequate" or "effective" legal assistance. No less than an accused in a criminal case, Jamie was entitled to "meaningful representation." Effective representation for Jamie included assistance by an attorney who had taken the time to prepare presentation of the law and the facts, and employed basic advocacy skills in support of her interests in the case .

Jamie did not receive the effective representation to which she was constitutionally entitled at the factfinding hearing. In a child protective proceeding under Family Court Act article 10, such as the instant case, where the attorney for the petitioner-child protective agency (here the County Attorney) presented the evidence in support of the petition in the first instance, it was the duty of Jamie's court-appointed Law Guardian to insure that the evidence sustaining her allegations of sexual abuse by respondent was fully developed. "As the child's advocate, the law guardian's interest is to insure that, to the greatest extent possible, all relevant facts, expert opinions and records are introduced into evidence. [The New York State Bar Association Law Guardian Representation Standards]* * * thus encourage the law guardian to be familiar with the possible evidentiary material, and to question and cross-examine witnesses whenever necessary for a full presentation * * * ". Here, the presentation of the evidence by the County Attorney clearly required more than a passive role on the part of Jamie's Law Guardian. In a case in which, foreseeably, the outcome inevitably would turn upon a determination of the credibility of Jamie or of respondent, the County Attorney failed to call the numerous witnesses to her out-of-court statements to confirm her testimony, expressly refused to explore the possibility of obtaining validation evidence from an expert witness, admissible to corroborate or bolster Jamie's testimony, and declined to conduct any cross-examination whatsoever of respondent. The Law Guardian did nothing to make up for these lapses in presentation of the evidence in support of Jamie's allegations. The Law Guardian called no witnesses and engaged in only the most perfunctory cross-examination of respondent, consisting of only three questions, none of which had any bearing on respondent's credibility.

The deficiencies noted cannot be explained as merely losing trial tactics. No conceivable forensic stratagem could justify the absence of preparation and advocacy skills shown here which in a criminal case would clearly have required reversal. The Law Guardian's failure to take an active role in the proceedings is alone sufficient to require reversal. Consequently, the order dismissing the petition should be reversed and the matter remitted to Family Court for further proceedings, including a new fact finding hearing.

* * *

Notes and Questions

1. *Questions about* Jamie TT. What was the basis for Jamie's claim for effective assistance of counsel? What did her trial attorney need to do to be "effective"?

2. *Right to counsel.* The Supreme Court has not extended the right to counsel to children in protection proceedings. Not all states provide attorneys in these proceedings, and some state courts have held that counsel is not constitutionally required. See, e.g., In re D.B. and D.S., 385 So.2d 83 (Fla.1980). Virtually all states, however, require appointment of a representative for the child. The Child Abuse Prevention and Treatment Act of 1974 (CAPTA) conditioned eligibility for certain federal funding on a state's providing a guardian ad litem "in every case involving an abused or neglected child which results in a judicial proceeding* * * ". 42 U.S.C. § 5106 (a)(6). CAPTA does not require that the guardian ad litem be an attorney and has been amended to specifically allow lay persons to be guardians ad litem.

3. *CASA programs.* Some states use trained lay volunteers, rather than attorneys, to represent children in abuse and neglect cases. These volunteers are frequently called Court Appointed Special Advocates, or CASAs. The CASA program began in 1977 in Seattle and has expanded across the country. In 1989 the ABA endorsed the combined use of CASA volunteers and attorneys for children in abuse and neglect cases. The Victims of Child Abuse Act of 1990 (Pub. L. No. 101–647, 104 Stat. 4789) included funding for CASA programs and CAPTA has been amended to specifically refer to CASA volunteers as permissible guardians ad litem.

CASA volunteers are used in a variety of models of representation. They may proceed independently, provide assistance to attorneys, or may serve in addition to attorneys, sometimes with separate counsel to advocate their position in court. For a recent decision involving the role of a CASA, see In re S.W., 903 P.2d 102 (Idaho 1995).

4. *Malpractice.* In abuse or neglect cases, should the child's attorney or guardian ad litem be subject to liability for malpractice or negligence if the representation is ineffective? In Marquez v. Presbyterian Hosp., 608 N.Y.S.2d 1012 (Sup.Ct.1994), the court concluded that the attorney (called a "law guardian" in New York) would be subject to liability in an appropriate case:

> The hybrid nature of the law guardian's role requires that in some cases liability for improper conduct be viewed under a standard different from that applicable to "counsel" for a party. A proper standard must serve two roles: (1) protect infants from malpractice and improper conduct and (2) protect law guardians from litigants' challenges of their proper exercise of discretion.

> In a legal malpractice case the plaintiff must prove (1) the existence of an attorney-client relationship, (2) negligence by the attorney (3) proximate cause between the negligence and the loss sustained and (4) actual damages. That standard properly protects the clients when attorneys deviate from the appropriate standard of care and protects attorneys in their exercise of professional judgment. That may well be an appropriate standard to apply to a law guardian in a case where the predominant role of the law guardian is that of "counsel". For example, when a law guardian is defending a delinquency proceeding or is representing an older child in a neglect proceeding the usual legal malpractice standard of care adequately properly [sic] protects the parties (see Matter of Jamie TT).

> However, when a law guardian is serving in a predominately guardian ad litem role, a different result should follow. People who exercise discretion and make value judgments in the "best interests" of their ward must be protected from needless collateral litigation which would undermine their good faith efforts. As the cases discussed above demonstrate, children who are incapable of intellectually expressing their views require that law guardians exercise independent judgment on their behalf. In order for that judgment to be truly independent, the law guardian must not be threatened by the possibility that differences of opinion with the infant's parents may give rise to tort litigation. For the

threat of even a baseless suit may serve to intimidate law guardians who should properly take aggressive positions adverse to the parents of the child.

* * *

The court concludes that the proper standard where there are very young children, and the guardian ad litem role predominates, is that liability should attach only if there is a showing that the law guardian failed to act in good faith in exercising discretion or failed to exercise any discretion at all. * * *

A test which looks solely at the law guardian's good faith protects the law guardian's exercise of that independent judgment which is implicit in a role which requires acts in another's "best interest." * * * The usual legal malpractice standard is simply inappropriate for law guardians acting as guardians ad litem. The usual standard places emphasis on the technical competence of "counsel" under the standard of care of attorneys and ignores the discretionary judgmental aspects of a law guardian's role. The usual malpractice standard places a law guardian, at least for a very young child, at substantial risk of the ultimate court decision. That is contrary to the strong public policy requiring a law guardian to exercise good faith in reaching an "independent" position on the child's behalf.

5. *Gross negligence.* Another court found that a paid guardian ad litem should be liable for damages for common law gross negligence. The court stated that a "paid guardian ad litem must answer to his ward if his negligent acts cause the ward damage," reasoning that the legislature had granted lay volunteer guardians ad litem immunity for simple negligence only and that surely a paid professional should be liable for gross negligence. Fleming v. Asbill, 42 F.3d 886 (4th Cir. 1994).

6. *Immunity.* The decisions in notes 4 and 5 are in the minority. Most courts have classified guardians ad litem as integral to the court and hence have conferred absolute quasi-judicial immunity: "A guardian ad litem serves to provide the court with independent information regarding the placement or disposition that is in the best interests of the child. This independent determination is crucial to the court's decision. The threat of civil liability would seriously impair the ability of the guardian ad litem to independently investigate the facts and to report his or her findings to the court. As a result, the ability of the judge to perform his or her judicial duties would be impaired and the ascertainment of truth obstructed." Ward v. San Diego County Dep't of Soc. Servs., 691 F.Supp. 238, 240 (S.D.Cal. 1988).

7. *Civil rights action.* Should the child's attorney be liable for damages under 42 U.S.C. § 1983? The attorney would probably be entitled to qualified immunity, Fleming v. Asbill, 42 F.3d 886 (4th Cir. 1994), or absolute immunity, Kurzawa v. Mueller, 732 F.2d 1456 (6th Cir. 1984).

IN THE INTEREST OF A.W.

Appellate Court of Illinois, 1993.
618 N.E.2d 729.

Presiding JUSTICE McNAMARA delivered the opinion of the court as modified upon the denial of rehearing:

Pursuant to Supreme Court Rule 308, on the basis that there was a substantial ground for a difference of opinion, we granted leave to Patrick T. Murphy, Cook County Public Guardian, to appeal the juvenile court's grant of a motion allowing A.W., a 13-year-old minor, to substitute private counsel in his place, in an abuse and neglect proceeding. On March 24, 1986, the Public Guardian was appointed as guardian ad litem and attorney for A.W., following an adjudication of wardship wherein the Department of Children and Family Services ("DCFS") was granted temporary custody. DCFS placed A.W. in the custodial care of her maternal grandmother, with whom she has lived until the present time.

The sole issue before this court is whether the juvenile court erred when it granted A.W.'s motion to substitute the law firm of Miller, Shakman, Hamilton & Kurtzon as attorney in place of the Public Guardian in the *pro bono* representation of A.W. Under the order, the Public Guardian continues to act as guardian *ad litem* for A.W. * * *

In March 1986, A.W., age six, reported that she had been sexually abused by her stepfather from the time she was two and one-half years old. A.W. had told her mother on several occasions that her stepfather had been touching her "private parts" and that he had put his penis inside her, but her mother refused to believe her. On March 4, 1987, the stepfather was convicted of aggravated criminal sexual assault and criminal sexual assault of A.W., and was sentenced to a term of eight years' imprisonment. His conviction was affirmed by this court on appeal.

While the stepfather was incarcerated, A.W. and her mother participated in therapy at the Human Effective Living Program ("H.E.L.P."). The staff therapist recommended that A.W. remain in the custody of her maternal grandmother, have no contact with the stepfather, and have only supervised visits with her mother. In the counseling report, the therapist noted that the mother did not believe her husband had abused A.W. DCFS subsequently terminated the therapy at H.E.L.P. and transferred her to another therapist at Salem House due to "concerns of the mother."

Upon his release from prison on November 2, 1990, the stepfather returned to live with A.W.'s mother and brother in the family residence. The social worker at Salem House noted that his return to the family seemed to have a profound effect on the mother because during the period of incarceration she began to accept the possibility that A.W. may have been sexually abused by her husband. However, upon his release from prison, the mother reverted to her previous stance, and believed that A.W. had lied about the sexual abuse in an attempt to receive more maternal attention. The therapy at Salem House was terminated on January 31, 1991, and the case was transferred back to H.E.L.P. because Salem House could not provide sex offender treatment for the stepfather.

When H.E.L.P. also proved unable to provide service to the stepfather, the case was transferred by DCFS to the Community Mental Health Council. The case manager noted that the mother remained in denial that her husband had molested her daughter, and that she appeared more empathetic toward her husband than to A.W. The stepfather also maintained that he was not guilty, and believed that he had been falsely charged and convicted by improperly procured evidence. The therapist recommended that the stepfather attend family group therapy focusing on his sexual abuse of A.W., and that he attend group therapy for sexual offenders three times per week. While he did attend group therapy, he did not attend the prescribed sex offenders' therapy sessions.

On December 19, 1991, the court ordered an unsupervised day visit by A.W. on Christmas Day with her mother and stepfather. Following the visit, the court ordered the family to participate in a joint therapeutic family counseling session with counselor Pamela Goodson, prior to December 31, 1991. Should Goodson so recommend, the parties were permitted an unsupervised overnight visit for New Year's Day. These visits transpired without incident. On January 29, 1992, over the objection of the Public Guardian, the court granted the mother's motion for unsupervised overnight visits on alternating weekends for A.W. during February 1992.

On March 5, 1992, Goodson submitted a report to the court recommending that A.W. begin weekly unsupervised visitation commencing in March. Assuming the success of those visits and subsequent therapeutic sessions, Goodson recommended that A.W. return home by June 1992. Goodson believed that A.W.'s anxiety "decreased tremendously as her visits with family increased" and that her level of comfort with her stepfather is "more than adequate for a successful transition back into the family unit."

Ellen Epstein, the assistant Public Guardian assigned to represent A.W., objected to the acceleration of unsupervised visits. She believed that A.W. would not be protected because both parents were in denial that she had been sexually abused, and the stepfather refused to participate in treatment for sex offenders.

A.W. became upset when unsupervised visitation was terminated in late March. In a letter to the judge dated March 27, 1992, A.W. stated:

"... I am very unhappy about not visiting my mom, dad and brother. Ellen Epstein [Public Guardian] is a great person but she is not doing what I really want and that is to be at home with my family."

Goodson's supervisor, Denise Snyder, met with Denise Kane, the Associate Director of the Citizens Committee On The Juvenile Court, and discussed the possibility of A.W. obtaining other representation. Thereafter, A.W. telephoned Barbara Shulman, an attorney associated with Miller Shakman, and told her that the Public Guardian was advocating a position contrary to her direction, and that she had repeatedly asked that office to advocate for visitation with her parents.

On April 21, 1992, a motion for substitution of counsel was filed in which Miller Shakman argued that it was A.W. who selected the firm to act as her counsel, and that she had an absolute right to choose her own attorney. The Public Guardian argued that while there is "no question that the child is both mature and competent," she had been manipulated by others to seek the change in counsel. Acknowledging its responsibility to act in the "best interest" of the child, the court ordered that a hearing be conducted to determine whether A.W. was coerced into making the motion for substitution of counsel.

In opening statement at trial, the Public Guardian stated that in many cases, the office of the Public Guardian would "step aside and gladly welcome the offer of additional counsel" both as lawyer and guardian *ad litem*. However, under the factual circumstances in this case, in which the therapist, mother and attorney conspired to coerce and manipulate the minor into changing counsel, the Public Guardian believed that he was the appropriate party to represent A.W.

At the evidentiary hearing, Shulman testified that she was first contacted by A.W., and that she made no promises regarding benefits she could obtain for her in the case. Denise Kane of the Citizens Committee On The Juvenile Courts testified that during March 1992 she had several conversations with Denise Snyder, a supervisor with the Community Mental Health Council. Snyder told Kane that A.W. was depressed because she felt that her viewpoint was not being represented, and that she really did want visitation to continue. Kane suggested to Snyder that she ask A.W. whether she wanted another lawyer to represent her. She suggested that the therapist, Goodson, present this option to A.W. If A.W. really wanted another attorney, Kane would try to find someone to represent her on a *pro bono* basis.

Pamela Goodson testified that she became A.W.'s therapist in the summer of 1991. She suggested to A.W. that she might want to seek alternative counsel pursuant to her supervisor's suggestion. Goodson telephoned Shulman, and made arrangements for A.W. to meet with Shulman.

Doctor Alan Ravitz, a child psychologist, was called as a witness by the Public Guardian, and opined that in the overwhelming majority of situations, a 12-year-old child does not have the capacity to choose an attorney. Doctor Ravitz stated that children of that age are psychologically immature, have a tendency toward impulsivity and have difficulty understanding the implications of their decisions. Too, children of this age have difficulty assessing the future results of immediate decisions due to their inability to defer gratification. Doctor Ravitz, however, had never interviewed A.W., and his opinion was not based upon the facts in this case.

The judge interviewed A.W. to ascertain her state of mind and mental condition, and whether she did want to retain substitute counsel. A.W. told the judge that she wanted Shulman to replace Ellen Epstein, one of the attorneys in the Office of the Public Guardian.

Thereafter, the judge granted the motion for substitution. The judge concluded that the evidence presented was not sufficient to show coercion or manipulation. Parenthetically, the judge noted that the Public Guardian would continue to act as guardian *ad litem*, and that his strong voice would still be heard on the ultimate issue in this case, which concerned the best interest of the minor.

The only question before us, which is one of first impression in Illinois, is whether A.W. may obtain counsel of her own choice in lieu of the Public Guardian. Miller Shakman does not request compensation, and is ready to represent A.W. *pro bono*.

We find it instructive to first conduct a review of the procedural due process rights accorded to minors pursuant to the Juvenile Court Act of 1987. Section 8015(1) sets forth the rights of the minor to representation during juvenile proceedings:

> "... [T]he minor who is the subject of the proceeding and his parents, guardian, legal custodian or responsible relative who are parties respondent have the right to be present, to be heard, to present evidence material to the proceedings, to cross-examine witnesses, to examine pertinent court files and records and also, although proceedings under this Act are not intended to be adversary in character, the right to be represented by counsel.

* * *

As stated in the prefatory provisions of the Act, the procedural rights assured to minors "shall be the rights of adults, unless specifically precluded by laws which enhance the protection of such minors." When these two sections are read together in a related manner, we find A.W.'s right to representation as a minor is clearly established, and that the right to representation afforded to minors is almost coextensive to that afforded to adults. We also observe that in Yellen v. Bloom (1945), this court held that a minor may engage private counsel in a civil case, and may make a valid contract by himself or through his next friend to hire an attorney to prosecute an action for injuries to a minor.

* * *

Other jurisdictions have also analyzed the issue of whether the court is obligated to respect the wishes of minors with respect to their choice of representation. In Wagstaff v. Superior Court, (1975), the Supreme Court of Alaska rejected the theory that the parents should choose the juvenile's attorney since they would be monetarily liable, and that a juvenile had no capacity to contract for the attorney's services. The

Wagstaff court held that the child may retain the attorney of his choice or, alternatively, ask the court to appoint an attorney for him. The court cautioned that in instances where the child has retained counsel, the court should respect the child's choice.

In a case factually analogous to the present case, the California Appellate court held that a minor initially represented by appointed counsel is entitled to seek substitution of retained counsel for dependency related hearings in order to effect the right to counsel of the minor's "own choice." (Akkiko M. v. Superior Court (1985)). * * *

* * * The Public Guardian warns that allowing the motion for substitution would "simply parrot the child's wishes" which often may not be in the child's best interest.

We are unpersuaded by the argument presented by the Public Guardian. We point to the significance of the fact that it is within the purview of the judge, and not the attorney, to assess the evidence and determine placement which truly reflects the child's best interest. In child custody hearings under the Juvenile Act, the best interest of the child is the standard, and the trial court is vested with wide discretion. The trial court's opportunity to observe the demeanor and conduct of the parties must be given great weight. Moreover, this court has held that juvenile counsel and the guardian *ad litem* have essentially the same obligations to the minor and to society.

We recognize that a minor's right to select substitute counsel is not absolute. However, in the present case, the judge conducted an extensive hearing, with both sides presenting evidence to address the issue of whether A.W. was coerced or manipulated into the decision to substitute private counsel for the Public Guardian. After hearing the evidence and interviewing A.W., the judge found insufficient evidence to support the Public Guardian's assertion that the decision to change counsel was not a volitional act made by A.W. As conceded by the Public Guardian prior to trial, A.W. was found to be mature and competent. We conclude, therefore, that the juvenile court did not err when it granted the motion for substitution of counsel.

We emphasize that nothing stated in this opinion suggests what the proper placement for A.W. should be. Nor do we hold, as the Public Guardian claims, that at the placement hearing Miller–Shakman is restricted to a mere parroting of A.W.'s views. The juvenile court shall conduct that hearing, with all parties present and participating fully, with one result in mind, the best interests of the minor child.

For the foregoing reasons, the judgment of the circuit court of Cook County is affirmed.

Judgment affirmed.

Notes and Questions

1. *Questions about* A.W. (a) Why was the Public Guardian unwilling to allow substitute counsel? What role remained for the Public Guardian after

A.W. secured private counsel, and how did this role differ from the Public Guardian's previous role? What is the role of A.W.'s new attorney? (b) How relevant are the concerns of Dr. Ravitz, the child psychologist, to the question of substituting counsel? Would the concerns be more relevant if A.W., rather than the judge, were deciding on her placement? (c) What effect will the appellate court's ruling have on information the juvenile court receives before deciding on A. W.'s placement?

2.   For a discussion of *A.W.* and the need to clarify the roles of the attorney and the guardian ad litem, see Diane Geraghty, Ethical Issues in the Legal Representation of Children in Illinois: Roles, Rules and Reforms, 29 Loy. U. Chi. L.J. 289 (1998). Some attorneys explicitly assume a dual role, advocating for their view of the child's best interests and also presenting the child's wishes, even when the child's position is in conflict with their own. See, e.g., In re Esperanza M., 955 P.2d 204 (N.M. Ct.App.1998)(denying motion to strike guardian ad litem's brief which properly presented both her view of the child's best interests and the child's contrary position).

S.S. v. D.M.

District of Columbia Court of Appeals, 1991.
597 A.2d 870.

ROGERS, CHIEF JUDGE.

Appellant S.S. assigns three errors by the trial judge in ordering the adoption of her six-year old son, J.S., by appellees D.M. and R.M., the child's maternal great aunt and her husband. She contends that the trial judge (1) erred in permitting the child's guardian *ad litem* to perform the dual roles of attorney and witness at the show cause hearing on why the petition for adoption should not be granted * * *.

* * *

II

Appellant contends that the trial judge erred in allowing the child's guardian *ad litem* to serve dual roles as attorney and witness at the show cause hearing on the adoption petition. By serving as a witness testifying from his personal knowledge and also acting as an attorney explaining and commenting on the evidence and examining witnesses, the guardian's credibility was enhanced in the eyes of the court, appellant maintains. She further maintains that allowing the child's attorney to testify as a fact witness violated the ethical rules prohibiting attorneys from acting as both advocates and witnesses in the same proceeding, and that these prohibitions exist precisely because of the prejudice to an opposing party that may result when the dual roles combine to enhance the attorney's credibility in the eyes of the factfinder. Because appellant did not object at trial to the guardian *ad litem* testifying as appellees' witness, our review is limited to a determination of whether the error resulted in a "miscarriage of justice."

We first review the testimony of the guardian *ad litem*, then the statutory framework, and finally the Rules of Professional Conduct.

A

The child's guardian *ad litem* testified, as a witness for appellees, that he was originally appointed as guardian *ad litem* for the child at the initial hearing in August 1985, when the child was at St. Anne's Receiving Home. The guardian *ad litem* explained that he had viewed the child as his client but that he had also acted in "a kind of protective role for him."[16] In the opinion of the guardian *ad litem*, appellees' petition for adoption should be granted in the child's best interests. Summarizing the reasons for his opinion, the guardian *ad litem* pointed to the child's view of appellees' home as his home, the child's development while residing with appellees, and the guardian's opinion that reunification is "not a viable goal in this case." The guardian began to explain why he had changed his mind from his original position that the mother had not neglected the child and that the child should be returned to her.

At this point the trial judge inquired of the guardian *ad litem* whether, during the neglect proceeding, he had been wearing "both your attorney hat and your guardian *ad litem* hat?" The guardian replied that since the child was only three years old at the time of the neglect proceeding, he had been acting as guardian *ad litem*. Yet in describing his conduct the guardian *ad litem* recounted that he had challenged the government's vague allegations of neglect, obtained two medical evaluations of appellant, and concluded then that as between government care and appellant's care, the child's best interests lay in being with appellant, particularly since one doctor had testified that appellant could benefit from therapy, which he was willing to provide. After the child was placed with appellees, however, the guardian *ad litem* became "a fan of Mrs. M," appellee great aunt, once he observed "the remarkable turnaround" in the child while under her care.

Thereafter, the trial judge asked the guardian *ad litem* a series of questions about the child: his physical condition when the guardian first met him, whether the guardian's observations of the child had been continuous to the present time, whether the child's physical problems persisted at the present time and how they had been abated; about appellees: the guardian's opinion of the suitability of appellees' home for the child, their financial ability to provide for the child, the child's relationship with appellee great uncle; and about reunification: the guardian's efforts to reunify appellant and the child, and the reason that reunification efforts ceased. Regarding reunification, the guardian *ad litem* described the three visits he had monitored between appellant and the child in late 1988 and early 1989, when appellant took umbrage at the child's view of appellees as his parents. The guardian *ad litem* also expressed his legal opinion that the termination of parental rights

---

16. In the latter role, the guardian ad litem drew a further distinction between representing the best interests of the child as he, the guardian ad litem, perceived them, and, where possible, representing the child's subjective desires; in the guardian's view, because of the tender age of the child throughout the relevant time period, the guardian ad litem, or protective role, predominated almost entirely.

statute allowed for a shift in emphasis from reunification to the child's need for stability and continuity of care. On cross-examination the guardian *ad litem* described the deteriorated relationship between appellant and appellee great aunt, and admitted he was unaware of the precise nature of appellee great uncle's "mental functioning."

B

The District of Columbia Code is not unlike the statutes in other jurisdictions which do not always clearly distinguish between the dual roles of a guardian *ad litem*. Commentary in the area has identified two principal roles, which may in practice overlap, the first being that of a neutral factfinder, and the second that of a zealous advocate. As neutral factfinder, the attorney's duties are to investigate the details of the case and to prepare a report summarizing the relevant facts for the presiding judge; as factfinder, the attorney does not recommend a particular disposition. As advocate, the attorney forms an opinion, either in consultation with the child or based on his or her own analysis, about the disposition which would promote the child's best interests and advocates that position before the court.

The District of Columbia Code provides that "[i]n any proceeding wherein the custody of a child is in question, the court may appoint a disinterested attorney to appear on behalf of the child and represent his best interests." With respect to any neglect or termination of parental rights proceeding, the Code provides for the appointment of counsel for the child, and that:

> The Superior Court shall in every case involving a neglected child which results in a judicial proceeding, including the termination of the parent and child relationship ... appoint a guardian *ad litem* who is an attorney to represent the child in the proceedings. The guardian *ad litem* shall in general be charged with the representation of the child's best interest.

The legislative history indicates that this statute was designed to bring the District of Columbia Code into conformity with federal law [the Child Abuse Prevention and Treatment Act of 1974] and that the Council of the District of Columbia contemplated an advocacy role for the guardian *ad litem*:

> * * * Given the complexities and the adversary nature of the proceedings involved in neglect litigation, your committee feels it is important that this guardian be an attorney who can function in the court and who can, in addition to advocating the child's best interests, act as the child's counsel.

* * *

The statutes as well as the testimony of the guardian *ad litem* indicate that the trial court appointed a guardian *ad litem* to serve as an advocate for the child in the neglect proceeding. The guardian *ad litem* continued as an advocate, according to his testimony, almost to the time of the disposition in the neglect proceeding. Later, while monitoring three of appellant's visits with the child, the guardian *ad litem* may have functioned more like a factfinding guardian *ad litem*. Once the adoption proceeding began, however, he resumed his role as advocate. But as a witness for appellees he also appears, from the trial judge's questions about the guardian's observations of the parties, to have assumed the role of neutral factfinder from the commencement of the neglect proceeding. After completing his testimony, the guardian *ad litem* again resumed his advocacy role.

There may well be overlapping functions for a guardian *ad litem* who is appointed during a neglect proceeding when subsequent events result in either a termination of parental rights or an adoption proceeding. The definition of the precise roles of the attorney and the guardian *ad litem* for children is still evolving and not without difficulty. But what happened here went beyond a mere overlapping of the dual roles of a guardian *ad litem*; the advocate guardian became a witness for one of the parties to facts and opinions on the ultimate issues. For this purpose the guardian's roles as advocate and as neutral factfinder are distinct, and the D.C. Rules on Professional Conduct make clear that there is reason to keep them separate.

C

Rule 3.7 of the D.C. Rules on Professional Responsibility[d] states the traditional prohibition:

(a) A lawyer shall not act as advocate at a trial in which the lawyer is likely to be a necessary witness except where:

(1) The testimony relates to an uncontested issue;

(2) The testimony relates to the nature and value of legal services rendered in the case; or

(3) Disqualification of the lawyer would work substantial hardship on the client.

The commentary on the rule recites the basic reason for prohibiting an attorney from being both attorney and witness, namely, to avoid conflicts that arise when an attorney puts his or her own credibility at issue in litigation. Such conflicts may prejudice the client when the attorney's testimony is impeached on cross-examination, or may prejudice the opposing party, when the attorney's testimony is given undue weight by the factfinder as a result of his dual role. * * *

Appellant argues persuasively that an attorney, as an advocate of one position, usually has an interest in the outcome and does not make legal arguments from the witness stand. When the same person acts as attorney and witness, the attorney puts his or her credibility on the line and, as an officer of the court, may well be viewed less critically than a

---

d. The District of Columbia Rule is identical to Rule 3.7 of the ABA Model   Rules of Professional Conduct (1989).

lay witness. Appellant maintains, therefore, that the attorney's credibility is enhanced in a contested proceeding when the attorney is allowed to testify and comment on the evidence. Further, because of the presumption that a guardian *ad litem* acts solely in the best interests of the child, appellant maintains that the testimony of a guardian *ad litem* is likely to be given even greater credibility by the trier of fact since the guardian *ad litem* is viewed as an unbiased witness without a stake in the litigation in the same sense as an attorney for a party to an adversary proceeding.

Specifically, appellant contends that she was prejudiced precisely because the guardian's testimony was accorded the type of undue weight which the attorney-witness prohibitions were designed to avoid. She observes that the trial judge described the guardian as "[giving] voice to [the child's] perceived best interests," thereby presenting her with "the difficult dilemma of having to argue against his credibility." Her position was made even more difficult, she continues, by the substance of the guardian's testimony in which he indicated that he originally supported reunification between the mother and child, but changed his view when he observed the progress of the child under appellees' care. Furthermore, during closing arguments, the guardian *ad litem* stated to the trial judge, "You have heard my testimony," thereby as attorney relying on his evidence as a witness.

The issues on which the guardian *ad litem* testified were clearly in dispute and went to the heart of the adoption proceeding. Not only did he describe his personal observations, he offered lay opinions on the best interests of the child and the likelihood of reunification. Accordingly, because the guardian *ad litem*, who had been appointed as an advocate for the child, was called as a witness for one of the opposing parties, new counsel should have been appointed to represent the child. The circumstances suggest no substantial hardship to the child; while the guardian *ad litem* had probably established a relationship with the child, the child was very young and another lawyer could still serve effectively as an advocate for the child in the adoption proceeding. The question remains whether there was a miscarriage of justice.

* * *

[T]he findings of the trial judge make clear that the judge did not uncritically adopt the lay opinions of the guardian *ad litem*. * * * In sum, the judge's findings and conclusions did not emphasize evidence that was only offered by the guardian *ad litem*, but made an informed, independent judgment based on the entire record regarding the child's best interests. Furthermore, appellant's counsel had the opportunity to object to the guardian *ad litem* appearing as a witness and did not. We conclude there was not a miscarriage of justice.

* * *

Notes and Questions

1. *Questions about* S.S. v. D.M. (a) What role(s) did the guardian ad litem for J.S. take? (b) Do you think that the guardian ad litem for J.S. should have testified? (c) Compare the different roles taken by representatives for A.W. and J.S. Which do you prefer and why?

2. *Confidentiality.* If the child's guardian ad litem testifies, are attorney-child communications privileged? Some courts protect the privilege. See, e.g., Nicewicz v. Nicewicz, 1995 WL 390800 (Ohio Ct. App.1995) (guardian ad litem, who was an attorney, allowed to testify about conclusions and recommendations, but asserted the privilege with regard to confidential communications with the child); In re Order Compelling Production of Records of Maraziti, 559 A.2d 447 (N.J. App.Div.1989)(communications between attorney and defendant's daughters were protected by attorney-client privilege). Other courts, however, do not protect the privilege. See e.g., Deasy–Leas v. Leas, 693 N.E.2d 90 (Ind.App.1998) (no specific statutory privilege protects communications between a guardian ad litem and her client in a custody case, and the attorney-client privilege does not apply; a court may limit discovery in its discretion, however, based on the child's best interests); Ross v. Gadwah, 554 A.2d 1284 (N.H. 1988)(privilege does not apply to guardian ad litem, even when the guardian is an attorney).

3. *Role at trial.* Does the guardian ad litem's obligation to testify depend on the role he or she assumes at trial? See e.g., In re J.E.B., 854 P.2d 1372, 1374–75 (Colo.Ct.App.1993):

> The requirement that a guardian ad litem make recommendations to the court may be satisfied either (1) by presenting his or her opinions based upon the guardian's independent investigation, or (2) by advocating a specific result based upon the evidence which has been presented before the court, or (3) by some combination of these two approaches. Determination of the issue presented here, whether a guardian ad litem may be examined and cross-examined, depends on the manner in which the guardian chooses to proceed in fulfilling the statutory requirements of the position.

> Insofar as the guardian ad litem chooses to present his or her recommendations as an opinion based on an independent investigation, the facts of which have not otherwise been introduced into evidence, the guardian functions as a witness in the proceedings and, thus, should be subject to examination and cross-examination as to the bases of his or her opinion and recommendation.

> If, on the other hand, the guardian ad litem's recommendations are based upon the evidence received by the court from other sources, then they are analogous to arguments made by counsel as to how the evidence should be viewed by the trier of fact. Opinions and recommendations so based and presented are not those of a witness, but are merely arguments of counsel and examination and cross-examination concerning these should not be permitted.

4. *Parents' attorney.* The role of the parents' attorney in child abuse and neglect cases is challenging but not ambiguous. The parents' attorney represents the client's objectives and should do so in a competent and

forceful manner. For a particularly egregious example of an attorney who did not provide effective assistance, see Appeal in Gila County Juvenile Action, 637 P.2d 740 (Ariz. 1981)(in a termination of parental rights proceeding, parent's attorney did not meet with the client, did not allow her to testify, called no witnesses favorable to her, and did not cross-examine adverse witnesses). For thoughtful analyses of issues the parents' attorney may confront, see Bruce A. Boyer, Ethical Issues in Representation of Parents in Child Welfare Cases, 64 Fordham L. Rev. 1621 (1996); Kathleen A. Bailie, Note, The Other "Neglected" Parties in Child Protective Proceedings: Parents in Poverty and the Role of the Lawyers Who Represent Them, 66 Fordham L. Rev. 2285 (1998).

PROBLEM 3–2

Mary's mother is an alcoholic. A neighbor called the child abuse hotline and reported that Mary, age 12, was left alone for long periods without food in the house and had bruises from beatings by her mother. The Department of Social Services has taken Mary into custody. You have been appointed to represent Mary and by statute must "represent the child and her interests." Mary's mother has entered a residential treatment program for alcoholism. The social worker assigned to the case has told you that Mary's mother is unlikely to stop drinking and that her alcoholism is severe. The social worker has told you that the Department is investigating whether to place Mary in the home of her Aunt Ruth, who lives nearby and has a daughter, Ann, about Mary's age. No other relative placements are available.

When you meet Mary, you ask her whether she would like to live with her Aunt Ruth while her mother is in treatment. She responds that Ann has told her that her stepfather (Ruth's husband, George) has sexually abused her on numerous occasions. Mary dislikes George and is afraid of him. You learn from court records that George had pleaded guilty to criminal sexual assault of a minor six years ago, prior to his marriage to Ruth.

When Mary is faced with the possibility that she will be placed in a foster care home with strangers, Mary says she would much prefer living with Ruth. She had been in foster care for six months when she was 8 and again when she was 10, and hated it. "Anything is better than that," she says.

At the dispositional hearing for Mary, the Department of Social Services recommends that Mary be placed with Ruth, unaware that George is a threat to her safety. What do role do you take and what do you recommend?

When you first met with Mary, you explained the nature of your role. What would you have told her about lawyer-client confidentiality?

IN RE JEFFREY R.L.[e]

Supreme Court of West Virginia, 1993.
435 S.E.2d 162.

* * *

By the very nature of the painful issues involved, abuse and neglect cases are troublesome to this Court. Despite our efforts to give the highest priority to child abuse and neglect cases, we have yet to find viable solutions to all of the problems which arise in these cases. As a result, we continue to explore stronger approaches to facilitate the fair and expeditious handling of child abuse and neglect cases.

The Juvenile Justice Committee has brought to this Court's attention the problems which commonly arise with the representation of children by guardians *ad litem* in abuse and neglect proceedings. Quite often children do not get adequate representation because the guardians *ad litem* have not been given proper direction as to their role in representing the child in abuse and neglect proceedings. Thus, to further our goal of protecting the interests of children who suffer from abuse and neglect, the Juvenile Justice Committee has proposed that this Court adopt guidelines for guardians *ad litem* to follow in order to provide children in abuse and neglect proceedings with adequate representation.

In suggesting the guidelines, the Juvenile Justice Committee represents that it has relied upon our state *Code, Rules of Professional Conduct, Rules of Civil Procedure for Trial Courts of Record* and case law. The Juvenile Justice Committee has also consulted other sources such as: (1) the Department Advisory Committee of the Fourth Department Law Guardian Program in New York, *Guidelines for Law Guardians/Abuse and Neglect Proceedings*; (2) the National Association of Counsel for Children, *Guidelines for Guardians Ad litem in Abuse and Neglect Cases*; and (3) the New York State Bar Association's study, Jane Knitzer & Merrill Sobie, *Law Guardians in New York State: A Study of the Legal Representation of Children* (1984).

As a brief background, we believe that two studies which were performed, one in North Carolina[21] and the other in New York,[22] to evaluate programs that provide children with attorneys in protection proceedings, illustrate why there is concern about the performance of guardians *ad litem* in child abuse and neglect cases. First, the North Carolina study found, among other things, that experienced attorneys who knew how to represent their child clients and worked hard, spoke

---

e. This case is also discussed in the section on termination of parental rights in the chapter on abuse and neglect.

21. See Robert Kelly & Sarah Ramsey, Do Attorneys for Children in Protection Proceedings Make a Difference? A Study of the Impact of Representation Under Conditions of High Judicial Intervention, 21 J.Fam.L. 405 (1983).

22. See Jane Knitzer & Merrill Sobie, Law Guardians In New York State—A Study of the Legal Representation of Children (1984).

with their clients, and involved themselves in the negotiating and factfinding, had a beneficial influence in the outcome of the case. However, the North Carolina study found that these experienced, hard-working attorneys were in the minority. Among the findings of the New York study were that law guardians are uncertain about what is expected of them and that they "feel that they need assistance in their work, in particular, regular briefings on case law and legislation, and access to independent social work and mental health professionals. The results of both studies lead to the conclusion that there should be "greater accountability in the performance of individual attorneys, . . . systematic and continuing evaluations of program outcomes, and . . . enhanced efforts geared toward implementing and testing new approaches to representing children in protection proceedings."

* * *

All of the guidelines we have reviewed attempt to provide guardians *ad litem* with comprehensive standards * * * so that there is little question as to the attorney's responsibilities in representing children. * * **

* * *

In summary, each child in an abuse and neglect case is entitled to effective representation of counsel. * * * Therefore, this Court adopts these guidelines, effective within sixty days of the date of this opinion, to further ensure the adequate representation of children in abuse and neglect cases by court-appointed guardians *ad litem*. By adopting the proposed guidelines in this case, we are providing guardians *ad litem* with fairly comprehensive standards which they can follow so that they may conduct an independent investigation of the case and present the child's position to the court. The guardians *ad litem* may use their discretion in acting under the guidelines because the applicability of each of the guidelines is dependent upon the facts of each case.

In addition to the guidelines adopted herein, we believe attorneys who act as guardians *ad litem* should participate in special continuing legal education relating to the representation. * * *

* * *

Notes and Questions

1. How effective do you think the combination of guidelines and training will be in improving the level of representation?

2. *The New York study: the role of appointed counsel.* Where the family does not retain private counsel, children may be represented in family court by a legal services agency or by private counsel the court appoints from a panel. The study conducted by Dr. Jane Knitzer and Professor Merril Sobie demonstrated the gulf between the law on the books and the law in practice. Among other things, the Knitzer–Sobie study found that most panel law guardians did not represent many children each year and thus had difficulty developing expertise in representing children; that only one-quarter of these

law guardians viewed themselves as specialists in juvenile law; and that more than half reported little interest in substative juvenile law. The study also found that almost 70% of the panel law guardians had no special screening, orientation or co-counsel experience before joining the panel; that many law guardians received no training after appointment to the panel; and that most law guardians did not receive updates on case law and legislation, and had no access to independent social workers and mental health professionals during their representation. Jane Knitzer and Merril Sobie, Law Guardians in New York State—A Study of the Legal Representation of Children (1984).

Under these circumstances, the quality of representation generally remained low. Forty-five percent of the authors' courtroom observations reflected either seriously inadequate or marginally inadequate representation; 27% reflected acceptable representation, and only 4% reflected effective representation. (Twenty-four percent of the observations lacked sufficient information to be coded.). Id. at 6–8. Lack of preparation and lack of contact with the represented children were major problems:

> In 47% of the observations it appeared that the law guardian had done no or minimal preparation. In 5% it was clear that the law guardian had not met with the client at all. In 37% of the cases observers could not tell whether the law guardian had met with the client before the court proceeding. Further, in 35% of the cases, the law guardians did not talk to, or made only minimal contact with their clients during the court proceedings.

Id. at 8. The authors reported patterns of ineffective representation:

> The first pattern involves a lack of preparation or investigation even when there are clear questions of fact, as in serious abuse cases; the second, representation in which the law guardian is present, but otherwise inactive, unprepared and unresponsive to the client. In addition, ineffective representation is characterized by violations of statutory or due process rights; almost 50% of the transcripts included appealable errors made either by law guardians or made by judges and left unchallenged by the law guardians. * * *

> To a lesser extent, there is also evidence that law guardians are unfamiliar with the substantive statutes governing different proceedings, particularly proceedings related to voluntary placements (including reviews) and PINS proceedings involving educational issues. Further, substantial numbers of law guardians assume virtually no role at dispositional proceedings. Instead, they rely almost totally upon others. Ineffective law guardians also have only perfunctory, if any, relationships with the children they represent.

Id. at 9–10.

3. *North Carolina study.* In a footnote, *Jeffrey R. L.* noted several useful lessons from the North Carolina study:

> That attorneys had little effect overall is understandable if circumstances surrounding the guardian's role are considered. First, there was much confusion about the role of the guardian ad litem. . . . This confusion not only prevented the guardian ad litem from having a clear

goal, but it was also a source of confusion to the judge who may have resented, criticized, or ignored a guardian ad litem who was taking on responsibilities that the judge felt were inappropriate.... The attorney survey showed that 53% felt that judges expected them to assume an adversarial role in representing their client's position, while 41% felt that judges did not have this expectation, at best an ambivalent situation.... The condition of ambivalence with respect to the expectations of the attorney was not aided by the fact that guardians typically had received no specialized training relevant to abuse and neglect cases, either during law school or thereafter.

Another, and perhaps more critical, factor in limiting attorney effectiveness was that both guardians and judges seemed to assume that the guardian should play only a minor role. Court records from our sample indicated that attorneys spent a median of only five hours per case. Since this figure includes all court time, the time left for investigation, negotiation, or consultation is negligible. Not surprisingly, guardians indicated that they concurred with the department of social services recommendations in 88% of their cases. Additionally, attorneys usually did not follow their cases after the dispositional hearing to see if treatment plans were being carried out. Attorneys, it appears, were a presence rather than an influence in the court's handling of the cases.

Quoting 21 J. Fam. L. at 451–52.

4. *Additional studies.* National studies of representation of children in abuse and neglect cases have also reported a number of problems. See CSR, Inc., National Study of Guardian ad Litem Representation (1988); U.S. Dep't of Health & Human Services, Final Report on the Validation and Effectiveness Study of Legal Representation Through Guardian Ad Litem (1994). For a comparison of trained volunteers, law students, and attorneys representing children in a Michigan county, see Donald N. Duquette and Sarah H. Ramsey, Representation of Children in Child Abuse and Neglect Cases: An Empirical Look at What Constitutes Effective Representation, 20 Mich. J. L. Reform 341 (1987). For recommendations on evaluating and monitoring attorneys for children in abuse and neglect cases, see Robert F. Kelly & Sarah H. Ramsey, Monitoring Attorney Performance and Evaluating Program Outcomes: A Case Study of Attorneys for Abused and Neglected Children, 40 Rutgers L. Rev. 1217 (1988); for consideration of conditions that can strengthen, or weaken, representation for children, see Danald C. Bross, The Evolution of Independent Legal Representation for Children, 1 J. Center for Children & Cts 7 (1999). For a study of representation of children in England, that includes interviews with the child clients, see Judith Masson and Maureen W. Oakley, Out of Hearing: Representing Children in Care Proceedings (1999).

5. *Guidelines.* In 1996 the ABA adopted Standards of Practice for Lawyers Who Represent Children in Abuse and Neglect Cases. For the text of the Standards see *<http://www.abanet.org/child/childrep.html>*. For discussion of the Standards, see Linda Elrod et al., Representing Children Standards of Practice Committee, Proposed Standards of Practice for Lawyers Who Represent Children in Abuse and Neglect Cases, 29 Fam.L.Q.375 (1995). As *Jeffery R. L.* notes, a number of guidelines have been adopted. For additional

discussion, see the special issue of the Fordham Law Review on Ethical Issues in the Representation of Children, 64 Fordham L. Rev. 1281–74 (1996).

PROBLEM 3–3

Assume that the United Nations Convention on the Rights of the Child will soon be ratified by the United States Senate. Your state bar association is developing guidelines for attorneys representing children in abuse and neglect cases and has asked you what the attorneys' role should be to comply with the Convention. Article 12 of the Convention requires the following:

> 1. States Parties shall assure to the child who is capable of forming his or her own views the right to express those views freely in all matters affecting the child, the views of the child being given due weight in accordance with the age and maturity of the child.

> 2. For this purpose, the child shall in particular be provided the opportunity to be heard in any judicial and administrative proceedings affecting the child, either directly, or through a representative or an appropriate body, in a manner consistent with the procedural rules of national law.

What is your response to the State Bar?

NOTE ON THE CHILD'S COUNSEL
IN ADOPTION PROCEEDINGS

Should children be represented in adoption proceedings? Generally representation is not required, but can be provided at the court's discretion. If there are special circumstances or a dispute, a representative would seem to be appropriate and necessary. The Uniform Adoption Act requires appointment of a guardian ad litem for a minor adoptee in contested proceedings. The guardian ad litem's role is "to encourage the court and the contestants to pay attention to the needs of the minor, including the need for expeditious resolution of the dispute." Unif. Adoption Act § 3–210 cmt.

In the absence of a dispute, for example, a guardian ad litem was not needed when the biological mother's lesbian partner petitioned to adopt the child, who was conceived through artificial insemination. The court reasoned that because no guardian ad litem was appointed "in adoptions by married couples or single persons except where the matter was contested or the report of the social worker raised a concern with respect to whether the proposed adoption was in the infant's best interests," there was no reason to treat this uncontested adoption petition any differently. In re Adoption of J., 642 N.Y.S.2d 814 (Sur.Ct.1996).

Frequently, termination of parental rights may lead to an adoption. Because termination severs the child-parent relationship, state constitutions or statutes may require appointment of a representative for the child. See e.g., In re S.A.W., 856 P.2d 286 (Okla.1993); Adoption of D.R.W., 875 P.2d 433 (Okla. Civ. App. 1994)(independent counsel for the child required by statute and state constitution); but compare In re Kapcsos, 360 A.2d 174, 178 (Pa. 1976)(counsel for termination of parental rights under the adoption act not required, and there is no constitutional right to counsel for the child "provided that the child's interest is adequately protected by the court and the parties in the case").

D. Counsel's Role in Delinquency and Status Offense Cases

As discussed in Chapter 1, In re Gault gives children the due process right to counsel during the adjudicatory phase of delinquency proceedings. The Court stated that:

> A proceeding where the issue is whether the child will be found to be "delinquent" and subjected to the loss of his liberty for years is comparable in seriousness to a felony prosecution. The juvenile needs the assistance of counsel to cope with problems of law, to make skilled inquiry into the facts, to insist upon regularity of the proceedings, and to ascertain whether he has a defense and to prepare and submit it. The child "requires the guiding hand of counsel at every step in the proceedings against him."

In re Gault, 387 U.S. 1 (1967).

Debate continues, however, about counsel's appropriate role and about precisely what stages of delinquency proceedings require appointment of counsel.

IN THE INTEREST OF K.M.B

Appellate Court of Illinois, 1984.
462 N.E.2d 1271.

MILLS, PRESIDING JUSTICE:

K.M.B., a 13-year-old female, appeals the circuit court's order placing her in the Salem Children's Home. She contends that she was denied her constitutional right to counsel during the dispositional hearing.

We disagree and affirm.

THE FACTS

On October 1, 1982, K.M.B. was found to be delinquent and adjudicated a ward of the court. She was placed on probation for 24 months. On April 18, 1983, Judge Witte found that K.M.B. had wilfully violated the conditions of her probation and revoked her probation. Elizabeth Robb, an assistant public defender, served as K.M.B.'s guardian ad litem throughout all of these proceedings.

At the dispositional hearing, Robb again appeared on behalf of K.M.B. Robb informed Judge Witte that K.M.B. had requested her to withdraw as counsel because—contrary to K.M.B.'s wishes—Robb wanted to recommend that K.M.B. be placed in a juvenile home. K.M.B.

wished to remain in her mother's home. K.M.B.'s mother also asked Judge Witte to replace Robb as K.M.B.'s counsel.

Judge Witte replied that Robb was employed by the county as an attorney to represent K.M.B. and also to use her professional judgment to protect K.M.B.'s best interest. Judge Witte stated:

> "I have no reason to believe that Mrs. Robb would not help her client [K.M.B.] present all the information and all of her, and her position as to the best she may, and if she wants to make a different recommendation that's certainly her professional responsibility and obligation."

Judge Witte refused to replace Robb as K.M.B.'s counsel. He did, however, appoint counsel for K.M.B.'s mother and father and continued the dispositional proceeding for a later hearing.

At the second dispositional hearing, the State introduced into evidence a predispositional hearing report of juvenile court officer Diane McKimmey. In her report, McKimmey evaluated K.M.B.'s entire background including the condition of K.M.B.'s mother's home. K.M.B.'s mother is single and unemployed. She lives with three of her children—including K.M.B.—in Bloomington, supports herself and the children with Aid to Dependent Children payments, and receives no child support from K.M.B.'s father.

McKimmey noted that DCFS had received numerous complaints concerning the mother's residence. Those complaints included: loud parties into the early morning hours, underage drinkers, the uncleanliness of the home, and the number of residents in the home who are not members of the mother's family. McKimmey expressed her concern that K.M.B.'s mother did not provide an adequate parental role for K.M.B. McKimmey recommended that K.M.B. be placed in the Salem Children's Home.

At the end of the hearing, Robb told the court that K.M.B. desired to remain in her mother's home. Robb then continued:

> "I don't think that there's any question that placement is necessary at this time. I think that this situation has just deteriorated to such a degree that to keep the Minor in this * * * type of living situation * * * we are doing an extreme disservice to her * * *. I certainly believe that * * * the factors which have caused the situation * * * are certainly as a result of many, many factors, unemployment of [K.M.B.'s mother], no support provided by [K.M.B.'s father], having to deal with a number of children on a very little income, trying to, to work, provide, be a single parent, and deal with someone, with a child who has obviously some serious problems which affect her ability to learn and her ability to interact with other individuals, * * * I don't think any person is to blame as much as the environment and economic situation are the cause and factor.

I just don't see any other solution than placement * * * in a very structured situation where there is a reinforcement of things taught in a school, in the living environment in order to try and address the deteriorating situation which is occurring in her home."

Judge Witte then ordered Juvenile Court Services to assume guardianship of K.M.B. and to place her in the Salem Children's Home.

THE LAW

On appeal, K.M.B. argues that she was denied her constitutional right to counsel because her attorney, Robb, recommended placement outside of the home even though she, K.M.B., desired to stay in her mother's home. We cannot agree.

The seminal case on a minor's right to counsel is In re Application of Gault (1967). In Gault, the United States Supreme Court found that the Due Process Clause of the fourteenth amendment to the United States Constitution requires that juveniles be represented by counsel during proceedings to determine delinquency.

The responsibility of the court-appointed juvenile counsel, however, is different than that of other court-appointed counsel. The juvenile counsel must not only protect the juvenile's legal rights but he must also recognize and recommend a disposition in the juvenile's best interest, even when the juvenile himself does not recognize those interests. As our supreme court stated in In re Beasley (1977):

"Although such a proceeding [under the Juvenile Court Act] retains certain adversary characteristics, it is not in the usual sense an adversary proceeding, but it is one to be administered in a spirit of humane concern for and to promote the welfare of the minor as well as to serve the best interests of the community."

The United States Supreme Court in Gault explicitly recognized the unique role of the juvenile's counsel:

"Recognition of the right to counsel involves no necessary interference with the special purposes of juvenile court procedures; indeed, it seems that counsel can play an important role in the process of rehabilitation."

It is not always possible for a juvenile's counsel to carry out his unique responsibility to protect the juvenile's best interest without alienating the juvenile. A delinquent juvenile's wishes are often not in his best interest. Although the juvenile's counsel should consider the juvenile's wishes and inform the court of those wishes, the counsel has an obligation to protect the juvenile's best interest. If protecting a juvenile's best interest requires that the counsel make a recommendation contrary to the juvenile's wishes, then the counsel has, as Judge Witte stated, a "professional responsibility and obligation" to make that recommendation.

In the present case, Robb did exactly that. She considered K.M.B.'s wish to remain in her mother's home and she informed the court of

K.M.B.'s desire. Then after considering the juvenile court officer's report, Robb stated that in her opinion it was in K.M.B.'s best interest to be placed in a structured home instead of remaining with her mother. Robb then recommended that K.M.B. be placed in the Salem Children's Home.

Robb's recommendation did not deprive K.M.B. of her right to counsel. Instead, the record reveals that Robb's recommendation was based on her professional evaluation of K.M.B.'s best interest and indicates to us not only that K.M.B. received counsel but that she received very conscientious counsel.

Attorney Robb, in fact, is to be highly commended.

Affirmed.

Notes and Questions

1. *Questions on* K.M.B. (a) Was K.M.B.'s attorney an advocate or a neutral fact-finder? (b) How did the roles of DCFS and K.M.B.'s attorney differ? (c) Would a "best interests" approach at the adjudicatory stage be considered adequate under legal representation *Gault*?

2. The *K.M.B.* position on the attorney's role is controversial and presents a minority view. Generally attorneys for children in delinquency cases are expected to take direction from their child clients as they would from adult clients. This approach is endorsed most strongly at the adjudication rather than the disposition stage of the proceeding, however.

The IJA/ABA Standards Relating to Counsel for Private Parties provide that counsel for the alleged delinquent "should ordinarily be bound by the client's definition of his or her interests with respect to admission or denial of the facts or conditions alleged. It is appropriate and desirable for counsel to advise the client concerning the probable success and consequences of adopting any posture with respect to those proceedings." Institute of Judicial Administration, American Bar Association, Standards Relating to Counsel for Private Parties, § 3.1 (b)(ii)[a](1980). The comment to the Standard states that:

> [E]ven a youthful client will be mature enough to understand, with advice of counsel, at least the general nature of the proceedings, the acts with which he or she has been charged, and the consequences associated with the pending action. On this basis a juvenile client can decide whether to accede to or contest the petition. That, in essence, is what is required of the defendant in criminal proceedings and should suffice for juvenile court purposes. Although counsel may strongly feel that the client's choice of posture is unwise, and perhaps be right in that opinion, the lawyer's view may not be substituted for that of a client who is capable of good judgment * * *

See also Randy Hertz et al, Trial Manual for Defense Attorneys in Juvenile Court, § 2.03 (1991); Katherine Hunt Federle, Overcoming the Adult–Child Dyad: A Methodology for Interviewing and Counseling the Juvenile Client in Delinquency Cases, 26 J. Fam. L. 545 (1987–1988).

The conflict between defending the client from delinquency charges and doing what is "best" for the child can still cause frustration, however. Consider these comments by a former juvenile defender indicate:

   * * * *Gault* and similar cases seem to guarantee a juvenile representation not very different from that afforded to an adult: The lawyer looks out for the client by defending the client, by seeking to avoid a finding of guilt, mitigating the sentence, and the like. Protection of the client's rights is the lawyer's credo. Yet, even though *Gault* tells the juvenile court to respect these rights, reality can take a very different tack: The child's rights are respected in form only, with paramount importance given to finding ways to get the child "on the right track."

   This conflict seemed to be at the root of much of my anger and frustration. I would show up, ready for battle on behalf of my client in the usual sense (even if I was also armed with even more programmatic and social work-type alternatives than I normally would be with an adult client). The court knew it needed me there, that it had to put up with me to a certain extent. But the judges often made it clear to me that the legal niceties were not what counted, and that if I wanted to have a role in what this was really about I should try to contribute to what we were going to "do" with my client. In contrast to my own conception of my role as advocate for the defendant, honed over hundreds of adult cases, the court had another: Lawyer as hood ornament, a decorative accoutrement that served no real function, but that was required by legal convention. This idea was captured neatly by the judge's actions when I stood up in court * * * and was told, in effect: "That's all very nice, but we're here to discuss how to help your client." Unless I was prepared to address the judge's agenda, I would have no real role at all. I was in a court not primarily of law but of social work, a court of programs and of group homes, a court of results. Adjudication meant little, perhaps nothing.

   And yet, in the months and years since, I have often asked myself this question: If we say that the juvenile court's goal is to do what is in the best interest of the child, was the judge really wrong in taking this approach? The judge may have been little more than a super social worker in a robe, but was that not what the law commanded the judge to do? In other words, acknowledging a level of tension between the best interests doctrine and the teachings of *Gault*, how could a judge not often ignore law and procedure * * * in favor of doing what was "necessary" to help the child? It seems that the basic philosophy of the court commits all involved—even defense counsel—to a nonlegal, helping approach, under which a lawyer defending a juvenile client could conceivably stand up and say: "Your Honor, my client tells me he wants to go home, but it's obvious to me he needs to be incarcerated. I urge the court to do that." Little wonder that a defense lawyer might feel puzzled, frustrated, relegated to a role of form over substance. Simply put, no one in the system wants counsel assigned to represent juvenile offenders to act as a "real" lawyer would.

David A. Harris, The Criminal Defense Lawyer in the Juvenile Justice System, 26 U. Tol. L. Rev. 751, 762–763 (1995).

3. *The Katzenbach Commission.* While *Gault* was pending before the Supreme Court, the President's Commission on Law Enforcement and Administration of Justice (the Katzenbach Commission) issued its comprehensive report. The Commission concluded that no single action holds more potential for achieving procedural justice for the child than provision of counsel. The Commission explained:

> The rights to confront one's accusers, to cross-examine witnesses, to present evidence and testimony of one's own, to be unaffected by prejudicial and unreliable evidence, to participate meaningfully in the dispositional decision, to take an appeal have substantial meaning for the overwhelming majority of persons brought before the juvenile court only if they are provided with competent lawyers who can invoke those rights effectively. The most informal and well-intentioned of judicial proceedings are technical; few adults without legal training can influence or even understand them; certainly children cannot.

President's Commission on Law Enforcement and Administration of Justice: The Challenge of Crime in a Free Society 86 (1967).

4. *The quality of representation.* A shockingly high proportion of alleged delinquents are still tried without lawyers. Barry C. Feld, Justice for Children (1993); Janet E. Ainsworth, Re–Imagining and Reconstructing the Legal Order: The Case for Abolishing the Juvenile Court, 69 N.C. L. Rev. 1083, 1126 (1991). Unrepresented juveniles, Professor Ainsworth suggests, may be the lucky ones. "Over and over again, studies have shown that juveniles with lawyers fare worse in juvenile court than those proceeding without counsel, being more likely to be incarcerated and jailed for longer periods than if represented pro se." She explains:

> These statistics reveal only the correlation between legal representation and more severe dispositions, and not why this disadvantage exists. One possibility is that lawyers hurt their clients through sheer incompetence and inadequacy in their advocacy. Another is that lawyers in juvenile court may deliberately solicit harsher penalties, believing that such dispositions are in their clients' best interests in the long run. Still another explanation is that juvenile court judges may display conscious or unconscious antagonism toward the idea of attorneys in juvenile court, and take out their hostility on the represented clients. Or it may be that the juvenile court judge has prejudged the case and predetermined the likely sentence before the proceedings began, and to save the system time and money, encourages waiver of counsel in those cases where the probable sanction is comparatively light. What is clear, however, is that all of these factors find factual support in current studies of the juvenile court.

> [T]rials in juvenile court are frequently "only marginally contested" marked by "lackadaisical defense efforts." Defense counsel generally make few objections, and seldom move to exclude evidence on constitutional grounds. Defense witnesses rarely are called, and the cross-examination of prosecution witnesses is "frequently perfunctory and reveals no design or rationale on the part of the defense attorney." Closing arguments are sketchy when they are made at all. Watching these trials, one gets the overall impression that defense counsel prepare

minimally or not at all. A New York State Bar Association study estimated that in forty-five percent of all juvenile trials, counsel was "seriously inadequate"; in only five percent could the performance of defense counsel be considered "effective representation."

One explanation for the abysmal performance of defense counsel is that lawyers in juvenile court are all too frequently both inexperienced and overworked. Particularly in jurisdictions where juveniles have no right to jury trial, public defender offices often assign their greenest attorneys to juvenile court to season them. Supervision from senior attorneys is not always what might be desired, and caseloads in these high volume courts are crushing. Moreover, in a forum without jury trials, there is a tendency for lawyers to cut corners in these cases of comparatively low public visibility, a tendency often tacitly encouraged by judges anxious to process cases as expeditiously as possible. Under these circumstances, it is no wonder that juvenile bench trials are seldom models of zealous defense advocacy.

In addition, defense lawyers who routinely practice in juvenile court face tremendous institutional pressures to cooperate in maintaining a smoothly functioning court system. The defense lawyer who is seen as obstreperous in her advocacy will be reminded subtly, or overtly if necessary, that excessive zeal in representing her juvenile clients is inappropriate and counter-productive. If she ignores these signals to temper her advocacy, the appointed defense lawyer is vulnerable to direct attacks, such as having her fees slashed or being excluded from the panel of lawyers from which the court makes indigent appointments. Seldom are such crude measures necessary, however. For most defense lawyers, withstanding the psychological debilitation attendant upon being the sustained focus of judicial and prosecutorial disapproval is hopeless.

Perhaps the most pervasive and insidious reason for less than zealous defense advocacy is the ambiguity felt by many juvenile court lawyers concerning their proper role. The legacy of decades of paternalistic parens patriae ideology is still evident in the attitudes of many defense lawyers, who cannot help thinking of themselves as charged, at least in part, with a responsibility to act in their clients' long term best interests rather than scrupulously to safeguard their legal rights. Despite the clear ethical mandate to represent juveniles on the same terms and with the same zeal as they would adults, many defenders nevertheless find themselves deeply torn between their professional obligation to press their clients' legitimate legal claims and their paternalistic inclination to help the court address their clients' often desperate social needs. Even lawyers who have not internalized this role conflict may face external pressure from judges and probation officers to conform to a guardian-like role.

Id. at 1126–30.

5. *Ineffective assistance of counsel.* A juvenile may seek to upset an adverse delinquency determination by claiming ineffective assistance of retained or appointed counsel. "[T]he right to counsel is the right to the effective

assistance of counsel." McMann v. Richardson, 397 U.S. 759, 771 n. 14 (1970).

Ineffectiveness claims generally challenge counsel's performance in the particular case. Strickland v. Washington, 466 U.S. 668, 688, 694,, held that a party asserting such failure must show (1) that counsel's representation fell below an objective standard of reasonableness, and (2) a "reasonable probability that, but for counsel's unprofessional errors, the result of the proceeding would have been different." In relatively rare circumstances, however, "the likelihood that any lawyer, even a fully competent one, could provide effective assistance is so small that a presumption of prejudice is appropriate without inquiry into the actual conduct of the trial." United States v. Cronic, 466 U.S. 648, 659–60 (1984).

In the ordinary case that turns on inquiry rather than presumption, the party claiming ineffectiveness may prevail only by pinpointing counsel's specific errors. Ineffectiveness claims by delinquents and adults alike usually fail in these cases, largely because "[j]udicial scrutiny of counsel's performance must be highly deferential." Strickland at 689, "a court must indulge a strong presumption that counsel's conduct falls within the wide range of reasonable professional assistance" *Strickland,* 466 U.S. at 689. In juvenile and general jurisdiction court alike, ineffectiveness claims frequently involve Monday morning quarterbacking by clients challenging counsel's ultimately unsuccessful trial strategy. The reviewing court must make "every effort * * * to eliminate the distorting effects of hindsight, to reconstruct the circumstances of counsel's challenged conduct, and to evaluate the conduct from counsel's perspective at the time." Strickland, 466 U.S. at 689.

In In re A.V., 674 N.E.2d 118, 120–21 (Ill. App.Ct. 1996), the adjudicated delinquent established ineffectiveness under the *Strickland* test. The record indicated that counsel misunderstood the applicable standards of proof in the consolidated delinquency and parole violation hearing. Counsel were two third-year law students with limited experience in the actual practice of criminal law, who tried the case under the supervision of attorneys from the law school's clinic.

Strickland also held that counsel owes the client a duty of loyalty, including a duty to avoid conflicts of interest. 466 U.S. at 688. In delinquency proceedings, appellate courts sometimes find ineffective assistance by counsel who violated ordinary conflicts standards. See, e.g., In re Jason S., 511 N.Y.S.2d 722 (N.Y.App.Div.1987) (juvenile deprived of effective assistance because court-appointed counsel represented several youths involved in the matter); In re Delfin A., 506 N.Y.S.2d 215, 217 (N.Y.App.Div. 1986) (juvenile, charged with sodomy while in foster care in a residential facility, was denied effective assistance of counsel because the residential facility had also retained his counsel in the proceedings against the juvenile, and because his counsel also represented the juvenile's two alleged accomplices whose statements concerning the incident differed from the juvenile's).

In Evitts v. Lucey, 469 U.S. 387, 396–99 (1985), the Court held that due process is offended by ineffective assistance of counsel on the first appeal as of right. The holding has been applied on juveniles' first appeals from delinquency adjudications. See, e.g., State v. Berlat, 707 P.2d 303, 307 (Ariz.1985).

6. *Appeals.* What should the child's counsel do if an adjudicated delinquent wants to appeal, but counsel feels that no meritorious grounds for appeal exist? Because the minor is under a legal disability, the minor cannot proceed pro se. In In re D.A.S., 951 S.W.2d 528 (Tex.App.1997), the court held that the attorney appointed to represent the minor on appeal could (1) file a brief for the minor, (2) move for substitute counsel, or (3) move to dismiss the appeal with the motion signed by the child's legal guardian.

7. *Scope of representation.* A narrow reading of *Gault* would grant alleged delinquents a due process right to counsel only at adjudication and only if secure detention is a possibility. Some states provide for counsel at all stages of a delinquency proceeding, however. See, e.g., Ga. Code Ann. § 15–11–30(b); Ohio Rev. Code Ann. § 2151.352. "Other states simply provide that a juvenile is entitled to be represented by counsel, without specifying whether this right extends to all stages of the proceedings or whether it applies to all forms of conduct for which the juvenile might be before the court. Still others provide for a more limited right to counsel, requiring the court to appoint counsel only where the juvenile requests counsel and is financially unable to retain counsel of his or her own choice." Samuel M. Davis, The Role of the Attorney in Child Advocacy, 32 U. Louisville J. Fam. L. 817 (1994).

8. *Lawyer's fees.* May the court require a child's parents to pay the fees for the child's lawyer? A state might require reimbursement by statute, although the decision to appoint counsel could not constitutionally depend on parents' willingness to pay. Opinion of the Justices, 431 A.2d 144 (N.H. 1981). A lawyer might also be able to claim that fees were a necessity, and hence were part of a parent's support obligation (see Chapter 9).

IN RE W.C.

Supreme Court of Illinois, 1995.
657 N.E.2d 908.

JUSTICE FREEMAN delivered the opinion of the court:

Pursuant to the Juvenile Court Act of 1987, the State filed a delinquency petition in the circuit court of Cook County, alleging respondent, W.C., is accountable for the first degree murder of Carey Long. * * *

* * *

ISSUES

We are asked to decide: * * * whether respondent's waiver of the right to remain silent and to counsel was knowing and intelligent such that his statement to police was properly admitted into evidence; * * *

FACTUAL BACKGROUND

On May 28, 1992, Carey L. Long, "Skip," aged 29 years and a drug abuser, was fatally shot in the face and back by Othenio Lucas, "Pooh-Pooh," aged 17 years, a reputed drug dealer. Shortly after the shooting, Long's six-foot, one-inch, 180-pound body was found by police lying in the rear courtyard area of an apartment building. On May 29, 1992, police interviewed John Crafton pursuant to their investigation of Long's death. As a result of the interview, police learned that W.C. had been present at the scene of the shooting and in the company of William Hodges, "Juan," aged 14 years. W.C. was then 13 years old, five feet, two inches tall and weighed 90 to 100 pounds. Based on the information obtained from Crafton, police went to W.C.'s home and requested that his mother bring him to the police station.

W.C. and his mother, accompanied by two police officers with whom the mother was familiar, arrived at the police station at around 6 p.m. W.C. was taken into temporary custody by officers at the station, and he and his mother were taken to an interview room. Once there, Detectives Cliff Gehrke and Joseph Fine read *Miranda* warnings to W.C. directly from their police manual. According to the officers, W.C. indicated to them that he understood his rights by responding "I understand" to each *Miranda* query. W.C. agreed to talk and gave an oral statement in the presence of his mother, the detectives and police youth officer Deanna Hall. Although W.C. initially began to relate a false version of events, his mother soon directed him to tell the truth, and W.C. related an apparently truthful version. Gehrke took notes. At some point, Fine left the interview room to contact an assistant State's Attorney. At another point, W.C. and his mother had an opportunity to privately talk when both officers left the room.

After a brief period, Assistant State's Attorney Diane Sheridan entered the interview room and repeated *Miranda* warnings to W.C. According to the State, Sheridan explained the warnings to W.C. and he indicated that he understood them. As Sheridan took notes, W.C. repeated his prior oral statement. Sheridan then left the room briefly to reduce her notes to a formal written statement. She subsequently returned to the room and read the written statement aloud to W.C. and his mother because W.C.'s mother was upset and neither she nor W.C. possessed the ability to read the document. * * *

* * *

The social investigation report indicated that W.C. had received three station adjustments and that three charges once brought against him had been dropped with leave to reinstate. W.C.'s school records indicated that he was in sixth grade, had received failing grades throughout his entire education and had never been evaluated for special educational services. Dr. Diane Stone, a Chicago board of education school psychologist, testified at the transfer hearing that W.C. was illiterate and moderately mentally retarded with an IQ of 48, which Stone stated was the equivalent developmentally of a six to eight-year-old. A psychological examination summary, prepared by a court psychologist, also described W.C. as being moderately mentally retarded, stuttering, and possessing the emotional maturity of a six to seven-year-old.

* * *

The adjudication phase commenced in the juvenile division. W.C.'s counsel filed a motion to suppress his statement on the basis that he did not knowingly and intelligently waive his rights to remain silent and have an attorney present.

* * * In addition, Dr. Stone testified as W.C.'s expert in determining the cognitive developmental and language skills levels of children and adolescents. Based on psychological, achievement and language skills tests she administered to W.C., it was Stone's opinion that he was unable at the time of his arrest to understand *Miranda* warnings. Two police officers, who had arrested W.C. on two previous occasions, also testified that they had read W.C. *Miranda* warnings on those occasions, and that he had indicated that he understood the warnings, in one instance even refraining from asking or answering further questions. Sheridan testified that she gave W.C. an explanation of the *Miranda* warnings before questioning him and that he indicated that he understood them. Officer Fine confirmed Sheridan's testimony. W.C. testified by responding in few words, by not remembering and with inconsistency. The circuit court denied the motion to suppress W.C.'s statement.

At the adjudicatory hearing, the State's evidence consisted of the testimony of an investigating police officer concerning his observations of Long's body at the crime scene, the stipulated testimony of the medical examiner as to the cause of death, the medical examiner's report and W.C.'s written statement. Other than W.C.'s written statement, there was no incriminatory evidence. W.C. did not testify and presented no evidence. * * *

The social investigation report was supplemented for the dispositional determination. In the report, the Juvenile Detention Center confirmed that W.C. was a nonreader, functioned academically at the second-grade level, had a very small sight vocabulary and a comprehension level between second and third grade. W.C. was also reported as being unable to tell time because he could not remember the difference between the hour and minutes. W.C. was adjudicated a ward of the court.

After considering recommendations that W.C. be placed on probation in either a therapeutic day center or a residential treatment center, the circuit court ordered W.C. transferred to the custody of the Department of Corrections. * * *

ANALYSIS

* * *

II

Waiver of *Miranda* Rights

Respondent claims that his written statement should not have been allowed into evidence because he did not validly waive his right to remain silent and the attendant right to the presence of an attorney.

Specifically, respondent claims that he lacked the mental capacity to understand the *Miranda* warnings he received, and thus he could not have knowingly and intelligently waived his constitutional rights.

* * *

* * * Our appellate court has held that the crucial test to be used in determining whether an accused knowingly and intelligently waived his rights is whether the words in the context used, considering the age, background and intelligence of the individual being interrogated, impart a clear understandable warning of all of his rights.

* * *

The record reveals the following. Dr. Stone testified that she administered the WISC III, the Process Assessment for Learning, the Bender Visual–Motor Gestalt, the Wide Range Achievement Test and various other tests to W.C. She also performed a clinical interview and reviewed his school records. In total, Stone estimated that she spent 28 hours with W.C. over a period of several days. W.C. scored below third grade in reading and spelling and at the beginning of third grade in math. W.C.'s vocabulary and comprehension levels were at the second-grade level. W.C., nevertheless, functioned academically at the first to second-grade levels and was for all practical purposes illiterate. W.C.'s level of comprehension and understanding of the English language as spoken to him was on a kindergarten to first-grade level. W.C. could understand English when spoken in very short sentences with one or two syllable words.

Stone also testified that W.C.'s IQ was 47 or 48, indicating moderate mental retardation, which was the chronological age equivalent of a six to seven-year-old. The court's psychologist agreed with this assessment. Stone believed, however, that W.C. might be able to function at a mildly retarded level, which is within an IQ range of 60 to 70. She believed his IQ score was depressed due to his being overwhelmed by and uncomprehending of his situation. In her opinion, it was fair to say that W.C. was also stressed when he was detained at the police station.

Stone testified that she also tested W.C.'s ability to read and comprehend the Dolch word list comprised of 50 words that first graders should know. W.C. was able only to comprehend concrete words such as "pretty" and "green." Based on W.C.'s performance on the test, Stone formed an opinion concerning whether W.C. would have understood the *Miranda* warnings contained in his written statement.

According to Stone, W.C. would not have understood the words "remain," "against," "during," "formal," "hire" and would absolutely not have understood the word "appointed." He would not understand the concept of "present" as meaning being there with him. He would not know the word "right" as an entitlement as opposed to being the opposite of "wrong."

According to Stone, W.C.'s ability to comprehend and think on an abstract level was extremely low. In Stone's opinion, W.C. would not have been able to understand that he had a right to remain silent during questioning and that if he gave up that right, anything he said could be used against him in a court of law. Neither would W.C., under the police questioning, have understood that he had a right to an attorney, the attorney's presence and that one could be appointed for him. For W.C., the information was too abstract. Stone concluded that W.C. was incapable on May 30, 1992, of understanding the *Miranda* rights enumerated in his written statement and the consequences of waiving them when he spoke with police and the State's Attorney.

Police Officer Mark Mizula testified that, in 1991, W.C., aged 12 years, was taken into temporary custody by police and brought to the police station where Mizula worked. Mizula testified that he read W.C. the *Miranda* warnings, asked him whether he understood each warning, and W.C. indicated that he did. Mizula did not ask W.C. to explain what it meant to remain silent or any of the other *Miranda* warnings.

Police Officer Alfred Thome testified that, in 1990, he and his partner took W.C. into temporary custody at age 11, and Thome's partner read W.C. *Miranda* warnings from the police manual. Thome testified that W.C. stated that he understood, and when the officers asked W.C. if he wished to ask any questions, W.C. replied that he did not. At the station, Thome reread W.C. the warnings. According to Thome, W.C. again said he understood, did not request any explanation and did not appear confused. When asked whether he wanted to answer questions, W.C. indicated that he did and answered. Thome did not ask W.C. whether he knew how to read and write or understood the meaning of various terms in the *Miranda* warnings.

Sheridan testified that in this case she advised W.C. that he did not have to talk with her if he did not want to, and that anything he told her, she would tell a judge. Sheridan also testified that she explained to W.C. that she was a lawyer and that "a lawyer is a person who helps people," but that she was "a lawyer working with the police and he could have a lawyer who helps him, who could be present, if he wanted one." Sheridan also stated that she told W.C. that if he could not afford a lawyer, one could be "appoint[ed]" for him. According to Sheridan, W.C. responded to this information by saying either "yes" or "okay." Sheridan then asked W.C. if he wanted to tell her what had happened and he responded affirmatively.

Sheridan testified that she had no trouble communicating with W.C. and that he communicated very well and his answers were appropriate to her questions. Sheridan did not think that W.C. was moderately retarded, nor did she have any idea that his mental functioning was that of a five or six-year-old. To Sheridan, W.C. appeared to be a normal 13-year-old who had "some" difficulty reading. W.C. never said that he did not understand his rights. Neither did W.C.'s mother ever say that she or W.C. did not understand. According to Sheridan, W.C. reflected that he understood her by his eye contact, demeanor and communication skills. Sheridan did not ask W.C. to explain what his "rights" meant.

Police Officer Joseph D. Fine testified that he read W.C. the *Miranda* warnings from the police manual before Sheridan arrived. W.C. responded affirmatively without any question, request to explain, or any statement indicating that he did not understand. Fine confirmed Sheridan's testimony regarding her interactions with W.C. Fine did not notice anything unusual about W.C. and he only learned that W.C. could not read when there was discussion regarding the reduction of his statement to writing. Fine, nonetheless, felt that W.C. was "street smart."

W.C. testified. When asked what was a public defender, W.C. answered, "Somebody that helps you." When asked what was a lawyer, W.C. responded with the query, "Somebody that will help you?" When asked what the first sentence of the *Miranda* warning meant, W.C. answered, "That I can—that I commit a crime or something." In response to the admonishment that one has the right to talk to, have present and be appointed an attorney, W.C. replied that it meant that the "State going to give me a lawyer." When asked what the word "right," spelled "right," meant, W.C. indicated by scribbling with his right hand. When asked what he had believed a lawyer was when he was first questioned by police in this case, W.C. responded, "That they were trying to get you locked up."

The following exchange also appears of record:

"Q. And then he told you, do you understand, [W.C.], anything you say could be used against you, in a court of law, and you said yes. Right?

A. Yes.

Q. And then he told you, do you understand you have a right to have a lawyer present with you, during questioning, and you said?

A. No.

Q. You told him, no?

A. Yes.

Q. Which one of the officers did you tell that to? Could you describe him?

A. He got on glasses, I think.

Q. So you told him, no. What did you say to him when he told you that?

A. I can't hear you.

Q. You told him, 'I can't hear you', you can't hear me?

A. I can't hear you.

Q. When the officer told you, 'Do you understand you have a right to have a lawyer with you, during questioning' you told him, no?

A. I don't remember him telling me this.

> Q. Do you remember him telling you, if you can't afford a lawyer, the court will appoint one for you free of charge. You can get a lawyer, free of charge.
>
> A. No.
>
> Q. Did you ever ask the officers to explain anything to you?
>
> A. No; because they were explaining it to me, anyway.
>
> Q. So you already knew and understood what they were saying?
>
> A. Yes. They were telling me."

For the most part, W.C.'s responses to examination consisted of either a "yes" or "no," few words, or a failure to remember. W.C.'s mother testified to basically the same account that she gave at the transfer hearing. The circuit court denied the motion to suppress.

In this case, there was no question that the evidence of the objective circumstances surrounding W.C.'s waiver supported a knowing and intelligent waiver of rights. The evidence showed that on two previous occasions W.C. had received *Miranda* warnings and had once delayed speaking with police after receiving the warnings. In this case, W.C. received at least one standard verbal *Miranda* warning, a simplified verbal explanation and was read a standard written warning. Neither W.C. nor his mother stopped the questioner, asked for explanation or indicated that W.C. did not understand. W.C. responded affirmatively in response to queries regarding whether he understood. To witnesses, his demeanor and communication skills conveyed that he understood the warnings. Notably, however, these same witnesses' evaluative observations did not detect, in the least, W.C.'s substantial intellectual limitations which are apparent from even the cold record.

There was a question, however, whether given the evidence of W.C.'s age, intelligence and mental capacities, he yet possessed the ability to understand the simplified warnings given by Sheridan. "If intelligent knowledge in the *Miranda* context means anything, it means the ability to understand the very words used in the warnings." We agree with respondent that if one lacks that ability, the repetition of the advice even accompanied by a statement of agreement indicates very little.

The evidence of W.C.'s mental ability presented at the hearing was twofold, consisting of Stone's testimony of her extensive examination of W.C., a court psychologist's summary, the social investigation report, and the testimony of W.C., himself. Stone's testimony, the summary and the report left little doubt that W.C. did not possess the ability to understand the words and terms contained in standard *Miranda* warnings, regardless of how he presented himself to the authorities. Stone testified that W.C.'s intellectual abilities and emotional development were those of a primary-school-level child. The court's own psychologist agreed. It is not so clear from this evidence, however, that W.C. would have been unable to understand Sheridan's explanation of the *Miranda* warnings.

Sheridan explained the *Miranda* warnings to W.C. in concrete, nonabstract terms: he did not have to talk; she was a lawyer, but she was a lawyer working with police, who would tell a judge what he told her; and he could have a lawyer to help him if he wanted one, even if he could not afford one. According even to the evidence detailing W.C.'s quantifiable intellectual limitations, he might have been able to understand the explanation offered by Sheridan. In this regard, as a court of review, we are not prepared to say that the trial court's firsthand assessment of W.C. was wanting. A trial court sits in an uniquely advantageous position when evaluating a witness' subjective mental capabilities. Accordingly, we conclude that the circuit court's determination that W.C.'s waiver was valid was not against the manifest weight of the evidence.

* * *

Notes and Questions

1. How did the court assess W.C.'s ability to understand the *Miranda* warnings? Do you agree with the court's approach?

2. How meaningful is *Gault*, if a child like W.C. can waive his right to counsel? Should there be a presumption that minors, or minors under a certain age, cannot understand the *Miranda* warnings? For extensive discussion of these issues, see Chapter 11.

3. How do you reconcile *K.M.B.*'s view of minors' competence with *W.C's.*?

NOTE ON COUNSEL FOR THE CHILD IN
STATUS OFFENSE PROCEEDINGS

Recall from Chapter 1 that a status offense proceeding charges conduct sanctionable only because the person committing it is a minor. A number of states grant alleged status offenders a statutory right to counsel. Under a narrow reading of *Gault*, due process would not require appointment of counsel in status offense proceedings, because that decision concerned only delinquency proceedings and because status offense dispositions should not result in placement in secure detention. In practice, children charged with offenses often are not represented. Barry C. Feld, Justice for Children 82, 256 (1993). When the failure to provide counsel has been the subject of an appeal, some courts have focused on whether the alleged status offender might have been taken into custody. In re Walker, 191 S.E.2d 702 (N.C.1972) Rogers v. State, 491 So.2d 987 (Ala.Crim.App.1985). See generally, Donald T. Kramer, Legal Rights of Children, § 20.07 (2nd ed. 1994).

The role of counsel for the alleged status offender is subject to debate. Should the attorney treat the child like an adult client when setting the objectives for representation, or should the attorney advocate for the child's best interests? Probably the majority view would have the attorney advocate for the child's wishes rather than best interests, but this choice may depend on the child's age and ability. The IJA–ABA

Standards Relating to Counsel for Private Parties treat counsel for children in status offense proceedings and delinquency proceedings alike. Counsel "should ordinarily be bound by the client's definition of his or her interests with respect to admission or denial of the facts or conditions alleged." Standard 3.1 (b)(ii)[a]. The Standards also state that "where it is locally permissible to so adjudicate very young persons [as delinquents or status offenders], and in child protective proceedings, the respondent may be incapable of considered judgment in his or her own behalf." In the face of incapacity, the Standards recommend appointment of a guardian ad litem for the child. Standard 3.1 (b)(ii)[c].

Attorneys for alleged status offenders should consider whether the child's home circumstances are such that a child protective proceeding, targeting the parents, rather than a status offense proceeding, targeting the child, would be more appropriate. With the client's permission, an abuse or neglect report could be made to child protective services. For an example of a status offense case becoming a child protective case, see In re Leif Z. in Chapter 10.

PROBLEM 3–4

You have been appointed to represent 13–year-old Jim in a delinquency proceeding. Jim has been taken into police custody before for shoplifting and theft. This time he was caught stealing tires from a gas station. His home situation is very bad and is likely to get worse. His father is absent, his mother has had a series of abusive boyfriends and does not pay any attention to Jim, and his older brother, a notorious drug-dealer, has just come back home after a state prison term. You think Jim will soon be selling and using drugs. He is failing seventh grade for the second time and sees drug-pushing as a source of money and prestige.

You think Jim would benefit greatly from placement in a new state school designed to give kids like him a real chance at success. It is a detention facility, but it is in a new campus-style building with excellent staff. Its mission is to treat each child as an individual and concentrate on his or her life skills, self-esteem and education. You think this facility would literally be a lifesaver for Jim.

Jim, however, wants probation so he can continue to live at home. You think that if you mention Jim's home situation at the dispositional hearing, the judge will place him in the new facility, but that if you emphasize Jim's youth and relatively minor offense record, the judge will give him probation.

What do you do at the dispositional hearing?

Chapter 4

ABUSE AND NEGLECT

SECTION 1. INTRODUCTION

As Chapter 1 demonstrated, parents have a constitutionally supported right to rear their children as they see fit, but the state may limit this right to protect the child's health or safety. The state's parens patriae authority to protect children allows the state to remove children from their parents' custody when the state's interest is sufficiently compelling. When a parent has severely beaten a child, intervention and removal seem clearly appropriate. But the state has also used its authority in questionable ways to remove children from parents whose lifestyles are viewed as immoral or whose income is insufficient to provide a "proper" home. Even when removal is needed, children too often receive woefully inadequate state-provided care, such as long-term foster care with minimal services and multiple placements. Hence, a major problem in abuse and neglect cases is determining whether the state should intervene.

Three major systems regulate families when child abuse or neglect is an issue. The first is the criminal law, which has been used since the 1600's to prosecute parents who abuse and neglect their children (see Chapter 6). The second is the welfare system, which intervened in poor families where children were considered neglected. Earlier in our history, the poor laws, modeled on the Elizabethan poor laws, gave overseers of the poor authority to remove pauper children from their families and bind them out as apprentices or send them to poorhouses or asylums. The modern welfare system is not as intrusive, but government aid still brings oversight and regulation of family life (see Chapter 9). The third major system of regulation is the civil child protection system, the focus of this chapter.

The civil child protection system reportedly began in New York City in 1874, in response to the case of Mary Ellen, a child severely beaten by her stepmother. Because no child protection system existed, her case was brought by the President of the New York Society for the Prevention of Cruelty to Animals, who argued "The child is an animal. If there is no justice for it as a human being, it shall at least have the rights of the stray cur in the street. It shall not be abused." Robert W. Ten Bensel et al., Children in a World of Violence: The Roots of Child Maltreatment in The Battered Child 3 (Mary Edna Helfer et al., eds., 5th ed. 1997), quoting Jacob Riis, Children of the Poor (1894).

Working as a police reporter, Riis wrote about the trial: "I saw a child brought in, carried in a horse blanket, at the sight of which men wept aloud, and I heard the story of Mary Ellen told again, that stirred the soul of a city and roused the conscience of a world that had forgotten; and, as I looked, I knew I was where the first chapter of the children's rights was being written." Id. at 16. In response to her case and growing public concern about child abuse, the New York Society for the Prevention of Cruelty to Children was established and New York enacted a child protection statute. The Society and similar groups in other states took an active role in investigating abuse and neglect and placing children in institutions and foster care. When the juvenile court system began in 1899, child protection cases were a major part of the caseload.

More recently, in the early 1960's child abuse attracted the attention of the media, the public, the medical profession, and lawmakers because of reports on the battered child syndrome. The "battered child syndrome" is a term used in an influential article by Dr. C. Henry Kempe and his colleagues. See C. Henry Kempe et al., The Battered Child Syndrome, 181 J.A.M.A. 17 (1962). In addition to describing characteristics of the injuries, the article identified other characteristics of the syndrome:

> The battered child syndrome may occur at any age, but, in general, the affected children are younger than 3 years. In some instances the clinical manifestations are limited to those resulting from a single episode of trauma, but more often the child's general health is below par, and he shows evidence of neglect including poor skin hygiene, multiple soft tissue injuries, and malnutrition. One often obtains a history of previous episodes suggestive of parental neglect or trauma. A marked discrepancy between clinical findings and historical data as supplied by the parents is a major diagnostic feature of the battered child syndrome.* * *

Earlier researchers had identified characteristics of injuries to children that show that the injuries are deliberate rather than accidental, but their findings had not received popular attention.

In response to public concern, states enacted laws that required physicians to report abuse to the state. In 1974 Congress enacted the federal Child Abuse Prevention and Treatment Act, which provided funding to the states for child abuse and neglect programs, established standards for child abuse and neglect reporting and investigation, required appointment of guardians ad litem for the child in abuse and neglect cases, and established the National Center on Child Abuse and Neglect.

The battered child syndrome is dramatic evidence of abuse, but children can be at risk even though they do not show any obvious injuries. Malnutrition or poor hygiene, for example, can indicate a "maltreatment syndrome that may develop into severe physical injury." The Maltreated Child (Vincent J. Fontana and Douglas J. Besharov, eds. 5th ed. 1996) Child maltreatment frequently results from the interactions of personal and social factors. Particularly significant factors are "poverty, ethnicity, neighborhood dysfunction, mental health problems, substance abuse, and the presence of children with special needs." U.S. Advisory Board on Child Abuse and Neglect, Child Abuse and Neglect: Critical First Steps in Response to a National Emergency x (1990)

There is no doubt that abuse and neglect can have long-term, harmful effects on children. After reviewing research in the area, the U.S. Advisory Board on Child Abuse and Neglect concluded that:

> Maltreated children are more likely than their peers to have significant depression. They also are more apt to engage in violent behavior, especially if they have been subjected to physical abuse, and their social and moral judgments often are impaired. Maltreated children also tend to lag behind their peers in acquiring new cognitive and social skills, so that their academic achievement is chronically delayed.

> Often these effects are long-lasting and even intergenerational. For example, the rate of depression among adult women who report having been sexually abused as children is quite high. Adult survivors of sexual abuse also are especially likely to report concerns about their sexual adequacy. Similarly, aggressiveness is a remarkably persistent personality trait in abused boys and often is part of a pattern of continuing antisocial behavior. Although most maltreated children do not become maltreating parents, the risk of their doing so is markedly greater than if they had not been abused themselves.

> Infants or young children are at greater risk of serious physical harm as a result of abuse or neglect. For evidence, one need only look at the costs accrued in intensive care units when infants are shaken or beaten, when young children suffer serious injuries when they are left unsupervised, and when infants "fail to thrive", and their survival and development are threatened by a lack of weight gain and emotional nurturance as a result of neglect.

Id. at 5.

Unfortunately, child abuse and neglect reports are numerous and have increased to record numbers:

> In 1990, the U.S Advisory Board on Child Abuse and Neglect concluded that child abuse and neglect was a national emergency. According to the study, reports of child maltreatment steadily increased over the years, from about 60,000 cases reported in 1974 to 1.1 million in 1980. Reports then doubled to about 2.4 million during the 1980's. More recently, HHS [the Department of Health and

Human Services] reported that between 1990 and 1994, the number of children that were the subject of reports of abuse and neglect rose approximately 14 percent, to over 2.9 million. Although reasons for the high number of reports are complex, research indicates that the number has risen, in part, due to (1) increased child maltreatment by drug-dependent caretakers, as a result of the cocaine epidemic during the 1980's, (2) the mandate for certain groups of professionals to report suspected maltreatment, and (3) the stresses of poverty among families. Since HHS began collecting data in 1990, neglect has been the predominant type of maltreatment. * * * HHS recently reported that for the first time, a leveling off—in both the annual number of reports nationwide and the annual number of confirmed cases—is occurring. However, some state and local officials told us they are concerned about the effect welfare reform will have on the number of CPS [child protective services] reports.

General Accounting Office, Child Protective Services: Complex Challenges Require New Strategies (1997).

The U.S. Advisory Board on Child Abuse and Neglect also noted that the actual incidence of maltreatment was far greater than the number of reported cases, because surveys consistently show large numbers of abuse cases go unreported.

The systems for protecting children from abuse and neglect are complex. States may have four sets of laws dealing with abuse and neglect—reporting statutes, child protective statutes, criminal statutes, and social services statutes. The definitions of abuse and neglect may differ for each statute. In addition, the federal government has long been involved in child protection and child welfare and has exercised extensive control over state systems through mandates tied to federal funding. The following table provides a summary of major federal legislation in this area:

Figure 4-1
U.S. Child Protection Legislation at a Glance[a]

- *Child Welfare Services Program, Title IV–B of the Social Security Act (1935)* provides grants to states to support preventive and protective services to vulnerable children and their families. Initially, most funds went to foster care payments; since 1980, federal law has encouraged prevention of out-of-home placement.

- *Foster care payments under the Aid to Dependent Children program, Title IV–A of the Social Security Act (1961)* provide federal funds to help states make maintenance payments for children who are eligible for cash assistance and who live in foster care. Such payments go to foster parents to cover the costs of children's food, shelter, clothing, supervisions, travel home for visits, and the like. In 1980, this program was transferred to a new Title IV–E of the Social Security Act.

a.   From 8 The Future of Children 1, 28   (Spring, 1998).

- *The Child Abuse Prevention and Treatment Act (CAPTA), Public Law 93–247 (1974)* provides limited funding to states to prevent, identify, and treat child abuse and neglect. It created the National Center on Child Abuse and Neglect, developed standards for receiving and responding to reports of child maltreatment, and established a clearinghouse on the prevention and treatment of abuse and neglect. Changes in 1996 reinforced the act's emphasis on child safety.

- *The Social Services Block Grant, Title XX of the Social Security Act (1975)* provides funds the states can use for social services to low-income individuals. A significant but unknown proportion of these funds pays for services related to child protection, including prevention, treatment programs, and foster care and adoption services.

- *The Indian Child Welfare Act, Public Law 95–608 (1978)* strengthens the role played by tribal governments in determining the custody of Indian children, and specifies that preference should be given to placements with extended family, then to Indian foster homes. Grants to allow tribes and Indian organizations to deliver preventive services were authorized, but have not been funded.

- *The Adoption Assistance and Child Welfare Act, Public Law 96–272 (1980)* requires states that seek to maximize federal funding to establish programs and make procedural reforms to serve children in their own homes, prevent out-of home placement, and facilitate family reunification following placement. This act also transferred federal foster care funding to a new Title IV–E of the Social Security Act, and it provides funds to help states pay adoption expenses for children whose special needs make adoption difficult.

- *The Family Preservation and Support Initiative, Public Law 103–66 (1993)* gives funds to the states for family preservation and support planning and services. The aim is to help communities build a system of family support services to assist vulnerable children and families prior to maltreatment, and family preservation services to help families suffering crises that may lead to the placement of their children in foster care.

- *The Adoption and Safe Families Act, Public Law 105–89 (1997)* reauthorizes and increases funding for the Family Preservation and Support program, while changing its name to "Promoting Safe and Stable Families." This law also requires states to move children in foster care more rapidly into permanent homes, by terminating parental rights more quickly and by encouraging adoptions.

Sources: U.S. House of Representatives, Committee on Ways and Means. 1996 green book: Background material and data on programs within the jurisdiction of the Committee on Ways and Means. Washington D.C.: U.S. Government Printing Office, 1996; Pecora, P.J., Whittaker, J.K., Maluccio, A.N., et. al. The child welfare challenge: Policy, practice and research. New York: Aldine de Gruyter, 1992, pp. 13–30.

Note

1. *Additional references.* For a comprehensive text on child abuse and neglect, including historical materials, see The Battered Child (Mary Edna Helfer, Ruth S. Kempe, and Richard Krugman, eds., 1997); and 8 The Future of Children, Protecting Children from Abuse and Neglect (Spring, 1998). For historical materials, see Joseph N. Hawes, The Children's Rights Movement (1991); Marilyn L. Holt, The Orphan Trains (1992); Jacobus TenBroek, Family Law and the Poor (Joel F. Handler, ed. 1971); Judith Areen, Intervention Between Parent and Child: A Reappraisal of the State's Role in Child Neglect and Abuse Cases, 63 Geo.L.J. 887 (1975); Lela B. Costin, Unraveling the Mary Ellen Legend: Origins of the "Cruelty" Movement, 1991 Social Service Review 203 (1991). Mason P. Thomas, Jr., Child Abuse and Neglect, Part I: Historical Overview, Legal Matrix, and Social Perspectives, 50 N.C.L. Rev. 293 (1972). For a helpful overview of the child protective system with a social welfare and policy emphasis, see Peter J. Pecora et al., The Child Welfare Challenge (1992). For National Clearinghouse on Child Abuse and Neglect annotated bibliographies on selected publications, 1990–95 on a variety of topics, see < http://biblioline.nisc.com >. For incidence statistics, see Office of Juvenile Justice and Delinquency Prevention, Juvenile Offenders and Victims: 1999 National Report (1999); National Center on Child Abuse and Neglect, Third National Incidence Study of Child Abuse and Neglect (1996) available at < www.calib.com/nccanch >.

SECTION 2.   DISCOVERING ABUSE AND NEGLECT: REPORTING STATUTES

The identification of the battered child syndrome in 1962 was a catalyst for laws requiring physicians to report suspected child abuse and neglect. By 1967 all states had adopted reporting laws. Over time other professionals, such as teachers and social workers, also became "mandated reporters." States have expanded the kinds of maltreatment that must be reported as well, in part because of federal requirements. State laws vary, however, with regard to who must report, what must be reported, what penalties may be imposed for failure to report, and civil liabilities related to reporting.

The variations in state reporting laws make it difficult to determine the incidence and prevalence of child abuse and neglect. Section 14 of the Child Abuse Prevention and Treatment Act of 1974 required states receiving funding under the Act to enact reporting laws that use a broad definition of maltreatment, specifically including mental injury and sexual abuse. The Child Abuse Prevention, Adoption, and Family Services Act of 1988 was even more inclusive, defining maltreatment as "the physical or mental injury, sexual abuse or exploitation, negligent treatment, or maltreatment of a child by a person who is responsible for the child's welfare, under circumstances which indicate that the child's health or welfare is harmed or threatened."

Very few of the reported cases actually end up in court. As the following article excerpt explains, screening is an important part of the reporting process.

JANE WALDFOGEL, RETHINKING THE PARADIGM FOR CHILD PROTECTION

8 The Future of Children 104, 106 (Spring, 1998).

* * *

The prioritizing of CPS [child protective services] reports begins at the point of screening. Nationwide, CPS hot lines screen out about half of the reports they receive. The remainder are assigned to a caseworker for investigation. The primary purpose of the investigation is to establish the safety of the child victim and the identity of the adult perpetrator. The family's need for services may also be assessed, but this is secondary to the main purpose of the investigation. From the perspective of the family, the investigation is an intrusive and adversarial process. At the first contact, the investigator informs the family of the allegations and may warm them that anything they say can be used against them if the case is taken to court. At the end of the investigation, the caseworker decides whether the allegations in the report are substantiated and what steps are necessary to protect the child from further harm.

As Figure 4–2 shows, more than 70% of all reported cases nation-wide are closed by the end of the investigation, either because the report was screened out by the hot line worker (approximately 50% of reported cases) or because the investigator recommended closing the case (about 20% of reported cases). The investigator will recommend that a case be closed if the evidence of abuse or neglect is insufficient to remove the child or to compel the family to participate in in-home services involuntarily, or if a family is considered low risk and hence a lower priority for services than other cases. In making these decisions, then, CPS takes into account not only the child's need for protection and the family's need for services but also, implicitly, the services available.

The remaining cases, about 30% of those originally reported to CPS, stay open for a period of time so the caseworker can assess the family and develop a plan for services. Service plans typically call for "ongoing treatment" or "protective oversight" (intermittent calls or visits by a caseworker), and may include other services such as family counseling or day care for a preschool-age child. In about one-third of these cases—less than 10% of those originally reported to CPS—the risk of severe maltreatment is so high that case is taken to court, which may assign custody of the children to the state, authorize the removal of the children and their placement into substitute care, or terminate parental rights altogether.

* * *

FIGURE 4–2

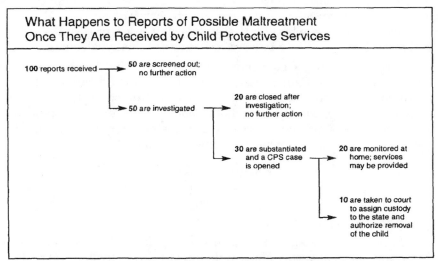

> What Happens to Reports of Possible Maltreatment
> Once They Are Received by Child Protective Services
>
> 100 reports received → 50 are screened out; no further action
>
> → 50 are investigated → 20 are closed after investigation; no further action
>
> 30 are substantiated and a CPS case is opened → 20 are monitored at home; services may be provided
>
> 10 are taken to court to assign custody to the state and authorize removal of the child

Sources: Author estimates from data in Wiese, D., and Daro, D. *Current trends in child abuse reporting and fatalities: The results of the 1994 annual fifty-state survey.* Working paper no. 808. Chicago: National Committee to Prevent Child Abuse, 1995; and U.S. Department of Health and Human Services, National Center on Child Abuse and Neglect. *Child maltreatment, 1993; Reports from the states to the national child abuse and and neglect data system,* Washington, DC; U.S. Government Printing Office, 1995.

The state must investigate a child abuse report within specified time limits, and maintain records of reports in the state's central registry. Valmonte v. Bane describes the operation of a state registry, but also illustrates some problems these central registries create.

* * *

VALMONTE v. BANE

United States Court of Appeals, Second Circuit, 1994.
18 F.3d 992.

ALTIMARI, CIRCUIT JUDGE:

* * *

Valmonte brought her claim against the Commissioner of the New York State Department of Social Services and the Commissioner of the Orange County Department of Social Services (collectively "the appellees" or "the state") alleging that their inclusion of her name on the New York State Central Register of Child Abuse and Maltreatment ("the Central Register" or "the list") violated her Fourteenth Amendment right of due process. Valmonte's amended complaint raised numerous challenges to the statutory scheme of the Central Register.

* * *

The major issue presented in this appeal is whether the state's maintenance of a Central Register that identifies individuals accused of child abuse or neglect, and its communication of the names of those on the list to potential employers in the child care field, implicates a protectible liberty interest under the Fourteenth Amendment. If so, we must also determine whether the state's statutory procedures established to protect the liberty interest are constitutionally adequate.

For the reasons stated below, we hold that the dissemination of information from the Central Register to potential child care employers, coupled with the defamatory nature of inclusion on the list, does implicate a liberty interest. We also hold that the procedures established violate due process, primarily because the risk of error in evaluating the allegations against those included on the list is too great. * * *

BACKGROUND

* * *

I.   Statutory Scheme

Valmonte is challenging the state's system for collecting and storing information about allegedly abusive and neglectful individuals. Article 6, Title 6 of the New York Social Services Law governs the recording and investigation of reports of suspected maltreatment of children, and the administrative review process by which substantiated reports may be reviewed. The Central Register maintains reports of child abuse as part of a larger system to ensure the safety of children in New York, and is maintained by both the state and various county departments of social services.

A.   Reporting and Initial Placement on Register

The Central Register procedures are triggered by reports to the Central Register of suspected child abuse. The state DSS maintains a telephone hotline with a toll-free telephone number that is staffed full-time in order to receive complaints. State law places an affirmative duty on designated individuals such as health care workers, social workers, law enforcement agents, judicial officers, and education employees to report to the Central Register whenever they have reasonable cause to suspect that a child is maltreated. Calls to the hotline can be made, however, by any individuals, not only those with affirmative duties of reporting.

Upon receiving a complaint of suspected child abuse, hotline operators must determine whether the allegations, if true, would be legally sufficient to constitute child abuse. If so, the operator records the complaint on paper and relays it to the appropriate county or local DSS. The local DSS is responsible for investigating all complaints of suspected child maltreatment, and must investigate the truth of the charges and complete an investigation within 60 days.

At the conclusion of the investigation, the local department must determine whether the complaint is "unfounded" or "indicated." Unfounded reports are expunged from the Central Register and all records destroyed. If the local DSS finds that there is "some credible evidence" to support the complaint, the complaint is marked "indicated" and the individual who is the subject of the report is listed on the Central Register. The Central Register accepts the findings of the county department, without making an independent determination.

B.   Confidentiality of Central Register Determinations

As noted earlier, the information in the Central Register is generally confidential. The names of individuals on the Central Register are not publicly available, although there are numerous exceptions for, among others, public agencies, law enforcement personnel, and judicial officers.

More significant, for purposes of this case, are the statutory provisions requiring certain employers in the child care field to make inquiries to the Central Register to determine whether potential employees are among those listed. The purpose of these provisions is to ensure that individuals on the Central Register do not become or stay employed or licensed in positions that allow substantial contact with children, unless the licensing or hiring agency or business is aware of the applicant's status. Numerous state agencies, private businesses, and licensing agencies related to child care, adoption, and foster care are required by law to inquire whether potential employees or applicants are on the Central Register. For purposes of simplicity, this group will be referred to as "employers," even though licensing agencies are included within that designation.

When such employers make an inquiry, the state DSS will inform the potential employer if the individual is the subject of an indicated report on the Central Register. The state DSS will not inform the employer of the nature of the indicated report, but only that the report exists. If the potential employee is on the list, the employer can only hire the individual if the employer "maintain[s] a written record, as part of the application file or employment record, of the specific reasons why such person was determined to be appropriate" for working in the child or health care field.

* * *

II.   Valmonte's Case

Valmonte became entangled in this system on November 30, 1989, when she slapped her eleven year-old daughter Vanessa on the side of her face with an open hand. Valmonte states in her complaint that she slapped Vanessa because Vanessa had been caught stealing and other forms of discipline had not been successful. An unidentified employee at Vanessa's school made a complaint to the child abuse hotline that Valmonte had mistreated her daughter. Subsequently, child abuse investigators working for the Orange County DSS concluded that Valmonte had engaged in "excessive corporal punishment," marked the complaint against her as "indicated," and commenced child protective proceedings against her.

The New York state family court subsequently dismissed the child protective proceedings against Valmonte on the condition that the Valmonte family receive counselling. This dismissal, however, had no impact on Valmonte's inclusion on the Central Register.

During this time, Valmonte requested expungement of her indicated report from the state DSS. This request was denied. Valmonte then exercised her right to an administrative hearing before an agent of the state DSS. The state DSS again denied expungement, finding some credible evidence to support the allegations.

Subsequently, Valmonte brought an action in the district court challenging the constitutionality of the Central Register statutory scheme under 42 U.S.C. § 1983. The complaint contained numerous procedural due process claims, substantive due process claims, and appended related state law claims.* * *

* * *

DISCUSSION

I.   Does Disclosure Violate a Liberty Interest?

* * *

The central issue in this case is whether Valmonte has sufficiently alleged the deprivation of a protected liberty interest. Valmonte's strongest argument on this issue is that the state's dissemination of information from the list to potential employers in the child care field not only stigmatizes those on the list but also denies them employment in their chosen field.

* * *

The Central Register does not simply defame Valmonte, it places a tangible burden on her employment prospects. Valmonte has alleged that because of her inclusion on the Central Register, and because all child care providers must consult that list, she will not be able to get a job in the child-care field. In other words, by *operation of law*, her potential employers will be informed specifically about her inclusion on the Central Register and will therefore choose not to hire her. Moreover, if they do wish to hire her, those employers are required by law to explain the reasons why in writing.

* * *

We hold that Valmonte has adequately stated a cause of action for deprivation of a liberty interest not merely because of the defamatory aspect of the Central Register, but because that defamation occurs in conjunction with a statutory impediment to employment. In this case, we find that the requirement that puts burdens on employers wishing to hire individuals on the list results in a change of that individual's status significant enough to satisfy the "plus" requirement of the "stigma plus" test.

II.   Procedural Due Process

Even though the Central Register implicates Valmonte's liberty interest, Valmonte still must show that the procedural safeguards of her interest established by the state are insufficient to protect her rights. Valmonte argues that the existing procedures violate due process by prohibiting expungement of a subject's indicated record if there is "any credible evidence" to support the allegation and only holding the county DSS to a higher "preponderance of the evidence" standard *after* a subject loses an opportunity for employment.

To summarize, the statutory framework for the Central Register sets out the following procedural steps for the placement of an individual's name on the list:

1.   Hotline

Phone call to Central Register hotline, which requires the operator to make a determination on the complaint about whether to pass it on to the appropriate county DSS.

2.   Investigation

County DSS investigation, which must be completed in 60 days, and must determine whether a complaint is "unfounded" or "indicated" based on "some credible evidence."

3.   State DSS Review Upon Request

If "indicated," the subject of the report has 90 days to request that the report be expunged. If a request is made, the state DSS has to conduct a review, determining whether there is "some credible evidence" for the allegations.

4.   Administrative Hearing

If the expungement request is denied, an administrative hearing is held where the local DSS must prove the allegations by "some credible evidence."

5.   * * * If the expungement request is again denied, the subject can [request judicial review of the denial.]

6.   Second Administrative Hearing

This is only for those who are denied employment based on their placement on the list. The hearing is to determine whether the person's record will be sealed in the future, although the name would still be on the list. The standard of proof in this hearing is "fair preponderance of the evidence."

The standards for evaluating the constitutionality of these procedures are clear. In Mathews v. Eldridge (1976), the Supreme Court articulated a three-factor test for evaluating administrative procedures, requiring examination of: (1) the nature of the private interest affected by the official action; (2) the risk of error and the effect of additional procedural safeguards; and (3) the governmental interest. We must balance these factors to determine "when, under our constitutional system, judicial-type procedures must be imposed upon administrative action to assure fairness."

* * *

A. Private Interest

Valmonte's argument in support of her private interest at stake is basically her argument in support of her liberty interest; that is, her interest in securing future employment in the child care field free from the defamatory label placed upon her by the state. * * *

B. Countervailing State Interest

Valmonte does not seriously challenge that the state, as parens patriae, has a significant interest in protecting children from abuse and maltreatment. * * *

C. Risk of Erroneous Deprivation

The deciding factor in this case, the one that clearly shows the inadequacy of the procedural protections established by the state, is the enormous risk of error that has been alleged by Valmonte and acknowledged by the appellees. As noted earlier, the state only requires that the local DSS meet the "some credible evidence" standard in order to initially include a subject on the Central Register or to keep the subject on the list at the non-deprivation administrative hearing. It is only later, at the post-deprivation hearing, when the subject has already been denied employment due to his or her inclusion on the Central Register, that the local DSS is required to prove the allegations against the subject by a "fair preponderance of the evidence."

The distinction between the two standards is significant. Valmonte points out that, according to her figures, nearly 75% of those who seek expungement of their names from the list are ultimately successful. Half of that number obtain expungement only after they have lost employment or prospective employment because of their inclusion on the Central Register. This means that roughly one-third of those initially placed on the Central Register are eventually removed once the local DSS is required to prove the charges against the subject by a fair preponderance of the evidence. The fact that only 25% of those on the list remain after all administrative proceedings have been concluded indicates that the initial determination made by the local DSS is at best imperfect.

* * *

Considering the minimal standard of proof, and the subjective nature of the inquiry, it is not altogether surprising 75% of those who seek expungement are ultimately successful. Another fact adduced at oral argument and noted in the record is that there are roughly 2,000,-000 individuals on the rolls of the Central Register. This staggering figure has been cited to us by Valmonte, but it was not contested at oral argument. We find it difficult to fathom how such a huge percentage of New Yorkers could be included on a list of those suspected of child abuse and neglect, unless there has been a high rate of error in determinations.

The appellees, remarkably, do not challenge these figures, but argue that there is no real deprivation in cases where individuals contest the initial inclusion on the Central Register. According to the appellees, the subjects are not deprived of anything if their names are taken off the list. Moreover, they assert that the fact that reports are eventually expunged demonstrates that the state's procedures are working to correct mistakes in the original determination.

This is an inherently contradictory argument by the state. To argue that the extraordinarily high percentage of reversals supports the fairness of the system, as a desirable feature of that system, is a curious defense of administrative procedures. One does not normally purchase a car from a dealer who stresses that his repair staff routinely services and repairs the model after frequent and habitual breakdowns. If 75% of those challenging their inclusion on the list are successful, we cannot help but be skeptical of the fairness of the original determination.

D.   Balancing

We hold that the high risk of error produced by the procedural protections established by New York is unacceptable. While the two interests at stake are fairly evenly balanced, the risk of error tilts the balance heavily in Valmonte's favor. The crux of the problem with the procedures is that the "some credible evidence" standard results in many individuals being placed on the list who do not belong there. Those individuals must then be deprived of an employment opportunity solely because of their inclusion on the Central Register, and subject to the concurrent defamation by state officials, in order to have the opportunity to require the local DSS to do more than merely present some credible evidence to support the allegations.

* * *

CONCLUSION

* * * Although we recognize the grave seriousness of the problems of child abuse and neglect, and the need for the state to maintain a Central Register for ensuring that those with abusive backgrounds not be inadvertently given access to children, we find the current system unacceptable.

Notes and Questions

1.   After *Valmonte*, what changes to the New York central registry would you propose? Would the report on Ms. Valmonte still be on the registry under your proposal? Should a child who is the subject of an abuse report have a right to a review of a determination that the report is "unfounded"?

2.   As a general matter, child welfare agencies do not intervene until parents fall below a rather low-threshold of competence. Many children are

left with inadequate (or less than adequate) parents. As a general matter, why do you think the threshold is low?

3.   Why do you think medical, social service, educational and law enforcement personnel are mandated reporters?

4.   *Registry access.* Would you favor legislation specifically allowing adult-run youth programs such as Boy Scouts and Little Leagues to check the registry before hiring someone or taking on a volunteer? If these programs are allowed to inspect the registry, does this, in effect, create an obligation that they do so?

5.   *Immunity.* Reporting laws generally provide some type of immunity for persons reporting suspected abuse. Some states provide qualified immunity for reports made in good faith. For a discussion of different approaches, see Elmore v. Van Horn, 844 P.2d 1078 (Wyo.1992). California has granted absolute immunity to mandated reporters, even for false and reckless reports, not only for state law claims but also for 42 U.S.C. § 1983 claims. The § 1983 immunity was granted on the ground that immunity was authorized under the Federal Child Abuse Treatment and Adoption Reform Act, 42 U.S.C. §§ 5105 et seq, § 5106a(b)(1)(B). See, e.g., Thomas v. Chadwick, 224 Cal. App. 3rd 813, 274 Cal.Rptr. 128 (1990). Immunity may not be granted, however, if a mandated reporter fails to follow the reporting act procedures, but instead discloses abuse to a private party. See, e.g., Searcy v. Auerbach, 980 F.2d 609 9th Cir. (1992) (psychologist who reported suspected abuse to child's father not entitled to immunity in mother's malpractice action because he did not follow the reporting act procedures). For a comprehensive treatment of mandated reporting, see Seth C. Kalichman, Mandated Reporting of Suspected Child Abuse: Ethics, Law and Policy (American Psychological Assn. 1993).

What advice would you give a person who wishes to report abuse, but is not a mandated reporter?

6.   *Failure to report.* Should a mandated reporter's failure to report result in criminal or civil liability for the abuse suffered by the child? Should the reporter be held liable for a negligent failure to report, or only for intentional failure? In Landeros v. Flood, 551 P.2d 389 (Cal. 1976), the child plaintiff was required to show that the defendant "in fact observed her various injuries and in fact formed the opinion that they were caused by other than accidental means..." to establish that the physician had violated the reporting statutes and was negligent. Violation was a misdemeanor, but the court held that the criminal statute did not automatically result in a civil cause of action, and that "the ramifications of creating a tort liability must be weighed against the consequences of resultant potential over-reporting." See also Vance v. T.R.C., 494 S.E.2d 714 (Ga. Ct. App. 1997) (no private cause of action against physician for violating reporting statute). But cf. Nash v. Perry, 944 S.W.2d 728 (Tex. App. 1997)(violation of reporting statute may be negligence per se); Williams J. Coleman, 488 N.W.2d 464 (Mich. App. 1992) ($900,000 verdict for failure to report that was proximate cause of child's death).

7.   *Unsubstantiated reports.* In 1995 an estimated 65% of reports were labeled "unfounded" after investigation. The investigative process places heavy demands on agency resources and is intrusive and traumatic to the

family. Vague, overly broad reporting laws are one cause of these inappropriate reports. See Douglas J. Besharov, Commentary 1: How We Can Better Protect Children from Abuse and Neglect, in 8 The Future of Children 120 (Spring, 1998). On the other hand, narrowing reporting criteria might leave some children at risk. Further, even when a report is not substantiated, the investigation could identify services that would benefit the family. Finally, it is important to distinguish between unsubstantiated reports and deliberately false reports. Some research reports that relatively few (16%) of reports are false. Jeanne M. Giovannoni, Unsubstantiated Reports: Perspectives of Child Protection Workers in Child & Youth Servs. 51 (1991). Some recent reform proposals suggest that narrowing reporting criteria and the scope of child protective services should be accompanied by expanding the responsibility of other agencies and community resources to assist in preventing child abuse. Jane Waldfogel, Rethinking the Paradigm for Child Protection, 8 The Future of Children 104 (Spring, 1998).

8. *Professional ethics codes and abrogation of privilege.* Mandatory reporting can conflict with professional ethics codes related to client confidentiality. Therapists and researchers may be required to report under state law, yet may feel ethically bound to remain silent. For a comprehensive discussion of the impact of reporting laws on attorney-client confidences, see Robert P. Mosteller, Child Abuse Reporting Laws and Attorney–Client Confidences: The Reality and the Specter of Lawyer as Informant, 42 Duke L.J. 203 (1992). Professor Mosteller concludes that, with the possible exception of Mississippi, state reporting laws do not abrogate the attorney-client privilege and require attorneys to report.

9. *Future crimes.* Even if they are not required to report, may lawyers reveal child abuse under the "future crimes" exception to an ethics rule such as Rule 1.6 of the American Bar Association Model Rules of Professional Conduct? Consider this analysis by Professor Mosteller, id. at 249–52:

> The degree of knowledge necessary to justify disclosure of future criminality has been a very troublesome issue for the drafters of ethics rules, and not surprisingly, different knowledge standards have been required by the courts and bar associations. Some authorities have demanded a relatively rigorous knowledge standard to prevent erosion of the protections afforded to confidential communications. Others have been somewhat less demanding; one recent ethics opinion requires that the lawyer must conclude only that the future crime was "reasonably likely."

> Regardless of the standard of knowledge used, all types of child abuse should not be treated identically under the "future crimes" exception. Some conduct constituting abuse under often exceptionally broad statutory definitions, which may include any non-accidental injury, involves no special likelihood of repetition. Other conduct, in contrast, reflects either a special psychological propensity for the violent treatment of children or perhaps an even more powerful drive to commit sexual abuse. In these latter situations, the level of probability may be sufficiently high to constitute a degree of knowledge of future criminal conduct authorizing disclosure regardless of the standard used. However, expert advice from the psychiatric/psychological community will

often be necessary for a proper decision. Moreover, such determinations cannot be reached categorically. They must instead be reached through careful examination of the circumstances of each case, and even then, unfortunately, results will often be unclear.

With regard to child abuse, the determination that the client will commit a future crime is difficult not only because it is based entirely on past conduct without a statement of intent, but also because the disclosure required to prevent the future crime will frequently be unusual. Because the lawyer does not know of any specific planned criminal episode, the action required to prevent the crime will be quite general and potentially expansive in scope. In some cases, referral to the relevant social services agency for either treatment or punishment will be sufficient. In others, prevention may require permanent removal of the client from the presence of a particular child or all children, which may mean in turn that the client must be incarcerated. In either situation, the lawyer must reveal what she knows about the past conduct in order to prevent future criminality; and revelations that are so explicitly backward-looking are unusual, if not unprecedented, as satisfying the ethical duty to thwart a future wrong. However, despite these difficulties, ethics panels in a number of jurisdictions have rather freely offered the "future crimes" exception as authorization for disclosure of a client's act of child abuse.

Once established, this precedent has substantial promise for application and misuse in other areas. For example, a legal aid attorney may learn that her client, who is facing eviction from his housing project for the burglary of a neighboring apartment, is addicted to drugs, is unemployed, and has committed similar burglaries to support his drug habit. Not only is the likelihood of that client's committing future crimes of the same type extremely high, but the conduct necessary to prevent such future crimes is as difficult to target precisely in this area as it is in the area of child abuse.

* * *

10. *Investigations and due process.* Must a social service investigator have "probable cause" before requiring an examination of children or a home? Probable cause is not required because the search is not criminal, but rather is an administrative search, done in an emergency to protect the child's safety. See, e.g., E.Z. v. Coler, 603 F. Supp. 1546 (N.D.Ill.1985) aff'd sub nom. Darryl H. v. Coler, 801 F.2d 893 (7th Cir.1986). The investigator must have an "objectively reasonable suspicion of abuse" before removing a child from the home. See, e.g., Croft v. Westmoreland County Children and Youth Servs., 103 F.3d 1123 (3d Cir.1997). For a comprehensive discussion of due process issues in investigations, see Mark Hardin, Legal Barriers in Child Abuse Investigations: State Powers and Individual Rights, 63 Wash. L. Rev. 493 (1988). For a discussion of the need for due process protections when a parent "voluntarily" consents to removal of a child from the home, see Katherine C. Pearson, Cooperate or We'll Take Your Child: The Parents' Fictional Voluntary Separation Decision and a Proposal for Change, 65 Tenn. L. Rev. 835 (1998).

11. *The privilege against compulsory self-incrimination.* May a parent be required to assist the state in determining whether a child has been abused? The Fifth Amendment privilege against compulsory self-incrimination, which applies to the states as a matter of Fourteenth Amendment due process, may present a barrier to civil proceedings or criminal prosecutions alleging abuse or neglect.

The privilege surfaced in the civil abuse-neglect context in Baltimore City Dep't of Social Servs. v. Bouknight, 493 U.S. 549 (1990). On a finding that the natural mother had committed serious recurring acts of physical abuse against her infant son, the juvenile court asserted jurisdiction by adjudicating the child to be a "child in need of assistance." The adjudication placed the child under the court's continuing oversight. Shortly afterwards, the mother regained custody after signing a court-approved protective supervision order, which she later violated in nearly every respect. After reports of further serious abuse, the juvenile court ordered the mother to produce the child or reveal his whereabouts. She refused on the ground that compliance would violate her privilege against compulsory self-incrimination. She contended that the act of producing the child would amount to testimony concerning her control and possession of him. The juvenile court held her in contempt.

The Supreme Court held that the Fifth Amendment privilege did not shield the mother from the obligation to comply with the production order. The Court assumed, without deciding, that the limited testimonial assertion inherent in producing the child would be sufficiently incriminating to trigger the privilege. But the Court invoked the privilege's "required records" exception. This exception removes Fifth Amendment protection from production of records that claimants must keep for the public benefit pursuant to "an essentially non-criminal and regulatory area of inquiry." Id. at 556–57. *Bouknight* held that the challenged production order fell within the recognized exception because the mother was the child's custodian pursuant to a juvenile court order that had required production of the child as part of a non-criminal regulatory scheme: "Once [the child] was adjudicated a child in need of assistance, his care and safety became the particular object of the State's regulatory interests.... By accepting care of [the child] subject to the custodial order's conditions ..., [the mother] submitted to the routine operation of the regulatory system and agreed to hold [the child] in a manner consonant with the State's regulatory interests and subject to inspection by the [social services agency]." Id. at 559. The Supreme Court, however, left open the possibility that in later criminal proceedings against the mother, the privilege might limit the state's ability to use the testimonial aspects of her act of production. Id. at 561.

Bouknight and the Fifth Amendment privilege are discussed in William Wesley Patton, The World Where Parallel Lines Converge: The Privilege Against Self–Incrimination in Concurrent Civil and Criminal Child Abuse Proceedings, 24 Ga. L. Rev. 473 (1990); Irene Merker Rosenberg, *Bouknight*: Of Abused Children and the Parental Privilege Against Self–Incrimination, 76 Iowa L. Rev. 535 (1991).

12. *Additional references.* John E. B. Myers and Wendell D. Peters, Child Abuse Reporting Legislation in the 1980's (1987); Catherine M. Brooks et al.,

Child Abuse and Neglect Reporting Laws: Understanding Interests, Understanding Policy, 12 Behavioral Sciences and the Law 49 (1994).

PROBLEM 4–1

An elementary school teacher sees the Chairman of the School Board hit his fourth-grade daughter four times with an open hand on her buttocks in the school parking lot. When he hits her, he puts his arm far back and the teacher can see the child's body sway with each hit. The child comes into school crying. The teacher, who is a mandated reporter, immediately calls you and asks your advice about whether she should report what she saw. What do you advise?

SECTION 3. THE CHILD PROTECTION SYSTEM: A COMPOSITE CASE

How does a child protection case begin and what happens to it? The article and chart that follow give an overview of the complex system that has evolved for dealing with abuse and neglect cases. These materials illustrate the multiplicity of agencies, courts and professionals involved in these cases. Obviously there must be extensive cooperation and ability to communicate despite differences in training and objectives among these entities. Not surprisingly, this cooperation and ability are often lacking. The child's lawyer can play an important role in advocating for the child's interests, encouraging cooperation and bridging gaps in communication.

DEP'T OF HEALTH & HUMAN SERVICES, U.S. ADVISORY BOARD ON CHILD ABUSE AND NEGLECT, CHILD ABUSE AND NEGLECT: CRITICAL FIRST STEPS IN RESPONSE TO A NATIONAL EMERGENCY 26–31 (1990).

It should come as no surprise that the many elements of the child protection system increase the complexity of the problem. Families in which maltreatment is suspected or is known to have occurred find themselves the objects of action (or inaction) by numerous public agencies that often are poorly coordinated and may have conflicting purposes.

This point can be best understood through a composite case example. Although not all cases involve injuries as severe as those in the following example, the facts presented herein illustrate how the child protection system frequently works.

J. is a 2 year-old boy who is brought to a hospital at 4:00 p.m. complaining of severe abdominal pain. His mother says that he was fine when she left for work at noon, but that at 3:00 p.m. she received a call from her babysitter (also her boyfriend), saying "Something's wrong with J." She gives no history of trauma.

J. is examined, found to have abdominal bleeding, and rushed to the operating room, where multiple injuries to his stomach, liver, bowel and kidneys are diagnosed. Many bruises of different ages are found on his body. The surgeon suspects that J. has been abused and calls the local CPS [child protective services] hotline.

The CPS caseworker, who has two months experience, comes to the hospital to investigate. The mother says that she does not know what happened but that J. has been bruising easily. The boyfriend says that J. fell from his bunkbed onto a toy. No one else was home at the time.

This story is not unique. Instead of a young child with an abdominal injury, it could have been an infant in a coma from a brain hemorrhage, a 5–year-old who told her mother that she had been molested, or a 4–month-old who had gained only 1–1/2 pounds since birth. While procedures will vary among local jurisdictions, each of the following may need to occur if the CPS caseworker seeks to protect J.:

1. The surgeon must be willing to state (and perhaps testify) that a fall from a bunkbed onto a toy would *not* cause the injuries that he saw, and that they were most likely the result of a beating.

2. The mother must be interviewed privately to assess her possible involvement in the abuse and her willingness to protect her child from further harm; she must acknowledge that her child is not safe with her boyfriend.

3. If the mother cannot protect J., or if she instead protects her boyfriend, then the CPS caseworker may have to call the police for a detention order or a judge for a protective or emergency custody order.

4. A juvenile court petition must be filed and a temporary custody hearing must be held within 24–72 hours.

5. The CPS caseworker must brief the attorney who will present the case for the State or County in juvenile court.

6. If the judge awards temporary custody to the State or County, placement with a relative or in foster care must be arranged.

7. Meanwhile, law enforcement is likely to begin an investigation that may lead to criminal charges.

8. A prosecutor will consider the filing of criminal charges.

9. A juvenile court adjudicatory hearing will be held, at which the juvenile court judge will determine whether abuse has occurred.

10. Psychological and social evaluations of the child, mother, and boyfriend are likely to be ordered by the juvenile court in order to develop a treatment plan as part of the disposition of the civil child abuse proceeding.

11. The CPS caseworker will compile all relevant medical, social, and psychological data for presentation to the court.

12. At the juvenile court dispositional hearing, the juvenile court judge will order a treatment plan that might include parenting classes for J.'s mother and her boyfriend (unless he is arrested), individual counseling for the mother and her boyfriend, a therapeutic nursery program for J., and supervised visitation between the mother and her child.

13. An attorney, court-appointed special advocate (CASA), or guardian ad litem may be appointed by the court to represent the child and monitor his progress in treatment.

14. If treatment fails, termination of the parent-child relationship may ensue, and an adoption worker will try to place J. in an adoptive home.

15. In the meantime, if the assistant district attorney decides to file criminal charges against the boyfriend, a lengthy process of pretrial hearings, trial, and sentencing may occur.

This example, as presented, is a rather simple one. In reality, it could be much more complex.

1. A large number of other agencies working directly with the family could be involved: the housing authority, a substance abuse agency, a local day care center, a WIC (Supplemental Food Program for Women, Infants, and Children) program, an adult education program, a vocational rehabilitation program.

2. Even agencies that never see the family, such as the Medicaid payment agency, could be involved.

3. The identity of the perpetrator could be unclear and the subject of a multitude of investigatory interviews.

4. The juvenile and criminal courts could be working at cross-purposes. Protection of the child, preservation of the family unit, rehabilitation of the parents, and punishment of the perpetrator are not necessarily compatible.

5. The CPS caseworker who "manages" the child's and family's progress through the maze of steps and agencies may also be handling 25 to 100 other cases at the same time.

6. Several prosecuting and defense attorneys could be involved in the array of legal proceedings.

7. The CPS caseworker may "burn out" and leave her job while the case is in progress.

In reality, it would be very rare for any individual working within the child protection system to be involved throughout the duration of the case. Rarely would there be an individual who provides continuity of care to the child and family for years. Although many states and communities have taken steps to improve coordination, such coordination still is an episodic response to a chronic difficulty.

In short, the child protection system is a complex web of social service, legal, law enforcement, mental health, health, educational, and volunteer agencies. Although CPS is the agency that is mandated by law to provide protection to maltreated children, it is just one part of the network. An assessment of society's response to child abuse and neglect must consider the child protection system as a whole. Unfortunately, such an assessment reveals critical problems throughout the child protection system.

As noted above, the composite case is atypical in that it involves serious physical injuries. A majority of substantiated cases involve ne-

FIGURE 4–3[b]

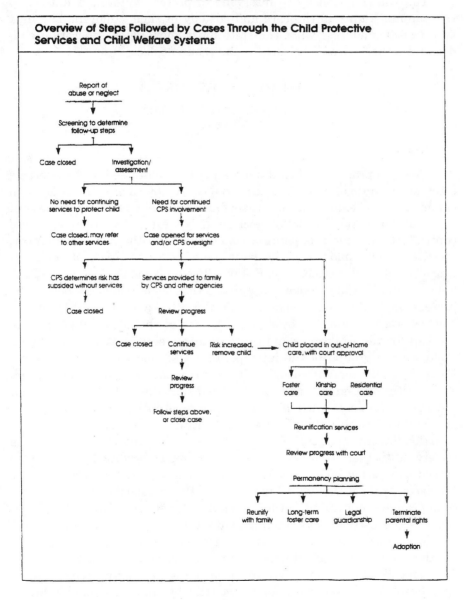

Overview of Steps Followed by Cases Through the Child Protective Services and Child Welfare Systems

b. From 8 The Future of Children 1, 31.

glect, rather than severe physical abuse. Diana J. English, The Extent and Consequences of Child Maltreatment, 8 The Future of Children 39 (Spring, 1998). Note that the chart above portrays only the civil child protection process, but that there might be concurrent criminal proceedings as well.

SECTION 4.   LIMITS ON INTERVENTION

The state's authority to intervene to protect children is limited by the parents' rights to the care and custody of their children. The next two decisions address what the state must show when separating children from their parents because of abuse and neglect.

IN RE KNOWACK

Court of Appeals of New York, 1899.
53 N.E. 676.

BARTLETT, J.

This is a proceeding based upon a petition addressed to the supreme court of the state of New York [the trial court] by Charles Knowack and Johanna, his wife, praying that their four children, now in the custody of the Children's Aid Society of Rochester, be restored to their care and control. At the time this petition was verified, on the 22d of December, 1897, the four children of the petitioners—the only issue of the marriage—were aged, respectively, Frank, 12 years; Gustave, 11 years; Emil, 8 years; and Freddie, 6 years. It appears that some two years before the present application was made, and on the 5th day of June, 1895, these children were committed by a police justice of the city of Rochester to the care of the Children's Aid Society, under section 291 of the Penal Code, on the ground of the intemperance and neglect of their parents. Each child was committed by a separate commitment, which was headed 'Destitution Commitment,' and recited that the child 'was found not having any home or other place of abode, or proper guardianship, being in a state of want and suffering, and destitute of means of support, in violation of statute,' etc. The child was to remain in charge of the society 'until therefrom discharged in manner prescribed by law, not to exceed the period of its minority.' * * * So far as this record discloses the facts, the petitioners do not dispute the regularity of the original commitments, nor does the Children's Aid Society controvert the allegations in the petition and accompanying affidavits. The petitioners aver that whatever ground might have existed on the 5th day of June, 1895, for the removing of the children from their care and custody has been fully and absolutely removed; and that since the last-named day they have been sober, industrious, and have tried by all means possible to live honorable and respectable lives. It further appears that the father and mother are both earning good weekly wages for persons in their position; that they are in comfortable financial circumstances, and have a substantial bank account with the Rochester Savings Bank of the city of Rochester, and own good and valuable chattels and securities; that they are free from all debts, and are in comparatively independent circumstances for persons in their station in life. The petitioners further aver that they are in every way able, willing, and desirous of caring for their four children, who are now a charge upon the poor fund of the city of Rochester for their food, clothing, and care, and that all the facts touching their willingness, ability, and desire are more fully set forth and confirmed by the affidavits attached to the petition. The petitioners further show that they have made frequent demands of the president and other officers of the Children's Aid Society for the return of their children, and that they even offered that the children be returned to them on trial, to be taken away again without resort to law, whenever the petitioners' conduct might seem to the officers of the society to justify such proceeding, but the officers have at all times refused to comply with these demands and requests. It further appears that the children are all anxious and desirous of returning to the home of their parents. Annexed to the petition are a number of affidavits of third parties, corroborating, in detail, the allegations that the petitioners are sober, industrious, and for a long time have been living honorable and respectable lives. The truth of the allegations of the petition and affidavits is admitted; the Children's Aid Society, in substance, demurring to these facts. * * *

* * *

The single question presented by this appeal is whether the supreme court of the state of New York * * * has power to intervene in this case, and restore these children to the custody and care of their parents. It certainly is a most startling doctrine that a child, who is a public charge and has been committed for such reasons as are disclosed in this case, cannot be restored to parental care and control, where conditions have changed and are such that neither in law nor morals the separation of parent and child should be continued. We are not now called upon to decide what effect legal adoption in good faith by third parties would have on an application like this. The Children's Aid Society stands in this proceeding upon the bald proposition of law already stated, that without its consent to their release these children are to remain in the custody of this institution during their minorities. As the youngest child was only 3 1/2 years of age when thus committed, it would be subjected to legal custody for a period of more than 17 years. * * * Stripped of all form and technicality, we have this situation: Intemperate parents are deemed to be unfit custodians of their children, and the state steps in and cares for and supports them for the time being. It now appears that the parents have reformed, are living honorable lives, and are abundantly able to care for their children. It seems self-evident that public policy and every consideration of humanity demand the restoration of these children to parental control. If the court of chancery can interfere and take the child from the custody of its parents, it can also intervene and restore it to their care, in the exercise of the same discretionary power.* * *

* * *

IN RE JUVENILE APPEAL

Supreme Court of Connecticut, 1983.
455 A.2d 1313.

SPEZIALE, CHIEF JUSTICE.

This is an appeal by the defendant, mother of five children, from the order of the Superior Court for juvenile matters granting temporary custody of her children to the plaintiff commissioner of the department of children and youth services.

The defendant and her six children lived in a small apartment in New Haven. They had been receiving services from the department of children and youth services (hereinafter DCYS) as a protective service family [1] since 1976, and were supported by the Aid to Families with Dependent Children program.[2] Michelle Spicknall, a DCYS caseworker, was assigned to the defendant's case in January 1979. In the next nine months she visited the defendant's home twenty-seven times. She considered the family situation "marginal," but noted that the children were "not abused [or] neglected." It was Spicknall's opinion that the children were very happy and active, and that they had a "very warm" relationship with their mother.

During the night of September 4–5, 1979, the defendant's youngest child, nine month old Christopher, died. The child was brought by ambulance to Yale–New Haven Medical Center where resuscitation was unsuccessfully attempted by his pediatrician, Dr. Robert Murphy. No cause of death could be determined at that time, but the pediatrician noticed some unexplained superficial marks on Christopher's body.

Because of Christopher's unexplained death, the plaintiff commissioner of children and youth services seized custody of the defendant's five remaining children on September 5, 1979, under authority of the "96–hour hold" provision * * * which permits summary seizure if the commissioner has probable cause to believe that a child is "suffering from serious physical illness or serious physical injury or is in immediate physical danger from his surroundings, and that immediate removal from such surroundings is necessary to insure the child's safety.... "

On September 7, 1979, in the Juvenile Court for New Haven, DCYS filed petitions of neglect under General Statutes § 46b–129(a) for each of

---

1. A protective services family is one which has come to the attention of DCYS as having a potential for abuse, neglect, abandonment, or sexual exploitation. DCYS then investigates the family and, where appropriate, provides "support systems to bolster family functioning."

2. Aid to Families with Dependent Children is a federal-state grant-in-aid program * * *.

the defendant's children. Accompanying each petition was an affidavit for orders of temporary custody asking that the court issue temporary ex parte orders to keep the five children in DCYS custody under authority of § 46b-129(b)(2).[5] The petitions alleged, in addition to Christopher's unexplained death, that the defendant's apartment was dirty, that numerous roaches could be found there, that beer cans were to be found in the apartment, that the defendant had been observed drinking beer, that on one occasion the defendant may have been drunk, that a neighbor reported that the children once had been left alone all night,[6] and that the two older children had occasionally come to school without having eaten breakfast. On the basis of these allegations, on September 7, 1979, the court granted, ex parte, temporary custody to the commissioner pending a noticed hearing on temporary custody set for September 14, 1979, within ten days of the ex parte order as required by § 46b-129(b)(2). The court also set October 1, 1979, for a hearing on the neglect petitions.

At the September 14 temporary custody hearing, DCYS presented testimony of Spicknall confirming and elaborating on the conditions of the defendant's home and on the defendant's beer drinking. Christopher's pediatrician testified concerning Christopher's treatment and physical appearance when the child was brought to the hospital on September 5. The doctor also testified that, although the pathologist's report on the autopsy was not complete, the external marks on Christopher's body were not a cause of death, that no internal injuries were found, and that the child had had a viral lung infection. He also explained, on cross-examination, the term "sudden infant death syndrome" and its pathology. At the conclusion of the state's case, the court found "probable cause" and ordered temporary custody of the children to remain with the plaintiff commissioner of children and youth services.

The defendant appealed to this court claiming that General Statutes § 46b-129(b) violates the due process clause of the fourteenth amendment both because it is an impermissible infringement on her right to family integrity, and because the statute is unconstitutionally vague. * * *

* * *

5. General Statutes § 46b–129(b) provides: "If it appears from the allegations of the petition and other verified affirmations of fact accompanying the petition, or subsequent thereto, that there is reasonable cause to find that the child's or youth's condition or the circumstances surrounding his care require that his custody be immediately assumed to safeguard his welfare, the court shall either (1) issue an order to the parents or other person having responsibility for the care of the child or youth to show cause at such time as the court may designate why the court shall not vest in some suitable agency or person the child's or youth's temporary care and custody pending a hearing on the petition, or (2) vest in some suitable agency or person the child's or youth's temporary care and custody pending a hearing upon the petition which shall be held within ten days from the issuance of such order on the need for such temporary care and custody. * * *

6. The report was allegedly made by an upstairs neighbor of the defendant. At the hearing, the neighbor denied having made such a report at any time.

I
Constitutionality of General Statutes § 46b–129(b)

A. FAMILY INTEGRITY

The Connecticut legislature has declared: "The public policy of this state is: To protect children whose health and welfare may be adversely affected through injury and neglect; to strengthen the family and to make the home safe for children by enhancing the parental capacity for good child care; to provide a temporary or permanent nurturing and safe environment for children when necessary; and for these purposes to require the reporting of suspected child abuse, investigation of such reports by a social agency, and provision of services, where needed, to such child and family." General Statutes § 17–38a(a).

In administering this policy, courts and state agencies must keep in mind the constitutional limitations imposed on a state which undertakes any form of coercive intervention in family affairs. The United States Supreme Court has frequently emphasized the constitutional importance of family integrity. * * * It must be stressed, however, that the right to family integrity is not a right of the parents alone, but "encompasses the reciprocal rights of both parents and children. It is the interest of the parent in the 'companionship, care, custody and management of his or her children,' and of the children in not being dislocated from the 'emotional attachments that derive from the intimacy of daily association,' with the parent.". This right to family integrity includes "the most essential and basic aspect of familial privacy—the right of the family to remain together without the coercive interference of the awesome power of the state."

B. CRITERIA FOR COERCIVE INTERVENTION BY THE STATE

Where fundamental rights are concerned we have a two-part test: "[1] regulations limiting these rights may be justified only by a 'compelling state interest,' and ... [2] legislative enactments must be narrowly drawn to express only the legitimate state interests at stake." Roe v. Wade (1973). The state has a substantial interest in protecting minor children; intervention in family matters by the state is justified, however, only when such intervention is actually "in the best interests of the child," a standard long used in this state.

Studies indicate that the best interests of the child are usually served by keeping the child in the home with his or her parents. * * * The love and attention not only of parents, but also of siblings, which is available in the home environment, cannot be provided by the state. Unfortunately, an order of temporary custody often results in the children of one family being separated and scattered to different foster homes with little opportunity to see each other. Even where the parent-child relationship is "marginal," it is usually in the best interests of the child to remain at home and still benefit from a family environment.

The defendants' challenge to the temporary custody statute, § 46b-129(b), must be addressed in light of the foregoing considerations. The defendant contends that only when the child is "at risk of harm" does the state's interest become a compelling one, justifying even temporary removal of the child from the home. We agree.

In custody proceedings, any criteria used to determine when intervention is permissible must take into account the competing interests involved. The parent has only one interest, that of family integrity; and the state has only one compelling interest, that of protecting minor children. The child, however, has two distinct and often contradictory interests. The first is a basic interest in safety; the second is the important interest, discussed above, in having a stable family environment. Connecticut's child welfare statutes recognize both the conflicting interests and the constitutional limitations involved in any intervention situation. Thus, under the criteria of General Statutes § 17–38a(e), summary assumption of temporary custody is authorized only when there is probable cause to believe that "the child is suffering from serious physical illness or serious physical injury or is in immediate physical danger from his surroundings, and that immediate removal from such surroundings is necessary to insure the child's safety.... "

The language of § 17–38a(e) clearly limits the scope of intervention to cases where the state interest is compelling, as required by the first part of the test from Roe v. Wade. Intervention is permitted only where "serious physical illness or serious physical injury" is found or where "immediate physical danger" is present. It is at this point that the child's interest no longer coincides with that of the parent, thereby diminishing the magnitude of the parent's right to family integrity; and therefore the state's intervention as parens patriae to protect the child becomes so necessary that it can be considered paramount. A determination that the state interest is compelling does not alone affirm the constitutionality of the statute. More is needed. The second part of the due process analysis of Roe v. Wade, requires that statutes affecting fundamental rights be "narrowly drawn to express only the legitimate state interests at stake." General Statutes § 17–38a(e) meets this part of the test by requiring, in addition to the compelling need to protect the child, that the assumption of temporary custody by the commissioner be immediately "necessary to insure the child's safety." This phrase requires that various steps short of removal from the home be used when possible in preference to disturbing the integrity of the family. The statute itself mentions supervised in-home custody, but a wide range of other programs short of removal are a part of existing DCYS procedure.

The challenged statute, § 46b–129(b), does not contain the "serious physical illness or serious physical injury" or "immediate physical danger" language of § 17–38a(e). We note, however, that § 46b–129(b) does limit the temporary custody order to those situations in which "the child or youth's condition or the circumstances surrounding his care require that his custody be immediately assumed to safeguard his welfare." It is axiomatic that statutes on a particular subject be "considered as a whole, with a view toward reconciling their separate parts in order to render a reasonable overall interpretation.... * * * Because we hold that General Statutes § 46b–129(b) may be applied only on the basis of the criteria enunciated in § 17–38a, we reject the defendant's claim that § 46b–129(b) is unconstitutional.

In the instant case, no substantial showing was made at the temporary custody hearing that the defendant's five children were suffering from either serious physical illness or serious physical injury, or that they would be in immediate physical danger if they were returned to the defendant's home. The DCYS caseworker admitted at trial, as did the state's counsel at argument before this court, that without the unexplained death of Christopher there was no reason for DCYS to have custody of the other children. The medical evidence at the hearing indicated no connection between Christopher's death and either the defendant or the conditions in her home. While the final autopsy report was not available at the hearing, the pediatrician testified that the marks on Christopher's body were not related to the child's death. There was, therefore, no evidence before the court to indicate whether his death was from natural causes or was the result of abuse. Yet with nothing before it but subjective suspicion, the court granted the commissioner custody of the defendant's other children. It was error for the court to grant to the commissioner temporary custody when no immediate risk of danger to the children was shown.

It appears from this record that DCYS has not heeded the suggestion of this court that the agency bears a responsibility of continuing review of cases it is litigating. * * * In this case, at some time shortly after the orders of temporary custody were granted, the state received the final autopsy report which effectively exonerated the defendant from any wrongdoing in Christopher's death. The reason for the custody order then no longer existed. It was then incumbent on DCYS to reunite the family. "In this situation, the state cannot constitutionally 'sit back and wait' for the parent to institute judicial proceedings. It 'cannot ... [adopt] for itself an attitude of "if you don't like it, sue." ' "[13]

Petitions for neglect and for temporary custody orders * * * "are particularly vulnerable to the risk that judges or social workers will be tempted, consciously or unconsciously, to compare unfavorably the material advantages of the child's natural parents with those of prospective adoptive parents [or foster parents]."

13. We recognize that there are three parties to litigation in the Superior Court for juvenile matters—DCYS, the parent, and the child (through a guardian ad litem * * *) and that any of these parties could have moved to terminate this litigation in a number of ways. We are saying only that DCYS, acting as parens patriae, had a duty to do so.

* * * We are even more concerned that the attorney for the children took no steps to protect their interests in family integrity by insisting on a resolution of the neglect petitions, and failed to represent their interests before this court. This court, therefore, is appreciative of the fact that the interests of the children have been ably represented by the Connecticut Civil Liberties Union as amicus curiae on this appeal.

This case clearly shows that these dangers do exist; it is shocking that the defendant's children have been in "temporary" custody for more than three years. This is a tragic and deplorable situation, and DCYS must bear full responsibility for this unwarranted and inexcusable delay. Too often the courts of this state are faced with a situation where, as here, litigation has continued for years while the children, whose interests are supposed to be paramount, suffer in the insecurity of "temporary" placements. The well-known deleterious effects of prolonged temporary placement on the child, which we have discussed above, makes continuing review by DCYS of all temporary custody and commitment cases imperative. Where appropriate, the agency can and must take unilateral action either to reunite families or to terminate parental rights as expeditiously as possible to free neglected children for placement and adoption in stable family settings.

The failure of DCYS properly to administer § 46b–129 does not, however, affect its constitutionality. The statute is constitutional because when it is read together with § 17–38a, as it must be, it is justified by a compelling state interest and is narrowly drawn to express only that legitimate state interest.

* * *

[Reversed on other grounds and remanded with direction to set aside the orders of temporary custody].

Notes and Questions

1. What was the basis for the court's return of the children in *Knowack*? Using the ruling in *Juvenile Appeal,* what arguments could you make for return?

2. In *Juvenile Appeal,* what showing was the state required to make in order to remove a child from home? What argument can you make that removal is a remedy of last resort, and may not be used when state services for the family would make the child's home safe?

3. *Void for vagueness.* Statutes often define child abuse and neglect broadly. The Alabama statute reviewed in Roe v. Conn, 417 F.Supp. 769, 773, 780 (M.D.Ala.1976), for example, defined "neglected child" as "any child, who, while under sixteen years of age * * * has no proper parental care or guardianship or whose home, by reason of neglect, cruelty, or depravity, on the part of his parent or parents, guardian or other person in whose care he may be, is an unfit or improper place for such child." The court held that as applied, the statute was void for vagueness. "[N]ot only is the statutory definition of neglect circular (a neglected child is any child who has no proper parental care by reason of neglect), but it is couched in terms that have no common meaning. When is a home an "unfit" or "improper" place for a child? Obviously, this is a question about which men and women of ordinary intelligence would greatly disagree. Their answers would vary in large measure in relation to their differing social, ethical, and religious views. [T]hese terms are too subjective to denote a sufficient warning to those individuals who might be affected by their proscription."

Compare the Alabama statute to the following definitions that were part of a consent decree following a successful challenge to Kentucky removal practices:

A. "Dependent child" means any child who is under improper care, control, or guardianship that is not due to the negligence of the parent or guardian, provided that the child is not an abused or neglected child.

B. "Abused or neglected child" means a child whose health or welfare is harmed or threatened with harm when his parent, guardian, or other person who has the permanent or temporary care, custody, or responsibility for the supervision of the child: inflicts or allows to be inflicted upon the child physical or mental injury to the child by other than accidental means; commits or allows to be committed an act of sexual abuse upon the child; willfully abandons or exploits such child; does not provide the child with adequate care and supervision, food, clothing and shelter, education, or medical care necessary for the child's well-being; provided, however, that a parent or guardian legitimately practicing his religious beliefs who thereby does not provide specified medical treatment for a child, for that reason alone shall not be considered a negligent parent or guardian. This exception, however, shall not preclude a court from ordering that medical services be provided to the child, where his health requires it.

C. "Physical harm" means physical pain or any impairment of physical condition.

D. "Emotional harm" means an injury to the mental or psychological capacity or emotional stability of a child as may be evidenced by a substantial and observable impairment in his ability to function within a normal range of performance and behavior with due regard to his culture, which injury may be directly attributable to the failure, refusal or incapacity of the parent or guardian to exercise a minimum degree of parental care and supervision toward the child.

E. "Serious injury" means physical injury which creates a substantial risk of death or which causes serious and prolonged disfigurement, prolonged impairment of health or prolonged loss or impairment of the function of any bodily organ.

Siereveld v. Conn, 557 F.Supp. 1178 (E.D.Ky.1983).

4. *Reference.* Peggy Cooper Davis and Gantam Barua, Custodial Choices For Children at Risk: Bias, Sequentiality, and the Law, 2 U.Chi.L.Sch. Roundtable 139 (1995).

PROBLEM 4–2

Mary, age four, lives in a rural area with her mother, her mother's boyfriend, and his wife in a back-to-nature commune with no electricity, no phone, and no indoor plumbing. Mary's mother, Sue, has an annual income of $40,000 from a trust fund created by her grandfather, but she gives all but $5000 per year to charity. Mary is in good health and she and her mother have a warm and loving relationship. Most of Mary's clothes and toys were purchased at second-hand shops and her diet is very basic. She has never seen a movie or television, or used a computer. The state statute provides that:

(i) "Neglected child" means a minor:

(A) whose parent, guardian, or custodian has abandoned or subjected the minor to mistreatment or abuse;

(B) who lacks proper parental care by reason of the fault or habits of the parent, guardian, or custodian;

(C) whose parent, guardian, or custodian fails or refuses to provide proper or necessary subsistence, education, or medical care, including surgery or psychiatric services when required, or any other care necessary for health, safety, morals, or well-being; or

(D) who is at risk of being a neglected or abused child because another minor in the same home is a neglected or abused child as defined in this chapter.

The Department of Social Services petition alleges that Mary is neglected because of "her mother's immoral lifestyle, namely an on-going sexual relationship with a man to whom she is not married and who is cohabiting with his wife; and further because she is not provided proper and necessary food, shelter, clothing and education necessary for her health, safety and well-being." Is Mary neglected under the statute? How would you interpret the statute to help insure its constitutionality?

PROBLEM 4–3

Marina left her sixteen-month-old son, Joey, at the home of a babysitter, Mrs. Jones, at 5:00 p.m. on February 16th, but did not return to pick him up that night, as had been planned. The next morning Mrs. Jones called child protective services (CPS) and reported that she had not heard from Marina, but that Marina's boyfriend had told her that Marina was "passed out drunk." CPS sent a police officer to Marina's home, but the officer got no response when she knocked at the door. When the CPS worker arrived at Mrs. Jones's home, Mrs. Jones told him that she had called Marina's mother, who said that she would pick up Joey at noon. The CPS worker nonetheless told Mrs. Jones to deliver Joey to the police station, which she did and a police officer then delivered Joey to a county shelter home. Joey's grandmother arrived at the police station shortly after the officer left with Joey. She asked for Joey's return and was told that she should get a lawyer and file a petition for custody.

On March 1st, Marina received a letter with a notice of a custody hearing to be held on March 15th and a copy of an Order of Temporary Custody that placed Joey with child protective services.

Were Marina's due process rights violated by the actions of child protective services and the police officer?

SECTION 5.   PATTERNS OF ABUSE AND NEGLECT

This section provides decisions that illustrate major categories of abuse and neglect. Additional materials are found in Chapter 6, Criminal Abuse and Neglect, and Chapter 8, Medical Decision–Making.

A.   *Neglect*

IN RE S.T.

Utah Court of Appeals, 1996.
928 P.2d 393.

WILKINS, JUDGE:

N.T. and T.T. appeal the juvenile court's order terminating their parental rights to their four children. * * *

BACKGROUND

N.T. (father) and T.T. (mother) are the natural parents of four children: C.T., M.T., H.T., and S.T. The children are now nine, eight, seven, and six years old.

The Division of Child and Family Services (DCFS) initially became involved with appellants and their children in June 1989, when a DCFS worker visited appellants' home to investigate a child abuse/neglect referral. C.T., M.T., and H.T. were two and one-half years, one year, and one month old, respectively. S.T. had not yet been born. The worker found the house dirty and cluttered. The floor was covered with food and soiled diapers, and dirty dishes, with aged, crusted food, were piled in the kitchen. The worker reported the children, especially the baby, were so thin they appeared malnourished.

DCFS offered to provide family preservation services, which included counseling to help appellants organize and properly care for their children, visits from a homemaker, and family aid. Appellants declined the services, but on several occasions met with a counselor from the preservation unit, and accepted a vacuum cleaner and cleaning supplies. Appellants were also offered the services of the Family Support Center (Center), a twenty-four-hour crisis nursery designed to provide care for children at risk of abuse or neglect, and to provide services for families in need. DCFS encouraged appellants to use the Center, in part, so they could monitor the children's condition. DCFS directed the workers and volunteers to vigilantly record their observations and to report anything, however minor, that suggested abuse or neglect.

Appellants frequently left the children at the Center.[1] Although the Center requires parents to provide clean clothes, diapers, and bottles for

---

1. When appellants had custody of their children from 1989 through 1993, they frequently used the services of the Center. The record shows that appellants left the children with the Center twenty-three days and nine nights between April and September 1989, eighty-six times between February and December 1991, and 160 times in 1992. In addition, appellants extensively used the Kid's Corral, a day care facility, between August 3 and October 18, 1991.

the children, reports detail that the children often arrived with bottles containing sour milk and nipples with old, crusty formula. The children's clothing was often wet and dirty; sometimes the children had dried food caked in their hair and soiled bottoms. Severe diaper rashes and sores were also a constant problem. Various workers documented that the children often arrived sick with a bad cough, cold, or fever, and in some instances, head lice. The children had dark circles under their eyes and appeared extremely thin. Several reports noted bruises, burns, cuts, and bumps on the children's bodies. Some reports even noted black eyes. The children almost always arrived hungry. Because sometimes after eating, one of them would vomit or complain of a stomach ache, the Center's volunteers closely monitored the children to make sure they did not eat too much at one time.

Volunteers reported the children also exhibited significant emotional problems. At times they had bouts of uncontrollable, incessant crying, or exhibited anger towards anyone they came in contact with. The children generally seemed starved for attention, sometimes demanding to be held and other times acting withdrawn. Reports also indicated the children appeared developmentally delayed. For instance, at two years and eight months, C.T. only spoke two or three words; at fourteen months, M.T. could not stand by herself.

After receiving two more referrals in August 1989, the DCFS worker revisited appellants' home. The state of the home had not changed. The baby, H.T., appeared lethargic and very thin. The worker instructed appellants to clean the home and take H.T. to a doctor. The worker made repeat visits to the home throughout August and September. While the living conditions improved slightly, appellants never obtained medical care for H.T. After several failed promises, the DCFS worker made an appointment and transported H.T. to the doctor. The doctor found that H.T., then four months old, had only gained three pounds since birth. Because H.T.'s birth weight was average, she had since become underweight. The doctor diagnosed H.T. with "failure to thrive."

C.T. and M.T. were also evaluated by a pediatrician. C.T., at two years and nine months, was malnourished, anemic, and twenty-five to thirty percent underweight. The pediatrician noted that it is unusual to see children with inadequate nutrition because many commonly available foods are fortified. C.T. had not had any of the eleven immunizations required for children his age. In addition, C.T. also had significant developmental delays in all areas, including an eight-month delay in social skills, a twelve-month delay in motor skills, and an eighteen-month delay in expressive language skills. An average two-and-one-half year old has a vocabulary of fifty plus words; C.T. only knew two.

M.T., who was sixteen months old, was also malnourished, anemic, and significantly underweight, in addition to lacking the required immunizations. M.T. also showed severe delays in the same areas, having a four-month delay in motor skills, an eight-month delay in language, and an eight-month delay in social skills.

On November 6, 1989, appellants admitted to the State's first petition alleging neglect. DCFS took custody of the children and placed them in foster care. Appellants began their first treatment plan, which required them to secure adequate housing, maintain a clean home, participate in parenting classes, attain a psychological evaluation, and participate in weekly counseling. Father was also required to find meaningful employment.

Appellants, however, did not begin working on the treatment plan until March 1990. Even then, appellants never consistently attended counseling or parenting classes, and on several occasions were resistant to homemaking services. Appellants did meet with a family counselor in April 1990, who diagnosed both mother and father with depression. In addition, father's aptitude test resulted in a score within the range of borderline intellectual functioning; on the same test, mother scored in the ranges of average and high average.

The children resided with a foster family from November 1989 to October 1990. While appellants made little progress with the treatment plan, the children made marked developmental improvements with the foster family. After eight months of attention, stimulation, and diligent effort by the foster mother, C.T. spoke in five to six-word sentences, recognized basic shapes and colors, sang songs, rode a bicycle, held himself on a swing, and interacted well with siblings and other foster children. M.T. started talking and learned to walk and run. H.T. gained nineteen ounces the first twenty days, and after eight months, gained nine pounds, thirteen ounces.

Appellants' fourth child, S.T., was born on June 12, 1990. DCFS did not remove the child from the home. Instead, DCFS created a second treatment plan and, despite appellants' sporadic attendance at parenting and counseling classes, returned C.T., M.T., and H.T. to appellants' care in November 1990.

In March 1991, DCFS investigated another referral. The worker reported a burn on M.T.'s palm which precisely and clearly spelled "IF". Appellants claimed M.T. was burned on the stove while a babysitter was with the children; the babysitter knew nothing of the burn. The worker also reported that the children, dressed only in diapers and underpants, had an offensive odor about them. The apartment was unsanitary and had an offensive smell. Appellants reasoned that it was due to their pet messing and urinating on the floor. While noticing food and garbage on the floor, the worker observed S.T. and M.T. pick a stale piece of bread and a cookie off the floor and put them in their mouths.

In April 1991, appellants admitted to a second petition filed by the State requesting protective supervision for the children. Again, DCFS offered reunification services to help appellants improve their personal functioning and parenting skills. DCFS offered a weekly family aide counselor, homemaking services, personal counseling, weekly supervised home visits, and use of the Center. Believing the best way to keep the children safe was to provide the family with the maximum amount of day care possible, the DCFS worker also authorized 180 hours of day care at the Kid's Corral.

Appellants, however, never consistently used the offered counseling and homemaking services. They refused to answer the door to the family aide and homemaking counselors on several occasions, failed to keep several medical appointments set up for the children, and failed to change the messy, cluttered state of the home. Mother did, at times, make an effort to participate in parenting classes.

While appellants sporadically used the reunification services, they continued to frequently use the Center and the day care facility. Reports, detailing the volunteers' observations of the children, showed little sign of improvement. The children still arrived dirty, wet, hungry, and sick with colds, coughs, and fevers. They often had bruises, burns, or bumps, and appeared thin with dark circles under their eyes. On several occasions, they did not want to leave when appellants came to pick them up. In addition, M.T., H.T., and S.T., three and one-half, two and one-half, and one and one-half years of age, respectively, were all on bottles, in spite of the fact M.T. and H.T. had been weaned from bottles by their foster mother.

In October 1991, appellants were evicted from their home due to unpaid rent and destruction of property. As a result, they voluntarily placed their children in DCFS's custody. Another medical examination of the children revealed the children were frail and very underweight for their age and height. Despite the medical evidence of neglect, the children were again returned to appellants' care.

During the first six months of 1992, DCFS received no new referrals on appellants. Appellants were working regularly with the family aide and appeared to be meeting the children's needs. During this time, a doctor explained that C.T.'s tonsils may be a cause of his failure to gain weight and thus suggested they be removed. However, appellants failed to make an appointment for several months. In fact, appellants made no effort to seek medical help until DCFS required mother to set the appointment as a condition to DCFS closing the case. In addition, despite being diagnosed with occasional physical illnesses, chronic fatigue, depression, and anxiety, appellants have never been diligent in seeking medical attention for themselves, or in using DCFS's services.

C.T. began kindergarten in July 1992. Concerned because C.T. had attended only three of twenty school days, the school psychologist visited mother at home. The psychologist explained that C.T. lacked school-readiness skills and that he could not progress when he did not attend school. Mother agreed to make an effort to send C.T. to school every day. The school psychologist made seven more visits between August 1992 and January 1993, each time admonishing mother to send C.T. to school and discussing the available educational services. While mother agreed to join Participating Partners, a program designed to assist developmentally delayed children, father adamantly refused.

In October 1992, pursuant to two new referrals, the DCFS worker revisited appellants' home. The worker found appellants' living conditions had not improved; the home was filthy and unsanitary. The worker again noted that mother had missed several doctor appointments set for the children and that C.T. continued to miss school. Mother again promised to clean the home, take the children to the doctor, and make sure C.T. attended school.

In November 1992, after DCFS's prompting, mother finally took the children to a doctor. The doctor diagnosed C.T. with a slight case of pneumonia, M.T. with two ear infections, and H.T. with rheumatic fever, which resulted in heart valve damage. C.T. also continued to miss school. Between July 1992 and January 1993, C.T. missed forty-eight of the ninety-six school days.

On January 12, 1993, a DCFS worker went to appellants' home and found it posed a threat to the health and safety of the children. Animal feces, cigarette butts, stale food, and dirty diapers littered the floor, all within easy reach of the children. There were no clean linens on the dirty mattresses, and the home had a noxious odor. As a result, DCFS filed a third neglect petition; the juvenile court found the petition to be true. The children were again removed and placed in foster care. Again, reunification services were offered in an attempt to reunite the family.

Between June and September 1993, DCFS provided supervised visitation during which the children regularly visited with appellants. During this time, the children appeared to be bonded to their parents. C.T. related memories he had of appellants and comfortably discussed missing them. He was depressed, in part, because he was homesick and wanted to go home. Several supervised visits went well, and often the children had a difficult time leaving their parents. One DCFS worker reported the children were "always excited to see their parents." In August 1993, DCFS began short unsupervised visits between appellants and the children. After three weekend visits, the children experienced a dramatic escalation in the expression of unusual fears. The fears increased and coincided with the children's knowledge that they would be returning home.

Reunification services continued until indications of possible abuse occurring during the weekend visits prompted new investigations. In January 1994, appellants were warned of the probable termination of their parental rights if existing circumstances did not change.

The State filed a petition to terminate appellants' parental rights on July 15, 1994. A thirteen-day trial was held. On March 24, 1995, the juvenile court terminated appellants' parental rights, finding: (1) appellants are unfit, substantially neglectful, and incompetent parents; (2) father is unable to care for the children's immediate and continuing physical or emotional needs for extended periods of time; (3) appellants continuously fail to meet the children's physical, emotional, and educational needs and to assume daily routine child care responsibilities, despite extraordinary services offered them since 1989; (4) appellants are unable or unwilling to correct the circumstances, conduct, or conditions leading to the removal of the children, notwithstanding reasonable and appropriate efforts by DCFS to return the children home; (5) the children's family identity is with their foster family, and the foster parents can provide stability and security for the children; (6) the children are special needs children who require extraordinary parental involvement, and the foster parents are more capable than appellants to provide them with the love, nurturing, guidance, and education they will require; and (7) it is in the best interest of C.T., M.T., H.T., and S.T. that appellants' parental rights be permanently terminated.

* * *

While appellants have made an attempt to marshal the evidence, they have not established clear error in the juvenile court's findings. After reviewing the record, we conclude there is ample evidence to support the juvenile court's findings that appellants are unfit, neglectful, unable or unwilling to change the conditions requiring the removal of their children, and unable to meet the children's physical, emotional, and educational needs.

The evidence reveals that while in appellants' care, the children lived in unhealthy and unsanitary conditions. The children were dirty, hungry, underweight, malnourished, and developmentally delayed. In addition, appellants frequently missed doctor appointments scheduled for the children, and only because of DCFS's prompting did the children receive medical care. Appellants were unable to consistently send C.T. to school and would not participate in educational programs offered to improve C.T.'s academic deficiencies. Despite the reunification services offered by DCFS, including several treatment programs, homemaking services, personal counseling, parenting classes, day care services, and the services of a family aide, appellants failed to make any substantial effort to change their living conditions or improve their parenting skills. Appellants also were unable or unwilling to seek medical help or psychological services for themselves to enable them to adequately care and provide for their children.

The evidence further shows that while in the care of their foster parents, the children gained weight and made marked developmental improvements in their language, social, and motor skills. The facts also establish that when the children were returned to appellants, they regressed physically, emotionally, and developmentally.

Since 1993, C.T., M.T., H.T., and S.T. have lived with the same foster family they were originally placed with in 1989. The children have expressed a desire to continue living with their foster parents. In addition, C.T. has discussed being adopted by them. These children deserve a stable, structured environment with parents able to nurture, love, and provide for their special needs. Appellants' passive parenting style cannot accommodate the children's basic needs, let alone the extraordinary care these children require. Thus, the evidence also supports the finding that termination of appellants' parental rights, and the children's continued placement with their foster family, is in the children's best interests. Because the evidence of neglect and parental unfitness is so abundant, we are convinced that no mistake has been made.

* * *

We acknowledge the love appellants have for their children, as found by the juvenile court. Yet, the evidence shows that for over seven years, appellants have made no substantial effort to change their conduct or living conditions to provide these children with basic necessities and stability, and the children show a remarkable lack of developmental and emotional progress when in appellants' care. As a result, it is the judgment of the people of Utah, as expressed by statutes enacted by the legislature, that under these difficult circumstances, termination of appellants' parental rights is necessary. * * *

Notes and Questions

1. *Questions about* S.T. (a) What services did the family receive? (b) Do you think the state's actions were proper in this case? (c) Should the state have done more to help the family or less, perhaps terminating parental rights earlier? (d) Should the state have been more concerned about the nonaccidental burn on MT's hand? If you were appointed to represent M.T., how would you find out the answer to this question?

2. *State variations.* State categories and definitions of maltreated children vary. Utah, for example, distinguishes among abused, dependent and neglected children. Classify the *S.T.* children under Utah Code Annotated § 78–3a–103 (1999) which follows:

(a) "Abused child" includes a minor less than 18 years of age who has suffered or been threatened with nonaccidental physical or mental harm, negligent treatment, sexual exploitation, or who has been the victim of any sexual abuse.

(h) "Dependent child" includes a minor who is homeless or without proper care through no fault of his parent, guardian, or custodian.

* * *

(q)(i) "Neglected child" means a minor:

(A) whose parent, guardian, or custodian has abandoned or subjected the minor to mistreatment or abuse;

(B) who lacks proper parental care by reason of the fault or habits of the parent, guardian, or custodian;

(C) whose parent, guardian, or custodian fails or refuses to provide proper or necessary subsistence, education, or medical care, including surgery or psychiatric services when required, or any other care necessary for health, safety, morals, or well-being; or

(D) who is at risk of being a neglected or abused child as defined in this chapter because another minor in the same home is a neglected or abused child as defined in this chapter.

(ii) The aspect of neglect related to education, described in Subsection (1)(q)(i)(C), means that, after receiving notice that a minor has been frequently absent from school without good cause, or that the minor has failed to cooperate with school authorities in a reasonable manner, a parent or guardian fails to make a good faith effort to ensure that the minor receives an appropriate education.

* * *

3. *Failure to thrive.* The *S.T.* parents were held responsible for their children's "failure to thrive." Failure to thrive, or growth deficiency, is a condition in which the child's weight and linear growth have fallen below standard measures or have significantly dropped without a physical cause. Children who are not treated can suffer permanent physical, cognitive, and behavioral problems. Early studies identified maternal deprivation and neglect as causes of failure to thrive. Later the importance of family, social and economic stresses were identified. More recently, studies have identified child behavior and temperament as important "failure to thrive" factors. "A diminished parental sense of competence may result from the demands of raising a child who adapts poorly to his or her environment, has an overall difficult behavioral style, and/or is malnourished/growth deficient." William G. Bithoney et al., "Parental Stress and Growth Outcome in Growth-deficient Children," 96 Pediatrics 707(1995)

Expert testimony is used to establish "failure to thrive". See, e.g., In re S.H.A., 728 S.W.2d 73, 76–78 (Tex. App.1987) in which the expert recommended placing the child in foster care:

> Part of the diagnosis was that the child was a "failure to thrive" child, and Dr. Paul Prescott was called in as a consultant on the child's case. Dr. Prescott testified that failure to thrive "means a child is not living up to his own growth potential." He said that the "failure to thrive" syndrome is best explained as a "symptom," like a headache or backache; there are "five-hundred and some odd causes of failure to thrive," including organic, nutritional, and psychosocial causes, such as where a mother has failed to nurture the child in some way.

> Dr. Prescott stated that once failure to thrive is diagnosed, medical causes are ruled out first. Here, the child's failure to thrive was not due to medical reasons. Dr. Prescott testified that the cause of this child's failure to thrive was malnutrition. Dr. Prescott could not, however, positively exclude the possibility of emotional causes of the child's failure to thrive. The failure to thrive syndrome, in a child of this age, can have long-term effects, such as decreased intelligence, learning disabilities, permanently stunted growth, and increased risk of infection. Dr. Prescott testified that it is common for one child in a family of several children to suffer from failure to thrive. He stated that "if there is no medical reason, and it's malnutrition, that's actually more worrisome, because we then start calling it the maternal deprivation syndrome. Then you get into emotional deprivation. And for some reason,

this one child is being scapegoated." Dr. Prescott testified that the maternal deprivation syndrome may be based on purely nutritional problems, but that only one child "is neglected, for who knows what reason."

Dr. Prescott stated that his diagnosis of malnutrition as the cause of this child's failure to thrive was in part based on the child's comparative weight gain over three time periods. During the child's May hospitalization, he gained about 1 1/2 to 1 3/4 ounces in weight each day. During the child's June hospital stay, he gained almost 3 ounces in weight each day. During the thirty-day period between hospital stays, the child gained an average of 1/4 ounce in weight per day while he was at home. An average child of this age gains about 1/2 ounce per day.

4. *Emotional harm.* Failure to thrive can be classified as emotional neglect or abuse when it is due to maternal deprivation. Should other kinds of emotional harm be the basis for intervention and, if yes, how should emotional harm be defined? Should the focus be on the condition of the child (e.g., Minn. St. § 3626.556(10) (neglect means "a pattern of behavior which contributes to impaired emotional functioning of the child which may be demonstrated by a substantial and observable effect in the child's behavior, emotional response, or cognition that is not within the normal range for the child's age and stage of development, with due regard to the child's culture") or on parental behavior (e.g., D.C. Code § 16–2401(23) (ennumerated acts include "habitually tormenting, vexing, or afflicting a child"). An emotional neglect case can be brought under more general statutory language such as "an environment injurious to the child's welfare."

Should a threat of emotional harm to the children justify intervention or must actual harm be shown? According to In re Matthew S., 49 Cal.Rptr.2d 139 (Cal.Ct.App.1996), a threat of harm is sufficient:

* * *

Alexandra S. had these delusions: her son's penis had been mutilated, he was being treated a UCLA while she was on a trip to South America, she murdered the treating physician when she returned to find her son in a "septic state" at the hospital. Acting on these delusions, she took her thirteen year old son to a urologist, * * *, for an examination on September 2, 1994. He found no evidence of injury whatsoever to her son's penis, and her son stated he had no such injury. * * * [The son] said that his mother makes confusing statements. For example, his mother says she was married to Gregory Harrison (the actor) who was murdered by the Mafia. When Alexandra S. was told that Mr. Harrison is alive, she suggested that his murder and funeral were staged. * * *

* * *

Substantial evidence supports the court's finding [that the child was at risk of suffering serious emotional damage] even though there are notable positive aspects in the home environment. Neither of the children feel threatened by their mother. Matthew S. likes school and is a good student. His grades have improved since he returned to his mother's [Alexandra's] home, and he appears to be "reasonably well-adjusted." Matthew S. and Sarah S. appear to have a warm close relationship with their mother. This is why the Department recommends the children not be removed from the home.

Although the children have not as yet suffered harm at their mother's hands, substantial evidence points to potential serious emotional harm. It is problematic that Alexandra S.'s delusions could result in some catastrophic event giving rise to a substantial risk that Matthew S. could suffer serious physical harm or illness as the Department postulates. * * *

Alexandra S. brings a foreboding sense of dread, danger and catastrophe to the lives of her children. Although Matthew S. so far has been able to deal with his mother's delusions, he is confused by them. As Hillsinger points out, Matthew S. is forced to shoulder a tremendous burden. He has a close loving relationship with his mother, but he "remains silent. He does not speak up for an apology, not out of a fear of retaliation, but out of a fear he will aggravate his mother's emotional problems. This is a lot of self-control to expect from a thirteen year old." Hillsinger also pointed out that at this time in his life, Matthew S. did not have the capacity "to escape from [his mother's] generalized and overwhelming sense that everybody is in immediate danger from some obscure and threatening force." * * *

The dissent felt the evidence was speculative and did not support a finding of future emotional harm.

5. *Additional references.* James Garbarino et al., The Psychologically Battered Child (1986); Psychological Maltreatment of Children and Youth (Brassard et al., eds. 1987); N.A. Polansky et al., Damaged Parents: An Anatomy of Child Neglect (1981); Neglected Children: Research, Policy and Practice (H. Dubowitz, ed. 1999).

PROBLEM 4–4

For the last several years, Shane has been subjected to an unrelenting torrent of verbal abuse by his father directed at his sexual identity. Specifically, he has been regularly called a "fag," "faggot," and "queer". In desperation, the boy pleaded with his mother to intervene on his behalf and prevail upon his father to cease making these accusations. However, the mother's efforts were abortive, resulting only in a repetition of the taunts by the father with the added assertion that they were true.

Nor were these accusations limited to the home. On one particular occasion, the respondent father humiliated the boy by calling him a "fag" while they were shopping in a store.

It should be noted that, in addition to the verbal indignities to which he was subjected, Shane was frequently forced to remove his father's shoes and massage his feet. The boy complied without protest since he was constantly in fear of his father. This fear was well-founded since the father has a history of assaultive behavior in the home.

The respondent father seeks to justify his verbal abuse of Shane as a form of legitimate parental discipline designed to cure the child of certain unspecified "girlie" behavior. He stated that it would be embarrassing to him if Shane were "queer". [Facts quoted from In re Shane T., 453 N.Y.S.2d 590, 593 (N.Y.Fam.Ct.1982)]

Would you recommend that a petition be filed alleging emotional abuse?

B. Abuse

1. The Battered Child Syndrome

Unfortunately parents not only neglect their children's needs, but they also beat, break bones, tie up, torture and murder their children. Decisions and news reports have litanies of abuse such as these alleged to have been inflicted on five-year-old Rafael B. by his mother:

a–1 On June 19, 1995, while in the care and custody of his mother, Deborah [S], * * * Rafael [B.] was found to have the following injuries:

a) Old fracture of the right ankle.

b) New fracture of the right elbow.

c) Large scar under the left eye.

d) Broken blood vessels in the left eye.

e) Swelling and bruising to both sides of face.

f) Swollen right eye.

g) Swelling to the right upper lip.

h) Two missing front teeth.

i) Gash under the chin with multiple bruising.

j) Multiple bruises and scars in various degrees of healing to both legs, especially the knees.

k) Circular scar around left ankle.

l) Multiple bruises in various stages of healing on the stomach.

m) Two bruises on the chest.

n) Circular scar around right wrist.

o) Multiple bruises and scars down the length of the left arm.

p) Bruising under right arm.

q) Eight healed scalp lacerations.

r) Multiple bruises on buttocks.

a–2 The mother has willfully withheld food from Rafael for extended periods of time.

a–3 According to medical opinion, Rafael's injuries were inflicted non-accidentally over a prolonged period of time.

a–4 On several occasions, since April 1995, the mother has willfully concealed Rafael from Child Protective Services and law enforcement during investigations of alleged abuse in order to avoid detection of his injuries.

* * *

i–1 The mother has confined * * * Rafael, to his room for prolonged periods of time.

i–2 The mother allows Rafael to sit in his own waste for extended periods.

i–3 On numerous occasions, the mother has tied Rafael's ankles and wrists together to restrain him and has put a sock in his mouth to prevent him from screaming.

i–4 The mother has confined Rafael in a darkened closet for extended periods of time.

i–5 The mother has confined Rafael to his crib by placing a board across the top held down by a weight. While confined to his crib, the mother has jabbed Rafael with a screwdriver through the crib's slats.

Deborah S. v. Superior Ct., 50 Cal.Rptr.2d 858, 860(1996)

Sadly, Rafael had been adjudged a "dependent" child three years earlier, after having sustained "five fractures and multiple bruising while in the care and custody of his parents," but the state did not permanently remove him from the home and the abuse continued. When the department of social services again initiated proceedings alleging that Rafael was a dependent child, the department included Rafael's siblings in the action based primarily upon the severity of abuse to Rafael.

The multiple injuries Rafael received are characteristic of the battered child syndrome. Because the battered child syndrome indicates that the child's injuries were not accidental, it is useful for both physicians and prosecutors to establish that a child's injuries were caused by abuse. Expert testimony can be used to establish that a child suffers from the battered child syndrome in both civil and criminal cases:

> * * * [T]he battered child syndrome has become a well-recognized medical diagnosis. The diagnosis is dependent on inferences, not a matter of common knowledge, but within the area of expertise of physicians whose familiarity with numerous instances of injuries accidentally caused qualifies them to express with reasonable probability that a particular injury or group of injuries to a child is not accidental or is not consistent with the explanation offered therefor but is instead the result of physical abuse by a person of mature strength.

> Expert testimony that a child was a victim of "battered child syndrome" has been held admissible and not an invasion of the jury's domain, even though by this diagnosis the physician draws an

inference of non-accidental injury, a function usually left for the jury.

The use of the term "battered child syndrome" by a physician does not, of course, necessarily indicate any wrongdoing by a particular defendant. * * *

State v. Mulder, 629 P.2d 462, 463 (Wash.1981).

Expert testimony on the battered child syndrome also has been used in a very different way, namely as a defense to prosecution of the child. For a discussion of the approaches taken by various states to the use of the syndrome as a defense, see State v. Nemeth, 694 N.E.2d 1332 (Ohio 1998). In State v. Janes, 822 P.2d 1238, 1243 (Wash.1992), the court permitted such expert testimony to assist the jury in evaluating the reasonableness of the stepchild's perception that he "was in imminent danger of death or serious bodily harm at the time he killed his stepfather." The court stated:

> Neither law nor logic suggests any reason to limit to women recogni-
> tion of the impact a battering relationship may have on the victim's
> actions or perceptions. We have noted in other contexts that chil-
> dren are both objectively and subjectively more vulnerable to the
> effects of violence than are adults. For that reason, the rationale
> underlying the admissibility of testimony regarding the battered
> woman syndrome is at least as compelling, if not more so, when
> applied to children. Children do not reach the age of majority until
> they are 18 years of age. Until then, they have virtually no indepen-
> dent ability to support themselves, thus preventing them from
> escaping the abusive atmosphere. Further, unlike an adult who may
> come into a battering relationship with at least some basis on which
> to make comparisons between current and past experiences, a child
> has no such equivalent life experience on which to draw to put the
> battering into perspective. There is therefore every reason to believe
> that a child's entire world view and sense of self may be conditioned
> by reaction to that abuse.

For examples and additional information, see Paul Mones, When a Child Kills: Abused Children Who Kill their Parents (1991).

2. Shaken Baby Syndrome

The "shaken baby syndrome" was identified in the early 1970's. The syndrome is caused by a parent who severely shakes an infant, resulting in whiplash type injuries. No external injury is seen, but the shaking can cause death or severe brain injury. See, e.g., Luke J. Haseler, et al., Evidence from Proton Magnetic Resonance Spectroscopy for a Metabolic Cascade of Neuronal Damage in Shaken Baby Syndrome. 99 Pediatrics 4 (1997). The syndrome can be very difficult to prove because typically there are no witnesses to the shaking and identifying the time of the incident may be difficult. See, e.g., Jody Tabner Thayer, The Latest Evidence for the Shaken Baby Syndrome, 12–SUM Crim. Just. 15 (1997). Physical abuse of a pregnant woman can result in harm to the fetus that is similar to the "shaken baby syndrome." Robert P. Stephens et al., Bilateral subdural hematomas in a newborn infant, 99 Pediatrics 619 (1997).

3. The Target Child

Some parents single out one child for abuse. Two recent notorious New York City cases fit this pattern. Elisa Izquierdo's mother tortured her and beat her to death in 1995, for example, and was sentenced to 15 years to life in prison. Her five other children were not physically abused.

Five-year-old Daytwon Bennett's mother beat and starved him. He weighed only 30 pounds and had scars all over his body when he died in 1997. His four siblings had not been physically harmed. He lived with them in a well-kept, immaculately clean apartment. His family was involved with the social services department because of prior abuse of Daytwon. A caseworker had visited the home 13 times in the nine months before Daytwon's death.

Social workers investigating abuse may see the unharmed children and either be unaware of the existence of another child, or assume the missing child is safe because the other children appear well. Because of allegations that the City had not reacted properly to multiple reports of abuse of Elisa, her death resulted in laws designed to make New York child protective services records more open and agencies more publicly accountable.

4. Why Do Parents Abuse Their Children?

The question, "why do parents abuse their children," is complex. First, are we asking about the population generally or only about parents in the child protection system? What definition of abuse is being used? Are neglect and emotional abuse included or just physical abuse? Is a parent "abusive" if the parent is too poor or depressed to care adequately for a child?

Based on a 1995 survey of parents, forty-four children in every one thousand are physically abused by their parents. Diane J. English, The Extent and Consequences of Child Maltreatment in Protecting Children from Abuse and Neglect, 8 The Future of Children 39 (1998). Another self-report study found that 63% of parents had used psychological aggression on their children. Taken together, self-report studies suggest that "several million children suffer physical or sexual abuse yearly, and that psychological abuse is even more common." Id. at 43. Note that these studies do not include neglect.

When data about substantiated abuse and neglect cases are analyzed, however, a different picture is presented than that based on the self-report studies of parents. In 1994, 1.6 million cases were investigated and one-third were substantiated; 53% of the substantiated cases were neglect, 24% physical abuse, 14% sexual abuse and 5% emotional abuse. Id. at 44.

The articles that follow address the question of causation, looking at different populations. Dr. Gelles' article is based on his assessment of what we know when we look at the population as a whole and seek to predict which parents will be abusive. Dr. English primarily examines families who are involved with child protective services because of substantiated child abuse and neglect. Dr. Taylor and her colleagues report on a study of court child protection cases involving severe mistreatment to determine whether the parents had intellectual or emotional impairments.

RICHARD J. GELLES, FAMILY VIOLENCE: WHAT WE KNOW AND CAN DO, UNHAPPY FAMILIES: CLINICAL AND RESEARCH PERSPECTIVES ON FAMILY VIOLENCE 1, 5–7(ELI. H. NEWBERGER AND RICHARD BOURNE, EDS., 1985).

["Family violence" means physical abuse and includes kicking, biting, punching, hitting or trying to hit with an object, beating, threatening with a gun or knife, or using a gun or knife."]

* * *

It is generally agreed now that, at most, 10% of wife abuse and child abuse cases are attributable to mental illness and character disorders or, in other words, to "kinds of people." The other 90% of the abusers defy clinical classification as suffering from individual aberrations. They are not different psychologically from most people.

Generally four factors are found to be related to family violence. Note, "found to be related," should be understood as a probability statement, not a determining statement. The first factor is that family violence is, in many cases, transmitted intergenerationally. An abused child's chances of becoming an abusive adult are, in some instances, a thousand times greater than a nonabused child. However, the base rate of child abuse is not especially high, 3.6%; so a thousand times greater does not mean that every abused child grows up to be an abusive parent. In terms of my own research findings, there is only about a 50% chance that an abused child will become an abusive parent. For a social scientist, that is a strong association. For a clinician, that is too weak to base a prediction on. It is important for clinicians to realize that although the social scientists jump for joy over strong associations, strong associations do not necessarily make predictive instruments.

The second factor is that abuse of all kinds is more likely to occur in lower socioeconomic families. Families below the poverty line have rates of wife and child abuse which exceed the rates of those making $25,000 or more per year by a factor of two. But again, all poor people are not abusers, and abuse can be found in some fairly well-to-do families.

The third factor is that abusive families of all kinds are characterized by significant social isolation which can be identified by noticing how few organizations in the community abusive families belong to, how little contact they have with neighbors and relatives and families, and how many moves they make. Abusive families typically do not live in the same neighborhood for a long time. One of the factors that we have found very strongly related was living in a house in a neighborhood less than two years.

The fourth factor is social stress. The higher the social stress the greater the chance that the family will be abusive.

* * *

Causal explanations are few to be found. People abuse family members because they can. There are rewards to be gained from being abusive: the immediate reward of getting someone to stop doing something; of inflicting pain on someone as revenge; of controlling behavior; or of having power. All of these rewards are evident in other social settings. Why don't people beat up their neighbors when they return the lawn mower broken? Why don't people beat up their boss, when he makes them stay late on the night they have show tickets which cannot be returned? Why don't people beat up their annoying co-workers? The motivation is there and is, perhaps, as strong as the motivation in families. They do not because the costs are too high. Beating up a boss could result in being kicked back, fired or having the police called. The police are known to respond faster when people are beating up a stranger than when they are beating up a family member. Beat up a stranger and the result could be assault charges or incarceration. Very few of those controls operate in families. A person does not lose his job for beating his wife or beating his children. The risk of official social control is rarely run; judges are despondent when faced with a choice of leaving a family intact or criminally prosecuting the abuser. The tradition in families is for a more powerful person to beat on someone less powerful, someone who cannot return and inflict even physical costs.

* * *

DIANA J. ENGLISH, THE EXTENT AND CONSEQUENCES OF CHILD MALTREATMENT

8 The Future of Children 39, 45–47 (Spring, 1998)

While knowing how many children are abused and neglected is critical to policy development, understanding the factors that contribute to maltreatment and that shape its consequences for children is crucial to the development of prevention and treatment approaches. For instance, the likelihood that an individual child will experience abuse or neglect may be influenced by characteristics of the parent or caregiver, the family's socioeconomic situation, or the child. Caregiver characteristics such as psychological impairment, experience of child abuse or domestic violence, and attitudes toward parenting contribute directly to the occurrence of maltreatment. Aspects of the family's social and economic situation (such as unemployment, poverty, or social isolation) affect maltreatment both directly and indirectly, though their effects on parents' psychological well being. Finally, characteristics of the child (such as age and gender) may increase the potential for abuse or re-abuse, or may intensify the harmful consequences of maltreatment.

Caregiver Characteristics

A wide variety of characteristics of the child's parents or caregivers have been linked to an increased likelihood of child abuse or neglect. For instance, individual attributes such as low self-esteem, poor impulse control, aggressiveness, anxiety, and depression often characterize maltreating parents or caregivers. Inaccurate knowledge of child development, inappropriate expectations of the child, and negative attitudes toward parenting contribute to child-rearing problems, as well. However, because cultural groups differ in the child-rearing and disciplinary practice they consider appropriate, cultural norms must also be factored in when judgements are made about child maltreatment and responses to it.

Domestic violence involving the child's caregiver is a problem that is more likely to contribute to physical abuse than neglect. As stated earlier, date from a 1985 national survey indicated that between 1.5 and 3.3 million children in the United States witness domestic violence each year. Not only is the experience of witnessing violence likely to be psychologically harmful, but several studies have found that male batterers are more likely than other men to physically abuse their children. Women who are victims of domestic violence are also more likely to be reported for maltreating their children.

Substance abuse by the parent or caregiver is strongly associated with child maltreatment. Current estimates indicate that between 50% and 80% of families involved with child protective services are dealing with a substance abuse problem. The use of crack cocaine, which rose rapidly in the late 1980's, has increased referrals to CPS agencies and has resulted in cases of both abuse and neglect that are more complex and challenging for caseworkers to handle.

Socioeconomic Characteristics

From the earliest history of child protection, concerned citizens have identified poverty as an environmental factor that contributes to child maltreatment. In recent times, researchers have focused on the relationship between child maltreatment and both poverty and single-parent-hood. Although child abuse and neglect occur in families of all income brackets, cases of child maltreatment are drawn disproportionately from lower-income families. Studies suggest that sexual abuse and emotional abuse, specifically, are not closely related to socio-economic status. However, the 1993 National Incidence Study found family income to be the strongest correlate of incidence across categories of child maltreatment. Poverty was especially related to serious neglect and severe violence toward children.

No one fully understands the links between poverty and maltreatment. The stress and frustrations of living in poverty may combine with attitudes toward the use of corporal punishment to increase the risk of physical violence. For instance, researchers have found that unemployment can lead to family stress and to child abuse. When a family lacks the basic resources needed to provide for a child, neglect is likely, although researchers suggest that dynamics over and above poverty (such as disorganization and social isolation) differentiate neglecting families form others. Indeed, most poor people do not mistreat their children. The effects of poverty appear to interact with other risk factors such as unrealistic expectations, depression, isolation, substance abuse, and domestic violence to increase the likelihood of maltreatment.

Child Characteristics

Studies suggest that younger children, girls, premature infants, and children with more irritable temperaments are more vulnerable to abuse and neglect. Girls are more likely to suffer from sexual abuse than are boys, but other types of maltreatment affect both sexes about equally. Maltreated infants and young children are significantly more likely to be reported to CPS [child protective services] agencies than are older children. About 16 per 1,000 children under age one were involved in substantiated reports in 1994, compared to only 9 per 1,000 adolescents ages 16 to 18. The youngest children, whose bodies are fragile, more often die from maltreatment: 45% of the maltreatment-related fatalities from 1993 to 1995 involved infants, and 85% involved children under age five.

* * *

CAROL TAYLOR ET AL., DIAGNOSED INTELLECTUAL AND EMOTIONAL IMPAIRMENT AMONG PARENTS WHO SERIOUSLY MISTREAT THEIR CHILDREN: PREVALENCE, TYPE, AND OUTCOME IN A COURT SAMPLE

15 Child Abuse and Neglect 389 (1991).

* * *

A prominent and troublesome issue in assessing the potential risk to a child living with a previously abusive or severely neglectful family is the mental health of the parents. When hearing of a parent who batters or seriously neglects a child, one might assume that the parent is emotionally disturbed or even "crazy" however, to date, findings conflict about whether parental mental illness and mental retardation are important variables associated with severe mistreatment of children. Further, there is little data on the types and extent of diagnosed psychopathology in a population of parents known to have abused or severely neglected their children. The judicial system in particular, having the responsibility to decide whether a parent's custody conflicts with a child's right to be protected, is frequently compelled to adjudicate these cases with insufficient information about such important factors as the parents' psychiatric status, including the ability to employ good judgment, the capacity to exercise control of anger, and the willingness to accept services or treatment.

* * *

In this court-referred sample, more than half of the parents who had seriously mistreated their children were diagnosed as having emotional disorders and/or low IQ. When records documenting alcohol or substance abuse only (i.e., no diagnosed emotional or mental limitations were added, fully three-quarters of these families had at least one parent who met DSM [Diagnostic and Statistical Manual of Mental Disorders, 1987] criteria for a diagnosed disorder.* * *

* * *

Despite the high incidence of serious emotional disorders, low IQ, and substance abuse, none of these factors alone or in combination significantly predicted type of mistreatment, higher risk of being a repeat case with DSS or the Court, or greater likelihood of their children being permanently removed by the court. * * *

* * *

The parents with more serious psychiatric impairments (those with personality/character disorders, severe affective disorders and those at risk for psychosis) were not significantly more likely than neurotically disordered parents to pose a high risk to their children, to have engaged in one form of mistreatment over another, to have had higher rates of prior agency involvement, or to have rejected court-ordered services more often. What diagnosis did predict was which parents kept their children. Four-fifths of character-disorder and psychotic-risk parents had their children permanently removed, in sharp contrast to the one-fifth of neurotically disordered parents who lost their children. The severe affective disorder group fell in between. The determining factor in returning a child to parental custody, on a case by case basis, was the parents' compliance with court-ordered services.

Although overwhelmingly the evidence in the research literature reveals that parents who seriously mistreat their children have little ability to empathize, suffer from low self-esteem, are significantly depressed, and are often characterologically impulsive, these personality-trait descriptors tell us little about predicting a given individual's capacity to accept proper intervention or treatment and to respond flexibly and adaptively to required changes in his or her own behavior. social isolation) differentiate neglecting families from others. Indeed, most poor people do not mistreat their children. The effects of poverty appear to interact with other risk factors such as unrealistic expectation, depression, isolation, substance abuse, and domestic violence to increase the likelihood of maltreatment.* * *

* * *

Notes and Questions

1. *Populations, sub-populations and inferences.* In discussing causes of abuse, a common mistake is to look at characteristics of a sub-population, such as the characteristics of parents with children in the child protective system, and assume that people in the general population with these characteristics will also abuse their children. We cannot make an inference about a larger group based on a sub-population of that group, unless we know that the sub-population was selected to be representative of the larger group through, for example, random selection. Two examples may help illustrate this point.

(a) Assume that a study reports that 90% of the children in foster care in your county because of physical abuse by a parent were abused by parents who themselves reported being abused as children. Could you assume that 90% of children abused by their parents will abuse their children when they become parents?

(b) Assume that ninety percent of the players in the National Basketball Association (NBA) played basketball in college. Does this mean that 90% of college basketball players will join the NBA?

For a general reference on research methods, see John B. Williamson, The Research Craft: An Introduction to Social Science Research Methods (2d ed. 1982).

2. *Expert testimony.* Expert testimony on family characteristics sometimes associated with child abuse has been disallowed in criminal cases. In Commonwealth v. Day, 569 N.E.2d 397, 398–99 (Mass.1991), the expert, Dr. Eli Newberger, testified that "five family characteristics are sometimes associated with child abuse":

> (1) stress derived from economic hardship and conflict between the parents; (2) isolation of the family; (3) violence against the mother; (4) obtaining medical care from different physicians and hospitals; and (5) singling out of a particular child for abuse. Dr. Newberger also testified, over repeated objections by defense counsel, about the presence of "risk factors" in child abuse cases such as a "repeated pattern" of partners of single mothers who sometimes "offend against [the] children" while the mothers are at work. Dr. Newberger added that another "pattern" recognized in child abuse cases is when a single parent, usually the mother, has several partners who bring alcohol and drugs into the household. Dr. Newberger stated that more than 60% of the cases of child abuse reported to the department "involved" the use of drugs.

The court excluded Dr. Newberger's testimony about the "family characteristics" and "patterns" found in child abuse cases because it consisted of profile evidence irrelevant and highly prejudicial in that particular case.

C. Corporal Punishment

IN RE C. CHILDREN

Supreme Court, Appellate Division, 1992.
583 N.Y.S.2d 499.

MEMORANDUM BY THE COURT.

In a child protective proceeding [the Family Court] * * * found that the respondent [mother] had abused her child Antoine and had neglected her child Katoine,* * * [and] placed the children in the custody of the Commissioner of Social Services of the City of New York until the end of the 1990–1991 school year, at which time the children would be returned to the respondent on the condition that she undergo counseling.

* * *

The subjects of the instant abuse and neglect proceeding are the respondent's two infant children, Antoine and Katoine, who were six years old and two years old respectively, at the time the proceeding was commenced. On or about December 5, 1990, Antoine was observed at school with a large scar or bruise and scratches on his face. He told a caseworker from the Child Welfare Administration that his mother beat him with a belt buckle whenever he did anything wrong, and that he had a mark on his face and a bruise on his back where he had been hit.

The caseworker spoke with respondent, who admitted that she routinely used a belt to discipline her two children. In fact, she showed the caseworker two different belts, each with a buckle, the larger of which was used on Antoine and the smaller of which was used on Katoine. She admitted striking Antoine in the face with the buckle while attempting to discipline him for pushing his brother and telling lies. She claimed that she accidentally left a mark on Antoine's cheek, just under the eye. When the caseworker suggested other methods of discipline, the respondent insisted that belt beatings were the only effective means of punishment and indicated that she intended to continue disciplining her children in this fashion.

The caseworker observed that Antoine had some old marks on his arm and nose. The two children were brought to a hospital where each was observed to have old and new bruises on his body.

The Family Court found that the mark on Antoine's face had not been inflicted accidentally or inadvertently and concluded that the child had been abused * * *. The court also found that Katoine was a neglected child. We affirm.

A child need not sustain a serious injury in order to justify a finding that he or she has been abused. It is sufficient to show that the child was subjected to a substantial risk of physical injury which would be likely to cause serious or protracted disfigurement, or protracted impairment of his physical or emotional health. Here, the respondent subjected Antoine to a substantial risk of serious physical injury by the excessive use of a belt, with a buckle, striking a blow that landed perilously close to the child's eye. She compounded the danger to the child by thereafter insisting that she would continue to inflict such punishment in the future. The evidence was clearly sufficient to establish that Antoine was an abused child.

The evidence also supports the Family Court's finding that Katoine was a neglected child because of the excessive corporal punishment inflicted upon him.

Notes and Questions

1. *Questions about* C. Children. (a) Should the children have been removed from the home in this case? (b) If the children had bruises only on their buttocks, would you have advocated removal? (c) If the children are returned to the mother at the end of the school year, how will the state determine whether the abuse continues?

2. *Restatement (Second) of Torts.* Under § 147 of the Restatement, a parent "is privileged to apply such reasonable force or to impose such reasonable confinement upon his child as he reasonably believes to be necessary for its proper control, training, or education." In determining the reasonableness of punishment, the following factors in § 150 are to be considered:

   (a) whether the actor is a parent;

   (b) the age, sex and physical and mental condition of the child;

   (c) the nature of his offence and his apparent motive;

   (d) the influence of his example upon other children of the same family or group;

   (e) whether the force or confinement is reasonably necessary and appropriate to compel obedience to a proper command;

   (f) whether it is disproportionate to the offense, unnecessarily degrading, or likely to cause serious or permanent harm.

Would you use these factors to decide whether corporal punishment was abusive?

RABOIN v. NORTH DAKOTA DEPARTMENT OF HUMAN SERVICES

Supreme Court of North Dakota, 1996.
552 N.W.2d 329.

SANDSTROM, JUSTICE.

* * *

The Raboins were married in 1983 and live in Fargo with their six children, all of whom were under 11 years of age at the time of these proceedings. It is undisputed the Raboins' children are healthy, happy, and well-adjusted. As a last resort for disciplining the children, the Raboins impose corporal punishment by spanking the children on the buttocks with a plastic spoon or leather belt a predetermined number of "whacks," according to the seriousness of the misconduct.

In October 1994, Cass County Social Services received a report from a person expressing concern the Raboins were striking their children with objects as a form of discipline. The Department * * * investigated the report of suspected child abuse through the Cass County Social Services office. On November 21, 1994, the social worker who conducted the investigation filed a written report * * * concluding there was probable cause to believe child abuse had occurred.* * *

* * *

The term "abused child" is defined under N.D.C.C. § 50–25.1–02(2): " 'Abused child' means an individual under the age of eighteen years who is suffering from serious physical harm or traumatic abuse caused by other than accidental means by a person responsible for the child's health or welfare * * *."

The term "harm" is defined under N.D.C.C. § 50–25.1–02(4), which provides in relevant part:

" 'Harm' means negative changes in a child's health which occur when a person responsible for the child's health and welfare:

"a.   Inflicts, or allows to be inflicted, upon the child, physical or mental injury, including injuries sustained as a result of excessive corporal punishment. . . ."

Having reviewed the entire record in this case, we conclude there is no evidence from which a reasonable person could conclude the Raboins have committed child abuse as defined by these statutes. There is simply no evidence the Raboin children have suffered serious physical harm or traumatic abuse from the spankings administered by their parents in disciplining them.

A

An assessment worker with Cass County Social Services, investigated the alleged abuse by the Raboins and filed a written report. The assessment worker relates Brandon, age 10 and the oldest child, told her he was swatted on the butt twenty times "five years ago" because he swore a lot and as a result he "received a black and blue mark for a couple minutes." Brandon also told her none of his brothers or sisters have ever had bruises or marks as a result of being disciplined by their parents. The second oldest child, Andrew, age 9, told Brown he received seventeen whacks on the butt for kicking his little sister. He said he had bruises from this but was unable to describe for Brown what the bruises looked like. Brown's report does not mention any other incidents which even suggest any of these children have ever suffered serious physical harm or emotional trauma from the spankings.

At the administrative hearing, Jim and Kim Raboin both testified they have never administered corporal punishment out of anger or in rage against their children. Kim Raboin testified both parents give their children "a lot of love" so the children know they are "accepted" and give them "structure" and "affection" with lots of "verbal praise." They set clear rules and boundaries for the children and use corporal punishment only as a last resort when the children refuse to heed the parents' numerous verbal warnings or occasional pinch on the back of the neck to let them know the boundaries have been crossed. Corporal punishment is administered only on a child's buttocks with the use of a wooden or plastic spoon or belt. Both parents testified they have never observed any bruises, welts, cuts, abrasions, or any other lasting evidence of the spankings other than some temporary reddening of the skin. Besides the very vague and nondescript statements by Brandon and Andrew to Brown about some slight bruising, there is no evidence to contradict Jim and Kim Raboins' testimony.

The regional representative of Child Protection Services for the Southeast Human Service Center, testified he had no reason to doubt the Raboin children are healthy and well-adjusted. He said with the number of whacks administered on occasion to some of the children "there may have been bruises on [the] children at some point," but he did not testify he had personal knowledge any of the Raboin children were bruised by the spankings.

Although the Department may not have been comfortable with the Raboins' disciplinary practices, we conclude a reasonable person could not find on this record probable cause the Raboins abused their children. There is no evidence from which a reasonable person could conclude any of these children ever suffered serious physical harm or traumatic abuse as a result of the parents' spankings. Even if we infer from Brandon and Andrew's statements to the investigator each of them had experienced slight bruising on the buttocks from a past spanking, these spankings fall far short of the statutory definition of child abuse. A reasonable person could not conclude a slight bruise on the buttocks is a serious "negative change[ ] in a child's health." N.D.C.C.§ 50–25.1–02(4).[2]

* * *

IV

We conclude the Department's finding of probable cause of abuse is not supported by a preponderance of the evidence and this application of the statute by the Department is not in accord with the law. The judgment of the district court affirming the decision of the Department is therefore reversed, and the case is remanded with directions the district court order the Department to vacate the probable cause finding against the Raboins. * * *

NEUMANN, JUSTICE, concurring specially.

I have joined the majority's opinion, but write separately to remind myself that what is legally sufficient often is, and must be, less than what is socially desirable.

---

2. The use of reasonable force by a parent to punish a child is expressly authorized under N.D.C.C. S 12.1–05–05(1): "The use of force upon another person is justified under any of the following circumstances: ... a parent ... may use reasonable force upon the minor for the purpose of safe-guarding or promoting his welfare, including prevention and punishment of his misconduct, and the maintenance of proper discipline.... The force used must not create a substantial risk of death, serious bodily injury, disfigurement, or gross degradation."

I suspect corporal punishment, regularly and consistently applied, can only diminish a child's sense of self-worth, and thereby unnecessarily limit the resources that child can bring to life's battles. Because all of us as parents and as citizens want to equip our children in the best ways possible to meet their future, a future that is ours as well, I believe the regular use of corporal punishment is a practice to be avoided.

But, if corporal punishment is a practice that ideally should be avoided, such perfection in parenting is not a standard to which we fallible, struggling, impatient humans can or should be held as a matter of law. Accordingly, our legislature has defined "child abuse" and "harm" to forbid only excessive corporal punishment that results in injury. It is that legislative definition which this court is obligated to apply, and which the majority has properly applied in this case. We should understand, however, that while avoiding physical or mental injury to our children is the most that is demanded of us by the law, it is the least we owe our children. Fortunately for our children and for ourselves, most parents—including, I think, the petitioners in this case—strive to be better than the minimum the law demands of us.

Notes and Questions

1. Do you think that the Raboin children were "abused children" under the North Dakota statute quoted in the case? Should the statutory definition of "abused child" should be broadened? How do you explain the different results in *Raboin* and *C. Children*?

2. *Domestic violence statutes.* Should a child be able to get a protection order against a parent under a state's domestic violence statutes? Are there advantages to such a proceeding from the child's point of view? What is the difference between corporal punishment and domestic violence? Consider the approach taken in Beermann v. Beermann, 559 N.W.2d 868 (S.D.1997):

> Erica Beermann is the daughter of divorced parents, Barbara Beermann DeJong and defendant Kevin Beermann. On September 15, 1995, Erica, then 14 years of age, was visiting her father in his home. During an argument between the two, Kevin picked her up, dropped her, picked her up again and threw her into a chair. He screamed and swore at her, all the while holding her in the chair by her shoulders.

> One week later, Erica went to court seeking a temporary protection order under the "Protection From Domestic Abuse" chapter of the South Dakota Code.

* * *

> The trial court suggested two alternatives to proceeding under the domestic abuse statutes. First, the court stated Erica's mother could seek to modify the visitation order. * * * One problem with that solution, at least in Erica's case, is that she never sought to modify or end her father's visitation rights.

> Another problem is that modification must be sought by the custodial parent, who may be unwilling or financially unable to seek such relief. In contrast, a victim can fill out the standard preprinted forms for

a temporary restraining order without assistance from counsel, and can obtain the order without paying costs by filing an affidavit of indigency. Moreover, relief via visitation modification would take much longer than a temporary restraining order, which the court can issue upon application.

The trial court also suggested the remedy in Chapter 26–8A of the South Dakota Code ("Protection of Children From Abuse or Neglect"). Relief under this chapter may be inadequate for the reasons stated above; most significantly, there is none of the immediacy available under the domestic abuse laws. In contrast, under Chapter 26–8A, the victim must first file a complaint, or wait for one to be filed on her behalf, and then wait for an investigation to be conducted and a report to be compiled. The circumstances under which a law enforcement or court services officer may take immediate action without a court order are extreme and involve the actual taking of temporary custody.

Erica did not seek such extraordinary measures; the order she requested was to insure nonviolence during visitation. When a court issues a protection order, it puts the would-be abuser on notice that his or her actions will be scrutinized. * * *

We conclude that the "Protection From Domestic Abuse" statutes were enacted to provide an immediate and affordable solution to family members, regardless of age, who are subjected to domestic abuse. * * *

What if Erica wanted to end visitation with her father? See Bacon v. Bacon, 567 N.W. 2d 414 (Iowa 1997)(Father prohibited from seeing his daughter for one year, but father did not question whether domestic abuse statute applied to child.)

2. *Research.* A recent review of the research on parental corporal punishment concluded that "there are not enough quality studies that document detrimental outcomes of nonabusive physical punishment to support advice or policies against this age-old parental practice." Robert E. Larzelere, The Short and Longterm Consequences of Corporal Punishment, 98 Pediatrics 824 (1996). On the other hand, some researchers emphasize the flaws in the research and tend to think a connection exists between corporal punishment and violence. Murray A. Straus, Spanking and the Making of a Violent Society, 98 Pediatrics 837 (1996). Others suggest that other forms of discipline are more appropriate and equally effective as corporal punishment and that these should be used instead. Anthony M. Graziano, et al., Subabusive Violence in Child Rearing in Middle–Class Families, 98 Pediatrics 845 (1996).

Sometimes opposition to corporal punishment can be extreme. In a review of historian Philip Greven's Spare the Rod: The Religious Roots of Punishment and the Psychological Impact of Physical Abuse (1991), Kenneth Silverman summarizes Mr. Greven's conclusions about the psychological effects of corporal punishment:

> By his account, the severity of damage ranges from apathy to obsessiveness, paranoia and extreme dissociation. He concludes that fear of the rod does not make children obedient and law-abiding, as its religious proponents maintain, but can incite them to delinquency,

criminality and domestic violence. Its consequences are therefore felt throughout the secular culture as well. In fact, Mr. Greven links physical punishment of children to specific kinds of political behavior: authoritarianism; "the persistent 'conservatism' of American politics"; "the passive acceptance, even the welcoming of the annihilation of the planet as a wrathful Father's ultimate scourging of this wayward children."

Book Review, N.Y. Times, 5 February 17, 1991 at 5.

4. *The international picture.* Sweden outlawed parental corporal punishment in 1979. The law carried no penalties, but a 1988 study found that public education had resulted in substantial compliance with the law. See Adrienne Ahlgren Haeuser, Swedish Parents Don't Spank, 63 Mothering 42 (1992). A number of other countries, including Norway, Denmark, Finland and Austria, have also prohibited parental corporal punishment. Corporal punishment in schools had been banned much earlier. The Committee on the Rights of the Child, which supervises implementation of the United Nations Convention on the Rights of the Child, has condemned corporal punishment in both families and institutions. (As chapter 1 reported, the United States has not ratified the Convention.) For additional information on the laws of countries prohibiting corporal punishment and international law, see Susan H. Bitensky, Spare the Rod, Embrace our Humanity: Toward a New Legal Regime Prohibiting Corporal Punishment of Children, 31 U. Mich. J. L. Ref. 353 (1998).

After a jury had acquitted a stepfather who corporally punished his stepson on the grounds that the corporal punishment was reasonable, the boy and his biological father applied to the European Commission on Human Rights. The commission found the United Kingdom responsible for a breach of Article 3 of the European Convention on Human Rights (prohibition of torture and inhuman or degrading treatment or punishment), because English law did not provide sufficient protection for the child. See Sharon Detrick, European Court of Human Rights: Judgment in the Case of *A v. the United Kingdom*, 6 Int'l. J. of Children's Rts. 335 (1998).

5. *Public schools.* May public schools use corporal punishment? Should they? In Ingraham v. Wright, 430 U.S. 651 (1977), the Supreme Court considered whether corporal punishment constituted cruel and unusual punishment in violation of the Eighth Amendment and, if it were permissible, whether the Due Process Clause of the Fourteenth Amendment required prior notice and an opportunity to be heard. The Court concluded that the Eighth Amendment did not apply to public schools and that notice and hearing were not required. The Court indicated that the common law remedies were adequate if punishment was excessive.

The trend in public schools has been away from the use of corporal punishment. In 1974 it was explicitly permitted in a vast majority of states. Now more than half the states prohibit its use. Leonard P. Edwards, Corporal Punishment in the Legal System, 36 Santa Clara L. Rev. 983 (1996). The American Academy of Pediatrics has urged "(1) the legal prohibition by all states of corporal punishment in schools and (2) the employment of alternative measures of managing student behavior." American Academy of Pediatrics, Corporal Punishment in Schools, 88 Pediatrics 173 (1991).

6. *Additional references.* Murray A. Straus, Beating the Devil Out of Them: Corporal Punishment in American Families (1994); Dean M. Herman, A Statutory Proposal to Prohibit the Infliction of Violence Upon Children, 19 Fam. L. Q. 1 (1985); Mary Kate Kearney, Substantive Due Process and Parental Corporal Punishment: Democracy and the Excluded Child, 32 San Diego L. Rev. 1 (1995); David Orentlicher, Spanking and Other Corporal Punishment of Children by Parents: Overvaluing Pain, Undervaluing Children, 35 Hous. L. Rev. 147 (1998); Jerry R. Parkinson, Federal Court Treatment of Corporal Punishment in Public Schools: Jurisprudence That Is Literally Shocking to the Conscience, 39 S.D. L. Rev. 276 (1994); Irene M. Rosenberg, A Study in Irrationality: Refusal to Grant Substantive Due Process Protection Against Excessive Corporal Punishment in the Public Schools, 27 Hous. L. Rev. 399 (1990). See also Project, Corporal Punishment: Special Issue, 17 Children's Legal Rights J. 2 (1997).

PROBLEM 4–5

Alice is eight years old. She lives with her mother, but visited her father regularly in accordance with the visitation schedule ordered when her parents divorced. Her father called her the day before his visitation day and told her that she was to take a bath and wash her hair before he picked her up, because he wanted her to be well-groomed for a photo-taking session at a church function the next day. When he picked her up, she had neither bathed nor washed her hair. Her father told her that she would be disciplined. When they arrived at his house, he struck her three times on the buttocks with a wooden spoon. She was wearing denim jeans at the time. Two red, oval marks were observed by the child's mother a few hours after the spanking and by the school nurse the next day. Only one faint mark could be seen five days later. Under state law "child abuse" is: "Any nonaccidental physical injury * * * suffered by a child as the result of the acts or omissions of a person responsible for the care of the child." The Department of Social Services regulations define physical injury as: "damage to any bodily tissue to the extent that the tissue must undergo a healing process in order to be restored to a sound and healthy condition * * *." The agency handbook for child protective services workers states that "physical injuries that require a healing process include, but are not limited to, * * * bruises, hyperemia (reddening of the surface tissue) lasting twenty-four hours or more."

Did Alice's father abuse her?

PROBLEM 4–6

The following bill is being considered by your state legislature:

The Legislature hereby finds that each year within the state there have been at least 50 child deaths, 2000 permanent injuries to children, and 20,000 serious injuries to children, all caused by parents or caretakers. The Legislature further finds that over ninety percent of these death and injuries are inflicted upon children less than five years old. The Legislature further finds that often parents and caretakers inflict these deaths and injuries believing that the child deserves corporal punishment. The Legislature further finds that many parents and caretakers have not been informed about the dangers of hitting or shaking children under five years of age.

Therefore, the Legislature hereby declares that parents and caretakers shall not use corporal punishment upon or otherwise strike any child under five years of age for the purpose of punishment. There is no criminal penalty attached to this legislation.

The Legislature further instructs the Department of Health to develop and implement an educational program which will provide all parents and caretakers with information on how to raise and control young children without the use of physical discipline. This educational program shall be implemented in all counties and shall be offered free of charge.

[Quoted from Leonard P. Edwards, Corporal Punishment in the Legal System, 36 Santa Clara L. Rev. 983, 1023 (1996).]

You have been asked whether the law would be constitutional and whether it represents good policy. What is your response?

D. *Sexual Abuse*

Child sexual abuse was not acknowledged as a serious problem until the 1970's when the women's movement and the Child Abuse Prevention and Treatment Act raised public awareness of this form of abuse. Sexual abuse cases are a relatively small percentage of the overall child protective services caseload (14%), but surveys of adults have indicated that there may be as many as a million child abuse victims. Diana J. English, The Extent and Consequences of Child Maltreatment, 8 The Future of Children 39, 43 (Spring 1998).The term "child sexual abuse" "covers a wide range of acts. In general, legal and research definitions of child sexual abuse require two elements: (1) sexual activities involving children and (2) an 'abusive condition' such as coercion or a large age gap between the participants, indicating a lack of consensuality." David Finkelhor, Current Information of the Scope and Nature of Child Sexual Abuse, 4 The Future of Children 31, 32 (Summer/Fall 1994). Usually the abuser is known to the victim. Men are more likely than women to be the abusers. Girls are at higher risk of sexual abuse, although boys may be less likely to report because of the shame of being a victim and concerns about being labeled homosexual.

1. Failure to Protect

IN RE T.G.

Supreme Court of South Dakota, 1998.
578 N.W.2d 921.

PER CURIAM.

* * *

FACTS

The evidence indicates that: thirty-year-old Mother is the product of an abusive childhood. She lived with her alcoholic mother until she was four years old. She recalls being thrown, starved and locked in cupboards by her mother, and abused by her mother's boyfriends. Her mother "sold" her to adoptive parents for $1500 and these parents began sexually abusing her at age seven. Mother gave birth to her first child when she was thirteen. The child, fathered by adoptive father, was placed for adoption. Mother was placed in a residential home until she graduated from high school after completing a special education curriculum. When she was eighteen, she gave birth to her second child, the product of a rape. The baby died the day after birth.

Mother and Father* lived together from 1986 and 1993 when Mother left due to his violence, drug use, and schizophrenia. They had four children. Older Daughter was born in 1987 and Younger Daughter was born in 1988. They are the children involved in this appeal. Two younger children are awaiting adoption.

During the time that Mother and Father lived together the Department of Social Services (DSS) substantiated a neglect referral that Older Daughter failed-to-thrive. Services appropriate to Mother's level of understanding were provided. DSS received five other referrals regarding physical abuse of the children, but was not able to substantiate the allegations.

In 1993, shortly after she left Father, Mother and her two daughters began living with Stepfather, whom Mother married in 1996. Stepfather, now thirty-two, was also sexually molested as a child and began using marijuana and alcohol when he was fourteen. In 1987 he was sentenced to four years in the penitentiary for sexually molesting a seven-year-old girl.

Between 1994 and 1997 DSS received three referrals that Stepfather was sexually molesting both daughters. He and the children denied it. A 1995 report, however, substantiated that the girls had been sexually abused by someone outside of the home. Despite her knowledge of this,

* Father voluntarily terminated his parental rights and is not involved in this appeal.

Mother later allowed a man that she knew had sexually abused a friend's children take her daughters on a three day trip.

On February 9, 1997, Mother told a girlfriend that Stepfather had sexually molested Older Daughter. The friend took Mother and daughters to the sheriff's office where statements were taken. When Mother insisted on returning to Stepfather, the friend refused to allow the children to go with her.

A social worker and law enforcement official interviewed each daughter and the friend the next day. Both daughters described how Stepfather had touched them in their private parts and told them that he would kill them or go to the penitentiary if they told. The friend told of hearing Mother tell Older Daughter not to tell what happened and overheard Stepfather tell Mother to coach the children on what to say so he would not return to prison. A week later, a medical examination of both daughters found physical evidence of sexual abuse.

Stepfather denied abusing the girls, threatening them, or asking Mother to cover up the abuse. He admitted giving Older Daughter a "hickey" the night before the abuse was reported. He also admitted that he wrestled with the girls until he got an erection on occasions when Mother refused to have sex with him.

Mother admitted that Stepfather had given Older Daughter a "hickey," but claimed it was accidental. She believed that the situation had been exaggerated. She did remember, however, that Stepfather asked her to perform fellatio on him in front of her daughters after he had played with them.

Mother and Stepfather entered into separate Family Service Agreements with DSS. Stepfather's cooperation with DSS was minimal but he did complete a psychological evaluation. The conclusion provided that Stepfather's prognosis was poor due to his low mental functioning and great amount of minimization. The evaluator believed he should not have contact with any children and that these children would be at great risk if returned to his home since Mother was unable or unwilling to protect them.

Mother's FSA had five objectives. She was to attend and complete an individual parenting class. This class was taught by a woman who knew Mother's limitations because she had worked with her on failure-to-thrive issues. Mother was eventually dropped from the program because she missed nine weeks; normally parents are dropped after three misses. Mother did complete a psychological evaluation and did begin counseling, with sporadic attendance. She was not consistent in attending co-dependency meetings. Although she did attend twenty-one of twenty-eight visitations with her daughters, her interaction was minimal, and harsh, and she cut visits short. During this period, her relationship with Stepfather was volatile. Ultimately she chose to remain with him and bear his child. She remains ambivalent as to whether Stepfather had sexual contact with her daughters.

Oldest Daughter was a failure-to-thrive child. She was first sexually abused at age seven. She now functions in the mildly retarded range of intelligence; her full scale IQ is 59. She is intensely jealous of her sister, idealizes her mother, and struggles with rejection because of her lack of friends. She does not deny Stepfather's abuse of her. Younger Daughter's full scale IQ is 104. Due to a learning disability, her skills range from low average to superior. Depression is a major factor in her functioning and she expresses a strong need for security, support and affection. She refuses to discuss sexual abuse by Stepfather and denies substantiated abuse by another.

Both girls miss their mother and are protective of her. Their therapist noted that termination of Mother's parental rights would be painful for these girls, as it would for most children. Because of the abuse and neglect that they have experienced throughout their lives, the therapist believed that a permanent or foster home would provide the stability and security that Mother's home lacked. In addition, daughters were doing well in foster care where the caregivers were able to focus on the children's needs rather than their own needs as mother did.

The trial court concluded that the least restrictive alternative available was the termination of Mother's parental rights.

DECISION

* * *

The trial court found that the children were abused and that Mother ignored the abuse, and, when aware of it, concealed it and attempted to have the children do so. Because Mother did not physically or sexually abuse daughters, she contends that there is no evidence to support these findings.

"The mother's contention that some type of physical abuse or neglect are [sic] required to justify termination is spurious." A court may terminate parental rights "if the court finds, by clear and convincing evidence, that the least restrictive alternative available commensurate with the best interests of the child with due regard for the rights of the parents, the public and the state so requires." There is no statutory requirement for physical abuse. In addition, a child "[w]ho is subject to sexual abuse, sexual molestation or sexual exploitation by the child's parent, guardian, custodian or any other person responsible for the child's care "is an abused or neglected child.

In this case, while Mother did not physically or sexually abuse her daughters she knew of the substantiated report of sexual abuse and allowed her daughters to travel with a known sexual abuser. She knew that Stepfather had been convicted of molesting a child, and chose to live with him and expose her daughters to him. She was aware of allegations that Stepfather was abusing her daughters, and did nothing to alleviate the situation. While she did tell a friend that Stepfather sexually abused daughters, she immediately backtracked and attempted to stop the children from discussing the abuse with authorities. This evidence supports the trial court's findings; they are not clearly erroneous.

* * *

The trial court also found that Mother "has chosen a relationship with a child molester, who has molested her children, over the welfare of her children." Mother contends that DSS should have mandated the severance of her relationship with Stepfather.

The trial court, DSS, and her own attorney continually warned Mother that her continuing relationship with Stepfather was jeopardizing her ability to regain her children. At one point during these proceedings the trial court even ordered Stepfather to have no contact with Mother, except by logged telephone calls, and no contact with daughters. While the latter was successful, the former was not because Mother continually went back to Stepfather. Because of Mother's ongoing choice, DSS attempted to work with Stepfather, but he steadfastly refused to cooperate. Even as she was faced with the prospect of having her parental rights terminated, Mother chose to stay with Stepfather.

* * *

The record is clear that Mother is incapable of placing her children's significant needs beyond those of her own. When aware of the sexual abuse throughout their young lives, Mother ignored it, attempted to conceal it, and failed to protect the children from it. She chose a sexual abuser over her own daughters, despite DSS attempts to help her. Daughters have significant problems which need consistent, stable help if they are ever to have a chance at independent living. Mother cannot provide this.

* * *

Notes and Questions

1. Should the mother's rights have been terminated in the case? Should the state terminate because the mother associates with persons who have a history of abusing other children? See In re Interest of Joshua M., State v. Lona F., 558 N.W.2d 548 (Neb.1997) (the mother's associations with the man who fathered her oldest daughter when he was 36 and she was 15, and with a man who was imprisoned for abusing her oldest daughter and was the father of her three other children, were grounds for termination).

What if the mother associates with someone who abuses her? Should a battered woman be held responsible for failure to protect her children, if she does not remove herself and the children from the batterer? Some courts have allowed a mother to use a battered woman syndrome defense when the state seeks to terminate her rights for failure to protect her children. See, e.g., In re Betty J.W., 371 S.E.2d 326 (W.Va.1988). Should the law insist that the mother protect her children when she cannot even protect herself?

2. *Sexual abuse prevention programs.* Since the 1980's, a number of states have implemented school-based sexual abuse prevention programs for pre-

school and elementary school children. The programs are intended to teach children personal safety skills and to help them recognize abuse. Evaluations of these programs have not shown that they are effective in preventing child sexual abuse, primarily because of methodological problems in the evaluations. Ethical issues present obstacles to measuring program effectiveness. "These include the issue of denying a comparison group of children a potentially beneficial education program. Ethical considerations also arise in trying to measure accurately whether young children can use what they have learned to resist offenders. Some argue that exposing young children to a simulated abusive episode, while potentially a good measure of children's capability to respond to an actual assault, may be unduly traumatic, or may desensitize children to dangerous situations." U.S. General Accounting Office, Preventing Child Sexual Abuse 3 (1996).

3. *Additional references.* Special Issue: Sexual Child Abuse, 19 Criminal Justice and Behavior 4 (1992); Lynne Henderson, Without Narrative: Child Sexual Abuse, 4 Va. J. Soc. Pol'y & L. 479 (1997); Kristian Miccio, In the Name of Mothers and Children: Deconstructing the Myth of the Passive Battered Mother and the "Protected Child" in Child Neglect Proceedings, 58 Albany L. Rev. 1087 (1995).

PROBLEM 4–7

Mr. and Mrs. Henry allowed their thirteen-year-old daughter, Susan, and her nineteen-year-old boyfriend to have a sexual relationship and he was allowed to share her bedroom. The six-year age difference between Susan and her adult boyfriend puts the sexual relationship within the criminal code definition of "criminal sexual conduct." Have the Henrys neglected Susan by failing to protect her from sexual abuse?

2. *Proving the Case*

IN RE NICOLE V.

Court of Appeals of New York, 1987.
518 N.E.2d 914.

SIMONS, JUDGE.

In these two child protective proceedings [discussion of the second case is omitted] parents have been charged with sexually abusing their children. The proof of abuse rests principally on out-of-court statements of each child, evidence which is not legally sufficient to make a fact finding of child abuse unless corroborated in accordance with the requirements of section 1046(a)(vi) of the Family Court Act.[1] The common

---

1. Family Court Act § 1046(a)(vi) provides that in any hearing under article 10: "(vi) previous statements made by the child relating to any allegations of abuse or neglect shall be admissible in evidence, but if uncorroborated, such statements shall not be sufficient to make a fact-finding of abuse or neglect. Any other evidence tending to support the reliability of the previous statements, including, but not limited to the types of evidence defined in this subdivision shall be sufficient corroboration. The testimony of the child shall not be necessary to make a fact-finding of abuse or neglect". * * *

issue presented is whether the corroborative evidence in each proceeding is sufficient under the statute.

In Matter of Nicole V., Bronx County Family Court made a fact finding that Nicole V.'s father, respondent Lawrence V., had sexually abused his daughter, then 3 1/2 years old, and prohibited him from visiting her without supervision for 18 months. On his appeal, respondent challenges the sufficiency of the evidence to support the finding of abuse, claiming the court erroneously received testimony from Nicole's therapist to "validate" and corroborate Nicole's out-of-court statements. * * *

I

In recent years preventing the sexual abuse of children in family settings has become a major social and judicial concern. Such abuse is difficult to detect because the acts are predominantly nonviolent and usually occur in secret rendering the child the only witness. Moreover, once abuse is uncovered it is difficult to fix blame, not only because of the lack of evidence but also because of the reluctance or inability of victims to testify.

In an effort to alleviate these problems, the Legislature, in 1969, enacted the Child Protective Proceedings Act. Its purpose is to protect children from injury or mistreatment while ensuring that the State's intervention on behalf of the child, against the wishes of a parent, comports with the parent's due process rights. Child protective proceedings do not, of themselves, permanently sever parental rights or result in criminal sanctions. They are civil in nature and a finding of abuse or neglect need only be supported by a preponderance of the evidence. Upon making such a finding Family Court may interfere with a parent's right to continue care and custody of a child for an initial 18–month period, subject to renewal, by putting into effect a wide variety of remedies which include various levels of supervision or removal of the child from the parent's home Because the accused parent is not subject to criminal sanctions in a child protective proceeding, the Legislature has provided that the usual rules of criminal evidence do not apply. Unsworn out-of-court statements of the victim may be received and, if properly corroborated, will support a finding of abuse or neglect (Family Ct.Act § 1046[a][vi]). Corroboration is not required because statements of children are generally unreliable but because the out-of-court statements are hearsay and the statute requires some further evidence to establish their reliability. * * *

As amended, section 1046(a)(vi) states a broad flexible rule providing that out-of-court statements may be corroborated by "[a]ny other evidence tending to support" their reliability. The amendment also provides that corroboration may include, but is not limited to, the types of evidence defined in other paragraphs of section 1046(a). Thus, corroboration may come in the form of proof that the parent abused one of his other children; proof that the injuries were of such nature that they would not ordinarily be sustained but for the acts or omissions of the parent; proof that the parent abuses drugs or alcohol to the extent that it would produce in him a state of stupor, unconsciousness, intoxication, hallucination, disorientation, incompetence or irrationality; hospital or agency reports suggesting the parent committed the act or omission; and evidence regarding the emotional health of the parent. The statute provides that the evidence listed in these subdivisions may be sufficient, standing alone, to support a fact finding of abuse or neglect, but in those cases in which it is not, evidence of the types listed may provide corroboration for a child's out-of-court statements. The types of evidence listed in the section are only illustrative; additional kinds may also be deemed adequate on a case-by-case basis. Thus, courts have found sufficient corroboration in admissions by the parent, even though subsequently recanted, evidence that the child was afflicted with a sexually transmitted disease or evidence that the child had become pregnant. Of course, Family Court Judges presented with the issue have considerable discretion to decide whether the child's out-of-court statements describing incidents of abuse or neglect have, in fact, been reliably corroborated and whether the record as a whole supports a finding of abuse.

II

Applying these concepts to the evidence presented in the two proceedings before us, we conclude the statutory requirements of corroboration are satisfied in both and the orders should, therefore, be affirmed.

A

In Matter of Nicole V., petitioner presented three witnesses at the fact-finding hearing: the child's mother, Linda V.; the child's caseworker from Special Services for Children, Ms. Champ; and the child's therapist, Ms. Lemp. Each witness testified to out-of-court hearsay statements made by Nicole describing incidents of sexual abuse by respondent in which he played "secret games" with her, involving hand to vagina contact, hand to chest contact, hand to anus contact, penis to vagina contact, and incidents in which he put "white paste" from his genital area in Nicole's mouth and "all over her". There was also other evidence. Ms. Lemp testified that Nicole's behavior was symptomatic of a sexually abused child. Nicole's mother testified that Nicole developed vaginal rashes after weekend visits with respondent; that Nicole's behavior changed after weekend visits with respondent; and that, on one occasion after Nicole returned from a visit with respondent, the mother noticed blood on the washcloth after washing Nicole's vaginal area. Finally, petitioner submitted a certified medical report stating that Nicole's hymen had been ruptured.

Respondent testified on his own behalf and denied the allegations of abuse. He contends on appeal that Nicole's out-of-court statements describing incidents of sexual abuse were not sufficiently corroborated.

Specifically, he contends that the opinion testimony of Nicole's therapist was not corroborative evidence within the meaning of the statute.

Under familiar rules, expert opinions are admissible on subjects involving professional or scientific knowledge or skill not within the range of ordinary training or intelligence. The psychological and behavioral characteristics and reactions typically shared by victims of abuse in a familial setting are not generally known by the average person and the courts have become increasingly more receptive to admitting expert testimony on the subject. * * *

The sexually abused child syndrome is * * * a recognized diagnosis based upon comparisons between the characteristics of individuals and relationships in incestuous families, as described by mental health experts, and the characteristics of the individuals and relationships of the family in question. Expert diagnoses on the subject have thus been accepted by some of our courts to validate out-of-court statements, particularly when an independent expert is employed for the purpose. * * * We conclude expert testimony was properly used to satisfy the corroboration requirements of section 1046(a)(vi) in this case.

The validation evidence came from Nicole's therapist, Ms. Lemp. She testified Nicole's behavior led her to conclude Nicole had been sexually abused. Her opinion was formed during at least 10 therapy sessions spanning four months and was based on the nature of Nicole's statements, their consistency over a period of time and her observation of Nicole's behavioral patterns. Ms. Lemp explained that among the symptoms manifested by children who are sexually abused in an intra-familial setting are: age-inappropriate knowledge of sexual behavior, manifested verbally, in play activities or through drawings; enuresis in a toilet trained child; regressive behavior and withdrawal; and severe temper tantrums or depression inappropriate for children of like age. She identified classic symptoms of child abuse in Nicole: her uncommunicative, withdrawn demeanor, a typical avoidance mechanism adopted by persons suffering from posttraumatic stress, and her knowledge of sexual activity far beyond the norm for 3 1/2-year-old children. There was no other basis in reality, for example, for Nicole's statements of "white glue" or "paste" coming from her father's genital area or the placing of his penis in her vagina. Those statements by Nicole demonstrated specific knowledge of sexual activity.

Ms. Lemp was also able to observe Nicole's display of extreme anger—far exceeding the temper tantrums normally seen in young children—and her fearful behavior exhibited through nightmares and sleep disturbances; she testified that such reactions were symptomatic of an abused child. She found it significant that Nicole repeated her claims to various people over a period of time in a consistent manner because, she stated, children "do not have the skill at lying that adults do" and thus "cannot be consistent [about lying] for a period of several months to several different people".

Respondent contends that validation evidence, even if admissible to corroborate a child's hearsay statement, must be received from independent experts in psychiatry or psychology and Ms. Lemp's testimony did not qualify for the purpose because she was a social worker hired by Nicole's mother to treat her.

Ms. Lemp's qualifications to testify were conceded by respondent, however, after it was established that she had a Bachelor's degree in deviant behavior and social control and a Master's degree in social work, that she was the director of two Bronx County offices of the Victim Services Agency and had counseled sexually abused children and their families for 2 1/2 years and that she was the chairperson of the education committee of the New York City Task Force Against Sexual Abuse.

Nor was her testimony unavailable for corroboration because she was treating Nicole. An expert's relationship to the party offering her does not disqualify the witness from giving opinion evidence and any bias Ms. Lemp may have had could be addressed on cross-examination. Moreover, Nicole's statement was also corroborated by evidence that she suffered from vaginal rashes, depression and sleep disturbances, that blood was found in her vaginal area and by a certified medical report stating that she had no hymen. There may be circumstances when the court, in its discretion, finds it desirable to use the assistance of an independent expert but in this case not only was the testimony of Ms. Lemp sufficient to corroborate Nicole's out-of-court statements and establish a prima facie case, there was also additional corroboration which supported Family Court's fact finding. Accordingly, the order of the Appellate Division should be affirmed.

* * *

Notes and Questions

1. *Difficulties of proof.* Sexual abuse of children is often difficult to prove because of a lack of physical proof and because there are no adult witnesses, or at least none willing to testify. Requiring the children to testify can be very traumatic for them. In addition, some children would not be willing to give accurate information, would not be considered competent or would make poor witnesses. Hence a court may have to base its decision on other grounds, such as parental unfitness, even when there is evidence of sexual abuse. See, e.g., Adoption of Quentin, 678 N.E.2d 1325 (Mass.1997).

For discussion of the use of the Child Sexual Abuse Accommodation Syndrome in criminal trials, see chapter 6, Criminal Abuse and Neglect.

2. *False accusations.* False allegations of child sexual abuse by one parent against another are a problem in divorce cases and other family disputes. See, e.g., In the Interest of E.A., 552 N.W.2d 135 (Iowa 1996) (finding that father's allegations of abuse were not substantiated and noting that the case "has characteristics of dysfunction consistent with a relationship of domestic violence with the main issue of power and control contributing to this allegation of sexual abuse and subsequent investigation").

3. *Repressed memories of sexual abuse.* Claims of childhood sexual abuse present particularly vexing statute of limitations issues. In the past decade or so, numerous adults have alleged that they were sexually abused as children years earlier, but that they had repressed memories of the abuse and had recalled the abuse only shortly before filing suit. Typically the civil damage claims (such as assault, battery, or negligent or intentional infliction of emotional distress) carry limitations periods ranging from only one to three years. Facing dismissal for untimeliness, some plaintiffs have sought to invoke provisions which toll the statute of limitations while a would-be plaintiff suffers from mental disability that deprives him of capacity to sue. Other plaintiffs have sought to invoke discovery rules, which would toll the statute of limitations until the plaintiff discovered, or should reasonably have discovered, the abuse, the injury, or the causal relationship between them. In the absence of a statute specifically tolling or postponing operation of the limitations period for claims alleging repressed memories of childhood sexual abuse, plaintiffs met with mixed results.

The scientific community remains divided on whether memories can truly be repressed and, if so, whether repressed memories are likely to be accurate in actions alleging childhood sexual abuse. See, e.g., Sheila Taub, The Legal Treatment of Recovered Memories of Child Sexual Abuse, 17 J. Leg. Med. 183 (1996). Nevertheless about half the states have enacted discovery statutes that permit plaintiffs to allege such abuse within a specified period after recalling the abuse or the injury, regardless of the time that has passed since the abusive acts themselves. Suits filed decades after the alleged acts may thus be timely. Section 340.1(a) of the California Civil Procedure Code, for example, provides: "In any civil action for recovery of damages suffered as a result of childhood sexual abuse, the time for commencement of the action shall be within eight years of the date the plaintiff attains the age of majority or within three years of the date the plaintiff discovers or reasonably should have discovered that psychological injury or illness occurring after the age of majority was caused by the sexual abuse, whichever period expires later."

To complicate matters further, some states with discovery statutes also have general statutes of repose, which establish an outer limit on the time within which suits may be brought even under a discovery provision. The question may arise whether these general repose provisions affect the operation of specific discovery statutes relating to alleged childhood sexual abuse.

3. Preventing Sexual Abuse

The first article excerpt that follows proposes broad societal changes in an effort to prevent child abuse. The second reviews the research on whether there is a cycle of sexual abuse, with child victims becoming abusive adults. The high recidivism rates among sexual abusers are discussed in the Chapter 6, Criminal Abuse and Neglect.

DAVID FINKELHOR, SEXUAL ABUSE AND PHYSICAL ABUSE: SOME CRITICAL DIFFERENCES IN UNHAPPY FAMILIES

21, 25–27 (Eli. H. Newberger and Richard Bourne, eds. 1985).

Sexual abuse prevention is even more difficult than physical abuse prevention. The model that has been applied in physical abuse has been that of alienated and ineffective parents; social interventions that improve a family's economic conditions and build networks of social support can be fairly effective in the prevention of physical abuse.

But sexual abuse is a more complicated problem. It grows out of a set of contradictions in our culture concerning sexuality, and these contradictions are not abating. They are, in fact, growing more intense. We see evidence of it in the proliferation of child pornography, the increasing sexualization of children in the media, and the distancing of men from children that results from the rising rate of divorce.

In sexual abuse, the offenders are mostly men, both inside and outside the family. The implication is that more than being a problem of alienated and ineffective parenting, sexual abuse needs to be seen as a problem of male sexual socialization.

Why is it that the offenders are so overwhelmingly men? I would like to suggest three things that account for this; all of them have to do with differences between male and female socialization. First, women in our society get trained in the distinction between sexual and nonsexual affection. Partly as preparation for being the caretakers of children, women learn about nonsexual affection. With men, physical affection is withdrawn at an earlier age and only given back later on in adolescence through sex. Thus, men tend to seek fulfillment of all affectionate, nurturant or dependency needs through sexual channels. They are not comfortable with nonsexual affection.

A second difference is that men are socialized to focus sexual arousal around specific sexual acts divorced from any relationship context, whereas women tend to be more focused on the relationship in which the sexual act takes place. This makes it easier for men to sexualize relationships with children. The child has the right set of orifices to provide sexual gratification for the man. The fact that it is an inappropriate relationship may be somewhat distracting but not distracting enough to inhibit the man from seeking sexual gratification there. Women, on the other hand, find the inappropriateness of that relationship so distracting that they are unable to have sexual fantasies or arousal.

Thirdly, there is something that I call attraction gradient: we train men to be attracted to persons who are smaller, younger, less powerful than themselves, and we train women to be attracted to persons who are larger, older and more powerful than themselves. On that gradient it is much less of a contortion for a man to find a child to be appropriate sexual object than it is for a woman.

Now there are some implications here about larger social arrangements, implications for kinds of social changes that may have long term effects on the prevention of sexual abuse. First of all, some people might draw the conclusion that what we need to do is keep men away from children entirely. And although that may seem like a far-fetched conclusion to draw, I think it is implicit in some ideas that we have, for instance, that girls are preferable to boys as baby-sitters, and that men do not make good single parents and should not be given custody of children. Lurking behind those ideas is the imagery about men sexually abusing children. But, in fact, the implication should be the opposite: if we want men to learn the distinction between nonsexual and sexual affection, we need to get men more involved in the intimate process of bringing up children. I have a speculation, for which I have no evidence: that men who are actively involved in diapering children, for example, rarely sexually abuse them.

Secondly, I think that as we bring men up to be attracted to women who are their social equals, we are going to have a reduction in the number of men who need as their sexual partner someone who is smaller, less powerful, and younger than themselves. This will have the effect of reducing sexual abuse.

Closing on this note, I look forward to a time when men take more equal responsibility for the care of children and learn how to enjoy relationships with children without sexualizing them. I see this as an important step toward raising a generation of men who are not offenders against, but defenders of, the well-being of children.

U.S. GENERAL ACCOUNTING OFFICE, CYCLE OF SEXUAL ABUSE: RESEARCH INCONCLUSIVE ABOUT WHETHER CHILD VICTIMS BECOME ADULT ABUSERS 2–3 (1996).

Studying the relationship between early sexual victimization and later perpetration of sexual abuse is methodologically difficult. If researchers take a retrospective approach, and ask adult sex offenders whether they experienced childhood sexual abuse, there are problems of selecting a representative sample of offenders, finding an appropriate comparison group of adults who have not committed sex offenses but are similar to the study group in other respects, minimizing errors that arise when recalling traumatic events from the distant past, and dealing with the possibility that offenders will purposely overreport childhood abuse to gain sympathy or underreport abuse to avoid imputations of guilt. A prospective approach—selecting a sample of children who have been sexually abused and following them into adulthood to see whether they become sexual abusers—overcomes some of the problems of the retrospective approach, but it is a costly and time-consuming solution . In addition, researchers choosing the prospective approach still face the challenge of disentangling the effects of sexual abuse from the effects of other possible problems and stress-related factors in the backgrounds of these children (e.g., poverty, unemployment, parental alcohol abuse, or other inadequate social and family functioning). This requires the selection of appropriate comparison groups of children who have not been sexually abused and children who have faced other forms of maltreatment, as well as the careful measurement of a variety of other explanatory factors.

* * *

Nevertheless, overall, the retrospective studies, prospective studies, and research reviews indicated that the experience of childhood sexual victimization is quite likely neither a necessary nor a sufficient cause of adult sexual offending. The two prospective studies concluded that the majority of victims of sexual abuse during childhood did not become sex offenders as adults. Therefore, childhood sexual victimization would not necessarily lead to adult sexual offending. In addition, the majority of retrospective studies concluded that most adult sex offenders against children did not report that they were sexually victimized as children.

* * *

E. *Newborns With Positive Toxicologies*

IN RE DANTE M.

Court of Appeals of New York, 1995.
661 N.E.2d 138.

SMITH, JUDGE.

The issue before this Court is whether a finding of neglect as to a newborn and the newborn's older sibling may be based solely on the newborn's positive toxicology for a controlled substance. We conclude that more than a positive toxicology is generally required for a neglect determination. We affirm in this case because, as the Appellate Division concluded, there is additional evidence in the record supporting the Family Court's findings of neglect.

Appellant gave birth to her son Dante in November 1990. Both mother and son tested positive for cocaine. After learning of the positive toxicologies, the Nassau County Department of Social Services (DSS) brought a petition pursuant to section 1022 of the Family Court Act to temporarily remove Dante from appellant's care. Family Court conducted a hearing on the removal petition on November 21, 1990.

At the hearing, DSS presented evidence that Dante was born with a positive toxicology for cocaine and a low birth weight. DSS also presented evidence that appellant had a history of cocaine abuse, had been admitted to several drug rehabilitation centers, and that appellant's mother had custody of two of appellant's children because appellant's drug use rendered her incapable of caring for them. Appellant's mother informed DSS that she had observed appellant high on cocaine in the last weeks of appellant's pregnancy with Dante. Appellant told DSS that she smoked a cigarette at a Halloween party at the end of her pregnancy which may have contained cocaine.

Appellant did not present any witnesses at the removal hearing, but argued that DSS had failed to sustain its burden of proof because no toxicology report or witnesses to recent drug abuse had been produced. Appellant's counsel also argued that appellant had not admitted to recent, intentional, drug use. Family Court dismissed the petition and directed the hospital to release Dante to appellant's custody. That removal proceeding is not before us.

DSS subsequently brought this consolidated child protective proceeding against appellant on behalf of Dante, appellant's son, and Dantia (born in 1987), appellant's daughter. At the fact-finding hearing, DSS introduced into evidence two medical reports showing a positive toxicology for cocaine from Dante and positive toxicology for cocaine and opiates from appellant. DSS also presented evidence of appellant's prior history of drug abuse and appellant's admission that she may have smoked a cigarette containing cocaine, while she was pregnant with Dante, at a Halloween party.

Appellant presented two experts who testified that appellant provided a clean, well-ordered environment for her children, that appellant interacted appropriately with her children and that four random urine samples taken from appellant tested negative for controlled substances. The experts opined that appellant had not been a regular user of controlled substances since the latter half of the 1980's. The experts also testified that appellant was voluntarily receiving counseling at a general education and support program run by the Family Service Association. Appellant did not testify at the fact-finding hearing.

Dante's medical records reveal a primary diagnosis of prematurity, even though they also indicate 38–39 weeks of gestation, with a low birth weight (4 pounds, 14 ounces) for his gestation period. Dante remained in the Neonatal Intensive Care Unit for the duration of his stay at the Nassau County Medical Center. He was released to the custody of his mother on November 21, 1990, after the Family Court refused to order removal.

The medical records also contain a note from the medical center's social worker documenting a phone call from appellant's aunt at the beginning of November, before Dante's birth, alerting the social worker to appellant's drug use and expressing concern about Dante's health. The records further contain a discharge assessment form indicating a discharge diagnosis of prematurity and advising follow-up care in the high-risk clinic.*

* Expert testimony would be particularly   helpful in cases such as these, where medi-

Family Court found that Dante's positive toxicology for cocaine constituted sufficient evidence for a finding of neglect as to Dante and Dantia. The Family Court further found that a presentment agency need not produce any evidence for a finding of neglect other than a positive toxicology for a controlled substance in the newborn. Appellant was permitted to retain custody of Dante and Dantia and placed under the supervision of DSS for a one-year period. The Appellate Division affirmed, relying on additional evidence in the record for its factual findings of neglect.

Section 1012(f)(i)(B) of the Family Court Act defines a "neglected child" as a child less than 18 years of age "whose physical, mental or emotional condition has been impaired or is in imminent danger of becoming impaired" because of a parent's failure to exercise a minimum degree of care "by misusing a drug or drugs." Thus, the statute sets forth two predicates for a finding of neglect: actual physical, emotional or mental impairment, or the imminent danger of such impairment.

Although physical impairment is not defined by statute, section 1012(h) of the Family Court Act defines "impairment of emotional health" and "impairment of mental or emotional condition" as "a state of substantially diminished psychological or intellectual functioning in relation to, but not limited to, such factors as failure to thrive, control of aggressive or self-destructive impulses, ability to think and reason, or acting out or misbehavior". The Practice Commentaries to section 1012 use that statutory definition as a model to define "impairment of a physical condition" and arrive at the following formulation: "a state of substantially diminished physical growth, freedom from disease, and physical functioning in relation to, but not limited to, fine and gross motor development and organic brain development."

The imminent danger standard is not specifically defined by statute, but clearly reflects the judgment of the Legislature that a finding of neglect may be appropriate even when a child has not been actually impaired, in order to protect that child and prevent impairment. Consequently, the imminent danger of impairment to a child is an independent and separate ground on which a neglect finding may be based.

A report which shows only a positive toxicology for a controlled substance generally does not in and of itself prove that a child has been physically, mentally or emotionally impaired, or is in imminent danger of being impaired. Relying solely on a positive toxicology result for a neglect determination fails to make the necessary causative connection to all the surrounding circumstances that may or may not produce impairment or imminent risk of impairment in the newborn child. The Family Court thus erred in concluding that Dante's positive toxicology alone was sufficient for the findings of neglect. A positive toxicology report, however, in conjunction with other evidence, may support a neglect finding. Even though here, the trial court did not make any findings linking the

cal records must be interpreted, especially when a question exists as to whether a newborn exhibited drug withdrawal symptoms after birth.

positive toxicology to physical impairment, the record contains other evidence which supports the findings of neglect on the ground that appellant's children were placed in imminent danger of impairment by appellant's drug use, and justifies the limited DSS intervention which was ordered.

Dante was born prematurely, with low birth weight and a positive toxicology for cocaine. Dante required a specialized level of care and spent his entire hospital stay in the Neonatal Intensive Care Unit. After discharge from the hospital, Dante required a high degree of follow-up care at the high-risk clinic. Appellant had a history of being unable to care for her children because of her drug use and was observed high on cocaine during the end of her pregnancy with Dante. Although two experts opined that appellant had not regularly used drugs since the second half of the 1980's, appellant's mother and aunt stated that appellant had been high during the end of her pregnancy with Dante.

A trier of fact may draw the strongest inference that the opposing evidence permits against a witness who fails to testify in a civil proceeding. Appellant did not testify at the fact-finding hearing. Consequently, it may be inferred that appellant knowingly used cocaine during her pregnancy. Appellant's use of cocaine during her pregnancy, considered in conjunction with her prior, demonstrated inability to adequately care for her children while misusing drugs provided a sufficient basis to conclude, at the least, that Dante was in imminent danger of impairment. Moreover, that same evidence indicated a substantial impairment of judgment leading to a conclusion of neglect.

Appellant's conduct and lack of judgment created an imminent danger of impairment as to Dantia, who was under appellant's care during that time period. Proof of neglect as to one child is admissible on the issue of neglect as to another . Appellant's neglect of Dante could be considered in determining whether appellant neglected Dantia. Consequently, the Appellate Division had sufficient grounds to sustain the neglect findings as to Dante and Dantia.

The fact that appellant had a series of negative toxicology tests subsequent to Dante's birth, and that social workers testified at the fact-finding hearing that appellant was currently providing a good home were relevant in this proceeding to the disposition, and not to whether appellant previously neglected the children by her acts or omissions. It should be emphasized that there is no issue here of the removal of either Dante or Dantia from the care of appellant. Nevertheless, the record supported the need to insure the adequacy of care provided to both children. The limited supervision ordered by the Family Court achieved this goal with an appropriate level of State intervention. * * *

Notes and Questions

1.   Would a parent's continued use of illegal drugs when a child is an infant, without more, support a neglect finding under *Dante M.*, or must a direct adverse impact on the child be shown?

2. *The delicate balance.* Does *Dante M.* strike the right balance between child protection and parents' rights? Other jurisdictions treat a positive toxicology at birth as abuse or neglect. In Minnesota, for example, "[n]eglect includes prenatal exposure to a controlled substance * * * used by the mother for a nonmedical purpose, as evidenced by withdrawal symptoms in the child at birth, results of a toxicology test performed on the mother at delivery or the child at birth, or medical effects or developmental delays during the child's first year of life that medically indicate prenatal exposure to a controlled substance." Minn. Stat.§ 626.556(2)(c).

Should an abuse or neglect finding depend upon the current state of medical knowledge about potential harm to the child? When crack cocaine use was increasing rapidly, the mass media predicted that thousands of children would be born with severe emotional and physical problems. Some recent research, however, has not supported these fears and suggests that the mother's substance abuse after the child is born and severe poverty may be more harmful than cocaine use during pregnancy. 15 Harvard Mental Health Letter, Cocaine Before Birth, Dec. 1, 1998; Barbara Bennett Woodhouse, Poor Mothers, Poor Babies, Law, Medicine and Crack, in Child, Parent and State 111 (S. Randall Humm et al. eds., 1994).

3. *"Difficult" children.* A mother's use of drugs or alcohol can damage the child's health. Unfortunately "difficult" children are more likely to be abused and neglected. See, e.g., Lewis v. Department of Health and Rehabilitative Servs., 670 So.2d 1191, 1192 (Fla.Dist.Ct.App.1996):

> M.L. was born when the mother was 16 years old. Because the mother consumed alcohol during the pregnancy, M.L. was born with Fetal Alcohol Syndrome ("FAS") and was diagnosed with failure to thrive syndrome. The FAS caused the child to have a small stature, a small head, heart problems, and developmental delay. The child is expected to suffer from mental retardation, hyperactivity, temper tantrums and small stature as he matures. M.L. also has epilepsy, and he appears near death during seizures. HRS filed a petition for dependency alleging that M.L. was at significant risk of imminent abuse or neglect because the mother was unable to care for him or address his special medical needs.* * *

4. *Substance abuse during pregnancy.* Should the criminal justice system regulate the conduct of pregnant women? The National Institute on Drug Abuse estimates that "45,000 mothers inhaled or ingested cocaine at least once during pregnancy in 1994, 35,000 smoked crack, 757,000 drank alcohol, and 320,000 smoked tobacco." 15 Harvard Mental Health Letter, Cocaine Before Birth, December 1, 1998.

Nationwide, criminal prosecutions under endangerment and abuse statutes have generally failed because courts have held that a fetus is not a "child" within the meaning of these statutes, or that prosecution for prenatal substance abuse was outside legislative intention. See, e.g., State v. Kruzicki, 561 N.W.2d 729 (Wis.1997); State v. Gray, 584 N.E.2d 710, 711 (Ohio 1992); Commonwealth v. Welch, 864 S.W.2d 280 (1993); but see, e.g., Whitner v. State, 492 S.E.2d 777 (S.C.1997) (criminal child neglect statute included a pregnant woman's use of crack cocaine after the fetus had become viable). Prosecutions have also failed under statutes proscribing distribution or delivery of drugs to a child. See, e.g., State v. Luster, 419 S.E.2d 32 (Ga.1992). Courts have also rebuffed prosecutors' efforts to invoke these statutes on the theory that the mother passed the drugs not to the fetus, but to the child during the brief moment when the child left the womb before the umbilical cord was severed. See, e.g., Sheriff v. Encoe, 885 P.2d 596 (Nev.1994); Johnson v. State, 602 So.2d 1288, 1290 (Fla.1992).

Perhaps because of reliance on statutory interpretation, most courts have not wrestled with constitutional questions raised by commentators, such as whether prosecution of addicted mothers would violate their equal protection or privacy rights or whether prosecution would constitute cruel and unusual punishment. See, e.g., Margaret P. Spencer, Prosecutorial Immunity: The Response to Prenatal Drug Abuse, 25 Conn. L. Rev. 393, 410–26 (1993). There is an extensive debate on whether drug-using pregnant women should face criminal prosecution. For succinct statements on the positions of the opposing sides, see Doretta Massardo McGinnis, Prosecution of Mother's of Drug–Exposed Babies: Constitutional and Criminal Theory in Child, Parent, and State 84 (S. Randall Humm et al. eds. 1994) and Paul A. Logli, Prosecution of Mother's of Drug–Exposed Babies: A Response to McGinnis, in the same volume at 127. Some states have decided to use the civil, rather than criminal, system. Wisconsin recently amended its child protection statutes to include "unborn child abuse" and to allow a court to require in-patient treatment of drug-using mothers if necessary to protect the fetus. Wis. Stat. Ann. § 48.133. South Dakota now allows pregnant drug abusers to be confined to treatment centers. S.D. Codified Laws § 34–20A–63.

As discussed in the first section in this chapter, reporting statutes require medical personnel to report suspected abuse or neglect; several states also require hospitals to perform toxicology tests on newborns and to report positive results to child welfare agencies. See, e.g., Okla. Stat. Ann. tit. 21 § 846(A)(2). It has been argued that minority and poor female substance abusers are considerably more likely to be reported to authorities than other women. *See*, e.g., Dorothy E. Roberts, Punishing Drug Addicts Who Have Babies: Women of Color, Equality, and the Right of Privacy, 104 Harv. L. Rev. 1419 (1991). Many medical associations have gone on record opposing prosecution of mothers who deliver babies harmed by substance abuse during pregnancy, concerned that the threat of prosecution deters many expectant mothers from seeking drug treatment and general prenatal care. *See*, e.g., Am. Med. Ass'n, Bd. of Trustees, Legal Interventions During Pregnancy: Court–Ordered Medical Treatments and Legal Penalties for Potentially Harmful Behavior by Pregnant Women, 264 JAMA 2663, 2667 (1990) (adopted by the AMA House of Delegates). The AMA asserts that reliance on criminal prosecution would be counterproductive: "[T]he number of women who are convicted and incarcerated for potentially harmful behavior is likely to be relatively small in comparison with the number of women who would be prompted to avoid medical care altogether. As a result, the potential well-being of many infants may be sacrificed in order to preserve the health of a few." For additional discussion see Barry M. Lester et al., Keeping Mothers and Their Infants Together: Barriers and Solutions, 22 N.Y.U. Rev. L. & Soc. Change 425 (1996). In addition to fear of incarceration, health care providers also report that pregnant substance abusers fear loss of child custody: "Women * * * fear that if their children are placed in foster care, they will never get the children back." U.S. Gen'l Accounting Office, Drug–Exposed Infants: A Generation at Risk 9 (1990).

PROBLEM 4–8

Seventeen-year-old April gave birth to her son Jason in March. The doctor who delivered Jason said that April appeared intoxicated at the delivery, and that April had said that she had been drinking all during her pregnancy. Jason was premature and was born with apnea of prematurity, or breathing difficulties, which required monitoring. Because he was born prematurely with a low birth weight of two pounds and fifteen ounces due to probable alcoholism and smoking by April during her pregnancy, the hospital reported his situation to the Department of Social Services (DSS).

Because of his health problems Jason spent his first six weeks of life in the hospital. April visited him regularly and spoke often of her devotion to him. Nurses who observed her visits said that she appeared to be happy and to have bonded with Jason. April cooperated with DSS on a voluntary basis and participated in a two-day detoxification program. April did not have a permanent home, however, and stayed with various friends and relatives during the six weeks. Neither the hospital nor DSS knew where she was, although she called and visited often. When Jason was ready to be discharged, she told the hospital she was moving to a condominium in a nearby town. The hospital was concerned because she had not given them her address and had indicated she would not have a phone. Because Jason was going to be released from the hospital on a monitor and needed numerous follow-up visits, the hospital was concerned about April's ability to schedule visits without a phone and to care for him, particularly if she was drinking.

DSS filed a neglect petition, alleging that Jason was neglected because his mother provided an "environment that was injurious to his welfare." At the hearing on the neglect petition, April argued that Jason had never been in her custody and thus that she could not have provided an "injurious environment." She further argues that a court may not base its neglect finding on "anticipatory neglect," or a belief that she would neglect Jason if she had custody of him. You represent DSS. What is your response?

SECTION 6. DUTY TO INVESTIGATE

DESHANEY v. WINNEBAGO COUNTY DEPARTMENT OF SOCIAL SERVICES

Supreme Court of the United States, 1989.
489 U.S. 189.

CHIEF JUSTICE REHNQUIST delivered the opinion of the Court.

Petitioner is a boy who was beaten and permanently injured by his father, with whom he lived. Respondents are social workers and other local officials who received complaints that petitioner was being abused by his father and had reason to believe that this was the case, but nonetheless did not act to remove petitioner from his father's custody. Petitioner sued respondents claiming that their failure to act deprived him of his liberty in violation of the Due Process Clause of the Fourteenth Amendment to the United States Constitution. We hold that it did not.

I

The facts of this case are undeniably tragic. Petitioner Joshua DeShaney was born in 1979. In 1980, a Wyoming court granted his parents a divorce and awarded custody of Joshua to his father, Randy DeShaney. The father shortly thereafter moved to Neenah, a city located in Winnebago County, Wisconsin, taking the infant Joshua with him. There he entered into a second marriage, which also ended in divorce.

The Winnebago County authorities first learned that Joshua DeShaney might be a victim of child abuse in January 1982, when his father's second wife complained to the police, at the time of their divorce, that he had previously "hit the boy causing marks and [was] a prime case for child abuse." The Winnebago County Department of Social Services (DSS) interviewed the father, but he denied the accusations, and DSS did not pursue them further. In January 1983, Joshua was admitted to a local hospital with multiple bruises and abrasions. The examining physician suspected child abuse and notified DSS, which immediately obtained an order from a Wisconsin juvenile court placing Joshua in the temporary custody of the hospital. Three days later, the county convened an ad hoc "Child Protection Team"—consisting of a pediatrician, a psychologist, a police detective, the county's lawyer, several DSS caseworkers, and various hospital personnel—to consider Joshua's situation. At this meeting, the Team decided that there was insufficient evidence of child abuse to retain Joshua in the custody of the court. The Team did, however, decide to recommend several measures to protect Joshua, including enrolling him in a preschool program, providing his father with certain counseling services, and encouraging his father's girlfriend to move out of the home. Randy DeShaney entered into a voluntary agreement with DSS in which he promised to cooperate with them in accomplishing these goals.

Based on the recommendation of the Child Protection Team, the juvenile court dismissed the child protection case and returned Joshua to the custody of his father. A month later, emergency room personnel called the DSS caseworker handling Joshua's case to report that he had once again been treated for suspicious injuries. The caseworker concluded that there was no basis for action. For the next six months, the caseworker made monthly visits to the DeShaney home, during which she observed a number of suspicious injuries on Joshua's head; she also noticed that he had not been enrolled in school, and that the girlfriend had not moved out. The caseworker dutifully recorded these incidents in her files, along with her continuing suspicions that someone in the

DeShaney household was physically abusing Joshua, but she did nothing more. In November 1983, the emergency room notified DSS that Joshua had been treated once again for injuries that they believed to be caused by child abuse. On the caseworker's next two visits to the DeShaney home, she was told that Joshua was too ill to see her. Still DSS took no action.

In March 1984, Randy DeShaney beat 4-year-old Joshua so severely that he fell into a life-threatening coma. Emergency brain surgery revealed a series of hemorrhages caused by traumatic injuries to the head inflicted over a long period of time. Joshua did not die, but he suffered brain damage so severe that he is expected to spend the rest of his life confined to an institution for the profoundly retarded. Randy DeShaney was subsequently tried and convicted of child abuse.

Joshua and his mother brought this action under 42 U.S.C. § 1983 in the United States District Court for the Eastern District of Wisconsin against respondents Winnebago County, DSS, and various individual employees of DSS. The complaint alleged that respondents had deprived Joshua of his liberty without due process of law, in violation of his rights under the Fourteenth Amendment, by failing to intervene to protect him against a risk of violence at his father's hands of which they knew or should have known. The District Court granted summary judgment for respondents.

The Court of Appeals for the Seventh Circuit affirmed holding that petitioners had not made out an actionable § 1983 claim * * *.

* * *

II

The Due Process Clause of the Fourteenth Amendment provides that "[n]o State shall ... deprive any person of life, liberty, or property, without due process of law." Petitioners contend that the State deprived Joshua of his liberty interest in "free[dom] from ... unjustified intrusions on personal security," by failing to provide him with adequate protection against his father's violence. The claim is one invoking the substantive rather than the procedural component of the Due Process Clause; petitioners do not claim that the State denied Joshua protection without according him appropriate procedural safeguards, but that it was categorically obligated to protect him in these circumstances.

But nothing in the language of the Due Process Clause itself requires the State to protect the life, liberty, and property of its citizens against invasion by private actors. The Clause is phrased as a limitation on the State's power to act, not as a guarantee of certain minimal levels of safety and security. It forbids the State itself to deprive individuals of life, liberty, or property without "due process of law," but its language cannot fairly be extended to impose an affirmative obligation on the State to ensure that those interests do not come to harm through other means. * * * Its purpose was to protect the people from the State, not to ensure that the State protected them from each other. The Framers were content to leave the extent of governmental obligation in the latter area to the democratic political processes.

Consistent with these principles, our cases have recognized that the Due Process Clauses generally confer no affirmative right to governmental aid, even where such aid may be necessary to secure life, liberty, or property interests of which the government itself may not deprive the individual. * * * If the Due Process Clause does not require the State to provide its citizens with particular protective services, it follows that the State cannot be held liable under the Clause for injuries that could have been averted had it chosen to provide them. As a general matter, then, we conclude that a State's failure to protect an individual against private violence simply does not constitute a violation of the Due Process Clause.

Petitioners contend, however, that even if the Due Process Clause imposes no affirmative obligation on the State to provide the general public with adequate protective services, such a duty may arise out of certain "special relationships" created or assumed by the State with respect to particular individuals. Petitioners argue that such a "special relationship" existed here because the State knew that Joshua faced a special danger of abuse at his father's hands, and specifically proclaimed, by word and by deed, its intention to protect him against that danger. Having actually undertaken to protect Joshua from this danger—which petitioners concede the State played no part in creating—the State acquired an affirmative "duty," enforceable through the Due Process Clause, to do so in a reasonably competent fashion. Its failure to discharge that duty, so the argument goes, was an abuse of governmental power that so "shocks the conscience," as to constitute a substantive due process violation.

We reject this argument. It is true that in certain limited circumstances [involving prisoners and involuntarily committed mental patients] the Constitution imposes upon the State affirmative duties of care and protection with respect to particular individuals. * * *

* * *

But these cases afford petitioners no help. Taken together, they stand only for the proposition that when the State takes a person into its custody and holds him there against his will, the Constitution imposes upon it a corresponding duty to assume some responsibility for his safety and general well-being. The rationale for this principle is simple enough: when the State by the affirmative exercise of its power so restrains an individual's liberty that it renders him unable to care for himself, and at the same time fails to provide for his basic human needs—e.g., food, clothing, shelter, medical care, and reasonable safety—it transgresses the substantive limits on state action set by the Eighth Amendment and the Due Process Clause. The affirmative duty to protect arises not from the State's knowledge of the individual's predicament or from its expressions of intent to help him, but from the limitation which it has imposed on his freedom to act on his own behalf. In the substantive due process analysis, it is the State's affirmative act of restraining the individual's freedom to act on his own behalf—through incarceration, institutionalization, or other similar restraint of personal liberty—which is the "deprivation of liberty" triggering the protections of the Due Process Clause, not its failure to act to protect his liberty interests against harms inflicted by other means.

* * * Petitioners concede that the harms Joshua suffered occurred not while he was in the State's custody, but while he was in the custody of his natural father, who was in no sense a state actor.[9] While the State may have been aware of the dangers that Joshua faced in the free world, it played no part in their creation, nor did it do anything to render him any more vulnerable to them. That the State once took temporary custody of Joshua does not alter the analysis, for when it returned him to his father's custody, it placed him in no worse position than that in which he would have been had it not acted at all; the State does not become the permanent guarantor of an individual's safety by having once offered him shelter. Under these circumstances, the State had no constitutional duty to protect Joshua.

It may well be that, by voluntarily undertaking to protect Joshua against a danger it concededly played no part in creating, the State acquired a duty under state tort law to provide him with adequate protection against that danger. But the claim here is based on the Due Process Clause of the Fourteenth Amendment, which, as we have said many times, does not transform every tort committed by a state actor into a constitutional violation. A State may, through its courts and legislatures, impose such affirmative duties of care and protection upon its agents as it wishes. But not "all common-law duties owed by government actors were ... constitutionalized by the Fourteenth Amendment." Because, as explained above, the State had no constitutional duty to protect Joshua against his father's violence, its failure to do so—though calamitous in hindsight—simply does not constitute a violation of the Due Process Clause.

Judges and lawyers, like other humans, are moved by natural sympathy in a case like this to find a way for Joshua and his mother to receive adequate compensation for the grievous harm inflicted upon them. But before yielding to that impulse, it is well to remember once again that the harm was inflicted not by the State of Wisconsin, but by Joshua's father. The most that can be said of the state functionaries in this case is that they stood by and did nothing when suspicious circumstances dictated a more active role for them. In defense of them it must also be said that had they moved too soon to take custody of the son

---

9. Had the State by the affirmative exercise of its power removed Joshua from free society and placed him in a foster home operated by its agents, we might have a situation sufficiently analogous to incarceration or institutionalization to give rise to an affirmative duty to protect. Indeed, several Courts of Appeals have held * * * that the State may be held liable under the Due Process Clause for failing to protect children in foster homes from mistreatment at the hands of their foster parents. We express no view on the validity of this analogy, however, as it is not before us in the present case.

away from the father, they would likely have been met with charges of improperly intruding into the parent-child relationship, charges based on the same Due Process Clause that forms the basis for the present charge of failure to provide adequate protection.

The people of Wisconsin may well prefer a system of liability which would place upon the State and its officials the responsibility for failure to act in situations such as the present one. They may create such a system, if they do not have it already, by changing the tort law of the State in accordance with the regular lawmaking process. But they should not have it thrust upon them by this Court's expansion of the Due Process Clause of the Fourteenth Amendment.

Affirmed.

JUSTICE BRENNAN, with whom JUSTICE MARSHALL and JUSTICE BLACKMUN join, dissenting.

"The most that can be said of the state functionaries in this case," the Court today concludes, "is that they stood by and did nothing when suspicious circumstances dictated a more active role for them." Because I believe that this description of respondents' conduct tells only part of the story and that, accordingly, the Constitution itself "dictated a more active role" for respondents in the circumstances presented here, I cannot agree that respondents had no constitutional duty to help Joshua DeShaney.

It may well be, as the Court decides that the Due Process Clause as construed by our prior cases creates no general right to basic governmental services. That, however, is not the question presented here; indeed, that question was not raised in the complaint, urged on appeal, presented in the petition for certiorari, or addressed in the briefs on the merits. No one, in short, has asked the Court to proclaim that, as a general matter, the Constitution safeguards positive as well as negative liberties.

This is more than a quibble over dicta; it is a point about perspective, having substantive ramifications. In a constitutional setting that distinguishes sharply between action and inaction, one's characterization of the misconduct alleged under § 1983 may effectively decide the case. Thus, by leading off with a discussion (and rejection) of the idea that the Constitution imposes on the States an affirmative duty to take basic care of their citizens, the Court foreshadows—perhaps even preordains—its conclusion that no duty existed even on the specific facts before us. This initial discussion establishes the baseline from which the Court assesses the DeShaneys' claim that, when a State has—"by word and by deed"—announced an intention to protect a certain class of citizens and has before it facts that would trigger that protection under the applicable state law, the Constitution imposes upon the State an affirmative duty of protection.

The Court's baseline is the absence of positive rights in the Constitution and a concomitant suspicion of any claim that seems to depend on such rights. From this perspective, the DeShaneys' claim is first and foremost about inaction (the failure, here, of respondents to take steps to protect Joshua), and only tangentially about action (the establishment of a state program specifically designed to help children like Joshua). And from this perspective, holding these Wisconsin officials liable—where the only difference between this case and one involving a general claim to protective services is Wisconsin's establishment and operation of a program to protect children—would seem to punish an effort that we should seek to promote.

I would begin from the opposite direction. I would focus first on the action that Wisconsin has taken with respect to Joshua and children like him, rather than on the actions that the State failed to take.* * *

* * *

Wisconsin has established a child-welfare system specifically designed to help children like Joshua. Wisconsin law places upon the local departments of social services such as respondent (DSS or Department) a duty to investigate reported instances of child abuse. While other governmental bodies and private persons are largely responsible for the reporting of possible cases of child abuse, Wisconsin law channels all such reports to the local departments of social services for evaluation and, if necessary, further action. Even when it is the sheriff's office or police department that receives a report of suspected child abuse, that report is referred to local social services departments for action; the only exception to this occurs when the reporter fears for the child's immediate safety. In this way, Wisconsin law invites—indeed, directs—citizens and other governmental entities to depend on local departments of social services such as respondent to protect children from abuse.

The specific facts before us bear out this view of Wisconsin's system of protecting children. Each time someone voiced a suspicion that Joshua was being abused, that information was relayed to the Department for investigation and possible action. When Randy DeShaney's second wife told the police that he had " 'hit the boy causing marks and [was] a prime case for child abuse,' "the police referred her complaint to DSS. When, on three separate occasions, emergency room personnel noticed suspicious injuries on Joshua's body, they went to DSS with this information. When neighbors informed the police that they had seen or heard Joshua's father or his father's lover beating or otherwise abusing Joshua, the police brought these reports to the attention of DSS. And when respondent Kemmeter, through these reports and through her own observations in the course of nearly 20 visits to the DeShaney home, compiled growing evidence that Joshua was being abused, that information stayed within the Department—chronicled by the social worker in detail that seems almost eerie in light of her failure to act upon it. (As to the extent of the social worker's involvement in, and knowledge of, Joshua's predicament, her reaction to the news of Joshua's last and most devastating injuries is illuminating: " 'I just knew the phone would ring some day and Joshua would be dead.' ")

Even more telling than these examples is the Department's control over the decision whether to take steps to protect a particular child from suspected abuse. While many different people contributed information and advice to this decision, it was up to the people at DSS to make the ultimate decision (subject to the approval of the local government's Corporation Counsel) whether to disturb the family's current arrangements. When Joshua first appeared at a local hospital with injuries signaling physical abuse, for example, it was DSS that made the decision to take him into temporary custody for the purpose of studying his situation—and it was DSS, acting in conjunction with the corporation counsel, that returned him to his father. Unfortunately for Joshua DeShaney, the buck effectively stopped with the Department.

In these circumstances, a private citizen, or even a person working in a government agency other than DSS, would doubtless feel that her job was done as soon as she had reported her suspicions of child abuse to DSS. Through its child-welfare program, in other words, the State of Wisconsin has relieved ordinary citizens and governmental bodies other than the Department of any sense of obligation to do anything more than report their suspicions of child abuse to DSS. If DSS ignores or dismisses these suspicions, no one will step in to fill the gap. Wisconsin's child-protection program thus effectively confined Joshua DeShaney within the walls of Randy DeShaney's violent home until such time as DSS took action to remove him. Conceivably, then, children like Joshua are made worse off by the existence of this program when the persons and entities charged with carrying it out fail to do their jobs.

It simply belies reality, therefore, to contend that the State "stood by and did nothing" with respect to Joshua. Through its child-protection program, the State actively intervened in Joshua's life and, by virtue of this intervention, acquired ever more certain knowledge that Joshua was in grave danger. * * *

* * *

As the Court today reminds us, "the Due Process Clause of the Fourteenth Amendment was intended to prevent government 'from abusing [its] power, or employing it as an instrument of oppression.' "My disagreement with the Court arises from its failure to see that inaction can be every bit as abusive of power as action, that oppression can result when a State undertakes a vital duty and then ignores it. Today's opinion construes the Due Process Clause to permit a State to displace private sources of protection and then, at the critical moment, to shrug its shoulders and turn away from the harm that it has promised to try to prevent. Because I cannot agree that our Constitution is indifferent to such indifference, I respectfully dissent.

JUSTICE BLACKMUN, dissenting.

Today, the Court purports to be the dispassionate oracle of the law, unmoved by "natural sympathy." But, in this pretense, the Court itself retreats into a sterile formalism which prevents it from recognizing either the facts of the case before it or the legal norms that should apply to those facts. As Justice BRENNAN demonstrates, the facts here involve not mere passivity, but active state intervention in the life of Joshua DeShaney—intervention that triggered a fundamental duty to aid the boy once the State learned of the severe danger to which he was exposed.

The Court fails to recognize this duty because it attempts to draw a sharp and rigid line between action and inaction. But such formalistic reasoning has no place in the interpretation of the broad and stirring Clauses of the Fourteenth Amendment. * * *

* * *

Poor Joshua! Victim of repeated attacks by an irresponsible, bullying, cowardly, and intemperate father, and abandoned by respondents who placed him in a dangerous predicament and who knew or learned what was going on, and yet did essentially nothing except, as the Court revealingly observes "dutifully recorded these incidents in [their] files." It is a sad commentary upon American life, and constitutional principles—so full of late of patriotic fervor and proud proclamations about "liberty and justice for all"—that this child, Joshua DeShaney, now is assigned to live out the remainder of his life profoundly retarded. Joshua and his mother, as petitioners here, deserve—but now are denied by this Court—the opportunity to have the facts of their case considered in the light of the constitutional protection that 42 U.S.C. § 1983 is meant to provide.

Notes and Questions

1. *Questions about* DeShaney. (a) What actions did the state take in reaction to complaints about abuse of Joshua? (b) Why was there no violation of Joshua's constitutional rights? Do you agree with the Court's distinction between action and inaction by the state? Do you agree with the majority that when the state returned Joshua "to his father's custody, it placed him in no worse position than that in which he would have been had it not acted at all?"

2. *Aftermath*. Randy DeShaney was convicted of child abuse and sentenced to two to four years in prison. He was freed on parole after serving less than two years. Andrea Neal, State Didn't Have to Protect Abused Child, Detroit Free Press, Feb. 23, 1989, at 1A.

3. *Tort claim*. The DeShaney majority notes that a state tort law claim might be available to Joshua, but even if the state allows such a claim, establishing liability may be very difficult. Boland v. State, 638 N.Y.S. 2d 500 (1996), involved the erroneous routing of a hotline call reporting abuse. Before the case was investigated, the child who was the subject of the report was seriously beaten and died. To establish state liability the claimant father needed to first show that there was a special relationship between the child who was killed and the governmental entity. This burden was met because the state's "detailed and comprehensive statutory scheme at issue * * * was designed to protect a discrete and limited class of individuals," namely the

claimant's children. Id. at 506. Further, the claimant had to show that the governmental official negligently failed to perform a ministerial act, in this instance the routing of the hotline call to the correct child protective office. The claimant succeeded in establishing this. Id. at 243. Finally, the claimant had to show that the state's negligence was the proximate cause of the child's death. This would require the claimant "to establish that had the hotline report been correctly routed in the first instance, a timely investigation would have ensued, with the investigator assigned to the case interviewing the stepmother and the children prior to the infliction of [the victim's] fatal injuries and, based upon such interview, concluding that the stepmother posed such an imminent danger to the children's health that they would have been summarily removed from the home." Boland v. State, 693 N.Y.S.2d 748 (N.Y.A.D. 1999). The claimant could not meet this last requirement and therefore could not establish state liability.

4. *The ominous numbers.* Unfortunately the lack of intervention that resulted in Joshua's injuries is all too likely to happen again. A U.S. General Accounting Office 1997 study on selected child protective services offices across the country describes the current situation:

> Increases in the number of maltreatment cases, the changing nature of family problems, and long-standing systemic weaknesses have placed the CPS [Child Protective Services] system in a state of crisis and undermined its ability to fully carry out the responsibilities for abused and neglected children. First, child maltreatment reports have risen steadily across the country. The caseload of CPS units have grown correspondingly, and CPS units often cannot keep pace with this workload. Second, these caseloads are increasingly composed of families whose problems have grown more troubling and complicated, with substance abuse a common and pervasive condition. Finally, systemic weaknesses–such as difficulty maintaining professional and skilled workforce, inconsistently implementing policies and procedures, a lack of automated case management in recordkeeping systems, and poor working relationships between CPS and the courts–have further weakened CPS units. The combined effect of difficult caseloads and systemic weaknesses (1) overburdens caseworkers and dilutes the quality of their responses to families and (2) may further endanger the lives of children coming to the attention of CPS.

CPS policies were a major problem:

> In CPS, where staff are sometimes dealing with life-and-death issues, the knowledge of and consistent application of appropriate policies and procedures are critical. CPS policies and procedures–such as those that define acceptable levels of risk to the child and those that outline the time frames, methods, and protocols for sharing information with local service providers, as well as documentation requirements for collecting evidence during the investigation–are important safeguards for children. These policies and procedures provide structure in the stressful environment in which caseworkers function and reduce the probability of making serious mistakes. Clear policies and procedures can also provide important guidance when staff receive inadequate or inconsistent supervision.

In some of the sites we visited, however, CPS staff were unable to consistently apply existing policies. For example, a 1995 state review of New York City's CPS operations found numerous problems in implementing policies, such as inadequate safety assessments for all children within the home in over 20 percent of the cases, inadequate investigations in over 50 percent of the cases, excessive time frames for conducting investigations in 50 percent of the cases, and missing service plans in 18 percent of open cases for which abuse was validated. Moreover, the review identified a lack of supervisory involvement in determining the validity of alleged maltreatment in 21 percent of the cases. Bronx and Manhattan Field Office managers, supervisors, and caseworkers reported that they lack knowledge on policies and procedures, in part, because policies change frequently, no procedures manual exists, and information is inconsistently distributed to all staff.

U.S. Gen'l Accounting Office, Child Protective Services: Complex Challenges Require New Strategies 6–7, 11 (1997).

Do caseworkers have too much discretion and too little liability for errors related to removing children from their parents? What remedy would you suggest for a child harmed by the problems identified in the GAO report?

5. *Immunity for wrongful removal?* Should a parent have a § 1983 cause of action against caseworkers and the department of social services attorney for bringing a dependency action that wrongfully results in the child's removal from the parents' custody? In Ernst v. Child and Youth Services, 108 F.3d 486 (3d Cir. 1997), the Third Circuit held:

> * * * [T]he public policy considerations supporting absolute immunity for prosecutors are equally applicable to child welfare workers acting in a quasi-prosecutorial capacity in dependency proceedings. Like a prosecutor, a child welfare worker must exercise independent judgment in deciding whether or not to bring a child dependency proceeding, and such judgment would likely be compromised if the worker faced the threat of personal liability for every mistake in judgment. Certainly, we want our child welfare workers to exercise care in deciding to interfere in parent-child relationships. But we do not want them to be so overly cautious, out of fear of personal liability, that they fail to intervene in situations in which children are in danger.

6. *Additional references.* Laura Oren, The State's Failure to Protect Children and Substantive Due Process: *DeShaney* in Context, 68 N.C.L. Rev. 659 (1990); Affirmative Constitutional Obligations of Government Officials, The Supreme Court, 1988 Term, 103 Harv. L. Rev. 167 (1989).

SECTION 7. THE PROSECUTOR'S ROLE

In an abuse and neglect case, does the prosecutor represent the department of social services, the prosecutor's view of the best interests of the child or the state as a whole? The department, according to West Virginia ex rel. Diva P. v. Kaufman, 490 S.E.2d 642 (W.Va.1997), which held that the legislature made the department the state's representative. The county prosecutor thus did not have authority to litigate abuse and neglect cases independently of the department. The chief justice concurred:

> From a very pragmatic view, this issue was particularly hard for me because over the course of almost sixteen years on the bench, I have seen the department fail to protect children and fail to advocate vociferously for them on many occasions.[1] In addition, although guardians ad litem are appointed to represent children, most of them until relatively recently, did not do much aggressive advocacy either, frequently not even appearing on appeal on behalf of the children.[2]

> Furthermore, I believe strongly that the community at large (all of us in the corporate sense) have an interest and a responsibility in abuse and neglect proceedings which could and probably should be represented by prosecuting attorneys. Thank goodness, we as a society have stopped looking at child abuse as a "family problem" and now recognize that it's everyone's business. But as I have said in other contexts, it is up to courts to interpret the law, not create it. As much as I would like to make the policy decision that prosecuting attorneys have the right and responsibility to represent the public interest in protecting abused and neglected children when their position conflicts with the department's, I do not believe the law as currently constituted permits them that role. * * *

> There cannot be too much advocacy for children. The public has a legitimate interest in protecting abused and neglected children, and the prosecutors are very logical representatives to carry out that mission if the Legislature chooses to modify the law to accord them that responsibility.

Questions

1. Should the legislature amend the law to allow the prosecutor to proceed independently of the department? Would Joshua DeShaney have benefitted from a proactive prosecutor who took a broad view of the prosecutor's role?

SECTION 8.   THE REASONABLE EFFORTS REQUIREMENT

How much effort should the state make to keep families together before removing children from their homes? Where should we draw the line between parental and governmental responsibility for children? The governmental response to these questions has resembled a pendulum,

---

1. A September 1996 legislative audit of the Child Protective Services Division (CPS) for the 1995 fiscal year, involving a twelve-county survey, found that despite the requirement that it conduct a face-to-face interview with the child or children within 14 days of being notified of suspected abuse or neglect, CPS failed to conduct any such interview in 46% of the cases. In 29% of cases, CPS conducted the interview within 14 days, in 15% of the cases, CPS conducted the interview within 15 to 90 days, and in 10% of the cases, CPS took over 90 days to interview the alleged victims.

2. [This and other cases] * * * precluding prosecutors from an independent role in abuse and neglect, impel me to re-emphasize that, now more than ever, guardians ad litem * * * must be strong advocates for the children they represent.

moving from emphasis on parental responsibility to emphasis on government responsibility and back again. When the emphasis is on government responsibility, removal is more difficult because the government has assumed the obligation to provide services to try to keep families together.

IN RE N.M.W.

Court of Appeals of Iowa, 1990.
461 N.W.2d 478.

HABHAB, JUDGE.

Appellant, B.W., appeals the adjudication of the juvenile court determining N.M.W. to be a child in need of assistance (CINA) and the subsequent dispositional order directing continued foster care of N.M.W. We affirm.

The child in question is a girl born in July 1983. Her parents are not married to each other. She lived with her mother from the date of her birth until 1989.

The family has had involvement with the Department of Human Services since at least 1984. Over the years, the Department has prepared several abuse reports. The primary concern has been extreme filth in the mother's home, although there have also been concerns about inadequate food in the home, inadequate supervision of the child, and refusal of services by the mother.

On April 12, 1989, N.M.W. was found in front of a house a block from B.W.'s residence. When the police were unable to locate her home, they took N.M.W. to the police station. N.M.W. informed the authorities her mother had told her to go outside. B.W. claimed the child had just taken off without her knowledge. From statements made by law enforcement officers concerning the condition of B.W.'s apartment, a child protective worker visited B.W.'s apartment.

When the worker, who was accompanied by a police officer, approached the apartment, the stench of cat feces and urine became noticeable. Inside the apartment, the worker discovered the entire front room to be strewn with a collection of garbage, clothing, and other general clutter. Ashtrays were found filled to overflowing with some knocked over. Windows and screens were missing and garbage materials were embedded in the carpet. A side closet was packed with a mixture of clutter and refuse. A bedroom was filthy with garbage. Additionally, two litters of cats were living under the bed. Apparently a total of eleven to twelve cats lived in the apartment.

The same squalid conditions existed in the kitchen. The floor was filthy and the garbage container was left uncovered. The refrigerator had smeared food on parts of it and was empty of food except for milk, eggs, and ketchup. Dishes were stacked in the sink, on the counter, and on the table. Also, a cat box filled with cat excrement was found in the kitchen. In the bathroom, the cats had defecated along the bathtub and some of

N.M.W.'s clothing was stuck to the feline fecal material. Because of the filthy apartment, N.M.W. stayed with a friend of B.W.

On April 14, 1989, the child protective worker returned to B.W.'s apartment. The same squalid conditions still existed. Likewise, the conditions had not improved by April 17, 1989, when the worker again returned to the home. The worker returned again on April 20th to find B.W. had made limited improvement. Later visits to B.W.'s home found the unsanitary conditions unabated.

Following hearing on the matter, the juvenile court made a CINA determination as to N.M.W. At the initial hearing, the State presented evidence concerning three prior child abuse reports. The three reports had formed the basis for a prior CINA proceeding in which the juvenile court had dismissed the petition.

* * *

I.

Initially, B.W. argues the trial court erred in finding the existence of sufficient evidence to establish N.M.W. as a child in need of assistance. Iowa Code section 232.2(6)(g) defines CINA as an unmarried child:

> Whose parent, guardian, or custodian fails to exercise a minimal degree of care in supplying the child with adequate food, clothing or shelter and refuses other means made available to provide such essentials.

We find clear and convincing record evidence to support the juvenile court's determination that N.M.W. is a child in need of assistance.

The chronic unsanitary conditions of B.W.'s apartment are of sufficient magnitude to form the basis for a CINA adjudication. We take judicial notice of the health hazards of having animal fecal materials scattered throughout one's living quarters. While the record does not disclose any adverse health effects of this environment on N.M.W., the child's well being demands that action be taken to prevent actual harm.

B.W. also asserts the juvenile court erred in considering B.W.'s past actions which formed the basis for prior CINA proceedings. We disagree. In considering what the future holds for a child if returned to the parent, the Iowa Supreme Court noted * * *

> Insight for this determination can be gained from evidence of the parent's past performance, for that performance may be indicative of the quality of the future care that parent is capable of providing.

We find no error in permitting such evidence as long as there is other clear and convincing evidence that forms the basis of the current CINA proceeding. We find such other clear and convincing evidence independent of the prior CINA proceedings.

* * *

III.

Finally, B.W. challenges the juvenile court's decision at the dispositional hearing to place N.M.W. with the Iowa Department of Human Services. We find no error in this order. B.W. was given numerous opportunities to clean and sanitize her apartment, but failed to rectify the situation. The juvenile court quite appropriately informed her that she could resume custody of N.M.W. when she removed the pets and cleaned the apartment. B.W.'s choice in this case was either her cats or her child; so far she has chosen her cats. We find no error in the juvenile court's dispositional order.

IV.

There are certain parts of the dissent that need addressing. The dissenter claims she is concerned because the majority decision may be interpreted as setting standards for housekeeping that need to be met before we allow parents to keep their children. We fail to find anything in the opinion to justify such concern. Our concern in its simplified term is with the child's welfare and best interests. We just do not believe that this child should be compelled to live under [these] circumstances * * *

* * *

We, too, agree that parents who devote time and attention to their children, who allow their children to have pets and projects in their home are contributing substantially to their children's emotional development. But that is a much different setting than requiring a child to live in the stench of cat feces and urine. It is also much different than to require a child to live in a home that is strewn with a collection of garbage, clothing, and other general clutter. It is also different than requiring the child to live in a home where the cats defecated along the bathtub where some of the child's clothing was stuck to the feline fecal material.

We have no quarrel with the position of the dissenter that recommends that the State take a more active role in assisting the mother in cleaning this home so that the child may be returned. We encourage it. But until that time, is it really fair to the child to require the child to return to the mother's home as it is presently constituted? We think not.

The juvenile court, who had the first-hand opportunity to observe and talk with the mother, explained the options available to her. When we give meaningful consideration to the best interest of this child and couple the circumstances with the help given by the State, we do not believe the options to be insurmountable.

* * *

SACKETT, JUDGE (dissenting).

I dissent. Over twelve months ago N.M.W., a happy, healthy five-year-old child was removed from her biological mother's care and placed in foster care where she remains today. The majority has determined the child must remain in foster care.

The reason for the removal, and the decision the child should remain in foster care, is that the mother is an inadequate housekeeper and does not keep what the majority terms a sanitary house. I agree with the majority that the record clearly supports a finding this mother is an extremely poor housekeeper. I agree with the majority it would be in the child's best interests to live in a cleaner house. However, the house could have been cleaned without taking the child from her mother. I do not, however, feel removal from the parental home was in the child's best interests and feel the matter should be remanded to direct reasonable efforts be utilized to allow the child to return home. Houses can be cleaned, but the trauma a child experiences when he or she is removed from the only parental home he or she has ever known can cause emotional scars that can last a lifetime.

There is strong authority that parenting deficiencies may best be addressed by leaving the child in the home, that removals from biological families are traumatic for children, and that foster care placement is wrought with problems. Additionally, the difficulties I see occur with foster placements convince me the state, despite conscientious efforts by dedicated persons, is ill-equipped to parent.

Our legislature has recognized that children are best served by remaining in their home and requires reasonable efforts be made to allow them to remain there. Federal legislation providing states' reimbursement for foster care directs that reasonable efforts be made to allow a child to remain in his or her home, and a state's failure to do so can result in the loss of funds for foster care reimbursement.

To apply reasonable efforts first requires identifying the problem. The problems identified by the majority are the poor housekeeping conditions in the home, and the inability of the mother to correct these deficiencies. After identifying the problem, the next step is to look at the family as a unit and determine what it takes to correct this problem.

If this mother came from a higher economic level, she could do as many parents do who have neither the desire or ability to clean their houses. She could hire a cleaning service. I would consider reasonable efforts to entail granting this mother assistance with cleaning her house and keeping it clean. A few hours of cleaning service would have cost the state less than the judicial time and court appointed attorney fees spent to litigate the adequacy of this woman's housekeeping skills through the state's appellate courts. And most importantly, the child would not have suffered the trauma of removal and the insecurities that come in foster care.

The majority decision also concerns me because it may be interpreted as setting standards for housekeeping that need to be met before we allow parents to keep their children. If I were convinced: (1) only people in clean houses were good parents, (2) for a child to be healthy it is necessary for him or her to be raised in a sanitary house, and (3) a child suffers less by being removed from his or her parents than from growing up in a dirty house, I could agree with the majority. I am not convinced of these things. I consider parents who devote time and attention to their children, who allow their children to have pets and projects in their home, and who welcome their children's friends in their home are contributing substantially to their children's emotional development. Parents who seek to direct their financial and emotional resources in these directions may have few resources left to keep a sanitary house.

If we concentrate too much on sanitary houses, we may take children away from good and adequate parents, and we may use energies and resources that would best be directed to helping families and to identifying children who suffer serious abuse.

Notes and Questions

1. *Questions about* N.M.W. If you represent N.M.W. and she wants to stay with her mother, what arguments would you make on her behalf? Do you think staying with her mother is in N.M.W.'s best interests? Do you agree with the dissent that the state should have simply paid for housekeeping assistance?

2. *Family reunification.* After years of debate and documentation of the harm done to children by removal from their homes and placement in foster care, Congress passed the Adoption Assistance and Child Welfare Act of 1980. The Act was intended to require states to keep children in their own homes when possible and, when removal was necessary, to require states to move aggressively to reunite the family. If reunification was not possible within a reasonable time, the child should be placed in an adoptive home in most circumstances. The Act makes eligibility for specified federal funding contingent on a state's meeting a requirement that "in each case, reasonable efforts will be made (A) prior to the placement of the child in foster care, to prevent or eliminate the need for removal of the child from his home, and (B) to make it possible for the child to return to his home." 42 U.S.C. § 671(a)(15)(1991).

To what extent are "reasonable efforts" constitutionally required?

3. *The Adoption and Safe Families Act of 1997.* By 1997 Congress had become concerned that the states were making too much, rather than too little, effort to reunite families. The Adoption and Safe Families Act of 1997 requires states to meet stringent time requirements for moving children out of foster care and into adoptive homes. It also specifies that reasonable efforts are not required in some cases:

"(D) reasonable efforts * * * shall not be required to be made with respect to a parent of a child if a court of competent jurisdiction has determined that—

"(i) the parent has subjected the child to aggravated circumstances (as defined in State law, which definition may include but need not be limited to abandonment, torture, chronic abuse, and sexual abuse);

"(ii) the parent has—

"(I) committed murder * * * of another child of the parent;

"(II) committed voluntary manslaughter * * * of another child of the parent;

"(III) aided or abetted, attempted, conspired, or solicited to commit such a murder or such a voluntary manslaughter; or

"(IV) committed a felony assault that results in serious bodily injury to the child or another child of the parent; or

"(iii) the parental rights of the parent to a sibling have been terminated involuntarily; * * *

42 U.S.C. (a)(15)D.

4. *Services not required.* Parental rights may be terminated to all children in the household because of severe abuse of one, without the state providing reunification services. In *Deborah S.*, supra page 320, the trial judge ruled that services were not required, and noted, "I can't for the life of me figure * * * what reunification services that we could offer to these people that would make them parents that one would feel safe in sending any living creature back into their home."

5. *Extent of services.* At what point is it "reasonable" for the state to refuse to provide services? Must a state, for example, provide housing for homeless families? Homelessness is a significant factor in foster care placements. The Supreme Court of Rhode Island ruled that a social services agency can be ordered to provide housing as part of a reasonable efforts requirement when "the court first finds that family reunification cannot be achieved because of a family's homelessness." The court rejected the agency's arguments that the "[l]egislature did not create or envision it as a housing or income-maintenance agency and * * * that if the Family Court is allowed to order it to make rental-subsidy payments, critical moneys and energies will be diverted from its primary mission of preserving and reunifying families." In re Nicole G., 577 A.2d 248, 249 (R.I.1990). See also, e.g., In re Burns, 519 A.2d 638 (Del.1986)(state should have provided housing as part of reasonable efforts). See also Washington State Coalition for the Homeless v. Department of Soc. and Health Servs., 949 P.2d 1291 (Wash.1997).

6. *The parents' cooperation.* A treatment plan for the abused child's family may require the parents to admit responsibility for the abuse. Family therapy may be required before a child will be returned to the family, for example, and an important step in family therapy may be having parents admit how the abuse occurred. Without the parents' confession, the department of social services might not allow family reunification on the ground that lack of acceptance of responsibility means the family situation would be unsafe for the child. Parents who in fact did not abuse their child face a cruel dilemma. They must either confess to an offense they did not commit or continue to have their child kept out of their home. See Blanca P. v. Superior Ct., 53 Cal.Rptr.2d 687 (1996); George J. Alexander, Big Mother: The State's Use of Mental Health Experts in Dependency Cases, 24 Pac.L.J. 1465 (1993).

7. *Additional references.* Michael J. Bufkin, The Reasonable Efforts Requirement: Does It Place Children at Increased Risk of Abuse or Neglect, 35 U. Louisville J. Fam. L. 355 (1996–97); Christine H. Kim, Putting Reason Back Into the Reasonable Efforts Requirements in Child Abuse and Neglect

Cases, 1999 U. Ill. L. Rev. 287 (1999); Shawn L. Raymond, Where Are the Reasonable Efforts to Enforce the Reasonable Efforts Requirement? Monitoring State Compliance under the Adoption Assistance and Child Welfare Act of 1980, 77 Tex. L. Rev. 1235 (1999).

PROBLEM 4–9

Foster care in State X costs $12,000 per child and a welfare grant for a family of three is $10,000 for one year. Eight-year-old Sally and her five-year-old brother John live with their mother, Sue Smith. Ms. Smith lost her minimum wage job because of downsizing and is unemployed. She is not eligible for unemployment compensation because she had the job for too short a time. She has exceeded the state's five-year lifetime limit on welfare benefit eligibility. There is no food in their apartment, both children have ear infections that need treatment, and the family has received an eviction notice for non-payment of rent. The state statute provides the following: "Child neglect ... means ...the failure on the part of a person responsible for the care of a child to provide for the adequate food, shelter, clothing or other care necessary for the child's health and welfare when financially able to do so or when offered financial or other reasonable means to do so."

You represent the Department of Social Services which wants the children adjudicated neglected, removed from the home, and placed in foster care. The mother's attorney argues that the statute, the "reasonable efforts" requirement, and the U.S. Constitution forbid removal and require the state to provide aid in the home. What is your response?

SECTION 9.   TERMINATION OF PARENTAL RIGHTS

When the state's efforts to keep a family together fail, the state may move to terminate parental rights. The goal of termination typically is to free the child for permanent placement, with adoption usually preferred. Termination generally severs all parent-child ties, particularly when the child is being freed for adoption by strangers. After termination the child usually has no right to support or inheritance from the parent, and the parent has no right to see the child or know where the child goes.

Because termination is such a drastic remedy, the Supreme Court has been sympathetic to parents' arguments that termination proceedings should have more due process protections than the usual civil case. Making termination of parental rights more difficult, however, is not necessarily good for children. Children may end up in a series of foster homes, unable to return home but not free for adoption. In response to the plight of these children and to the overloaded and expensive foster care system, Congress passed the Adoption Assistance and Child Welfare Act of 1980. As mentioned above, a major purpose of the Act was to force states to actively try to reunify families and, when reunification failed, to terminate parental rights and place the children in permanent homes. The new Adoption and Safe Families Act of 1997 imposes deadlines and quotas on the states to expedite termination of parental rights and locate adoptive homes when the family cannot be reunited quickly.

This section examines constitutionally required due process protections for parents and considers grounds for termination in addition to those seen in earlier cases in this Chapter. While studying termination, consider what will happen to children whose ties to their parents are severed. Will their lives be improved? Is termination in the child's best interests, and what does "best interests" mean? The foster care and adoption chapters will examine what happens to children who are removed from their parents.

A.　Due Process Protections for Parents

SANTOSKY v. KRAMER

Supreme Court of the United States, 1982.
455 U.S. 745.

JUSTICE BLACKMUN delivered the opinion of the Court.

Under New York law, the State may terminate, over parental objection, the rights of parents in their natural child upon a finding that the child is "permanently neglected." N.Y.Soc.Serv.Law §§ 384–b.4.(d), 384–b.7.(a). The New York Family Court Act § 622 requires that only a "fair preponderance of the evidence" support that finding. Thus, in New York, the factual certainty required to extinguish the parent-child relationship is no greater than that necessary to award money damages in an ordinary civil action.

Today we hold that the Due Process Clause of the Fourteenth Amendment demands more than this. Before a State may sever completely and irrevocably the rights of parents in their natural child, due process requires that the State support its allegations by at least clear and convincing evidence.

I

A

New York authorizes its officials to remove a child temporarily from his or her home if the child appears "neglected," within the meaning of Art. 10 of the Family Court Act. Once removed, a child under the age of 18 customarily is placed "in the care of an authorized agency," usually a state institution or a foster home. At that point, "the state's first obligation is to help the family with services to ... reunite it...." But if convinced that "positive, nurturing parent-child relationships no longer exist," the State may initiate "permanent neglect" proceedings to free the child for adoption.

The State bifurcates its permanent neglect proceeding into "factfinding" and "dispositional" hearings. At the factfinding stage, the State must prove that the child has been "permanently neglected." * * * The

Family Court judge then determines at a subsequent dispositional hearing what placement would serve the child's best interests.

At the factfinding hearing, the State must establish, among other things, that for more than a year after the child entered state custody, the agency "made diligent efforts to encourage and strengthen the parental relationship." The State must further prove that during that same period, the child's natural parents failed "substantially and continuously or repeatedly to maintain contact with or plan for the future of the child although physically and financially able to do so." Should the State support its allegations by "a fair preponderance of the evidence," the child may be declared permanently neglected. That declaration empowers the Family Court judge to terminate permanently the natural parents' rights in the child. Termination denies the natural parents physical custody, as well as the rights ever to visit, communicate with, or regain custody of the child.

New York's permanent neglect statute provides natural parents with certain procedural protections.[2] But New York permits its officials to establish "permanent neglect" with less proof than most States require. Thirty-five States, the District of Columbia, and the Virgin Islands currently specify a higher standard of proof, in parental rights termination proceedings, than a "fair preponderance of the evidence." * * * The question here is whether New York's "fair preponderance of the evidence" standard is constitutionally sufficient.

B

Petitioners John Santosky II and Annie Santosky are the natural parents of Tina and John III. In November 1973, after incidents reflecting parental neglect, respondent Kramer, Commissioner of the Ulster County Department of Social Services, initiated a neglect proceeding under Fam.Ct.Act § 1022 and removed Tina from her natural home. About 10 months later, he removed John III and placed him with foster parents. On the day John was taken, Annie Santosky gave birth to a third child, Jed. When Jed was only three days old, respondent transferred him to a foster home on the ground that immediate removal was necessary to avoid imminent danger to his life or health.

In October 1978, respondent petitioned the Ulster County Family Court to terminate petitioners' parental rights in the three children.[4] Petitioners challenged the constitutionality of the "fair preponderance of the evidence" standard specified in Fam.Ct.Act § 622. The Family Court Judge rejected this constitutional challenge and weighed the evidence under the statutory standard. While acknowledging that the Santoskys had maintained contact with their children, the judge found those visits "at best superficial and devoid of any real emotional content." After

2. Most notably, natural parents have a statutory right to the assistance of counsel and of court-appointed counsel if they are indigent.

4. Respondent had made an earlier and unsuccessful termination effort in September 1976.* * *

deciding that the agency had made " 'diligent efforts' to encourage and strengthen the parental relationship," he concluded that the Santoskys were incapable, even with public assistance, of planning for the future of their children. The judge later held a dispositional hearing and ruled that the best interests of the three children required permanent termination of the Santoskys' custody.[5]

Petitioners appealed, again contesting the constitutionality of § 622's standard of proof. The New York Supreme Court, Appellate Division, affirmed.* * *

The New York Court of Appeals then* * * dismissed petitioners' appeal * * *.

II

Last Term in Lassiter v. Department of Social Services (1981), this Court, by a 5–4 vote, held that the Fourteenth Amendment's Due Process Clause does not require the appointment of counsel for indigent parents in every parental status termination proceeding. The case casts light, however, on the two central questions here—whether process is constitutionally due a natural parent at a State's parental rights termination proceeding, and, if so, what process is due.

In *Lassiter*, it was "not disputed that state intervention to terminate the relationship between [a parent] and [the] child must be accomplished by procedures meeting the requisites of the Due Process Clause." * * *

The fundamental liberty interest of natural parents in the care, custody, and management of their child does not evaporate simply because they have not been model parents or have lost temporary custody of their child to the State. Even when blood relationships are strained, parents retain a vital interest in preventing the irretrievable destruction of their family life. If anything, persons faced with forced dissolution of their parental rights have a more critical need for procedural protections than do those resisting state intervention into ongoing family affairs. When the State moves to destroy weakened familial bonds, it must provide the parents with fundamentally fair procedures.

* * *

III

In parental rights termination proceedings, the private interest affected is commanding; the risk of error from using a preponderance standard is substantial; and the countervailing governmental interest favoring that standard is comparatively slight. Evaluation of the three [Matthews v. Eldridge, 1976] factors compels the conclusion that use of a

---

5. Since respondent Kramer took custody of Tina, John III, and Jed, the Santoskys have had two other children, James and Jeremy. The State has taken no action to remove these younger children. At oral argument, counsel for respondents replied affirmatively when asked whether he was asserting that petitioners were "unfit to handle the three older ones but not unfit to handle the two younger ones."

"fair preponderance of the evidence" standard in such proceedings is inconsistent with due process.

A

"The extent to which procedural due process must be afforded the recipient is influenced by the extent to which he may be 'condemned to suffer grievous loss.' " * * *

Lassiter declared it "plain beyond the need for multiple citation" that a natural parent's "desire for and right to 'the companionship, care, custody, and management of his or her children' " is an interest far more precious than any property right. When the State initiates a parental rights termination proceeding, it seeks not merely to infringe that fundamental liberty interest, but to end it. "If the State prevails, it will have worked a unique kind of deprivation. . . . A parent's interest in the accuracy and justice of the decision to terminate his or her parental status is, therefore, a commanding one."

* * *

* * * Once affirmed on appeal, a New York decision terminating parental rights is final and irrevocable. Few forms of state action are both so severe and so irreversible.

Thus, the first *Eldridge* factor—the private interest affected—weighs heavily against use of the preponderance standard at a state-initiated permanent neglect proceeding. We do not deny that the child and his foster parents are also deeply interested in the outcome of that contest. But at the factfinding stage of the New York proceeding, the focus emphatically is not on them.

The factfinding does not purport—and is not intended—to balance the child's interest in a normal family home against the parents' interest in raising the child. Nor does it purport to determine whether the natural parents or the foster parents would provide the better home. Rather, the factfinding hearing pits the State directly against the parents. The State alleges that the natural parents are at fault. The questions disputed and decided are what the State did—"made diligent efforts," and what the natural parents did not do—"maintain contact with or plan for the future of the child." The State marshals an array of public resources to prove its case and disprove the parents' case. Victory by the State not only makes termination of parental rights possible; it entails a judicial determination that the parents are unfit to raise their own children.

At the factfinding, the State cannot presume that a child and his parents are adversaries. After the State has established parental unfitness at that initial proceeding, the court may assume at the dispositional stage that the interests of the child and the natural parents do diverge. But until the State proves parental unfitness, the child and his parents share a vital interest in preventing erroneous termination of their natural relationship. Thus, at the factfinding, the interests of the child and his natural parents coincide to favor use of error-reducing procedures.

* * *

B

Under Mathews v. Eldridge, we next must consider both the risk of erroneous deprivation of private interests resulting from use of a "fair preponderance" standard and the likelihood that a higher evidentiary standard would reduce that risk. Since the factfinding phase of a permanent neglect proceeding is an adversary contest between the State and the natural parents, the relevant question is whether a preponderance standard fairly allocates the risk of an erroneous factfinding between these two parties.

In New York, the factfinding stage of a state-initiated permanent neglect proceeding bears many of the indicia of a criminal trial. The Commissioner of Social Services charges the parents with permanent neglect. They are served by summons. The factfinding hearing is conducted pursuant to formal rules of evidence. The State, the parents, and the child are all represented by counsel. The State seeks to establish a series of historical facts about the intensity of its agency's efforts to reunite the family, the infrequency and insubstantiality of the parents' contacts with their child, and the parents' inability or unwillingness to formulate a plan for the child's future. The attorneys submit documentary evidence, and call witnesses who are subject to cross-examination. Based on all the evidence, the judge then determines whether the State has proved the statutory elements of permanent neglect by a fair preponderance of the evidence.

At such a proceeding, numerous factors combine to magnify the risk of erroneous factfinding. Permanent neglect proceedings employ imprecise substantive standards that leave determinations unusually open to the subjective values of the judge. In appraising the nature and quality of a complex series of encounters among the agency, the parents, and the child, the court possesses unusual discretion to underweigh probative facts that might favor the parent. Because parents subject to termination proceedings are often poor, uneducated, or members of minority groups such proceedings are often vulnerable to judgments based on cultural or class bias.

The State's ability to assemble its case almost inevitably dwarfs the parents' ability to mount a defense. No predetermined limits restrict the sums an agency may spend in prosecuting a given termination proceeding. The State's attorney usually will be expert on the issues contested and the procedures employed at the factfinding hearing, and enjoys full access to all public records concerning the family. The State may call on experts in family relations, psychology, and medicine to bolster its case. Furthermore, the primary witnesses at the hearing will be the agency's own professional caseworkers whom the State has empowered both to investigate the family situation and to testify against the parents.

Indeed, because the child is already in agency custody, the State even has the power to shape the historical events that form the basis for termination.

The disparity between the adversaries' litigation resources is matched by a striking asymmetry in their litigation options. Unlike criminal defendants, natural parents have no "double jeopardy" defense against repeated state termination efforts. If the State initially fails to win termination, as New York did here, it always can try once again to cut off the parents' rights after gathering more or better evidence. Yet even when the parents have attained the level of fitness required by the State, they have no similar means by which they can forestall future termination efforts.

Coupled with a "fair preponderance of the evidence" standard, these factors create a significant prospect of erroneous termination. * * *

* * *

The Appellate Division approved New York's preponderance standard on the ground that it properly "balanced rights possessed by the child ... with those of the natural parents.... " By so saying, the court suggested that a preponderance standard properly allocates the risk of error between the parents and the child. That view is fundamentally mistaken.

The court's theory assumes that termination of the natural parents' rights invariably will benefit the child. Yet we have noted above that the parents and the child share an interest in avoiding erroneous termination. Even accepting the court's assumption, we cannot agree with its conclusion that a preponderance standard fairly distributes the risk of error between parent and child. Use of that standard reflects the judgment that society is nearly neutral between erroneous termination of parental rights and erroneous failure to terminate those rights. For the child, the likely consequence of an erroneous failure to terminate is preservation of an uneasy status quo. For the natural parents, however, the consequence of an erroneous termination is the unnecessary destruction of their natural family. A standard that allocates the risk of error nearly equally between those two outcomes does not reflect properly their relative severity.

C

Two state interests are at stake in parental rights termination proceedings—a parens patriae interest in preserving and promoting the welfare of the child and a fiscal and administrative interest in reducing the cost and burden of such proceedings. A standard of proof more strict than preponderance of the evidence is consistent with both interests.

"Since the State has an urgent interest in the welfare of the child, it shares the parent's interest in an accurate and just decision" at the factfinding proceeding. As parens patriae, the State's goal is to provide the child with a permanent home. Yet while there is still reason to believe that positive, nurturing parent-child relationships exist, the parens patriae interest favors preservation, not severance, of natural familial bonds. * * *

IV

The logical conclusion of this balancing process is that the "fair preponderance of the evidence" standard prescribed by Fam.Ct.Act § 622 violates the Due Process Clause of the Fourteenth Amendment. * * * [A]t a parental rights termination proceeding, a near-equal allocation of risk between the parents and the State is constitutionally intolerable. The next question, then, is whether a "beyond a reasonable doubt" or a "clear and convincing" standard is constitutionally mandated.

* * * [I]n the Indian Child Welfare Act of 1978, Congress requires "evidence beyond a reasonable doubt" for termination of Indian parental rights, reasoning that "the removal of a child from the parents is a penalty as great [as], if not greater, than a criminal penalty. . . . " Congress did not consider, however, the evidentiary problems that would arise if proof beyond a reasonable doubt were required in all state-initiated parental rights termination hearings.

Like civil commitment hearings, termination proceedings often require the factfinder to evaluate medical and psychiatric testimony, and to decide issues difficult to prove to a level of absolute certainty, such as lack of parental motive, absence of affection between parent and child, and failure of parental foresight and progress. The substantive standards applied vary from State to State. Although Congress found a "beyond a reasonable doubt" standard proper in one type of parental rights termination case, another legislative body might well conclude that a reasonable-doubt standard would erect an unreasonable barrier to state efforts to free permanently neglected children for adoption.

A majority of the States have concluded that a "clear and convincing evidence" standard of proof strikes a fair balance between the rights of the natural parents and the State's legitimate concerns. We hold that such a standard adequately conveys to the factfinder the level of subjective certainty about his factual conclusions necessary to satisfy due process. We further hold that determination of the precise burden equal to or greater than that standard is a matter of state law properly left to state legislatures and state courts.

* * *

It is so ordered.

JUSTICE REHNQUIST, with whom THE CHIEF JUSTICE, JUSTICE WHITE, and JUSTICE O'CONNOR join, dissenting.

* * *

State intervention in domestic relations has always been an unhappy but necessary feature of life in our organized society. For all of our experience in this area, we have found no fully satisfactory solutions to the painful problem of child abuse and neglect. We have found, however, that leaving the States free to experiment with various remedies has produced novel approaches and promising progress.

* * *

This case presents a classic occasion for such solicitude. New York has enacted a comprehensive plan to aid marginal parents in regaining the custody of their child. The central purpose of the New York plan is to reunite divided families. Adoption of the preponderance-of-the-evidence standard represents New York's good-faith effort to balance the interest of parents against the legitimate interests of the child and the State. These earnest efforts by state officials should be given weight in the Court's application of due process principles. * * *

* * *

[T]he State seeks not only to protect the interests of parents in rearing their own children, but also to assist and encourage parents who have lost custody of their children to reassume their rightful role. Fully understood, the New York system is a comprehensive program to aid parents such as petitioners. Only as a last resort, when "diligent efforts" to reunite the family have failed, does New York authorize the termination of parental rights. The procedures for termination of those relationships which cannot be aided and which threaten permanent injury to the child, administered by a judge who has supervised the case from the first temporary removal through the final termination, cannot be viewed as fundamentally unfair. The facts of this case demonstrate the fairness of the system.

The three children to which this case relates were removed from petitioners' custody in 1973 and 1974, before petitioners' other two children were born. The removals were made pursuant to the procedures detailed above and in response to what can only be described as shockingly abusive treatment.[10] At the temporary removal hearing held before the Family Court on September 30, 1974, petitioners were represented by counsel, and allowed the Ulster County Department of Social Services (Department) to take custody of the three children.

Temporary removal of the children was continued at an evidentiary hearing held before the Family Court in December 1975, after which the

---

10. Tina Apel, the oldest of petitioners' five children, was removed from their custody by court order in November 1973 when she was two years old. Removal proceedings were commenced in response to complaints by neighbors and reports from a local hospital that Tina had suffered injuries in petitioners' home including a fractured left femur, treated with a home-made splint; bruises on the upper arms, forehead, flank, and spine; and abrasions of the upper leg. The following summer John Santosky III, petitioners' second oldest child, was also removed from petitioner's custody. John, who was less than one year old at the time, was admitted to the hospital suffering malnutrition, bruises on the eye and forehead, cuts on the foot, blisters on the hand, and multiple pin pricks on the back. Jed Santosky, the third oldest of petitioners' children, was removed from his parents' custody when only three days old as a result of the abusive treatment of the two older children.

court issued a written opinion concluding that petitioners were unable to resume their parental responsibilities due to personality disorders. Unsatisfied with the progress petitioners were making, the court also directed the Department to reduce to writing the plan which it had designed to solve the problems at petitioners' home and reunite the family.

A plan for providing petitioners with extensive counseling and training services was submitted to the court and approved in February 1976. Under the plan, petitioners received training by a mother's aide, a nutritional aide, and a public health nurse, and counseling at a family planning clinic. In addition, the plan provided psychiatric treatment and vocational training for the father, and counseling at a family service center for the mother. Between early 1976 and the final termination decision in April 1979, the State spent more than $15,000 in these efforts to rehabilitate petitioners as parents.

Petitioners' response to the State's effort was marginal at best. They wholly disregarded some of the available services and participated only sporadically in the others. As a result, and out of growing concern over the length of the children's stay in foster care, the Department petitioned in September 1976 for permanent termination of petitioners' parental rights so that the children could be adopted by other families. Although the Family Court recognized that petitioners' reaction to the State's efforts was generally "non-responsive, even hostile," the fact that they were "at least superficially cooperative" led it to conclude that there was yet hope of further improvement and an eventual reuniting of the family. Accordingly, the petition for permanent termination was dismissed.

Whatever progress petitioners were making prior to the 1976 termination hearing, they made little or no progress thereafter. In October 1978, the Department again filed a termination petition alleging that petitioners had completely failed to plan for the children's future despite the considerable efforts rendered in their behalf. This time, the Family Court agreed. The court found that petitioners had "failed in any meaningful way to take advantage of the many social and rehabilitative services that have not only been made available to them but have been diligently urged upon them." In addition, the court found that the "infrequent" visits "between the parents and their children were at best superficial and devoid of any real emotional content." The court thus found "nothing in the situation which holds out any hope that [petitioners] may ever become financially self sufficient or emotionally mature enough to be independent of the services of social agencies. More than a reasonable amount of time has passed and still, in the words of the case workers, there has been no discernible forward movement. At some point in time, it must be said, 'enough is enough.' "

In accordance with the statutory requirements set forth above, the court found that petitioners' failure to plan for the future of their children, who were then seven, five, and four years old and had been out of petitioners' custody for at least four years, rose to the level of permanent neglect. At a subsequent dispositional hearing, the court terminated petitioners' parental rights, thereby freeing the three children for adoption.

As this account demonstrates, the State's extraordinary 4–year effort to reunite petitioners' family was not just unsuccessful, it was altogether rebuffed by parents unwilling to improve their circumstances sufficiently to permit a return of their children. At every step of this protracted process petitioners were accorded those procedures and protections which traditionally have been required by due process of law. Moreover, from the beginning to the end of this sad story all judicial determinations were made by one Family Court Judge. After four and one-half years of involvement with petitioners, more than seven complete hearings, and additional periodic supervision of the State's rehabilitative efforts, the judge no doubt was intimately familiar with this case and the prospects for petitioners' rehabilitation.

It is inconceivable to me that these procedures were "fundamentally unfair" to petitioners. Only by its obsessive focus on the standard of proof and its almost complete disregard of the facts of this case does the majority find otherwise. * * *

B

In addition to the basic fairness of the process afforded petitioners, the standard of proof chosen by New York clearly reflects a constitutionally permissible balance of the interests at stake in this case. The standard of proof "represents an attempt to instruct the factfinder concerning the degree of confidence our society thinks he should have in the correctness of factual conclusions for a particular type of adjudication." In this respect, the standard of proof is a crucial component of legal process, the primary function of which is "to minimize the risk of erroneous decisions."

In determining the propriety of a particular standard of proof in a given case, however, it is not enough simply to say that we are trying to minimize the risk of error. Because errors in factfinding affect more than one interest, we try to minimize error as to those interests which we consider to be most important. * * *

* * *

On one side is the interest of parents in a continuation of the family unit and the raising of their own children. The importance of this interest cannot easily be overstated. Few consequences of judicial action are so grave as the severance of natural family ties. Even the convict committed to prison and thereby deprived of his physical liberty often retains the love and support of family members. * * *

On the other side of the termination proceeding are the often countervailing interests of the child. A stable, loving homelife is essential to a child's physical, emotional, and spiritual well-being. It requires no citation of authority to assert that children who are abused in their youth generally face extraordinary problems developing into responsible, productive citizens. The same can be said of children who, though not physically or emotionally abused, are passed from one foster home to another with no constancy of love, trust, or discipline. If the Family Court makes an incorrect factual determination resulting in a failure to terminate a parent-child relationship which rightfully should be ended, the child involved must return either to an abusive home or to the often unstable world of foster care. The reality of these risks is magnified by the fact that the only families faced with termination actions are those which have voluntarily surrendered custody of their child to the State, or, as in this case, those from which the child has been removed by judicial action because of threatened irreparable injury through abuse or neglect. Permanent neglect findings also occur only in families where the child has been in foster care for at least one year.

In addition to the child's interest in a normal homelife, "the State has an urgent interest in the welfare of the child." Few could doubt that the most valuable resource of a self-governing society is its population of children who will one day become adults and themselves assume the responsibility of self-governance. "A democratic society rests, for its continuance, upon the healthy, well-rounded growth of young people into full maturity as citizens, with all that implies." Prince v. Massachusetts (1944). Thus, "the whole community" has an interest "that children be both safeguarded from abuses and given opportunities for growth into free and independent well-developed ... citizens."

When, in the context of a permanent neglect termination proceeding, the interests of the child and the State in a stable, nurturing homelife are balanced against the interests of the parents in the rearing of their child, it cannot be said that either set of interests is so clearly paramount as to require that the risk of error be allocated to one side or the other. Accordingly, a State constitutionally may conclude that the risk of error should be borne in roughly equal fashion by use of the preponderance-of-the-evidence standard of proof. This is precisely the balance which has been struck by the New York Legislature: "It is the intent of the legislature in enacting this section to provide procedures not only assuring that the rights of the natural parent are protected, but also, where positive, nurturing parent-child relationships no longer exist, furthering the best interests, needs, and rights of the child by terminating the parental rights and freeing the child for adoption."

III

For the reasons heretofore stated, I believe that the Court today errs in concluding that the New York standard of proof in parental-rights termination proceedings violates due process of law. The decision disregards New York's earnest efforts to aid parents in regaining the custody of their children and a host of procedural protections placed around parental rights and interests. The Court finds a constitutional violation only by a tunnel-vision application of due process principles that altogether loses sight of the unmistakable fairness of the New York procedure.

Even more worrisome, today's decision cavalierly rejects the considered judgment of the New York Legislature in an area traditionally entrusted to state care. The Court thereby begins, I fear, a trend of federal intervention in state family law matters which surely will stifle creative responses to vexing problems. Accordingly, I dissent.

Notes and Questions

1. *Questions about* Santosky. (a) What grounds for termination of parental rights did the state use? (b) What do you think will happen to the Santosky children if their parents' rights are terminated? Do you agree with *Santosky's* majority that "for the child, the likely consequence of an erroneous failure to terminate is preservation of an uneasy status quo"?

2. *Aftermath.* On remand from the Supreme Court, the appellate court reviewed the trial court record and, using the more stringent burden of proof, affirmed the termination of the Santoskys' parental rights. In re John AA, 453 N.Y.S.2d 942 (App.Div.1982).

3. *Reunite or terminate.* The Adoption Assistance and Child Welfare Act of 1980 sought to reduce the number of children in foster care. Intensive services would be provided to try to keep children in their homes. If children were removed, the state was to provide intensive services to reunite the family. If reunification failed, however, the state was to terminate parental rights so the children could be placed in adoptive homes. If a state used a "clear and convincing" standard of proof when the children were removed from their home, would this justify a lower standard of proof at termination? In a footnote the Court said that it would not consider the New York statutory procedures as a "package."

What happens to a child in foster care if the state has not complied with the "reasonable efforts" requirement? May parental rights be terminated? For an argument that termination of parental rights statutes should not require the state to prove that reasonable efforts have been made to reunite the family, but rather should focus on whether the parent can provide a permanent home for the child within a reasonable time, see David J. Herring, Inclusion of the Reasonable Efforts Requirement in Termination of Parental Rights Statutes: Punishing the Child for the Failure of the State Child Welfare System, 54 U. Pitt. L. Rev. 139 (1992).

In a termination proceeding, should a court be required to assess the child's prospects for adoption? See In the Matter of the Welfare of J.M., 574 N.W.2d 717, 724 (Minn. 1998)(holding that the termination statute did not require findings on the likelihood of adoption, and noting that while "no one can predict with complete accuracy if or when the * * * children will be adopted, we also recognize the absolute certainty that if * * * parental rights are not terminated, the * * * children will never be adopted").

A NOTE ON LASSITER v. DEPARTMENT OF SOCIAL SERVICES AND RIGHT TO COUNSEL

In Lassiter v. Department of Social Servs., 452 U.S. 18 (1981), the Court held, in a 5–4 vote, that due process does not require appointment of counsel for indigent parents in all termination proceedings. Instead, whether counsel must be appointed is determined on a case by case basis. The Court used the three factors identified in Mathews v. Eldridge, 424 U.S. 319 (1976), to evaluate the due process claim, namely "the private interests at stake, the government's interest, and the risk that the procedures used will lead to erroneous decisions." With regard to the parents' interests, the Court noted that its decisions "have by now made plain beyond the need for multiple citation that a parent's desire for and right to the 'companionship, care, custody and management of his or her children' is an important interest that 'undeniably warrants deference and, absent a powerful countervailing interest, protection.'" The parent's interest was not strong enough to prevail, however:

> The dispositive question * * * is whether the three *Eldridge* factors, when weighed against the presumption that there is no right to appointed counsel in the absence of at least a potential deprivation of physical liberty, suffice to rebut that presumption and thus to lead to the conclusion that the Due Process Clause requires the appointment of counsel when a State seeks to terminate an indigent's parental status. * * * [T]he parent's interest is an extremely important one (and may be supplemented by the dangers of criminal liability inherent in some termination proceedings); the State shares with the parent an interest in a correct decision, has a relatively weak pecuniary interest, and, in some but not all cases, has a possibly stronger interest in informal procedures; and the complexity of the proceeding and the incapacity of the uncounseled parent could be, but would not always be, great enough to make the risk of an erroneous deprivation of the parent's rights insupportably high.

> If, in a given case, the parent's interests were at their strongest, the State's interests were at their weakest, and the risks of error were at their peak, it could not be said that the *Eldridge* factors did not overcome the presumption against the right to appointed counsel, and that due process did not therefore require the appointment of counsel. But since the *Eldridge* factors will not always be so distributed, and since "due process is not so rigid as to require that the significant interests in informality, flexibility and economy must always be sacrificed," neither can we say that the Constitution requires the appointment of counsel in every parental termination proceeding. We therefore * * * leave the decision whether due process calls for the appointment of counsel for indigent parents in termination proceedings to be answered in the first instance by the trial court, subject, of course, to appellate review.

Justice Stevens' *Lassiter* dissent suggests that the Court treated children as property:

A woman's misconduct may cause the State to take formal steps to deprive her of her liberty. The State may incarcerate her for a fixed term and also may permanently deprive her of her freedom to associate with her child. The former is a pure deprivation of liberty; the latter is a deprivation of both liberty and property, because statutory rights of inheritance as well as the natural relationship may be destroyed. Although both deprivations are serious, often the deprivation of parental rights will be the more grievous of the two. The plain language of the Fourteenth Amendment commands that both deprivations must be accompanied by due process of law.

Without so stating explicitly, the Court appears to treat this case as though it merely involved the deprivation of an interest in property that is less worthy of protection than a person's liberty.

A NOTE ON M.L.B. v. S.L.J. AND RIGHT TO APPEAL

In M.L.B. v. S.L.J., 519 U.S. 102 (1996), a mother's parental rights were terminated and her appeal of the termination was dismissed because she lacked $2,352.36 to pay the record preparation fees. The Supreme Court considered the following question: "May a State, consistent with the Due Process and Equal Protection Clauses of the Fourteenth Amendment, condition appeals from trial court decrees terminating parental rights on the affected parent's ability to pay record preparation fees?" The Court held that "just as a State may not block an indigent petty offender's access to an appeal afforded others, so Mississippi may not deny M. L. B., because of her poverty, appellate review of the sufficiency of the evidence on which the trial court found her unfit to remain a parent."

In reaching this decision the Court considered the importance of family life and the unique nature of termination of parent rights actions:

Choices about marriage, family life, and the upbringing of children are among associational rights this Court has ranked as "of basic importance in our society," rights sheltered by the Fourteenth Amendment against the State's unwarranted usurpation, disregard, or disrespect. M. L. B.'s case, involving the State's authority to sever permanently a parent-child bond, demands the close consideration the Court has long required when a family association so undeniably important is at stake. We approach M. L. B.'s petition mindful of the gravity of the sanction imposed on her and in light of two prior decisions most immediately in point: Lassiter v. Department of Social Servs. of Durham Cty (1981), and Santosky v. Kramer (1982).

Id. at 116.

Both *Lassiter* and *Santosky* yielded divided opinions, but *M. L. B.* was unanimously of the view that "the interest of parents in their relationship with their children is sufficiently fundamental to come within the finite class of liberty interests protected by the Fourteenth Amendment," and that "[f]ew consequences of judicial action are so grave as the severance of natural family ties."

B.   When Should Parental Rights Be Terminated?

CHAMPAGNE V. Welfare Division
Supreme Court of Nevada, 1984.
691 P.2d 849.

Springer, Justice.

This opinion considers * * * appeals in which the parental rights of fathers and mothers have been permanently terminated by judicial decree. Severance of parental rights is an exercise of awesome power, a power which we "question closely" as we consider the four cases before us.

TERMINATION OF PARENTAL RIGHTS; APPLICABLE LAW

NRS 128.110 authorizes the courts to terminate the legal relationship of parent and child "upon finding grounds" set out in the statute. NRS 128.105[1] provides that a termination order "may be made on the grounds that the termination is in the child's best interest in light of the considerations set forth in this section * * * "The "considerations" set forth in the section include abandonment, neglect, unfitness of the parent, child abuse and a rather hazy, probably redundant consideration phrased as "[o]nly token efforts by the parent" to avoid or prevent abandonment, neglect, unfitness or abuse. Whatever "token efforts" might mean, we read NRS 128.105 as a whole to mean that termination of parental rights is to be based on substantial abandonment, neglect, parental unfitness or child abuse.

By NRS 128.106 the court is given direction in "determining neglect or unfitness of a parent" in that the courts are required to consider certain conditions which relate to "suitability as a parent."

1. NRS 128.105 provides:

128.105 Grounds for terminating parental rights: Basic considerations. An order of the court for termination of parental rights may be made on the grounds that the termination is in the child's best interest in light of the considerations set forth in this section and NRS 128.106 to 128.108, inclusive:

1. Abandonment of the child;

2. Neglect of the child;

3. Unfitness of the parent;

4. Risk of serious physical, mental or emotional injury to the child if he were

returned to, or remains in, the home of his parent or parents;

5. Only token efforts by the parent or parents:

(a) To support or communicate with the child;

(b) To prevent neglect of the child;

(c) To avoid being an unfit parent;

(d) To eliminate the risk of serious physical, mental or emotional injury to the child; or

6. With respect to termination of parental rights of one parent, the abandonment by that parent.

From a reading of the foregoing sections and Chapter 128 as a whole we conclude that there are two kinds of grounds necessary to be considered in termination proceedings. One relates to parental conduct or incapacity and the parent's suitability as a parent; the other relates to the best interest of the child.

Putting it another way: there must be jurisdictional grounds for termination—to be found in some specific fault or condition directly related to the parents—and dispositional grounds—to be found by a general evaluation of the child's best interest.

We borrow from Ketcham and Babcock[3] to state the general proposition in these terms: "The jurisdictional question is whether the biological parent, by behavior, has forfeited all rights in the child. The dispositional question is whether terminating parental rights would be in the best interest of the child. The first question focuses on the action, or inaction, of the natural parent. The second focuses on the placement which will be most beneficial to the child. If it is first decided that the parent has forfeited his rights in the children, then the court moves on to the second question. On the other hand, if it is decided that the biological parent's behavior does not violate minimum standards of parental conduct so as to render the parent unfit, then the analysis ends and termination is denied. In these latter instances, the court never reaches the question of whether the child's future well-being would be better served by placement with the substitute or psychological parent."

Jurisdictional Grounds

The jurisdictional aspect of termination proceedings focuses on the "fundamental liberty interests of the natural parents in the care, custody, and management of their child," and this interest "does not evaporate simply because they have not been model parents or have lost temporary custody of the child to the State." Santosky v. Kramer (1982). * * *

Because of the sacredness of parental rights a higher standard of proof, that of "at least clear and convincing evidence," is required before the children can be judicially taken away. Also, the degree and duration of parental fault of incapacity necessary to establish jurisdictional grounds for termination is greater than that required for other forms of judicial intervention.

For example, a judicial determination that a child has been neglected may call for varying degrees of state intervention, ranging from mild reprimand to permanent termination of parental rights. Neglect is a relative term applied to a child who "lacks the proper parental care by reason of [parental] fault." NRS 128.014. Although it is difficult to define "proper," it is probably true that all parents are at one time or another guilty of neglecting to give their children "proper" care. To provide a jurisdictional basis for termination, neglect must be serious

3. Ketcham and Babcock, Statutory Grounds for the Involuntary Termination of Parental Rights, 29 Rutgers L.Rev. 530 (1976). * * *

and persistent and be sufficiently harmful to the child so as to mandate a forfeiture of parental rights. In such a case a parent may be adjudged to be unsuitable to maintain the parental relationship and, therefore, to deserve to lose it.

The same principles apply to the jurisdictional ground of unfitness. Unfitness is the other side of the neglect coin. Neglect defines a condition of the child; unfitness describes a condition of the parent. A neglected child is one who does not receive "proper "care; an unfit parent is one who fails to provide a child with "proper "care. Again: all parents are guilty of failure to provide proper care on occasion; and a parent does not deserve to forfeit the sacred liberty right of parenthood unless such unfitness is shown to be severe and persistent and such as to render the parent unsuitable to maintain the parental relationship.

In like manner, abuse of a child may or may not render a parent unsuitable to be a parent. NRS 128.105 lists as a ground or consideration for termination "[r]isks of serious physical, mental or emotional injury to the child if he were returned to, or remains in the home.... " Such a risk may be mitigated, and a child may be safely returned to the home; or the risk may be of such magnitude and persistency as to render the parent unsuitable and justify forfeiture of parental rights.

Failure of Parental Adjustment

Our discussion of jurisdictional grounds cannot be complete without adding to abuse and neglect, unfitness and abandonment, another ground revealed in the interstices of NRS Chapter 128. It is difficult to give this ground a name or designation, but, essentially, it consists in a parent's being unable or unwilling within a reasonable period of time to remedy substantially conditions which led to a child's out-of-the-home placement, notwithstanding reasonable and appropriate efforts on the part of the state and others to return the child.

The new ground, finding its way into law in the 1981 legislative session, has its mediate origin in the Juvenile Justice Standards Project, Standards Relating to Abuse and Neglect, Standard 8. These standards, adopted jointly by the American Bar Association and the Institute of Judicial Administration, are in turn largely based on theories published in a book entitled Beyond the Best Interests of the Child.[6]

---

6. A full understanding of this jurisdictional ground for termination cannot be gained without understanding the general trend toward diminishing the value of parental autonomy in its balance with the child's interest to a stable and nurturing environment. This means a shift of emphasis from the jurisdictional to the dispositional basis for termination, that is to say, away from parents' rights toward children's interests. This is particularly true in cases of long term foster placements in which a relationship of "psychological" parent and child has been established. This trend can be traced to certain psychoanalytically-based theories announced in 1973 by the publication Beyond the Best Interests of the Child, by Joseph Goldstein, Anna Freud, and Albert Solnit. The authors claim to present proposals for reforming the child welfare system in a manner that is supported by psychoanalytic theory.

Goldstein, Freud, and Solnit base their program on two fundamental beliefs: that the law should make the child's not the parent's needs paramount and that permanency of relationship is the first and most

The gist of the new ground, which might be abbreviated as "failure of parental adjustment" finds its matrix in NRS 128.107 and 128.108, which enumerate "specific considerations" applicable when a child is not in the physical custody of a parent or when the child has been placed in a foster home.

These "specific considerations" form a number of heterogeneous matters to be considered "in determining whether parental rights should be terminated." The list includes factors of both jurisdictional and dispositional import. For example, in assessing the duties of a parent who has been separated from his or her child, the court must consider the services provided or offered to the parent "to facilitate a reunion with the child" and the effort of the parent to adjust "circumstances, conduct or conditions" to justify the child's return home within a "reasonable length of time."

The idea of permanently taking a child from a parent by reason of the parent's failing to adjust to "circumstances, conduct or conditions" prescribed by the state is an idea that is new to public family law. The idea is part of what have been called "permanency programs" (see footnote 6) which can be traced to the early 1970's. These programs call

important developmental need of a child. Under their theory the state should not disrupt the relationship of a child who has been removed from his home when the child has developed a relationship with what the authors term a "psychological parent." The theory has brought about the institution of "permanency programs" which promote termination of parental rights followed by adoption as being the best means of satisfying the children's psychological needs. Accordingly, a foster parent who has established a relationship with a child would take precedence over a natural parent, even if the natural parent has lost custody of the child through no fault of his own.

The influence of Goldstein, Freud, and Solnit and "permanency planning" is evidenced in NRS 128.106 and NRS 128.107, added to the Nevada Revised Statutes in 1981. This statute provides that in cases of foster placement where the welfare agency's goal is to have the foster parents adopt the child, the court must consider whether the child "has become integrated" into the foster family to the extent that his familial identity is with that family. The court is even required to compare the real parents with the foster parents to see who can best "give the child love, affection and guidance and to continue the education of the child ... and the capacity ... to provide the child with food, clothing and medical care ... [and the] moral fitness, physical and mental health" of real parents versus new parents. Under the mentioned psychoana-

lytic theory, poor and marginally adequate parents are always under a threat of permanently losing their children. It is very difficult for such parents to avoid, at some time or another, finding that they have failed to meet the standards of parenting which the more fortunate of us have grown to respect. If they are so unlucky as to come in contact with agencies of the state and to suffer temporary loss of custody of their children, they are likely to find themselves in a classic "Catch–22" situation, thus: contact with their children is made difficult or impossible; they are thrust into "counseling" and parenting programs in which they have little chance of success; the children are likely to have grown used to neater, cleaner, and more intelligent, possibly more permissive parents, with whom, although they still love their natural parents, they have developed some degree of attachment.

The last step in this scenario is when the natural parents are told that their children now have some nice, new parents, a scenario not too distant from what is presented in at least one of the cases before us.

* * * We agree that children's interests should be paramount; but their interests cannot displace established liberty interests of natural parents. Children cannot be taken from poor parents and placed permanently in the home of substitute parents simply because their "emotional needs" would be better served or because they might have a cleaner, neater, or richer environment.

for increased efforts to keep children in their natural families, mandatory periodic review of out-of-home placements and, significantly, termination of parental rights to free children for adoption when it appears that parents will be unable to resume custody within a reasonable period of time.

Certainly no one can quarrel with the idea of promoting permanency and stability in the lives of children. Still, we must remember that poverty, sickness, and other such eventualities may result in the separation of children of a loving and quite suitable parent. There is always the risk that passage of time might result in a situation in which a child develops new relationships—becomes "integrated" into a foster family or otherwise becomes estranged from natural parents. Caution must be exercised not to allow termination proceedings to be carried out absent a showing of unsuitability on the part of the parent by reason of the parent's fault or incapacitation. We must be extremely careful in concluding that a parent has crossed the line of unsuitability. This is true because of the vast power differential between the state and the welfare client, the paucity of truly efficacious "services" that are or can be made available to the client, the usually greatly diminished contact between welfare client-parents and the removed child and the oft-seen ineptitude of the so-called "inadequate" parent.

On the other hand, there does come a time when society must give up on a parent. A child cannot be kept in suspense indefinitely. If a child is removed from the home, a parent must exercise reasonably diligent efforts to seek the child's return. A parent's failure to make such efforts may, under our statutory scheme, result in the court's finding that the parent is unsuitable by reason of unfitness or neglect in the form of failing or refusing to adjust after the child was removed. The parent, however, still must be shown to be at fault in some manner. The parent cannot be judged unsuitable by reason of failure to comply with requirements and plans that are unclear or have not been communicated to the parent, or which are impossible for the parent to abide by. Failure of parental adjustment may provide a jurisdictional basis for termination, but it is fraught with difficulties and must be applied with caution.

Dispositional Grounds

In order to justify termination of parental rights the court must, after finding jurisdictional grounds for termination, find dispositional grounds—that the child's interest would be served by termination. It is certainly possible for the court to find that a parent was unsuitable and still not be able to find the requisite dispositional grounds for termination. For example, the Juvenile Justice Standards Relating to Abuse and Neglect, Standard 8.4(c), provides that a court should not order termination (as it did here in the case of Billy Murphy) where, because of the nature of a child's problems, the child is placed in a residential treatment facility, and continuation of parental rights does not interfere with proper or necessary permanent placement efforts. The Standards recognize that even where jurisdictional grounds exists, there are cases in which termination is not indicated. As in the case of Billy Murphy, if a disturbed child is placed in a treatment center, there is no point in depriving him of whatever support the natural parents might give. Another example would be when an older child (ten or older by Standard 8.4) expresses the wish not to have parental rights terminated. In these and in a number of other possible examples, jurisdictional grounds may exist and the parent may deserve to have parental rights terminated, but the interest of the child is not necessarily best served by the termination. The test is this: If under no reasonable circumstances the child's best interest can be served by sustaining the parental tie, dispositional grounds for termination exist.

Each case must be considered on its own terms. The court may consider "[w]hether additional services would be likely to bring about a lasting parental adjustment . . . within a predictable period of time," NRS 128.107(4); it may consider the physical, mental, or emotional conditions and needs of the child, including the child's desires, NRS 128.107(2); or it may conclude that the natural parents are so depraved or so disinterested that it appears that even having no parents is better than having this kind of parent. The overlying dispositional issue is that of the welfare of the child; and, as said, when it appears that the child's interest will not be served by preserving the relationship, the relationship should be terminated.

* * *

MELVIN MURPHY and JEENEAN GERTRUDE SNYDER MURPHY

This is a case in which the district court found that Mr. and Mrs. Murphy were unfit parents, that they had neglected their children, and that they "would always continue" to neglect their children.

There are three children involved. Billy, now 13, is a serious behavioral problem who had to be removed from the home and placed in a residential program for behaviorally disturbed children. The two other children are girls, Tanya and Angela, now 12 and 10. The girls have suffered from learning disabilities and some difficulties in school and in social development. The three children have been placed in three different residential placements.

The separation of the girls from their parents and from each other seems to have been precipitated by the visit and report of a volunteer worker who described the Murphy home as "filthy."

The volunteer made only the one visit to the Murphy home because "[h]e wouldn't go into the area they are in now." Nevertheless, after this one visit he recommended that parental rights be terminated as soon as possible. This report prompted a neglect complaint which was filed against the Murphys on April 23, 1981. The following day, a juvenile court services officer removed Tanya and Angela from the Murphy home. The juvenile officer testified that the action was based on the supposed mental deficiency of the parents accompanied by "destitution bordering on marginal environmental neglect." Interestingly, the officer stated that he had "seen more filthy homes" than the Murphy residence. He also testified that when he removed Tanya and Angela, they "appeared to be all right. Their dress was normal. Their clothes might have been a little larger than would have been normal, and they appeared to be ... not in hunger pains or anything like that."

Following a juvenile court hearing on June 16, 1981, the girls were made wards of the court. On June 23, 1981, they were both placed in Child Haven. On February 12, 1982, the state filed a petition to terminate the Murphys' parental rights as to all three children. Following a hearing on June 25 and 28, 1982, the district court terminated the Murphys' parental rights.

It does not appear from the record that termination in this case can be upheld on the basis of the jurisdictional ground of neglect. There is no contention or finding that the Murphys were in any way at fault (other than in being poor and wanting in neatness and cleanliness). They are not unfit, neglecting, abusing, or abandoning parents; and any supportable jurisdictional ground would have to have been based on a finding of parental unsuitability based on the parents' supposed incapacity to raise their children in an acceptable manner.

There are only two possibilities of finding the Murphys to be unsuitable in the stated manner; and both possibilities exist because of the language of NRS 128.106, which, as mentioned above, sets out "conditions which may diminish suitability as a parent." The two possibilities are found in subsections 1 and 7 of NRS 128.106.

The condition mentioned in subsection 1 is "[e]motional illness, mental illness or mental deficiency which renders the parent consistently unable to care for the immediate and continuing physical or psychological needs of the child for extended periods of time."

There are a number of reasons why this condition does not apply to the Murphy family. First, it is noted that the only suggestion in the record of mental deficiency relates to Mr. Murphy and not Mrs. Murphy. The record reflects that Mrs. Murphy, who is unquestionably mentally competent, is the "primary care giver." Thus, the family as a unit is competent to care for the children; and even if Mr. Murphy were of questionable intelligence, it makes no real difference under the circumstances of this case. The only evidence relating to mental retardation of Melvin Murphy is found in the testimony of the director of Outreach Services, an agency responsible for services to the mentally retarded. The director, who has degrees in education and counseling, mentioned off-handedly that "although he fits our criteria, he [Mr. Murphy] isn't the primary care giver." This is the only evidence relating to Mr. Murphy's mental capacity. The record does not disclose the degree, if any, of Mr. Murphy's supposed mental incapacity. There is no proof in the record that Mr. Murphy's mental condition renders him in any way unable to care for his children, much less "consistently unable" to care for them "for extended periods of time." Mr. Murphy's ill-described mental condition cannot provide jurisdictional grounds for termination.

The second possible condition relates to the possibility of a finding of jurisdictional grounds based on failure of parental adjustment. Under subsection 7 of NRS 128.106, the "[i]nability of appropriate public or private agencies to reunite the family despite reasonable efforts on the part of the agencies" can be considered as a factor which tends to "diminish suitability as a parent."

One of the state's witnesses characterized the Murphy's home thus: "[T]his lifestyle is not significantly different than that of other families in their income bracket and who live in the apartment complex." The court expressly found that the Murphys were "cooperative with public agencies" and that "they love their children;" still, the court went on to say that "the public agencies have become frustrated at the failure to solve the problems keeping this family apart."

To dissolve a loving, cooperative family because of a welfare agency's "frustration" appears on its face to be a bit Herodian; but this aside, the main problem with this case is that on this record the Murphys do not appear to have been given a fair chance to cooperate with the supposed efforts to "reunite the family." In this case, the many "plans" proposed to the Murphys failed to specify relevant criteria to determine successful completion.* * *

It is true that Billy Murphy has a serious behavioral problem which necessitated his removal from the home so that this disorder could be attended to professionally. No one is waiting in the wings to adopt him and whisk him off to a loving, middle class family. Billy is exactly the kind of child who needs the support of his family and who should not have his parents' rights terminated.

It is also true that the two girls were having problems in school and with problems of social adjustment. These problems appear to have been relieved somewhat after their removal from the home; but, here again there is no evidence that their lot would be improved, without their consent, by the permanent loss of their natural parents.

Because of these latter conclusions it is also very doubtful that dispositional, "child's-best-interest" grounds are present; but this need not be decided, for there are clearly no jurisdictional grounds for termination. The Murphys have not been clearly or otherwise shown to be unsuitable parents by reason of neglect, unfitness, or other fault or incapacity which would justify taking their children away from them forever.

The termination order must be reversed. This court is not sufficiently informed to pass judgment on the optimum placement of the children at this time. The matter must be remanded for this purpose. The children have been split up and taken from their parents. Billy may need continued residential treatment, but he still needs his parents. The two girls have been placed out of the home for such a period of time that reunification with their parents will probably be difficult; but the parents should have a chance, and the children should have a chance to have the family brought together. If this cannot be done, it is possible that termination proceedings could be later completed in conformance with this opinion.

* * *

PAUL CHAMPAGNE and PAMELA CHAMPAGNE

Paul and Pamela Champagne were formerly, but are no longer, husband and wife. At the time of the hearing, held on April 6, 1981, they were living together. There are six children involved in the proceeding. Paul Champagne is the natural father of Steven, Crystal, and Jon Paul Champagne. Pamela Champagne is the natural mother of all six of the named children.

* * *

Propriety of Termination

The Champagnes claim that there is no substantial evidence to support termination of their parental rights. There is.

Both neglect and its mirror image, parental unfitness, are well-established in the record of this case.

The Champagnes have police records involving narcotics, burglary, and child abuse. The children were frequently left unattended. Mr. Champagne, it appears, has an unbridled temper, particularly while under the influence of drugs or alcohol. He also has been a chronic alcohol and substance abuser.

A careful reading of this record discloses that by reason of the habits of the Champagnes' the children suffered serious and continued neglect. The record reveals parents who are unfit and who because of their unfitness and substantial neglect have become clearly unsuitable as parents.

On the issue of abandonment, the record further shows that the Champagnes did not, although they were required to do so, support the children during the two years they were in state custody. This and the general course of conduct engaged in by the Champagnes supports the jurisdictional finding of abandonment in this case.

A jurisdictional basis for termination can also be found in the Champagnes' failure to adjust in a timely fashion to a well-formulated case plan. In November, 1979, the welfare division entered into a service agreement with the parents. The state presented six witnesses, two juvenile court officers, three welfare division social workers and a mental health counselor, all had been involved in the effort to reunite the Champagnes with their children. All six of these witnesses testified that in the circumstances of this case they believed that termination of appellants' parental rights was in the best interest of the children.

Ample jurisdictional grounds have been established for the termination order. Dispositional grounds are also well-established. We have here children who for years have had to put up with drunkenness and an unacceptable family life. The children have advised welfare workers that they want a new life and that they want a new mother and father that they can count on. "I want a Mom and Dad like everyone else," one child was heard to say. Under these circumstances, we cannot say that the district judge abused his discretion in finding that the best interests of these children would be served by terminating parental rights. There is good cause appearing in the record to conclude that under no reasonable circumstances could the children's interests be served by sustaining the parental relationship. The termination order is therefore affirmed.

* * *

SUMMARY AND CONCLUSION

Termination of parental rights is essentially, of course, a statutory proceeding; but the statute does not say it all. Overlying constitutional considerations, constantly recurring statutory amendments, and the rapidly evolving nature of present-day social theory and public policy make judicial interpretation an inevitable and indispensable part of critical legal operation. Today we * * * set forth general principles applicable to the process of severing the legal ties of parenthood.

We have held that one who institutes termination proceedings must be able to prove clearly and convincingly that there are both jurisdictional and dispositional grounds for termination. This means, first, that the parent must have provided some cause for the termination. Specific grounds—abandonment, abuse, neglect, unfitness, certain forms of incapacity or failure to adjust—must support a conclusion of parental unsuitability before termination of parental rights can be justified.

Jurisdictional grounds are not enough; it still must be shown that the child's interest would be better served by termination than continuation of the natural parent's relationship; or, as we put it, if under no reasonable circumstances the child's best interest can be served by sustaining the parental tie, the second requirement, the dispositional ground, has been fulfilled.

This approach to a difficult and emotionally charged field of law seems to us to strike the best and fairest balance between sometimes opposing interests of parent and child. Termination of parental rights is an extreme measure. Often guardianship, wardship, and juvenile court custody decrees can be employed to serve and protect the interests and welfare of children at risk. If the "capital punishment of welfare law" must be invoked, it should be done only under the strictest of conditions as set forth in this opinion.

Notes and Questions

1. *Questions about* Champagne. (a) What are the grounds for termination of parental rights in Nevada? (b) Can parental rights be terminated based on

a parent's failure to adjust to state prescribed "circumstances, conduct or conditions?" How does the court interpret these termination grounds so that they will not violate parents' constitutional rights? (c) When does an analysis of the child's best interests become relevant?

2. In a footnote, *Champagne* distinguished between parents who are "unsuitable" and deserve to have their rights terminated and parents who are merely "inadequate," like the Murpheys. The court quoted at length from Michael Wald, State Intervention on Behalf of 'Neglected' Children: A Search for Realistic Standards, 27 Stan.L.Rev. 985, 1021–24 (1975):

Inadequate Parenting

While no empirical studies provide a statistical breakdown of the reasons for intervention in neglect cases, probably the largest category of cases involves persons thought to be "inadequate parents." All commentators agree that the great majority of neglect cases involve very poor families who are usually receiving welfare. Most of the parents are not merely poor, however. In addition to the problems directly caused by the poverty—poor housing, inadequate medical care, poor nutritional practices—many of these parents can be described as extremely "marginal" people, that is they are continually at the borderline of being able to sustain themselves—economically, emotionally, and mentally.

Their plight is reflected in their home situations. Their homes are often dirty and run-down. Feeding arrangements are haphazard. One or both parents may ... be retarded, which may affect the quality of their child care....

Such parents may provide little emotional support for their children. While the children may not be physically abused, left unattended, dangerously malnourished, or overtly rejected, they may receive little love, attention, stimulation, or emotional involvement.... It is certainly very tempting to intervene to help such children. Intervention might be justified both to protect the children by providing them with an environment in which they can better reach their potential and to protect the state, since it is claimed that such children will probably end up as delinquents, criminals, or welfare recipients. Without intervention, we may be perpetuating a "culture of poverty."

Despite the appeal of these arguments, parental "inadequacy" in and of itself should not be a basis for intervention, other than the offer of services available on a truly voluntary basis. The term "inadequate home" or "inadequate parent" is even harder to define than emotional neglect. There is certainly no consensus about what types of "inadequate" behavior would justify intervention. Given the vagueness of the standard, almost unlimited intervention would be possible.

.... In fact, by focusing solely on parental behavior, child-care workers often ignore the many strengths a given child may be deriving from his environment. As I have stressed, the complexity of the process by which a child relates to any environment defies any attempt to draft laws solely in terms of environmental influences.

Moreover, there is every reason to be extremely pessimistic about the utility of coercive intervention. The services necessary to help these families are generally unavailable. More day-care centers, homemakers, health facilities, and job training programs would all be needed if intervention were to mean anything more than periodic visits by a social worker. Such visits themselves are costly, have not been shown to be effective, and may be resented by the parent who will blame the child for the outside meddling.

Even when "inadequate" parents seek help, agencies often lack the resources or ability to alleviate undesirable home conditions. The chances of success are even lower when the family resists intervention. Few communities have sufficient personnel and programs to permit meaningful intervention, even in cases involving physical abuse or severe emotional damage. It is highly questionable whether limited resources ought to be expended on families with less severe problems, unless the families request services or accept them voluntarily.

Furthermore, when parents do not respond to the treater, the next step is to remove the children. Yet there is no evidence demonstrating that children from such families are helped through placement.

In an ideal world, children would not be brought up in "inadequate" homes. However, our less than ideal society lacks the ability to provide better alternatives for these children. The best we can do is to expand the social welfare services now offered families on a voluntary basis.

* * *

IN RE JEFFREY R.L. [c]

Supreme Court of Appeals of West Virginia, 1993.
435 S.E.2d 162.

* * *

The first issue we shall address is whether the circuit court erred in failing to terminate the parental rights of Jeffrey R.L.'s parents, and whether the circuit court abused its discretion by returning custody of Jeffrey R.L. to his mother without sufficient evidence to support the ruling. The guardian ad litem asserts that the conditions giving rise to the abusive behavior cannot be substantially corrected when the perpetrator of the abuse has not been identified, and that the best interests of the child preclude returning his custody to either parent. Gail L. [Jeffrey R.L.'s mother] contends that: (1) there is insufficient evidence in the record to support termination of her parental rights; (2) there is no evidence that she was the abuser; and (3) she has fulfilled all of the requirements placed upon her by the circuit court and the DHHR [Department of Health and Human Resources]. The DHHR contends that Jeffrey R.L. should not have been returned to his mother's custody until the perpetrator of the abuse had been identified and a determina-

---

c. *Jeffrey R. L.* is considered in Chapter 3 also.

tion of Gail L.'s ability to provide a safe environment for her son has been made.

In the Court's analysis of child abuse and neglect cases, we must take into consideration the rights and interests of all of the parties in reaching an ultimate resolution of the issues before us. Although the rights of the natural parents to the custody of their child and the interests of the State as parens patriae merit significant consideration by this Court, the best interests of the child are paramount. Thus, as an initial matter, we emphasize that the health, safety, and welfare of Jeffrey R.L. must be our primary concern in analyzing the facts and issues before us.

* * *

While this Court has repeatedly recognized the constitutionally-protected right of the natural parent to the custody of his or her minor children, we have also emphasized that such right is not absolute.* * *

* * *

W.Va.Code, 49–1–3(a)(1) [1992] defines an "[a]bused child" as "a child whose health or welfare is harmed or threatened by: (1) A parent, guardian or custodian who knowingly or intentionally inflicts, attempts to inflict, or knowingly allows another person to inflict, physical injury, or mental or emotional injury, upon the child or another child in the home [.]" This Court has recognized * * * that a parent who "takes no action in the face of knowledge of the abuse" to the child can have his or her parental rights terminated * * *.

A parent's rights to custody of his or her child may also be terminated where there is no reasonable likelihood that the conditions of abuse and neglect can be substantially corrected * * *

* * *

Relying upon the well-established principles stated above, we shall now review the facts before us in the present case. To begin with, during the first three months of his life, Jeffrey R.L. was in the care of his mother, father and maternal grandparents. At the helpless age of approximately three months, Jeffrey R.L. was brought to the hospital when his maternal grandparents showed Gail L. that he was not moving his right arm in the same manner he was moving his left. X-rays revealed that Jeffrey R.L. suffered fifteen fractures to his skull, clavicle, ribs, arms and legs.[15] It is undisputed that Jeffrey R.L. suffered these extensive injuries as a result of physical abuse, and the physicians diagnosed him as suffering from battered child syndrome.

Yet, his mother, Gail L., gave several possible explanations for the injuries to Jeffrey R.L. She stated that he could have suffered these

15. * * * Dr. Corder testified that great force would be necessary to fracture Jeffrey R.L.'s ribs, and that the other fractures he sustained were consistent with a "twisting, torsion, shaking of limbs[.]"

injuries while he was rolling around in his crib. However, the crib was found by the social worker to be well-padded. Gail L. also stated that his injuries could be the result of a genetic bone disease from which her grandfather suffered. Yet, after several tests were performed at West Virginia University Hospital, there was no indication that Jeffrey R.L. suffered from any bone disease. Furthermore, Gail L. offered the explanation that Jeffrey R.L. suffered his injuries during birth, despite the fact that the evidence in the record reveals Gail L. experienced a normal vaginal delivery. None of the evidence in the record supports any of Gail L.'s explanations of Jeffrey R.L.'s injuries.

Although Gail L. admitted to the circuit court at the hearing held on November 20, 1991, that some trauma had occurred to Jeffrey R.L., absent from the record is any evidence which would indicate that Gail L. made any attempts to identify her child's abuser. In fact, * * * Mr. Trainor, in his psychological report dated October 3, 1991, found that Gail L. showed "no emotionality about the loss of her child or apparent concern over [his] injuries except for some resentment over the way they had been treated by the physicians and by the Department of Human Services." He also observed that Gail had an "apparent lack of serious motivation to uncover" Jeffrey R.L.'s abuser. Although her grandfather had alleged that Jeffrey R.L.'s father had confessed to him and to a social worker that he had abused Jeffrey R.L., that allegation appears to be without foundation.

Even in the face of knowledge of her son's abuse, there is no indication in the record that Gail L. made any attempts to identify her son's abuser. At the time Jeffrey R.L. suffered these extreme injuries, he was under his mother's care and the care of those individuals with whom she entrusted him. Gail L. is aware of those individuals who cared for her child during the first three months of his life when he was subject to physical abuse; yet, she has never attempted to identify his abuser. Nearly two and one-half years have passed since Jeffrey R.L. suffered his injuries. By failing to even attempt to identify his abuser during this two and one-half-year period, Gail L. has not shown that she is fully committed to the welfare of her child.

Establishing the identity of the person or persons who inflicted these injuries on Jeffrey R.L. is crucial to his health, safety and welfare. [Mr. Trainor and three other experts] have all stated that Jeffrey R.L. should not be returned to either parent until the perpetrator of his abuse has been identified. Yet, despite the fact that the perpetrator has not been identified, the circuit court returned custody of Jeffrey R.L. to his mother.[d] We find that the circuit court clearly erred in returning Jeffrey R.L. to his mother before the perpetrator who inflicted such extensive physical abuse on this helpless infant has been identified.

d. Gail L. and her husband Jeffrey L. had separated by the hearing and Jeffrey L. indicated that he desired "to remain mute" on the issue of whether Jeffrey R. L. should have been returned to his mother.

There is no reasonable likelihood that the conditions of abuse can be substantially corrected because the perpetrator of Jeffrey R.L.'s physical abuse has not been identified. Jeffrey R.L., due to his young age and physical condition, needs consistent close interaction with fully committed adults. Jeffrey R.L.'s health, safety and welfare would be seriously threatened if he were to be placed back into the environment where he suffered extensive physical injuries when his abuser has not been identified. Therefore, because it appears that Jeffrey R.L.'s abuser will never be identified, this Court will not place him back into the environment where he suffered his abuse.

We find that: (1) continuation in Jeffrey R.L.'s home is not in his best interests because his abuser has not been identified; (2) reunification between Jeffrey R.L. and his parents is not in his best interests because his parents have not identified his abuser; and (3) the state department made reasonable efforts to reunify the family, drafted a treatment plan Gail L. refused to sign, arranged for Gail L. and Jeffrey L. to complete a parental training program, and monitored the case. Rather than prolong these proceedings, we believe there is clear and convincing evidence before us to warrant terminating parental rights.
* * *

In summary, we hold that parental rights may be terminated where there is clear and convincing evidence that the infant child has suffered extensive physical abuse while in the custody of his or her parents, and there is no reasonable likelihood that the conditions of abuse can be substantially corrected because the perpetrator of the abuse has not been identified and the parents, even in the face of knowledge of the abuse, have taken no action to identify the abuser. Accordingly, the parental rights of Gail L. and Jeffrey L. to their son, Jeffrey R.L., are hereby terminated.[20] The guardian ad litem shall continue to represent Jeffrey R.L. until he is adopted or placed into a permanent home. If the guardian ad litem is unable to continue representing Jeffrey R.L., another guardian ad litem will be appointed.

* * *

Notes and Questions

1. How expansive should "non-cooperation" be as a ground for termination? In a case after *Jeffrey R.L.*, West Virginia terminated the rights of parents present when a child, not their own, died from the shaken baby syndrome. The parents would not cooperate with authorities to identify the

20. The guardian ad litem before this Court asserts that Jeffrey R.L.'s interests were not adequately represented before the circuit court. She points out that the attorney representing the child did not call any witnesses, did not place any exhibits into evidence, and did not confer with the treating physician or with the foster parents until this petition was filed with this Court. She also asserts that at the hearing in December of 1992, the attorney represented to the circuit court that he had yet to decide whether the child should be placed back with his family. However, because we are terminating parental rights in this case and adopting standards for guardians ad litem to adhere to in the future, we need not further address this issue.

perpetrator. West Virginia Dep't. of Health and Human Resources v. Doris S., 475 S.E.2d 865 (W.Va. 1996).

2. *Termination required.* The Adoption and Safe Families Act of 1997, 42 U.S.C. § 675, requires the state to initiate termination of parental rights proceedings in some cases:

> (E) in the case of a child who has been in foster care under the responsibility of the State for 15 of the most recent 22 months, or, if a court of competent jurisdiction has determined a child to be an abandoned infant (as defined under State law) or has made a determination that the parent has committed murder of another child of the parent, committed voluntary manslaughter of another child of the parent, aided or abetted, attempted, conspired, or solicited to commit such a murder or such a voluntary manslaughter, or committed a felony assault that has resulted in serious bodily injury to the child or to another child of the parent, the State shall file a petition to terminate the parental rights of the child's parents (or, if such a petition has been filed by another party, seek to be joined as a party to the petition), and, concurrently, to identify, recruit, process, and approve a qualified family for an adoption, unless—
>
>> "(i) at the option of the State, the child is being cared for by a relative;
>>
>> "(ii) a State agency has documented in the case plan (which shall be available for court review) a compelling reason for determining that filing such a petition would not be in the best interests of the child; or
>>
>> "(iii) the State has not provided to the family of the child, consistent with the time period in the State case plan, such services as the State deems necessary for the safe return of the child to the child's home, if reasonable efforts * * * are required to be made with respect to the child.".

3. *Termination presumptions.* When, if at all, should the state presume that termination of the parent-child relationship is in the child's best interests? Some states have presumptions, such as those listed in Idaho Code § 16–2005:

> The court may grant termination as to a parent:
>
> (1) Who caused the child to be conceived as a result of rape, incest, lewd conduct with a minor child under sixteen (16) years, or sexual abuse of a child under the age of sixteen (16) years,
>
> (2) Who murdered or intentionally killed the other parent of the child; or
>
> (3) Who has been incarcerated and has no possibility of parole.
>
> There is a rebuttable presumption that termination of the parent-child relationship in any of the circumstances provided [above] is in the best interest of the child.

Compare the Idaho presumptions to the Adoption and Safe Families Act provisions discussed in the preceding note. Would you amend the Idaho statute? Would you make the presumptions conclusive rather than rebuttable?

4. *The parent's incarceration.* What should the state do when a single parent of a young child is incarcerated for a lengthy time for a crime that did not directly affect the child? Is there a basis for intervention if the parent has relatives who can take the child or who can afford to pay for private care?

Although incarceration per se may not be allowed as a basis for termination of parental rights, imprisonment can be a factor the court considers. In Vance v. Lincoln County Dep't of Public Welfare, 582 So.2d 414 (Miss.1991), for example, the Mississippi Supreme Court upheld the termination of the parental rights of a mother who had been sentenced to concurrent sentences of 50 and 30 years for murder and armed robbery. Mississippi law permits termination of parental rights "when there is some other substantial erosion of the relationship between the parent and child which was caused at least in part by the parent's * * * prolonged imprisonment." Id. Efforts to place the children with relatives had failed.

5. *Abuse of a sibling.* Should abuse of a sibling be a basis for termination of rights to other children? As mentioned earlier, some parents abuse one child, the target child, and other children are not physically harmed. Abuse of a sibling is considered probative of how the parents might treat other children. See, e.g., In re Dittrick, 263 N.W.2d 37 (Mich. 1977). Courts hold that abuse of a child is prima facie evidence of imminent danger to the child's sibling in the same circumstances; such evidence may be sufficient predicate for an order to remove the sibling. See, e.g., In the Interest of M.R.F., 907 S.W.2d 787, 796, (Mo.Ct.App. 1995); In the Interest of W.J.D., 756 S.W.2d 191, 196 (Mo.Ct.App. 1988). In extreme cases, the court may terminate parental rights to a child based entirely on proof of abuse of a sibling, even where no evidence is adduced concerning injury to the child and where all evidence concerns the sibling. See, e.g., In the Interest of M.H., 859 S.W.2d 888, 894 (Mo.Ct.App. 1993).

The child protective impulse is self-evident. "The past abuse of another sibling is evidence of a home environment that is currently dangerous to the child." In the Interest of D.G.N., 691 S.W.2d 909, 911 (Mo. 1985). "The importance of intervention . . ., even though no damage to the second infant is manifest, lies in the knowledge that neglect or abuse by a parent with a propensity toward it is often triggered by the child's growth." In re A.A., 533 S.W.2d 681, 681 (Mo.Ct.App. 1976), quoted with approval in In the Interest of D.G.N., 691 S.W.2d 909, 912 (Mo. 1985).

In light of its child protective purpose, abuse and neglect jurisdiction attaches even in the absence of an allegation that the child has been, or is likely to be, directly harmed; the reasoned belief that circumstances might cause harm sustains jurisdiction. See, e.g., In Interest of K.H., 652 S.W.2d 166 (Mo.Ct.App. 1983). Where the parent fails to provide the minimum quality of care the community will tolerate, the court may exercise neglect jurisdiction even without finding that a dangerous situation presently exists. See, e.g., In the Interest of M.A.T., 934 S.W.2d 2, 4 (Mo.Ct.App. 1996) ("When faced with a potentially harmful situation, the juvenile court does not have to wait until harm is done before it can act.") See also, e.g. In the

Interest of J.J., 718 S.W.2d 235, 237 (Mo.Ct.App. 1986) (court is "not required to 'test' the parents by subjecting the infant child to the potentially harmful environment.... in their home).

6. *Americans with Disabilities Act.* Does the Americans with Disabilities Act (42 U.S.C. §§ 12131–12134) entitle a mentally retarded or mentally ill parent to special consideration in a termination of parental rights proceeding? In a recent Vermont decision, In re B.S., 693 A.2d 716 (Vt. 1997), the court rejected the mother's contention that her parental rights were terminated improperly because the state did not reasonably accommodate her disability, mental retardation:

> [T]he ADA does not directly apply to TPR proceedings. The goals of the ADA are "to assure equality of opportunity, full participation, independent living, and economic self-sufficiency" for persons with disabilities. The act encompasses three areas: employment, public services, and public accommodations offered by private entities. Title II, which deals with public services, provides that "no qualified individual with a disability shall, by reason of such disability, be excluded from participation in or be denied the benefits of the services, programs, or activities of a public entity." TPR proceedings are not "services, programs or activities" within the meaning of Title II of the ADA. Thus, the anti-discrimination requirement does not directly apply to TPR proceedings.

> Even if the ADA applied directly to TPR proceedings, there is no specific discrimination against disabled persons in the TPR process. Mental retardation is not, by itself, a ground for terminating parental rights. In deciding whether to terminate parental rights, the court must determine the best interests of the child in accordance with four [statutory] criteria * * *: (1) the interaction and interrelationship of the child with the child's natural parents, foster parents, siblings, and others who may significantly affect the child's best interests, (2) the child's adjustment to home and community, (3) the likelihood the natural parent will be able to resume parental duties within a reasonable period of time, and (4) whether the natural parent has played and continues to play a constructive role in the child's welfare. A mentally retarded parent is capable of meeting these criteria.

* * *

7. *Teenage parents.* Should a teenage mother be given more time than an adult to develop parenting abilities? No, according to In re McCrary, 600 N.E.2d 347 (Ohio 1991), which held that a maximum two-year time limit on reunification did not violate the due process rights of the minor, who gave birth when she was fifteen. The minor urged that the time limits should not begin to operate until she reached age 18 and argued that "a minor parent often lacks the social and emotional maturity necessary to rear a child * * *." Id. at 351. The court of appeals concluded that allowing the infant "at such a developmentally critical stage of its life to languish in a state of temporary custodianship* * *is simply unacceptable." Id. at 353. (The termination order was reversed on a procedural ground).

What should be expected of teenage parents? Should they be expected to get a job, find appropriate housing, and support themselves and their child? Should they get a full-time job or continue in school?

8. *Additional references.* Raymond C. O'Brien, An Analysis of Realistic Due Process Rights of Children versus Parents, 26 Conn. L. Rev. 1209 (1994); Michael S. Wald, State Intervention on behalf of Neglected Children: Standards for Removal of Children from their Homes, Monitoring the Status of Children in Foster Care, and Termination of Parental Rights, 28 Stan. L. Rev. 625 (1976).

IN RE ADOPTION OF B.O.

Court of Appeals of Utah, 1996.
927 P.2d 202.

DAVIS, ASSOCIATE PRESIDING JUDGE:

Appellant challenges the trial court's order terminating his parental rights in the context of an adoption proceeding. We affirm.

BACKGROUND

Born on April 16, 1984 in Morgan, Kentucky, B.O. is the natural daughter of appellant [father] and L.M. [mother]. Appellant and L.M. were married and living together at the time of B.O.'s birth; however, the couple separated approximately four months later. Thereafter, L.M. assumed physical custody of B.O. and relocated to Sandy, Utah. Appellant eventually relocated to California. L.M. and appellant divorced, and appellant was ordered to pay $25.00 per week in child support.

In Sandy, B.O. resided with her maternal grandparents and her aunt, appellee S.G., after L.M. relinquished physical custody of B.O. During this time, S.G. provided B.O.'s day-to-day care. In December 1991, appellees S.G. and C.G. married. At that time, S.G. moved from her mother's home to live with appellee C.G.; B.O. continued living with her maternal grandmother. Shortly thereafter, once appellees had settled into their new home, B.O. moved in with appellees and has been in their care and custody ever since. Thus, S.G. has been B.O.'s primary caretaker for the past eleven years, meeting B.O.'s day-to-day needs. Moreover, S.G. and C.G. have now filled parental roles for B.O. for nearly three years.

At all relevant times, appellant had knowledge of both an address and telephone number through which he could contact B.O. Moreover, appellees, as well as B.O.'s maternal grandparents, have encouraged B.O. to maintain a relationship with appellant. However, over the past eleven years, appellant has visited B.O. on only two occasions. Appellant's most recent visit occurred in 1992 when L.M. took B.O. to California to see her father. Thus, in the eleven years following his divorce from L.M., appellant initiated only one visit with B.O. At trial, appellant testified that he believed one visit every several years, coupled with one or two phone calls per year, was sufficient to adequately provide B.O. with a father figure.

In addition to this infrequent visitation schedule, appellant placed but one phone call or mailed one card to B.O. every four to six months. Appellant's Christmas and birthday correspondence to B.O. routinely arrived late, if at all. Appellant also made numerous unfulfilled promises to visit B.O. and/or send her special gifts without ever explaining his reasons for breaking them. Moreover, appellant concedes that he is at least $2000 in arrears of his child support obligation. He also had not paid child support as ordered under his divorce decree for at least two years, and as many as five years, prior to the trial on this matter. Appellant resumed paying child support in June 1995, at least three months after the adoption petition was filed in the present case. Finally, appellant testified that he is unaware of who has been responsible for B.O.'s care during the past eleven years.

Appellees filed their Petition for Adoption on February 23, 1995. * * * On November 29, 1995, the trial court entered its findings of fact and conclusions of law. Based on the facts adduced at trial, the trial court's conclusions of law stated:

1. [Appellees] have proven by clear and convincing evidence that [appellant] has made only token efforts to support and/or communicate with [B.O.];

2. [Appellant] is an unfit parent as provided in U.C.A. § 78–3a–401 et seq. (1953) as amended;

3. It is in the best interests and welfare of [B.O.] that the parental rights of [appellant] be terminated.

Accordingly, on November 29, 1995, the trial court also entered an order terminating appellant's parental rights. Finally, the trial court entered a Decree of Adoption on December 7, 1995, declaring appellees the legal parents of B.O. and relieving appellant "of any parental duties and all responsibilities for [B.O.]." This appeal followed.

* * *

Constitutionality Of Section 78–3a–407(6)(a)

[A]ppellant presents a facial challenge to the constitutionality of section 78–3a–407(6), claiming that the statute "is violative of [appellant's] fundamentally protected rights under Amendments IX and XIV of the Constitution of the United States, and * * * the Constitution of Utah." In doing so, appellant presents a laundry list of United States and Utah Supreme Court decisions in support of his assertion that "Utah Code Ann. § 78–3a–407(6), which permits termination upon either token efforts to support or communicate with [B.O.], is a standard insufficient to overcome [appellant's] countervailing and constitutionally protected parental rights." We agree with appellant's assertion that "a parent has a fundamental right to maintain a relationship with his or her child." This right is by now well established by both United States and Utah precedent. See generally Santosky v. Kramer (1982); In re J.P., 648 P.2d 1364 (Utah 1982).

Citing J.P., appellant claims that section 78–3a–407(6) "does not rise to a showing of unfitness, abandonment, or substantial neglect as is required" to overcome his fundamental right to maintain a relationship with B.O. In J.P., the Utah Supreme Court decided whether an involuntary termination of parental rights, based solely on a showing of the best interest of the child, was violative of a mother's constitutionally protected parental rights. Holding in the affirmative, the supreme court concluded:

> The Utah Constitution recognizes and protects the inherent and retained right of a parent to maintain parental ties to his or her child * * * and that the United States Constitution recognizes and protects the same right under the Ninth and Fourteenth Amendments. We further conclude that, under both Constitutions, a [parent] is entitled to a showing of unfitness, abandonment, or substantial neglect before [his or] her parental rights are terminated.

This showing of unfitness, abandonment, or substantial neglect must be by clear and convincing evidence. However, the court adhered to the notion that the child's welfare remains the paramount consideration, noting,

> The principle that "the welfare of the child is the paramount consideration" means that parental rights, though inherent and retained, are not absolute; that the state, as parens patriae, has the authority and obligation to assume a parental role after the natural parent has been shown to be unfit or dysfunctional; and that parental prerogatives cannot, at that extreme point, frustrate the state in discharging its duty.

Since J.P. was decided, several decisions have affirmed the termination of parental rights based on a parent's failure to communicate and/or pay child support. For instance, in State ex rel. J.R.T. v. Timperly, 750 P.2d 1234 (Utah App.1988), this court affirmed a juvenile court termination order based on abandonment where the father had failed to contact his child over a sixteen month period. In doing so, this court relied on the two-pronged abandonment test * * *. Under this test, the court considers, "first, whether the parent's conduct evidenced a conscious disregard for his or her parental obligations, and second, whether that disregard led to the destruction of the parent-child relationship." Under this test, "[a]bandonment may be proven by either the parent's objective conduct or the parent's expressed subjective intent." Because the father "offered no evidence of contact nor any reasonable excuse for his extended lack of contact with the child," the * * * court affirmed the juvenile court's termination order.

* * *

Recently, in State ex rel. E.R., 918 P.2d 162 (Utah App.1996), this court reaffirmed the holding that "abandonment will be upheld 'based solely on a parent's lack of visitation and communication.' "In E.R., "after sending [E.R. a] gift in January 1994 and after he knew how to contact [E.R.], defendant never sent cards or gifts to E.R. to let her know that she had a father who was interested in establishing a parent/child relationship with her." * * * [T]his court noted that "defendant had 'an obligation . . . to vigorously pursue the fruits' of his parental rights, but failed to do so." Moreover, "[a] lack of visitation and communication with a party's child or children evidences a conscious disregard of parental obligations, which leads 'to the destruction of the parent-child relationship.' "Thus, the termination of E.R.'s father's parental rights was affirmed on abandonment grounds where the father had failed to communicate with his child.

Accordingly, although not decided in the context of constitutional challenges, our review of Utah case law yields numerous instances where the termination of parental rights, usually on abandonment grounds, was affirmed based on a parent's failure to communicate with his or her child. Thus, failure to communicate, by itself, has repeatedly been held to support a showing of abandonment in overcoming a parent's fundamental right to maintain a relationship with his or her child. Accordingly, we reject appellant's contention that section 78–3a–407(6)(a) is unconstitutional because it "permits termination upon either token efforts to support or communicate with the child."[8]

Moreover, appellant presents no justification for us to differentiate between the abandonment cases relied upon by the trial court, or those cited herein, and the token efforts grounds upon which his parental rights were terminated.[9] "Token" is defined as "merely simulated; slight or of no real account." The abandonment cases discussed previously, and the facts of many of those cases in particular, amply demonstrate instances in which parents took "slight or no real account" of their parental duties, thus justifying the termination of their parental rights. In light of these cases and the absence of specific "token efforts" precedent, we cannot say that the trial court abused its discretion by utilizing abandonment cases in reaching its token efforts conclusion.

8. We note that the trial court found that appellees had "proven by clear and convincing evidence that [appellant] . . . made only token efforts to support and/or communicate with [B.O.]." (Emphasis added). Thus, the trial court added the conjunctive "and" to the "support or communicate" language of section 78–3a407(6)(a), thereby signifying the dual grounds under that section upon which the trial court terminated appellant's parental rights. Because we find the failure to communicate portion of section 78–3a–407(6)(a) is adequate, in and of itself, to overcome appellant's fundamental parental rights, we do not address his challenge to the failure to support portion of the statute.

9. Though the trial court relied on token efforts, unfitness, and best interests grounds in terminating appellant's parental rights, we note that the trial court's findings of fact also present a prima facie case of abandonment, codified at Utah Code Ann. § 78–3a–407(1) (Supp.1995), as defined in Utah Code Ann. § 78–3a–408(1)(b) (Supp.1995):

(1) In determining whether a parent or parents have abandoned a child, it is prima facie evidence of abandonment that the parent or parents:

. . . .

(b) have failed to communicate with the child by mail, telephone, or otherwise for six months or failed to have shown the normal interest of a natural parent, without just cause.

Accordingly, appellant's challenge to the constitutionality of section 78–3a–407(6) also fails.

* * *

Questions

1. Do you agree that the rights of B.O.'s father should have been terminated? Should his rights be terminated if he failed to communicate with his child for six months without just cause or should a longer time period be needed? Should his rights be terminated if he always paid child support in a timely manner in the amount specified by the court?

PROBLEM 4–10

When Nancy gave birth to her son Eric in August she was living with Dan, Eric's father. Dan moved out two months after Eric was born. Nancy had previously given birth to a child whom she voluntarily had given up for adoption. A year after Eric was born, Nancy left him with her sister who agreed to look after him. A month later, in September, she was diagnosed with breast cancer and underwent surgery, radiation and chemotherapy. In that same month Dan took Eric from Nancy's sister and lived with various members of his family for several months until he gave Eric to another couple, Mr. and Mrs. Edwards. Eric lived with the Edwards for three months and then in May they petitioned for legal custody, which they were granted. Nancy had no contact with Eric from September to May. She said that she did not get along with Dan and his family and that she did not always know where Eric was. Dan says he told her where Eric was and offered to arrange visits, but Nancy did not want any. In May she found out that Eric was with the Edwards and started visiting him on a regular basis. In June the Edwards filed a petition for termination of Nancy's parental rights. Dan voluntarily relinquished his rights. The Edwards want to adopt Eric.

At the termination hearing a friend of Nancy's testified that when Eric lived with Nancy, he had observed Eric lying on the floor with a roach crawling on his face. He testified further that he had observed Nancy giving Eric a milk bottle "with contents looking similar to cottage cheese." Another friend testified that she had seen cat litter and cat feces near Eric. One witness testified that she had recently visited Nancy and saw cat feces on the kitchen floor. A family therapist, Kent Harris, who was employed by the court to do a home study, testified that Nancy's home was clean and neat and that all cat owners had cat feces on their floor at some time. He further testified that Nancy's breast cancer had changed her and she wanted to be a better parent. He testified, "I can't predict the future, but I do know that when people face death and trauma they change. Sometimes you see a man who has been drinking all his life and then the doctor says 'You're going to die if you don't stop drinking,' and he stops. Pain is life's best teacher and that's what's happened to Nancy."

Under state law a parent's rights can be terminated if (1) the parent has abused or neglected the child or (2) the parent has willfully abandoned the child for a least six consecutive months immediately preceding the filing of the termination petition.

You are the judge. Would you terminate Nancy's parental rights?

SECTION 10.   SOCIAL CLASS, ETHNIC AND RACIAL BIAS

A.   *Overview*

U.S. ADVISORY BOARD ON CHILD ABUSE AND NEGLECT, CHILD ABUSE AND NEGLECT: CRITICAL FIRST STEPS IN RESPONSE TO A NATIONAL EMERGENCY 18–19 (1990)

* * *

Poverty

Although child maltreatment occurs in all socioeconomic and cultural groups in society, its reported incidence is disproportionately large within those groups that are least powerful and subjected to the most stressors. Data have shown that the higher the poverty rate is in a neighborhood, the higher the rate of maltreatment will be. Although reporting bias and class-related variations in public authorities' knowledge about families may account for some of the relationship between social class and child maltreatment rates, the evidence is strong that poverty makes child maltreatment much more likely. A national incidence survey showed that child maltreatment was seven times more likely in families with incomes under $15,000 (in 1986) than in families with higher incomes.

Ethnicity

Reflecting the high rates of poverty among ethnic minorities, minority children enter the child protection system in disproportionately large numbers. Upon entering the child protection system, minority families are especially likely to be subjected to intrusive interventions.

In responding to suspected maltreatment in minority families, the child protection system sometimes has difficulty taking into account cultural differences. Such differences are manifest in the allocation of responsibility for childrearing, the discipline of children, and ways in which nurturance and healing are provided. A further difficulty for the child protection system is that society sometimes misperceives some cultural practices involving children as abusive.

When maltreatment is identified, it is often difficult for the child protection system to respond in a fully competent manner. In this context the term "competence" implies a manner which is congruent with cultural expectations and which utilizes strengths and supports that are consistent with cultural norms (e.g., reliance on extended families).

Responses by child protection system personnel to maltreatment in minority families do not always reflect an understanding of the connection between racism and child maltreatment. Nor do they always reflect an understanding that the use of traditional legal interventions often does not "fit" within a particular culture.

Notes

1. *The Indian Child Welfare Act.* The assimilation policy of the Bureau of Indian Affairs that resulted in the removal of large numbers of Native American children from their homes and placement with non-Indian parents was discussed in Chapter 1. This history of a high rate of placement with few returns and the accompanying cultural dislocation has resulted in hostile feelings toward foster care and child protective service workers among many Native Americans. Charles Horejsi, Bonnie Heavy Runner Craig, & Joe Pablo, Reactions by Native American Parents to Child Protective Agencies: Cultural and Community Factors, 71 Child Welfare 329 (1992). As noted in Chapter 1, the Indian Child Welfare Act was intended to keep Native American children in Native American homes.

2. *Bias in reporting.* Some studies have shown that class and race, rather than severity of injuries to the child, determine who is reported to child protective services by hospital staff, with significant underreporting of white and more affluent families. Eli H. Newberger, The Helping Hand Strikes Again: Unintended Consequences of Child Abuse Reporting, 12 J. of Clinical Child Psychology 307, 309–310 (1983). The author notes that "the data suggest that the reporting process contributes to the widespread mythology that these problems are confined to people who are poor who are members of ethnic minorities. This myth that families who abuse their children are different from the rest of us, has led this country to identify child abuse and neglect as 'poor people's problems,' for which we have created traditionally poor quality programs which may met out punishment in the guise of help."

B. Understanding Cultural Context

KAREN AILEEN HOWZE, MAKING DIFFERENCES WORK: CULTURAL CONTEXT IN ABUSE AND NEGLECT PRACTICE FOR JUDGES AND ATTORNEYS 7–8 (1996).

A new Methodology is needed

* * * [A]buse and neglect proceedings require more than an unbiased view of the people before the court. Judges, commissioners, referees and lawyers who have spent many years in the family courts of this nation agree that creating a balance between culture and the adjudication and review process is difficult. **The critical first step requires that the scope of relevant facts be expanded to include the total life experiences of adults and children before the court.**

* * *[T]he people who come before the courts bring their cultural and social precepts. From family to family, case to case, differences rule. Even if families appear on the surface to be similar, the combinations of cultural and subcultural context are too numerous to expect uniformity.

Ultimately, judicial officers assigned to abuse and neglect cases must understand that matters of culture often affect decisions concerning children and their families.

Ultimately, the judicial officers must hold the attorney for the child and counsel for the parents accountable for ensuring that matters of culture are recognized and introduced into the case when and where relevant.

The reality remains: norms that are set today will no longer be applicable or valid tomorrow. Instead, social workers and the legal profession **must develop a more disciplined method of questioning the facts in each case to determine whether cultural and subcultural factors may be at play** throughout each phase of abuse and neglect proceedings.

But first, a few principles:

> **Cultural context encompasses more than race and ethnicity**. Other areas that must be explored in each case: economic status, literacy, language, immigration status, mental and physical disabilities, education, gender, age and sexual orientation.

> **Culture does not shape the law within the abuse and neglect framework.** Rather the cultural contexts of the families before the court provide a backdrop upon which judges, attorneys and social service agencies can determine the levels of service, the types of services and the anticipated impact of such services on the outcome of each case.

> **Cultural context requires an understanding and knowledge of when and how cultural factors affect the way families work.** The understanding is developed by examining each family as an unique entity working within its own environment. That environment is affected by race, economics, language, disabilities.

> **Learning a few generalizations about the characteristics of African Americans, Hispanics, Asians, Native Americans, or the poor does not meet the requirements for working within cultural context**. Rather, learning to question why parents or children respond the way they do will lead to an effective use of cultural context.

> **The cultural context must be explored through methodical questioning.** The facts of abuse and neglect must be balanced against the law with a constant eye on the impact of culture and subculture in shaping the case outcome.

* * *

Notes

1. For an argument that the child protective system is more concerned with controlling women than protecting children, see Annette R. Appell, Protecting Children or Punishing Mothers: Gender, Race and Class in the Child Protection System, 48 S.C.L. Rev. 577 (1997).

2. Cultural factors also play a role in criminal prosecutions. For additional material, see Chapter 6, Criminal Abuse and Neglect.

3. *Additional references.* For a discussion of cross-cultural conflicts and a recommendation for a middle ground between cultural relativism and cultural imperialism, see Françoise Baylis and Jocelyn Downie, Child Abuse and Neglect: Cross–Cultural Considerations in Feminism and Families 173 (Hilde Lindemann Nelson ed., 1997).

SECTION 11. FINDING A CURE

JAMES M. GAUDIN, EFFECTIVE INTERVENTION WITH NEGLECTFUL FAMILIES
20 Crim. Just. & Behav. 66 (1993).

* * *

The conclusions that can be drawn from most of the outcome studies of interventions with neglectful families are limited by the lack of rigor in the research. The studies are limited by small, nonrandom sampling of reported neglect cases, inconsistent definitions of neglect across studies, failure to specify subtypes of neglect, absence of control groups, use of unreliable measures, and failure to evaluate outcomes of discrete components of interventions. A small number of outcome studies on behavioral interventions with very small, nonrandom samples of neglectful parents and children have used single-subject, time series designs to demonstrate the effectiveness of these interventions in remedying specific skill deficits in neglectful parents.

The empirical support for the effectiveness of specific interventions with neglectful parents and children is thus very limited. Research on interventions with neglectful families is needed that is characterized by (a) clear operational definitions of neglect, (b) specification of subtypes of neglect treated, (c) inclusion of control groups, (d) specification of outcomes for discrete interventions or elements of intervention within multiservice models, (e) random samples, (f) inclusion of male family members, and (g) controlled studies of interventions with pre-school, school-age, and adolescent victims of neglect to remedy cognitive and social skill deficits.

Existing studies indicate that most interventions to remedy child neglect have been effective less than 50% of the time. One review of demonstration projects offers evidence that therapeutic group child care for preschool victims of abuse and neglect and group interventions with adolescents are successful in improving the children's functioning 70% of the time. Multiservice models that use family counseling, parent groups, and trained paraprofessionals to supplement skilled professional problem-solving counseling offer the best chances of success. Behavioral, skills-training interventions have been successful in remedying specific deficits of neglectful mothers, interventions with neglectful families that continue for a least one year are the most successful in many studies.

Finally, because child neglect is so highly associated with poverty, effective interventions to prevent or remedy child neglect in the United States must be supported by social and economic programs needed to remedy the poverty that places one out of five children at nine times the risk of neglect as children from families with higher, more adequate incomes.

DAVID WOLFE, PREVENTION OF CHILD NEGLECT: EMERGING ISSUES

20 Criminal Justice and Behavior 90, 104–05, 107–09 (1993).

The Importance Of Matching Services To The Needs Of Parents, Children And Families: What Works For Whom?

* * * [N]o *particular* method of intervention is likely to lead to desirable outcomes for even a majority of families, especially by the time child maltreatment has been identified. From a cost-benefit perspective, the cost of remediating serious child-rearing concerns is prohibitive.

These costs may be reduced by placing greater emphasis on preparing parents for their child-rearing role well in advance of the emergence of problems, and having a wider range of appropriate services available. Such a model requires staff who are trained to assist with families at a level that is most beneficial, rather than attempting to detect and intervene after the fact. Staff would have to be sensitive to individual, community, and cultural preferences, as well as socio-economic limitations, that constitute the majority of disadvantaged families, and be willing to tolerate such differences for the purpose of establishing a basis for improving the parent-child relationship. This approach requires more investment in family development at an earlier point in time, but holds considerable promise in reducing the costs and failures of the current reactive system.

On what basis should early intervention services be provided and matched to families? There is an urgent need to match interventions to the needs of each family as best as possible. Although this seems obvious, the literature shows repeated attempts to design and implement a particular strategy to any given sample of maltreating parents, with little regard to the needs of each participant (especially cultural and ethnic minorities* * *). Whereas some parents require information and assistance in basic child rearing, many others require social support, childcare respite, and/or personal counseling. Yet the interventions persist in attempting to fit the patient to the cure, rather than the reverse. Although the expanding multiservice programs are promising in this regard, they lack thorough evaluation and follow-up, and tend to have weak or inadequate research designs.

* * *

Moreover, few prevention or intervention programs have been directed at the developmental needs of abused and neglected children. Rather, treatment has been predominately aimed at adults. Although our understanding of the developmental impact of these programs has grown, efforts to remediate and/or prevent such problems have been slow to develop. Neglected children, in particular, suffer major psychological consequences that have been inadequately addressed by current approaches.

* * *

The Need For A Multiservice, Public Health Model Of Ongoing Support For Families

Given its prevalence, child maltreatment can be compared to other major threats to public health, such as AIDS, childhood diseases, poverty, and home safety. Therefore, it makes sense in the long run to address the causes of this problem from a public health vantage point, rather than tertiary intervention. Evidence for the effectiveness of such a model can be found in reports from Scandinavian countries. Sweden, Finland, and Denmark all have nationwide programs that resemble the family support programs being explored in the United States. * * *

* * *

* * * [A] public health approach to the prevention of child abuse and neglect is a promising strategy that merits serious consideration. Such a strategy would not undermine existing efforts at treatment and early intervention, but rather would be designed to approach the widespread problem of child maltreatment from a broader, more fundamental vantage point.

DOUGLAS J. BESHAROV, CHILD ABUSE AND NEGLECT REPORTING AND INVESTIGATION: POLICY GUIDELINES FOR DECISION MAKING
22 Family Law Quarterly 1, 3–4, 14–15 (1988).

* * *

The "Child Protective Mission"

Child abuse and child neglect are serious national problems. Only firm and effective government intervention protects many children from serious injury and even death.

The Role of Child Protective Services

The responsibility to receive and investigate reports of suspected child abuse and neglect is primarily assigned to a single, statutorily created public agency, usually called the "Child Protective Service Agency" (or CPS). To protect children from abuse or neglect, Child Protective Service Agencies perform the following functions: report taking, screening, investigation, initial risk assessment, crisis intervention, report disposition, case planning and implementation, and case closure.

The objective of Child Protective Service Agencies is to protect children from abuse and neglect. They do so by strengthening families so that children can remain within or be returned to their families; by temporarily removing children from situations of immediate danger; and by pursuing the termination of parental rights and assuring the child permanency in a substitute family if the custodial family cannot be preserved without serious risk to the child.

The Wider Role of Community-based Services

Nevertheless, the protection of children from abuse and neglect is a community-wide concern. Child protective services must be provided as an integral component of a larger array of child welfare services designed to enhance the well-being of children and of an even broader continuum of human services designed to help meet the needs of children and families. Special responsibility is placed on child welfare, law enforcement, medical and public health, and educational agencies and professionals.

Across the nation, however, Child Protective Service Agencies are being pushed to respond to the absence of other, more appropriate services. Child abuse hotlines, for example, are receiving thousands of "reports" that, at base, are not about child abuse or child neglect, but are really requests for needed family-oriented social services. Many of these reports involve adolescent behavioral problems (such as truancy, delinquency, school problems, substance abuse, and sexual acting out); children who need specialized education or treatment; and chronic parent-child conflicts with no indication of abuse or neglect. Some of these reports result in the family receiving much needed services , but most do not. In any event, these additional, inappropriate calls to CPS hotlines significantly increase the number of unsubstantiated cases.

In effect, callers are trying to use Child Protective Service Agencies to fill gaps in what should be a comprehensive child welfare system. To prevent this misdirection of scarce resources and to reduce the number of unsubstantiated cases, Child Protective Service Agencies must develop policies and procedures that specify the kinds of calls that are appropriate and that should be accepted for investigation.

* * *

Conclusion

* * *

1. Child Protective Services should be defined as a program limited to abused or neglected children and their families within a broader child welfare service system, not as *the* child welfare program.

2. The community, not the Child Protective Service Agency alone, has the primary and ultimate responsibility for preventing and treating child abuse and neglect. The community and professionals do not satisfy this obligation merely by reporting cases.

3. Child Protective Service Agencies should be assigned investigatory responsibility only over intrafamilial or quasifamilial child maltreatment, broadly defined to include parents, guardians, foster parents, and other persons (such as boyfriends or girlfriends) continuously or regularly in the child's home.

4. Investigating nonfamilial abuse and neglect should be the responsibility of law enforcement, licensing, or other agencies with the expertise and authority to investigate such cases, not of the Child Protective Service Agency. Furthermore, such units must be independent of the agency or facility being investigated, so that there is no conflict of interest.

5. Consistent with the need to safeguard the welfare of endangered children, every effort must be made to protect parental rights.

6. Definitions of child abuse and neglect and implementing rules should be redrafted to be more specific and to clarify the types of cases that should be reported—and not reported—to the Child Protective Service Agency.

7. Involuntary Child Protective Service intervention should be authorized only if (1) the parent has engaged in seriously harmful behavior toward the child, whether or not actual harm resulted; or (2) the parent is suffering from a severe mental disability that *demonstrably* prevents the parent from adequately caring for the child.

8. Decision makers do not have specific and widely accepted guidelines that would help ensure uniform and more appropriate reporting and case disposition. More specific operational definitions and decision-making criteria must be developed for each stage of the child protective process.

9. Public and professional education should provide clear information about what to report (and not to report), give descriptions and examples of reportable conditions, explain what to expect when a report is made, and give information on appropriate alternative resources for other child and family problems. Professionals should be asked to give more specific information than the general public when making a report.

10. "Behavioral indicators" of child abuse, especially of sexual abuse, have a valid place in decision making. However, the lists of behavioral indicators not being circulated, standing on their own and without an accompanying full history of past and present behaviors, should not be the basis of a report.

11. State law should allow for, and guidelines should support, the screening of reports by qualified staff in order to limit the Child Protective Service Agency's involvement in inappropriate cases.

12. The extent of Child Protective Service Agency intervention should vary with the degree of harm or threatened harm to the child and the certainty of the evidence. Guidelines to assess both should be developed.

13. Reporters should not be expected to decide if abuse or neglect has occurred before making a report. Thus, a certain number of unsubstantiated investigations is necessary to ensure adequate child protection.

14. Uniform categories and definitions of investigative findings should be developed. They should accurately reflect the disposition and the services provided in cases that are not substantiated.

Notes and Questions

1. *Program evaluation and implementation.* Should "reasonable efforts" under the Adoption Assistance and Child Welfare Act of 1980 mean that a state must provide services that are *appropriate* for a family, or merely *available* services? If a program has not been properly evaluated, or if its evaluation shows that it has a success rate of less than 50%, should parents be required to participate in the program? What are the barriers to adequate program evaluation and implementation of successful programs?

2. *Scope of child protective services.* How should "success" in child abuse and neglect reporting and investigation be measured? Does a high number of unsubstantiated reports indicate that the reporting laws are too broad? Should the scope of reporting laws be reduced and mandatory state intervention be limited to the most serious cases? How should the impact of poverty on children be taken into account when designing child protective services programs?

3. *Additional references.* David T. Ellwood, Poor Support: Poverty in the American Family (1988); Irwin Garfinkel, Assuring Child Support: An Extension of Social Security (1992); National Commission on Children, Beyond Rhetoric: A New American Agenda for Children and Families; Lisbeth B. Schorr & Daniel Schorr, Within Our Reach: Breaking the Cycle of Disadvantage (1989); Aroloc Sherman, Children's Defense Fund, Wasting America's Future (1994); Douglas J. Besharov, Gaining Control Over Child Abuse Reports, Public Welfare 34 (Spring, 1990); David Finkehor, Is Child Abuse Overreported? The Data Rebut Arguments for Less Intervention, Public Welfare 22 (Winter 1990); Martha S. Hill & Jodi R. Sandfort, Effects of Childhood Poverty on Productivity Later in Life: Implications for Public Pollicy, 17 Children Youth Servs. Rev. 91 (1995); Alice C. Shotton, Making Reasonable Efforts in Child Abuse and Neglect Cases: Ten Years Later, 26 Cal. W. L. Rev. 223 (1990); Stephen Sugarman, Financial Support of Children and the End of Welfare as We Know It, 81 Va. L. Rev. 2423 (1995).

Chapter 5

FOSTER CARE

What happens to abused or neglected children when a court decides they cannot remain at home safely? Children whose families lack the resources to provide other care may be placed in government funded foster care. The foster care placement is intended to be temporary, with the children being returned to their parents or, if return is not possible, placed for adoption or in some other permanent arrangement. Foster children are placed in private homes licensed and supervised by the state, or in group homes or institutions. If the child is placed with relatives rather than strangers, the foster care is called kinship care. This Chapter explores the rights and responsibilities of children, parents, foster parents and the government in this complex system of care.

SECTION 1.   THE CURRENT STATUS OF FOSTER CARE

Introduction

Foster care remains a valuable resource for providing homes for children, but there is general agreement that foster care is not a good long-term option because placements are impermanent. Major federal and state efforts to reduce the number of children in foster care have not been successful, however. Instead, the number of children in foster care has been increasing. As of March 1998, 520,000 children were in foster care nationwide. Children's Bureau, Administration on Children, Youth and Families, U.S. Dep't of Health and Human Services, Foster Care and Adoption Statistics Current Reports, available at <http://www.acf.dhhs.gov/programs/cb/stats/afcars>. Twenty-nine percent of these children were in kinship care and fifty percent were in foster care with non-relatives. Fifteen percent were in institutions or group homes. Only two percent were in pre-adoptive homes. The remaining four percent were in a variety of other placements. Children's median length of stay in foster care was 21 months. Id.

Minority children are substantially overrepresented in foster care. Based on information from twenty-one states with recent data available, 62% of foster care children are children of color.

Almost half of American foster children are African–American, and African–American foster children usually wait for adoption longer than white children do. Whatever the minority group in a given area—Hispanic, African–American, or native American—that minority is nearly always overrepresented in the foster care population. Latino children constitute roughly 12% of the child population nationwide, but 14% of the children in out-of-home placement. In Texas, a state with a high percentage of Latinos, while Latino children make up 21% of the overall child population and 21% of the child maltreatment victims, they represent close to 30% of the children in placement. In large urban areas—Detroit, New York, and Chicago, for example—children of color may constitute 80–90% of the child welfare population.

Donald N. Duquette, et al., We Know Better Than We Do: A Policy Framework for Child Welfare Reform, 31 U. Mich. J.L. Ref. 93, 96 (1997).

The median age of foster children has been decreasing also. Between 1983 and 1990, the children entering foster care who were under age one increased by two-thirds. These infants stayed longer in foster care than any other age group. See U.S. General Accounting Office, Child Welfare: Complex Needs Strain Capacity To Provide Services (1995).

U.S. GENERAL ACCOUNTING OFFICE, CHILD WEL-FARE: COMPLEX NEEDS STRAIN CAPACITY TO PROVIDE SERVICES 7–15 (1995).[a]

* * *

Children are also entering care from families more troubled than in the past and with greater emotional, behavioral, and medical needs. Such families today more often face economic hardship, substance abuse, homelessness, mental or physical illness, or the imprisonment of a family member. In Los Angeles County, New York City and Philadelphia county in 1991, over half of the preschool-age foster children were estimated to have serious health related problems, including developmental delays, low birth weight, heart problems, and human immunodeficiency virus (HIV) infection. An estimated 62 percent of the preschool-age foster children were at risk of serious health problems due to prenatal drug exposure, more than double the 29 percent risk of such problems in 1986.

Children with these complex needs require a variety of community-based services and a level of care not required in the past. A California study found that foster children were 10 times more likely to use mental health services than other children on Medicaid and that they were hospitalized for mental conditions almost twice as long. For this reason, while foster children constituted only 4 percent of California children on

a. Figures and references to them are omitted.

Medicaid they accounted for 40 percent of all Medicaid mental health expenditures.

Children who leave foster care are increasingly returned home when caseworkers consider it safe. About 67 percent of children leaving care in 1990 returned to their families, up from 56 percent in 1983. Meanwhile, the percentage of children adopted declined from 12 to 8 percent.

Although foster care is a relatively short-term experience for many children, some children remain in care for extended periods. Of the children leaving care in 1990, for example, 50 percent had been in foster care for 8 months or less. However, of those remaining in care, over 25 percent had been in foster placements for at least 3 years. Foster children for whom adoption is ultimately planned spend an average of 4 to 6 years in foster care, according to a 1991 report on adoptions in 20 states.

The shorter the initial stay in foster care, the more likely it appears that children who are reunited with their parents will reenter care. In Los Angeles County and New York City, for example, 32 percent of children whose initial stay in foster care was less than 1 year later returned to care, compared with 16 percent of children whose initial stay was 1 year or longer.

Youths who leave foster care at age 18 because they are no longer eligible may experience unstable and troubled lives. A study conducted 2.5 to 4 years after youths left foster care found that 46 percent had not completed high school, 38 percent had not held a job for more than 1 year, 25 percent had been homeless for at least one night, and 60 percent of young women had given birth to a child. Forty percent had been on public assistance, incarcerated, or a cost to the community in some other way.

* * *

U.S. GENERAL ACCOUNTING OFFICE, FOSTER CARE: STATE EFFORTS TO IMPROVE THE PERMANENCY PLANNING PROCESS SHOW SOME PROMISE 1, 4–6 (1997)

* * *

The mid–1980's through the mid–1990's witnessed dramatic increases in the number of children placed in foster care to protect them from abuse and neglect at home. From fiscal year 1984 to 1995, the foster care population rose from an estimated 276,000 children to 494,000. In 1995, states received more than $2.8 billion in federal assistance for approximately half of these 494,000 children in foster care.[1] The Congressional

---

1. Under title IV–E of the Social Security Act, federal matching funds are provided to states for foster care maintenance costs for children from families eligible for Aid to Families With Dependent Children (AFDC). Although legislation passed in 1996 eliminated the AFCD program, children who meet the 1995 eligibility criteria for AFCD

Budget Office estimates that by 2001, federal costs will rise to $4.8 billion with caseloads of federally assisted foster care children increasing by almost 26 percent. Longer stays in foster care have contributed to these rising costs. Many of these children are among the nation's most at risk for future problems, having suffered the effects of both physical and emotional abuse, and poverty.

* * *

State child welfare systems consist of a complicated network of policies and programs designed to protect children. Today, these systems must respond to growing numbers of children from families with serious and multiple problems. Many of these families also need intensive and long-term interventions to address these problems. With growing case-loads over the past decade, the systems' abilities to keep pace with the needs of troubled children and their families has been greatly taxed. In addition, the continued growth in caseloads expected over the next few years will give child welfare agencies little relief.

When parents or guardians are unable to care for their children, state child welfare agencies face the difficult task of providing temporary placements for children while simultaneously working with a wide array of public and private service providers, as well as the courts, to determine the best long-term placement option. The permanency planning process is guided by federal statute and typically occurs in stages requiring considerable time. Finding an appropriate placement solution is extremely difficult because it often involves numerous steps and many different players.

In each case, states must make reasonable efforts to prevent the placement of a child in foster care. If the child must be removed from the home, states are required under the Adoption Assistance and Child Welfare Act to take appropriate steps to make the child's safe return home possible. Once removed, if reunification with the parents cannot be accomplished quickly, a child will be placed in temporary foster care while state child welfare agencies and community service providers continue to work with the parents in hope of reunification. To be eligible for federal funding, the state must demonstrate to the appropriate court that it has made reasonable efforts to prevent out-of-home placement and to reunify the family. Federal law further requires that placement be as close as possible to the parent's home in the most family-like setting possible.

* * *

For abused and neglected children, living with their parents may be unsafe. Yet foster care is not an optimal situation, especially not as a permanent solution. State child welfare agencies and the courts are confronted with the dilemma of whether to reunite families as quickly as possible or keep the children in foster care with the expectation of future

will continue to be eligible for title IV–E assistance. The states incur all foster care costs for children not eligible for federal support.

reunification. They must also determine at what point to abandon hope of reunification, terminate the parents' rights, and initiate a search for an adoptive home or other permanent placement for the child. If children are reunited with their families too quickly, they may return to foster care because the home environment may still be unstable. On the other hand, when children remain in foster care too long, it is difficult to reestablish emotional ties with their families. Furthermore, the chances for adoption can be reduced because the child is older than the most desirable adoption age or has developed behavioral problems.

Determining an appropriate placement option for children quickly is of twofold importance. First, finding permanent placements for children removed from their families is critical to ensure their overall well-being. Children without permanent homes and stable caregivers may be more likely to develop emotional, intellectual, and behavioral problems. A second reason for placing children more quickly is the financial costs of children remaining in foster care. * * * While some options for permanent placements, such as providing long-term support to a relative to care for a child, may not realize cost savings, other options, such as adoption, will reduce foster care costs. Title IV–E payments, between fiscal years 1984 and 1996, increased from $435.7 million to an estimated $3.1 billion.

* * *

KAREN SPAR, CONGRESSIONAL RESEARCH SERVICE, ADOPTION PROMOTION LEGISLATION IN THE 105TH CONGRESS 1–4 (97–491, NOV. 1997)

* * *

More than half a million children are currently in foster care. Although the number of foster children has almost doubled since the mid 1980's, the number of these children who are adopted each year has remained at approximately 20,000 throughout this period. Most children who enter foster care eventually return to their families, but concern has developed in recent years about the growing number of children who cannot return home. This concern prompted the 105th Congress to consider legislation with two primary goals: (1) to ensure that consideration of children's safety is paramount in child welfare decisions, so that children are not returned to unsafe homes; and (2) to ensure that necessary legal procedures occur expeditiously, so that children may be placed for adoption or another permanent arrangement quickly and do not linger in foster care.

* * *

Most provisions in the new law [the Adoption and Safe Families Act] amend Titles IV–B and IV–E of the Social Security Act, which authorize grants to states for child welfare activities, including foster care and adoption assistance. To receive federal funds (almost $5 billion in

FY1998), states must comply with requirements designed to ensure that services are provided to the families of children who are at risk, so that children can remain safely with their families or return home after they have been placed in foster care. States also must conduct administrative and court hearings on every child's case according to a prescribed timetable, and establish a permanent placement plan for each child.

The Adoption and Safe Families Act establishes significant new procedural requirements to promote safety and expedite permanency, which the Congressional Budget Office (CBO) has estimated will save federal money by shortening the time that some children spend in foster care. At the same time, the new law also contains some spending provisions. These include financial incentive payments to states that increase their numbers of adoptions from foster care; a requirement that states provide health insurance to special needs adopted children who are not eligible for federal subsidies; a provision that continues eligibility for federal subsidies to special needs children whose adoptions are disrupted; and a reauthorization and expansion of the family preservation program under Title IV–B. CBO has estimated the net cost of P.L. 105–89 at $40 million over a 5–year period. To offset these costs, the law reduces spending for the contingency fund under the Temporary Assistance for Needy Families (TANF) block grant.

Child Safety and "Reasonable Efforts" to Preserve Families

The Adoption and Safe Families Act requires that a child's health and safety be of "paramount" concern in any efforts made by the state to preserve or reunify the child's family. States continue to be required to make "reasonable efforts" to avoid the need to place children in foster care, and to return them home if they are removed, but the new law establishes exceptions to this requirement. Specifically, states are not required to make efforts to preserve or reunify a family if a court finds that a parent had killed another of their children, or committed felony assault against the child or a sibling, or if their parental rights to another child had previously been involuntarily terminated.

In addition, the new law establishes that efforts to preserve or reunify a family are not required if the court finds that a parent had subjected the child to "aggravated circumstances." Each state will define these circumstances in state law, although the Act cites abandonment, torture, chronic abuse, and sexual abuse as examples. Moreover, the new law does not preclude judges from using their discretion to protect a child's health and safety in any case, regardless of whether the specific circumstances are cited in federal law.

* * *

"Reasonable Efforts" to Promote Adoption

If efforts to preserve or reunify a family are not required because the court has found that an exception to this requirement exists, as described above, the Adoption and Safe Families Act requires that a permanency hearing (formerly called "dispositional" hearing) be held for the child within 30 days of that court finding. In these cases, or whenever a child's permanency plan is adoption or another alternative to family reunification, the new law requires states to make reasonable efforts to place the child in a timely manner in accordance with the permanency plan, which may include placement for adoption, with a guardian, or in another planned permanent arrangement. States also must document specific efforts made to place the child for adoption. These provisions are intended to shorten the length of time that children spend in foster care, once a court has determined that family reunification is not feasible or likely.

The new law also specifies that efforts to preserve or reunify a family can be made concurrently with efforts to place the child for adoption or guardianship. This practice is referred to as "concurrent planning" and allows states to develop a back-up plan, to save time in case efforts to restore the original family are unsuccessful.

* * *

Permanency Hearings and Termination of Parental Rights

Prior to enactment of the Adoption and Safe Families Act, federal law required that every foster child must have a judicial hearing, known as "dispositional" hearing, within 18 months of their placement in care to determine their future status. The new law requires this hearing to occur within 12 months of placement, and changes the name to "permanency" hearing. The law revises the list of permanency goals (which had included long-term foster care) to include returning home, referral for adoption and termination of parental rights, guardianship, placement with a relative, or, as a last resort, another planned, permanent living arrangement. [The Act] also requires that foster parents, preadoptive parents, and relative caregivers be given notice and an opportunity to be heard at reviews and hearings.

One of the most significant provisions of the new law requires states to initiate proceedings to terminate parental rights (TPR) for certain foster children; there was no comparable provision in prior law. Specifically, [the Act] requires states to initiate TPR proceedings for children who have been in foster care for 15 of the most recent 22 months, or for infants determined under state law to be abandoned, or in any case where the court has found that a parent has killed another of their children or committed felony assault against the child or a sibling. States can opt *not* to initiate such proceedings if the child is in a relative's care, or if the state agency has documented in the child's case plan a compelling reason to determine that TPR would not be in the child's best interest, or if the state had not provided necessary services to the family.

* * *

SECTION 2.   THE COURT'S ROLE IN PERMANENCY
PLANNING

During the 1970's, child advocates became concerned about children left in foster care "limbo," not only having no permanent home, but also being moved from foster home to foster home. Multiple placements and the lack of a permanent family were considered harmful to children. The result was permanency planning, which was intended to move children out of foster care into permanent homes. Because of a loss of confidence in the ability of child welfare systems to manage foster care, courts were given a major role in insuring implementation of permanancy planning.

MARK HARDIN, CHILD PROTECTION CASES
IN A UNIFIED FAMILY COURT

32 Fam. L. Q. 147 (1998).

* * *

Permanency planning, as required under federal and state law, has redefined and expanded the role of the court in child protection cases. For example, to reinforce the obligations placed on caseworkers to try to avoid the need for placement, courts now determine whether workers had made reasonable efforts to prevent placement. Courts now conduct periodic hearings to oversee the agency's case plan for the child and to assure permanent placements of children in foster care. Courts must conduct hearings to make timely decisions whether to return children home or to place them in new legally permanent homes.

This national trend toward expanded judicial responsibilities in child protection cases has continued from the 1970s to the present. Throughout those years, there have been continuing amendments of federal and state laws and state and local court rules to add to judicial responsibilities. For example, as recently as November, 1997 new amendments [the Adoption and Safe Families Act] to federal law impose, among other things, stricter and earlier "permanency hearings" to shorten the length of stay in foster care.

As a result of continually expanding judicial responsibilities (and of enhanced procedural protections for parents and children), child protection cases have become more complex. Courts are now far more heavily involved in decision making for foster children than in the past. * * * As described below, the expanded court functions have also led to a more elaborate and distinctive court process in child protection cases.

Performance of these new functions in child protection cases results in far more court hearings in each case. [The figure that follows] illustrates the new hearings in child protection cases, contrasting current practice with common practice in 1976.

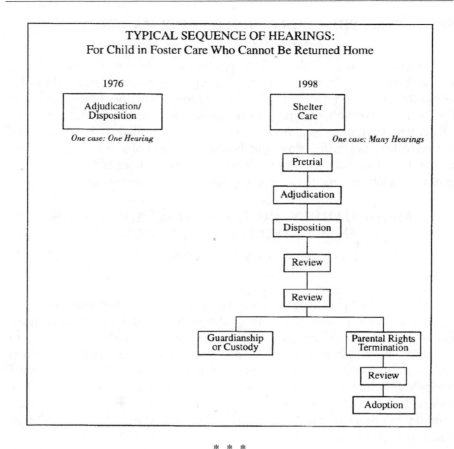

TYPICAL SEQUENCE OF HEARINGS:
For Child in Foster Care Who Cannot Be Returned Home

1976

Adjudication/
Disposition

One case: One Hearing

1998

Shelter
Care

One case: Many Hearings

Pretrial

Adjudication

Disposition

Review

Review

Guardianship
or Custody

Parental Rights
Termination

Review

Adoption

* * *

B.   Stages of the Court Process

* * *

Many courts now hold a separate "disposition hearing," following the adjudication (trial). The disposition hearing is an early stage of the court process in which the court determines who is to have custody (legal responsibility) of the child and what will be the plan to rehabilitate the parents and protect the child. While in the past, courts typically simply decided whether to transfer custody to the state and authorize foster care, courts are now expected to review the long-term goal and short term plan for the child. In many states, the court is expected to approve or modify a written case plan submitted by the child protection agency.

Agency case plans set forth, among other things, the goals of state intervention, tasks to be performed by parents and the child protection agency to achieve the goals, and timetables for their accomplishment. Case plans often identify the providers of various services for the child and family and address basic logistical issues in ensuring that the services be provided. In addition, they often set forth arrangements for parent-child visits and, where applicable, visits among siblings. Before permanency planning, not only was there no separate disposition hearing but also at the conclusion of the adjudication hearing the court would simply decide, without further discussion, whether or not to transfer custody of the child to the agency for placement into foster care.

After disposition, many state courts conduct periodic review hearings to ensure that a child does not remain too long in foster care. Federal law allows such hearings to be conducted either by courts or by other administrative bodies, including, but not limited to, child protection agencies. At minimum, whether conducted by agencies or courts, these hearings review progress under the current case plan, make corrections in the plan, and revise timetables to achieve case goals.

The frequency of progress review hearings varies. While judicial review hearings must take place at least every three months in a few states and at least every six months in some others, many states require them at longer intervals, alternating judicial and non judicial reviews. Before permanency planning, there were no regular judicial or other forms of reviews.

Federal law also requires a different type of post disposition hearing, now known as a "permanency hearing." The "permanency hearing" is designed to be a decision point by which the final direction of the case is decided. The permanency hearing was created because of the tendency of judges to be indecisive at routine progress review hearings, and of agencies to continue to pursue goals of family reunification for years.

Recent amendments to federal law are designed to tighten the timing and procedures in permanency hearings. For example, if a child has not been returned home by the time of the permanency hearing * * * and return continues to be unsafe, the permanency hearing now must decide on the new permanent goal for the child. In addition, if the judge decides that the new case goal is adoption, the judge is also to order the agency to file a petition to terminate parental rights. Thus, a permanency hearing must determine the permanent status of the child. This new federal requirement and others will place major new demands on courts hearing child protection cases and make the need for court reform even more pressing.

If a child cannot be returned home following the permanency hearing, there may be a termination of parental rights proceeding to free the child for adoption. In this hearing the court must decide whether there is clear and convincing evidence to support the statutory grounds for termination, basically to show that the child cannot safely return home. If legal grounds exist, the court must decide whether termination actually will benefit the child, e.g., whether adoption is a practical solution for the child. Following termination of parental rights, will be hearings concerning the child's adoption.

* * *

Notes and Questions

1. *Improving the courts.* Unfortunately courts and social service agencies frequently lack the resources necessary to cope with the increased responsibilities placed on them by new federal and state requirements. A recent U.S. Gen. Accounting Office study found that "[s]erious systemic problems continue to plague the juvenile dependency court system." The states studied reported:

> a lack of cooperation between the courts and child welfare agencies as well as difficult personnel and data management issues that jeopardize the courts' ability to ensure that a child's stay in the foster care system is as brief as possible and that the permanent placement decided upon is in the best overall interest of the child. Despite their shared involvement in the child welfare system, courts and child welfare agencies often do not work well together. For example, some judges mistrust the judgments of caseworkers and routinely order additional clinical assessments to compensate for what the judges perceive as professional inadequacies. In addition, courts face numerous difficulties, including increased caseloads, short tenures for judges and attorneys assigned to juvenile dependency courts, insufficient training of judges and attorneys in child welfare law and concepts, and information systems that do not adequately track the progress of individual cases or monitor the courts' compliance with statutory time frames for achieving permanent placements.

U.S. Gen. Accounting Office, Juvenile Courts: Reforms Aim to Better Serve Maltreated Children 2 (1999).

Fortunately, a number of states have initiated reforms to respond to court problems. Many of these reform efforts resulted from the National Council of Juvenile and Family Court Judges (NCJFCJ) Permanency Planning Project for Children, which began in 1980, primarily with private funds. Reform efforts are described in Mark Hardin, Judicial Implementation of Permanency Planning Reform: One Court that Works (1992) and Mark Hardin, et al., A Second Court that Works: Judicial Implementation of Permanency Planning Reforms (1995).

2. *Resource Guidelines.* As part of its continuing court improvement efforts, the NCJFCJ developed a bench book for judges, Resource Guidelines: Improving Court Practice in Child Abuse and Neglect Cases (1995). Judges, court administrators, attorneys and child welfare experts developed the Guidelines which were endorsed by the American Bar Association and the Conference of Chief Justices in 1995. NCJFC, Child Victims Project Model Courts Status Report, 1997–98.

3. *The need for effective intervention.* Is the emphasis on keeping families together wise, or would children be better off in foster care? In an effort to answer this question, law professor Michael Wald and his colleagues compared the physical, academic, social, and emotional development of abused and neglected children who remained in their homes to similar children who were placed in foster care. To their surprise, they did not find a clear indication that one approach was better than the other. What they did find, however, is more disturbing—namely that children in both settings had significant problems. They concluded that extensive, long-term services were

needed to assist abused and neglected children . They caution that "[u]nless we find more effective interventions and, even more important, ways of preventing abuse and neglect, many children will * * *continue 'weeping in the play time of others.' " Michael S. Wald, et al., Protecting Abused and Neglected Children 200 (1988). Because Wald's study involved only a small number of California children, its findings are tentative, but nonetheless valuable because of the extensive information collected on the children in the study. The authors also make a compelling case for the need for more interdisciplinary research on children.

4. *Criticisms of permanency planning.* The permanency planning model required by federal law has been criticized for exaggerating the harms caused by foster care and also for other reasons. Successful reunification often requires extensive, long-term services and when these are not provided the child is at risk. Critics also note that termination may harm children by depriving them of contact with their parents, and that many children "freed" for adoption are never placed successfully in adoptive homes. See Marsha Garrison, Parents' Rights vs. Children's Interests: The Case of the Foster Child, 22 N. Y. Rev. L. & Soc. Change 371 (1996).

Professor Garrison has proposed that termination based on length of stay in foster care should not be permitted until the child has been in foster care for at least three years. She notes that many parents regain their children within this time. In addition, since the availability of a permanent home is not a prerequisite for bringing a termination action, the child may not benefit from termination. Marsha Garrison, Child Welfare Decisionmaking: In Search of the Least Drastic Alternative, 75 Geo. L. J. 1745 (1987).

With the increased emphasis on permanency, the foster care rolls should include relatively few children waiting for adoptive homes after termination of parental rights. A study conducted after the passage of the Adoption Assistance and Child Welfare Act of 1980, however, determined that the number of children awaiting adoption had increased rather than decreased. Using foster care data from Michigan and New York, Professor Martin Guggenheim estimated the number of children in foster care who were available for adoption, but not yet adopted. In both states he found this number was substantially larger in 1992 than it was five years earlier. (He does not indicate whether the percentage increased, however.) For both states combined, he estimates that 9% of the total 1992 foster care population consists of children available for adoption. He recommended that:

> [P]arental rights ought to be terminated only when three conditions exist. First, there must be grounds for termination. Most states currently require a legal finding by clear and convincing evidence that, despite diligent efforts by an agency to reunify parent and child, reunification is not possible and the prospects for reunification in the future are so dim that the child's best interests require contemplating freeing the child for adoption. However, this ought to be only preconditional. In addition, courts should inquire into the child's best interests and not presume, merely because statutory grounds exist to terminate parental rights, the child's interests are served by doing so. A careful inquiry into the child's best interests should be conducted. If a court finds both that there are grounds to terminate and that the child's best interests would be served

by being adopted, then courts should reach the third condition for termination: adoptability. If the prospects for a child's adoption after termination are extremely poor or non-existent, an order of termination should rarely be entered.

Martin Guggenheim, The Effects of Recent Trends to Accelerate the Termination of Parental Rights of Children in Foster Care–An Empirical Analysis in Two States, 29 Fam. L. Q. 121, 136 (1995).

As discussed above, the Adoption and Safe Families Act of 1997 requires states to petition for termination of parental rights if the child has been in foster care for 15 of the most recent 22 months (with some exceptions). According to the GAO study, "[s]ome practitioners believe this provision will increase the number of termination of parental rights hearings that must be held as well as the overall court calendar time needed, since these hearings can take several days to conduct." U.S. Gen. Accounting Office, Juvenile Courts: Reforms Aim to Better Serve Maltreated Children 8 (1999). The Department of Health and Human Services estimated that approximately 34% of the children in foster care would be in this category as of March 1998. Id. The Act also provides incentives to the states to increase adoptions of foster children. For an extensive critique of the Act, see Robert M. Gordon, Drifting Through Byzantium: The Promise and Failure of the Adoption and Safe Families Act of 1997, 83 Minn. L. Rev. 637 (1999).

5. *The supply of foster parents.* While the number of children needing foster care has increased, the supply of foster parents unfortunately has decreased. One reason for the shortage is the low reimbursement foster parents receive. Foster care parents are paid an average of $8 to $15 per day, and in some states foster parents who are relatives of the child receive no payment. Additional reasons for the decrease in available foster homes are (1) that the foster children have significant physical and emotional problems and thus are more difficult to manage, (2) that support services are inadequate, and (3) that women have more employment opportunities outside the home than in the past. U.S. Gen. Accounting Office, Child Welfare: Complex Needs Strain Capacity to Provide Services (1995). One response to this shortage is to engage professional foster care parents who are paid a salary in addition to receiving board payments for their foster children. Typically these foster parents would provide specialized foster care, "care of children with behavioral, developmental, or medical needs above and beyond those of average children in out-of-home care." Mark F. Testa and Nancy Rolock, Professional Foster Care: A Future Worth Pursuing?, 78 Child Welfare 108 (1999).

6. *The perspective of foster children.* For descriptions of foster care from the foster child's perspective, see Survivors of the System: Foster Child United at <http://www.azstarnet.com/~marier/sos/index1.html>.

7. *Additional references.* Foster Children in the Courts (Mark Hardin, ed. 1980); Robert H. Mnookin, Foster Care—In Whose Best Interests? 43 Harv. Educ. Rev. 599 (1973).

SECTION 3.   THE CHILD'S RIGHT TO A "FAMILY"

SMITH v. ORGANIZATION OF FOSTER FAMILIES FOR EQUALITY AND REFORM

Supreme Court of the United States, 1977.
431 U.S. 816.

MR. JUSTICE BRENNAN delivered the opinion of the Court.

Appellees, individual foster parents[1] and an organization of foster parents, brought this civil rights class action pursuant to 42 U.S.C. § 1983 * * * on their own behalf and on behalf of children for whom they have provided homes for a year or more. They sought declaratory and injunctive relief against New York State and New York City officials, alleging that the procedures governing the removal of foster children from foster homes * * * violated the Due Process and Equal Protection Clauses of the Fourteenth Amendment. The District Court appointed independent counsel for the foster children to forestall any possibility of conflict between their interests and the interests asserted by the foster parents. A group of natural mothers of children in foster care[5] were

1. Appellee Madeleine Smith is the foster parent with whom Eric and Danielle Gandy have been placed since 1970. The Gandy children, who are now 12 and 9 years old respectively, were voluntarily placed in foster care by their natural mother in 1968, and have had no contact with her at least since being placed with Mrs. Smith. The foster-care agency has sought to remove the children from Mrs. Smith's care because her arthritis, in the agency's judgment makes it difficult for her to continue to provide adequate care. A foster-care review proceeding * * * resulted in an order, subsequent to the decision of the District Court, directing that foster care be continued and apparently contemplating, though not specifically ordering, that the children will remain in Mrs. Smith's care.

Appellees Ralph and Christiane Goldberg were the foster parents of Rafael Serrano, now 14. His parents placed him in foster care voluntarily in 1969 after an abuse complaint was filed against them. It is alleged that the agency supervising the placement had informally indicated to Mr. and Mrs. Goldberg that it intended to transfer Rafael to the home of his aunt in contemplation of permanent placement. This effort has apparently failed. A petition for foster-care review * * * filed by the agency alleges that the Goldbergs are now separated, Mrs. Goldberg having moved out of the house, taking her own child but leaving Rafael. The child is now in a residential treatment center, where Mr. Goldberg continues to visit him.

Appellees Walter and Dorothy Lhotan were foster parents of the four Wallace sisters, who were voluntarily placed in foster care by their mother in 1970. The two older girls were placed with the Lhotans in that year, their two younger sisters in 1972. In June 1974, the Lhotans were informed that the agency had decided to return the two younger girls to their mother and transfer the two older girls to another foster home. The agency apparently felt that the Lhotans were too emotionally involved with the girls and were damaging the agency's efforts to prepare them to return to their mother. The state courts have ordered that all the Wallace children be returned to their mother. We are told that the children have been returned and are adjusting successfully.

5. Intervenor Naomi Rodriguez, who is blind, placed her newborn son Edwin in foster care in 1973 because of marital difficulties. When Mrs. Rodriguez separated from her husband three months later, she sought return of her child. Her efforts over the next nine months to obtain return of the child were resisted by the agency, apparently because it felt her handicap prevented her from providing adequate care. Eventually, she sought return of her child in the state courts, and finally prevailed, three years after she first sought return of the child. The other named intervenors describe similar instances of voluntary placements during family emergencies followed by lengthy and frustrating attempts to get their children back.

granted leave to intervene on behalf of themselves and others similarly situated.

A divided three-judge District Court concluded that "the pre-removal procedures presently employed by the State are constitutionally defective," holding that "before a foster child can be peremptorily transferred from the foster home in which he has been living, be it to another foster home or to the natural parents who initially placed him in foster care, he is entitled to a hearing at which all concerned parties may present any relevant information to the administrative decisionmaker charged with determining the future placement of the child" * * * We reverse.

I

A detailed outline of the New York statutory system regulating foster care is a necessary preface to a discussion of the constitutional questions presented.

A

The expressed central policy of the New York system is that "it is generally desirable for the child to remain with or be returned to the natural parent because the child's need for a normal family life will usually best be met in the natural home, and . . . parents are entitled to bring up their own children unless the best interests of the child would be thereby endangered." But the State has opted for foster care as one response to those situations where the natural parents are unable to provide the "positive, nurturing family relationships" and "normal family life in a permanent home" that offer "the best opportunity for children to develop and thrive."

Foster care has been defined as "[a] child welfare service which provides substitute family care for a planned period for a child when his own family cannot care for him for a temporary or extended period, and when adoption is neither desirable nor possible." Thus, the distinctive features of foster care are, first, "that it is care in a *family*, it is noninstitutional substitute care," and, second, "that it is for a *planned* period either temporary or extended. This is unlike adoptive placement, which implies a *permanent* substitution of one home for another."

Under the New York scheme children may be placed in foster care either by voluntary placement or by court order. Most foster care placements are voluntary. They occur when physical or mental illness, economic problems, or other family crises make it impossible for natural parents, particularly single parents, to provide a stable home life for their children for some limited period. Resort to such placements is almost compelled when it is not possible in such circumstance to place the child with a relative or friend, or to pay for the services of a homemaker or boarding school.

Voluntary placement requires the signing of a written agreement by the natural parent or guardian, transferring the care and custody of the child to an authorized child welfare agency. Although by statute the terms of such agreements are open to negotiation, it is contended that agencies require execution of standardized forms. The agreement may provide for return of the child to the natural parent at a specified date or upon occurrence of a particular event, and if it does not, the child must be returned by the agency, in the absence of a court order, within 20 days of notice from the parent.

The agency may maintain the child in an institutional setting, but more commonly acts under its authority to "place out and board out" children in foster homes. Foster parents, who are licensed by the State or an authorized foster-care agency, provide care under a contractual arrangement with the agency, and are compensated for their services. The typical contract expressly reserves the right of the agency to remove the child on request. Conversely, the foster parent may cancel the agreement at will.

The New York system divides parental functions among agency, foster parents, and natural parents, and the definitions of the respective roles are often complex and often unclear. The law transfers "care and custody" to the agency, but day-to-day supervision of the child and his activities, and most of the functions ordinarily associated with legal custody, are the responsibility of the foster parent. Nevertheless, agency supervision of the performance of the foster parents takes forms indicating that the foster parent does not have the full authority of a legal custodian.[18] Moreover, the natural parent's placement of the child with the agency does not surrender legal guardianship, the parent retains authority to act with respect to the child in certain circumstances. The natural parent has not only the right but the obligation to visit the foster child and plan for his future; failure of a parent with capacity to fulfill the obligation for more than a year can result in a court order terminating the parent's rights on the ground of neglect.

Children may also enter foster care by court order. The Family Court may order that a child be placed in the custody of an authorized child-care agency * * * if it is found that the child has been abused or neglected by his natural parents. In addition, a minor adjudicated a juvenile delinquent, or "person in need of supervision" may be placed by the court with an agency. The consequences of foster-care placement by court order do not differ substantially from those for children voluntarily placed, except that the parent is not entitled to return of the child on demand * * *; termination of foster care must then be consented to by the court.

---

18. "The agency sets limits and advances directives as to how the foster parents are to behave toward the child—a situation not normally encountered by natural parents. The shared control and responsibility for the child is clearly set forth in the instruction pamphlets issued to foster parents." Agencies frequently prohibit corporal punishment; require that children over a certain age be given an allowance; forbid changes in the child's sleeping arrangements or vacations out of State without agency approval; require the foster parent to discuss the child's behavioral problems with the agency. Furthermore, since the cost of supporting the child is borne by the agency, the responsibility, as well as the authority, of the foster parent is shared with the agency.

B

The provisions of the scheme specifically at issue in this litigation come into play when the agency having legal custody determines to remove the foster child from the foster home, either because it has determined that it would be in the child's best interests to transfer him to some other foster home, or to return the child to his natural parents in accordance with the statute or placement agreement. Most children are removed in order to be transferred to another foster home. The procedures by which foster parents may challenge a removal made for that purpose differ somewhat from those where the removal is made to return the child to his natural parent.

[Soc. Serv. Law §] 383(2) provides that the "authorized agency placing out or boarding [a foster] child . . . may in its discretion remove such child from the home where placed or boarded." Administrative regulations implement this provision. The agency is required, except in emergencies, to notify the foster parents in writing 10 days in advance of any removal. The notice advises the foster parents that if they object to the child's removal they may request a "conference" with the Social Services Department. The department schedules requested conferences within 10 days of the receipt of the request. The foster parent may appear with counsel at the conference, where he will "be advised of the reasons [for the removal of the child], and be afforded an opportunity to submit reasons why the child should not be removed." The official must render a decision in writing within five days after the close of the conference, and send notice of his decision to the foster parents and the agency. The proposed removal is stayed pending the outcome of the conference.

If the child is removed after the conference, the foster parent may appeal to the Department of Social Services for a "fair hearing," that is, a full adversary administrative hearing, * * * the determination of which is subject to judicial review * * *; however, the removal is not automatically stayed pending the hearing and judicial review.

This statutory and regulatory scheme applies statewide. In addition, regulations promulgated by the New York City Human Resources Administration, Department of Social Services Special Services for Children (SSC) provide even greater procedural safeguards there. * * *

One further preremoval procedural safeguard is available. Under Soc.Serv.Law § 392, the Family Court has jurisdiction to review, on petition of the foster parent or the agency, the status of any child who has been in foster care for 18 months or longer.* * *

C

Foster care of children is a sensitive and emotion-laden subject, and foster-care programs consequently stir strong controversy. The New York regulatory scheme is no exception. New York would have us view the scheme as described in its brief:

"Today New York premises its foster care system on the accepted principle that the placement of a child into foster care is solely a temporary, transitional action intended to lead to the future reunion of the child with his natural parent or parents, or if such a reunion is not possible, to legal adoption and the establishment of a new permanent home for the child."

Some of the parties and *amici* argue that this is a misleadingly idealized picture. They contend that a very different perspective is revealed by the empirical criticism of the system presented in the record of this case and confirmed by published studies of foster care.

From the standpoint of natural parents, such as the appellant intervenors here, foster care has been condemned as a class-based intrusion into the family life of the poor. It is certainly true that the poor resort to foster care more often than other citizens. For example, over 50% of all children in foster care in New York City are from female-headed families receiving Aid to Families with Dependent Children. Minority families are also more likely to turn to foster care; 52.3% of the children in foster care in New York City are black and 25.5% are Puerto Rican. This disproportionate resort to foster care by the poor and victims of discrimination doubtless reflects in part the greater likelihood of disruption of poverty-stricken families. Commentators have also noted, however, that middle-and upper-income families who need temporary care services for their children have the resources to purchase private care. The poor have little choice but to submit to state-supervised child care when family crises strike.

The extent to which supposedly "voluntary" placements are in fact voluntary has been questioned on other grounds as well. For example, it has been said that many "voluntary" placements are in fact coerced by threat of neglect proceedings and are not in fact voluntary in the sense of the product of an informed consent. Studies also suggest that social workers of middle-class backgrounds, perhaps unconsciously, incline to favor continued placement in foster care with a generally higher-status family rather than return the child to his natural family, thus reflecting a bias that treats the natural parents' poverty and lifestyle as prejudicial to the best interests of the child. This accounts, it has been said, for the hostility of agencies to the efforts of natural parents to obtain the return of their children.

Appellee foster parents as well as natural parents question the accuracy of the idealized picture portrayed by New York. They note that children often stay in "temporary" foster care for much longer than contemplated by the theory of the system. The District Court found as a fact that the median time spent in foster care in New York was over four years. Indeed, many children apparently remain in this "limbo" indefinitely. The District Court also found that the longer a child remains in foster care, the more likely it is that he will never leave: "[T]he probability of a foster child being returned to his biological parents declined markedly after the first year in foster care." It is not surprising then that many children, particularly those that enter foster care at a very early age and have little or no contact with their natural parents during extended stays in foster care, often develop deep emotional ties with their foster parents.

Yet such ties do not seem to be regarded as obstacles to transfer of the child from one foster placement to another. The record in this case indicates that nearly 60% of the children in foster care in New York City have experienced more than one placement, and about 28% have experienced three or more. The intended stability of the foster-home management is further damaged by the rapid turnover among social work professionals who supervise the foster-care arrangements on behalf of the State. Moreover, even when it is clear that a foster child will not be returned to his natural parents, it is rare that he achieves a stable home life through final termination of parental ties and adoption into a new permanent family.

The parties and amici devote much of their discussion to these criticisms of foster care, and we present this summary in the view that some understanding of those criticisms is necessary for a full appreciation of the complex and controversial system with which this lawsuit is concerned. But the issue presented by the case is a narrow one. Arguments asserting the need for reform of New York's statutory scheme are properly addressed to the New York Legislature. The relief sought in this case is entirely procedural. Our task is only to determine whether the District Court correctly held that the present procedures preceding the removal from a foster home of children resident there a year or more are constitutionally inadequate. To that task we now turn.

II

A

Our first inquiry is whether appellees have asserted interests within the Fourteenth Amendment's protection of "liberty" * * *.

* * *

The appellees' basic contention is that when a child has lived in a foster home for a year or more, a psychological tie is created between the child and the foster parents which constitutes the foster family the true "psychological family" of the child. That family, they argue, has a "liberty interest" in its survival as a family protected by the Fourteenth Amendment. Upon this premise they conclude that the foster child cannot be removed without a prior hearing satisfying due process. Appointed counsel for the children, however, disagrees, and has consistently argued that the foster parents have no such liberty interest independent of the interests of the foster children, and that the best interests of the children would not be served by procedural protections beyond those already provided by New York law. The intervening natural parents of children in foster care, also oppose the foster parents, arguing that recognition of the procedural right claimed would undercut both the substantive family law of New York, which favors the return of children to their natural parents as expeditiously as possible, and their constitutionally protected right of family privacy, by forcing them to submit to a hearing and defend their rights to their children before the children could be returned to them.

* * *

* * * "[T]o determine whether due process requirements apply in the first place, we must look not to the 'weight' but to the nature of the interest at stake.... We must look to see if the interest is within the Fourteenth Amendment's protection of liberty and property."

We therefore turn to appellees' assertion that they have a constitutionally protected liberty interest—in the words of the District Court, a "right to familial privacy,"—in the integrity of their family unit. This assertion clearly presents difficulties.

B

It is, of course, true that "freedom of personal choice in matters of ... family life is one of the liberties protected by the Due Process Clause of the Fourteenth Amendment." Cleveland Board of Education v. La-Fleur (1974). There does exist a "private realm of family life which the state cannot enter," Prince v. Massachusetts, (1944), that has been afforded both substantive and procedural protection. But is the relation of foster parent to foster child sufficiently akin to the concept of "family" recognized in our precedents to merit similar protection? Although considerable difficulty has attended the task of defining "family" for purposes of the Due Process Clause, we are not without guides to some of the elements that define the concept of "family" and contribute to its place in our society.

First, the usual understanding of "family" implies biological relationships, and most decisions treating the relation between parent and child have stressed this element. * * * And Prince v. Massachusetts, stated:

> "It is cardinal with us that the custody, care and nurture of the child reside first in the parents, whose primary function and freedom include preparation for obligations the state can neither supply nor hinder."

A biological relationship is not present in the case of the usual foster family. But biological relationships are not exclusive determination of the existence of a family. The basic foundation of the family in our society, the marriage relationship, is of course not a matter of blood relation. Yet its importance has been strongly emphasized in our cases:

> "We deal with a right of privacy older than the Bill of Rights—older than our political parties, older than our school system. Marriage is a coming together for better or for worse, hopefully enduring, and intimate to the degree of being sacred. It is an association that promotes a way of life, not causes; a harmony in living, not political faiths; a bilateral loyalty, not commercial or social projects. Yet it is

an association for as noble a purpose as any involved in our prior decisions." Griswold v. Connecticut, (1965).

Thus the importance of the familial relationship, to the individuals involved and to the society, stems from the emotional attachments that derive from the intimacy of daily association, and from the role it plays in "promot[ing] a way of life" through the instruction of children, Wisconsin v. Yoder (1972), as well as from the fact of blood relationship. No one would seriously dispute that a deeply loving and interdependent relationship between an adult and a child in his or her care may exist even in the absence of blood relationship. At least where a child has been placed in foster care as an infant, has never known his natural parents, and has remained continuously for several years in the care of the same foster parents, it is natural that the foster family should hold the same place in the emotional life of the foster child, and fulfill the same socializing functions, as a natural family.[52] For this reason, we cannot dismiss the foster family as a mere collection of unrelated individuals. Cf. Village of Belle Terre v. Boraas, (1974).

But there are also important distinctions between the foster family and the natural family. First, unlike the earlier cases recognizing a right to family privacy, the State here seeks to interfere, not with a relationship having its origins entirely apart from the power of the State, but rather with a foster family which has its source in state law and contractual arrangements. * * * Here, however, whatever emotional ties may develop between foster parent and foster child have their origins in an arrangement in which the State has been a partner from the outset. While the Court has recognized that liberty interests may in some cases arise from positive-law sources, in such a case, and particularly where, as here, the claimed interest derives from a knowingly assumed contractual relation with the State, it is appropriate to ascertain from state law the expectations and entitlements of the parties. In this case, the limited recognition accorded to the foster family by the New York statutes and the contracts executed by the foster parents argue against any but the most limited constitutional "liberty" in the foster family.

A second consideration related to this is that ordinarily procedural protection may be afforded to a liberty interest of one person without derogating from the substantive liberty of another. Here, however, such a tension is virtually unavoidable. Under New York law, the natural parent of a foster child in voluntary placement has an absolute right to the return of his child in the absence of a court order obtainable only

---

52. The briefs dispute at some length the validity of the "psychological parent" theory propounded in J. Goldstein, A. Freud, & A. Solnit, Beyond the Best Interests of the Child (1973). That book, on which appellee foster parents relied to some extent in the District Court, is indeed controversial. See, e. g., Strauss & Strauss, Book Review, 74 Colum.L.Rev. 996 (1974); Kadushin, Beyond the Best Interests of the Child: An Essay Review, 48 Soc.Serv.Rev. 508, 512 (1974). But this case turns, not on the disputed validity of any particular psychological theory, but on the legal consequences of the undisputed fact that the emotional ties between foster parent and foster child are in many cases quite close, and undoubtedly in some as close as those existing in biological families.

upon compliance with rigorous substantive and procedural standards, which reflect the constitutional protection accorded the natural family. Moreover, the natural parent initially gave up his child to the State only on the express understanding that the child would be returned in those circumstances. These rights are difficult to reconcile with the liberty interest in the foster family relationship claimed by appellees. It is one thing to say that individuals may acquire a liberty interest against arbitrary governmental interference in the family-like associations into which they have freely entered, even in the absence of biological connection or state-law recognition of the relationship. It is quite another to say that one may acquire such an interest in the face of another's constitutionally recognized liberty interest that derives from blood relationship, state-law sanction, and basic human right an interest the foster parent has recognized by contract from the outset. Whatever liberty interest might otherwise exist in the foster family as an institution, that interest must be substantially attenuated where the proposed removal from the foster family is to return the child to his natural parents.

As this discussion suggests, appellees' claim to a constitutionally protected liberty interest raises complex and novel questions. It is unnecessary for us to resolve those questions definitively in this case, however, for like the District Court, we conclude that "narrower grounds exist to support" our reversal. We are persuaded that, even on the assumption that appellees have a protected "liberty interest," the District Court erred in holding that the preremoval procedures presently employed by the State are constitutionally defective.

III

Where procedural due process must be afforded because a "liberty" or "property" interest is within the Fourteenth Amendment's protection, there must be determined "what process is due" in the particular context. * * *

It is true that "[b]efore a person is deprived of a protected interest, he must be afforded opportunity for some kind of a hearing * * *." Only last Term, the Court held that "identification of the specific dictates of due process generally requires consideration of three distinct factors: First, the private interest that will be affected by the official action; second, the risk of an erroneous deprivation of such interest through the procedures used, and the probable value, if any, of additional or substitute procedural safeguards; and finally, the Government's interest, including the function involved and the fiscal and administrative burdens that the additional or substitute procedural requirement would entail." Mathews v. Eldridge, (1976). Consideration of the procedures employed by the State and New York City in light of these three factors requires the conclusion that those procedures satisfy constitutional standards.

Turning first to the procedure applicable in New York City, [the regulation] provides that before a child is removed from a foster home for transfer to another foster home, the foster parents may request an "independent review." * * * Such a procedure would appear to give a more elaborate trial-type hearing to foster families than this Court has found required in other contexts of administrative determinations. The District Court found the procedure inadequate on four grounds, none of which we find sufficient to justify the holding that the procedure violates due process.

First, the court held that the "independent review" administrative proceeding was insufficient because it was only available on the request of the foster parents. In the view of the District Court, the proceeding should be provided as a matter of course, because the interests of the foster parents and those of the child would not necessarily be coextensive, and it could not be assumed that the foster parents would invoke the hearing procedure in every case in which it was in the child's interest to have a hearing. Since the child is unable to request a hearing on his own, automatic review in every case is necessary. We disagree. As previously noted, the constitutional liberty, if any, sought to be protected by the New York procedures is a right of family privacy or autonomy, and the basis for recognition of any such interest in the foster family must be that close emotional ties analogous to those between parent and child are established when a child resides for a lengthy period with a foster family. If this is so, necessarily we should expect that the foster parents will seek to continue the relationship to preserve the stability of the family; if they do not request a hearing, it is difficult to see what right or interest of the foster child is protected by holding a hearing to determine whether removal would unduly impair his emotional attachments to a foster parent who does not care enough about the child to contest the removal. * * * Moreover, automatic provision of hearings as required by the District Court would impose a substantial additional administrative burden on the State. * * *

Second, the District Court faulted the city procedure on the ground that participation is limited to the foster parents and the agency and the natural parent and the child are not made parties to the hearing. This is not fatal in light of the nature of the alleged constitutional interests at stake. When the child's transfer from one foster home to another is pending, the interest arguably requiring protection is that of the foster family, not that of the natural parents. * * *

Much the same can be said in response to the District Court's statement:

> "[I]t may be advisable, under certain circumstances, for the agency to appoint an adult representative better to articulate the interests of the child. In making this determination, the agency should carefully consider the child's age, sophistication and ability effectively to communicate his own true feelings."

But nothing in the New York City procedure prevents consultation of the child's wishes, directly or through an adult intermediary. We assume, moreover, that some such consultation would be among the first steps that a rational factfinder, inquiring into the child's best interests, would pursue. Such consultation, however, does not require that the child or an appointed representative must be a party with full adversary powers in all preremoval hearings.

The other two defects in the city procedure found by the District Court must also be rejected. One is that the procedure does not extend to the removal of a child from foster care to be returned to his natural parent. But as we have already held, whatever liberty interest may be argued to exist in the foster family is significantly weaker in the case of removals preceding return to the natural parent, and the balance of due process interests must accordingly be different. * * *

* * *

Outside New York City, where only statewide procedures apply, foster parents are provided not only with the procedures of a preremoval conference and postremoval hearing * * * but also with the preremoval *judicial* hearing available on request to foster parents who have in their care children who have been in foster care for 18 months or more, Soc. Serv. L § 392. * * *

* * * We do not think that the 18–month limitation on § 392 actions renders the New York scheme constitutionally inadequate. The assumed liberty interest to be protected in this case is one rooted in the emotional attachments that develop over time between a child and the adults who care for him. But there is no reason to assume that those attachments ripen at less than 18 months or indeed at any precise point. Indeed, testimony in the record, as well as material in published psychological tests, suggests that the amount of time necessary for the development of the sort of tie appellees seek to protect varies considerably depending on the age and previous attachments of the child. * * * If New York sees 18 months rather than 12 as the time at which temporary foster care begins to turn into a more permanent and family-like setting requiring procedural protection and/or judicial inquiry into the propriety of continuing foster care, it would take far more than this record provides to justify a finding of constitutional infirmity in New York's choice.

* * *

Finally, the § 392 hearing is available to foster parents, both in and outside New York City, even where the removal sought is for the purpose of returning the child to his natural parents. Since this remedy provides a sufficient constitutional preremoval hearing to protect whatever liberty interest might exist in the continued existence of the foster family when the State seeks to transfer the child to another foster home, a fortiori the procedure is adequate to protect the lesser interest of the foster family in remaining together at the expense of the disruption of the natural family.

We deal here with issues of unusual delicacy, in an area where professional judgments regarding desirable procedures are constantly and rapidly changing. In such a context, restraint is appropriate on the part of courts called upon to adjudicate whether a particular procedural scheme is adequate under the Constitution. Since we hold that the procedures provided * * * are adequate to protect whatever liberty interest appellees may have, the judgment of the District Court is

Reversed.

MR. JUSTICE STEWART, with whom THE CHIEF JUSTICE and MR. JUSTICE REHNQUIST join, concurring in the judgment.

The foster parent-foster child relationship involved in this litigation is, of course, wholly a creation of the State. New York law defines the circumstances under which a child may be placed in foster care, prescribes the obligations of the foster parents, and provides for the removal of the child from the foster home "in [the] discretion" of the agency with custody of the child. The agency compensates the foster parents, and reserves in its contracts the authority to decide as it sees fit whether and when a child shall be returned to his natural family or placed elsewhere. Were it not for the system of foster care that the State maintains, the relationship for which constitutional protection is asserted would not even exist.

The New York Legislature and the New York courts have made it unmistakably clear that foster care is intended only as a temporary way station until a child can be returned to his natural parents or placed for adoption.* * *

In these circumstances, I cannot understand why the Court thinks itself obliged to decide these cases on the assumption that either foster parents or foster children in New York have some sort of "liberty" interest in the continuation of their relationship. Rather than tiptoeing around this central issue, I would squarely hold that the interests asserted by the appellees are not of a kind that the Due Process Clause of the Fourteenth Amendment protects.

* * *

Notes and Questions

1. *Questions about* OFFER. (a) How does the state portray the foster care system? How does this portrayal differ from the one offered by the parents and foster parents? (b) What is the "liberty" interest that the foster parents assert and what is its basis? (c) Do foster children have an interest in a hearing independent of their foster parents' interest? (d) When would a hearing be constitutionally required? If a child had lived with a foster parent for two years, would a hearing be constitutionally required before the state could transfer the child to another foster home? What if the child was being returned to a parent following a two-year voluntary placement?

2. *Background.* Smith v. OFFER was filed by Marcia Lowry of the Children's Rights Project of the New York Civil Liberties Union. The case was studied extensively by Professors David Chambers and Michael Wald as part of a larger study of the use of test-case litigation to promote children's welfare. Chambers and Wald discovered that the case began because of foster

mother Madeleine Smith's persistence, and they recorded how she managed to get representation:

> Madeline Smith is a black woman in her fifties who lives on the second story of an old rowhouse in Queens under the plane traffic of LaGuardia Airport. In February 1970, not long after the death of a daughter who was in her twenties, Mrs. Smith learned about foster parenting and approached the Catholic Guardian Society, a private agency authorized by the City to place children. Mrs. Smith suffered from arthritis in her legs but was interested in providing a home for young children she might eventually adopt. The Guardian Society arranged for the placement with her of two black children, Eric and Danielle Gandy. Danielle was almost two; Eric was four. Eric was believed to be slightly retarded; there was also some evidence that he had been abused in an earlier placement. Both had lived in a series of institutions and foster homes since birth. Mrs. Smith took them into her home and for the next three and a half years cared for them together with her adolescent grandson. Some time after Eric and Danielle came into her home, Mrs. Smith took in a third foster child from another family.

> In Mrs. Smith's view, the Gandy children thrived. She was their "Ma." In the late fall of 1973, however, Mrs. Graber, a new agency worker, concluded that Mrs. Smith's arthritis had become so severe that she could no longer care adequately for the children. A doctor for Mrs. Smith had in fact certified her as disabled for the purposes of government benefits. Mrs. Graber claimed that one result of Mrs. Smith's crippled condition was that the home was not clean enough. Mrs. Smith believes that it was not her arthritis or her house-cleaning, but, at least in part, her refusal to be sufficiently deferential to Mrs. Graber that prompted the decision. In any event, the third child was removed from the home. Mrs. Smith protested this removal to the City agency, but following an informal hearing, the decision was upheld.

> After deliberating for some time, the Catholic Guardian Society decided to remove the Gandy children as well. The Accountability Team for the New York City Department of Children's Services, which had responsibility for reviewing these decisions, concurred. To this day, some workers from the City believe that the decision to remove was sensible. The Society then ordered Mrs. Smith to prepare the children to leave within a few days.

> Mrs. Smith had known that her social worker was deliberating about he removal. During this period, she learned about the Children's Rights Project and started calling Lowry's office. However, Lowry did not become involved until the decision to remove had been made. She recalls:

>> My secretary at this point kept coming in and saying, "Well, there's this really nice lady on the phone and she thinks that the Agency is after her or something, and what can we do?" And I said, "Well, we don't take individual cases but refer her to Legal Services." And she kept calling back when that didn't work out. Finally one day she called and she spoke to my secretary and she said, "I've gone to court and I've asked for an adjournment so I can get a

lawyer, but the Agency has told me they're going to take the children this week and I'm just frantic."... My secretary, who screened out a lot of calls and had very good sense, said to me, "You really have to do something".... So I spoke to Mrs. Smith.

That was the critical moment. We too have met Mrs. Smith. It seems quite unlikely that anyone could speak to this powerful, loving woman and say "no." She is energetic, competent, and has an infectious personality. She conveys a deep love and understanding of Eric and Danielle. When she spoke to Lowry, she was absolutely determined to keep "her babies." The question for Lowry was not whether to help but how.

David L. Chambers and Michael S. Wald, Smith v. OFFER, in Robert H. Mnookin, In the Interests of Children 78–79 (1985).

The *OFFER* case had a happy ending for the Gandy children. The agency decided not to remove the children from Mrs. Smith, and she was allowed to adopt them in 1971.

3. *The children's counsel.* Ironically, Lowry ended up representing the foster parents, rather than the children, because the trial judge decided that the children needed separate counsel. Over Lowry's objection, the judge appointed Helen Buttenweiser, who had strong ties to private foster care agencies, to represent the seven named foster children and the class of children who had been in foster care for more than one year, a class which included thousands of children.

What position should the children's attorney, Buttenweiser, have taken and how should she have arrived at that position? In their extensive study of *OFFER*, Chambers and Wald suggest that she had several choices:

> She could have investigated closely the cases of the three foster families who were plaintiffs, interviewed the seven children (the two Gandy children, the Serrano child, and the four Wallace girls) and either advocated the positions they desired or advocated what she concluded was in their best interests. Second, she could have ignored the particular named children and advocated what she determined was in the best interests of the general run of children in long-term foster care. Third, she could have a middle course—bringing to the court the needs (or desires) of the seven particular children as well as her view of the needs of the thousands of others. Or, finally, she could have abstained from advocating any position at all and have simply adopted the role of ensuring that the court had before it all the relevant considerations.

> At the time of appointing Buttenwieser, Judge Carter gave her no guidance as to which of these roles he expected her to serve. Without hesitation she adopted the second course of speaking for the generality of children in foster care, regardless of their proposed destination. Her thirty years' experience told her what she believed she needed to know about foster children's needs in this setting and the position she should take. * * *[S]he did not meet then—or later—with her seven named clients, deciding that it would be a "trap" to become embroiled in arguing about the fates of a few children when the real issues at stake were so much broader.

Id. at 92–93.

4. *The children's interest.* How could the foster parents have standing to rely on a right of the foster children to a liberty interest in their foster family, if the children's counsel has said that the children do not have such a right and oppose the relief that the foster parents want? The Court answered this question in footnote 44:

> This argument misunderstands the peculiar circumstances of this lawsuit. Ordinarily, it is true, a party would not have standing to assert the rights of another, himself a party in the litigation; the third party himself can decide how best to protect his interests. But children usually lack the capacity to make that sort of decision, and thus their interest is ordinarily represented in litigation by parents or guardians. In this case, however, the State, the natural parents, and the foster parents, all of whom share some portion of the responsibility for guardianship of the child, are parties, and all contend that the position they advocate is most in accord with the rights and interests of the children. In this situation, the District Court properly appointed independent counsel to represent the children, so that the court could have the benefit of an independent advocate for the welfare of the children, unprejudiced by the possibly conflicting interests and desires of the other parties. It does not follow, however, that that independent counsel, who is not a guardian *ad litem* of the children, is solely authorized to determine the children's best interest.

> * * * We believe it would be most imprudent to leave entirely to court-appointed counsel the choices that neither the named foster children nor the class they represent are capable of making for themselves, especially in litigation in which all parties have sufficient attributes of guardianship that their views on the rights of the children should at least be heard.

5. *Voluntary placements.* The *OFFER* record indicated that as many as 80% of the children in foster care in New York City were voluntarily placed. What sorts of parents might voluntarily place their children in foster care? In footnote 10 the Court suggested an answer:

> [T]ypical parents in this situation might be "[a] divorced parent in a financial bind, an unwed adolescent mother still too immature to rear a child, or a welfare mother confronted with hospitalization and therefore temporarily incapable of caring for her child." A leading text on child-care services suggests that "[f]amily disruption, marginal economic circumstances, and poor health" are principal factors leading to placement of children in foster care. Other studies suggest, however, that neglect, abuse, abandonment and exploitation of children, which presumably account for most of the children who enter foster care by court order, are also involved in many cases of voluntary placement.

As *OFFER* notes, "voluntary" placements may actually be the result of coercion by departments of social services. Under the Adoption Assistance and Child Welfare Act, even voluntary placements must be reviewed by a court if they extend past specified time limits.

6. *Psychological parent. OFFER* footnote 52 mentions that the parties disputed the validity of the "psychological parent" theory presented in Beyond the Best Interests of the Child. (For the definition of "psychological parent," see note 3 on page 190.) The concept of psychological parent can arise in termination of parental rights cases when a child has lived for a substantial period with a foster parent and develops a strong emotional attachment to the foster parent. Should a child's strong attachment to a foster parent be a basis for terminating parental rights? In addressing this question, the New Jersey Supreme Court stated that: "In cases in which [the state] seeks termination of parental rights, not on grounds of current unfitness but because of potential harm to the child based on separation from a foster parent with whom the child has bonded, the quality of the proof adduced must be consistent with the interests at stake. * * * To show that the child has a strong relationship with the foster parent or might be better off if left in their custody is not enough. [The state] must prove by clear and convincing evidence that separating the child from his or her foster parents would cause serious and enduring emotional or psychological harm." In re J.C., J.C., and J.M.C., 608 A. 2d 1312, 1320 (N.J.1992). The court used this stringent test in part because of controversy over the validity of the psychological parent concept and concern about its misuse to favor agencies and foster parents over low-income parents. For discussion of the misuse of psychological parent theory in termination of parental rights cases, see the symposium issue, Ties That Bind: The Impact of Psychological and Legal Debates on the Child Welfare System, 22 N.Y.U. Rev. L. & Soc. Change 295 (1996). See also the symposium issue, The Impact of Psychological Parenting on Child Welfare Decision–Making, 12 N.Y.U. Rev. L. & Soc. Change 485 (1983–84). For a study of the courts' use of psychological parenting theory, see Peggy C. Davis, 'There is a Book Out...,' An Analysis of Judicial Absorption of Legislative Fact, 100 Harv. L. Rev. 1539 (1987).

7. *Class actions.* For thoughtful discussions of the appropriate role of counsel for children in children's class actions, see Martha Matthews, Ten Thousand Tiny Clients: The Ethical Duty of Representation in Children's Class Action Cases, 64 Fordham Law Review 1435 (1996), and Christopher Dunn, The Ethical Legitimacy of Class–Action, Institutional–Reform Litigation on Behalf of Children: A Response to Martha Matthews, id. at 1991.

IN RE ASHLEY K

Appellate Court of Illinois, 1991.
571 N.E.2d 905.

* * *

There were several errors committed in the circuit court. The first error was perhaps the most significant because it precipitated Ashley into a mess that strains believability. Ashley was placed with the Procopios on June 7, 1984. More than five years later, on August 28, 1989, the circuit court made its first dispositional ruling when it transferred custody of Ashley to her biological mother and father. This was a violation of federal law. The fact that the circuit court acted either in total ignorance or in total disregard of the federal law behooves us to expatiate freely on the subject.

In response to the inadequacies in our country's system for child welfare and foster care, in 1980 the federal government adopted the Adoption Assistance and Child Welfare Act. The Act amended Title IV of the Social Security Act and sought to provide the states with fiscal incentives to encourage a more active and systematic monitoring of children in the foster care system.

* * *

* * * For a state to receive its share of any funds appropriated under the Act, the Act provides that the state must certify, inter alia, that it has implemented and is operating "a case review system * * * for each child receiving foster care under the supervision of the state."

* * *

As is evident from the language of the Act, every child that is placed in foster care in a participating state must have a dispositional hearing no later than 18 months after the original placement to determine, among other things, whether the child should be returned to the parents, continue in foster care for a specified period or be placed for adoption. Illinois has certified that it has implemented and is operating a case review system under the Act and is a participating state under the Act. The circuit court of Cook County is therefore required to comply with the Act's provisions.

* * *

When one considers the central purpose of the Act, it is plain that the 18–month requirement for a dispositional hearing contemplates a dispositional ruling within a reasonable time thereafter. Also, when one considers the central purpose of the Act it is clear that it is critical for reviewing courts in Illinois to make certain that the time requirements for a dispositional hearing and ruling be complied with in individual cases.

* * *

In the present case, the circuit court's August 29, 1989 dispositional order transferring Ashley's custody to her biological mother and father was made five years and four months after Ashley's original placement. This dispositional ruling was clearly not made within any reasonable time after a dispositional hearing as required under the Act. The circuit court therefore erred in not complying with the federal law.

The fact that the federal law was not complied with in this case is not an insignificant factor in Ashley's life. Rather, it is the center of the cause of the anguish that now encircles her life. If there had been a dispositional hearing in December 1985 (18 months after Ashley's placement) and a dispositional ruling within a reasonable time thereafter, a permanent decision would have been made for her future at a time which would have avoided the turmoil and problems she has suffered and may suffer the rest of her life.

The August 29, 1989 circuit court order vacated the appointment of the DCFS as guardian of Ashley and transferred custody of Ashley to her biological mother and father. The salient facts at that time are as follows:

(1) Ashley was five years and four months old.

(2) Ashley had lived with the Procopios as her *de facto* parents virtually all of her life in a home environment that was stable, loving and caring.

(3) A report in the record states: "There is no doubt about the fact that the Procopios have done a beautiful job with Ashley. Not only have they nursed her through her addiction, but they have provided a rich, stimulating environment for her where, until recently, she was secure and happy."

(4) In her entire lifetime, Ashley had never lived with her biological mother and father, and she had never spent an entire week with them.

(5) Ashley's biological mother was a heroin and cocaine addict during the time that she was pregnant with Ashley, and Ashley's biological father was also a drug addict at the time.

(6) As a result of her biological mother's drug addiction during pregnancy, Ashley was born with withdrawal and tremors from heroin and cocaine.

(7) Ashley's biological mother was prostituting during the time she was pregnant with Ashley.

(8) While Ashley's biological mother and father were living together, Ashley's biological mother was using prostitution to support herself, a daughter, son and Ashley's biological father. She was engaged in prostitution while Ashley's father was at home with her daughter and son.

(9) Ashley's biological mother had a criminal conviction for child neglect involving Ashley's sister.

(10) While Ashley's biological mother and father were living together, they were spending $300 per day on drugs while they were not working because they were just "too sick."

(11) During Ashley's lifetime, Ashley's biological mother had a conviction for forgery; Ashley's biological father also had a conviction for forgery.

(12) On May 3, 1984, the circuit court adjudged that Ashley was a neglected and dependent minor.

(13) During the first 16 months of Ashley's life, she was visited by her biological mother three times and twice by her biological father.

(14) On May 5, 1985, the circuit court adjudged that Ashley's biological mother and father were unfit parents.

(15) Although Ashley's biological mother and father were allowed visitation with Ashley in 1985, they saw her on only seven occasions for the entire year because, according to Ashley's biological mother, "it was hard for her to be with Ashley at this time as she was often sick from drugs."

(16) Ashley's biological mother was arrested for prostitution on May 15, 1984; arrested for prostitution on June 25, 1984; arrested for possession of stolen property on May 29, 1984; arrested for possession of stolen property on August 28, 1984; arrested for prostitution on November 13, 1984; and arrested for prostitution in March 1986.

(17) In the entire year of 1986, Ashley's biological mother and father visited her only on January 7, and 11 months later on December 1.

(18) On February 18, 1986, Ashley's older sister and brother were taken into protective custody and Ashley's biological mother was charged with abandonment.

(19) On December 9, 1986, the circuit court adjudged Ashley's biological mother to be an unfit parent and the DCFS received guardianship of Ashley's older sister and brother. In 1986, Ashley's older sister and brother were placed in a foster home because Ashley's biological mother was unfit as a parent.

(20) On September 28, 1987, Sonia Yballe, M.D., child psychiatrist at Mount Sinai Hospital, evaluated Ashley and filed a report on October 12, 1987, which states: "Recommendation: (1) Ashley should return home to her foster parents, Mr. and Mrs. Procopio."

(21) There is unrefuted testimony that while she was living with Ashley's mother and father, Ashley's sister was made to hold "a packet of drugs in her mouth during a police raid for her mother."

(22) Ashley's biological mother and father had intermittent "dirty" urine from drugs as late as 1988.

(23) Ashley's biological mother and father filed their petition to have custody of Ashley transferred to them for the first time on December 29, 1988, almost five years after Ashley was born.

(24) Paul Fitzgerald, a psychologist, treated Ashley for eight months and testified as follows on January 31, 1989: "It would not be in her best interest to be separated from her foster family whom she regards at this point as her real family. It would be a traumatic event for her. It is the one thing she seems to fear the most which is provoking a great deal of anxiety at this point."

(25) On January 31, 1989, Dr. David Zinn, a psychiatrist and director of the program in Adolescent Psychiatry at Northwestern Memorial Hospital, testified: "I believe it is in Ashley's best interest to remain in the Procopios' home."

(26) On March 30, 1989, Dr. Zinn signed an affidavit which states: "It is my professional opinion that Ashley would suffer grave and irreparable psychological harm if she would be returned home to her biological parents; the biological parents have not shown that they have the psychological strengths to adequately raise Ashley; because the biological parents continue to deny that their actions were the cause of Ashley's coming into foster care, and psychological rehabilitation has not occurred; and I treat adolescents impaired because of these kinds of trauma as children, and view the possibility of Ashley's removal from her family and return to the biological parents as a disastrous outcome."

(27) There was no testimony or report of any kind from a psychiatrist or from any other medical doctor to contradict the conclusions and recommendations of the two psychiatrists, Yballe and Zinn. Nor was there any testimony or report from any psychologist to contradict the conclusions and recommendations of Paul Fitzgerald.

(28) Ashley's biological mother and father had literally never nurtured, trained, or had anything whatsoever to do with Ashley's education or upbringing for the first five years of Ashley's life.

(29) Ashley's biological mother and father were not married and did not contemplate marriage.

The above facts are to be weighed against the following facts:

(1) Gerry Davis, a social worker for DCFS, testified on January 31, 1989, as follows:

Q. Mr. Davis, I am going to direct your attention to the DCFS service plan that was set up for my client. In that service plan, have the natural parents completed all the tasks required by your agency?

A. Yes.

Q. And in so doing, have they remained drug free to your knowledge?

A. Yes.

* * *

Q. And do you feel that the original reason for this placement of Ashley, neglect and substance abuse, are still existing?

A. I believe that they are no longer existing.

(2) Brenda Massey, who has a Bachelor of Science degree and is employed by the Garfield Counseling Center, testified on January 31, 1989, that Ashley's mother has "a 10–year history of substance abuse," and that she believed that "the first time Ashley's mother has been really free of drugs" was "as of July 1988, when she became drug free." Brenda Massey also testified:

Q. And do you think that at this time the mother would be ready, willing and able to assume control of Ashley?

A.   Yes, I think so.

(3) Jerry Okubo, who is employed as a social worker for Hephzibah, testified on January 31, 1989, as follows:

Q.   And what are you recommending with regards to Ashley today?

A.   That D.C.F.S. guardianship be vacated and Ashley to go to the home of the birth parents.

Q.   And did you feel there is any risk of harm to the child if she is returned to her natural parents today?

A.   No, I do not.

We fail to see how the facts taken as a whole could possibly be construed to favor transferring the custody of Ashley to her biological mother and father on August 29, 1989. When the facts are construed in favor of the biological mother and father, at best they merely demonstrate that although they have had a 10–year history of drug abuse, repeated prostitution, child neglect, child abandonment, forgery convictions, adjudications of being unfit parents and other anti-social behavior, they had stopped using drugs for about 13 months, from July 1988 to August 29, 1989, and that they had completed a DCFS service plan within that same 13–month time frame. Moreover, they are still not married.

* * *

In addition, the record demonstrates that in reaching their conclusions the DCFS, Hephzibah and the circuit court narrowly focused on whether in the last 13 months the biological parents finally began to show an interest in Ashley's well-being and whether they had stopped using drugs during that 13–month period, rather than on the best interest of Ashley.

* * *

In the present case, we conclude that on August 29, 1989, the facts leave no doubt that it was not in the best interest of Ashley to transfer her custody to her biological mother and father. The August 29, 1989 circuit court order transferring custody of Ashley to her biological mother and father is palpably against the manifest weight of the evidence and an abuse of discretion, and must be reversed.

* * * We remand the case for a new hearing on the petition of the biological mother and father to transfer custody of Ashley to them. The hearing and decision shall be had and made posthaste. Until a decision is made, however, Ashley shall continue to live with her biological mother and father unless the circuit court finds that exigent circumstances dictate otherwise.

At the new hearing on the petition of the biological mother and father to transfer custody of Ashley to them, the circuit court shall base its decision solely on the best interest of Ashley. * * *

PROCOPIO v. JOHNSON

United States Court of Appeals, Seventh Circuit, 1993.
994 F.2d 325.

CUDAHY, CIRCUIT JUDGE.

The plaintiffs, hoping to adopt a child, became foster parents to a little girl born to an active drug addict. They nursed her through chronic narcotic withdrawal and cared for her for five years. When the birth parents successfully sought to have custody of the girl returned to them, the plaintiffs sued, asserting a violation of 42 U.S.C. § 1983 in addition to state law claims.

I.

The lamentable story of Ashley K.'s childhood began on April 27, 1984, when Ashley was born to a drug-addicted woman who had used heroin and cocaine and prostituted herself during the pregnancy. On May 3, 1984, Ashley was found to be a neglected and dependent minor and was placed in the custody of the Illinois Department of Children and Family Services (DCFS).

About the same time, the plaintiffs, Joseph and Marjorie Procopio, contacted defendant Lutheran Child and Family Services (LCFS) to inquire about how they might adopt a child. LCFS informed the Procopios that they would have a better chance to adopt if they became licensed foster parents. The Procopios complied, received their foster parents license in April 1984 and became foster parents to Ashley about a month later. Apparently LCFS and DCFS officials repeatedly led the Procopios to believe that almost no significant barriers would prevent their adoption of Ashley and that she was "97% adoptable."

During the first 16 months of Ashley's life, she was visited by her mother three times and her father twice.[2] Ashley's mother, who had a significant arrest record for theft, child neglect, prostitution, forgery and possession of stolen property, was reported using heroin in March 1985. The DCFS nevertheless developed a service plan on April 25, 1985, to work toward the goal of returning Ashley to her parents and to maintain an older sister and brother in the family home as well. On May 8, 1985, however, the state circuit court found Ashley's parents, who remained unmarried but who had lived together since 1980, unfit to care for her and granted guardianship to the DCFS. Ashley continued to experience withdrawal tremors and high fevers, but was otherwise progressing well with the Procopios. The September 4, 1985, update of the DCFS service plan continued to indicate a goal of returning Ashley to her biological parents.

In February 1986, Ashley's mother, who was completing a methadone drug treatment program, was charged with child abandonment, and

---

2. Despite having visiting privileges, Ashley's mother and father saw her on only seven occasions during 1985. In 1986, they visited her only twice, although at least 16 appointments for visitation were scheduled.

her son and older daughter were taken into protective custody. She was arrested for prostitution in March 1986. On December 9, 1986, the circuit court found her to be an unfit parent, and the DCFS received guardianship of the two older children.

Two days later Ashley's mother entered an in-patient drug program, but left the program in March 1987 prior to completion. She enrolled instead in an outpatient methadone maintenance program. In June 1987 Ashley's mother purchased a house with her own mother; Ashley's father, who lived in the house with Ashley's mother and grandmother, also entered a methadone maintenance program.

Ashley's biological parents filed a juvenile court petition on December 29, 1988, seeking custody of Ashley. Although various psychological reports recommended that Ashley should remain with the Procopios, DCFS supported her return to her biological parents. In April 1989, DCFS began working with defendant Hephzibah Children's Association[b] on a plan to effect Ashley's move. In July 1989, DCFS took Ashley from the Procopios and placed her with Hephzibah. At this point Ashley's parents had not used drugs for more than a year and had completed a DCFS service plan. On August 29, 1989, the juvenile court returned custody of Ashley to her natural parents.

On August 29, 1992, the Procopios filed a three-count complaint in federal court against the DCFS, DCFS directors, Hephzibah and LCFS. This case presents a story of what must have been a severe and prolonged emotional trauma to Ashley, but the problem presented to the federal courts is a narrower one than that. The Procopios asserted one federal claim under 42 U.S.C. § 1983 alleging violation of their Fourteenth Amendment due process rights and two state claims alleging fraudulent misrepresentation and intentional infliction of emotional distress. Concluding that the Procopios failed to demonstrate that their long-term foster relationship with Ashley or the DCFS's assurances of adoption created a liberty interest, the district court dismissed the section 1983 claim for failure to state a claim upon which relief can be granted. The court declined to exercise supplemental jurisdiction over the remaining state claims and dismissed them as well. The Procopios appeal.

II.

We review the district court's dismissal of the plaintiffs' claims de novo. The Procopios' § 1983 action requires them to prove that they have a liberty interest in their family relationship with Ashley that the state could not impair without due process.[4] If they demonstrate such an interest, they then must show that the process accorded them was not constitutionally adequate. The Procopios contend that their liberty interest in their family relationship with Ashley derives from Illinois state

---

b. Hephzibah was a child welfare agency that worked with DCFS.

4. Section 1983 provides a federal cause of action for "the deprivation of any rights, privileges, or immunities secured by the Constitution and [federal] laws."

law and from the federal statutory scheme governing reimbursement for various state and child welfare services, the Adoption Assistance and Child Welfare Act of 1980. We address these in turn.

The power of the state to regulate biological family relationships is limited. How far that limitation extends to nonbiological families is less clear. The Supreme Court has recognized that biological relationships are not the "exclusive determination of the existence of a family" and that emotional attachments play a role as well. Smith v. Organization of Foster Families for Equality & Reform (1977). But the Court has stopped short of deciding that foster family arrangements achieve the status of a liberty interest that states cannot disrupt without due process.[5] The scope of the liberty interest at stake, according to the Court, is appropriately ascertained from the parties' expectations and entitlements as they are set out in state law.

The Procopios contend that two different state law provisions support their claim that their relationship with Ashley amounts to a liberty interest. First, they argue that the Illinois Adoption Act confirms that foster parents are to be preferred above all others as the foster child's permanent family. * * *

We agree with the district court that this statutory language does not suffice to create a liberty interest in the Procopios' family relationship. Notwithstanding the preference state law grants to foster families seeking to adopt their foster children, this priority does not rise to the level of an entitlement or expectancy. State law still requires that foster families who wish to adopt obtain the permission of the natural parents, or of the legal guardian if the natural parents' rights have been terminated, as they were here. Even given that permission, the Juvenile Court has the "sole discretion" to make the "final determination" about the adoption. Ashley's guardian, the DCFS, never granted that consent, nor did the Procopios receive juvenile court approval of their adoption of Ashley.[6]

Second, the Procopios claim that the Illinois Juvenile Court Act of 1987, supports an expectancy of a permanent relationship with Ashley. The Act's statement of purpose indicates that, where possible, a minor removed from his or her family should be placed "in a family home so that he or she may become a member of the family by legal adoption or otherwise."

5. Smith found it unnecessary to resolve the question because the procedures employed by the state were adequate to protect whatever liberty interests the plaintiffs might have. The Court did note, however, that "[w]hatever liberty interest might otherwise exist in the foster family as an institution, that interest must be substantially attenuated where the proposed removal from the foster family is to return the child to his natural parents."

6. However imprudent or unauthorized any of the defendants' assurances to the Procopios may have been, we do not believe such promises transform the Procopios' expectation of adopting Ashley into an entitlement. Such a liberty interest derives from state law; the defendants' promises were not supported by state law, and certainly not in any "explicitly mandatory language." * * *

We are not persuaded that this language in the Juvenile Court Act serves to create a liberty interest in the Procopios' family relationship. As the language preceding the quoted passage makes clear, the Act strives foremost to secure appropriate care and guidance for each child "in his or her own home" and to "strengthen the minor's family ties whenever possible." Indeed, when guardianship is not feasible within the child's own home, the Act does advocate placing the child in a "family home" that affords the equivalent of parental care and discipline. Yet the Act's opening policy statement introduces this option as a subordinate alternative to the expressly preferred course of maintaining children in their own (original) home. Further, although the Act unmistakably endorses efforts to provide a home-like environment to children whose parents' custodial rights have been suspended or terminated, the legislature's articulation of this aim neither nullifies the state's ultimate prerogative to terminate the foster family unit nor otherwise confirms any legally cognizable expectancy in the foster family's permanence.

* * *

The Procopios also argue that section 1983 provides a remedy for the defendants' violation of federal law-in this case the Adoption Assistance and Child Welfare Act of 1980 (AACWA).* * *

* * *

* * * We * * * conclude that under the circumstances of the case before us, the procedural guarantees embodied in * * * the AACWA do not give rise to a constitutional liberty interest.[c]

Because we hold that the Procopios have not established that state or federal law creates a liberty interest in Ashley's foster family relationship, we need not consider whether the procedures the state afforded them were constitutionally adequate.

III.

Although the Procopios' plight is a sympathetic one, their long-term foster relationship with Ashley does not create an interest within the Fourteenth Amendment's protection of liberty * * *.

Notes and Questions

1. *Questions about* Procopio. (a) Why couldn't the Procopios establish a liberty interest in their relationship with Ashley? If they had been able to establish a liberty interest, would they have been entitled to a hearing before or after Ashley was returned to her parents? (b) Should Ashley have been represented in the Procopios' appeal ? What would you argue if you were representing Ashley? (c) Does Ashley have a constitutionally protected interest in staying with the Procopios?

2. *Question about* Ashley K. The appellate court left Ashley with her biological parents, pending the outcome of the remand, and the trial court on

---

c. The court also held that the Procopios' AACWA claim was precluded by Suter v. Artist M. [*Suter* is discussed in Section 4, infra.]

remand awarded permanent custody of Ashley to her biological parents. Instead, should the appellate court have removed Ashley from her biological parents and ordered DCFS to place her with the Procopios?

3. *The foster parents' lawyer.* In 1997, the President of the American Bar Association reported that children frequently languish in foster care, deprived of permanent adoptive homes, partly because of "a shortage of qualified lawyers who can help [foster] families on a pro bono or reduced-fee basis" in their efforts to terminate parental rights and proceed toward adoption: "Sometimes the [adoption] process is too cumbersome, fraught with legal barriers that seem impossible to overcome. * * * Sometimes the adoption process seems daunting to potential parents because of the legal complexities. Often these families-in-waiting feel they do not have the resources to locate and retain an attorney to assist them." N. Lee Cooper, Free the Children, A.B.A. J., May 1997, at 8.

For a fascinating account of a foster mother's struggle to adopt her foster children and reflections on the task of lawyering, see Jane M. Spinak, Reflections on a Case (Of Motherhood), 95 Columbia L. Rev. 1990 (1995).

4. *Model court.* The Circuit Court of Cook County, which heard *Ashley K.*, is now part of the National Council of Juvenile and Family Court Judges Child Victims Model Court Project. The number of children in out-of-home placement decreased from 58,000 children in 1995 to 31, 534 in 1998. There is a new emphasis on expediting adoptions, as well as a number of other changes. NCJFCJ, Child Victims Project Model Courts Status Report, 1997–98, 21–22 (1998). The judge who originally ordered Ashley K. returned to her biological parents was subsequently removed from hearing custody or child abuse and neglect cases. Bob Greene, For Sarah the Final Chapter Begins, Chicago Tribune, September 15, 1991, at 1.

PROBLEM 5–1

Carrie was young, unemployed, and unhappily married when her second daughter, Liz, was born. She had mainly left her first daughter in the care of her parents. Liz was born by cesarean section in 1992. Carrie asked some good friends, the Millers, who had helped her out on numerous occasions, to look after Liz until she recovered from the cesarean. After Carrie had recovered, she did not take responsibility for Liz but instead left her with the Millers. She visited every weekend the first year of Liz's life, but her visits grew more infrequent, with more than a month passing between visits. Because Carrie moved around a lot, the Millers did not always know where she was. Other than some old clothes and occasional food stamps, Carrie provided no financial assistance for Liz. The Millers thought about applying to become foster parents or taking some other legal step, but did not because they had heard negative things about foster care and were afraid that a legal proceeding might scare Carrie into removing Liz. In 1995 Carrie filed for divorce from her husband so she could marry the man she was living with. As part of the dissolution action, the court awarded custody of Liz to Carrie. Her former husband did not want custody. The Millers intervened and petitioned for custody and were granted standing because they had physical custody of Liz, who was still living with them. At the custody hearing, Carrie testified that she had never intended to allow the Millers to keep Liz permanently. Who should get custody—the Millers or Carrie? What, if any, visitation would you allow? Would your answers be different if the Millers had become licensed foster parents shortly after they took Liz?

PROBLEM 5–2

Andy was abandoned by his mother shortly after his birth. His father had no interest in him. Fourteen days later the state placed him with Ms. Perez, a licensed foster care parent. Over the next three years, Andy's caseworker observed a strong bond developing between Andy and Ms. Perez and Andy's biological mother visited him only a few times. Andy's placement goal was changed from reunification with his mother to adoption by Ms. Perez. His biological mother's rights were terminated, and Ms. Perez entered into an Adoption Placement Agreement with the agency.

Ms. Perez had another foster child living with her, Tim, age three. While Ms. Perez was out, Tim's caseworker dropped by unannounced on March 18th. He found Andy and Tim home alone with Ed, Ms. Perez's 12–year-old nephew who also lived with her. Ed was a special needs child, and the caseworker thought that Ed could not manage the other two children. Ed seemed very stressed and incapable of controlling the children, who were running around and going in and out of the apartment. The caseworker tried to locate Ms. Perez or determine whether there was an adult in charge by asking neighbors, but to no avail. He called his supervisor who told him to remove the two children. The children were then put in new foster homes.

Ms. Perez did not receive official notice of the removal until June 15th and was not allowed to visit Andy until June 27th. At a hearing held in July, it was determined that Ms. Perez had not abused or neglected Andy and he was returned to her home. The adoption proceedings were resumed in January, and the adoption was finalized in August.

Ms. Perez then sued the agency on behalf of herself and her son Andy for a violation of their due process rights because of the lack of notice of removal, the lack of a pre-removal hearing, the lack of an adequate post-removal hearing to contest removal, and the lack of an adequate hearing on the denial of visitation. The agency moved for summary judgment, claiming that Ms. Perez had no liberty interest protected under 14th Amendment due process, or assuming she did, that she received all the due process that she was constitutionally entitled to. Will Ms. Perez prevail?

SECTION 4. THE CHILD'S RIGHT TO SERVICES AND PROTECTION FROM HARM

SUTER v. ARTIST M.

Supreme Court of the United States, 1992.
503 U.S. 347.

CHIEF JUSTICE REHNQUIST delivered the opinion of the Court.

This case raises the question whether private individuals have the right to enforce by suit a provision of the Adoption Assistance and Child Welfare Act of 1980 (Adoption Act or Act), either under the Act itself or through an action under 42 U.S.C. § 1983. * * *

The Adoption Act establishes a federal reimbursement program for certain expenses incurred by the States in administering foster care and adoption services. * * *

To participate in the program, States must submit a plan to the Secretary of Health and Human Services for approval by the Secretary. * * * As relevant here, the Act provides:

"(a) Requisite features of State plan

"In order for a State to be eligible for payments under this part, it shall have a plan approved by the Secretary which—

. . .

"(3) provides that the plan shall be in effect in all political subdivisions of the State, and, if administered by them, be mandatory upon them;

. . .

"(15) effective October 1, 1983, provides that, in each case, reasonable efforts will be made (A) prior to the placement of a child in foster care, to prevent or eliminate the need for removal of the child from his home, and (B) to make it possible for the child to return to his home...."

Petitioners in this action are Sue Suter and Gary T. Morgan, the Director and the Guardianship Administrator, respectively, of the Illinois Department of Children and Family Services (DCFS). DCFS is the state agency responsible for, among other things, investigating charges of child abuse and neglect and providing services to abused and neglected children and their families. * * *

Respondents filed this class-action suit seeking declaratory and injunctive relief under the Adoption Act. They alleged that petitioners * * * failed to make reasonable efforts to prevent removal of children from their homes and to facilitate reunification of families where removal had occurred. This failure occurred, as alleged by respondents, because DCFS failed promptly to assign caseworkers to children placed in DCFS custody and promptly to reassign cases when caseworkers were on leave from DCFS. The District Court, without objection from petitioners, certified two separate classes seeking relief, including all children who are or will be wards of DCFS and are placed in foster care or remain in their homes under a judicial protective order. The District Court denied a motion to dismiss filed by petitioners, holding, as relevant here, that the Adoption Act contained an implied cause of action and that suit could also be brought to enforce the Act * * *.

* * *

The Court of Appeals affirmed. Relying heavily on this Court's decision in Wilder v. Virginia Hospital Assn. (1990), the Court of Appeals held that the "reasonable efforts" clause of the Adoption Act could be enforced through an action under § 1983. That court * * * also found that the Adoption Act created an implied right of action such that private individuals could bring suit directly under the Act to enforce the provisions relied upon by respondents. We granted certiorari, and now reverse.

* * *

In Maine v. Thiboutot, (1980), we first established that § 1983 is available as a remedy for violations of federal statutes as well as for constitutional violations. We have subsequently recognized that § 1983 is not available to enforce a violation of a federal statute "where Congress has foreclosed such enforcement of the statute in the enactment itself and where the statute did not create enforceable rights, privileges, or immunities within the meaning of § 1983."

* * * [In Pennhurst State School and Hospital v. Halderman, (1981)] we noted that it was well established that Congress has the power to fix the terms under which it disburses federal money to the States. As stated in Pennhurst:

"The legitimacy of Congress' power to legislate under the spending power thus rests on whether the State voluntarily and knowingly accepts the terms of the 'contract.' There can, of course, be no knowing acceptance if a State is unaware of the conditions or is unable to ascertain what is expected of it. Accordingly, if Congress intends to impose a condition on the grant of federal moneys, it must do so unambiguously."

* * *

Did Congress, in enacting the Adoption Act, unambiguously confer upon the child beneficiaries of the Act a right to enforce the requirement that the State make "reasonable efforts" to prevent a child from being removed from his home, and once removed to reunify the child with his family? We turn now to that inquiry.

* * * [T]o obtain federal reimbursement, a State [is required to] have a plan which "provides that, in each case, reasonable efforts will be made ... to prevent or eliminate the need for removal of the child from his home, and ... to make it possible for the child to return to his home...." As recognized by petitioners, respondents, and the courts

below, the Act is mandatory in its terms. However, in the light shed by Pennhurst, we must examine exactly what is required of States by the Act. Here, the terms of § 671(a) are clear: "In order for a State to be eligible for payments under this part, it shall have a plan approved by the Secretary." Therefore the Act does place a requirement on the States, but that requirement only goes so far as to ensure that the State have a plan approved by the Secretary which contains the 16 listed features.

Respondents do not dispute that Illinois in fact has a plan approved by the Secretary which provides that reasonable efforts at prevention and reunification will be made. Respondents argue, however, that § 1983 allows them to sue in federal court to obtain enforcement of this particular provision of the state plan. This argument is based, at least in part, on the assertion that 42 U.S.C. § 671(a)(3) requires that the State have a plan which is "in effect." This section states that the state plan shall "provid[e] that the plan shall be in effect in all political subdivisions of the State, and, if administered by them, be mandatory upon them." But we think that "in effect" is directed to the requirement that the plan apply to all political subdivisions of the State, and is not intended to otherwise modify the word "plan."

In *Wilder*, the underlying Medicaid legislation similarly required participating States to submit to the Secretary of Health and Human Services a plan for medical assistance describing the State's Medicaid program. But in that case we held that the Boren Amendment actually required the States to adopt reasonable and adequate rates, and that this obligation was enforceable by the providers. We relied in part on the fact that the statute and regulations set forth in some detail the factors to be considered in determining the methods for calculating rates.

In the present case, however, the term "reasonable efforts" to maintain an abused or neglected child in his home, or return the child to his home from foster care, appears in quite a different context. No further statutory guidance is found as to how "reasonable efforts" are to be measured. This directive is not the only one which Congress has given to the States, and it is a directive whose meaning will obviously vary with the circumstances of each individual case. How the State was to comply with this directive, and with the other provisions of the Act, was, within broad limits, left up to the State.

Other sections of the Act provide enforcement mechanisms for the "reasonable efforts" clause of 42 U.S.C. § 671(a)(15). The Secretary has the authority to reduce or eliminate payments to a State on finding that the State's plan no longer complies with § 671(a) or that "there is a substantial failure" in the administration of a plan such that the State is not complying with its own plan. The Act also requires that in order to secure federal reimbursement for foster care payments made with respect to a child involuntarily removed from his home the removal must be "the result of a judicial determination to the effect that continuation [in the child's home] would be contrary to the welfare of such child and (effective October 1, 1983) that reasonable efforts of the type described in section 671(a)(15) of this title have been made." While these statutory provisions may not provide a comprehensive enforcement mechanism so as to manifest Congress' intent to foreclose remedies under § 1983, they do show that the absence of a remedy to private plaintiffs under § 1983 does not make the "reasonable efforts" clause a dead letter.

* * *

Careful examination of the language relied upon by respondents, in the context of the entire Act, leads us to conclude that the "reasonable efforts" language does not unambiguously confer an enforceable right upon the Act's beneficiaries. The term "reasonable efforts" in this context is at least as plausibly read to impose only a rather generalized duty on the State, to be enforced not by private individuals, but by the Secretary in the manner previously discussed.

* * *

We conclude that 42 U.S.C. § 671(a)(15) neither confers an enforceable private right on its beneficiaries nor creates an implied cause of action on their behalf.

[Justices Blackmun and Stevens dissented]

Notes and Questions

1.   What approaches, other than litigation, could the plaintiffs have used to get what they wanted? Why might the state be out of compliance with the federal requirements?

2.   In 1994 Congress limited *Suter* by amending the Social Security Act. The amendment states:

> In an action brought to enforce a provision of this chapter, such provision is not to be deemed unenforceable because of its inclusion in a section of this chapter requiring a State plan or specifying the required contents of a State plan. This section is not intended to limit or expand the grounds for determining the availability of private actions to enforce State plan requirements other than by overturning any such grounds applied in Suter v. Artist M., but not applied in prior Supreme Court decisions respecting such enforceability; provided, however, that this section is not intended to alter the holding in Suter v. Artist M. that section 671(a)(15) of this title is not enforceable in a private right of action.

42 U.S.C. § 1320a–10.

3.   Before the Supreme Court's *Suter,* decision, Illinois entered into an expansive consent order that detailed its responsibility under the Adoption Assistance and Child Welfare Act. The consent order was continued post-*Suter*, partly because of the Social Security Act amendment that limited *Suter*. See Norman v. McDonald, 930 F.Supp. 1219 (N.D.Ill.1996).

PROBLEM 5–3

As discussed in this section, the Adoption and Safe Families Act of 1997 places even more stringent requirements on the states. It requires states to hold a permanency planning hearing within 12 months of a child's placement. The Act also specifies situations in which "reasonable efforts" to reunify the family are not required and, when they are not, requires a permanency planning hearing within 30 days. The Act also requires that termination of parental rights petitions must be filed, with exceptions for relative placements and some other situations, when a child has been in state care for 15 of the most recent 22 months. The Act does not provide additional resources for courts and agencies that must implement the permanency requirements. What argument can you make that these requirements will be enforceable under 42 U.S.C. § 1983?

LASHAWN A. v. KELLY

United States District Court, District of Columbia, 1995.
887 F.Supp. 297.

THOMAS F. HOGAN, DISTRICT JUDGE.

Four years ago, this Court heard more than two weeks of testimony and accepted more than 1000 admissions in a trial which exposed the desperate condition of the District of Columbia child welfare system. The Court then issued a 102–page opinion reaching "[t]he inescapable conclusion" that the system was operated in violation of federal law, District law, and the United States Constitution.[1]

Once the Court entered this finding of liability, the parties and court-appointed Monitor worked before a backdrop of further legal proceedings to plan and implement reforms which would alleviate the violations. Four years and two mayoral administrations later, however, many if not most of the problems remain. Children are routinely denied the protections and services that local and federal law require. Because all reasonable alternative measures of change have been exhausted, the Court today grants the plaintiffs' motion for contempt and imposition of a full receivership.

I. PROCEDURAL HISTORY

This case began with the filing of a class action on behalf of abused and neglected children in the District of Columbia, including both children within the District's custody and those who remained in private custody but were known to the District's Department of Human Services (DHS). Several District of Columbia officials, including the mayor, were named in their official capacities. After a bench trial in February 1991, the Court issued a Memorandum Opinion on April 18, 1991.

The opinion detailed widespread problems within the District of Columbia child welfare system and held that the defendants operated the

---

1. LaShawn A. v. Dixon, 762 F.Supp. 959, 960–61 (D.D.C.1991).

system in a manner that violated the federal and local statutory rights of all the children in the plaintiff class. The Court also held that the defendants violated the Fifth Amendment rights of those plaintiff children in the foster care custody of the District of Columbia.

After the finding of liability, the parties worked together to plan a course of remedial action. After a few months, the plaintiffs and defendants reached agreement on the specifics of needed reform. On August 27, 1991, the Court granted the parties' joint motion for entry into judgment of a Remedial Order incorporating this agreement. The Court then adopted the Monitor's Implementation Plan which laid out the steps necessary to comply with the Remedial Order. The defendants, in accordance with the terms of the Remedial Order, then appealed the judgment of liability, arguing alternatively that the Court erred in finding federal statutory and constitutional liability and that the Court should have abstained from exercising jurisdiction because the plaintiffs' claims were more appropriately addressed by the District of Columbia courts.

On October 1, 1993, the Court of Appeals issued a remand, concluding that

> Because the district court's judgment is independently supportable by District of Columbia law, we affirm the court's decision in favor of the children in this case. It appears that each provision of the remedial order reflects the requirements of District of Columbia statutes and regulations, as well as of federal statutes. Nevertheless, because the order was drafted to conform with federal as well as with District law, there are scattered references in the order to federal law that are inappropriate in light of our confirmation of the decision entirely on the basis of local law.
>
> We therefore remand to the district court, with instructions to fashion an equally comprehensive order based entirely on District of Columbia law, if possible. If there are any portions of the consent decree that depend entirely on a federal statute, the district court should consider the impact of Suter v. Artist M. on those provisions before it includes them in the revised consent decree.[3]

After reviewing the parties' briefs and hearing arguments on necessary modifications, the Court issued a second Remedial Order on January 27, 1994, which incorporated the minor changes requested by the Court of Appeals. The Monitor thereafter developed a Revised Implementation Plan, which the Court ordered incorporated into the new Remedial Order.

* * *

Since the entry of the initial Remedial Order, the Center for the Study of Social Policy has acted as a court-appointed Monitor. The

---

3. LaShawn A. ex rel. Moore v. Kelly, 990 F.2d 1319, 1326 (D.C.Cir.1993), cert.   denied, 510 U.S. 1044 (1994).

Monitor proposed detailed implementation plans for both remedial orders and regularly reports to the Court on the status of compliance with the Court's orders. The Monitor also assists the parties with negotiations when consent agreements are developed for the Court's consideration.

On April 4, 1995, the plaintiffs filed their third motion for contempt and also requested the imposition of a full receivership to cover all areas of the District's child welfare system. The Court now considers this motion.

II. REMEDIAL HISTORY

The remedial phase of this case has been marked by repeated cycles of noncompliance and sluggish progress, frustration and requests for court intervention, promises to improve, and further noncompliance after a flurry of attempts to make short-term changes. This pattern has convinced the Court that the defendants either cannot or will not make the fundamental changes necessary to improve the plight of abused and neglected children.

The framework of the entire post-trial effort was the Remedial Order. This was not a set of restrictions that the Court unilaterally imposed upon the defendants. The parties developed its terms by consent and the then-mayor of the District of Columbia expressed her personal commitment to carrying out the plan. The Court entered the consent agreement as the Remedial Order.

On December 22, 1992, the plaintiffs filed their first contempt motion when the defendants were tardy in complying with a provision of the Remedial Order requiring that the District conduct a case review of all individuals in the child welfare system. However, once the motion was filed, the parties were able to agree that the defendants would immediately focus on five key areas—"building blocks"—which were necessary precursors to further reform. On April 30, 1993, the plaintiffs withdrew the contempt motion and stated that they were "gratified with the progress and the hard work" that the defendants had devoted to the building block areas. This was perhaps the high point in the District's compliance history.

On March 22, 1994, the plaintiffs filed their second contempt motion and supplemented it with a memorandum filed on July 21, 1994. The plaintiffs alleged noncompliance with nearly every section of the Remedial Order. This time, the plaintiffs requested that the Court appoint a receiver to solve all of the compliance problems. However, by the time they appeared before the Court on September 16, 1994, the parties had drafted a "consent agreement" stretching out the deadlines in many areas and the plaintiffs had agreed to hold in abeyance the request for a full receiver. Nonetheless, the plaintiffs maintained that receiverships for Resource Development and Corrective Action were necessary, and repeated their request for a finding of contempt. The Court, not eager to engender resentment among the defendants and their employees, declined to grant the plaintiff's motion for a finding of contempt and held it in abeyance, even though "contempt may well [have been] justified." The Court therefore entered an order imposing the two limited receiverships and adopting the consent agreement on October 4, 1994.

By November 23, 1994, it was clear to the Court that the defendants would be unable to meet the consent agreement's deadlines with respect to Protective Services. Therefore, the Court imposed a third limited receivership in that area.

At this point, faced with increasing resistance on the part of the defendants, the Court was forced to begin issuing a series of piecemeal orders directing compliance with extant orders when it became apparent that the defendants had no plans to comply. See November 23, 1994 Order (requiring defendants to provide Monitor with copy of federal revenue maximization consultant's contract and establishing deadline for minor amendment of contract); November 23, 1994 Order (requiring defendants to formally adopt policies and procedures); February 16, 1995 Order (establishing deadline for defendants to issue management information system Request For Proposals).

By February 10, 1995, the newly appointed Receivers had informed the court that extremely basic resources were absent or in short supply, thus making it almost impossible for various sectors of the child welfare system to function. The Court therefore entered an order adopting the Receivers' Emergency Resource Plan to address these pressing needs. The plan required the provision of such essentials as diapers, copy paper, printed intake forms, automobile maintenance, telephones, and food vouchers.

Finally, on April 4, 1995, after learning that the Receivers were encountering resistance and hostility to their court-ordered efforts, and after compiling a 32–page list of over 130 areas in which they alleged the defendants had missed deadlines or were in noncompliance, the plaintiffs filed a third motion for contempt and again requested that the Court impose a full receivership. The motion has been fully briefed and was argued on May 15, 1995.

III.   PRESENT VIOLATIONS: FINDINGS OF FACT

Various recent submissions from the parties, Monitor, and Receivers show that the defendants remain in noncompliance with many court-ordered requirements. It is important to note that most of these requirements, including those set forth in the Remedial Order and October 4, 1994 consent agreement, have been voluntarily proposed by the defendants. Instances of noncompliance are set forth below.

A.   Adoption

Activity in this area has nearly ground to a halt, even though adoption provides welcome stability for children and an end to foster care expenses for the defendants. The Monitor reports that

> [a]doptions activity has now declined to levels that existed before the implementation of the ... Remedial Order. During [the first quarter

of 1995] . . . no children's adoptive placements were finalized by the Court. . . . A total of 151 children have been awaiting adoptive placement for more than 9 months, with 92 of these children expected to be adopted by their foster care parents. As of the end of the quarter, there were 104 adoptive homes studies that were incomplete after 150 days. These data are a cause for serious concern. . . . The Adoptions Branch has been operating without a permanent Chief since October, 1994 and there is a critical need to restore forceful leadership to this area.

The plaintiffs express equally strong warnings about the state of adoptions activity. Because the defendants were totally inactive in pursuing an adoption for one of the named plaintiffs, the plaintiffs' counsel themselves performed many of the defendants' responsibilities in an attempt to move the process forward. Counsel had to exert "an enormous amount of pressure" on the defendants just to get the child's picture taken for the adoption search. When the defendants did not proceed, counsel, who are not experts in the adoption field, compiled a list of adoption agencies that could help with the search. Even after the defendants received the list, they said they were unable to reach the agencies. Plaintiffs' counsel then attempted to contact the agencies and succeeded. Finally, after this massive intervention by counsel into the defendants' professional sphere, the defendants signed a contract with an agency to assist with the search, but the plaintiffs remain unconvinced that the matter will proceed. It is therefore not surprising to learn that the defendants are out of compliance with many requirements in the adoptions area.

[The court then reviewed noncompliance in policies and procedures, adoptions branch staffing, termination of parental rights staffing, prompt home studies, and monitoring and improvement.]

* * *

B.　Staffing

1.　*Total Number of Social Workers.* The Court ordered the defendants to ensure the employment of 316 social workers by December 31, 1994. The defendants report that only 290 social workers were in place as of April 18, 1995. As the Monitor points out, the figures showing noncompliance here understate the actual shortage, since the present requirement was calculated based on the total number of children in the child welfare system in December 1993. In the meantime, the number of children in the system has increased and the total number of necessary social workers will rise accordingly.

Serious problems can occur when staffing shortages lead to high caseloads. In its April 1991 opinion, the Court found that the extra responsibility made the social workers unable to

> initiate timely investigations, provide needed services, ensure appropriate placements, prepare case plans, visit with foster children and

parents, recruit foster and adoptive families, monitor foster homes and institutions, and claim all federal funding to which the CFSD should be entitled.

* * *

2. *Administrative Supports.* The Monitor and defendants agree that the defendants are not in compliance with the court-ordered requirement that they develop and implement a plan to provide the required administrative supports to staff. This requirement is reiterated in the Emergency Resources Plan adopted by the Court on February 10, 1995. The Monitor reports that even though many of the requirements of the Emergency Resources Plan were initially met,

> the Receivers and workers continue to report ongoing problems related to the availability of administrative supports (e.g., difficulty accessing supplies, forms, and vouchers for client services, lack of attention to basic office cleanliness and maintenance, lack of working word processors, phones that were once operable ceasing to work, and the ever-present problem of too few working automobiles). The response to the February 10 Court Order addressed the immediate crises and some systems were put in place to avert future crises of the same nature. However, the Receivers report that maintenance of equipment and lack of basic staff resources is an ongoing problem.

The Receivers concur, and note that "[e]ach box of xerox paper secured for staff and each time a fax machine receives toner is a major victory," but that the cost of pursuing these basic resources is "high both in time and in steadily accumulating frustration." This level of noncompliance is dismal. Without administrative supports that most professionals take for granted, the social workers cannot be expected to fulfill their most basic responsibilities, let alone take the extra steps needed to reform the present system.

3. *Other Staffing Requirements.* * * *

Furthermore, the defendants admit that they are not in compliance with requirements that all social workers have a current and valid license. More importantly, they admit that over half of their supervisory units do not meet the required supervisor-to-staff ratio. * * *

C. Training

The Monitor notes and the defendants admit that the defendants are in noncompliance with the court-ordered requirement that they develop and implement training for contract agencies focused on the needs of child-care and group home providers. * * *

D. Management Information System

Federal law requires any child welfare agency receiving federal funds to maintain an information system from which the status, location, and goals for the placement of all foster care children may be readily determined. 42 U.S.C. § 627(a)(2)(A). In 1991, the Court observed that

> such a system is also mandated by reasonable professional standards and, this Court believes, by basic common sense. Defendants have admitted that [its current information system] is not adequate. [The system] cannot provide accurate information on the number of children in emergency care, how long they have been in that status, and when they are reaching the 90–day deadline for remaining in that status. [The system] is also unable to accurately identify the physical location of all of the children in foster care. Additionally, it does not contain accurate information concerning vacancies in foster homes, nor does it contain accurate information regarding which social workers are assigned to which children.

* * *

> Based on the foregoing, the Court finds that [the information system] is clearly inadequate for keeping track of the children in the District's foster care. The Court can only wonder how an agency that cannot track the location of the children in its custody can possibly comply with the remaining requirements of federal and District law, much less with reasonable professional standards.

> Unfortunately, this situation remains largely unremedied. * * *

E.   Administrative Review and Quality Assurance

1.   *Administrative Review.* As noted in the Court's original liability opinion, federal and District law both require that periodic reviews be conducted to determine the continued appropriateness of each child's placement. Obviously, this requirement prevents children from languishing in inappropriate situations as their circumstances change. The Court ordered the defendants to provide an administrative review for all children in care within 180 days of their entering the Department's physical and legal custody and every 180 days thereafter. * * *

[The court found that defendants were not in substantial compliance with the administrative review requirements or in the quality assurance process requirement. Additional areas of noncompliance were licensing, monitoring, and contract review, legal representation and court relationships, revenue maximization, and services to families and children].

* * *

J.   Out-of-home Care

The defendants are not in compliance with at least ten requirements in this area. First, and most essentially, the Court required the defendants to centralize placement activity in one placement office. * * * The Monitor explains that "placement workers still rely on personal knowledge and relationships in making placements," and that the centralized office does not receive reliable listings of available placements. The Monitor also notes that

> [t]he lack of appropriate placements has reached crisis proportions with approximately 20 children for whom no placements are now available. The Placement Office staff are under extreme stress and are often forced to move children multiple times to a series of inappropriate placements.

Second, the Monitor reports that the defendants are not in compliance with the Court's order to develop procedures and resources available to serve as a placement transition fund. * * *

Third, the defendants are out of compliance with the Court's requirement that they hire a full-time employee to develop and coordinate supports for foster parents. * * *

Fourth, the defendants have not achieved full compliance with licensing standards for the number of children in foster care homes. * * *

Fifth, the Court required the defendants to increase foster parent payment rates * * * by April 1, 1994. The defendants have not done so and have not provided any information to the Monitor on progress in this area.

Sixth, the defendants have failed to implement a wide variety of support services for foster parents. * * *

Seventh, the Monitor states that the defendants are not in compliance with certain sections of the Remedial Order regarding the case planning process and supervision of placements. * * *

Eighth, the Court required the defendants to establish and fill a full-time position to coordinate kinship care. * * *

Ninth, the Court required the defendants to develop and implement policies and procedures for regarding the placement of children with kinship providers. * * *

Tenth, the Court required the defendants to develop and implement a licensure process for kinship homes. * * *

IV.   PRACTICAL EFFECTS OF VIOLATIONS: FINDINGS OF FACT

Though the above review of the defendants' noncompliance mentions the practical effects of these problems, further illustration is in order. Three documents recently submitted to the Court show that the defendants' noncompliance can have devastating outcomes.

A.   Child Fatality

On February 4, 1995, a three-year old child was beaten and choked to death by a relative who was caring for the child. Because the deceased was known to the District's child welfare system, the Monitor reviewed the circumstances surrounding the fatality and prepared a Memorandum on April 4, 1995 which was forwarded to the parties and the Court.

The Monitor concluded that the death "could have been prevented" and that "no one adequately discharged a protective function" on behalf of the deceased or other children in the household. Though the defendants had received a report of neglect as early as October 1992, they missed "numerous clues, indications, and opportunities" to avoid this tragedy.

The Monitor found that the defendants erred in several ways, including by not adequately assessing the child's risk at an early stage; not dealing appropriately with the child's mother; not performing regular visits; allowing the case to remain unassigned to any social worker for several periods of time; not providing adequate supervision and training for workers involved with the case; and not coordinating services provided by other parts of the District government.

Furthermore, the Monitor concluded that the defendants' internal review of the fatality was "unsatisfactory on all accounts." The defendants failed to convene a timely review panel; failed to involve the required high-level management in the review; failed to produce a report with sufficiently documented and detailed information; failed to produce the report promptly; and failed to address problems raised by the review.

The widespread problems and inadequate internal response to this terrible event provide stark evidence that the defendants are unable or unwilling to comply with the Court's orders and alleviate the problems raised at trial. The Court cannot expect the defendants to respond to the more mundane but pressing matters involved in some of the remedial provisions (such as increasing staffing and making policy statements available) if they do not respond adequately to this clearly identifiable, highly publicized tragedy.

B.   Emergency Overnight Placements

Over the past several weeks, the Receivers have grown increasingly aware that children are being placed in a large number of successive temporary placements over short periods of time. The Resource Development Receiver investigated this issue and completed a report on May 18, 1995.

The report found that in April 1995, twenty-four children had multiple placements "driven by a drastic shortage of placement resources." One child experienced six different placements in two weeks. Other examples include a child moved three times in three days and another moved four times in four days. When children are shuttled around in this manner, many suffer. The children are traumatized and social workers are overburdened.

The Receiver identified several causes for this practice. In addition to the general shortage of placement resources, which must be addressed by systematic resource development, other problems worsen the situation:

—The computerized daily list of placement options is not accurate and makes placement difficult.

—Social workers are unsure whether day care is available when there is a chance to place a child in a home where day care is required.

—Foster parents and licensed vendors who can provide care are becoming reluctant to participate because they are not being paid and services have not been provided.

—Placement is not centralized and lacks "even basic computer support." Social workers must routinely make 25 phone calls to secure a placement.

—Few new foster care families have been approved in the last several months even though there have been numerous applicants.

The Receiver has identified short-term solutions for some of these problems and will proceed with the Resource Development Workplan in order to achieve long-term progress. However, the report buttresses the above evidence of systemic difficulty and shows how these problems can have harmful effects on children.

C.   Receivers' Report

On May 18, 1995, the Receivers submitted a joint report detailing the operation of the limited receiverships over the past few months. Though there are signs of progress, the Receivers also tell of epidemic inaction, resistance, frustration, and poor attitudes.

For example, the Protective Services Receiver states that children often remain overnight at the defendants' offices at 625 H Street N.E. The report tells of at least four children who slept at the facility in the month of May alone. The Receiver believes that "agency leadership does not demand the best from its staff," and that placements are not so difficult to find that children must remain in the offices. Foster parents also leave their children with the building's security guards during the day and this practice "is allowed and even condoned by some foster care workers who are desperate to keep homes, no matter how inadequate the foster parent may be." The Receiver concludes that

> [o]ne of the goals of this Receiver was to point out problems which could provide the basis for moving to solutions. The District has refused most efforts to help and in some instances has actively worked against the Receivership. For this, I have no choice but to support the concept of a General Receivership.

The Corrective Action Receiver concurs and maintains "that there is such an atmosphere of passivity and even detachment within the FSA that it is difficult to see how client and service problems can be effectively addressed." The Receiver notes that it is difficult to retain workers because they are frustrated with pay cuts, furloughs, lack of basic administrative supports, and unclear pronouncements on the permanency of contract jobs. One social worker responded to a January 13,

1995 survey distributed by the Receivers thus: "I need 'an experienced capable supervisor. I have been here eight months. I am now the senior member of the unit. Since that time, three social workers, ones with the most experience, have left the unit. Please help. This is dangerous.' " A May 12, 1995 letter from a supervisor to the Receiver painted an equally pathetic picture:

> We sincerely appreciate your cooperation in helping us to expeditiously obtain toner for our printer. However, as I mentioned in our conversation, we ask that you continue in your endeavor to assist us in acquiring other much needed supplies and materials, i.e.: Telephone lines, space, supplies, standardized forms, typewriter, summer camp activities for children and training for parents.

Though the Receivers have graciously and valiantly risen to address the "severe level of dysfunction in the agency" that surprised even them, the Court did not appoint these three professionals with the idea that they would spend their time tracking down office supplies. It is apparent that the defendants will not act of their own accord to assist the limited receivers with reform.

* * * After detailing various other problems reviewed above, the Receiver concludes from personal experience that "the environment is as dismal now as it was in the very beginnings of judicial intervention."

V. SUMMARY OF FINDINGS OF FACT

As the above recital of woes demonstrates, the defendants are radically out of compliance with the Court's orders. * * * The Court further finds that the problems in the District of Columbia's child welfare system are so widespread and persistent that the limited receiverships will not suffice to accomplish reform.

VI. CONCLUSIONS OF LAW

A. Contempt

Civil contempt does not have a punitive goal. It is "a remedial sanction designed to obtain compliance with a court order or to compensate for damage sustained as a result of noncompliance." Contempt is appropriate if clear and convincing evidence shows noncompliance, regardless of the intent of the contemnor.

1. *Good Faith.* The defendants argue that good faith and substantial compliance are defenses to contempt allegations. However, the cases they cite from this circuit * * * do not control.

In any case, the defendant's good faith is arguable at best. The remedial history outlined above demonstrates that the defendants have repeatedly attempted last-minute adjustments or compromises in an attempt to avoid sanctions. Because this pattern has persistently recurred since 1991, the Court must question whether the defendants truly intend to cooperate in the remedial efforts. Additionally, the defendants' recent actions cast an extremely bad light on their alleged good intentions. On March 30, 1995, the Mayor transmitted a bill to the District of Columbia City Council that sought to abolish private rights of action to enforce local statutory responsibilities to care for and protect abused and neglected children. * * *

* * *

2.   *Substantial Compliance.* Whether or not substantial compliance is a defense to contempt is irrelevant, for the defendants have not substantially complied with the Court's orders. * * *

Therefore, the Court holds that the defendants are in civil contempt of court for failing to comply with numerous provisions of the Court's orders. At this time, the Court will not impose any fines upon the defendants, and instead will take the measures outlined below.

B.   Full Receivership

* * *

The defendants make several arguments opposing the imposition of a full receivership. First, they state that the facts do not support the need for a full receivership because they have made and are continuing to make substantial progress. While it is true that the defendants have made some progress in various areas, the above factual findings show the urgent need for a new, more fundamental approach to change. * * *

* * *

The defendants also argue that the present Receivers be given more time to work before a full receivership is imposed. Because the Receivers themselves endorse the idea of a full receivership and because noncompliance is rampant in areas outside of the present Receivers' purview, this argument is unavailing. In fact, recent successes within the areas of receivership provide hope that change could occur elsewhere were a full receivership to be in place. * * *

Finally, the defendants argue that they have proposed a viable restructuring plan that would improve the state of the child welfare system and obviate the need for a receivership. * * * Four years ago the Court was told that the defendants had a "plan" to rebuild the agency. Now, facing contempt and full receivership, the defendants again put forth a proposed solution. There is no reason to believe this plan has more chance of success than the one the defendants presented at trial and quickly abandoned.

Therefore, the Court today imposes a full receivership over the child welfare system for the District of Columbia. As the accompanying order illustrates, the parties and Monitor shall attempt to agree upon the terms of a proposed order setting forth the steps necessary to effectuate this receivership. The parties have fully briefed the issue of the appropriate extent of the Receiver's powers, but the Court will defer resolution of this matter until after receipt of the proposed order. Obviously, the

Receiver will have to be granted broad powers to effectuate the fundamental changes needed.

* * *

VIII. CONCLUSION

Today is a sad day for the District of Columbia and an even sadder day for the children of the District of Columbia. The defendants should be extremely uncomfortable with their present level of compliance and are undoubtedly disappointed to learn of the imposition of the receivership. The Court does not take these steps lightly. It has repeatedly expressed its reluctance to impose contempt sanctions and to interfere in the operations of local government by imposing broad receiverships or issuing flurries of micromanaging orders. The plaintiffs have also expressed their reluctance to seek a finding of contempt. However, as the Court has warned the defendants with increasing frequency, it cannot tolerate widespread noncompliance with its orders. Notwithstanding the Court's warnings, outright hostility has replaced grudging acceptance. The pattern of delay and inaction that has characterized this case for the last few years must end now.

Abused and neglected children in the District of Columbia are not receiving the services and protection which are their desert and legal entitlement. The young child who was killed in February did not receive life-saving intervention. Boys and girls who must sleep in the defendants' office building do not receive the attention or resources necessary to provide them with a home for the night. Children who are shuttled from one emergency placement to another do not receive the continuity that their young psyches require. Perhaps most sadly of all, children awaiting adoption do not receive the expeditious help of the defendants in beginning a safer, more stable, and maybe even happier life.

At the time of the Cuban missile crisis, President John F. Kennedy noted that the Chinese character for crisis is a composite of two other characters meaning "danger" and "opportunity." The crisis now before the Court has just those elements. It is all too evident that the plaintiff children face great danger in the present system, and the Court intends for its ruling to provide the children and the defendants with the opportunity to begin again. Let us hope that the defendants respond to this opportunity.

MARISOL A. v. GIULIANI

United States District Court, S.D.N.Y., 1996.
929 F.Supp. 662

ROBERT J. WARD, DISTRICT JUDGE.

* * *

BACKGROUND

Plaintiffs are eleven children all of whom have suffered, and some of whom continue to be at risk of, severe abuse and neglect. These children allege that defendants, who are officials with responsibility for the Child Welfare Administration of the City of New York ("CWA") now renamed the New York City Administration for Children's Services ("ACS"), mishandled plaintiffs' cases and, through defendants' actions or inactions, deprived plaintiffs of their rights under the First, Ninth, and Fourteenth Amendments to the United States Constitution, under Article XVII of the New York State Constitution, as well as under numerous federal and state statutes.

The factual allegations of the complaint portray a child welfare program in crisis and collectively suggest systemic deficiencies of gross proportions. The eleven children who seek to represent the proposed class have endured a wide range of abuses and all reflect the dire situation facing children in the system. In their complaint, the named plaintiffs allege the following facts:

Marisol A. is a five-year old who was born two days after her mother, Ms. A., was arrested on charges of dealing drugs. CWA placed Marisol with Ms. C. during and subsequent to Ms. A.'s incarceration but, in 1994, CWA restored Marisol to her mother's custody despite her criminal history and reports that she was abusing Marisol during visitations. CWA failed to assess properly the appropriateness of this placement and took no steps to supervise or monitor Ms. A.'s home. Upon regaining custody, Ms. A. confined Marisol to a closet for several months, deprived her of sustenance resulting in her eating her own feces and plastic garbage bags to survive, and both physically and sexually abused her to the point of injury. During this period, Ms. A.'s sister and Ms. C. filed multiple reports of abuse with CWA to no avail. A housing inspector familiar with the signs of abuse discovered Marisol during a chance visit and reported the situation to the police. Despite Ms. C.'s eagerness to adopt Marisol, CWA has not begun the process of terminating Ms. A.'s parental rights and has not provided Marisol with counseling or support services.

Lawrence B. died on February 18, 1996 of AIDS-related illness at the age of nineteen. Lawrence's mother died of AIDS in or around 1985 leaving him an orphan and he entered the foster care system in 1995, at age seventeen, pursuant to a voluntary agreement signed by his aunt who could no longer care for him. After taking custody, CWA failed to assess Lawrence's medical condition for almost two months and then shuttled him from one inappropriate placement to another. Lawrence first spent seven months in a diagnostic facility and then was transferred to a group home that lacked the medical staff needed to monitor his condition. In fact, CWA neglected even to inform the agency of Lawrence's HIV-positive status. Finally, CWA placed Lawrence in a group home aimed to assist teenagers in making the transition to independent living. CWA again failed to alert that agency to Lawrence's medical condition. Even when the agency notified CWA that Lawrence needed hospice care, CWA suggested that the staff simply take him to the hospital when necessary. Despite his deteriorating health, CWA recommended continued placement in the group home and maintained a goal of independent living in his case plan until his death.

Thomas C. is a fifteen-year old who has been in foster care since he was seven. In those eight years, Thomas endured numerous placements including a hospital, a diagnostic center, and a residential treatment center ("RTC"). In 1993, without adequate investigation, CWA approved Thomas' placement with Rev. D., a minister Thomas met at the RTC, who took him to South Carolina. There Rev. D. sexually abused Thomas who subsequently ran away. In 1994, Thomas was returned to the RTC where he now resides. He has since attempted suicide twice and has run away from the RTC only to return after facing hardship and abuse on the streets. CWA has failed to determine the appropriateness of the RTC placement, to pursue the possibility of adoption, or to provide Thomas with counseling.

Shauna D. is a two-year old who lives with Ms. D., her drug-addicted mother. CWA has failed to investigate reports of suspected abuse despite the fact that Ms. D. has already lost custody of her six other children. In September 1995, Ms. M., a friend who had been caring for Shauna, filed for formal custody. In November 1995, however, Ms. D. forcibly took Shauna from Ms. M.'s home. Despite repeated calls from Shauna's law guardian, her CWA caseworker has failed to investigate adequately reports of abuse or to ensure that Ms. D. is in a drug rehabilitation program.

Ozzie E. is a fourteen-year old who suffers from seizure disorder, brain lesions, and behavioral problems. In 1995, Ozzie's father placed him in foster care after finding himself unable to care for Ozzie. Although Ozzie and his mother, Ms. E., both want to be reunited, he remains in a group home because CWA has failed to provide any family preservation services to enable Ms. E. to care for him. Although CWA acknowledges that the group home is not equipped to address Ozzie's neurological problems, the agency has taken no steps to return Ozzie to his mother.

Darren F. and David F. are seven-year old twins who have been in foster care since they were one. In 1990, CWA placed the twins with their grandmother who was too old to care for them and from whom they were removed after she allowed their drug-addicted mother to live with them. In 1991, CWA placed the twins, who already were evidencing signs of psychological trauma, with Ms. R. who made efforts to address the children's special needs. Despite Ms. R.'s requests, CWA failed to provide the twins with treatment as their behavior deteriorated. Finally, a psychiatrist recommended that, because of their young age, they remain with Ms. R. but enroll in a day treatment center. CWA, however, placed the twins in an inappropriate residential center where they remain today and has risked their chance to be adopted by Ms. R.

Bill G. is a fourteen-year old who is mentally retarded and suffers from a mild form of cerebral palsy. His sister, Victoria G., is ten. In 1985, CWA placed them together in the home of Ms. H. pursuant to a finding of parental neglect. The children's permanency goal was to return to their parents, Mr. and Mrs. G., and the case plan outlined steps for their parents to follow in that regard. CWA, however, failed to monitor the parents' progress and the children remained with Ms. H. even after her legal authority had lapsed. In 1989, Mr. and Mrs. G. agreed to voluntary placement but, during their infrequent visits, beat the children. Despite all of these factors, CWA still failed to obtain a termination of parental rights and has considered returning them to their father after they have spent more than ten years in Ms. H.'s care.

Brandon H. is a seven-year old who was placed in foster care at birth because his mother was twelve at the time and in foster care herself. In early 1992, CWA placed Brandon with Ms. W. but did not file a petition seeking termination of parental rights until later that year. The court terminated those rights in 1994 but, despite Ms. W.'s willingness to adopt him, CWA still has not even taken steps to transfer Brandon's case to the agency's adoption division. CWA thus allows Brandon to remain in foster care without addressing his need for permanency.

Steven I. is a sixteen-year old who has developed severe psychiatric and emotional problems after spending his entire life in foster care. Steven exhibits violent behavior and, by age twelve, Steven had attempted to rape a nine-year old girl, had stabbed other children with pencils, and had lit several fires. After CWA ignored a recommendation that Steven receive long-term residential treatment, his behavior deteriorated to the point that, at age fifteen, he was committed to New York Hospital as a "sexual predator." Upon his release, CWA placed him in an inappropriate group home from which he ran away in 1994. He now lives on the streets and CWA has failed to locate him or to provide him with any treatment.

In support of their claims, plaintiffs specifically allege that defendants fail to:

(1) appropriately accept reports of abuse and neglect for investigation;

(2) investigate those reports in the time and manner required by law;

(3) provide mandated preplacement preventive services to enable children to remain at home whenever possible;

(4) provide the least restrictive, most family-like placement to meet children's individual needs;

(5) provide services to ensure that children do not deteriorate physically, psychologically, educationally, or otherwise while in CWA custody;

(6) provide children with disabilities, including HIV/AIDS, with appropriate placements;

(7) provide appropriate case management or plans that enable children to return home or be discharged to permanent placements as quickly as possible;

(8) provide services to assist children who are appropriate for adoption in getting out of foster care;

(9) provide teenagers adequate services to prepare them to live independently once they leave the system;

(10) provide the administrative, judicial, or dispositional reviews to which children are entitled;

(11) provide caseworkers with training, support, or supervision; and

(12) maintain adequate systems to monitor, track, and plan for children.

Plaintiffs bring this action pursuant to 42 U.S.C. § 1983 * * *. They allege that defendants have violated and continue to violate their rights under the First, Ninth, and Fourteenth Amendments to the United States Constitution; the Adoption Assistance and Child Welfare Act of 1980 ("Adoption Assistance Act") * * *; the Child Abuse Prevention and Treatment Act ("CAPTA"); provisions of the Medicaid Act, the Americans with Disabilities Act of 1990 ("ADA"); § 504 of the Rehabilitation Act of 1973 ("Rehabilitation Act"); * * * [and the New York State Constitution and New York laws]. Plaintiffs seek injunctive or declaratory relief as needed to remedy defendants' alleged violations and, further, request the appointment of a receiver with full authority to oversee and direct the implementation of all the injunctive relief granted by the court, to restructure the New York City child welfare system, and to take all steps necessary to ensure that the child welfare system operates in full compliance with all applicable law. * * *

Before this Court are motions by both City and State defendants for an order dismissing the bulk of plaintiffs' federal constitutional and statutory claims as well as plaintiffs' state law claims. Also before the Court is plaintiffs' motion * * * for an order certifying this action as a class action on behalf of:

> [a]ll children who are or will be in the custody of the New York City Child Welfare Administration ("CWA"), and those children who, while not in the custody of CWA, are or will be at risk of neglect or abuse and whose status is known or should be known to CWA[.]

Finally, City defendants have moved for an order bifurcating this action.

DISCUSSION

I. Motions to Dismiss

* * *

A. Plaintiffs' Federal Constitutional Claims

Defendants ask this Court to dismiss plaintiffs' first cause of action which alleges violations of their rights derived from the First, Ninth, and Fourteenth Amendments to the United States Constitution. Although plaintiffs' first cause of action contains more specific language, their federal constitutional claims can be divided loosely into two significant categories: (1) violation of plaintiffs' substantive due process right to protection from harm while in state custody; and (2) violation of plaintiffs' right not to be deprived of entitlements created by New York State law without due process.

1. Substantive Due Process Claims

Defendants move to dismiss the first significant component of plaintiffs' first cause of action in which they assert that defendants have, through their actions or inactions, violated plaintiffs' substantive due process right to be free from harm. Defendants argue that, unlike the custodial plaintiffs whose claims defendants do not challenge, those children who are not in ACS custody have no federal substantive due process right to be protected from harm in light of the Supreme Court's decision in DeShaney v. Winnebago County Dep't of Social Servs. (1989). Defendants assert, therefore, that non-custodial plaintiffs fail to state a substantive due process claim upon which relief can be granted. This Court agrees. Indeed, plaintiffs concede that "[t]he non-custodial plaintiffs' constitutional claim is limited to their right not to be denied the protections and benefits of the detailed state law regarding child protection without due process." The following analysis of plaintiffs' substantive due process claims, therefore, applies only to custodial plaintiffs.

Under certain circumstances, the federal Constitution imposes upon the government an affirmative duty to provide services and care to individuals in state custody. The Supreme Court first recognized this obligation by granting incarcerated prisoners the right to adequate medical care pursuant to the Eighth Amendment. See Estelle v. Gamble (1976). Shortly thereafter, the Court extended this analysis and required the state to ensure the safety of involuntarily committed mental patients pursuant to the substantive component of the Fourteenth Amendment's Due Process Clause. See Youngberg v. Romeo (1982). The Court, interpreting this line of cases, has noted that "[t]aken together, they stand ... for the proposition that when the State takes a person into its custody and holds him there against his will, the Constitution imposes upon it a corresponding duty to assume some responsibility for his safety and general well-being." Under the *Youngberg* line of cases, therefore, the government must provide to those individuals in its custody reasonably safe conditions of confinement and general freedom from undue bodily restraint.

* * * This Court agrees with the decision of other courts to extend to children in foster care a substantive due process right to protection from harm.

The parties agree that custodial plaintiffs have a constitutional right to be free from harm. The issue facing this Court with respect to custodial plaintiffs, therefore, is not whether they are entitled to protection from harm but, rather, how broad that protection must be. The

Supreme Court has held that the right to be free from harm encompasses the right to essentials of care including adequate food, shelter, clothing, and medical attention. Additionally, the state must provide reasonably safe conditions of confinement. Custodial plaintiffs, however, ask this Court to take an expansive view and recognize a substantive due process right to be free not only from physical harm but also from psychological, emotional, and developmental harm. Defendants, on the other hand, urge this Court to take a narrower approach to custodial plaintiffs' substantive due process claims.

The Court is inclined, at this juncture, to take a broad view of the concept of harm in the context of plaintiffs' substantive due process claims. Clearly, the state is required to protect children in its custody from physical injury. This Court further finds that custodial plaintiffs have a substantive due process right to be free from unreasonable and unnecessary intrusions into their emotional well-being. * * *

a.   Right to Appropriate Conditions and Duration of Foster Care

As a key element of their substantive due process claims, plaintiffs allege that defendants have violated "their right to be housed in the least restrictive, most appropriate and family-like placement." In support of their motions to dismiss, however, defendants argue that custodial plaintiffs do not have a Fourteenth Amendment due process right to the least restrictive, optimal level of care or placement and, therefore, that children who are kept in foster care longer than necessary or who are denied services to enable them to reunite with their families fail to state a claim.

Courts generally agree that the Fourteenth Amendment does not require the state to provide children in foster care with an optimal level of care or treatment. * * *

Individuals in state custody, however, do have a constitutional right to conditions of confinement which bear a reasonable relationship to the purpose of their custody. * * * The goal of the child welfare system is "to further the best interest of children by helping to create nurturing family environments without infringing on parental rights." Plaintiffs thus are entitled to conditions and duration of foster care which are reasonably related to this goal. Additionally, as noted above, defendants have an affirmative obligation to provide custodial plaintiffs with adequate food, shelter, clothing, medical care, and reasonable safety.

This Court is satisfied that the right to be free from harm encompasses the right alleged by plaintiffs to appropriate conditions and duration of foster care. Indeed, the crux of plaintiffs' latter claim is that defendants' failure to provide safe and appropriate placements has caused them to suffer impermissible harm. Custodial plaintiffs have alleged sufficient facts to support the claim that they have been deprived of even adequate or appropriate conditions of foster care including certain basic necessities which defendants are obligated to provide. Thus, to the extent that custodial plaintiffs can establish that the conditions and duration of foster care are so inadequate as to violate plaintiffs' Fourteenth Amendment due process right to be free from harm, they are entitled to do so and defendants' motions to dismiss are denied.

b.   Right to Family Integrity

Another key element of plaintiffs' substantive due process claims is the allegation that defendants have violated "their right not to be deprived of a family relationship absent compelling reasons." While defendants acknowledge the constitutional foundation for the right to family integrity, they argue that this right is not implicated on the facts set forth in the complaint. Specifically, defendants assert that (1) plaintiffs fail to allege that defendants were wrongfully removing children from their biological parents and (2) any alleged failure of defendants to provide services to reunite biological family members does not rise to the level of a constitutional violation.

* * * Although the Supreme Court has held the parent-child relationship to be constitutionally protected, courts nevertheless have been loathe to impose a constitutional obligation on the state to ensure a particular type of family life or to create such an obligation "through the penumbral constitutional . . . right to familial privacy." In fact, the only courts to apply the concept of family integrity to the child welfare context have done so when children in foster care were denied visitation with siblings and parents.

Plaintiffs in the instant case do not allege facts suggesting that they have been denied such visitation rights but, rather, challenge defendants' general failure to provide services that function to preserve the family unit. Courts have held, however, that plaintiffs "do not have a constitutional right to rely on an agency to strengthen and reunite their families even if that agency has a statutory duty to do so." Thus, plaintiffs cannot argue that defendants have violated their right to family integrity and, to the extent that custodial plaintiffs allege a substantive due process right to associate with their biological family members, their claims must be dismissed.

Nevertheless, plaintiffs do have a constitutional right to protection from harm as noted above. Plaintiffs' family integrity claims are closely related to those pertaining to the duration of foster care and, by extension, fall within the concept of harm for substantive due process purposes. Indeed, plaintiffs suggest that defendants unnecessarily place children in foster care and allow children properly in foster care to languish without taking steps to reunite them with their biological family where appropriate. Once again, this Court is persuaded that plaintiffs have stated facts sufficient to support a claim that they have been impermissibly harmed in violation of the Fourteenth Amendment by defendants' failure to provide reasonable services and placements that protect custodial plaintiffs' right of association with their biological family members. Custodial plaintiffs, therefore, are entitled to show that defendants' actions or inactions regarding plaintiffs' familial relationships have caused them harm as defined by the Court. Defendants' motions to dismiss this portion of plaintiffs' first cause of action, therefore, are denied.

2.   Procedural Due Process Claims

Defendants further move to dismiss the second significant component of plaintiffs' first cause of action in which they assert that defendants have deprived plaintiffs of government services to which they have a statutory entitlement without due process of law. * * *

* * *

The Supreme Court has specifically declined to address whether state child welfare statutes give children an entitlement to protective services "which would enjoy due process protection against state deprivation...." DeShaney v. Winnebago County Dep't of Social Servs. (1989). * * * Lower courts faced with this question are divided.

* * *

Title 6 [of New York Social Services Law] sets forth a specific scheme for child protection the purpose of which is

> to encourage more complete reporting of suspected child abuse and maltreatment and to establish in each county of the state a child protective service capable of investigating such reports swiftly and competently and capable of providing protection for the child or children from further abuse or maltreatment and rehabilitative services for the child or children and parents involved.* * *

Each relevant provision of Title 6 contains the mandatory language necessary to elevate the benefit to an entitlement. * * * The Court finds, therefore, that New York's Child Protective Services laws are more than mere procedural guidelines and, in fact, give plaintiffs an entitlement to protective services of which they may not be deprived without due process of law.

An entitlement to child protective services thus having been established, the Court is unwilling at this juncture to dismiss plaintiffs' procedural due process claims.* * *

B.   Plaintiffs' Federal Statutory Claims

* * *

1.   Claims Pursuant to the Social Security Act

Defendants ask the Court to dismiss plaintiffs' second, third, and fifth causes of action brought pursuant to various provisions of the Social Security Act ("SSA") * * * on the ground that these provisions do not provide for a private right of action to enforce their requirements. Defendants do not argue that plaintiffs fail to state violations of these provisions but, rather, move to dismiss on the basis that plaintiffs are not entitled to pursue these claims in federal court.

When deciding whether a private right of action exists to enforce a federal funding statute, courts are bound by any expression of clear intent on the part of Congress to create such a right. Where no unambiguous statement of intent exists, courts must determine if the statute creates enforceable rights, privileges, or immunities. [In Wilder v. Virginia Hosp. Assoc. (1990)], the Supreme Court set forth three factors for courts to consider: (1) whether " 'the provision in question was intend[ed] to benefit the putative plaintiff' "; (2) whether the provision "reflects merely a 'congressional preference' for a certain kind of conduct rather than a binding obligation on the governmental unit"; and (3) whether "the interest the plaintiff asserts is 'too vague and amorphous' such that it is 'beyond the competence of the judiciary to enforce.' "

Once these three factors have been met, the burden shifts to the state actor to show Congressional intent to the contrary. * * *

a.   The Adoption Assistance Act Claims

* * *

Whether a private right exists to enforce provisions of the Adoption Assistance Act has been the subject of recent debate in both the judicial and legislative branches of government. In 1992, the Supreme Court considered whether a private individual could bring a § 1983 claim to enforce § 671(a)(15) of the Adoption Assistance Act. See Suter v. Artist M. (1992). The Court asked whether "Congress, in enacting the Adoption Act, unambiguously confer[red] upon the child beneficiaries of the Act a right to enforce the requirement that the State make 'reasonable efforts' to prevent a child from being removed from his home, and once removed to reunify the child with his family." Departing from earlier precedent, the Court held that § 671(a)(15) was too vague and amorphous to provide a cause of action under § 1983 and that Congress did not intend "to create the private remedy sought by plaintiffs." In the following years, several other courts applied *Suter* to find that no private right of action exists to enforce this statute. Defendants rely on this line of cases in support of their motions to dismiss.

In 1994, however, Congress expressed its disapproval of the Supreme Court's decision in *Suter* and amended the SSA. * * *

* * *

This Court does not read the Amendment as a clear expression of Congress' intent to create a private right of enforcement. Rather, this Court is persuaded that Congress has expressed its intent to require courts to apply pre-*Suter* case law to determine the private enforceability of SSA provisions other than § 671(a)(15).[8] Courts that recently have considered this issue have adopted this approach. Accordingly, only the narrow holding in *Suter* remains and this Court "must 'rewind the clock'

---

8.   It is undisputed that the Amendment reaffirms the Supreme Court's decision in Suter that no private right exists to enforce § 671(a)(15) and plaintiffs do not allege violations of that provision.

and look to cases prior to *Suter* to determine the enforceability'' of the provisions at issue in the instant case. The Court must now apply the factors set forth in Wilder to decide whether plaintiffs are entitled to pursue their claims under § 1983.

[The Court then applied the Wilder factors and concluded that they had been met.]

* * *

* * * Additionally, this Court finds no evidence that Congress has indicated its intent to preclude private plaintiffs from seeking to enforce provisions of the Adoption Assistance Act other than § 671(a)(15). For the foregoing reasons, defendants' motions to dismiss plaintiffs' claims pursuant to provisions of the Adoption Assistance Act are hereby denied.

b.   CAPTA Claims

Plaintiffs further allege violations of two provisions of CAPTA which govern federal grants to states for child abuse and neglect prevention and treatment programs. The first, 42 U.S.C. § 5106a(b)(2), requires a state, as a condition of federal funding, to initiate a prompt investigation into all reports of abuse or neglect and to take immediate steps to protect children whom the state believes have suffered or are at risk of suffering abuse or neglect. The second, 42 U.S.C. § 5106a(b)(3), requires a state to have in effect administrative procedures, personnel, training procedures, facilities, and related programs and services "to ensure that the State will deal effectively with child abuse and neglect cases" in order to be eligible for federal funds.

* * *

* * * [t]his Court is persuaded that plaintiffs are entitled to claim alleged violations of CAPTA pursuant to § 1983. In so doing, the Court has considered and now rejects the notion that the discretionary nature of the regulation renders CAPTA too vague for the court to enforce. * * *

* * *

[The court's discussion of plaintiffs' ADA and Rehabilitation Act Claims, state law claims and motion for class certification and of defendants' motion for bifurcation is omitted.]

CONCLUSION

For the foregoing reasons, defendants' motions to dismiss * * * are denied to the extent that (1) custodial plaintiffs may pursue their substantive due process claims based on alleged violations of their right to be free from harm and all plaintiffs may pursue their procedural due process claims based on alleged violations of various provisions of New York's Child Protective Services laws * * * (2) plaintiffs may pursue their federal statutory claims based on the Adoption Assistance and

Child Welfare Act, * * * the Child Abuse Prevention and Treatment Act, the Americans with Disabilities Act, and the Rehabilitation Act. * * *

Notes and Questions

1. *Questions about* LaShawn A. (a) Why was the child welfare system ultimately so unresponsive to the monitor in *LaShawn A.?* Why might the political system want the monitor to fail? (b) After the child welfare system was in receivership, to whom can the receiver complain if the agency still does not comply with the court orders? (c) Who will pay for improvements in the agency?

2. LaShawn A. *aftermath.* Six months after the receivership was imposed, the receiver said that his plans had "ground to a halt" because he lacked control of his agency's budget. Vernon Loeb, Progress on Foster Care Stalled by Budget Delay, Receiver Says, Washington Post, Feb. 29, 1996 at J01. City officials had not transferred funds for the receivership into an account he could access and were challenging the legality of the receivership (an effort that was not successful). LaShawn A. v. Barry, 1996 WL 679301, 107 F.3d 923 (D.C.Cir.) (1996). The mayor's budget response to the receivership was an initiative to prevent it from "unduly increasing costs," even though the budget the receiver requested was more than 20% below what was spent the year before. Loeb, supra.

3. *Questions about* Marisol A. What are the sources for the rights the plaintiffs assert in *Marisol A.?* What remedies do the *Marisol A.* plaintiffs want?

4. Marisol A. *settlement.* Some attorneys who represented the *LaShawn A.* plaintiffs also represented the *Marisol A.* plaintiffs. In part because of the lack of progress in the District of Columbia foster care system, the *Marisol A.* attorneys decided to settle in December, 1998. Another important factor was that New York City had been working hard to improve its child protection system since the 1995 beating death of six-year-old Elisa Izquierdo by her mother. Elisa's story made headlines because of the appalling "pattern of error, omission and illegality" that characterized the child protective services response to reports of her abuse. Nina Bernstein and Frank Bruni, She Suffered in Plain Sight But Alarms Were Ignored, N.Y.Times, Dec. 12, 1995 at 1. Also, her story seemed particularly poignant because she had come to the attention of "a real prince," Prince Michael of Greece, who had promised to pay her private school tuition through the 12th grade. Id. After Elisa's death, New York City child welfare services became a separate agency that reported directly to the mayor. Nicholas Scopetta, who had been active with the Children's Aid Society and had years of government experience, gave up a lucrative law practice to head the new agency. Dale Russakoff, The Protector, The New Yorker, April 21, 1997 at 58. Interestingly enough, Scopetta and his two brothers had been removed from their home when he was five and spent five years in foster care. Id.

In the *Marisol A.* settlement, the City agreed to be guided for two years by an advisory panel of experts, who would have free access to city officials and their records. If the City failed to act in good faith, the experts would testify against the City in subsequent litigation. For the plaintiffs, the settlement meant "gaining unprecedented independent scrutiny of the agency and a sharper legal case against the City if it should renege on its commitment." Rachel L. Swarns, Finding Common Ground on Child Welfare, N. Y. Times, Dec. 6, 1998 at 49, 51. There were advantages for the City also. With 40,000 children in foster care, the City could concentrate on improving the child welfare system, rather than litigating. Further, the City avoided the potentially inflexible mandates a court might impose and additional negative publicity. Id.

5. *Successful child advocacy projects.* As of 1996, twenty-one states had been sued because of inadequate child welfare programs. Congressional Testimony Before the House Comm. on Ways and Means, 1996 WL 10829094 (June 27, 1996) (statement of Select Comm. Chr. Hon. George Miller). *LaShawn A.* clearly shows that litigation alone cannot reform such programs.

Sheryl Dicker, an attorney and child advocate, studied a variety of successful child advocacy projects. She identified four ingredients of successful advocacy present in all the case studies:

> * * *(1) Advocates must propose concrete solutions to the problems they address; (2) advocates must use a variety of strategies over a prolonged period to achieve their goals; (3) advocates must find a "partner" inside government to achieve successful implementation of reforms; (4) advocates must work toward enabling parents or children to "call the shots" or to be empowered to make decisions affecting their lives.

> To varying degrees, the advocates also made use of the media to highlight the problems they sought to remedy. While the media were a powerful tool for the exposure of a problem, the process of negotiation was generally shielded from the glare of publicity.

> All of the advocates lobbied their state legislatures to pass legislation or make additional budget allocations, or got executive agencies to develop new government policies. Some of the case studies illustrate other strategies, including the production of analytical studies, the use of community organizing, and the filing of administrative complaints to secure the cutoff of federal funds. Finally, the successful advocates all seem to have been sufficiently flexible to change strategies as dictated by political circumstances.

> Another common thread is the presence of an "inside/outside" relationship between the advocates and governmental officials as a necessary ingredient for successful implementation. * * * Full implementation, however, always required the presence of a skilled administrator with the necessary management tools to enforce new government policies and practices. Without these cooperative or reluctant inside partners, the often brilliant advocacy strategies would have produced only paper victories.

Sheryl Dicker, Stepping Stones: Successful Advocacy for Children 7–8 (1990).

For an additional case study, see Ellen Borgersen and Stephen Shapiro, *G.L. v. Stangler*: A Case Study in Court–Ordered Child Welfare Reform, 1997 J. Disp. Resol. 189.

SECTION 5. LIABILITY FOR HARM

KARA B. v. DANE COUNTY

Supreme Court of Wisconsin, 1996.
555 N.W.2d 630.

JON P. WILCOX, JUSTICE.

* * *

The relevant facts are not in dispute. In 1989 and 1990, Kara B. and Mikaela R. were adjudged to be children in need of protection or services in separate juvenile court proceedings, and were placed in the temporary custody of the Dane County Department of Social Services for foster home placement. Kara B., a seven year old girl, was placed in a licensed foster home operated by Roxanne Smit on March 28, 1989, and remained there until July 14, 1990. Mikaela R., an eleven year old girl, was placed in the Smit home on June 11, 1990. She remained there until December 18, 1990, when she fled after being sexually assaulted at knifepoint by two men in the basement of the home. The men were known to have a history of physically and sexually abusing children. In the course of investigating the assault, police contacted Kara B., who told them that she too had been sexually abused by Smit and by a man who had lived in the foster home during the course of her stay there.

In separate actions brought under 42 U.S.C. § 1983 and state-law negligence and professional malpractice claims, Kara B. and Mikaela R. sued Dane County for damages resulting from physical and sexual abuse that occurred during their separate stays in the Smit foster home. In the case brought by Kara B., the circuit court, Judge Mark A. Frankel, granted Dane County's motion for summary judgment dismissing the § 1983 claims. The court concluded that the Dane County public officials were entitled to qualified immunity because Kara B. had not shown that the public officials had violated a clearly established constitutional right. In Mikaela R.'s case, a second circuit court, Judge Gerald C. Nichol, denied Dane County's motion for summary judgment. This decision was based on the circuit court's determination that the Dane County public officials were not entitled to qualified immunity because they had a clearly established constitutional duty to protect Mikaela R. while she was in the Smit home, and that a reasonable jury could have found that the Dane County public officials had violated that duty.

The court of appeals held that: (1) the Dane County public officials were not entitled to qualified immunity from the 42 U.S.C. § 1983 claims brought by Kara B. and Mikaela R. because the public officials were accused of violating a clearly established right, (2) the public officials' conduct should be assessed based on a professional judgment standard, and (3) Dane County was not entitled to qualified immunity. Dane County petitioned for review and we granted the petition on January 16, 1996.

I.

The doctrine of qualified immunity protects public officials from civil liability if their conduct does not violate a person's clearly established constitutional or statutory right. Qualified immunity is designed to allow public officials to perform their duties without being hampered by the expense or threat of litigation. * * *

Qualified immunity does not protect public officials who have allegedly violated someone's clearly established constitutional right. This, in part, stems from the fact that officials may reasonably anticipate that violation of a clearly established constitutional right will give rise to liability. * * * The parties dispute whether the constitutional right of foster children to safe and secure placement in a foster home was clearly established in 1989. * * *

* * *

* * * Consequently, we must determine whether, in March 1989, existing case law had clearly established a constitutional right for a foster child to be placed in a safe and secure foster home to such an extent that a reasonable public official would have been put on notice that violation of such a right could lead to liability.

The examination begins with Estelle v. Gamble (1976). In *Estelle*, the Supreme Court considered whether various prison officials had subjected a prisoner to cruel and unusual punishment in violation of the Eight Amendment by inadequately treating his injuries. * * * This case established that the state owes a constitutional duty to prisoners arising from the fact that prisoners are in the state's custody.

The extension of this duty to foster children was first alluded to in Doe v. New York City Dep't of Social Services (2d Cir.1981).* * *

In 1982, the Supreme Court extended the state's duty to involuntarily committed mental patients. Youngberg v. Romeo (1982). The *Youngberg* Court held that a committed individual had constitutionally protected liberty interests under the Due Process Clause of the Fourteenth Amendment to reasonably safe conditions of confinement, freedom from unreasonable bodily restraints, and such minimally adequate training as reasonably might be required by these interests. The reasoning used by the Court in reaching its decision suggests that foster children should be entitled to a similar constitutional right.

* * *

The Eleventh Circuit recognized such an extension of *Youngberg* in Taylor by and through Walker v. Ledbetter (1987). The *Taylor* court held that "a child involuntarily placed in a foster home is in a situation so analogous to a prisoner in a penal institution and a child confined in a mental health facility that the foster child may bring a section 1983 action for violation of fourteenth amendment rights." In so holding, the Taylor court relied on the reasoning of *Youngberg:*

The liberty interest in this case is analogous to the liberty interest in Youngberg. In both cases, the state involuntarily placed the person in a custodial environment, and in both cases, the person is unable to seek alternative living arrangements.

Although we do not believe it impossible, or even improbable, that a reasonable social worker would have been aware of the natural application of *Youngberg* to foster children, we do not believe that prior to DeShaney v. Winnebago County Dep't of Social Services, the constitutional right to reasonably safe and secure placement in a foster home had reached the level of clearly established. We also do not believe that *DeShaney*, if viewed in isolation from the cases that preceded it, is sufficient to clearly establish such a constitutional right. However, when *Estelle*, *Youngberg*, *Taylor*, *Doe*, and *DeShaney* are read together a constitutional right is clearly established.

In *DeShaney*, the mother of a child who had been beaten brought a § 1983 action against social workers and local officials who, although having received complaints that the boy was being abused by the father, had not removed him from the father's custody. The Supreme Court held that the state does not owe a duty to protect a child who was abused by his natural father. The reasoning employed by the Court to reach this decision clearly illustrates that foster children do have constitutional rights under the Due Process Clause. The Court based its holding on the fact that the state's duty only arises when it takes a person into its custody and so deprives that person of the ability to care for himself:

> Taken together [*Youngberg* and *Estelle*] stand only for the proposition that when the State takes a person into custody and holds him there against his will, the Constitution imposes upon it a corresponding duty to assume some responsibility for his safety and general well-being.... The rationale for this principle is simple enough: when the State by the affirmative exercise of its power so restrains an individual's liberty that it renders him unable to care for himself, and at the same time fails to provide for his basic human needs—e.g. food, clothing, shelter, medical care, and reasonable safety—it transgresses the substantive limits on state action set by the Eighth Amendment and the Due Process Clause.

When this reasoning is examined in the context of *Estelle*, *Youngberg*, *Taylor*, and *Doe*, it is apparent that the *DeShaney* decision completed the clear establishment of a constitutional right to safe and secure placement in a foster home. There can be no doubt that the explicit holding of *DeShaney*—that the state assumes responsibility for an individual's safety when that individual is taken into custody by the state—provided public officials with adequate notice.

The *DeShaney* Court also made specific reference to foster homes:

> Had the State by affirmative exercise of its power removed Joshua from free society and placed him in a foster home operated by its agents, we might have a situation sufficiently analogous to incarceration or institutionalization to give rise to an affirmative duty to

protect. Indeed several Courts of Appeals have held, by analogy to *Estelle* and *Youngberg*, that the State may be held liable under the Due Process Clause for failing to protect children in foster homes from mistreatment at the hands of their foster parents. We express no view on the validity of this analogy, however, as it is not before us in the present case.

This footnote, although not determinative on its own, illustrates that the Court considered the effect of its holding on the rights of foster children. The footnote should have also served as a warning to social workers that they should carefully examine the holding of *DeShaney*. If the Dane County public officials had considered the holding of *DeShaney* and the trend established by *Estelle*, *Youngberg*, *Taylor*, and *Doe* when they took Kara B. and Mikaela R. into custody, they would have certainly expected to assume some responsibility for their safety.

Dane County points out that the *DeShaney* Court did not directly confront the application of the state's duty to those in its custody to the foster home setting.[2] We do not discount this fact; however, it was not necessary for the circuit court to directly consider the issue to clearly establish a constitutional right.

In addition to arguing that *DeShaney* does not clearly establish a constitutional right, Dane County asserts that Doe v. Bobbitt (7th Cir.1989) would have led a reasonable public official to believe that no constitutional right to safe and secure placement in a foster home existed in 1989. Although the *Bobbitt* case does not strengthen the clear establishment of a constitutional right by *DeShaney, Youngberg, Estelle, Doe*, and *Taylor*, it also does not destroy it.

* * *

The *Bobbitt* court was called on to determine whether foster children had a clearly established constitutional right in 1984; the issue in this case is whether such a right was clearly established in 1989. * * *

* * *

The impact of *Bobbitt* is further weakened by the Seventh Circuit's decision in *K.H.* In *K.H.*, the court was called on to determine whether foster children had a clearly established right in 1986. The Seventh Circuit stated that its own decision in *Bobbitt* was limited to cases in which the child was placed with a relative. * * *

* * *

2. Another argument that could be made, but was not raised, is that even though *DeShaney* completed the establishment of a clear constitutional right, the one month between the *DeShaney* decision and the placement of Kara B. in the Smit home was not a sufficient period for a reasonable public official to acquire notice. The relevant date for determining if a clearly established constitutional right existed is the date on which the foster child left the foster home. A social worker's duty does not end when a child is placed in a foster home. If this were the case, a child could be left in an abusive foster home for years without hope of rescue. Thus, the insufficient notice argument must fail as Kara B. spent almost sixteen months in the Smit home. Certainly, more than seventeen months need not elapse before a reasonable public official would have notice of the holding of a case affecting his liability.

In sum, we believe that the trend beginning with *Estelle* and ending with *DeShaney* created a clearly established right. The first significant steps toward establishing this right were taken by the Supreme Court in *Estelle* and *Youngberg*. The *Doe* court then recognized a constitutional right of foster children. The *Taylor* court moved the right closer to being clearly established by the explicit extension of the *Youngberg* reasoning to foster children. The Supreme Court provided the final link in *DeShaney*. Accordingly, we conclude that Kara B. and Mikaela R. had a clearly established constitutional right under the Due Process Clause to safe and secure placement in a foster home.

II.

The next issue that we address is the appropriate scope of the public officials' constitutionally imposed duty to place foster children in a safe and secure environment. Constitutional issues are questions of law that this court reviews without deference to the holdings of the lower courts.

Dane County argues that a deliberate indifference standard should be used to evaluate whether the foster children's rights were violated. The plaintiffs assert that a professional judgment standard is appropriate. We hold that those entrusted with the task of ensuring that children are placed in a safe and secure foster home owe a constitutional duty that is determined by a professional judgment standard.

It is undisputed that a deliberate indifference standard is imposed on public officials for claims brought by prisoners based on the Eighth Amendment. Under this standard, liability is imposed when public officials exhibit deliberate indifference to a risk to the prisoner that was actually known to them. * * * However, in *Youngberg,* the Supreme Court asserted that the professional judgment standard is appropriate for public officials charged with the care of institutionalized mentally retarded individuals.

The *Youngberg* Court defined the professional judgment standard as follows:

> [T]he decision, if made by a professional, is presumptively valid; liability may be imposed only when the decision by the professional is such a substantial departure from accepted professional judgment, practice, or standards as to demonstrate that the person responsible actually did not base the decision on such a judgment.

The Court reasoned that this standard was appropriate because "[p]ersons who have been involuntarily committed are entitled to more considerate treatment and conditions of confinement than criminals whose conditions of confinement are designed to punish."

* * *

We agree that *Youngberg* is more closely analogous to claims involving foster children than *Estelle*. We also find compelling the argument that foster children should be entitled to greater rights than prisoners. Accordingly, we conclude that the duty of public officials to provide foster children with a safe and secure placement is based on a professional judgment standard.

* * *

The decision of the court of appeals is affirmed.

Notes and Questions

1. *Standard of liability. Kara B.* adopts a professional judgment standard, but some courts use a deliberate indifference standard. See, e.g., White v. Chambliss, 112 F. 3rd 731 (4th Cir.1997). Even when a professional judgment standard is used, it may be more limited than *Kara B.'s* approach. See, e.g., K.H. ex rel. Murphy v. Morgan, 914 F.2d 846, 854 (7th Cir.1990) ("[O]nly if without justification based either on financial constraints or on considerations of professional judgment they [agents of the state] place the children in hands they know to be dangerous or otherwise unfit do they expose themselves to liability"). What standard do you think should be used for children in foster care?

2. *A conservative stance.* The conservative Fourth Circuit has substantially limited state liability for harm to foster children under 42 U.S.C. § 1983. Relying on *DeShaney's* footnote 9 (quoted in *Kara B.*), the court distinguished between voluntary placements in foster care and those in which the state had affirmatively exercised its power to remove the child. Milburn v. Anne Arundel County Dep't of Soc. Serv., 871 F.2d 474 (4th Cir.1989).

In a more recent decision involving an involuntary foster placement, the Fourth Circuit held that the child's liberty interests had not been violated because the plaintiffs (a) had failed to show that the state knew the foster home was dangerous but ignored the danger when the child was placed, and (b) had failed to establish liability for failure to protect the child once she had been placed. "[G]iven the state of this circuit's law on the issue and the absence of controlling Supreme Court authority, we cannot say that a right to affirmative state protection for children placed in foster care was clearly established at the time of [the child's] death." (The child died in January, 1992). White v. Chambliss, 112 F.3d 731 (4th Cir.1997). The court also held that the state had no affirmative obligation to protect individuals against private violence and that foster parents were not state agents. Id.

3. *Voluntary vs. involuntary placements.* A number of commentators have argued that the state's duty of care should not depend on whether the foster placement was voluntary or involuntary. A "voluntary" foster care placement may not be truly voluntary when the state coerces the parent with threats of child protective proceedings or when the parent has no alternatives and needs temporary care for a child. Further, the voluntary/involuntary distinction refers to the parents' decision, not the child's. Because children may not voluntarily leave foster care, a foster child's right to a safe placement should not turn on whether the parents placed them in foster care willingly or unwillingly. See Karen M. Blum, *DeShaney*: Custody, Creation of Danger, and Culpability, 27 Loy. L.A. L. Rev. 435 (1994); Kevin M. Ryan, Stemming the Tide of Foster Care Runaways: A Due Process Perspective, 42 Cath. U.L.Rev. 271 (1993); Laura Oren, *DeShaney's* Unfinished Business: The Foster Child's Due Process Right to Safety, 69 N.C. L. Rev. 112 (1990).

4. *State actor*. Is the foster parent a state actor for purposes of a § 1983 suit? Generally no, and hence the foster parent would not be individually liable. See, e.g., Walker v. Johnson, 891 F.Supp. 1040, 1051 (M.D.Pa. 1995) (foster parents not state actors because "1) the care of foster children is not a power exclusively reserved to the state; 2) the [state] does not exercise coercive power over foster parents, and relegates to them, for the most part, day-to-day parenting decisions; and 3) there is not a sufficiently close nexus between the state and the challenged action").

5. *State tort liability*. Should the state be held liable for foster parents' negligence, or would such liability place too great a burden on the state? Unless a statute imposes state responsibility, most courts hold that the state is not liable, because they find no agency, respondeat superior, or vicarious liability. See, e.g., Stanley v. State Indust., Inc., 630 A.2d 1188 (N.J. 1993). But see Nichol v. Stass, 697 N.E.2d 758, 762–63 (Ill. 1998). Unless barred by sovereign immunity, however, courts are willing to hold the state liable in tort for a child's injuries when the state has negligently placed the child with foster parents who were known to be abusive. Id.

Foster parents have been considered state employees in other contexts. See, e.g., Hunte v. Blumenthal, 680 A.2d 1231 (Conn. 1996) (foster parents were "employees," not independent contractors, and thus were entitled to defense and indemnification in wrongful death action brought against them by the estate of a foster child who died in their care); Ga. Code Ann. § 50–21–22 (foster parents are employees for purposes of state tort claims).

6. *Protections for foster parents*. Should the foster parents be treated as "parents" in a tort suit by a child injured while in their care? Some statutes provide immunity that is coextensive with parental immunity. See, e.g., Spikes v. Banks, 586 N.W.2d 106 (Mich.App.1998)

Should the state protect foster parents by providing insurance or indemnification? For a discussion of the inadequacy of damage actions, see Michael B. Mushlin, Unsafe Havens: The Case for Constitutional Protection of Foster Children from Abuse and Neglect, 23 Harv. C. R.-C. L. L.Rev. 199 (1988). What system would best protect the interests of foster children and foster parents alike? See Karen Cavanaugh and Daniel Pollack, Liability Protections for Foster Parents, Kan. J. L. and Pub. Pol'y 78 (1997).

PROBLEM 5–4

Fourteen-year-old Annie ran away from home and was placed in a foster home in September. While there she entered a sexual relationship with the seventeen-year-old son of the foster parents. In March her foster mother informed Annie's social worker that Annie and her son had become sexual partners, but nothing was done. In June Annie was found to be two months pregnant and she was transferred to an institution in July. Annie sues under § 1983, alleging that the state had violated her 14th Amendment rights to liberty and substantive due process of law because she had a right to be protected from conditions under which she might become pregnant. Should she prevail?

SECTION 6. TYPES OF PLACEMENTS

A. *Foster Parents*

1. *Kinship Care: Relatives as Foster Parents*

Under federal foster care requirements, states "shall consider giving preference to an adult relative over a non-related caregiver when determining a placement for a child, provided that the relative caregiver meets all relevant State child protection standards." 42 U.S.C. § 671 (a)(19). As the following materials indicate, kinship foster care has become an important option.

U.S. GENERAL ACCOUNTING OFFICE, CHILD WELFARE: COMPLEX NEEDS STRAIN CAPACITY TO PROVIDE SERVICES 21–22 (1995).

When foster care is necessary, states have increasingly placed children with relatives in what is called kinship care. The proportion of foster children placed with relatives grew from 18 percent to 31 percent between 1986 and 1990 in 25 states, including California and New York. The proportions were even higher in some metropolitan areas, such as New York City, where about half of foster children were in kinship care in the early 1990s. African American children are especially likely to be placed in kinship care. * * *

States have increased their use of kinship care for a variety of reasons: to maintain children's ties to their families; encourage long-term placements; meet federal standards of care; offset shortages of traditional foster homes; and, in some cases, save on costs by offering lower payments. Kinship care is less costly than traditional foster homes in those states where relatives are ineligible for state foster care payments. Although relatives might be eligible for assistance from AFDC, AFDC levels are significantly lower than state foster care maintenance payments.

Kinship care, however, poses several challenges. First, children's access to needed services may be more limited because kinship foster parents are more likely to live in impoverished communities and lack experience accessing needed services than other foster parents. Second, children may be more vulnerable to repeated neglect or abuse because they are more at risk of unsupervised visits with parents or other relatives from whose care they were removed. Third, child welfare agencies do not always monitor or supervise kinship care placements as much as traditional foster care placements. Finally, children in kinship care tend to stay in foster care longer than other foster children because, for various reasons, child welfare agencies are less likely to arrange alternative placements, such as guardianship or adoption. In those states where relatives receive AFDC rather than foster care payments, AFDC costs may offset savings that might have resulted from lower reimbursement rates when children remain in kinship care for prolonged periods.

Notes and Questions

1. *Complex relationships.* Kinship care placements often involve complex family structures. A study in kinship care in Cook County, Illinois, concluded that:

> A broad view of the family is required to understand fully the complexity of relationships, the caregiving burden, and the resource drain experienced by the kinship networks of children in kinship foster care. The caregiving relationships arranged within kinship systems of children in state custody are varied and often quite intricate. Most of the children selected for this study had siblings and were living in the same kinship foster home with at least one sibling. Many of the children also had siblings living at home with their parents, with other relatives, and in nonrelated foster care. In addition, the kinship foster homes in which these children lived had several children and adults living in them. In addition to the kinship foster child's siblings, the caregivers' biological children and other children related to the caregivers were also living in many of the homes. Over three-quarters of the kinship foster homes had more than five persons living in them and 55% of the children lived in kinship foster homes with at least three other children under 18 years of age.

Faith Johnson Bonecutter and James P. Gleason, Broadening Our View: Lessons From Kinship Foster Care, 5 J. of Multicultural Social Work 99, 105 (1997).

> The study found that 67% of the caregivers were grandparents or great-grandparents. Over half the caregivers worked outside the home and slightly more than 25% received SSI disability or retirement income. The median experience of the caseworkers working with the kinship homes was less than two years; only 12% had master's degrees. Id. at 103, 105.

2. *Special rules?* Should kinship foster families be governed by the same rules as other foster families? Should they be subject to the same licensing rules? Should the permanency planning goals, usually reunification or adoption, be the same? For suggestions for special rules, with case examples, see Madeleine L. Kurtz, The Purchase of Families Into Foster Care: Two Case Studies and the Lessons They Teach, 26 Conn. L. Rev.1454 (1994).

3. *Constitutional rights and funding.* Although kinship care is looked upon favorably in federal policy , some states have provided no funding or only reduced rate funding for relative foster homes compared to non-relative foster homes. What arguments could you make that a child has a constitutional right to stay with kin rather than strangers in foster care and thus that kinship care should be fully funded? Consider the following:

> In Lipscomb v. Simmons [884 F.2d 1242 (9th Cir.1989), *rev'd,* 962 F.2d 1374 (9th Cir.1992)(en banc)] the plaintiffs challenged an Oregon statute that authorized funds for the foster care of children but did not provide funds to children placed in foster care with relatives. Plaintiffs argued—and the state conceded—that children have a fundamental right to live with family members, including members of extended families. The state contended, however, that it has no constitutional obligation to fund the exercise of fundamental rights. The Ninth Circuit

panel viewed the issue in a different light. It determined that once the state develops a "special relationship" with the children by placing them in foster care, it assumes a duty to secure their constitutional liberty. By denying aid to foster children placed with relatives, Oregon's statutory scheme burdened plaintiffs' fundamental liberty interest in family autonomy. The panel concluded that Oregon must provide foster care funds for children who live with relatives if it funds non-relative foster care.

In a closely divided decision, the Ninth Circuit sitting en banc, reversed the panel determination. The court viewed the issue as the state suggested: as an attempt to impose an affirmative obligation to provide assistance. Having reframed the issue in this manner, the majority found no constitutional infirmities and upheld the statutory scheme. The court said:

> The barrier to plaintiffs' exercise of any fundamental right is that their relatives either lack or are unwilling to spend the money to take care of them. Because Oregon has no affirmative obligation to fund plaintiffs' exercise of a right to maintain family relationships free from governmental interference, we decline to apply heightened scrutiny. . . .

Daan Braveman and Sarah Ramsey, When Welfare Ends: Removing Children from the Home for Poverty Alone, 70 Temple Law Review 447, 464 (1997).

Foster care can be funded with federal money, state money, or a combination of state and federal funds. When a foster home is funded with federal money, federal statutes require equal funding for kin and non-kin care. Miller v. Youakim, 440 U.S. 125 (1979).

4. *The influence of race.* Discouragingly, some research indicates that race negatively influences caseworkers' decisions and the families they serve. One study, for example, asked child protection service administrators to study brief vignettes of child maltreatment and to indicate levels of risk and types of interventions:

> The vignettes were varied by race and the scores compared. There was no consistency in decision-making. For example, in one vignette a three-year-old was left unsupervised and ingested some cocaine. In the Caucasian vignette, the child was more likely to remain at home under supervision. In the African American vignette, the child was more likely to enter out-of-home care under supervision. The facts were the same; the race valued and influenced the choice made. * * *

Carol W. Williams, Personal Reflections on Permanency Planning and Cultural Competency, 5 Journal of Multicultural Social Work 9, 10(1997).

Another study found that "clients who perceive themselves as ethnic or racial minorities expected to be negatively evaluated by the public systems that serve them. They expected and feared condescension, discrimination and a lack of understanding of them, their background and culture and what it signifies." Id. In another study, child protective service workers did not have high expectations for change in African American families, and the agency gave the families the services that were available, rather than what was needed. Id. at 11.

5. *Criticism.* Some critics of funded kinship care view it not only as a needless drain on scarce financial resources, but also as a disincentive to family reunification. They suggest that when a grandmother, for example, gets paid more for keeping her grandchildren in kinship foster care than the children's mother would get from welfare, there is a financial incentive to keep the children in foster care. In an opinion article written while she was a judge in Manhattan Family Court, the well-known "Judge Judy" posits an example of a grandmother who cares for her daughters' four children, receiving generous foster care payments because two of the children are special needs children: "Her drug-addicted daughter drops by occasionally to see her and ask for money, which she gets. With more money in the household, there is no incentive for mom to become drug-free; she does not risk losing contact with her children." Judith B. Sheindlin, Paying Grandmas to Keep Kids in Limbo, N. Y. Times, Aug. 29, 1994, Op–ed at A11.

PROBLEM 5–5

You are providing legal assistance to a legislative committee that is reviewing the state child welfare system. An important child welfare official has testified that the increase in agency regulations has harmed child welfare practice, particularly kinship care. She has stated that from a social work perspective, the increase in child welfare procedural requirements is partly responsible for:

> the narrow view of family and the lack of involvement of members of the child's kinship network in child welfare decision-making. Legal responsibility for a child is defined by the child's legally sanctioned relationship to a parent figure. Legal definitions of problems and legal solutions to problems are narrow. While legal mandates tend to be narrow in their focus, they have multiplied geometrically in recent years both through legislation and litigation. Child welfare caseworkers are bombarded with an overwhelming number of specific legal mandates with which they must comply and for which they and their supervisors are held accountable. * * * A broad view of family and creative solutions to family problems is not only difficult in such a context, but is actually discouraged by it. [quote from Faith Johnson Bonecutter and James P. Gleason, Broadening Our View: Lessons From Kinship Foster Care, 5 J. of Multicultural Soc. Work 99, 107 (1997)]

You are asked to respond to this criticism from a parents' rights perspective. What would you say?

2. *Racial and Ethnic Matching*

When making a foster care placement, how much weight should a caseworker or judge place on racial or ethnic matching in relation to other best interest factors? When children are placed in foster homes that are culturally very different from their parents' homes, cultural differences may become an obstacle to reuniting the family. See, e.g., In re Luis, 554 A. 2d 722 (Conn. 1989) (because child had grown up as non-

Hispanic child in Anglo–American foster home, his relationship with his Hispanic mother had suffered). Professor Twila Perry recommends that racial matching be a substantial factor in the initial placement of children for foster care or adoption. "There it is a proper consideration because that context presents the least conflict between the child's racial needs, his needs for permanence, and his interests in avoiding litigation. It is also the setting where, in considering race, the least damage is done to the interests of affected parties." Twila L. Perry, Race and Child Placement: The Best Interests Test and the Cost of Discretion, 29 J. Fam. L. 51 (1990). Professor Perry has criticized the use of the best interest test to resolve racial matching issues in subsequent decisions, however:

> When race becomes a factor, child placement issues, which are already complex, difficult, and painful, take on an added dimension. The problem of subjectivity for which the best interests rule has long been criticized is present and this is further complicated by constitutional considerations, political issues, and the practical realities of our foster care and adoption systems. * * *

> Although the best interests test seems reasonable in theory, it is problematic in practice. When the law permits race to be considered as a part of the best interests test in child placement decision-making, courts may overemphasize that factor at the expense of competing concerns.

Id. at 126.

Strong arguments have been made for and against the position that racial or ethnic matching is necessary. In 1972, for example, the National Association of Black Social Workers published a strong statement opposing transracial adoption for black children. As noted in Chapter 1, opposition to adoption of Native American children by non-Indians was an impetus for the Indian Child Welfare Act. Much of the literature on matching concerns adoption and is discussed in Chapter 7, Adoption.

3. Religious Matching

Should a parent's religious preferences be considered when the child is placed in foster care? Most states do consider the parents' preferences in making a foster care placement, but do not feel bound to find a foster home that matches the parents' preference. The free exercise rights of the parents and child are observed, "[s]o long as the state makes reasonable efforts to assure that the religious needs of the children are met * * *." Wilder v. Bernstein, 848 F.2d 1338, 1347 (2d Cir.1988).

Religious matching is also discussed in Chapter 7, Adoption.

B. Institutional Care

Two issues emerge in recent writings about children and institutional care. One is whether children whose parents cannot support them should be placed in institutions. The second is what should happen to children who need institutional care because of mental illness or some other cause.

1. Placements and Poverty

Most children in the child welfare system come from families below the poverty line. Although the recent debate over welfare reform, which included proposals for orphanages and special group homes, focused new attention on the issue, the question of what to do with the children of the poor has been debated for years. The following excerpt provides a brief history of the way the welfare system has vacillated between providing help for poor children in their homes and removing them from home. The article focused on New York, which presents a fairly typical picture of the early child welfare systems.

SARAH RAMSEY AND DAAN BRAVEMAN, "LET THEM STARVE": GOVERNMENT'S OBLIGATION TO CHILDREN IN POVERTY

68 Temple L. Rev. 1607, 1608 (1995).

* * *

The treatment of the poor in the United States has its roots in the Elizabethan Poor Laws. Like the English system, the poor laws in the United States gave the overseers of the poor authority to remove pauper children from their families and to bind them out as apprentices or send them to poorhouses. This was the beginning of our family law for the poor, a separate system of family law that allowed for extensive government regulation of poor families.

* * *

A. Almshouses

In the late 1700s and early 1800s, the poor were cared for primarily through "outdoor relief." Outdoor relief could take the form of either financial or other assistance provided in the poor's own homes, or of a "boarding out" system which placed the poor in the homes of more prosperous members of the community. The boarding out system sometimes resembled an auction, with the lowest bidder getting the boarder whose care was paid for by local government funds. Children, as well as adults, were auctioned. In other instances, poor children of all ages, including infants, were apprenticed or placed out, with the keeper assuming the cost of caring for the child.

In the early 1800s, a few almshouses were established in New York, especially in cities where increasing numbers of poor immigrants had begun to overwhelm earlier relief systems. In 1824, the Secretary of State, John Yates, submitted a study of poor relief to the legislature. The Yates report criticized the abuses of the boarding out system and of outdoor relief. Specifically, the report noted that the keepers maintained the poor as cheaply as possible in order to benefit from their labor. Moreover, outdoor relief was viewed as perpetuating poverty because it made the life of the poor too easy. Indeed, it was believed that the poor would become accustomed to the dole and would no longer look for work. There was also concern that the poor needed to be removed from the temptations which existed in their communities. Institutions, it was argued, would keep them away from taverns and gambling halls.

* * *

The rehabilitative design also did not include strengthening the family relationships of poor persons. The absence of this goal is not surprising given the societal attitudes toward poverty. Poverty, it was believed, was a status brought on by loose morals, a lack of thrift and industry, overindulgence in alcohol, and an unwillingness to work. Although there was recognition that some poor persons could not work because of ill health or other legitimate reasons, the poor as a class were heartily condemned. As a result, there was no reason to keep a poor family intact; to do so perpetuated and encouraged the very immorality intended to be corrected by the almshouses.

* * *

By the 1850s there were numerous reports that the almshouses had failed to meet expectations which had accompanied their construction. In 1857, a New York state legislative committee reported that the almshouses were "badly constructed, ill arranged, ill warmed, and ill ventilated." * * * The "stagnant atmosphere" of the poorhouse was perceived as even more harmful to children than adults. One report observed: "Evil associations surround the child, its conscience is weakened, and its moral life almost extinguished, often in a comparatively brief period. Thus reared, it goes into the world, too frequently an object rather shunned than welcomed; indifferent; without hope, self-respect, courage or sense of duty."

* * *

By the mid-nineteenth century, many reformers recognized that almshouses were a failure, both for children and adults. The belief in institutions remained strong, however, and the solution was to improve the institutions rather than to abolish them. * * *

B.   The Asylums

* * *

The asylums were seen as a vast improvement over the almshouses, designed to provide proper food, clothing, housing, religious instruction, and job training for children. * * *

Removal from parents was an important part of the plan for preventing these children from becoming paupers. As stated by the President of the State Convention of Superintendents for the Poor:

> The children have no chance of ever making themselves self-supporting or of being a credit to society, and the only way they can be

saved and brought to lead lives of usefulness is by taking them away from their debased parents. Instead of being a hardship, it is really a benefit to the children, as well as to the parent. We should consider it our duty to separate such families as would if left together, become an injury to society.

* * *

While the asylums represented an improvement over the almshouses, they nevertheless had critics. The most prominent critic was Charles Loring Brace, who maintained that any institutional care would harm children. Brace argued that the asylum did not prepare a child for real life and suggested that a child would survive better in the outside world if left to fend for himself rather than placed in an asylum:

> As a poor boy, who must live in a small house, he ought to learn to draw his own water, to split his wood, kindle his fires, and light his candle; as an "institutional child," he is lighted, warmed, and watered by machinery.... His virtue seems to have an alms-house flavor; even his vices do not present the frank character of a thorough street-boy; he is found to lie easily, and to be very weak under temptation; somewhat given to hypocrisy, and something of a sneak. And, what is very natural, *the longer he is in the Asylum, the less likely he is to do well in outside life.*

* * *

Like the earlier reformers, Brace advocated removal of children from their families and placement in an environment that would teach them economic self-sufficiency. However, Brace believed that children between the ages of two and ten should be placed with families rather than kept in institutions. Many of the asylum managers in fact agreed with Brace, and worked with him and the Children's Aid Society which placed out at least 150,000 children between 1853 and 1929.

* * *

At the turn of the century, the pendulum began to swing back to "outdoor relief," with the 1908 White House Conference on Dependent Children stressing that aid should be given to enable mothers to keep their children. By the 1920s, six states, including New York, had aid-to-mothers programs that were designed to keep children with their families. In 1935 Congress adopted the Social Security Act. Although the Social Security Act was aimed primarily at providing employment related benefits, it also provided means-tested federal support for single parent families, the elderly, and the disabled. Benefit programs gradually expanded with a major increase in the 1960s. Medicaid and the Food Stamp program were added, as well as a number of other in-kind programs such as Head Start and various housing programs. Thus, until the recent "reform" proposals, the trend had been toward keeping children with their families when possible by providing various kinds of "outdoor" relief. The policy of keeping children with their families was also supported by federal legislation that made state receipt of funding contingent upon adoption of policies that required the state, whenever possible, to provide services in the home rather than remove the child from the home.

* * *

Notes and Questions

1. *Orphanages and welfare reform.* In 1994 when the most recent debate over welfare was heating up, Speaker of the House Newt Gingrich made the controversial suggestion that poor children might be better off in orphanages than at home with their mothers on welfare. One critic of orphanages responded this way:

> The thing to understand about orphanages, as they figure in the national fantasy life that is politics, is that they aren't about orphans. They aren't even about what some commentators are calling 'social orphans'—victims of extreme abuse or neglect; runaways and throwaways; kids who've spent years bounced around between relatives and foster care and are too old or traumatized to be adopted. * * *

* * *

> * * * [T]he reason we are suddenly talking about orphanages is not because we are thinking about waifs and strays and child abuse. It's because we are thinking about welfare. Orphanages were the answer Newt Gingrich gave to the question, What will happen to the babies if you ban welfare for single teenage mothers? * * *

> The orphanage is about depriving women of their children not because those women are unfit parents—abusive, violent, neglectful, crazy, criminal, dangerous, incestuous, out of their minds on drugs or alcohol—but because they are young, unmarried and poor. That's it! It's about "restigmatizing illegitimacy" * * *.

Katha Pollitt, Subject to Debate, The Nation, Feb. 13, 1995, at 192.

2. *Free boarding schools.* Another view is that the orphanages of the past really were not so bad after all. They provided food, shelter, education and job placement. They were "a way of life for children to get the benefits of middle-class life despite having parents who had not entered that status." James Q. Wilson, Bring Back the Orphanage, Wall St. J., Aug. 22, 1994 at A 10. According to Wilson, institutional care should be seriously considered as an alternative to family reunification or foster care, because "[n]ot all families are worth preserving" ; further, foster parents are hard to supervise and "cannot handle the kind of children they are now getting." Id.

Nicolas Scopetta, the Commissioner of the New York City Administration for Children Services, spent four of his five years in foster care in an institution, Woodycrest. Dale Russakoff, The Protector, The New Yorker, April 21, 1997 at 58. His description of Woodycrest makes "it sound almost like a boarding school." Id. at 65. The institution was privately supported and children spent summers at a camp on the New Jersey shore. In reflecting on his childhood, Scopetta commented that being placed in foster care left "lots of scars," but that "the alternative of staying at home for those years could have been much worse." Id. at 68.

3. *The threat to young children.* Concern about proposals to reinstate orphanages promoted a response from physicians, who oppose institutional care for young children because, as pioneering pediatrician Henry Dwight Chapin concluded in 1908,"the collecting of many little children under one roof is not good for them, no matter how well managed the institution." Deborah A. Frank, et al., Infants and Young Children in Orphanages: One View from Pediatrics and Child Psychiatry, 97 Pediatrics 569 (1996).

The Frank article reviewed the research in five areas: "(1) infectious morbidity, (2) nutrition and growth, (3) cognitive development, (4) socioaffective development, and (5) physical and sexual abuse." The authors concluded that "infants and young children are uniquely vulnerable to the medical and psychosocial hazards of institutional care, negative effects that cannot be reduced to a tolerable level even with massive expenditure. Scientific experience consistently shows that, in the short term, orphanage placement puts young children at increased risk of serious infectious illness and delayed language development. In the long term, institutionalization in early childhood increases the likelihood that impoverished children will grow up into psychiatrically impaired and economically unproductive adults. "Id. Even with a ratio of one caregiver for every three infants, children were developmentally behind lower class infants reared at home or in foster care. The authors also pinpointed a heightened danger of abuse.

Institutions for children are currently regulated differently by each state. Despite strong opposition by the AAP [American Academy of Pediatrics], many states still permit corporal punishment in schools and do not explicitly forbid it in day care. Some commentators stress instilling "discipline" in children of lower-class parents as a rationale for establishing orphanages. Whether corporal punishment currently would be accepted as discipline in newly established orphanages, which presumably also would be state regulated, cannot be determined from published proposals.

In contrast to corporal punishment, sexual abuse of children is never socially sanctioned. Nonetheless, there are numerous graphic published accounts of sexual abuse of school aged and adolescent boys and girls in secular and religious orphanages, often involving many children and multiple staff members. There is little documentation of sexual abuse in orphanages caring for infants and preschoolers; they lack the verbal capacity to report.

Physical and sexual abuse is more likely to occur in residential institutions than in low-income families but is far less likely to be reported to authorities or to be acted upon if reported. Although the presumption of truthfulness is in favor of the child in investigations of presumed intrafamilial abuse, it is routinely in favor of the care givers in institutions. In contrast to noninstitutionalized children, for whom families monitor school or day care while school and day care personnel monitor families, institutionalized children do not have extensive contact with adults independent of the settings where the abuse occurred. Moreover, staff members of an abusing institution are often hesitant to report abuse because of fear of job loss or discrediting the institution or the public body that funds it For example, Harris documented that more than 80 people in secular law enforcement and social service positions and in the Catholic religious hierarchy knew of sexual and physical abuse of children placed by the provincial government in the Mount Cashel orphanage in Newfoundland but continued to protect the institution. The abuse continued for nearly a decade after it was first revealed.

See also Craig N. Shealy, From *Boys Town* to *Oliver Twist*: Separating Fact From Fiction in Welfare Reform and Out-of-home Placement of Children and Youth, 50 American Psychologist 565 (1995).

2. *Types of Facilities*

If a court has decided a child cannot be returned home, the court must decide whether the state's proposed placement is the least restrictive (most family like), most appropriate setting available in close proximity to the parents' home, consistent with the child's best interests and special needs. 42 U.S.C. § 675(5)(A). Foster families or kinship care are considered less restrictive than institutional care. "Institutional care" covers a range of placements. Residential treatment facilities are for children who "have been neglected, have negative and disruptive behavior patterns, have been in trouble with the law, do not respond to less restrictive forms of treatment, and need considerable structure in their lives in order to make further progress." Donald T. Kramer, Legal Rights of Children § 30.05 (2d ed. 1994). Depending on their needs, children may be placed in group homes, shelter facilities, or even hospitals. Usually group homes and shelter facilities are small and non-secure, and are located in a community setting so residents will attend local schools and participate in community events. Id. at § 30.04. The distinctions between types of facilities are often blurred. A small facility that provides mental health treatment may be called a "group home" or a "residential treatment facility," for example. Or a "group home" may provide supervision, but no treatment. An institutional placement, such as a group home, also may be used for transitional care of older children to prepare them for independent living as adults, or for children who cannot function in a family setting. National Council of Juvenile and Family Court Judges, Resource Guidelines: Improving Court Practice in Child Abuse and Neglect Cases 58(1995).

Some institutions that were orphanages have become residential treatment centers. Perhaps the most famous of these is Boys Town, which now provides residential treatment for boys and girls. Boys Town now has facilities in several locations, but at its original site just outside Omaha, Nebraska, children in this privately owned, non-profit facility live in relatively luxurious surroundings with comfortable houses, flower gardens and swimming pools. Mary Lou Weisman, When Parents Are Not in the Best Interests of the Children, Atlantic Monthly, July, 1994, at 42. Most facilities do not offer a setting like Boys Town, but residential treatment is expensive nonetheless. A year in residential treatment in New York, a high-cost state for child protective care, is $49,225 compared to $14,235 for foster care or $33,580 for specialized foster care. In Kansas, residential care costs $26,000 and foster care, $4500 annually. Id.

Cost is an important issue in choice of care:

> The children who enter the child-welfare system are almost always from the bottom of the socioeconomic ladder and therefore at the mercy of bureaucrats, policymakers, social workers, and judges. Where do people with money send their emotionally disturbed children when they can no longer tolerate them at home? If they don't ship them off to a tough uncle who owns a dude ranch in Colorado, or check them into a psychiatric hospital, chances are they enroll them in boarding schools described in their brochures as suitable "for the child who has special educational and emotional needs." The cost? About $36,000 a year, the price of many residential treatment centers and group homes, although private boarding schools do not pay for a student's clothing, medical and dental treatment, vocational training, or other extracurricular needs. * * *

Id.

C. Guardianship

Generally the permanency plan for foster children who cannot be reunited with their parents is termination of parental rights, followed by adoption. For some children, however, adoption is unlikely because of their special needs or a desire to continue contact with a biological parent. Children near the age of majority may stay in foster care or move to independent living. For children in kinship foster care, the foster parents may not want to adopt because they do not want to terminate the parental rights of the biological parent, their relative. The Adoption and Safe Families Act of 1997 permits "legal guardianship" as part of a permanency plan. The Act does not provide incentives for use of guardianships, however, although it does provide adoption incentives. The following materials expand upon the guardianship information provided in Chapter 2 by providing more detail about the limits of guardianship orders and their advantages and disadvantages.

GUARDIANSHIP PETITION OF LUPE C.

Court of Appeals of New Mexico, 1991.
812 P.2d 365.

DONNELLY, JUDGE.

[Pam and Lupe C. (appellees) are husband and wife. Pam C. is an aunt of the child who is the subject of the guardianship petition. On February 13, 1990, they filed a petition seeking to remove custody of the child from the mother and requesting that they be appointed the child's guardians. They alleged "that the mother had substantial physical, mental, and emotional problems that made her a danger to herself and others, including the child, and that rendered her unable to adequately care for the child." After an ex parte hearing, the trial court (district court) appointed a guardian ad litem for the child and issued a temporary order directing that the child be removed from the mother's custody, and be immediately placed with Pam and Lupe C., as guardians.]

* * *

On March 23, 1990, a hearing was held on the merits of the appellees' petition for guardianship. The mother was represented by counsel at this hearing. At the outset of the hearing, over the objection of the mother, the district court ruled that the guardianship proceedings were governed by Section 45–5–204(A), a provision of the Probate Code, and not by the Children's Code or related statutes. Conflicting testimony was presented concerning the mental and emotional condition of the mother and the mother's ability to care for the child. At the conclusion of the hearing, the district court entered a decision directing that the child should remain with the guardians under an order of guardianship.

The court's decision found, among other things, that "[a]ll parental rights of custody of [the mother] have been suspended by circumstances in that at this time [the mother] is unable to provide [the child] with a fit and suitable home environment," that "[the mother] has neglected [the child] in that at this time she is unable to furnish him with necessary emotional support and proper guidance," and that "[i]t is in the best interest of [the child] that he be temporarily placed in the home of [appellees] under their guardianship with visitation with his mother."

Based upon its findings the district court entered an order appointing appellees as temporary guardians of the minor child "until such time as this Court finds that [the mother] can provide [a] suitable home environment." The order further provided that the mother's rights of visitation were continued in accordance with the previous order of the court, and that the parties were ordered to participate in counseling and mediation.

DISCUSSION

* * *

B.   Sources of Authority for the Appointment of a Guardian

In New Mexico there are four principal sources of law authorizing the appointment of a guardian for a minor. * * *

First, our supreme court has held that the district court sitting as a court of equity has inherent power concerning issues of custody of minors. This power, however, is usually exercised when there is no other parent or individual to act for the child. While equity may have the power to take custody away from a parent, it will do so only in extreme circumstances. This inherent power is limited to situations where there is no other available or adequate remedy at law. * * *

Second, our statutes relating to marriage and its dissolution empower the district court to "make such an order for the guardianship, care, custody, maintenance and education of the minor children ... as may seem just and proper." * * * This statute gives the district court relatively broad powers with respect to the children of a marriage that is being dissolved. However, in this case there is no dissolution action before the district court.

Our concern in this case is with the relationship between the court's third and fourth sources of power involving custody and guardianship issues relating to minors, the Probate Code and the Children's Code. * * *

1. The Probate Code

* * * The primary purpose of the Probate Code is to control the distribution and settlement of decedents' estates, and, with respect to minors, to simplify and clarify the law relating to their affairs.

The Probate Code provides three different mechanisms for the appointment of a guardian for an unmarried minor. First, a parent may, by an acknowledged power of attorney, delegate to another person any of the parent's powers regarding the care, custody, or property of the minor child. This delegation may not last for more than six months. Second, a parent may make a testamentary appointment of a guardian for a minor child, although the child has some power to object to the appointment. Third, the court may appoint a guardian for an unmarried minor "if all parental rights of custody have been terminated or suspended by circumstances or prior court order." The district court in this case determined that the mother's rights to custody had been suspended by circumstances because she had neglected the child.

We find nothing in either the purposes of the Probate Code or the language of this section indicating a legislative intent that Section 45–5–204 permits a child to be removed from the custody of a parent who in fact has the child in his or her custody.

Section 45–5–204 is identical to Section 5–204 of the Uniform Probate Code. The drafting committee's Comment to Section 5–204, promulgated by the National Conference of Commissioners on Uniform State Laws, states:

> Nothing in this Article is intended to deal with the status of a so-called natural guardian, with the authority of a parent over a child, or with authority over a child or children that may be conferred by other state laws.

> The court [under the Probate Code] is not authorized to appoint a guardian for one for whom a parent has custodial rights or for one who has a parental guardian.

Uniform Probate Code § 5–204 (Comment), 8 U.L.A. 444, at 445 (1983). Similarly, as observed by R. Wellman, in 2 Uniform Probate Code Practice Manual, at 511 (1977):

Under the [Uniform Probate] Code, the power of the court to appoint a guardian for a minor is narrowly limited. The court may make such an appointment only if: (1) the minor is unmarried; (2) all parental rights of custody have been terminated or suspended by circumstances or prior court order; and (3) no testamentary appointment as guardian has been accepted. . . . It should be remembered, however, that the court has no power to appoint a guardian at all if the minor has a living parent entitled to his custody or a guardian appointed by the will of a parent [who] is willing to act. The parents and their testamentary appointees have, therefore, priority over everyone whom the court might appoint unless the parents have been deprived of custody. . . .

Other states that have adopted this section of the Uniform Probate Code have interpreted the phrase "suspended by circumstances" in a restricted manner. * * *

We apply a similar construction. A parent's right to custody is not "suspended by circumstances" if in fact the parent has lawful custody, is present, and has not voluntarily relinquished physical custody of the child.

2.   The Provisions of the Children's Code

* * *

Like the Probate Code, the Children's Code includes a provision identifying its purposes and policies. The Children's Code has as its central focus children who are alleged to be delinquent, in need of supervision, abused, or neglected. With respect to neglected children, the legislative purposes contained in the Children's Code emphasize a legislative objective of keeping the family together whenever possible, and separating the child from his parents and family only when necessary for his welfare, and providing services to assist the child and the family.

* * *

The Children's Code contains provisions authorizing the appointment of a permanent guardian for a child under certain circumstances. Unlike a neglect proceeding, which must be commenced by the children's court attorney, permanent guardianship proceedings may be initiated by a prospective guardian. The parent is entitled to appointed counsel, and the court may appoint a guardian ad litem for the child. However, the circumstances under which the children's court may appoint a permanent guardian for the child are substantially the same as those that must be shown in order to terminate parental rights. Thus, the appointment of a guardian under the Children's Code requires substantially more than a showing of neglect. To appoint a guardian for the child, the children's court must find not only that the child has been neglected, but that the "conditions and causes of the neglect . . . are unlikely to change in the foreseeable future despite reasonable efforts by the department or other appropriate agency to assist the parent in adjusting the conditions which render the parent unable to properly care for the child...."

* * *

3.   Considering the Statutes Together to Determine the Meaning of Section 45–5–204(A)

The guardians argue that we should read Section 45–5–204 of the Probate Code broadly to provide an alternate means of proceeding with respect to neglected children. Such reading would, however, dispense with the rights guaranteed to parents under the Children's Code, and would allow the district court to enter orders of guardianship unlimited in time, and not be subject to the requirement of periodic review. Similarly, this result would not require efforts to remedy the causes of neglect and return the child to his home.

We do not believe that the legislature intended that the Probate Code be used in this manner. As evidenced by its statement of purpose, the Children's Code provides the mechanism whereby a child can be removed from the custody of a parent where the parent in fact is invested with and is currently exercising custody of the child.

Applying the statutes and rationale discussed above to the facts herein, we determine that the district court erred in applying the provisions of the Probate Code to appellees' application for guardianship and in adjudicating the child to be neglected under procedural provisions outside the provisions of the Children's Code. * * *

* * *

Questions

1.   (a) What must be shown before a guardian may be appointed under the New Mexico Children's Code? Under the Probate Code? (b) Why did the trial court's action infringe on the mother's rights? (c) In *Phillip B.* (Chapter 2 at 180) the biological parents lost in the guardianship proceeding even though they had won in the neglect proceeding. Under New Mexico law, how would *Phillip B.* be decided?

MERYL SCHWARTZ, REINVENTING GUARDIAN-SHIP: SUBSIDIZED GUARDIANSHIP, FOSTER CARE, AND CHILD WELFARE

22 N. Y. Rev. L. & Soc. Change 441, 446–47, 456–58, 478–80 (1996).

* * * Foster care can be a problematic home for some children who must remain there on a long-term basis. It is particularly problematic in those states where the long-term placement is treated like an ordinary foster care placement, subject to regular agency supervision where foster parents have limited powers to act on behalf of the child. This type of placement is also known as "substitute care."

Generally, when a child is in substitute care, the child is in the custody of the state or a licensed child welfare agency. The power to make decisions on behalf of the child is divided between the child welfare agency, which has legal custody, the parents, who retain guardianship, and the foster parents, who have physical custody. Foster parents act at the behest of the child welfare agency. Without prior approval from the agency, however, they cannot make any decisions beyond those to feed and clothe the child. Consequently, the relationship between foster parent and foster child is restricted, both practically and possibly psychologically, by the foster parents' inability to exercise real decision making power.

Moreover, when a child is in foster care, the child welfare agency is required to continue to monitor the foster child and the foster family. Monthly caseworker visits can be intrusive, they remind the child and the foster family that they are not a "real" family. No placement in foster care is "permanent" even if the agency is unable to remove the child without a court order.

* * *

Some long term foster care statutes minimize these problems by both expanding the powers of the foster parents and reducing those of the child welfare agency and courts. A long term foster care statute that meets the above concerns would place a child in long term foster care when neither reunification nor adoption are possible without requiring the termination of parental rights. Such a statute would allow ongoing visitation with the biological parents. Foster parents would be invested with significant decision-making power, while oversight by the child welfare agency and the courts would be reduced. This scheme would allow a case worker to recognize that although reunification is not in the best interest of the child, continued contact with a parent is, and adoption would preclude that possibility.

Unfortunately, long-term foster care in most states is really the same as ordinary foster care. It remains subject to the same criticisms raised almost 20 years ago that foster care was not serving the needs of the children it intended to protect. Tension continues to exist in a system designed for the temporary out of home care of children and one being used to provide permanent care for the same children.

* * *

I. A Compromise in Subsidized Guardianship

For a growing group of children in foster care, the termination of parental rights that must accompany adoption is itself an obstacle to securing a permanent home. The limits of adoption become more pronounced as the number of parents who seek to continue some form of relationship with their children grows, the number of older children in foster care rises, and the use of kinship foster care increases. In states where all three trends are apparent, the number of children locked into long-term foster care will continue to rise unless something else is done.

Guardianship presents another option. It is available in most states and is recognized by the 1980 Adoption Assistance and Child Welfare Act. Yet, guardianship remains virtually unused as a permanency plan for children in foster care. It appeared as a goal in only about three percent of the cases in twenty-nine states surveyed by the U.S. Department of Health and Human Services in 1988. The primary reason guardianship is not used is the lack of a subsidy to support children under the plan.

II. Subsidized Guardianship as a Permanency Goal for Children in Foster Care

The appointment of a guardian for a child is not a new idea. It has been discussed in the context of foster care since as long ago as 1935. In 1949, the Social Security Administration's Children's Bureau devoted an entire publication to the subject. The Adoption Assistance and Child Welfare Act of 1980 lists guardianship as a permanency goal for children needing long term out of home care, second only to adoption. Indeed, the specific child welfare laws of some states provide for the use of guardianship as a final disposition in a child protective proceeding. Nevertheless, guardianship is rarely used for children in foster care.

The primary reason that guardianship is not widely used is the lack of a subsidy to support the children after they are discharged from foster care. In the small number of states that properly subsidize it, guardianship provides an additional path to permanence for children in foster care who cannot be reunited with their parents. As the experience of these states shows, subsidized guardianship can provide a useful alternative to both long-term foster care and adoption; one responsive to the needs of children, parents and caregivers.

A. What Is Subsidized Guardianship?

Subsidized guardianship can provide a permanent home for children in foster care who cannot be reunited with their parents and for whom adoption is an inappropriate goal. A guardian can meet a child's need for a stable and legally secure relationship in a family-like setting.

The guardian can be a relative or other suitable individual, including a foster parent. Once appointed by a court, the guardian has legal authority to make virtually all decisions on behalf of a child. A guardian is said to stand in the shoes of the parent and is charged with protecting the child's health and welfare.

Appointment of a guardian does not require the termination of parental rights. Transfer of guardianship from parents to another adult relieves the parents of their right to custody and their obligation of care, but parents retain the right to visit, and to consent to adoption. They are also responsible for child support.

The appointment of a guardian for a child who is in foster care, relieves the agency of its authority over the child, unless a new complaint of abuse or neglect is made at a later time. The dissolution of the relationship between foster child and foster parent, and the substitution of the relationship between guardian and ward ends the oversight of both the court and agency, even if the new guardian was the foster parent. A foster parent who becomes the child's legal guardian no longer has to take time off from work to go to court when the placement is reviewed and is freed from the monthly visits of a caseworker. The substitution of guardianship for foster care should relieve the stress inevitable in a temporary relationship and allow a deeper bond to grow.

In essence, guardians are substitute parents. They have complete control over the care and custody of their wards including responsibility for their health, welfare and education. Unlike foster parents, they need not ask an agency for permission to vaccinate the child or to visit the zoo in a nearby county. In contrast to long-term foster care, guardianship cements the bond between the child and the caregiver, localizes authority over the child, and endows the relationship with an expectation of continuity.

* * *

Notes

1. *Permanency.* Some research suggests that guardianships may be more permanent than non-relative foster care and that more research should be done on guardianship as a permanency planning option. Because guardianships are not often used, the barriers to implementation should also be studied. See, e.g., Alfreda P. Iglehart, Kinship Foster–Care: Placement, Service and Outcome Issues, 16 Children and Youth Servs. Rev. 107 (1994).

2. *Subsidies.* In 1997 only ten states provided subsidized guardianships. Of these, some did not support kinship guardianships or provided a lower level of support for kinship guardianships. In Wisconsin, for example, the subsidy for a guardian is less than foster care or Temporary Assistance for Needy Families benefits. Wis. Stat. Ann. § 48.57 (3m); Note, The Policy of Penalty in Kinship Care, 112 Harv. L. Rev. 1047 (1999).

PROBLEM 5–6

Jane is the mother of three children, Linda, age three, Mary, age seven months, and Jackie, age nine. When the younger children were found to have been sexually abused by Jackie, Jane voluntarily placed them with the Department of Social Services. Jane then entered an inpatient substance abuse program. The two younger children were put in a foster care home; Jackie was placed in a group home. More than two years later the state petitioned to terminate Jane's parental rights to the two younger children. The evidence at the termination hearing established that the children were doing well in foster care and that Jane was unfit to have custody because of her low intelligence, mental illness, and drug and alcohol addictions. A licensed clinical psychologist, Dr. Ann Smith, evaluated all the children and testified at the hearing. She stated that Jane did not have the capacity to parent her children because of her "severe and long-standing psychiatric difficulties." Dr. Smith recommended that parental rights not be terminated, but rather that the children be given a permanent placement that would allow the mother visitation. Dr. Smith testified that "in the absence of some real risk from a parent, a total cutoff from biological parents is unnecessary." She also stated that there was not a risk in this case and that the children would not be unduly stressed by the visitation.

State law provides that "when reasonable efforts to maintain or reunify a family have failed, the Department of Social Services shall act in a timely fashion to provide the child with a permanent environment. With regard to a child who is three years or younger, if the goal is not to return the children home, the goal for the child shall be adoption unless there are extenuating circumstances that justify long-term foster care or guardianship."

You are the judge. Do you terminate parental rights?

PROBLEM 5–7

Mrs. Williams is a 60 year-old grandmother caring for two school age children, Melissa age 6 and Adam, age 7. They are the children of her drug-addicted daughter. The foster care worker placed the children with Mrs. Williams two years ago when child protective services removed them from her daughter's care because of neglect. Mrs. Williams is in poor health and receives $350 per month in disability payments. She also works part-time when she can and usually earns about $200 per month. She receives foster care payments of $416 per month for each child. Because of the renewed emphasis on permanency, the caseworker wants to terminate parental rights. She wants Mrs. Williams to adopt the children or become their legal guardian; otherwise, the caseworker will try to find another adoptive family for the children. The state does not subsidize guardianships. The Temporary Assistance for Needy Families benefits for the two children would be $250 per month.

What are the advantages and disadvantages of guardianship for Mrs. Williams, the children and the state?

Chapter 6

CRIMINAL ABUSE AND NEGLECT

Earlier chapters have emphasized civil processes designed to protect children and regulate the conduct of persons who care for or interact with them. In this chapter, criminal law moves to the foreground. Much of the chapter is intimately related to chapters 4 and 5 because it concerns prosecutions for conduct that would support a civil abuse or neglect proceeding against a parent or guardian, or that might support a foster placement. As you proceed, you should analyze the relative roles of civil and criminal enforcement in child protection. When should authorities prosecute under the criminal law instead of (or in addition to) pursuing a civil remedy? These questions figure prominently in Commonwealth v. Ogin and State v. Crawford, the chapter's first two decisions.

SECTION 1. ABUSE, NEGLECT AND CHILD ENDANGERMENT

States have enacted a range of criminal statutes that may be invoked against persons who inflict physical or emotional violence on children. Some of these statutes (such as ones proscribing murder, manslaughter or assault) apply when the victim is "any person," and thus permit prosecution when the victim happens to be a child. But complementing these general-application crimes are an array of crimes applicable only when the victim is a child. These child-specific crimes carry a variety of names, such as child abuse, criminal neglect, cruelty to children, or endangering the welfare of a child. *Ogin* and *Crawford* review convictions under both general and specific statutes.

COMMONWEALTH v. OGIN

Superior Court of Pennsylvania, 1988.
540 A.2d 549.

Beck, Judge:

This is a consolidated appeal by a mother and father who were convicted by a jury and sentenced for using excessive force against their baby daughter. The issue is whether the evidence adduced at trial supports the jury verdict that appellants are guilty of simple assault and endangering the welfare of children. We find that the evidence is sufficient to establish appellants' guilt, and we affirm.

* * *

One day during the summer of 1983, Commonwealth witness Ann Marie Blaine observed appellants' children April and Glynn Jr. playing outside the building where the family lived. At this time, Glynn Jr. was three years old and April was approximately seventeen months old. Glynn Jr. rode his Big Wheel down to the end of the block and April followed him. Appellant Debby Ogin ran after the children, told them to stay in front of the building, and slapped April on the rear end. Soon afterward, Glynn Jr. rode down an alley and April again followed him. Debby ran after the children and grabbed April. Blaine testified on direct examination:

A. Debby was dragging April.

Q. You say dragging. Can you describe for the jury what you mean by that?

A. She had her by the one arm and was dragging her. Her feet were touching the ground. She was stumbling to try to walk. And she flung her like an old rag doll against the building. She said, I told you to sit there.

Q. When you say she flung her against the building, please, describe to the jury exactly what Debby Ogin did to her daughter.

A. She had her by the arm. She come around the building with the child by the arm and she threw her up against the building by one arm.

Q. What part of April's body hit that building?

A. The whole back of her. And she—when she hit the building, she kind of stumbled over and hit the steps. And they're cement steps there.

. . .

Q. What happened after April had been thrown against the wall?

A. The child was screaming for quite a few minutes, and then Debby took her and put her inside the stairway and shut the door.

The witness also stated that she observed a small red mark that resembled a brushburn on the side of April's face.

The second incident occurred the following winter. On December 20, 1983, Debby Ogin took her children to see a Santa Claus at the local firehouse. They were accompanied by Audrey Wampole, a neighbor, and by Ann Marie Blaine. Wampole held April for the first hour they waited and then set her down. April approached her mother and gestured that she wanted to be picked up. Debby Ogin responded by slapping April with the back of her hand causing April to stumble. Ten minutes later, April approached her mother and reached out her arms to be picked up. Debby Ogin again hit April in the face with the back of her hand, this time with "extreme force". April fell and hit her back against a brick wall. Afterward, Blaine noticed a lump on the back of the child's head.

The third incident took place in February, 1984, and involved Glynn Wildoner, April's father. Doris Whitmire, Mr. Wildoner's cousin, testified that she was with his family one evening at dinner time. She saw Debby Ogin take spaghetti off the stove and place it on a plate on the kitchen table. Glynn Wildoner moved the plate in front of April. When April did not eat it, Wildoner reached out, put his hand under the plate, and pushed the hot food up into the child's face. April began crying. Her face swelled and she sustained small burn marks which dissipated after a few days.

Appellants were tried by a jury * * *. Ogin was convicted of two counts of simple assault and two counts of endangering the welfare of children, and was sentenced to two years probation. Wildoner was convicted of one count of simple assault and one count of endangering the welfare of children and was sentenced to two years special probation consecutive to a sentence he was then serving for unrelated criminal conduct. This appeal followed. * * *

I.

We begin by considering appellants' challenge to their convictions for simple assault. Section 2701 of the Crimes Code provides that a person is guilty of assault if he "attempts to cause or intentionally, knowingly, or recklessly causes bodily injury to another...." Section 2301 of the Crimes Code defines bodily injury as "[i]mpairment of physical condition or substantial pain." Appellants argue that April's injuries were not sufficiently serious to support an inference that appellants either impaired her physical condition or caused her substantial pain. We disagree.

* * *

[O]ne can infer that April suffered substantial pain from the fact: 1) that she was grabbed by the arm and flung against a building and then screamed for several minutes; 2) that she was struck in the face with extreme force causing her to fall against a wall; and 3) that she cried after having hot food shoved in her face. These incidents are serious matters; we are not dealing here with "temporary hurts resulting from trivial contacts which are a customary part of modern day living." Accordingly, appellants' argument that the Commonwealth failed to establish the elements of simple assault is without merit.

II.

Appellants also allege that they were improperly convicted of endangering the welfare of children. Section 4304 of the Crimes Code provides:

A parent, guardian, or other person supervising the welfare of a child under 18 years of age commits a misdemeanor of the second degree if he knowingly endangers the welfare of the child by violating a duty of care, protection or support.

Appellants contend that they did not fail to provide a duty of protection. We conclude that this argument is without merit. Section 4304 is a comprehensive provision designed to penalize those who knowingly breach a legal duty to protect the well-being of children who are entrusted to their care. * * *

* * * Section 4304 was drawn broadly to cover a wide range of conduct in order to safeguard the welfare and security of children. It is to be given meaning by reference to the common sense of the community and the broad protective purpose for which it was enacted.

Parents have a responsibility to advance the physical, mental, and emotional health of their children, and extreme acts or grave omissions which adversely affect a child may come within the scope of the statute. This will sometimes include actions which the parent allegedly undertook in order to punish the child for bad behavior. In the instant case, we cannot say that the jury erred by finding that appellants breached a statutory duty to protect their daughter April. April was a very young child when the appellants flung her, struck her, and burned her in the manner graphically described by the Commonwealth witnesses. One may conclude that these incidents were traumatic and created a danger of lasting physical harm notwithstanding the fact that April fortuitously did not sustain serious injury. In short, a jury could find that appellants' acts were so contrary to "the common sense of the community" as to rise to the level of criminal liability.

Appellants also contend that by failing to provide a duty of protection, they did not *knowingly* endanger April's welfare as required by section 4304. The jury reasonably could have found otherwise based upon an assessment of the Commonwealth's evidence and of appellants' own testimony at trial. Although defense counsel presented evidence that appellants were of low intelligence and had repeatedly experienced difficulties with raising their children, both Ogin and Wildoner took the stand and insisted that they were capable of fulfilling their parental responsibilities. Appellants denied that they had ever mistreated April in the ways described by the Commonwealth witnesses. They testified that they believed it was wrong to beat children, and that they never disciplined their children except by hitting them on the rear end without great force or by taking away their toys. The jury could have credited the Commonwealth's version of the events, and could have believed so much of the defense testimony as indicated that appellants knew that the conduct in question posed a threat to a child's welfare. Thus, the elements of the crime of endangering the welfare of children were established.

III.

Appellants' final argument is that even if their actions would otherwise have been criminal, they are entitled to the defense of justification based upon their status as the victim's parents. We agree with appellants that parents may not ordinarily be prosecuted for disciplining their children. We do not agree that under the facts of this case appellants' actions were justified.

It is well-established that parents have a privilege to subject their children to corporal punishment when the children misbehave. This is so because our society recognizes the primary role of parents in preparing children to assume the obligations and responsibilities of adults, and because there is a need to ensure that the state through its criminal justice system does not unduly interfere with the private realm of family life. Nevertheless, there are limits regarding the type and severity of the corporal punishment which a parent may impose. The law long ago abandoned the view that children are essentially chattels of their parents without independent legal rights. Moreover, it is now clear that child abuse is a serious and widespread problem; the state has a powerful interest in preventing and deterring the battering of children.

In 1972, the legislature balanced these competing interests by adopting section 509 of the Crimes Code. This section provides in relevant part:

The use of force upon or toward the person of another is justifiable if:

(1) The actor is the parent or guardian or other person similarly responsible for the general care and supervision of a minor or a person acting at the request of such parent, guardian or other responsible person and:

(i) the force is used for the purpose of safeguarding or promoting the welfare of the minor, including the preventing or punishment of his misconduct; and

(ii) the force used is not designed to cause or known to create a substantial risk of causing death, serious bodily injury, disfigurement, extreme pain or mental distress or gross degradation.

We conclude that appellants' conduct was not authorized by this provision.

Appellants contend that the Commonwealth's evidence showed that they were attempting to discipline April for her misconduct on each of the occasions when they used force. We will assume arguendo that section 509(1)(i) was satisfied. We must therefore consider whether or not the force which appellants employed was in excess of that permitted by section 509(1)(ii). Section 509(1)(i) and (ii) involve independent requirements and appellants are not entitled to a justification defense unless they complied with both standards. This point is underscored by the commentary to section 3.08 of the Model Penal Code. Model Penal Code section 3.08 is virtually identical to Pennsylvania Crimes Code

Section 509 and it is the source from which Pennsylvania Crime Code Section 509 was derived. The commentary states:

> The law has universally allowed a privilege for the exercise of domestic authority, sometimes articulated in the penal statutes, though often without a definition of its scope. Older decisions tended to treat the motive of the actor as decisive, though extreme measures naturally could be taken to refute benevolent intent. Modern authority has tended towards a more objective test of moderation. The Model Code formulation requires a true parental purpose, while forbidding extreme force however well-intentioned is its use.[5]

It is thus clear that a defendant's actions are not legally justified simply because he may sincerely believe that the best way of safeguarding or promoting a child's welfare is to inflict a cruel and patently excessive punishment.

After considering appellants' conduct in light of the standard established by section 509(1)(ii), we hold that the evidence is sufficient to support a finding that appellants exceeded their privilege to administer corporal punishment. We note that when applying the justification statute, the court should focus not only on the degree of force exerted by the parent but also on the age and the physical and mental condition of the child who has been disciplined. April was two years old or younger when her mother flung her into a building, when her mother struck her with such force that she fell backward into a brick wall, and when her father pushed hot food in her face. Under these circumstances, a jury could have fairly concluded beyond a reasonable doubt that appellants used force which was known to create at least a "substantial risk of . . . extreme pain or mental distress" within the meaning of section 509(1)(ii). Therefore, appellants' defense of justification was properly rejected.

Judgments of sentence affirmed.

CAVANAUGH, JUDGE, concurring:

Under the evidence in this case I am constrained to concur in the result reached by the majority. I am concerned however that this case be read as a precedent for facile resort to the criminal justice system as a vehicle for enforcement of a prosecutor's personal notions as to parental responsibility.

If the conduct engaged in by appellants is not condoned by the professionals within our agencies that promote the welfare of children,

---

5. This approach is in accord with the majority rule in American jurisdictions.

Some courts have taken the view that the test of illegality is the infliction of permanent injury by means of the punishment administered, or that it proceeded from malice and was not in the exercise of a corrective authority, and they have accordingly held that a parent, or one in loco parentis, is not criminally liable merely because the punishment inflicted was excessive. The decided preponderance of authority, however, is that a parent, or one in loco parentis, in punishing children, must not exceed the bounds of moderation, and must not be cruel or merciless, and that any act of punishment in excess of such limits is unlawful, and this rule has been incorporated in some statutory provisions.

the means by which that conduct is best altered is not through the imposition of criminal convictions. While the evidence in this case is strongly suggestive that appellants are not fully suited to their parental tasks, I believe that other forms of legal intervention are available to protect the interest of the juveniles involved before invocation of the criminal law and its unavoidably devastating effect on the hope of resolving appellants' problems in parenting.

* * *

The record reveals that all three of appellants' children were removed from the home upon their arrest on the instant charges. The children's wellbeing, if threatened by living with their parents, was protected through the system that is designed to safeguard their interests. Less than ideal circumstances, resulting from poverty and mental deficiency of their parents, may have caused the children of Debby Ogin and Glynn Wildoner to be among those considered to be less privileged by our society. However, branding her parents with criminal convictions will do no more to improve April's chances of happiness in childhood and of normal development as an adjusted and secure adult than would a conviction of April herself for being a part of the family unit.

Notes and Questions

1. *Interagency cooperation.* When we consider the respective roles of civil and criminal enforcement, we necessarily anticipate that child protective agencies and law enforcement agencies will cooperate with one another. Professor Douglas J. Besharov reports that "many child protective agencies and law enforcement agencies across the nation have developed working arrangements to call upon the other for help in meeting their responsibilities toward children." These arrangements recognize that abuse and neglect are "community problems requiring a cooperative response by law enforcement, child protective, and other local agencies," and that no single agency has "all the tools that are needed": "Child protective agencies seek to protect children through the provision of services or the removal of children from the home. Law enforcement seeks to protect children through the arrest of offenders and criminal prosecution. These approaches are complementary, not incompatible. Depending on the situation, either agency may benefit from the assistance of the other." Douglas J. Besharov, Combating Child Abuse: Guidelines for Cooperation between Law Enforcement and Child Protective Agencies, 24 Fam. L.Q. 209, 218, 221 (1990).

Professor Besharov's report made a number of recommendations designed to improve cooperation between law enforcement and child protective agencies, including these: the respective agencies should collaborate to reduce the risk of "children falling between the cracks as each agency thinks the other is investigating a particular case"; law enforcement should be required to report suspected intrafamilial child abuse and neglect to the child protective agency because the immediate and long-term needs of all children in the family may warrant attention even if a prosecution is brought; all cases falling under the language of criminal abuse and neglect laws, and all cases involving severe danger to the child, should be reported to law enforcement; nonfamilial child abuse and neglect cases should not be processed by child protective agencies, which are equipped to assist children threatened by family or household members and not by strangers; arrest should be an important child protective device in cases involving serious injury to the victim, use or threatened use of a weapon, violation of a protection order, or other imminent danger to the victim; and the respective agencies should coordinate their investigations to increase effectiveness and avoid duplication. Id. at 243–45.

Only a small percentage of substantiated child maltreatment cases result in criminal prosecutions. See, e.g., Douglas J. Besharov, Child Abuse: Arrest and Prosecution Decision–Making, 24 Am. Crim. L. Rev. 315, 319 (1987) (less than 5%).

2. *Abusive discipline. Ogin* put parental discipline to the test. The precise number of abuse cases resulting from discipline by parents or caregivers cannot be determined, but Professor Kandice K. Johnson believes the number is significant: "First, it is clear that most children who suffer from abuse do so at the hands of their parents or other caregiver. Statistics indicate that approximately twelve percent of abuse cases result from acts by individuals who are not related to the child. Thus, most abuse can be attributed to adults who are responsible for the well-being of the child. Second, there is widespread acceptance of the use of corporal punishment in our society. Societal acceptance of corporal punishment is reflected by the legal recognition of the parental force privilege and by studies conducted from the 1950s through the 1990s that consistently indicate that greater than ninety percent of American parents use physical force to punish their children. If the use of physical force on children is condoned by most parents and if most children are abused by their caregivers, it is reasonable to speculate that there may be some relationship between abuse and discipline." Kandice K. Johnson, Crime or Punishment: The Parental Corporal Punishment Defense–Reasonable and Necessary, or Excused Abuse?, 1998 U. Ill. L. Rev. 413, 420.

"The reported cases tell us that in the name of discipline children are beaten with belts, electrical cords, sticks, coat hangers, bats, and studded weapons. They are locked in rooms without food or heat and forced to carry excrement or to eat urine-soaked food. They have plastic bags placed over their heads, are knocked into walls, are scalded, or emersed in freezing water. * * * They are injured, they are scarred, and they die." Id. at 481–82.

Abusive discipline frequently has appalling results. For just one recent example, consider Mitchell v. State, 503 S.E.2d 293, 295 (Ga.Ct.App. 1998), which upheld the father's convictions for cruelty to children and battery. The father "disciplined his eight-year-old son for bed wetting by forcing him to sit naked in a bathtub filled with very hot water and bleach (or some other caustic chemical) to wash his soiled bed linens. Mitchell himself admitted to a police officer he placed the child in the liquid for disciplinary reasons. The child suffered severe burns to his feet, buttocks, and knuckles. Mitchell did not allow the boy to receive medical treatment for the open, oozing lesions until five days later when required to do so by investigating police." The court of appeals rejected the father's contention that the trial court improperly allowed the boy's treating physician to rule out diaper rash as the cause of the buttocks burns. Id.

Abusive discipline leads to the child's death with disturbing frequency. In State v. Elliott, 475 S.E.2d 202, 207 (N.C.1996), for example, the mother's live-in boyfriend was convicted of murder and felony child abuse for killing her two-year-old daughter, Brandie Jean Freeman:

> * * * Soon after moving into their home in November of 1992, defendant began taking care of Brandie while her mother was at work. Ms. Linker [the mother] permitted defendant to discipline Brandie; and the evidence suggested that Brandie sustained bruises, black eyes, and other injuries while in defendant's care. After Ms. Linker became concerned that defendant was spanking Brandie too hard, defendant began using the "punishment position," a form of discipline described by witnesses as requiring Brandie to lie on her stomach with her arms and legs raised for ten to twenty minutes.

> On the morning of 3 January 1993, * * * Brandie woke defendant and told him that she had "poopied" in her pants. This made defendant angry. Defendant cleaned and changed the victim and told her to assume the punishment position. Defendant went to the kitchen to get a glass of water for himself. When defendant returned Brandie was in the punishment position with her head raised. Defendant grabbed Brandie by the hair on the back of her head and slammed her head to the floor six or seven times.

> Defendant asked the child if she was okay, and Brandie attempted to raise her arm and put it around defendant's neck. When defendant failed to get any further response from Brandie, he shook her, slapped her, and hit her in what he claimed was an effort to obtain a response. As part of this effort, defendant took Brandie to the bathroom, where he ran water over her and continued to hit and slap the child repeatedly. [Brandie died in the hospital the next day.].

Does section 509 of Pennsylvania's Crimes Code, quoted in *Ogin*, provide clear guidelines for distinguishing between appropriate parental discipline and criminally sanctionable discipline?

3. *Parental privilege.* The Model Penal Code's privilege formulation, quoted in *Ogin*, extends beyond parents to other caretakers in a variety of circumstances. State formulations vary in reach and scope. In State v. Dodd, 518 N.W.2d 300, 301 (Wis.1994), for example, the court denied the privilege to the mother's live-in boyfriend convicted for abusing the child. Wisconsin's criminal code affords the privilege "[w]hen the actor's conduct is reasonable discipline of a child by a person responsible for the child's welfare." Wis. Stat. § 939.45(5)(b). The term "person responsible for the child's welfare" "includes the child's parent, stepparent or guardian * * * or any other person legally responsible for the child's welfare in a residential setting." Wis. Stat. § 939.45(5)(a)(3). The court held that the boyfriend was not legally responsible.

4. Under Pennsylvania's endangerment statute, must the prosecutor prove the defendant knew the child was under eighteen? Would a prosecution fail

if the child did not actually suffer injury or death by reason of the alleged conduct?

5. *The potential defendant class.* Pennsylvania's child endangerment statute operates against "a parent, guardian, or other person supervising the welfare of a child under 18 years of age." Most endangerment statutes similarly extend beyond persons having "legal" custody or control of the child. See, e.g., State v. Perruccio, 471 A.2d 632 (Conn. 1984) (teacher); State v. Deringer, 1985 WL 7238 (Ohio Ct. App.) (babysitter); City of Columbus v. Wolfinger, 1996 WL 52898 (Ohio Ct. App.) (day care worker); State v. DeBoucher, 660 P.2d 471 (Ariz. Ct. App. 1982) (boarding school director).

6. *Vagueness.* The breadth of Pennsylvania's endangerment statute is typical because these protective statutes are designed to enable authorities to prosecute a wide range of physical and emotional maltreatment of children. On the one hand, these criminal statutes must be strictly construed in the defendant's favor. On the other hand, breadth enables courts to interpret endangerment statutes consistent with their evident protective purpose.

Breadth has its bounds, however, and some questionable conduct cannot fit under even broad statutory formulations. Where the fit seems difficult to make, constitutional challenge remains available under the void-for-vagueness doctrine.

Due process requires that a penal statute "define the criminal offense with sufficient definiteness that ordinary people can understand what conduct is prohibited and in a manner that does not encourage arbitrary and discriminatory enforcement." Kolender v. Lawson, 461 U.S. 352, 357 (1983). A vagueness challenge urges that the statute fails this test either facially or as applied to the particular defendant.

Where the conduct at issue appears particularly harmful to children and is arguably within the endangerment statute's proscriptions, courts normally reject vagueness challenges. See, e.g., State v. Payne, 695 A.2d 525 (Conn. 1997) (defendant used threats to force children to expose their genitals and urinate into a cup in a public place); State v. Mahurin, 799 S.W.2d 840, 842 (Mo. 1990) (defendants nearly starved their child to death); State v. Nivert, 1995 WL 608415 (Ohio App.) (defendants caused about fifteen broken bones throughout their four-month-old boy's body); People v. Wilkenson, 635 N.E.2d 463 (Ill. Ct. App. 1994) (defendant held knife to her child's throat while yelling that she was going to kill the child).

Vagueness challenges to endangerment statutes, however, sometimes succeed where the harm caused by the defendant's conduct seems open to fair question. See, e.g., State v. Schriver, 542 A.2d 686 (Conn. 1988) (defendant grabbed fully clothed thirteen-year-old girl while uttering sexually suggestive comment).

7. *Using children in drug trafficking.* Adults sometimes use children, particularly young children, as couriers or runners in illicit drug trafficking. The adults and children themselves often believe the children are effectively immune from the law's reach, especially where they are below the age of transfer to criminal court and the participants do not expect harsh juvenile court treatment. The adults would be reachable under endangerment statutes. Because of the harm to children who are used to commit crime and the

dangers inherent in the drug trade, however, Congress and many state legislatures have specifically criminalized adults' knowing use of children in such transactions and have provided for enhanced penalties. See, e.g., 21 U.S.C. § 861(a); Wis. Stat. § 961.455.

8. *Minors as defendants.* May a minor be convicted under a child endangerment or criminal abuse statute? What if the defendant is younger than the victim? See, e.g., K.B.S. v. State, 725 So.2d 448, 449 (Fla.Dist.Ct.App.1999) (under a statute operating against "[a] person who knowingly or willfully abuses a child," the court affirmed a delinquency adjudication against a fourteen-year-old for abusing a nine-year-old; the court noted that the statute would also operate against a nine-year-old who abused a fourteen-year-old).

9. *Abandonment.* Where child endangerment rises to the level of total neglect, a parent or guardian may face prosecution for abandonment. See, e.g., Ga. Code § 19–10–1(b). One commentator reports, however, that at least with respect to older children, abandonment statutes are "close to a dead letter" and abandonment by parents is "shockingly common." Gregory A. Loken, "Thrownaway Children" and Throwaway Parenthood, 68 Temp. L. Rev. 1715, 1718, 1728 (1995). As discussed in Chapter 10, more than a million children each year run away from home and live on the streets, frequently to escape physical, emotional or sexual abuse, alcoholic or drug addicted parents, divorce, sickness, poverty or school problems. Many runaways (more than a fifth and as many as 46%, depending on the study) are more aptly labeled "throwaways" because they are directly told to leave the household, because they have been away from home and a caretaker refused to allow them back, because they have run away but the caretaker makes no effort to recover them or does not care whether they return, or because they are abandoned or deserted. Criminal abandonment statutes are rarely, if ever, invoked against throwaways' parents. Id. at 1728 n.71.

PROBLEM 6–1

You are a member of the court that heard oral argument in *Ogin*, and Judges Beck and Cavanaugh have circulated their respective draft opinions. Which opinion would you join? What factors should child protective agencies and law enforcement agencies consider when they determine whether abuse or neglect should be the subject of civil proceedings, criminal prosecution, or both?

PROBLEM 6–2

You are a Pennsylvania prosecutor. Under the state's child endangerment statute (quoted in *Ogin*), could you secure a conviction of parents or other covered persons who knowingly commit the following conduct?:

    a) Driving a motor vehicle under the influence of drugs or alcohol with a child passenger.

    b) Possessing crack cocaine while driving a van with a child as a passenger.

c) Waiting two days to secure doctor's appointment for a child who had suffered a broken nose manifested by marked swelling and discoloration.

d) Transporting a child in a stolen vehicle.

e) Unlawfully selling fireworks to a child.

f) Murdering the child's mother during a domestic dispute and leaving her body in a pool of blood on the kitchen floor, where the child could find the body the next morning.

h) On a hot summer day, leaving a three-month-old child in a parked motor vehicle with the windows rolled up and the doors locked.

i) Committing forcible sexual abuse against the mother in the child's presence.

j) After the seven-year-old son threw a temper tantrum in shopping center's parking lot and refused to enter the car because the mother refused to buy him a toy, driving off and leaving the child alone in the parking lot for a few minutes before returning to pick him up.

PROBLEM 6–3

A fifteen-year-old boy's parents allow him periodically to have his fifteen-year-old girlfriend stay overnight at the house. The two sleep upstairs, and the girl becomes pregnant with the boy's child. The boy's parents permit the sleepovers because they fear their son will engage in promiscuous behavior on the outside unless the parents are home to supervise. Would you prosecute the parents under a statute providing that "[a] person is guilty of endangering the welfare of a child when * * * [h]e knowingly acts in a manner likely to be injurious to the physical, mental or moral welfare of a child less than sixteen years old"? If you were the indicted parents' lawyer, what defenses would you raise?

STATE v. CRAWFORD

Supreme Court of North Carolina, 1991.
406 S.E.2d 579.

MEYER, JUSTICE.

In 1988, six-year-old Christopher West lived with his mother, Angela West, his younger brother, Shaun, and his sister, Sara, in a Burlington apartment. Defendant, Angela West's boyfriend, moved in with them in September of that year. On 1 October 1988, Christopher awoke early and broke a house rule by taking food from the kitchen without permission. The State produced evidence at trial that showed defendant had developed a pattern of using extraordinary disciplinary methods intended to punish and humiliate Christopher for disobeying rules. On the following day, Christopher awoke with a minor rash, which defendant attributed to sherbet Christopher had eaten. Defendant attempted to "flush out

[Christopher's] system" by coercing him to drink large quantities of water over the next two to three hours. Christopher complained, but defendant continued to coerce him to drink. Finally, the water intake caused Christopher to scream, convulse, and lose his eyesight. After being taken to the hospital unconscious, where he was diagnosed as suffering from water intoxication, Christopher was pronounced brain dead and was removed from a respirator the next day. A jury found defendant guilty of first-degree murder [by torture] and of felony child abuse.[a] After a sentencing hearing and upon its finding of no aggravating circumstances, the jury recommended a sentence of life imprisonment. The trial court sentenced defendant to life imprisonment for first-degree murder and arrested judgment on the conviction for felony child abuse. We find no error.

The State's evidence tended to show the following: In the spring of 1987, defendant and Angela West met through a mutual friend and, by the summer, were dating regularly. After defendant left his job in February 1988, he spent more time with Angela West and soon began to fill the role of disciplinarian of the children as well.

The State introduced testimony describing a number of incidents involving extraordinary disciplinary methods to show by circumstantial evidence an absence of mistake and an intent by defendant to punish Christopher on 2 October 1988. Defendant testified that certain of his disciplinary techniques were inappropriate but contends that they were done in good faith, and, in any event, he agreed to stop using inappropriate disciplinary measures after meeting with an investigator from the Department of Social Services (DSS) in May of 1988.

Testimony as to defendant's disciplinary techniques was as follows. In the late winter of 1988, at Angela West's request, defendant punished Christopher for allegedly starting a fire in nearby woods. Defendant affixed a sign around Christopher's neck which read, "I sat [sic] the woods on fire, and I lied to my mama." Christopher was required to stand outside with the sign around his neck for between ten and twenty minutes and to recite aloud the words on the sign. When Christopher would try to go back into the apartment, defendant would push him back outside.

Defendant testified to paddling the children on the soles of their feet in order to conceal bruising, to giving the children cold showers "to cool them down" when "they were in an excited state," to putting hot sauce on their tongues, and to washing their mouths out with soap. The latter two disciplinary methods were to prevent "lying and cussing." Other testimony indicated that Christopher had such a physical reaction to the soap used that his mouth "puffed up."

Additionally, a neighbor testified that in the late spring or early summer of 1988, she saw Christopher wearing a diaper, carrying a baby

a. N.C. Gen. Stat. § 14–17 defines "first degree murder" to include "[a] murder which shall be perpetrated by means of poison, lying in wait, imprisonment, starving, torture, or by any other kind of willful, deliberate, and premeditated killing * * *."

bottle, and crying. When asked at the time about why Christopher was wearing a diaper, defendant responded that "he was being punished, because he was a sissy."

One of Angela West's friends, who visited the apartment frequently, testified that she saw Christopher disciplined on more than one occasion by being required to stand in the corner. When Christopher cried, defendant would taunt him by saying, "Look at the baby. Chris is a little baby."

Another witness testified that defendant asked her if she had ever seen anyone drink hot sauce before. Christopher cried and screamed in fright when defendant said this; then, as the visitor left, she heard Christopher screaming, crying, and saying it was "hot" as defendant poured the hot sauce into a glass. Another witness testified that defendant had told her that Christopher learned from humiliation.

Defendant's extraordinary punishment procedures were not limited to Christopher. Evidence presented at trial indicated that Sara had been forced to sleep in a urine-soaked bed, which was "his way of teaching [her] not to wet the bed," and in another instance, defendant put Sara's urine-soaked underwear on her head. When these instances of punishment occurred, Sara was two or three years old. Finally, a witness testified that in the summer of 1988, defendant forced Shaun to stand with his face up against a tree in the park. A school counselor testified that defendant told her that he was on a "mission" to help Angela West with disciplinary problems. Defendant denies that he made such a statement.

DSS began an investigation of the West family on 9 May 1988. A DSS investigator visited the West home, where defendant stated that Christopher was a bully and needed discipline. Defendant related a number of his disciplinary methods to the investigator, who reported defendant to the police. He was arrested in June for misdemeanor child abuse of the West children. However, on 2 August 1988, those charges were dismissed.

West entered a service agreement on 16 May 1988 with DSS. The agreement in this instance provided that defendant would have no contact with any of the West children. The agreement expired in August 1988 and was not renewed. Defendant was asked to submit to a mental health evaluation, due to the misdemeanor child abuse charges against him, but did not do so on the advice of his attorney. Christopher, however, was examined by a pediatrician, who found no indication of mental instability or mental illness.

Defendant moved in with the West family in September while still unemployed and looked after Christopher's brother Shaun. Shaun had been removed from kindergarten, defendant contends, to prevent him from being expelled. There were at least two meetings at approximately that same time with DSS in which the agency continued to press, to no avail, for removal of the children from the home.

On 1 October 1988, while Angela West was at work and defendant was home alone with the three children, defendant discovered that biscuits were missing from the kitchen and confronted Shaun and Christopher about breaking the house rule that forbade them from going downstairs to the kitchen before an adult was awake to accompany them. Shaun admitted breaking the rule and implicated Christopher. Defendant spanked the boys on the buttocks and required them to stand in the corner. When Angela West returned home, the children were still standing in the corner, having been spanked a second time for not standing quietly. At that time, West and defendant noted a mild rash or reddish mark on Christopher's forehead and face. West restricted the boys to their room for the day.

The next morning, defendant awoke late. After following defendant downstairs, Shaun told defendant that Christopher had vomited during the night at least twice. Defendant noted that Christopher's rash was worse. Upon learning that Christopher had eaten sherbet on the previous morning, defendant concluded that Christopher had food poisoning. West wanted to take Christopher to the hospital, but defendant convinced her otherwise. Defendant testified that he was afraid to take Christopher to the hospital for fear that he would be accused of child abuse, and the children would be taken away.

Defendant suggested to West that the best course to take would be to "flush out [Christopher's] system." Defendant urged Christopher to drink large quantities of water. Christopher vomited dozens of times on the couch, in the bathroom, and in a bucket placed nearby. Nonetheless, defendant continued to ply him with water, despite Christopher's complaining of a headache and of sleepiness. In all, during this treatment Christopher ingested a large quantity of water (defendant testified on one occasion three pitchers and on another to four or five quarts; one physician testified "a little bit more than four quarts"; and another physician estimated "eight to nine quarts"). Finally, Christopher screamed loudly. His eyes widened, and he began convulsing. He fell to the floor and exclaimed that he could not see.

Angela West ran next door to a phone, and a neighbor called for an ambulance. Defendant took Christopher to the hospital, although an ambulance arrived within minutes after his departure. A witness testified that defendant stopped for several minutes at an intersection on the way to the hospital.

At the hospital, Christopher experienced two more seizures, his condition deteriorated, and he was transferred to Duke University Medical Center. The next day, Christopher was pronounced brain dead and was disconnected from a respirator. Although not the cause of death, an autopsy revealed recent bruising to Christopher's head, thigh, and buttocks, some of which, an expert testified, were not of the type that result from normal childhood activity. When police officers searched the West apartment, they found, on the coffee table in the living room near where Christopher drank the water, among other things, a half-filled pitcher of water, a bottle of hydrogen peroxide, a bottle of "Safety Bowl, non-acid restroom and bowl cleaner," and an empty bottle of Lysol toilet bowl cleaner.

The defense introduced evidence to show an absence of intent to harm Christopher.

* * *

The State's theories on both the charges of felony child abuse and of first-degree murder by means of torture and by premeditation and deliberation were that defendant forced Christopher to consume the large quantity of water to punish and ultimately kill Christopher for having eaten sherbet without permission. The defense contended that defendant forced Christopher to drink the water to "flush out his system," and therefore Christopher's death was an accident or, at most, involuntary manslaughter. * * *

* * *

II.

* * *

Murder by Torture

The trial court instructed the jury on murder by torture as follows:

Now, I charge that for you to find the defendant guilty of first degree murder by means or [sic] torture, the state must prove two things beyond a reasonable doubt.

First, that the defendant intentionally tortured the victim.

* * *

Second, the state must prove that the torture was a proximate cause of the victim's death. * * *

* * *[D]efendant * * * contends that the State did not present adequate evidence of torture. The record indicates otherwise. Torture was defined by the trial court in pertinent part as "the course of conduct by one ... which intentionally inflicts grievous pain and suffering upon another for the purpose of punishment, persuasion, or sadistic pleasure." We note first that, based on the evidence of a pattern of extraordinary disciplinary methods, the jury could have inferred an intent to cause Christopher grievous pain. There was also adequate evidence of "grievous pain and suffering." Through expert testimony, evidence was presented that Christopher's stomach was distended to accommodate large quantities of water and that this "is very painful." Moreover, Christopher vomited "dozens" of times as he was urged to drink more and more water. Other testimony indicated that the fluid that filled Christopher's lungs would have created a sensation similar to suffocation and that the swelling of his brain that resulted from the ingestion of water created a tremendous headache, which culminated in a scream, followed by blindness. Lastly, based on defendant's past pattern of punishing Christopher, there was adequate evidence for the jury to find that defendant's acts were for the purpose of punishment. We hold here that the State presented adequate evidence of torture.

Murder With Premeditation and Deliberation

Defendant also contends that the State failed to present sufficient evidence of premeditation and deliberation to submit an instruction to the jury. We disagree. * * *

* * *

In this case, there is ample evidence to support the instructions on murder with premeditation and deliberation. Previous ill will by defendant toward Christopher was shown through testimony of extraordinary disciplinary procedures intended to oppress and humiliate Christopher. The manner of killing, which involved the painful ingestion of large quantities of water over a two-to three-hour period, indicates a particularly brutal method of killing. In addition, evidence indicated that Christopher suffered from bruises to the head and buttocks, possibly inflicted during this two-to three-hour period. * * *

* * *

IV.

Defendant next contends that the torture statute is unconstitutionally vague. We do not find it so. Essentially, defendant argues that a reasonable person of ordinary intelligence would not be on notice that his conduct was a crime.

A common understanding of torture would put a person of ordinary understanding on notice that coercing a six-year-old to drink quart after quart of water over a two-to three-hour period, despite his vomiting dozens of times and complaining of headaches, would constitute torture for purposes of the murder statute. * * *

* * *

Notes and Questions

1. *Criminal vs. civil enforcement (again).* Using *Ogin* as a vehicle, Problem 6–1 invited exploration of the respective roles of criminal and civil enforcement in child protection. Does *Crawford* provide reason for reexploration?: (a) Did the civil child protection system (the Department of Social Services) fail Christopher West in the early summer of 1988 by investigating the household, securing a three-month service agreement with Crawford, but not insisting on the children's removal from the home? Or did the criminal justice system fail Christopher when misdemeanor child abuse charges against Crawford were dismissed three months before the boy died of murder by torture?,

(b) Regardless of what child protective authorities do in the civil arena, should prosecutors pursue criminal charges against parents and other caretakers on relatively "minor" abuse charges where it appears the abuse may escalate? Do Professor Besharov's recommendations, stated in note 1 following *Ogin*, provide helpful guidelines?

2. *Issue preclusion (collateral estoppel)*. Does the issue preclusion (collateral estoppel) doctrine preclude criminal prosecution of the defendant for the same incident that resulted in an earlier civil neglect finding? In People v. Roselle, 643 N.E.2d 72 (N.Y. 1994), the family court found that the defendant had neglected his three-year-old daughter by placing her in a bathtub of scalding hot water, causing severe burns to her buttocks and right foot. Defendant was then indicted, among other things, for assault and endangering the welfare of a child in the scalding incident.

"When an issue of fact or law is actually litigated and determined by a valid and final judgment, and the determination is essential to the judgment, the determination is conclusive in a subsequent action between the parties, whether on the same or a different claim." Restatement (Second) of Judgments § 27. *Roselle* held that the neglect proceeding did not preclude the criminal action because "no legally cognizable identity of issues exists between the child protective proceeding, which seeks to safeguard the child, and a criminal action, which yields a final determination conclusive of defendant's penal responsibility." 643 N.E.2d at 76.

3. *Contributing to the delinquency of a minor*. Most states have statutes criminalizing conduct that might lead a juvenile to commit delinquent acts. Massachusetts, for example, punishes "[a]ny person who shall be found to have caused, induced, abetted, or encouraged or contributed toward the delinquency of a child, or to have acted in any way tending to cause or induce such delinquency." Mass. Gen. Laws ch. 119 § 63. These statutes are generally used to punish adult conduct detrimental to the juvenile's welfare. See, e.g., State v. Eno, 727 A.2d 981, 982 (N.H.1999) (defendant teacher-coach provided alcohol to student, had a sexual relationship with her, and urged another student to withhold information about the relationship); State v. Barr, 984 P.2d 185 (N.M.App.1999) (31–year-old defendant drove juveniles to a home and burglarized it); State v. Howard, 578 N.W.2d 211 (Wis.1998) (mother recruited her daughter to assist her in shoplifting). Because the statutes usually operate against "any person" who commits the proscribed conduct, however, they can also reach a juvenile's conduct detrimental to another juvenile. See, e.g., In re Lomeli, 665 N.E.2d 765, 766 (Ohio Ct. App. 1995).

Under the Massachusetts statute quoted above, may the defendant be convicted if the affected juvenile did not commit a delinquent act, or was never charged or adjudicated a delinquent? Should contributing-to-delinquency statutes extend this far?

A NOTE ABOUT PARENTAL–LIABILITY STATUTES

In an effort to combat juvenile crime, several states and localities now authorize prosecution of parents following misconduct by their children. These parental liability statutes proceed a significant step further than endangerment and contributing-to-delinquency statutes. Some parental liability statutes criminalize particular parental acts or omissions. In Florida, for example, a parent or other adult can be prosecuted for allowing children to gain access to their firearms if the children kill or injure someone with them. See Fla. Stat. § 784.05. Oregon, however, recently enacted broader legislation authorizing prosecution of parents for "failure to supervise" their children who commit a crime or specified status offense:

(1) A person commits the offense of failing to supervise a child if the person is the parent, lawful guardian or other person lawfully charged with the care or custody of a child under 15 years of age and the child:

(a) Commits an act that brings the child within the [delinquency] jurisdiction of the juvenile court;

(b) Violates a curfew law of a county or any other political subdivision; or

(c) Fails to attend school as required [by law]. * * *

* * *

(3) In a prosecution of a person for failing to supervise a child under subsection (1)(a) of this section, it is an affirmative defense that the person:

(a) Is the victim of the act that brings the child within the jurisdiction of the juvenile court; or

(b) Reported the act to the appropriate authorities.

(4) In a prosecution of a person for failing to supervise a child under subsection (1) of this section, it is an affirmative defense that the person took reasonable steps to control the conduct of the child at the time the person is alleged to have failed to supervise the child.

* * *

(6) If a person pleads guilty or is found guilty of failing to supervise a child under this section and if the person has not previously been convicted of failing to supervise a child, the court:

(a) Shall warn the person of the penalty for future convictions of failing to supervise a child and shall suspend imposition of sentence. * * *

(7)(a) If a person pleads guilty or is found guilty of failing to supervise a child under this section and if the person has only one prior conviction for failing to supervise a child, the court, with the consent of the person, may suspend imposition of sentence and order the person to complete a parent effectiveness program approved by the court. Upon the person's completion of the parent effectiveness program to the satisfaction of the court, the court may discharge the person. If the person fails to complete the parent effectiveness program to the satisfaction of the court, the court may impose a sentence authorized by this section.

(b) There may be only one suspension of sentence under this subsection with respect to a person. * * *

(9) Failing to supervise a child is a violation punishable by a fine of not more than $1,000.

Or. Rev. Stat. § 163.577. As failure-to-supervise statutes gain popularity at the state and local levels, their constitutionality and efficacy are matters of spirited debate. Courts generally reject challenges that the statutes are void-for-vagueness, overbroad, violate substantive due process, or constitute cruel and unusual punishment. See, e.g., Naomi R. Cahn, Pragmatic Questions About Parental Liability Statutes, 1996 Wis. L. Rev. 399, 412–15.

Do parental liability statutes reflect sound policy? If a child commits a crime or status offense, do authorities send the child the right message by prosecuting the parent? Why not simply make the child accountable for his or her own conduct, either in a delinquency or status offense proceeding or a criminal prosecution? Regardless of whether the parent has a reasonableness defense, does prosecution diminish the parent in the eyes of the child and siblings? What if the parent holds tenuous employment necessary to the family's economic well being, but loses that employment because of the prosecution? Who should define what constitutes "reasonable" parenting? If the parent fails to control the child and asserts that failure stems from inability to exert control, would a civil neglect proceeding better enable authorities to treat the family? Should treatment be available to the family without a criminal prosecution? Should the criminal law play a role in encouraging parents to supervise their children?

The wisdom of parental liability statutes may turn on one's beliefs about parents' capacity to influence their children's behavior, and about the law's capacity to influence parental behavior. One commentator, supporting these statutes in principle, asserts that "a parent's influence over child behavior is ordinarily decisive. Parental example, tender loving care, moral tutoring, reprimands and withdrawals of customary privileges or treats for misconduct are virtually fail-safe methods of preventing juvenile crime." This commentator acknowledges that "[s]anctions for malparenting are no panacea for the worrisome incidence of juvenile crime," but concludes that some parents "need the specter of punishment to concentrate the mind wonderfully on the responsibilities of parenthood." Bruce Fein, Impose Penalties for Malparenting?, Wash. Times, June 5, 1995, at A16.

Professor Naomi R. Cahn, however, criticizes parental liability statutes for assuming that "parents can, do, and should control their child," that "children and parents enjoy such a relationship that parental liability will have an impact on the child's actions," and that the family is a cause of the child's criminal activity. She believes that "parents may have no such control and therefore responsibility is irrelevant, that parental liability may decrease family harmony, and that punishment alone may be ineffective. There is a dramatic difference between our aspirations for parental liability and control, and the reality of many children's lives. The family is not always a benign influence on children; consequently, children may have good reason not to trust, or to reject their parents. Correspondingly, even where there are harmonious relationships, children may no longer be capable of being influenced by their parents. A second problem is that the laws tend to have a disproportionate impact on single-parent households, further penalizing poor, often African–American women who are already over-burdened and who are acting in the most responsible manner of which they are capable, and yet who cannot meet middle-class defined parenting norms." Id. at 415–16.

In the absence of parental liability statutes, when can parents be prosecuted arising from their children's criminal conduct? See generally Abraham Abramovsky, Parent's Liability for Crimes of Children, N.Y.L.J., July 7, 1989, at 3.

Parents' civil liability for their children's torts is discussed in Chapter 9, Financial Responsibility and Control.

PROBLEM 6–4

If you were a state legislator, would you vote to enact a "failure to supervise" criminal statute identical to Oregon's in your state? If you would support such legislation in principle but are uneasy with some of the Oregon provisions, what additions or deletions would you recommend?

A NOTE ABOUT THE "CULTURAL DEFENSE" TO ABUSE, NEGLECT OR ENDANGERMENT PROSECUTIONS

Where a parent or other person commits acts or omissions that would support prosecution for abuse, neglect or child endangerment, should guilt be excused or punishment mitigated on the ground that the acts or omissions were products of the defendant's cultural background that differs from mainstream American culture? Should juvenile courts weigh cultural differences in determining whether to find a child abused or neglected in civil proceedings?

The "cultural defense" has arisen periodically as the American population grows more diverse through immigration from nations with a variety of cultural and religious traditions. A group of scholars has posited the tension between pluralism and child protection. See Richard A. Shweder et al., The Free Exercise of Culture, 51 Items (Dec. 1997) (Social Science Research Council), available at <http://www.ssrc.org> (visited Nov. 15, 1999). On the one hand, "[w]e are not an assimilative society, but a facilitative, pluralistic one, in which we must be willing to abide by someone else's unfamiliar or even repellent practice because the same tolerant impulse protects our own idiosyncracies." Id., quoting Michael H. v. Gerald D., 491 U.S. 110, 141 (1989) (Brennan, J., dissenting). On the other, "[c]ultural differences are beautiful, but they have nothing to do with the law. We can't possibly have a set of laws for Americans, a set of laws for immigrants, and a set of laws for tourists." Shweder et al., quoting an official with the New York State Administration for Children's Services.

Shweder and his colleagues pinpoint several cultural practices that potentially clash with mainstream American views of child protection, including shaming and corporal punishment, parent/child co-sleeping arrangements, male facial scarification and arranged teenage marriage.

Female genital mutilation has also hit the headlines in recent years. Congress and a few states have outlawed this form of circumcision performed on young girls (usually between the ages of four and eight) in several African nations to protect their virginity and prevent promiscuity by reducing sexual desire. See, e.g., 18 U.S.C. § 116. Steeped in culture and tradition, the procedure reportedly is sometimes performed in the United States by families that have emigrated from these nations. In the most extreme form, the girls' clitorises are cut off and their genital lips are stitched together, leaving only a small opening (sometimes the size of a match head or the tip of the small finger) for passage of urine and menstrual blood. The result may be permanent physical and psychological damage, such as infections, severe hemorrhaging, inability to have intercourse later without further cutting, interference with orgasm, bleeding during labor, difficulties during delivery without further cutting, infertility, incontinence, and lifelong reduction of sexual pleasure. See Karungari Kiragu, Female Genital Mutilation: A Reproductive Health Concern, 23 Population Reps. S1 (Oct. 1995).

Which cultural practices, if any, should United States authorities tolerate in the name of cultural diversity? As you formulate your own position, consider these events:

a.   In May of 1997, New York City police arrested a Danish tourist for leaving her 14–month-old daughter in a baby carriage outside a restaurant where she dined inside with the daughter's father. The child was placed in foster care, and the parents were jailed for two nights, charged with child endangerment.

Danish parents reportedly were astonished at news coverage of the arrests. "Come on, we do this all the time," a Danish woman told the Associated Press as she sat in a Copenhagen cafe while her 7–month-old son dozed out of reach. "We go in for a cup of coffee, sit so we can see the stroller, go out and check once in a while and that's it." An editor at Denmark's largest newspaper said parents routinely leave babies in their strollers on Copenhagen streets because parents are reluctant to take them into noisy, smoke-filled restaurants. "We'd rather they take their nap enjoying the fresh air," the editor reported.

Asserted cultural differences, however, did not move New York authorities. "To leave a child unattended for an hour on a city street in New York is pretty inappropriate," the city's Commissioner for Children's Services said. "I don't think you should expect the Police Department to make inquiries about whether this is acceptable in Denmark." See Mirta Ojito, Danish Mother Is Reunited With Her Baby, N.Y. Times, May 15, 1997, at B3; Tony Marcano, Toddler, Left Outside Restaurant, Is Returned to Her Mother, N.Y. Times, May 14, 1997, at B3.

b.   In early 1996, Boston police arrested a Somali man for kicking and punching his sixteen-year-old stepdaughter to keep her from going out alone late at night with her boyfriend in violation of religious customs. The girl reportedly had been quarreling with her parents for almost a year over the boy and her desire to "act like American girls." According to a family friend, "It's the conflict of a girl in a permissive society and a family which wants to be able to promote their values." See Jason B. Johnson, Culture Clash Blamed as a Girl's Stepfather Faces Assault Charges, Boston Herald, Feb. 3, 1997, at 7. The incident is typical of prosecutions and child welfare proceedings that have arisen when recent immigrants from cultures that encourage corporal punishment of children find themselves in an American culture that has grown to disdain such discipline. See, e.g., Celia W. Dugger, A Cultural Reluctance to Spare the Rod; Newcomers Say Americans Spoil Children, N.Y. Times, Feb. 29, 1996, at B1.

c.   In January of 1985, a Japanese woman who had lived in the United States for more than a dozen years attempted to drown herself and her two young children, aged six months and four years, in the ocean at Santa Monica, California after she learned her husband had been unfaithful. She was rescued, but the children drowned. She said she had attempted parent-child suicide, a traditional practice that occurs frequently in Japan in the face of humiliation. The Japanese–American community immediately rallied to her cause. The Los Angeles county district attorney initially stated, "It doesn't matter if you kill out of love or kill out of hate. * * * We have the right to demand that people who live in our society abide by our own rules." See Leslie Pound, Mother's Tragic Crime Exposes a Culture Gap, Chicago Tribune, June 10, 1985, at 1. The mother was charged with first degree murder but was allowed to plead guilty to voluntary manslaughter after the prosecution concluded that "[b]ased on the unusual facts of this case, a significant quantity of psychiatric evidence indicates that [her] state of mind was less than that required for a murder conviction." See Michael D. Harris, U.P.I., Oct. 18, 1985. She received five years probation, and she and her unfaithful husband reconciled and moved to Los Angeles. T.W. McGarry, Japanese Mom's Life After Suicide Attempt, S.F. Chronicle, June 16, 1988, at B6.

PROBLEM 6–5

You are a prosecutor, and the three arrests described in this note occurred in your jurisdiction. Would you prosecute against the Danish tourist, the Somali father, or the Japanese mother, or would you seek some other resolution? If the latter, what resolution would you seek? Would your view of the Danish tourist's conduct change if a stranger had seized the toddler from the carriage and killed her?

SECTION 2. SEXUAL ABUSE

The American Academy of Pediatrics defines "sexual abuse" as "the engaging of a child in sexual activities that the child cannot comprehend, for which the child is developmentally unprepared and cannot give informed consent, and/or that violate the social and legal taboos of society. The sexual activities may include all forms of oral genital, genital, or anal contact by or to the child, or nontouching abuses, such as exhibitionism, voyeurism, or using the child in the production of pornography. Sexual abuse includes a spectrum of activities ranging from violent rape to a gentle seduction." American Acad. of Pediatrics, Guidelines for the Evaluation of Sexual Abuse of Children, 87 Pediatrics 254 (1991).

Endangerment, criminal child abuse, and general criminal sex abuse statutes can usually reach much sexual exploitation of children. Child sexual abuse statutes, however, operate specifically against such exploitation and ordinarily carry significantly greater penalties. These specific statutes are the subject of this section.

A. *The Nature of the Problem*

WILLIAM WINSLADE ET AL., CASTRATING PEDOPHILES CONVICTED OF SEX OFFENSES AGAINST CHILDREN: NEW TREATMENT OR OLD PUNISHMENT?

51 SMU L. Rev. 349, 357–60 (1998).

* * *

Many persons now in prison were placed there based upon convictions for "violent sex offenses," including rape and sexual assault. The U.S. Department of Justice reports that 9.7% of state prisoners in 1994 were violent sex offenders. The self-reports of state prisoners convicted of rape or sexual assault indicate that two-thirds were "child victimizers" (victims aged seventeen years or less), and fifty-eight percent of those said their victims were twelve years or younger. Additionally, in one study of crime data reported to police in three states, fifteen percent of rape victims were under age twelve, and twenty-nine percent of rape victims were between the ages of twelve and seventeen. The U.S. Department of Justice also reports that ninety percent of rape victims under age twelve knew the offender, and that two-thirds of victims eighteen to twenty-nine years old had a prior relationship with their rapist. Startlingly, while the average annual growth in the number of prisoners since 1980 has been about 7.6%, the number of prisoners sentenced for violent sexual assault other than rape increased by an annual average of nearly fifteen percent, faster than any other category except drug trafficking.

More recent reports appear to confirm that typical rape or sexual assault victims are children or adolescent girls, and that one of the most notable risk factors for rape or sexual assault, especially for girls, is the presence of a stepfather as part of the household. Girls raised with stepfathers are over seven times more likely to be sexually abused by them than girls raised in households with their natural fathers. Although studies suggest that girls rather than boys are at a higher risk for sexual abuse, with two to four girls for every boy sexually assaulted, boys are believed to be underrepresented and may therefore be at greater risk of sexual assault than is now known. This underrepresentation may be due to the "male enculturation" process, which may make boys less likely to admit to victimization, especially since sexual abuse for boys can carry the stigma of homosexuality. Girls are considered more willing than boys to disclose sexual abuse, and girls often serve as a third-party conduit through which sexual abuse of their brothers is discovered. Unlike girls, however, boys are more frequently subject to anal abuse and have more physical indicators of abuse; they are also more likely to be forcefully abused, to be victimized outside the family, and to be abused by younger offenders, typically older adolescents.

Another distinctive feature of child sexual offending is that a single child molester may have many victims or may victimize the same child many times over, committing hundreds of sexual acts on many children. One study found that self-reported child molesters had an average of seventy-two victims, but given the tendency of offenders to minimize their number of offenses, this number may be even higher. Another study indicates that pedophiles who are interdicted but who go untreated will often repeat their offending behavior—sex offense recidivism rates for untreated pedophiles who engage in incest are between four and ten percent, while sex offense recidivism rates for untreated, non-familial child sexual abusers are between ten and forty percent. Sex offense recidivism rates for male sex offenders are reportedly as high as fifty percent, and depend upon such factors as demographic characteristics, criminal history and legal disposition of the offender, the offender's particular paraphilia, amenability of the offender to treatment, and the amount of community and family support available to the offender.

All told, it is estimated that between 100,000 and 500,000 children in the United States are sexually molested each year. Between 1980 and 1992, the number of child sexual abuse cases tripled, from 37,336 cases in 1980 to 128,556 in 1992. This increase has been attributed to an increase in actual identification and reporting of child sexual abuse rather than an increase in the actual occurrence of child sexual abuse. Generally, however, the actual scope of child sexual abuse is not known but only estimated because the majority of sexually abused children never come to the attention of child protection agencies or professionals. Additionally, the nature of sexual abuse, including "the secrecy and shame surrounding it, the criminal prohibitions against it, and the young age and dependent status of its victim[s]," serves to limit identification, disclosure, and reporting of child sexual abuse. In essence, child sexual abuse may be a much larger problem than it appears.

* * *

DONALD C. BROSS, TERMINATING THE PARENT–CHILD RELATIONSHIP AS A RESPONSE TO CHILD SEXUAL ABUSE

26 Loy. U. Chi. L.J. 287, 291–93 (1995).

* * *

Researchers have extensively documented the short-term effects of child sexual abuse. One study reported that the majority of intrafamilial victims of child sexual abuse suffer "initial effects," including sleep disorders, eating disturbances, fears, phobias, depression, guilt, shame, and anger. Using standard mental health measures, other researchers found that seventeen percent of sexually abused children aged four to six met the criteria for "clinically significant pathology."[21] The results were even more dramatic for those in the seven to thirteen-year-old age group, forty percent of whom met the criteria for clinically significant pathology. In addition, researchers found substantially elevated levels of aggression and antisocial behavior in victims of childhood sexual abuse, as well as other short-term effects on sexual and social functioning.

Long-term effects on victims of child sexual abuse include self-destructive ideation and behaviors. Other effects include increased rates of anxiety, tension, nightmares, and sleeplessness. Studies also report that victims experience dissociation,[27] feelings of isolation, and lower self-esteem. Another study of long-term consequences of sexual abuse found that sixty-four percent of the incest survivors complained of fear of or conflict with husbands or sexual partners as compared to forty percent of the control group. Thirty-nine percent of the survivors never married. Researchers also link Post–Traumatic Stress Disorder (PTSD) to experiences of childhood incest. In one study, seventeen women in treatment, an average of seventeen years after their final incest experiences, met the criteria for PTSD.[30] Researchers have since found that PTSD is common among childhood sexual abuse survivors. In some of those victims who did not exhibit PTSD symptoms, researchers have observed other long-term interpersonal effects. For example, studies show that the patterns of human relationships or attachments which a child acquires

---

21. "Clinically significant pathology" is a conclusive term meaning that a reasonable therapist would recommend treatment for such children.

27. "Dissociation is a process that produces a discernible alteration in a person's thoughts, feelings, or actions so that for a period of time certain information is not associated or integrated with other information as it normally or logically would be."

30. PTSD is particularly debilitating as can be surmised from the following reported symptoms:

The reexperiencing of the trauma as evidenced by at least one of the following: (1)

recurrent and intrusive recollections of the event; (2) recurrent dreams of the event; (3) sudden acting or feeling as if the traumatic event were reoccurring, because of an association with an environmental or ideational stimulus.

. . .

The numbing or responsiveness to or reduced involvement with the external world, beginning some time after the trauma, as shown by at least one of the following: (1) markedly diminished interest in one or more significant activities; (2) feelings of detachment or estrangement from others; (3) constricted affect.

in early life tend to reappear in adult life, so that avoidant personalities, dependency, self-defeating personality disorder, and borderline personality disorder are overrepresented among sexually abused subjects.[32]

Research on general child maltreatment, including sexual abuse, suggests that poor educational performance, health problems, and low levels of achievement in adult life are additional long-term consequences for some victims. Citing various studies, the American Humane Association reports that abused or neglected children were fifty-three percent more likely to be arrested as juveniles, thirty-eight percent more likely to be arrested as adults, and thirty-eight percent more likely to be arrested for a violent crime.

Preliminary results of increased research on the effects of child sexual abuse indicate short-term and continuing effects stem from abusive sexual experiences of children. These results suggest legal intervention is warranted based on the severity of the effects alone.

* * *

B. The Basis for Criminal Intervention

DONALD C. BROSS, TERMINATING THE PARENT– CHILD RELATIONSHIP AS A RESPONSE TO CHILD SEXUAL ABUSE

26 Loy. U. Chi. L.J. 287, 293–96 (1995).

* * *

Legal intervention [against child sexual abuse] can occur through a variety of proceedings. The two primary methods are through criminal prosecution of the abuser and civil protection proceedings under child abuse and neglect laws. The choice between pursuing a remedy in one proceeding over another may depend on the facts of the particular case, a particular strategy, or the purposes for the proceedings themselves.

For example, commentators report several factors which indicate whether child sexual abuse will result in criminal prosecution, including the seriousness of the abuse, whether the abuse occurs inside rather than outside the family,[36] and the presence of maternal support. In some cases, the State may be justified in seeking both criminal prosecution and termination of the parent-child legal relationship.

---

32. "Avoidant personalities" involve a "pervasive pattern of social discomfort, fear of negative evaluation, and timidity." "Dependency" is a "pervasive pattern of dependent and submissive behavior." Individuals with "self-defeating personality disorder" are repeatedly involved in relationships or situations that are self-defeating and avoid or sabotage pleasurable experiences. "Borderline personality disorder" involves a "pervasive pattern of instability of self-image, interpersonal relationships, and mood."

36. Proportionately, more cases of extrafamilial child sexual abuse are prosecuted than cases of parental or familial abuse. Other factors increasing the likelihood of prosecution include: the presence of oral-genital abuse, the use of force, the duration of the abuse, and the presence of physical or eyewitness evidence.

If the facts do not indicate a clear choice of proceedings, then strategy may play a key role in deciding whether and how to intervene legally. For example, the standard of proof may influence the choice between a civil or criminal intervention.[39] Furthermore, especially in termination cases, a child advocate may want to seek civil terminations in tandem with criminal prosecutions, especially given the greater likelihood for delay or reversal in criminal proceedings. Finally, if a child advocate relies on the possibility of a favorable criminal ruling to support a subsequent termination order, a child advocate loses the opportunity to present facts inadmissible in a criminal trial but admissible in civil proceedings.[41]

In other instances, the choice between criminal prosecution of child sexual abuse and civil protection proceedings depends upon the different purposes of the proceedings. Criminal law's goal is to punish and deter crimes against children by holding an individual perpetrator accountable. In contrast, civil child protection proceedings almost never result, even indirectly, in the imprisonment of the perpetrator. Rather the purpose of a child protection proceeding is to assure the safety of a particular child. The civil system achieves this safety through treatment of the child, parents, or family; through placement of the child in foster care if the home is not safe; or through freeing the child for adoption if such a result is unavoidable.

Indeed, in some instances, permanently freeing the child for adoption may guarantee the child long-term freedom from sexual abuse better than a short criminal sentence for the perpetrator. The effects of short jail time or other sentences are particularly uncertain when the convicted familial offender does not receive treatment or when treatment is unsuccessful. Especially when treatment of the offender is not accomplished or is unsuccessful, terminating the parent-child legal relationship through civil proceedings is usually the best long-term solution.

Despite the ability of the legal system to protect the child, child sexual abuse rarely results in the initiation of legal proceedings. A study of three counties, which included 833 substantiated reports of all types of intrafamilial child maltreatment, found that only four percent of the reports led to filings in criminal court, and only twenty-one percent of the incidents led to filings of civil dependency and neglect proceedings.

---

39. For example, the amount of evidence that would uphold a civil termination ruling may fall far below the standard of proof required for a criminal proceeding. This is because in a criminal proceeding, the prosecutor must prove that the criminal abuse occurred beyond a reasonable doubt, while in a civil proceeding, the proof must be by preponderance of the evidence.

* * *

41. For child protection agency lawyers and guardians ad litem who believe that termination is justified, the lesson appears to be not to rely on any aspect of the criminal process to achieve termination. By immediately proceeding with the juvenile or family court process to termination where appropriate, all the court proceedings affecting the child's life are processed simultaneously instead of sequentially. This is particularly important in the lives of children for whom time is always of the essence.

Thus, legal proceedings only occur in a small percentage of substantiated incidents of child abuse and neglect.

* * *

FERRIS v. SANTA CLARA COUNTY

United States Court of Appeals, Ninth Circuit, 1989.
891 F.2d 715.

DAVID R. THOMPSON, CIRCUIT JUDGE:

Appellant Sam Ferris appeals pro se the district court's grant of summary judgment in an action for injunctive relief and damages under 42 U.S.C. § 1983. Ferris alleged his civil rights were violated when he was arrested and convicted under state laws that proscribe certain sexual activities with minors. Ferris contends the statutes are unconstitutional and that the district court erred in striking his proposed second amended complaint. We have jurisdiction under 28 U.S.C. § 1291 and we affirm.

Facts

Ferris was arrested and charged with violating California Penal Code §§ 261.5 (one count), 288a(b)(1) (four counts), and 288a(b)(2) (two counts).[1] Ferris entered a plea of *nolo contendere* to all charges. He was sentenced to six months in the County jail and placed on probation. All charges resulted from Ferris' relations with two minor females, aged fifteen and seventeen. * * *

Analysis

* * *

Ferris argues that the statutes under which he was convicted deny him substantive due process, because they violate his right to engage in consensual sexual activities with females between the ages of fourteen and eighteen. In essence, Ferris argues he has a privacy right protected by the Constitution to engage in this conduct.

Even if we assume that Ferris may have a constitutional right to engage in consensual sexual activities with females, the State may nonetheless regulate this conduct insofar as it pertains to minors.

* * *

---

1. Section 261.5 provides:

Unlawful sexual intercourse is an act of sexual intercourse accomplished with a female not the wife of the perpetrator, where the female is under the age of 18 years.

Subsections (1) and (2) of section 288a(b) provide:

(b)(1) Except as provided in Section 288, any person who participates in an act of oral copulation with another person who is under 18 years of age shall be punished by imprisonment in the state prison, or in a county jail for a period of not more than one year.

(2) Except as provided in Section 288, any person over the age of 21 years who participates in an act of oral copulation with another person who is under 16 years of age shall be guilty of a felony.

* * * [The challenged California statutes] are aimed at protecting youth from physical and psychological harm as a result of specified sexual activities. California has a compelling interest in safeguarding its youth in this manner. * * *

* * *

Notes and Questions

1. *State sex crimes against children.* State codes define a number of sex crimes that operate only against sexual activity with minor victims. Chapter 948 of the Wisconsin statutes provides a representative sample. For example, Wis. Stat. § 948.02 criminalizes "sexual assault of a child." First degree sexual assault of a child occurs when the defendant "has sexual contact or sexual intercourse with a person who has not attained the age of 13 years"; second degree sexual assault of a child occurs when the defendant "has sexual contact or sexual intercourse with a person who has not attained the age of 16 years." Section 948.025 ("engaging in repeated acts of sexual assault of the same child") is a sentencing enhancement provision for repeated offenders.

Section 948.06 criminalizes "incest with a child." Section 948.07 ("child enticement") operates against any person who, with intent to commit any of the specified sex acts, causes or attempts to cause a child under 18 to go into any vehicle, building, room or secluded place. Section 948.09 operates against any person who "has sexual intercourse with a child who is not the defendant's spouse and who has attained the age of sixteen years." Section 948.10 operates against any person who "for purposes of sexual arousal or sexual gratification, causes a child to expose genitals or pubic area or exposes genitals or pubic area to a child" who is not the defendant's spouse.

2. *Federal legislation.* Most prosecutions of sex crimes against children (like most prosecutions generally) occur in state courts, but Congress has also enacted a number of such crimes. See, e.g., 18 U.S.C. § 2241(c) (crossing state lines with intent to engage in a sexual act with a child under twelve; in the special maritime and territorial jurisdiction of the United States or in a federal prison, knowingly engaging in a sexual act with a person under 12 or knowingly engaging in a sexual act by force or threat of force with person between 12 and 16 who is at least four years younger than the defendant); 18 U.S.C. § 2243(a) (sexual abuse of a minor in the special maritime and territorial jurisdiction of the United States or in a federal prison); 18 U.S.C. § 2423 (interstate transportation of a minor with intent to engage in criminal sexual activity; interstate travel with intent to engage in a sexual act with a minor).

3. *"Statutory" and "forcible" rape.* Defendant Ferris was convicted of "statutory rape," an offense sometimes called by such names as indecent liberties with a child, lewd and lascivious activities with a child, or carnal knowledge of a child. Force is not an element of statutory rape; the key element is the victim's age. The prosecutor may prevail on proof that the proscribed sexual conduct took place between the defendant and the under-age victim. The victim is deemed incapable of consent, as a matter of law, if he or she is below the age specified in the statute (the so-called "age of consent"), or if more than a specified minimum age differential exists

between the victim and the defendant. Purported consent would thus not be a defense, regardless of anything the young victim might have said or indicated to the perpetrator. *Ferris* holds that a state may constitutionally remove any consent defense.

To be distinguished from statutory rape is "forcible rape," which depends on proof that the victim submitted to sexual activity because of the defendant's physical force or threat of physical force. Forcible rape statutes generally criminalize conduct against "any person," and thus reach forcible conduct against child victims.

4. *State constitutional challenges.* Defendant Ferris unsuccessfully raised federal constitutional challenges to his convictions. Based on a compelling state interest in protecting children, courts also reject challenges to sex crime statutes under state constitutional privacy guarantees. See, e.g., State v. Cunningham, 712 So.2d 1221 (Fla.Dist.Ct.App.1998) (24–year-old defendant); State v. J.A.S., 686 So.2d 1366 (Fla.Dist.Ct.App.1997) (15-year-old defendants).

5. *Gender neutrality.* Statutory rape laws once sought to "protect girls under the age of eighteen years from conscienceless men, as far as possible." State v. Henderson, 114 P. 30, 32 (Idaho 1911). Nowadays these laws "attempt to prevent the sexual exploitation of persons deemed legally incapable of giving consent." State v. Stiffler, 788 P.2d 220, 222 (Idaho 1990).

Statutory and forcible rape laws now carry gender-neutral language in virtually all states. The typical statutory rape prosecution still involves a male offender and an underage female victim, but prosecution of females for statutory rape of underage male victims remains possible. (Problem 6–6 below concerns such a case.). Prosecution may even be possible where the perpetrator and the underage victim are of the same gender. Cf. State v. Buch, 926 P.2d 599 (Haw. 1996) (third-degree sexual assault).

In Michael M. v. Superior Ct., 450 U.S. 464 (1981) (plurality opinion), the Court held that equal protection was not offended by California's statutory rape law that operated only when the victim was female. (Even as the Court rendered its decision, the statute was an oddity because thirty-seven states already had enacted gender-neutral statutory rape laws, 450 U.S. at 492 (Brennan, J., dissenting)). *Michael M.'s* plurality concluded that at least one purpose of California's law was to advance the state's strong interest in helping prevent teenage out-of-wedlock pregnancies. 450 U.S. at 471.

In People v. Liberta, 474 N.E.2d 567, 576 (N.Y.1984), the court struck down a forcible rape statute that exempted females from criminal liability. (At the time, New York was one of only ten jurisdictions without a gender-neutral forcible rape statute.). *Liberta* distinguished *Michael M.* on the ground that the primary purpose of forcible rape statutes is not prevention of pregnancies, but rather punishment for violence, which can offend the dignity of men and women alike.

6. *Mistake of age.* What if the defendant contends that he reasonably believed the fourteen-year-old victim was nineteen? In most states, statutory rape and other sex crimes are strict-liability crimes (that is, crimes not

requiring proof of mens rea, or a culpable mental state), even though strict liability crimes are the exception rather than the rule in American criminal jurisprudence. Mistake of age is no defense, regardless of the victim's appearance, sexual sophistication or verbal misrepresentations about age, and regardless of the defendant's efforts to ascertain the victim's age.

Only about a third of the states permit a mistake-of-age defense in some form in sex crime prosecutions. Some states make the defense available with respect to crimes charging sexual relations with older underage victims but not with younger ones. See, e.g., Colo. Rev. Stat. § 18–3–406(2) (line of demarcation is fifteen); People v. Salazar, 920 P.2d 893, 896 (Colo.Ct.App. 1996) (denying defense to defendant who claimed he reasonably believed his 11–year-old victim was 17). Other states make the defense available with respect to less serious sex crimes but not more serious ones. See, e.g., Minn. Stat. §§ 609.344–609.345 (defense available for some crimes under third-degree and fourth-degree criminal sexual conduct). In either circumstance, the defendant must prove the reasonableness of his belief concerning the victim's age. See, e.g., Or. Rev. Stat. § 163.325(1), (2). In at least four states without sex crime statutes expressly creating the mistake-of-age defense, the highest courts have held that the statutes by implication require proof of a mens rea regarding the victim's age and thus make the mistake-of-age defense available. See Garnett v. State, 632 A.2d 797, 803 (Md. 1993) (citing decisions). Courts have rejected constitutional challenges to strict liability statutory rape statutes. See, e.g., United States v. Brooks, 841 F.2d 268, 269–70 (9th Cir.1988).

Where the underage victim was a willing participant in the non-forcible sexual activity and reasonably appeared older than the age of consent, should the state charge the defendant with a crime as serious as rape, which ordinarily carries a long prison sentence and considerable public obloquy? Should the answer depend on the victim's actual age? What policies underlie the legislative decision to withhold the consent defense? Where the statute provides no consent defense, does defense counsel have any way to urge the jury to consider the victim's willingness and appearance?

7. *Marriage.* The marital rape exemption once prevailed, providing as a matter of law that a husband could not be convicted of raping or committing other sex crimes on his wife. By statute or court decision, virtually all states have largely or entirely abolished the exemption with respect to forcible rape and other sex crimes for which force is an element. See, e.g, Developments in the Law: Legal Responses to Domestic Violence, 106 Harv. L. Rev. 1498, 1533–34 (1993).

Marriage, however, remains a defense to most statutory rape and other non-forcible sex crimes which impose liability based on the victim's age. See, e.g., Kan. Stat. § 21–3505. The rationale is that because marriage emancipates a child, the law should not intrude on the marital relationship unless the defendant has resorted to force. A marital exception to statutory rape laws is unlikely to affect sexual relations with particularly young minors because such minors normally do not marry, even under statutes permitting marriage with parental consent or court approval.

8. *Emancipation*. If the sex crime victim is below the age of consent, the defendant may not avoid liability by establishing that the victim was emancipated. See, e.g., State v. Plude, 621 A.2d 1342 (Conn. Ct. App. 1993).

9. *Adolescent perpetrators*. If two fourteen-year-olds (each below the age of consent) have sexual relations with each other, has each one committed statutory rape of the other? Can a perpetrator be prosecuted where he or she is within the age group the statute protects?

Most statutes proscribing sexual conduct with an underage child operate broadly against "any person," or against "whoever" engaged in the conduct. A defendant of any age would thus be subject to prosecution. Some statutory rape laws apply only where the difference in the ages of the perpetrator and the underage victim is at least a specified minimum. See, e.g., N.C. Gen. Stat. § 14–27.2(a)(1) (first-degree rape) (victim under thirteen and defendant at least twelve and at least four years older than the victim).

Courts uphold application of statutory rape laws against minor perpetrators, or against both minor participants on the ground that "each is the victim of the other." In re T.W., 685 N.E.2d 631, 635 (Ill. Ct. App. 1997).

10. *Prosecutorial discretion and child perpetrators?* The propriety of prosecution may be a threshold issue when the alleged sex crime perpetrator is a child. The National Task Force on Juvenile Sex Offending recommends that "[p]rosecution should be a component of most interventions in juvenile sex offenses," because criminal sanction provides "support for the victim's rights, a means to insure victim and community safety, and a mechanism to facilitate prevention of further victimization." The Revised Report from the National Task Force on Juvenile Sex Offending, 1993 of The National Adolescent Perpetrator Network, 44 Juv. & Fam. Ct. J. 3, 13, 18–19, 21 (1993 No. 4). The Task Force recognizes, however, that court-imposed supervision without prosecution may be appropriate for prepubescent children who engage in sexual behavior. Id. at 21.

Another commentator urges circumspection where the children are particularly young and the sexual behavior is "consensual" in the ordinary use of the term: "[I]t is generally conceded that a certain amount of sexual discovery and experimentation is part of the normal process of growing up. The adults involved in juvenile proceedings should be sensitive to this and the fact that such cases, by their nature, involve very young children who might be easily damaged." Henry J. Hall, I California Juv. Ct. Prac.: Delinquent Minors 3–4 (1995 update).

In Scott E. v. State, 931 P.2d 1370, 1375 (Nev.1997), the juvenile court adjudicated eleven-year-old Scott a delinquent and placed him on three years' probation for "lewdness with a child under fourteen," a class A felony if committed by an adult. The charges were that Scott "touched" his eight-year-old female step-cousin "on the top of her clothes" on her "personal spot," and twice exposed his penis and had her touch his penis. The state supreme court vacated the adjudication on procedural grounds.

Justice Charles E. Springer chided the prosecutor for "bring[ing] criminal charges against pre-adolescent children charged with engaging in consensual sex games" that may have amounted to nothing more than "playing doctor." Id. n.1, 1376 n.5. "Is this really the kind of case that calls for the filing of formal criminal charges against this little boy relating to the commission of sex crimes? What good can possibly come out of forcing these two young children to testify against each other and to testify formally in a court of law concerning childish sex games? Why make Scotty into an adjudicated sex criminal even if these charges had been true? * * * If either Scott or his cousin were in need of some kind of juvenile court services by reason of supposed sexual aberrations * * *, then some kind of child protection proceedings might have been justified, but not sex offender charges against one of the participants only." Id. at 1376–77.

Chief Justice Miriam Shearing took issue with Justice Springer: "Juvenile court is supposed to teach juveniles the difference between appropriate and inappropriate behavior with the hope of preventing their getting into the adult criminal system. This purpose cannot be accomplished if all sexual activity between children is dismissed as mere games or a waste of time." Id. at 1375. See also, e.g., In re T.S., 515 S.E.2d 230, 233 (N.C.App.1999) (reversing delinquency adjudication of nine-year-old boy for exposing himself to his three-year-old female playmate; state failed to prove he acted "for the purpose of arousing and gratifying sexual desire," an essential element of the "indecent liberties with children" statute that was the petition's basis).

Which view do you agree with? Would your answer be different if 11-year-old Scott had used force against his 8–year-old step-cousin?

11. *Would statutory rape prosecutions help control the rate of teenage out-of-wedlock pregnancies?* In 1998, 32.8% of births were born to single mothers, a substantial number of whom were teenagers. See Bernard Guyer et al., Annual Summary of Vital Statistics—1998, 104 Pediatrics 1229, tbl. 5 (Dec. 1999). The National Center for Health Statistics reported that the United States adolescent birth rate fell in 1998 to a near-record-low; girls between fifteen and seventeen had the lowest birth rate in forty years, and girls between ten and fourteen had the lowest birth rate since 1969. See Marc Lacey, Teen–Age Birth Rate in U.S. Falls Again, N.Y. Times, Oct. 27, 1999, at A14. The U.S. adolescent birth rate, however, remains the highest of all developed countries by far. See American Acad. of Pediatrics, Adolescent Pregnancy–Current Trends and Issues: 1998, 103 Pediatrics 516 (1999). According to one observer, "[o]ur lowest state has a[n adolescent birth] rate equal to about the highest rate in the developed world." See Lacey, supra.

In 1995, a comprehensive nationwide study conducted by the Alan Guttmacher Institute reported that at least half of unwed teenage mothers are impregnated by men twenty or older. See Jennifer Steinhauer, Study Cites Adult Males for Most Teen–Age Births, N.Y. Times, Aug. 2, 1995, at A10. Some studies have placed the figure even higher, finding that almost two of every three births to unwed teenage mothers result from intercourse with men over twenty. See American Acad. of Pediatrics, Adolescent Pregnancy, supra.

By having sexual relations with girls below the age of consent, most of the adult men were committing statutory rape or another sex crime. To reduce the number of teenage out-of-wedlock births and to enforce child-support obligations, some voices have urged prosecution of adult men who impregnate unwed teenagers. The 1996 Welfare Reform Act called on states and local jurisdictions to "aggressively enforce statutory rape laws." 42 U.S.C. § 14016.

Calls for prosecution have produced spirited debate. Professor Michelle Oberman, for example, supports prosecution on the ground that statutory rape laws "reflect a consensus that minors are not mature enough to make major decisions because they are vulnerable to coercion and exploitation." Michelle Oberman, Statutory Rape Laws: The Risk of Psychological Harm to Girls is Too Great, 82 A.B.A.J. 86 (Aug. 1996).

Professor Richard Delgado, however, asserts that "[e]xcept in the case of the very young, who of course should be protected from sexual predators, statutory rape laws * * * can only be applied unevenly—and they are." He concludes that authorities apply these laws "principally against two groups: men, frequently older, who have sex with girls from 'good homes'; and minority men, who are punished if they commit the crime of having sex with white women or impregnate a woman of color under circumstances that add to the welfare rolls." Richard Delgado, Statutory Rape Laws: Selective Enforcement Targets "Unpopular" Men, 82 A.B.A.J. 86, 87 (Aug. 1996).

12. *Incest*. Where a person engages in sexual relations with a minor family member such as a sibling or a son or daughter, the person may face prosecution for incest. State incest statutes reach blood relationships, but they are not uniform in their treatment of non-blood relationships (such as step or adoptive relationships). Section 230.2 of the Model Penal Code, for example, would criminalize sexual relations between adoptive parents and their adoptive children, but not between other family members related by adoption or between step relations.

13. *The Internet*. "As the use of the Internet becomes commonplace in the classroom and in the home, prosecutors have become inundated with calls from local police departments, families, and educators who report a wide variety of offenses against youngsters who have had contact with potential molesters." Virginia Kendall, The Lost Child: Congress's Inability to Protect Our Teenagers, 92 Nw. U. L. Rev. 1307, 1307 (1998). A federal prosecutor explains that "[t]hese molesters usually meet children in teen 'chat rooms' where the child and the adult speak freely in 'real time' without any of the personal barriers that hamper social relationships: age differences, beauty, disability, race, and social class. * * * In practice, this means that molesters, who were once ostracized and limited in their ability to nurture relationships with minors due to the lack of opportunities to communicate freely with them in unsupervised settings, now develop relationships based on daily contact with children over the Internet. Within months, sometimes even weeks, these molesters are able to nurture the relationship to a point where the molester can travel to see the minor or arrange for the minor to travel to the molester." Id.

In an effort to reach molesters who use the Internet to converse with children and arrange meetings, Congress has enacted 18 U.S.C. § 2423(b), which makes it a crime to travel in interstate commerce to engage in any of a wide range of sexual acts with a person under eighteen. The section has been upheld against challenges that it exceeds Congress' commerce clause authority or impermissibly burdens the fundamental right to interstate travel. See, e.g., United States v. Brockdorff, 992 F.Supp. 22, 24–25 (D.D.C. 1997).

A 1999 Roper survey found that 20% of parents in on-line households do not supervise their children's Internet use at all, 52% of the parents supervise use only moderately, 71% of the parents with children 14 or older have stopped monitoring their children's Internet use, and 48% of the parents allow their children access to the Internet every day or as much as they want. Mike Snider, Study: Kids Lacking Net Supervision, USA Today, May 27, 1999, at 1A.

Some state legislative efforts to control use of the Internet by potential sex abusers have encountered constitutional roadblocks. See, e.g., ACLU v. Miller, 977 F.Supp. 1228 (N.D.Ga.1997) (granting preliminary injunction against enforcement of state law prohibiting Internet transmissions which falsely identify sender); American Libraries Ass'n v. Pataki, 969 F.Supp. 160 (S.D.N.Y.1997) (granting preliminary injunction enjoining enforcement of state law that made it a crime to use a computer to disseminate obscene material to minors; plaintiffs demonstrated a likelihood of success on the merits of their claim that the act violated the Commerce Clause).

PROBLEM 6–6

In 1997, Mary Kay LeTourneau, a 35–year-old Seattle, Washington schoolteacher, made national headlines when she gave birth to a baby girl fathered by a 13–year-old student in her sixth grade class. The two first met when he was in her second grade class four years earlier. The boy stated that he and his teacher had had sex about six times in the year of the pregnancy, usually in her home or in the back seat of her car. The teacher pleaded guilty to child rape and was released from prison for treatment after serving six months of an eight-year prison sentence. A month after her release, she was returned to prison when police found her and the boy in a parked car with the windows steamed up at 3 a.m. outside a bungalow where she was staying. A search of the car turned up groceries, baby and young men's clothes, a strongbox containing more than $6000 in cash, and the teacher's passport. Within a few months, she bore the boy's second child.

The boy told a reporter that he had initiated the relationship, and that "[a]ll that matters was that we loved each other." Frank Bruni, In an Age of Consent, Defining Abuse by Adults, N.Y. Times, Nov. 9, 1997, § 4, at 3. Interviewed on television, he reiterated that he was a willing participant, that the two had exchanged rings and planned the pregnancies to reaffirm their bond, and that he loved the teacher and was despondent over her arrest and imprisonment. He said he loved LeTourneau and denied he was a victim. "No matter how long I have to wait," he said, "I'll be there because our love is so special that nothing can stand in its way." Jean Sonmor, Prisoner of Love Teacher Stews in Prison While Her Heart Aches for a 14–Year-old Sex Partner, Toronto Sun, May 10, 1998, at 32.

You are the prosecutor in the LeTourneau statutory rape case. The boy insists that he consented to the sexual activity, and that the state has no business intruding in the two participants' private affairs. Would you prosecute the teacher? Why should the state have authority to prosecute the adult defendant over the minor's insistence that the conduct was indeed consensual?

C. Proving the Case

"Child abuse is one of the most difficult problems to detect and prosecute, in large part because there often are no witnesses except the victim." Pennsylvania v. Ritchie, 480 U.S. 39, 60 (1987). This section provides a flavor of sexual abuse prosecutions and explores the difficulties the state may face in the effort to prove guilt beyond a reasonable doubt consistent with the presumption of innocence and other constitutional guarantees.

1. Difficulties of Proof

LISA R. ASKOWITZ AND MICHAEL H. GRAHAM, THE RELIABILITY OF EXPERT PSYCHOLOGICAL TESTIMONY IN CHILD SEXUAL ABUSE PROSECUTIONS

15 Cardozo L. Rev. 2027, 2028, 2033–34 (1994).

For more than a decade now, courts have grappled with the distinctive evidentiary problems of child sexual abuse prosecutions. Unlike other prosecutions, child sexual abuse prosecutions rarely are supported by physical or medical evidence or a nonparticipant eyewitness to the crime. Unlike other complainants, the child sexual abuse victim generally is not forceful, convincing, nor consistent in her allegations. The case usually comes down to a credibility match between the child and the defendant, and expert psychological testimony offered by the prosecution often is the determinative factor.

* * *

Child sexual abuse prosecutions present distinctive evidentiary problems. Typically, these cases pit the word of a young, often traumatized child against that of a seemingly respectable adult. Because most child sexual abuse occurs in private, the child victim usually is the only eyewitness. The prosecution's case may be severely hampered if the child is found incompetent to testify, or if the prosecutor or the child's family determines that the child should not testify because of the additional trauma to the child that may result.

If the child does testify, the effectiveness of her testimony often is limited by several factors. A testifying child must face the defendant, the jury, and the public in court under intense direct and cross-examination. The child's cognitive and verbal abilities may not enable her to give "consistent, spontaneous, and detailed reports of her sexual abuse." Additionally, several years may have elapsed between the abusive incident(s) and the time of trial. The longer the interval, the less likely the child will appear credible.

If the prosecution is successful, the child may feel "guilt and blame" for testifying against the defendant, who may be a parent or relative. If the defendant is acquitted, the child may feel "a sense of hopelessness" and face possible reprisals by the offender.

Prosecutors face another dilemma in offering the child victim as a witness if the child has delayed reporting the abuse or has recanted her allegations. Contrary to the general expectation that a sexually abused child would seek help, the child often does not report the abuse out of fear of being blamed for the incident or fear that no one will be able to protect her from retaliation by the abuser. Furthermore, a child who must testify against a trusted adult, such as a parent or relative, may experience feelings of "anger, fear, and ambivalence," and "may retract ... her story because of family pressures or insensitivities in the legal process." Jurors may interpret delayed, inconsistent, or unconvincing disclosure or recantation as evidence of fabrication, especially if defense counsel suggests this conclusion on cross-examination of the child victim or in argument.

In addition to the particular problems facing sexually abused children as witnesses are those commonly facing all child witnesses. Children often are confused by dates, times, and frequencies of events. Children also can become confused and can be led to contradict previous statements if questions are not phrased in age-appropriate language. Jurors may interpret a child's apparent confusion, hesitancy, and inconsistency as indicating unreliability. Jurors may believe that a child has memory deficits, is suggestible, cannot distinguish between fact or fantasy, or is likely to fabricate her experiences.

All of these problems are compounded by the lack of corroborative physical or medical evidence in most child sexual abuse cases. Physical or medical evidence is found in only ten to fifteen percent of confirmed sexual abuse cases. Sometimes such evidence is unavailable because the abuser used "threats and intimidation, rather than actual violence, to induce the child victim's submission." Moreover, the nature of the abuse itself (e.g., fondling) frequently will not produce lasting physical changes in the child's body.

Faced with these unique problems, prosecutors increasingly have relied on mental health professionals to bolster child sexual abuse cases with expert psychological testimony. * * *

* * *

2. The Child Victim's Testimony

ROBERT P. MOSTELLER, REMAKING CONFRONTATION CLAUSE AND HEARSAY DOCTRINE UNDER THE CHALLENGE OF CHILD SEXUAL ABUSE PROSECUTIONS

1993 U. Ill. L. Rev. 691, 691–94.

Child sexual abuse is a major and growing problem in the United States. Recognizing the significance and emotional power of the problem, state legislatures have responded with an impressive array of legislative innovations that admit out-of-court statements of child victims and attempt to shield children from emotional and psychological trauma resulting from participation in judicial proceedings. * * *

The frequent association of *reform* with children's issues is easily understood. First, we as a society care intensely about the treatment of children, and as a result, child welfare has been a paramount concern of state legislatures throughout this century. Mistreatment of children, particularly sexual abuse, is especially horrendous. All agree that action is required and perpetrators must be apprehended and punished. Second, because children obviously differ from adults, society is willing to rethink procedures and evidentiary rules. We begin almost with a presumption that the ground rules should be different. Thus, the initial inquiry is what changes to make in the process rather than whether it should be altered at all. That inquiry, in turn, quickly moves to how fundamental the modifications should be. Third, proof in child cases is often problematic. Children frequently have difficulty testifying effectively as a result of their different and somewhat limited abilities to remember, conceptualize, and communicate, and because of fear and the obstacles presented by the courtroom setting.

States have experimented with new hearsay[2] exceptions that admit out-of-court statements by children and with new procedures for receiving testimony from children in court. In the area of hearsay, one approach has been to identify specific crimes—principally sexual abuse—and, regarding those crimes, to admit the hearsay statements of children below a specified age if the statements are deemed generally trustworthy. This approach authorizes the admission of a broad array of statements of a child victim of sexual abuse, limited solely by the Confrontation Clause.[3]

---

2. Rule 801(c) of the *Federal Rules of Evidence* provides a simple and widely used definition of hearsay: "a statement, other than one made by the declarant while testifying at the trial or hearing, offered in evidence to prove the truth of the matter asserted." Conceptually, hearsay is not admissible, see Fed. R. Evid. 802, unless it falls within one of the many hearsay exceptions.

3. The Sixth Amendment to the United States Constitution states, inter alia: "In all criminal prosecutions, the accused shall enjoy the right ... to be confronted with the witnesses against him; to have compulsory process for obtaining witnesses in his favor...." The first of these rights is called the Confrontation Clause, and the second, the Compulsory Process Clause.

To shield children from trauma, statutes and the case law have treated the trauma that would result from testifying as bases for finding a child unavailable to be called as a witness. In these situations, hearsay statements under this new exception may constitute the only evidence from the child, and the defense may be prohibited from questioning the child, who is physically available and could provide some information to the jury if cross-examined. In combination, the ability to introduce effective hearsay statements while simultaneously shielding the child creates powerful and pernicious incentives for the prosecutor. If the hearsay conveys the child's story well, as it frequently will, the prosecution has strong motivation to develop evidence and arguments that the child cannot be called as a witness. Assuming these developments continue, we can expect to see fewer instances of children testifying in sexual abuse cases in the future. As a result, defendants' rights under both the Confrontation Clause and the Compulsory Process Clause will be seriously compromised.

A number of states have experimented with a second much more controversial hearsay exception. This exception permits the prosecution to produce ex parte videotaped statements by the child before trial and admit them as an alternative to the child's direct examination. This procedure has some potential for shielding children from trauma, but its chief purpose is to enhance the effectiveness of the state's proof.

The production at trial of ex parte videotaped testimony is a particularly ominous hearsay innovation because of recent developments in confrontation analysis that may admit hearsay statements regardless of their reliability if the prosecution simply makes the child physically available without calling her as a witness. Under this view, the Confrontation Clause is satisfied by the *opportunity* for the defense to call and to cross-examine the witness in front of the jury. In addition, other recent Confrontation Clause authority suggests that where cross-examination is attempted, the chance to cross-examine need not be very meaningful to be constitutionally sufficient. These developments are particularly troubling where states have legislated the automatic competency of child victims of sexual abuse, as a number have done. The stage is thus set to reduce confrontation to a hollow formalism and to admit statements where meaningful cross-examination is, as a practical matter, impossible.

Legislatures have authorized new methods of presenting testimony to shield children from the trauma of testifying. First, through videotaped recordings, children testify in the presence of the defendant but do so by way of a deposition taken in a less formal and more comfortable environment than the typical courtroom. Second, using either videotaped recording or live closed circuit television, children testify outside the courtroom *and* outside the presence of the defendant upon a specified showing that trauma would otherwise interfere with effective testimony.

Adding complication, all of the above techniques can be "mixed and matched" as desired. For example, where a statute specifies that the child victim must testify for her hearsay statement to be admitted, it may permit such testimony to be received through an electronic medium and/or outside the defendant's physical presence.

Child abuse hearsay provides a major testing ground for both hearsay rules and the Confrontation Clause. * * * The general child sexual abuse exception imposes no explicit categorical requirements to establish trustworthiness, but rather uses an open-textured approach under which all reliable hearsay is admitted. * * * Similarly, the innovation of ex parte videotaped statements challenges the core concepts of the Confrontation Clause. If the clause imposes no restraint on such statutory innovations, the meagerness of its basic protection will be starkly established. * * *

Notes and Questions

1. *"General child hearsay" exception statutes.* In recent years, about half the states have enacted "general child hearsay" exception statutes, which permit admission of a particularly young sexual abuse victim's out-of-court statements that appear trustworthy. Missouri's statute provides an example: "A statement made by a child under the age of twelve relating to [a sexual abuse offense], performed with or on a child by another, not otherwise admissible by statute or court rule, is admissible in evidence in criminal proceedings in the courts of this state as substantive evidence to prove the truth of the matter asserted if: (1) The court finds, in a hearing conducted outside the presence of the jury that the time, content and circumstances of the statement provide sufficient indicia of reliability; and (2)(a) The child testifies at the proceedings; or (b) The child is unavailable as a witness; or (c) The child is otherwise physically available as a witness but the court finds that the significant emotional or psychological trauma which would result from testifying in the personal presence of the defendant makes the child unavailable as a witness at the time of the criminal proceeding." Mo. Rev. Stat. § 491.075.

The "general child hearsay" exception statute may specify factors the court must consider in determining trustworthiness. Where the statute is silent, courts examine such factors as (1) the spontaneity and consistent repetition of the child's statement, (2) the child's mental state, (3) the child's motive to fabricate, and (4) the child's use of terminology or description not normally within the knowledge of a child of that age. See, e.g., State v. Redman, 916 S.W.2d 787, 791 (Mo. 1996). Where the child makes the statements in an interview, the court examines the interviewer's experience and looks at whether the interviewer used leading questions. See, e.g., State v. Worrel, 933 S.W.2d 431, 434–35 (Mo.Ct.App.1996). Whether statute or case law provides the standard, however, the trial court has broad discretion to determine trustworthiness based on the facts of the case, and appellate review is by the deferential abuse-of-discretion standard. See State v. Gillard, 986 S.W.2d 194, 196 (Mo.Ct.App.1999). General child hearsay statutes normally do not reach statements made by non-victim child witnesses. See, e.g., State v. Merrill, 990 S.W.2d 166, 170 (Mo.Ct.App.1999).

2. *The "unavailable" child witness.* Normally a declarant's mere absence from the trial does not establish the declarant's unavailability. The party seeking to invoke the hearsay exception must also establish that the declar-

ant could not be present or testify because of death or physical mental illness or infirmity, or that the party could not procure the declarant's attendance by process or other reasonable means. Fed R. Evid. 804(a). The Missouri statute quoted in note 1, however, illustrates the relaxed approach taken by the "general child hearsay" exception statutes. The child's significant emotional or psychological trauma can render the child "unavailable" even if he or she is sitting at home a mile away and thus is not unavailable in the sense in which evidence law generally understands the term. The child's trustworthy hearsay statement would be admissible, and the defendant would not have an opportunity to question the child who could otherwise be produced.

3. *The victim's ex parte videotaped statement.* A handful of states have enacted statutes permitting admission of a videotaped interview of the child victim, without a showing that the child presently suffers from significant emotional trauma and without contemporaneous cross-examination. Any later testimony by the child may be in person, or it may be by videotape or closed-circuit television hookup in accordance with the child witness protection statute. Kan. Stat. § 22–3433(a) provides a typical example:

> In any criminal proceeding in which a child less than 13 years of age is alleged to be a victim of the crime, a recording of an oral statement of the child, made before the proceeding began is admissible in evidence if:
>
> (1) The court determines that the time, content and circumstances of the statement provide sufficient indicia of reliability;
>
> (2) no attorney for any party is present when the statement is made;
>
> (3) the recording is both visual and aural and is recorded on film or videotape or by other electronic means;
>
> (4) the recording equipment is capable of making an accurate recording, the operator of the equipment is competent and the recording is accurate and has not been altered;
>
> (5) the statement is not made in response to questioning calculated to lead the child to make a particular statement or is clearly shown to be the child's statement and not made solely as a result of a leading or suggestive question;
>
> (6) every voice on the recording is identified;
>
> (7) the person conducting the interview of the child in the recording is present at the proceeding and is available to testify or be cross-examined by any party;
>
> (8) each party to the proceeding is afforded an opportunity to view the recording before it is offered into evidence, and a copy of a written transcript is provided to the parties; and
>
> (9) the child is available to testify.

The Kansas statute further provides that if a recording is admitted under the section, "any party to the proceeding may call the child to testify and be cross-examined, either in the courtroom or as provided by" the child witness protection statute. Id. A few videotape-interview statutes, however, do not specify whether the child must merely be available to testify or whether he or she must actually testify if called.

Courts have disagreed about whether statutes providing for admission of ex parte videotaped interviews comport with the Sixth Amendment Confrontation Clause. See, e.g., State v. Schaal, 806 S.W.2d 659 (Mo.1991) (yes); People v. Bastien, 541 N.E.2d 670 (Ill.1989) (no).

IDAHO v. WRIGHT

Supreme Court of the United States, 1990.
497 U.S. 805.

JUSTICE O'CONNOR delivered the opinion of the Court.

This case requires us to decide whether the admission at trial of certain hearsay statements made by a child declarant to an examining pediatrician violates a defendant's rights under the Confrontation Clause of the Sixth Amendment.

I

Respondent Laura Lee Wright was jointly charged with Robert L. Giles of two counts of lewd conduct with a minor under 16, in violation of Idaho Code § 18–1508 (1987). The alleged victims were respondent's two daughters, one of whom was 5 1/2 and the other 2 1/2 years old at the time the crimes were charged.

Respondent and her ex-husband, Louis Wright, the father of the older daughter, had reached an informal agreement whereby each parent would have custody of the older daughter for six consecutive months. The allegations surfaced in November 1986 when the older daughter told Cynthia Goodman, Louis Wright's female companion, that Giles had had sexual intercourse with her while respondent held her down and covered her mouth, and that she had seen respondent and Giles do the same thing to respondent's younger daughter. The younger daughter was living with her parents—respondent and Giles—at the time of the alleged offenses.

Goodman reported the older daughter's disclosures to the police the next day and took the older daughter to the hospital. A medical examination of the older daughter revealed evidence of sexual abuse. One of the examining physicians was Dr. John Jambura, a pediatrician with extensive experience in child abuse cases. Police and welfare officials took the younger daughter into custody that day for protection and investigation. Dr. Jambura examined her the following day and found conditions "strongly suggestive of sexual abuse with vaginal contact," occurring approximately two to three days prior to the examination.

At the joint trial of respondent and Giles, the trial court conducted a voir dire examination of the younger daughter, who was three years old at the time of trial, to determine whether she was capable of testifying. The court concluded, and the parties agreed, that the younger daughter was "not capable of communicating to the jury."

At issue in this case is the admission at trial of certain statements made by the younger daughter to Dr. Jambura in response to questions he asked regarding the alleged abuse. Over objection by respondent and Giles, the trial court permitted Dr. Jambura to testify before the jury as follows:

"Q. [By the prosecutor] Now, calling your attention then to your examination of [the younger daughter] on November 10th. What— would you describe any interview dialogue that you had with [her] at that time? Excuse me, before you get into that, would you lay a setting of where this took place and who else might have been present?

"A. This took place in my office, in my examining room, and, as I recall, I believe previous testimony I said that I recall a female attendant being present, I don't recall her identity.

"I started out with basically, 'Hi, how are you,' you know, 'What did you have for breakfast this morning?' Essentially a few minutes of just sort of chitchat.

"Q. Was there response from [the daughter] to that first—those first questions?

"A. There was. She started to carry on a very relaxed animated conversation. I then proceeded to just gently start asking questions about, 'Well, how are things at home,' you know, those sorts. Gently moving into the domestic situation and then moved into four questions in particular, as I reflected in my records, 'Do you play with daddy? Does daddy play with you? Does daddy touch you with his pee-pee? Do you touch his pee-pee?' And again we then established what was meant by pee-pee, it was a generic term for genital area.

"Q. Before you get into that, what was, as best you recollect, what was her response to the question 'Do you play with daddy?'

"A. Yes, we play—I remember her making a comment about yes we play a lot and expanding on that and talking about spending time with daddy.

"Q. And 'Does daddy play with you?' Was there any response?

"A. She responded to that as well, that they played together in a variety of circumstances and, you know, seemed very unaffected by the question.

"Q. And then what did you say and her response?

"A. When I asked her 'Does daddy touch you with his pee-pee,' she did admit to that. When I asked, 'Do you touch his pee-pee,' she did not have any response.

"Q. Excuse me. Did you notice any change in her affect or attitude in that line of questioning?

"A. Yes.

"Q. What did you observe?

"A. She would not—oh, she did not talk any further about that. She would not elucidate what exactly—what kind of touching was taking place, or how it was happening. She did, however, say that daddy does do this with me, but he does it a lot more with my sister than with me.

"Q. And how did she offer that last statement? Was that in response to a question or was that just a volunteered statement?

"A. That was a volunteered statement as I sat and waited for her to respond, again after she sort of clammed-up, and that was the next statement that she made after just allowing some silence to occur."

On cross-examination, Dr. Jambura acknowledged that a picture that he drew during his questioning of the younger daughter had been discarded. Dr. Jambura also stated that although he had dictated notes to summarize the conversation, his notes were not detailed and did not record any changes in the child's affect or attitude.

The trial court admitted these statements under Idaho's residual hearsay exception, which provides in relevant part:

"Rule 803. Hearsay exceptions; availability of declarant immaterial.—The following are not excluded by the hearsay rule, even though the declarant is available as a witness.

* * *

"(24) Other exceptions. A statement not specifically covered by any of the foregoing exceptions but having equivalent circumstantial guarantees of trustworthiness, if the court determines that (A) the statement is offered as evidence of a material fact; (B) the statement is more probative on the point for which it is offered than any other evidence which the proponent can procure through reasonable efforts; and (C) the general purposes of these rules and the interests of justice will best be served by admission of the statement into evidence."

* * *

The Supreme Court of Idaho held that the admission of the inculpatory hearsay testimony violated respondent's federal constitutional right to confrontation because the testimony did not fall within a traditional hearsay exception and was based on an interview that lacked procedural safeguards. * * *

We granted certiorari and now affirm.

II

* * *

From the earliest days of our Confrontation Clause jurisprudence, we have consistently held that the Clause does not necessarily prohibit the admission of hearsay statements against a criminal defendant, even though the admission of such statements might be thought to violate the literal terms of the Clause. * * *

Although we have recognized that hearsay rules and the Confrontation Clause are generally designed to protect similar values, we have also been careful not to equate the Confrontation Clause's prohibitions with the general rule prohibiting the admission of hearsay statements. The Confrontation Clause, in other words, bars the admission of some evidence that would otherwise be admissible under an exception to the hearsay rule.

In *Ohio* v. *Roberts* [1980], we set forth "a general approach" for determining when incriminating statements admissible under an exception to the hearsay rule also meet the requirements of the Confrontation Clause. We noted that the Confrontation Clause "operates in two separate ways to restrict the range of admissible hearsay." "First, in conformance with the Framers' preference for face-to-face accusation, the Sixth Amendment establishes a rule of necessity. In the usual case . . ., the prosecution must either produce, or demonstrate the unavailability of, the declarant whose statement it wishes to use against the defendant." Second, once a witness is shown to be unavailable, "his statement is admissible only if it bears adequate 'indicia of reliability.' Reliability can be inferred without more in a case where the evidence falls within a firmly rooted hearsay exception. In other cases, the evidence must be excluded, at least absent a showing of particularized guarantees of trustworthiness." * * *

Applying the *Roberts* approach to this case, we first note that this case does not raise the question whether, before a child's out-of-court statements are admitted, the Confrontation Clause requires the prosecution to show that a child witness is unavailable at trial—and, if so, what that showing requires. The trial court in this case found that respondent's younger daughter was incapable of communicating with the jury, and defense counsel agreed. The court below neither questioned this finding nor discussed the general requirement of unavailability. For purposes of deciding this case, we assume without deciding that, to the extent the unavailability requirement applies in this case, the younger daughter was an unavailable witness within the meaning of the Confrontation Clause.

The crux of the question presented is therefore whether the State, as the proponent of evidence presumptively barred by the hearsay rule and the Confrontation Clause, has carried its burden of proving that the younger daughter's incriminating statements to Dr. Jambura bore sufficient indicia of reliability to withstand scrutiny under the Clause. * * *

In *Roberts*, we suggested that the "indicia of reliability" requirement could be met in either of two circumstances: where the hearsay statement "falls within a firmly rooted hearsay exception," or where it is supported by "a showing of particularized guarantees of trustworthiness."

We note at the outset that Idaho's residual hearsay exception, under which the challenged statements were admitted, is not a firmly rooted hearsay exception for Confrontation Clause purposes. Admission under a firmly rooted hearsay exception satisfies the constitutional requirement of reliability because of the weight accorded longstanding judicial and legislative experience in assessing the trustworthiness of certain types of out-of-court statements. The residual hearsay exception, by contrast, accommodates ad hoc instances in which statements not otherwise falling within a recognized hearsay exception might nevertheless be sufficiently reliable to be admissible at trial. Hearsay statements admitted under the residual exception, almost by definition, therefore do not share the same tradition of reliability that supports the admissibility of statements under a firmly rooted hearsay exception. Moreover, were we to agree that the admission of hearsay statements under the residual exception automatically passed Confrontation Clause scrutiny, virtually every codified hearsay exception would assume constitutional stature, a step this Court has repeatedly declined to take.

* * *

Although we agree with the court below that the Confrontation Clause bars the admission of the younger daughter's hearsay statements, we reject the apparently dispositive weight placed by that court on the lack of procedural safeguards at the interview. Out-of-court statements made by children regarding sexual abuse arise in a wide variety of circumstances, and we do not believe the Constitution imposes a fixed set of procedural prerequisites to the admission of such statements at trial. The procedural requirements identified by the court below, to the extent regarded as conditions precedent to the admission of child hearsay statements in child sexual abuse cases, may in many instances be inappropriate or unnecessary to a determination whether a given statement is sufficiently trustworthy for Confrontation Clause purposes. Although the procedural guidelines propounded by the court below may well enhance the reliability of out-of-court statements of children regarding sexual abuse, we decline to read into the Confrontation Clause a preconceived and artificial litmus test for the procedural propriety of professional interviews in which children make hearsay statements against a defendant.

The State responds that a finding of "particularized guarantees of trustworthiness" should instead be based on a consideration of the totality of the circumstances, including not only the circumstances surrounding the making of the statement, but also other evidence at trial that corroborates the truth of the statement. We agree that "particularized guarantees of trustworthiness" must be shown from the totality of the circumstances, but we think the relevant circumstances include only those that surround the making of the statement and that render the declarant particularly worthy of belief. * * *

* * * Our precedents have recognized that statements admitted under a "firmly rooted" hearsay exception are so trustworthy that adversarial testing would add little to their reliability. Because evidence possessing "particularized guarantees of trustworthiness" must be at least as reliable as evidence admitted under a firmly rooted hearsay exception, we think that evidence admitted under the former requirement must similarly be so trustworthy that adversarial testing would add little to its reliability. Thus, unless an affirmative reason, arising from the circumstances in which the statement was made, provides a basis for rebutting the presumption that a hearsay statement is not worthy of reliance at trial, the Confrontation Clause requires exclusion of the out-of-court statement.

The state and federal courts have identified a number of factors that we think properly relate to whether hearsay statements made by a child witness in child sexual abuse cases are reliable. [citing decisions concerning spontaneity and consistent repetition, mental state of the declarant, use of terminology unexpected of a child of similar age, and lack of motive to fabricate]. Although these cases (which we cite for the factors they discuss and not necessarily to approve the results that they reach) involve the application of various hearsay exceptions to statements of child declarants, we think the factors identified also apply to whether such statements bear "particularized guarantees of trustworthiness" under the Confrontation Clause. These factors are, of course, not exclusive, and courts have considerable leeway in their consideration of appropriate factors. We therefore decline to endorse a mechanical test for determining "particularized guarantees of trustworthiness" under the Clause. Rather, the unifying principle is that these factors relate to whether the child declarant was particularly likely to be telling the truth when the statement was made.

As our discussion above suggests, we are unpersuaded by the State's contention that evidence corroborating the truth of a hearsay statement may properly support a finding that the statement bears "particularized guarantees of trustworthiness." To be admissible under the Confrontation Clause, hearsay evidence used to convict a defendant must possess indicia of reliability by virtue of its inherent trustworthiness, not by reference to other evidence at trial. * * *

In short, the use of corroborating evidence to support a hearsay statement's "particularized guarantees of trustworthiness" would permit admission of a presumptively unreliable statement by bootstrapping on the trustworthiness of other evidence at trial, a result we think at odds with the requirement that hearsay evidence admitted under the Confrontation Clause be so trustworthy that cross-examination of the declarant would be of marginal utility. * * * [W]e think the presence of corroborating evidence more appropriately indicates that any error in admitting the statement might be harmless, rather than that any basis exists for presuming the declarant to be trustworthy.

* * * Corroboration of a child's allegations of sexual abuse by medical evidence of abuse, for example, sheds no light on the reliability of the child's allegations regarding the identity of the abuser. There is a very real danger that a jury will rely on partial corroboration to mistakenly infer the trustworthiness of the entire statement. * * *

Finally, we reject respondent's contention that the younger daughter's out-of-court statements in this case are *per se* unreliable, or at least presumptively unreliable, on the ground that the trial court found the younger daughter incompetent to testify at trial. * * * [T]he Confrontation Clause does not erect a *per se* rule barring the admission of prior statements of a declarant who is unable to communicate to the jury at the time of trial. Although such inability might be relevant to whether the earlier hearsay statement possessed particularized guarantees of trustworthiness, a *per se* rule of exclusion would not only frustrate the truth-seeking purpose of the Confrontation Clause, but would also hinder States in their own "enlightened development in the law of evidence."

III

* * * We think the Supreme Court of Idaho properly focused on the presumptive unreliability of the out-of-court statements and on the suggestive manner in which Dr. Jambura conducted the interview. Viewing the totality of the circumstances surrounding the younger daughter's responses to Dr. Jambura's questions, we find no special reason for supposing that the incriminating statements were particularly trustworthy. The younger daughter's last statement regarding the abuse of the older daughter, however, presents a closer question. According to Dr. Jambura, the younger daughter "volunteered" that statement "after she sort of clammed-up." Although the spontaneity of the statement and the change in demeanor suggest that the younger daughter was telling the truth when she made the statement, we note that it is possible that "[i]f there is evidence of prior interrogation, prompting, or manipulation by adults, spontaneity may be an inaccurate indicator of trustworthiness." Moreover, the statement was not made under circumstances of reliability comparable to those required, for example, for the admission of excited utterances or statements made for purposes of medical diagnosis or treatment. Given the presumption of inadmissibility accorded accusatory hearsay statements not admitted pursuant to a firmly rooted hearsay exception, we agree with the court below that the State has failed to show that the younger daughter's incriminating statements to the pediatrician possessed sufficient "particularized guarantees of trustworthiness" under the Confrontation Clause to overcome that presumption. * * *

JUSTICE KENNEDY, with whom THE CHIEF JUSTICE, JUSTICE WHITE, and JUSTICE BLACKMUN join, dissenting.

The issue is whether the Sixth Amendment right of confrontation is violated when statements from a child who is unavailable to testify at trial are admitted under a hearsay exception against a defendant who stands accused of abusing her. The Court today holds that it is not, provided that the child's statements bear "particularized guarantees of trustworthiness." I agree. My disagreement is with the rule the Court invents to control this inquiry and with the Court's ultimate determination that the statements in question here must be inadmissible as violative of the Confrontation Clause. * * *

* * *

I see no constitutional justification for this decision to prescind corroborating evidence from consideration of the question whether a child's statements are reliable. It is a matter of common sense for most people that one of the best ways to determine whether what someone says is trustworthy is to see if it is corroborated by other evidence. In the context of child abuse, for example, if part of the child's hearsay statement is that the assailant tied her wrists or had a scar on his lower abdomen, and there is physical evidence or testimony to corroborate the child's statement, evidence which the child could not have fabricated, we are more likely to believe that what the child says is true. Conversely, one can imagine a situation in which a child makes a statement which is spontaneous or is otherwise made under circumstances indicating that it is reliable, but which also contains undisputed factual inaccuracies so great that the credibility of the child's statements is substantially undermined. Under the Court's analysis, the statement would satisfy the requirements of the Confrontation Clause despite substantial doubt about its reliability. * * *

* * *

In this case, the younger daughter's statements are corroborated in at least four respects: (1) physical evidence that she was the victim of sexual abuse; (2) evidence that she had been in the custody of the suspect at the time the injuries occurred; (3) testimony of the older daughter that their father abused the younger daughter, thus corroborating the younger daughter's statement; and (4) the testimony of the older daughter that she herself was abused by their father, thus corroborating the younger daughter's statement that her sister had also been abused. These facts, coupled with the circumstances surrounding the making of the statements acknowledged by the Court as suggesting that the statements are reliable, give rise to a legitimate argument that admission of the statements did not violate the Confrontation Clause. * * *

Notes and Questions

1. The *Wright* prosecutor sought to introduce the child's statements under the state's residual hearsay exception, which the Court held was not a "firmly rooted" exception and thus could be invoked only where the child's statement showed "particularized guarantees of trustworthiness." Does the relatively new "general child hearsay" exception (discussed above in the Mosteller article and the ensuing note) constitute a firmly rooted hearsay exception under *Wright's* formulation, or is the child's statement admissible only when supported by such a showing?

2. *Traditional hearsay exceptions.* A child sexual abuse victim's hearsay statements may be admissible under a number of traditional hearsay exceptions that are staples of the evidence class. The most prominent are the

excited utterance exception and the exception for statements for purposes of medical diagnosis or treatment. Professor Mosteller reports that the two exceptions have been used "innovatively" to admit children's hearsay in sex abuse cases. Robert P. Mosteller, Remaking Confrontation Clause and Hearsay Doctrine Under the Challenge of Child Sexual Abuse Prosecutions,1993 U. Ill. L. Rev. 691, 706; Robert P. Mosteller, Child Sexual Abuse and Statements For the Purpose of Medical Diagnosis or Treatment, 67 N.C. L. Rev. 257 (1989).

3. *Potential for manipulation during the interview.* This section surveys various statutory innovations that test the Confrontation Clause's outer limits in an effort to facilitate admission of child sexual abuse victims' statements or testimony. These innovations stem largely from the sense that children's reports of sexual abuse are generally reliable because children would not persistently lie about sensitive sexual matters and would not have the knowledge of such matters necessary to sustain a lie. The Court's recitation of Dr. Jambura's interview with the young victim, however, suggests that an adult questioner (such as a physician, child welfare agency employee, or police officer) can sometimes lead a child to give answers the questioner wants to hear. Scholarship and empirical research on the suggestibility of child interviewees reveal sharp disagreements about the circumstances under which young sex abuse victims can or should necessarily be believed. See, e.g., Thomas D. Lyon, The New Wave in Children's Suggestibility Research: A Critique, 84 Cornell L. Rev. 1004 (1999), which cites and discusses much of the literature. The suggestibility issue is significant in light of Supreme Court decisions limiting the defendant's Sixth Amendment right to face-to-face confrontation and preserving a greater role for the child's hearsay testimony.

PROBLEM 6–7

You have just been appointed defense counsel to John Jones, who stands accused of molesting his five-year-old stepdaughter. You learn that the victim has been interviewed by a child psychologist employed by the department of family services, and you assume the prosecutor will call the psychologist to testify about what the child told her. What questions would you ask the psychologist before trial, and what questions would you ask her on cross-examination?

MARYLAND v. CRAIG

Supreme Court of the United States, 1990.
497 U.S. 836.

JUSTICE O'CONNOR delivered the opinion of the Court.

This case requires us to decide whether the Confrontation Clause of the Sixth Amendment categorically prohibits a child witness in a child abuse case from testifying against a defendant at trial, outside the defendant's physical presence, by one-way closed circuit television.

I

In October 1986, a Howard County grand jury charged respondent, Sandra Ann Craig, with child abuse, first and second degree sexual offenses, perverted sexual practice, assault, and battery. The named victim in each count was a 6–year-old girl who, from August 1984 to June 1986, had attended a kindergarten and prekindergarten center owned and operated by Craig.

In March 1987, before the case went to trial, the State sought to invoke a Maryland statutory procedure that permits a judge to receive, by one-way closed circuit television, the testimony of a child witness who is alleged to be a victim of child abuse. To invoke the procedure, the trial judge must first "determin[e] that testimony by the child victim in the courtroom will result in the child suffering serious emotional distress such that the child cannot reasonably communicate." Once the procedure is invoked, the child witness, prosecutor, and defense counsel withdraw to a separate room; the judge, jury, and defendant remain in the courtroom. The child witness is then examined and cross-examined in the separate room, while a video monitor records and displays the witness' testimony to those in the courtroom. During this time the witness cannot see the defendant. The defendant remains in electronic communication with defense counsel, and objections may be made and ruled on as if the witness were testifying in the courtroom.

In support of its motion invoking the one-way closed circuit television procedure, the State presented expert testimony that the named victim as well as a number of other children who were alleged to have been sexually abused by Craig, would suffer "serious emotional distress such that [they could not] reasonably communicate," if required to testify in the courtroom. * * *

[The trial court rejected Craig's objection that the one-way closed circuit television procedure violated the Confrontation Clause, and permitted the children to testify by the procedure on a finding that face-to-face testimony would have caused them the requisite emotional distress. The Maryland Court of Special Appeals affirmed Craig's convictions on all counts.].

The Court of Appeals of Maryland reversed and remanded for a new trial. * * *

* * *

II

The Confrontation Clause of the Sixth Amendment, made applicable to the States through the Fourteenth Amendment, provides: "In all criminal prosecutions, the accused shall enjoy the right ... to be confronted with the witnesses against him."

We observed in *Coy* v. *Iowa* [1988] that "the Confrontation Clause guarantees the defendant a face-to-face meeting with witnesses appearing before the trier of fact." This interpretation derives not only from the literal text of the Clause, but also from our understanding of its historical roots.

We have never held, however, that the Confrontation Clause guarantees criminal defendants the *absolute* right to a face-to-face meeting with witnesses against them at trial. Indeed, in *Coy* v. *Iowa*, we expressly "le[ft] for another day ... the question whether any exceptions exist" to the "irreducible literal meaning of the Clause: 'a right to *meet face to face* all those who appear and give evidence *at trial.*' "The procedure challenged in *Coy* involved the placement of a screen that prevented two child witnesses in a child abuse case from seeing the defendant as they testified against him at trial. In holding that the use of this procedure violated the defendant's right to confront witnesses against him, we suggested that any exception to the right "would surely be allowed only when necessary to further an important public policy"—*i.e.*, only upon a showing of something more than the generalized, "legislatively imposed presumption of trauma" underlying the statute at issue in that case. We concluded that "[s]ince there ha[d] been no individualized findings that these particular witnesses needed special protection, the judgment [in the case before us] could not be sustained by any conceivable exception." Because the trial court in this case made individualized findings that each of the child witnesses needed special protection, this case requires us to decide the question reserved in *Coy*.

The central concern of the Confrontation Clause is to ensure the reliability of the evidence against a criminal defendant by subjecting it to rigorous testing in the context of an adversary proceeding before the trier of fact. The word "confront," after all, also means a clashing of forces or ideas, thus carrying with it the notion of adversariness. * * *

* * * [T]he right guaranteed by the Confrontation Clause includes not only a "personal examination," but also "(1) insures that the witness will give his statements under oath—thus impressing him with the seriousness of the matter and guarding against the lie by the possibility of a penalty for perjury; (2) forces the witness to submit to cross-examination, the 'greatest legal engine ever invented for the discovery of truth'; [and] (3) permits the jury that is to decide the defendant's fate to observe the demeanor of the witness in making his statement, thus aiding the jury in assessing his credibility."

The combined effect of these elements of confrontation—physical presence, oath, cross-examination, and observation of demeanor by the trier of fact—serves the purposes of the Confrontation Clause by ensuring that evidence admitted against an accused is reliable and subject to the rigorous adversarial testing that is the norm of Anglo–American criminal proceedings.

We have recognized, for example, that face-to-face confrontation enhances the accuracy of factfinding by reducing the risk that a witness will wrongfully implicate an innocent person. See *Coy* ("It is always more difficult to tell a lie about a person 'to his face' than 'behind his back.' ... That face-to-face presence may, unfortunately, upset the truthful rape victim or abused child; but by the same token it may confound and undo the false accuser, or reveal the child coached by a malevolent adult"). We have also noted the strong symbolic purpose served by requiring adverse witnesses at trial to testify in the accused's presence.

Although face-to-face confrontation forms "the core of the values furthered by the Confrontation Clause," we have nevertheless recognized that it is not the *sine qua non* of the confrontation right.

For this reason, we have never insisted on an actual face-to-face encounter at trial in *every* instance in which testimony is admitted against a defendant. Instead, we have repeatedly held that the Clause permits, where necessary, the admission of certain hearsay statements against a defendant despite the defendant's inability to confront the declarant at trial. * * *

We have accordingly stated that a literal reading of the Confrontation Clause would "abrogate virtually every hearsay exception, a result long rejected as unintended and too extreme." Thus, in certain narrow circumstances, "competing interests, if 'closely examined,' may warrant dispensing with confrontation at trial." * * * Given our hearsay cases, the word "confronted," as used in the Confrontation Clause, cannot simply mean face-to-face confrontation, for the Clause would then, contrary to our cases, prohibit the admission of any accusatory hearsay statement made by an absent declarant—a declarant who is undoubtedly as much a "witness against" a defendant as one who actually testifies at trial.

In sum, our precedents establish that "the Confrontation Clause reflects a *preference* for face-to-face confrontation at trial," a preference that "must occasionally give way to considerations of public policy and the necessities of the case." "[W]e have attempted to harmonize the goal of the Clause–placing limits on the kind of evidence that may be received against a defendant—with a societal interest in accurate factfinding, which may require consideration of out-of-court statements." We have accordingly interpreted the Confrontation Clause in a manner sensitive to its purposes and sensitive to the necessities of trial and the adversary process. Thus, though we reaffirm the importance of face-to-face confrontation with witnesses appearing at trial, we cannot say that such confrontation is an indispensable element of the Sixth Amendment's guarantee of the right to confront one's accusers. * * *

* * *

That the face-to-face confrontation requirement is not absolute does not, of course, mean that it may easily be dispensed with. As we suggested in *Coy*, our precedents confirm that a defendant's right to confront accusatory witnesses may be satisfied absent a physical, face-to-face confrontation at trial only where denial of such confrontation is necessary to further an important public policy and only where the reliability of the testimony is otherwise assured.

III

Maryland's statutory procedure, when invoked, prevents a child witness from seeing the defendant as he or she testifies against the defendant at trial. We find it significant, however, that Maryland's procedure preserves all of the other elements of the confrontation right: The child witness must be competent to testify and must testify under oath; the defendant retains full opportunity for contemporaneous cross-examination; and the judge, jury, and defendant are able to view (albeit by video monitor) the demeanor (and body) of the witness as he or she testifies. Although we are mindful of the many subtle effects face-to-face confrontation may have on an adversary criminal proceeding, the presence of these other elements of confrontation—oath, cross-examination, and observation of the witness' demeanor—adequately ensures that the testimony is both reliable and subject to rigorous adversarial testing in a manner functionally equivalent to that accorded live, in-person testimony. * * * [W]e think these elements of effective confrontation not only permit a defendant to "confound and undo the false accuser, or reveal the child coached by a malevolent adult," *Coy,* but may well aid a defendant in eliciting favorable testimony from the child witness. Indeed, to the extent the child witness' testimony may be said to be technically given out of court (though we do not so hold), these assurances of reliability and adversariness are far greater than those required for admission of hearsay testimony under the Confrontation Clause. We are therefore confident that use of the one-way closed circuit television procedure, where necessary to further an important state interest, does not impinge upon the truth-seeking or symbolic purposes of the Confrontation Clause.

The critical inquiry in this case, therefore, is whether use of the procedure is necessary to further an important state interest. The State contends that it has a substantial interest in protecting children who are allegedly victims of child abuse from the trauma of testifying against the alleged perpetrator and that its statutory procedure for receiving testimony from such witnesses is necessary to further that interest.

* * *

We * * * conclude today that a State's interest in the physical and psychological well-being of child abuse victims may be sufficiently important to outweigh, at least in some cases, a defendant's right to face his or her accusers in court. That a significant majority of States have enacted statutes to protect child witnesses from the trauma of giving testimony in child abuse cases attests to the widespread belief in the importance of such a public policy. Thirty-seven States, for example, permit the use of videotaped testimony of sexually abused children; 24 States have authorized the use of one-way closed circuit television testimony in child abuse cases; and 8 States authorize the use of a two-way system in which the child witness is permitted to see the courtroom and the defendant on a video monitor and in which the jury and judge are permitted to view the child during the testimony.

* * *

Given the State's traditional and " 'transcendent interest in protecting the welfare of children,' " and buttressed by the growing body of academic literature documenting the psychological trauma suffered by child abuse victims who must testify in court, we will not second-guess the considered judgment of the Maryland Legislature regarding the importance of its interest in protecting child abuse victims from the emotional trauma of testifying. Accordingly, we hold that, if the State makes an adequate showing of necessity, the state interest in protecting child witnesses from the trauma of testifying in a child abuse case is sufficiently important to justify the use of a special procedure that permits a child witness in such cases to testify at trial against a defendant in the absence of face-to-face confrontation with the defendant.

The requisite finding of necessity must of course be a case-specific one: The trial court must hear evidence and determine whether use of the one-way closed circuit television procedure is necessary to protect the welfare of the particular child witness who seeks to testify. The trial court must also find that the child witness would be traumatized, not by the courtroom generally, but by the presence of the defendant. Denial of face-to-face confrontation is not needed to further the state interest in protecting the child witness from trauma unless it is the presence of the defendant that causes the trauma. In other words, if the state interest were merely the interest in protecting child witnesses from courtroom trauma generally, denial of face-to-face confrontation would be unnecessary because the child could be permitted to testify in less intimidating surroundings, albeit with the defendant present. Finally, the trial court must find that the emotional distress suffered by the child witness in the presence of the defendant is more than *de minimis, i.e.,* more than "mere nervousness or excitement or some reluctance to testify," We need not decide the minimum showing of emotional trauma required for use of the special procedure, however, because the Maryland statute, which requires a determination that the child witness will suffer "serious emotional distress such that the child cannot reasonably communicate," clearly suffices to meet constitutional standards.

To be sure, face-to-face confrontation may be said to cause trauma for the very purpose of eliciting truth, but we think that the use of Maryland's special procedure, where necessary to further the important state interest in preventing trauma to child witnesses in child abuse cases, adequately ensures the accuracy of the testimony and preserves the adversary nature of the trial. Indeed, where face-to-face confrontation causes significant emotional distress in a child witness, there is evidence that such confrontation would in fact *disserve* the Confrontation Clause's truth-seeking goal.

In sum, we conclude that where necessary to protect a child witness from trauma that would be caused by testifying in the physical presence of the defendant, at least where such trauma would impair the child's ability to communicate, the Confrontation Clause does not prohibit use of a procedure that, despite the absence of face-to-face confrontation, ensures the reliability of the evidence by subjecting it to rigorous adversarial testing and thereby preserves the essence of effective confrontation. Because there is no dispute that the child witnesses in this case testified under oath, were subject to full cross-examination, and were able to be observed by the judge, jury, and defendant as they testified, we conclude that, to the extent that a proper finding of necessity has been made, the admission of such testimony would be consonant with the Confrontation Clause.

IV

* * *

* * * [T]he Court of Appeals interpreted our decision in *Coy* to impose two subsidiary requirements. First, the court held that "§ 9–102 ordinarily cannot be invoked unless the child witness initially is questioned (either in or outside the courtroom) in the defendant's presence." Second, the court asserted that, before using the one-way television procedure, a trial judge must determine whether a child would suffer "severe emotional distress" if he or she were to testify by *two*-way closed circuit television. * * *

* * *

The Court of Appeals appears to have rested its conclusion at least in part on the trial court's failure to observe the children's behavior in the defendant's presence and its failure to explore less restrictive alternatives to the use of the one-way closed circuit television procedure. Although we think such evidentiary requirements could strengthen the grounds for use of protective measures, we decline to establish, as a matter of federal constitutional law, any such categorical evidentiary prerequisites for the use of the one-way television procedure. The trial court in this case, for example, could well have found, on the basis of the expert testimony before it, that testimony by the child witnesses in the courtroom in the defendant's presence "will result in [each] child suffering serious emotional distress such that the child cannot reasonably communicate." So long as a trial court makes such a case-specific finding of necessity, the Confrontation Clause does not prohibit a State from using a one-way closed circuit television procedure for the receipt of testimony by a child witness in a child abuse case. * * *

JUSTICE SCALIA, with whom JUSTICE BRENNAN, JUSTICE MARSHALL, and JUSTICE STEVENS join, dissenting.

Seldom has this Court failed so conspicuously to sustain a categorical guarantee of the Constitution against the tide of prevailing current opinion. The Sixth Amendment provides, with unmistakable clarity, that "[i]n all criminal prosecutions, the accused shall enjoy the right . . . to be confronted with the witnesses against him." The purpose of enshrining this protection in the Constitution was to assure that none of the many policy interests from time to time pursued by statutory law could overcome a defendant's right to face his or her accusers in court. * * *

* * *

The Court today has applied "interest-balancing" analysis where the text of the Constitution simply does not permit it. We are not free to conduct a cost-benefit analysis of clear and explicit constitutional guarantees, and then to adjust their meaning to comport with our findings. The Court has convincingly proved that the Maryland procedure serves a valid interest, and gives the defendant virtually everything the Confrontation Clause guarantees (everything, that is, except confrontation). I am persuaded, therefore, that the Maryland procedure is virtually constitutional. Since it is not, however, actually constitutional I would affirm the judgment of the Maryland Court of Appeals reversing the judgment of conviction.

Notes and Questions

1. *Questions about* Craig. (a) What purposes do child witness protection statutes seek to serve?,

(b) What must the prosecutor show to invoke a child witness protection statute?,

(c) *Craig* says the emotional trauma to the child must be more than de minimis, but does the Court provide helpful guidelines for determining the minimum showing of emotional trauma the prosecutor must make?,

(d) Can the prosecutor make the required showing without expert testimony?,

(e) How much weight may the trial court give expert testimony?,

(f) By what standard of proof must the prosecutor establish the requisite trauma (preponderance-of-the-evidence, clear-and-convincing-evidence, or beyond-a-reasonable-doubt)?,

(g) Where evidence is conflicting about whether the child would suffer trauma from testifying in the defendant's presence, do you think the prosecutor will have difficulty making the required showing?

2. *Other Supreme Court decisions.* In Coy v. Iowa, 487 U.S. 1012 (1988), the defendant was convicted of sexually assaulting two thirteen-year-old girls who were camping out in the backyard of the house next door. The girls testified that after they were asleep, the assailant entered their tent wearing a stocking over his head, shined a flashlight in their eyes and warned them not to look at him. Pursuant to statute, the trial court permitted the girls to testify with a large screen placed between the defendant and the witness during testimony; the screen enabled the defendant dimly to perceive the witnesses, but the witnesses could not see him.

The Supreme Court reversed the conviction on the ground that the defendant's "constitutional right to face-to-face confrontation was violated" because the trial court employed the screen with "no individualized findings that these particular witnesses needed special protection." 487 U.S. at 1021–22. Justice O'Connor's concurrence stated that Confrontation Clause rights are "not absolute but rather may give way in an appropriate case to other competing interests so as to permit the use of certain procedural devices designed to shield a child witness from the trauma of courtroom testimony." 487 U.S. at 1022.

See also White v. Illinois, 502 U.S. 346 (1992) (holding that the sixth amendment confrontation clause does not require that before admission of a child victim's testimony under the spontaneous declaration or medical examination exceptions to the hearsay rule, the prosecution must produce the declarant at trial or the trial court must find the declarant unavailable); Kentucky v. Stincer, 482 U.S. 730 (1987) (holding that excluding the defendant from a hearing to determine child witness' competency to testify does not violate the confrontation clause).

3. *Interdisciplinary collaboration.* *Craig* provides an excellent example of why children's lawyers sometimes must collaborate with other professionals. The state ordinarily must seek the input, and sometimes also the expert testimony, of psychologists and other mental health professionals when it urges the court to invoke the child witness protection statute.

Before discussing the particular child witness' emotional condition, what will the expert likely say about the state of psychological theory concerning the potential vulnerability of child witnesses generally? In an amicus brief filed in *Craig*, the American Psychological Association (APA) reported that "child victims may be more likely than adult victims to suffer substantial distress as a result of testifying in the physical presence of the defendant":

> * * * [Y]oung children's lack of cognitive sophistication may make the legal system even more difficult to understand than it is for adult victims. By the intermediate (late elementary) grades, most children have an appreciation of the nature and purpose of the adversary system and an understanding of many legal concepts. However, preschool and primary grade children often comprehend no more than the most rudimentary legal concepts (i.e., police and judge), if any. Moreover, children involved in sexual abuse cases are even less knowledgeable, on average, than their peers. Given the fact that ambiguity generally fosters anxiety, young children's lack of understanding of the legal process is likely to add to the stress that they experience when they testify.

> The stress of appearing in court and testifying in the presence of a defendant is added to the distress that many child victim-witnesses are already experiencing due to the trauma of the sexual abuse. * * * Although testimony in juvenile court does not appear to result in significant, lasting distress for most children, testimony in criminal court is, on average, associated with immediate as well as lasting distress.

* * *

There is reason to believe face-to-face confrontation is a significant factor in child victim-witnesses' distress. Indeed, research shows that the most frequent fear expressed by children awaiting testimony is a fear of facing the defendant. When children are interviewed while waiting to testify or after they emerged from the courtroom, most children regardless of age mention facing the defendant as the most negative and frightening issue. When asked how the legal process could have been made less stressful, children and parents most often mention use of closed-circuit television or videotaped testimony.

Not all children are adversely affected, however, and some professionals believe that, if handled supportively, some children may benefit from the experience of testifying against their abusers. * * *.

Nevertheless, children who must testify more than once, children who lack maternal support when the abuse was disclosed, children whose cases lack corroborative evidence (so that proof of the crime rests primarily on the child's testimony), children whose abuse was severe, and children who were particularly frightened of the defendant when they testified, are most likely to show adverse effects of testifying. Children who are more closely related to the defendant are also somewhat more distressed as a result of testifying than children who are less closely related to the defendant. Children with any of these characteristics are likely to be at particular risk of enduring emotional distress. * * *

The APA also argued in favor of child witness protection statutes because "in the presence of the defendant, many children are less communicative—and less accurate—witnesses":

[T]he presence of the defendant in and of itself may affect children's ability or willingness to describe events accurately. Children are more likely to refuse to identify a culprit when he is physically present than when his picture is presented in a photo lineup. Research studies indicate that correct identifications occur only half as often when children face the defendant as when they do not have to face the defendant. Children show noticeable signs of nervousness, fear, and anxiety when having to face the defendant. Thus children's anxiety adversely affects their performance, with fears leading children not to reveal what they know. Moreover, the same research shows that the absence of a face-to-face encounter does not increase children's errors of identification.

Even under the controlled conditions of research studies, children can be silenced by fear or apprehensiveness. For example, many children who witness or experience an event in the presence of a stranger or loved one can be easily silenced about the event when told by that person not to tell. Children's main error in such circumstances is the withholding of information.

In contrast, providing a supportive atmosphere can improve children's accuracy. Young children are less suggestible in response to leading questions, including questions about abuse-related actions, when interviewed in a reinforcing and supportive manner. Thus, testimony in a supportive atmosphere may decrease commission errors (false affirmations). The presence of a supportive person (a child's friend) leads to more accurate testimony.

One study indicated that children who testify in a simulated court-room in front of the defendant are more likely to omit information by saying "I don't know" and are also somewhat more likely to recall less correct information than children who testify in a private room without the defendant present, as in one-way closed circuit television arrangements. Testifying in court in front of the defendant results in less complete (and even somewhat less accurate) testimony compared to testimony taken in a more sheltered environment. Moreover, children who have to face the defendant and testify in court may then refuse to do so again at another time. Overall, laboratory studies indicate that the accuracy and completeness of children's testimony is adversely affected when child witnesses must confront the defendant or testify in an unsupportive atmosphere.

* * *

Maryland v. Craig, Brief for Amicus Curiae American Psychological Association in Support of Neither Party (1990). *Craig* cited the amicus brief and some of the studies it presented and was clearly influenced by it. The brief was drafted with the assistance of the APA's counsel, demonstrating that lawyers working pro bono or on retainer may sometimes influence the development of the law by participating in amicus briefs on important questions.

4. *Manner of examination.* Trial courts have considerable discretion to regulate the manner in which child witnesses are examined. In State v. Pollard, 719 S.W.2d 38 (Mo.Ct.App.1986), for example, a six-year-old sodomy victim began to cry while testifying. After a recess, the trial court allowed the victim's mother to sit inside the railing near the counsel table during the child's testimony. The court instructed the prosecutor to advise the mother not to communicate with the victim in any way. The court of appeals held that the defendant did not suffer prejudice because the court instructed the victim's mother not to communicate with him by gesture or otherwise, because the defendant did not indicate that she did so, and because the mother's presence did not unduly influence the victim. Id. at 42.

Whether or not the trial court invokes the protective procedures approved by *Craig*, cross-examination may be particularly stressful for child sexual abuse victims, as it may be for adult witnesses. In criminal cases, the Sixth Amendment right to confrontation includes the right to cross-examine. The trial judge may control and limit cross-examination of children, however, because courts "retain wide latitude * * * to impose reasonable limits on * * * cross-examination based on concerns about, among other things, harassment, prejudice, confusion of the issues, the witness's safety, or interrogation that is repetitive or only marginally relevant." Delaware v. Van Arsdall, 475 U.S. 673, 679 (1986).

5. *The presumption of innocence.* In Marx v. State, 987 S.W.2d 577 (Tex. Ct. Crim. App. 1999), the defendant was convicted of aggravated sexual assault after the 13–year-old victim and a 6–year-old witness testified by closed circuit television. The defendant argued that admission of the televised testimony violated due process by impairing his presumption of innocence. The contention was that the only reasonable inference the jury could draw was that the defendant "has abused the witness to such a degree, that

to allow the witness to testify in the ordinary manner, would traumatize the witness even further." Id. at 581. The court rejected the contention because the trial court's instruction—that the statute authorized the televised procedure "in these types of cases"–likely conveyed to the jury that the purpose of televised testimony was to protect children from the intimidating courtroom environment rather than from a guilty defendant. Id.

6. *Children's testimony in civil abuse and neglect cases.* Most child witness protection statutes apply not only to child victims who testify in criminal sexual abuse proceedings, but also to child victims who testify in civil abuse and neglect proceedings. Testimony may be equally traumatic regardless of the forum. The Sixth Amendment Confrontation Clause does not apply in civil proceedings, but the statutory procedure must comport with due process.

7. *State constitutional law. Craig's* Sixth Amendment holding does not foreclose challenges to child witness protection statutes under state constitutions whose confrontation clauses provide greater protections to criminal defendants. See, e.g., Brady v. State, 575 N.E.2d 981, 989 (Ind.1991) (holding that use of one-way closed circuit television violated the state constitution's confrontation clause, but that use of two-way closed television would not).

8. *Closing the courtroom.* The Sixth Amendment provides that a criminal defendant "shall enjoy the right to a * * * public trial." The right is not absolute, however, and courts have long exercised authority to exclude the public from sexual assault trials, particularly ones involving minor victims. See, e.g., Reagan v. United States, 202 F. 488, 490 (9th Cir. 1913) (in prosecution for rape of a child, court of appeals affirmed an order excluding spectators from the courtroom because the "unfortunate girl who was called upon to testify to the story of the defendant's crime and her shame" should not be compelled to appear before a "crowd of idle, gaping loafers, whose morbid curiosity would lead them to attend such a trial"). Several states have long had statutes permitting exclusion in sexual assault trials involving children.

The public also holds a constitutional right to open criminal trials. Where the objection to a closure order comes from the media or other members of the public rather than from the defendant, however, the objection implicates the First Amendment rather than the Sixth Amendment. In Globe Newspaper Co. v. Superior Ct., 457 U.S. 596 (1982), the Court struck down a state statute that mandated exclusion of the press and the general public during testimony of minor victims of specified sexual offenses. In an appeal by excluded members of the media, the state argued that mandatory exclusion protects minor sex crime victims from embarrassment. The Court found the state interest compelling but nonetheless held that mandatory exclusion violated the First Amendment. The Court held that "[i]n individual cases, and under appropriate circumstances, the First Amendment does not necessarily stand as a bar to the exclusion from the courtroom of the press and general public during the testimony of minor sex-offense victims." Id. at 611 n.27. The trial court, however, must "determine on a case-by-case basis whether closure is necessary to protect the welfare of a minor victim. Among the factors to be weighed are the minor victim's age, psychological maturity and understanding, the nature of the crime, the desires of the victim, and the interests of parents and relatives." 457 U.S. at 608.

Chief Justice Burger and Justice Rehnquist dissented on the ground that the First Amendment did not require case-specific determination: "Historically our society has gone to great lengths to protect minors *charged* with crime, particularly by prohibiting the release of the names of offenders, barring the press and public from juvenile proceedings, and sealing the records of those proceedings. Yet today the Court holds unconstitutional a state statute designed to protect not the *accused*, but the minor *victims* of sex crimes." 457 U.S. at 612. See also Press–Enterprise Co. v. Superior Ct., 478 U.S. 1, 9 (1986) (holding that First Amendment guarantees a qualified public right of access to a criminal trial's preliminary proceedings, including voir dire).

In jurisdictions that permit courts to exercise discretion to allow cameras in the courtroom to televise trials, should courts ever permit a child sex crime victim's testimony to be televised? See Karla G. Sanchez, Barring the Media From the Courtroom in Child Abuse Cases: Who Should Prevail?, 46 Buff. L. Rev. 217, 248–56 (1998).

9. *Federal legislation.* The Child Victims' and Child Witness' Protection Act of 1990, 18 U.S.C. § 3509, governs federal court testimony of children who are victims of physical, emotional or sexual abuse; children who are victims of child exploitation (child pornography or child prostitution); or children who witness a crime against another person. The Act authorizes the court to permit these children to testify by closed-circuit television where expert testimony provides the basis for a case-specific determination that the prospective witness would suffer substantial fear or trauma and be unable to testify or communicate reasonably because of the defendant's physical presence, and not merely because of a general fear of the courtroom. Id. § 3509(b)(1)(B). See, e.g., United States v. Moses, 137 F.3d 894, 898–99 (6th Cir. 1998).

10. *References.* Billie Wright Dziech and Charles B. Schudson, On Trial: America's Courts and Their Treatment of Sexually Abused Children (1989); Perspectives on Children's Testimony (Stephen J. Ceci et al. eds.,1989); Gail S. Goodman and Bette L. Bottoms, Child Victims, Child Witnesses: Understanding and Improving Testimony (1993); John E.B. Myers, Child Witness Law and Practice (1987); Michael H. Graham, The Confrontation Clause, the Hearsay Rule, and Child Sexual Abuse Prosecutions: The State of the Relationship, 72 Minn. L. Rev. 523 (1988); Jean Montoya, On Truth and Shielding in Child Abuse Trials, 43 Hastings L.J. 1259 (1992); Mark A. Small and Ira M. Schwartz, Policy Implications for Children's Law in the Aftermath of *Maryland v. Craig*, 1 Seton Hall Const. L.J. 109 (1990); Special Issue on Child Sexual Abuse, 23 Fam. L.Q. (1989); Symposium: Child Abuse, 28 Pac. L.J. 1 (1996); Symposium on Child Sexual Abuse Prosecutions: The Current State of the Art, 40 U. Miami L. Rev. 5 (1985); Symposium, Throwing Away the Key: Social and Legal Responses to Child Molesters, 92 Nw. L. Rev. 1197 (1998); Various authors, Sexual Abuse of Children, in 4 The Future of Children (Summer/Fall 1994).

PROBLEM 6–8

Defendant Bill Baxter was convicted of raping and sodomizing his daughter, who was between five and ten at the time of the assaults but fifteen by the time of trial. In an in camera interview with the victim at which no expert testimony was presented, the trial conducted the following inquiry:

"Q. Why is it that him being there in the room would make you unable to tell your side?

"A: I don't know. I just can't. I just can't be near him.

"Q. We've already talked about that you're not afraid of him, are you?

"A. No.

"Q. I know it's difficult to exactly put a finger on what it is about; but why do you think that you could tell when he's not in the room but you couldn't tell it with him in the room?

"A. I don't know. I just can't be near him. I don't know why. I just can't.

"Q. Do you think that if you were to try and you know if we had to take breaks or something, you would be able to do it?

"A. I don't know."

The trial court found "compelling need" to permit the victim to testify by close circuit television: "Because of factors which I cannot define but which go much further than anxiety or nervousness, compelling need exists for using one-way closed circuit television. I am convinced that due to the nature of the testimony and the witness' age, a face-to-face arrangement would inhibit the witness and cloud the jury's search for the truth."

You sit on the state court of appeals, which is reviewing Baxter's conviction. Was the trial court finding consistent with *Craig*?

3. Expert Testimony

JOHN E.B. MYERS ET AL., EXPERT TESTIMONY IN CHILD SEXUAL ABUSE LITIGATION
68 Neb. L. Rev. 1, 3–4, 32–144 (1989).

Child sexual abuse is often exceedingly difficult to prove. Molestation occurs in secret, and the child is usually the only eyewitness. While many children are capable witnesses, some cannot take the stand. Most children find the courtroom a foreboding place, and when a child is asked to testify against a familiar person, even a parent, the experience can be overwhelming. Consequently, children's testimony is sometimes ineffective. The problems engendered by ineffective testimony and lack of eyewitnesses are compounded by the paucity of physical evidence in many child sexual abuse cases. Faced with a vacuum of evidence, attorneys increasingly turn to physicians, psychiatrists, social workers, and psychologists to provide expert testimony regarding child sexual abuse.

* * *

IV. CATEGORIES OF EXPERT TESTIMONY ON CHILD SEXUAL ABUSE

* * *

A. Medical Evidence of Child Sexual Abuse

Expert medical testimony plays an important role in child sexual abuse litigation. While medical evidence of abuse is present in a relatively small percentage of cases, when such evidence exists, it is generally admissible. Furthermore, in some cases where there is no physical evidence, a physician may nevertheless assist the jury by informing it that lack of medical evidence does not mean a child was not abused.

* * *

B. Behavioral Science Testimony Describing Behaviors Commonly Observed in Sexually Abused Children

* * *

Many reactions have been observed in sexually abused children, including anxiety, regression, sleep disturbance, acting out, depression, nightmares, and enuresis [bedwetting], to name just a few. An examination of these behaviors quickly reveals that they are also associated with a wide range of psychological problems that have nothing to do with sexual abuse. For example, the fact that a child suffers nightmares, regression, and depression says little about sexual abuse. Myriad other circumstances cause such behaviors.

While some of the behaviors observed in sexually abused children are consistent with a number of problems, others are more strongly associated with personal or vicarious sexual experience. Examples of behaviors that have greater specificity for sexual abuse include age-inappropriate knowledge of sexual acts or anatomy, sexualization of play and behavior in young children, the appearance of genitalia in young children's drawings, and sexually explicit play with anatomically detailed dolls.

The presence in a young child of behaviors commonly observed in sexually abused children can be probative of abuse. Evidence of the behaviors is relevant because it has a tendency to prove that abuse occurred. Children with behaviors associated with sexual abuse—particularly sexual reactions—are more likely to have been abused than children without such behaviors. This conclusion does not ignore the fact that approximately twenty percent of sexually abused children demonstrate no observable behavioral reactions. Absence of behaviors does not disprove abuse, but presence of behaviors increases the likelihood of abuse. Evidence of behaviors is seldom dispositive, but evidence need not be dispositive to be logically relevant and admissible.

The probative value of expert testimony describing behaviors observed in young sexually abused children is highest when there is a coalescence of three types of behaviors: (1) a central core of sexual behaviors which are strongly associated with sexual abuse; (2) nonsexual behaviors which are commonly observed in sexually abused children; and (3) medical evidence of sexual abuse.

Probative value declines as sexual behaviors and medical evidence decrease in proportion to nonsexual behaviors. When the only evidence consists of a number of ambiguous, nonsexual behaviors, the evidence may lack any probative value, or probative worth may be outweighed by the potential for unfair prejudice or jury confusion.

When a child demonstrates no sexual behaviors, but does evidence signs of serious anxiety or post-traumatic stress disorder, expert testimony may still be relevant. In this scenario, however, testimony serves only to establish that the child may have experienced some type of traumatic event. Such testimony is not specific to sexual abuse.

In some cases, testimony describing behaviors observed in sexually abused children is a combination of expert and lay testimony. The testimony takes the following form: (1) expert testimony describing behaviors observed in sexually abused children as a class, coupled with (2) lay testimony establishing that the child in the case at hand demonstrates such behaviors. The lay testimony is usually provided by individuals who are familiar with the child's behavior, such as parents. Expert testimony of this type is limited to a description of sexually abused children as a class, and does not focus on the child in the case at hand. Indeed, the expert need have no knowledge of the particular child. The sole purpose of the expert testimony is to inform the fact finder of behaviors commonly seen in abused children. The testimony of lay witnesses is adduced to acquaint the jury with the behavior of the alleged victim. It is up to the jury to put two and two together, and to conclude that because the alleged victim demonstrates behaviors commonly seen in sexually abused children, the victim probably was abused.

In a proper case, an expert could step beyond a description of sexually abused children as a class, to describe behaviors observed in a particular child. Expert testimony that a particular child displays behaviors similar to those seen in sexually abused children as a class approaches an opinion that the child was sexually abused. Nevertheless, there is a meaningful distinction between expert testimony that a particular child was sexually abused, and expert testimony that a child demonstrates behaviors commonly observed in the class of sexually abused children. In the latter case, the expert does not offer a direct opinion on the ultimate question of whether abuse occurred.

* * *

In a substantial number of cases, courts approve expert testimony describing behaviors observed in sexually abused children. * * * [I]t seems most courts do not approve such testimony as substantive evidence of abuse. Rather, the testimony is permitted to rehabilitate children's credibility. * * *

* * *

Presence in a young child of behaviors observed in sexually abused children is sometimes probative of abuse. Expert testimony explaining such behaviors can assist the jury in understanding the evidence and determining facts in issue. Such evidence should be admitted unless its probative value is substantially outweighed by the potential for unfair prejudice or confusion of the jury. Such testimony should rarely be prejudicial, and the evidence is not so arcane or ambiguous as to confuse the fact finder.

* * *

C. Behavioral Science Testimony on Whether a Child Was Sexually Abused

* * *

Expert testimony which states in so many words that a child was sexually abused is not the only form of testimony relating to abuse. Expert testimony relating to sexual abuse occurs along a continuum. At one end of the continuum is a direct opinion that a child was sexually abused; that is, that a specific event happened in the past. At the other end of the continuum is an opinion that a child demonstrates age-inappropriate sexual knowledge or awareness. It is the direct opinion that abuse occurred which raises the most concern and disagreement among professionals. By contrast, there is considerable consensus that experts on child sexual abuse can determine whether children demonstrate age-inappropriate sexual knowledge or awareness, and that testimony to that effect is within the ambit of professional competence. Between the extremes of a direct opinion that abuse occurred, and testimony relating to age-inappropriate knowledge or awareness, other opinions are possible. For example, behavioral science experts on child sexual abuse are trained and experienced in diagnosing the symptoms and behaviors that are consistent with sexual abuse, and in ferreting out alternative explanations for such symptoms and behaviors. An expert could be permitted to testify that a child demonstrates symptoms and behaviors consistent with sexual abuse, and that, in the expert's opinion, no explanation other than sexual abuse seems plausible. Alternatively, an expert might testify that a child probably experienced age-inappropriate sexual contact. The latter opinion approaches a direct opinion that abuse occurred, however, and to the extent a direct opinion raises concern, so too might an opinion regarding age-inappropriate sexual contact. Because testimony cast in the form of a direct opinion that a child was sexually abused remains controversial, the present subsection focuses on the form of testimony in which the expert states that a child's symptoms and behavior are consistent with sexual abuse. This form of opinion lies near the middle of the continuum, and would win the endorsement of many experts on child sexual abuse.

* * *

* * * Based on present knowledge, expert behavioral science testimony on whether sexual abuse occurred raises the most troubling concerns in criminal jury trials. Because of disagreement among experts on child sexual abuse, and because of the consequences of criminal conviction, it may be appropriate in criminal jury trials to eschew behavioral science testimony cast in terms of a direct opinion that sexual abuse occurred. However, it may be proper to permit one or more of the alternative forms of expert testimony discussed earlier. In particular, it may be appropriate to permit a properly qualified expert to testify that a child demonstrates age-inappropriate sexual knowledge or awareness. Furthermore, it may also be proper to permit an expert to state that a child's symptoms and behavior are consistent with sexual abuse.

* * *

D. Behavioral Science Testimony to Rehabilitate a Child's Credibility Following Impeachment in Which the Defendant Asserts that Behaviors such as Recantation and Delay in Reporting Are Inconsistent with Allegations of Sexual Abuse

* * *

A substantial percentage of children are sexually abused at some point in their minority. Most victims never disclose their abuse. Of those who do, delay in reporting is very common.

* * *

* * * [T]he defendant may assert that a child should not be believed because the child did not report alleged abuse for a substantial period of time, or because the child retracted allegations of abuse. Such impeachment is legitimate. However, when the defense concentrates on delay and recantation, the question arises whether the state may offer expert rebuttal testimony to inform the jury that many sexually abused children delay reporting and recant. * * *

* * *

The great majority of courts approve such expert rebuttal testimony [including *J.Q.,* infra p. 588]. Expert testimony is admitted to explain why sexually abused children delay reporting their abuse, why children recant, why children's descriptions of abuse are sometimes inconsistent, why abused children are angry, and why some children want to live with a person who abused them.

While expert testimony is admissible to rehabilitate children's impeached credibility, courts circumscribe such testimony to be sure it is limited to rehabilitation, and is not used as substantive evidence of abuse. For example, expert testimony regarding delay and recantation goes far toward rehabilitating credibility. It is important to ensure, however, that jurors apprehend the limits of such testimony. Delay itself does not prove abuse, nor does recantation. One commentator remarked about recantation, that "[t]here is something fundamentally strange about saying that since the child denies that the event occurred, it must have occurred." Yet, there is a danger jurors may misconstrue expert testimony on delay and recantation as substantive evidence of abuse.
* * *

* * *

Expert testimony to rehabilitate a child's credibility is usually offered on rebuttal, following impeaching cross-examination of the child. Until some form of impeachment has occurred, such expert testimony constitutes improper bolstering. It is not always necessary for the state to await cross-examination, however. In some cases the defense makes plain as early as opening statement that the child should not be believed. Regardless of the timing or method of the defendant's attack on credibility, and regardless of whether the attack is aimed directly or indirectly at the child, expert rehabilitation testimony is properly admitted as soon as the assault is underway.

Courts are comfortable with expert testimony to rehabilitate a child's impeached credibility, and for good reason. The defense invites such rebuttal testimony by its attack on the child's credibility. The state has a legitimate need to inform the jury about the dynamics of child sexual abuse so that jurors can fairly and accurately evaluate the child's credibility.

E. Behavioral Science Testimony to Rehabilitate a Child's Credibility Following Impeachment in Which the Defendant Argues that Developmental Differences Between Adults and Children Render Children Less Credible Witnesses than Adults

* * *

Taken as a whole, the research and theory in the field of child development suggest that children, like adults, bring both strengths and weaknesses to the task of testifying. Children can demonstrate adultlike reliability when testifying about certain kinds of information, under certain conditions. In other situations, regarding other types of information, children perform less well than adults. To further complicate matters, there are conditions under which children perform better than adults. For example, children sometimes remember details that adults overlook. Thus, it would be quite wrong to suggest that children are uniformly less reliable witnesses than adults.

* * *

When the defense seeks to undermine a child's credibility by asserting that developmental differences between children and adults render children less credible than adults, it is sometimes appropriate to admit rebuttal evidence in the form of expert testimony. For example, the defense might argue that inconsistencies in a young child's description of abuse mean the child is lying. As jurors evaluate the child's impeached credibility, they could benefit from expert testimony informing them that inconsistency is developmentally normal in young children. Such information is beyond the ken of the average juror.

The defense may attempt to convince the jury that young children are so suggestible that their testimony should be regarded with skepticism. The defense may illustrate the point during cross-examination by plying the child with suggestive questions that lead the child into providing inaccurate information. The defense may point out that the child was interviewed numerous times, and that there was ample opportunity to plant the idea of abuse in the child's malleable young mind. Jurors may accept the argument that young children are dangerously suggestible. Faced with such impeachment, the state has a legitimate need to rehabilitate the child. The average juror is unaware of recent psychological research indicating that young children are not always more suggestible than older children and adults. To the extent the defense asserts the contrary, expert rebuttal testimony is proper.

A final example illustrates the occasional need for expert testimony to rehabilitate children's credibility. The defense may argue that young children cannot differentiate fact from fantasy, and that the child in the case at hand lives in a fantasy world. Counsel might turn to the jury and say, "Ladies and gentleman, can you believe the testimony of this young child, who admits that she has an imaginary friend named Julius the Rabbit, and that Julius talks to her?" Fantasy plays important part in children's lives, but the professional literature indicates that even young children can distinguish real from pretend. If counsel paints an inaccurate picture of a child's ability in this regard, expert rebuttal testimony is warranted.

There is little case law regarding the type of rebuttal testimony discussed in this subsection. However, lack of precedent should not dissuade courts from permitting expert rebuttal testimony designed to acquaint jurors with the developmental capabilities and limits of young children.

F. Behavioral Science Testimony that a Particular Child, or Sexually Abused Children as a Class, Generally Tell the Truth About Sexual Abuse

* * *

It is appropriate to prohibit expert testimony that a child told the truth on a particular occasion. There is considerable intuitive appeal to the notion that jurors defer too quickly to expert assessment of credibility. Furthermore, while qualified experts possess specialized knowledge regarding certain aspects of credibility, expert capacity to detect lying and coaching is too limited to justify admission of generalized credibility testimony.

While generalized credibility testimony is properly excluded, circumstances exist where narrowly tailored expert testimony may be proper to rebut certain attacks on credibility. For example, if the defense asserts or intimates strongly that children as a group lie about sexual abuse, it seems fair to permit rebuttal expert testimony. Such testimony could draw from the clinical and scientific literature for the conclusion that fabricated allegations of sexual abuse are rare. Such testimony should be limited to an opinion that deliberately false allegations are rare. The opinion should not be couched in terms of the percentage of children who tell the truth. Such quantification of credibility runs too high a risk of misleading or confusing the jury.

* * *

G. Expert Testimony Identifying the Perpetrator

* * * Nothing in the professional literature suggests that experts on child sexual abuse possess special knowledge or expertise that allows them to identify the perpetrator of sexual abuse. In the few cases that discuss such expert testimony, courts quite properly reject it.

H. Behavioral Science Testimony Describing the Profile of Persons who Abuse Children

* * *

* * * [S]ex offenders are a heterogeneous group with few shared characteristics apart from a predilection for deviant sexual behavior. Furthermore, there is no psychological test or device that reliably detects persons who have or will sexually abuse children. Thus, it is appropriate to conclude that under the current state of scientific knowledge, there is no profile of a "typical" child molester.

* * *

Note

The Child Sexual Abuse Accommodation Syndrome (CSAAS). In State v. J.Q., 617 A.2d 1196 (N.J. 1993), the court ordered a new trial for a father convicted of several acts of sexual penetration and oral sexual contact on his two daughters, aged five and seven. The girls did not report the acts to their mother for more than a year.

The appeal turned on application of the Child Sexual Abuse Accommodation Syndrome (CSAAS). The Syndrome offers explanations about why a sexually abused child would accept the abuse or delay reporting it to a parent or other authority figure, behavior which some adults might find unusual or even inconceivable. The Syndrome includes five behaviors most commonly observed in child sex abuse victims:

Secrecy. "[C]hild abuse happens only when the child is alone with the offending adult, and the experience must never be disclosed. That secrecy is frequently accompanied by threats: 'This is our secret; nobody else will understand.' 'Don't tell anybody.' 'Nobody will believe you.' 'Don't tell your mother; (a) she will hate you, * * * (c) she will kill you,' and the like. From the secrecy, the child gets the impression of danger and fearful outcome." (In *J.Q.*, the two victims testified that they had not reported the alleged abuse because defendant had told them that if they did, he would hit them and they would get into more trouble than he.).

Helplessness. "[T]he abused child's sense of helplessness is an out-growth of the child's subordinate role in an authoritarian relationship in which the adult is entrusted with the child's care, such as the parent-child relationship. The prevailing reality for the most frequent victim of child sexual abuse is a sense of total dependence on this powerful adult in the face of which the child's normal reaction is to 'play possum.' "

Entrapment and accommodation. "Because of the child's helplessness, the only healthy option left is to survive by accepting the situation. 'There is no way out, no place to run.' * * * 'The child cannot safely conceptualize that a parent might be ruthless and self-serving; such a conclusion is tantamount to abandonment and annihilation.' The roles of parent and child become reversed: it is the child who must protect the family. The abuser warns, 'If you ever tell, they could send me to jail and put all you kids in an orphanage.' "

Delayed, conflicted and unconvincing disclosure. "Most victims never disclose the sexual abuse—at least not outside the immediate family. * * * [F]amily conflict triggers disclosure, if ever, 'only after some years of continuing sexual abuse and an eventual breakdown of accommoda-tion mechanisms.' "

Retraction. " 'Whatever a child says about sexual abuse, she is likely to reverse it' appears to be a fact. The post-disclosure family situation tends to confirm the victim's worst fears, which encouraged her secrecy in the first place, *i.e.*, her mother is disbelieving or hysterical, her father threatened with removal from the home, and the blame for this state of affairs placed squarely on the *victim*. Once again, because of the re-versed roles, the child feels obligated to preserve the family, even at the expense of his or her own well being. The only 'good' choice, then, is to 'capitulate' and restore a lie for the family's sake."

617 A.2d at 1204–05. Admissibility of scientific evidence depends on whether the scientific community generally recognizes the evidence as reli-able. When testimony is based on interviews with the child, most authorities in the field consider the underlying theory and science of CSAAS valid as diagnostic tools to explain children's seemingly unusual reactions to sexual abuse. These authorities also recognize, however, that behaviors characteris-tic of the Syndrome may also characterize children's reactions to other

disorders having nothing to do with sexual abuse, such as extreme poverty or psychological abuse.

J.Q. held that CSAAS has a sufficiently reliable scientific basis to allow an expert witness to aid jurors in evaluating specific defenses to charges of child sexual abuse. The court ordered a new trial, however, because the expert exceeded this limited scope during the prosecution's case-in-chief by relating CSAAS to behavior she had observed in the two victims, and by stating that in her expert opinion, the two girls had been sexually abused.

CSAAS testimony has divided the courts that have ruled on its admissibility. The majority decisions illustrate courts' reluctance to admit expert testimony in child sexual abuse cases except for limited purposes. Like *J.Q.*, most decisions hold that the prosecutor may not use the syndrome in the case-in-chief as substantive evidence that abuse occurred. These decisions hold that CSAAS assumes that abuse occurred and may be introduced only to rehabilitate the child's credibility by explaining his or her coping mechanisms. The question, of course, remains whether juries can understand the court's limiting instructions when some evidence of abuse is offered and the defendant begins to appear reprehensible.

Contrast *J.Q.* with Commonwealth v. Dunkle, 602 A.2d 830 (Pa. 1992), which held CSAAS testimony inadmissible either as substantive evidence or to rehabilitate. *Dunkle* concluded that such testimony would inevitably bolster the child's credibility and thus remove the credibility issue from the jury, that expert CSAAS testimony is unnecessary because fact testimony enables lay jurors to understand children's reactions to sexual abuse, and that CSAAS testimony is inherently unreliable even to rehabilitate the child's credibility: "[O]ne cannot reliably say that a child exhibiting a certain combination of behaviors has been sexually abused rather than, for instance, physically abused, neglected, or brought up by psychotic or antisocial parents." Id. at 832–33.

D. *Prospective Restraints on the Offender*

Because protections provided by child witness protection statutes are far from complete, prosecutors concerned with forcing the victim to relive the trauma in a public forum may decide not to charge or may decide to accept a plea bargain. One study found that about three-quarters of the sample of child sex abusers entered into plea bargains that resulted in lesser sentences than could have been imposed after trial and conviction, and that the average prison sentence was nine years. See Lenore M.J. Simon, The Myth of Sex Offender Specialization: An Empirical Analysis, 23 New Eng. J. on Crim. & Civ. Confinement 387, 398 (1997).

Following a plea bargain, a dangerous defendant may return to the streets considerably sooner than if sentencing had followed trial and conviction. On the other hand, many sex offenders are not recidivists. What measures can the state take to protect future child victims from danger while enabling offenders to reintegrate themselves peaceably into the community after serving their sentences? The next two decisions, *Hendricks* and *Doe,* wrestle with this vexing question.

1. Civil Commitment

KANSAS v. HENDRICKS

Supreme Court of the United States, 1997.
521 U.S. 346.

JUSTICE THOMAS delivered the opinion of the Court.

In 1994, Kansas enacted the Sexually Violent Predator Act, which establishes procedures for the civil commitment of persons who, due to a "mental abnormality" or a "personality disorder," are likely to engage in "predatory acts of sexual violence." The State invoked the Act for the first time to commit Leroy Hendricks, an inmate who had a long history of sexually molesting children, and who was scheduled for release from prison shortly after the Act became law. Hendricks challenged his commitment on, *inter alia*, "substantive" due process, double jeopardy, and *ex post facto* grounds. The Kansas Supreme Court invalidated the Act, holding that its pre-commitment condition of a "mental abnormality" did not satisfy what the court perceived to be the "substantive" due process requirement that involuntary civil commitment must be predicated on a finding of "mental illness." * * * We * * * now reverse the judgment below.

I

A

The Kansas Legislature enacted the Sexually Violent Predator Act (Act) in 1994 to grapple with the problem of managing repeat sexual offenders. Although Kansas already had a statute addressing the involuntary commitment of those defined as "mentally ill," the legislature determined that existing civil commitment procedures were inadequate to confront the risks presented by "sexually violent predators." * * *

As a result, the legislature found it necessary to establish "a civil commitment procedure for the long-term care and treatment of the sexually violent predator." The Act defined a "sexually violent predator" as:

"any person who has been convicted of or charged with a sexually violent offense and who suffers from a mental abnormality or personality disorder which makes the person likely to engage in the predatory acts of sexual violence."

A "mental abnormality" was defined, in turn, as a "congenital or acquired condition affecting the emotional or volitional capacity which predisposes the person to commit sexually violent offenses in a degree constituting such person a menace to the health and safety of others."

As originally structured, the Act's civil commitment procedures pertained to: (1) a presently confined person who, like Hendricks, "has been convicted of a sexually violent offense" and is scheduled for release; (2) a person who has been "charged with a sexually violent offense" but has been found incompetent to stand trial; (3) a person who has been found "not guilty by reason of insanity of a sexually violent offense"; and (4) a person found "not guilty" of a sexually violent offense because of a mental disease or defect.

The initial version of the Act, as applied to a currently confined person such as Hendricks, was designed to initiate a specific series of procedures. The custodial agency was required to notify the local prosecutor 60 days before the anticipated release of a person who might have met the Act's criteria. The prosecutor was then obligated, within 45 days, to decide whether to file a petition in state court seeking the person's involuntary commitment. If such a petition were filed, the court was to determine whether "probable cause" existed to support a finding that the person was a "sexually violent predator" and thus eligible for civil commitment. Upon such a determination, transfer of the individual to a secure facility for professional evaluation would occur. After that evaluation, a trial would be held to determine beyond a reasonable doubt whether the individual was a sexually violent predator. If that determination were made, the person would then be transferred to the custody of the Secretary of Social and Rehabilitation Services (Secretary) for "control, care and treatment until such time as the person's mental abnormality or personality disorder has so changed that the person is safe to be at large."

In addition to placing the burden of proof upon the State, the Act afforded the individual a number of other procedural safeguards. In the case of an indigent person, the State was required to provide, at public expense, the assistance of counsel and an examination by mental health care professionals. The individual also received the right to present and cross-examine witnesses, and the opportunity to review documentary evidence presented by the State.

Once an individual was confined, the Act required that "[t]he involuntary detention or commitment ... shall conform to constitutional requirements for care and treatment." Confined persons were afforded three different avenues of review: First, the committing court was obligated to conduct an annual review to determine whether continued detention was warranted. Second, the Secretary was permitted, at any time, to decide that the confined individual's condition had so changed that release was appropriate, and could then authorize the person to petition for release. Finally, even without the Secretary's permission, the confined person could at any time file a release petition. If the court found that the State could no longer satisfy its burden under the initial commitment standard, the individual would be freed from confinement.

B

In 1984, Hendricks was convicted of taking "indecent liberties" with two 13-year-old boys. After serving nearly 10 years of his sentence, he was slated for release to a halfway house. Shortly before his scheduled release, however, the State filed a petition in state court seeking Hendricks' civil confinement as a sexually violent predator. On August 19,

1994, Hendricks appeared before the court with counsel and moved to dismiss the petition on the grounds that the Act violated various federal constitutional provisions. Although the court reserved ruling on the Act's constitutionality, it concluded that there was probable cause to support a finding that Hendricks was a sexually violent predator, and therefore ordered that he be evaluated at the Larned State Security Hospital.

Hendricks subsequently requested a jury trial to determine whether he qualified as a sexually violent predator. During that trial, Hendricks' own testimony revealed a chilling history of repeated child sexual molestation and abuse, beginning in 1955 when he exposed his genitals to two young girls. At that time, he pleaded guilty to indecent exposure. Then, in 1957, he was convicted of lewdness involving a young girl and received a brief jail sentence. In 1960, he molested two young boys while he worked for a carnival. After serving two years in prison for that offense, he was paroled, only to be rearrested for molesting a 7–year-old girl. Attempts were made to treat him for his sexual deviance, and in 1965 he was considered "safe to be at large," and was discharged from a state psychiatric hospital.

Shortly thereafter, however, Hendricks sexually assaulted another young boy and girl—he performed oral sex on the 8–year-old girl and fondled the 11–year-old boy. He was again imprisoned in 1967, but refused to participate in a sex offender treatment program, and thus remained incarcerated until his parole in 1972. Diagnosed as a pedophile, Hendricks entered into, but then abandoned, a treatment program. He testified that despite having received professional help for his pedophilia, he continued to harbor sexual desires for children. Indeed, soon after his 1972 parole, Hendricks began to abuse his own stepdaughter and stepson. He forced the children to engage in sexual activity with him over a period of approximately four years. Then, as noted above, Hendricks was convicted of "taking indecent liberties" with two adolescent boys after he attempted to fondle them. As a result of that conviction, he was once again imprisoned, and was serving that sentence when he reached his conditional release date in September 1994.

Hendricks admitted that he had repeatedly abused children whenever he was not confined. He explained that when he "get[s] stressed out," he "can't control the urge" to molest children. Although Hendricks recognized that his behavior harms children, and he hoped he would not sexually molest children again, he stated that the only sure way he could keep from sexually abusing children in the future was "to die." Hendricks readily agreed with the state physician's diagnosis that he suffers from pedophilia and that he is not cured of the condition; indeed, he told the physician that "treatment is bull——."

The jury unanimously found beyond a reasonable doubt that Hendricks was a sexually violent predator. The trial court subsequently determined, as a matter of state law, that pedophilia qualifies as a "mental abnormality" as defined by the Act, and thus ordered Hendricks committed to the Secretary's custody. * * * [The Kansas Supreme Court held that "the Act violates Hendricks' substantive due process rights."].

* * *

II

A

* * *

The challenged Act unambiguously requires a finding of dangerousness either to one's self or to others as a prerequisite to involuntary confinement. Commitment proceedings can be initiated only when a person "has been convicted of or charged with a sexually violent offense," and "suffers from a mental abnormality or personality disorder which makes the person likely to engage in the predatory acts of sexual violence." The statute thus requires proof of more than a mere predisposition to violence; rather, it requires evidence of past sexually violent behavior and a present mental condition that creates a likelihood of such conduct in the future if the person is not incapacitated. * * *

A finding of dangerousness, standing alone, is ordinarily not a sufficient ground upon which to justify indefinite involuntary commitment. We have sustained civil commitment statutes when they have coupled proof of dangerousness with the proof of some additional factor, such as a "mental illness" or "mental abnormality." These added statutory requirements serve to limit involuntary civil confinement to those who suffer from a volitional impairment rendering them dangerous beyond their control. The Kansas Act is plainly of a kind with these other civil commitment statutes: It requires a finding of future dangerousness, and then links that finding to the existence of a "mental abnormality" or "personality disorder" that makes it difficult, if not impossible, for the person to control his dangerous behavior. The precommitment requirement of a "mental abnormality" or "personality disorder" is consistent with the requirements of these other statutes that we have upheld in that it narrows the class of persons eligible for confinement to those who are unable to control their dangerousness. * * *

Hendricks nonetheless argues that our earlier cases dictate a finding of "mental illness" as a prerequisite for civil commitment * * *. He then asserts that a "mental abnormality" is not equivalent to a "mental illness" because it is a term coined by the Kansas Legislature, rather than by the psychiatric community. Contrary to Hendricks' assertion, the term "mental illness" is devoid of any talismanic significance. Not only do "psychiatrists disagree widely and frequently on what constitutes mental illness," but the Court itself has used a variety of expressions to describe the mental condition of those properly subject to civil confinement.

* * *

To the extent that the civil commitment statutes we have considered set forth criteria relating to an individual's inability to control his dangerousness, the Kansas Act sets forth comparable criteria and Hendricks' condition doubtless satisfies those criteria. The mental health professionals who evaluated Hendricks diagnosed him as suffering from pedophilia, a condition the psychiatric profession itself classifies as a serious mental disorder. * * * Hendricks' diagnosis as a pedophile, which qualifies as a "mental abnormality" under the Act, thus plainly suffices for due process purposes.

B

* * * [Hendricks] contends that where, as here, newly enacted "punishment" is predicated upon past conduct for which he has already been convicted and forced to serve a prison sentence, the Constitution's Double Jeopardy and *Ex Post Facto* Clauses are violated. We are unpersuaded by Hendricks' argument that Kansas has established criminal proceedings. * * *

* * *

As a threshold matter, commitment under the Act does not implicate either of the two primary objectives of criminal punishment: retribution or deterrence. The Act's purpose is not retributive because it does not affix culpability for prior criminal conduct. Instead, such conduct is used solely for evidentiary purposes, either to demonstrate that a "mental abnormality" exists or to support a finding of future dangerousness. * * * In addition, the Kansas Act does not make a criminal conviction a prerequisite for commitment–persons absolved of criminal responsibility may nonetheless be subject to confinement under the Act. An absence of the necessary criminal responsibility suggests that the State is not seeking retribution for a past misdeed. * * *

Moreover, unlike a criminal statute, no finding of scienter is required to commit an individual who is found to be a sexually violent predator; instead, the commitment determination is made based on a "mental abnormality" or "personality disorder" rather than on one's criminal intent. The existence of a scienter requirement is customarily an important element in distinguishing criminal from civil statutes. The absence of such a requirement here is evidence that confinement under the statute is not intended to be retributive.

Nor can it be said that the legislature intended the Act to function as a deterrent. Those persons committed under the Act are, by definition, suffering from a "mental abnormality" or a "personality disorder" that prevents them from exercising adequate control over their behavior. Such persons are therefore unlikely to be deterred by the threat of confinement. And the conditions surrounding that confinement do not suggest a punitive purpose on the State's part. The State has represented that an individual confined under the Act is not subject to the more restrictive conditions placed on state prisoners, but instead experiences essentially the same conditions as any involuntarily committed patient in the state mental institution. Because none of the parties argues that people institutionalized under the Kansas general civil commitment statute are subject to punitive conditions, even though they may be involuntarily confined, it is difficult to conclude that persons confined under this Act are being "punished."

Although the civil commitment scheme at issue here does involve an affirmative restraint, "the mere fact that a person is detained does not inexorably lead to the conclusion that the government has imposed punishment." The State may take measures to restrict the freedom of the dangerously mentally ill. This is a legitimate non-punitive governmental objective and has been historically so regarded. The Court has, in fact, cited the confinement of "mentally unstable individuals who present a danger to the public" as one classic example of nonpunitive detention. If detention for the purpose of protecting the community from harm *necessarily* constituted punishment, then all involuntary civil commitments would have to be considered punishment. But we have never so held.

Hendricks focuses on his confinement's potentially indefinite duration as evidence of the State's punitive intent. That focus, however, is misplaced. Far from any punitive objective, the confinement's duration is instead linked to the stated purposes of the commitment, namely, to hold the person until his mental abnormality no longer causes him to be a threat to others. If, at any time, the confined person is adjudged "safe to be at large," he is statutorily entitled to immediate release. * * *

* * *

Hendricks next contends that the State's use of procedural safeguards traditionally found in criminal trials makes the proceedings here criminal rather than civil. * * * The numerous procedural and evidentiary protections afforded here demonstrate that the Kansas Legislature has taken great care to confine only a narrow class of particularly dangerous individuals, and then only after meeting the strictest procedural standards. That Kansas chose to afford such procedural protections does not transform a civil commitment proceeding into a criminal prosecution.

Finally, Hendricks argues that the Act is necessarily punitive because it fails to offer any legitimate "treatment." Without such treatment, Hendricks asserts, confinement under the Act amounts to little more than disguised punishment. Hendricks' argument assumes that treatment for his condition is available, but that the State has failed (or refused) to provide it. The Kansas Supreme Court, however, apparently rejected this assumption, explaining:

> "It is clear that the overriding concern of the legislature is to continue the segregation of sexually violent offenders from the public. Treatment with the goal of reintegrating them into society is incidental, at best. The record reflects that treatment for sexually violent predators is all but nonexistent. * * *

* * * While we have upheld state civil commitment statutes that aim both to incapacitate and to treat, we have never held that the Constitution prevents a State from civilly detaining those for whom no treatment is available, but who nevertheless pose a danger to others. * * * To conclude otherwise would obligate a State to release certain confined individuals who were both mentally ill and dangerous simply because they could not be successfully treated for their afflictions. * * *

* * * Where the State has "disavowed any punitive intent"; limited confinement to a small segment of particularly dangerous individuals; provided strict procedural safeguards; directed that confined persons be segregated from the general prison population and afforded the same status as others who have been civilly committed; recommended treatment if such is possible; and permitted immediate release upon a showing that the individual is no longer dangerous or mentally impaired, we cannot say that it acted with punitive intent. We therefore hold that the Act does not establish criminal proceedings and that involuntary confinement pursuant to the Act is not punitive. Our conclusion that the Act is nonpunitive thus removes an essential prerequisite for both Hendricks' double jeopardy and *ex post facto* claims.

1

The Double Jeopardy Clause provides: "[N]or shall any person be subject for the same offence to be twice put in jeopardy of life or limb." Although generally understood to preclude a second prosecution for the same offense, the Court has also interpreted this prohibition to prevent the State from "punishing twice, or attempting a second time to punish criminally, for the same offense." * * *

Because we have determined that the Kansas Act is civil in nature, initiation of its commitment proceedings does not constitute a second prosecution. Moreover, as commitment under the Act is not tantamount to "punishment," Hendricks' involuntary detention does not violate the Double Jeopardy Clause, even though that confinement may follow a prison term. * * * If an individual otherwise meets the requirements for involuntary civil commitment, the State is under no obligation to release that individual simply because the detention would follow a period of incarceration.

* * *

2

Hendricks' *ex post facto* claim is similarly flawed. The *Ex Post Facto* Clause, which " 'forbids the application of any new punitive measure to a crime already consummated,' "has been interpreted to pertain exclusively to penal statutes. As we have previously determined, the Act does not impose punishment; thus, its application does not raise *ex post facto* concerns. Moreover, the Act clearly does not have retroactive effect. Rather, the Act permits involuntary confinement based upon a determination that the person *currently* both suffers from a "mental abnormality" or "personality disorder" and is likely to pose a future danger to the public. To the extent that past behavior is taken into account, it is used, as noted above, solely for evidentiary purposes. * * *

JUSTICE KENNEDY, concurring.

I join the opinion of the Court in full and add these additional comments.

* * *

It seems the dissent, too, would validate the Kansas statute as to persons who committed the crime after its enactment, and it might even validate the statute as to Hendricks, assuming a reasonable level of treatment. As all Members of the Court seem to agree, then, the power of the state to confine persons who, by reason of a mental disease or mental abnormality, constitute a real, continuing, and serious danger to society is well established. Confinement of such individuals is permitted even if it is pursuant to a statute enacted after the crime has been committed and the offender has begun serving, or has all but completed serving, a penal sentence, provided there is no object or purpose to punish. The Kansas law, with its attendant protections, including yearly review and review at any time at the instance of the person confined, is within this pattern and tradition of civil confinement. * * *

Notwithstanding its civil attributes, the practical effect of the Kansas law may be to impose confinement for life. At this stage of medical knowledge, although future treatments cannot be predicted, psychiatrists or other professionals engaged in treating pedophilia may be reluctant to find measurable success in treatment even after a long period and may be unable to predict that no serious danger will come from release of the detainee.

A common response to this may be, "A life term is exactly what the sentence should have been anyway," or, in the words of a Kansas task force member, "So be it." The point, however, is not how long Hendricks and others like him should serve a criminal sentence. With his criminal record, after all, a life term may well have been the only sentence appropriate to protect society and vindicate the wrong. The concern instead is whether it is the criminal system or the civil system which should make the decision in the first place. If the civil system is used simply to impose punishment after the State makes an improvident plea bargain on the criminal side, then it is not performing its proper function * * * [W]hile incapacitation is a goal common to both the criminal and civil systems of confinement, retribution and general deterrence are reserved for the criminal system alone. * * *

On the record before us, the Kansas civil statute conforms to our precedents. If, however, civil confinement were to become a mechanism for retribution or general deterrence, or if it were shown that mental abnormality is too imprecise a category to offer a solid basis for concluding that civil detention is justified, our precedents would not suffice to validate it.

JUSTICE BREYER, with whom JUSTICE STEVENS and JUSTICE SOUTER join, and with whom JUSTICE GINSBURG joins as to Parts II and III, dissenting.

I agree with the majority that the Kansas Sexually Violent Predator Act's "definition of 'mental abnormality' "satisfies the "substantive" requirements of the Due Process Clause. Kansas, however, concedes that Hendricks' condition is treatable; yet the Act did not provide Hendricks (or others like him) with any treatment until after his release date from prison and only inadequate treatment thereafter. These, and certain other, special features of the Act convince me that it was not simply an effort to commit Hendricks civilly, but rather an effort to inflict further punishment upon him. The *Ex Post Facto* Clause therefore prohibits the Act's application to Hendricks, who committed his crimes prior to its enactment.

I

* * *

A

* * * Because (1) many mental health professionals consider pedophilia a serious mental disorder; and (2) Hendricks suffers from a classic case of irresistible impulse, namely, he is so afflicted with pedophilia that he cannot "control the urge" to molest children; and (3) his pedophilia presents a serious danger to those children, I believe that Kansas can classify Hendricks as "mentally ill" and "dangerous" * * *.

* * *

III

* * *

To find a violation of [the *Ex Post Facto*] Clause here, however, is not to hold that the Clause prevents Kansas, or other States, from enacting dangerous sexual offender statutes. A statute that operates prospectively, for example, does not offend the Ex Post Facto Clause. Neither does it offend the *Ex Post Facto* Clause for a State to sentence offenders to the fully authorized sentence, to seek consecutive, rather than concurrent, sentences, or to invoke recidivism statutes to lengthen imprisonment. Moreover, a statute that operates retroactively, like Kansas' statute, nonetheless does not offend the Clause *if the confinement that it imposes is not punishment*—if, that is to say, the legislature does not simply add a later criminal punishment to an earlier one. * * *

* * *

Notes and Questions

1. *Questions about* Hendricks. (a) How many Justices voted to uphold the constitutionality of a properly drawn violent sexual predator civil commitment statute?,

(b) As a general matter, how many Justices would permit a state to apply such a statute that considers acts the defendant committed before enactment?,

(c) To pass constitutional muster, what procedural and substantive protections must a violent sexual predator civil commitment statute guarantee?,

(d) If the Supreme Court had held the Kansas act to be an ex post facto law as applied to Leroy Hendricks, what would have been the practical effect on state efforts to civilly commit persistent violent sexual offenders sentenced before enactment of the act?,

(e) Was Kansas trying to treat (and perhaps cure) Hendricks, or was it trying to punish him further, or both?,

(f) If a state truly wishes to treat a sex offender rather than merely extend his incarceration, should the civil commitment statute require provision of treatment throughout the period of incarceration?,

(g) If Leroy Hendricks has a mental abnormality beyond cure, will he ever be released?

2. Hendricks' *antecedents*. Sexual predator civil commitment statutes, including the Kansas statute upheld in *Hendricks*, were patterned on the statute enacted by Washington state in 1990 and upheld by its supreme court three years later. See Personal Restraint of Young, 857 P.2d 989 (Wash.1993). The Washington statute arose from public outcry after a particularly vicious sexual assault on a seven-year-old boy abducted while riding his bicycle near his Tacoma home. The victim was dragged into the woods, raped, stabbed, choked nearly to death, and left semiconscious in the dirt after the abductor cut off his penis. Earl Shriner, the 39-year-old abductor, had a long record of assaults on children, had been labeled a sexual psychopath by a psychiatrist, and had continued committing assaults each time he was released from prison. He had been released two years earlier after serving a ten-year sentence for assaulting two teenage girls. Before releasing him, corrections officials tried to have him civilly committed to a mental hospital, but commitment was rejected under the then-prevailing standards because he was not mentally ill and was not committing violent acts at the time. See Barry Siegel, Locking Up "Sexual Predators," L.A. Times, May 10, 1990, at 1.

A year before the assault on the seven-year-old bicyclist, Shriner had grabbed a 10–year-old boy, tied his hands behind his back, unbuttoned his pants and dragged him to a fence post, tied him to it and repeatedly beat him. The prosecutor charged Shriner with attempted statutory rape, but let him plead guilty to a reduced charge of unlawful imprisonment and serve only 67 days (reportedly because the victim would not testify against him). See Sickening Attack in Tacoma, Seattle Times, May 24, 1989, at A10; Peyton Whitely, Lack of Witnesses Tied Prosecutor's Hands, Seattle Times, May 25, 1989, at A8. For the attack on the young bicyclist, Shriner received 131½ years, enough, according to the judge, that he would have to serve at least 88 years even with time off for good behavior. See Kate Shatzkin, Shriner Gets 131 Years, Seattle Times, Mar. 26, 1990, at A1.

The Kansas statute itself resulted from public outrage about a violent sex crime. The state legislature acted within a year after a 19–year-old student was abducted, raped and murdered by a persistent sex offender who had been paroled nine months earlier after serving ten years for raping and sodomizing a woman. See Kyle Hughes, State Looks For Way to Keep Sex Predators Locked Up, Times–Union (Albany, N.Y.), Feb. 21, 1999, at E7.

3. *Plea bargaining.* Justice Kennedy states, "If the civil system is used simply to impose punishment after the State makes an improvident plea bargain on the criminal side, then it is not performing its proper function." Prosecutors, however, often accept plea bargains to lesser charges to spare child victims the trauma of in-court testimony, and to avoid other difficulties of proof. Because lesser charges may carry only a moderate sentence, should civil commitment play a meaningful role in protecting society from persons like Mr. Hendricks?

Incidentally, Leroy Hendricks himself received the sort of "improvident plea bargain" Justice Kennedy addressed. In 1984, Hendricks plea bargained to concurrent sentences of five to twenty years on two counts of taking indecent liberties with a child. The prosecutor dropped the third count and agreed not to request imposition of sentence under the Habitual Criminal Act, which would have authorized the court to sentence him to consecutive sentences totaling between 45 and 180 years, effectively a life sentence. As one Kansas Supreme Court justice put it, "Without violating the Constitution, the State could have incarcerated Hendricks until he exhaled his last breath and his spirit departed this earth, but it did not." In re Hendricks, 912 P.2d 129, 139 (Kan.1996) (Lockett, J., concurring).

When the 60–year-old Hendricks was due to be released in 1994 after serving only ten years despite a thirty-year record of child molestation, the same prosecutor's office that agreed to the 1984 plea bargain invoked the new sexually violent predator act. See Tom Malone, The Kansas Sexually Violent Predator Act–Post *Hendricks*, 67 J. Kan. B.A. 36, 38 (Mar. 1998). Do you agree with the commentator who, surveying the *Hendricks* record, criticized civil commitment laws as "crutches to compensate for light sentences and lazy prosecutors"? See Rael Jean Isaac, Put Sex Predators Behind Bars, Not on the Couch, Wall St. J., May 8, 1998, at A17.

4. *Stiff sentencing as an alternative to civil commitment.* Courts may incapacitate a person who commits a sex offense against a juvenile by imposing the fully authorized sentence, seeking consecutive rather than concurrent sentences, or invoking recidivist statutes. Many courts are doing just that, leading one commentator to conclude that "[s]tates that provide appropriate sentences for serious repeat violent offenders will not need to enact a predator law." John Q. LaFond, The Costs of Enacting a Sexual Predator Law, 4 Psychol. Pub. Pol'y & L. 468 (1998). But does reliance on stiff sentencing alone adequately protect children when prosecutors often must plea bargain down when, as reportedly occurred in Shriner's case, young victims are unwilling or unable to testify?

Some courts are carrying stiff sentencing to extremes that have raised a few judges' eyebrows. California Supreme Court Justice Stanley Mosk, for example, has criticized "the inordinately long sentences imposed by many courts" in child sex abuse cases:

* * * On August 23 of last year, a trial judge in Pomona, California, sentenced a convicted rapist to 515 years in prison. My court has denied petitions for habeas corpus in cases where defendants were sentenced to 129 years in prison, 98 years, 99 years and four months, and 111 years.

Even those sentences are commonplace. In 1990, the defendant in People v. Lewis was sentenced to 155 years plus two consecutive life terms running concurrently with two additional life terms. George Anthony Sanchez was given 406 years and Grace Dill received 405 years in prison, both for child molestation.

I wondered what judge would be the first to make the Guinness Book of World Records by imposing a prison sentence of 1,000 years. I wonder no more. An Oklahoma City judge put us all to shame. On December 23, 1994, the press reported that "[a] judge weary of criminals serving only a portion of their time yesterday sentenced a child rapist to 30,000 years in prison." * * *

Do you agree with Justice Mosk that "a sentence that on its face is impossible for a human being to serve is per se * * * 'cruel and unusual' punishment under the Eighth Amendment"? Justice Mosk believes that for persistent sex offenders "[t]he maximum sentence that should be imposed is one a defendant is able to serve: life imprisonment. In a particularly egregious case involving exceptionally numerous victims, the maximum conceivably could be life without possibility of parole. * * * Such sentences would serve the purposes of punishment, would be constitutional, and would avoid making the judicial process appear oblivious to life expectancy tables." See Stanley Mosk, States Rights–And Wrongs, 72 NYU L. Rev. 552, 556–59 (1997).

5. *The potential costs of sexual predator civil commitment statutes.* Several states are expected to enact sexual predator civil commitment statutes now that the *Hendricks* statute has survived constitutional challenge. Professor John Q. LaFond argues that states enacting civil commitment statutes will incur substantial direct costs for such features as (1) new bureaucracies to screen, evaluate and provide multilevel pre-release review of each of the few hundred sex offenders scheduled for release from prison each year, (2) trials to determine whether a particular sex offender is a predator subject to commitment (which cost about $100,000 per trial in Minnesota, largely because each side's efforts resemble the efforts expended in capital punishment trials), (3) annual costs for treating committed offenders in specialized and sometimes specially constructed facilities (which in 1998 ranged from $60,300 per offender in Wisconsin to $127,750 in Minnesota), (4) recordkeeping costs, and (5) costs of providing some individual offenders with less restrictive alternative placements and gradual-release programs when authorized by statute or ordered by a court. John Q. LaFond, The Costs of Enacting a Sexual Predator Law, 4 Psychol. Pub. Pol'y & L. 468, 476–85 (1998).

Professor LaFond expects commitment statutes to generate expensive ongoing litigation for several years. First, even though *Hendricks* has upheld the general constitutionality of the statutes, constitutional challenges to conditions of confinement and treatment, and to conditions for release, will likely continue. Courts may impose costly mandates in the name of constitutional right. Finally, if states ultimately use civil commitment statutes less often because they increase sentences, they will face litigation about conditions for releasing persons previously committed. Id. at 485–93.

Professor LaFond argues that the civil commitment statutes may ultimately be counterproductive because, among other things, they (1) would deter many sex offenders from seeking in-prison treatment which would generate information that could be used against them in a later civil commitment proceeding, (2) would adversely affect the success rate of in-prison treatment among inmates who believe the aim of state-provided therapy is to build a record for a later civil commitment proceeding rather than to seek to cure them, and (3) would burden the trial and appellate courts by discouraging plea bargaining to offenses that might trigger later civil commitment proceedings. Id. at 495–98.

6. *References*. Steven I. Friedland, On Treatment, Punishment, and the Civil Commitment of Sex Offenders, 70 U. Colo. L. Rev. 73 (1999); Eric S. Janus, Foreshadowing the Future of *Kansas v. Hendricks*: Lessons From Minnesota's Sex Offender Commitment Litigation, 92 Nw. U. L. Rev. 1279 (1998); Wayne A. Logan, The Ex Post Facto Clause and the Jurisprudence of Punishment, 35 Am. Crim. L. Rev. 1261 (1998); Michael L. Perlin, There's No Success Like Failure/and Failure's No Success at All: Exposing the Pretextuality of *Kansas v. Hendricks*, 92 Nw. U. L. Rev. 1247 (1998); Sex Offenders: Scientific, Legal, and Policy Perspectives,4 Psychol. Pub. Pol'y, and Law 3 (Mar./June 1998).

2. *Registration and Community Notification*

On July 29, 1994, seven-year-old Megan Kanka was abducted, raped and murdered by a neighbor who lived across the street from her family in suburban New Jersey. The confessed murderer enticed the child into his home with a promise to see his new puppy, then strangled her with a belt, covered her head with plastic bags, raped her as she lay unconscious, and left her body in a nearby park. Megan, her parents, local police, and other members of the community were unaware that the murderer had twice been convicted of sex offenses against young girls, and that he shared his house with two other men also previously convicted of sex crimes.

New Jersey's governor and legislature responded swiftly to intense public reaction to Megan's murder by enacting the Registration and Community Notification Laws, collectively called "Megan's Law," within three months. The legislature passed the measure after emergency suspension of its rules, with no hearings in one house and only brief hearings in the other. The bill required registration by persons who had committed designated crimes involving sexual assault and provided for dissemination of information about registrants.

Most other states enacted their own versions of Megan's Law within a year. In 1994, Congress enacted the Jacob Wetterling Crimes Against Children and Sexually Violent Offender Registration Act, 42 U.S.C. § 14071, which conditioned availability of a percentage of federal crime fighting funds on a state's creation of a sex offender registration program. The Act permitted, but did not mandate, community notification. When it became apparent that only a few states would mandate notification, the lawmakers in 1996 enacted a federal version of Megan's Law, which requires states also to enact community notification provisions as a condition for receiving their full share of federal funds. 42 U.S.C. § 14071(d). Within two days after its introduction, the 1996 legislation passed without amendment in the House, 418–0, and in the Senate by voice vote. See 142 Cong. Rec. S10664 (daily ed. May 9, 1996). Every state now has a registration statute, nearly all of which also mandate some form of community notification.

DOE v. PORITZ

Supreme Court of New Jersey, 1995.
662 A.2d 367.

WILENTZ, C.J.

* * * The question before us is whether two * * * bills, the Registration and Community Notification Laws, are constitutional. We hold that they are, but that the prosecutor's decision to provide community notification, including the manner of notification, is subject to judicial review before such notification is given, and that such review is constitutionally required. * * *

The essence of our decision is that the Constitution does not prevent society from attempting to protect itself from convicted sex offenders, no matter when convicted, so long as the means of protection are reasonably designed for that purpose and only for that purpose, and not designed to punish; that the community notification provided for in these laws, given its remedial purpose, rationality, and limited scope, further assured by our opinion and judicial review, is not constitutionally vulnerable because of its inevitable impact on offenders; that despite the possible severity of that impact, sex offenders' loss of anonymity is no constitutional bar to society's attempt at self-defense. The Registration and Notification Laws are not retributive laws, but laws designed to give people a chance to protect themselves and their children. They do not represent the slightest departure from our State's or our country's fundamental belief that criminals, convicted and punished, have paid their debt to society and are not to be punished further. They represent only the conclusion that society has the right to know of their presence not in order to punish them, but in order to protect itself. The laws represent a conclusion by the Legislature that those convicted sex offenders who have successfully, or apparently successfully, been integrated into their communities, adjusted their lives so as to appear no more threatening than anyone else in the neighborhood, are entitled not to be disturbed simply because of that prior offense and conviction; but a conclusion as well, that the characteristics of some of them, and the statistical information concerning them, make it clear that despite such integration, reoffense is a realistic risk, and knowledge of their presence a realistic protection against it.

The choice the Legislature made was difficult, for at stake was the continued apparently normal lifestyle of previously-convicted sex offenders, some of whom were doing no harm and very well might never do any harm, as weighed against the potential molestation, rape, or murder by others of women and children because they simply did not know of the presence of such a person and therefore did not take the common-sense steps that might prevent such an occurrence. The Legislature chose to risk unfairness to the previously-convicted offenders rather than unfairness to the children and women who might suffer because of their ignorance, but attempted to restrict the damage that notification of the public might do to the lives of rehabilitated offenders by trying to identify those most likely to reoffend and limiting the extent of notification based on that conclusion.

The legislative choice was undoubtedly influenced by the fact that if the law did not apply to previously-convicted offenders, notification would provide practically no protection now, and relatively little in the near future. The Legislature reached the irresistible conclusion that if community safety was its objective, there was no justification for applying these laws only to those who offend or who are convicted in the future, and not applying them to previously-convicted offenders. Had the Legislature chosen to exempt previously-convicted offenders, the notification provision of the law would have provided absolutely no protection whatsoever on the day it became law, for it would have applied to no one. The Legislature concluded that there was no justification for protecting only children of the future from the risk of reoffense by future offenders, and not today's children from the risk of reoffense by previously-convicted offenders, when the nature of those risks were identical and presently arose almost exclusively from previously-convicted offenders, their numbers now and for a fair number of years obviously vastly exceeding the number of those who, after passage of these laws, will be convicted and released and only then, for the first time, potentially subject to community notification.

I

The Legislative Purpose: Addressing the Problem of Repetitive Sex Offenders

The challenged laws before us in this case have two basic provisions. First, they require registration with law enforcement authorities of certain convicted sex offenders and spell out the offenses that trigger the registration requirement, registration of those convicted prior to their passage limited to offenders found to have repetitive and compulsive characteristics. Second, they provide for notice of the presence of such offenders in the community, the scope of that notice measured by the likelihood that such offenders will commit another sex offense: where the risk of such reoffense is low, only law enforcement authorities are notified; where it is moderate, institutions and organizations having the responsibility to care for and supervise children and women are notified;

and where the risk is high, those members of the public likely to encounter the offender are notified.

* * *

Based on statistical and other studies the Legislature could have found, and presumably did find, the following facts, essentially reflected in its statement of purpose, and its enactment of the laws:

* * * Studies report that rapists recidivate at a rate of 7 to 35%; offenders who molest young girls, at a rate of 10 to 29%, and offenders who molest young boys, at a rate of 13 to 40%. Further, of those who recidivate, many commit their second crime after a long interval without offense. In cases of sex offenders, as compared to other criminals, the propensity to commit crimes does not decrease over time.... [I]n one study, 48% of the recidivist sex offenders repeated during the first five years and 52% during the next 17 years * * *.

As Doe acknowledges, successful treatment of sex offenders appears to be rare. * * *

* * *

* * * As a group, sex offenders are significantly more likely than other repeat offenders to reoffend with sex crimes or other violent crimes, and that tendency persists over time. * * *

* * *

II
The Laws and the Attorney General's Guidelines

Despite complexities of detail, the Registration Law is basically simple. It requires registration of sex offenders convicted after its effective date and all prior-convicted offenders whose conduct was found to be repetitive and compulsive. The sex offenses that trigger the laws for those previously convicted are aggravated sexual assault, sexual assault, aggravated criminal sexual contact, kidnapping * * *, and for those convicted after their effective date, added to the foregoing are various laws concerning endangering the welfare of a child, luring or enticing, criminal sexual contact if the victim is a minor, and kidnapping, criminal restraint, or false imprisonment if the victim is a minor and the offender not the parent; and in all cases an attempt to commit any of the foregoing.

Registration requires, in the case of those no longer in custody—generally those who committed the offense before adoption of the laws—appearance at a local police station for fingerprinting, photographing, and providing information for a registration form that will include a physical description, the offense involved, home address, employment or school address, vehicle used, and license plate number. For those in custody, the procedure is effected at that location. The forms, information, fingerprints, and photographs (or copies) are centrally collected by the State Police and prosecutors. The registration requirement applies to all convicts, all juveniles, no matter what their age, found delinquent because of the commission of those offenses, and to all found not guilty by reason of insanity. The requirements apply as well to sex offenders convicted elsewhere who relocate to this state. Registrants whose conduct was repetitive and compulsive must verify their addresses with the local law enforcement agency quarterly, other registrants must do so annually. Upon relocation to another municipality, re-registration is required there, and, apparently, any change of address requires notice to the local law enforcement agency.

All of these are lifetime requirements unless the registrant has been offense-free for fifteen years following conviction or release from a correctional facility (whichever is later) and, on application to terminate these obligations, can persuade the court that he or she is not likely to pose a threat to the safety of others. Registration records are open to any law enforcement agency in the state, or any other state, or any federal law enforcement agency. Failure to comply with the Registration Law is a fourth-degree crime.

The Community Notification Law requires the local chief of police to give notification of the registrant's presence in the community, such notification is also required if the registrant changes address (presumably whether within or outside of the community although the statutory language refers only to the latter). The law provides for three levels of notification (referred to as Tiers One, Two and Three in the Guidelines) depending on the risk of reoffense.

(1) If risk of reoffense is low, law enforcement agencies likely to encounter the person registered shall be notified;

(2) If risk of reoffense is moderate, organizations in the community including schools, religious and youth organizations shall be notified in accordance with the Attorney General's Guidelines, in addition to the notice required by paragraph (1) of this subsection;

(3) If risk of reoffense is high, the public shall be notified through means in accordance with the Attorney General's Guidelines designed to reach members of the public likely to encounter the person registered, in addition to the notice required by paragraphs (1) and (2) of this subsection.

* * * Although the statute provides that the risk of reoffense, and therefore the extent (the level, the Tier) of notification shall be assessed by the prosecutors of the county of conviction and the county of residence together with any law enforcement officials that either deems appropriate, the Guidelines appear to require the final assessment to be made by one prosecutor, apparently the prosecutor of the county of residence. * * *

IV

Interpretation of Statute; Revision of Attorney General's Guidelines; Judicial Review

* * * Because we have concluded that despite its constitutionality, the statute sufficiently impinges on liberty interests to trigger both procedural due process and the fairness doctrine in our state, those subject to the statute are entitled to the protection of procedures designed to assure that the risk of reoffense and the extent of notification are fairly evaluated before Tier Two or Tier Three notification is implemented. * * * [W]e have concluded that judicial review through a summary proceeding should be available prior to notification if sought by any person covered by the law. * * *

[The court proceeded to describe the nature of the notice and opportunity to be heard the offender must receive, and the procedure that must be followed in the court hearing.]

In these proceedings, the State shall have the burden of going forward, that burden satisfied by the presentation of evidence that *prima facie* justifies the proposed level and manner of notification. Upon such proof, the offender shall have the burden of persuasion on both issues, that burden to remain with the offender. In other words, the court, assuming the State has satisfied its burden of going forward, shall affirm the prosecutor's determination unless it is persuaded by a preponderance of the evidence that it does not conform to the laws and Guidelines. * * *

The only issue for the court on the Tier level of notification is the risk of reoffense. In that sense the factors of the Guidelines noting the characteristics of prior offenses or of the offender are relevant only to the risk of reoffense, *i.e.*, the likelihood of its occurrence. That is the clear intent of the statute. All offenders required to register are, by statute, subject to at least Tier One notification, meaning that no matter how low the risk of reoffense, the Legislature has concluded Tier One notification is required. * * *

As for the manner of notification, the limitations set forth in our opinion are mandatory. For Tier Two notification, only those community organizations that own or operate an establishment where children gather under their care, or where women are cared for, shall qualify, and only those that are "likely to encounter" the offender as discussed in connection with Tier Three. The notice that goes out to such organizations shall specifically direct them *not* to notify anyone else, that being the acknowledged intent of the statute as interpreted by the Attorney General, an interpretation with which we agree. Organizations concerned with the welfare of children and women, but not having them under their custody or care, do not qualify, and as we understand the Guidelines, the Attorney General does not take a different position. There shall be no automatic inclusion of an organization simply because it is "registered." Tier Two notification can easily amount to the same notification as required for Tier Three if these limitations are not observed. * * *

As for the manner and extent of notification under Tier Three, "likely to encounter" clearly includes the immediate neighborhood of the offender's residence and not just the people next door. It presumably would include (since Tier Three includes Tier Two notification) all schools within the municipality, depending on its size, and we see no reason why it should not include schools and other institutions in adjacent municipalities depending upon their distance from the offender's residence, place of work, or school. * * *

We do not automatically exclude, however, notification to a group carefully selected to include only those "likely to encounter" the offender. There may be instances where the administrative difficulties of notification will warrant such a procedure. Furthermore, in certain instances the members of the public likely to encounter the offender may include children at a nearby school in which case it may be appropriate for the parents of such children to be notified, as well as the children, and that notification may most effectively be given at a meeting at the school that could include a description of safety measures that would enable the parents to reinforce whatever instructions the children may have been given by the school. * * *

We assume that the media will exercise responsibility in this matter in recognition of the critical societal interest involved. In particular, we assume that the media will not knowingly frustrate the explicit legislative goal of confining notification to those likely to encounter the offender. In other settings, all sectors of the media have voluntarily and on their own initiative, where they thought the public interest was served, consistently restrained their articles, coverage and reporting, *e.g.*, withholding the name of rape victims. * * *

V

Challenges Based on the Claim that the Laws Constitute Punishment

* * *

D

The laws, as we have described them above, when measured against the standards of the cases that determine whether a provision, statute or sanction constitutes punishment, leave no doubt that they are remedial. The legislative intent, based on the history of the legislation and the recitals in the laws themselves, is clearly and totally remedial in purpose and no challenge whatsoever is made to that proposition by any of the parties. They were designed simply and solely to enable the public to protect itself from the danger posed by sex offenders, such offenders widely regarded as having the highest risk of recidivism. * * * "There is no doubt that preventing danger to the community is a legitimate regulatory goal." * * * [The court thus rejected contentions that the Registration and Notification acts were ex post facto laws or inflicted double jeopardy.].

* * *

The law does not apply to all offenders but only to sex offenders, and as for those who may have committed their offenses many years ago, it applies only to those who were found to be repetitive and compulsive offenders, *i.e.*, those most likely, even many years later, to reoffend, providing a justification that strongly supports the remedial intent and nature of the law. It applies to those with no culpability, not guilty by reason of insanity, those who would clearly be excluded if punishment were the goal but included for remedial purposes. And it applies to juveniles, similarly an unlikely target for double punishment but included for remedial protective purposes.

The notification provisions are as carefully tailored as one could expect in order to perform their remedial function without excessively intruding on the anonymity of the offender. The division of notification into Tiers has that as its clear purpose, and the definition of the factors that determine the Tiers are those not only rationally related, but strongly related to the risk of reoffense and the consequent need for greater or lesser notification. The warnings against vigilantism, the requirements of confidentiality, the restriction of notification to those likely to encounter the offender, all point unerringly both at a remedial intent and remedial implementation.

* * *

Plaintiff's additional claims that the challenged provisions of Megan's Law violate the Bill of Attainder and Cruel and Unusual Punishment Clauses of the State and Federal Constitutions rest upon the premise that the provisions impose punishment. The Bill of Attainder Clause prohibits the legislature from determining guilt and inflicting punishment upon an individual or an easily ascertainable group of individuals without the protections of a judicial trial, and the Cruel and Unusual Punishment Clause prohibits the imposition of punishment which is "grossly disproportionate" to the offense involved. Because the challenged provisions do not constitute punishment, they do not violate any constitutional prohibition against punishment. * * *

[The court held that the registration and notification laws did not violate the plaintiff's federal or state constitutional rights (1) to privacy, because the state interest in public disclosure "substantially outweighs" the plaintiff's privacy interest, or (2) to equal protection, because the laws were rationally related to the legitimate state interest in protecting the public.]

* * *

Notes and Questions

1. *Aftermath.* On May 30, 1997, Megan Kanka's abductor was convicted of kidnapping, four counts of aggravated sexual assault, and two counts of felony murder. On June 20, he was sentenced to death. See William Glaberson, Killer in "Megan" Case Is Sentenced to Death, N.Y. Times, June 21, 1997, at A1. The state supreme court upheld the conviction and sentence. See State v. Timmendequas, 737 A.2d 55 (N.J.1999).

2. *The record in the courts.* Most courts have upheld the constitutionality of sex-offender registration/notification acts. See, e.g., Doe v. Attorney Gen'l, 686 N.E.2d 1007, 1009 n. 3 (Mass.1997) (citing decisions). Where the issue has been raised, however, courts have generally held that sex offenders must have opportunity for a pre-notification hearing to determine whether they pose a continuing threat to children and other persons in the community. See, e.g., Doe v. Pryor, 61 F.Supp.2d 1224 (M.D.Ala.1999); but see, e.g., Cutshall v. Sundquist, 193 F.3d 466 (6th Cir.1999) (hearing not required). Shortly after a federal judge upheld a constitutional challenge to New York's Megan's Law, a New York tabloid called him "the pervert's pal." Rogues Gallery of Junk Judges, N.Y. Daily News, Mar. 31, 1996, at 40 (editorial).

3. *Registration by delinquents.* Most state registration statutes apply only to perpetrators convicted in criminal court, but some statutes (including New Jersey's) also apply to adjudicated delinquents. The affected juveniles range from ones who commit forcible rape to B.G., a twelve-year-old adjudicated delinquent for reportedly groping his eight-year-old stepbrother while they were in the bathtub. In In re B.G., 674 A.2d 178, 185 (N.J.App.Div. 1996), the court held that the registration and notification requirements would continue even after the general effect of the delinquency adjudication terminated on B.G.'s eighteenth birthday. Courts have held that despite juvenile court confidentiality statutes, court records must be disclosed to the extent necessary to effectuate the registration requirement. See, e.g., Doe v. Attorney Gen'l, 680 N.E.2d 92, 95–96 (Mass.1997).

Challenges to the general constitutionality of juvenile registration and notification statutes, pressed on a variety of grounds, have been unavailing. See, e.g., In re C.D.N., 559 N.W.2d 431 (Minn.Ct.App.1997) (holding that mandatory registration did not violate delinquents' due process rights by imposing an "adult sanction" without granting them the right to a jury trial in juvenile court).

Should state registration and notification provisions reach delinquents?

4. *Is vigilantism a problem?* Doe v. Poritz recognized that community notification might invite violence and vigilantism against sex offenders who have served their sentences, and might leave these offenders unable to live free of threatened or actual violence. The court, however, perceived not "a society clamoring for blood, demanding the names of previously-convicted sex offenders in order to further punish them, but rather families concerned about their children who want information only in order to protect them." Dissenting Justice Gary S. Stein called the majority's confidence "simply unrealistic" and recited from the record several acts of violence against released sex offenders following public notification. 662 A.2d at 430–31 (Stein, J., dissenting).

5. *Capital punishment for rapists of children?* In Louisiana and Georgia, rape of a child is punishable by death even where the victim survives. See La. Rev. Stat. § 14:42(A)(4) (child under 12); Ga. Code § 16–6–1(b)(1) (child under 10). The Louisiana statute specifies that the defendant's lack of knowledge of the victim's age is not a defense.

In a prosecution charging a defendant with raping three girls between the ages of five and nine (including his daughter) when he knew he was HIV-positive, the Louisiana Supreme Court upheld the statute in State v. Wilson, 685 So.2d 1063 (La.1996), cert. denied sub nom. Bethley v. Louisiana, 520 U.S. 1259 (1997). The court rejected contentions that because the victim's death is not an element of rape, the death penalty constitutes cruel and unusual punishment under the Eighth Amendment and the state constitution. The court concluded that "[r]ape of a child less than twelve years of age is like no other crime," that children "need special protection," and that the capital punishment option deters commission of the crime. 685 So. 2d at 1067, 1073.

The state supreme court decision came on appeal from motions to quash indictments. When the Supreme Court denied certiorari, Justices Stevens, Ginsburg and Breyer stated that the Court could entertain certiorari petitions again after conviction and sentence. A decision on the merits would confront Coker v. Georgia, 433 U.S. 584, 592 (1977) (plurality opinion), which held that capital punishment for rape of the surviving adult victim constituted cruel and unusual punishment.

A 1997 poll reported that 65% of Americans supported the death penalty for child molesters. See John Q. Barrett, Death for Child Rapists May Not Save Children, Nat'l L.J., Aug. 18, 1997, at A21. Quite apart from Eighth Amendment jurisprudence, however, the Louisiana and Georgia legislation raise several intriguing questions, largely because the vast majority of child victims of sex crimes are attacked by family members or close family friends. Would the protracted proceedings that characterize death penalty litigation unduly traumatize child victims for years? Should child victims be put in the position of having to provide the key testimony that results in a death sentence? Would some rapists go free because some child victims and their parents, normally reluctant to testify in sex abuse cases, would refuse to testify in capital cases? Would statutory rape, already vastly underreported, become even more underreported because parents and their children would be even less willing to come forward if the death penalty were an option? Where a rapist has any awareness of the death penalty statute, would the statute remove the rapist's incentive to spare the life of his child victim, perhaps the only eyewitness against him? Because any sexual intercourse with a child twelve or under constitutes statutory rape, anyone who engages in nonforcible intercourse with an underage victim could be put to death; does the statute thus cast too wide a net? Does *Hendricks* suggest a better way to keep molesting recidivists off the streets? Or does the death penalty reflect justifiable public outrage at the rape of a child?

6. *Castration for rapists of children?* In 1996, California became the first state to mandate that some twice-convicted child molesters be chemically castrated shortly before parole, unless the molester elects surgical castration. Cal. Penal Law § 645(a). Montana, Florida and Texas have since enacted legislation that expressly sanctions surgical castration for persons convicted of specified sex offenses involving child victims. Florida, like California, requires courts to order castration of second offenders. Montana permits but does not require courts to order castration of particular classes of sex offenders. Texas permits physicians to perform surgical castration on some sex offenders, but does not require courts to order castration of any class of

sex offender. See William Winslade et al., Castrating Pedophiles Convicted of Sex Offenses Against Children: New Treatment or Old Punishment?, 51 SMU L. Rev. 349, 376–86 (1998). Professor Winslade believes castration of convicted sex offenders would be unconstitutional, at least unless the inmate voluntarily decides to undergo surgical castration, the inmate is free from coercion when deciding, and surgical castration is clinically indicated. Id. at 387.

Forced-castration orders and the ensuing constitutional showdown are not likely in California or Florida for several years. The states' mandates apply only to persons convicted after the legislation's effective dates (January 1, 1997 and October 1, 1997 respectively), and these persons would likely serve substantial prison terms before parole and castration become issues.

7. *References.* Megan's Law and the Protection of the Child in the On–Line Age, 35 Am. Crim. L. Rev. 1319 (1998) (debate); Symposium: Critical Perspectives on Megan's Law: Protection vs. Privacy, 13 N.Y.L. Sch. J. Hum. Rts. 1 (1996); Symposium on Megan's Law, 6 B.U. Pub. Int. L.J. 29 (1996); Symposium: The Treatment of Sex Offenders, 23 New Eng. J. on Crim. & Civ. Confinement 267 (1997); Comment, The Child Sex Offender Registration Laws: The Punishment, Liberty Deprivation, and Unintended Results Associated with the Scarlet Letter Laws of the 1990s, 90 Nw. U. L. Rev. 788, 849–56 (1996).

SECTION 3. CHILD PORNOGRAPHY

"Human dignity is offended by the pornographer. American law does not protect all human dignity; legally, an adult can consent to its diminishment. When a child is made the target of the pornographer-photographer, the statute will not suffer the insult to the human spirit, that the child should be treated as a thing." United States v. Wiegand, 812 F.2d 1239, 1245 (9th Cir. 1987). The last sentence's wisdom may seem self-evident today, but its constitutional basis remained uncertain into the early 1980s.

NEW YORK v. FERBER

Supreme Court of the United States, 1982.
458 U.S. 747.

JUSTICE WHITE delivered the opinion of the Court.

At issue in this case is the constitutionality of a New York criminal statute which prohibits persons from knowingly promoting sexual performances by children under the age of 16 by distributing material which depicts such performances.

I

In recent years, the exploitive use of children in the production of pornography has become a serious national problem. The Federal Government and 47 States have sought to combat the problem with statutes specifically directed at the production of child pornography. At least half of such statutes do not require that the materials produced be legally obscene. Thirty-five States and the United States Congress have also passed legislation prohibiting the distribution of such materials; 20 States prohibit the distribution of material depicting children engaged in sexual conduct without requiring that the material be legally obscene.

New York is one of the 20. In 1977, the New York Legislature enacted Article 263 of its Penal Law. Section 263.05 criminalizes as a class C felony the use of a child in a sexual performance:

> "A person is guilty of the use of a child in a sexual performance if knowing the character and content thereof he employs, authorizes or induces a child less than sixteen years of age to engage in a sexual performance or being a parent, legal guardian or custodian of such child, he consents to the participation by such child in a sexual performance."

A "[s]exual performance" is defined as "any performance or part thereof which includes sexual conduct by a child less than sixteen years of age." § 263.00(1). "Sexual conduct" is in turn defined in § 263.00(3):

> " 'Sexual conduct' means actual or simulated sexual intercourse, deviate sexual intercourse, sexual bestiality, masturbation, sado-masochistic abuse, or lewd exhibition of the genitals."

A performance is defined as "any play, motion picture, photograph or dance" or "any other visual representation exhibited before an audience." § 263.00(4).

At issue in this case is § 263.15, defining a class D felony:

> "A person is guilty of promoting a sexual performance by a child when, knowing the character and content thereof, he produces, directs or promotes any performance which includes sexual conduct by a child less than sixteen years of age."

To "promote" is also defined:

> " 'Promote' means to procure, manufacture, issue, sell, give, provide, lend, mail, deliver, transfer, transmute, publish, distribute, circulate, disseminate, present, exhibit or advertise, or to offer or agree to do the same." § 263.00(5).

A companion provision bans only the knowing dissemination of obscene material. § 263.10.

This case arose when Paul Ferber, the proprietor of a Manhattan bookstore specializing in sexually oriented products, sold two films to an undercover police officer. The films are devoted almost exclusively to depicting young boys masturbating. Ferber was indicted on two counts of violating § 263.10 and two counts of violating § 263.15, the two New York laws controlling dissemination of child pornography. After a jury trial, Ferber was acquitted of the two counts of promoting an obscene sexual performance, but found guilty of the two counts under § 263.15, which did not require proof that the films were obscene. * * *

The New York Court of Appeals [held] that § 263.15 violated the First Amendment. * * *

II

* * *

* * * This case * * * constitutes our first examination of a statute directed at and limited to depictions of sexual activity involving children. We believe our inquiry should begin with the question of whether a State has somewhat more freedom in proscribing works which portray sexual acts or lewd exhibitions of genitalia by children.

A

* * * [T]he Court squarely held in *Roth* v. *United States* (1957) that "obscenity is not within the area of constitutionally protected speech or press." * * *

Roth was followed by 15 years during which this Court struggled with "the intractable obscenity problem." Despite considerable vacillation over the proper definition of obscenity, a majority of the Members of the Court remained firm in the position that "the States have a legitimate interest in prohibiting dissemination or exhibition of obscene material when the mode of dissemination carries with it a significant danger of offending the sensibilities of unwilling recipients or of exposure to juveniles."

Throughout this period, we recognized "the inherent dangers of undertaking to regulate any form of expression." Consequently, our difficulty was not only to assure that statutes designed to regulate obscene materials sufficiently defined what was prohibited, but also to devise substantive limits on what fell within the permissible scope of regulation. In *Miller* v. *California* [1973], a majority of the Court agreed that a "state offense must also be limited to works which, taken as a whole, appeal to the prurient interest in sex, which portray sexual conduct in a patently offensive way, and which, taken as a whole, do not have serious literary, artistic, political, or scientific value." * * *

B

The *Miller* standard, like its predecessors, was an accommodation between the State's interests in protecting the "sensibilities of unwilling recipients" from exposure to pornographic material and the dangers of censorship inherent in unabashedly content-based laws. Like obscenity statutes, laws directed at the dissemination of child pornography run the risk of suppressing protected expression by allowing the hand of the censor to become unduly heavy. For the following reasons, however, we are persuaded that the States are entitled to greater leeway in the regulation of pornographic depictions of children.

First. It is evident beyond the need for elaboration that a State's interest in "safeguarding the physical and psychological well-being of a minor" is "compelling." "A democratic society rests, for its continuance, upon the healthy, well-rounded growth of young people into full maturity as citizens." *Prince* v. *Massachusetts.* Accordingly, we have sustained legislation aimed at protecting the physical and emotional well-being of youth even when the laws have operated in the sensitive area of constitutionally protected rights. In *Prince* v. *Massachusetts*, the Court held that a statute prohibiting use of a child to distribute literature on the street was valid notwithstanding the statute's effect on a First Amendment activity. * * * *

The prevention of sexual exploitation and abuse of children constitutes a government objective of surpassing importance. The legislative findings accompanying passage of the New York laws reflect this concern:

> "[T]here has been a proliferation of exploitation of children as subjects in sexual performances. The care of children is a sacred trust and should not be abused by those who seek to profit through a commercial network based upon the exploitation of children. The public policy of the state demands the protection of children from exploitation through sexual performances."

We shall not second-guess this legislative judgment. Respondent has not intimated that we do so. Suffice it to say that virtually all of the States and the United States have passed legislation proscribing the production of or otherwise combating "child pornography." The legislative judgment, as well as the judgment found in the relevant literature, is that the use of children as subjects of pornographic materials is harmful to the physiological, emotional, and mental health of the child. That judgment, we think, easily passes muster under the First Amendment.

Second. The distribution of photographs and films depicting sexual activity by juveniles is intrinsically related to the sexual abuse of children in at least two ways. First, the materials produced are a permanent record of the children's participation and the harm to the child is exacerbated by their circulation. Second, the distribution network for child pornography must be closed if the production of material which requires the sexual exploitation of children is to be effectively controlled. Indeed, there is no serious contention that the legislature was unjustified in believing that it is difficult, if not impossible, to halt the exploitation of children by pursuing only those who produce the photographs and movies. While the production of pornographic materials is a low-profile, clandestine industry, the need to market the resulting products requires a visible apparatus of distribution. The most expeditious if not the only practical method of law enforcement may be to dry up the market for this material by imposing severe criminal penalties on persons selling, advertising, or otherwise promoting the product. Thirty-five States and Congress have concluded that restraints on the distribution of pornographic materials are required in order to effectively combat the problem, and there is a body of literature and testimony to support these legislative conclusions.

Respondent does not contend that the State is unjustified in pursuing those who distribute child pornography. Rather, he argues that it is enough for the State to prohibit the distribution of materials that are legally obscene under the *Miller* test. While some States may find that this approach properly accommodates its interests, it does not follow that the First Amendment prohibits a State from going further. The *Miller* standard, like all general definitions of what may be banned as obscene, does not reflect the State's particular and more compelling interest in prosecuting those who promote the sexual exploitation of children. Thus, the question under the *Miller* test of whether a work, taken as a whole, appeals to the prurient interest of the average person bears no connection to the issue of whether a child has been physically or psychologically harmed in the production of the work. Similarly, a sexually explicit depiction need not be "patently offensive" in order to have required the sexual exploitation of a child for its production. In addition, a work which, taken on the whole, contains serious literary, artistic, political, or scientific value may nevertheless embody the hardest core of child pornography. "It is irrelevant to the child [who has been abused] whether or not the material . . . has a literary, artistic, political or social value." We therefore cannot conclude that the *Miller* standard is a satisfactory solution to the child pornography problem.

Third. The advertising and selling of child pornography provide an economic motive for and are thus an integral part of the production of such materials, an activity illegal throughout the Nation. * * * We note that were the statutes outlawing the employment of children in these films and photographs fully effective, and the constitutionality of these laws has not been questioned, the First Amendment implications would be no greater than that presented by laws against distribution: enforceable production laws would leave no child pornography to be marketed.

Fourth. The value of permitting live performances and photographic reproductions of children engaged in lewd sexual conduct is exceedingly modest, if not *de minimis.* We consider it unlikely that visual depictions of children performing sexual acts or lewdly exhibiting their genitals would often constitute an important and necessary part of a literary performance or scientific or educational work. As a state judge in this case observed, if it were necessary for literary or artistic value, a person over the statutory age who perhaps looked younger could be utilized. Simulation outside of the prohibition of the statute could provide another alternative. Nor is there any question here of censoring a particular literary theme or portrayal of sexual activity. The First Amendment interest is limited to that of rendering the portrayal somewhat more "realistic" by utilizing or photographing children.

Fifth. * * * When a definable class of material, such as that covered by § 263.15, bears so heavily and pervasively on the welfare of children engaged in its production, we think the balance of competing interests is clearly struck and that it is permissible to consider these materials as without the protection of the First Amendment.

C

There are, of course, limits on the category of child pornography which, like obscenity, is unprotected by the First Amendment. As with all legislation in this sensitive area, the conduct to be prohibited must be adequately defined by the applicable state law, as written or authoritatively construed. Here the nature of the harm to be combated requires that the state offense be limited to works that *visually* depict sexual conduct by children below a specified age. The category of "sexual conduct" proscribed must also be suitably limited and described.

The test for child pornography is separate from the obscenity standard enunciated in *Miller*, but may be compared to it for the purpose of clarity. The *Miller* formulation is adjusted in the following respects: A trier of fact need not find that the material appeals to the prurient interest of the average person; it is not required that sexual conduct portrayed be done so in a patently offensive manner; and the material at issue need not be considered as a whole. We note that the distribution of descriptions or other depictions of sexual conduct, not otherwise obscene, which do not involve live performance or photographic or other visual reproduction of live performances, retains First Amendment protection. As with obscenity laws, criminal responsibility may not be imposed without some element of scienter on the part of the defendant. * * *

D

* * *

We hold that § 263.15 sufficiently describes a category of material the production and distribution of which is not entitled to First Amendment protection. It is therefore clear that there is nothing unconstitutionally "underinclusive" about a statute that singles out this category of material for proscription. It also follows that the State is not barred by the First Amendment from prohibiting the distribution of unprotected materials produced outside the State.

III

* * *

B

* * *

* * * [W]e hold that § 263.15 is not substantially overbroad. We consider this the paradigmatic case of a state statute whose legitimate reach dwarfs its arguably impermissible applications. New York, as we have held, may constitutionally prohibit dissemination of material specified in § 263.15. While the reach of the statute is directed at the hard core of child pornography, the Court of Appeals was understandably concerned that some protected expression, ranging from medical textbooks to pictorials in the National Geographic would fall prey to the statute. How often, if ever, it may be necessary to employ children to engage in conduct clearly within the reach of § 263.15 in order to produce educational, medical, or artistic works cannot be known with certainty. Yet we seriously doubt, and it has not been suggested, that these arguably impermissible applications of the statute amount to more than a tiny fraction of the materials within the statute's reach. * * * Under these circumstances, § 263.15 is "not substantially overbroad and . . . whatever overbreadth may exist should be cured through case-by-case analysis of the fact situations to which its sanctions, assertedly, may not be applied." * * *

JUSTICE BLACKMUN concurs in the result.

JUSTICE O'CONNOR, concurring.

Although I join the Court's opinion, I write separately to stress that the Court does not hold that New York must except "material with serious literary, scientific, or educational value" from its statute. The Court merely holds that, even if the First Amendment shelters such material, New York's current statute is not sufficiently overbroad to support respondent's facial attack. The compelling interests identified in today's opinion suggest that the Constitution might in fact permit New York to ban knowing distribution of works depicting minors engaged in explicit sexual conduct, regardless of the social value of the depictions. For example, a 12–year-old child photographed while masturbating surely suffers the same psychological harm whether the community labels the photograph "edifying" or "tasteless." The audience's appreciation of the depiction is simply irrelevant to New York's asserted interest in protecting children from psychological, emotional, and mental harm.

* * *

JUSTICE BRENNAN, with whom JUSTICE MARSHALL joins, concurring in the judgment.

I agree with much of what is said in the Court's opinion. * * * [T]he State has a special interest in protecting the well-being of its youth. This special and compelling interest, and the particular vulnerability of children, afford the State the leeway to regulate pornographic material, the promotion of which is harmful to children, even though the State does not have such leeway when it seeks only to protect consenting adults from exposure to such material. I also agree with the Court that the "tiny fraction" of material of serious artistic, scientific, or educational value that could conceivably fall within the reach of the statute is insufficient to justify striking the statute on the grounds of overbreadth.

But in my view application of § 263.15 or any similar statute to depictions of children that in themselves do have serious literary, artistic, scientific, or medical value, would violate the First Amendment. As the Court recognizes, the limited classes of speech, the suppression of which does not raise serious First Amendment concerns, have two attributes. They are of exceedingly "slight social value," and the State has a compelling interest in their regulation. The First Amendment value of depictions of children that are in themselves serious contributions to art, literature, or science, is, by definition, simply not *"de minimis."* At the same time, the State's interest in suppression of such materials is likely to be far less compelling. For the Court's assumption of harm to the child resulting from the "permanent record" and "circulation" of the child's "participation" lacks much of its force where the depiction is a serious contribution to art or science. The production of materials of serious value is not the "low-profile, clandestine industry" that according to the Court produces purely pornographic materials. In short, it is inconceivable how a depiction of a child that is itself a serious contribution to the world of art or literature or science can be deemed "material outside the protection of the First Amendment."

* * *

Justice Stevens, concurring in the judgment [omitted].

Notes and Questions

1. *Questions about* Ferber. (a) What is "child pornography," according to *Ferber*?,

(b) *Ferber* upheld a New York statute that criminalized production or dissemination of depictions of sexual performances by children under sixteen. Would *Ferber* permit the age to be set at eighteen, as Congress did in the Child Protection Act of 1984?,

(c) How many Justices agreed with the core proposition that child pornography is not protected speech under the First Amendment?,

(d) The Supreme Court's First Amendment jurisprudence is replete with decisions protecting communication whose speaker or message, or both, are deplorable or even reprehensible to most people. Why, then, did *Ferber* take the extraordinary step of removing child pornography from the Amendment's protection?,

(e) By placing child pornography outside the First Amendment, did *Ferber* seek to protect the public, children, or both? What does *Ferber* say about child pornography's effect on persons who view it or on the community as a whole?,

(f) Under *Ferber*, may a person be convicted for publishing an article, or giving a talk, that describes children engaged in the sort of conduct involved in the films defendant Ferber sold?,

(g) Under *Ferber*, would the First Amendment permit prosecution of a defendant who produced or disseminated child pornography without a profit motive? Should the First Amendment protect such activity in the absence of a profit motive?,

(h) Would the New York statutes quoted in *Ferber* support a conviction if the photos of children engaged in sex acts were contained on a roll of undeveloped film in the defendant's camera?,

(i) In light of *Ferber*, would the First Amendment permit the state to prosecute persons who produce or disseminate a medical textbook containing photographs showing children's sex acts?

2. *Child nudity.* Ferber concerned a statute that prohibited "distribution of photographs and films depicting sexual activity by juveniles." In 1986, the Attorney General's Commission on Pornography stated that "[t]he distinguishing characteristic of child pornography, as generally understood, is that actual children are photographed while engaged in some form of sexual

activity, either with adults or with other children." Atty. Gen. Comm'n on Pornography, Final Rep. 405 (1986). In recent years, however, a number of commercial photographers have used nude and partially nude children in photo essays displayed in public exhibitions or published in books. At least one photographer regularly used her own children as nude models and received considerable remuneration for her widely distributed work. See Richard B. Woodward, The Disturbing Photography of Sally Mann, N.Y. Times Mag., Sept. 27, 1992, at 29.

The Supreme Court has not decided whether photographs and films of nude children or partially nude children, without sexual activity, constitute punishable child pornography, or whether such photographs or films constitute expression protected by the First Amendment. *Ferber's* footnote 18 stated that "nudity, without more is protected expression," but the statement was dictum because the Court was not reviewing a statute that presented the nudity issue. The Court repeated this dictum in Osborne v. Ohio, 495 U.S. 103, 112 (1990), which also did not present the issue. In Massachusetts v. Oakes, 491 U.S. 576 (1989), the Court granted certiorari to decide an overbreadth challenge to a state statute that prohibited adults from posing or exhibiting nude minors for purposes of visual representation or reproduction in any book, magazine, pamphlet, motion picture, photograph or picture. The statute excluded material "produced, processed, published, printed or manufactured for a bona fide scientific or medical purpose, or for an educational or cultural purpose for a bona fide school, museum or library." 491 U.S. at 579.

Oakes declined to determine the constitutional issue because after the Court granted certiorari, the state legislature amended the statute to punish only defendants who acted with "lascivious intent." Justice Brennan's dissent (joined by Justices Marshall and Stevens) argued that the unamended statute was impermissibly overbroad because its "blanket prohibition" of the described acts "without regard to the adult's intentions or the sexually explicit nature of the minor's conduct, nets a considerable amount of" conduct protected by the First Amendment, such as non-lewd artwork and parents' bathtub photographs of their infants and toddlers. 491 U.S. at 592–93, 597. Justice Scalia's dissent (joined by Justice Blackmun), however, concluded that the unamended statute was not impermissibly overbroad, and that its constitutionality did not depend on adult intentions or a finding of sexually explicit conduct: "Most adults, I expect, would not hire themselves out as nude models, whatever the intention of the photographer or artist, and however unerotic the pose. There is no cause to think children are less sensitive. It is not unreasonable, therefore, for a State to regard parents' using (or permitting the use) of their children as nude models, or other adults' use of consenting minors, as a form of child exploitation." 491 U.S. at 589 n.2.

In the absence of Supreme Court resolution, most lower courts have regarded photographs and films of nude children, without more, as expression protected by the First Amendment, but have upheld convictions under statutes that prohibit only such depictions made for sexual gratification. As thus limited, the depictions become child pornography proscribable under *Ferber.* See, e.g., People v. Batchelor, 800 P.2d 599, 601–03 (Colo.1990); State v. Young, 525 N.E.2d 1363, 1367–68 (Ohio 1988).

In determining whether depictions of nude children are "nudity without more" or are punishable, courts frequently apply the inclusive list of factors enunciated in United States v. Dost, 636 F.Supp. 828, 832 (S.D.Cal.1986), aff'd sub nom. United States v. Wiegand, 812 F.2d 1239, 1244 (9th Cir. 1987), a successful federal prosecution of defendants who photographed nude children in various provocative poses: "1) whether the focal point of the visual depiction is on the child's genitalia or pubic area; 2) whether the setting of the visual depiction is sexually suggestive, i.e., in a place or pose generally associated with sexual activity; 3) whether the child is depicted in an unnatural pose, or in inappropriate attire, considering the age of the child; 4) whether the child is fully or partially clothed, or nude; 5) whether the visual depiction suggests sexual coyness or a willingness to engage in sexual activity; 6) whether the visual depiction is intended or designed to elicit a sexual response in the viewer. Of course, a visual depiction need not involve all of these factors to be a 'lascivious exhibition of the genitals or pubic area.' The determination will have to be made based on the overall content of the visual depiction, taking into account the age of the minor."

3. *Proscribing private possession and viewing of child pornography.* Ferber upheld a statute that prohibited distribution of non-obscene child pornography. Neither New York's statute nor the facts of the case raised the question whether one may possess such material, and the Court did not speak to the question. In Osborne v. Ohio, supra, 495 U.S. 103, the Court upheld a statute that prohibited private possession and viewing of non-obscene child pornography (including private possession and viewing in one's own home), even without proof that the possessor intended to distribute the material. Stressing the need to protect children, the Court found that because "much of the child pornography market has been driven underground" since *Ferber*, "it is now difficult, if not impossible, to solve the child pornography problem by only attacking production and distribution." 495 U.S. at 111.

5. *Federal legislation.* The 1970 Report of the Commission on Obscenity and Pornography made no mention of the child pornography industry, and Congress did not act until the Protection of Children Against Sexual Exploitation Act of 1977 made child pornography a federal crime. (States also did not begin enacting child pornography legislation until the 1970s.)

Based on findings that the "highly organized, multimillion dollar" underground child pornography industry was interstate and international in scope, S. Rep. 95–438, at 5 (1977), the 1977 Act added three sections to the federal criminal code. The first section, now 18 U.S.C. § 2251, prohibited the use of minors in "sexually explicit" productions, and prohibited parents and guardians from allowing such use of their children. The second section, now 18 U.S.C. § 2252, made it a federal crime to transport, ship or receive in interstate commerce for the purpose of selling, any "obscene visual or print medium" if its production involved the use of a minor engaging in sexually explicit conduct. The third section, now 18 U.S.C. § 2256, as amended, contained definitions. "Minor" meant anyone under the age of sixteen years. "Producing" meant manufacturing or issuing "for pecuniary profit." "Sexually explicit conduct" comprehended five categories of activity: sexual intercourse, bestiality, masturbation, sado-masochistic abuse, and "lewd" exhibition of the genitals or pubic area. 92 Stat. 8 (1978), formerly 18 U.S.C.

§ 2253(2)(A)-(E). See, e.g., United States v. X–Citement Video, Inc., supra, 513 U.S. 64 (upholding constitutionality of § 2252).

Because of the need to prove obscenity and a pecuniary-profit motive, the 1977 Act yielded only a handful of prosecutions in its first five years of operation. Under § 2252 only 28 people were indicted and 23 convicted; under § 2251 convictions were "non-existent." H.R. Rep. 98–536, at 1, 2 (1984), reprinted in 1984 U.S.C.C.A.N. 492, 493. Relying on *Ferber*, the Child Protection Act of 1984, Pub. L. No. 98–292, 98 Stat. 204, prohibited distribution of nonobscene material depicting sexual activity by children and eliminated the "pecuniary profit" element. The 1984 Act clarified that obscenity was not the threshold by replacing the word "lewd" with the word "lascivious" in the definition of sexually explicit conduct. See, e.g., United States v. Knox, 32 F.3d 733, 736–37 (3d Cir.1994) (videotapes that focus on minor females' genitalia and pubic area may constitute a "lascivious exhibition of the genitals or pubic area" even though these body parts are covered by clothing; the Act does not require that the subjects be nude).

The 1984 Act also redefined "minor" to mean persons under eighteen, and legislated against possession by criminalizing the receipt in interstate or foreign commerce of materials showing minors engaged in sexually explicit conduct. Federal authorities could now move against a wide range of child pornography produced and disseminated by pedophiles who sought sexual gratification rather than profit. Indictments and convictions followed in large numbers. See H.R. Rep. 99–910, at 4–5 (1986), reprinted in 1986 U.S.C.C.A.N. 5952, 5954. Courts have held that the legislation does not exceed Congress' Commerce Clause authority. See, e.g., United States v. Winningham, 953 F.Supp. 1068, 1073–76 (D.Minn.1996).

Congressional legislation has continued. In 1986, for example, the lawmakers prohibited production and use of advertisements for child pornography and created a private civil remedy in favor of persons who suffer personal injury resulting from the production of child pornography. 18 U.S.C. §§ 2251(c), 2255.

The Child Pornography Prevention Act of 1996, Pub. L. No. 104–208, broadens the definition of child pornography to reach "any visual depiction, including * * * any * * * computer or computer-generated image or picture, whether made or produced by electronic, mechanical or other means * * * where such visual description is, or appears to be, of a minor engaging in sexually explicit conduct." 18 U.S.C. § 2256(8). The Act criminalizes computerized or "virtual" child pornography, which can take several forms: a photograph of a real child can be scanned, replicated and widely distributed on the Internet; a computer can manipulate, or "morph," an innocent picture of an actual child to create a sexually explicit picture; an obscene or nonobscene picture of an adult can be transformed into the image of a child; or the image of a nonexistent child (ranging from a simple cartoon character to a high-resolution image resembling a real child) can be generated wholly by computer graphics. "Through readily available desktop computer programs, one can even create a realistic picture of an imaginary child engaged in sexual activity and pass off that creation as an image of a real child." United States v. Hilton, 167 F.3d 61, 65 (1st Cir. 1999).

Because computerized child pornography need not use actual identifiable children, the 1996 Act is based squarely on the material's effect on viewers. Congress found that "[c]omputer generated images which appear to depict minors engaging in sexually explicit conduct are just as dangerous to the well-being of * * * children as material produced using actual children." Sen. Rep. No. 104–358, at 19 (1996). The lawmakers found danger because child pornography "stimulates the sexual appetites and encourages the activities of child molesters and pedophiles, who use it to feed their sexual fantasies," S. Rep.104–358, at 12 (1996), and because child molesters and pedophiles use child pornography "as a device to break down the resistance and inhibitions of their victims or targets of molestation, especially when these are children." Id. at 13. "A child who may be reluctant to engage in sexual activity with an adult, or to pose for sexually explicit photos, can sometimes be persuaded to do so by viewing depictions of other children participating in such activity." Id.

By focusing on viewers rather than on the child performers, the 1996 legislation raises an interesting constitutional question. Does the First Amendment permit Congress or the states to prohibit production, dissemination and possession of nonobscene sexually explicit computerized images not involving an actual identifiable child? Before the cyberspace age, *Ferber* granted states "greater leeway in the regulation of pornographic depictions of children," but removed child pornography from First Amendment protection because of its present and future harmful effects on the actual child performers, without discussing any effect child pornography might have on viewers. The Court specified in dictum that "the distribution of descriptions or other depictions of sexual conduct, not otherwise obscene, which do not involve live performance or photographic or other visual reproduction of live performances, retains First Amendment protection." Do you see any other passages in *Ferber* that indicate the Court considered only depictions of actual children?

Courts have split on the 1996 Act's constitutionality. See Free Speech Coalition v. Reno, 198 F.3d 1083 (9th Cir. 1999) (holding that the Act imposes content-based restrictions on protected speech, unsupported by a compelling state interest because the restricted images are not of real children); United States v. Hilton, 167 F.3d 61, 65 (1st Cir. 1999) (holding that the Act is a content-based regulation, but that child pornography in any form may be "freely regulated" because it is outside the First Amendment; the Act neither impinges substantially on protected expression nor is so vague as to offend due process).

5. *Photo processors*. Congress and a number of states require photo processors to report customers' sexual depictions of children on film. These statutes typically extend beyond films made by commercial customers and may reach parents and guardians who do nothing more than film their toddlers on bear skin rugs and the like. Processors are typically granted immunity from civil or criminal liability arising from filing a required report in good faith. See, e.g., 42 U.S.C. § 13031; Cal. Penal Code § 11166.

6. *References*. Debra D. Burke, The Criminalization of Virtual Child Pornography: A Constitutional Question, 34 Harv. J. Legis. 439 (1997); L. Steven Grasz and Patrick J. Pfaltzgraff, Child Pornography and Child

Nudity: Why and How States May Constitutionally Regulate the Production, Possession, and Distribution of Nude Visual Depictions of Children, 71 Temp. L. Rev. 609 (1998); John Quigley, Child Pornography and the Right to Privacy, 43 Fla. L. Rev. 347 (1991); Frederick Schauer, Codifying the First Amendment: *New York v. Ferber*, 1982 S. Ct. Rev. 285.

7. *Regulating media influences on children. Ferber* placed child pornography outside the First Amendment's protections. In recent years, however, First Amendment constraints have frequently upset legislative efforts to control children's access to violent or sexually suggestive influences in such media as television, movies, music and video games. Judicial scrutiny emanates from core propositions: (1) "Material limited to forms of violence is given the highest degree of [First Amendment] protection," Sovereign News Co. v. Falke, 448 F.Supp. 306, 394 (N.D.Ohio 1977); (2) "Sexual expression which is indecent but not obscene is protected by the First Amendment," Sable Communications of Cal., Inc. v. FCC, 492 U.S. 115, 126 (1989); and (3) "Minors are entitled to a significant measure of First Amendment protection, and only in relatively narrow and well-defined circumstances may government bar public dissemination of protected materials to them," Erznoznik v. City of Jacksonville, 422 U.S. 205, 212–13 (1975). A few representative decisions highlight the salient issues:

a. In Ginsberg v. New York, 390 U.S. 629 (1968), the Court affirmed the defendant retail store owners' convictions for selling a sixteen-year-old boy two magazines featuring photographs of nude women. The Court acknowledged that the magazines were not obscene for adults. The challenged statute, however, prohibited the sale to minors under seventeen of material defined to be obscene based on its appeal to children regardless of whether the material would be obscene for adults. The statute operated only against material that was "utterly without redeeming social importance for minors." Id. at 646.

Even before *Ginsberg*, obscenity was not entitled to First Amendment protection; *Ginsberg* left unprotected material that the legislature rationally found obscene as to minors. Writing for the majority, Justice Brennan concluded that the challenged statute's variable concept of obscenity did not violate minors' First Amendment rights because "the power of the state to control the conduct of children reaches beyond the scope of its authority over adults." Id. at 638 (citing Prince v. Massachusetts). Two state interests justified limiting minors' access to the material the legislature had rationally determined might be harmful: (1) Because "the parents' claim to authority in their own household to direct the rearing of their children is basic in the structure of our society, * * * [t]he legislature could properly conclude that parents and others, teachers for example, who have this primary responsibility for children's well-being are entitled to the support of laws designed to aid discharge of that responsibility," and (2) the state "has an independent interest in the well-being of its youth. * * *: 'While the supervision of children's reading may best be left to their parents, the knowledge that parental control or guidance cannot always be provided and society's transcendent interest in protecting the welfare of children justify reasonable regulation of the sale of material to them." Id. at 639–40.

Ginsberg stressed that the challenged statute did not prohibit persons from stocking the magazines and selling them to persons seventeen or older, including parents who might wish to purchase them for their underage children. Id. at 634–35, 639.

b.   In Reno v. ACLU, 521 U.S. 844, 849 (1997), the Court held that despite "the legitimacy and importance of the congressional goal of protecting children from harmful materials," two provisions of the Communications Decency Act of 1996 violated the First Amendment. Both provisions concerned communications on the Internet. The first provision prohibited the knowing transmission of obscene or indecent messages to any recipient under 18, and the second prohibited the knowing sending or displaying of patently offensive messages in a manner that is available to a person under 18.

The Court distinguished *Ginsberg* on the grounds that the statute reviewed in the 1968 decision did not prohibit parents from securing the assertedly objectionable material for their children, regulated only commercial transactions, reached only material "utterly without redeeming social importance for minors," and applied only to children under seventeen. Id. at 865–66. *Reno* held that the CDA, which contained none of these limitations, "effectively suppresses a large amount of speech that adults have a constitutional right to receive and to address to one another." "[T]he governmental interest in protecting children from harmful materials * * * does not justify an unnecessarily broad suppression of speech addressed to adults. * * * [T]he Government may not 'reduc[e] the adult population ... to ... only what is fit for children.' " Id. at 874–75.

c.   In Video Software Dealers Ass'n v. Webster, 968 F.2d 684 (8th Cir. 1992), the court of appeals struck down a state statute that prohibited the rental or sale of violent videos to minors and required dealers to display or maintain such videos in separate areas within their rental stores. In an effort to describe the proscribed class of videos, the statute adapted the Miller v. California obscenity test (which *Ferber* quotes in relevant part above). A video was violent if "(1) Taken as a whole and applying contemporary community standards, the average person would find that it has a tendency to cater or appeal to morbid interests in violence for persons under the age of seventeen; and (2) It depicts violence in a way which is patently offensive to the average person applying contemporary adult community standards with respect to what is suitable for persons under the age of seventeen; and (3) Taken as a whole, it lacks serious literary, artistic, political, or scientific value for persons under the age of seventeen." Id. at 687.

Webster rejected the state's threshold effort to invoke *Ginsberg*, holding that videos which depict violence without sexual conduct cannot be obscene for either minors or adults because obscenity encompasses only expression that depicts or describes sexual conduct. Id. at 688. Then the court of appeals held that the challenged statute was not narrowly tailored to promote an articulated, compelling state interest without unnecessarily interfering with First Amendment freedom of expression; the statute "covers all types of violence," including "animated violence in many cartoon shows, simulated violence in western and war movies, real violence in the boxing ring, or psychological violence in suspense stories or 'thrillers'." Id. at 689. The panel also found the statute unconstitutionally vague because it failed to specifically define the type of violent acts covered and forced courts to provide the definition only "on a video-by-video basis." Id. at 690.

See generally, e.g., Harry T. Edwards and Mitchell N. Berman, Regulating Violence on Television, 89 Nw. U. L. Rev. 1487 (1995); Richard P. Salgado, Regulating a Video Revolution, 7 Yale L. & Pol'y Rev. 516 (1989); Kevin W. Saunders, Media Violence and the Obscenity Exception to the First Amendment, 3 Wm. & Mary Bill of Rts. L. J. 107 (1994); Symposium: The Music and Obscenity Controversy, 15 Nova L. Rev. 118 (1991); Symposium: Should Cyberspace be a Free Speech Zone?: Filters, "Family Friendliness," and the First Amendment, 15 N.Y.L. Sch. J. Hum. Rts. 1 (1998); Michael J. Fucci, Facing the Future: An Analysis of the Television Ratings System, 6 UCLA Ent. L. Rev. 1 (1998); Eugene Volokh, Freedom of Speech, Shielding Children, Transcending Balancing, 1997 S. Ct. Rev. 141; R. Polk Wagner, Filters and the First Amendment, 83 Minn. L. Rev. 755 (1999); Edith Wise, A Historical Perspective on the Protection of Children From Broadcast Indecency, 3 Vill. Sports & Ent. L.J. 15 (1996).

Chapter 7

ADOPTION

SECTION 1. INTRODUCTION

JAMIL S. ZAINALDIN, THE EMERGENCE OF A MODERN AMERICAN FAMILY LAW: CHILD CUSTODY, ADOPTION, AND THE COURTS, 1796–1851

73 Nw. U. L. Rev. 1038, 1041–45 (1979).

* * *

Like many aspects of family law, the status of adoption can be traced back through early civilization. Adoption existed in ancient Greece and Rome, in portions of continental Europe that "received" Roman law in the fifteenth century, in the Middle East, in Asia, and in the tribal societies of Africa and Oceania. Adoption in history ordinarily served one or more purposes: preventing the extinction of a bloodline, preserving a sacred descent group, facilitating the generational transfer of a patrimony, providing for ancestral worship, or mending the ties between factious clans or tribes. In each case the adoption of an individual, most often an adult male, fulfilled some kin, religious, or communal requirement.

Yet, unlike most historical phenomena, the first instance of departure from the traditional model of adoption can be isolated by location, day, and year. On April 2, 1847, the Massachusetts House of Representatives ordered that the Committee on the Judiciary consider "the expediency of providing by law for the adoption of children." On May 13, 1851, the Committee reported to the House "A Bill for the Adoption of Children." There seems to have been little or no opposition. Eleven days later the Massachusetts legislature passed the first general "Act to Provide for the Adoption of Children" in America.

The Massachusetts adoption statute of 1851 was the first *modern* adoption law in history. It is notable for two reasons. First, it contradicted the most fundamental principles of English domestic relations law, and overruled centuries of English precedent and legislation which prohibited the absolute, permanent, and voluntary transfer of parental power to third persons. Second, the traditional status of adoption allocated benefits between the giver and taker, while the Massachusetts statute distinguished the adoptee as the prime beneficiary. The heart of the adoption transaction became the judicially monitored transfer of rights with due regard for the *welfare of the child* and the *parental qualifications* of the adopters.

Within the next twenty-five years, more than a score of states would enact some form of adoption law, and in most cases the Massachusetts statute served as a model. Strangely, it would seem, the passage of the first Massachusetts act attracted little public attention. Little or no debate over the issue occurred in the legislature, apparently no social reform movements advocated passage of the law, and, when the law did appear, few newspapers bothered to take note of the event. And for several years after the passage of the statute, few adopters took advantage of the law. There is, then, no clear explanation for why the legislature passed the law when it did. Nor at first glance would there seem to be any explanation for the casual reception accorded such an apparently radical statute.

The new law may have been part of the larger legislative trend of substituting private enactments with general statutes. Private laws granting divorce, legitimacy, incorporation, and change of name were becoming particularly cumbersome in the 1840's. And there is ample evidence that children throughout the United States were being "adopted" through private acts, especially those concerning change of name. A contemporary of the nineteenth century—and an advocate of statutory adoption—thought that the law would secure important rights to the adopters. A modern commentator, however, suggests that the first general adoption statute may have evolved out of a desire to protect the perceived right of inheritance of nonlegally adopted children.

Just why the Massachusetts legislature moved in 1851 may never be known. Perhaps all of these reasons prompted the lawmakers to action. At once they endeavored to protect the child and to endow his standing in the family with status, while conferring upon adopters the rights and duties of parents. The discretionary proceeding in the probate court was perceived as the soundest, most efficient method for effecting adoption.

* * *

Notes and Questions

1. *The array of state laws.* Today all states have statutes providing for adoption of children. The various acts, and the judicial decisions interpreting them, are marked by both similarities and significant differences. Efforts at nationwide uniformity have largely failed because "state legislatures appear inclined to retain the unique attributes of their respective bodies of family law." Lehr v. Robertson, 463 U.S. 248, 257 n. 11 (1983). Only five states have enacted substantial portions of the 1969 Revised Uniform Adoption

Act, and only one state (Vermont) has enacted substantial portions of the Uniform Adoption Act (1994). Several other states have enacted various provisions of these model acts verbatim or in modified form. Lawyers should remain aware that differences in statutory language from state to state may affect the outcome in cases presenting apparently similar facts.

Because of the similarities among adoption acts, however, lawyers should remain alert to other jurisdictions' decisional and statutory law, which may be persuasive authority. Where parties to an adoption proceeding reside in different states, conflict of laws rules may also require application of another jurisdiction's adoption law.

2. *The number of U.S. adoptions annually.* Between 2% and 4% of American families have an adopted child. See Kathy S. Stolley, Statistics on Adoption in the United States, in 3 The Future of Children 26 (1993). Courts grant at least 140,000 to 160,000 adoptions annually (that is, considerably more than a million each decade), though estimates remain necessarily inexact because the U.S. Bureau of the Census, other federal agencies, and most states do not systematically track the total number. Accurate records are maintained only of international adoptees who enter the United States with the cooperation of immigration authorities, and of "special needs" children who receive federal assistance. It is estimated that in 60% or more of adoptions of children annually, the adoptive parents are relatives of the child within the third or fourth degree of consanguinity or affinity; adoptions by nonrelatives of children born in the United States probably do not account for more than 20% to 30% of adoptions each year, percentages considerably smaller than the percentage of children adopted by nonrelatives before this generation. See Joan Heifetz Hollinger, Introduction to Adoption Law and Practice § 1.05[2] [a], [b], in 1 Hollinger, Adoption Law and Practice (1998).

3. *References.* The history of American adoption law is treated in Robert B. Hill, Informal Adoption Among Black Families (1977); Joseph Ben–Or, The Law of Adoption in the United States: Its Massachusetts Origins and the Statute of 1851, 130 New Eng. Hist. & Geneal. Reg. 259–72 (1976); Tim Hacsi, From Indenture to Family Foster Care: A Brief History of Child Placing, 74 Child Welfare 162 (1995); Leo A. Huard, The Law of Adoption: Ancient and Modern, 9 Vand. L. Rev. 743 (1956); Sanford N. Katz, Rewriting the Adoption Story, 5 Fam. Advoc. 9 (1982); Yasuhide Kawashima, Adoption In Early America, 20 J. Fam. L. 677 (1981–82); Stephen B. Presser, The Historical Background of the American Law of Adoption, 11 J. Fam. L. 443 (1971).

SECTION 2. WHO MAY ADOPT A CHILD?

IN THE INTEREST OF ANGEL LACE M.

Supreme Court of Wisconsin, 1994.
516 N.W.2d 678.

STEINMETZ, JUSTICE.

* * *

On February 17, 1992, Annette G. filed a petition to adopt Angel Lace M., the daughter of Annette's partner, Georgina G. * * * We hold that this adoption is not permissible under ch. 48, Stats. * * *

Angel was born on March 10, 1986. On September 20, 1988, Georgina and Terry M. adopted Angel. Georgina and Terry were married at the time of the adoption. They separated in February, 1990, and divorced in June of that same year. Aside from paying court-ordered child support, Terry has played no part in Angel's life since late 1990.

In June, 1990, Georgina and Angel began living with Annette. The two women have shared equally in raising Angel since that time. Georgina and Annette symbolically solemnized their commitment to each other by partaking in a marriage-like ceremony in Milwaukee on August 11, 1991.[1]

On February 17, 1992, Annette filed a petition in the Brown county circuit court to adopt Angel. * * *

* * * Terry signed a statement consenting to the termination of his parental rights and testified that his consent was both voluntary and knowing. The Community Adoption Center filed a report with the court recommending the adoption. In addition, a social worker from the center testified at the hearing that the termination of Terry's parental rights and the adoption of Angel by Annette would be in Angel's best interests.

* * *

The petitioners argue that the circuit court should have granted Annette's petition for adoption because the court found that the adoption is in Angel's best interests. *See* sec. 48.01(2), Stats.[3] There is no doubt that a court must find that an adoption is in the best interests of the child before the court may grant the petition for adoption. However, the fact that an adoption—or any other action affecting a child—is in the child's best interests, by itself, does not authorize a court to grant the adoption. * * *

Were we to allow a court to grant an adoption petition any time the adoption is in the best interests of the child, there would be no need for plethora of adoption statutes other than sec. 48.01(2), Stats. * * *

"Adoption proceedings, unknown at common law, are of statutory origin and the essential statutory requirements must be substantially met to validate the proceedings." Accordingly, before we apply the best interests standard in this case, we must determine whether Annette's

---

1. Wisconsin does not recognize same-sex marriages. Hence under the laws of Wisconsin, Georgina and Annette are not married. As a result, Annette is not Angel's stepparent.

3. Section 48.01(2), Stats., provides as follows:

(2) This chapter shall be liberally construed to effect the objectives contained in this section. The best interests of the child shall always be of paramount consideration, but the court shall also consider the interest of the parents or guardian of the child, the interest of the person or persons with whom the child has been placed for adoption and the interests of the public.

proposed adoption of Angel satisfies the statutory requirements for adoption. * * *

Section 48.82, Stats.[4] controls who may adopt a minor. * * * Annette does not qualify under sec. 48.82(1)(a) because she is not legally "the husband or wife" of Georgina who is the "parent of the minor." However, Annette does fit the description in sec. 48.82(1)(b) because she is "[a]n unmarried adult."

For the adoption to be valid, not only must Annette qualify as a party who may adopt Angel, but Angel must also be eligible for adoption. Section 48.81, Stats.,[5] controls who may be adopted. * * * Pursuant to sec. 48.81(1), a minor may only be adopted if her "parental rights have been terminated...."[6] Angel's adoptive father, Terry, has consented to the termination of his parental rights. Georgina's parental rights, on the other hand, remain intact.

The petitioners claim that sec. 48.81(1), Stats., is ambiguous. According to the petitioners, the statute could mean that Angel is eligible for adoption only if the rights of *both* of her parents have been terminated. Or, it could mean that she is eligible for adoption as long as the rights of *at least one* of her parents have been terminated. The petitioners ask this court to construe the statute liberally to further the best interests of Angel, pursuant to sec. 48.01(2), and accept the second interpretation of the statute.

Under this second interpretation of the statute—that a minor is eligible for adoption as long as the rights of *at least one* of her parents have been terminated—a minor would be eligible for adoption when the rights of only one of her parents are terminated. The minor would be eligible to be adopted even if the remaining parent is legally fit to raise the child alone and prefers to raise the child alone. Ostensibly, a

---

4. Section 48.82, Stats., provides as follows:

48.82 Who may adopt. (1) The following persons are eligible to adopt a minor if they are residents of this state:

(a) A husband and wife jointly, or either the husband or wife if the other spouse is a parent of the minor.

(b) An unmarried adult.

(3) When practicable and if requested by the birth parent, the adoptive parents shall be of the same religious faith as the birth parents of the person to be adopted.

(4) No person may be denied the benefits of this subchapter because of a religious belief in the use of spiritual means through prayer for healing.

(5) Although otherwise qualified, no person shall be denied the benefits of this section because the person is deaf, blind or has other physical handicaps.

(6) No otherwise qualified person may be denied the benefits of this subchapter because of his or her race, color, ancestry or national origin.

5. Section 48.81, Stats., provides as follows:

48.81 Who may be adopted. Any minor who meets all of the following criteria may be adopted:

(1) * * * [A] minor whose parental rights have been terminated [in Wisconsin] or in another state or a foreign jurisdiction.

(2) A minor who is present within this state at the time the petition for adoption is filed.

6. We first note that this statute is poorly worded. A minor does not have parental rights that may be terminated. Rather, her parents possess these rights. The legislature must have intended to state that a minor may be adopted if her "parents' rights have been terminated...."

complete stranger could petition to adopt a minor who is a member of this stable family; and, at least pursuant to sec. 48.81, Stats., the proposed adoption would be permissible. The legislature could not have intended to declare a minor eligible for adoption under those circumstances. This would be an absurd result. This court will not construe a statute so as to work absurd or unreasonable results. Hence, we hold that pursuant to sec. 48.81(1), a minor is not eligible for adoption unless the rights of both of her parents have been terminated.[8] Because Georgina's parental rights remain intact, Angel is not eligible to be adopted by Annette.

Section 48.92, Stats.,[9] also stands in the way of Annette's proposed adoption of Angel. This statute severs the ties between the birth parent and the adopted minor after a court enters the order of adoption. Pursuant to sec. 48.92(2), if the circuit court grants Annette's petition to adopt Angel, "all the rights, duties and other legal consequences of [Georgina's relationship with Angel] *shall* cease to exist." (emphasis added.) If the legislature had intended to sanction adoptions by nonmarital partners, it would not have mandated this "cut-off" of the "rights, duties and other legal consequences" of the birth parents in these adoptions.

* * *

For this court to find that ch. 48, Stats., sanctions the proposed adoption, we must accept the petitioners' interpretation of *both* secs. 48.81(1) and 48.92(2). The petitioners interpret sec. 48.81(1) as permitting a minor to be adopted as long as the rights of *at least one* of the minor's parents are terminated. If we accept this interpretation, then a minor who still has one parent could be adopted. Section 48.82(1)(a) clearly allows "[a] husband and wife jointly" to adopt a minor. The petitioners next interpret the "cut-off" provision of sec. 48.92(2) as directory. If we also accept this interpretation, then the above husband and wife could jointly adopt the above minor without severing the ties between the remaining birth parent and the minor. The minor would then have three parents. Subsequently, a court could terminate the rights of one of the three parents and a second husband and wife could

8. This holding obviously does not apply to stepparent adoptions. In a stepparent adoption, the minor is eligible to be adopted if the rights of one of her parents are terminated. Section 48.81, Stats., does not clearly provide for this exception in the case of stepparent adoptions. However, it is clear from surrounding statutes that the legislature intended to sanction stepparent adoptions. * * *

9. Section 48.92, Stats., provides as follows:

48.92 Effect of adoption. (1) After the order of adoption is entered the relation of parent and child and all the rights, duties and other legal consequences of the natural relation of child and parent thereafter exists between the adopted person and the adoptive parents.

(2) After the order of adoption is entered the relationship of parent and child between the adopted person and the adoptive person's birth parents, unless the birth parent is the spouse of the adoptive parent, shall be completely altered and all the rights, duties and other legal consequences of the relationship shall cease to exist. Notwithstanding the extinction of all parental rights under this subsection, a court may order reasonable visitation under s. 48.925. * * *

jointly adopt the minor, giving the minor four parents. This process could go on *ad infinitum*. Obviously, the petitioners' interpretations of secs. 48.81(1) and 48.92(2), read *in pari materia*, could lead to absurd results. This court will not construe a statute so as to work absurd or unreasonable results.

To avoid this absurd result and to harmonize the rules of statutory construction discussed above, we hold that the "cut-off" provision of sec. 48.92(2), Stats., is mandatory. Hence, Georgina would lose the "rights, duties and other legal consequences of" her relationship with Angel if the circuit court granted Annette's petition to adopt Angel. This result would frustrate rather than further the petitioners' intentions. We also hold that, pursuant to sec. 48.81(1), Angel is not eligible for adoption. Therefore, we conclude that the proposed adoption does not satisfy the essential requirements of the adoption statutes and is, in fact, prohibited by these statutes. The circuit court properly denied the petitions before it despite its finding that the adoption would be in Angel's best interests.

[The court then rejected contentions that the adoption act as construed violated the constitutional rights of Angel or Annette, or both.]

GESKE, JUSTICE (*concurring*.)

I join in the majority opinion because I believe that it correctly analyzes current Wisconsin law. Although the dissents accurately point out that sec. 48.01(2), Stats., directs us to liberally construe ch. 48 with "[t]he best interests of the child" in mind, we are still bound by the statutory requirements for adoption. Those requirements are not met in this case.

I write separately only to encourage the Wisconsin legislature to revisit ch. 48 in light of all that is occurring with children in our society. The legislators, as representatives of the people of this state, have both the right and the responsibility to establish the requirements for a legal adoption, for custody, and for visitation. This court cannot play that role. We can only interpret the law, not rewrite it.

* * *

HEFFERNAN, CHIEF JUSTICE (*dissenting*).

The issue addressed in this case is whether the Wisconsin statutes governing adoption allow Annette G. to adopt Angel, a child with whom she already has a functional parent-child relationship. The adoption statutes on their face do not address this issue. * * * Section 48.01(2), Stats., states that the children's code, of which the adoption statutes are a part, "shall be liberally construed to effect the objectives contained in this section." * * *

* * *

Because the best interests of the child is "paramount", it appears that the legislature deems liberal construction of the statutes particularly appropriate when such construction effectuates the best interests of the child unless the other concerns listed outweigh the child's best interests. * * *

In the present case everyone involved agrees that the adoption is in Angel's best interests. * * *

* * *

The first relevant section in the adoption statutes is sec. 48.82(1), Stats., which governs who may adopt. * * * Annette meets the sec. 48.82(1)(b) requirement—she is an unmarried adult.

The second relevant statute is sec. 48.81, Stats., which sets forth the criteria governing who may be adopted. * * *

The portion of sec. 48.81(1) stating that an eligible minor is one "whose parental rights have been terminated" is ambiguous. * * * Looking solely at sec. 48.81, this court need not employ the legislatively-mandated canon of liberal construction in order to conclude that this statute requires that the parental rights of only one parent be terminated in order for a child to be eligible for adoption in those situations in which the remaining parent supports the adoption. Stepparent adoption is a common form of adoption but would be prohibited if sec. 48.81 is read to require that both parents' parental rights must be terminated before an adoption can take place.

In a footnote, the majority states that [the adoption act], which expressly refers to stepparent adoption, and sec. 48.81(1), read *in pari materia*, clearly allow a minor to be adopted by a stepparent. I agree. However, this conclusion does not preclude further interpretation of sec. 48.81 to determine whether a child may be eligible for adoption in other circumstances in which the rights of only one parent have been terminated. If sec. 48.81 is construed utilizing the canon of liberal construction mandated by the legislature, a child may be eligible for adoption after the rights of only one parent have been terminated as long as the remaining legal parent supports the adoption. Such an adoption will still be subject to all of the additional statutory criteria. Because the legislature mandated liberal construction it is contrary to legislative intent to strictly construe sec. 48.81 as prohibiting adoption when only one parent's rights have been terminated with the exception of adoptions otherwise expressly allowed by the statutes. This court should utilize the guidance the legislature has provided.

The third relevant statute is sec. 48.92, Stats. [effect of adoption]. * * * Section 48.92 cannot be interpreted to prohibit the adoption in this case. Section 48.92 does not establish requirements that must be met in order for an adoption to occur; rather, it defines the legal status of the parties after the adoption has been approved. * * *

* * *

When interpreting sec. 48.81, governing who may be adopted, the majority employs the canon that a statute is not to be construed so as to work absurd or unreasonable results. Applying this canon, the majority concludes that if sec. 48.81 is interpreted to mean that a minor is eligible for adoption after the parental rights of only one parent have been terminated, then a child could be adopted by a second person even against the wishes of the child's present legal parent. The majority then concludes that a minor is not eligible for adoption unless the rights of both parents have been terminated.

The majority's concern about the hypothetical adoption is misplaced, particularly given its acknowledgement that other sections of the adoption statutes may prohibit the adoption. It seems highly unlikely that a court would find such an adoption to be in the best interests of the child. Moreover, such an adoption would undoubtedly be prohibited as a violation of the constitutionally protected liberty interest of the legal parent to control the upbringing of that parent's child. [citing Meyer v. Nebraska and Pierce v. Society of Sisters]. * * *

In interpreting sec. 48.92(2), the majority sets forth the hypothetical that if "shall" is directory then a court may grant adoption to two people without severing ties between the previous legal parent, leaving the minor with three parents. Again, the hypothetical posited by the majority would likely be precluded by the best interests standard. * * *

* * *

* * * The majority disregards Angel's interests. Annette and Angel have a functional parent-child relationship but the majority's conclusion that the relationship cannot be accorded legal protection leaves Angel in a vulnerable position. Annette, who is already Angel's *de facto* parent, will not have the right nor the obligation to maintain their relationship were Georgina to die or become incompetent or were Annette and Georgina to separate. * * * In the best interests of a young girl named Angel, this court should not close the door on her adoption.

BABLITCH, JUSTICE (*dissenting*).

I join the dissenting opinion filed by Chief Justice Heffernan. Respectfully, I write only to address the concurring opinion which strongly urges the legislature to address this issue. My experience as a former member of the legislature tells me this: that will not happen.

In some legislation the legislature, recognizing that the future will bring issues to the fore that it cannot anticipate at the time of passage of the bill, meets its obligation to the future by placing the burden on the courts to deal with those issues consistent with its expressed intent. This is just such an issue. That is why the dissent by the Chief Justice is so very correct.

* * *

[T]he legislature knew precisely what it was doing when it inserted into the adoption statutes the somewhat amorphous and vague directives to the courts that in interpreting these statutes, they "shall be liberally construed to effect the objectives contained in this section," and that "(t)he best interests of the child shall always be of paramount consideration. . . ." The legislature knew it could not anticipate all the situations that might arise in the future. It certainly knew, if by instinct only, that some of those issues would be very thorny indeed. And it most certainly knew, from experience alone, that future legislatures would be most reluctant to address the thorniest of them.

The legislature at times, as here, deliberately paints with a very broad and ambiguous brush. By design, it left the details to us, even the most controversial ones. We abdicate our responsibility by passing this back to the legislature, particularly when we know the likelihood of the legislature ever acting is minimal at best.

The legislature, by being deliberately ambiguous, is telling the courts, "We will not because we cannot spell out in detail every conceivable situation that might arise in the future, particularly the very sensitive ones. Look to the best interests of the child when these situations arise." As the dissent eloquently points out, everybody agrees what the best interests are here.

Notes and Questions

1. *The "best interests of the child"*. A child is adopted only when the court enters a final decree approving the adoption. The court enters the decree when it determines that adoption by a petitioner or petitioners with standing to adopt would be in the best interests of the child. The "best interests" standard necessarily vests considerable discretion in the court, and state legislatures have resisted efforts to constrain discretion by defining the term. In the absence of a comprehensive definition, what general factors should the court examine in determining whether a proposed adoption would be in the best interests of the child?

"[C]ourts have not demanded perfection in adoptive parents." In re Michael JJ, 613 N.Y.S.2d 715, 716 (App.Div. 1994). Adoption may be in the child's best interests, for example, even where the prospective adoptive parents have relatively modest means. See, e.g., State ex rel. St. Louis Children's Aid Society v. Hughes, 177 S.W.2d 474, 477 (Mo.1944) ("[T]he duty of the court [in adoption cases] is * * * to provide the *best* home that is available. By that is not meant the wealthiest home, but the home which * * * the court deems will best promote the welfare of the particular child.") (emphasis by the court).

An adoption petition is not necessarily defeated by the prospective adoptive parents' nondisclosure or misrepresentation to authorities in connection with the adoption. See, e.g., In re Baby Girl W., 542 N.Y.S.2d 415, 416 (App.Div. 1989) (approving adoption even though petitioners misrepresented their educational backgrounds, employment histories and financial condition during the preadoption investigation, and equivocated when asked to explain discrepancies; "the petitioners' character flaws are offset by their proven ability to care for the child").

Even a prospective adoptive parent's criminal record does not necessarily defeat the adoption petition. See, e.g., In re Alison "VV," 621 N.Y.S.2d 739, 739–40 (App.Div. 1995) (holding that the 34-year-old petitioner's convictions for disorderly conduct and hindering prosecution when she was seventeen years old did not preclude her from being considered as a prospective adoptive parent because she had engaged in no further criminal activity, had been steadily employed by the same employer for twelve years, had been certified as a foster parent and had had foster children placed in her home); In re Adoption of Jonee, 695 N.Y.S.2d 920 (Fam. Ct. 1999) (striking down a state statute requiring denial of the petition of a prospective adoptive parent previously convicted of any felony involving (1) child abuse or neglect, (2) spousal abuse, (3) a crime against a child, including child pornography, or (4) a crime involving violence, including rape, sexual assault or homicide, other than a crime involving physical assault or battery; the irrebuttable presumption violated due process).

The best-interests-of-the-child standard necessarily means that the ultimate question is whether the proposed adoption would serve the child's welfare, and not whether it would serve the welfare of the biological parents, the prospective adoptive parents or anyone else. For example, the standard would not consider pleas that infertile prospective adoptive parents need a child for their emotional wellbeing, or that prospective adoptive parents need a child to help shore up their shaky marriage. Remember this ultimate question as the chapter proceeds, particularly when we explore such matters as transracial and international adoption. Some critics charge that in recent years, adoption law has frequently focused not on the best interests of the child but on the interests of others such as childless couples, assertedly sometimes at the expense of the children involved.

2. *Determining standing and the best interests of the child. Angel Lace M.* wrestles with two threshold issues—whether a person has standing to petition to adopt a child and, if so, whether granting the adoption decree would be in the best interests of the child. One or both issues may produce considerable strain.

a. *Gays and lesbians.* One member of a gay or lesbian partnership may wish to adopt the other's child, who may have been conceived by artificial insemination or who may be the biological or adoptive child of the other's prior heterosexual marital or extramarital relationship. For decisions contrary to *Angel Lace M.,* see, e.g., In re Jacob, 660 N.E.2d 397 (N.Y.1995); Adoption of Tammy, 619 N.E.2d 315 (Mass.1993); Adoptions of B.L.V.B. and E.L.V.B., 628 A.2d 1271 (Vt.1993). Vermont's legislature codified the *B.L.V.B.* holding in 1996. See 15A V.S.A. § 1–102(b) (if the family unit consists of a biological parent and the parent's partner, and if the adoption is in the best interests of the child, the biological parent's partner may adopt the child without terminating the biological parent's rights).

As individuals or couples, gays or lesbians may also wish to adopt children of persons other than their partners. A same-sex partnership is not necessarily a homosexual partnership, but two states expressly prohibit homosexuals from adopting children. See Fla. Stat. § 63.042(3); N.H. Rev. Stat. § 170–B:4. New Hampshire's prohibition has been upheld on the ground that it "bears a rational relationship to the government's legitimate objective of providing adopted and foster children with appropriate parental role models." In re Opinion of the Justices, 530 A.2d 21, 26 (N.H.1987). Research about children adopted by gay and lesbian parents has been sparse, but research about children born to such parents does not support the proposition that the children suffer harm because of their parents' sexual preferences. See, e.g., Charlotte J. Patterson, Adoption of Minor Children by Lesbian and Gay Adults: A Social Science Perspective, 2 Duke J. Gender L. & Pol'y 191 (1995); Nancy D. Polikoff, This Child Does Have Two Mothers: Redefining Parenthood to Meet the Needs of Children in Lesbian–Mother and Other Non–Traditional Families, 78 Geo. L.J. 459, 561–67 (1990). But see Lynn D. Wardle, The Potential Impact of Homosexual Parenting on Children, 1997 U. Ill. L. Rev. 833 (suggesting that social science studies have ignored significant potential effects of gay childrearing on children, including increased development of homosexual orientation in children, emotional and cognitive disadvantages caused by the absence of opposite-sex parents, and economic security); Carlos A. Ball and Janice Farrell Pea, Warring With Wardle: Morality, Social Science, and Gay and Lesbian Parents, 1998 U. Ill. L. Rev. 253; Lynn D. Wardle, Fighting With Phantoms: A Reply to Warring With Wardle, 1998 U. Ill. L. Rev. 629.

In states other than Florida and New Hampshire, courts apply the best-interests-of-the-child standard to determine whether to grant adoption petitions filed by gays or lesbians, provided the statute confers standing to adopt. The Child Welfare League of America, a voluntary association of social service agencies, recommends that "[s]exual preferences should not be the sole criteria on which the suitability of prospective applicants is based." CWLA, Standard for Adoption Service, Standard 5.8 (rev. ed. 1988). The number of gays and lesbians who adopt is unknown because many applicants probably hide their sexual orientation from agencies and courts for fear that it will be held against them.

A number of courts have granted adoption petitions by homosexuals on findings that adoption was in the best interests of the child. See, e.g., In re Adoption of Charles B., 552 N.E.2d 884 (Ohio 1990) (granting adoption by single homosexual male of eight-year-old physically and mentally handicapped boy). In recent years, gays and lesbians have frequently adopted HIV-infected or other special needs children. See, e.g., Richard Lacayo, Nobody's Children, Time, Oct. 9, 1989, at 91.

A 1998 NBC News poll asked respondents: under what circumstances should a lesbian couple be allowed to adopt a child? Thirty percent thought the standard should be the same for everyone. Thirteen percent said lesbian couples should be allowed to adopt only where a suitable heterosexual couple cannot be found. Fifty percent said lesbian couples should not be allowed to adopt a child under any circumstances. (Seven percent of the respondents were not sure). NBC News Transcripts, Dateline NBC, Feb. 27, 1998, Question of the Week. In a 1993 poll, 70% of respondents objected to allowing gays and lesbians to adopt children. See Joseph P. Shapiro et al., Straight Talk About Gays, U.S. News & World Rep., July 5, 1993, at 42.

b. *Single persons*. Some states permit single persons to petition to adopt a child. See, e.g., Wis. Stat. § 48.82(1)(b). Most states require married couples to petition jointly unless the petitioner is the child's stepparent. See, e.g., Ariz. Rev. Stat. § 8–103. Two unmarried adults may be unable to petition jointly to adopt a child even if neither adult is a biological parent of the child. See, e.g., In re Jason C., 533 A.2d 32 (N.H.1987) (Souter, J.).

c. *Foster parents.* Nationwide a substantial number of adoptions each year are by the child's foster parents. Of the 26 states responding to the Child Welfare League of America 1995 survey, a majority reported that half or more of the children adopted that year were adopted by their foster parents. In many of the states, three-quarters or more of the children were adopted by their foster parents. See CWLA, Child Abuse and Neglect: A Look at the States 137 (1997).

Until relatively recently, public and private child placement agencies often required prospective foster parents, as a condition for receiving temporary custody of a child, to agree in writing not to seek to adopt the child. The evident purpose was to discourage development of emotional bonds between foster parent and child while the agency sought to reunify the child with the biological family or to find a permanent adoptive placement. Recent decisions, however, have refused to enforce no-adoption agreements where adoption by the foster parents was in the best interests of the child. See, e.g., Knight v. Deavers, 531 S.W.2d 252 (Ark.1976); C.S. v. S.H., 671 So.2d 260 (Fla.Dist.Ct.App.1996). Courts and child welfare professionals have come to recognize that where a child has spent much or most of his or her young life in foster care, arbitrary removal from the foster parents' home for adoption by strangers may cause the child added hardship from severing a secure relationship. The hardship may be particularly severe because many foster children suffer from severe emotional or physical disability to begin with, frequently exacerbated by multiple severed relationships before the adoption petition is filed.

Some states even grant a statutory preference to foster parents who have cared for the child for a specified period of time, though the court retains ultimate authority to grant or deny the adoption petition in the best interests of the child. See, e.g., N.Y. Social Servs. Law § 383(3) (where foster parent has had custody of an infant continuously for more than two years, the foster parent, if eligible, may apply to adopt the child; court gives application first consideration and first preference). Courts may grant the foster parent's petition even where a competing petitioner is the child's blood relative. See, e.g., Petition of Dep't of Social Servs., 491 N.E.2d 270 (Mass.App.Ct.1986) (three-year-old child's best interests served by adoption by foster parents with whom she had been placed when she was four days old rather than by the paternal aunt and uncle).

d. *Grandparents and other blood relatives.* Grandparents or other relatives sometimes seek to adopt a child whose biological parents have died, have had their parental rights terminated, or have become unable to care for the child because of mental disability, substance abuse or other cause. The child's relatives hold no due process right to adopt the child after the birth parents' deaths or after termination of the birth parents' parental rights. See, e.g., Mullins v. State, 57 F.3d 789 (9th Cir.1995). The relative's blood relation to the child, however, is a factor to consider in determining the best interests of the child. See, e.g., Dunn v. Dunn, 380 S.E.2d 836, 837 (S.C.1989). Some decisions create a preference in the relative's favor. See, e.g., In re Welfare of D.L., 486 N.W.2d 375, 379 (Minn.1992). In most states, however, the relative holds a preference only where the statute or applicable rule grants one. See, e.g., In re Adoption of Hess, 608 A.2d 10, 13 (Pa.1992). The preference usually depends on the duration of the relative's relationship with the child.

See, e.g., Fla. Stat. § 63.0425 (where child placed for adoption has lived with grandparent for at least six months, grandparent has priority to adopt the grandchild unless the deceased parent has indicated a different preference by will or unless the stepparent wishes to adopt).

In In re Peter L., 453 N.E.2d 480 (N.Y.1983), the court rejected the contention that in the absence of a statutory preference, a fit relative takes precedence, as a matter of law, over adoptive parents selected by the agency holding custody of the child. Writing for the court, Judge Hugh R. Jones explained that recognition of any such mandatory preference would "materially undermine the decision voluntarily made by the parent in determining to confer on the agency the power to act in her place in granting or withholding consent to adoption." 453 N.E.2d at 482. Also arguing against recognition was "the complexity which would be added to the process of adoption of a child surrendered to an agency if all such fit members of the child's extended family were to be recognized as possessing a prior claim to a child, the relinquishment of which would have to be obtained before a secure placement for adoption could be made." Id. In agency adoptions and private placements alike, however, courts show a marked inclination to honor the wishes of birth parents to place a child with otherwise fit relatives.

e. *Stepparents*. Most stepparents do not adopt their stepchildren because they cannot unless the parental rights of the noncustodial biological parent are terminated by consent or a contested proceeding. Nonetheless stepparent adoptions are the most common type of adoption today, accounting for more than half of all adoptions annually according to some estimates. See Joan Heifetz Hollinger, Aftermath of Adoption: Legal and Social Consequences § 13.02[3][b] & n.25, in 1 Hollinger, Adoption Law and Practice (1998). Most stepparent adoptions involve stepfathers adopting their wives' children born in or out of wedlock. Because an uncontested stepparent adoption generally gives the law's imprimatur to a family structure already in existence, most adoption acts exempt such adoptions from requirements relating to confidentiality, home studies, probationary periods, and similar matters. Some critics warn, however, that exemption and relaxation may prevent the court from discovering child abuse in the household.

Contested stepparent adoptions may be an entirely different matter. Where the custodial biological parent and the stepparent seek to establish grounds for terminating the parental rights of the noncustodial biological parent, prolonged family disruption may ensue, sometimes drawing in more distant family members.

What if the biological custodial parent dies and the surviving stepparent wishes to adopt the child? If no competing petition is filed, the court would likely approve the adoption unless the stepparent appears unfit. If a close relative also petitions to adopt the child, however, the stepparent may lose because he is a legal stranger to the child. The stepparent's position would appear most tenuous where the adoption act grants the relative a preference. On the other hand, the stepparent's position would appear stronger if the child has resided with him for a significant period and if uprooting would likely cause the child psychological harm. The best-interests-of-the-child standard would determine the outcome.

f. *Older petitioners.* Older persons frequently petition to adopt children. Courts determine these petitions in accordance with the best-interests standard because adoption statutes do not establish a maximum permissible age. See, e.g., Sonet v. Unknown Father, 797 S.W.2d 1, 5 (Tenn. Ct. App.1990) (woman approximately 70-years-old petitioned to adopt child who was nearly three-years-old; affirming denial of petition based on petitioner's age, her lack of parenting ability with no foreseeable improvement, and the child's failure to thrive in her care); In re Adoption of Christian, 184 So. 2d 657, 658 (Fla.Dist.Ct.App.1966) (reversing order that denied 68–year-old grandmother's petition to adopt her 13–year-old granddaughter; trial court had found the grandmother fit and suitable as an adoptive parent, but denied petition based solely on her age). Where the petitioners are the child's grandparents or other relatives, the factors discussed above may come into play.

The Child Welfare League of America takes the position that the adoptive parents' age, while not determinative, is nonetheless relevant to the best-interests calculus: "Physical condition and life expectancy of the applicants should be taken into consideration to protect the child against a repeated, foreseeable loss of parents through death or incapacitating illness. Also, it is important for applicants to be physically and emotionally capable of meeting the needs of children as they grow and develop." CWLA, Standards for Adoption Service, Standard 5.9 (rev. ed. 1988).

g. *Disabled petitioners. Angel Lace M.* quotes Wis. Stat. § 48.82(5): "Although otherwise qualified, no person shall be denied the benefits of this section because the person is deaf, blind or has other physical handicaps." A number of states have enacted similar statutes in recent years.

3. *Strict construction and liberal construction. Angel Lace M.* demonstrates that statutory meaning sometimes remains elusive. On the one hand, many decisions hold that "[a]doption statutes are in derogation of the common law and therefore must be strictly construed." Doe v. Brown, 489 S.E.2d 917, 920 (S.C.1997). Strict construction has long dominated interpretation of adoption statutes. See, e.g., Rush H. Limbaugh, The Adoption of Children in Missouri, 2 Mo. L. Rev. 300, 309 (1937).

On the other hand, many adoption statutes mandate that courts liberally interpret adoption statutes to further the best interests of the child. See, e.g., Wis. Stat. § 48.01(2), quoted in note 3 of *Angel Lace M.* The Illinois adoption act expressly displaces strict construction. See 750 Ill. Comp. Stat. 50/20 ("This Act shall be liberally construed, and the rule that statutes in derogation of the common law must be strictly construed shall not apply to this Act."). Other statutes, however, mandate liberal construction without such express displacement. Courts may experience perceptible difficulty applying strict construction and liberal construction in the same case.

Even if liberal construction affects interpretation of substantive adoption provisions, courts may insist on strict construction of procedural provisions, which are designed to protect children by enabling the court to base its decision on the most complete information available. Much adoption procedure is set out in the adoption act itself. Because adoption is a civil proceeding, the state's general civil procedure code applies as to procedural matters not explicitly addressed in the adoption code.

4. *The effect of adoption.* Adoption is "the legal equivalent of biological parenthood." Smith v. OFFER, 431 U.S. 816, 844 n. 51 (1977). Except in a stepparent adoption, a valid adoption extinguishes the parent-child relationship between the child and the biological parents and creates in its place a new relationship between the child and the adoptive parents. In a stepparent adoption, the parent-child relationship continues with the custodial biological parent, and the stepparent replaces only the biological parent whose rights have been terminated by consent or otherwise.

Adoptive parents acquire the constitutional rights of parenthood and family autonomy discussed elsewhere in this casebook. By creating a new parent-child relationship, the adoptive parents and the adoptee also secure new rights and obligations under a variety of federal and state laws, including the tax laws, workers' compensation laws, social security and other entitlement laws, welfare laws, inheritance laws, and family leave laws. See, e.g., Buchea v. United States, 154 F.3d 1114, 1116 (9th Cir. 1998) (girl could not sue for her biological father's wrongful death because she had previously been adopted by her maternal grandparents and thus was no longer the biological father's "child").

5. *Incest.* A major exception exists to the principle that a valid adoption extinguishes the child's legal relationship with the biological parents. Under incest statutes prohibiting marriage or sexual relations between parent and child, brothers and sisters, and other close relatives of the whole or half blood, proof that one of the parties had been validly adopted is not a defense. In State v. Sharon H., 429 A.2d 1321 (Del.Super.Ct.1981), for example, a half-sister and half-brother (born of the same mother but of different fathers) married. The sister had been adopted by a non-family-member when she was ten days old. *Sharon H.* rejected the couple's defense that the adoption rendered the otherwise incestuous marriage lawful. The court held that the legislature did not intend the adoption act provision to overcome the incest prohibitions.

6. *Minimum age.* In most states, a person must be eighteen or older to adopt a child, unless he or she is the child's stepparent or is married to an adult petitioner. See, e.g., Md. Code, Fam. Law § 5–309. A few states establish a higher minimum age. See, e.g., Colo. Rev. Stat. § 19–5–202 (twenty-one); Ga. Code § 19–8–3 (twenty-five). A few states prescribe no minimum age, leaving it to the courts to determine on a case-by-case basis whether adoption by a minor would be in the best interests of the child. See, e.g., Mich. Comp. Laws § 710.24.

Where the adoption act precludes minors from adopting a child but does not specify that a married minor may adopt, the act's silence does not necessarily disable married minors from adopting. Marriage emancipates a minor, and emancipation confers rights of adulthood.

7. *Posthumous adoption.* A prospective adoptive parent or the child may die during the pendency of the adoption proceeding but before the court enters the final adoption decree. Most adoption acts do not expressly state whether courts may enter the decree after a party's death. But see Utah Code § 78–30–14(7) (authorizing court to enter final adoption decree on adoptive parents' request where the child dies before expiration of the required probationary six-month residence in the adoptive parents' home).

In In re Adoption of Bradfield, 642 P.2d 214 (N.M.1982), the prospective adoptive parent filed a wrongful death action against the defendant physicians, whose malpractice allegedly caused the child's death during the pendency of adoption proceedings but before entry of the final decree. The state supreme court vacated the decree on the ground that the trial court had no jurisdiction to enter it posthumously: "The fundamental purpose of an adoption is to establish the relationship of parent and child between living human beings. The proceeding is distinctly personal in nature and, therefore, abates upon the death of either the adoptive parent or the child. The 'adoption does not become final until the order of the court * * *' and can never become final if either the adoptor or adoptee dies before the order is signed." Id. at 217.

8. *Adult adoption*. This chapter focuses on adoption of children, but most states also permit adoption of adults. Adult and child adoption are marked by similarities and differences:

a. Adult-adoption statutes generally do not apply the best-interests-of-the-child standard, but instead direct courts to presume competent adults can make decisions affecting their own rights and obligations. Some adoption statutes limit the circumstances in which adults may be adopted. See, e.g., Ohio Rev. Code § 3107.02(B) (an adult may be adopted (i) if "he is totally and permanently disabled"; (ii) if "he is determined to be a mentally retarded person"; or (iii) if "he had established a child-foster parent or child-stepparent relationship with the petitioners as a minor, and he consents to the adoption").

b. A minor may not be adopted unless the birth parents' parental rights have been terminated involuntarily or by consent. Most states provide that an adult may be adopted without consent of the adoptee's birth parents or termination of their parental rights.

c. Adult adoption, like adoption of minors, may occur only with court approval. Courts frequently approve adult adoptions that are motivated by a desire to create inheritance rights or other economic rights. See, e.g., In re Adoption of Berston, 206 N.W.2d 28 (Minn.1973) (approving 29-year-old man's adoption of his 53-year-old mother, which was designed to allow the mother to take as the adoptor's heir under a trust created by the adoptor's late father, who had divorced the mother). Courts withhold approval, however, where they find a fraudulent or otherwise improper economic purpose. See, e.g., In re Jones, 411 A.2d 910 (R.I. 1980) (refusing to approve adoption by older man of his 20-year-old paramour where the adoption would work to the economic detriment of the man's wife and family).

Courts may also withhold approval where the adoption appears motivated by desire to secure recognition of a sexual relationship. For example, in Adoption of Robert Paul P., 471 N.E.2d 424 (N.Y.1984), the court affirmed an order that denied a 57-year-old man's petition to adopt a 50-year-old man with whom he shared a homosexual relationship. In In re Elizabeth P.S., 509 N.Y.S.2d 746, 747–48 (Fam. Ct. 1986), the court distinguished *Robert Paul P.* and approved adoption of a 48-year-old woman by a 49-year-old nun because the nun had long cared for the would-be adoptee who had been sexually abused and abandoned as a child, because the would-be adoptee viewed the nun as her mother, and because the women's relationship was "totally devoid on any sexual overtones."

9. *Adoption of siblings.* Must siblings be adopted into the same home, or may the court separate siblings by approving adoptions into different homes? Neither the United States Supreme Court nor any state supreme court has articulated a constitutional right of sibling association, that is, a child's right not to be separated from his or her siblings in adoption. See, e.g., William Wesley Patton and Sara Latz, Severing Hansel from Gretel: An Analysis of Siblings' Association Rights, 48 U. Miami L. Rev. 745, 747 (1994). Nor does any state statute prohibit separate adoption of siblings or even create a rebuttable presumption against separation.

In the absence of constitutional or statutory directive, the touchstone in adoption cases remains the best interests of the child. "[A] sibling relationship is but one factor, albeit an important one, that a judge should consider in custody cases." Adoption of Hugo, 700 N.E.2d 516, 524 (Mass.1998). Courts hearing adoption petitions acknowledge that "[w]herever possible brothers and sisters should be kept together." Matter of L.B.T., 318 N.W.2d 200, 202 (Iowa 1982). The principle also applies to half-siblings. See, e.g., Crouse v. Crouse, 552 N.W.2d 413, 418 (S.D.1996). The Child Welfare League of America believes that "[b]rothers and sisters have the right to be placed together.": "Separation should occur rarely and should be seen as an exception to agency policy. A decision to separate siblings should be based on a carefully documented and reviewed determination that such a separation would beneficial to all the siblings involved. * * * On the rare occasion when siblings must be placed in separate families, it is advisable for them to maintain contact with each other, and only adoptive families who commit themselves to this contact should be selected." CWLA Standards for Adoption Service, Standard 4.11.

The rationale for avoiding separation of siblings is straightforward. "Young brothers and sisters need each other's strengths and association in their everyday and often common experiences, and to separate them, unnecessarily, is likely to be traumatic and harmful. The importance of rearing brothers and sisters together, and thereby nourishing their familial bonds, is also strengthened by the likelihood that the parents will pass away before their children." Obey v. Degling, 337 N.E.2d 601, 602 (N.Y.1975). "In the final analysis, when these children become adults, they will have only each other to depend on." In re Patricia A.W., 392 N.Y.S.2d 180, 187 (Fam. Ct. 1977).

Courts nonetheless separate 35,000 children from their brothers and sisters in foster and adoption homes each year. See Patton and Latz, supra, at 745, 754–60. Some courts have granted separated siblings visitation rights with each other. See, e.g., In re Adoption of Anthony, 448 N.Y.S.2d 377, 381 (Fam. Ct. 1982). Sometimes courts and authorities are torn between the desire to keep siblings together and the difficulty of finding adoptive parents willing and able to adopt siblings as a group; the court may subordinate the children's longterm interest in sibling association to their shortterm interest in permanency. Other factors may also appear. See, e.g., In re T.J.O., 527 N.W.2d 417 (Iowa Ct.App.1994) (termination of parental rights proceeding; siblings separated because they had never resided together and did not know one another); Morgan v. Department of Social Servs., 313 S.E.2d 350, 353–54 (S.C.Ct.App.1984) (ordering adoption by foster parents who had helped cure child of severe emotional problems, even though siblings had previously been adopted by other parents).

Concerning sibling adoption generally, see, e.g., Stephen P. Bank & Michael D. Kahn, The Sibling Bond (1982); Jane M. Leder, Brothers & Sisters: How They Shape Our Lives (1991); Sibling Relationships: Their Nature and Significance Across the Lifespan (Michael E. Lamb & Brian Sutton–Smith eds., 1982).

PROBLEM 7–1

You are the guardian ad litem of Mark, now four years old, who was placed in Department of Family Services (DFS) custody three days after he was born to a woman who had a history of psychiatric illness, and had tested positive for cocaine at the time of his birth. The boy had never lived with either of his biological parents. When Mark was two, his sister Karen, then four years old, was adopted by her foster mother, Mrs. F.

When DFS learned that Mark's first foster mother no longer wanted to adopt him, the agency persuaded Ms. F. to accept him as a foster child. Mark moved permanently to Ms. F.'s home shortly before Karen's adoption. DFS also learned that Mark's paternal aunt in a nearby state, Ms. A., was interested in adopting him. Perhaps because of prenatal exposure to cocaine, Mark had special needs and faced physical, mental, and developmental challenges, including difficulties with motor skills and speech. When he was a year old, the boy was diagnosed with "failure to thrive," and at sixteen months he began receiving services from a child development specialist. At the age of two, he began receiving early intervention services, including speech, physical and occupational therapies, to address his developmental and physical delays. He had behavioral and emotional difficulties, displaying a low tolerance for frustration and difficulty with transitions.

After living in Ms. F.'s foster home for about a year, Mark had bonded with her and called her "Mommy." He had also bonded with his sister and derived important support from her, despite her young age. Karen protected her younger brother and frequently translated his garbled speech to others. Ms. F. regularly took Mark to the many appointments scheduled for his multiple special needs, but there was no evidence that Ms. F. herself worked to improve his speech or address his developmental delays. Ms. F. derived her income from being a foster parent, but wanted to adopt Mark nonetheless. While Mark was living with her, Ms. F.'s household experienced a number of changes. Her two biological daughters, a biological granddaughter, and a foster child moved out of the home, and one foster child moved in.

In contrast to Ms. F., Mark's aunt planned to spend "a lot of quality time with him and working in areas where he needs help." The forty-three-year-old Ms. A. had raised her own fifteen-year-old son, who had special needs and developmental disabilities since birth, including a heart murmur, low birth weight, poor motor skills, speech delays, and visual difficulties that have required surgery. Her son's school achievement was below average, but his development had progressed over time and he had no behavioral problems.

Ms. A. had been "heavily, consistently, and directly" involved in her son's treatment. She had worked with him at home to reinforce the goals of his teachers and special needs providers. Ms. A. intends to do the same with Mark. She has conferred with psychologists and service providers to determine the most appropriate educational placement for Mark; the school psychologist, with whom she has a long-term working relationship, was available to provide additional assistance with Mark, if needed.

The court has heard expert testimony (1) that Mark is a fragile child for whom transitions are difficult; that he recovered from the disruption of the move from his first foster home; and that if he moved to his aunt's home in the nearby state, he would lose an important stable and structured environment, (2) that a child may be helped to compensate for, and adjust to, loss, (3) that Mark is attached to Ms. F. and to Karen, that these attachments are predictive of his ability to form future attachments, and that where such an attachment is disrupted, a child typically will go through a period of adjustment and might display behavioral disturbances, but that steps could be taken to assist a child through this process, and (4) that as Mark advances to the age of formal schooling, it will be important to minimize his developmental deficits so he can interact with peers and teachers to optimize his continuing growth and development.

As guardian ad litem, which person—Ms. F. or Ms. A.—would you recommend to the court as the better adoptive parent for Mark?

PROBLEM 7–2

Section 1–102 of the Uniform Adoption Act (1994) creates broad standing to adopt: "Subject to this [Act], any individual may adopt or be adopted by another individual for the purpose of creating the relationship of parent and child between them." If a prospective adoptive parent is married, his or her spouse must join the petition. § 3–301(b).

Under § 1–102, "[n]o one is categorically excluded * * * from being considered as a prospective adoptee or as a prospective adoptive parent." § 1–102 cmt. The drafters are explicit that "[m]arital status, like other general characteristics such as race, ethnicity, religion, or age, does not preclude an individual from adopting." Id. Parties with standing may adopt only where the Act's many requirements are satisfied. For example, a child would become available for adoption only where the birth parents consent to a direct adoptive placement, relinquish their parental rights to an agency, or have their parental rights terminated by a court. The court may approve the adoption only if it finds that the prospective adoptive parents are fit to adopt and that the adoption would be in the best interests of the child.

If you were a state legislator, would you vote to enact § 1–102 in your state?

A NOTE ABOUT "EQUITABLE ADOPTION"

Suppose an adult agrees to adopt a child but fails to complete the adoption process and secure an adoption decree. The child continues to live in the adult's household, and the adult raises and educates the child and holds him out as a member of the family. If the adult dies intestate, may the child inherit? Some states would answer in the negative, refusing to recognize an adoption for failure to comply with statutory directives. Denying inheritance from the adult may produce a harsh result, however, perhaps leaving the child in economic distress while property passes to more distant relatives by operation of law.

More than half the states recognize equitable adoption, sometimes also called adoption by estoppel, virtual adoption or de facto adoption. See, e.g., Lankford v. Wright, 489 S.E.2d 604, 605, 606 (N.C.1997). The equitable adoption doctrine enables courts to enforce agreements to adopt where the adult failed to complete the adoption process through negligence or design, and thus where no court order ever decreed the adoption. The agreement may be with the child, the child's birth parents, or someone in loco parentis.

Most claimants invoking the equitable adoption doctrine have sought to share in the intestate adult's estate. Courts have also applied the doctrine, however, in suits to recover damages for the adult's wrongful death, to recover support from the adult, to establish adoptive status under inheritance tax laws, or to recover life insurance, workers' compensation or other death benefits following the adult's death. The adult might also seek to invoke the doctrine, for example, in suits seeking workers' compensation benefits for the child's death, inheritance from the child, or damages for the child's wrongful death. In jurisdictions that recognize the doctrine, should courts be more willing to invoke it in a suit by the child than in a suit by the adult?

Equitable adoption does not confer adoptive status but, in accordance with the maxim that equity regards as done that which ought to be done, merely confers the benefit the claimant seeks. See, e.g., Lankford, supra, 489 S.E.2d at 606. Does this mean that a child may inherit from both the intestate adult and the intestate biological parents? See, e.g., Gardner v. Hancock, 924 S.W.2d 857, 859 (Mo.Ct.App.1996).

Contract law has been the basis of most decisions that recognize equitable adoption. The claimant must prove (1) the adult's express or implied agreement to adopt the child, (2) the child's reliance on the agreement, (3) performance by the child's biological parents in relinquishing custody, (4) performance by the child in living in the adults' home and acting as their child, and (5) partial performance by the adults in taking the child into their home and treating the child as their own. See, e.g., Lankford, supra, 489 S.E.2d at 606–07.

A handful of courts, however, reject the contract basis as an "unnecessary fiction" frequently harmful to the best interests of the child. Even in the absence of an express or implied agreement to adopt, these decisions find equitable adoption "when a close relationship, similar to parent-child, exists" and the parties have acted for years as if the child had been adopted. Atkinson v. Atkinson, 408 N.W.2d 516, 520 (Mich.Ct. App.1987). The distinction was determinative in O'Neal v. Wilkes, 439 S.E.2d 490 (Ga.1994), in which the child alleged an equitable adoption on the ground that the intestate foster parent and the child's paternal aunt had agreed to the adoption years earlier. The *O'Neal* majority held that the intestate's agreement to adopt was invalid because the aunt, with no authority to consent to the child's adoption, had no authority to enter into the agreement. The dissenter would have recognized the equitable adoption because the intestate and the claimant had lived in the same household as parent and child for several years.

In jurisdictions that recognize the equitable adoption doctrine based on contract law, the judicial embrace has nonetheless been lukewarm. Claimants are "rarely" successful in establishing the requisite agreement to adopt. J.N.H. v. N.T.H. II, 705 So.2d 448, 452 (Ala. Ct. Civ. App. 1997). Where a stepchild claims an equitable adoption by the stepparent, courts have denied the claim if the evidence demonstrates only a close stepchild/stepparent relationship. See, e.g., Weidner v. American Family Mut. Ins. Co., 928 S.W.2d 401, 403 (Mo.Ct.App.1996). Where the suit asserting equitable adoption seeks intestate succession or other economic advantage after the foster parent's death, courts are particularly wary of fraudulent claims. Most jurisdictions require the claimant to prove the agreement by a heightened standard of proof, such as clear, cogent and convincing evidence. See, e.g., Kisamore v. Coakley, 437 S.E.2d 585, 587 (W.Va.1993). The heightened standard may be satisfied without particular difficulty where the agreement is in writing, but alleged oral agreements without witnesses remain difficult to prove. In the absence of a writing, what sort of facts might the claimant show to establish an equitable adoption?

SECTION 3. ADOPTION INTERMEDIARIES AND THEIR REGULATION

A. *Agency Adoptions and Private Placements*

JANA B. SINGER, THE PRIVATIZATION OF FAMILY LAW

1992 Wis. L. Rev. 1443, 1444, 1478–86.

Over the past twenty-five years, family law has become increasingly privatized. In virtually all doctrinal areas, private norm creation and private decision making have supplanted state-imposed rules and structures for governing family-related behavior. This preference for private over public ordering has encompassed both the substantive legal doctrines governing family relations and the preferred procedures for resolving family law disputes.

* * *

[T]here has been a change in the perceived purpose of American adoption law, from promoting the welfare of children in need of parents—traditionally and unproblematically a "public" function—to fulfilling the needs and desires of couples who want children.

This shift in purpose is * * * evident in the increased popularity of so-called independent or private placement adoptions, in which prospective adoptive parents solicit available infants directly through newspaper ads and physician referrals.

* * *

1. Agency–Facilitated Adoption

American law recognizes two methods of placing children for adoption with non-relatives: agency placement and independent or private placement, sometimes referred to as "gray market" adoption. In an agency adoption, the biological parents generally relinquish their parental rights to a public or private adoption agency, after they have been counseled about their options for raising the child.[163] The agency is then responsible for placing the child with adoptive parents. Traditionally, in agency adoptions, the birth parents played little or no role in selecting adoptive parents and had no contact with the adoptive parents once they had been selected by the agency. This is changing, however, largely in response to competition from private placement adoption. Thus, many adoption agencies now permit birth parents to play a more active role in selecting an adoptive family. State laws relaxing the confidentiality of adoption records have also facilitated contact between the biological and the adoptive parents in agency adoptions.

Adoption agencies are also generally responsible for investigating the fitness of prospective adoptive parents. Traditionally, many adoption agencies restricted eligibility for adoption based on factors such as age, marital status, race, religion, financial stability and emotional health. These restrictions disqualified many prospective parents from participating in agency adoptions and discouraged others from even applying to agencies.

Once an agency approves prospective parents for adoption, those parents are typically placed on a waiting list until a suitable child becomes available for adoption. The waiting period for a healthy infant today can be as long as four to six years. When a possible child becomes available, the agency often performs additional studies on the biological

---

163. Frequently, if the biological parents are not married, the birth mother will have had some contact with the agency prior to the birth of her child. Although the mother may tentatively plan to relinquish her child during pregnancy, she will have to reaffirm her intention after the child's birth, since a mother's pre-birth consent to the adoption generally is not enforceable.

parents and adoptive parents in an effort to ensure the success of the adoption. Agencies also provide for the care of the child should problems arise in the adoption process, and may perform follow-up studies after placing the child in the adoptive home, to ensure that the child and family are adjusting well.

Adoption agencies are heavily regulated by the state. In all states, such agencies must be licensed and, in most, they must operate as nonprofit entities. Some adoption agencies are dedicated exclusively to the provision of adoption services; others are part of multi-service agencies or government entities. * * *

2. Independent or Private–Placement Adoption

Independent or private-placement adoptions occur without the assistance of a licensed adoption agency.[170] Instead, birth mothers and prospective adoptive parents deal directly with each other or, more commonly, through an intermediary such as a physician or a lawyer.[172] Often, potential adoptive parents seek out pregnant women who are considering adoption by placing advertisements in newspapers or magazines. These advertisements typically promise a loving and financially secure home for the baby, along with payment of the pregnant woman's medical and legal expenses.[173] Some lawyers specializing in private adoptions engage in similar advertising directed at expectant mothers. Couples seeking to adopt privately are also counseled to send their resumes to obstetricians and to post their resumes in public places, particularly on college campuses.

Over the past ten years, there has been a marked increase in private-placement adoptions, particularly for healthy white infants. A recent treatise on adoption asserts that today "[t]he overwhelming majority of healthy infants are adopted through private placements." Other commentators report that, in California and other states that

170. All but seven states apparently allow parents to place their children with unrelated prospective adopters, either through a direct private placement or with the assistance of an intermediary. In the seven states that do not allow private placement, only licensed state or private agencies are authorized to place children for adoption by non-relatives. Even in these states, however, birth parents may be able to arrange to have an agency place the child with someone selected by the parents, or to get a judicial or administrative waiver of the agency-placement requirement, if they can show that a waiver is in the best interests of the child.

172. Some states explicitly permit third party intermediaries to assist a birth parent in locating prospective adopters and in arranging for the actual physical transfer of the child. These states supposedly hold intermediaries to strict accounting requirements for their fees and expenses. Other states permit private placements by parents, but prohibit unlicensed intermediaries, including lawyers, from engaging in "child-placement" activities. Even in these states, however, it is considered appropriate for lawyers representing prospective adoptive parents to advise them on how to locate a child, and for lawyers representing birth parents to advise them on how to evaluate prospective adopters.

173. One such advertisement, in a South Carolina newspaper, read:

Adoption: Loving financially secure, college educated couple. Much love & happiness to give to adopted white newborn. We invite you to live with us. Share our vacations. Live like a queen. All expenses paid. Legal & confidential. Please consider this an opportunity for a new start for you in a booming area (Houston)....

allow private adoption, up to eighty percent of all newborn adoptions are handled privately. In the mid–1970s, by contrast, private adoptions accounted for less than a third of all infant placements.

Private-placement adoption differs from illegal baby-selling primarily in that payments to the birth mother are limited to her pregnancy-related expenses, and payments to the intermediary (if any) are restricted to the provision of professional services. The line between such permissible and impermissible payments, however, is often difficult to draw. State laws differ substantially on what qualifies as a compensable pregnancy-related expense on the part of the birth mother. Similarly, the distinction between legitimate professional services and illegal "child placement activities" on the part of an adoption intermediary is neither clear nor uniform across the country.

Despite the fine line between private-placement adoption and illegal baby selling, private adoption has become increasingly acceptable today, in both legal and nonlegal circles. * * *

[A] growing number of legal commentators view private adoption as superior to agency-facilitated placements, particularly for infants. Proponents of private adoption argue that, unlike agency placement, private adoption allows both the biological and the prospective adoptive parents to exercise control over the adoption process. The birth mother can decide which adoptive family will provide the best home for her child; the prospective adoptive parents can find out "specifically and in detail who their child was born to, what the family tree is like, and what the obtainable family health histories are." Because of this element of control, and because parties to independent adoptions knowingly "choose each other," proponents claim that private adoption results in "fewer regrets on the part of the birth parent(s) and a lower incidence of refusals to sign consents to adoption." Proponents also emphasize that private adoption appropriately minimizes state intervention into the private lives of both birth parents and adoptive families.

A minority of commentators are more skeptical of private adoption. They caution that placement (or facilitation of placement) of children by unlicensed intermediaries may not adequately protect the welfare of the parties involved in the adoption, particularly the child. They note that while agencies generally conduct extensive preplacement screening of potential adoptive parents, only an abbreviated form of post placement screening occurs in many private adoptions. Critics also argue that the limited supply of "adoptable" babies, in contrast to the great demand for them, inevitably generates pressure for unscrupulous intermediaries and parents to sell babies at whatever price desperate adoptive couples are willing to pay.

* * *

Notes and Questions

1. *Agency adoptions.* In an agency adoption, the birth mother consents to termination of her parental rights and relinquishes custody of the child to

the agency for adoption after receiving counseling about her options and the consequences of her decision. If the mother consents before the child's birth, she must reaffirm that consent after birth. The child remains in the agency's custody until placement with the adoptive parents. The agency makes efforts to locate the father and to secure his consent to termination of his parental rights, but does not deny services to birth mothers who refuse to name the father. If efforts to locate the father prove fruitless, the agency must move for involuntary termination. The agency's counseling of the birth mother should continue after placement. See CWLA, Standards for Adoption Service, Standards 2.1–2.6 (rev. ed. 1988).

Many adoption agencies evaluate, and exclude, prospective adoptive parents based on such factors as age, marital status, race, religion, financial stability and emotional health. At one time, discrimination based on outward appearances was encouraged because adoption was deemed an inferior way to constitute a family; if parents and child looked sufficiently alike and were within a particular age range, resemblance made it easier for the family to hide the adoption. Nowadays officially sanctioned discrimination is becoming the exception rather than the rule throughout American life, and Congress has even seemingly mandated an end to race matching in adoptive placement (see infra p. 715). Discrimination in adoptive placement resists eradication, however, because it frequently results from the agencies' exercise of discretion rather than from express rules and regulations. Where discrimination is charged, courts appear reluctant to second guess the agency determination, which is normally granted deference because of the agency's expertise. In light of society's general commitment to end official discrimination, what state interests support continued discriminatory treatment of prospective adoptive parents who are otherwise fit parents for a child in need of adoption?

According to data reported by 25 states to the Child Welfare League of America, 93% of children placed by agencies in 1995 were special-needs children. The definition of "special needs" differs from state to state, but all states' definitions include older children, children of racial or ethnic minority groups, children with siblings who should be placed together if possible, and children with mental, emotional or physical disabilities. See CWLA, Child Abuse and Neglect: A Look at the States 117 (1997). These disabilities are frequently congenital, but a substantial number of children in agency custody are victims of prolonged physical or emotional abuse.

As one might expect, agencies frequently experience considerable difficulty placing special needs children regardless of the cause of the disability. The CWLA reports that in light of "the urgent need for more adoptive families" for special-needs children, agencies have eased previously restrictive eligibility requirements. CWLA, Standards for Adoption Service, Standard 0.12 (rev. ed. 1988). As section 8 below discusses, agencies dealing with prospective adoptive parents may sometimes jeopardize the adoption's ultimate success by misrepresenting, or at least by being less than candid about, the child's disabilities.

2. *Private adoptions.* All states permit private adoptions by stepparents or other members of the child's family. All but a handful of states also permit private adoptions to adoptive parents unrelated to the child. Even in the

handful of states that prohibit non-relative private placements, parents may sometimes work with the agency to direct the child to a person they designate. See generally Stanley B. Michelman & Meg Schneider, The Private Adoption Handbook (1988).

The increasing volume of private adoptions is fueled partly by frustration with agencies' long waiting lists, restrictive guidelines, and sometimes intrusive investigations. The major reason for the increase, however, is the contemporary shortage of adoptable children without special needs, and the resulting intense competition for these children among desirous adoptive parents. The shortage stems from several factors. For one thing, abortion and birth control are more widely available to unmarried women than in the past. Unmarried birth mothers today are also much more likely to keep their babies because the stigma of single parenting and out-of-wedlock births has markedly diminished in the past generation. Stern condemnation of unwed motherhood is no longer the norm, and Professor Elizabeth Bartholet says that "most of the pressure" young unmarried mothers face nowadays is "to either abort or keep." Laura Mansnerus, Market Puts Price Tags on the Priceless, N.Y. Times, Oct. 26, 1998, at A1.

Sources indicate that 97% or more of unmarried women who deliver babies now choose to keep the child. See National Committee for Adoption, Adoption Factbook, United States Data, Issues, Regulations and Resources 64 (1989) (97%); Mansnerus, supra (98%). As a result, prospective adoptive couples outnumber healthy adoptable children by at least 20–1 and, according to some estimates, by as much as 40–1 or even higher. Adoption Factbook, supra, at 6 (20–1); Curt Suplee, The Ties that Bind: The Case for Open Adoption, Wash. Post, July 17, 1990, at B4 (40–1); William R. Greer, The Adoption Market: A Variety of Options, N.Y. Times, June 26, 1986, at C1 (as much as 100–1). The odds are particularly daunting for would-be adoptive parents disfavored by agencies, such as older couples and single persons.

3. *Federal and state subsidies for adopting special-needs children.* Child psychologists recognize that children freed for adoption thrive best in permanent adoptive homes rather than in prolonged foster or institutional care. For want of available adoptive homes, however, many special-needs children are deprived of permanency. See Katherine A. Nelson, On the Frontier of Adoption: A Study of Special Needs Adoptive Families (1985). The number of special-needs children entering the adoption system appears to be growing. Adoptive placement may be difficult because parents willing to adopt and nurture these children face sometimes imposing obstacles, including financial ones, not faced by parents who adopt other children. In an effort to facilitate adoption of special-needs children, federal and state law now provide financial assistance for parents willing to shoulder the responsibility:

> * * * Before the [federal] Adoption Assistance [and Child Welfare] Act [of 1980, 42 U.S.C. §§ 670–76], federal funding was available for foster care payments and services but not for adoption services. Throughout the 1970s, legislators and professionals became aware that the lack of federal subsidies was a disincentive to adoption, both for state governments which might be sponsoring adoption and for foster parents considering adoption. The Adoption Assistance Act, therefore,

established an adoption assistance program under the Social Security Act, providing federal funds for the adoption of special needs children.

The federal adoption assistance program is designed specifically for children with special needs. Under the program, adoptive parents who have entered into written agreements with the state are subsidized with the payment of nonrecurring adoption expenses, payments up to the amount it would cost the state to maintain the child in foster care, eligibility for Medicaid benefits, and certain social services. * * *

While the Adoption Assistance Act encourages permanent placement efforts at the state level, it delegates a great deal of responsibility to the states. Since the federal program complements rather than replaces state programs, the states are expected to maintain their own programs as well as direct and administer the federal program. * * *

* * *

The Adoption Assistance Act accomplished an important goal: the establishment of a federal subsidy program for the adoption of children with special needs. Before its passage, adoption professionals strongly advocated subsidies to facilitate special needs adoption, particularly when foster parents wished to adopt their foster children but hesitated because adoption meant the loss of their federal subsidy under the foster care program. Adoption subsidies also were seen as crucial for states, which had no incentive to promote adoption of special needs children since they would have to foot the bill for adoption subsidies. The federal program attempts to remedy both problems by placing adoptive parents of special needs children on equal footing with their foster care counterparts and by providing money to the states to implement this agenda. The AAA also encourages more families to adopt special needs children by eliminating a "means" test for eligibility. Finally, the AAA aims to contribute to the broader goal of finding permanent homes for special needs children earlier in the child welfare process.

Susan L. Brooks, Rethinking Adoption: A Federal Solution to the Problem of Permanency Planning For Children With Special Needs, 66 N.Y.U. L. Rev. 1130, 1144–50 (1991). The Adoption and Safe Families Act of 1997, Pub. L. No. 105–89, further seeks to promote adoption of special needs children. Among other things, the 1997 Act (1) provides incentive payments to states whose adoptions of foster children exceed the previous year's number (§ 201), (2) requires states to provide health insurance coverage for any special needs child with an adoption assistance agreement who the state determines would not be adopted without medical assistance (§ 306), (3) guarantees that special needs children will not lose eligibility for federal adoption assistance if their adoption is dissolved or their adoptive parents die (§ 307), (4) prohibits states from postponing or denying a suitable out-of-state adoptive placement while seeking in-state placement (§ 202), and (5) requires states to do criminal background checks on prospective foster and adoptive parents if the child has special needs that makes him eligible for federal adoption assistance, unless the state opts out of this requirement (§ 106).

4. *Investigations or home studies.* In agency adoptions and private placements alike, adoption acts require at least one investigation or home study. In some states, courts may waive this requirement for good cause. Many states do not impose the requirement where the prospective adoptive parent is the child's stepparent or other close relative.

The investigation or home study enables the court to determine whether the parents would be suitable for the child, helps the parents probe their capacity to be adoptive parents and the strength of their desire to adopt, and helps reveal factors about the parents or the child that might affect the adoption. The investigation or home study may also protect the child from a placement undesirable because of the parents' circumstances, such as a history of abuse or neglect or the parents' likely inability to cope with special needs the child might have.

In agency adoptions, the agency must make an investigation or home study before placing the child with the prospective adoptive parents, with the child sometimes placed in temporary foster care in the interim. The agency must follow up with a further inspection shortly after placement. In private placements, however, no investigation or home study normally takes place until after the parent or intermediary has made the placement, and sometimes not until long afterwards. See William M. Schur, Adoption Procedure § 4.12, in 1 Hollinger, Adoption Law and Practice (1998). Public concern about lax regulation of private placements has led some states to require that at least where the prospective adoptive parent is not the child's stepparent or other relative, a notice to adopt must be filed and an investigation or home study must be conducted before transfer of the child. Transfer may not be made until the parents are certified as qualified. See, e.g., N.Y. Dom. Rel. L. §§ 115, 115–c, 115–d. These requirements recognize that because of the child's need for continuity, a meaningful study may not be possible once transfer is made.

Except in stepparent adoptions and other unusual circumstances, the adoption does not become final until the child has been in the adoptive parents' custody for a probationary period which, depending on the state, may range from three months to a year. The court signs the final adoption order if circumstances warrant after a final home investigation. See, e.g., N.Y. Dom. Rel. L. § 116–1.

5. *Fees.* "Earlier in the century it was considered inappropriate to charge couples seeking to adopt lest the arrangement appear too commercial; charitable donations were routinely sought and accepted. Since the 1950s fees have been charged to defray the administrative costs incurred by agencies: the costs for counseling birth parents and adoptive parents, for providing temporary care for the child, for handling termination of parental rights actions and for supervising placements after they are made. These fees can run as high as $7000 to 10,000 or more, with the highest fees being charged by private agencies." Joan Heifetz Hollinger, Introduction to Adoption Law and Practice § 1.05[3][a], in 1 Hollinger, Adoption Law and Practice (1998). In private-placements, adoptive parents may pay as much as $20,000, including their legal fees and the birth mother's legal fees and maternity-related expenses. Id. § 1.05[3][b]. Some observers believe that in private placements smacking of black market transactions, "under the

table" payments may boost the amount considerably higher. "Baby selling" is discussed beginning at page 659.

A NOTE ON THE INTERSTATE COMPACT ON THE PLACEMENT OF CHILDREN

Children are frequently moved from one state to another for foster care or possible agency or private adoption. In light of the sometimes significant differences between state adoption laws, movement sometimes results from forum shopping as parties seek advantages in states with comparatively favorable provisions.

In an effort to provide greater protection to children moved interstate, all states have enacted the Interstate Compact on the Placement of Children (ICPC), first proposed in 1960. The Compact seeks to protect children transported interstate for foster care or possible adoption, and to maximize their opportunity to be placed in a suitable environment with persons able to provide the necessary and desirable level of care. ICPC Art. I(a). Most decisions hold that the ICPC applies to both private and agency adoptions. See, e.g., In re Baby Girl—, 850 S.W.2d 64, 68 n.6 (Mo. 1993) (citing decisions).

An interstate compact is an agreement between two or more states which is both a binding contract between the states and a statute in each state. A compact takes precedence over the state's other statutory law. See U.S. Const. art. I, § 10; United States Steel Corp. v. Multistate Tax Comm'n, 434 U.S. 452, 468 (1978). The ICPC's history began in the 1950s when state social service administrators explored problems that arose when children were sent or brought from one state to another for foster care or possible adoption. Existing state interstate-placement statutes were unilateral enactments which could not mandate interstate cooperation, supervision and continuing enforcement. Territorial limitations on state jurisdiction left a sending state powerless to ensure proper care and supervision in the receiving state.

Article III(a) of the Compact establishes Conditions for Placement: "No sending agency shall send, bring or cause to be sent or brought into any other party state, any child for placement in foster care or as a preliminary to a possible adoption unless the sending agency shall comply with each and every requirement set forth in this article and with the applicable laws of the receiving state governing the placement of children therein." Sending agencies must notify the receiving state's compact administrator before placing a child. The receiving state's authorities must investigate and, if they are satisfied, must notify the sending state that the proposed placement does not appear to be contrary to the child's interests. The child may not be sent or brought into the receiving state until such notification is given.

The "sending agency" may be either an entity or a natural person. The term "means a party state, officer or employee thereof; a subdivision of a party state, or officer or employee thereof; a court of a party state; a person, corporation, association, charitable agency or other entity which sends, brings or causes to be sent or brought any child to another party state." ICPC Art. II(b). Article VIII, however, excludes from the Compact's scope the sending of a child into the receiving state by "his parent, step-parent, grandparent, adult brother or sister, adult uncle or aunt or his guardian and leaving the child with any such relative or non-agency guardian in the receiving state."

The Compact defines "placement" to reach arrangements "for the care of a child in a family free or boarding home or in a child caring agency or institution," but not arrangements in "any institution caring for the mentally ill, mentally defective or epileptic or any institution primarily educational in character, and any hospital or other medical facility." ICPC Art. II(d). The sending agency retains jurisdiction over the child in matters relating to custody, supervision, care and disposition until the child is adopted, reaches majority, becomes self-supporting or is discharged with the receiving state's concurrence. The sending agency also continues to have financial responsibility for support and maintenance of the child during the period of the placement. ICPC Art. V(a).

The Compact provides two penalties for sending or bringing a child across state lines for foster care or possible adoptive placement in violation of its provisions. Violations are punishable under the child placement laws of either state, and may be grounds for suspending or revoking a license to place or care for children. ICPC Art. IV.

The Compact does not specify, however, whether violation may be a ground for dismissing the adoption petition. Only a few decisions have entered dismissal orders. See, e.g., In re Adoption of T.M.M., 608 P.2d 130, 134 (Mont.1980); Matter of Adoption of A.M.M., 949 P.2d 1155, 1159–62 (Kan.Ct.App.1997). Most decisions merely hold out the prospect of dismissal but ultimately refuse to make children pay for adult non-compliance. These majority decisions determine the appropriateness of adoption based on the best interests of the child; the adoption is unlikely to be upset where the child would be deprived of an established family relationship, or would be returned to foster care or the custody of a marginally fit parent who had previously consented to adoption. See, e.g., In re Adoption/Guardianship No. 3598, 701 A.2d 110, 124 (Md. 1997).

Where compliance with the ICPC is litigated, parties might seek redress in courts of the sending or receiving state. Determining the jurisdictionally proper court may implicate the Uniform Child Custody Jurisdiction Act (which has been enacted in all states) and the federal Parental Kidnapping Prevention Act.

Where an attorney overlooks or violates the ICPC in representing a party to the adoption, the attorney may face professional discipline, sanctions under the civil procedure code's bad-faith pleading rule, or reduction of fees otherwise awardable. See, e.g., In re Adoption of R.N.L., 913 P.2d 761 (Utah Ct.App.1996) (sanction for bad-faith pleading); In re Adoption of Calynn, 523 N.Y.S.2d 729 (Surr. Ct. 1987) (fee reduction).

Professor Bernadette W. Hartfield identifies counsel's noncompliance as a persistent barrier to the ICPC's effectiveness. Noncompliance may be unintentional because "[m]any persons, including attorneys, who are inexperienced in interstate adoptions are simply unaware of the existence of the ICPC and its provisions." Bernadette W. Hartfield, The Role of the Interstate Compact on the Placement of Children in Interstate Adoption, 68 Neb. L. Rev. 292, 303 (1989).

For several reasons, parties to an interstate adoption may intentionally choose not to comply with the ICPC. "First, one of the states might prohibit or impose greater restrictions on independent placements. Second, complying with the ICPC may be time consuming, and time may be of the essence if placement of the infant with the adoptive parents directly from the hospital is desired. Third, the penalties for noncompliance may be insufficient to deter intentional noncompliance * * *." Id. at 305. Parties may seek to avoid compliance with the ICPC by relocating the birth mother during pregnancy to a state with comparatively lax adoption regulations. Louisiana appears to be a favorite. "It is possible to find a birth mother anywhere in the country, send her to live in Louisiana, pay her expenses and fees to intermediaries, have her relinquish the child in Louisiana and finalize the adoption there, all while living elsewhere. And some couples who can afford it, most of them in the Northeast, do just that." Laura Mansnerus, Market Puts Price Tags on the Priceless, N.Y. Times, Oct. 26, 1998, at 1. Compact administrators might take the position that the adoption is interstate in nature and requires compliance with the ICPC (if they learn about the details at all), but weak sanctions provisions make successful evasion likely.

B. Baby Selling

STATE v. CLARK

Court of Appeals of Kansas, 1992.
826 P.2d 925.

PRAGER, CHIEF JUSTICE Retired:

* * *

* * * The defendant received a cash payment of $5,000 as consideration for his consent to the adoption of his baby girl. Defendant admitted that he wanted the money to cover some old bills, including some bad checks, traffic fines, and a phone bill, and to buy a car. Defendant admitted that the money was not to be used to pay any bill or expense incidental to the birth of the child or adoption proceedings.

The controlling statute is K.S.A.1991 Supp. 59–2121, which provides as follows:

"(a) Except as otherwise authorized by law, no person shall request, receive, give or offer to give any consideration in connection with an adoption, or a placement for adoption, other than:

(1) Reasonable fees for legal and other professional services rendered in connection with the placement or adoption not to exceed customary fees for similar services by professionals of equivalent experience and reputation where the services are performed, except that fees for legal and other professional services as provided in this section performed outside the state shall not exceed customary fees for similar services when performed in the state of Kansas;

(2) reasonable fees in the state of Kansas of a licensed child-placing agency;

(3) actual and necessary expenses, based on expenses in the state of Kansas, incident to placement or to the adoption proceeding;

(4) actual medical expenses of the mother attributable to pregnancy and birth;

(5) actual medical expenses of the child; and

(6) reasonable living expenses of the mother which are incurred during or as a result of the pregnancy.

(b) In an action for adoption, a detailed accounting of all consideration given, or to be given, and all disbursements made, or to be made, in connection with the adoption and the placement for adoption shall accompany the petition for adoption. Upon review of the accounting, the court shall disapprove any such consideration which the court determines to be unreasonable or in violation of this section and, to the extent necessary to comply with the provisions of this section, shall order reimbursement of any consideration already given in violation of this section.

* * *

Defendant * * * contends that the evidence was not sufficient to support the trial court's finding that the defendant was guilty of the crime of receiving unauthorized consideration in connection with an adoption for the reason that the State failed to prove that he failed to report all consideration received or that he failed to return any unauthorized payment following a judicial determination that the consideration was unauthorized.

We find no merit to this contention. We agree with the State that 59–2121(a) and (b) create separate crimes and that failure to report or reimburse any consideration given or received is not an element of the crime of intentionally and knowingly receiving or accepting clearly excessive fees or expenses in connection with an adoption under subsection (a).

* * *

In this case, the defendant did not contend that his conduct came within any of the six statutory exceptions. In his statements to the police, defendant clearly acknowledged that the $5,000 he requested and received was not for the purpose of paying any fees or expenses incidental to the birth of the child or the adoption proceedings. He indicated he was aware that his conduct was unlawful. His acts were committed knowingly and intentionally.

* * *

Affirmed.

Notes and Questions

1. *How effective are baby-selling prohibitions?* All states have enacted statutes prohibiting baby selling and baby brokering. The policy is that adoption should not be a commercial transaction in which the birth mother or intermediary sells a product. Some observers believe, however, that these statutes are ineffective in preventing a "black market" in healthy adoptable babies because desperate would-be adoptive parents may be willing to pay considerable sums to birth mothers and intermediaries regardless of statutory proscription.

Baby selling prosecutions are few and far between, in part because there is usually no complainant unless the birth mother has second thoughts. Proof beyond a reasonable doubt is difficult to establish because, as the Kansas statute quoted in *Clark* demonstrates, the line between proper and improper payments is often hazy at best. Sanctions imposed on birth parents are both quite rare and quite minor. Courts applying the best-interests test normally do not withhold approval of the adoption because unlawful payments usually surface, if at all, only in accountings reported well after the child has been placed. By that time, courts are loathe to upset the child's established relationship with loving adoptive parents.

2. *Child support arrearages.* A biological parent may marry, either after divorcing the other biological parent or after leaving that parent following the child's birth out of wedlock. The new spouse (the child's stepparent) may adopt the child only if the parental rights of the other biological parent are terminated. By creating a new parent-child relationship, adoption would excuse the terminated biological parent from any obligation to pay future child support. But to secure consent to termination, may the custodial birth parent and the new spouse agree to waive the right to any past child support the terminated birth parent owes? The Kansas baby selling statute is silent on the question, but other baby selling statutes frequently respond in the affirmative. See, e.g., S.C. Code § 16–3–160. Some decisions reach an affirmative answer even in the absence of statute. See, e.g., In Adoption of C.L.R., 352 N.W.2d 916, 919 (Neb.1984).

3. *Discipline of lawyer intermediaries.* Lawyers frequently act as intermediaries in private-placement adoptions, bringing together birth mothers (often unmarried teenagers) and prospective adoptive parents. Lawyers and other intermediaries must heed the baby selling statutes. In In re Thacker, 881 S.W.2d 307 (Tex.1994), the court upheld disciplinary sanctions imposed on a lawyer convicted of purchasing five children from the same mother, including a set of unborn twins.

The birth mother was a prostitute and a drug user who gave birth to her first child when she was fifteen and who commonly lived on the streets. Lawyer Thacker, the sole proprietor of a state-licensed adoption agency, found birth mothers who wanted to-relinquish their children for adoption and matched the children with adoptive parents. For her services, adoptive parents paid her a fee of $11,000 for a placement, or $2500 for a "hard-to-place" child. The birth mother would relinquish her parental rights in favor of the lawyer, who would then go to court with the adoptive parents and finalize the adoption. In affirming Thacker's baby-selling conviction, the court of appeals found that the lawyer paid the birth mother about $12,000 for the five children. Thacker v. State, 889 S.W.2d 380, 384–85 (Tex. Ct. App. 1994), denying writ of habeas corpus, 999 S.W.2d 56 (Tex. Ct. App.1999).

The court upheld the decision of state disciplinary authorities, which ordered the lawyer disbarred once the conviction became final. The court held that violation of the baby selling statute constitutes a crime involving moral turpitude, a predicate for disbarment.

Should states require a special license for lawyers and other intermediaries who facilitate private placements?

4. *Fraud by the birth parent.* The birth parent might incur liability for civil or criminal fraud if she promises her newborn to more than one prospective adoptive parent and accepts payments from each of them, knowing she cannot transfer the child to all. A few states have criminalized the practice. See, e.g., Cal. Penal Code § 273(c)-(d).

5. *Endangerment.* The sort of activity that preceded the attempted sale in *Clark* may support prosecution of the parent for child endangerment. See, e.g., State v. Luddy, 1997 WL 698271 (Conn.Super.Ct.1997).

6. *Should states prohibit private adoptions?* The Child Welfare League of America would outlaw private placements: "The placement of children with adopting parents is a function that should be delegated only to an organization that provides child welfare services as its primary purpose, and is subject to appropriate legal and community controls * * *. The knowledge and skills of individual professional practitioners who operate privately, whether they are social workers, doctors, lawyers, or religious counselors, cannot assure the comprehensive legal, medical, and social protections to which the various parties to an adoption are entitled." CWLA, Standards for Adoption Service, Standard 1.7 (rev. ed. 1988). Now that you have read the materials on agency adoptions, private placements and baby selling statutes, do you agree?

7. *Questions about* Clark. Does defendant Clark strike you as the sort of person who would be a good parent to his baby daughter? If not, should the state make him a felon? Wouldn't everyone be better off if the state encouraged him to consent to the child's adoption by a couple who are willing to pay him for the child, and who thus may be more devoted parents? Would a regulated adoption market serve the best interests of the children involved? Do you agree with this criticism of baby selling statutes: "Where there is a willing seller and an eager buyer, and the baby moves from an unwanted environment into a home with loving adoptive parents, where's the crime? ... If there is such a thing as a victimless crime, this is it"? Lynne McTaggart, The Baby Brokers: The Marketing of White Babies in America 317 (1980) (quoting Phyllis Schlafly).

Before you answer based on your feelings about "baby selling," recall that an adoption requires court approval and most require an investigation or home study of the attendant circumstances. Consider too the arguments of Judge Richard A. Posner. In a 1978 article, then-Professor Posner and his co-author proposed a free market approach to adoption. See Richard A. Posner and Elizabeth Landes, The Economics of the Baby Shortage, 7 J. Legal Stud. 323 (1978). Nearly a decade later, Judge Posner refined his proposal.

RICHARD A. POSNER, THE REGULATION OF THE MARKET IN ADOPTIONS
67 B.U. L. Rev. 59, 64–71 (1987).

* * *

II.   Characteristics of and Desirable Constraints on the Baby Market

A.   *The Question of Price*

For heuristic purposes (only!) it is useful to analogize the sale of babies to the sale of an ordinary good, such as an automobile or a television set. We observe, for example, that although the supply of automobiles and of television sets is rationed by price, not all the automobiles and television sets are owned by wealthy people. On the contrary, the free market in these goods has lowered prices, through competition and innovation, to the point where the goods are available to a lot more people than in highly controlled economies such as that of the Soviet Union. There is even less reason for thinking that if babies could be sold to adoptive parents the wealthy would come to monopolize babies. Wealthy people (other than those few who owe their wealth to savings or inheritance rather than to a high income) have high costs of time. It therefore costs them more to raise a child—child rearing still being a time-intensive activity—than it costs the nonwealthy. As a result, wealthy couples tend to have few rather than many children. This pattern would not change if babies could be bought. Moreover, since most people have a strong preference for natural, as distinct from adopted, children, wealthy couples able to have natural children are unlikely (to say the least) to substitute adopted ones.

It is also unlikely that allowing people to bid for babies with dollars would drive up the price of babies, thereby allocating the supply to wealthy demanders. Today we observe a high black-market price conjoined with an artificially low price for babies obtained from adoption agencies and through lawful independent adoptions. The "blended" or average price is hard to calculate; but probably it is very high. The low price in the lawful market is deceptive. It ignores the considerable queuing costs—most people would pay a considerable premium to get their adopted baby now, not five or ten years from now. And for people unable to maneuver successfully in the complex market created by the laws against baby selling, the price is infinite. Quality-adjusted prices in free markets normally are lower than black market prices, and there is no reason to doubt that this would be true in a free market for adoptions. Thus, while it is possible that "[i]nherent in the baby black market is the unfairness that results from the fact that only the affluent can afford to pay the enormous fees necessary to procure a baby," the words "black market" ought to be italicized. It is not the free market, but unwarranted restrictions on the operation of that market, that has raised the black market price of babies beyond the reach of ordinary people.

Thus far I have implicitly been speaking only of the market for healthy white infants. There is no shortage of nonwhite and of handicapped infants, and of any children who are no longer infants, available for adoption. Such children are substitutes for healthy white infants, and the higher the price of the latter, the greater will be the demand for the former. The network of regulations that has driven up the full price (including such nonmonetary components of price as delay) of adopting a healthy, white infant may have increased the willingness of childless couples to consider adopting a child of a type not in short supply, though how much (if at all) no one knows. The present system is, in any event, a grossly inefficient, as well as covert, method of encouraging the adoption of the hard-to-place child. If society wants to subsidize these unfortunate children, the burden of the subsidies should be borne, if not by the natural parents of these children, then by the taxpaying population at large—rather than by just the nation's childless white couples, who under the present unsystematic system bear the lion's share of the burden by being denied the benefits of an efficient method of allocating healthy white infants for adoption in the hope that this will induce them to adopt nonwhite, handicapped, or older children.

B. *The Question of Quality*

As soon as one mentions quality, people's hackles rise and they remind you that one is talking about a traffic in human beings, not in inanimate objects. The observation is pertinent, and at least five limitations might have to be placed on the operation of the market in babies for adoption. The first, already mentioned and already in place, is that the buyers can have no right to abuse the thing bought, as they would if the thing were a piece of steel or electronics. This really should go without saying. The laws against child abuse have never distinguished among different methods of acquiring custody of the child. * * *

If the laws against child abuse were perfectly efficacious, nothing more would have to be said on the subject. But they are not. The abuse occurs in secret, and the victim may be too young and too dependent to bring it to the attention of the authorities—or indeed to know what is going on. In addition, many child abusers may be so mentally or psychologically abnormal that they cannot be deterred even by very harsh penalties. In such a setting, preventive as well as punitive measures may be justified. Today, all adoptive parents are, in theory anyway, screened for fitness. Adoption agencies are charged with this responsibility, and if we moved toward a freer market in babies the agencies could be given the additional function of investigating and certifying prospective purchasers, who would pay the price of the service.

* * *

* * * Whatever screening is deemed necessary for persons who adopt through an agency or by independent adoption would also be necessary for persons who adopted children in a free(r) market. Freeing the adoption market from price regulation would leave the case for or against screening largely, perhaps entirely, unaffected.

The third limitation on a baby market concerns remedies for breach of contract. In an ordinary market a buyer can both reject defective goods and, if the seller refuses to deliver and damages would be an inadequate remedy for the refusal, get specific performance of the contract. Natural parents are not permitted to reject their baby, either when it is born or afterward, because it turns out to be handicapped or otherwise not in conformity with their expectations; no more should adoptive parents who buy their babies. Nor should the adoptive parents be able to force the natural mother to surrender the baby to them if she changes her mind, unless some competent authority determines that the baby would be better off adopted. For the welfare of the baby must be considered along with that of the contracting parties. Refusing to grant specific performance in circumstances in which it appears that forcing the sale go through would harm the baby is consistent with the basic equity principle that the third-party effects of equitable remedies must be considered in deciding whether to grant such a remedy or confine the plaintiff to damage remedies. The child is an interested third party whose welfare would be disserved by a mechanical application of the remedies available to buyers in the market for inanimate goods.

For the same reason (the child's welfare) neither natural nor adopting parents should be allowed to sell their children after infancy, that is, after the child has established a bond with its parents. Nor should the natural mother be allowed to take back the baby after adoption, any more than a seller of a conventional good or service can (except in extraordinary circumstances) rescind the sale after delivery and payment in accordance with his contract with the buyer, unless, once again, a competent authority decides that the baby's welfare would be increased. I shall not try to resolve the question whether, in any of these remedial settings, the welfare of the child should be paramount or should be balanced with that of the adult parties.

The last limitation on the baby market that I shall discuss relates to eugenic breeding. Although prospects still seem remote, one can imagine an entrepreneur in the baby market trying to breed a race of *Ubermenschen* who would command premium prices. The external effects of such an endeavor could be very harmful, and would provide an appropriate basis for governmental regulation.

I am not so sanguine about the operation of a baby market, even with the limitations I have discussed, that I am prepared to advocate the complete and immediate repeal of the laws forbidding the sale of babies for adoption. That such a market might give somewhat greater scope for child abusers and might encourage weird and potentially quite harmful experiments in eugenic breeding should be enough to give anyone pause. But to concentrate entirely on the downside would be a mistake. One million abortions a year is a serious social problem regardless of where one stands on the underlying ethical issues; so is a flourishing black market in babies combined with a severe shortage in the lawful market.

* * *

One reason people fear the operation of a free market in babies for adoption is that they extrapolate from experience with the illegal market. Critics who suggest that baby selling offers the promise of huge profits to middlemen—the dreaded "baby brokers"—fail to distinguish between an illegal market, in which sellers demand a heavy premium (an apparent, though not real, profit) in order to defray the expected costs of punishment, and a legal market, in which the premium is eliminated. Seemingly exorbitant profits, low quality, poor information, involvement of criminal elements—these widely asserted characteristics of the black market in babies are no more indicative of the behavior of a lawful market than the tactics of the bootleggers and rum-runners during Prohibition were indicative of the behavior of the liquor industry after Prohibition was repealed.

III.   The Objection From Symbolism and the Issue of Semantics

Even if partial deregulation of the baby market might make practical utilitarian sense along the lines just suggested, some will resist on symbolic grounds. If we acknowledge that babies can be sold, the argument goes, we open the door to all sorts of monstrous institutions—including slavery. We regularly resist this type of argument in analogous contexts, and I have difficulty understanding why it stubbornly persists in this one. * * * Allowing parents to sell their children into slavery would be a monstrous idea. Allowing the prospective mother of an illegitimate child to receive money in exchange for giving up the child for adoption, when described in shorthand as "baby selling," seems to many people uncomfortably close to the type of real baby selling that is found in slave societies—that was found in the slave societies of the South before the Civil War. No doubt it requires more thought than most people are willing to give to the problem to hold these quite different concepts separate in their minds. But if they are not held separate we may find ourselves condemned to perpetuate the painful spectacle of mass abortion and illegitimacy in a society in which, to a significant extent, children are not available for adoption by persons unwilling to violate the law.

* * *

The opponents of "baby selling" are unwilling to acknowledge that what we have today, even apart from the black market, is closer to a free market in babies than a free market in babies would be to slavery or torture (always bearing in mind that a free market in an economic sense is one in which due consideration is given the welfare of affected third parties, here the babies themselves). * * * [A]doption agencies do lawfully "sell" babies, and many charge thousands of dollars. Moreover, in independent adoptions, the mother herself may "sell" her baby, for it is not considered unlawful to use a part of the fee paid by the adoptive parents to defray the medical and other maintenance costs of the mother during pregnancy. It seems that to obtain lawfully a healthy, white infant (rarely available through adoption agencies), a couple must be prepared to lay out at least $5,000. Black-market prices of $25,000, even $50,000, have been rumored, but the equilibrium baby price in a free market (by which I do not mean an entirely unregulated market, for I suggested in Part II of this paper that the market should be regulated in various ways) might not exceed $5,000. As a matter of fact, though baby selling is everywhere unlawful, almost half the states have no specific restrictions on fees payable for adoption, and in many other states the restrictions are porous. No doubt many lawful and semi-lawful "baby sales" are taking place today at approximately free-market prices.

Two other important examples of legal baby selling should be mentioned. One is the "family compact" doctrine, which allows a woman to enter into an enforceable contract to give up her baby for adoption by a close relative. The other is surrogate motherhood, by which (at least in some states) a married couple in which the wife is infertile can make an enforceable contract with another woman whereby the latter agrees to be artificially inseminated with the husband's sperm and to carry the baby to term and give it up to the couple. In the first case the close family relative "buys" the baby, in the second the father (and his wife) "buys out" the natural mother's "share" in their joint product.

So we have legal baby selling today; the question of public policy is not whether baby selling should be forbidden or allowed but how extensively it should be regulated. I simply think it should be regulated less stringently than is done today.

Notes and Questions

1. *Debate about Judge Posner's proposal.* Since the appearance of his 1978 article, Judge Posner's baby-selling proposals have inspired sometimes strident criticism. See, e.g., Jane Maslow Cohen, Posnerism, Pluralism, Pessimism, 67 B.U. L. Rev. 105 (1987); Tamar Frankel & Francis H. Miller, The Inapplicability of Market Theory to Adoptions, 67 B.U. L. Rev. 99 (1987); Robin West, Submission, Choice, and Ethics: A Rejoinder to Judge Posner, 99 Harv. L. Rev. 1449, 1449 (1986). See also, e.g., Nancy C. Baker, Babyselling: The Scandal of Black–Market Adoption (1978). In his 1992 book, Sex and Reason, Judge Posner sought to refute criticisms of his position.

In 1984, however, Time magazine quoted a South Carolina judge: "Even if baby selling does exist, what's so horrible about that? If the child is going to a home with good parents who can give it all the love and security it will ever need, why should we care if the parents paid $50,000 for the privilege? The child is happy, the parents are happy, so what is the harm?" Newborn Fever: Flocking to An Adoption Mecca, Time, Mar. 12, 1984, at 31.

2. *The role of money.* If the thought of buying and selling babies offends sensibilities, does the law permit money to count for too much under the present adoption system? Consider these thoughts by Professor Elizabeth Bartholet:

> The parental screening system applies only to those who do not possess the money to buy their way around it. Prospective adopters with money can escape all but minimal screening. They can also exercise extensive choice among the children available for adoption, and it is they who are most likely to end up adopting the healthy infants who are most in demand. The more money prospective adopters have, the greater their ability to shop around and escape the strictures of the system.

> Without money, you are limited to the public adoption agency system, which deals primarily with the children in foster care and applies the classic screening and matching criteria. With money, you can venture into the private adoption agency world, where a great variety of screening systems are used and a much larger proportion of healthy infants and young children are available. Some private agencies screen and match according to the classic home study criteria, but others are much more sympathetic to nontraditional parents. Still others are willing to place children with virtually all adoptive applicants who satisfy minimal criteria. Prospective adopters can shop among the private agencies and select the one most sympathetic to their personal profile and most likely to provide the kind of child they are looking for. Fees vary significantly, with the agencies that are most open to nontraditional parents tending to charge higher fees.

> Money also gives access to the world of independent adoption, which accounts for roughly one third of all nonrelative adoption in this country. Here home studies are not required at all. Some intermediaries and some birth parents apply their own screening criteria, and nontraditional parents have a harder time adopting than young married couples do. But many of those who place children in the independent process do little or no screening, and those who are more selective have a wide variety of views on what qualities they are looking for. A great many parents who surrender infants at birth are attracted to independent adoption, so prospective adopters with enough money to explore the possibilities are able both to avoid classic screening and to find their way to a healthy newborn. The state subjects these parents to only the most minimal scrutiny in the court process that formalizes the adoption. Even when a postplacement home study is required, its purpose is to determine whether the adopter satisfies minimum fitness criteria, not to decide whether he or she ranks high enough to be assigned a particular child, as is the case in the agency process.

> Independent adoptions are allowed in all but a handful of states. Even those states that outlaw them as a formal matter and require home studies prior to adoptive placement permit a form of adoption that

enables those with money to bypass key aspects of the screening system. In what are known as identified adoptions, prospective adopters are allowed to find their own child as long as they satisfactorily complete a home study before taking the child home. Since they can generally exercise some choice as to who will do the study, and since they will not be compared with other potential adopters, they must satisfy only minimal standards for parental fitness.

Judged in terms of the very values it purports to serve, the screening system fails. Together with the rule against baby-buying, parental screening is supposed to ensure that children are assigned not to the highest bidder but to those deemed most fit to parent. The fact that money enables those deemed least fit to buy their way to the children who are most in demand makes a farce of the entire system.

Elizabeth Bartholet, Family Bonds: Adoption and the Politics of Parenting 73–74 (1993).

SECTION 4. THE CONSENT REQUIREMENT

A. *The Requirement of Informed and Voluntary Consent*

The general rule is that on a petition by persons with standing to adopt, the court may not proceed unless consents to adoption have been secured from all persons with a right to give or withhold consent. The required consents do not complete the adoption, but merely enable the court to order the adoption if it concludes all other requirements have been satisfied.

Knowing and voluntary consent (or, as some statutes call it, "release," "relinquishment" or "surrender") generally must be secured from both biological parents. A parent may execute a specific consent (authorizing adoption by particular named persons) or a general consent (authorizing adoption by persons chosen by the agency, an authorized intermediary, or the court). To preserve confidentiality, general consents are normally used in adoptions in which a child placement agency is the intermediary.

Consent is not required from a biological parent who has died, who a court determines is incompetent, whose parental rights have been terminated by consent or court order, or who has abandoned or neglected the child for a specified period. If the biological parent is incompetent, the court may appoint a guardian of the child's person, with authority to consider whether to consent in the parent's stead. In some states, the court in the adoption proceeding itself may determine whether to terminate parental rights; other states require that where contested or consensual termination is a predicate for adoption, the termination proceeding must take place before the adoption proceeding.

Because valid consent to adoption may terminate the parent-child relationship, statutes require formalities designed to bring home to the biological parent the gravity of consent. In almost all states, consent must be in writing. The adoption act may specify that the consent be signed before a judge, notary or other designated officer. A particular number of witnesses may be required. The consent may have to be under oath. See, e.g., Mass. Gen. Laws ch. 210 § 1.

In most states, consent to the adoption must also be secured from the child over a specified age. See, e.g., Cal. Fam. Code § 8602 (twelve or older). Some statutes authorize the court to dispense with the child's consent for good cause. See, e.g., N.M. Stat. § 32A–5–21 (ten or older unless the court finds the child does not have mental capacity to make the judgment). Why should consent of older adoptees be a condition of adoption? Should the court have authority to dispense with it in appropriate cases?

Where a child has been committed to the custody of a public or private child placement agency, the agency's consent may also be a factor. In a few states, agency refusal to consent operates as a veto, divesting the court of authority to grant the adoption. Many states make the agency's consent a prerequisite to adoption, but authorize judicial scrutiny by providing that the agency may not unreasonably withhold consent. See, e.g., Minn. Stat. § 259.24(1)(e), (7). Under the familiar judicial approach to review of agency decisionmaking, the court will likely accord deference to the agency determination because of the agency's expertise. Even where the consent statute seemingly makes agency consent mandatory without condition, many decisions hold that the agency's refusal to consent is nonetheless persuasive only. The court holds authority to grant the adoption if it finds the agency's refusal to consent is contrary to the best interests of the child. See, e.g., In re M.L.M., 926 P.2d 694, 697 (Mont.1996).

The right to consent (or withhold consent) to the adoption must be distinguished from the right to notice of the adoption proceeding. A person with the right to consent, such as a parent, may veto the adoption by withholding consent. The court may not enter the adoption decree until knowing and voluntary consent has been secured from all persons or agencies holding the right.

Notice of the adoption proceeding must be provided to persons whose consent to the adoption is required. The adoption act, however, may also require notice to other persons, who may address the court concerning the best interests of the child, but who do not hold the right to veto the adoption. To expedite the adoption process, some states provide that notice of the adoption proceeding need not be given to a person who has executed a valid consent to adoption. These provisions excusing notice may make good sense because the person has knowingly and voluntarily waived the right to veto the adoption and because his or her whereabouts may be unknown or difficult to ascertain; on the other hand, such provisions may encourage persons to secure consents from vulnerable birth parents under conditions approaching fraud or duress. Most states permit minor biological parents to execute valid out-of-court consents without the advice of their parents or guardians, other family members or counsel. To help reduce the adoption's vulnerability to later collateral attack, however, counsel for the adoptive parents may wish the minor to acknowledge her desires in open court.

Notes and Questions

1. *Revoking consent.* Most states specify that consent to adoption may not be executed until the child is born. See, e.g., Ariz. Rev. Stat. § 8–107(B) (not before child is 72 hours old). In some states this specification applies only to the birth mother; the birth father may consent before or after the child's birth. See, e.g., 23 Pa. Cons. Stat. § 2711(c). Why would a state distinguish between mothers and fathers in this respect?

In many states, consent may be revoked within the first few days after execution, or within the first few hours or days after the child's birth. The court may then have authority to determine whether revocation is in the best interests of the child.

What if *a prospective adoptive parent* signs the adoption petition and the consent to adopt but seeks to revoke consent before the court signs the final adoption decree? Should the court hold the parent to the consent and order the adoption over his or her objection? The question does not normally arise because adoptive parents are generally eager to complete the adoption process, except perhaps when they learn disturbing details about the child's physical or emotional condition before entry of the decree.

In In re Baby Boy C., 638 N.E.2d 963 (N.Y.1994), however, the husband sought to revoke his consent because he sued his wife for divorce after he signed the consent but before entry. The husband indicated he would take no part in raising the child. The Court of Appeals held that in the exercise of its equitable powers, the trial court may impose the adoption on the unwilling husband. The court should do so, however, "only in the rarest and most exceptional of circumstances where, due to the conduct of the adoptive parent in taking custody and processing the adoption, the child's interests would be severely and unavoidable prejudiced as a result of being deprived of *status* as the legal child of the adoptive parent." Id. at 966–67. The concurring judge would have held that "as a matter of law, a child's best interests are never served by forcing an unwilling and unfit person to assume the intimacy and responsibility of becoming a parent." Id. at 968.

PROBLEM 7–3

You are a state legislative aide, and the chair of the Child Welfare Committee has asked you to consider actions the legislature might take to expedite the adoption process for children awaiting entry into permanent homes. It has occurred to the chair that where consents have been secured by all persons with the right to grant or withhold consent, the court wastes time by ordering an investigation or home study and calendaring a proceeding to take testimony and evidence. To help assure swift determination of the child's status, would you favor legislation permitting the court to enter summary adoption decrees on unanimous consent?

B. *The Rights of Unwed Parents*

The child's biological mother has traditionally held the right to veto an adoption by withholding consent, unless consent was excused by operation of law. Because this right emanated from the mother's legal right to custody of the child, the right applied regardless of whether she was married to the father at conception and birth. The right was meaningful because the mother's identity is ordinarily ascertainable from the birth certificate or hospital records. Surrogate parenting and other developing reproductive techniques have sometimes strained traditional rules for determining motherhood, but these techniques appear in the decided minority of adoption cases.

Before Stanley v. Illinois in 1972, the father's right to notice of an adoption and to withhold consent was quite another story. Where the child was conceived or born during marriage, the father's identity and whereabouts were ordinarily ascertainable and his consent to adoption was normally required, again unless excused by operation of law. Unwed fathers, however, held no right to notice of the child's impending adoption and no right to veto the adoption under the federal constitution or under the constitutions or statutes of most states. An unwed father could not secure these rights by acknowledging the child as his own, by supporting the child, or by seeking to establish a relationship with the child or the mother. In most states, the unwed father held no legal relationship to the child.

1. *Constitutional Law*

STANLEY v. ILLINOIS

Supreme Court of the United States, 1972.
405 U.S. 645.

MR. JUSTICE WHITE delivered the opinion of the Court.

Joan Stanley lived with Peter Stanley intermittently for 18 years, during which time they had three children. When Joan Stanley died, Peter Stanley lost not only her but also his children. Under Illinois law, the children of unwed fathers become wards of the State upon the death of the mother. Accordingly, upon Joan Stanley's death, in a dependency proceeding instituted by the State of Illinois, Stanley's children were declared wards of the State and placed with court-appointed guardians. Stanley appealed, claiming that he had never been shown to be an unfit parent and that since married fathers and unwed mothers could not be deprived of their children without such a showing, he had been deprived of the equal protection of the laws guaranteed him by the Fourteenth Amendment. * * *

Stanley presses his equal protection claim here. The State continues to respond that unwed fathers are presumed unfit to raise their children and that it is unnecessary to hold individualized hearings to determine whether particular fathers are in fact unfit parents before they are separated from their children. We granted certiorari to determine whether this method of procedure by presumption could be allowed to stand in light of the fact that Illinois allows married fathers—whether divorced, widowed, or separated—and mothers—even if unwed—the benefit of the presumption that they are fit to raise their children.

I.

* * *

* * * Is a presumption that distinguishes and burdens all unwed fathers constitutionally repugnant? We conclude that, as a matter of due process of law, Stanley was entitled to a hearing on his fitness as a parent before his children were taken from him and that, by denying him a hearing and extending it to all other parents whose custody of their children is challenged, the State denied Stanley the equal protection of the laws guaranteed by the Fourteenth Amendment.

II

Illinois has two principal methods of removing nondelinquent children from the homes of their parents. In a dependency proceeding it may demonstrate that the children are wards of the State because they have no surviving parent or guardian. In a neglect proceeding it may show that children should be wards of the State because the present parent(s) or guardian does not provide suitable care.

The State's right—indeed, duty—to protect minor children through a judicial determination of their interests in a neglect proceeding is not challenged here. Rather, we are faced with a dependency statute that empowers state officials to circumvent neglect proceedings on the theory that an unwed father is not a "parent" whose existing relationship with his children must be considered. "Parents," says the State, "means the father and mother of a legitimate child, or the survivor of them, or the natural mother of an illegitimate child, and includes any adoptive parent," but the term does not include unwed fathers.

Under Illinois law, therefore, while the children of all parents can be taken from them in neglect proceedings, that is only after notice, hearing, and proof of such unfitness as a parent as amounts to neglect, an unwed father is uniquely subject to the more simplistic dependency proceeding. By use of this proceeding, the State, on showing that the father was not married to the mother, need not prove unfitness in fact, because it is presumed at law. Thus, the unwed father's claim of parental qualification is avoided as "irrelevant." * * *

* * *

The private interest here, that of a man in the children he has sired and raised, undeniably warrants deference and, absent a powerful countervailing interest, protection. It is plain that the interest of a parent in the companionship, care, custody, and management of his or her children "come[s] to this Court with a momentum for respect lacking when appeal is made to liberties which derive merely from shifting economic arrangements."

The Court has frequently emphasized the importance of the family. The rights to conceive and to raise one's children have been deemed "essential," *Meyer* v. *Nebraska* (1923), "basic civil rights of man," and "[r]ights far more precious ... than property rights." "It is cardinal with us that the custody, care and nurture of the child reside first in the parents, whose primary function and freedom include preparation for obligations the state can neither supply nor hinder." *Prince* v. *Massachusetts* (1944). * * *

Nor has the law refused to recognize those family relationships unlegitimized by a marriage ceremony. The Court has declared unconstitutional a state statute denying natural, but illegitimate, children a wrongful-death action for the death of their mother, emphasizing that such children cannot be denied the right of other children because familial bonds in such cases were often as warm, enduring, and important as those arising within a more formally organized family unit. *Levy* v. *Louisiana* (1968). "To say that the test of equal protection should be the 'legal' rather than the biological relationship is to avoid the issue. For the Equal Protection Clause necessarily limits the authority of a State to draw such 'legal' lines as it chooses."

These authorities make it clear that, at the least, Stanley's interest in retaining custody of his children is cognizable and substantial.

For its part, the State has made its interest quite plain: Illinois has declared that the aim of the Juvenile Court Act is to protect "the moral, emotional, mental, and physical welfare of the minor and the best interests of the community" and to "strengthen the minor's family ties whenever possible, removing him from the custody of his parents only when his welfare or safety or the protection of the public cannot be adequately safeguarded without removal ..." These are legitimate interests, well within the power of the State to implement. We do not question the assertion that neglectful parents may be separated from their children.

But we are here not asked to evaluate the legitimacy of the state ends, rather, to determine whether the means used to achieve these ends are constitutionally defensible. What is the state interest in separating children from fathers without a hearing designed to determine whether the father is unfit in a particular disputed case? We observe that the State registers no gain towards its declared goals when it separates children from the custody of fit parents. Indeed, if Stanley is a fit father, the State spites its own articulated goals when it needlessly separates him from his family. * * *

It may be, as the State insists, that most unmarried fathers are unsuitable and neglectful parents. It may also be that Stanley is such a parent and that his children should be placed in other hands. But all unmarried fathers are not in this category; some are wholly suited to have custody of their children. This much the State readily concedes, and nothing in this record indicates that Stanley is or has been a neglectful father who has not cared for his children. Given the opportunity to make his case, Stanley may have been seen to be deserving of custody of his offspring. Had this been so, the State's statutory policy would have been furthered by leaving custody in him.

* * *

[I]t may be argued that unmarried fathers are so seldom fit that Illinois need not undergo the administrative inconvenience of inquiry in any case, including Stanley's. The establishment of prompt efficacious procedures to achieve legitimate state ends is a proper state interest worthy of cognizance in constitutional adjudication. But the Constitution recognizes higher values than speed and efficiency. * * *

Procedure by presumption is always cheaper and easier than individualized determination. But when, as here, the procedure forecloses the determinative issues of competence and care, when it explicitly disdains present realities in deference to past formalities, it needlessly risks running roughshod over the important interests of both parent and child. It therefore cannot stand.[9] * * *

* * * The State's interest in caring for Stanley's children is *de minimis* if Stanley is shown to be a fit father. It insists on presuming rather than proving Stanley's unfitness solely because it is more convenient to presume than to prove. Under the Due Process Clause that advantage is insufficient to justify refusing a father a hearing when the issue at stake is the dismemberment of his family.

III

The State of Illinois assumes custody of the children of married parents, divorced parents, and unmarried mothers only after a hearing and proof of neglect. The children of unmarried fathers, however, are declared dependent children without a hearing on parental fitness and without proof of neglect. Stanley's claim in the state courts and here is that failure to afford him a hearing on his parental qualifications while extending it to other parents denied him equal protection of the laws. We have concluded that all Illinois parents are constitutionally entitled to a hearing on their fitness before their children are removed from their

---

9. We note in passing that the incremental cost of offering unwed fathers an opportunity for individualized hearings on fitness appears to be minimal. If unwed fathers, in the main, do not care about the disposition of their children, they will not appear to demand hearings. If they do care, under the scheme here held invalid, Illinois would admittedly at some later time have to afford them a properly focused hearing in a custody or adoption proceeding.

Extending opportunity for hearing to unwed fathers who desire and claim competence to care for their children creates no constitutional or procedural obstacle to foreclosing those unwed fathers who are not so inclined. The Illinois law governing procedure in juvenile cases provides for personal service, notice by certified mail, or for notice by publication when personal or certified mail service cannot be had or when notice is directed to unknown respondents under the style of "All whom it may Concern." Unwed fathers who do not promptly respond cannot complain if their children are declared wards of the State. Those who do respond retain the burden of proving their fatherhood.

custody. It follows that denying such a hearing to Stanley and those like him while granting it to other Illinois parents is inescapably contrary to the Equal Protection Clause.

* * *

MR. JUSTICE POWELL and MR. JUSTICE REHNQUIST took no part in the consideration or decision of this case.

MR. JUSTICE DOUGLAS joins in Parts I and II of this opinion.

MR. CHIEF JUSTICE BURGER, with whom MR. JUSTICE BLACKMUN concurs, dissenting.

* * *

No due process issue was raised in the state courts; and no due process issue was decided by any state court. * * *

* * *

In regard to the only issue that I consider properly before the Court, I agree with the State's argument that the Equal Protection Clause is not violated when Illinois gives full recognition only to those father-child relationships that arise in the context of family units bound together by legal obligations arising from marriage or from adoption proceedings. Quite apart from the religious or quasi-religious connotations that marriage has—and has historically enjoyed—for a large proportion of this Nation's citizens, it is in law an essentially contractual relationship, the parties to which have legally enforceable rights and duties, with respect both to each other and to any children born to them. Stanley and the mother of these children never entered such a relationship. * * * Stanley did not seek the burdens when he could have freely assumed them.

Where there is a valid contract of marriage, the law of Illinois presumes that the husband is the father of any child born to the wife during the marriage; as the father, he has legally enforceable rights and duties with respect to that child. When a child is born to an unmarried woman, Illinois recognizes the readily identifiable mother, but makes no presumption as to the identity of the biological father. It does, however, provide two ways, one voluntary and one involuntary, in which that father may be identified. First, he may marry the mother and acknowledge the child as his own; this has the legal effect of legitimating the child and gaining for the father full recognition as a parent. Second, a man may be found to be the biological father of the child pursuant to a paternity suit initiated by the mother; in this case, the child remains illegitimate, but the adjudicated father is made liable for the support of the child until the latter attains age 18 or is legally adopted by another.

* * *

The Illinois Supreme Court correctly held that the State may constitutionally distinguish between unwed fathers and unwed mothers. Here, Illinois' different treatment of the two is part of that State's statutory scheme for protecting the welfare of illegitimate children. In almost all cases, the unwed mother is readily identifiable, generally from hospital records, and alternatively by physicians or others attending the child's birth. Unwed fathers, as a class, are not traditionally quite so easy to identify and locate. Many of them either deny all responsibility or exhibit no interest in the child or its welfare; and, of course, many unwed fathers are simply not aware of their parenthood.

Furthermore, I believe that a State is fully justified in concluding, on the basis of common human experience, that the biological role of the mother in carrying and nursing an infant creates stronger bonds between her and the child than the bonds resulting from the male's often casual encounter. This view is reinforced by the observable fact that most unwed mothers exhibit a concern for their offspring either permanently or at least until they are safely placed for adoption, while unwed fathers rarely burden either the mother or the child with their attentions or loyalties. Centuries of human experience buttress this view of the realities of human conditions and suggest that unwed mothers of illegitimate children are generally more dependable protectors of their children than are unwed fathers. While these, like most generalizations, are not without exceptions, they nevertheless provide a sufficient basis to sustain a statutory classification whose objective is not to penalize unwed parents but to further the welfare of illegitimate children in fulfillment of the State's obligations as *parens patriae.*

Stanley depicts himself as a somewhat unusual unwed father, namely, as one who has always acknowledged and never doubted his fatherhood of these children. He alleges that he loved, cared for, and supported these children from the time of their birth until the death of their mother. He contends that he consequently must be treated the same as a married father of legitimate children. Even assuming the truth of Stanley's allegations, I am unable to construe the Equal Protection Clause as requiring Illinois to tailor its statutory definition of "parents" so meticulously as to include such unusual unwed fathers, while at the same time excluding those unwed, and generally unidentified, biological fathers who in no way share Stanley's professed desires.

Indeed, the nature of Stanley's own desires is less than absolutely clear from the record in this case. Shortly after the death of the mother, Stanley turned these two children over to the care of a Mr. and Mrs. Ness; he took no action to gain recognition of himself as a father, through adoption, or as a legal custodian, through a guardianship proceeding. Eventually it came to the attention of the State that there was no living adult who had any legally enforceable obligation for the care and support of the children; it was only then that the dependency proceeding here under review took place and that Stanley made himself known to the juvenile court in connection with these two children. Even then, however, Stanley did not ask to be charged with the legal responsibility for the children. He asked only that such legal responsibility be given to no one else. He seemed, in particular, to be concerned with the loss of the welfare payments he would suffer as a result of the designation of others as guardians of the children.

* * *

The Court today * * * invalidates a provision of critical importance to Illinois' carefully drawn statutory system governing family relationships and the welfare of the minor children of the State. And in so invalidating that provision, it ascribes to that statutory system a presumption that is simply not there and embarks on a novel concept of the natural law for unwed fathers that could well have strange boundaries as yet undiscernible.

Notes and Questions

1. *Whose rights mattered?* Joan Stanley, the biological mother, had died before the dependency proceeding, of course. (a) Whose constitutional rights did *Stanley* vindicate?, (b) What did *Stanley* say about whether the children had a constitutional right to their biological father's continued care and companionship unless he was found to be an unfit parent?

2. *Other questions about* Stanley. (a) Now that judicial acceptance of gender-based discrimination is the exception rather than the rule, what state interests justify treating unwed mothers differently from unwed fathers in the first place?,

> (b) Did *Stanley* guarantee rights of parenthood to all unwed fathers, or only to unwed fathers who, like Mr. Stanley, had maintained a relationship with their children?,

> (c) If *Stanley's* guarantees applied to all unwed fathers, what burdens would these guarantees place on adoption proceedings concerning non-marital children? What did the Court say about this burden?,

> (d) Once the Court determined that Mr. Stanley had a due process right to relief, why did the Court proceed to determine that he also had an equal protection right?,

> (e) In footnote 9, the Court suggests that publication notice would adequately protect an absent unwed father's rights. From your understanding of publication notice gleaned from the civil procedure course, do you find this suggestion persuasive? Should the Court have been concerned that publication notice would often embarrass the mother and child, without much likelihood of providing the absent father notice?

3. *Post-*Stanley *decisions.* Stanley was the first Supreme Court decision to address the constitutional rights of fathers with respect to their children born out of wedlock. The decision arose in a dependency proceeding, but observers quickly recognized its application to adoption.

Within a few years, the Court handed down two adoption decisions that distinguished between unwed fathers who, like Mr. Stanley, had maintained relationships with their children before claiming rights of parenthood and unwed fathers who had not maintained such relationships. See Quilloin v. Walcott, 434 U.S. 246 (1978), Caban v. Mohammed, 441 U.S. 380 (1979). These two decisions began to provide some answers to questions *Stanley* left open. The two are synthesized in *Lehr.*

LEHR v. ROBERTSON

Supreme Court of the United States, 1983.
463 U.S. 248.

JUSTICE STEVENS delivered the opinion of the Court.

The question presented is whether New York has sufficiently protected an unmarried father's inchoate relationship with a child whom he has never supported and rarely seen in the two years since her birth. The appellant, Jonathan Lehr, claims that the Due Process and Equal Protection Clauses of the Fourteenth Amendment, as interpreted in *Stanley* v. *Illinois* (1972), and *Caban* v. *Mohammed* (1979), give him an absolute right to notice and an opportunity to be heard before the child may be adopted. We disagree.

Jessica M. was born out of wedlock on November 9, 1976. Her mother, Lorraine Robertson, married Richard Robertson eight months after Jessica's birth. On December 21, 1978, when Jessica was over two years old, the Robertsons filed an adoption petition in the Family Court of Ulster County, New York. The court heard their testimony and received a favorable report from the Ulster County Department of Social Services. On March 7, 1979, the court entered an order of adoption. In this proceeding, appellant contends that the adoption order is invalid because he, Jessica's putative father, was not given advance notice of the adoption proceeding.

The State of New York maintains a "putative father registry." A man who files with that registry demonstrates his intent to claim paternity of a child born out of wedlock and is therefore entitled to receive notice of any proceeding to adopt that child. Before entering Jessica's adoption order, the Ulster County Family Court had the putative father registry examined. Although appellant claims to be Jessica's natural father, he had not entered his name in the registry.

In addition to the persons whose names are listed on the putative father registry, New York law requires that notice of an adoption proceeding be given to several other classes of possible fathers of children born out of wedlock—those who have been adjudicated to be the father, those who have been identified as the father on the child's birth certificate, those who live openly with the child and the child's mother and who hold themselves out to be the father, those who have been identified as the father by the mother in a sworn written statement, and those who were married to the child's mother before the child was six months old. Appellant admittedly was not a member of any of those classes. He had lived with appellee prior to Jessica's birth and visited her in the hospital when Jessica was born, but his name does not appear on Jessica's birth certificate. He did not live with appellee or Jessica after Jessica's birth, he has never provided them with any financial support, and he has never offered to marry appellee. Nevertheless, he contends that the following special circumstances gave him a constitutional right to notice and a hearing before Jessica was adopted.

On January 30, 1979, one month after the adoption proceeding was commenced in Ulster County, appellant filed a "visitation and paternity petition" in the Westchester County Family Court. In that petition, he asked for a determination of paternity, an order of support, and reasonable visitation privileges with Jessica. Notice of that proceeding was served on appellee on February 22, 1979. Four days later appellee's attorney informed the Ulster County Court that appellant had commenced a paternity proceeding in Westchester County; the Ulster County judge then entered an order staying appellant's paternity proceeding until he could rule on a motion to change the venue of that proceeding to Ulster County. On March 3, 1979, appellant received notice of the change of venue motion and, for the first time, learned that an adoption proceeding was pending in Ulster County.

On March 7, 1979, appellant's attorney telephoned the Ulster County judge to inform him that he planned to seek a stay of the adoption proceeding pending the determination of the paternity petition. In that telephone conversation, the judge advised the lawyer that he had already signed the adoption order earlier that day. According to appellant's attorney, the judge stated that he was aware of the pending paternity petition but did not believe he was required to give notice to appellant prior to the entry of the order of adoption. * * *

The Appellate Division of the Supreme Court affirmed [the order denying Lehr's petition to vacate the adoption order]. * * * The New York Court of Appeals also affirmed by a divided vote. * * *

Appellant has now invoked our appellate jurisdiction. He offers two alternative grounds for holding the New York statutory scheme unconstitutional. First, he contends that a putative father's actual or potential relationship with a child born out of wedlock is an interest in liberty which may not be destroyed without due process of law; he argues therefore that he had a constitutional right to prior notice and an opportunity to be heard before he was deprived of that interest. Second, he contends that the gender-based classification in the statute, which both denied him the right to consent to Jessica's adoption and accorded him fewer procedural rights than her mother, violated the Equal Protection Clause.

The Due Process Claim.

* * *

* * * We * * * first consider the nature of the interest in liberty for which appellant claims constitutional protection and then turn to a discussion of the adequacy of the procedure that New York has provided for its protection.

I

The intangible fibers that connect parent and child have infinite variety. They are woven throughout the fabric of our society, providing it with strength, beauty, and flexibility. It is self-evident that they are sufficiently vital to merit constitutional protection in appropriate cases. In deciding whether this is such a case, however, we must consider the broad framework that has traditionally been used to resolve the legal problems arising from the parent-child relationship.

* * *

* * * This Court has examined the extent to which a natural father's biological relationship with his child receives protection under the Due Process Clause in precisely three cases: *Stanley* v. *Illinois* (1972), *Quilloin* v. *Walcott* (1978), and *Caban* v. *Mohammed* (1979).

Stanley involved the constitutionality of an Illinois statute that conclusively presumed every father of a child born out of wedlock to be an unfit person to have custody of his children. The father in that case had lived with his children all their lives and had lived with their mother for 18 years. There was nothing in the record to indicate that Stanley had been a neglectful father who had not cared for his children. Under the statute, however, the nature of the actual relationship between parent and child was completely irrelevant. Once the mother died, the children were automatically made wards of the state. * * * [T]he Court held that the Due Process Clause was violated by the automatic destruction of the custodial relationship without giving the father any opportunity to present evidence regarding his fitness as a parent.

Quilloin involved the constitutionality of a Georgia statute that authorized the adoption, over the objection of the natural father, of a child born out of wedlock. The father in that case had never legitimated the child. It was only after the mother had remarried and her new husband had filed an adoption petition that the natural father sought visitation rights and filed a petition for legitimation. The trial court found adoption by the new husband to be in the child's best interests, and we unanimously held that action to be consistent with the Due Process Clause.

Caban involved the conflicting claims of two natural parents who had maintained joint custody of their children from the time of their birth until they were respectively two and four years old. The father challenged the validity of an order authorizing the mother's new husband to adopt the children; he relied on both the Equal Protection Clause and the Due Process Clause. Because this Court upheld his equal protection claim, the majority did not address his due process challenge. The comments on the latter claim by the four dissenting Justices are nevertheless instructive, because they identify the clear distinction between a mere biological relationship and an actual relationship of parental responsibility.

* * *

The difference between the developed parent-child relationship that was implicated in *Stanley* and *Caban*, and the potential relationship involved in *Quilloin* and this case, is both clear and significant. When an unwed father demonstrates a full commitment to the responsibilities of parenthood by "com[ing] forward to participate in the rearing of his child," *Caban*, his interest in personal contact with his child acquires substantial protection under the Due Process Clause. At that point it may be said that he "act[s] as a father toward his children." But the mere existence of a biological link does not merit equivalent constitutional protection. The actions of judges neither create nor sever genetic bonds. "[T]he importance of the familial relationship, to the individuals involved and to the society, stems from the emotional attachments that derive from the intimacy of daily association, and from the role it plays in 'promot[ing] a way of life' through the instruction of children ... as well as from the fact of blood relationship."

The significance of the biological connection is that it offers the natural father an opportunity that no other male possesses to develop a relationship with his offspring. If he grasps that opportunity and accepts some measure of responsibility for the child's future, he may enjoy the blessings of the parent-child relationship and make uniquely valuable contributions to the child's development.[18] If he fails to do so, the Federal Constitution will not automatically compel a State to listen to his opinion of where the child's best interests lie.

In this case, we are not assessing the constitutional adequacy of New York's procedures for terminating a developed relationship. Appellant has never had any significant custodial, personal, or financial relationship with Jessica, and he did not seek to establish a legal tie until after she was two years old.[19] We are concerned only with whether New York has adequately protected his opportunity to form such a relationship.

II

The most effective protection of the putative father's opportunity to develop a relationship with his child is provided by the laws that authorize formal marriage and govern its consequences. But the availability of that protection is, of course, dependent on the will of both

18. Of course, we need not take sides in the ongoing debate among family psychologists over the relative weight to be accorded biological ties and psychological ties, in order to recognize that a natural father who has played a substantial role in rearing his child has a greater claim to constitutional protection than a mere biological parent. New York's statutory scheme reflects these differences, guaranteeing notice to any putative father who is living openly with the child, and providing putative fathers who have never developed a relationship with the child the opportunity to receive notice simply by mailing a postcard to the putative father registry.

19. This case happens to involve an adoption by the husband of the natural mother, but we do not believe the natural father has any greater right to object to such an adoption than to an adoption by two total strangers. If anything, the balance of equities tips the opposite way in a case such as this. In denying the putative father relief in *Quilloin* v. *Walcott*, we made an observation equally applicable here:

"Nor is this a case in which the proposed adoption would place the child with a new set of parents with whom the child had never before lived. Rather, the result of the adoption in this case is to give full recognition to a family unit already in existence, a result desired by all concerned, except appellant. Whatever might be required in other situations, we cannot say that the State was required in this situation to find anything more than that the adoption, and denial of legitimation, were in the 'best interests of the child.' "

parents of the child. Thus, New York has adopted a special statutory scheme to protect the unmarried father's interest in assuming a responsible role in the future of his child.

After this Court's decision in *Stanley*, the New York Legislature appointed a special commission to recommend legislation that would accommodate both the interests of biological fathers in their children and the children's interest in prompt and certain adoption procedures. The commission recommended, and the legislature enacted, a statutory adoption scheme that automatically provides notice to seven categories of putative fathers who are likely to have assumed some responsibility for the care of their natural children. If this scheme were likely to omit many responsible fathers, and if qualification for notice were beyond the control of an interested putative father, it might be thought procedurally inadequate. Yet, as all of the New York courts that reviewed this matter observed, the right to receive notice was completely within appellant's control. By mailing a postcard to the putative father registry, he could have guaranteed that he would receive notice of any proceedings to adopt Jessica. The possibility that he may have failed to do so because of his ignorance of the law cannot be a sufficient reason for criticizing the law itself. The New York legislature concluded that a more open-ended notice requirement would merely complicate the adoption process, threaten the privacy interests of unwed mothers, create the risk of unnecessary controversy, and impair the desired finality of adoption decrees. Regardless of whether we would have done likewise if we were legislators instead of judges, we surely cannot characterize the state's conclusion as arbitrary.

Appellant argues, however, that even if the putative father's opportunity to establish a relationship with an illegitimate child is adequately protected by the New York statutory scheme in the normal case, he was nevertheless entitled to special notice because the court and the mother knew that he had filed an affiliation proceeding in another court. This argument amounts to nothing more than an indirect attack on the notice provisions of the New York statute. The legitimate state interests in facilitating the adoption of young children and having the adoption proceeding completed expeditiously that underlie the entire statutory scheme also justify a trial judge's determination to require all interested parties to adhere precisely to the procedural requirements of the statute. The Constitution does not require either a trial judge or a litigant to give special notice to nonparties who are presumptively capable of asserting and protecting their own rights. Since the New York statutes adequately protected appellant's inchoate interest in establishing a relationship with Jessica, we find no merit in the claim that his constitutional rights were offended because the family court strictly complied with the notice provisions of the statute.

The Equal Protection Claim.

* * *

The legislation at issue in this case * * * is intended to establish procedures for adoptions. Those procedures are designed to promote the best interests of the child, protect the rights of interested third parties, and ensure promptness and finality. To serve those ends, the legislation guarantees to certain people the right to veto an adoption and the right to prior notice of any adoption proceeding. The mother of an illegitimate child is always within that favored class, but only certain putative fathers are included. Appellant contends that the gender-based distinction is invidious.

As we have already explained, the existence or nonexistence of a substantial relationship between parent and child is a relevant criterion in evaluating both the rights of the parent and the best interests of the child. In *Quilloin* v. *Walcott*, we noted that the putative father, like appellant, "ha[d] never shouldered any significant responsibility with respect to the daily supervision, education, protection, or care of the child. Appellant does not complain of his exemption from these responsibilities. . . ." We therefore found that a Georgia statute that always required a mother's consent to the adoption of a child born out of wedlock, but required the father's consent only if he had legitimated the child, did not violate the Equal Protection Clause. Because, like the father in *Quilloin*, appellant has never established a substantial relationship with his daughter, the New York statutes at issue in this case did not operate to deny appellant equal protection.

We have held that these statutes may not constitutionally be applied in that class of cases where the mother and father are in fact similarly situated with regard to their relationship with the child. In *Caban* v. *Mohammed* (1979), the Court held that it violated the Equal Protection Clause to grant the mother a veto over the adoption of a four-year-old girl and a six-year-old boy, but not to grant a veto to their father, who had admitted paternity and had participated in the rearing of the children. The Court made it clear, however, that if the father had not "come forward to participate in the rearing of his child, nothing in the Equal Protection Clause [would] preclud[e] the State from withholding from him the privilege of vetoing the adoption of that child."

Jessica's parents are not like the parents involved in *Caban*. Whereas appellee had a continuous custodial responsibility for Jessica, appellant never established any custodial, personal, or financial relationship with her. If one parent has an established custodial relationship with the child and the other parent has either abandoned or never established a relationship, the Equal Protection Clause does not prevent a state from according the two parents different legal rights.

* * *

Justice White, with whom Justice Marshall and Justice Blackmun join, dissenting.

* * *

I

* * *

* * * As Jessica's biological father, Lehr either had an interest protected by the Constitution or he did not. If the entry of the adoption order in this case deprived Lehr of a constitutionally protected interest, he is entitled to notice and an opportunity to be heard before the order can be accorded finality.

According to Lehr, he and Jessica's mother met in 1971 and began living together in 1974. The couple cohabited for approximately 2 years, until Jessica's birth in 1976. Throughout the pregnancy and after the birth, Lorraine acknowledged to friends and relatives that Lehr was Jessica's father; Lorraine told Lehr that she had reported to the New York State Department of Social Services that he was the father. Lehr visited Lorraine and Jessica in the hospital every day during Lorraine's confinement. According to Lehr, from the time Lorraine was discharged from the hospital until August, 1978, she concealed her whereabouts from him. During this time Lehr never ceased his efforts to locate Lorraine and Jessica and achieved sporadic success until August, 1977, after which time he was unable to locate them at all. On those occasions when he did determine Lorraine's location, he visited with her and her children to the extent she was willing to permit it. When Lehr, with the aid of a detective agency, located Lorraine and Jessica in August, 1978, Lorraine was already married to Mr. Robertson. Lehr asserts that at this time he offered to provide financial assistance and to set up a trust fund for Jessica, but that Lorraine refused. Lorraine threatened Lehr with arrest unless he stayed away and refused to permit him to see Jessica. Thereafter Lehr retained counsel who wrote to Lorraine in early December, 1978, requesting that she permit Lehr to visit Jessica and threatening legal action on Lehr's behalf. On December 21, 1978, perhaps as a response to Lehr's threatened legal action, appellees commenced the adoption action at issue here.

* * *

Lehr's version of the "facts" paints a far different picture than that portrayed by the majority. The majority's recitation, that "[a]ppellant has never had any significant custodial, personal, or financial relationship with Jessica, and he did not seek to establish a legal tie until after she was two years old," obviously does not tell the whole story. Appellant has never been afforded an opportunity to present his case. The legitimation proceeding he instituted was first stayed, and then dismissed, on appellees' motions. Nor could appellant establish his interest during the adoption proceedings, for it is the failure to provide Lehr notice and an opportunity to be heard there that is at issue here. We cannot fairly make a judgment based on the quality or substance of a relationship without a complete and developed factual record. This case requires us to assume that Lehr's allegations are true—that but for the actions of the child's mother there would have been the kind of significant relationship that the majority concedes is entitled to the full panoply of procedural due process protections.

I reject the peculiar notion that the only significance of the biological connection between father and child is that "it offers the natural father an opportunity that no other male possesses to develop a relationship with his offspring." A "mere biological relationship" is not as unimportant in determining the nature of liberty interests as the majority suggests.

"[T]he usual understanding of 'family' implies biological relationships, and most decisions treating the relation between parent and child have stressed this element." The "biological connection" is itself a relationship that creates a protected interest. Thus the "nature" of the interest is the parent-child relationship; how well-developed that relationship has become goes to its "weight," not its "nature." Whether Lehr's interest is entitled to constitutional protection does not entail a searching inquiry into the quality of the relationship but a simple determination of the *fact* that the relationship exists—a fact that even the majority agrees must be assumed to be established.

* * * Any analysis of the adequacy of the notice in this case must be conducted on the assumption that the interest involved here is as strong as that of *any* putative father. That is not to say that due process requires actual notice to every putative father or that adoptive parents or the State must conduct an exhaustive search of records or an intensive investigation before a final adoption order may be entered. The procedures adopted by the State, however, must at least represent a reasonable effort to determine the identity of the putative father and to give him adequate notice.

II

In this case, of course, there was no question about either the identity or the location of the putative father. The mother knew exactly who he was and both she and the court entering the order of adoption knew precisely where he was and how to give him actual notice that his parental rights were about to be terminated by an adoption order. Lehr was entitled to due process, and the right to be heard is one of the fundamentals of that right, which " 'has little reality or worth unless one is informed that the matter is pending and can choose for himself whether to appear or default, acquiesce or contest.' "

* * *

The State asserts that any problem in this respect is overcome by the seventh category of putative fathers to whom notice must be given, namely those fathers who have identified themselves in the putative father register maintained by the State. Since Lehr did not take advantage of this device to make his interest known, the State contends, he was not entitled to notice and a hearing even though his identity, location and interest were known to the adoption court prior to entry of the adoption order. I have difficulty with this position. First, it represents a grudging and crabbed approach to due process. The State is quite willing to give notice and a hearing to putative fathers who have made themselves known by resorting to the putative fathers' register. It makes little sense to me to deny notice and hearing to a father who has not placed his name in the register but who has unmistakably identified himself by filing suit to establish his paternity and has notified the adoption court of his action and his interest. I thus need not question the statutory scheme on its face. Even assuming that Lehr would have been foreclosed if his failure to utilize the register had somehow disadvantaged the State, he effectively made himself known by other means, and it is the sheerest formalism to deny him a hearing because he informed the State in the wrong manner.

No state interest is substantially served by denying Lehr adequate notice and a hearing. The State no doubt has an interest in expediting adoption proceedings to prevent a child from remaining unduly long in the custody of the State or foster parents. But this is not an adoption involving a child in the custody of an authorized state agency. Here the child is in the custody of the mother and will remain in her custody. Moreover, had Lehr utilized the putative father register, he would have been granted a prompt hearing, and there was no justifiable reason, in terms of delay, to refuse him a hearing in the circumstances of this case.

The State's undoubted interest in the finality of adoption orders likewise is not well served by a procedure that will deny notice and a hearing to a father whose identity and location are known. As this case well illustrates, denying notice and a hearing to such a father may result in years of additional litigation and threaten the reopening of adoption proceedings and the vacation of the adoption. * * *

Notes and Questions

1. *Whose rights mattered?* (a) Whose constitutional rights determined *Lehr's* outcome?, (b) In determining whether the Constitution granted the unwed father the right to veto the adoption, what did *Lehr* say about whether the child had a constitutional right to her biological father's continued care and companionship unless he was found to be an unfit parent?, (c) What did *Lehr* say about the constitutional rights of the biological mother or the prospective adoptive stepparent?

2. *The interests at stake.* (a) What are the respective *interests* of the unwed father, the mother, the child and the state when an adoption petition is filed with respect to an out-of-wedlock child? See, e.g., Eric G. Andersen, Children, Parents, and Nonparents: Protected Interests and Legal Standards, 1998 BYU L. Rev. 935, 969–74. Might any of these interests be disserved by focusing solely on the unwed father's constitutional *rights*?, (b) According to *Lehr*, how substantial a relationship with the child must the unwed father develop before he earns the constitutional right to withhold consent to the adoption?

3. Lehr's *holding*. According to *Lehr*, what steps must the unwed father take to assure himself the rights to notice of the child's adoption proceeding

and to withhold consent? In New York and other states that have enacted putative fathers' registries, what must an unwed father prove to win entitlement to veto the child's adoption? What rights does the father have if he registers but does not develop the appropriate relationship with the child (or the mother), or vice versa?

4. *More on* Quilloin *and* Caban. The Court set the stage for *Lehr* in *Quilloin* and *Caban*, both of which concerned unwed fathers' efforts to veto adoptions despite the statute that gave unwed fathers no veto right. Before the stepfather's adoption petition was filed, Mr. Quilloin had never sought custody or visitation of his 11–year-old son, had supported the boy only irregularly, and had had several contentious visits with him. Even when the adoption petition was filed, Mr. Quilloin sought only visitation and not custody. The Court held that *Stanley* did not compel the state to enable Mr. Quilloin to veto the adoption because he had "never exercised actual or legal custody over the child, and thus ha[d] never shouldered any significant responsibility with respect to the daily supervision, education, protection, or care of the child." 434 U.S. 246, 256 (1978).

Mr. Caban, on the other hand, had lived with his two children as their father and had supported them for several years until he and their mother separated. He continued to see the children often after the separation and continued to raise them. The Supreme Court held that *Stanley* granted Mr. Caban a constitutional right to veto the children's adoption because his "substantial relationship" with his children was different from Mr. Quilloin's "failure to act as a father." 441 U.S. 380, 389 n. 7 (1979).

5. *Domestic violence.* May an adoption proceed without notice to the unwed father, and without his consent, if the mother's refusal to identify him stems from her reasonable fear of physical violence if she does identify him? See In re Karen A. B., 513 A.2d 770 (Del.1986).

6. *Divorced fathers' notice rights.* Lehr held that the unwed father did not have a due process right to notice of his child's adoption. Does due process require that a *divorced* father be given notice of his child's impending adoption by the stepfather? See Armstrong v. Manzo, 380 U.S. 545 (1965). Consider also the holding in Mullane v. Central Hanover Bank & Trust Co., 339 U.S. 306 (1950), a staple of the first-year civil procedure course.

7. *Must the unwed father have maintained a relationship with the mother?* Chapter 2 presented Michael H. v. Gerald D., 491 U.S. 110 (1989) (plurality opinion), in which a sharply divided Court rejected the constitutional claims of an unwed father who had concededly maintained a relationship with his young child. Recall that Michael H., the unwed father, had asserted his interest in raising and providing for young Victoria ever since her birth, had contributed to her support, and had lived with the biological mother, Carole D. (though only intermittently). Michael and Carole had conceived the child, however, while she was married to another man, Gerald D., to whom she remained married at the time of the litigation. When Carole and Gerald tried to end Michael's contact with the girl, Michael unsuccessfully sought a hearing to determine his paternity.

Blood tests showed a 98.07% certainty that Michael was the girl's father, but *Michael H.* upheld the constitutionality of a California statute that conclusively presumed that a child born of a woman living with her husband is a child of the marriage. (The statute permitted the presumption to be challenged only by the woman or her husband, and only in limited circumstances.). The Court produced five opinions, none of which garnered a majority. Much of the Justices' disagreement stemmed from their divergent syntheses of *Stanley* and its progeny.

Justice Scalia's plurality opinion concluded that Michael, the "adulterous natural father," did not assert a liberty interest necessary to trigger due process at all:

> * * * Michael reads the landmark case of *Stanley* v. *Illinois* and the subsequent cases of *Quilloin* v. *Walcott, Caban* v. *Mohammed,* and *Lehr* v. *Robertson* as establishing that a liberty interest is created by biological fatherhood plus an established parental relationship—factors that exist in the present case as well. We think that distorts the rationale of those cases. As we view them, they rest not upon such isolated factors but upon the historic respect—indeed, sanctity would not be too strong a term–traditionally accorded to the relationships that develop within the unitary family. In *Stanley,* for example, we forbade the destruction of such a family when, upon the death of the mother, the State had sought to remove children from the custody of a father who had lived with and supported them and their mother for 18 years. * * *

> Thus, the legal issue in the present case reduces to whether the relationship between persons in the situation of Michael and Victoria has been treated as a protected family unit under the historic practices of our society, or whether on any other basis it has been accorded special protection. We think it impossible to find that it has. In fact, quite to the contrary, our traditions have protected the marital family (Gerald, Carole, and the child they acknowledge to be theirs) against the sort of claim Michael asserts.

* * *

> In *Lehr* v. *Robertson,* a case involving a natural father's attempt to block his child's adoption by the unwed mother's new husband, we observed that "[t]he significance of the biological connection is that it offers the natural father an opportunity that no other male possesses to develop a relationship with his offspring," and we assumed that the Constitution might require some protection of that opportunity. Where, however, the child is born into an extant marital family, the natural father's unique opportunity conflicts with the similarly unique opportunity of the husband of the marriage; and it is not unconstitutional for the State to give categorical preference to the latter. * * * In accord with our traditions, a limit is also imposed by the circumstance that the mother is, at the time of the child's conception and birth, married to, and cohabitating with, another man, both of whom wish to raise the child as the offspring of their union. It is a question of legislative policy and not constitutional law whether California will allow the presumed parenthood of a couple desiring to retain a child conceived within and born into their marriage to be rebutted.

* * *

491 U.S. at 121–24, 128–30. The Chief Justice joined the plurality opinion. Justices O'Connor and Kennedy also joined the plurality, but refused to join a lengthy footnote which imposed history-based limits on due process analysis. Justice Stevens concurred separately in the judgment.

Justice Brennan's forceful dissent, joined by Justices Marshall and Blackmun, chastised the plurality for upholding a statute that "stubbornly insists that Gerald is Victoria's father in the face of evidence showing a 98 percent probability that her father is Michael." Justice Brennan read the *Stanley* line of decisions differently than the plurality did:

> * * * Though different in factual and legal circumstances, [*Stanley*, *Quilloin*, *Caban* and *Lehr*] have produced a unifying theme: although an unwed father's biological link to his child does not, in and of itself, guarantee him a constitutional stake in his relationship with that child, such a link combined with a substantial parent-child relationship will do so. "When an unwed father demonstrates a full commitment to the responsibilities of parenthood by 'com [ing] forward to participate in the rearing of his child,' . . . his interest in personal contact with his child acquires substantial protection under the Due Process Clause. At that point it may be said that he 'act[s] as a father toward his children.' " *Lehr*. This commitment is why Mr. Stanley and Mr. Caban won; why Mr. Quilloin and Mr. Lehr lost; and why Michael H. should prevail today. Michael H. is almost certainly Victoria D.'s natural father, has lived with her as her father, has contributed to her support, and has from the beginning sought to strengthen and maintain his relationship with her.

* * *

> The evidence is undisputed that Michael, Victoria, and Carole did live together as a family; that is, they shared the same household, Victoria called Michael "Daddy," Michael contributed to Victoria's support, and he is eager to continue his relationship with her. Yet they are not, in the plurality's view, a "unitary family," whereas Gerald, Carole, and Victoria do compose such a family. The only difference between these two sets of relationships, however, is the fact of marriage. The plurality, indeed, expressly recognizes that marriage is the critical fact in denying Michael a constitutionally protected stake in his relationship with Victoria * * *. However, the very premise of *Stanley* and the cases following it is that marriage is not decisive in answering the question whether the Constitution protects the parental relationship under consideration. These cases are, after all, important precisely because they involve the rights of unwed fathers. It is important to remember, moreover, that in *Quilloin*, *Caban*, and *Lehr*, the putative father's demands would have disrupted a "unitary family" as the plurality defines it; in each case, the husband of the child's mother sought to adopt the child over the objections of the natural father. Significantly, our decisions in those cases in no way relied on the need to protect the marital family. Hence the plurality's claim that *Stanley*, *Quilloin*, *Caban*, and *Lehr* were about the "unitary family," as that family is defined by today's plurality, is surprising indeed.

* * *

491 U.S. at 142–45. Justice White (joined by Justice Brennan) also dissented, concluding that as the child's biological father, Michael had a liberty interest that could not be denied without due process of law:

* * *

Like Justices BRENNAN, MARSHALL, BLACKMUN, and STEVENS, I do not agree with the plurality opinion's conclusion that a natural father can never "have a constitutionally protected interest in his relationship with a child whose mother was married to, and cohabiting with, another man at the time of the child's conception and birth." Prior cases here have recognized the liberty interest of a father in his relationship with his child. In none of these cases did we indicate that the father's rights were dependent on the marital status of the mother or biological father. The basic principle enunciated in the Court's unwed father cases is that an unwed father who has demonstrated a sufficient commitment to his paternity by way of personal, financial, or custodial responsibilities has a protected liberty interest in a relationship with his child.

* * *

As the Court has said: "The significance of the biological connection is that it offers the natural father an opportunity that no other male possesses to develop a relationship with his offspring. If he grasps that opportunity and accepts some measure of responsibility for the child's future, he may enjoy the blessings of the parent-child relationship and make uniquely valuable contributions to the child's development." *Lehr*. It is as if this passage was addressed to Michael. Yet the plurality today recants.

* * *

491 U.S. at 157–58, 163. Professor Deborah L. Forman observes that "the Supreme Court's definition of fatherhood after *Michael H.* is far from clear and undoubtedly reflects the ambivalence society and the individual Justices feel about unwed fathers." She concludes that the decisions from *Stanley* to *Michael H.* yield these principles: "First, the biological connection itself does not make a man a father. To qualify as a father, the man must also establish a social relationship with the child. Second, the satisfaction of the biology plus formula is necessary but not sufficient to establish fatherhood. Whether a man will be recognized as a father will depend to a great extent on the nature of the relationship he has maintained with the mother and whether his recognition would disrupt any existing formal family units." Deborah L. Forman, Unwed Fathers and Adoption: A Theoretical Analysis in Context, 72 Tex. L. Rev. 967, 977–78 (1994).

Professor Janet L. Dolgin goes a step further, arguing that after *Michael H.*, "[a] biological father does protect his paternity by developing a social relationship with his child, but this step demands the creation of a family, a step itself depending upon an appropriate relationship between the man and his child's mother." The father must have established a marriage or marriage-like relationship with the mother. Janet L. Dolgin, Just a Gene: Judicial Assumptions About Parenthood, 40 UCLA L. Rev. 637, 650, 671

(1993). Professor Forman responds that by suggesting the Court might reach a different conclusion about the adulterous father's rights where the marital parents did not wish to raise the child themselves, Justice Scalia "arguably undercuts" Professor Dolgin's interpretation. According to Professor Forman, the suggestion indicates that the court "would recognize a liberty interest in a man in Michael's position even though he had never formed a more traditional family with the mother and child than Michael did with Carol and Victoria." 72 Tex. L. Rev. at 977.

A few state statutes confer rights on only unwed fathers who develop a relationship with both the child and the mother. See, e.g., Kan. Stat. § 59–2136(h)(4), (5); Wis. Stat. § 48.415(6)(a)(2), 6(b). See also, e.g., In re Adoption of Baby E.A.W., 658 So.2d 961 (Fla.1995) (holding that an unwed father's emotional abuse of the mother during pregnancy can constitute abuse under the state adoption act, a predicate for waiver of the right to consent to the adoption); In re Adoption of Doe, 543 So.2d 741 (Fla.1989) (holding that an unwed father's prebirth conduct toward the mother can constitute abandonment under the state adoption act, a predicate for waiver of the right to consent to the adoption).

PROBLEM 7–4

You are a state legislator. In light of *Lehr* and *Michael H.*, would you vote to enact this statute?:

> In an adoption case, the juvenile court may terminate the rights of a child's unmarried father if it finds that termination is in the best interests of the child and when it appears by clear and convincing evidence that: * * * the child's unmarried mother has voluntarily terminated her rights and the child's father, knowing he is the child's father, has provided no financial or emotional support to the mother during the pregnancy or at the birth of the child.

A NOTE ABOUT PUTATIVE FATHER REGISTRIES

A number of states have created putative father registries after *Lehr* upheld their general constitutionality. Where a man believes he is or may be a child's father, registry statutes place the burden on the man to register (usually with the state department of health or similar agency) if he wishes to receive notice of a prospective adoption. Once the man receives notice, he may seek to establish paternity and assert his right to veto the adoption.

New York's registry statute at issue in *Lehr* established no time limit within which the putative father must register to preserve his claim of right. In some states, however, the statute requires him to register before the child is born or within a specified short period after birth. See, e.g., Ariz. Rev. Stat. § 8–106.01B (any time before the child's birth but not later than 30 days after birth). Failure to register within the specified period may constitute waiver not only of the right of notice but also of the right to contest the adoption. See, e.g., id. § 8–106.01E.

Registry statutes are generally strictly construed against the putative father, both to avoid the lengthy custody battles the registries are designed to prevent, and to protect the unwed mother from "the terrible limbo of growing attachment and love for the child, awaiting either the outcome of a judicial proceeding with its attendant notoriety or the decision of the amorous Hamlet in the wings, pondering whether he should assume his responsibility." Shoecraft v. Catholic Social Servs. Bureau, Inc., 385 N.W.2d 448 (Neb.1986). Strict construction has been upheld against constitutional attack. See, e.g., In re Adoption of Reeves, 831 S.W.2d 607, 608 (Ark. 1992) (holding that the putative father who failed to register waived his parental rights even though he had established a "significant relationship" with the child).

In Sanchez v. L.D.S. Social Servs., 680 P.2d 753, 755–56 (Utah 1984), the putative father had repeatedly asked the mother to marry him, had publicly acknowledged paternity throughout the pregnancy and had personally informed the adoption agency of his opposition to adoption and his desire for custody, and had attempted to sign the child's birth certificate before the child left the hospital (but was prevented from doing so by the natural mother's failure to consent). During the pregnancy, he did not know of the registry's existence and the agency did not advise him of its existence. He filed a notice of paternity within hours after learning of the registry during consultation with an attorney. The filing came when the child was less than a week old and before any adoption petition had been filed, but it was late because the four-day-old child had already been relinquished to an agency. Id. at 756. The court rejected the putative father's constitutional challenge with a stern lecture: "Marriage is the institution established by society for the procreation and rearing of children. Those who conceive children outside the bonds of marriage may be loving parents, but experience teaches that the number of illegitimate children born each year contribute disproportionately to many of the serious social problems with which society must cope. It is not too harsh to require that those responsible for bringing children into the world outside the established institution of marriage should be required either to comply with those statutes that accord them the opportunity to assert their parental rights or to yield to the method established by society to raise children in a manner best suited to promote their welfare." Id. at 755.

A persistent problem is that most men never learn of the registry's existence. Most unwed fathers are not lawyers, and it is not normal practice to consult a lawyer about childbirth. A few states have amended their registry statutes to maximize publicity in places likely to be frequented by unwed fathers, such as hospitals, local health departments and other such health facilities, motor vehicle department offices, and schools and universities. Regardless of the extent of publicity, however, the putative father's lack of knowledge of the registry's existence does not excuse noncompliance with the registration provisions. Noncompliance is likewise not excused because the unwed father asserts he did not know about the pregnancy or the birth. See, e.g., 750 Ill. Comp. Stat.

50/12.1(g). The rationale is that men "are aware that sexual intercourse may result in pregnancy, and of the potential opportunity to establish a family." In re Clausen, 502 N.W.2d 649, 687 (Mich.1993) (Levin, J., dissenting).

Despite the statutory purpose to enable unwed fathers to protect their rights, registries are not foolproof. For one thing, each registry is a particular state's enactment, without reach or effect in other states. Assume two teenagers conceive a child while on summer vacation in state A, and then return to their homes in states B and C respectively. With the help of her parents, the teenage mother in state C then places the child for adoption in state D, asserting that she does not know the father's identity or whereabouts. If each of these states has a putative father registry, where should the father register? What if the father has no idea that adoption proceedings are pending in state D? What are the chances that registration will provide him notice of the adoption proceedings? Would a system of interstate cooperation, which would enable putative fathers to search the registries of all states after registering in their own state, help provide actual notice to men who truly want to assert their parental rights?

For a critique of the operation of putative father registry statutes, see Deborah L. Forman, Unwed Fathers and Adoption: A Theoretical Analysis in Context, 72 Tex. L. Rev. 967, 1001–07 (1994).

PROBLEM 7–5

After you complete the children and the law course, a friend confides that he has had intercourse with a woman and that she is now pregnant. Your friend asks whether he should register with the putative father registry, and what the legal consequences would be if he does register? What advice would you provide?

2. Strains on the Constitutional Law

From *Stanley* to *Michael H.,* the Supreme Court's unwed-father decisions concerned children who were at least a few years old when the dispute arose, and children whose existence and whereabouts the fathers had known about since birth. The decisions do not explicitly answer two recurring questions:

(a) *Newborn adoptions.* Many transfers of children to nonrelative adoptive parents occur at birth or within days (but not years) thereafter. What are the unwed father's constitutional rights to veto an adoption at the child's birth, when the unwed father will have had no opportunity yet to "develop a relationship" with the child?

(b) *The "thwarted" unwed father.* What are the unwed father's constitutional rights where the biological mother, seeking to thwart his efforts to develop the requisite relationship with the child, places the child for adoption at birth or shortly afterwards after hiding the child from the father, after untruthfully asserting that she does not know the father's identity or whereabouts, after refusing to name the father, after forging his signature on consent documents, or after knowingly naming the wrong man? See, e.g., Martha Shirk, Unwed Youth Fought Years For His Baby: Secret Adoption Cut Him Out, St. Louis Post–Dispatch, Feb. 13, 1994, at 1.

The National Council for Adoption estimates that less than 1% of adoptions annually are contested. Potential for contests lurks, however, because the biological father cannot be located in at least half of all adoption cases. See Jon D. Hull, The Ties that Traumatize, Time, April 12, 1993, at 48–49. Headlines periodically remind us of the passions and hardship that may follow a newborn adoption marked by evident fraud or misrepresentation by one birth parent, by the prospective adoptive parents or by an intermediary. Bitter dispute may accompany the unwed father's assertion of parental rights after transfer of the child or entry of the adoption decree.

These contested adoptions sternly test some of the propositions raised in Chapter 2. The following opinions chronicle the "Baby Richard" case, which determined the rights of an unwed father temporarily thwarted by the mother's deception. The case dominated the headlines for more than three years and aroused the national consciousness because, despite adoption's goal to serve the best interests of the child, the youngster appeared victimized by adult manipulation and systemic breakdown. As you proceed, ask whether the law's focus on the unwed father's constitutional rights may sometimes disserve the best interests of the child, and whether the child and the other actors should hold countervailing constitutional rights. You should also ask whether children, often pawns in contested adoption dramas, might sometimes be better served if the law abandoned its general unwillingness to recognize that a child might have more than one mother or more than one father.

IN RE PETITION OF DOE

Supreme Court of Illinois, 1994.
638 N.E.2d 181.

JUSTICE HEIPLE delivered the opinion of the court:

John and Jane Doe filed a petition to adopt a newborn baby boy. The baby's biological mother, Daniella Janikova, executed a consent to have the baby adopted four days after his birth without informing his biological father, Otakar Kirchner, to whom she was not yet married.

The mother told the father that the baby had died, and he did not find out otherwise until 57 days after the birth. The trial court ruled that the father's consent was unnecessary because he did not show sufficient interest in the child during the first 30 days of the child's life. The appellate court affirmed with one justice dissenting. We granted leave to appeal and now reverse.

Otakar and Daniella began living together in the fall of 1989, and Daniella became pregnant in June of 1990. For the first eight months of her pregnancy, Otakar provided for all of her expenses.

In late January 1991, Otakar went to his native Czechoslovakia to attend to his gravely ill grandmother for two weeks. During this time, Daniella received a phone call from Otakar's aunt saying that Otakar had resumed a former romantic relationship with another woman.

Because of this unsettling news, Daniella left their shared apartment, refused to talk with Otakar on his return, and gave birth to the child at a different hospital than where they had originally planned. She gave her consent to the adoption of the child by the Does, telling them and their attorney that she knew who the father was but would not furnish his name. Daniella and her uncle warded off Otakar's persistent inquiries about the child by telling him that the child had died shortly after birth.

Otakar found out that the child was alive and had been placed for adoption 57 days after the child was born. He then began the instant proceedings by filing an appearance contesting the Does' adoption of his son. As already noted, the trial court ruled that Otakar was an unfit parent under section 1 of the Adoption Act because he had not shown a reasonable degree of interest in the child within the first 30 days of his life. Therefore, the father's consent was unnecessary under section 8 of the Act.

The finding that the father had not shown a reasonable degree of interest in the child is not supported by the evidence. In fact, he made various attempts to locate the child, all of which were either frustrated or blocked by the actions of the mother. Further, the mother was aided by the attorney for the adoptive parents, who failed to make any effort to ascertain the name or address of the father despite the fact that the mother indicated she knew who he was. Under the circumstances, the father had no opportunity to discharge any familial duty.

In the opinion below, the appellate court, wholly missing the threshold issue in this case, dwelt on the best interests of the child. Since, however, the father's parental interest was improperly terminated, there was no occasion to reach the factor of the child's best interests. That point should never have been reached and need never have been discussed.

Unfortunately, over three years have elapsed since the birth of the baby who is the subject of these proceedings. To the extent that it is relevant to assign fault in this case, the fault here lies initially with the mother, who fraudulently tried to deprive the father of his rights, and secondly, with the adoptive parents and their attorney, who proceeded with the adoption when they knew that a real father was out there who had been denied knowledge of his baby's existence. When the father entered his appearance in the adoption proceedings 57 days after the baby's birth and demanded his rights as a father, the petitioners should have relinquished the baby at that time. It was their decision to prolong this litigation through a lengthy, and ultimately fruitless, appeal.

The adoption laws of Illinois are neither complex nor difficult of application. Those laws intentionally place the burden of proof on the adoptive parents in establishing both the relinquishment and/or unfitness of the parents and, coincidentally, the fitness and the right to adopt of the adoptive parents. In addition, Illinois law requires a good-faith effort to notify the natural parents of the adoption proceedings. These laws are designed to protect natural parents in their preemptive rights to their own children wholly apart from any consideration of the so-called best interests of the child. If it were otherwise, few parents would be secure in the custody of their own children. If best interests of the child were a sufficient qualification to determine child custody, anyone with superior income, intelligence, education, etc., might challenge and deprive the parents of their right to their own children. The law is otherwise and was not complied with in this case.

Accordingly, we reverse.

BOB GREENE, SUPREME INJUSTICE FOR A LITTLE BOY

Chicago Tribune.
Sunday, June 19, 1994, page 1.

There may be a worse place in the nation to live than Illinois if you are a child in desperate trouble, but it's hard to imagine where.

The Illinois Supreme Court made that very clear last week. In a unanimous decision, the justices sent a 3–year-old boy who has lived happily all his life with his adoptive parents back to the boy's biological father and to the mother who had represented the child as being dead. The mother and her then-boyfriend had had a fight when she gave up the child for adoption; they made up, got married, and decided to pursue the biological father's legal action to get the boy out of his adoptive home.

Until the state's Supreme Court made its decision last week, it looked as if Richard was going to be allowed to continue on with a life that is, by every account, a good and loving one. That is because, in an Illinois Appellate Court decision last August, Judge Dom J. Rizzi wrote for the court:

"Richard is not a piece of property with property rights belonging either to his biological or adoptive parents. Richard 'belongs' to no one but himself. . . . It is his best interest and corollary rights that come before anything else, including the interests and rights of biological and adoptive parents. . . .

"A child's best interest . . . is not to be balanced against any other interest. . . . Courts are here to protect children—not to victimize them."

That is the ruling that the state Supreme Court overturned last week. Supreme Court Justice James D. Heiple wrote: "Laws are designed to protect natural parents in their preemptive rights to their own children wholly apart from any consideration of the so-called best interests of the child."

And thus a boy who is well along on the course of a happy life is being sent to live with people he has never met—one of whom, the woman who gave birth to him, cared so much about him that she announced that he was dead.

All seven state Supreme Court justices went along with the decision that will remove Richard from the only home he has ever known. The justices are among the most powerful people in the state * * *.

They had a wide range of options available to them in this case; there were many ways they could have disagreed with some of the lower courts' findings, and still have ruled that the child's future in the only home he knows could continue. Instead they rejected Judge Rizzi's opinion that "Courts are here to protect children—not to victimize them." Instead they went with Justice Heiple's diminution of the "so-called best interests of the child."

Justice Heiple, astonishingly, wrote that "The adoption laws of Illinois are neither complex nor difficult of application." But of course he is wrong; the interpretation of the law in this particular adoption case is wrenchingly complex, because by taking Richard from his home and giving him to the biological father (who by all accounts always wanted him), the Supreme Court is also giving him to the woman who willingly placed him for adoption, declaring him to be dead. It would be interesting to see the seven Supreme Court justices explain this to Richard on the day he is taken from his home and handed, like a prize, to strangers.

Even the attorney for the biological father told me when we first talked last year that if he won the case for his client, "It will be just awful for the child." Surely the Supreme Court justices know that. Yet in taking meticulous care of the rights of the biological father (and the woman who is now his wife), they made no effort at all to do anything to help that little boy. Where is justice for him? He is totally faultless here, and he is the one who must pay most dearly. Where is mercy?

Judge Rizzi, in another part of the Appellate Court opinion that the state Supreme Court overturned, wrote: "There comes a point when we should not be ignorant as judges of what we know as men and women."

So much for that. Richard has to be taken from his home. In a column about the case that appeared here last August, it was noted: "In the end, a judge is the only person a child in peril has to count on. If a judge's humanity fails, who will hear the child's cry?"

Not the justices of the Illinois Supreme Court. Damn them all.

IN RE PETITION OF DOE

Supreme Court of Illinois, 1994.
638 N.E.2d 181 at 187.

JUSTICE HEIPLE, writing in support of the denial of rehearing:

* * *

I have been a judge for over 23 years. In that time, I have seldom before worked on a case that involved the spread of so much misinformation, nor one which dealt with as straightforward an application of law to fact.

As was made clear in the majority opinion, a conspiracy was undertaken to deny the natural father any knowledge of his son's existence. It began when the biological mother, 8 1/2 months pregnant, was misinformed that the father, her fiance, had left her for another woman. She left their shared home and, at the encouragement of a social worker, agreed to give up her child. The social worker called her personal attorney, who contacted the adoptive mother (that attorney's friend and employee). At the behest of the adoptive parents and their attorney, the mother gave birth at a different hospital than she and the father had planned to avoid the father's intervention; the mother surrendered the baby to strangers four days after his birth; and then falsely told the father that the child had died. All of this occurred in the space of less than three weeks.

The father did not believe the mother, and he immediately began an intensive and persistent search and inquiry to learn the truth and locate the child. On the 57th day following the child's birth, the father learned of his son's existence and of the pending adoption. On that day, he hired a lawyer and contested the adoption of his son by strangers. One may reasonably ask, What more could he have done? What more should he have done? The answer is that he did all that he could and should do.

The majority opinion pointed out that the adoptive parents should have relinquished the baby at that time. That is to say, on the 57th day. Instead of that, however, they were able to procure an entirely erroneous ruling from a trial judge that allowed the adoption to go forward. The father's only remedy at that stage was a legal appeal which he took. He is not the cause of the delay in this case. It was the adoptive parents' decision to prolong this litigation through a long and ultimately fruitless appeal. Now, the view has been expressed that the passage of time warrants their retention of the child; that it would not be fair to the child to return him to his natural parents, now married to each other, after the adoptive parents have delayed justice past the child's third birthday.

* * *

In 1972, the United States Supreme Court, in the case of *Stanley v. Illinois*, ruled that unmarried fathers cannot be treated differently than unmarried mothers or married parents when determining their rights to the custody of their children. The courts of Illinois are bound by that decision. * * *

* * *

The best interest of the child standard is not to be denigrated. It is real. However, it is not triggered until it has been validly determined that the child is *available* for adoption. And, a child is not available for adoption until the rights of his natural parents have been properly terminated. Any judge, lawyer, or guardian *ad litem* who has even the most cursory familiarity with adoption laws knows that. Justice Rizzi, if he is to be taken at face value, does not know that.

Columnist Bob Greene apparently does not care. Rather, columnist Greene has used this unfortunate controversy to stimulate readership and generate a series of syndicated newspaper columns in the Chicago Tribune and other papers that are both false and misleading. In so doing, he has wrongfully cried "fire" in a crowded theatre, and has needlessly alarmed other adoptive parents into ill-founded concerns that their own adoption proceedings may be in jeopardy. In support of his position, Greene has stirred up contempt against the Supreme Court as an institution, concluding one of his columns by referring to all of the Justices with the curse, "Damn them all."

* * *

In support of his objective, Greene brings to bear the tools of the demagogue, namely, incomplete information, falsity, half-truths, character assassination and spurious argumentation. He has conducted a steady assault on my abilities as a judge, headlining one of his columns "The Sloppiness of Justice Heiple." Another was entitled "Supreme Injustice for a Little Boy." He has shown my picture in his columns with bylines reading, respectively, "Justice Heiple: Ruling takes boy from home," and "James D. Heiple: No justice for a child."

Make no mistake about it. These are acts of journalistic terrorism. These columns are designed to discredit me as a judge and the Supreme Court as a dispenser of justice by stirring up disrespect and hatred among the general population.

Lest we forget the place from which he comes, let us remind ourselves that Greene is a journalist with a product to sell. He writes columns for a living. His income is dependent on writing and selling his columns to newspapers. He cannot secure either sales or earnings by writing on subjects that lack impact or drama. So, he must seek out subjects that are capable of generating wide public interest. An adoption case involving two sets of parents contesting for the custody of a three-year-old boy is a ready-made subject for this type of journalist. So far, so good.

The trouble with Greene's treatment of the subject, however, is that his columns have been biased, false and misleading. They have also been destructive to the cause of justice both in this case and in the wider perspective. Part of Greene's fury may be attributable to the fact that he staked out his views on this case in a published column that appeared on August 22, 1993. Subsequently, on June 16, 1994, the Supreme Court had the audacity to base its decision on the law rather than on his newspaper column. So much for his self-professed moralizing.

That Greene has succeeded to a limited degree cannot be denied. I have, indeed, received several pieces of hate mail with such epithets as idiot, jerk, etc. The Governor, in a crass political move, announced his attempt to intervene in the case. And the General Assembly, without meaningful debate or consideration, rushed into law a constitutionally infirm statute with the goal of changing the Supreme Court's decision.

Both the Governor and the members of the General Assembly who supported this bill might be well advised to return to the classroom and take up Civics 101. The Governor, for his part, has no understanding of this case and no interest either public or private in its outcome. The legislature is not given the authority to decide private disputes between litigants. Neither does it sit as a super court to review unpopular decisions of the Supreme Court. We have three branches of government in this land. They are designated as the legislative, the executive and the judicial. Legislative adjudication of private disputes went by the wayside generations ago. Moreover, this case cannot be decided by public clamor generated by an irresponsible journalist. Neither can it be decided by its popularity or lack thereof. This case can only be decided by a court of law. That is a judicial function pure and simple. For the Supreme Court to surrender to this assault would be to surrender its independence, its integrity and its reason for being. In so doing, neither justice to the litigants nor the public interest would be served. Under the circumstances, this case looms even larger than the child or the two sets of contesting parents.

* * *

As for the child, age three, it is to be expected that there would be an initial shock, even a longing for a time in the absence of the persons whom he had viewed as parents. This trauma will be overcome, however, as it is every day across this land by children who suddenly find their parents separated by divorce or lost to them through death. It will not be an insurmountable trauma for a three-year-old child to be returned, at last, to his natural parents who want to raise him as their own. It will work itself out in the fullness of time. As for the adoptive parents, they will have to live with their pain and the knowledge that they wrongfully deprived a father of his child past the child's third birthday. They and their lawyer brought it on themselves.

This much is clear. Adoptive parents who comply with the law may feel secure in their adoptions. Natural parents may feel secure in their right to raise their own children. If there is a tragedy in this case, as has been suggested, then that tragedy is the wrongful breakup of a natural family and the keeping of a child by strangers without right. We must remember that the purpose of an adoption is to provide a home for a child, not a child for a home.

Notes and Questions

1. *Aftermath*. Within a week after the June 12 decision, the state legislature met in emergency session and swiftly amended the adoption act in an effort to reverse the decision. The Governor, who had sought to intervene in the case, quickly signed the emergency legislation, dubbed the "Baby Richard Law."

Effective July 3, 1994, the legislation requires, among other things, separate determinations of parenthood and custody when an adoption is denied or revoked on appeal. Where the best interests of the child mandate, the legislation permits the court to decree the parenthood of the biological parents but to grant custody to others, such as the would-be adoptive parents. See 750 Ill. Comp. Stat. 50/20. The legislation also creates a putative father registry, which entitles an unwed father to notice of adoption only if he registers before the child's birth or within thirty days after birth. See 750 Ill. Comp. Stat. 50/12.1.

The Baby Richard saga outlasted the state supreme court's July 12 denial of the rehearing motion brought by the prospective adoptive parents and the child's guardian ad litem. The governor quickly excoriated the court, wondering aloud "how the justices who prevailed in this case will be able to sleep at night." The governor called it "a dark day for justice and human decency in Illinois. The highest court in the state has committed a travesty" by ordering the child "brutally, tragically torn away from the only parents he has ever known—parents who by all accounts loved and nurtured him from the second he joined their family." According to the Governor, "[t]his young child should have found a champion—a protector—in the highest court of this state. Instead, he found justices who betrayed their obligations to him and to the people who placed them in their lofty positions." What Two Justices Wrote and How Edgar Responded, Chicago Tribune, July 13, 1994, at § 1, 17.

On January 25, 1995, the state supreme court heard oral arguments on the habeas corpus petition of Otakar Kirchner, the biological father, and ordered the adoptive parents, Kim and Jay Warburton, to surrender the child "forthwith," without a best-interests hearing under the new legislation. See Edward Walsh, Justices Refuse to Delay Transfer of "Baby Richard," Wash. Post, Feb. 14, 1995, at A3. The governor called the decision "incredibly inhumane," "outrageous" and "heartless." Kevin McDermott, Dad Gets "Baby Richard": State High Court Rules Against Adoptive Parents, State Journal–Register (Springfield, Ill.), Jan. 26, 1995, at 1. The United States Supreme Court denied the Warburtons' motion to stay the order. See O'Connell v. Kirchner, 513 U.S. 1303 (1995) (Stevens, Circuit Justice); O'Connell v. Kirchner, 513 U.S. 1138 (1995) (full Court by 7–2 vote).

On February 28, 1995, the Illinois Supreme Court issued the full opinion granting Otakar's habeas corpus petition. The court denied the Warburtons a custody hearing under the new legislation because the court's June 16 decision was final before the legislation's July 3 effective date. In re Kirchner, 649 N.E.2d 324 (Ill.1995) (per curiam). Baby Richard had his fourth birthday two weeks after the court issued the full opinion. Amid a sea of reporters, protesters and neighbors on April 30, the boy was turned over to his biological parents, including the father he had never met. See Janan Hanna, Wrenching Day for "Richard," Boy Begins Trip in Tears, Ends It Calmly, Chicago Tribune, May 1, 1995, at 1. Two months later, the United States Supreme Court declined to review the state supreme court's February 28 decision. Doe v. Kirchner, 515 U.S. 1152 (1995).

The specter of further court battles surfaced in 1997 when the biological mother, Daniella Kirchner, petitioned to be declared the child's legal mother. The petition sought to overcome an unusual predicament that could serve as grist for a devious law professor's final examination. Daniella's 1991 signed consent to the boy's adoption was assertedly irrevocable. If this were true, Otakar was the child's legal father after he won the earlier court battle but Daniella was no longer the legal mother. Otakar said his wife filed the petition because "if anything happens to me, the whole case is open." "Richard" Inquiry Halted By Bilandic, Chicago Tribune, July 29, 1997, at 1. By the time Daniella filed the petition, Otakar had reportedly separated from her to live with another woman in a nearby motel, leaving the child in her custody even though she was legally a non-parent to him. See Janan Hanna, Legal Door Could Reopen in "Richard" Case, Chicago Tribune, Jan. 21, 1997, at 1.

Evidently Daniella and her lawyer thought her petition would pass unnoticed, but they were wrong. Asserting that Daniella's only option was to try to adopt the child, the Warburtons sought to intervene with a petition for visitation, a best-interests hearing, and appointment of an attorney for the child. Rather than risk reopening the proceedings, Daniella quickly sought to dismiss her petition. Despite a civil plaintiff's general right to voluntarily dismiss a petition, the trial judge refused to allow her to dismiss, saying, "I think when you put this case back in court, you put everything back on the table." Janan Hanna, High Court Slams Door Again on "Richard," Chicago Tribune, Aug. 5, 1997, at 1. The judge ordered an agency evaluation of the boy's home life with Daniella and scheduled a hearing on the agency report. The state supreme court quickly ordered the trial court to dismiss Daniella's petition, but the adoptive parents' counsel remained undaunted: "[W]e do have some things in the arsenal of things we can do, but we want to think it through and make sure it would be in [the child's] best interest." Id.

Otakar proceeded to sue Bob Greene, alleging that the columnist defamed him and the boy by writing that the boy was being "broken like a dog," and that his return to the Kirchners was "a crime" that police, courts and child welfare agencies should prevent. The state court of appeals affirmed dismissal of the complaint. Kirchner v. Greene, 691 N.E.2d 107 (Ill. App. Ct. 1998).

2. *Whose rights mattered?* (a) In the final analysis, whose constitutional rights determined the outcome in the sordid Baby Richard affair?, (b) According to the state supreme court, what constitutional rights did the biological mother or the prospective adoptive parents hold? (c) Should Baby Richard have had a due process right to a hearing into whether his best interests precluded removal from the only home and "parents" he had ever known? Should it have mattered that the boy had developed a psychological bond to the would-be adoptive family with the lower courts' blessing?

3. *Due process rights for adoptees?* Courts have not been hospitable to claims that children hold constitutional rights in adoption proceedings. Recall *Angel Lace M.*, for example, which held that Wisconsin's adoption code did not grant the biological mother's companion standing to petition to adopt the child despite the parties' concessions that the adoption would have been in the child's best interests. The state supreme court rejected claims

that the code deprived the child of a due process liberty interest in having her best interests be the paramount factor in the decision: "An interest will only qualify as a liberty interest if it is both fundamental and traditionally protected by our society. The right to have a child's best interests be the paramount consideration in the adoption proceedings is neither fundamental nor traditionally protected by our society. Adoption itself is not even a fundamental right. It certainly follows that a legislative directive to construe adoption statutes with the child's best interests of paramount consideration is not a fundamental right. Furthermore, because adoption is a relatively recent statutory development, we cannot conclude that adoption has traditionally been protected by our society." 516 N.W.2d at 685.

Consider, however, the concurring justice's approach in Matter of John E. v. Doe, 564 N.Y.S.2d 439 (App.Div.1990). The biological father sought to regain custody of a child conceived during a "doubly adulterous" affair—both he and the biological mother were married to other people at conception and throughout the pregnancy. By the time the case reached the appellate court, the three-year-old child had lived with the adoptive parents ever since they had taken custody pursuant to a prearranged adoption when the child was four days old. The trial court heard testimony that the adoptive parents had given the child love, physical comfort and emotional security; that the child would suffer "devastating" psychological damage if he were removed from the only home he had ever known; and that the biological father provided virtually no financial support during the pregnancy or after the child's birth, did not previously acknowledge his paternity or take steps to establish legal responsibility for the child, and planned to have the child raised by his adult daughter, who operated a day care center.

By interpreting the relevant statutes, *John E.* held that the biological father's consent to the adoption was not required and allowed the adoption to proceed. The concurrence, however, pressed a constitutional basis for decision: the case threatened "a wrenching uprooting that so palpably disserves [the child] that it amounts to a denial of *his* constitutional right to liberty, on a scale certainly no less than the [biological father's] asserted liberty interest. The [biological father] can better survive defeat in this litigation than can [the child]." Id. at 446–47. See also, e.g, Suellyn Scarnecchia, A Child's Right to Protection From Transfer Trauma in a Contested Adoption Case, 2 Duke J. Gender L. and Pol'y 42, 46 (1995) (arguing that a child has a right to due process protections when "state action, in the form of a transfer of custody, is likely to cause substantial harm to the child").

4. *Applying* Stanley *and its progeny.* By making the unwed father's constitutional rights the touchstone for decision, the Illinois Supreme Court in *Petition of Doe* applied these decisions as most courts have done in the absence of a putative father registry. Trouble frequently arises when a court, upholding the thwarted father's right to an opportunity to develop a relationship with the child, enables the father to veto an adoption a few months, or even a few years, after the child's transfer to the prospective adoptive parents. Most decisions hold or assume that the court may constitutionally determine the best interests of the child only after all necessary consents to adoption have been secured. The putative father does not lose the right to withhold consent if he acts promptly after discovering the child's whereabouts. In addition to *Petition of Doe*, see, e.g., In re Clausen, 501 N.W.2d

193 (Mich.Ct.App.), aff'd, 502 N.W.2d 649 (Mich.1993); In Adoption of Kelsey S., 823 P.2d 1216, 1236 (Cal.1992).

On the other hand, some decisions have recited the thwarted father's opportunity right, but have denied his effort to veto the adoption where the child appeared well adjusted to the adoptive home. These decisions either (1) have applied a strict test and found that on the facts of the case, the father had not been sufficiently diligent in grasping the opportunity to develop a relationship with the child, or (2) have found the best interests of the child determinative at the expense of the thwarted father's opportunity right. See, e.g., In re Baby Boy C., 581 A.2d 1141, 1145 (D.C.App.1990) (holding that even if the thwarted father is a presumptively fit parent, his opportunity right may be defeated by clear and convincing evidence that the adoption would be in the best interests of the child); Robert O. v. Russell K., 604 N.E.2d 99, 103 (N.Y.1992) (holding that "an unwed father who has promptly done all that he could to protect his parental interest is entitled to constitutional protection," but "promptness is measured in terms of the baby's life and not by the onset of the father's awareness").

5. *Reevaluating exclusive parenthood.* Chapter 2 treated the law's general unwillingness to recognize that a child may have more than one mother or more than one father. Should the law recognize dual parenthood in unusual circumstances in which a court determines that exclusive parenthood would disserve the best interests of the child? Would Baby Richard's interests have been better served if the trial court, after factfinding hearings, could have found that the biological parents and the adoptive parents each had much to offer him, and that forcing an "all or nothing" choice between the two adult couples might well cause the boy lasting emotional harm?

The law has taken tentative steps toward recognizing the prospect of dual parenthood in contested adoption cases such as Baby Richard's. As discussed in note 1, Illinois' emergency Baby Richard legislation permits the court to decree parenthood in one set of parents and custody in another when an adoption is denied or revoked on appeal. The Uniform Adoption Act (1994) would similarly permit courts to order that parental rights remain with the biological parent(s), but that custody remain in the would-be adoptive parents. Where the court denies an adoption petition, the Act requires the court to make an independent custody determination in accordance with the best interests of the child. 9 U.L.A. Ann. §§ 2–408(e)-(f), 2–409(e)-(f), 3–704, 2–408 cmt. The official Comment explains that "the Act does not treat a minor as an object that 'belongs' to the parent or would-be parent and has to be shifted back and forth in the event 'ownership' rights are changed or reinstated. The fact that a birth parent's status as a legal parent may be restored or recognized * * * is *not* a determination that the minor must be placed in that parent's custody." Id. § 2–408 cmt. (emphasis in original). The Act expressly recognizes the prospect that in some cases, "the individuals who had hoped to adopt may be granted custody even though they cannot become the legal adoptive parents." Id. § 3–704 cmt.

The Illinois Baby Richard legislation and the Uniform Adoption Act would thus permit courts to divest biological parents of custody without a finding that they are unfit parents. Justice Heiple called the legislation "constitutionally infirm." Question indeed remains whether such divestment is constitutional in light of *Stanley, Lehr* and the parental prerogatives recognized in such decisions as *Meyer, Pierce* and *Prince* presented in Chapter 1.

A number of commentators have urged reevaluation of prevailing constitutional doctrine and the law's general unwillingness to recognize dual parenthood. See, e.g., Naomi R. Cahn, Reframing Child Custody Decisionmaking, 58 Ohio St. L.J. 1, 53 (1997) ("[W]here there is a conflict between different adults, any of whom could arguably be classified as parents, then we may not benefit them or the child by somewhat arbitrarily designating one or two as those who can exercise parental rights. Instead, where each of them has declared a willingness to assume responsibility for the child, and each has a legal connection based either on biology or already having cared for the child for a significant period of time (including, I think, gestation), then we may want to recognize all of them as parents."); Joan Heifetz Hollinger, Adoption and Aspiration: The Uniform Adoption Act, the DeBoer–Schmidt Case, and the American Quest For the Ideal Family, 2 Duke J. Gender L. and Pol'y 15, 37 (1995) (suggesting that prospective adoptive parents should have a "constitutionally protected liberty interest in the survival of their adoptive family" when they "take custody of a child only after they have a reasonable basis for expecting that they will become the child's permanent legal parents"); Judith T. Younger, Responsible Parents and Good Children, 14 Law and Ineq. 489, 507 (1996) (arguing that courts should "separat[e] the question of parental rights from the question of custody and mak[e] the custody determination depend on a standard reflecting the child's interests"; if the child is in a family that is functioning well with respect to the child, "the child should stay where it is").

6. *Feminist Critiques of* Stanley *and its progeny.* Professor Katharine K. Baker argues that the law should divest the unwed father of all right to veto a potential adoption, and should vest the birth mother with "complete decisionmaking authority based on her disproportionate physical and emotional investment in the child": "To require [the] mother * * * to tell the biological father about the child so that he could develop his own relationship with the child, completely discounts the work that mother did in carrying and bearing the child. It also gives her a remarkable incentive to abort the child. * * * Whatever the biological father's desire to invest, the mother invested first and to a greater degree. The father has done and can do nothing to make his claim to a relationship any weightier at birth than it is prior to birth when the mother still has the right to abort. If the law need not respect his desire for connection pre-birth, the law need not respect his desire post-birth either. He has done nothing to earn it." Katharine K. Baker, Property Rules Meet Feminist Needs: Respecting Autonomy By Valuing Connection, 59 Ohio St. L.J. 1523, 1587–88 (1998).

Professor Mary L. Shanley, however, argues that maternal autonomy does not provide a "fully satisfactory" basis for determining the rights of unwed parents. Professor Shanley too would depart from *Stanley* and its progeny because "almost all arguments for unwed biological fathers' rights are based on a notion of gender-neutrality that is misleading, due not only to women's biological experience of pregnancy but also to the inequality inherent in the social structures in which sexual and reproductive activity currently takes place." But she believes that a society "interested in protecting the possibility of intimate association and family life for all its members should articulate norms that ground parental claims in a mixture of genetic relationship, assumption of responsibility, and provision of care to the child (including gestation)." Mary L. Shanley, Unwed Fathers' Rights, Adoption, and Sex Equality: Gender–Neutrality and the Perpetuation of Patriarchy, 95 Colum. L. Rev. 60, 64–65 (1995).

7. *Expedited proceedings.* Who should bear the blame for the delay of more than three years that Baby Richard endured? The court system certainly moved at glacial speed. Because psychologists regularly report that children need continuity and established relationships, the adoptive parents may have felt that delay would work in their favor, despite the unfavorable constitutional law. It has been suggested that to avoid unnecessary delay in contested adoption cases, adoption acts should provide for expedited trial and appellate hearings and decisions. See, e.g., Annette R. Appell and Bruce A. Boyer, Parental Rights vs. Best Interests of the Child: A False Dichotomy in the Context of Adoption, 2 Duke J. of Gender L. and Pol'y 63, 83 (1995).

Anecdotal evidence suggested that the Baby Richard case, and well-publicized cases like it, have frightened many adoptive parents and perhaps deterred other adults from seeking to adopt. Before one feels too sorry for adoptive parents who appear crushed when the unwed father seeks to assert his parental rights to a child adopted in secrecy, however, one might consider concurring Justice McMorrow's observation that adoptive parents proceed with known risk whenever they adopt a child whose birth mother asserts she does not know the father's identity or whereabouts. Indeed, while Daniella was pregnant with Richard, the Warburtons and their counsel evidently were fully aware that she knew the biological father's identity and whereabouts, and that she planned to lie to him about the child's survival. See In re Doe, supra, 627 N.E.2d at 657–58 (Tully, J., dissenting). As the Baby Richard case demonstrates, the innocent child may be the loser in such intrigues.

8. *Civil remedies for the thwarted father?* Daniella may have committed fraud by lying to the father about the child's survival. The birth mother might also commit fraud by knowingly naming the wrong man as the father or by untruthfully asserting that she does not know the father's identity or whereabouts. In the absence of fraud, she might otherwise seek to thwart the father's efforts to maintain a relationship with the child.

Birth mothers' fraud or concealment may be grounds for civil penalties in favor of the state or civil damages in favor of injured parties. See, e.g., Kessel v. Leavitt, 511 S.E.2d 720, 734 (W.Va.1998) (holding that a newborn child's biological father could maintain a fraud action against the mother, her attorney and her parents and brother for concealing information about the child's location and adoption, and could sue the attorney, and the mother's parents and brother for tortious interference with parental rights; affirming judgment for $2 million compensatory damages and $5.85 million punitive damages); Smith v. Malouf, 722 So. 2d 490, 497–98 (Miss.1998) (holding that the newborn child's father stated claims for intentional infliction of emotional distress and conspiracy against the mother and her parents who sought to prevent the father from exercising his parental rights).

Section 7–105(f) of the Uniform Adoption Act provides for a civil penalty against a biological parent who knowingly misidentifies the other biological parent with intent to deceive the other parent, the adoptive parents or the adoption agency.

9. *Children conceived by sexual assaults.* May the state terminate the father's parental rights on the ground that the child was conceived during a forcible rape or other nonconsensual sex crime committed by the father? Several states authorize termination where the child is conceived by such violence. See, e.g., N.M. Stat. § 32A–5–19(c) (consent to adoption not required from biological father of child conceived by rape or incest). Courts hold or assume that the federal and state constitutions impose no barrier to such terminations. See, e.g., In re Adoption of Kelsey S., 823 P.2d 1216, 1237 n. 14 (Cal.1992).

What if the child is conceived during a statutory rape in the absence of force? A number of decisions uphold the criminal conduct as a ground for termination, regardless of whether the man seeks to petition for custody or to develop a relationship with the child. See, e.g., Pena v. Mattox, 84 F.3d 894 (7th Cir. 1996); In re R.P., 216 Ga. App. 799, 456 S.E.2d 107 (1995). Other courts disagree. See, e.g., In re Craig "V," 500 N.Y.S.2d 568, 569 (App.Div.1986) (holding that the unwed father was not seeking to benefit from his wrongdoing but was seeking to assume his support obligation; court could consider the father's conduct when determining the best interests of the child at the custody hearing).

PROBLEM 7–6

On January 14, Sue Mathis gave birth to a healthy baby girl whom she immediately placed for adoption when the child was two days old. The 28-year-old unwed mother lied by naming her current boyfriend, Bill Boyd, as the father. Bill promptly signed a consent to the adoption. Anita and Bob Allen took custody of the child and filed a petition to adopt her three weeks later. The court promptly terminated the parental rights of Sue and Bill. The state has no putative father registry.

Shortly thereafter, Sue began dating her old boyfriend, Mike O'Leary. Sue then admitted to Mike that he was the girl's biological father, and DNA tests conclusively established his paternity. Mike had previously fathered two children out of wedlock with other women and did not support or have further significant relations with them, and he had little contact with Sue during this pregnancy. Mike intervened in the Allens' adoption proceeding, seeking return of the child on the ground that he is the biological father and had never consented to the adoption. The bench trial was held when the child was nearly a year old, and the court ordered that the Allens return the child to Mike, whom she has never met. The case finally reached the state supreme court when the child was two years old. What would you argue if you represented the Allens? If you represented Mike? How would you decide the case if you were a judge of the state supreme court?

PROBLEM 7–7

You are counsel to a couple who wish to adopt a newborn, and you have established contact with a pregnant teenager who wishes to place her child for adoption privately. What precautions can you take to reduce the risk of collateral attack on the adoption decree after it is entered?

10. *References.* Elizabeth Buchanan, The Constitutional Rights of Unwed Fathers Before and After *Lehr v. Robertson*, 45 Ohio St. L.J. 313 (1984); Linda R. Crane, Family Values and the Supreme Court, 25 Conn. L. Rev. 427 (1993); Scott A. Resnik, Seeking the Wisdom of Solomon: Defining the Rights of Unwed Fathers in Newborn Adoptions, 20 Seton Hall Legis. J. 363 (1996); Elizabeth S. Scott and Robert E. Scott, Parents as Fiduciaries, 81 Va. L. Rev. 2401 (1995); Robin L. West, The Ideal of Liberty: A Comment on *Michael H. v. Gerald D.*, 139 U. Pa. L. Rev. 1373 (1991).

SECTION 5. OPEN ADOPTION

In an "open adoption," the child has continuing post-decree relations with the biological parents or other relatives. The continuing relations may include contact through visitation, correspondence, telephone calls, or otherwise. Open adoptions were not unknown in past decades, particularly where the adoptive parents were the child's foster parents, relatives or family friends, or where an older child had established pre-adoption relationships with family members. See, e.g., In re McDevitt, 162 N.Y.S. 1032 (App.Div.1917). Indeed, informal adoption, frequently with arrangements for openness, was the norm for the first several decades after Massachusetts enacted the first modern adoption act in 1851. Only in the early years of the twentieth century did states begin to insist on mandated sealing of adoption records to insure confidentiality and complete severance of the legal and social relationship between the adoptee and the biological parents.

In recent years, the shortage of readily adoptable children has helped increase the prevalence of open adoptions resulting from agreements between biological parents and adoptive parents. The shortage has provided leverage to birth mothers who seek a future right of contact with the child before consenting to a private placement adoption. See, e.g., Harold D. Grotevant, Openness in Adoption: Exploring Family Connections (1998); Cynthia Crossen, In Today's Adoptions, The Biological Parents Are Calling the Shots, Wall St. J., Sept. 14, 1989, at 1. Indeed, some adoption agencies facing loss of business now accommodate birth mothers who seek open arrangements and might opt for private adoption in the absence of such accommodation. Because the *Stanley* line of decisions gives many unwed fathers a constitutional right to withhold consent to adoption, unwed fathers concerned about adoption arrangements may also have a voice.

The growth of privately arranged open adoptions has also resulted from the changing demographics of adoption. In recent years, smaller percentages of adoptions have involved newborns and greater percentages have involved children over the age of two, including considerably older children and other children with special needs. More and more children have been adopted by their stepparents, relatives and foster parents. The result is that in a growing number of adoptions, the biological parents, adoptees and adoptive parents know one another's identities and whereabouts before the petition is filed. For better or worse, the child may have had a relationship with his or her parents and other relatives that cannot be undone by a stroke of the judge's pen.

Where practical necessity or private arrangement does not produce openness, however, confidentiality and complete severance of prior legal relationships may still be the bywords. The next decision determines whether the court may order an open adoption over the adoptive parents' objection.

IN RE ADOPTION OF C.H.

Supreme Court of Minnesota, 1996.
554 N.W.2d 737.

STRINGER, JUSTICE.

* * *

C.H. was born on October 10, 1987 and A.H. was born on January 12, 1989. In 1991, the children's paternal aunt Alesia Hunter became concerned that the children were being neglected by their biological parents and reported her concerns to the Chisago County Department of Human Services. The following year Mrs. Hunter and her husband Thomas Hunter accepted custody of both children but A.H. began to exhibit rather severe behavioral problems. Therefore, after about six months, A.H. was placed with her grandparents (Alesia Hunter's parents) Samuel and Lorraine Holmes so that she could receive more "one on one" attention. The children remained so placed for the next year.

In the spring of 1993, the Hunters and the Holmeses (collectively the "Hunter/Holmes") discussed with Lori Karp, a Chisago County Social Worker, the prospect of terminating parental rights to the children and placing them for adoption. Shortly thereafter, the children's biological parents voluntarily terminated their parental rights. The biological parents, who now reside in Wisconsin, have not contacted the children and did not participate in the adoption proceedings. All actions and decisions of the Hunter/Holmes family subsequent to the termination have been made in concert by the four Hunter/Holmes.

The Hunter/Holmes did not initially seek to adopt the children themselves, but, prior to the termination of parental rights, they expressed to Ms. Karp the qualities they desired in an adoptive family, including a willingness to maintain contact between the children and their natural relatives. Ms. Karp reviewed the state adoption list and identified John and Marie Cummings as meeting all the criteria specified by the Hunter/Holmes. The Cummings then met with the Hunter/Holmes and Ms. Karp and discussed an open adoption. On August 23, 1993, Alesia and Thomas Hunter and John and Marie Cummings signed an "agreement for continued contact" which provided for a minimum of three visits per year between the children and their natural relatives and also provided for telephone and mail correspondence. That same day, the Cummings assumed custody of C.H. and A.H. on a foster care basis while their petition to adopt, filed in June 1994, was considered.

Upon arriving at the Cummings home, the children were placed in pre-school programs. The four Hunter/Holmes visited in October and there were several telephone contacts between the children and the Hunter/Holmes. Shortly after the October visit, however, C.H.'s school teacher alerted Marie Cummings to behavioral changes in C.H. and suggested that contact with the Hunter/Holmes be temporarily cut off. In December 1993, Marie Cummings decided that contact with the children's relatives was causing the children distress so she terminated such contacts and arranged for a psychologist to counsel the children. In the following months, the parties, with the involvement of social workers and the psychologist, negotiated regarding the terms of visitation but to no avail, and the parties gradually became estranged. The Cummings filed a petition to adopt C.H. and A.H. in June 1994 and the Hunter/Holmes' each filed their own petition to adopt the children. * * *

* * *

The court concluded that it was in the best interests of the children that the adoption petition of the Cummings be granted subject to an open adoption arrangement whereby the Hunter/Holmes would be allowed to correspond with the children and visit with them several times each year and entered its order accordingly. On the Hunter/Holmes' appeal, the court of appeals reversed, holding that * * * Minnesota does not recognize open adoptions.

* * *

Adoption is a creation of statute and therefore the court's authority in matters relating to adoption is limited to the authority set forth by statute. The policy of this state with respect to the relationship of the children to biological parents and to adoptive parents is very clear: after the adoption petition is granted, for all purposes the children are deemed to be the children of the adoptive parents without conditions, qualifications or exceptions.

Upon adoption, the child shall become the legal child of the adopting persons and they shall become the legal parents of the child with all the rights and duties between them of birth parents and legitimate child * * *. After a decree of adoption is entered the birth parents of an adopted child shall be relieved of all parental responsibilities for the child, and they shall not exercise or have any rights over the adopted child or the child's property. The child shall not owe the birth parents or their relatives any legal duty nor shall the child

ADOPTION Ch. 7

inherit from the birth parents or their kindred except as provided in subdivision 1a.

Minn.Stat. § 259.59, subd. 1 (1994). Implicit, if not explicit, in this statutory declaration is that, in granting an adoption petition, the court has no authority to impose conditions—an adoption petition is either granted or it is denied. There is no middle ground in our statutory scheme.[3] * * * While visitation with the biological family might be in a child's best interests, that is a decision the legislative policy directs should be made by the child's adoptive parents, not by the courts.

We recognize that it is not uncommon for a biological family to make informal arrangements with the adoptive parents as to the children's relationship with the biological family after the adoption. For many children such an arrangement providing for continued contact with the biological family may well be in the children's best interests, particularly when a complete severance of the relationship with the birth family would be traumatic or would prevent a harmonious adjustment to the adoptive family. In reaching our conclusion in this important matter, we are mindful of these considerations and it is not our intention to suggest that there is a legal impediment or state policy disapproving of such arrangements. We simply hold that until such time as the legislature determines that state policy favors open adoptions and specifically authorizes such arrangements, it is beyond the power of a court granting an adoption petition to mandate continuing visitation with the biological family.

* * *

Notes and Questions

1. *Court-ordered visitation.* Visitation is usually central to an open-adoption arrangement. Some adoption acts authorize courts to order visitation between an adopted child and legal strangers, usually the biological parents or other close relatives, when visitation would be in the best interests of the child. See, e.g., Wis. Stat. § 48.92(2), quoted in note 9 of *Angel Lace M.,* supra. Other statutes, however, expressly preclude visitation orders following adoption. See, e.g., Colo. Rev. Stat. § 19–1–116(1)(b).

Where the adoption act is silent about visitation, courts disagree about whether it may be ordered in the best interests of the child. Decisions permitting courts to exercise inherent equitable or parens patriae authority to enter visitation orders include In re S.A.H., 537 N.W.2d 1, 7 (S.D.1995) (holding that the court may order visitation with persons who previously acted in a custodial or parental role for the child when three factors indicate,

---

3. Minn.Stat. § 257.022 (1994) provides further indicia that a court does not have the authority to order an open adoption. While the statute allows a court to grant visitation rights to parents or grandparents of a child after a dissolution of marriage, legal separation, annulment or determination of parentage if it finds that such visitation would be in the best interests of the child, the statute provides an exception for adopted children:

This section shall not apply if the child has been adopted by a person other than a stepparent or grandparent. Any visitation rights granted pursuant to this section prior to the adoption shall be automatically terminated upon such adoption.

by clear and convincing evidence, that such an arrangement would be in the best interests of the child: (1) the child's psychological need to know his or her ancestral, ethnic and cultural background, (2) the effect of open adoption on the child's integration with the adoptive family, and (3) the effect open adoption will have on the pool of prospective adoptive parents). Decisions such as *C.H.* preclude courts from exercising inherent authority to enter post-adoption visitation orders on the ground that the adoption act terminates all rights and relationships between the adoptee and persons other than the adoptive parents.

Where a court grants biological parents or others visitation rights with respect to an adopted child, the decision may test the law's general refusal, discussed in Chapter 2, to recognize that a child may have more than one mother or more than one father. Such decisions may also raise constitutional questions in light of the parental prerogatives of the adoptive parents, who succeed to the biological parents' prerogatives by operation of the adoption law. See, e.g., in People ex rel. Sibley v. Sheppard, 429 N.E.2d 1049, 1052–53 (N.Y.1981), (rejecting a constitutional challenge to a statute permitting courts to order post-adoption visitation with grandparents in the best interests of the child).

Proponents of court-mandated openness argue that the prospect of visitation may facilitate adoption of some children who desperately need adoptive homes, particularly special-needs children. The openness option may help overcome judicial reluctance to order an adoption where complete severance of ties with biological parents or other close relatives may not be in the child's best interests. The option may also help overcome a birth parent's reluctance to consent to termination of parental rights, and thus may enable the child to secure an adoptive home without lengthy contested termination proceedings. Openness may also benefit an older child who has had a relationship with the biological parents or other close relatives. Finally, an open adoption arrangement may enable disputing parties to settle a contested adoption proceeding without the trauma the child might otherwise suffer when birth parents and adoptive parents each hold out until the bitter end for an "all or nothing" outcome.

On the other hand, court mandated openness may deter many adoptive parents from adopting for fear they must "share" the child or might later lose the child. Openness also would sometimes produce continued relationships with abusive or neglectful parents. Openness may also leave the child confused by loyalties to more than one set of parents. Some adoption professionals have called for further research into the effect of open adoptions on children. See, e.g., Marianne Berry, Risks and Benefits of Open Adoption, in 3 The Future of Children 125 (Spring 1993).

The two children in *C.H.* were seven and five when the adoption petition was filed. Were their best interests necessarily served when the courts ordered complete severance of all relationship with their grandparents and aunt and uncle, with whom they had spent most of their young lives? Might their interests have been better served if the court had flexibility to explore various options and fashion the adoption order that best reflected their relationships with the various adults in their lives?

2. *Enforceability of private agreements. C.H.* says that "it is not uncommon for a biological family to make informal arrangements with the adoptive parents as to the children's relationship with the biological family after the adoption." The state supreme court disclaimed any "intention to suggest that there is a legal impediment or state policy disapproving of such arrangements," but held that "it is beyond the power of a court granting an adoption petition to mandate continuing visitation with the biological family." Would *C.H.* permit the court to order specific performance of a private open adoption agreement where the court did not incorporate the agreement in the final adoption decree?

States differ on the specific-enforcement question. In Michaud v. Wawruck, 551 A.2d 738 (Conn.1988), for example, the court held that a written visitation agreement between the biological mother and the adoptive parents would be specifically enforced where the agreement was in the best interests of the child. On the other hand, Hill v. Moorman, 525 So.2d 681 (La.Ct.App. 1988), held that the adoptive parents' written agreement to allow the birth mother reasonable visitation with the child was unenforceable as contrary to public policy because it would impair the adoptive parents' right to the child.

3. *Duress or undue influence.* Where one or both biological parents consent to *termination of parental rights* in return for a promise of continued post-adoption contact with the child, is the consent invalid as a product of duress or undue influence? The issue surfaced in In re Welfare of D.D.G., 558 N.W.2d 481 (Minn.1997). The cocaine-addicted father contended that he agreed to voluntary termination of his parental rights only after county authorities promised they would impose open-adoption conditions on whoever adopted the child, presumably the child's grandparents. The state supreme court warned that "while the law does not bar informal open adoption arrangements made at the time of adoption, such arrangements should not be made at the time of termination." The court expressed concern that "even informal open adoption arrangements made at the time of termination will be used primarily as a settlement inducement, rather than an agreement to promote the best interests of the child." Id. at 485 & n.1.

4. *References.* Jeanne W. Lindsay, Open Adoption: A Caring Option (1987); Lois R. Melina & Sharon K. Roszia, The Open Adoption Experience (1993); Carol Amadio & Stuart L. Deutsch, Open Adoption: Allowing Adopted Children to "Stay in Touch" With Blood Relatives, 22 J. Fam. L. 59 (1983); Annette R. Appell, Blending Families Through Adoption: Implications for Collaborative Adoption Law and Practice, 75 B.U. L. Rev. 997, 1008–13 (1995); Annette Baran & Reuben Pannor, Perspectives on Open Adoption, in 3 The Future of Children 119 (Spring 1993); Marianne Berry, Adoptive Parents' Perceptions of, and Comfort with, Open Adoption, 72 Child Welfare 231 (1993); Lawrence W. Cook, Open Adoption: Can Visitation with Natural Family Members Be in the Child's Best Interest?, 30 J. Fam. L. 471 (1991– 92); Harriet E. Gross, Open Adoption: A Research–Based Literature Review and New Data, 72 Child Welfare 269 (1993); Margaret M. Mahoney, Open Adoption in Context: The Wisdom and Enforceability of Visitation Orders For Former Parents Under Uniform Adoption Act § 4–113, 51 Fla. L. Rev. 89 (1999); Candace M. Zierdt, Make New Parents But Keep the Old, 69 N.D. L. Rev. 497 (1993).

SECTION 6.   CULTURAL AND RELIGIOUS IDENTITY

A. *Transracial Adoption*

In 1996 Congress enacted the Small Business Jobs Protection Act (SBJPA), which contained provisions seeking to end the practice of matching adoptive parents with children of the same race. The relative silence that accompanied the bill's enactment provided a sharp contrast to the passion that has marked the "transracial adoption" (TRA) debate for several years.

The SBJPA prohibits private and public child placement agencies from denying any person the opportunity to become an adoptive or foster parent, or from delaying or denying the placement of a child for adoption or into foster care, "on the basis of the race, color, or national origin of the adoptive or foster parent, or the child." 42 U.S.C. § 1996b(1). Violations are actionable under title VI of the Civil Rights Act of 1964. Id. § 1996b(2).

The SBJPA repealed the Howard M. Metzenbaum Multiethnic Placement Act of 1994, 42 U.S.C. § 5115 (1994). The 1994 Act was grounded in congressional testimony that race-matching had delayed or effectively prevented adoption or foster placement of minority children, consigning many to long-term temporary care. The effect seemed harshest on children who were older or who had special emotional or physical needs that made them difficult to place.

Even Senator Metzenbaum favored repeal when it became evident that the Act's compromise language might validate the very practice that he and other race-matching opponents sought to eradicate. The SBJPA, however, will likely not mute discussion about transracial adoption. For example, new legislation does not prohibit agencies from delaying or denying adoptive or foster placement on the ground that the prospective adoptive or foster parents lack the sensitivity needed to raise a child in a multiracial family. Besides, "[t]here is * * * a big difference between the prohibiting of a deeply ingrained practice and its actual disappearance." Randall Kennedy, How Are We Doing With *Loving*? Race, Law, and Intermarriage, 77 B.U. L. Rev. 815, 821 (1997).

A 1997 memorandum issued by the U.S. Department of Health and Human Services does little to clarify lingering doubts about the role of race in foster and adoptive placements. The memorandum instructed that " 'the best interests of the child' remains the operative standard" in such placements, and that decisions based on race are subject to strict scrutiny review in the courts. But the Department invited continued litigation: "Any decision to consider the use of race as a necessary element of a placement decision must be based on concerns arising out of the circumstances of the individual case. * * * [T]he law cannot anticipate in advance every factual situation which may present itself. However-er, * * * only the most compelling reasons may serve to justify considerations of race and ethnicity as part of a placement decision." Dep't of HHS Memorandum to OCR Regional Managers and ACF Regional Directors, June 4, 1997, quoted in 1 Hollinger, Adoption Law and Practice § 3–B.05, at 3B–22 to 3B–05.

The term "transracial adoption" would describe any adoption in which the parents and child are of different races, including adoptions in which the child is white. As a practical matter, however, nearly all transracial adoptions involve white parents and black or biracial children. Professor Twila L. Perry has called the ongoing TRA debate "interesting" because only a relatively small number of transracial adoptions are completed each year. "Issues such as affirmative action or housing discrimination," she writes, "are of far greater centrality to the relationship between Blacks and whites than transracial adoption. In addition, health care, education, the homicide rate among African American male teenagers, rates of incarceration, and infant mortality, for example, are matters of far greater urgency for the African American community than transracial adoption." Twila L. Perry, The Transracial Adoption Controversy: An Analysis of Discourse and Subordination, 21 N.Y.U. Rev. L. and Soc. Change 33, 35 (1994).

In 1987, the adoption of black children by white parents represented only 1 percent of all adoptions in the United States, numbering a few hundred children. See Rita James Simon and Howard Altstein, Adoption, Race and Identity: From Infancy Through Adolescence 14 (1992). According to data obtained in 1994 by the Child Welfare League of America from 22 states, about 4% of adoptions completed by public agencies in those states involved adoptions of a child of one race by parents of another race. See CWLA, Child Abuse and Neglect: A Look at the States 148 (1997).

The two entries that follow, the first by a TRA opponent and the second by a proponent, demonstrate the sensitivities that underlie the continuing debate.

RUTH–ARLENE W. HOWE, TRANSRACIAL ADOPTION (TRA): OLD PREJUDICES AND DISCRIMINATION FLOAT UNDER A NEW HALO[a]

6 B.U. Pub. Int. L.J. 409, 417–20, 440–41, 466, 470–72 (1997).

* * *

* * * By according no legitimacy to the group interests of African–Americans and focusing just on the individual rights of African–American children, [TRA proponents] assure a supply of children to meet the market demands of white adults seeking to parent whatever children they select. These actions rob African–Americans of the privilege and responsibility of caring for their own children. No group can be assured continued existence and vitality if it does not bear and rear its own children.

Today's children are the adults of the future. The quality of care and nurture that a child receives, and the kinds of interactions the family

---

a All footnote references have been omitted [ed.].

unit has with individuals and groups, shapes not only the child's future adult self, but determines future group memberships and affiliations. The ability of "caring and loving" white adoptive parents within the private confines of their households to nurture an African–American child is not doubted. But, the family is not the only group that plays an important role in shaping one's perspectives of self and of the world. Personal identity is derived from the way in which one is perceived and treated by others.

Thus, while I do not assert that white adoptive parents can never successfully rear an African–American child, I do maintain that they should strive to ensure that the child's reference groups, such as the extended family and those created by interactions in school, the neighborhood, and at work, include positive relationships with African–Americans. * * *

A disproportionately large number of African–American children enter and remain in the foster care system for longer periods than any other group of children. They also enter at younger ages and are more likely than white children to be denied a permanent family because appropriate services are often unavailable or in short supply. TRA advocates claim adoption should be "colorblind" and that same-race placement preferences actually victimize African–American children in foster care. This, however, creates a diversionary "smokescreen" that both obfuscates important systemic problems and creates additional barriers to meeting the needs of African–American children in a manner that does not affront the African–American community. Elimination of race from all placement decision-making sets the stage for anachronistic recommodification of young African–American children and provides no strong assurance that the needs of older children, never the preferred choice of adoptive applicants, will be appropriately met. White adults who seek healthy infants now have an opportunity to "garner the market" on the only expanding "crop" of healthy newborns—biracial infants being relinquished by unwed white birth mothers, hesitant to be single parents rearing their children in today's society.

* * *

I strongly reject the assertion of TRA proponents that not enough African–American homes exist to care for those children in need of substitute care. Instead, the child welfare community is accountable for not delivering culturally competent services in ways that provide African–American children with needed homes. The child welfare community has completely disregarded the National Urban League's Black Pulse Survey's finding that three million heads of black households are interested in formally adopting a black child. This number far exceeds the total number of Black children legally free for adoption so that it is simply unreasonable to presume that from such a large pool of potential adopters, appropriate same-race placements could not be made. * * *

* * *

Regrettably, most child welfare professionals did not aggressively implement any of the culturally sensitive services or strategies advocated by Seaton Manning in 1960. Public and private agencies have been exceedingly slow to recognize the profoundly complex relationship between race, ethnicity and child welfare service outcomes. To render more effective and meaningful services, agencies should diversify their staff and forge solid working partnerships with organizations and institutions within the African-American community. * * *

* * *

While considering the purpose, function and efficacy of TRA for African–American children, an analogy is drawn between current TRA proponents and the slave trader/merchants of Gorée. I believe this comparison is appropriate. It dramatizes two important paradigm shifts that have occurred in adoption: (1) a shift in focus from meeting the needs of a child for a home to satisfying the interests of adults; and (2) a heightened dominance of lawyers as the key professional players. These developments are especially troubling for the African–American community.

* * *

The immediate family is not the only group that plays an important role in shaping an African–American child's perspectives on self and the world. Because of the noted continuing social realities, prejudices and biases that have prevented African–Americans from being fully accepted in this society as "equals," the need for strong, positive affiliations with other African–Americans is self-evident. Wholesale TRA of African–American babies by business entrepreneurs poses the threat of placing these children only with those able to pay higher prices than prospective African–American applicants, with no guarantee that the adopters are racially and culturally competent to help prepare the child for the challenges that he will encounter because of his appearance. The present status of the law opens up the possibility that prospective African–American applicants will be discriminated against, out-bid in the market place, or screened out by agency staff applying traditional criteria to find them unacceptable.

* * *

* * * TRA is * * * a form of "cultural genocide." Widespread, unregulated occurrences of private placements of infants of African–American descent with non-African–American adoptive parents place these children at risk of alienation from their natural reference group. It poses a threat to the future vitality and unity of African–Americans. The greatest harm one can inflict on any group is the oblivion that awaits a people denied the opportunity to rear its own children. * * *

RANDALL KENNEDY, ORPHANS OF SEPARATISM: THE PAINFUL POLITICS OF TRANSRACIAL ADOPTION

The American Prospect 38 (Spring 1994).

No issue more highlights feelings of ambivalence over the proper place of racial distinctions in American life than the delicate matter of transracial adoptions. Opponents of such adoptions insist that allowing white adults to raise black children is at worst tantamount to cultural genocide and at best a naive experiment doomed to failure. In most states, custom reflects and reinforces these beliefs; public policy, formally or informally, discourages cross-racial adoptions or foster placements, to the point where thousands of children are denied placement in loving homes.

* * *

[I]ncreasingly large numbers of children bereft of functioning parents are flooding social welfare agencies. Agencies are charged with maintaining these young refugees from destroyed families and either placing them in the temporary care of foster parents or the permanent care of adoptive parents. * * *

Like most social catastrophes in the United States, this one weighs most heavily upon racial minority communities: the percentage of minority children in need of foster care or adoptive homes is far greater than their percentage of the population. In Massachusetts, approximately 5 percent of the population is black, yet black children constitute nearly half of the children in need of foster care or adoptive homes. In New York City, 75 percent of the nearly 18,000 children awaiting adoption are black. Nationwide, there are about 100,000 children eligible for adoption; 40 percent are black. While two years and eight months is the median length of time that children in general wait to be adopted, the wait for black children is often twice that long.

* * *

Racial matching is a disastrous social policy both in how it affects children and in what it signals about our current attitudes regarding racial distinctions. * * *

[G]iven that racial matching mirrors and reinforces the belief that same race child placements are better and therefore preferable to transracial arrangements, some adults seeking to become foster or adoptive parents are likely to steer clear of transracial parenting. Some adults who would be willing to raise a child regardless of racial differences find themselves unwilling to do so in the face of social pressures that stigmatize transracial adoption as anything from second-best to cultural genocide. What this means in practice is that racial matching narrows the pool of prospective parents, which in turn either delays or prevents the transmission of children in need of parents to adults able and willing to serve as parents. How much misery this adds to our pained country is difficult to calibrate. That racial matching adds a substantial amount of misery, however, is inescapable.

The other level on which racial matching is disastrous has to do with its diffuse, long-term moral and political consequences. Racial matching reinforces racialism. It strengthens the baleful notion that race is destiny. It buttresses the notion that people of different racial backgrounds really are different in some moral, unbridgeable, permanent sense. It affirms the notion that race should be a cage to which people are assigned at birth and from which people should not be allowed to wander. It belies the belief that love and understanding are boundless and instead instructs us that our affections are and should be bounded by the color line regardless of our efforts.

* * *

There is no rationale sufficiently compelling to justify preferring same-race child placements over transracial placements. One asserted reason for favoring same-race placements (at least in terms of black children) is that African–American parents can, on average, better equip African–American children with what they will need to know in order to survive and prosper in a society that remains, in significant degree, a pigmentocracy. This rationale is doubly faulty.

First, it rests upon a racial generalization, a racial stereotype, regarding the relative abilities of white and black adults in terms of raising African–American children. Typically (and the exception does not apply here), our legal system rightly prohibits authorities from making decisions on the basis of racial generalizations, even if the generalizations are accurate. Our legal system demands that people be given individualized consideration to reflect and effectuate our desire to accord to each person respect as a unique and special individual. * * * Thus, even if one believes that, on average, black adults are better able than white adults to raise black children effectively, it would still be problematic to disadvantage white adults, on the basis of their race, in the selection process.

Second, there is no evidence that black foster or adoptive parents, on average, do better than white foster or adoptive parents in raising black children. The empirical basis for this claim is suspect; there are no serious, controlled, systematic studies that support it. Nor is this claim self-evidently persuasive. Those who confidently assert this claim rely on the hunch, accepted by many, that black adults, as victims of racial oppression, will generally know more than others about how best to instruct black youngsters on overcoming racial bias. A counter-hunch, however, with just as much plausibility, is that white adults, as insiders to the dominant racial group in America, will know more than racial minorities about the inner world of whites and how best to maneuver with and around them in order to advance one's interests in a white-dominated society.

To substantiate the claim that black adults will on average be better than white adults in terms of raising black children, one must stipulate a baseline conception of what constitutes correct parenting for a black child—otherwise, one will have no basis for judging who is doing better than whom. * * * There exists * * * no consensus on how best to raise a black child (or, for that matter, any other sort of child) or on what constitutes a proper sense of self worth or on what constitutes an appropriate racial identity or on how one would go about measuring any of these things. * * *

* * *

* * * What parentless children need are not "white," "black," "yellow," "brown," or "red" parents but *loving* parents.

* * *

Notes and Questions

1. *A bit of history.* The first recorded adoption in the United States of a black child by white parents took place in 1948. See Joyce A. Ladner, Mixed Families: Adopting Across Racial Boundaries 59 (1977). Professor Margaret Howard has identified seven reasons why transracial adoptions increased in the 1950s and 1960s: (1) growing numbers of children entered the child placement system when medical professionals identified the battered child syndrome in the early 1960s and states began enacting abuse reporting statutes; (2) despite the theoretically temporary nature of foster care, it became apparent that many children languished in foster care for several years or until they reached majority; (3) foster care came to be seen as more likely than permanent placement to harm children's psychological development; (4) the number of healthy white infants available for adoption declined dramatically with the increased availability of contraception, the legalization of abortion, and the growing number of single mothers who kept their babies as the stigma of out-of-wedlock births declined; (5) the social work profession departed from matching, the belief that adopted children adjust best with adoptive parents who share their physical, mental, racial and religious characteristics; (6) the number of minority children needing adoption exceeded the number of available adoptive homes; and (7) the change in social attitudes about racial integration led more white families to seek transracial adoption and more agencies to facilitate it. See Margaret Howard, Transracial Adoption: Analysis of the Best Interests Standard, 59 Notre Dame L. Rev. 503, 505–16 (1984).

Until the 1960s, some states prohibited transracial adoption as race mixing. Courts eventually declared these prohibitions unconstitutional. See, e.g., Compos v. McKeithen, 341 F.Supp. 264, 268 (E.D.La.1972). The decisions followed on the heels of Loving v. Virginia, 388 U.S. 1 (1967), which struck down state laws that prohibited interracial marriage.

In 1972, the National Association of Black Social Workers sternly condemned transracial adoption as "cultural genocide":

> * * * Black children should be placed only with Black families whether in foster care or for adoption. Black children belong, physically,

psychologically and culturally in Black families in order that they receive the total sense of themselves and develop a sound projection of their future. Human beings are products of their environment and develop their sense of values, attitudes and self concept within their family structures. Black children in white homes are cut off from the healthy development of themselves as Black people.

Our position is based on:

1. the necessity of self-determination from birth to death, of all Black people.

2. the need of our young ones to begin at birth to identify with all Black people in a Black community.

3. the philosophy that we need our own to build a strong nation.

The socialization process for every child begins at birth. Included in the socialization process is the child's cultural heritage which is an important segment of the total process. This must begin at the earliest moment; otherwise our children will not have the background and knowledge which is necessary to survive in a racist society. This is impossible if the child is placed with white parents in a white environment.

National Assoc. of Black Social Workers, Position Paper (Apr. 1972), quoted in Rita James Simon and Howard Altstein, Transracial Adoption 50–52 (1977). The ensuing nationwide decline in the number of transracial adoptive placements is generally attributed to this position paper, though Professor Howe attributes the decline also to reduced federal subsidies to social services agencies. Howe, supra, 6 B.U. Pub. Int. L.J. at 465.

2. Palmore. In Palmore v. Sidoti, 466 U.S. 429 (1984), the white divorced wife lost custody of her young daughter after the wife remarried a black man. On the motion to modify the order granting custody to the wife, the trial court found neither birth parent unfit but stated that placement with the birth father was now in the best interests of the child: "[D]espite the strides that have been made in bettering relations between the races in this country," the trial court determined, "it is inevitable that [the child] will, if allowed to remain in her present situation and attains school age and thus more vulnerable to peer pressures, suffer from the social stigmatization that is sure to come." 466 U.S. at 431, 104 S. Ct. at 1881 (quoting the trial court).

Concluding that the trial court "was entirely candid and made no effort to place its holding on any ground other than race," the Supreme Court held that the decision violated equal protection. 466 U.S. at 432, 104 S. Ct. at 1881. The Court expressly addressed the child's prospects in a biracial household: "It would ignore reality to suggest that racial and ethnic prejudices do not exist or that all manifestations of those prejudices have been eliminated. * * * The Constitution cannot control such prejudices but neither can it tolerate them. Private biases may be outside the reach of the law, but the law cannot, directly or indirectly, give them effect." 466 U.S. at 433. The Supreme Court has not decided whether *Palmore* precludes judicial enforcement of race-matching in adoption cases, and the Supreme Court has not determined the issue.

3. *References.* For further discussion of transracial adoption since enactment of the SBJPA, see, e.g., R. Richard Banks, The Color of Desire: Fulfilling Adoptive Parents' Racial Preferences Through Discriminatory State Action, 107 Yale L.J. 875 (1998); Jane Maslow Cohen, Race–Based Adoption in a Post–*Loving* Frame, 6 B.U. Pub. Int. L.J. 653 (1997); Rita J. Simon & Howard Altstein, The Relevance of Race in Adoption Law and Social Practice, 11 Notre Dame J.L. Ethics & Pub. Pol'y 171 (1997); Symposium on Transracial Adoption, 6 B.U. Pub. Int. L.J. 381 (1997). Earlier discussions include Lucille J. Grow and Deborah Shapiro, Black Children, White Parents: A Study of Transracial Adoption (1974); Joyce A. Ladner, Mixed Families: Adopting Across Racial Boundaries (1977); Elizabeth Bartholet, Where Do Black Children Belong? The Politics of Race Matching in Transracial Adoption, 139 U. Pa. L. Rev. 1163 (1991); Mark C. Rahdert, Transracial Adoption—A Constitutional Perspective, 68 Temp. L. Rev. 1687 (1995).

B. *Native American Adoption*

Congress' rejection of race-matching in the Small Business Jobs Protection Act of 1996 stands in contrast to the lawmakers' recognition of tribal identity in the Indian Child Welfare Act of 1978, 25 U.S.C. § 1901 et seq. The Act, which is discussed more fully in Chapter 1, provides that "[i]n any adoptive placement of an Indian child under State law, a preference shall be given, in the absence of good cause to the contrary, to a placement with (1) a member of the child's extended family; (2) other members of the Indian child's tribe; or (3) other Indian families." 25 U.S.C. § 1915(b). The SBJPA expressly exempts the ICWA from its provisions.

An estimated 1,000 to 2,500 Native American children are adopted each year. See Joan Heifetz Hollinger, Introduction to Adoption Law and Practice § 1.05[2][e], in 1 Hollinger, Adoption Law and Practice (1998). The ICWA seeks to protect the best interests of Indian children, and to promote the security, survival and stability of Indian families and tribes. 25 U.S.C. § 1902. The Act recognizes children as tribal resources. 25 U.S.C. § 1901(1), (3).

C. *Religion*

By statute in some states and case law in others, courts are mandated or authorized to consider the religion of the prospective adoptive parent and of the child (or the child's birth parents) in determining whether to approve the adoption. Religious-matching raises two fundamental questions.

Religious differences.   The first question is whether the court may deny an adoption on the ground that the adoptive parent and the child (or the child's birth parents) are of different religions. Courts generally hold that where the statute requires religious matching when "feasible" or "practicable" but does not create an inflexible rule requiring matching as a matter of law, religion may be considered in determining the best interests of the child. See, e.g., Petition of Gally, 107 N.E.2d 21, 25

(Mass.1952). Where the child is too young to express a religious preference, courts consider the birth parents' religious preferences for the child, but such preferences too are not determinative. See, e.g., Cooper v. Hinrichs, 140 N.E.2d 293, 297 (Ill.1957). Religious differences are less significant where the birth parents consent to adoption by a petitioner of a different faith. See, e.g., Adoption of Anonymous, 261 N.Y.S.2d 439 (Fam. Ct. 1965).

Should the child's age affect the weight the court gives to the adoptive parents' different religion? Consider, for example, a twelve-year-old who has practiced a religion for as long as the child can remember. The Child Welfare League of America believes that "[c]hildren who have already established some identification with a particular religious faith of their own should have the right to have such identification respected in any adoptive placement. Efforts should be made to place the child within that religious faith." CWLA, Standards for Adoption Service, Standard 2.8 (rev. ed. 1988). On the other hand, where the adoptive child is a newborn or infant, why should the court consider religion at all in determining whether to grant adoption by an otherwise qualified petitioner? Do you agree with the court in Petitions of Goldman, 121 N.E.2d 843, 846 (Mass.1954): "[A] child too young to understand any religion, even imperfectly, nevertheless may have a religion. * * * [T]he statute was intended to apply to such children, and * * * the words 'religious faith * * * of the child' mean the religious faith of the parents, or in case of 'dispute' the faith of the mother"?

Should the religious-matching question depend on the availability of adoptive parents of the child's or birth parents' faith? If a child languishing in foster care is difficult to place because of a physical or mental disability, religious matching may not be "practicable" if no such other adoptive parents appear. See, e.g., Frantum v. Dep't of Pub. Welfare, 133 A.2d 408 (Md.1957) (denying adoption by Lutheran petitioners of physically disabled infant whose birth mother wished him to be raised as a Catholic; denial was without prejudice to renewal of petition if the infant was not adopted by others in six months); Petition of Gally, supra, 107 N.E.2d at 24 (holding that religious matching was not "practicable" where it was unlikely that the physically disabled two-year-old would be adopted by anyone other than the petitioners). On the other hand, where prospective adoptive parents of the same religion as the child or birth parents are available, religious differences may be a factor in determining the best interests of the child. See, e.g., Petitions of Goldman, supra, 121 N.E.2d at 844–45.

Belief in a Supreme Being. The second fundamental question is whether a court may deny an adoption because a prospective adoptive parent does not believe in a Supreme Being. Some decisions consider a parent's failure to believe in God as indicating inability or unwillingness to direct the child's religious and moral upbringing. However, In re Adoption of E, 279 A.2d 785 (N.J.1971), is typical of decisions holding that without other facts, a court may not find failure to believe in God controlling. On the one hand, "[s]incere belief in and adherence to the tenets of a religion may be indicative of moral fitness to adopt in a particular case." "On the other hand, we do not believe that any reasonable man no matter how devout in his own beliefs, would contend that morality lies in the exclusive province of one or of all religions or of religiosity in general." Id. at 792–93.

Religious-matching statutes invite challenges that they violate the First Amendment by establishing a religion or by prohibiting the free exercise of religion. Where religious matching is merely one factor but is not controlling, courts reject these challenges on the ground that the statute seeks only to determine the best interests of the child. See, e.g., Dickens v. Ernesto, 281 N.E.2d 153 (N.Y.1972). Some courts have held, however, that the First Amendment is violated when courts invoke religious matching as the sole ground for denying an adoption. See, e.g., Adoption of E, supra, 279 A.2d at 793–96 (establishment and free exercise clauses); Orzechowski v. Perales, 582 N.Y.S.2d 341, 347–48 (Fam. Ct. 1992) (establishment clause).

SECTION 7.   INTERNATIONAL ADOPTION

ELIZABETH BARTHOLET, INTERNATIONAL ADOPTION: PROPRIETY, PROSPECTS AND PRAGMATICS

13 J. Am. Acad. Matrim. Law. 181 (1996).

I.   Introduction

International adoption is a very important part of the total adoption picture. How various nations of the world shape the rules governing international adoption will define to a great degree adoption's future role as a parenting alternative. This is because the world divides into essentially two camps for adoption purposes, one consisting of countries with low birthrates and small numbers of children in need of homes, and the other consisting of countries with high birthrates and huge numbers of such children. * * * In the poorer countries of the world, war, political turmoil, and economic circumstances contribute to a situation in which there are very few prospective adopters in comparison with the vast number of children in need of homes.

For the infertile people who want to parent, international adoption constitutes the major alternative to infertility treatment and infertility "by-pass" arrangements such as donor insemination and surrogacy. * * * [T]he single person or the over–40 couple, whose adoption opportunities in the United States are significantly limited, can expand their options by looking abroad. From the child's perspective, international adoption is also advantageous. For most of the homeless children of the world, international adoption represents the only realistic opportunity for permanent families of their own.

Controversy surrounds the topic of international adoption. To some, it presents in extreme form problematic issues they see at the heart of all adoption. It can be viewed as the ultimate form of exploitation, the taking by the rich and powerful of the children born to the poor and powerless. It does tend to involve the adoption by the privileged classes in the industrialized nations, of the children of the least privileged groups in the poorest nations, the adoption by whites of black-and brown-skinned children from various Third World nations, and the separation of children not only from their birth parents, but from their racial, cultural, and national communities as well.

To others, however, international adoption is a particularly positive form of adoption. Prospective parents reach out to children in need, rather than fighting over the limited number of healthy infants available for adoption in this country. The fact that these families are built across lines of racial and cultural difference can be seen as a good thing, both for the parents and children involved and for the larger community. These are families whose members must learn to appreciate one another's differences, in terms of racial and cultural heritage, while at the same time experiencing their common humanity. * * * [T]he evidence indicates that they succeed in doing so. * * * *

International adoption now comprises roughly one-sixth of all non-relative adoptions in this country. Worldwide, there are an estimated 15,000 to 20,000 international adoptions per year.

Increasing interest in international adoption has collided with a new hostility to such adoption. The politics are similar to those involved in the debate about transracial adoption in this country. Political forces in the "sending countries" have been condemning in increasingly loud voices the practice of giving their countries' children to the imperialist North Americans and other foreigners. The notion that there is something shameful in sending homeless children abroad rather than taking care of "one's own" has gained widespread acceptance. The future trajectory for international adoption is unclear.

* * *

III. Foreign Laws and Policies

Although there is great variation among nations in the way they deal with international adoption, few countries have designed their laws in a way that facilitates the placement of children in need of homes with adoptive parents in other countries. Islamic countries prohibit all adoption, whether foreign or domestic. Some countries prohibit international adoption, and others place special restrictions on it. And although today most countries allow such adoption, their laws and policies are not designed to accommodate its unique features, and therefore effectively prevent many prospective parents who would be interested in adopting across borders from doing so.

When international adoption is allowed, the foreign country applies its law to decide what children are available for adoptive placement. It decides whether adoptive parents must come to the child's country to be screened and to process the adoption, or whether the child can be sent abroad for adoption. Requirements that the adoption take place in the child's country of origin add significantly to the financial and other costs of an international adoption, particularly when lengthy or uncertain periods of time abroad are involved, or multiple trips. Many Latin American countries require that adoptive parents from abroad go through essentially the same process as is required in the context of a domestic adoption. The process that might not be unduly burdensome for the person who lives locally may be overwhelmingly difficult for the foreigner who will be required to leave home and family and job to live abroad for the duration of the adoption, which may range from two weeks to several months.

IV.   United States Laws and Policies

* * * The United States' restrictive approach to immigration, together with the complications of the federal system, mean that would-be adoptive parents face a particularly challenging series of hurdles in accomplishing a foreign adoption. They must satisfy the laws and policies of their home state and of the United States government, in addition to those of the foreign country at issue. Because of the absence of coordination among these jurisdictions, the parents and their future child will be screened repeatedly, subject to overlapping and often inconsistent standards.

At the state level, prospective parents must initially satisfy their home state's requirements with respect to parental fitness, since a satisfactory home study is a prerequisite under federal law for all international adoptions.

At the federal level, immigration rules must be satisfied before a child placed by a foreign country for adoption will be permitted to enter the United States with its adoptive parents. These rules allow the issuance of the "preferential visas" that permit the immediate entry of foreign-born adoptees[10] only where adoptive parents can demonstrate that they have fulfilled all requirements under the applicable laws of the parents' home state and of the child's country of origin. These requirements create additional levels of significantly duplicative processing.

In 1994 INS regulations were revised to impose somewhat more stringent requirements for assessing the ability of prospective adoptive parents to provide an appropriate home and parenting. * * * The thrust and tone of the new restrictions are extremely negative, as exemplified by the requirement that prospective adoptive parents be disqualified if there is evidence of "child-buying" activity.

A.   *The Orphan Restriction*

In addition, Congress has severely limited the scope of foreign adoption by permitting entry only to foreign adoptees who fit a narrow

10. Without the preferential visa the foreign-born adoptee would be subject to the regular quota system limiting immigrants and would typically not be eligible for entry for many years.

"orphan" definition. For an adoptee to qualify, both parents must have died or have abandoned the child, or the "sole or surviving" parent must be unable to care for the child. Children may be disqualified simply because they appear to have two living "parents," even if the only evidence of the father's existence is a name on a birth certificate and even if the parents are demonstrably unable or unwilling to care for the child and are interested in adoptive placement. Moreover, children who have already been adopted in foreign countries in accordance with the laws of those countries, are permitted to enter the United States with their legal adoptive parents only if they are found to satisfy the orphan definition.

* * *

The orphan restriction causes many problems. It prevents the adoption of many children who are in need of homes and free for adoption under the laws of their own country. It means that birth parents may feel compelled to abandon their children rather then surrender them in an orderly way, in the hope of making them eligible for adoption in the United States. And it can add significantly to the emotional difficulties involved when the adoption takes place abroad. The visa decision will not be made until the parents have completed the adoption and are ready to return home. And the facts that determine whether a child satisfies the orphan definition often cannot be known until late in the adoptive process. Adoptive parents must therefore go through the entire process of becoming the child's emotional and legal parents without knowing for sure whether at the end they will be permitted to bring the child home with them to the United States.

B. *Unnecessary Adoption and Citizenship Requirements*

After a child has been brought into the United States, additional legal steps are required to fully protect the child and regularize the new parent-child relationship. A United States adoption is necessary if the child has not been adopted abroad and is advisable even if such an adoption has taken place. A foreign adoption decree is not entitled to the same "full faith and credit" accorded a decree issued by courts within the United States. A United States adoption is therefore important to guarantee the child fully protected legal status as an adoptee. In addition, the United States decree will generally be necessary to obtain a United States birth certificate. * * * Although a second adoption in the United States is usually no more than a formality, state law requirements will have to be satisfied. Only a few states have designed their adoption laws to facilitate recognition of foreign adoption decrees.

For most adoptive parents, the final step in the foreign adoptive process involves helping their child acquire United States citizenship. Foreign adoptees do not become citizens by virtue of their adoption by United States citizens. They must apply for citizenship, a process that ordinarily takes from six months to a year. This final bureaucratic hurdle appears to have no substantive meaning. Quite clearly the goal is not to determine which of these foreign-born infants and young children are fit to become United States citizens, but simply to provide citizenship status for all foreign-born adoptees who apply.

From start to finish international adoption involves an enormous amount of process with very little substance. Parent and child must be screened on multiple occasions by numerous agencies, dozens of documents must be accumulated, notarized, certified, stamped with official stamps, copied, and translated. For prospective parents with sufficient resources and determination, international adoption can be accomplished. There are many who are able and willing to endure a great deal for the opportunity to adopt. Moreover, many United States adoption agencies have established ongoing programs with foreign agencies, and for parents who are able to work through these programs, a foreign adoption may be no more difficult than many domestic adoptions. But the bureaucratic process creates very significant costs in financial and other terms. The expenses generally range upwards of $10,000, with many international adoptions costing $15,000 to $30,000 even when no major obstacles arise. Prospective parents can easily devote years of their lives to adoptive efforts that turn out to be futile. The children who are eventually adopted will generally have spent significant periods of their young lives in orphanages or other institutions waiting for adoptive placement. Most important, large numbers who could have been adopted will not be since, for most prospective adoptive parents, the barriers are too great to surmount.

* * *

V.   International Law and the Hague Convention

There is very little international law governing adoption across borders. Most of what exists is designed primarily to protect against potential abuses in international adoption, rather than to facilitate such adoption.

The United Nations has in recent years taken some significant action, with the passage by the General Assembly of the Declaration on Social and Legal Principles Relating to Adoption and Foster Placement of Children Nationally and Internationally in 1986, and the Convention on the Rights of the Child in 1989 [hereinafter U.N. Adoption Declaration and the U.N. Convention, respectively]. These documents recognize the legitimacy of international adoption and demonstrate the international community's support for a number of basic principles regarding such adoption, for example, that there should be safeguards against abduction and against trafficking for profit and that there should be guarantees of citizenship and other appropriate legal status for the children when adopted. But these documents do not establish standards for the processing of international adoptions, and they relegate such adoptions to "last resort" status, with the preferred options being adoption or foster care or other "suitable" care in the child's country of origin.

Some countries have, in the past few decades, developed bilateral treaties or other agreements designed to govern adoption between a particular sending and a particular receiving country. But most of the significant intercountry cooperation that exists today occurs not on the governmental but on the adoption agency level.

In the Spring of 1993 the Hague Conference on Private International Law adopted, by unanimous vote of the 55 countries present at the final Conference proceedings, the final text of a proposed "Convention on Protection of Children and Co-operation in Respect of Intercountry Adoption" [hereinafter Convention], designed to cover all adoptions between countries that become party to it. This represents a very important development in the realm of international adoption law. Almost all the countries significantly involved today in sending or receiving children for international adoption were involved in drafting and approving the text of the Convention. The Convention will, to the degree it becomes operable, establish as a matter of international law specific standards and procedures governing international adoption, thus going far beyond the kinds of general principles incorporated in the United Nations declarations discussed above. And the Convention represents a far more enthusiastic endorsement of international adoption as a good solution for children without parents than any previous international agreement.

* * *

VI. Real Problems and Mythical Concerns

The problems that should be seen as central to the international adoption debate are the misery and deprivation that characterize the lives of huge numbers of the children of the world. Millions of children die regularly of malnutrition and of diseases that should not kill. Millions more live in miserably inadequate institutions or on the streets. Their situations vary: some institutions are worse than others; some "street children" maintain a connection with a family while others are entirely on their own. But there can be no doubt that overwhelming numbers of children in the poor countries of the world are living and dying in conditions which involve extreme degrees of deprivation, neglect, exploitation, and abuse. These are the real problems of the children of the world. International adoption should be seen as an opportunity to solve some of these problems for some children. It should be structured to maximize this positive potential by facilitating the placement of children in need of nurturing homes with people in a position to provide those homes.

International adoption can, of course, play only a very limited role in addressing these problems. Solutions lie in reallocating social and economic resources both among countries and within countries, so that more children can be cared for by their birth families. But, given the fact that social reordering on a grand scale is not on the immediate horizon, international adoption clearly can serve the interests of at least those children in need of homes for whom adoptive parents can be found.

A. *Adoption and Underlying Social Ills*

Some have suggested that international adoption programs might conflict with programs designed to improve the lives of the millions of children now in need, or with efforts to accomplish the kind of social reordering that might help the children of the future. For example, some argue that instead of promoting and pursuing adoption, governments and individuals in the well-off, industrialized countries should devote increased resources to more cost-effective programs designed to promote the well-being of children in their native lands. These efforts could include improving foster care arrangements, sponsoring orphanages, and supporting various UNICEF projects.

Such efforts, however, are not inconsistent with supporting foreign adoption. Indeed, the opposite is true. Foreign adoption programs are likely to increase awareness in the United States and other receiving countries of the problems of children in the sending countries. Those who adopt have reason to identify, through their children, with the situations of other children not lucky enough to have found homes. Foreign adoption is thus likely to help create a climate more sympathetic to wide-ranging forms of support for children abroad.

Another argument voiced against international adoption is that it might relieve pressure within some sending countries to deal with social problems that need attention. But this argument also collapses upon analysis. Sending children abroad for adoption tends to highlight rather than to hide the fact that there are problems at home. Indeed, it seems likely that a major reason for the hostility exhibited by many sending countries toward foreign adoption relates to their governments' embarrassment at having domestic problems spotlighted by this public confession of their inability to take care of their children.

Although speculative arguments can always be mounted, it is unlikely that adoption of a relatively small number of the world's homeless children will interfere with efforts to assist those other children who remain in their native countries. The nations of the world are in general agreement that "the best interests of the child" should be the paramount principle governing the placement of children outside their biological families. Given the real problems confronting the world's children, it should be clear that this principle requires laws and policies designed to facilitate the international placement of children in need of homes.

B. *The Risk of Abuse and Exploitation*

Care should be taken, of course, to prevent international adoption from creating new problems. Adoption must not be used to break up viable birth families, and those who want to adopt must not be allowed to use their financial advantage to induce impoverished birth parents to surrender their children. There is a need for the laws that prohibit baby buying, and for rules governing the process by which a child is removed from one parent to be given to another. The rules should ensure that the birth parents have voluntarily surrendered or abandoned their child, or have had their parental rights terminated for good reason.

* * *

D. *Loss of Roots Versus Opportunities for Better Lives*

* * *

The empirical studies that have focused on international adoption provide no basis for concern as to the welfare of the vast majority of international adoptees and their families. The studies show these children and their families functioning well, and comparing well on various measures of emotional adjustment with other adoptive families, as well as with biologic families. This is rather strikingly positive evidence since most international adoptees have had problematic preadoptive histories that could be expected to cause difficulties in adjustment. The studies show that adoption has for the most part been extraordinarily successful in enabling even those children who have suffered extremely severe forms of deprivation and abuse in their early lives, to recover and flourish.

* * *

There has been no focus in the studies on determining what special positives might inhere in international adoption for the children, their adoptive families, or the larger society. But some studies hint at the rich quality of the experience involved in being part of an international adoptive family, and the special perspective its members may develop on issues of community. One major nationwide study found that one-half of the international adoptees involved felt that as a result of their status, "they may be bridge-builders between the nations." * * *

[T]here is no real conflict between the interests of the sending and those of the receiving nations. International adoption simply serves a symbolic function for those in power. Sending countries can talk of their homeless children as "precious resources," but it is clear that the last thing these countries actually need is more children to care for. At the same time, the well-off countries of the world have no burning need for these children. Their governments might be willing to permit the entry of adoptees from abroad to enable those struggling with infertility to parent, but international adoption is not seen as serving any strong national interest. So the homeless children end up as "resources" that the receiving countries of the world are quite willing to forgo to improve relations abroad.

* * *

VIII.   Conclusion

* * *

The nations of the world should move beyond political hostilities and symbolic acts to focus on the real needs of children. If they did, they would accept international adoption as a good solution for at least some group of the world's homeless children and could begin to restructure their laws and policies so as to facilitate rather than impede such adoption. One side benefit would be that many more of the infertile who want to parent would be given the opportunity to do so through adoption. These people now feel under significant pressure to pursue biological parenthood through high-tech infertility treatment or complicated surrogacy arrangements—pressure that makes little sense in a world suffering in myriad ways from overpopulation. Another side benefit would be enrichment of our understanding of the meaning of family and of community.

Notes and Questions

1. *The present situation.* International adoption, largely unknown in the United States before World War II, began in earnest with returning soldiers and with media coverage of the plight of children and other refugees during and immediately after the conflict. The Korean and Vietnam wars produced heightened interest.

International adoption is no longer a product solely of war. In fiscal year 1997, United States citizens adopted 13,621 children from abroad, including significant numbers from China, Korea and Eastern European nations, including the former Soviet Union. The White House has estimated that this number exceeds the number of international adoptions completed by citizens of all other nations combined. See White House, Office of the Press Secretary, June 11, 1998. One commentator reports that while international adoption accounts for only about 5% to 6% of all adoptions annually, it is "increasing more rapidly than any other type of adoption." See Joan Heifetz Hollinger, Introduction to Adoption Law and Practice § 1.05[2] [c], in 1 Hollinger, Adoption Law and Practice (1998). The steady increase appears to result from the shortage of readily adoptable children in the United States and, according to some observers, from the growth of open adoption in the United States.

2. *The Hague Convention.* As of June, 1998, the United States and thirty-one other nations had signed the Hague Convention, seventeen nations had ratified it, and one nation had acceded to it. The United States has not yet ratified it, though the White House has transmitted implementing legislation to Congress. White House, Office of the Press Secretary, June 11, 1998. Because United States citizens comprise the vast majority of adoptive parents in international adoptions, this nation's decision whether to ratify the Convention would appear particularly critical to the ratification decisions of other nations and to the ultimate effort of the international effort.

SECTION 8.　POST–ADOPTION DISPUTES

Juvenile court judges frequently report that uncontested adoptions tend to be a refreshing aspect of their dockets. In sharp contrast to the family breakdown and personal tragedy that permeate the court calendar, everyone generally leaves the courthouse happy after an uncontested adoption. The child secures a permanent home consistent with his or her best interests, sometimes escaping actual or incipient mistreatment or deprivation. Unless the biological parents have suffered involuntary termination of parental rights, adoption is completed with their knowing and voluntary consent. The adoptive parents realize their dreams of parenthood, and perhaps also their quest to provide an heir to carry on the family name. Where the adoptive parent is the child's stepparent or other close relative, adoption may formalize an existing family relationship.

Sometimes, however, courtroom happiness may be evanescent. A relatively small percentage of adoptions fail, frequently when the child manifests severe physical or emotional problems previously unknown to the adoptive parents. The Child Welfare League of America states that "[t]o make decisions and provide informed consent to * * * add to the family via adoption, * * * adoptive parents should receive full and complete information from the agency pertinent to that decision." Standards for Adoption Service, Standard 0.9 (rev. ed. 1988). Adoption law faces its greatest challenge when a party sues to annul an adoption or to recover damages for negligence or fraudulent misrepresentation by an adoption agency or other intermediary that has allegedly failed to adhere to this principle.

GIBBS v. ERNST

Supreme Court of Pennsylvania, 1994.
647 A.2d 882.

Montemuro, Justice.

* * *

* * * The Complaint alleges the following facts: in early 1983, appellees Jayne and Frank Gibbs, who were already foster parents, inquired of [defendant] Concern [Professional Services for Children and Youth, a state-licensed private child placement agency] about the availability of a healthy Caucasian infant for adoption, and were informed that there was a two year waiting list for healthy Caucasian infants. Appellees were actively encouraged by agency representatives to apply for the adoption of an older child, and were told that it would be easier to adopt a "hard to adopt due to age" child, and that if the child had been physically or sexually abused, Concern would disclose fully the history of these occurrences. Appellees were invited to look through a book containing photographs of older children available for adoption, along with brief positive descriptions of the children.

In May of 1983, appellees submitted a dual application for adoption of a healthy Caucasian infant and a "hard to adopt due to age" child. * * * [T]hey specifically requested a child who was "hard to place due to age," but who had no history of sexual or physical abuse or any mental or emotional problems.

In late August or early September 1984, appellees were informed by Concern that they had been chosen to adopt Michael, a five year old boy from Northampton County.[1] In addition to his age, appellees were told by Concern that Michael was presently repeating kindergarten, that he was Caucasian, and that he had been in foster care, but for only two years and only with one family. Appellees were further informed by Concern that Michael was hyperactive, behind in his school work, had been verbally abused by his mother and that the major problem was neglect by his mother. Concern specifically denied any history of physical or sexual abuse. In October of 1984, appellees were introduced to Michael and his caseworkers at Concern. They were given information about Michael's foster family, and were once again informed by Concern that there was no history of sexual or physical abuse. Later that same afternoon, appellees met with Brenda Messa, a caseworker at [defendant Northhampton County] Children and Youth's offices [a state adoption agency] in Easton, Pennsylvania where they requested a more detailed social and medical history of Michael.

During the first weekend of November, 1984, Michael was placed for adoption with appellees who filed a Report of Intention to Adopt with the Orphan's Court of Berks County. Shortly thereafter, Concern forwarded certain documents identified as Michael's medical file, consisting of records of Michael's birth and the medical history of his natural mother. Appellees once again requested more information about Michael's psychological and emotional history.

Concern supervised Michael's placement with appellees and, although he had educational problems, Michael seemed much calmer and passed first grade. In September of 1985, Concern consented to the finalization of the adoption. Prior to finalization, appellees met with Concern and specifically asked whether there was anything in Concern's file that had not been disclosed to them. They were assured by Concern that they had been given everything Children and Youth had provided to Concern; but were told that Children and Youth had "promised additional information," and that there was a "communication problem" with Children and Youth. Concern agreed to check all records to make sure everything was made available to appellees prior to the finalization of the adoption.

On October 21, 1985, a final order was entered in the Court of Common Pleas of Berks County granting the adoption of Michael J. Gibbs. Immediately thereafter, Michael began experiencing severe emotional problems. He became violent and aggressive toward younger children, attempting to amputate the arm of a five year old; attempting to suffocate his younger cousin; attempting to kill another cousin by hitting him over the head with a lead pipe; deliberately placing Clorox in a cleaning solution causing Ms. Gibbs to burn her hands badly; and starting a fire which seriously injured a younger cousin.

---

    1. We note that Michael was born on May 21, 1977, making him, in fact, more than seven years old in August/September of 1984.

After Michael's admission and evaluation at the Philadelphia Child Guidance Center, appellees were advised that little chance existed of any change in his violent behavior. Michael's conduct deteriorated further, and he was admitted to a special program for adopted children at the Northwestern Institute where he remained until he was transferred by court order to the Eastern State School and Hospital. On or about September 15, 1989, Michael was declared dependent by the Family Division of the Philadelphia Court of Common Pleas, and was placed in the custody of the Department of Human Services.

In September of 1989, a caseworker from the Department of Human Services informed appellees for the first time that Michael had been severely abused, both physically and sexually as a young child. Records in the possession of Northwestern Institute revealed that Michael had been in ten different foster placements before he was freed for adoption; that during his first six years Michael's mother repeatedly placed him in and then removed him from foster care; that there was a long, serious history of abuse, both physical and sexual, by his biological parents; that Michael had been neglected by his biological mother; that Michael had an extensive history of aggressiveness and hostility towards other children; and that Michael's mother at one time attempted to cut off his penis. At no time prior to the finalization of the adoption did Concern or Children and Youth disclose this information although it was in their possession and had been requested.

* * * [A]ppellees commenced this action * * * for Wrongful Adoption and * * * for Negligent Placement of Adoptive Child. * * *

* * *

Most authorities have recognized that causes of action for wrongful adoption are no more than an extension of common law principles to the adoption setting. * * *

In determining whether these traditional common law causes of action should be applied to the adoption context in our Commonwealth, we are well aware of the competing interests involved. On one side is the interest of prospective parents in obtaining as much information as possible about the child they are to adopt. Adoption experts are virtually unanimous in the belief that complete and accurate medical and social information should be communicated to adopting parents. Providing full and complete information is crucial because the consequences of non-disclosure can be catastrophic; ignorance of medical or psychological history can prevent the adopting parents and their doctors from providing effective treatment, or any treatment at all. Moreover, full and accurate disclosure ensures that the adopting parents are emotionally and financially equipped to raise a child with special needs. Failure to provide adequate background information can result in the placement of children with families unable or unwilling to cope with physical or mental problems, leading to failed adoptions.[6] For these reasons, a policy

6. It can be argued that adoptive parents are entitled to no notice of medical problems, since natural parents receive no advance warning of a child's special needs.

in favor of full and accurate disclosure of a child's medical history improves the chances of a successful placement and promotes public confidence in the institution of adoption.

On the other side of the ledger, adoption agencies and intermediaries are justifiably concerned lest any undue burden placed upon them should ultimately reduce the number of successful adoptions. In deciding to apply traditional common law causes of action to the adoption context, we have paid particular attention to the obligations placed upon adoption agencies so as not to diminish their effectiveness in placing children. We are * * * convinced that agencies, on occasion, do fail to provide prospective parents with complete and accurate information, and, worse, occasionally supply information which is both false and misleading. Mindful of the seriousness of this problem and its potentially devastating consequences, we hold that the traditional common law causes of action grounded in fraud and negligence do apply to the adoption setting.

* * *

Appellants correctly assert that adoption is a statutorily created mechanism, unknown at common law. It is also true that the Adoption Act must be strictly construed, and that exceptions to the Act may not be judicially created. However, we find nothing in the Act to be inconsistent with the application of traditional common law principles to the adoption setting. * * *

The complaint suggests several common law theories of recovery. The first such cause of action is intentional misrepresentation or fraud, which contains the following elements: (1) a representation; (2) which is material to the transaction at hand; (3) made falsely, with knowledge of its falsity or recklessness as to whether it is true or false; (4) with the intent of misleading another into relying on it; (5) justifiable reliance on the misrepresentation; and (6) the resulting injury was proximately caused by the reliance.[12]

* * *

However, the risks assumed by adoptive parents are, in truth, very different from those of adoptive parents. Biological parents, theoretically at least, are aware of their medical histories and can decide to have a child with knowledge of, e.g., an increased risk of genetic abnormality. Adoptive parents, without full and accurate information, have no way of knowing if the adoptee has a risk of a genetic problem. This Court is also mindful that adoptive parents are performing a valuable social service in providing a family to otherwise unwanted children. In light of this contribution to society, it is only equitable to conclude that adoptive parents should not be asked to assume unwittingly the same risks as natural parents.

12. The tort of intentional non-disclosure has the same elements as the tort of intentional misrepresentation except that in a case of intentional non-disclosure the party intentionally conceals a material fact rather than making an affirmative misrepresentation. The tort of intentional non-disclosure has been recognized in the adoption setting by other state courts. Such fraud arises where there is an intentional concealment calculated to deceive. We need not decide whether actions for the closely related tort of intentional non-disclosure or concealment should be allowed in the adoption setting, since close examination of appellees' complaint reveals that they have not pleaded such a cause of action.

* * * We now hold, in accord with the unanimous decisions of our sister jurisdictions, that the cause of action for intentional misrepresentation is equally applicable in the adoption context. Such application will further the goal of providing prospective parents with full and accurate information about the child, and, at the same time will inhibit adoption agencies from providing false information. Adopting parents will then be able to make informed choices about adoption, ensuring that they have the emotional and financial resources to care properly for the child they have consented to adopt. This truthfulness in the adoption process will, thus, result in fewer failed adoptions and enhance public confidence in the process. We * * * believe that it would be a "travesty of justice" to allow adoption agencies to engage in deceitful and fraudulent conduct with impunity. * * * *

Upon review of the complaint, we find that appellees clearly plead the elements of intentional misrepresentation * * *, and we hold that they should be able to proceed to trial on this cause of action.

The complaint also suggests that negligent misrepresentation provides grounds for recovery. The elements which must be proven for such a wrong to be shown are: (1) a misrepresentation of a material fact; (2) the representor must either know of the misrepresentation, must make the misrepresentation without knowledge as to its truth or falsity or must make the representation under circumstances in which he ought to have known of its falsity; (3) the representor must intend the representation to induce another to act on it; and (4) injury must result to the party acting in justifiable reliance on the misrepresentation. Thus, negligent misrepresentation differs from intentional misrepresentation in that to commit the former, the speaker need not know his or her words are untrue, but must have failed to make reasonable investigation of the truth of those words. * * * *

We are fully aware that application of the tort of negligent misrepresentation presents more of a burden on adoption agencies than the tort of intentional misrepresentation, which requires only that adoption agencies refrain from fraudulent and deceitful conduct. Negligent misrepresentation, however, requires that the adoption agency make reasonable efforts to determine whether its representations are true. Nevertheless, we believe that this admittedly heavier burden is tempered in several ways. First, agencies are only under the obligation to make *reasonable* efforts to determine if their statements are true. Thus, adoption agencies need not offer warranties or guarantees as to the information they provide. Second, * * * agencies may refrain from making any representations at all if they find that the burden of reasonable investigation is too harsh. While we adopt the traditional common-law cause of action of negligent misrepresentation in the adoption setting today, we in no way imply that adoption agencies are insurors or warrantors of a child's health. The tort we now recognize is not similar to, nor can it be compared with products liability or contractual warranties. Adoption agencies must merely use reasonable care to insure that the information they communicate is accurate, and the parents must show that any negligently communicated information is causally related to their damages. We believe that this tort is sufficiently restricted by the common law notion of foreseeability as found in the concepts of duty and proximate cause to prevent it from becoming in any way a guarantee or warranty of a child's future health.

An important element of duty is foreseeability; thus, the liability of adoption agencies is limited to those conditions reasonably predictable at the time of placement. * * * Accordingly, under the traditional principles of negligence, the duty of adoption agencies for the purposes of negligent misrepresentation will only apply where the condition of the child was foreseeable at the time of placement so that the agency is blameworthy in making a misrepresentation.

Upon reviewing appellees' complaint, we find that they have plead a cause of action for negligent misrepresentation. * * * We therefore hold that appellees should be able to proceed to trial on the theory of negligent misrepresentation.

The complaint also suggests a cause of action against Concern and Children and Youth for negligently failing to disclose relevant information about Michael that they had in their possession at the time of the adoption. As discussed *supra*, any cause of action in negligence must be premised on a duty owed by one party to the other. After a careful review of the law of this Commonwealth we find that an adoption agency has a duty to disclose fully and accurately to the adopting parents all relevant non-identifying information in its possession concerning the adoptee.

* * *

The adoption agency-adopting parent connection is, or should be, one of trust and confidence, differing significantly from a business arrangement in which two parties to a transaction may maintain silence in order to negotiate the stronger position, and are under no obligation to divulge information which may weaken that position. Rather, this relationship is a singular one in that the parties act not as adversaries, but in concert to achieve a result desired by both sides, the creation of a viable family unit. * * * "[A] duty to disclose exists because of a fiduciary or similar relationship of trust and confidence between the parties. An adoption is not an arms-length sale of widgets." We thus conclude that a duty to disclose is created by this unique association.

* * *

We find that the creation of a duty in this instance will further the interests of parents by providing them with as much factual and valid information as possible about the child they are to adopt without placing an undue burden on adoption agencies, as they are required only to make reasonable efforts to disclose fully and accurately the medical history they have already obtained. Only where adoption intermediaries disclose information negligently will they be liable. Thus, the only burden on adoption intermediaries is the obligation to make a reasonable investigation of their records, and to make reasonable efforts to reveal fully and accurately all non-identifying information in their possession to the adopting parents. We do not believe that this responsibility constitutes an undue burden in light of the important interests served by its performance.

* * * [W]e hold that appellees should be able to proceed to trial on this cause of action.

Finally, appellees' complaint suggests a cause of action for failing to investigate Michael's mental and physical health. We can find no authority in Pennsylvania for the creation of a duty of reasonable investigation as a matter of common law, nor have any of our sister states recognized a duty to investigate. [The court then found no such authority explicit or implicit in the adoption act.].

* * *

[J]udicial imposition of such a duty [to investigate] would be, in our estimation, an undue burden on adoption agencies. We find that although the Act requires a good faith effort to obtain medical history information on the part of adoption intermediaries,[15] the requirement of a comprehensive investigation into the background of a child in order to avoid liability would strain the resources of adoption intermediaries and reduce the number of adoptions. Accordingly, appellees may not proceed to trial on the theory of breach of a duty to investigate * * *.

* * *

Notes and Questions

1. *"Wrongful adoption."* Burr v. Board of County Comm'rs, 491 N.E.2d 1101 (Ohio 1986), was the first decision to impose liability on an adoption intermediary for nondisclosure of information about the adopted child's physical or mental condition. A number of jurisdictions have now permitted recovery for fraud or negligence, or both. Courts generally avoid the term "wrongful adoption" because "the question of whether to recognize causes of action for 'wrongful adoption' simply requires the straightforward application and extension of well-recognized common-law actions, such as negligence and fraud, to the adoption context and not the creation of new torts." Mallette v. Children's Friend & Serv., 661 A.2d 67, 69 (R.I.1995). The measure of compensatory damages sought is normally the extraordinary costs of raising the child in light of the fraudulently or negligently concealed physical or mental condition.

15. Several commentators have asserted that recognizing a duty to disclose information, but refusing to recognize a duty to investigate creates, in the words of one author, a "perverse incentive structure" under which agencies will operate on a less information less liability basis. We believe that the good faith requirement to obtain medical information implicit in the Adoption Act prevents such an effect in this Commonwealth.

One observer reports that instances of fraudulent misrepresentation by adoption agencies and other intermediaries have declined (though not disappeared) since *Burr*, but that nondisclosure and inadequate disclosure smacking of negligence persist. See Liane Leshne, Wrongful Adoption: Fewer Secrets and Lies, But Agencies Still Fail at Full Disclosure, Trial, Apr. 1999, at 14. Before *Burr* opened the courts to adoptive parents' tort suits, the situation appeared disturbing. In California alone, sixty-nine adoptions were reportedly annulled from 1983 to 1987 on the ground that public agencies had misrepresented the child's physical or emotional condition before entry of the court's adoption order. See Dianne Klein, "Special" Children: Dark Past Can Haunt Adoptions, L.A. Times, May 29, 1988, at 1. One study found that disclosure had not been given to more than half the parents who had adopted a sexually abused child, to a third of the parents who had adopted a physically abused child, and to a third of the parents who had adopted a learning disabled child. See Richard P. Barth & Marianne Berry, Adoption and Disruption: Rates, Risks, and Responses 108–10 (1988).

Lawsuits are likely to continue because the adoption docket includes greater numbers of emotionally and physically disabled foster children and of international adoptees. Complete information about foster children is sometimes unavailable because of poor recordkeeping, rapid turnover of social welfare agency personnel, and frequent movement of the child from home to home. Private adoption agencies frequently do not receive full information from foster care authorities. International adoptees may have been anonymously abandoned by their parents or may have come from poorly administered orphanages that did not maintain adequate medical histories. See Leshne, supra.

2. *Annulling adoptions.* In *Gibbs,* state authorities had removed the child from the adoptive parents' custody before the parents filed suit. Where there has been no such removal, however, the adoptive parents may seek to annul the adoption rather than merely seek damages. Annulment makes the adoption a nullity ab initio, and thus frees the adoptive parents of the rights and obligations that adoption creates; a damage action, on the other hand, leaves the adoptive family intact but awards compensatory or punitive damages, or both, for the defendant's fraud or negligence. Suits to annul adoptions tend to arise in three situations. An adopting stepparent may seek annulment when he or she later divorces the natural parent; the adoptive parents may find the child ungovernable and beyond their effective control; or the child may manifest undisclosed severe emotional or physical disabilities unknown to the parents when they adopted.

Except where the adoptive parents appear defrauded or where other extreme circumstances appear, courts normally deny annulment as contrary to the best interests of the child. An annulment order is particularly unlikely where the child has been in the adoptive home for a substantial period, or where the child's likely alternative is a return to state custody. "[P]ublic policy disfavors a revocation of an adoption because an adoption is intended to bring a parent and child together in a permanent relationship, to bring stability to the child's life, and to allow laws of intestate succession to apply with certainty to adopted children." In re Adoption of T.B., 622 N.E.2d 921, 924 (Ind.1993). Because "the law abhors the idea of being able to 'send the child back' ", id., a number of decisions indicate that only a strong showing of fraud will establish grounds for annulment. See, e.g., In re Kevin G., 643 N.Y.S.2d 590 (App.Div.1996). Many courts hold that a party may annul an adoption only where entitlement to annulment is established by clear and convincing evidence. See, e.g., In re Lisa Diane G., 537 A.2d 131, 132–33 (R.I.1988).

Adoption codes normally establish a short period within which finalized adoptions may be challenged. See, e.g., Md. Code, Fam. Law § 5–325 (one year). The period is not tolled because of the child's minority because tolling would defeat the purpose of the short period, which is to produce finality and thus to protect children from the psychological trauma occasioned by disrupted lives. See, e.g., Wimber v. Timpe, 818 P.2d 954, 957 (Or.Ct.App.1991).

The limitations statutes, however, frequently reach only challenges for procedural irregularities or defects in the adoption proceeding itself. See, e.g., Md. Code, Fam. Law § 5–325 (one year). A few states also expressly create a limitations period for fraud challenges. See, e.g., Colo. Rev. Stat. § 19–5–214(1). Other states have enacted broad statutes of limitations that reach all challenges. See, e.g., 10 Okla. Stat. § 58.

Where the adoption code's statute of limitations reaches only procedural irregularities or defects, courts usually permit challenges for fraud or other substantive irregularity under the state's civil procedure statute or rules relating to vacatur of final judgments generally. The state statute or rules may be based on Fed. R. Civ. P. 60(b), which permits vacatur on a showing, among other things, of fraud, misrepresentation or other misconduct of an adverse party or voidness of the judgment. See, e.g., Green v. Sollenberger, 656 A.2d 773 (Md.1995). Under general limitations doctrines, the limitations period for a fraud claim may be tolled until the allegedly defrauded party discovered or should reasonably have discovered the fraud. See, e.g., Mohr v. Commonwealth, 653 N.E.2d 1104, 1109 (Mass.1995).

3. *Exculpatory clauses.* *Gibbs* discusses the strong policy reasons for requiring adoption intermediaries to disclose medical and other vital information to prospective adoptive parents. Many adoption acts now require such disclosure. In light of these reasons and acts, should courts enforce agreements that would eliminate or sharply reduce the duty to disclose? See, e.g., Ferenc v. World Child, Inc., 977 F.Supp. 56, 60–61 (D.D.C.1997) (enforcing exculpatory clause).

4. *Fraud by one adoptive parent on the other.* If one adoptive parent fraudulently induces the other to complete the adoption, may the defrauded parent annul the adoption? In In re Adoption of B.J.H., 564 N.W.2d 387 (Iowa 1997), the court held that the wife had defrauded the husband, a holding normally sufficient to vacate a civil judgment. The court further held, however, that an adoption decree may be vacated for fraud only where vacatur would be in the best interests of the child. *B.J.H.* found vacatur consistent with best interests here because the husband had had no psychological or emotional relationship with the children since the filing of the adoption decree. Id. at 393.

Does *B.J.H.* mean that even a parent defrauded by a spouse must maintain the adoptive relationship if annulment would be contrary to the best interests of the child?

5. *References.* D. Marianne Brower Blair, Getting the Whole Truth and Nothing But the Truth: The Limits of Liability for Wrongful Adoption, 67 Notre Dame L. Rev. 851 (1992); Pat McDonald–Nunemaker, Wrongful Adoption: The Development of a Better Remedy in Tort, 12 J. American Acad. Matrim. Law. 391 (1994); Note, When Love is Not Enough: Toward a Unified Wrongful Adoption Tort, 105 Harv. L. Rev. 1761 (1992).

PROBLEM 7–8

Six years after adopting a 15–year-old girl, John and Mary Smith divorce. Shortly after the divorce becomes final, the daughter moves to vacate the adoption decree so she and John can marry without violating the state incest statute. Father and daughter seek to marry to legitimate their newborn infant, whom they conceived while John and Mary were still married. Indeed the parties conceded that father and daughter had had sexual relations several times before they conceived the child. You are the judge and you have concluded that state law permits you to annul an adoption at this late date. Would you grant the daughter's motion to vacate the adoption order as to one or both of her adoptive parents?

SECTION 9. ADOPTEES' RIGHTS TO "LEARN THEIR ROOTS"

Entry of an adoption decree extinguishes the existing parent-child relationship, and creates a new parent-child relationship between adoptive parent and child. To effect this complete severance and to serve the parties' interests, states in the 1920s began to enact statutes sealing records in agency adoptions. "Secrecy enables the natural parent to place the child for adoption with a respectable agency with the assurance that his or her identity will not become public knowledge. The natural parent is then afforded an opportunity to restructure his or her life after a most traumatic episode. The confidentiality proviso allows adoptive parents, having taken a child into their home, to raise that child free from interference from the natural parents and without any apprehension that the birth status of their child will be used to harm themselves or the child. * * * The confidentiality shield protects the adoptee from any possible stain of illegitimacy and permits the formation of a relationship with the new parents that hopefully can 'bloom and grow forever,' free of the threat of outside interference that can be posed by the appearance of a natural, well-intended parent who just wishes to drop by and see or talk to his or her offspring." In re Christine, 397 A.2d 511, 513 (R.I.1979). By serving these interests, secrecy assertedly also serves a state interest in encouraging parties to participate in the adoption process.

When the court decrees an adoption, the child is issued a new birth certificate naming the adoptive parents as the only parents and the child assumes their surname. The original birth certificate and all other court records are permanently sealed and may be released only on court order for good cause (or in some states, on consent of the adoptive parents, the biological parents, and the adoptee). In the absence of the severe necessity that establishes good cause, the biological parents may not learn the identity or whereabouts of the child or adoptive parents, and the adoptive parents and the child may not learn the identities or whereabouts of the biological parents. An adoptee inquisitive about his or her heritage may learn only what the adoptive parents reveal, and they may not know very much themselves.

The good-cause requirement is a formidable hurdle that permits disclosure of identifying information (that is, information which includes the birth parents' name, birth date, place of birth and last known address) only where the adoptee shows an urgent need for medical, genetic or other reasons. Even without such a showing, most states mandate or allow disclosure to adoptive families of an adopted child's health and genetic information, which can be critical in an age of rapid advances in medicine and genetic counseling. Some states also grant adoptees, when they reach majority, the right to nonidentifying information concerning their biological parents (that is, information about the parents' physical description, age at the time of adoption, race, nationality, religious background, and talents and hobbies, without revealing the parents' identities).

A vast array of statutes and rules help assure confidentiality. Adoption proceedings are not open to the public. Adoption records are exempt from state freedom of information acts or open records laws. The adoption agency, the attorneys and other participants face criminal or contempt sanction for making unauthorized disclosure. See, e.g., Or. Rev. Stat. § 109.440. Logistics may also matter. The Child Welfare League of America recommends that in agency adoptions, "[t]he adoptive family selected should live in a locality where there is a reasonable assurance that the child cannot be identified by the birth parents, unless such identification and contact were a part of an adoption plan agreed to by both the birth and adoptive parents before the adoption." Standards for Adoption Service, Standard 4.10.

Confidentiality statutes impede or thwart the efforts of many adoptees to locate their birth parents. The adoption act's mandate that the child assume a new identity and a new life, however, cannot extinguish the desire of many adoptees for disclosure. Recent years have witnessed the growth of advocacy and support groups to assist adoptees' efforts to locate their birth families, to lobby for legislation easing confidentiality standards, and to challenge the constitutionality of sealed-records statutes.

Notes and Questions

1. *Questions about sealed records.* (a) Are the interests of the natural parents, adoptive parents and the state sufficiently strong to thwart an adoptee's request for disclosure of identifying information?,

(b) Given the recent growth in open adoptions, do confidentiality statutes continue to serve a worthwhile purpose when adult adoptees seek disclosure of their sealed adoption records?,

(c) Given the contemporary shortage of healthy adoptable children and the long waiting lists of desirous adoptive parents, does the state still have a strong interest in sealing records to protect the sensibilities of prospective adoptive parents?,

(d) Does the state deny adoptees personal autonomy when it creates an adoption process by operation of law and denies them information concerning their heritage? Or does the state do enough when it assures release of non-identifying information needed for medical or other such purposes?

2. *The range of petitioners.* Adult adoptees are not the only persons who seek disclosure of adoption records. Biological mothers also frequently move for disclosure in an effort to see the child or learn his or her whereabouts. (Biological fathers usually do not make these requests). See, e.g., In re Christine, 397 A.2d 511 (R.I.1979). See also, e.g., Marvin A. v. Denise A., 615 N.Y.S.2d 249 (Fam. Ct. 1994) (motion by child's former foster father).

3. *Psychological need.* In Matter of Linda F.M. v. Department of Health, 418 N.E.2d 1302, 1304 (1981), the adoptee unsuccessfully sought release of her forty-year-old adoption records. She alleged that her inability to discover her natural parents' identity had caused psychological problems because "I feel cut off from the rest of humanity. * * * I want to know who I am. The only person in the world who looks like me is my son. I have no ancestry. Nothing." *Linda F.M.* acknowledged that "desire to learn about one's ancestry should not be belittled," but held that "mere desire to learn the identity of one's natural parents cannot alone constitute good cause, or the requirement * * * would become a nullity." The court did state that "concrete psychological problems, if found by the court to be specifically connected to the lack of knowledge about ancestry, might constitute good cause." 418 N.E.2d at 1304.

4. *Medical necessity.* In Golan v. Louise Wise Servs., 507 N.E.2d 275 (N.Y.1987), the 54-year-old movant had been adopted when he was less than fifteen months old. Suffering from a heart condition that produced a heart attack before the trial court heard the disclosure motion, he and his attending physicians asserted that genetic information would assist treatment and help enable the physicians to evaluate the severity of his condition. The movant asserted that without this information, the Federal Aviation Administration would not certify him to continue his career as a commercial pilot because the risk posed by his condition was unknown. The record also showed that Golan's son, an Air Force instructor pilot, would benefit from medical data concerning his ancestors. Both of Golan's adoptive parents were deceased, and his biological mother and father would have been 75 and 80 years old respectively if they were still alive.

The adoption agency supplied movant Golan with all the medical and historical information it possessed concerning his biological parents, except his biological father's name and hometown and the name of the college the biological father allegedly attended. (Golan already knew his birth mother's name.). The court denied the disclosure motion, which sought to examine and reproduce any records or reports relating to his biological parents. The court balanced "the medical danger in which adopted children may be placed in the absence of their genetic histories," with the fact that "as virtually any adopted person advances in age, his or her genetic history will be desirable for treatment of a variety of ailments including, for example, heart attack, diabetes and cancer." The court concluded that "[a] rule which automatically gave full disclosure to any adopted person confronted with a medical problem with some genetic implications would swallow New York's strong policy against disclosure as soon as adopted people reached middle age." Id. at 279.

5. *Constitutionality of sealed-records statutes.* Federal and state courts have rebuffed a variety of challenges to the constitutionality of statutes that mandate confidentiality of adoption records in the absence of good cause for disclosure. Even where the court acknowledges that the adult adoptee has an interest in disclosure, the state is found to have a rational basis for upholding the birth parents' interest in privacy, the adoptive parents' interest in finality, and the state's interest in fostering adoption. See, e.g., ALMA Society Inc. v. Mellon, 601 F.2d 1225 (2d Cir. 1979); In re Assalone, 512 A.2d 1383, 1390–91 (R.I. 1986).

6. *Registry statutes.* Most states have enacted registry statutes, which provide for release of identifying information where the birth parents, the adoptive parents and the adult adoptee all register their desire for release. Passive registry statutes allow parties to register their desires, and active registry statutes authorize state authorities to seek out parties' desires when one party expresses a desire for disclosure. See, e.g., Colo. Rev. Stat. § 25–2–113.5 (passive); Or. Rev. Stat. § 109.503 (active). In states without registry statutes, the parties' "unanimous" consent to disclosure may still be insufficient to establish "good cause" and overcome the state's interest in secrecy. See, e.g., In re Estate of McQuesten, 578 A.2d 335, 339 (N.H.1990).

7. *Legislation conferring the right.* A handful of states grant adult adoptees an absolute right to their original birth certificates, e.g., Alaska Stat. § 18.50.500, or to the court records of their adoption proceeding, e.g., 9 S.D. Cod. Laws § 25–6–15. In Doe v. Sundquist, 2 S.W.3d 919 (Tenn.1999), the court upheld the constitutionality of legislation that allowed disclosure of sealed adoption records to adoptees twenty-one years of age or older. The court held that the legislation did not violate the state constitution by impairing the vested rights of birth parents who had surrendered children under the prior law, or by violating the rights to familial and procreational privacy and to nondisclosure of personal information.

8. *Open adoptions.* Confidentiality statutes lose their force when the court orders an open adoption, or specifically enforces a private agreement for such an arrangement. As a practical matter, confidentiality may also be impossible where the birth mother insists on maintaining contact with the child as a condition of her consent, where the adoption is otherwise concluded informally before the parties seek the decree, or where the child has had a pre-adoption relationship with the biological parents or other relatives.

9. *Public opinion.* Large numbers of Americans apparently view adoption disclosure with favor. In a 1997 poll conducted by Princeton Survey Research Associates, 68% of respondents said contact between birth parents and adoptees after a search was usually a good thing for the adoptee, 56%

said it was usually a good thing for the birth parent, and 44% said it was good for the adoptive parents. See Tamar Lewin, U.S. Is Divided on Adoption, Survey of Attitudes Asserts, N.Y. Times, Nov. 9, 1997, at 16.

10. *Practical impossibility*. An adoptee's desire to learn his or her roots may prove to be a practical impossibility. Poor recordkeeping at some adoption agencies may make any sustained search fruitless, particularly after the passage of decades. Children adopted from orphanages overseas, sometimes after surreptitious abandonment by their biological parents, may have been subject to no recordkeeping in their native lands; an abandoned child might not even have a birth certificate or other proof of exact date of birth.

11. *References*. Paul Sachdev, Unlocking the Adoption Files (1989); Arthur Sorosky, Annette Baran & Reuben Pannor, The Adoption Triangle: The Effects of the Sealed Record on Adoptees, Birth Parents, and Adoptive Parents (1979); Katarina Wegar, Adoption, Identity, and Kinship: The Debate Over Sealed Birth Records (1997); Elton B. Klibanoff, Genealogical Information in Adoption: The Adoptee's Quest and the Law, 11 Fam L.Q. 185 (1977); Demosthenes A. Lorandos, Secrecy and Genetics in Adoption Law and Practice, 27 Loy. U. Chi. L.J. 277 (1996).

Chapter 8

MEDICAL DECISION–MAKING

At common law, a minor generally lacks the capacity to consent to medical treatment. Therefore, except in emergencies, a physician who provides treatment to a minor without obtaining parental consent can be sued for battery. Not surprisingly there are a number of exceptions to this rule, one of which you have already studied in Bellotti v. Baird in Chapter 1. As you read the material in this chapter, consider whether you would advocate for changes in the allocation of decision-making authority among children, parents and the state.

SECTION 1.   DECISION–MAKING AUTHORITY

IN RE E.G.

Supreme Court of Illinois, 1989.
549 N.E.2d 322.

JUSTICE RYAN delivered the opinion of the court:

Appellee, E.G., a 17–year-old woman, contracted leukemia and needed blood transfusions in the treatment of the disease. E.G. and her mother, Rosie Denton, refused to consent to the transfusions, contending that acceptance of blood would violate personal religious convictions rooted in their membership in the Jehovah's Witness faith. * * *

* * *

In February of 1987, E.G. was diagnosed as having acute nonlymphatic leukemia, a malignant disease of the white blood cells. When E.G. and her mother, Rosie Denton, were informed that treatment of the disease would involve blood transfusions, they refused to consent to this medical procedure on the basis of their religious beliefs. As Jehovah's Witnesses, both E.G. and her mother desired to observe their religion's prohibition against the "eating" of blood. Mrs. Denton did authorize any other treatment and signed a waiver absolving the medical providers of liability for failure to administer transfusions.

As a result of Denton's and E.G.'s refusal to assent to blood transfusions, the State filed a neglect petition in juvenile court. At the initial hearing on February 25, 1987, Dr. Stanley Yachnin testified that E.G. had approximately one-fifth to one-sixth the normal oxygen-carrying capacity of her blood and consequently was excessively fatigued and incoherent. He stated that without blood transfusions, E.G. would likely die within a month. Dr. Yachnin testified that the transfusions, along with chemotherapy, achieve remission of the disease in about 80% of all patients so afflicted. Continued treatment, according to Dr. Yachnin, would involve the utilization of drugs and more transfusions. The long-term prognosis is not optimistic, as the survival rate for patients such as E.G. is 20 to 25%.

Dr. Yachnin stated that he discussed the proposed course of treatment with E.G. He testified that E.G. was competent to understand the consequences of accepting or rejecting treatment, and he was impressed with her maturity and the sincerity of her beliefs. Dr. Yachnin's observations regarding E.G.'s competency were corroborated by the testimony of Jane McAtee, the associate general counsel for the University of Chicago Hospital. At the conclusion of this hearing, the trial judge entered an order appointing McAtee temporary guardian, and authorizing her to consent to transfusions on E.G.'s behalf.

On April 8, 1987, further hearings were held on this matter. E.G., having received several blood transfusions, was strong enough to take the stand. She testified that the decision to refuse blood transfusions was her own and that she fully understood the nature of her disease and the consequences of her decision. She indicated that her decision was not based on any wish to die, but instead was grounded in her religious convictions. E.G. further stated that when informed that she would undergo transfusions, she asked to be sedated prior to the administration of the blood. She testified that the court's decision upset her, and said: "[I]t seems as if everything that I wanted or believe in was just being disregarded."

Several other witnesses gave their opinions extolling E.G.'s maturity and the sincerity of her religious beliefs. One witness was Dr. Littner, a psychiatrist who has special expertise in evaluating the maturity and competency of minors. Based on interviews with E.G. and her family, Dr. Littner expressed his opinion that E.G. had the maturity level of an 18 to 21 year old. He further concluded that E.G. had the competency to make an informed decision to refuse the blood transfusions, even if this choice was fatal.

On May 18, 1987, the trial court ruled that E.G. was medically neglected, and appointed a guardian to consent to medical treatment. The court felt this was in E.G.'s best interests. The court did state, however, that E.G. was "a mature 17–year-old individual," that E.G. reached her decision on an independent basis, and that she was "fully aware that death [was] assured absent treatment." The court noted that it considered E.G.'s maturity and the religion of her and her parents, and that it gave great weight to the wishes of E.G. Nevertheless, the court felt that the State's interest in this case was greater than the interest E.G. and her mother had in refusing to consent to treatment. * * *

* * *

The paramount issue raised by this appeal is whether a minor like E.G. has a right to refuse medical treatment. In Illinois, an adult has a common law right to refuse medical treatment, even if it is of a life-sustaining nature. This court has also held that an adult may refuse life-saving blood transfusions on first amendment free exercise of religion grounds. An infant child, however, can be compelled to accept life-saving medical treatment over the objections of her parents. In the matter before us, E.G. was a minor, but one who was just months shy of her eighteenth birthday, and an individual that the record indicates was mature for her age. Although the age of majority in Illinois is 18, that age is not an impenetrable barrier that magically precludes a minor from possessing and exercising certain rights normally associated with adulthood. Numerous exceptions are found in this jurisdiction and others which treat minors as adults under specific circumstances.

In Illinois, * * * [a statute] grants minors the legal capacity to consent to medical treatment in certain situations. For example, a minor 12 years or older may seek medical attention on her own if she believes she has venereal disease or is an alcoholic or drug addict. Similarly, an individual under 18 who is married or pregnant may validly consent to treatment. Thus, if E.G. would have been married she could have consented to or, presumably, refused treatment. Also, a minor 16 or older may be declared emancipated under the Emancipation of Mature Minors Act and thereby control his or her own health care decisions. These two acts, when read together in a complementary fashion, indicate that the legislature did not intend that there be an absolute 18–year-old age barrier prohibiting minors from consenting to medical treatment.

In an analogous area of law, no "bright line" age restriction of 18 exists either. Under the Juvenile Court Act, individuals much younger than 18 may be prosecuted under the Criminal Code, if circumstances dictate. Furthermore, to be convicted of many of the offenses in the Criminal Code, a trier of fact would have to find that a minor had a certain mental state at the time the alleged crime was committed. Implied in finding this mental state would be an acknowledgment that a minor was mature enough to have formulated this mens rea. Consequently, the Juvenile Court Act presupposes a "sliding scale of maturity" in which young minors can be deemed mature enough to possess certain mental states and be tried and convicted as adults. This act reflects the common law, which allowed infancy to be a defense to criminal acts. The infancy defense at common law was "based upon an unwillingness to punish those thought to be incapable of forming criminal intent and not of an age where the threat of punishment could serve as a deterrent." When a minor is mature enough to have the capacity to formulate criminal intent, both the common law and our Juvenile Court Act treat the minor as an adult.

Another area of the law where minors are treated as adults is constitutional law, including the constitutional right of abortion. The United States Supreme Court has adopted a mature minor doctrine, which allows women under the age of majority to undergo abortions without parental consent. In the abortion rights context, the Court has noted: "Constitutional rights do not mature and come into being magically only when one attains the state-defined age of majority. Minors, as well as adults, are protected by the Constitution and possess constitutional rights." Moreover, children enjoy the protection of other constitutional rights, including the right of privacy, freedom of expression, freedom from unreasonable searches and seizures, and procedural due process. * * * While we find the language from the cases cited above instructive, we do not feel, as the appellate court did, that an extension of the constitutional mature minor doctrine to the case at bar is "inevitable." These cases do show, however, that no "bright line" age restriction of 18 is tenable in restricting the rights of mature minors, whether the rights be based on constitutional or other grounds. Accordingly, we hold that in addition to these constitutionally based rights expressly delineated by the Supreme Court, mature minors may possess and exercise rights regarding medical care that are rooted in this State's common law.

The common law right to control one's health care was also the basis for the right of an incompetent patient to refuse life-sustaining treatment through a surrogate * * *. We see no reason why this right of dominion over one's own person should not extend to mature minors. * * *

* * *

The trial judge must determine whether a minor is mature enough to make health care choices on her own. * * * We feel the intervention of a judge is appropriate for two reasons.

First, Illinois public policy values the sanctity of life. When a minor's health and life are at stake, this policy becomes a critical consideration. A minor may have a long and fruitful life ahead that an immature, foolish decision could jeopardize. Consequently, when the trial judge weighs the evidence in making a determination of whether a minor is mature enough to handle a health care decision, he must find proof of this maturity by clear and convincing evidence.

Second, the State has a *parens patriae* power to protect those incompetent to protect themselves. "[I]t is well-settled that the State as *parens patriae* has a special duty to protect minors and, if necessary, make vital decisions as to whether to submit a minor to necessary treatment where the condition is life threatening, as wrenching and distasteful as such actions may be." The State's *parens patriae* power pertaining to minors is strongest when the minor is immature and thus incompetent (lacking in capacity) to make these decisions on her own. The *parens patriae* authority fades, however, as the minor gets older and disappears upon her reaching adulthood. The State interest in protecting a mature minor in these situations will vary depending upon the nature of the medical treatment involved. Where the health care issues are potentially life threatening, the State's *parens patriae* interest is greater than if the health care matter is less consequential.

Therefore, the trial judge must weigh these two principles against the evidence he receives of a minor's maturity. If the evidence is clear and convincing that the minor is mature enough to appreciate the consequences of her actions, and that the minor is mature enough to exercise the judgment of an adult, then the mature minor doctrine affords her the common law right to consent to or refuse medical treatment. * * * The right must be balanced against four State interests: (1) the preservation of life; (2) protecting the interests of third parties; (3) prevention of suicide; and (4) maintaining the ethical integrity of the medical profession. Of these four concerns, protecting the interests of third parties is clearly the most significant here. The principal third parties in these cases would be parents, guardians, adult siblings, and other relatives. If a parent or guardian opposes an unemancipated mature minor's refusal to consent to treatment for a life-threatening health problem, this opposition would weigh heavily against the minor's right to refuse. In this case, for example, had E.G. refused the transfusions against the wishes of her mother, then the court would have given serious consideration to her mother's desires.

Nevertheless, in this case both E.G. and her mother agreed that E.G. should turn down the blood transfusions. They based this refusal primarily on religious grounds, contending that the first amendment free exercise clause entitles a mature minor to decline medical care when it contravenes sincerely held religious beliefs. Because we find that a mature minor may exercise a common law right to consent to or refuse medical care, we decline to address the constitutional issue.

* * *

[The supreme court ordered that the neglect finding against Rosie Denton be expunged.]

Justice Ward, dissenting:

I must respectfully dissent. I consider the majority has made an unfortunate choice of situations to announce, in what it calls a case of first impression, that a minor may with judicial approval reject medical treatment, even if the minor's death will be a medically certain consequence. The majority cites decisions where a minor was permitted to exercise what was called a common law right to consent to medical treatment. The safeguarding of health and the preservation of life are obviously different conditions from one in which a minor will be held to have a common law right, as the majority puts it, to refuse medical treatment and sometimes in effect take his own life. That violates the ancient responsibility of the State as *parens patriae* to protect minors and to decide for them, as the majority describes, vital questions, including whether to consent to or refuse necessary medical treatment. * * *

Unless the legislature for specific purposes provides for a different age, a minor is one who has not attained legal age. It is not disputed that E.G. has not attained legal age. It is fundamental that where language is clear there is no need to seek to interpret or depart from the plain language and meaning and read into what is clear exceptions or limitations. The majority nevertheless would in effect define a minor in these grave situations to be one who has not attained legal age unless it is a "mature" minor who is involved. If so this protection that the law gives minors has been lost and the child may make his own decision even at the cost of his life. * * *

I am sure that in a host of matters of far lesser importance it would not be held that a minor however mature could satisfy a requirement of being of legal age. It would not be held that a minor was eligible to vote, to obtain a driver's or a pilot's license, or to enlist in one of the armed services before attaining enlistment age.

* * *

Notes and Questions

1. *Questions about* E.G. (a) Does the court decide that a mature minor has a right to be heard or a right to decide about medical treatment? What would the dissent allow?

(b) What if the mother changes her mind and consents to the treatment, but E.G. still does not want it? Would the court uphold the child's wishes against the parent's contrary wishes? Would such a decision be constitutional? (c) What are the differences between the common law mature minor concept and the *Bellotti* mature minor doctrine?

2. *Assessment of competence.* How should a judge assess a minor's competence to make life-sustaining treatment decisions? Professor Jennifer Rosato proposes that "[g]enerally, the trial judge should determine whether the minor understands the illness and treatment alternatives, which include the possibility of death. The judge also should assess whether the minor has the capacity for rational decision making and whether the minor has the ability to make and communicate a choice." She proposes that in making this determination the judge should consider a number of factors such as the child's age, the child's understanding of death, and the child's reasons for refusing treatment. In addition, the judge should consider the probability of success of the proposed medical procedure as a means of accommodating the interests of parents and the state in preserving the child's life. Jennifer L. Rosato, The Ultimate Test of Autonomy: Should Minors Have a Right to Make Decisions Regarding Life–Sustaining Treatment?, 49 Rutgers L. Rev. 1, 64–65 (1996). Are these appropriate factors for the court to consider? Is a judge capable of assessing a minor's competence?

3. *Mature minor exception.* Not all jurisdictions recognize a common law mature minor exception to the requirement of parental consent for medical care for a child. In O.G. v. Baum, 790 S.W.2d 839 (Tex.Ct. App.1990), the court refused to adopt a mature minor exception. The case involved a 16–year-old child who was severely injured in a train accident and needed surgery to save his arm. The parents and child were Jehovah's Witnesses and refused to consent to a blood transfusion that might be needed during surgery. The court appointed a temporary conservator with authority to consent to the blood transfusion. Should the courts or the legislature decide whether a state will have a mature minor exception? When a child is too young to meet a mature minor test but old enough to have some understanding of the proposed medical treatment, should the court consider the child's views about the proposed medical treatment as part of a "best interests" determination? Should the child be represented? See In re Green, 292 A.2d 387 (Pa. 1972) and R.C. v. State Dep't of Human Resources, 587 So.2d 335 (Ala. Civ. App.1991).

4. *Immature minor.* How much control should a parent have over medical treatment for an immature child? When a parent refuses needed medical treatment, the state may bring a medical neglect proceeding. The trial court in *E.G.,* for example, had ruled that E.G. was medically neglected and had appointed a guardian who had consented to transfusions. The state's authority to take decision-making control from a parent has long been recognized. See, e.g., Jehovah's Witnesses v. King County Hosp., 278 F.Supp. 488 (W.D.Wash.1967), aff'd, 390 U.S. 598 (1968). The scope of this authority is explored in section 2 of this Chapter, medical neglect.

When a parent requests medical treatment for the child, should the parents' informed consent be all that is needed or should the parents' consent be reviewed by a court in some circumstances? Should court approval be required when the medical treatment is for another's benefit, such as an organ donation? (see section 4, infra.) Should court approval be required when the treatment is unusual, particularly risky or experimental? See, e.g., In re A.M.P., 708 N.E.2d 1235 (Ill.App. Ct. 1999) (Court should review parents' consent to electroconvulsive therapy (ECT) and, after providing the child with an opportunity to be heard and receiving input from a health care professional, authorize treatment only if it is in the child's best interests and is the least intrusive treatment available. The evidence included testimony about the risks of ECT and the "dearth of literature on the use of ECT on younger patients." The treatment was authorized.)

A rare psychological disorder, Munchausen syndrome by proxy, causes a parent to report and even induce medical problems to gain sympathy and attention from medical personnel. Children have undergone numerous, unnecessary medical procedures and have even died because of the parent's actions. These cases can be so extreme that they have resulted in the termination of parental rights, In re S.R., 599 A.2d 364 (Vt.1991), and murder convictions against the parents, People v. Phillips, 175 Cal.Rptr. 703 (Ct.App.1981).

5. *Forced medical treatment.* How would a parent or a court force an older child to undergo medical treatment? In a case involving a 15-year-old boy who refused a biopsy because of his "phobia for needles," the child's mother

filed a status offense petition alleging him to be a person in need of supervision. In re Thomas B., 574 N.Y.S.2d 659 (Fam.Ct.1991). The court ordered the child to cooperate with the hospital in obtaining treatment and directed the sheriff's department "to take all necessary steps to enforce the order, including but not limited to transporting the [child] to the hospital, restraining him, if necessary, and supervising the [child] while he is in the hospital." Id. at 661.

An older child's persistent resistance to medical treatment and the practical difficulties of requiring it may eventually convince parents or other authorities to stop treatment. For example, 16-year-old Billy Best ran away from home after 2½ months of chemotherapy for Hodgkin's disease. He returned home after 3 months in response to his family's pleas and promises from his parents and physicians that he would not be forced to receive additional chemotherapy. See Jennifer L. Rosato, The Ultimate Test of Autonomy: Should Minors Have a Right to Make Decisions Regarding Life Sustaining Treatment?, 49 Rutgers L. Rev. 1 (1996). Note that adults have the right to refuse medical treatment, even life-sustaining treatment, for themselves. Cruzan v. Director, Missouri Dep't of Health, 497 U.S. 261 (1990).

6. *Physician's role.* What is the physician's role with regard to the child's consent, particularly with elective surgery? Should a parent's consent be sufficient to authorize cosmetic plastic surgery on a child, for example? Some commentators recommend these guidelines: "It would seem reasonable to defer an elective procedure until the patient (the child) is capable of active participation in the consent process. The physician must be guided by the nature of the proposed procedure, its risk, benefits, and the indications for its initiation, including data on outcomes with other children. The agreement of the child would be a valuable and desirable reinforcement for such decisions." Michael A. Grodin and Joel J. Alpert, Informed Consent and Pediatric Care, in Children's Competence to Consent 93, 101 (Gary B. Melton, et al. eds., 1983). An American Academy of Pediatrics guideline recommended that "in all elective cases written consent to surgery or treatment should be obtained from any minor 13 years of age or older in addition to that of the parent." Id. at 95.

7. *Emancipation.* What are the differences between the common law "mature minor" concept for medical decision-making and emancipation?

8. *General medical emancipation statutes.* Many states have general medical emancipation statutes that enable some categories of minors to consent to medical care, such as married minors, minors on active military duty, and minors who meet the common law definition of emancipation. Also some states have codified the emergency exception and the common law mature minor rule expressed in *E.G.* See Jennifer Rosato, The Ultimate Test of Autonomy: Should Minors Have a Right to Make Decisions Regarding Life–Sustaining Treatment?, 49 Rutgers L. Rev. 1, 29–30 (1996). Does the following statute give too much decision-making authority to children? "A minor who understands the nature and purpose of the proposed examination or treatment and its probable outcome, and voluntarily requests it may consent to medical care." See Nev. Rev. Stat. Ann § 129.030 (2).

9. *Limited medical emancipation statutes*. Most states also have categories of medical care that a minor can receive without parental consent. Frequently these limited medical emancipation statutes cover health problems that minors might want to conceal from their parents and hence might not seek to have treated if parental consent were required, such as drug abuse, alcohol abuse, pregnancy or venereal disease. Under these statutes consent to treatment need not be secured from the child's parent or guardian, though the statutes may relieve the child's parent of the obligation to pay for the treatment. See, e.g., Mich. Stat. Ann. § 333.5127 (venereal disease or HIV), § 333.6121 (drug abuse), § 333.9132 (prenatal and pregnancy care); Ohio Rev. Code Ann. § 3709.241 (venereal disease), § 3719.012 (drug or alcohol abuse).

HIV testing and treatment present special problems. The cost of treatment is extremely high, treatment should be started early, and counseling is recommended, so involving parents may be necessary if a minor tests positive for HIV. If the HIV infection was contacted through drug use or homosexual activity (a high risk for gay teenage boys), children may be particularly afraid to involve their parents. William Adams, "But Do You Have to Tell My Parents?" The Dilemma for Minors Seeking HIV–Testing and Treatment, 27 J. Marshall L. Rev. 493 (1994).

10. *Minor parents*. Should minor parents have capacity to consent to medical care for their children? If not, who should have that authority? If yes, should they also be able to make decisions about their own medical care? What does the New Jersey statute below allow?

> The consent to the performance of medical or surgical care and procedure by a hospital or by a physician licensed to practice medicine and surgery executed by a married person who is a minor, or by a pregnant woman who is a minor, on his or her behalf or on behalf of any of his or her children, shall be valid and binding, and, for such purposes, a married person who is a minor or a pregnant woman who is a minor shall be deemed to have the same legal capacity to act and shall have the same powers and obligations as has a person of legal age.

> Notwithstanding any other provision of the law, an unmarried, pregnant minor may give consent to the furnishing of hospital, medical and surgical care related to her pregnancy or her child, and such consent shall not be subject to disaffirmance because of minority. The consent of the parent or parents of an unmarried, pregnant minor shall not be necessary in order to authorize hospital, medical and surgical care related to her pregnancy or her child.

N.J.Rev. Stat. § 17A–1.

13. *Additional reference*. Jan C. Costello, Making Kids Take Their Medicine: The Privacy and Due Process Rights of De Facto Competent Minors, 31 Loy. L.A. L. Rev. 907 (1998).

PROBLEM 8–1

Jim, a 14-year-old boy, refuses treatment for acute gonorrhea because of his religious belief in faith healing. His parents think he should be treated. If left untreated, the disease could cause arthritis, sterility and even death. Because the disease is contagious, Jim poses a public health risk. Treatment consists of penicillin injections and oral antibiotics. Under the state's limited medical emancipation statute, Jim can consent to treatment for gonorrhea. May he also refuse treatment or may the state treat him without his consent?

PROBLEM 8–2

Your state is considering legislation on living wills, which allow persons to delineate the types of medical treatment that will be withheld if they become incapacitated, and durable proxies for health care, which allow the appointment of an agent to make medical decisions in accord with the wishes of the grantor. Should these desires be available to adults only or to children as well?

PROBLEM 8–3

Benny was born with an enlarged liver and spleen and had had two liver transplants by the time he was twelve. He has to take anti-rejection drugs so his body will not reject the transplanted liver. The drugs cause side effects that include severe migraine headaches, ballooning of his face and hallucinations. He cannot go to school regularly, play with his friends or read for more than a few minutes. He is now age fourteen, and he has decided that he no longer wants to take the drugs, preferring to live a few months without pain rather than to continue fighting death. His parents have acquiesced in his decision, but the state has brought a neglect action based on his doctor's complaint. A child psychologist who evaluated Benny reports that Benny is well-informed about his illness and treatment options, that he realizes that the doctors are sure that if he stops taking the anti-rejection medication he will die, and that he has decided that his death, or a miraculous cure, is in God's hands. The physician's report indicates that Benny risks death even if he continues to take the medication and that he may need a third liver transplant. If he got a third transplant, he would have a 50% chance of survival and would probably have to continue taking anti-rejection medication. The state suggests that it is possible that a new drug, with fewer side effects, will be developed. If you were the judge, would you require Benny to continue taking the medication?

PROBLEM 8–4

Fred is just five months away from turning eighteen. He has cancer and needs blood transfusions before chemotherapy can be used. Fred and his parents are Jehovah's Witnesses and refuse to consent to blood transfusions. Fred has never been away from home, has always consulted with his parents when making decisions, and thinks of himself as a child. The state allows children to consent to medical care in a number of areas, including in-patient treatment for alcohol or substance abuse and for pregnancy-related decisions. If Fred were treated, there is a 75% chance that his disease would go into remission for a period ranging from a few months to several years, and a 25–30% chance of a cure. If you were the judge, would you allow Fred to make the medical decision on his own as a mature minor?

PROBLEM 8–5

You are president of the local Little League baseball program. The program is expanding and will now include games that are out of town, some up to 100 miles away. You are considering requiring parents to execute forms consenting to medical treatment for their child. You have a copy of the standard form a local summer camp uses which was developed with the American Academy of Pediatrics. It states, "I hereby give permission to the medical personnel selected by the camp director to order X-rays, routine tests, and treatment; to release any records necessary for insurance purposes; and to provide or arrange necessary related transportation for me/or my child. In the event I cannot be reached in an emergency, I hereby give permission to the physician selected by the camp director to secure and administer treatment, including hospitalization, for the person named above." What would you put in your Little League program's consent form? Should the program require one?

PARHAM v. J. R.

Supreme Court of the United States, 1979.
442 U.S. 584.

Mr. Chief Justice Burger delivered the opinion of the Court.

The question presented in this appeal is what process is constitutionally due a minor child whose parents or guardian seek state administered institutional mental health care for the child and specifically whether an adversary proceeding is required prior to or after the commitment.

I

Appellee J. R., a child being treated in a Georgia state mental hospital, was a plaintiff in this class action based on 42 U.S.C. § 1983, in the District Court for the Middle District of Georgia. Appellants are the State's Commissioner of the Department of Human Resources, the Director of the Mental Health Division of the Department of Human Resources, and the Chief Medical Officer at the hospital where appellee was being treated. Appellee sought a declaratory judgment that Georgia's voluntary commitment procedures for children under the age of 18, violated the Due Process Clause of the Fourteenth Amendment and requested an injunction against their future enforcement.

* * * After considering expert and lay testimony and extensive exhibits and after visiting two of the State's regional mental health hospitals, the District Court held that Georgia's statutory scheme was unconstitutional because it failed to protect adequately the appellees' due process rights.

To remedy this violation, the court enjoined future commitments based on the procedures in the Georgia statute. It also commanded Georgia to appropriate and expend whatever amount was "reasonably necessary" to provide nonhospital facilities deemed by the appellant state officials to be the most appropriate for the treatment of those members of plaintiffs' class, who could be treated in a less drastic, nonhospital environment.

Appellants challenged all aspects of the District Court's judgment.
* * *

(b) J. L., a plaintiff before the District Court who is now deceased, was admitted in 1970 at the age of 6 years to Central State Regional Hospital in Milledgeville, Ga. Prior to his admission, J. L. had received out-patient treatment at the hospital for over two months. J. L.'s mother then requested the hospital to admit him indefinitely.

The admitting physician interviewed J. L. and his parents. He learned that J. L.'s natural parents had divorced and his mother had remarried. He also learned that J. L. had been expelled from school because he was uncontrollable. He accepted the parents' representation that the boy had been extremely aggressive and diagnosed the child as having a "hyperkinetic reaction of childhood."

J. L.'s mother and stepfather agreed to participate in family therapy during the time their son was hospitalized. Under this program, J. L. was permitted to go home for short stays. Apparently his behavior during these visits was erratic. After several months, the parents requested discontinuance of the program.

In 1972, the child was returned to his mother and stepfather on a furlough basis, i. e., he would live at home but go to school at the hospital. The parents found they were unable to control J. L. to their satisfaction, and this created family stress. Within two months, they requested his readmission to Central State. J. L.'s parents relinquished their parental rights to the county in 1974.

Although several hospital employees recommended that J. L. should be placed in a special foster home with "a warm, supported, truly involved couple," the Department of Family and Children Services was unable to place him in such a setting. On October 24, 1975, J. L. (with J. R.) filed this suit requesting an order of the court placing him in a less drastic environment suitable to his needs.

(c) Appellee J. R. was declared a neglected child by the county and removed from his natural parents when he was three months old. He was placed in seven different foster homes in succession prior to his admission to Central State Hospital at the age of 7.

Immediately preceding his hospitalization, J. R. received outpatient treatment at a county mental health center for several months. He then began attending school where he was so disruptive and incorrigible that he could not conform to normal behavior patterns. Because of his abnormal behavior, J. R.'s seventh set of foster parents requested his removal from their home. The Department of Family and Children Services then sought his admission at Central State. The agency provided the hospital with a complete sociomedical history at the time of his admission. In addition, three separate interviews were conducted with J. R. by the admission team of the hospital.

It was determined that he was borderline retarded, and suffered an "unsocialized, aggressive reaction of childhood." It was recommended unanimously that he would "benefit from the structured environment" of the hospital and would "enjoy living and playing with boys of the same age."

J. R.'s progress was re-examined periodically. In addition, unsuccessful efforts were made by the Department of Family and Children Services during his stay at the hospital to place J. R. in various foster homes. On October 24, 1975, J. R. (with J. L.) filed this suit requesting an order of the court placing him in a less drastic environment suitable to his needs.

(d) Georgia Code § 88–503.1 (1975) provides for the voluntary admission to a state regional hospital of children such as J. L. and J. R. Under that provision, admission begins with an application for hospitalization signed by a "parent or guardian." Upon application, the superintendent of each hospital is given the power to admit temporarily any child for "observation and diagnosis." If, after observation, the superintendent finds "evidence of mental illness" and that the child is "suitable for treatment" in the hospital, then the child may be admitted "for such period and under such conditions as may be authorized by law."

Georgia's mental health statute also provides for the discharge of voluntary patients. Any child who has been hospitalized for more than five days may be discharged at the request of a parent or guardian. Even without a request for discharge, however, the superintendent of each regional hospital has an affirmative duty to release any child "who has recovered from his mental illness or who has sufficiently improved that the superintendent determines that hospitalization of the patient is no longer desirable."

Georgia's Mental Health Director has not published any statewide regulations defining what specific procedures each superintendent must employ when admitting a child under 18. Instead, each regional hospital's superintendent is responsible for the procedures in his or her facility. There is substantial variation among the institutions with regard to their admission procedures and their procedures for review of patients after they have been admitted.* * *

* * *

The District Court nonetheless rejected the State's entire system of providing mental health care on both procedural and substantive grounds. The District Court found that 46 children could be "optimally cared for in another, less restrictive, non-hospital setting if it were available." These "optimal" settings included group homes, therapeutic camps, and home-care services. The Governor of Georgia and the chairmen of the two Appropriations Committees of its legislature, testifying in the District Court, expressed confidence in the Georgia program and informed the court that the State could not justify enlarging its budget during fiscal year 1977 to provide the specialized treatment settings urged by appellees in addition to those then available.

Having described the factual background of Georgia's mental health program and its treatment of the named plaintiffs, we turn now to examine the legal bases for the District Court's judgment.

II

In holding unconstitutional Georgia's statutory procedure for voluntary commitment of juveniles, the District Court first determined that commitment to any of the eight regional hospitals constitutes a severe deprivation of a child's liberty. The court defined this liberty interest in terms of both freedom from bodily restraint and freedom from the "emotional and psychic harm" caused by the institutionalization. Having determined that a liberty interest is implicated by a child's admission to a mental hospital, the court considered what process is required to protect that interest. It held that the process due "includes at least the right after notice to be heard before an impartial tribunal."

* * *

III

In an earlier day, the problems inherent in coping with children afflicted with mental or emotional abnormalities were dealt with largely within the family. Sometimes parents were aided by teachers or a family doctor. While some parents no doubt were able to deal with their disturbed children without specialized assistance, others especially those of limited means and education, were not. Increasingly, they turned for assistance to local, public sources or private charities. Until recently, most of the states did little more than provide custodial institutions for the confinement of persons who were considered dangerous.

As medical knowledge about the mentally ill and public concern for their condition expanded, the states, aided substantially by federal grants, have sought to ameliorate the human tragedies of seriously disturbed children. Ironically, as most states have expanded their efforts to assist the mentally ill, their actions have been subjected to increasing litigation and heightened constitutional scrutiny. Courts have been required to resolve the thorny constitutional attacks on state programs and procedures with limited precedential guidance. In this case, appellees have challenged Georgia's procedural and substantive balance of the individual, family, and social interests at stake in the voluntary commitment of a child to one of its regional mental hospitals.

The parties agree that our prior holdings have set out a general approach for testing challenged state procedures under a due process claim. Assuming the existence of a protectible property or liberty interest, the Court has required a balancing of a number of factors:

"First, the private interest that will be affected by the official action; second, the risk of an erroneous deprivation of such interest through the procedures used, and the probable value, if any, of additional or substitute procedural safeguards; and finally, the Government's interest, including the function involved and the fiscal and administrative burdens that the additional or substitute procedural requirement would entail."

In applying these criteria, we must consider first the child's interest in not being committed. Normally, however, since this interest is inextricably linked with the parents' interest in and obligation for the welfare and health of the child, the private interest at stake is a combination of the child's and parents' concerns. Next, we must examine the State's interest in the procedures it has adopted for commitment and treatment of children. Finally, we must consider how well Georgia's procedures protect against arbitrariness in the decision to commit a child to a state mental hospital.

(a) It is not disputed that a child, in common with adults, has a substantial liberty interest in not being confined unnecessarily for medical treatment and that the state's involvement in the commitment decision constitutes state action under the Fourteenth Amendment. We also recognize that commitment sometimes produces adverse social consequences for the child because of the reaction of some to the discovery that the child has received psychiatric care.

This reaction, however, need not be equated with the community response resulting from being labeled by the state as delinquent, criminal, or mentally ill and possibly dangerous. The state through its voluntary commitment procedures does not "label" the child; it provides a diagnosis and treatment that medical specialists conclude the child requires. In terms of public reaction, the child who exhibits abnormal behavior may be seriously injured by an erroneous decision not to commit. Appellees overlook a significant source of the public reaction to the mentally ill, for what is truly "stigmatizing" is the symptomatology of a mental or emotional illness. The pattern of untreated, abnormal behavior—even if nondangerous—arouses at least as much negative reaction as treatment that becomes public knowledge. A person needing, but not receiving, appropriate medical care may well face even greater social ostracism resulting from the observable symptoms of an untreated disorder.

However, we need not decide what effect these factors might have in a different case. For purposes of this decision, we assume that a child has a protectible interest not only in being free of unnecessary bodily restraints but also in not being labeled erroneously by some persons because of an improper decision by the state hospital superintendent.

(b) We next deal with the interests of the parents who have decided, on the basis of their observations and independent professional recommendations, that their child needs institutional care. Appellees argue that the constitutional rights of the child are of such magnitude and the likelihood of parental abuse is so great that the parents' traditional interests in and responsibility for the upbringing of their child must be subordinated at least to the extent of providing a formal adversary hearing prior to a voluntary commitment.

Our jurisprudence historically has reflected Western civilization concepts of the family as a unit with broad parental authority over minor children. Our cases have consistently followed that course; our constitutional system long ago rejected any notion that a child is "the mere creature of the State" and, on the contrary, asserted that parents generally "have the right, coupled with the high duty, to recognize and prepare [their children] for additional obligations." Surely, this includes a "high duty" to recognize symptoms of illness and to seek and follow medical advice. The law's concept of the family rests on a presumption that parents possess what a child lacks in maturity, experience, and capacity for judgment required for making life's difficult decisions. More important, historically it has recognized that natural bonds of affection lead parents to act in the best interests of their children.

As with so many other legal presumptions, experience and reality may rebut what the law accepts as a starting point; the incidence of child neglect and abuse cases attests to this. That some parents "may at times be acting against the interests of their children" * * * creates a basis for caution, but is hardly a reason to discard wholesale those pages of human experience that teach that parents generally do act in the child's best interests. The statist notion that governmental power should supersede parental authority in all cases because some parents abuse and neglect children is repugnant to American tradition.

Nonetheless, we have recognized that a state is not without constitutional control over parental discretion in dealing with children when their physical or mental health is jeopardized. Moreover, the Court recently declared unconstitutional a state statute that granted parents an absolute veto over a minor child's decision to have an abortion. Appellees urge that these precedents limiting the traditional rights of parents, if viewed in the context of the liberty interest of the child and the likelihood of parental abuse, require us to hold that the parents' decision to have a child admitted to a mental hospital must be subjected to an exacting constitutional scrutiny, including a formal, adversary, pre-admission hearing.

Appellees' argument, however, sweeps too broadly. Simply because the decision of a parent is not agreeable to a child or because it involves risks does not automatically transfer the power to make that decision from the parents to some agency or officer of the state. The same characterizations can be made for a tonsillectomy, appendectomy, or other medical procedure. Most children, even in adolescence, simply are not able to make sound judgments concerning many decisions, including their need for medical care or treatment. Parents can and must make those judgments. * * *

* * *

In defining the respective rights and prerogatives of the child and parent in the voluntary commitment setting, we conclude that our precedents permit the parents to retain a substantial, if not the dominant, role in the decision, absent a finding of neglect or abuse, and that the traditional presumption that the parents act in the best interests of their child should apply. We also conclude, however, that the child's rights and the nature of the commitment decision are such that parents cannot always have absolute and unreviewable discretion to decide whether to have a child institutionalized. They, of course, retain plenary authority to seek such care for their children, subject to a physician's independent examination and medical judgment.

(c) The State obviously has a significant interest in confining the use of its costly mental health facilities to cases of genuine need. The Georgia program seeks first to determine whether the patient seeking admission has an illness that calls for inpatient treatment. To accomplish this purpose, the State has charged the superintendents of each regional hospital with the responsibility for determining, before authorizing an admission, whether a prospective patient is mentally ill and whether the patient will likely benefit from hospital care. In addition, the State has imposed a continuing duty on hospital superintendents to release any patient who has recovered to the point where hospitalization is no longer needed.

The State in performing its voluntarily assumed mission also has a significant interest in not imposing unnecessary procedural obstacles that may discourage the mentally ill or their families from seeking needed psychiatric assistance. The parens patriae interest in helping parents care for the mental health of their children cannot be fulfilled if the parents are unwilling to take advantage of the opportunities because the admission process is too onerous, too embarrassing, or too contentious. * * *

The State also has a genuine interest in allocating priority to the diagnosis and treatment of patients as soon as they are admitted to a hospital rather than to time-consuming procedural minuets before the admission. One factor that must be considered is the utilization of the time of psychiatrists, psychologists, and other behavioral specialists in preparing for and participating in hearings rather than performing the task for which their special training has fitted them. Behavioral experts in courtrooms and hearings are of little help to patients.

The amici brief of the American Psychiatric Association et al. points out * * * that the average staff psychiatrist in a hospital presently is able to devote only 47% of his time to direct patient care. One consequence of increasing the procedures the state must provide prior to a child's voluntary admission will be that mental health professionals will be diverted even more from the treatment of patients in order to travel to and participate in—and wait for—what could be hundreds—or even thousands—of hearings each year. Obviously the cost of these procedures would come from the public moneys the legislature intended for mental health care.

(d) We now turn to consideration of what process protects adequately the child's constitutional rights by reducing risks of error without unduly trenching on traditional parental authority and without undercutting "efforts to further the legitimate interests of both the state and the patient that are served by" voluntary commitments. We conclude that the risk of error inherent in the parental decision to have a child institutionalized for mental health care is sufficiently great that some kind of inquiry should be made by a "neutral factfinder" to determine whether the statutory requirements for admission are satisfied. That inquiry must carefully probe the child's background using all available sources, including, but not limited to, parents, schools, and other social agencies. Of course, the review must also include an interview with the child. It is necessary that the decisionmaker have the authority to refuse to admit any child who does not satisfy the medical standards for admission. Finally, it is necessary that the child's continuing need for commitment be reviewed periodically by a similarly independent procedure.

We are satisfied that such procedures will protect the child from an erroneous admission decision in a way that neither unduly burdens the states nor inhibits parental decisions to seek state help.

Due process has never been thought to require that the neutral and detached trier of fact be law trained or a judicial or administrative officer. * * * Thus, a staff physician will suffice, so long as he or she is free to evaluate independently the child's mental and emotional condition and need for treatment.

It is not necessary that the deciding physician conduct a formal or quasi-formal, hearing. A state is free to require such a hearing, but due process is not violated by use of informal traditional medical investigative techniques. * * * What is best for a child is an individual medical decision that must be left to the judgment of physicians in each case. We do no more than emphasize that the decision should represent an independent judgment of what the child requires and that all sources of information that are traditionally relied on by physicians and behavioral specialists should be consulted.

* * *

Here, the questions are essentially medical in character: whether the child is mentally or emotionally ill and whether he can benefit from the treatment that is provided by the state. * * *

Although we acknowledge the fallibility of medical and psychiatric diagnosis, we do not accept the notion that the shortcomings of specialists can always be avoided by shifting the decision from a trained specialist using the traditional tools of medical science to an untrained judge or administrative hearing officer after a judicial-type hearing. Even after a hearing, the nonspecialist decisionmaker must make a medical-psychiatric decision. Common human experience and scholarly opinions suggest that the supposed protections of an adversary proceeding to determine the appropriateness of medical decisions for the commitment and treatment of mental and emotional illness may well be more illusory than real.

Another problem with requiring a formalized, factfinding hearing lies in the danger it poses for significant intrusion into the parent-child relationship. Pitting the parents and child as adversaries often will be at odds with the presumption that parents act in the best interests of their child. It is one thing to require a neutral physician to make a careful review of the parents' decision in order to make sure it is proper from a medical standpoint; it is a wholly different matter to employ an adversary contest to ascertain whether the parents' motivation is consistent with the child's interests.

* * *

It has been suggested that a hearing conducted by someone other than the admitting physician is necessary in order to detect instances where parents are "guilty of railroading their children into asylums" or are using "voluntary commitment procedures in order to sanction behavior of which they disapprov[e]." Curiously, it seems to be taken for granted that parents who seek to "dump" their children on the state will inevitably be able to conceal their motives and thus deceive the admitting psychiatrists and the other mental health professionals who make and review the admission decision. * * * It is unrealistic to believe that trained psychiatrists, skilled in eliciting responses, sorting medically relevant facts, and sensing motivational nuances will often be deceived about the family situation surrounding a child's emotional disturbance. Surely a lay, or even law-trained, factfinder would be no more skilled in this process than the professional.

By expressing some confidence in the medical decisionmaking process, we are by no means suggesting it is error free. * * * In general, we are satisfied that an independent medical decisionmaking process, which includes the thorough psychiatric investigation described earlier, followed by additional periodic review of a child's condition, will protect children who should not be admitted; we do not believe the risks of error in that process would be significantly reduced by a more formal, judicial-type hearing. The issue remains whether the Georgia practices, as described in the record before us, comport with these minimum due process requirements.

* * *

We are satisfied that the voluminous record as a whole supports the conclusion that the admissions staffs of the hospitals have acted in a neutral and detached fashion in making medical judgments in the best interests of the children. The State, through its mental health programs, provides the authority for trained professionals to assist parents in examining, diagnosing, and treating emotionally disturbed children. Through its hiring practices, it provides well-staffed and well-equipped hospitals and—as the District Court found—conscientious public employees to implement the State's beneficent purposes.

* * *

IV

(a) Our discussion in Part III was directed at the situation where a child's natural parents request his admission to a state mental hospital. Some members of appellees' class, including J. R., were wards of the State of Georgia at the time of their admission. Obviously their situation differs from those members of the class who have natural parents. While the determination of what process is due varies somewhat when the state, rather than a natural parent, makes the request for commitment, we conclude that the differences in the two situations do not justify requiring different procedures at the time of the child's initial admission to the hospital.

For a ward of the state, there may well be no adult who knows him thoroughly and who cares for him deeply. Unlike with natural parents where there is a presumed natural affection to guide their action, the presumption that the state will protect a child's general welfare stems from a specific state statute. * * *

* * *

Since the state agency having custody and control of the child in loco parentis has a duty to consider the best interests of the child with respect to a decision on commitment to a mental hospital, the State may constitutionally allow that custodial agency to speak for the child, subject, of course, to the restrictions governing natural parents. On this record, we cannot declare unconstitutional Georgia's admission procedures for wards of the State.

(b) It is possible that the procedures required in reviewing a ward's need for continuing care should be different from those used to review the need of a child with natural parents. As we have suggested earlier, the issue of what process is due to justify continuing a voluntary commitment must be considered by the District Court on remand. In making that inquiry, the District Court might well consider whether wards of the State should be treated with respect to continuing therapy differently from children with natural parents.

The absence of an adult who cares deeply for a child has little effect on the reliability of the initial admission decision, but it may have some effect on how long a child will remain in the hospital. * * * For a child without natural parents, we must acknowledge the risk of being lost in the shuffle." Moreover, there is at least some indication that J. R.'s commitment was prolonged because the Department of Family and Children Services had difficulty finding a foster home for him. * * *

V

It is important that we remember the purpose of Georgia's comprehensive mental health program. It seeks substantively and at great cost to provide care for those who cannot afford to obtain private treatment and procedurally to screen carefully all applicants to assure that institutional care is suited to the particular patient. The State resists the complex of procedures ordered by the District Court because in its view they are unnecessary to protect the child's rights, they divert public resources from the central objective of administering health care, they risk aggravating the tensions inherent in the family situation, and they erect barriers that may discourage parents from seeking medical aid for a disturbed child.

On this record, we are satisfied that Georgia's medical factfinding processes are reasonable and consistent with constitutional guarantees. Accordingly, it was error to hold unconstitutional the State's procedures for admitting a child for treatment to a state mental hospital. The judgment is therefore reversed, and the case is remanded to the District Court for further proceedings consistent with this opinion.

Reversed and remanded.

Mr. Justice Stewart, concurring in the judgment.

* * *

Under our law, parents constantly make decisions for their minor children that deprive the children of liberty, and sometimes even of life itself. Yet surely the Fourteenth Amendment is not invoked when an informed parent decides upon major surgery for his child, even in a state hospital. I can perceive no basic constitutional differences between commitment to a mental hospital and other parental decisions that result in a child's loss of liberty.

* * *

To be sure, the presumption that a parent is acting in the best interests of his child must be a rebuttable one, since certainly not all parents are actuated by the unselfish motive the law presumes. Some parents are simply unfit parents. But Georgia clearly provides that an unfit parent can be stripped of his parental authority under laws dealing with neglect and abuse of children.

* * *

Mr. Justice Brennan, with whom Mr. Justice Marshall and Mr. Justice Stevens join, concurring in part and dissenting in part.

* * *

I

Rights of Children Committed to Mental Institutions

Commitment to a mental institution necessarily entails a "massive curtailment of liberty," and inevitably affects "fundamental rights." Persons incarcerated in mental hospitals are not only deprived of their physical liberty, they are also deprived of friends, family, and community. Institutionalized mental patients must live in unnatural surroundings under the continuous and detailed control of strangers. They are subject to intrusive treatment which, especially if unwarranted, may violate their right to bodily integrity. Such treatment modalities may include forced administration of psychotropic medication aversive conditioning, convulsive therapy, and even psychosurgery. Furthermore, as the Court recognizes, persons confined in mental institutions are stigmatized as sick and abnormal during confinement and, in some cases, even after release.

Because of these considerations, our cases have made clear that commitment to a mental hospital "is a deprivation of liberty which the State cannot accomplish without due process of law." * * *

These principles also govern the commitment of children. "Constitutional rights do not mature and come into being magically only when one attains the state-defined age of majority. Minors as well as adults are protected by the Constitution and possess constitutional rights.

Indeed, it may well be argued that children are entitled to more protection than are adults. The consequences of an erroneous commitment decision are more tragic where children are involved. Children, on the average, are confined for longer periods than are adults. Moreover, childhood is a particularly vulnerable time of life and children erroneously institutionalized during their formative years may bear the scars for the rest of their lives. Furthermore, the provision of satisfactory institutionalized mental care for children generally requires a substantial financial commitment that too often has not been forthcoming. Decisions of the lower courts have chronicled the inadequacies of existing mental health facilities for children.

In addition, the chances of an erroneous commitment decision are particularly great where children are involved. Even under the best of circumstances psychiatric diagnosis and therapy decisions are fraught with uncertainties. These uncertainties are aggravated when, as under the Georgia practice, the psychiatrist interviews the child during a period of abnormal stress in connection with the commitment, and without adequate time or opportunity to become acquainted with the patient. These uncertainties may be further aggravated when economic and social class separate doctor and child, thereby frustrating the accurate diagnosis of pathology.

These compounded uncertainties often lead to erroneous commitments since psychiatrists tend to err on the side of medical caution and therefore hospitalize patients for whom other dispositions would be more beneficial. The National Institute of Mental Health recently found that only 36% of patients below age 20 who were confined at St. Elizabeths Hospital actually required such hospitalization. Of particular relevance to this case, a Georgia study Commission on Mental Health Services for Children and Youth concluded that more than half of the State's institutionalized children were not in need of confinement if other forms of care were made available or used.

II

Rights of Children Committed by Their Parents

A

Notwithstanding all this, Georgia denies hearings to juveniles institutionalized at the behest of their parents. Georgia rationalizes this practice on the theory that parents act in their children's best interests and therefore may waive their children's due process rights. Children incarcerated because their parents wish them confined, Georgia contends, are really voluntary patients. I cannot accept this argument.

In our society, parental rights are limited by the legitimate rights and interests of their children. "Parents may be free to be become martyrs themselves. But it does not follow they are free, in identical circumstances, to make martyrs of their children before they have reached the age of full and legal discretion when they can make that choice for themselves." * * *

* * *

Additional considerations counsel against allowing parents unfettered power to institutionalize their children without cause or without any hearing to ascertain that cause. The presumption that parents act in their children's best interests, while applicable to most child-rearing decisions, is not applicable in the commitment context. Numerous studies reveal that parental decisions to institutionalize their children often are the results of dislocation in the family unrelated to the children's mental condition. Moreover, even well-meaning parents lack the expertise necessary to evaluate the relative advantages and disadvantages of inpatient as opposed to outpatient psychiatric treatment. Parental decisions to waive hearings in which such questions could be explored, therefore, cannot be conclusively deemed either informed or intelligent. In these circumstances, I respectfully suggest, it ignores reality to assume blindly that parents act in their children's best interests when making commitment decisions and when waiving their children's due process rights.

B

This does not mean States are obliged to treat children who are committed at the behest of their parents in precisely the same manner as other persons who are involuntarily committed. The demands of due process are flexible and the parental commitment decision carries with it practical implications that States may legitimately take into account. While as a general rule due process requires that commitment hearings precede involuntary hospitalization, when parents seek to hospitalize their children special considerations militate in favor of postponement of formal commitment proceedings and against mandatory adversary pre-confinement commitment hearings.

First, the prospect of an adversary hearing prior to admission might deter parents from seeking needed medical attention for their children. Second, the hearings themselves might delay treatment of children whose home life has become impossible and who require some form of immediate state care. Furthermore, because adversary hearings at this juncture would necessarily involve direct challenges to parental authority, judgment, or veracity, preadmission hearings may well result in pitting the child and his advocate against the parents. This, in turn, might traumatize both parent and child and make the child's eventual return to his family more difficult.

Because of these special considerations, I believe that States may legitimately postpone formal commitment proceedings when parents seek inpatient psychiatric treatment for their children. Such children may be admitted, for a limited period, without prior hearing, so long as the admitting psychiatrist first interviews parent and child and concludes that short-term inpatient treatment would be appropriate.

* * *

C

I do not believe, however, that the present Georgia juvenile commitment scheme is constitutional in its entirety. Although Georgia may postpone formal commitment hearings, when parents seek to commit their children, the State cannot dispense with such hearings altogether.* * *

The informal postadmission procedures that Georgia now follows are simply not enough to qualify as hearings—let alone reasonably prompt hearings.* * *

The special considerations that militate against preadmission commitment hearings when parents seek to hospitalize their children do not militate against reasonably prompt postadmission commitment hearings.* * *

* * *

* * *No legitimate state interest would suffer if the superintendent's determinations were reached through fair proceedings with due consideration of fairly presented opposing viewpoints rather than through the present practice of secret, *ex parte* deliberations.

* * *

III

Rights of Children Committed by Their State Guardians

Georgia does not accord prior hearings to juvenile wards of the State of Georgia committed by state social workers acting in loco parentis. The Court dismisses a challenge to this practice on the grounds that state social workers are obliged by statute to act in the children's best interest.

I find this reasoning particularly unpersuasive. With equal logic, it could be argued that criminal trials are unnecessary since prosecutors are not supposed to prosecute innocent persons.

* * *

* * * I believe that, in the absence of exigent circumstances, juveniles committed upon the recommendation of their social workers are entitled to preadmission commitment hearings. As a consequence, I would hold Georgia's present practice of denying these juveniles prior hearings unconstitutional.

* * *

Notes and Questions

1. *Questions about* Parham. (a) What justification does the Court use for giving parents so much control over civil commitment decisions for their children? Do you agree with the Court's rationale? (b) Do you agree with the majority that "what is best for the child is an individual medical decision that must be left to the judgment of physicians in each case"? (c) What does the Court mean by an "erroneous" commitment—the commitment of a healthy child or the commitment of a child who needs mental health treatment, but not institutionalization?

2. *The scope of "errors," due process, and the role of lawyers.* Professor James Ellis suggests that the "scope of the universe of 'errors' is crucial to the due process issue in *Parham.* If the only errors involve cases in which the system has mistakenly institutionalized a child who does not have mental health problems, it becomes easier to agree with the Court that minimal procedures may be adequate." James W. Ellis, Some Observations on the Juvenile Commitment Cases: Reconceptualizing What the Child Has at Stake, 31 Loy. L.A. Rev. 929, 931 (1998). If the errors involve confining a child in an institution when a less drastic form of treatment is appropriate, however, then a formal hearing has more value. He also argues that hearings should be provided all children, not just children who are sufficiently mature to make autonomous decisions; the focus of the hearing for immature children would be on "putting the state to its proof and testing the adequacy of its assertion that the child needs to be placed in an institution." Id. at 936.

Professor Ellis also notes that "[a]ccess to counsel experienced in the mental disability field * * * would surely be of great assistance in identifying the inappropriateness of the proposed commitment and in identifying alternatives for treatment in a noninstitutional setting. * * * Chief Justice

Burger's disdain for the assistance that such lawyers could provide is even more at odds with reality than his naïve assumption that the mental health system, left to its own devices, will seldom if ever confine the wrong children." Id. at 932.

Unfortunately, children are confined to institutions when a less drastic form of treatment would be appropriate. In Alabama, for example, an investigation found that the "the vast majority of the 115 children residing at the Eufaula facility are not in need of the type of restrictive and isolated environment Eufaula currently provides, and * * * could be more appropriately served in less restrictive, community-based programs, closer to their homes and families." Wyatt v. Poundstone, 892 F.Supp. 1410, 1414 (M.D.Ala.1995).

3. *Mature minors.* As *E.G.* pointed out, the common law allowed mature minors to make their own decisions about medical treatment without their parents' consent. Should a mature minor be provided the same protections as an adult in a civil commitment? Does the Court assume that a minor who may need psychiatric care is not "mature"?

Can you reconcile *Parham* with Bellotti v. Baird (discussed in Chapter 1)? Does the Court give minors more control over their liberty interest in the abortion decision than over their liberty interest in being free from confinement? If so, is the distinction justifiable?

Ironically *Parham* was handed down on the same day as Fare v. Michael C. (discussed in Chapter 11, Delinquency), which held that children were capable of waiving their right to remain silent and their right to counsel in a delinquency proceeding.

4. *Inappropriate commitments.* In recent years children have been admitted to inpatient mental health facilities at dramatically increasing rates. Critics suggest that many of these children do not belong in these facilities because they do not have severe mental disorders. Instead they are "troublesome" children who exhibit behavior that is distressing to their families or communities. This inappropriate use of inpatient facilities has resulted from "a combination of factors, including laissez-faire judicial policies, insurance coverage favoring inpatient treatment, the rise of corporate medicine, a mental health establishment willing to assume control over troublesome youth, and the symbolic appeal of a medical care perspective on deviance * * *" Lois A. Weithorn, Mental Hospitalization of Troublesome Youth: An Analysis of Skyrocketing Admission Rates, 40 Stanford L. Rev. 773, 826 (1988). For a comprehensive reform proposal and a critique of *Parham*, see Dennis Cichon, Developing a Mental Health Code for Minors, 13 T.M. Cooley L. Rev. 529 (1996).

5. *Due process.* Should states provide more protection for children than *Parham* requires? California provides an administrative hearing to children age 14 or older if they object to placement in a mental health facility. In re Roger S., 569 P.2d 1286 (Cal.1977). New Jersey requires a court hearing before a final commitment order can be made. The court may order commitment only if it finds that the minor has a mental illness, that the mental illness causes the child to be dangerous to himself, others or property; and that the minor is "in need of intensive psychiatric treatment that can be provided at a psychiatric facility * * * and which cannot be provided in the home, the community or on an outpatient basis * * *." N.J.R.Ct. 4: 74–7A.

In New Jersey, "Before a parent can commit the child for hospitalization, two clinical certificates stating that the child requires commitment are needed; at least one must be prepared by a psychiatrist. Following a review of the certifications, the court may temporarily commit the child, pending a formal hearing, which must be held within 14 days of admission of a minor * * *. The court must review the child's commitment every three months until the child is discharged or reaches the age of majority. The child is also entitled to legal representation by a guardian ad litem." Cecilia Zalkind, Having the Final Say: Children and Medical Treatment, 175 Mar. N.J. Law. 14 (1996).

For a survey of state civil commitment procedures, see James Kevin Walding, What Ever Happened to *Parham* and *Institutionalized Juveniles*: Do Minors Have Procedural Rights in the Civil Commitment Area?, 14 Law & Psych. Rev. 281 (1990) and Cichon, supra note 4.

6. *Additional references*. Children, Mental Health and the Law (N. Dickon Reppucci et al. eds., 1984); Frances J. Lexcen and N. Dickon Reppucci, Effects of Psychopathology on Adolescent Medical Decision–Making, 5 U. Chi. L. Sch. Roundtable 63 (1998); Richard E. Redding, Children's Competence to Provide Informed Consent for Mental Health Treatment, 50 Wash. & Lee L. Rev. 695 (1993). For a discussion of *Parham* and *Bellotti* as mechanisms for distributing decision-making authority over children, see Ira C. Lupu, Mediating Institutions: Beyond the Public/Private Distinction: The Separation of Powers and the Protection of Children, 61 U.Chi.L.Rev. 1317 (1994). For a discussion of *Parham* and social science, see Gail S. Perry and Gary B. Melton, Precedential Value of Judicial Notice of Social Facts: Parham as an Example, 22 J. Fam. L. 633 (1983–84).

A NOTE ON SAFE CONDITIONS

When children are confined in state institutions, the Fourteenth Amendment requires that they be provided with safe conditions. Youngberg v. Romeo, 457 U.S. 307 (1982). In litigation involving conditions at Eufaula Adolescent Center, an Alabama residential treatment facility, the state argued that children who were voluntarily admitted had no due process right to safe conditions. The court disagreed with the state's definition of "voluntary," however. "To be at an institution voluntarily means that the child may leave the institution if he or she wants. * * * Children at the Center may not simply check themselves out." Wyatt v. Poundstone, 892 F.Supp. 1410, n. 65 (M.D.Ala.1995).

The conditions at the Eufaula Adolescent Center, the subject of the *Wyatt* litigation, present a grim picture of the harm that can befall institutionalized children:

> The Eufaula Adolescent Center is a secure, residential treatment facility located in a remote and rural part of Barbour County, Alabama. Formerly a military base, it is comprised of several buildings—two dorms, a recreational and gym area, a school, an administration building with professional offices, and a security building. The area is surrounded by a chain link fence. The physical plant of

the children's dorms—old military style barracks—is "Spartan" and outdated. Furthermore, its remote location makes it difficult for families to visit their children and participate in therapy, and difficult to recruit qualified staff.

* * *

[T]he evidence reflects that several of the Center's severe and pervasive problems from the 1980s and the early 1990s still remain. To be sure, the Center, because of its nature, will always have somewhat of a dual personality: on the one hand, the Center is a mental-illness facility and, as such, must provide treatment to its residents; and, on the other hand, because its residents also suffer from conduct disorders, it must also provide a "secure environment." The critical question, however, is whether, in spite of these recent improvements, the facility is still unnecessarily "penal" in nature * * * and not sufficiently therapeutic, safe, and free from abuse. The court finds, as is shown below, that the defendants have failed to correct adequately the safety and abuse problems at the Center.

* * *

[C]hildren at the Eufaula Adolescent Center are unnecessarily subjected to abuse and unsafe conditions, and they do not feel safe. This danger is reflected in three particular areas: (1) gang activity; (2) staff abuse of children; and (3) the use of improper restraint techniques.

1. Gang Activity

Gang activity is current and widespread at the Center. Many children credibly attested: "There are gangs here [at the Center]. They hit and kick and beat up on kids." "The gangs are known to jump on kids they don't like and to hit and punch kids that are not members of their gang." Gang members are sent on "missions" where they "get higher ranks for beating other people up." Or the mission may involve "males mak[ing] the female do sex acts with them."

The gangs create fear in the children at the Center. As one child attested, "The gangs scare me . . . I feel threatened for my physical safety here. This is not a safe place for kids to be." And children will join gangs in order to feel safer and avoid being beat up. As one child stated, "I joined a gang because I kept getting hit and I thought once I joined people would leave me alone." In order to identify with a gang, a child may tattoo himself or herself with a gang symbol.

The gang activity is not only current and widespread, it has been longstanding and within the defendants' knowledge for some time. * * *

* * *

The evidence of pervasive and serious gang activity at the Center and the defendants' reaction to the evidence leads the court to three important inferences. First, the defendants' tolerance of the destructive activity is indicative of the fact that they view the activity as natural to the facility and not worthy of any remedial effort, and of the further fact that they thus still view the Center as substantially penal rather then therapeutic in nature. Second, unless serious problems are brought out into the open before the court and public, it is likely that the defendants will not address them. And third, absent direct and continuing judicial oversight, it is likely that the defendants will not remedy a serious problem, even once brought out into the open; they will often deny it without adequate inquiry.

2.   Staff Abuse

The administration at Eufaula Adolescent Center does not respond appropriately to evidence and allegations of staff abuse of children. Indeed, the evidence supports the conclusion that the Center, through inaction as well as action, has condoned and allowed continued abuse of children. The Center has a large number of abuse and neglect allegations, with an excessive number of children and staff being involved in multiple incidents of abuse and neglect. During the period from November 1990 to August 1993, 42 staff members at the Center were involved in multiple abuse and neglect investigations, representing a total of 240 incidents. Five of the Center staff were involved in eleven or more abuse and neglect incidents each. These numbers indicate that appropriate action is not taken to insure staff do not abuse their positions of control and authority over children, who, of course, are naturally vulnerable.

Several examples are illustrative of this problem. Mr. M. was involved in 13 different investigations from September 1992 to January 1993. Shortly after beginning work, he physically abused a child by pushing him against a wall and injuring his head. The only remedial action taken was verbal counseling and a one-day suspension without pay. Additional complaints were filed against Mr. M. and investigated, six for physical abuse and two for verbal abuse. The Center found insufficient evidence to determine whether there had been actual physical abuse in the six physical abuse complaints; and the Center found that two instances of verbal abuse had occurred. During one of the verbal abuse incidents, Mr. M. teased and taunted a child, making inappropriate and unprofessional comments concerning a child's mother. In the other instance, Mr. M. called a boy a "white cracker," a "pecker head," and a "4–eyed bitch," and told the boy, "suck my dick." For the verbal abuse, the Center sent a reprimand letter for one instance and issued a verbal warning for the other. The Center allowed Mr. M. to continue working with children after a substantiated instance and multiple allegations of physical abuse and instances of verbal abuse, potentially placing children in danger and certainly not providing appropriate care. Not until March 1993 did the Center terminate him.

Another staff member, a mental health worker, had sexual relationships with a child at the Center. The Department's Bureau of Special Investigations found evidence "sufficient to establish reason to believe and probable cause to believe" that Mr. H. engaged in sexual intercourse with a 15–year-old girl in a bathroom stall. Prior to this incident, Mr. H. had been investigated regarding five other incidents of physical abuse and sexual misconduct at the Center. In fact, Mr. H. had allegedly engaged in "digital intercourse" with the same woman on August 9, 1993. A staff member reported this incident to the director of the Center on August 18, but he failed to act or limit Mr. H.'s contact with children despite Mr. H.'s previous extensive record of sexual misconduct and the fact that the report mentioned that Mr. H. and this girl were planning to have intercourse in the bathroom.

* * * The director * * * took no personnel action against Mr. H. until October 30, when he reassigned Mr. H. to the boys' dorm, and, on November 5, when he placed Mr. H. on mandatory annual leave. One week later, he allowed Mr. H. to resign. * * *

Equally disturbing is the defendants' failure to administer to the victim any follow-up counseling specifically designed to address this incident. Although her clinical record reflects that her therapists in individual and group sessions addressed this incident, it does not indicate that she received any special therapy or additional therapy after the incident was reported. The court is further disturbed by the Center's failure to aid the victim in any manner in pursuing criminal charges.* * *

In summary, the court finds that the Center does not respond appropriately to serious instances of staff abuse. * * *

3.   Use of Improper Force to Restrain Children

Staff improperly uses dangerous physical force to restrain children at the Center. These include: hammerlocks, bending a child's thumb back while holding the child in a hammerlock, placing forearms against a child's neck while the child is against a wall, and using knees in a child's back to pin the child on the ground. Some of the children have sustained welts, scrapes, and bruises as a result of improper restraint practices. The administration at the Center has not taken action to redress such abuse. Although the defendants report that one staff member who used improper force to restrain children has been fired, this is only one staff member and does not address the institutional problem. This would require training staff to restrain children in a proper way, and not tolerating the failure to do so. The Center has a history of tolerating such abuse. There are proper and safe methods for restraining even the most volatile individuals and these should be used. Failure to use proven and safe methods should not be tolerated and should be firmly addressed.

* * *

Id. at 1412–1419. [The court issued a preliminarily injunction to require the defendants to provide for the safety of the residents.]

PROBLEM 8–6

Jana lived with her mother after her parents divorced. When she became a teenager, she and her mother frequently argued. Their disagreements became more intense when sixteen-year-old Jana started dating a man who was twenty-five. Jana's mother decided Jana needed psychiatric treatment to learn to control her emotions and her sexual urges and committed her to a private psychiatric facility, Dreamhaven, over Jana's strenuous objection. With her father's help, after she is released, Jana sues Dreamhaven under 42 U.S.C. § 1983 for false imprisonment and violation of her civil rights. You represent Dreamhaven. What is your defense?

PROBLEM 8–7

As part of an HIV/AIDS education program, a school district decided to make condoms available to high school students without charge. Some parents who object to the condom distribution program have asked for your assistance. What arguments can they make to challenge the program?

SECTION 2. MEDICAL NEGLECT

A. *Determining Neglect*

NEWMARK v. WILLIAMS/DCPS[a]
Supreme Court of Delaware, 1991.
588 A.2d 1108.

MOORE, JUSTICE.

Colin Newmark[1], a three year old child, faced death from a deadly aggressive and advanced form of pediatric cancer known as Burkitt's Lymphoma.* * *

* * *

[Dr. Rita Meek, a board certified pediatric hematologist-oncologist who treated Colin,] recommended that the hospital treat Colin with a heavy regimen of chemotherapy.

Dr. Meek opined that the chemotherapy offered a 40% chance of "curing" Colin's illness. She concluded that he would die within six to

---

    a. DCPS is the Delaware Division of Child Protective Services.

    1. We have used pseudonyms to protect the privacy of Colin and his family.

eight months without treatment. The Newmarks * * * advised Dr. Meek that they would place him under the care of a Christian Science practitioner and reject all medical treatment for their son. Accordingly, they refused to authorize the chemotherapy. * * *

[Although the court stated that there "was no doubt that the Newmarks sincerely believed, as part of their religious beliefs, that the tenets of their faith provided an effective treatment," the court did not base its decision on a spiritual treatment exemption.]

III.

Addressing the facts of this case, we turn to the novel legal question whether, under any circumstances, Colin was a neglected child when his parents refused to accede to medical demands that he receive a radical form of chemotherapy having only a forty percent chance of success. Other jurisdictions differ in their approaches to this important and intensely personal issue. Some courts resolved the question on an *ad hoc* basis, without a formal test, concluding that a child was neglected if the parents refused to administer chemotherapy in a life threatening situation. The California Court of Appeals in In re Ted B., (1987), employed the best interests test to determine if a child was neglected when his parents refused to permit treatment of his cancer with "mild" chemotherapy following more intense treatment. Ted B. weighed the gravity, or potential gravity of the child's illness, the treating physician's medical evaluation of the course of care, the riskiness of the treatment and the child's "expressed preferences" to ultimately judge whether his parents' decision to withhold chemotherapy served his "best interests." Finally, the Supreme Judicial Court of Massachusetts, in Custody Of A Minor, utilized a tripartite balancing test which weighed the interests of the parents, their child and the State to determine whether a child was neglected when his parents refused to treat his leukemia with non-invasive chemotherapy.

In the present case, the Family Court did not undertake any formal interest analysis in deciding that Colin was a neglected child under Delaware law. Instead, the trial court used * * * [an] ad hoc approach * * *. Specifically, the Family Court rejected the Newmarks' proposal to treat Colin by spiritual means under the care of a Christian Science practitioner. The trial judge considered spiritual treatment an inadequate alternative to chemotherapy. The court therefore concluded that "[w]ithout any other factually supported alternative" the Newmarks' decision to refuse chemotherapy "constitute[d] inadequate parental care for their son who is in a life threatening situation and constitute[d] neglect as defined in the Delaware statute."

* * * While we do not recognize the primacy of any one of the tests employed in other jurisdictions, we find that the trial court erred in not explicitly considering the competing interests at stake. The Family Court failed to consider the special importance and primacy of the familial relationship, including the autonomy of parental decision making au-

thority over minor children. The trial court also did not consider the gravity of Colin's illness in conjunction with the invasiveness of the proposed chemotherapy and the considerable likelihood of failure. These factors, when applied to the facts of this case, strongly militate against governmental intrusion.

A.

Any balancing test must begin with the parental interest. The primacy of the familial unit is a bedrock principle of law. We have repeatedly emphasized that the parental right is sacred which can be invaded for only the most compelling reasons.

Courts have also recognized that the essential element of preserving the integrity of the family is maintaining the autonomy of the parent-child relationship.* * * Parental autonomy to care for children free from government interference therefore satisfies a child's need for continuity and thus ensures his or her psychological and physical well-being.

Parental authority to make fundamental decisions for minor children is also a recognized common law principle. * * * Thus, the common law recognizes that the only party capable of authorizing medical treatment for a minor in "normal" circumstances is usually his parent or guardian.

Courts, therefore, give great deference to parental decisions involving minor children. In many circumstances the State simply is not an adequate surrogate for the judgment of a loving, nurturing parent. As one commentator aptly recognized, the "law does not have the capacity to supervise the delicately complex interpersonal bonds between parent and child."

B.

We also recognize that parental autonomy over minor children is not an absolute right. Clearly, the State can intervene in the parent-child relationship where the health and safety of the child and the public at large are in jeopardy. Accordingly, the State, under the doctrine of parens patriae, has a special duty to protect its youngest and most helpless citizens.

* * *

The basic principle underlying the parens patriae doctrine is the State's interest in preserving human life. Yet this interest and the parens patriae doctrine are not unlimited. In its recent Cruzan opinion [Cruzan v. Director, Missouri Dep't of Health (1990)], the Supreme Court of the United States announced that the state's interest in preserving life must "be weighed against the constitutionally protected interests of the individual."

The individual interests at stake here include both the Newmarks' right to decide what is best for Colin and Colin's own right to life. We have already considered the Newmarks' stake in this case and its relationship to the parens patriae doctrine. The resolution of the issues here, however, is incomplete without a discussion of Colin's interests.

C.

All children indisputably have the right to enjoy a full and healthy life. Colin, a three year old boy, unfortunately lacked the ability to reach a detached, informed decision regarding his own medical care. This Court must therefore substitute its own objective judgment to determine what is in Colin's "best interests."

There are two basic inquiries when a dispute involves chemotherapy treatment over parents' religious objections. The court must first consider the effectiveness of the treatment and determine the child's chances of survival with and without medical care. The court must then consider the nature of the treatments and their effect on the child.

The "best interests" analysis is hardly unique or novel. Federal and State courts have unhesitatingly authorized medical treatment over a parent's religious objection when the treatment is relatively innocuous in comparison to the dangers of withholding medical care. See Application of President & Directors of Georgetown College, Inc., 331 F.2d 1000, 1007 (D.C.Cir.)(1964) (better than 50% chance of saving life with blood transfusion); * * * In re Cabrera, 552 A.2d 1114, 1115 (1989) (blood transfusion 90% effective to treat illness); In re D.L.E., 645 P.2d 271, 275 (Colo.1982) (authorization of medication to prevent epileptic seizures)* * *. Accordingly, courts are reluctant to authorize medical care over parental objection when the child is not suffering a life threatening or potential life threatening illness. See In re Green, 448 Pa. 338 (1972) (court refused to authorize corrective spine surgery on minor); In re Seiferth, 309 N.Y. 80 (1955) (no authorization to correct cleft palate and harelip on fourteen year old minor); but cf. In re Sampson, (N.Y.Fam.Ct. 1970), aff'd, 278 N.E.2d 918 (1972) (authorizing corrective surgery on minor where parents' only objection was blood transfusion).

The linchpin in all cases discussing the "best interests of a child", when a parent refuses to authorize medical care, is an evaluation of the risk of the procedure compared to its potential success. This analysis is consistent with the principle that State intervention in the parent-child relationship is only justifiable under compelling conditions. The State's interest in forcing a minor to undergo medical care diminishes as the risks of treatment increase and its benefits decrease.

Applying the foregoing considerations to the "best interests standard" here, the State's petition must be denied. The egregious facts of this case indicate that Colin's proposed medical treatment was highly invasive, painful, involved terrible temporary and potentially permanent side effects, posed an unacceptably low chance of success, and a high risk that the treatment itself would cause his death. The State's authority to intervene in this case, therefore, cannot outweigh the Newmarks' parental prerogative and Colin's inherent right to enjoy at least a modicum of human dignity in the short time that was left to him.

IV

Dr. Meek originally diagnosed Colin's condition as Burkitt's Lymphoma. She testified that the cancer was "a very bad tumor" in an advanced disseminated state and not localized to only one section of the body. She accordingly recommended that the hospital begin an "extremely intensive" chemotherapy program scheduled to extend for at least six months.

The first step necessary to prepare Colin for chemotherapy involved an intravenous hydration treatment. This process, alone, posed a significant risk that Colin's kidneys would fail. Indeed, these intravenous treatments had already begun and were threatening Colin's life while the parties were arguing the case to us on September 14, 1990. Thus, if Colin's kidneys failed he also would have to undergo dialysis treatments. There also was a possibility that renal failure could occur during the chemotherapy treatments themselves. In addition, Dr. Meek recommended further pretreatment diagnostic tests including a spinal tap and a CAT scan.

* * *

The physicians planned to administer the chemotherapy in cycles, each of which would bring Colin near death. Then they would wait until Colin's body recovered sufficiently before introducing more drugs. Dr. Meek opined that there was no guarantee that drugs alone would "cure" Colin's illness. The doctor noted that it would then be necessary to radiate Colin's testicles if drugs alone were unsuccessful. Presumably, this would have rendered him sterile.

Dr. Meek also wanted the State to place Colin in a foster home after the initial phases of hospital treatment. Children require intensive home monitoring during chemotherapy. For example, Dr. Meek testified that a usually low grade fever for a healthy child could indicate the presence of a potentially deadly infection in a child cancer patient. She believed that the Newmarks, although well educated and financially responsible, were incapable of providing this intensive care because of their firm religious objections to medical treatment.

Dr. Meek ultimately admitted that there was a real possibility that the chemotherapy could kill Colin. In fact, assuming the treatment did not itself prove fatal, she offered Colin at "best" a 40% chance that he would "survive." Dr. Meek additionally could not accurately predict whether, if Colin completed the therapy, he would subsequently suffer additional tumors.

A.

No American court, even in the most egregious case, has ever authorized the State to remove a child from the loving, nurturing care of his parents and subject him, over parental objection, to an invasive regimen of treatment which offered, as Dr. Meek defined the term, only a forty percent chance of "survival." For example, the California Court of Appeals ruled in *Eric B.*, that the State could conduct various procedures as part of an "observation phase" of chemotherapy over the objection of his parents. The treatment included bone scans, CT scans, spinal taps and biopsies. The court specifically found that "[t]he risks entailed by the monitoring are minimal. The court also noted that the child would enjoy a 60% chance of survival with the treatments.

* * *

The Supreme Judicial Court of Massachusetts took custody away from parents who refused to administer "mild" cancer fighting drugs after the child had already undergone more "vigorous" treatment. The trial judge, in that case, specifically found that aside from some minor side effects, including stomach cramps and constipation, the chemotherapy "bore no chance of leaving the child physically incapacitated in any way." The trial court also ruled that the chemotherapy gave the child not only a chance to enjoy a long life "but also a 'substantial' chance for cure."

The Ohio Court of Appeals awarded custody of a minor suffering from Osteogenic Sarcoma to the state when his parents consented to chemotherapy, but later refused to authorize an operation to partially remove his shoulder and entire left arm. Although amputation is ultimately the most invasive type of surgery, there was at least a 60% chance in *Willmann* that the child would survive with the operation. The court also significantly noted that the child remained at home while receiving the lower court's mandated chemotherapy treatments.

B.

The aggressive form of chemotherapy that Dr. Meek prescribed for Colin was more likely to fail than succeed. The proposed treatment was also highly invasive and could have independently caused Colin's death. Dr. Meek also wanted to take Colin away from his parents and family during the treatment phase and place the boy in a foster home. This certainly would have caused Colin severe emotional difficulties given his medical condition, tender age, and the unquestioned close bond between Colin and his family.

In sum, Colin's best interests were served by permitting the Newmarks to retain custody of their child. Parents must have the right at some point to reject medical treatment for their child. Under all of the circumstances here, this clearly is such a case. The State's important and legitimate role in safeguarding the interests of minor children diminishes in the face of this egregious record.

Parents undertake an awesome responsibility in raising and caring for their children. No doubt a parent's decision to withhold medical care is both deeply personal and soul wrenching. It need not be made worse by the invasions which both the State and medical profession sought on this record. Colin's ultimate fate therefore rested with his parents and their faith.[13]

The judgment of the Family Court is, REVERSED.

Notes and Questions

1. *Decision guidelines.* Part III of *Newmark* describes three approaches that courts have used to decide whether a child is medically neglected: ad hoc, best interests of the child, and a tripartite balancing test that "weighs the interests of the parents, their child, and the State." Which approach does *Newmark* use? What facts are determinative? Which approach do you prefer and why?

2. *Childhood immunization against disease.* Parent is required to provide immunizations for diseases such as poliomyelitis, mumps, measles, and diphtheria. Although the parents' consent is necessary, a child whose parents refuse consent can be adjudicated neglectful and a court may order immunization. A number of states provide an exception to the immunization requirement for parents whose religious beliefs are opposed to immunization, although some state courts have declared the exception to be unconstitutional. See Brown v. Stone, 378 So.2d 218 (Miss. 1979) (the immunization exception violated the Equal Protection Clause.)

To promote immunizations, Congress adopted the Childhood Vaccine Injury Act of 1986 (42 U.S.C. § 300aa–1) which provides limited immunity for manufacturers of vaccines and for physicians who administer them. It also provides a system of recovery for injuries and deaths that is intended to be faster and easier than tort suits. The Act also states that "it shall be the ethical obligation of any attorney who is consulted by an individual with respect to a vaccine-related injury or death to advise such individual that compensation may be available under the program for such injury or death." § 300aa–10 (b).

The overall immunization rates for children age 19 to 35 months has been rising for the basic 4:3:1:3 series (four diphtheria, tetanus and pertussis vaccines, three oral polio vaccines, and one measles vaccine and 3 Haemophilus influenzae type b (Hib) vaccines). In 1997, the rate was 76% for all children and 71% for children with family incomes below the poverty level. White non-Hispanic children were more likely to receive the vaccine series than black, non-Hispanic or Hispanic children. Federal Interagency Forum on Child and Family Studies, America's Children: Key National Indicators of Well–Being 27 (1999). By the time they enter school, 98% of U.S. children are immunized completely. This figure suggests the efficacy of state statutes requiring proof of immunization as a condition of registering a child for school. See Caroline Breese Hall, Adolescent Immunization: The Access and Anchor for Health Services?, 95 Pediatrics 936 (1995).

3. *Screening and genetic testing.* Screening newborns for some diseases such as phenylketonuria (PKU) is required in many states and is done without parental consent, although some states allow parents to object for religious reasons. The justification for the state assuming this decision-

---

13. Tragically, Colin died shortly after   we announced our oral decision.

making authority is that if PKU is diagnosed early, it is curable, and the consequences of non-treatment are serious and include mental retardation.

For some diseases, such as Huntington's disease, however, testing is more problematic because there is no known cure and symptoms usually do not develop until adulthood. The disease is fatal, with progressive physical and mental deterioration. Although the blood test used to detect Huntington's disease is very accurate, it cannot determine what the progress of the disease will be. Children, and even adults, may not wish to know whether they have the disease and thus face certain death years in the future. In addition, test results might be revealed to the patient's insurance company. For articles on genetic testing of children, see Julie Holland, Should Parents be Permitted to Authorize Genetic Testing for Their Children?, 31 Fam. L. Q. 321 (1997); Mary Z. Pelias and Susan H. Blanton, Genetic Testing in Children and Adolescents: Parental Authority, the Rights of Children, and Duties of Geneticists, 3 U. Chi. L Sch. Roundtable 525 (1996); Carol Isaacson Barash, Commentary: Genetic Testing in Children and Adolescents: Parental Authority, the Rights of Children, and Duties of Geneticists, 3 U. Chi. L Sch. Roundtable 545 (1996).

If parents with a history of Huntington's disease in their family wanted their 10–year-old son to be tested, for estate planning purposes, should their consent be sufficient? Should the child be told the results of the test?

4. *Additional references*. Joseph Goldstein, Medical Care for the Child at Risk: On State Supervention of Parental Autonomy, 86 Yale L.J. 645 (1977); Daniel B. Griffith, The Best Interests Standard: A Comparison of the State's Parens Patriae Authority and Judicial Oversight in Best Interests Determinations for Children and Incompetent Patients, 7 Issues in L. & Med. 283 (1991); Lainie Friedman Ross and Timothy J. Aspinwall, Religious Exemptions to the Immunizations Statutes: Balancing Public Health and Religious Freedom, 25 J. Law, Medicine and Ethics 202 (1997); Walter Wadlington, Medical Decisionmaking For and By Children: Tensions Between Parent, State, and Child, 1994 U. Ill. L. Rev. 311.

PROBLEM 8–8

Seven-year-old John was diagnosed with Hodgkin's disease, which is usually fatal if left untreated. His physician recommended radiation treatments with subsequent chemotherapy, if needed. After extensive study, John's parents became convinced that John should be treated with nutritional or metabolic therapy, including injections of laetrile, and planned to take him to a clinic in Jamaica where this treatment was available. The medical community did not support this form of treatment generally, because of a lack of evidence that the treatment was effective. John's parents, however, had found a licensed physician in their state who favored this unconventional treatment. This physician, Dr. Smith, was willing to take charge of John's care and stated that he did not rule out more conventional treatment if John's condition worsened. The Department of Social Services petitioned to have John declared neglected. The evidence at trial showed that John's parents were loving parents who were deeply concerned about their child's welfare. The expert evidence showed that the conventional medical community strongly favored radiation-chemotherapy regimen and considered the proposed nutritional therapy to be equivalent to no treatment at all, at best. Dr. Smith testified that he considered nutritional therapy, with laetrile, to be a successful method of treatment. All the physicians agreed that the nutritional therapy had fewer potential harmful side effects than radiation or chemotherapy. Should John be adjudicated neglected so that he can receive radiation and possible chemotherapy?

B. Spiritual Treatment Exemptions

1. The Death of Ian Lundman : The Facts

LUNDMAN v. McKOWN

Court of Appeals of Minnesota, 1995.
530 N.W.2d 807.

* * *

Ian Lundman died at age 11 from juvenile-onset diabetes following three days of Christian Science care. A medical professional would have easily diagnosed Ian's diabetes from the various symptoms he displayed in the weeks and days leading up to his death (particularly breath with a fruity aroma). Although juvenile-onset diabetes is usually responsive to insulin, even up to within two hours of death, the Christian Science individuals who cared for Ian during his last days failed to seek medical care for him—pursuant to a central tenet of the Christian Science religion. This wrongful death action followed.

We begin the morning of May 6, 1989, when, after having been ill and lethargic intermittently for several weeks, 11–year-old Ian Lundman complained to his mother that he was again not feeling well, specifically that he had a stomachache. Ian's mother, appellant Kathleen McKown (mother), noticed that Ian had lost a "noticeable" amount of weight, had a fruity aroma on his breath, and lacked his normal energy. Consistent with the tenets of the Christian Science church, which she espoused, mother began treating Ian through prayer. Throughout the day, Ian continued to complain of a stomachache.

When Ian again complained to his mother about not feeling well the next morning (day two), she became more concerned. Because the Christian Science Church recommends that a journal-listed practitioner be hired when a parent is concerned about a child's health, mother contacted appellant Mario Tosto regarding Ian's condition. As a "journal-listed" practitioner, Tosto appears in a Christian Science publication as someone who is specially trained to provide spiritual treatment through prayer. Mother hired Tosto to begin praying for Ian.

When, despite his illness, Ian attended Sunday School that morning, his Sunday School teacher observed that he appeared tired. Ian's mother was concerned about his low energy level and his continued need to eat mints to mask his breath odor. She noted during an afternoon visit to his grandmother's home that the usually-active Ian lacked energy to do anything but lie on the sofa. Ian also vomited while at his grandmother's home.

Ian was unable to sleep the night of May 7, and several times in the early morning hours of May 8 (day three) he complained of illness, seeking his mother's help and comfort and stating that he did not want to be alone. Ian's fear of being alone caused mother to have still greater concern. At this point, the downward spiral of Ian's health accelerated. He was unable to keep any food down that morning; Ian's visible weight loss, coupled with his inability to eat, caused mother to fear that her son might die.

Seeking further outside help, mother and appellant William McKown (her husband and Ian's stepfather) made several telephone calls on day three. First, pursuant to church directives, mother contacted appellant James Van Horn, who served as the one-person Christian Science Committee on Publications (CoP) for Minnesota. Learning that she intended to rely on Christian Science care, Van Horn verified that mother had contacted a journal-listed practitioner; and he later notified appellant The First Church of Christ Scientist (First Church) in Boston, that a child of a Christian Scientist was seriously ill. (First Church is known as the "mother" church of Christian Science.)

Second, mother called a Christian Science nursing home, appellant Clifton House, and a nurse advised her to give Ian small quantities of liquids. Third, William McKown (who is also a Christian Scientist) made a follow-up call to Van Horn because, fearing that Ian might be suffering from a contagious disease, he wanted Van Horn to give him telephone numbers for state or local health departments. (The church, as a regular practice, alerts Christian Scientists to the legal requirement to report contagious disease.) Fourth, William McKown called Clifton House again and told the nurse that Ian was not drinking the liquids that had previously been suggested.

Ian's condition worsened throughout day three; by that afternoon he was unable to eat, drink, or even communicate with others, and he could not control his bladder. He had to be carried to join his family at dinner, and at one point, looking at his mother and not recognizing her, said, "My name is Ian, too." This disorientation reinforced her concern that Ian's condition was life-threatening.

At approximately 8:00 p.m., mother called Clifton House, seeking to have Ian admitted. But Clifton House regulations prohibit admitting anyone under 16, so mother decided that she would take Ian to North Memorial Hospital. Mother dismissed the idea of seeking medical help, however, when Ellen Edgar, the on-duty nurse at Clifton House, proposed hiring a private Christian Science nurse to come to the McKown home. Edgar told mother that she would try to have a Christian Science nurse who took in-home cases call the McKowns.

Edgar subsequently called appellant Quinna Lamb, a journal-listed Christian Science nurse and, at the time, off-duty from Clifton House. Edgar told Lamb about Ian and asked if she was available. Lamb told Edgar that she knew the McKowns and would offer her services to them. Lamb subsequently called mother, who accepted Lamb's offer and hired her to provide home nursing services.

When she arrived at the McKowns' home at about 9:00 p.m., Lamb called Van Horn, notifying him that she was now assisting in Ian's care. This was the third call to Van Horn, and last until after Ian's death. Lamb then commenced caring for Ian and reading hymnals to him. Throughout the evening, mother and Lamb also contacted Tosto by telephone concerning Ian's worsening condition. Although he assisted mother and Lamb in caring for Ian earlier in the evening, William McKown went to sleep about 11:00 p.m.

At approximately 2:36 a.m. on May 9 (day four), Ian died.

* * *

2. *The Criminal Case*

STATE v. McKOWN

Supreme Court of Minnesota, 1991.
475 N.W.2d 63.

On May 9, 1989, 11–year-old Ian Lundman died at his home in Independence, Minnesota. Ian's death was apparently caused by diabetic ketoacidosis, a complication of diabetes mellitus. Ian was occasionally ill in the weeks preceding his death and became seriously ill two or three days before he died.

Kathleen McKown, Ian's mother, and William McKown, Ian's step-father, are Christian Scientists. In accord with their religious beliefs, Ian was treated with Christian Science spiritual healing methods throughout his final illness. He did not receive conventional medical care at any time during that illness.

In late September and early October, 1989, the Hennepin County Attorney presented evidence related to Ian Lundman's illness and death to the Hennepin County Grand Jury. The grand jurors heard testimony from medical doctors indicating that Ian's diabetes was apparently treatable through conventional medicine and that his condition probably could have been stabilized as late as two hours before he died. The jurors also heard testimony regarding the nature and practice of Christian Science healing, and regarding the specific healing methods used in treating Ian Lundman.

Following this testimony, the county attorney instructed the grand jury as to the definition of second degree manslaughter. Having heard this instruction, two of the jurors asked, "Can you explain child neglect at all. Is there any sort of * * * statute that would apply?" The county attorney replied, "Well, I can read you the statute. There's a criminal, it's Minnesota Statute 609.378 * * *.'' He then read the entire child neglect statute aloud to the jurors, and asked, "Did that answer your question, ma'am?" The juror who posed the question responded, "Mm-hmm."[3] After deliberating, the grand jury returned indictments charging both Kathleen and William McKown with second degree manslaughter.[4]

The McKowns moved the District Court for the Fourth Judicial District, the Honorable Eugene J. Farrell presiding, to dismiss the indictments against them for lack of probable cause, because the indictments violated due process of law and their rights to freely exercise their religious beliefs, and because the grand jury was improperly instructed with respect to the McKowns' duty of care. The district court dismissed the indictments. It concluded that the child neglect statute and the second degree manslaughter statute were in pari materia, such that the spiritual treatment and prayer exception to the child neglect statute also operated as a defense to the charge of second degree manslaughter. The court determined that the McKown's rights had been prejudiced because the grand jury was not instructed as to the effect of the spiritual healing and prayer exception. It also concluded that the indictments violated due process of law in that the child neglect statute informed individuals that they might rely on spiritual healing and prayer without violating that statute, but did not state that doing so might expose them to other criminal charges if the treatment failed.

* * *

The state appealed to this court for reinstatement of the indictments charging respondents with second degree manslaughter. It contends that the court of appeals was correct in concluding that the spiritual healing and prayer exception to the child neglect statute does not apply to the second degree manslaughter statute because the two provisions are not in pari materia. It argues that both the trial court and the court of appeals were incorrect, however, in concluding that the indictments violate due process of law.

3. .The child neglect provision read to the jurors is found at Minn.Stat. § 609.378 (1988):

(a) A parent, legal guardian, or caretaker who wilfully deprives a child of necessary food, clothing, shelter, health care, or supervision appropriate to the child's age, when the parent, guardian, or caretaker is reasonably able to make the necessary provisions and which deprivation substantially harms the child's physical or emotional health, * * * is guilty of neglect of a child and may be sentenced to imprisonment for not more than one year or to payment of a fine of not more than $3,000, or both.

* * *

If a parent, guardian, or caretaker responsible for the child's care in good faith selects and depends upon spiritual means or prayer for treatment or care of disease or remedial care of the child, this treatment shall constitute "health care" as used in clause (a).

4. .Minn.Stat. § 609.205 (1988) reads:

[a] person who causes the death of another by any of the following means is guilty of manslaughter in the second degree and may be sentenced to imprisonment for not more than seven years or to payment of a fine of not more than $14,000, or both: (1) by the person's culpable negligence whereby the person creates an unreasonable risk, and consciously takes chances of causing death or great bodily harm to another * * *.

I

The trial court concluded that the child neglect statute and the second degree manslaughter statute are *in pari materia*, requiring that they be interpreted in light of one another. We disagree.

"Statutes 'in pari materia' are those relating to the same person or thing or having a common purpose." * * *

* * * [T]he child neglect and second degree manslaughter statutes are not in pari materia and thus, the spiritual treatment and prayer exception to the former cannot be imported into the latter. The child neglect provision applies specifically to individuals with legal responsibility for a child who wilfully neglect that responsibility and thereby cause the child substantial physical or emotional harm. The statute defining second degree manslaughter, however, permits the state to prosecute anyone who causes the death of another by exposing that person to an unreasonable risk of death or great bodily injury. The two statutes are therefore clearly based on separate and distinct purposes. Further, nothing in the language of either provision suggests they are so closely related as to require they be interpreted in light of one another, and neither contains an explicit mandate to construe them together.

* * *

We therefore conclude that the child neglect statute and the second degree manslaughter statute are not *in pari materia*. The doctrine of *in pari materia* is simply an interpretive tool this court relies on in certain instances to determine the meaning of ambiguous statutory language. Because neither statute is ambiguously worded, we have no need of the doctrine in this instance. Further, because the statutes at issue are not so closely related in either language or purpose as to suggest that they ought be interpreted together, application of the doctrine here would be inappropriate.

II

Both the trial court and the court of appeals concluded the indictments issued against respondents violate the constitutional guarantee of due process of law. We agree.

The essence of respondents' argument is not that either the manslaughter statute or the child neglect statute is so vaguely worded as to make it unreasonably difficult to discern what conduct each prohibits. Rather, respondents contend the child neglect statute misled them in that it unequivocally stated they could, in good faith, select and depend upon spiritual means or prayer without further advising them that, should their chosen treatment method fail, they might face criminal charges beyond those provided in the child neglect statute itself. In short, respondents argue that the child neglect statute does not go far enough to provide reasonable notice of the potentially serious consequences of actually relying on the alternative treatment methods the statute itself clearly permits. Neither the United States Supreme Court nor this court has directly addressed a similar due process claim. * * *

* * *

* * * This concern that individuals be given unambiguous notice of the boundaries within which they must operate directly contravenes the state's contention that nothing in the spiritual treatment and prayer exception to the child neglect provision reasonably suggests immunity from all prosecution. The exception is broadly worded, stating that a parent may in good faith "select and depend upon" spiritual treatment and prayer, without indicating a point at which doing so will expose the parent to criminal liability.[8] The language of the exception therefore does not satisfy the fair notice requirement inherent to the concept of due process.

Further, the indictments issued against respondents violate the long-established rule that a government may not officially inform an individual that certain conduct is permitted and then prosecute the individual for engaging in that same conduct.

The spiritual treatment and prayer exception to the child neglect statute expressly provided respondents the right to "depend upon" Christian Science healing methods so long as they did so in good faith. Therefore the state may not now attempt to prosecute them for exercising that right. By virtue of this conclusion, we do not introduce the proposition that conduct complying with one statute *necessarily* complies with all other statutes absent explicit notice to the contrary. Further, we do not here conclude that the state could never prosecute an individual whose good faith reliance on spiritual methods of treatment results in the death of a child. Rather, we hold that in this particular instance, where the state has clearly expressed its intention to permit good faith reliance on spiritual treatment and prayer as an alternative to conventional medical treatment, it cannot prosecute respondents for doing so without violating their rights to due process.[9]

---

8. As the court of appeals indicated, at least one other state has attempted to avoid the problem presented in this case by statutorily establishing a point beyond which parents may not rely solely on spiritual means of treatment. Okla.Stat. Tit. 21, § 852 (1988), provides:

Nothing in this section shall be construed to mean a child is endangered for the sole reason the parent or guardian, in good faith, selects and depends upon spiritual means alone through prayer, in accordance with the tenets and practice of a recognized church or religious denomination, for the treatment or cure of disease or remedial care of such child; provided, that medical care shall be provided where permanent physical damage could result to such child * * *.

9. The Church of Christ, Scientist, as amicus curiae, argues that prosecuting respondents for relying on Christian Science healing methods in the treatment of their son constitutes a violation of the right to freely exercise religious beliefs guaranteed by both the federal and state constitutions. Because of our disposition of this appeal, however, we need not address this issue.

Also participating as amicus curiae, the Minnesota Civil Liberties Union contends that the spiritual treatment and prayer exception violates the first amendment's prohibition against state-established religion. Although we find the MCLU's arguments persuasive, our disposition based on due process grounds makes it unnecessary for us to consider the establishment clause issue at this time.

We therefore conclude that the indictments issued against respondents, charging them with second degree manslaughter in the death of Ian Lundman, violate the constitutional guarantee of due process of law and must be dismissed.

* * *

Notes and Questions

1. *Questions about* McKown. (a) Does the Free Exercise Clause bar prosecution of parents for not providing medical care for their children because of their religious beliefs? Could the legislature repeal the statute's religious exemption clauses? (b) How could the statute be amended to resolve the "void for vagueness" problem? Does the Oklahoma statute quoted in footnote 8 achieve this resolution? (c) If Ian had been age 15 and had wanted Christian Science treatment only, would his parents be able to use the mature minor doctrine as a defense in a criminal prosecution for his death?

2. *Fair notice.* Did *McKown* adequately analyze the issue of whether the parents had fair notice that faith healing could result in criminal liability? Professor Rosato suggests not:

> [T]he court should have considered the disparate purposes of the child neglect and manslaughter statutes—purposes that are constructively known to an ordinary person exercising due care to know the law. The court also failed to consider how the defendants' First Amendment rights were implicated, which is a relevant inquiry for determining the degree of notice required. Furthermore, the court went too far in suggesting that "unambiguous notice" of the prohibited conduct is required to satisfy due process. Unambiguous notice is not required. Although due process requires statutes to provide a standard that an ordinary person can follow, due process does not require the legislature to state explicitly what conduct is prohibited as well as what conduct is not prohibited. Such a standard would impose an onerous burden on the legislature.

Jennifer L. Rosato, Putting Square Pegs in a Round Hole: Procedural Due Process and the Effect of Faith Healing Exemptions on the Prosecution of Faith Healing Parents, 29 U.S.F. L. Rev. 43, 107 (1994).

3. *Establishment Clause.* The First Amendment not only protects the "free exercise" of religion (the Free Exercise Clause), but it also prohibits "laws respecting an establishment of religion" (the Establishment Clause). Do statutory religious exemptions violate of the Establishment Clause? This issue was addressed, but not decided in *Newmark*, supra at 1113: "At least one state court has ruled that a statutory exemption to a criminal abuse and neglect statute * * * violated both the Establishment Clause and the Equal Protection Clause of the Fourteenth Amendment. See State v. Miskimens, 490 N.E.2d 931 (Ohio Ct. Com. Pl. 1984). *Miskimens* found that the statute 'hopelessly involved' the state in issues involving religious beliefs and served no 'legitimate purpose.'"

4. *Criminal convictions.* Manslaughter and felony child endangerment prosecutions have been allowed in other cases. See, e.g., Walker v. Superior Ct., 763 P.2d 852 (Cal. 1988). The Supreme Court denied certiorari in both

Walker and *McKown*. What sentence should be imposed on parents who are convicted in these cases? Prosecutors may sympathize with the parents and recommend community service or fines, rather than prison. One prosecutor stated: "[T]hese people are nice, middle-class, and well-intentioned. They're not drug-crazed psychotics...." David Margolick, Death and Faith. Law and Christian Science, N.Y. Times, Aug. 6, 1990 A1, A16, col. 2.

3. *The Civil Case*

LUNDMAN v. McKOWN

Court of Appeals of Minnesota, 1995.
530 N.W.2d 807.

DAVIES, JUDGE.

* * *

In April 1991, respondent Douglass G. Lundman, Ian's natural father, was appointed trustee of Ian's estate and commenced this wrongful death action on behalf of himself and Ian's older sister Whitney. Lundman filed suit against the appellants: William and Kathleen McKown; Quinna Lamb; Mario Tosto; James Van Horn; Clifton House, Inc.; and The First Church of Christ, Scientist. The complaint alleged, among other things, negligence in failing to provide, obtain, or recommend medical treatment for Ian.

Following a seven-week trial in July and August 1993, the jury returned a special verdict finding all appellants negligent and dividing liability as follows: Kathleen McKown, 25 percent; William McKown, 10 percent; Tosto, 10 percent; Lamb, 5 percent; Clifton House, 20 percent; Van Horn, 20 percent; and First Church, 10 percent. After awarding $5.2 million in compensatory damages, the jury, in a separate proceeding against the church alone, awarded $9 million in punitive damages.

Appellants moved for J.N.O.V., a new trial, or remittitur of damages. The trial court denied all posttrial motions except for a remittitur of the compensatory damages from $5.2 million to $1.5 million. Judgment was entered and this appeal followed.

* * *

ANALYSIS

I.

PUNITIVE DAMAGES

We first address appellant church's challenge to the award of punitive damages.

Punitive damages serve to punish wrongdoers and deter others from similar conduct. In those instances where deterrence will not be achieved, punitive damages should not be awarded. Respondent argues that the punitive damages award is a permissible deterrent because it "persuade[s] the First Church not to interfere in the direct care of seriously-ill children."

For three independent reasons we hold that punitive damages may not be imposed. First, there is no evidence that the church directly interfered in Ian's care and insufficient evidence as a matter of law that it interfered by agency through his caregivers. Hence, there is no past conduct by the church of the kind justifying punitive damages. The punitive damage award must be reversed on that ground alone.

Second, even were we to recognize an agency relationship, the punitive damages award would still fall because it is unconstitutional, as the church and two amici assert. They question the constitutionality of imposing punitive damages on a church to force it to abandon teaching its central tenet. We find the argument compelling.

In closing argument in the action for punitive damages, respondent's attorney compared the church's involvement to a weed, arguing:

> I see weeds on the lawn and I can sit there and pick at the surface of weeds all day long, but until you dig underneath and get the root of the weed, the weed will come back again and again and again.

Respondent's attorney explained why respondent sought punitive damages only from the church:

> [I]t is with the First Church that you go below the surface of these policies. If you want to establish a change, if you want to deter and make a difference, it is against the First Church that [a] punitive damage award will make a difference.

As these statements suggest, the main conduct of the church on which the punitive damages award was based is its espousal and promotion of spiritual treatment as a means of care, and on its concomitant failure to train Christian Science practitioners and nurses to perform or seek medical diagnoses.

The church's espousal of spiritual treatment is, however, entitled to substantial free exercise protection. The constitutional right to religious freedom includes the authority of churches to independently decide matters of faith and doctrine.

We do not grant churches and religious bodies a categorical exemption from liability for punitive damages. But under these facts, the risk of intruding—through the mechanism of punitive damages—upon the forbidden field of religious freedom is simply too great.

A third, independent reason the punitive damages award must be reversed is that it violates the Minnesota statute on punitive damages. That statute requires "clear and convincing evidence" that the defendant showed a "deliberate disregard" for the rights or safety of others. * * *

Here, the punitive damages award must be reversed because it is unchallenged that all defendants, including the church, acted in good faith. And there is no "clear and convincing evidence" that the church acted in "deliberate disregard" of Ian's rights. The church's only contact with Ian was when Van Horn told officials of the church in Boston that a Christian Science parent in Minnesota was using spiritual care for her seriously-ill child. Knowledge of illness is insufficient, by itself, to support an award of punitive damages.

We also note that the church teaches its members to "obey" all laws, including the reporting of contagious disease to local authorities. This, too, suggests the church lacked the malice required under Minnesota law for the imposition of punitive damages.

II.
CONSTITUTIONAL ISSUES ON COMPENSATORY DAMAGES

Appellants raise two constitutional challenges to the award of compensatory damages.

A. Freedom of Religion

Appellants first argue that the religious freedoms guaranteed by the Minnesota and United States constitutions preclude an award of compensatory damages.

1.   Absolute Freedom of Belief Does Not Extend to Conduct

Appellants generally argue that permitting this case to proceed improperly placed the Christian Science religion on trial and that allowing the jury to evaluate the reasonableness of appellants' conduct—which conformed to their genuine religious beliefs—amounted to an evaluation of those beliefs.

We disagree. Although one is free to believe what one will, religious freedom ends when one's conduct offends the law by, for example, endangering a child's life.* * *

* * * Appellants are free to believe what they will—and to teach and preach what they believe. But, when beliefs lead to conduct, the conduct is subject to regulation. Here, regulation is necessary for the protection of children and appellants' conduct, though rooted in religion, is subject to state regulation.

But even conduct—when religiously driven—enjoys some constitutional protection, so we next evaluate the constitutionality of a tort-liability sanction against appellants' conduct.

2.   Balancing Test Applied to Conduct

Minnesota courts balance the state's interest against the actor's free-exercise interest in religious-based conduct.[3] Where, as here, it is undisputed that the religious belief is sincerely held and that the religious belief would be burdened by the proposed regulation, the balancing test requires proof of a compelling state interest. Here, appel-

---

3. Minnesota's Constitution provides greater protection than does the U.S. Con-   stitution. Accordingly, we need not discuss federal constitutional law

lants concede that Minnesota has a compelling interest in protecting the welfare of children, and case law supports that conclusion.

There must also be no less-restrictive means to accomplish the state's goal, here to ensure the safety of children. * * *

* * *We do not believe that the Minnesota legislature sought to limit its rights as parens patriae by simply exempting spiritual healers from criminal child neglect statutes or by exempting Christian Scientists from laws that forbid practicing medicine without a license.

Although we agree that Minnesota statutes include some accommodation to the Christian Science religion, the statutes should not be read as authorizing reliance on prayer as a sole treatment for seriously-ill children under all circumstances or (by implication) as proscribing civil lawsuits. The statutes simply indicate the legislature's willingness to tolerate this religious practice—up to a point. We reject appellants' argument that the Minnesota legislature has sanctioned prayer alone to treat a child battling a life-threatening disease.

Appellants also argue that there are two less-restrictive alternatives that would serve Minnesota's interest in protecting children: mandated notice to public authorities when a seriously-ill child is being treated by spiritual means, and criminal prosecution of a custodial parent in case of death.

But the first alternative—a reporting requirement—does not always work and therefore is not a preclusive alternative. See Hermanson v. State (Fla.Dist.Ct.App.1990) (seven-year-old diabetic died in spite of Florida's criminally sanctioned reporting requirements), rev'd, 604 So.2d 775 (Fla.1992); see also Walker v. Superior Court, 763 P.2d 852, 871 (1988) (authorities generally will not learn of faith healing unless and until someone dies).

Likewise, criminal liability is not a preclusive less-restrictive alternative because it is fallible and requires that the state, rather than private parties, expend resources to bring forth a corrective response.

It is appropriate that disputes involving the consequences of religious-based conduct be brought before the civil courts where, as here, the underlying lawsuit is not a vehicle for attacking religious belief. * * *

* * *

III.

SUBSTANTIVE ISSUES RELATING TO NEGLIGENCE

The basic elements of a negligence claim are (1) the existence of a duty, (2) breach of that duty, (3) injury proximately caused by the breach, and (4) damages. Appellants challenge the existence of a duty of care and a breach of that duty.

A.   Duty of Care

* * *

Generally, there is a duty to aid another only if a "special relationship" exists between the parties. A special relationship exists where one party has custody of another under circumstances that deprive the other of normal opportunities of self-protection. That is,

> "the plaintiff is typically in some respect particularly vulnerable and dependent upon the defendant who, correspondingly, holds considerable power over the plaintiff's welfare."

A special relationship may also arise where one accepts responsibility to protect another, although there was no initial duty.

Kathleen McKown does not dispute that she owed a duty of care to her son. A custodial parent has a special relationship to a dependent and vulnerable child that gives rise to duty to protect the child from harm. The other appellants argue, however, that they had no duty of care and that the trial court erred as a matter of law in holding that they each had special relationships with Ian. We examine the duty of each of these appellants separately.

1.   William McKown

William McKown argues that he owed no legal duty to Ian because he was a stepparent and because Kathleen McKown was solely responsible for making decisions about Ian's health care. Although we recognize that, as a stepparent, William McKown usually had no "final word" control over Ian's health care, we disagree that his relationship as a stepparent did not impose a duty of care.

The record indicates that William McKown acted consistent with a special relationship existing between Ian and him. During Ian's last days, William McKown was fully aware of the gravity of Ian's condition, was frequently present as an on-the-scene caregiver, and attempted to assist Ian in several ways. He made telephone calls on Ian's behalf—calling Van Horn, when he feared Ian might be suffering from a contagious disease, and Clifton House, when Ian was unable to drink liquids or eat food. Because Ian could not walk or talk, William McKown carried Ian from his bed to the table in an attempt to offer him food and liquid (as suggested by Clifton House) and companionship. Finally, although he did not remain awake through the night when Ian died, William McKown testified that he spent most of that evening "in the doorway [to Ian's room] making sure I could be summoned for help, if necessary." These facts support the finding that William McKown knew of Ian's helplessness and the gravity of his situation, that he accepted a responsibility to protect Ian, and that a special relationship existed between the two.

Independent of William McKown's conduct during Ian's final illness, we believe there also is a presumption that "custodial" stepparents (and "visitation" stepparents during visitation) assume special-relationship duties to stepchildren. The partnership involved in marriage is presumed to extend to care of children, absent some most unusual disclaimer. There was no disclaimer in this case.

This special relationship may, to a significant extent, be viewed as a responsibility delegated to him by, or subject to veto by, Kathleen McKown. But even so, he could not hide behind the natural parent. Regardless of who had ultimate authority in overseeing Ian's care, William McKown, bearing an in loco parentis responsibility for Ian's well-being, was obligated to put Ian's interests first—above and beyond Kathleen McKown's interest in exercising her religious beliefs.

Our holding is not intended to affect the legal responsibilities of stepparents to their stepchildren in different factual situations. Rather, our recognition of a duty is based on our conclusion that a stepparent may not avoid responsibility by simply pointing to the natural parent and proclaiming that the parent had legal control over and full responsibility for the child.

Here, the law required that William McKown step forward to rescue Ian.

2. Quinna Lamb

Appellant Quinna Lamb, the Christian Science nurse hired by Kathleen McKown to care for Ian in the McKown home, argues that she did not have a duty of care.

We disagree. Both indicia of a "special relationship" apply: Lamb had significant "custody or control" of Ian under circumstances where Ian lacked even his limited minor's capacity for self-protection—that is why mother hired Lamb—and she accepted the responsibility to care for Ian and to protect him by providing professional services in return for cash wages.

When she arrived, Lamb found Ian lying in his own urine, unable to walk, talk, or breath normally.[5] Lamb immediately began providing

---

5. Lamb's notes on the night of Ian Lundman's death indicate her knowledge of Ian's grave condition:

9:00 p.m.—Arrived. Boy had urinated—prepared bed—dad carried—light e.c. [evening care] p.c. [patient care] given—P[atient] had juice earlier—eyes rolled back—P[atient] awakened when moved—seemed aware of people—breathing labored.

10:10—siphoned water.

10:50—turned P[atient] onto R[ight side]—siphoned water.

11:15—Pract[itioner Tosto] called—report given—onto back.

11:30—P[atient] vomiting brownish fluid—called Pract[itioner]—vomiting ceased.

12:30—labored breathing.

12:50—moistened lips [with] Vaseline—P[atient] wet—p.c. [patient care] given.

1:00—P[atient] swallowing—facial spasms—called Pract[itioner]—report given.

1:05—immediate [change]—symptoms gone—labored breathing.

2:05—taking big breaths every other breath, gritting teeth.

2:10—called Pract[itioner]—report shallow, irregular breathing—eyes fixed.

2:20—called Pract[itioner]—P[atient] color white—passing possible.

2:36—P[atient] stopped breathing.

2:50—N[urse] called Pract[itioner].

Christian Science nursing services: she read hymns and prayers to Ian, comforted him, cleaned him and his bedding, and attended to his physical care during the final critical hours of his life. During a good part of her involvement, though it was brief, a telephone call to involve a provider of conventional medical care would likely have led to the administration of insulin and would likely have saved Ian's life.

Lamb argues against finding a duty because advising medical treatment is antithetical to Christian Science nursing, which was what she was hired to provide. But in other situations Christian Scientists are instructed to cooperate with public officials—even when that cooperation runs contrary to Christian Science doctrine. Specifically, Christian Scientists have been instructed, ever since founder Mary Baker Eddy wrote on the question, to promptly notify local health officials whenever they know or have reason to believe that an individual has a communicable disease and "the law so requires."

Indeed, one Christian Science manual can be read to imply that situations may arise where medical treatment may be required. Christian Science parents are warned of limitations on their right to impose Christian Science care on their children:

> The rights of Christian Scientists to select Christian Science treatment for their children in lieu of medical treatment will continue to be respected by public officials so long as [the officials] are assured that effective care is being given our children.

Christian Science Comm. on Publication for Minnesota, Legal Rights and Obligations of Christian Scientists in Minnesota 5 (1976). Conversely, therefore, Christian Science parents are at least warned that their right to withhold conventional medical treatment is not absolute; parents are warned that when officials are not confident that effective care is being given, the right to select Christian Science treatment may end. That advice—or warning—logically extends beyond parents. Ian's situation was an instance where Christian Science professionals should have been aware of the requirement that they yield to the law of the community. We reject Lamb's argument that she had no professional duty except to persist in following pure Christian Science doctrine.

We also reject Lamb's argument that she is exempt from civil liability because the mother controlled what type of care Ian would receive. Lamb was alone with Ian from 1:00 until 2:00 a.m. while Kathleen McKown slept, and Lamb also held herself out as a professional Christian Science nurse with special training, skill, and experience in caring for others (albeit through Christian Science means). Regardless of who had ultimate authority in overseeing Ian's care, Lamb was obligated during her engagement to make Ian's welfare her paramount interest; she could not yield to a parent's directions; protecting a child's life transcends any interest a parent may have in exercising religious beliefs. Furthermore, Lamb's argument fails because William and Kathleen

3:02—husband called 911/M.E. [medical   examiner] and C.O.P. [Van Horn].

McKown, too, were required to abandon the unlawful stance that Lamb now claims they imposed on her.

In the common law tradition, our holding today serves as notice to all professional Christian Science caregivers—be they practitioners, nurses, or others—that they cannot successfully disavow their professional duty to a child by deferring to the parent as the ultimate decision-making authority.

3. Mario Tosto

Appellant Mario Tosto, the practitioner hired by Kathleen McKown to pray for Ian, generally argues that he did not owe a duty to Ian beyond Christian Science prayer for Ian's recovery (something he did from his own home).

Again, we disagree, and affirm the trial court conclusion that Tosto owed a broader duty to Ian. * * *

* * *

Tosto argues that his control of Ian's care was subject to Kathleen McKown's ultimate authority. He argues that he was engaged by her only for Christian Science care, and that it runs counter to Christian Science teachings to acknowledge the need for medical care or to call for such care. But like Lamb, he could not hide behind mother. He had a responsibility on these facts to acknowledge that Christian Science care was not succeeding and to persuade mother to call in providers of conventional medicine or, persuasion failing, to override her and personally call for either a doctor or the authorities.

[The court found that neither James Van Horn nor Clifton House had a legal duty of care toward Ian.]

* * *

6. First Church

Following special jury verdicts that Tosto and Lamb were "agents of the church," and that their acts were "authorized by the church," the trial court ruled that the church, as principal, owed a duty toward Ian.

As the church concedes, its Christian Science publications certainly "inspired Kathy to care for Ian as she did." But there is no evidence supporting a finding that the church acted as principal to Tosto or Lamb—there was never any agreement between them that manifested either consent or a right of control.

* * *

* * * We hold, therefore, that the jury could not lawfully find that First Church was a principal in an agency relationship relating to Ian's care; the trial court erred in imputing a duty of care to the church. To

rule otherwise would make too much of the consequences of the church's adherence to and promotion of its core tenet.

* * *

B. Standard of Care

The second element of negligence challenged by appellants is whether the individual defendants breached their respective duties of care. We examine this question only in relation to the appellants who had a duty of care.

* * *

We nonetheless agree with appellants that to apply the standard of care of a reasonable person, while not taking account of religious belief, is inappropriate under the facts presented. Our conclusion is based on our recognition that an individual's right to religious autonomy is a core ideal of both the state and federal constitutions; we must defend the right of any citizen to hold whatever religious beliefs he or she may choose. This is especially true where, as here, the undisputed facts demonstrate that appellants genuinely believed that Christian Science care was appropriate in treating Ian.

But appellants' *personal* rights to freely practice religion are not the only rights to be considered. It is crucial to distinguish between an adult's right to practice religion by refusing medical treatment for his or her *own* illness and the right to practice religion by refusing to seek or provide medical treatment for *another* person—especially when the other person is a child. As stated by the United States Supreme Court in Prince v. Massachusetts:

> Parents may be free to become martyrs themselves. But it does not follow they are free, in identical circumstances, to make martyrs of their children before they have reached the age of full and legal discretion when they can make that choice for themselves.

Although *Prince* did not involve the use of spiritual prayer to care for a child (it concerned the use of a nine-year-old girl to sell religious magazines in violation of child labor laws), its reasoning applies, and its language is hauntingly relevant.

To grant appellants an outright exemption from negligence liability based on their religious beliefs would insulate Christian Scientists from tort liability in cases involving children; we will not embrace a negligence standard that would ignore the rights of Ian Lundman. The right to hold one's own religious beliefs cannot include the right to persist to act in conformity with those beliefs to the point of imminent danger to a child. So, though we apply a standard of care taking account of "good-faith Christian Scientist" beliefs, rather than an unqualified "reasonable person standard," we hold that reasonable Christian Science care is circumscribed by an obligation to take the state's (and child's) side in the tension between the child's welfare and the parents' freedom to rely on spiritual care.

A parent may exercise genuinely held religious beliefs. But the resulting conduct, though motivated by religious belief, must yield when—judged by accepted medical practice—it jeopardizes the life of a child. Religious practices must bend to the state's interest in protecting the welfare of a child whenever the child might die without the intervention of conventional medicine.

We note that this circumscribed qualification on the reasonable person standard of care is easier stated than applied; slippery-slope concerns arise. Questions will be raised regarding the age at which a child may free others of responsibility to turn to conventional medicine, how ill a child must be before conventional medicine must be called on, how to deal with serious but less than life-threatening illness, and how to deal with an adult deprived of the capacity to choose. We decline to draw any bright-line rules. Our decision is based on the specific facts presented in this case (and generally undisputed by the parties): that the patient was a child, and that the defendants had a genuine, good-faith belief in their religion. Under these facts, a reasonable person—who is a good-faith Christian Scientist—standard of care applies to appellants' actions in caring for Ian. But under that standard, when the Christian Scientist appellants were put to a choice between fidelity to religious belief or serious injury and potential death to the child—judged by the law's general acceptance of conventional medicine—the child's right to life prevails.

C.   Breach and Causation

We next examine whether the evidence demonstrates that appellants failed to follow the reasonable person standard of care where the accommodation to their Christian Scientist beliefs is circumscribed by the limitation described above. * * *

We hold as a matter of law, therefore, that the four duty-bound defendants breached the standard of care for a *reasonable* Christian Scientist, who was obligated—with knowledge of a child's grave illness—to seek the assistance of conventional medicine. Further, their separate breaches of duty proximately caused Ian's death.

* * *

V.

REMITTITUR

* * *

Appellants * * * argue that the award of $1.5 million in compensatory damages is improper because Minnesota courts have previously not awarded more than $1 million for the death of a child. But, on this question, past cases represent history, not controlling law. At one time, the highest recovery was a few thousand dollars.

Appellants also argue there was only "weak" evidence regarding respondent's loss of companionship, and that the trial court failed to address facts regarding his late child support payments. But there is evidence supporting the trial court's findings that Lundman was a "very loving father" and that he had followed Ian's growth in "great detail." The evidence also supports the finding that Whitney Lundman had a close, loving relationship with Ian. Hence, the award of $1.5 million was not an abuse of discretion.

DECISION

The trial court erred in denying the First Church of Christ Scientist's motion for J.N.O.V. or remittitur of the punitive damage award; that award was unconstitutional. The trial court erred in denying motions for J.N.O.V. made by appellants James Van Horn, Clifton House, and the First Church of Christ, Scientist; they had no duty to Ian. The court properly granted appellants' motions for remittitur of the compensatory damage award from $5.2 million to $1.5 million. Appellants' alternative motions for a new trial were properly denied. Judgment in the amount of $1.5 million against Kathleen McKown, William McKown, Quinna Lamb, and Mario Tosto is affirmed.

* * *

Notes and Questions

1. *Questions about* Lundman. (a) Why was the punitive damage award reversed? (b) In considering what a "reasonable Christian Scientist" would do, did the court violate the First Amendment by entangling itself in religious matters, making decisions about Christian Science requirements? (c) Do you agree with the court that the lawsuit was not "a vehicle for attacking religious belief?" (d)The court indicates that the religious exemption was intended to "tolerate this religious practice—up to a point" but not to preclude civil lawsuits. Where is that "point"? If Ian had been given insulin in time to save his life, but he had suffered serious permanent damage because of the delay in treatment, would a tort claim for intentional injury be allowed?

2. *American Academy of Pediatrics* . The Committee on Bioethics of the American Academy of Pediatrics has issued a statement on religious objections to medical care which states in part:

> The American Academy of Pediatrics (AAP) recognizes that religion plays a major role in the lives of many children and adults in the United States and is aware that some in the United States believe prayer and other spiritual practices can substitute for medical treatment of ill or injured children. Through legislative activity at the federal and state levels, some religious groups have sought, and in many cases attained, government recognition in the form of approved payment for this "nonmedical therapy" and exemption from child abuse and neglect laws when children do not receive needed medical care. The AAP opposes such payments and exemptions as harmful to children and advocates that children, regardless of parental religious beliefs, deserve effective

medical treatment when such treatment is likely to prevent substantial harm or suffering or death.

Committee on Bioethics, American Academy of Pediatrics, Religious Objections to Medical Care, 99 Pediatrics 279 (1997).

3. *Background of religious exemption statutes.* Before the Child Abuse Prevention and Treatment Act of 1974 (CAPTA), few states had religious exemption statutes. Although CAPTA did not require a religious exemption, regulations promulgated under the Act required states to include one in their definitions of harm. Ann MacLean Massie, The Religion Clauses and Parental Health Care Decision–Making for Children: Suggestions for a New Approach, 21 Hastings Const. L. Q. 725, 734 (1994).

Thirty-three states passed religious exemption statutes after CAPTA. Although the federal regulations were amended in 1983 to permit, but not require, a religious exemption, few states have repealed their statutes. Jennifer L. Rosato, Putting Square Pegs in a Round Hole: Procedural Due Process and the Effect of Faith Healing Exemptions on the Prosecution of Faith Healing Parents, 29 U. S.F. L.Rev. 43, 61 (1994).

The scope and location of these exemptions vary from state to state, but are primarily grouped in three types of statutes:

First, they are found in statutes adjudicating whether a child is neglected, dependent, deprived, or in need of services. The typical exemption provides that a child who is provided faith healing will not, for that reason alone, be consider an abused or neglected child for the purpose of proceedings in which the judge determines whether the child is abused or neglected.

Second, faith healing exemptions are found in child abuse and neglect reporting statutes. Typically, reporting statutes impose criminal penalties on designated persons who fail to report suspected incidents of child abuse or neglect; these statutes do not address the parents' liability for failing to care for their children. Exemptions in reporting statutes generally state that, for purposes of the reporting statute, the failing to provide medical care is not considered abuse or neglect if the parent is providing faith healing. One plausible interpretation of such an exemption is that if a child is sick and being provided faith healing in good faith, the failure to provide medical care should not even be reported as a suspected incident of abuse or neglect.

A third location of faith healing exemptions is in a number of criminal statutes, prohibiting harm to children, including endangering the welfare of a child, criminal nonsupport, permitting abuse of a child, child abuse, contribution to deprivation or neglect, injury to children, neglect of a dependent, cruelty to juveniles, omission to provide for a child, unlawful neglect, and ill-treatment of children. * * *

Id. at 51–53.

4. Raboin *revisited.* In Raboin v. North Dakota Dep't of Human Services (Chapter 4 at 331), the parents argued that their disciplinary methods were based on their religious beliefs.

Kim Raboin testified she and Jim believe the teachings of the Bible require parents to administer corporal punishment, when necessary, to "train our children in the way they should go so that when they are old, they won't depart." The Raboins claim[ed] the Department is interfering with their constitutional right to freely practice their religious beliefs and that the Department's probable cause determination also violates [the statute] which, at the time of these proceedings, provided in relevant part: "Probable cause to believe that child abuse or neglect is indicated may not be determined where the suspected child abuse or neglect arises solely out of conduct involving the legitimate practice of religious beliefs by a parent or guardian. . . ."

552 N.W.2d 329, 335 (1996). Because the court determined that the evidence did not support a finding of child abuse, the court did not address this argument.

5. *Additional references.* Seth M. Asser and Rita Swan, Child Fatalities from Religious–Motivated Medical Neglect, 101 Pediatrics 625 (1998); James G. Dwyer, The Children We Abandon: Religious Exemptions to Child Welfare and Education Laws as Denials of Equal Protection to Children of Religious Objectors, 74 N.C.L. Rev. 1321 (1996); Rita Swan, On Statutes Depriving a Class of Children of Rights to Medical Care: Can this Discrimination Be Litigated?, 2 Quinnipiac Health L. 73 (1998); Jennifer Trahan, Constitutional Law: Parental Denial of a Child's Medical Treatment for Religious Reasons, 1989 Ann. Surv. Am. L. 307 (1990).

PROBLEM 8–9

David, age 15, has severe epilepsy. Both David and his mother believe that his condition will be cured through faith healing and do not want medical treatment for him. His epilepsy has caused permanent injury through a stroke. He has frequent seizures that severely impair his brain functioning, and he would probably choke if he had a seizure while eating. Medication would control the seizures. The state has petitioned for a determination that David is a neglected child because his mother fails and refuses to provide the medical care and medication necessary for his health and that his life is in immediate danger.

David and his mother argue that they can refuse medical treatment because their state has a spiritual treatment exemption in the neglect law. A neglected child is defined as "a child whose physical, mental or emotional health and well-being is threatened or impaired because of inadequate care and protection by the child's custodian." The exemption states: "No child who in good faith is under treatment solely by spiritual means through prayer in accordance with the tenets and practices of a recognized church or religious denomination by a duly accredited practitioner thereof shall for that reason alone be considered a neglected child for purposes of this chapter." If you represented the state, how would you interpret the statute to argue that David is neglected?

PROBLEM 8–10

Three-year-old Ed was diagnosed with retinal blastoma or eye cancer. With his parents' consent, his left eye was surgically removed. Subsequent to the surgery, tests indicated that not all the cancer had been removed. Ed's physician recommended chemotherapy. Ed's parents, who were Christian Scientists, refused to consent to chemotherapy, indicating that Ed would receive Christian Science treatment only. The Department of Social Services petitioned to have Ed declared medically neglected. The trial court ordered the chemotherapy because of the life-threatening nature of Ed's disease. Ed remained with his parents and they complied with the court order. When Ed's chemotherapy was almost finished, his physician recommended that he be monitored for an additional two years, because the cancer had a 40% chance of recurring. The monitoring would consist of examinations every six weeks and a bone scan every six months. If a recurrence were detected, additional treatment would be recommended. Ed's physician believes that Ed would be at risk without the monitoring, even though there was no present indication of cancer. Ed's parents oppose the monitoring, indicating that Ed should receive only Christian Science treatment. Should a court require the monitoring?

PROBLEM 8–11

Six-year-old Andy Smith was brought to the hospital emergency room by his mother. He was dead on arrival. A strangulated inguinal hernia caused his death; his intestine had slipped through his abdominal wall, with subsequent loss of blood supply, obstruction, and infection. His symptoms prior to his death probably were severe and lasted for some time. Because of Andy's death, the Department of Social Services (DSS) investigated the Smith's home. The remaining six Smith children were healthy, well fed, and properly clothed. The house was clean and well kept. The parents said they did not get medical care for Andy because of their religious beliefs. DSS filed a petition to remove the remaining children, based on the death of their sibling, Andy. Should the children be removed?

SECTION 3. WITHHOLDING MEDICAL CARE

A. *Infants*

Kathleen Knepper, Withholding Medical Treatment From Infants: When Is It Child Neglect?
33 U. Louisville J. Fam. L. 1, 12–26 (1995).

* * *

III. BABY DOES REVISITED

On April 9, 1982, an infant was born in Indiana with Down's syndrome and a blockage of his digestive tract. The infant's physicians recommended corrective surgery for the blockage. However, the infant's parents refused to consent to the surgery. The hospital brought the matter to the attention of the juvenile court, which declined to intervene. The Indiana Court of Appeals denied a request for an immediate hearing and the Indiana Supreme Court rejected a petition for a writ of mandamus. The infant died while the hospital sought a stay in the United States Supreme Court, and on November 7, 1983, the Supreme Court denied certiorari. Although the infant died within weeks of the start of court proceedings, the matter gained national attention.

As a result of a directive from then-President Ronald Reagan, federal authorities, through the Department of Health and Human Services (Department), initiated efforts to prevent a situation like this from recurring. The Department sought to enact regulations under section 504 of the Rehabilitation Act that would require hospitals to provide medically-indicated treatment to handicapped infants, such as Baby Doe of Indiana. Commentators have observed that the Department approached the issue with "military zeal," even absent evidence of abuse by medical personnel.

Federal efforts began with a notice to health care providers, informing them that the Department believed that withholding medical treatment from newborns might violate section 504 of the Rehabilitation Act. * * *

* * *

The United States Supreme Court reviewed [litigation over the section 504 regulations] in Bowen v. American Hospital Association (1986). In the majority opinion, the Supreme Court examined the preexisting state law framework that governed the provision of medical care to handicapped infants. The Court described this as a system that vests decision-making responsibility in the parents in the first instance, subject to review by the state acting as parens patriae in exceptional cases. The Court noted that parents' withholding of consent to treatment does not equate to hospitals' discriminatory denial of treatment, and were a hospital to provide treatment or perform surgery without such consent, this would constitute a tortious act. The Court reasoned that because of this finding, the regulations were not needed to prevent hospitals from denying treatment to handicapped infants. The regulations also were flawed because they failed to clarify the relationship between the reporting requirements for handicapped infants and those for non-handicapped infants. While the Department inferred that discriminatory non-reporting of such cases was occurring, the Court was not persuaded that this would constitute a violation of section 504, rather than a failure to adhere to the reporting requirements of state law. The Court noted that no section 504 violation would have occurred in the Baby Doe of Indiana case, because the hospital had been prepared to provide the surgery that would have saved the child's life. Finding no colorable basis for a section 504 violation, the Supreme Court held that the attempted rulemaking exceeded the Department's statutory authority.

Rather than abandoning its efforts, the federal government shifted its enforcement arena. The federal government established rules under the Child Abuse Prevention and Treatment Act, which remain in effect. This regulatory scheme provides a framework within which the failure to provide medical treatment to an infant may be a form of child neglect, enforceable under state laws by state child welfare agencies through the juvenile courts. While the regulations embody no direct enforcement power, they make the states' receipt of certain federal aid contingent upon the states' adherence to these regulations.[109]

* * *

IV. THE CURRENT STATUS OF NEONATAL CARE

The federal regulations must be considered in their present social and medical context. Within the last decade, the debate over the provision of medical care has intensified as improvements in medical technology have made it possible to keep many critically ill patients alive almost indefinitely. Nowhere are the results of these technological advances felt more intensely than in neonatal nurseries, where treatment is often experimental and where the prognosis for recovery and the long-term quality of life that an affected infant can be expected to experience are uncertain.* * *

In turn, as has been observed by a former president of the American Academy of Pediatrics, "this has created an ethical dilemma for families, physicians, and society as a whole. Criteria must be established to provide a framework for decision making in the care of critically ill patients. Nowhere is the need more urgent than in the newborn intensive care unit." Another physician has described these concerns more graphically: "The dramatic increase of technical power in neonatal medicine has made possible an unprecedented form of extremism. This change, I suggest, is nothing less than a radical social revolution."

Among the factors in this so-called social revolution are the number of babies born to young families living in poverty, the number born to single parents and the number born into lives of poverty, poor housing, violence and substance abuse. Babies born under these conditions are

---

109. 42 U.S.C.§ 5106(a) (1994). Included in the regulations is a provision that indicates that, in order for a state to qualify for federal assistance, the state shall:

   have in place for the purpose of responding to the reporting of medical neglect (including instances of withholding of medically indicated treatment from disabled infants with life-threatening conditions), procedures or programs, or both (within the State child protective services system), to provide for (i) coordination and consultation with individuals, designated by and within appropriate health-care facilities, (ii) prompt notification by individuals designated by and within appropriate health-care facilities of cases of suspected medical neglect (including instances of withholding of medically indicated treatment from disabled infants with life-threatening conditions), and (iii) authority, under State law, for the State child protective service system to pursue any legal remedies, including the authority to initiate legal proceedings in a court of competent jurisdiction, as may be necessary to prevent the withholding of medically indicated treatment from disabled infants with life-threatening conditions.

42 U.S.C. § 5101(g) (1994).

more likely than other babies to be at medical risk, which has been defined as follows:

A child is classified as a medical risk if, among other things, he or she is born premature or at a low birthweight; has a chronic disease such as asthma; has a life-threatening condition such as Sudden Infant Death Syndrome (SIDS) or a breathing problem; has a congenital defect such as Down's syndrome; or is born affected by drugs or alcohol.

* * *

* * * [N]eonatal intensive care units are one of the most costly high technology areas of medicine. The cost of neonatal hospital care ranges between $20,000 and $100,000 per infant, with long-term potential costs associated with a lifetime of health and custodial needs of these individuals resulting in costs as high as $300,000 to $400,000 per individual. A 1992 estimate placed the overall cost of neonatal care at $5.6 billion annually. A more conservative estimate placed the cost at $500 million annually. Even as hospitals and physicians experience increased pressures due to the costs associated with providing care to these infants, courts generally have not considered the financial implications of their decisions regarding the medical treatment to be provided to these children. One physician has expressed the frustrations of medical practitioners this way:

When I completed my residency in pediatric surgery in 1962, newborn babies who could not breathe spontaneously died; babies who could not feed died; most babies who weighed less than three pounds died. Generous federal funding of research in neonatology, coupled with grants to support training of the new breed of neonatal physicians, surgeons, and intensivists, brought increased survival.... Now comes both 'cost containment' and a confusing and contradictory bundle of legislation and court decisions posing a host of economic, legal, and ethical dilemmas for families, doctors, and hospitals.... Physicians are squeezed between the increasing costs of liability insurance and diminishing reimbursement under private and government fee schedules. Additional pressures on physicians have been generated by the succession of Baby Doe regulations....

Decisions about providing medical care to infants are relatively easy when the cases arise at the extremes of the treatment continuum: to wit, allowing an infant to die who has a terminal, incurable defect and for whom prolonging life constitutes prolonged suffering and requiring treatment for an otherwise normal child who has a surgically correctable but life threatening condition. Cases that arise within these treatment extremes create greater difficulties in application. The professional custom has been to treat aggressively infants who are born with serious birth defects or complications, even under circumstances that raise questions about the efficacy of doing so given the infant's prognosis. * * *

In the intensive care nursery ... the choice is among 'least worst' alternatives.... What troubles many pediatricians is the deeply felt sense that they are compelled to use their skills toward ends they believe are perverse: to forcibly keep alive infants who are so damaged that, even if they survive, they cannot be expected to become participants in society.[b]

* * *

Although the thrust of the so-called Baby Doe regulations tends to be consistent with the professional custom of treating aggressively infants with physical illnesses or impairments, the technological, social, economic and ethical milieu within which the regulations are set may be expected to affect their interpretation and implementation. Much concern has been expressed about the impact of the regulations upon treatment decisions, with an apparent underlying fear that the regulations cause federal and state officials to intrude inappropriately in these decisions.

V. ANALYSIS OF THE CURRENT REGULATORY SCHEME

* * *

The federal regulations create a presumption that the failure to treat aggressively an impaired infant is a form of child neglect, and they assume that a child's physical and mental impairments should not, as such, enter into these treatment decisions. The seminal concern in their implementation is, in fact, not centrally one of establishing child neglect per se , but is an ethical matter regarding the judgments that should be reached when deciding whether to authorize—and indeed to insist upon—a particular course of medical treatment for an infant. While failing to address the relationship between their interpretation and implementation and similar nontreatment decisions regarding older children, the medical questions that arise in their application are not unlike those that arise in cases involving older children and adults.

The implementation of the regulations creates obvious tension between the common law right of family autonomy and the enforcement of state child neglect laws. Physicians are given a central role in the regulatory scheme, as they must consider whether they should refer individual cases of parental refusal to authorize medical care to state child welfare agencies as a form of child neglect. As such, problems exist in the interpretation and application of the regulations. "The controversy over impaired infant care continues ... despite these 'Baby Doe' regulations."

* * *

b. Rasa Gustaitis, Right to Refuse Life–Sustaining Treatment, 81 Pediatrics 317, 318 (1988).

Notes and Questions

1.   The Baby Doe CAPTA regulations, 45 CFR § 1340.15 (b)(1999), provide the following:

(1) * * * The term "medical neglect" includes, but is not limited to, the withholding of medically indicated treatment from a disabled infant with a life-threatening condition.

(2) The term "withholding of medically indicated treatment" means the failure to respond to the infant's life-threatening conditions by providing treatment (including appropriate nutrition, hydration, and medication) which, in the treating physician's (or physicians') reasonable medical judgment, will be most likely to be effective in ameliorating or correcting all such conditions, except that the term does not include the failure to provide treatment (other than appropriate nutrition, hydration, or medication) to an infant when, in the treating physician's (or physicians') reasonable medical judgment any of the following circumstances apply:

(i) The infant is chronically and irreversibly comatose:

(ii) The provision of such treatment would merely prolong dying, not be effective in ameliorating or correcting all of the infant's life-threatening conditions, or otherwise be futile in terms of the survival of the infant; or

(iii) The provision of such treatment would be virtually futile in terms of the survival of the infant and the treatment itself under such circumstances would be inhumane.

(3)* * * (ii) The term "reasonable medical judgment" means a medical judgment that would be made by a reasonably prudent physician, knowledgeable about the case and the treatment possibilities with respect to the medical conditions involved.

What is the main purpose of these regulations? Can a hospital be held liable for providing life sustaining medical care to a newborn without a court order or the parents' consent? In a tort case in a Texas district court, Miller v. Woman's Hospital, 92–07830, parents were awarded forty million dollars because the hospital ignored the parents' instructions to refrain from providing life support for premature infant. Jury Awards $42 Million for 'Wrongful Birth,' Nat'l L. J., Feb. 2, 1998 at A8.

2.   *Medical abuse.* If doctors conclude that continuing a child's treatment and life support systems is futile and cruel, can the hospital get a court order allowing treatment to be discontinued over the parents' objections? Generally the parents' decision to continue treatment controls. See, e.g., In re Jane Doe, 418 S.E.2d 3 (Ga.1992). A doctor who removes life supports from a child without parental consent may be liable in a wrongful death action, even if the child was terminally ill and in the process of dying. See, e.g., Velez v. Bethune, 466 S.E.2d 627 (Ga.Ct.App.1995).

An extreme example of continuing care over the objections of treating physicians involved Baby K., who was born anencephalic, and was considered to be unconscious and unable to think, feel or develop. Her father consented to cessation of treatment, but her mother did not, and the child was kept alive for over two years. See Mary Crossley, Infants with Anencephaly, the

ADA, and the Child Abuse Amendments, 11 Issues in Law and Medicine 379 (1996); Mark A. Bonanno, The Case of Baby K: Exploring the Concept of Medical Futility, 2 Annals of Health L. 151 (1995). Crossley provides the following definition of anencephaly:

> Anencephaly is the congenital absence of major portions of the brain, skull, and scalp, characterized by a large opening in the skull accompanied by the absence or severe disruption of the cerebral hemispheres. Although the etiology of anencephaly is usually unknown, the condition begins to develop during the first month of gestation. Infants with anencephaly are believed to be permanently unconscious, but may exhibit brain stem functions in varying degrees. Resulting behaviors may include responses to noxious stimuli, feeding reflexes, respiratory reflexes and eye movements, but infants with anencephaly presumably cannot suffer because of their lack of cerebral material.* * * Most infants with anencephaly die within the first days after birth, with only a low percentage of cases surviving beyond one week of birth.

Crossley, supra, at n. 1.

In *Baby K.* the hospital brought a declaratory judgment action to allow it to refuse to provide treatment it considered futile or inhumane. The hospital's position was supported by the infant's guardian ad litem and the father. The court denied the hospital's request, finding that the Emergency Medical Treatment and Active Labor Act, the Rehabilitiation Act of 1973, and the American with Disabilities Act prohibited the hospital from denying care. The court also relied on the "constitutional and common law presumption" that parents should make medical decisions about their children and that when parents conflict the court should yield to "the presumption in favor of life." The court did not consider the CAPTA amendments because the state was not a party to the case (Child protective services was not involved.) In re Baby K., 832 F.Supp. 1022 (E.D.Va.1993).

3. *Terminating life-support for abused children.* If an abusive parent refuses to consent to termination of life support for a severely abused child because the parent will be charged with homicide when the child dies, may a court order termination of life support over the parent's objection? In In re L.V., Case No. 03283360 (Milwaukee Co. Cir. Ct. Oct., 1998), the court appointed a temporary guardian for the Baby L.V. to make the life-support decision because the mother's conflict of interest was so great that she could not make decisions based predominantly on the child's interests. For discussion of the case, see Miriam S. Fleming, Case Study of Child Abuse and a Parent's Refusal to Withdraw Sustaining Treatment, 26 SPG Hum.Rts. 12 (1999).

Is a court order to terminate a child's life-support over the parents' objections equivalent to an order terminating parental rights? In In re Tabatha R., 564 N.W.2d 598 (Neb.1997), amended by 566 N.W.2d 782 (Neb.1997), an infant was placed in the custody of the Department of Health and Human Services (DHHS) after suffering severe brain injury from a vigorous shaking while with her parents. DHHS was authorized to consent to medical care. The court decided that the DHHS decision to withdraw life support and not resuscitate Tabatha was likely to result in her death and was "essentially severing the relationship between the infant and the parents and was functionally equivalent to a termination of the parents' parental rights." In re Tabatha R., 587 N.W.2d 109, 113 (Neb.1998) (Tabatha II). The trial court thus could not issue the withdrawal order unless it found, "by clear and convincing evidence," that "the parents' rights should be terminated." Id.

4. *Brain death.* When a child has met a state's definition of brain death, a hospital may disconnect life support systems without parental consent or a court order. In re Long Island Jewish Medical Center, 641 N.Y.S.2d 989 (N.Y. Sup. Ct.1996). Under New York law the hospital was required prior to make reasonable efforts to notify next of kin before the determination of death and removal of life supports.

5. *Additional references.* For a comprehensive discussion of the impact of disability laws on medical decision-making, including analysis of *Baby K.* , see Philip G. Peters, Jr., When Physicians Balk at Futile Care: Implications of the Disability Rights Laws, 91 Nw. L. Rev. 798 (1997). For a detailed discussion of the impact on the medical community of governmental regulation of treatment of new borns by a neonatologist, see Frank I. Clark, Withdrawal of Life–Support in the Newborn: Whose Baby is It?, 23 Sw. U. L. Rev. 1 (1993). For a discussion of the application of the Child Abuse Prevention and Treatment Act regulations to babies born with HIV infection or exposure to crack, see James Boggs, Jr. and Deborah Hall Gardner, Aids Babies, Crack Babies: Challenges to the Law, 7 Issues in Law and Medicine 3 (1991). For additional information, see: Mark A. Bonnanno, The Case of Baby K: Exploring the Concept of Medical Futility, 4 Annols Health L. 151 (1995); Phoebe A. Haddon, Baby Doe Cases: Compromise and Moral Dilemma, 34 Emory L. J. 545 (1985); Dale L. Moore, Challenging Parental Decisions to Overtreat Children, 5 Health Matrix 311 (1995); Erin A. Neely, Medical Decision–Making for Children: A Struggle for Autonomy, 49 SMU L.Rev. 133 (1995); Nancy K. Rhoden, Treatment Dilemmas For Imperiled Newborns: Why Quality of Life Counts, 58 Cal. L. Rev. 1285 (1985); David M. Smolin, Praying for Baby Rena: Religious Liberty, Medical Futility, and Miracles, 25 Seton Hall L. Rev. 960 (1995); Robyn S. Shapiro & Richard Barthel, Infant Care Review Committee: An Effective Approach to the Baby Doe Dilemma? 37 Hastings L. J. 827 (1986).

B. Older Children

ROSEBUSH v. OAKLAND COUNTY PROSECUTOR

Court of Appeals of Michigan, 1992.
491 N.W.2d 633.

MacKenzie, Presiding Justice.

This is an appeal from an order allowing petitioners, the parents of Joelle Rosebush, to authorize the removal of life-support systems for their minor daughter. Although the issues raised in this appeal were rendered technically moot upon Joelle's death, appellate review is nevertheless appropriate because the issues involve questions of public significance that may recur and yet evade review.

I

Joelle Rosebush was born on May 20, 1976. On January 12, 1987, she was involved in a traffic accident. Her spinal cord was severed at the C–1 level, just below the skull, and she went into cardiac arrest. The spinal cord injury left Joelle completely and irreversibly paralyzed from the neck down and unable to breathe without a respirator. The lack of oxygen during cardiac arrest destroyed most, if not all, of Joelle's cerebral functions, and left her in a persistent vegetative state. It was uncontroverted that Joelle would never regain consciousness and would never be able to breathe on her own. Joelle's brain stem was not destroyed, however, and her injuries did not leave her "brain dead" as defined under Michigan law.

Joelle was hospitalized at William Beaumont Hospital of Royal Oak until June, 1987. In spite of the prognosis of no recovery and Joelle's steadily deteriorating condition, petitioners, hopeful of future improvement in Joelle's condition, rejected the option of discontinuing life-support at that time. Joelle was then moved to the Neurorehabilitation Center at the Georgian Bloomfield Nursing Home. By March 1988, it became clear to petitioners that Joelle's condition had not improved and that she would never progress from her vegetative condition. Petitioners then decided to authorize the removal of life-support systems. This decision was made after consultation with Joelle's treating physicians, the staff of the Neurorehabilitation Center, the family's Catholic priest, and the family's attorney.

In March 1988, Joelle's medical case manager sought the assistance of doctors at Children's Hospital of Michigan—Detroit in effectuating petitioners' decision to discontinue life-support. The bio-ethics committee at Children's Hospital subsequently authorized Joelle's transfer to that facility for further evaluation. The transfer was blocked, however, after staff members at the Neurorehabilitation Center contacted respondent, who obtained an ex parte temporary restraining order, and later a preliminary injunction, prohibiting Joelle's transfer or the removal of life-support systems.

Following seven days of trial, the court dissolved the preliminary injunction and authorized petitioners "to make any and all decisions regarding the medical treatment received by their daughter, including but not limited to, the authority to order the removal of the ventilator that sustains Joelle's respiratory functions." Joelle died on August 13, 1988, shortly after her respirator was deactivated.

II

A

Courts variously have found a right to forego life-sustaining medical treatment on the basis of three sources: (1) the common-law right to freedom from unwanted interference with bodily integrity, (2) the constitutional right to privacy or liberty, or (3) statute. We hold that, in Michigan, there is a right to withhold or withdraw life-sustaining medical treatment as an aspect of the common-law doctrine of informed consent. The trial court did not err in determining that petitioners had the legal authority to order the removal of life-support systems.

B

Michigan recognizes and adheres to the common-law right to be free from nonconsensual physical invasions and the corollary doctrine of informed consent. Accordingly, if a physician treats or operates on a patient without consent, the physician has committed a battery and may be required to respond in damages.

The logical corollary of the doctrine of informed consent is that the patient generally possesses the right not to consent, that is, the right to refuse medical treatment and procedures. Thus, a competent adult patient has the right to decline any and all forms of medical intervention, including lifesaving or life-prolonging treatment.

The right to refuse lifesaving medical treatment is not lost because of the incompetence or the youth of the patient. However, because minors and other incompetent patients lack the legal capacity to make decisions concerning their medical treatment, someone acting as a surrogate must exercise the right to refuse treatment on their behalf.

It is well established that parents speak for their minor children in matters of medical treatment. Because medical treatment includes the decision to decline lifesaving intervention, it follows that parents are empowered to make decisions regarding withdrawal or withholding of lifesaving or life-prolonging measures on behalf of their children.

C

Having determined that minors have the same right to decline life-sustaining treatment as their competent adult counterparts, and that parents may act as surrogate decision makers to exercise that right, we next consider what restrictions, if any, should be placed on the parents' decision-making authority and what role, if any, the courts should play in the decision-making process. We hold that the decision-making process should generally occur in the clinical setting without resort to the courts, but that courts should be available to assist in decision making when an impasse is reached. We further hold that, in making decisions for minors or other incompetent patients, surrogate decision makers should make the best approximation of the patient's preference on the basis of available evidence; if such preference was never expressed or is otherwise unknown, the surrogate should make a decision based on the best interests of the patient.

D

Our research has found two cases involving the discontinuation of life-sustaining treatment for minor children who were in a persistent vegetative state. In In re Guardianship of Barry (Fla. App. 1984), the parents petitioned to terminate life-support systems for their ten-month-old son, who was permanently comatose. The circuit court granted the petition, and the Florida Court of Appeals affirmed. * * *

The *Barry* court rejected the state's request that judicial review be required before life-support methods may be withheld from a minor who is not brain dead:

> [W]here, as here, the question concerns a young child, we do not think the parents must always qualify as legal guardians and seek judicial sanctions to discontinue these extraordinary measures. A decision by parents supported by competent medical advice ... should ordinarily be sufficient without court approval. Of course, diagnosis should always be confirmed by at least two physicians. We must remember that the conscience of society in these matters is not something relegated to the exclusive jurisdiction of the court.
>
> Although judicial intervention need not be solicited as a matter of course, still the courts must always be open to hear these matters on request of the family, guardian, affected medical personnel, or the state. In cases where doubt exists, or there is a lack of concurrence among family, physicians, and the hospital, or if an affected party simply desires a judicial order, then the court must be available to consider the matter. Medical personnel and hospitals may well consider the suggestion made by Dr. Solomon in his testimony that an advisory committee should be available to assist families and physicians in these matters.

In In re LHR [Ga., 1984] the parents of an infant in an irreversible chronic vegetative state sought to remove life-support systems from the child, and the hospital treating the child sought a declaratory judgment regarding whether life-support activity could be terminated. The Supreme Court of Georgia concluded that it could, stating:

> We conclude that the right to refuse treatment or indeed to terminate treatment may be exercised by the parents or legal guardian of the infant after diagnosis that the infant is terminally ill with no hope of recovery and that the infant exists in a chronic vegetative state with no reasonable possibility of attaining cognitive function. The above diagnosis and prognosis must be made by the attending physician. Two physicians with no interest in the outcome of the case must concur in the diagnosis and prognosis. Although prior judicial approval is not required, the courts remain available in the event of disagreement between the parties, any case of suspected abuse, or other appropriate instances.
>
> In the narrow case before us no hospital ethics committee need be consulted. This in no way forecloses use of such a committee if this is the choice of the hospital, physician or family. Once the diagnosis is made that the infant is terminally ill with no hope of recovery and in a chronic vegetative state with no possibility of attaining cognitive function, the state has no compelling interest in maintaining life. The decision to forego or terminate life-support

measures is, at this point, simply a decision that the dying process will not be artificially extended. While the state has an interest in the prolongation of life, the state has no interest in the prolongation of dying, and although there is a moral and ethical decision to be made to end the process, that decision can be made only by the surrogate of the infant. Since the parents are the natural guardians of the infant, where there are parents no legal guardian and no guardian ad litem need be appointed.

We conclude that the decision whether to end the dying process is a personal decision for family members or those who bear a legal responsibility for the patient. We do not consider this conclusion an abdication of responsibility of the judiciary. While the courts are always available to protect the rights of the individual, the condition of this individual is such that the decision is one to be made by the family and the medical community. As previously noted, the courts remain open to assist if there is disagreement between decision makers or question of abuse.

We agree with the principles set forth in *Barry* and In re LHR. After the trial court's decision in this case, our Legislature enacted M.C.L. § 700.496; M.S.A. § 27.5496, which allows competent adults to appoint a patient advocate to make medical-treatment decisions, including the withdrawal of life-sustaining treatment, on their behalf. While the statute provides for judicial intervention under certain limited circumstances, we believe that this legislation demonstrates that the overriding public policy of this state is to respect the roles played by the patient, family, physicians, and spiritual advisors in the making of decisions regarding medical treatment, as well as the policy that courts need not delve into that decision-making process unless necessary to protect the patient's interests. Although the legislation applies only to competent adults, we are satisfied that the public policy of judicial nonintervention also extends to decisions concerning the medical treatment of incompetent persons and minors. We therefore hold that, in general, judicial involvement in the decision to withhold or withdraw life-sustaining treatment on behalf of a minor or other incompetent patient need occur only when the parties directly concerned disagree about treatment, or other appropriate reasons are established for the court's involvement.

E

While the decision of a competent adult patient regarding the cessation of life-sustaining measures will generally control that patient's care, a different standard must necessarily guide the surrogate of an incompetent patient, including the parent of an immature minor child, where the incompetent or the minor has never expressed his wishes. Two basic standards have evolved for surrogates to decide whether to withdraw or withhold consent to life-sustaining treatment: the "substituted judgment" standard and the "best interests" standard.

Under the substituted judgment standard, the surrogate exercising an incompetent patient's rights must make the decision whether to forego life-sustaining treatment on the basis of what the patient would have decided had the patient been able to do so. * * *

Under the proper circumstances—where a patient was formerly competent or is a minor of mature judgment—the substituted judgment standard is an appropriate test. However, as applied to immature minors and other never-competent patients, the substituted judgment standard is inappropriate because it cannot be ascertained what choice the patient would have made if competent. We therefore conclude that, where the patient has never been competent, the decision-making test that better guides the surrogate is the best interests standard.

The best interests standard was summarized in In re Guardianship of Grant [Wash.1988] as follows:

> There will be many situations where it cannot be ascertained what choice the patient would make if competent. In such cases, the guardian must make a good-faith determination of whether the withholding of life sustaining treatment would serve the incompetent patient's best interests. The following is a nonexclusive list of the factors which should be considered in making this determination:

> [E]vidence about the patient's present level of physical, sensory, emotional, and cognitive functioning; the degree of physical pain resulting from the medical condition, treatment, and termination of the treatment, respectively; the degree of humiliation, dependence, and loss of dignity probably resulting from the condition and treatment; the life expectancy and prognosis for recovery with and without treatment; the various treatment options; and the risks, side effects, and benefits of each of those options.

The trial court in this case properly recognized the best interests standard as an appropriate standard to use in deciding whether to remove life-support systems for Joelle.

* * *

Notes and Questions

1. *Questions about* Rosebush. (a) What standards can be used to make a decision about withdrawing life-sustaining treatment for a minor? What factors are determinative in the choice of a standard? How do these differ from the decision-making standards in *Parham*? (b) *Rosebush* states that a substituted judgment standard is inappropriate for minors because "it cannot be ascertained what choice the patient would have made if competent." What does this suggest about the parents' right to decide when the child is mature? (c) When is judicial review needed to determine if a child's life-support systems are to be withdrawn? Does *Rosebush* sufficiently protect the child? (d) Does the *Rosebush* best interests standard offer the same

degree of protection afforded infants under the Child Abuse Amendments of 1984 discussed by Knepper? Should medical neglect laws and regulations treat infants be treated differently than older children?

2. *Withholding treatment from a minor.* The parents of a 17-year-old child suffering from muscular dystrophy and related serious illness executed a "do not resuscitate" (DNR) order, which was "generally understood to direct hospital personnel to not assist or intervene when the patient is confronted with a life-threatening situation." Belcher v. Charleston Area Med. Center, 422 S.E.2d 827, n. 3 (1992). After the child died, the parents sued the hospital, alleging that the child's consent to the DNR order was required. The court recognized the common law mature minor exception to parental consent and remanded the case for determination of whether the child was mature. The court concluded that

> except in very extreme cases, a physician has no legal right to perform a procedure upon, or administer or withhold treatment from a patient without the patient's consent, nor upon a child without the consent of the child's parents or guardian, unless the child is a mature minor, in which case the child's consent would be required. Whether a child is a mature minor is a question of fact. Whether the child has the capacity to consent depends upon the age, ability, experience, education, training, and degree of maturity or judgment obtained by the child, as well as upon the conduct and demeanor of the child at the time of the procedure or treatment. The factual determination would also involve whether the minor has the capacity to appreciate the nature, risks, and consequences of the medical procedure to be performed, or the treatment to be administered or withheld. Where there is a conflict between the intentions of one or both parents and the minor, the physician's good faith assessment of the minor's maturity level would immunize him or her from liability for the failure to obtain parental consent.

Id. at 838.

PROBLEM 8–12

Sixteen-year-old Bill was in an auto accident that left him in a persistent vegetative state. Two weeks before the accident, Bill and his brother visited a friend in the hospital who was in a coma following an accident. Bill said, "I don't ever want to get like that. I would want somebody to let me leave." After reading about an accident in the newspaper, he also had told his mother, "If I can't be myself, let me go to sleep." Bill's physician and another doctor have testified that Bill will never recover. Bill's parents want to remove his life support.

You're the judge. What do you decide and what is the basis for your decision? What would you decide if Bill had spoken out in opposition to terminating life support in the two instances described above, but his parents wanted them removed?

SECTION 4. BONE MARROW AND ORGAN DONATION

CURRAN v. BOSZE

Supreme Court of Illinois, 1990.
566 N.E.2d 1319.

JUSTICE CALVO delivered the opinion of the court:

Allison and James Curran are 3 1/2-year-old twins. Their mother is Nancy Curran. The twins have lived with Ms. Curran and their maternal grandmother since their birth on January 27, 1987.

The twins' father is Tamas Bosze. Ms. Curran and Mr. Bosze have never been married. As a result of an action brought by Ms. Curran against Mr. Bosze concerning the paternity of the twins, both Mr. Bosze and the twins underwent a blood test in November of 1987. The blood test confirmed that Mr. Bosze is the father of the twins. On February 16, 1989, Mr. Bosze and Ms. Curran entered into an agreed order (parentage order) establishing a parent-child relationship. The parentage order states that Ms. Curran "shall have the sole care, custody, control and educational responsibility of the minor children." Section B, paragraph 4, of the order provides:

> "In all matters of importance relating to the health, welfare and education of the children, Mother shall consult and confer with Father, with a view toward adopting and following a harmonious policy. Mother shall advise Father of which school the children will attend and both parents shall be given full access to the school records of the children."

Section M of the parentage order provides that the court retain jurisdiction over the parties and subject matter for the purposes of enforcing the agreed order.

Mr. Bosze is the father of three other children: a son, age 23; Jean Pierre Bosze, age 12; and a one-year-old daughter. Ms. Curran is not the mother of any of these children. Each of these children has a different mother. Jean Pierre and the twins are half-siblings. The twins have met Jean Pierre on two occasions. Each meeting lasted approximately two hours.

Jean Pierre is suffering from acute undifferentiated leukemia (AUL), also known as mixed lineage leukemia. * * * Jean Pierre was treated with chemotherapy and went into remission. Jean Pierre experienced a testicular relapse in January 1990, and a bone marrow relapse in mid-June 1990. [His doctor] has recommended a bone marrow transplant for Jean Pierre.

Mr. Bosze asked Ms. Curran to consent to a blood test for the twins in order to determine whether the twins were compatible to serve as bone marrow donors for a transplant to Jean Pierre. Mr. Bosze asked Ms. Curran to consent to the twins' undergoing a bone marrow harvesting procedure if the twins were found to be compatible. After consulting with the twins' pediatrician, family members, parents of bone marrow donors and bone marrow donors, Ms. Curran refused to give consent to the twins' undergoing either the blood test or the bone marrow harvesting procedure.

On June 28, 1990, Mr. Bosze filed an emergency petition in the circuit court of Cook County. The petition informed the court that Jean Pierre "suffers from leukemia and urgently requires a [bone] marrow transplant from a compatible donor. Without the transplant he will die in a short period of time, thereby creating an emergency involving life and death." The petition stated that persons usually compatible for serving as donors are parents or siblings of the recipient, and Jean Pierre's father, mother, and older brother had been tested and rejected as compatible donors.

According to the petition, "[t]he only siblings who have potential to be donors and who have not been tested are the children, James and Allison." The petition stated Ms. Curran refused to discuss with Mr. Bosze the matter of submitting the twins to a blood test to determine their compatibility as potential bone marrow donors for Jean Pierre. The petition stated the blood test "is minimally invasive and harmless, and no more difficult than the paternity blood testing which the children have already undergone." According to the petition, there would be no expense involved to Ms. Curran.

In the petition, Mr. Bosze requested the court find a medical emergency to exist and order and direct Ms. Curran to "forthwith produce the parties' minor children * * * at Lutheran General Hospital * * * for the purpose of compatibility blood testing." Further, Mr. Bosze requested in the petition that "if the children, or either of them, are compatible as donors, that the Court order and direct that [Ms. Curran] produce the children, or whichever one may be compatible, for the purpose of donating bone marrow to their sibling."

* * *

[The twins and Jean Pierre were joined in the lawsuit and were provided with guardians ad litem. The trial court denied Mr. Bosze's petition for emergency relief. He appealed.]

I

Mr. Bosze and the guardian *ad litem* for Jean Pierre strenuously argue that the doctrine of substituted judgment * * * should be applied in this case to determine whether or not the twins would consent, if they were competent to do so, to the bone marrow donation if they, or either of them, were compatible with Jean Pierre. The doctrine of substituted judgment requires a surrogate decisionmaker to "attempt[ ] to establish, with as much accuracy as possible, what decision the patient would make if [the patient] were competent to do so." Mr. Bosze and the guardian ad litem for Jean Pierre contend the evidence clearly and convincingly establishes that the twins, if competent, would consent to the bone marrow harvesting procedure.

Ms. Curran and the guardian *ad litem* for the twins vigorously object to the application of the doctrine of substituted judgment in this case. It is the position of Ms. Curran and the guardian ad litem for the twins that it is not possible to establish by clear and convincing evidence whether the 3 1/2-year-old twins, if they were competent—that is, if they were not minors but were adults with the legal capacity to consent— would consent or refuse to consent to the proposed bone marrow harvesting procedure. According to Ms. Curran and the guardian ad litem for the twins, the decision whether or not to give or withhold consent to the procedure must be determined by the best-interests-of-the-child standard. Ms. Curran and the guardian ad litem for the twins argue that the evidence reveals it is not in the best interests of the children to require them to submit to the bone marrow harvesting procedure.

* * *

Under the doctrine of substituted judgment, a guardian of a formerly competent, now incompetent, person may look to the person's life history, in all of its diverse complexity, to ascertain the intentions and attitudes which the incompetent person once held. There must be clear and convincing evidence that the formerly competent, now incompetent, person had expressed his or her intentions and attitudes with regard to the termination of artificial nutrition and hydration before a guardian may be authorized to exercise, on behalf of the incompetent person, the right of the incompetent person to terminate artificial sustenance.

* * *

The doctrine of substituted judgment requires clear and convincing proof of the incompetent person's intent before a court may authorize a surrogate to substitute his or her judgment for that of the incompetent. Any lesser standard would "undermin[e] the foundation of self-determination and inviolability of the person upon which the right to refuse medical treatment stands." A guardian attempting to prove what a 3 1/2-year-old child would or would not do in a given set of circumstances at a given time in the distant future would have to rely on speculation and conjecture.

Neither justice nor reality is served by ordering a 3 1/2-year-old child to submit to a bone marrow harvesting procedure for the benefit of another by a purported application of the doctrine of substituted judgment. Since it is not possible to discover that which does not exist, specifically, whether the 3 1/2-year-old twins would consent or refuse to consent to the proposed bone marrow harvesting procedure if they were competent, the doctrine of substituted judgment is not relevant and may not be applied in this case.

II

Several courts from sister jurisdictions have addressed the issue whether the consent of a court, parent or guardian, for the removal of a kidney from an incompetent person for transplantation to a sibling, may be legally effective. These cases have been addressed by the parties. While not mandatory authority to this court, these cases are illustrative of the complexities involved when otherwise healthy minors or incompetent persons, who lack the legal capacity to give consent, are asked to undergo an invasive surgical procedure for the benefit of a sibling.

* * *

In Hart v. Brown (Conn. Super. Ct. 1972) the parents of identical twins, age 7 years and 10 months, sought permission to have a kidney from the healthy twin transplanted into the body of the seriously ill twin who was suffering from a kidney disease. The parents brought a declaratory judgment action, as parents and natural guardians of the twins, seeking a declaration that they had the right to consent to the proposed operation. Guardians ad litem for each of the twins were appointed. Defendants in the declaratory judgment action were the physicians and the hospital at which the proposed kidney transplantation operation was to take place; the defendants had refused to use their facilities unless the court "declare[d] that the parents and/or guardians ad litem of the minors have the right to give their consent to the operation upon the minor twins."

* * *

The *Hart* court reviewed the medical testimony presented concerning the kidney transplant which "indicate[d] that scientifically this type of procedure is a 'perfect' transplant. The court also noted that a psychiatrist examined the proposed donor and testified the proposed donor "has a strong identification with her twin sister." * * *

Both guardians *ad litem* gave their consent to the procedure. Both parents gave their consent to the procedure. A clergy person testified that the natural parents were "making a morally sound decision." The *Hart* court found the testimony of the parents showed they reached their decision to consent "only after many hours of agonizing consideration." The twin who would serve as the kidney donor "ha[d] been informed of the operation and insofar as she may be capable of understanding she desires to donate her kidney so that her sister may return to her."

The *Hart* court stated:

"To prohibit the natural parents and the guardians ad litem of the minor children the right to give their consent under these circumstances, where there is supervision by this court and other persons in examining their judgment, would be most unjust, inequitable and injudicious. Therefore, natural parents of a minor should have the right to give their consent to an isograft kidney transplantation procedure when their motivation and reasoning are favorably reviewed by a community representation which includes a court of equity.

It is the judgment of this court that [the parents] have the right, under the particular facts and circumstances of this matter, to give their consent to the operations."

Although purporting to apply the doctrine of substituted judgment, the Hart court did not inquire as to what the 7 1/2-year-old minors would do if the minors were competent. The Hart court instead determined that "the natural parents would be able to substitute their consent for that of their minor children after a close, independent and objective investigation of their motivation and reasoning."

* * *

In each of the foregoing cases where consent to the kidney transplant was authorized, regardless whether the authority to consent was to be exercised by the court, a parent or a guardian, the key inquiry was the presence or absence of a benefit to the potential donor. Notwithstanding the language used by the courts in reaching their determination that a transplant may or may not occur, the standard by which the determination was made was whether the transplant would be in the best interest of the child or incompetent person.

* * *

We hold that a parent or guardian may give consent on behalf of a minor daughter or son for the child to donate bone marrow to a sibling, only when to do so would be in the minor's best interest.

As sole custodian of the twins, Ms. Curran "may determine the child[ren]'s upbringing, including but not limited to, [the] education, health care and religious training, unless the court, after hearing, finds, upon motion by the noncustodial parent, that the absence of a specific limitation of the custodian's authority would clearly be contrary to the best interests of the child[ren]."

* * *

Mr. Bosze believes Ms. Curran's decision to withhold consent for the twins to donate bone marrow is wrong. Mr. Bosze argued that under the doctrine of substituted judgment, the twins, if competent, would consent to donate bone marrow. Mr. Bosze presented evidence which he contended proved Ms. Curran was wrong in withholding consent. This evidence, and the evidence presented by Ms. Curran, is sufficient for this court to determine whether, under the facts of this case, it is in the best interests for the twins, or either of them, to donate bone marrow to their half-brother. Mr. Bosze, as the noncustodial parent, has the burden of persuading the court that the withholding of consent by the twins' custodial parent to the proposed bone marrow harvesting procedure is clearly contrary to the best interests of the children.

III

In the case at bar, the circuit court heard extensive testimony from physicians concerning the status of Jean Pierre's condition, and the risks and benefits of donating bone marrow. The physicians also testified concerning consent by a parent or guardian for bone marrow harvesting from a minor child.

* * *

The evidence reveals three critical factors which are necessary to a determination that it will be in the best interests of a child to donate bone marrow to a sibling. First, the parent who consents on behalf of the child must be informed of the risks and benefits inherent in the bone marrow harvesting procedure to the child.

Second, there must be emotional support available to the child from the person or persons who take care of the child. The testimony reveals that a child who is to undergo general anesthesia and the bone marrow harvesting procedure needs the emotional support of a person whom the child loves and trusts. A child who is to donate bone marrow is required to go to an unfamiliar place and meet with unfamiliar people. Depending upon the age of the child, he or she may or may not understand what is to happen. The evidence establishes that the presence and emotional support by the child's caretaker is important to ease the fears associated with such an unfamiliar procedure.

Third, there must be an existing, close relationship between the donor and recipient. The evidence clearly shows that there is no physical benefit to a donor child. If there is any benefit to a child who donates bone marrow to a sibling it will be a psychological benefit. According to the evidence, the psychological benefit is not simply one of personal, individual altruism in an abstract theoretical sense, although that may be a factor.

The psychological benefit is grounded firmly in the fact that the donor and recipient are known to each other as family. Only where there is an existing relationship between a healthy child and his or her ill sister or brother may a psychological benefit to the child from donating bone marrow to a sibling realistically be found to exist. The evidence establishes that it is the existing sibling relationship, as well as the potential for a continuing sibling relationship, which forms the context in which it may be determined that it will be in the best interests of the child to undergo a bone marrow harvesting procedure for a sibling.

* * *

Ms. Curran has refused consent on behalf of the twins to the bone marrow transplant because she does not think it is in their best interests to subject them to the risks and pains involved in undergoing general anesthesia and the harvesting procedure. While Ms. Curran is aware that the risks involved in donating bone marrow and undergoing general anesthesia are small, she also is aware that when such risk occurs, it may be life-threatening.

* * *

It is a fact that the twins and Jean Pierre share the same biological father. There was no evidence produced, however, to indicate that the twins and Jean Pierre are known to each other as family.

Allison and James would need the emotional support of their primary caregiver if they were to donate bone marrow. The evidence establishes that it would not be in a 3 1/2-year-old child's best interests if he or she were required to go to a hospital and undergo all that is involved with the bone marrow harvesting procedure without the constant reassurance and support by a familiar adult known and trusted by the child.

Not only is Ms. Curran presently the twins' primary caretaker, the evidence establishes she is the only caretaker the twins have ever known. Ms. Curran has refused to consent to the twins' participation in donating bone marrow to Jean Pierre. It appears that Mr. Bosze would be unable to substitute his support for the procedure for that of Ms. Curran because his involvement in the lives of Allison and James has, to this point, been a limited one.

The guardian ad litem for the twins recommends that it is not in the best interests of either Allison or James to undergo the proposed bone marrow harvesting procedure in the absence of an existing, close relationship with the recipient, Jean Pierre, and over the objection of their primary caretaker, Ms. Curran. Because the evidence presented supports this recommendation, we agree.

Mr. Bosze argued that the twins should be required to submit to the Human Leukocyte Antigen (HLA) blood test necessary to determine whether they or either of them is compatible as bone marrow donors for Jean Pierre. * * *

* * * Since there is no reason to order the HLA blood test if it is not appropriate for the twins to donate bone marrow, the circuit court properly refused to bifurcate these issues.

This court shares the opinion of the circuit court that Jean Pierre's situation "evokes sympathy from all who've heard [it]." No matter how small the hope that a bone marrow transplant will cure Jean Pierre, the fact remains that without the transplant, Jean Pierre will almost certainly die. The sympathy felt by this court, the circuit court, and all those who have learned of Jean Pierre's tragic situation cannot, however, obscure the fact that, under the circumstances presented in the case at bar, it neither would be proper under existing law nor in the best interests of the 3 1/2-year-old twins for the twins to participate in the bone marrow harvesting procedure.

* * *

Notes and Questions

1. *Questions about* Curran. What must Mr. Bosze show to get the court to order testing of the twins for the bone marrow donation? If Ms. Curran had consented, what would have to be shown to get the court's approval?

2. *Aftermath.* Jean Pierre died at home on November 19, 1990. Rachael M. Dufault, Comment, Bone Marrow Donations by Children: Rethinking the Legal Framework in Light of *Curran v. Bosze*, 24 Conn. L.Rev. 211 (1991).

3. *Altruism.* Should the best interests standard include the desire of a child to act altruistically? See Jennifer K. Robbennolt et al., Advancing the Rights of Children and Adolescents to be Altruistic: Bone Marrow Donation by Minors, 9 J. L. & Health 213 (1994–95)(recommending that courts consider the selflessness of potential minor donors and the minor's wishes, as well as other factors).

4. *Court intervention.* When should court approval be required for bone marrow or organ donation? See Janet B. Korins, *Curran v. Bosze:* Toward a Clear Standard for Authorizing Kidney and Bone Marrow Transplants Between Minor Siblings, 16 Vt. L.Rev. 499 (1992)(recommending that court approval not be required except in cases "involving a very young donor whose custodial parents disagree on the question of consent").

5. *Donating blood.* Most states confer capacity on seventeen year-olds to donate blood without the consent of their parents or guardians. See, e.g., Cal. Health and Safety Code § 1607.5(a). The statutes generally apply only when the donor receives no compensation. See, e.g., Minn. Stat. Ann. § 145.41; N.Y. Pub. Health L. § 3123; N.C. Gen. Stat. § 130A–411; Tex. Stat. § 162.015. Florida permits seventeen-year-olds to donate unless the parent specifically objects in writing. Fla. Stat. Ann. § 743.06. Mississippi permits seventeen-year-olds to donate blood for compensation without parental consent. Miss. Code Ann. § 41–41–15(1). Without discussing the matter of compensation, Oregon permits persons sixteen or older to donate blood without parental consent. Or. Rev. Stat. § 109.670.

6. *Anatomical gifts.* Every state has enacted either the Uniform Anatomical Gift Act (1968) or the Uniform Anatomical Gift Act (1987). Section 2(a) of the 1968 Act provides, and section 2(a) of the 1987 Act recommends, that only persons eighteen or older have capacity to make an anatomical gift (a donation of all or part of the body to take effect on or after death). 8A U.L.A. (Master ed. 1993 & Supp. 1996).

Most states have enacted the eighteen-year-old minimum age for anatomical gifts. Id. (Tables of adopting jurisdictions). Nebraska and Wyoming, however, permit "any individual of sound mind" to make an anatomical gift. See Neb. Rev. Stat. § 71–4802(1); Wyo. Stat. § 35–5–102(a) In Maine and New Mexico, the minimum age is sixteen. See Me. Rev. Stat. Ann. tit. 22 § 2902(1); N.M. Stat. Ann. § 24–6A–2. A few states permit persons under eighteen to make anatomical gifts with the written consent of a parent or guardian. See, e.g., Minn. Stat. Ann. § 525.9211(a); Ohio Rev. Code Ann. § 2108.02(A).

PROBLEM 8–13

A couple in their mid–40's decided to have a baby to provide a potential bone-marrow donor for their teen-age daughter who had leukemia. Although there was only a 25% chance that the baby would be a compatible donor, the baby, a girl, was compatible and was able to donate at 14 months. The girls' parents were criticized for treating the infant as "a medicine chest baby" who had no choice about being a donor. The parents said the child was a "blessing from God" who would have been loved even if she did not have bone-marrow compatible with her sister's.

Should the parents' consent to the bone marrow transplant be sufficient or should the hospital require a court order?

PROBLEM 8–14

Your state is considering adopting one of the two statutes that follow. Do you think either is a better approach than the rule applied in *Curran*? What would be the outcome of *Curran* under the statutes?

STATUTE I

Any minor who is 14 years of age or older, or has graduated from high school, or is married, or having been married is divorced or is pregnant, may give effective consent to the donation of his or her bone marrow for the purpose of bone marrow transplantation. A parent or legal guardian may consent to such bone marrow donation on behalf of any other minor.

OR

STATUTE II

§ 1. Donation of bone marrow by a minor

* * *

(2) Prohibition on donation of bone marrow by a minor. Unless the conditions under sub. (3) or (4) have been met, no minor may be a bone marrow donor in this state.

(3) Consent to donation of bone marrow by a minor under 12 years of age. If the medical condition of a brother or a sister of a minor who is under 12 years of age requires that the brother or sister receive a bone marrow transplant, the minor is deemed to have given consent to be a donor if all of the following conditions are met:

(a) The physician who will remove the bone marrow from the minor has informed the parent, guardian or legal custodian of the minor of all of the following:

1.   The nature of the bone marrow transplant.

2.   The benefits and risks to the prospective donor and prospective recipient of performance of the bone marrow transplant.

3.   The availability of procedures alternative to performance of a bone marrow transplant.

(b) The physician of the brother or sister of the minor has determined all of the following, has confirmed those determinations through consultation with and under recommendation from a physician other than the physician under par. (a) and has provided the determinations to the parent, guardian or legal custodian under par. (e):

1.   That the minor is the most acceptable donor who is available.

2.   That no medically preferable alternatives to a bone marrow transplant exist for the brother or sister.

(c) A physician other than a physician under par. (a) or (b) has determined the following and has provided the determinations to the parent, guardian or legal custodian under par. (e):

1.   The minor is physically able to withstand removal of bone marrow.

2.   The medical risks of removing the bone marrow from the minor and the long-term medical risks for the minor are minimal.

(d) A psychiatrist or psychologist has evaluated the psychological status of the minor, has determined that no significant psychological risks to the minor exist if bone marrow is removed from the minor and has provided that determination to the parent, guardian or legal custodian under par. (e).

(e) The parent, guardian or legal custodian, upon receipt of the information and the determinations under pars. (a) to (d), has given written consent to donation by the minor of the bone marrow.

[The remainder of the statute provides that children twelve or older can consent with some limits.]

SECTION 5.   EXPERIMENTATION

When should medical experimentation on children be allowed? Should parental consent be sufficient or must the child benefit from the experiment? In response to criticism about unethical medical research on children and adults, the predecessor to the U.S. Department of Health and Human Services promulgated regulations on the protection of human subjects in federally funded research in 1974. In 1983 additional regulations were promulgated that specifically dealt with research on children. See Leonard H. Glantz, The Law of Human Experimentation with Children in Children as Research Subjects: Science, Ethics and Law 103 (Michael A. Grodin and Leonard H. Glantz eds. 1994). These regulations require parental permission and the assent of the children except when the children are of such limited capability that they cannot be consulted or when the "procedure involved in the research holds out a prospect of direct benefit that is important to the health or well-being of the children and is available only in the context of the research * * *." 45 CFR § 46.408. The regulations divide research into four categories, depending on the degree of risk to the child and whether the research will directly benefit the child participant. Research on children who are wards of the state or any other institution is very restricted. The regulations exclude some research such as research in educational settings on instructional strategies and aptitude tests, but most research, including social science research, is included. Id. at 123–24.

IN RE NIKOLAS E.

Supreme Judicial Court of Maine, 1998.
720 A.2d 562.

WATHEN, CHIEF JUSTICE.

The guardian ad litem of Nikolas E. appeals from a judgment entered in the District Court denying the child protection petition brought by the Department of Human Services (hereinafter referred to as the "State"). The State sought custody of Nikolas for the limited purpose of approving medical treatment for his HIV condition.[1] * * *

The facts presented at trial may be briefly summarized as follows: Nikolas is a four-year-old boy who is HIV positive. Nikolas's mother and father, who are also HIV positive, are divorced and Nikolas lives with his mother who has sole responsibility for his medical care. In January of 1997, Nikolas's sister died at the age of four from complications with AIDS. Nikolas and his mother are under the care of their family physician, Jean Benson, M.D. After learning of a clinical trial program for children with HIV, Dr. Benson referred Nikolas and his mother to a specialist in pediatric infectious diseases, Dr. John Milliken of Bangor. Both the mother and Nikolas's deceased sister had been treated in the past by Dr. Milliken.

In September of 1997, Dr. Milliken examined Nikolas and met with his mother. He recommended a drug therapy known as highly aggressive anti-retroviral therapy (HAART). Based upon developments in her own illness and her experience with the drug therapy that accompanied the tragic and painful death of her daughter, the mother expressed her distrust of the drug therapy and declined to permit her son to participate at that time. Dr. Milliken, weighing in his mind whether the mother's refusal to provide the therapy to Nikolas constituted neglect, waited for nearly two months before writing his recommendations to Dr. Benson. In November, with updated medical information recommending that all children with HIV infection should be treated for that disease, Dr.

---

1. Human Immunodeficiency Virus (HIV) is a retrovirus that causes Acquired Immunodeficiency Syndrome (AIDS). The virus invades and eventually kills different cells in the blood and in body tissues, particularly white blood cells known as CD4+ cells. When the CD4+ count drops below 200 cells/mm3 of blood or when CD4+ cells comprise less than 14% of his or her total lymphocytes, a person is regarded as having AIDS.

Milliken sent a report to Dr. Benson and provided a copy to the State. In the report he explained his recommendations for treatment and his concern about the mother's decision to forego treatment within the context of her own disease. He suggested that the mother could be offered "a voluntary release of parental rights with residential custody for her," and that medical decisions could be removed from her.

As a result of Dr. Milliken's report, the State met with the mother and discussed her treatment plans for Nikolas. Because of differing opinions offered by Dr. Benson and Dr. Milliken, the State arranged for the mother and Nikolas to consult with Dr. Kenneth McIntosh, Chief of the Division of Infectious Diseases at Children's Hospital in Boston, Massachusetts. Dr. McIntosh is head of the AIDS program at the hospital and professor of pediatrics at Harvard Medical School. He provided the mother with information regarding treatment and suggested that Nikolas would benefit from HAART therapy. Specifically, the therapy would involve giving Nikolas daily dosages of three different kinds of drugs—two nucleoside analogue reverse transcriptase inhibitors, in this case, d4T and 3TC, and one protease inhibitor, in this case, nelfinavir, for an extended period of time, possibly for his lifetime. Dr. McIntosh saw no irrationality on the part of the mother, and he confirmed that he had never reported parents to child protective agencies for failing to accept his recommendations regarding therapy.

Later, the mother returned to Dr. McIntosh on her own to discuss the risks and long term effects of the proposed therapy. The District Court summarized the information she obtained on this visit as follows:

> Dr. McIntosh gave her all the information currently available from the limited experience the medical community has had in this treatment for children and could not give her any definitive information concerning long term effects. This drug treatment regimen is still in the evolving stages. Because of stepped-up FDA approval of drugs and programs in this area due to public and political pressure nation-wide, all ongoing AIDS treatment programs (especially for children), when compared to traditional methods of approving medical drugs and treatment protocols, are experimental. In effect, treatment is being provided to sufferers of this illness at the same time as statistics and efficacy studies are being conducted. The various regimens are changing constantly, and it is expected that new and more effective drugs and treatment protocols will emerge each year, if not sooner. It can be fairly said that the HAART regimen was still in experimental stages when [the mother] first consulted with Dr. Milliken. The CDC published its guidelines for children's HIV treatment over six months later, making this regimen conventional state of the art.
>
>   .   .   .
>
> Dr. McIntosh's [sic] feels that because Nikolas's blood tests (viral load count and CD4 cell count) meet the CDC guidelines qualifying him for aggressive drug therapy, the child may well benefit from

such treatment. However, this benefit cannot be quantified. No good estimation can be given either on whether or how much longer Nikolas will survive solely because he participates. Dr. McIntosh is of the opinion that no child should be started on this program unless his parents are fully accepting and in support of the treatment.

The court concluded that the long term effects of the drug therapy were essentially unknown and observed that the mother, although she had not agreed to the therapy at the time of hearing, stated clearly that her mind was not closed on the issue. The court stated that "[a]lthough she would rather spare Nikolas the effects and risks of this treatment, if his health begins to deteriorate significantly, she will reconsider and would now, if ordered, comply with treatment."

Against this factual background, the State in May of 1998, filed a petition for a child protection order, seeking custody of Nikolas so he could receive the treatment recommended by Dr. McIntosh. A guardian ad litem was appointed * * * and a hearing was held on the petition in September. The court denied the petition and the matter is now before us on an expedited appeal.

I. Standing

As a preliminary matter, the mother argues that the guardian lacks standing to prosecute an appeal in a child protection action. * * * The mother also argues that * * * only an "aggrieved party" may bring an appeal * * * and that neither Nikolas nor his guardian is a party to the child protection hearing.

* * *

* * *[C]ontrary to the mother's argument, the child has a significant interest in child protection proceedings and is a party to the proceedings. Because the child is a minor, a guardian ad litem is appointed and either the child or the guardian can ask for an attorney to be appointed. In this case, the guardian is an attorney and acts in both capacities. Accordingly, the guardian, as the legal representative of Nikolas, is an aggrieved party and, as such, has standing to prosecute this appeal.

II. Circumstances of jeopardy

The guardian argues that the State made a showing sufficient to establish that, by withholding medical treatment, the mother subjected Nikolas to "serious abuse or neglect." * * *

* * *

Although the court did not explicitly articulate and discuss all of the competing interests—the interests of the parent, the interests of the state, and the best interests of the child—and did not expressly balance the benefits and risks of treatment against the benefits and risks of delaying treatment, the court's findings implicitly reflect that the appropriate factors were weighed. The court found, for example, that although the State produced opinion evidence that Nikolas would benefit from treatment, the State did not produce evidence to persuade the court that there was a quantifiable benefit. The court also was unable to determine the likely effects of the treatment on the child. The court accepted as accurate that the drugs used in the therapy "are very potent and cause often unpleasant side effects." The court also found that the State was unable to produce evidence of the likely long-term side effects because the treatment is essentially new and experimental. The court also found that "removal of Nikolas from his home would have a severe and detrimental effect on his well-being." Implicit in the court's conclusion that the mother's decision does not constitute serious parental neglect is the express finding that the court is unpersuaded of the overall efficacy of the proposed treatment despite the recommendations of the physicians. Thus, the court did not apply an improper legal standard in reaching its decision.

The guardian argues that the evidence compels the conclusion that the medical treatment is beneficial and that the mother's refusal constitutes jeopardy. She argues that the court's finding that the mother's refusal is rational and reasoned is contrary to the weight of the evidence and that the court plainly erred in assessing the evidence concerning the treatment of AIDS.

* * *

Viewing Dr. McIntosh's testimony as the strongest evidence offered in favor of the State's position, it falls short of compelling a finding of serious child abuse or neglect. Even though there is significant evidence from Dr. McIntosh that he believes, based on the clinical trials, his expertise in this field, and his examination of Nikolas, that Nikolas would benefit from this treatment, there is also competent evidence from Dr. McIntosh that the theories on AIDS are still evolving, that this treatment has not been given for a long period of time, that the information on effects and prognosis are being studied on the children receiving treatment and therefore the longterm effects cannot be identified and that, although he believes a cure along the same lines as the present therapies is not likely, a person could lessen the chances of getting a good response to subsequent medications because of a resistance that could be built up from the therapy in question. The State concedes that Dr. McIntosh's testimony alone is sufficient to support either factual conclusion. We agree. Thus, the court was not clearly erroneous in remaining unpersuaded that jeopardy had been established.

We emphasize that the decision required the trial court to weigh the interests of the State, the child, and the parents, and to balance the benefits and risks of treatment against the benefits and risks of declining treatment. If the child's health should change, if the treatment efficacy should be demonstrated to be better than it is now known to be, or if better treatment options should become available, that balance could shift in favor of treatment. Neither the parents nor the State should assume that the trial court's decision, affirmed by our opinion today, is necessarily the final word on treatment for Nikolas.

Notes and Questions

1. *Questions on* Nikolas E. (a) What was the basis for the mother's objection to HAART treatment for Nikolas? (b) What did the state have to show at trial to get a child protection order?

2. *Distinguishing between research and medical care.* Physicians are assumed to be acting in their patients' best interests. Researchers have a different goal—namely the discovery of scientifically useful knowledge. Sometimes, however, the line between medical care and research is hard to determine. Is a physician who promotes a new technique experimenting or providing medical care? When is research "beneficial"? How would you answer these questions with regard to the treatment of Baby Fae?

> Baby Fae was born on October 12, 1984, suffering from hypoplastic left heart syndrome, a condition where the left side of the heart is too weak to pump blood. The result is usually death. There was a surgical procedure available at the time called the Norwood procedure that had a forty percent rate of success when performed by its originator, Dr. William Norwood. Heart transplantation was also a possible treatment for this condition. Even when the Norwood Procedure was not totally successful, it could extend a child's life long enough to find a human donor heart. In the Baby Fae case, however, Dr. Leonard Bailey proposed performing a xenograft in which he would transplant a heart from a baboon to the child. The parents agreed to this. Nine days after the procedure, Dr. Bailey predicted that Baby Fae might celebrate her twentieth birthday. Baby Fae died eleven days later. Dr. Bailey and his institution received substantial criticism. Commentators questioned whether he had adequately informed the parents about the Norwood Procedure. It appears that a newborn heart was available for transplantation but that Dr. Bailey did not look for a donor heart. Also the consent form was inadequate and possibly misleading. * * *

Children as Research Subjects: Science, Ethics and Law 127 (Michael A. Grodin and Leonard H. Glantz eds., 1994). Interestingly enough, the procedure had been reviewed by the hospital and was later reviewed by federal officials for compliance with research rules. Although the consent form was criticized, the use of the procedure was not and there was no suggestion that the operation should have been tried first on consenting adults rather than on a child.

> The Baby Fae treatment is a good illustration of the substantial discretion that parents and their physician have in deciding to provide, rather than withhold, treatment for a child. Because the heart transplant was considered to be beneficial treatment rather than research, neither the physician nor the hospital felt that court approval was needed.

3. *The impact of the Baby Doe amendments.* The distinction between research and medical care in the treatment of newborns is especially problematic because physicians may feel the Baby Doe CAPTA amendments require the use of new, experimental treatments. Stephan A. Newman, Baby Doe, Congress and the States: Challenging the Federal Standard for Im-

paired Infants, 15 Am. J.L. & Med. 1 (1989). According to Professor Newman:

> The federal infant Doe rule ignores the problems posed by innovative medical treatments. If such treatments, lying in the twilight zone between pure experimentation and conventional medical therapy, present a hope of survival that is not futile (or virtually futile and inhumane), these treatments are arguably required under the rule despite any parental objection. This interpretation of the rule may seem quite plausible to a court or administrative official, particularly if medical professionals do not admit the full extent of their untested, risk-prone, uncertain and stressful interventions. Physicians' inclinations, it has often been noted, tend toward aggressive treatment. Doctors may represent their treatment choices as "conventional" rather than "experimental." Those already oriented toward medical intervention may see their decisions as "medically indicated" (in the words of the statute) rather than as personal or professional preferences for innovation or experimental rescue attempts. It is also part of human nature to justify what one wants to do by portraying it as necessary and good for others.

Id. at 36–37

4. *Additional reference.* For a critique of the federal regulations and discussion of past debates on medical research on children, see Lainie Friedman Ross, Children as Research Subjects: A Proposal to Revise the Current Federal Regulations Using a Moral Framework, 8 Stan. L. & Pol. Rev. 159 (1997).

SECTION 6.   WHO PAYS FOR THE CHILD'S MEDICAL CARE?

MADISON GENERAL HOSPITAL v. HAACK

Supreme Court of Wisconsin, 1985.
369 N.W.2d 663.

Abrahamson, Justice.

* * *

Madison General Hospital, the plaintiff, sued Debra Haack (nee Debra Hughes), Bruce Haack (Debra Haack's husband) * * * for $2,319.08, the unpaid balance of a hospital bill totaling $4,613.91. This unpaid balance was for medical services rendered to Debra Haack in connection with the birth of her infant. Medicaid had paid the portion of the bill directly related to the care of the infant.

The issue presented is whether either Debra Haack, who was an unwed minor at the time the medical expenses were incurred, or Bruce Haack, who is the father of the infant and was an unwed adult at the time the medical expenses were incurred, or both are liable for the hospital charges for the medical care of Debra Haack relating to the delivery of the infant by caesarean section and relating to postoperative treatment.

* * *

The facts giving rise to this appeal are undisputed. When Debra Hughes, accompanied by her mother, was admitted to the hospital on February 3, 1976, she was 16 years old, apparently was living with her parents, and had no financial assets of her own. She was 34 weeks pregnant and suffering from severe labor convulsions. She delivered the infant by caesarean section on February 16, 1976, and, after postoperative treatment, was released on February 22, 1976.

On April 12, 1976, Bruce Haack and Debra Hughes (hereafter referred to as Debra Haack) were married. [T]he child "thereby became legitimated and enjoy[ed] all the rights and privileges of legitimacy" as if the child had been born during the marriage of the parents.

The hospital attempted to collect from Medicaid the cost of the delivery and the cost of the care of Debra Haack, but Medicaid covered only the costs associated with care of the infant. The hospital then attempted to collect the remainder of its bill from Donald J. Hughes's health insurer. The insurer did not pay. The hospital then commenced this action to collect payment from Debra Haack, Bruce Haack, and Donald J. Hughes. The hospital did not commence action against Dorothy Hughes, Debra Haack's mother. The hospital never served Donald J. Hughes, and the suit against him was dismissed.

We will consider first Debra Haack's liability for the remaining portion of the hospital bill and then Bruce Haack's liability. Since Debra Haack's father was not served with the summons and complaint and Debra Haack's mother was not named as a defendant, the liability of Mr. and Mrs. Hughes for the medical expenses in question is not directly before the court. Mr. and Mrs. Hughes's liability is, however, relevant to a determination of Debra Haack's liability and will be considered in that context.

Debra Haack's liability. The hospital urges several theories under which Debra Haack may be held liable for payment of the medical expenses. First, the hospital asserts that Debra Haack is liable under the common law doctrine that when a minor contracts for necessaries, the minor cannot disaffirm the contract. Emergency medical services are generally considered necessaries, and this point is not in dispute in this case.

* * *

* * * In light of the circuit court's finding that the minor did not enter into an express or implied in fact contract, we conclude that the common law doctrine that a minor may be liable for necessaries furnished on the credit of the minor is not applicable here.

The essence of the hospital's argument is that Debra Haack is liable for the medical expenses under a theory of unjust enrichment, that is, a quasi-contractual obligation imposed by law. Express contracts and contracts implied in fact rest on the assent of the parties; a quasi-contractual obligation does not. A quasi-contractual obligation is imposed by law on grounds of justice and equity to prevent unjust enrichment. The law may require a person enriched by a benefit to compensate the person furnishing the benefit when it would be inequitable to allow retention of the benefit without payment.

The hospital asserts that Debra Haack received medical care necessary to save her life and the life of her infant; that she knew and appreciated that such care was necessary; that she accepted the care which the hospital was required to render, and that she has refused to pay for these benefits. These facts, argues the hospital, satisfy the elements of a cause of action in equity for unjust enrichment.

The hospital's theory of Debra Haack's liability under the doctrine of unjust enrichment, however, overlooks the fact that when a minor has not contracted for necessaries, the law has traditionally imposed a quasi-contractual liability on a minor's father, not on the minor, under the doctrine of necessaries. * * * A parent's quasi-contractual obligation, under the doctrine of necessaries, arises because a third party has fulfilled the legal obligation of the parent to support the minor. Traditionally the law imposed the duty of support for the minor on the male parent. Today the wife shares with the husband the legal duty of support for the family.

In this case Mr. and Mrs. Hughes were under a duty to provide their daughter with medical services. * * *

The hospital, however, asserts that Debra Haack is liable for payment for medical services because her parents defaulted in paying for the medical services. * * * The cases, however, are not clear in their statement of this rule or its application.[4]

* * *

Even if we were to conclude that a minor should be liable for medical expenses when a parent neglects, fails, refuses, or is unable to pay, we would conclude that the record in this case is insufficient to establish the parents' neglect, failure, refusal, or inability to pay. There is no evidence that the hospital ever sought payment from Mrs. Hughes. With regard to Mr. Hughes we know only that he apparently resided at the same address as Debra Haack at the time the medical services were rendered, that the hospital was unsuccessful in collecting payment from his health insurer, that the hospital may have mailed some bills to him, that he apparently left Wisconsin after the infant's birth, and that the hospital filed suit more than four years after the medical services had been rendered and failed to obtain service on him.

4. In Gardner v. Flowers, 529 S.W.2d 708 (Tenn.1975), for example, the Tennessee court purported to be following "what appears to be" the majority rule holding "that the inability of parents to pay for essential medical treatment for an infant renders such treatment a necessary for which the infant is liable." The cases the Gardner court cites for this proposition, however, generally deal with the failure of the person seeking recovery against the minor to prove the parents' inability to pay or with cases in which the minor's estate includes a reimbursement for medical expenses

On the basis of this record, we conclude that Debra Haack is not liable to the hospital for the medical services furnished to her. She was not a party to an express contract or to one implied in fact and therefore any rules regarding a minor's liability under a contract for necessaries are inapplicable. Her parents, not she, would be liable under the common law doctrine of necessaries or unjust enrichment. Although some jurisdictions may impose liability on a minor when a parent does not meet the obligations imposed upon them by law under the doctrine of necessaries, the record in this case does not justify allowing recovery from Debra Haack under this theory.

There is a sense of uneasiness attached to following traditional common law and concluding that Debra Haack need not pay for the medical services she received. She appears to be profiting at the expense of the hospital, which did its best for her welfare. We expressed a similar uneasiness in a prior holding that a minor who disaffirms a contract for the purchase of an item which is not a necessary may recover the purchase price without liability for use, depreciation, damage or other diminution in value. We recognize that the laws relating to the capacity of infants to contract balance society's interests in protecting the minor and the family against interests in protecting innocent creditors. Similarly the doctrine of necessaries and the various exceptions thereto make this balance. We have been unwilling to modify the traditional rules governing infants' contractual liability, saying modification is best left to the legislature. We similarly conclude in this case that the balance made in the common law rules regarding the immunity and the quasi-contractual liability of a minor for necessaries should not be modified at this time.

Bruce Haack's liability. We turn now to the question of Bruce Haack's liability for the medical expenses incurred by Debra Haack at the time of the birth of the infant. Presented with the hospital's accounting and the nature of the Medicaid reimbursement, the circuit court found that the expenses at issue were for the care of Debra Haack, and not for the care of the infant.

* * *

* * * [T]he issue is whether there are any grounds under which liability may be imposed on him for Debra Haack's medical expenses. In deciding this question we consider two fact situations that "might have occurred," and the legal consequences that would have followed from each of them. First, Bruce and Debra Haack might have married prior to the birth of their infant. In this event, Bruce Haack probably would have been liable for the expenses under the doctrine of necessaries.* * *

Second, Bruce Haack and Debra Hughes might not have married, in which case Debra Hughes could have instituted paternity proceedings against Bruce Haack. In 1976 the circuit court would have been required to order Bruce Haack "to pay all expenses incurred for lying-in and attendance of the mother during pregnancy...." * * * The public policy underlying these paternity statutes is that the father of the infant should bear responsibility for expenses incurred as a result of a pregnancy in which he participated.

Considering the policies underlying both the doctrine of necessaries and the paternity statute, we conclude that it would be inequitable and against public policy to allow Bruce Haack to escape liability for Debra Haack's medical care arising from her pregnancy merely because the marriage took place after the birth of the infant instead of before the birth.

* * *

Notes and Questions

1. *Questions about* Haack. (a) Under what circumstances would Debra Haack be liable for her own medical bills incurred while she was a minor? (b) On what basis would the court hold the parents of Debra Haack (a minor) responsible for her medical bills?

2. *The child's obligation.* As discussed in Section 1, above, most states allow minors to consent to specified types of medical care. The minor's agreement may also serve as a contract for payment for the medical services that the minor may not disaffirm. Parents might be obligated to pay for the treatment as well, but some medical consent statutes obligate parents or guardians to pay only if they consented to the treatment. See, e.g., Mo. Rev. Stat. § 431.062.

What is the purpose of statutes that do not relieve nonconsenting parents or guardians of obligation to pay for the treatment? What purpose underlies statutes which obligate parents or guardians to pay only if they have consented to the treatment?

3. *State responsibility for payment.* When parents are indigent, should the state or the treating physician be able to decide what treatment will be available for a child with a fatal illness? Is there a constitutional basis for requiring the state to pay for medical care for children or is the obligation purely statutory? See Miller v. Whitburn, 10 F.3d 1315 (7th Cir.1993)(The state may deny payment for an organ transplant that has been classified by the state as experimental).

4. *Insurance.* Many children go without medical care because the children have no health insurance coverage and their parents cannot afford to pay for medical care, even though most of the parents are employed. In 1997, 15% of all children (10.7 million) had no health insurance, public or private. Hispanic children are less likely to have insurance than white, non-Hispanic or black children. Federal Interagency Forum on Child and Family Statistics, America's Children: Key National Indicators of Well–Being 18 (1999).

The lack of health insurance results in multiple problems. Children without health insurance "are more likely to suffer from health problems because they have fewer physician visits each year, and they are less likely to receive adequate preventive services and immunizations. A majority of uninsured children with asthma and one-third of those with recurring ear infections never see a doctor during the year. Poor health and misdiagnosed or untreated conditions can interfere with a child's ability to attend school regularly or to participate in recreational or other social activities that enhance development." Annie E. Casey Foundation, Kids Count Data Book, 1999.

Is the present allocation of health care resources inefficient and unfair to children? According to Professors Kopelman and Palumbo:

> Reliance on choice and market forces has already left many children in the United States without basic health services. * * * In particular, children from poor and working poor families bear the worst of such inequalities. * * *American children living in low-income families get sicker more and stay sicker longer. They are two to three times more likely than children in high-income homes to be of low birth weight, to get asthma and bacterial meningitis, to lack immunizations and to suffer from lead poisoning; poor children are also three to four times as likely as other children to become seriously ill and get multiple illnesses when they become sick. Moreover, the main health problems of children in the U.S. arise from a failure to provide basic and inexpensive care for children, including their allergies, asthma, dental pathology, hearing loss, vision impairments and many chronic disorders.

Loretta M. Kopelman and Michael G. Palumbo, The U.S. Health Delivery System: Inefficient and Unfair to Children, 23 Am. J. L. and Med. 319 (1997). See also, Sara Rosenbaum, Rationing Without Justice: Children and the American Health System, 140 U. Pa. L. Rev. 1859 (1992).

5. *Medicaid*. Medicaid (Title XIX of the Social Security Act, 42 U.S.C. §§ 1396a) is a cooperative federal-state public assistance program that pays for "necessary medical services" for eligible children of low income families, described as "categorically needy." Parents of Medicaid eligible children often are employed, but their wages are low. A state need not participate in Medicaid, but if it chooses to do so it must comply with federal Medicaid. To be eligible for federal funds, a state must have a federally approved plan for providing medical assistance, and the plan must include certain categories of medical services for qualified recipients. The state plan must contain "reasonable standards" for determining eligibility for aid and must provide methods and procedures "necessary to safeguard against unnecessary utilization" of care. Unfortunately an estimated 4.7 million Medicaid-eligible children are not enrolled in Medicaid. Thomas M. Selden et al., Medicaid's Problem Children: Eligible but Not Enrolled, 17 Health Affairs 192 (1998). Reasons for this lack of coverage include the complexity of the application process and regulations and the demeaning effect of having to apply for a welfare benefit.

For a brief but comprehensive overview of the Medicaid provisions that affect children, see Donald T. Kramer, Legal Rights of Children § 32.01–32.23 (2nd ed., 1994). Kramer notes that the Medicaid statutes and regulations are "complex and convoluted" and cites a section that contains one continuous sentence, with 62 subsections, that spans 21 pages of the United States Code "before it finally crescendos to the end with a period." (Id. § 32.03 n.31).

6. *Children's Health Insurance Program*. In spite of expansions in Medicaid, an estimated 10.7 million children were uninsured in 1997, as note 4 mentions. These uninsured children are children of the working poor, whose

parents earn too little to afford private health insurance, but too much to qualify for Medicaid.

In response to the problem of uninsured children, the federal government enacted the Children's Health Insurance Program under Title XXI of the Social Security Act in 1997. 42 U.S.C.A. § 1397aa. This federal program, known as "CHIP," was enacted to help states create and expand insurance programs for low income children. The program allocates funds to each state based on its share of the nation's uninsured children with family incomes below 200 percent of the poverty level. The program does provide for exceptions to the 200 percent eligibility. The states that wish to participate may expand Medicaid, create or expand a non-Medicaid program, or use a combination of both. Each state must submit a plan that sets forth how it will use the funds to provide health care assistance to needy children. CHIP has great potential in helping poor children, however, the states are still faced with the same outreach and enrollment challenges encountered by the Medicaid program. For a discussion on how the states are responding to CHIP, see Brian K Bruen and Frank Ullman, Children's Health Insurance Programs: "Where States Are, Where They Are Headed," New Federalism Series (Urban Institute), A–20, 1: 1–9 (1998).

Chapter 9

FINANCIAL RESPONSIBILITY AND CONTROL

SECTION 1. THE CHILD SUPPORT OBLIGATION

A parent's child support obligation has a variety of sources. A child support claim can be part of a divorce action, a paternity action, a neglect action, a criminal proceeding, a merchant's suit for reimbursement for necessaries furnished a child, or a state suit for reimbursement for welfare expenditures. In addition, some states have family expense statutes that are similar to the necessaries doctrine and allow creditors to sue parents for goods provided to children. This Chapter begins with Haxton v. Haxton, a decision that presents the historical development of the child support obligation in the United States and describes its complexity. The Chapter then considers the scope of individual and government responsibility for supporting children, the child's responsibilities to obey in exchange for support, and problems in formulating and enforcing child support awards. The final sections of this Chapter address financial responsibility and control in relation to contract, property and tort law and statutes of limitation.

A. *Historical Background*

HAXTON v. HAXTON
Supreme Court of Oregon, 1985
705 P.2d 721.

ROBERTS, JUSTICE.

The issue is whether ORS 109.010 provides a cause of action for support against his parent for an adult who is mentally handicapped to the extent that his handicap prevents him from securing employment. That statute provides:

> "Parents are bound to maintain their children who are poor and unable to work to maintain themselves; and children are bound to maintain their parents in like circumstances."

The parents were married on December 20, 1958, and were divorced in August 1978. The decree of dissolution awarded custody of the couple's four children to mother and provided for support payments by father for all four children. Two children are over the age of 18 and father's support obligations for these two children have terminated. The parents have a minor son, for whom father is currently providing support. Another child, James, a party to this litigation, is mentally retarded. At the time of trial, James was 20 years old, residing with his mother, unemployed and not attending school. The trial court found from expert testimony that James' disability prevented him from securing employment.

Mother first filed an action to modify the decree of dissolution to increase the support payments for the minor son and to require father to provide support for James. Two months later, mother filed a separate action for James' support in her own name, and later amended the complaint to an action in James' own name with mother as guardian ad litem. Both actions were consolidated for trial. * * *

* * *

* * * Both parties agree that the trial court's authority, if any, for the award must be found in ORS 109.010.

Father argues that "children," as used in this statute, means minor children, that is, those under the age of 18. He asserts that, although the statute may be a codification of the common law duty imposed on parents to support their children, the duty extended only to minor children. * * *

Mother contends that the word children connotes a relationship, not a temporary status by virtue of age. She points out that, by statute, the obligation of support is reciprocal. Children are both beneficiaries of the parents' duty and providers of support to their parents. Mother reasons from this that the term children logically cannot be limited to unemancipated minors. * * *

B. Origins of Familial Obligations of Support

The rights and responsibilities of family members toward each other are regulated by many of our statutes. Parental support obligations toward minor children after dissolution are addressed in [various statutes]. The criminal code prohibits child abandonment and neglect by those adults, most often the parents, with a responsibility to maintain the child. Our laws punish a parent's failure to support a child financially. * * *

Of particular relevance to the present case is the development of two civil statutes, ORS 416.061 and ORS 109.010, both of which address the duty of close family members, defined differently in the two statutory schemes, to support indigent relatives. Both statutes set forth a similar duty of support. However, their historical antecedents, purposes and development indicate that these statutes were enacted to address separate social concerns. ORS chapter 416, the relative responsibility law, has its origins in the Elizabethan poor laws of 1601. These laws constituted one of the first systems of public welfare for the poor. ORS 109.010 represents private familial obligations that developed in America independently of England.

C. Statutory Duty of Support

The Elizabethan poor laws, including the provision requiring family members to support their needy relatives, provided a model for the systems of public support found in most American jurisdictions, including our own and those of New York. The Elizabethan poor laws came into being in response to the demise of the power and wealth of religious institutions, which has assumed the burden to support the poor, and the subsequent unrest manifested in widespread vagrancy and begging that unassuaged poverty engendered. Professor tenBroek writes that the poor laws culminated the process of shifting the burden to alleviate poverty "from the ecclesiastical, private and voluntary to the civil, public and compulsory."[a]

In the Elizabethan system, support of the poor was achieved by taxation and was regulated at the county level. As a corollary, these statutes included features intended to reduce the burden on the public treasury. For example, the poor laws mandated forced labor at fixed wages for all paupers capable of working. They relocated the poor to the parishes of their birth and limited their mobility. They provided criminal sanctions for vagrancy, begging and refusing to work if able. Finally, they compelled financially able relatives to contribute to the support of family members who were public charges. * * *

This law found its way into the American statutes regulating public support of the poor * * *.

D. Common Law Duty of Support

While it is doubtful that English common law recognized enforceable familial obligations of support apart from the Elizabethan poor laws,[4] such was not the case in the United States. Early American cases recognized the parents', specifically the father's, duty to support his children. The duty of support, which was examined in a variety of contexts, was often said to exist as a matter of common law and independently of statute. See Hillsborough v. Deering, 4 N.H. 86, 95 (1827) (child's right to support from parent derives from common law and exists independently of statute); Godfrey v. Hays, 6 Ala. 501, 502

---

a. Jacobus tenBroek, California's Dual System of Family Law: Its Origin, Development and Present Status, Part I, 16 Stan. L. Rev. 257, 282 (1964).

4. Early commentators speak of the parents' natural duty to support their children. 1 Blackstone, Commentaries on the Laws of England, (Cooley ed 1899). However, there is little indication that the English common law conferred a legally enforceable duty between parents and children, or other relatives, to support and maintain each other. See Field, The Legal Relations of Infants, Parent and Child, and Guardian and Ward 57 (1888); Browne, Elements of the Law of Domestic Relations 72 (1883).

(1844) (father obliged to support son and in exchange entitled to earnings of son); McGoon v. Irvin, 1 Pin. 526, 532 (Wis.1845) (parents have legal obligation to maintain and support children; must reimburse third person for necessaries provided to child); Thompson and Waters v. Dorsey, 4 Md.Ch. 149, 151 (1853) (father's estate must reimburse third person who supplied necessaries to child because parents are bound to maintain their children.] * * *

* * * [One case] made explicit reference to the difference between the English common law, which did not recognize a parental duty of support, and the American common law, which recognized such a duty. The court noted the uncertainty or nonexistence of the English common law duty but was "not prepared to say" that this rule has been adopted in this country * * *. [Another case] acknowledged the minority American position, similar to England's, that no duty of support existed outside of statute but applied the "settled" state law that such a duty existed and was enforceable.

All cases involved minor children. However, * * * [another] elaborated in dictum that the duty of support should also extend into the child's adulthood "if from physical debility and impaired health, the boy is unable to earn a livelihood, and must depend upon others for support * * *." * * * [And another case] reasoned that the parental obligation of support is not grounded in the duty of the child to serve the parent but on the inability of the child to care for itself. Therefore, the parent has a "legal as well as * * * moral duty" to support his child "when [she is] unable, from infancy, disease or accident, to earn her own necessary support * * *."

* * *

II. *Codification of Familial Obligations of Support*

* * *

These two separate duties of familial support appeared in the first code of Oregon. When the code commission presented its report on the draft code to the Oregon Territorial Legislature in 1853, the duty now found in ORS 109.010 was placed among the civil laws, and the relative responsibility law, now ORS 416.061, was set forth under the heading "Support of the Poor" * * *. The laws were enacted in this format. The placement of two duties of familial support in different sections of the code, one public in nature, the other civil and private, mirrors the independent development of the duties of support in the United States.

The relative responsibility statute, and the overall scheme of public support for the poor of which it is a part have been amended throughout the years but the basic premise that certain relatives are liable to relieve the public burden of support of the poor has remained unchanged.* * * [D]espite the change in form and structure from the early Elizabethan poor laws, the purpose of relieving the burden for support of the poor through enforcement actions against relatives brought by the government on behalf of the public remains the same.

* * *

C. Conclusion

A duty of support appears among our earliest laws. No limitations were placed on the enforcement of that duty when it was first enacted, nor have any been imposed with subsequent amendments. We hold that a statutory duty of parental support exists and may be enforced in a direct action by this mentally handicapped adult child against his parent. The trial court below properly allowed the child to maintain an action against his father and awarded support.

Notes and Questions

1. *Questions about* Haxton. (a) As *Haxton* notes, the poor laws developed in England which imposed no common law duty to support a child. Why were the poor laws necessary in the United States? (b) If James' father had stopped paying support and James had received welfare benefits from the state, is it likely that the state could proceed against the father for reimbursement for the welfare benefits?

2. *Government assistance.* Should parents be required to support disabled children past the age of majority or should such support be a public expense? If a disabled adult is eligible for government assistance, such as federal Supplemental Security Income (SSI) that provides assistance to adults who are unable to work, should a parent's support obligation be reduced proportionately? No, according to the Supreme Court of Mississippi, reasoning that it was sound policy not to burden the public, when the parents were able to provide for the child's support. Hammett v. Woods, 602 So.2d 825 (Miss. 1992). What policy arguments would you make in rebuttal?

Minor children are also eligible for SSI benefits, but the eligibility requirements have been the subject of litigation and controversy. See, e.g., Sullivan v. Zebley, 493 U.S. 521 (1990) (Department of Health and Human Services Regulations for determining if a child was "disabled" for SSI eligibility were too restrictive and violated the Social Security Act.)

3. *Post secondary support and college education.* How long should parents be required to support children who could be self-supporting? At twenty-one, most children have completed high school and many have nearly completed college. Children are likely either to have entered, or to be on the verge of entering, a trade or occupation. At eighteen, on the other hand, a child might not even have completed high school. Many states have enacted statutes that extend the parental support obligation beyond eighteen, particularly when the child is pursuing higher education. In effect, these statutes define emancipation for support purposes. See, e.g., Mo. Rev. Stat. Ann. § 452.340.

a. Unmarried parents. A number of jurisdictions require divorced parents not only to provide support, but to pay for a child's post-secondary education if they are financially able to do so. More recently, never-married parents also have been required to provide support for a child over the age of majority who is in college. See, e.g., Jones v. Williams, 592 So.2d 608

(Ala.1991) ("We further note that the characterization of Darlene as an illegitimate child is irrelevant to the disposition of this case. It is firmly established in this State that parental obligations do not differ with regard to whether the parents of the child are married.")

b. *Married Parents.* Should married parents also be expected to provide for a child's college education? Could the following rationale be used to allow children to bring a support action against their married parents?

> In the past, a college education was reserved for the elite, but the vital impulse of egalitarianism has inspired the creation of a wide variety of educational institutions that provide post-secondary education for practically everyone. State, county and community colleges, as well as some private colleges and vocational schools provide educational opportunities at reasonable costs. Some parents cannot pay, some can pay in part, and still others can pay the entire cost of higher education for their children. In general, financially capable parents should contribute to the higher education of children who are qualified students. In appropriate circumstances, parental responsibility includes the duty to assure children of a college and even of a postgraduate education such as law school.

> In evaluating the claim for contribution toward the cost of higher education, courts should consider all relevant factors, including (1) whether the parent, if still living with the child, would have contributed toward the costs of the requested higher education; (2) the effect of the background, values and goals of the parent on the reasonableness of the expectation of the child for higher education; (3) the amount of the contribution sought by the child for the cost of higher education; (4) the ability of the parent to pay that cost; (5) the relationship of the requested contribution to the kind of school or course of study sought by the child; (6) the financial resources of both parents; (7) the commitment to and aptitude of the child for the requested education; (8) the financial resources of the child, including assets owned individually or held in custodianship or trust; (9) the ability of the child to earn income during the school year or on vacation; (10) the availability of financial aid in the form of college grants and loans; (11) the child's relationship to the paying parent, including mutual affection and shared goals as well as responsiveness to parental advice and guidance; and (12) the relationship of the education requested to any prior training and to the overall long-range goals of the child.

Newburgh v. Arrigo, 443 A.2d 1031 (N.J.1982).

Constitutional issues. The Pennsylvania Supreme Court has held that a statute allowing post-majority support orders for education costs of children who were not in intact families, violated equal protection under the Fourteenth Amendment because it treated "similarly situated young adults, i.e. those in need of financial assistance," differently based on the marital status of their parents without a rational reason. There was a thoughtful dissent. Curtis v. Kline, 666 A.2d 265 (Pa.1995). But see Marriage of Kohring, 999 S.W.2d 228 (Mo.1999) (statute permitting child support awards for college expenses for children of divorced or unmarried parents did not violate equal protection).

4. Inheritance. Should the parent's obligation to support a child continue past the parent's death? Despite the increased emphasis on child support collection, parents may disinherit their minor children in all states but Louisiana, which follows the civil law tradition of allowing disinheritance only for cause. A surviving, disinherited spouse may receive a forced share of the estate, but in these days of multiple marriages and single parenthood, the widow might not be the mother of all the testator's children and hence would have no obligation to support them. When a parent dies intestate, a surviving spouse and the decedent's children typically receive the estate under intestate succession laws, but children take equally, without regard to age. Why could this be unfair to minor children?

Should inheritance laws provide for support of all minor children or at least for minor children who do not live with both parents? When a parent is paying child support should courts be authorized to order the payor to purchase life insurance or provide some other security for payment of support for the duration of the child's minority? Some courts have continued the support obligation after the obligor's death, sometimes by finding a contractual obligation in a separation agreement that promises support until the child reaches the age of majority.

For a comprehensive discussion of existing law and proposals for reform, see Ralph C. Brashier, Disinheritance and the Modern Family, 45 Case W. L. Rev. 83 (1994), and Deborah A. Batts, I Didn't Ask to be Born: The American Law of Disinheritance and a Proposal for Change to a System of Protected Inheritance, 41 Hastings L. J. 1197 (1990). (Professor Batts' article also discusses the forced heirship and family maintenance systems used in a number of foreign countries.)

B. Scope of Obligation

1. Biological Relationship as the Obligation's Source

STATE EX REL. HERMESMANN v. SEYER

Supreme Court of Kansas, 1993.
847 P.2d 1273.

HOLMES, CHIEF JUSTICE:

* * *

The facts, as best we can determine them from an inadequate record, do not appear to be seriously in dispute.

Colleen Hermesmann routinely provided care for Shane Seyer as a baby sitter or day care provider during 1987 and 1988. The two began a sexual relationship at a time when Colleen was 16 years old and Shane was only 12. The relationship continued over a period of several months and the parties engaged in sexual intercourse on an average of a couple of times a week. As a result, a daughter, Melanie, was born to Colleen on May 30, 1989. At the time of the conception of the child, Shane was 13 years old and Colleen was 17. Colleen applied for and received financial assistance through the Aid to Families with Dependent Children program (ADC) from SRS [The Kansas Department of Social and Rehabilitation Services].

On January 15, 1991, the district attorney's office of Shawnee County filed a petition requesting that Colleen Hermesmann be adjudicated as a juvenile offender for engaging in the act of sexual intercourse with a child under the age of 16, Shanandoah (Shane) Seyer, to whom she was not married, in violation of K.S.A.1992 Supp. 21–3503. Thereafter, Colleen Hermesmann entered into a plea agreement with the district attorney's office, wherein she agreed to stipulate to the lesser offense of contributing to a child's misconduct. On September 11, 1991, the juvenile court accepted the stipulation, and adjudicated Colleen Hermesmann to be a juvenile offender.

On March 8, 1991, SRS filed a petition on behalf of Colleen Hermesmann, alleging that Shane Seyer was the father of Colleen's minor daughter, Melanie. The petition also alleged that SRS had provided benefits through the ADC program to Colleen on behalf of the child and that Colleen had assigned support rights due herself and her child to SRS. The petition requested that the court determine paternity and order Shane to reimburse SRS for all assistance expended by SRS on Melanie's behalf.* * **

* * *

The district judge, upon judicial review of the hearing officer's order, determined that Shane was the father of Melanie Hermesmann and owed a duty to support his child.* * *

The court found that the issue of Shane's consent was irrelevant and ordered Shane to pay child support of $50 per month. The court also granted SRS a joint and several judgment against Shane and Colleen in the amount of $7,068, for assistance provided by the ADC program on behalf of Melanie through February 1992. The judgment included medical and other birthing expenses as well as assistance paid after Melanie's birth. * * *

* * *

Shane asserts as his first issue that, because he was a minor under the age of 16 at the time of conception, he was legally incapable of consenting to sexual intercourse and therefore cannot be held legally responsible for the birth of his child. Shane cites no case law to directly support this proposition. Instead, he argues that Colleen Hermesmann sexually assaulted him, that he was the victim of the crime of statutory rape, and that the criminal statute of indecent liberties with a child should be applied to hold him incapable of consenting to the act.

What used to be commonly called "statutory rape" is now included in the statutory crime of indecent liberties with a child. The statute, K.S.A.1992 Supp. 21–3503, reads in pertinent part:

> "(1) Indecent liberties with a child is engaging in any of the following acts with a child who is under 16 years of age:

(a) Sexual intercourse."

Both the administrative hearing officer and the district court determined that whether Shane consented to sexual intercourse was not a relevant issue in a civil paternity and child support proceeding.

SRS maintains that Shane was not the victim of the crime of statutory rape. SRS points out that while Colleen was originally charged in juvenile proceedings with a violation of K.S.A.1992 Supp. 21–3503, she later stipulated to a lesser charge of contributing to a child's misconduct. While SRS is technically correct in asserting that Colleen was never found guilty of violating 21–3503, its entire case is based upon the fact that Shane is the father of the child. As it is undisputed that Shane was under the age of 16 when conception occurred, and throughout the entire time the sexual relationship continued, the argument of SRS is specious at best. The admitted facts established, without doubt, all of the elements necessary to prove a crime under K.S.A.1992 Supp. 21–3503(1)(a), and the fact that Colleen was able to plea bargain for a lesser offense does not preclude Shane from alleging he was a "victim" of statutory rape.

Although the issue of whether an underage alleged "victim" of a sex crime can be held liable for support of a child born as a result of such crime is one of first impression in Kansas, other jurisdictions have addressed the question.

In In re Paternity of J.L.H., (Wis.1989), J.J.G. appealed from a summary judgment in a paternity proceeding determining that he was the father of J.L.H. and ordering him to pay child support equal to 17 percent of his gross income. J.J.G. was 15 years old when the child was conceived. On appeal, he asserted that the child's mother, L.H., sexually assaulted him, contrary to Wis.Stat. § 940.225(2)(e) (1979) (the Wisconsin statutory rape statute in effect at the time), and that, as a minor, he was incapable of consent under the sexual assault law. The court rejected this argument and stated:* * *

> "If voluntary intercourse results in parenthood, then for purposes of child support, the parenthood is voluntary. This is true even if a fifteen-year old boy's parenthood resulted from a sexual assault upon him within the meaning of the criminal law."

Although the question of whether the intercourse with Colleen was "voluntary," as the term is usually understood, is not specifically before us, it was brought out in oral argument before this court that the sexual relationship between Shane and his baby sitter, Colleen, started when he was only 12 years old and lasted over a period of several months. At no time did Shane register any complaint to his parents about the sexual liaison with Colleen.

In Schierenbeck v. Minor, (Colo.1961), Schierenbeck, a 16-year-old boy, appealed the adjudication in a dependency proceeding that he was the father of a child born to a 20–year-old woman. On appeal, Schierenbeck cited a Colorado criminal statute which defined rape in the third degree by a female of a male person under the age of 18 years. In discussing the relevance of the criminal statute, the court stated:

"Certain it is that his [Schierenbeck's] assent to the illicit act does not exclude commission of the statutory crime, but it has nothing to do with assent as relating to progeny. His youth is basic to the crime; it is not a factor in the question of whether he is the father of [the child].

" 'The putative father may be liable in bastardy proceedings for the support and maintenance of his child, even though he is a minor.... If Schierenbeck is adjudged to be the father of [the child] after a proper hearing and upon sufficient evidence, he should support [the child] under this fundamental doctrine." * * *

The Kansas Parentage Act specifically contemplates minors as fathers and makes no exception for minor parents regarding their duty to support and educate their child. * * *

* * *

As previously stated, Shane does not contest that he is the biological father of the child. As a father, he has a common-law duty, as well as a statutory duty, to support his minor child. This duty applies equally to parents of children born out of wedlock.

Under the statutory and common law of this state, Shane owes a duty to support his minor child.* * * We conclude that the issue of consent to sexual activity under the criminal statutes is irrelevant in a civil action to determine paternity and for support of the minor child of such activity.* * *

For Shane's next issue, he asserts that it is not sound public policy for a court to order a youth to pay child support for a child conceived during the crime of indecent liberties with a child when the victim was unable to consent to the sexual intercourse. He claims that while the Kansas Parentage Act creates a State interest in the welfare of dependent relatives, the policy behind the Parentage Act is not to force a minor, who is unable to consent to sexual intercourse, to support a child born from the criminal act.

* * *

This State's interest in requiring minor parents to support their children overrides the State's competing interest in protecting juveniles from improvident acts, even when such acts may include criminal activity on the part of the other parent. Considering the three persons directly involved, Shane, Colleen, and Melanie, the interests of Melanie are superior, as a matter of public policy, to those of either or both of her parents. This minor child, the only truly innocent party, is entitled to support from both her parents regardless of their ages.

As his third issue, Shane asserts that the district court erred in finding he and Colleen were jointly and severally liable for the child support. He argues that, as Colleen was the perpetrator of the crime of statutory rape, she alone should be held responsible for the consequences of the act * * *. * * *

* * *

* * * Nowhere does the law in this state suggest that the mother's "wrongdoing" can operate as a setoff or bar to a father's liability for child support. Under the facts as presented to this court, the district court properly held that Shane owes a duty of support to Melanie and properly ordered that Shane and Colleen were jointly and severally liable for the monies previously paid by SRS.

* * *

The judgment of the district court is affirmed.

Notes and Questions

1. Should Shane be held responsible for child support if Colleen coerced him into sexual relations? If Colleen had been an adult and had been convicted of statutory rape?

2. What if Colleen had tricked Shane into having unprotected sexual intercourse? See, e.g., Pamela P. v. Frank S., 449 N.E.2d 713 (N.Y.1983) (father alleged that mother misrepresented her use of contraception, but was held liable for support; both parties were adults). Does the tricked party have any legal recourse against the other parent?

3. How long must Shane support his child? Should the obligation be tolled until Shane reaches the age of majority? Should the infant's grandparents be held liable? Some states impose a support obligation on grandparents if both parents are underage. See, e.g., Mo. Stat. § 210.847.

4. Could Shane and Colleen have entered into an agreement that released Shane from financial responsibility for the child and terminated his parental rights? See Casbar v. Dicanio, 666 So.2d 1028 (Fla.Dist.Ct.App.1996) (parties may not contract away the minor child's right to seek support; parental rights termination must be according to statutory requirements, not by private agreement.)

BRAD MICHAEL L. v. LEE D.

Court of Appeals of Wisconsin, 1997.
564 N.W.2d 354.

SCHUDSON, JUDGE.

* * *

I. FACTUAL BACKGROUND

Brad was born to Catherine L., on November 7, 1977. Catherine was unmarried at the time and Brad's paternity was never established. In 1992, however, Catherine, concerned about Brad's potential college costs, wrote to Lee informing him that he was Brad's father and asking that his "name be placed on the birth certificate as his father." She wrote:

I love Brad very much and want the best for him. I plan on him attending college. I do work but don't make enough to afford college. I'm not asking you for any money, please know that. I tried to enroll him on my tribal roll (Menominee) so that he would be eligible for grants for college. Unfortunately he doesn't have enough Menominee blood to qualify. I want to try to enroll him on your (Stockbridge) tribal roll.

After receiving no response from Lee, Catherine contacted Milwaukee County's Child Support Enforcement office. Catherine learned that the statute of limitations barred her and the State from bringing a paternity action, but Brad, under § 893.88, Stats., could do so. The Legal Aid Society of Milwaukee as guardian ad litem, then filed Brad's paternity action.

After blood tests established a 99.96% probability of Lee's paternity, he admitted his paternity but testified that he had had no knowledge of Brad's existence. Ultimately, the parties stipulated that Lee had not known of Brad for the first fifteen years of his life. In the fifteen years since Brad's birth, Lee had married and fathered two children. With his wife, he had successfully maintained a farm and logging business.

The trial court ordered Lee to pay $500 monthly for future support. The trial court order further provided that "[t]he child support order may be later modified ... to pay for Brad's subsequent education if Brad's academic performance and attitude warrant." The trial court, however, denied past support concluding that application of § 767.51(4), Stats., would violate the *Ex Post Facto* Clause of the United States Constitution and, further, would be unfair to Lee because he had not known of Brad and had had no opportunity to develop a relationship with him.

* * *

III.   PAST CHILD SUPPORT–AUTHORITY

* * *

* * * The statute in no way suggests that the limitation is further qualified by a condition that the father know of the child's birth. Thus, if § 767.51(4) applies to support for children born before its enactment, Lee would be responsible for Brad's support for all years following his birth, whether or not Lee knew of his birth.

* * *

We disagree with the trial court's conclusion that retroactive application of § 767.51(4), Stats., violates Lee's protection against *ex post facto* laws. * * * As the supreme court recently reiterated, however, "It is well established that the constitutional prohibition on ex post facto laws applies only to penal statutes." * * *

Moreover, the general rule requiring prospective application of substantive legislation is to ensure that informed people can conduct themselves according to legal expectations and requirements. Lee, aside from asserting his lack of knowledge of Brad, cannot claim that he could not conduct himself according to law. Even before the enactment of § 767.51(4), Stats., Wisconsin law required support payment from the time of a child's birth, without any condition connected to a father's knowledge of the birth * * *

Thus, the trial court decision was simply incorrect in stating that "[i]t goes against the basic concepts of justice to impose liability on an individual where, from the time the action accrued to the time the action was filed, the individual was not liable." Lee always *was liable*; he just did not know of his liability.

* * *

IV. PAST CHILD SUPPORT–FACTOR

Brad next argues that the trial court erred in deviating from the § 767.51(5), Stats., percentage standards by considering an impermissible factor—that Lee, because of lack of knowledge of Brad, "was not," in the trial court's words, "given the opportunity to provide for the child nor to visit with the child." Brad is correct.

Section 767.51(5), Stats., specifies the factors a trial court must consider when deviating from the child support percentage standard. The factors are:

(a) The needs of the child.

The physical, mental and emotional health needs of the child, including any costs for health insurance * * *

(b) The standard of living and circumstances of the parents, * * *

(c) The relative financial means of the parents.

(d) The earning capacity of each parent, based on each parent's education, training and work experience and based on the availability of work in or near the parent's community.

(e) The need and capacity of the child for education, including higher education.

(f) The age of the child.

(g) The financial resources and the earning ability of the child.

(gm) Any physical custody arrangement ordered or decided upon.

(gp) Extraordinary travel expenses incurred in exercising the right to periods of physical placement.

(h) The responsibility of the parents for the support of others.

(i) The value of services contributed by the custodial parent.

(im) The best interests of the child.

(j) Any other factors which the court in each case determines are relevant to the best interests of the child.

Although a trial court has discretion to deviate from the percentage standard when setting past support, it does not have discretion to ignore the statutorily specified factors on which it may base such a deviation, or to substitute others. * * *

* * *

We understand the trial court's equitable concerns, given Lee's lack of knowledge of Brad. Indeed, his lack of knowledge for fifteen years may very well have resulted in various life-style decisions that, in turn, affected Lee's "standard of living and circumstances," "relative financial means," "earning capacity," and "responsibility ... for the support of others". To acknowledge that such factors must be considered, however, is not to say that Lee's lack of knowledge and resulting inability to visit and provide for Brad, standing alone, may justify a deviation from the percentage standards. As Brad correctly argues:

There is nothing in [§] 767.51(5), Stats.[,] limiting a father's past support liability to the period beginning on the day he learned that he was the child's father. The child cannot be held responsible nor should the child be punished simply because the father was not aware of his child's birth nor because the paternity action was not begun earlier. * * *

* * *

VII. CONCLUSION

Accordingly, we affirm the order of paternity but remand for further proceedings to properly determine past support for the approximate fifteen years preceding the paternity action, and "future" support for the approximate three years from the commencement of that action to the time of Brad's adulthood.

* * *

Questions

What was Catherine's goal when she contacted the Child Support Enforcement Office? When Brad was born, should his mother have been required to identify Brad's father and to petition for child support? Should she be required to do so if Brad received welfare benefits from the state?

2. *Stepparents and In Loco Parentis*

COMMONWEALTH EX REL. McNUTT v. McNUTT
Superior Court of Pennsylvania, 1985.
496 A.2d 816.

DEL SOLE, JUDGE:

* * *

James McNutt married Florence McNutt, the Appellee, on December 28, 1969. At the time of the marriage, Florence McNutt had one child, Melissa, who was two months old. Florence was Melissa's natural mother but James was not her natural father. The whereabouts of the natural father are unknown. The parties had a child during the marriage, Martin, born in 1973. In 1974 or 1975, the parties visited a lawyer to discuss the possibility of James McNutt adopting Melissa, but Mr. McNutt did not proceed with the adoption. At the time of the parties' divorce in 1977, James McNutt agreed to pay $150 a month for the support "of their minor child". Neither Melissa's nor Martin's name appears in this separation agreement. The Appellant continues to visit both children after the divorce and Melissa continues to call him "Daddy". In 1982, Florence McNutt brought a complaint in support, seeking to increase support payments, arguing that the Appellant's payments were for both children, not just for Martin. The trial court found that the Appellant had acted in loco parentis toward Melissa and was therefore responsible for her support. McNutt does not appeal the trial court's support order for Martin in the amount of $150 a month but he appeals that part of the order requiring him to pay $75 a month in favor of Melissa on the grounds that he is not her father and therefore is not liable for her support.

The trial court found that the Appellant acted in loco parentis both before and after the dissolution of the marriage and this is a finding of fact we will not disturb. We do not agree however that the Appellant's past and continued love and devotion to his former stepchild carry with it the duty to financially support Melissa.[1] This would be carrying the common law concept of in loco parentis further than we are willing to go. There is authority in other jurisdictions for the proposition that a stepparent who stands in loco parentis may be held liable for the support of a child during the marriage. However, this obligation does not survive the dissolution of the marriage of the child's natural parent and stepparent. The general rule is that no legal duty rests upon the stepparent to support after the termination of the marriage.

If we were to hold that a stepparent acting in loco parentis would be held liable for support even after the dissolution of the marriage then all persons who gratuitously assume parental duties for a time could be held legally responsible for a child's support. It is not uncommon for a grandparent, an aunt or uncle or an older sibling to assume responsibilities for parenting when the natural parents are absent. These acts of generosity should not be discouraged by creating a law which would require anyone who begins such a relationship to continue financial support until the child is eighteen years old.

The Appellant has continued his caring relationship with Melissa even though his marriage to her mother has ended. He does not assume the benefit however, of claiming her as a dependent on his tax return. Nor would he, under the intestate laws of Pennsylvania, share in

---

1. A stepfather, by definition, is the "husband of one's mother." Since Mr. McNutt is no longer the husband of Melis- sa's mother, he is no longer her stepfather. See Black's Law Dictionary.

Melissa's estate if she were to die while she is a minor. We cannot extend the law so far as to hold a former stepparent financially responsible for a child whom he loves and cares for but has not adopted.

* * *

Notes and Questions

1. *Stepparents' obligation to support stepchildren.* Generally, stepparents do not have a direct obligation to support their stepchildren. In the few states that do require them to provide support, the obligation usually is more limited than that imposed on biological parents. The stepparents' obligation may be secondary to that of the biological parent, or the obligation may be imposed only if the stepchild would otherwise be a public charge. North Dakota continues a stepparent support obligation after the end of the marriage of the biological parent and stepparent, but that obligation is imposed only if the stepparent has received the stepchild into the stepparent's family and the stepchild continues to reside there. Although the stepparent's legal obligation to support is limited, most wage-earning stepparents probably do contribute to the support of their stepchildren while they are married to the custodial parent.

The in loco parentis doctrine can also be a basis for a support obligation. Hence, a stepparent who is in loco parentis can be considered responsible for the support of a stepchild. Since the in loco parentis relationship can be terminated at will, however, the stepparent can avoid continued financial responsibility by simply declaring that the in loco parentis relationship no longer exists. Therefore, the doctrine tends to be relevant only to matters related to prior support. For example, a stepparent's claim for reimbursement for expenses related to the child could be denied if the stepparent was in loco parentis.

Stepparents also may be required to support stepchildren if the facts present a particularly compelling situation for ordering support. Thus, stepparents who promised support, treated the child as their own, and discouraged biological parent-child contact could be required to pay support based on equitable doctrines such as estoppel. However, sympathetic facts do not always produce support awards.

Even though stepparents may not be legally obligated to support children directly, major welfare programs have taken stepparents' income into account in determining a child's welfare eligibility and grant amount, thus making stepparents indirectly responsible for the support of a child. The income of a wage-earner who marries a welfare recipient with children, for example, may be deemed available for the support of the children, resulting in a reduction or loss of the welfare grant. Stepparents can also be indirectly responsible for the support of stepchildren when their income is taken into account in determining the financial resources of their spouses (the biological parents) in child support determinations. See Sarah H. Ramsey, Stepparents and the Law, in Stepparenting: Issues in Theory, Research and Practice (Kay Pasley and Marilyn Ihinger–Tallman eds., 1994)

2. Should stepparents be expected to support stepchildren? If yes, should they have more rights with regard to the stepchild? For a comprehensive

discussion of stepparents rights and responsibilities, see Margaret M. Mahoney, Stepfamilies and the Law (1994). For a discussion of support issues see Sarah Ramsey and Judith Masson, Stepparent Support of Stepchildren: A Comparative Analysis of Policies and Problems in the American and English Experience, 36 Syracuse L. Rev. 659 (1985).

PROBLEM 9–1

Your state legislature is considering adopting the following statute:

1. A stepparent shall support his or her stepchild to the same extent that a natural or adoptive parent is required to support his or her child so long as the stepchild is living in the same home as the stepparent. However, nothing in this section shall be construed as abrogating or in any way diminishing the duty a parent otherwise would have to provide child support, and no court shall consider the income of a stepparent, or the amount actually provided for a stepchild by a stepparent, in determining the amount of child support to be paid by a natural or adoptive parent.

2. A natural or adoptive parent shall be liable to a stepparent for the sum of money expended by a stepparent for the support of a stepchild when that sum of money was expended because of the neglect or refusal of the natural or adoptive parent to pay any part of or all of the court-ordered amount of support.

3. This section shall not abrogate or diminish the common law right which a stepparent may possess to recover from a natural or adoptive parent the expense of providing necessaries for a stepchild in the absence of a court order for child support determining the amount of support to be paid by a natural or adoptive parent.

4. This section shall not be construed as granting to a stepparent any right to the care and custody of a stepchild or as granting a stepchild any right to inherit from a stepparent under the general statutory laws governing descent and distribution.

5. This section shall apply without regard to whether public assistance is being provided on behalf of the stepchild or stepchildren in question.

6. This section shall be construed to apply only to support obligations incurred on or after [the date the legislation is adopted], notwithstanding that a marriage giving rise to the support obligation occurred prior to [the date the legislation is adopted].

7. This section shall not be construed to render a child ineligible for public assistance on the basis of the child's not being deprived of parental support, but it shall be construed to permit the inclusion of the income of a stepparent in the determination of eligibility for benefits and in the determination of the amount of the assistance payment.

8.   In the determination of eligibility for benefits and in the determination of the amount of the assistance payment under [the state welfare statute] that portion of the stepparent's income, as defined by the division of family services in the administration of aid to families with dependent children, shall be considered.

Do you recommend adoption of the new law?

C. *The Government's Obligation*

A number of government programs that assist low-income families with children are generally described as "welfare" programs. The largest program that provides cash benefits is Temporary Assistance to Needy Families (TANF), which was established by the Personal Responsibility and Work Opportunity Reconciliation Act of 1996 (PRWORA). TANF replaced the Aid to Families with Dependent Children (AFDC) program, a cash benefits program that began in 1935 as part of the Social Security Act. TANF is a cooperative federal-state program, a mix of federal and state regulations and funding, as AFDC was.

Unlike AFDC, however, TANF is not an entitlement program with open-ended funding. Instead, TANF funds are limited so that eligible families might nonetheless be denied aid if the funds have been exhausted. In addition, families are eligible for TANF funds for not more than five years, and states may, and have, reduced the eligibility time limit to less than five years. Also, states have more discretion under TANF to set eligibility requirements than they had under AFDC.

In addition to cash programs, multiple in-kind programs provide services or goods rather than money. Some programs like the Special Supplemental Food Program for Women, Infants, and Children (WIC), the school nutrition programs (breakfast and lunch), child health insurance programs, and Head Start are aimed specifically at children. Others, such as Food Stamps, Medicaid, and housing assistance programs, assist low-income persons generally.

Despite these programs, the United States has an appallingly high number of children living below the federal poverty line. About one-fifth of America's children live in poverty, a much higher number than in other developed countries. Generally, neither the federal nor state governments have a legal obligation to provide for poor children. Some state constitutions require support for the poor, but the United States Constitution has not been interpreted to require either the federal government or the states to provide for the poor. An argument can be made that international law requires government support of needy children, but enforcement is difficult.

What should be the government's response to children living in poverty? One possibility is to provide more assistance for the child or the child's family. As the recent controversy surrounding the passage of PRWORA showed, however, it is difficult to assist children without also assisting their parents—and many politicians and citizens believe that their parents do not deserve government help or that the "help" provided has been counterproductive. Another possibility is removing children from their homes because of neglect and placing them in state supported care, such as foster care, or freeing them for adoption. This approach is discussed in Chapter 4 on Abuse and Neglect.

Another approach, which has its foundation in the Elizabethan Poor Laws discussed in *Haxton*, is to find private individuals who can be made to support the child. Federal attention to collecting child support from absent parents is part of this effort. In addition, embedded in the eligibility requirements for assistance are relative responsibility requirements. The income of stepparents and grandparents often can be taken into account when determining eligibility and grant amount, for example, even though the relative may not be required legally to support the child under state law. Indeed, as the following decision illustrates, the state may use child support that is paid for one child to reduce the amount of a welfare grant to other children in the same household. The decision involves the AFDC program rather than TANF, but the AFDC eligibility rules and structure are still used to determine Medicaid eligibility and, depending on the state, TANF eligibility as well.

BOWEN v. GILLIARD

Supreme Court of the United States, 1987.
483 U.S. 587.

JUSTICE STEVENS delivered the opinion of the Court.

As part of its major effort to reduce the federal deficit through the Deficit Reduction Act of 1984, 98 Stat. 494, [DEFRA] Congress amended the statute authorizing Federal Aid to Families with Dependent Children (AFDC)to require that a family's eligibility for benefits must take into account, with certain specified exceptions, the income of all parents, brothers, and sisters living in the same home. The principal question presented in this litigation is whether that requirement violates the Fifth Amendment to the United States Constitution when it is applied to require a family wishing to receive AFDC benefits to include within its unit a child for whom child support payments are being made by a noncustodial parent.

I

* * *

Because the 1984 amendment forced families to include in the filing unit children for whom support payments were being received, the practical effect was that many families' total income was reduced.[6] * * *

---

6. For example, under the July 1985 levels of payment in North Carolina, a family of four with no other income would have received $269. A child's support income of $100 would therefore reduce the family's AFDC payment to $169 if that child was included in the filing unit. The family would have a net income of $269. But if the family were permitted to exclude the child from the unit and only claim the somewhat smaller benefit of $246 for a family of three, it could have collected that amount plus the

Thus, the net effect of the 1984 amendments for a family comparable to [the plaintiff's] would include * * *: (1) the addition of the child receiving support would enlarge the filing unit and entitle the family to a somewhat larger benefit; (2) child support would be treated as family income and would be assigned to the State, thereby reducing the AFDC benefits by that amount * * *.

* * *

The District Court was undoubtedly correct in its perception that a number of needy families have suffered, and will suffer, as a result of the implementation of the DEFRA amendments to the AFDC program. Such suffering is frequently the tragic byproduct of a decision to reduce or to modify benefits to a class of needy recipients. Under our structure of government, however, it is the function of Congress—not the courts—to determine whether the savings realized, and presumably used for other critical governmental functions, are significant enough to justify the costs to the individuals affected by such reductions. The Fifth Amendment "gives the federal courts no power to impose upon [Congress] their views of what constitutes wise economic or social policy," by telling it how "to reconcile the demands of . . . needy citizens with the finite resources available to meet those demands." Unless the Legislative Branch's decisions run afoul of some constitutional edict, any inequities created by such decisions must be remedied by the democratic processes. The District Court believed that the amendment at issue did conflict with both the Due Process Clause and the Takings Clause of the Fifth Amendment. We consider these arguments in turn, and reject them.

III

The precepts that govern our review of appellees' due process and equal protection challenges to this program are similar to those we have applied in reviewing challenges to other parts of the Social Security Act:

> "[O]ur review is deferential. 'Governmental decisions to spend money to improve the general public welfare in one way and not another are ''not confided to the courts. The discretion belongs to Congress unless the choice is clearly wrong, a display of arbitrary power, not an exercise of judgment."

> This standard of review is premised on Congress' "plenary power to define the scope and the duration of the entitlement to . . . benefits, and to increase, to decrease, or to terminate those benefits based on its appraisal of the relative importance of the recipients' needs and the resources available to fund the program."

* * *

Appellees argue (and the District Court ruled), however, that finding that Congress acted rationally is not enough to sustain this legislation. Rather, they claim that some form of "heightened scrutiny" is appropri-

excepted child's $100 and have a net income   of $346.

ate because the amendment interferes with a family's fundamental right to live in the type of family unit it chooses.[16] We conclude that the District Court erred in subjecting the DEFRA amendment to any form of heightened scrutiny. That some families may decide to modify their living arrangements in order to avoid the effect of the amendment, does not transform the amendment into an act whose design and direct effect are to "intrud[e] on choices concerning family living arrangements." * * *

* * *

IV

Aside from holding that the amendment violated the Due Process Clause of the Fifth Amendment and its equal protection component, the District Court invalidated the DEFRA amendments as a taking of private property without just compensation. The court based this holding on the premise that a child for whom support payments are made has a right to have the support money used exclusively in his or her "best interest." Yet, the court reasoned, the requirements (1) that a custodial parent who applies for AFDC must include a child's support money in computing family income, and (2) that the support must be assigned to the State, effectively converts the support funds that were once to be used exclusively for the child's best interests into an AFDC check which, under federal law, must be used for the benefit of all the children. Therefore, the District Court held that the State was "taking" that child's right to exclusive use of the support money. * * *

* * *

The law does not require any custodial parent to apply for AFDC benefits. Surely it is reasonable to presume that a parent who does make such an application does so because she or he is convinced that the family as a whole—as well as *each* child committed to her or his custody—will be better off with the benefits than without. In making such a decision, the parent is not taking a child's property without just compensation; nor is the State doing so when it responds to that decision by supplementing the collections of support money with additional AFDC benefits.

V

Writing for a unanimous Court, [in Dandridge v. Williams (1970)] Justice Stewart described the courts' role in cases such as this:

> "We do not decide today that the . . . regulation is wise, that it best fulfills the relevant social and economic objectives that [Congress] might ideally espouse, or that a more just and humane system could

---

16. For example, the District Court had before it an affidavit from one mother who stated that she had sent a child to live with the child's father in order to avoid the requirement of including that child, and the support received from the child's father, in the AFDC unit.

not be devised. Conflicting claims of morality and intelligence are raised by opponents and proponents of almost every measure, certainly including the one before us. But the intractable economic, social, and even philosophical problems presented by public welfare assistance programs are not the business of this Court. The Constitution may impose certain procedural safeguards upon systems of welfare administration. But the Constitution does not empower this Court to second-guess ... officials charged with the difficult responsibility of allocating limited public welfare funds among the myriad of potential recipients."

The judgment of the District Court is

Reversed.

JUSTICE BRENNAN, with whom JUSTICE MARSHALL joins, dissenting.

Government in the modern age has assumed increasing responsibility for the welfare of its citizens. This expansion of responsibility has been accompanied by an increase in the scale and complexity of the activities that government conducts. Respect for the enormity of the administrative task that confronts the modern welfare state, as well as for the scarcity of government resources, counsels that public officials enjoy discretion in determining the most effective means of fulfilling their responsibilities.

The very pervasiveness of modern government, however, creates an unparalleled opportunity for intrusion on personal life. In a society in which most persons receive some form of government benefit, government has considerable leverage in shaping individual behavior. In most cases, we acknowledge that government may wield its power even when its actions likely influence choices involving personal behavior. On certain occasions, however, government intrusion into private life is so direct and substantial that we must deem it intolerable if we are to be true to our belief that there is a boundary between the public citizen and the private person.

This is such a case. The Government has told a child who lives with a mother receiving public assistance that it cannot both live with its mother and be supported by its father. The child must either leave the care and custody of the mother, or forgo the support of the father and become a Government client. The child is put to this choice not because it seeks Government benefits for itself, but because of a fact over which it has no control: the need of *other* household members for public assistance. A child who lives with one parent has, under the best of circumstances, a difficult time sustaining a relationship with both its parents. A crucial bond between a child and its parent outside the home, usually the father, is the father's commitment to care for the material needs of the child, and the expectation of the child that it may look to its father for such care. The Government has thus decreed that a condition of welfare eligibility for a mother is that her child surrender a vital connection with either the father or the mother.

The Court holds that the Government need only show a rational basis for such action. This standard of review has regularly been used in evaluating the claims of applicants for Government benefits, since "a noncontractual claim to receive funds from the public treasury enjoys no constitutionally protected status." Plaintiff child support recipients in this case, however, are children who wish not to receive public assistance, but to continue to be supported by their noncustodial parent. Their claim is *not* that the Government has unfairly denied them benefits, but that it has intruded deeply into their relationship with their parents. More than a mere rational basis is required to withstand this challenge, and, as the following analysis shows, the Government can offer no adequate justification for doing such damage to the parent-child relationship.

* * *

IV

* * *

"Happy families," wrote Tolstoy, "are all alike; every unhappy family is unhappy in its own way." L. Tolstoy, Anna Karenina . Contemporary life offers countless ways in which family life can be fractured and families made unhappy. The children who increasingly live in these families are entitled to the chance to sustain a special relationship with both their fathers and their mothers, regardless of how difficult that may be. Parents are entitled to provide both daily emotional solace and to meet their child's material needs; the fact that in some families a different parent may take on each role does not diminish the child's right to the care of both parents. The Government could not prohibit parents from performing these duties, and what it cannot do by direct fiat it should not be able to do by economic force. The Government has decreed that the only way a child can live with its mother and be supported by its father is if the mother is wealthy enough not to require public assistance. A child cannot be held responsible for the indigency of its mother, and should not be forced to choose between parents because of something so clearly out of its control. No society can assure its children that there will be no unhappy families. It *can* tell them, however, that their Government will not be allowed to contribute to the pain.

I dissent.

JUSTICE BLACKMUN, dissenting. [omitted].

Notes and Questions

1. *Questions about* Bowen. What level of scrutiny did the majority use and how did the Court decide on that level? If a heightened level of scrutiny was used, what arguments would you make that the government should prevail nonetheless?

2. *Welfare recipients.* One of the named class plaintiffs, Beaty Mae Gilliard, fits an inaccurate stereotype of the welfare mother. She was a single parent with seven children and had been on welfare for over 20 years. In fact in 1993 only 10% of families receiving AFDC had more than 3 children. Forty-three percent of the families receiving AFDC had only one child, and 30% had two children. Most families who received AFDC benefits managed to leave the program within two years. Illness, unemployment, or other problems caused some to return to the AFDC program, but a majority of AFDC families received no more than a total of 3 years of benefits. Center on Social Welfare Policy and Law, Welfare Myths: Fact or Fiction? (1996).

3. *Benefit levels.* The dollar amounts of benefits may seem surprisingly low for students unfamiliar with welfare programs. In fact, AFDC payments, even when combined with food stamps, did not bring a family above the federal poverty line. The 1994 median AFDC benefit for a family of three was $366 per month, with the highest benefit (excluding Alaska and Hawaii) of $610 in Vermont and the lowest of $120 in Mississippi. In 1994 the federal poverty level for a family of three was $12,320 annual income. For more detail, see Center on Social Welfare Policy and Law, Welfare Myths: Fact or Fiction? (1996).

4. *Poverty and neglect.* The 1996 Federal Poverty Guideline for a family of 8 was $26,080. The estimated median income for a four-person family in 1997 was $47,012. If the minimum wage is $5.35 and Ms. Gilliard works 40 hours per week for 50 weeks a year, she would earn $10,700. How much income do you think the Gilliard family needs on an annual basis? What should happen if Ms. Gilliard cannot earn that amount of money?

5. *Government assistance.* Should the state provide child support assistance to parents if a child has severe (and expensive) health problems; if a child has extraordinary mathematical ability; if a mother gives birth to triplets? Should the state provide grants to all parents to assist in childrearing? The United States is the only Western industrialized nation that does not provide a universal, financial benefit for families with children, typically called a child allowance. Although children can be claimed as a personal exemption on income tax, the resulting reduction in taxable income is more valuable for families in high income brackets and provides no benefit for a family whose income is so low that no taxes are owed. National Commission on Children, Beyond Rhetoric: A New American Agenda for Children and Families (1991). For an in-depth discussion of United States tax policies and practice see Allan J. Samansky, Tax Policy and the Obligation to Support Children 57 Ohio St. L.J. 329 (1996) and Annie L. Alstott, Comments on Samansky, "Tax Policy and the Obligation to Support Children," 57 Ohio St. L.J. 381 (1996). For an argument that government should not "subsidize the reproductive choices of parents who want more than two children" or subsidize daycare, see Edward B. Foley, Social Injustice and Child Poverty, 57 Ohio St. L.J. 485 (1996). For post-TANF analyses of the impact of welfare policies on children, see the symposium issue on welfare reform, 60 Ohio St. L. J. 1177–1617 (1999). For discussion of the lack of a United States governmental obligation to support poor children, see Sarah Ramsey and Daan Braveman, "Let Them Starve": Government's Obligation to Children in Poverty, 68 Temple Law Review 1607 (1995). For an argument that government does have an affirmative obligation, see Kay P. Kindred, God Bless the Child:

Poor Children, *Parens Patriae*, and a State Obligation to Provide Assistance, 57 Ohio St. L.Rev. 519 (1996).

Article 27(1) of the U.N. Convention on the Rights of the Child requires state parties to "recognize the right of every child to a standard of living adequate for the child's physical, mental, spiritual, moral and social development." For a comprehensive discussion of the meaning of Article 27 and implementation issues, see Implementing the U.N. Convention on the Rights of the Child (Arlene Bowers Andrews & Natalie Hevener Kaufman eds., 1999.) (As noted in Chapter 1, the United States has not yet ratified the Convention.)

6. *Child support and reduction of child poverty.* Unfortunately, child support studies have indicated that because of noncustodial parents' low income, higher awards and improved enforcement will not substantially reduce the number of children living in poverty. Some researchers and policymakers have recommended institution of a child support assurance program that would use public money to make up the difference between an obligor parent's low child support payment and a minimum standard of need for the child. For these and other proposals, see Children and Poverty, 7 The Future of Children 1–160 (Summer/Fall 1997); Irwin Garfinkel, Assuring Child Support: An Extension of Social Security (1992); David T. Ellwood, Poor Support: Poverty in the American Family (1988); and National Commission on Children, Beyond Rhetoric: A New American Agenda for Children and Families (1991).

7. *Food security.* For the twelve-month period ending April 1995, approximately 88.1% of the nation's approximately 100 million households were "food secure" (that is, they had access to sufficient nutritionally adequate and safe food obtainable through normal channels, without resorting to emergency food supplies, scavenging, stealing or other coping strategies).

About 11.9 million households, however, experienced some degree of "food insecurity" during this period. About 7.8% of the nation's households (7.8 million households) were "food insecure without hunger" (that is, they had a reduced quality diet, but with little or no reported reduction in household members' food intake). About 3.3% of the nation's households were "food insecure with moderate hunger" (that is, adult household members' food intake was reduced so the adults repeatedly experienced the physical sensations of hunger, but without observed reductions in children's food intake). About 0.8% (800,000 households) were "food insecure with severe hunger" (that is, children and adults had experienced reduced food intake and hunger). Food insecurity tends to be concentrated in population groups that have comparatively high poverty rates, such as female-headed households, households with children, black and Hispanic households, and households in central city areas. See U.S. Dep't of Agriculture Food Security Measurement Project, Household Food Security in the United States 1995, Executive Summary i-ix (Sept. 1997).

8. *Housing.* In 1995, 36% of households with children had one or more of three housing problems—physically inadequate housing, crowded housing or housing that cost more than 30% of household income.

Among families with children, inadequate housing (housing with severe or moderate physical problems) has become slightly less common in recent years. In 1995, 7% of households with children experienced physical housing problems, down from 9% in 1978. Crowded housing (housing in which there is more than one person per room) has also become slightly less common. The percentage of households with children in crowded housing decreased from 9% in 1978 to 7% in 1995.

These improvements in housing conditions, however, have been accompanied by rising housing costs. The percentage of households with children that paid more than 30% of their income for housing rose from 15% in 1978 to 28% in 1995. The percentage of these households with severe cost burdens (paying more than half of income for housing) rose from 6% to 12%. Where a family spends such significant percentages of income for housing, insufficient resources may remain to meet other basic needs.

In 1995, 12% of households with children had severe housing problems, either severe housing cost burdens or severe physical problems with their housing. Such problems are particularly prevalent among very low-income renters. In 1995, 32% of very low-income renters with children (2.1 million households) reported severe housing problems, particularly severe rent burden. Federal Interagency Forum on Child and Family Statistics, America's Children: Key National Indicators of Well-Being 15 (1999).

The following note describes the problems associated with homelessness.

A NOTE ON HOMELESS CHILDREN

"Tonight many thousands of children will find a place to sleep without a decent bed, shelter or roof. They will sleep in the trunks of old cars, and in parks I wouldn't walk through in daylight, and in abandoned buildings in inner-city combat zones." John Grisham, Somewhere for Everyone, Newsweek, Feb. 9. 1998, at 14.

The American Academy of Pediatrics has painted a bleak picture of the effect homelessness has on families with children:

> Families with children are the fastest growing subgroup of the homeless population nationally and represent more than half of the homeless population in many cities. Lack of a permanent dwelling deprives children of one of the most basic necessities for proper growth and development and poses unique risks for homeless children that compromise their health status. * * *

BACKGROUND

> * * * Each year an estimated 2.5 to 3 million people lack access to a conventional dwelling or residence, and it is estimated that families with children account for up to 43% of the homeless population. Although there is disagreement concerning the exact number of homeless persons, there is consensus that the numbers are large and continuing to grow. In 1994, requests for emergency shelter increased in 30 major cities by an average of 13%, with 9 of 10 of the cities reporting an increase in requests from families. In 87% of those cities, emergency shelters may have to turn away homeless families with children because of limited resources; 73% of

the surveyed cities identified homeless families with children as a group for whom shelter and other services were particularly lacking. There were 1900 shelters counted by HUD in 1984; by 1988, there were 5400 shelters. In 1984, 21% of the homeless requiring emergency shelter were families; that percentage increased to 40% in 1988.

Several societal problems contribute to the increasing rate of homelessness among American families, including lack of affordable housing; decreases in availability of rent subsidies; unemployment, especially among those who have held only marginal jobs; personal crises such as divorce and domestic violence; cutbacks in public welfare programs; substance abuse; deinstitutionalization of the mentally ill; and increasing rates of poverty. Although traditionally the homeless population has predominantly been made up of single adults, today families with children account for up to 43% of the homeless population. In some cities, children account for an average of 60% of homeless family members * * *, and in New York, NY, and Trenton, NJ, children are estimated to account for as much as 75% of homeless family members. Of the 30 cities surveyed by the US Conference of Mayors, 27 (90%) reported increases of families with children among the homeless population.

Most homeless children are temporarily housed with their families in shelters and missions operated by religious organizations and public agencies. However, in many cities, public agencies contract with private hotels to provide temporary housing to homeless people. A 1990 study of public shelter use in New York, NY, and Philadelphia, PA, showed a disproportionate impact of homelessness on minorities, especially black families. In both cities about 7% of black children had spent time in a public shelter between 1990 and 1992, in contrast to less than 1% of white children. * * *

HEALTH AND OTHER PROBLEMS ASSOCIATED WITH HOMELESSNESS

Common acute problems in homeless children include upper respiratory tract infections, scabies, lice, tooth decay, ear infections, skin infections, diaper rash, and conjunctivitis. In addition, the incidence of trauma-related injuries, developmental delays, and chronic disease, e.g., sinusitis, anemia, asthma, bowel dysfunction, eczema, visual deficits, and neurologic deficits is notably higher for homeless children than for others. * * *

It is estimated that 30% to 50% of the nation's 220,000 to 280,000 school-age homeless children do not attend school. Of those in school, sporadic attendance, grade repetition, and below-average performance (designated as having special needs) are common. The rate of developmental problems is two to three times higher in homeless children than in poor children who are not homeless.

Although iron deficiency anemia is found to be two to three times more common in homeless children than in children who are not homeless, the most prevalent nutritional problem appears to be obesity. Since refrigeration storage and cooking facilities are not available, fast-food restaurants and convenience stores are often the most common sources for food for homeless individuals. As a result, their diets often contain an excessive amount of carbohydrates and fats. Hunger is another common problem, with a significant number of homeless children lacking sufficient caloric intake.

Access to health care, particularly preventive health care, is impaired for homeless families. Health becomes a lower priority as parents struggle to meet the family's daily demands for food and shelter. Families are so often relocating that there is no opportunity to develop an ongoing relationship with a health care provider. When there is an acute problem, hospital emergency rooms, visiting public health nurses, and clinics usually are relied on to provide episodic and fragmented care. Continuity of care is nonexistent and care is rarely comprehensive, resulting in high rates of underimmunization and other unmet health needs.

Living in a shelter not only separates families from their usual sources of support in the community but also imposes severe hardships in carrying out daily sustenance activities. Despite the fact that families with children are the fastest growing segment of the homeless population, 53% of shelters in 30 major surveyed cities often cannot house families together. Rarely are homeless families housed in their originating neighborhoods. Schooling for children is therefore interrupted and often the family is separated from social networks and institutional support systems, such as day care and health care. Within temporary living situations, refrigeration storage, cooking facilities, opportunities for privacy, bathrooms, quiet quarters for reading and studying, storage space, telephones, and appropriate bedding may be unavailable. Sanitation, safety, and stability are often lacking. These impediments create unique health and social problems for homeless children.

Because young people living on the street often resort to "survival" sex (exchanging sexual activity for shelter, food, protection, or drugs), they are at significant risk of HIV infection, as well as other sexually transmitted diseases. Moreover, the incidence of pregnancy, alcohol and drug abuse, mental illness, and poor nutrition in this population is very high. * * *

AAP, Committee on Community Health Services, Health Needs of Homeless Children and Families, 98 Pediatrics 789 (1996).

The very fact of homelessness has a demoralizing effect on children. "[H]omeless children suffer the loss associated with separation from their home, furniture, belongings, and pets; the uncertainty of when they will eat their next meal and where they will sleep during the night;

the fear of who might hurt them or their family members as they live in strange and frequently violent environments; the embarrassment of being noticeably poor; and the frustration of not being able to do anything to alleviate their (or their family's) suffering. To assume that a child could push all of such suffering aside * * * may in some cases be unrealistic." Deborah M. Thompson, Breaking the Cycle of Poverty: Models of Legal Advocacy to Implement the Educational Promise of the McKinney Act for Homeless Children and Youth, 31 Creighton L. Rev. 1209, 1218 (1998).

Homelessness may also have a devastating effect on a child's ability to attend and benefit from public education. Children ashamed of being homeless often resist going to school, afraid that they are marked by their dirty clothes, their mode of transportation, their lack of supplies, their inability to invite friends home after school, or simply afraid that teachers and the other children know they are homeless. Unfortunately, in many schools other students do tease and taunt homeless children. Teachers sometimes unwittingly make it worse by singling out homeless children for special attention. Lisa K. Mihaly, Homeless Families: Failed Policies and Young Victims, CDFs Child, Youth, and Family Futures Clearinghouse at 8 (Jan. 1991).

In 1995, state school authorities reported at least eleven reasons why so many homeless children remain unserved by public school systems: (1) homeless children may lack private transportation to or from their temporary residence, and may be unable to afford public transportation; (2) most homeless shelters limit the length of time a family may remain (frequently measured in days), making enrollment in school seem not worthwhile in any one place; (3) the family must move repeatedly from shelter to shelter, forcing a homeless child to attend as many as five or six schools in a single year, leaving the child discouraged from attending at all; (4) homeless parents may be so preoccupied with finding food, shelter, and employment, and so dispirited with the family's circumstances, that they sacrifice pursuit of their children's education; (5) enrolling the child in school may be thwarted because parents cannot produce the child's birth certificate, or academic, health and immunization records, and cannot figure out how to obtain them from public agencies; (6) homeless families concerned with keeping a roof over their heads and food on the table may not be able to afford school supplies and decent clothing; (8) homeless children are more likely than other children to suffer from behavior problems or drug use; (9) homeless children or their parents may suffer from ill health or mental illness; (10) many school districts enroll only children whose families are permanent residents of the district or who pay tuition, and children of homeless parents may be unable to provide a lease, utility bill or other acceptable proof of residence; and (11) homeless families may lack information on the requirements or location of local schools. U.S. Dep't of Education, A Report to Congress: A Compilation and Analysis of

Reports Submitted by States in Accordance with Section 722(D)(3) of the Education for Homeless Children and Youth Program 3 (July 1995).

Other barriers to public education might also be identified. Homeless parents may be reluctant to press the public school system for fear that by coming forward, they might trigger a neglect proceeding by social service authorities. Children living in shelters or on the street have neither the space nor the peace and quiet needed to do homework. Homeless parents may be only semi-literate themselves, and thus unable to help children with their studies. Older children may be called on to supervise younger siblings while the parents seek employment or support for the family.

Because of the many formidable social and legal barriers encountered by homeless children, Congress enacted the Stewart B. McKinney Homelessness Assistance Act of 1987, the first federal legislation to address the plight of the homeless. With the homeless population more visible than ever before in the 1980s, the comprehensive Act recognized that the Federal Government has a clear responsibility and an existing capacity to fulfill a more effective and responsible role to meet the basic human needs and to engender respect for the human dignity of the homeless. 42 U.S.C. § 11301(a)(6). The Act provides grants to state educational agencies to insure that each child of a homeless individual and each homeless youth has equal access to the same free, appropriate public education, including a public preschool education, as provided to other children and youth. 42 U.S.C. § 11431(1). Participating states must review and take measures to revise any laws, regulations, practices, or policies that may act as a barrier to the enrollment, attendance, or success in school of homeless children and youth. 42 U.S.C. § 11431(2).

Based on the child's best interests determined on a case-by-case basis, the Act requires the local education agency either (1) to continue the child's education in the child's school of origin for the rest of the academic year (or for the following academic year if the family becomes homeless between academic years), or (2) to enroll the child in the school district where the child is actually living, even if the place of residence is a public or private shelter or some temporary structure such as an automobile. Id. § 11432(g)(3)(a). The agency then must eliminate the barriers to enrolling and retaining the child in that school, such as transportation difficulties; immunization requirements; residency requirements; lack of birth certificates, school records or other documentation; and guardianship issues. Id. § 11432(g)(1)(F). In making the best-interests determination, the agency must comply, to the extent feasible, with the request made by a parent or guardian regarding school selection. Id. § 11432(g)(3)(B).

Once a homeless child arrives at school, the Act requires that he or she be provided services comparable to those other students receive, including special education, gifted and talented programs, vocational education, school meals programs and programs for students with limited proficiency in English. Id. § 11432(g)(4). The agency must maintain the student's records so they may be provided in a timely fashion a new school district if the family relocates. Id. § 11432(g)(5).

As the 1996 American Academy of Pediatrics article reports, a third to a half of homeless children still do not attend school. "More than a decade after the passage of the McKinney Act, many of the barriers to school-aged homeless children have been removed in local school districts receiving McKinney education program funding. For example, most states have revised their laws, regulations, and policies regarding residency requirements to improve homeless children's access to education. * * * [N]ational compliance with the requirements of the McKinney Program has improved significantly." Nevertheless, a gulf remains between the law on the books and the law in practice because the McKinney Act program remains woefully underfunded, and problems remain in translating new state policies into standard practice at the local school level. Deborah M. Thompson, Breaking the Cycle of Poverty: Models of Legal Advocacy to Implement the Educational Promise of the McKinney Act for Homeless Children and Youth, 31 Creighton L. Rev. 1209, 1230 (1998). See also Susan D. Bennett, Heartbreak Hotel: The Disharmonious Convergence of Welfare, Housing and Homelessness, 1 Md. J. Contemp. Legal Issues 27, 54–57 (1990).

As the American Academy of Pediatrics article indicates, large numbers of homeless children suffer from physical and emotional disabilities. These children may also have rights under the Individuals with Disabilities Education Act (IDEA), and related legislation which is discussed in Chapter 1.

PROBLEM 9–2

Susan Combs and Larry Hill started living together, and Susan gave birth to a son, Larry, Jr., a year later. Larry supported the entire family. Unfortunately, Larry abused Susan and drugs, and Susan left him a year after Larry, Jr. was born. Larry was ordered to pay $500 per month in child support and paid for about six months and then stopped. Susan left the state with Larry, Jr. and concealed their whereabouts from Larry for five years. For two years of those years she received public assistance, but then managed to become self-supporting.

When she lost her job due to a recession, she applied for welfare again. To be eligible she had to put in a claim for child support. The state child support enforcement agency located Larry and charged him for $33,000 in past child support and has attached his wages for future child support payments. The state wants $12,000 reimbursement for the two years of welfare support that Susan received, and the rest would go to Susan. Larry now knows where Susan lives and she has agreed to a liberal visitation schedule.

Should Larry be required to pay the child support arrearage? Should both Susan and the state recover?

C. The Child's Responsibilities

OELER v. OELER

Supreme Court of Pennsylvania, 1991.
594 A.2d 649.

ZAPPALA, JUSTICE.

This appeal presents a question of first impression of whether a parent can be compelled to support a minor child who unilaterally chooses to reside in her own apartment.* * *

As do most domestic cases, this one has a long court-related history beginning in 1974 when the parties separated and continuing since then with various support-related proceedings. At the time of separation, the parties had three minor children, two sons and one daughter. When this most recent controversy arose, both sons were in college and no longer the subject of the existing support order entered on April 1, 1975. Only Paula, age 17, remained a subject of the original support order which had been modified due to various changes in circumstances.

Although the record is void of any custody orders, it appears undisputed that at least prior to 1985, the father had primary physical custody of his daughter, Paula. Based upon this order, Paula lived with her father from January, 1985 through May, 1986. Because the father resided outside of the Allen High School jurisdiction, the father paid Paula's tuition to enable her to continue to attend that high school. Notwithstanding the existing order and without modifying that order, Paula moved back with her mother in June of 1986, where she remained until late December of 1987.

On or about December 29, 1987, the parties entered into a support stipulation, which was incorporated into an order of court of the same date. According to the stipulation, the father's support obligation for Paula was set at $900.00 per month retroactive to June 15, 1987. Furthermore, in accordance with the parties' stipulations, the court included the following provisions in its order of December 29, 1987:

1. Should actual physical custody of Paula Oeler change from the Plaintiff to Defendant or any third party in the future, this Order shall be automatically subject to review.

2. In the event that Paula Oeler shall no longer be in actual physical custody of the Plaintiff, the Defendant, Richard Oeler, shall begin immediately to pay ... $300.00 per month.

Apparently, on the same day the court was entering this modified support order, the mother was relocating to New Haven, Connecticut. Based upon this move and the fact that Paula no longer resided with the mother, on December 31, 1987 the father filed for a modification of his support payments in accordance with paragraph 2 of the December 29, 1987 Order of Court.

At some point prior to the mother's move, the father was advised by his daughter that her mother intended to relocate to Connecticut to pursue an internship at Yale University Art Gallery. The father then advised his daughter that she was welcome to reside with him in order to complete her high school education at Allen High School. During their conversation, Paula indicated to her father that she and her mother intended to make arrangements for Paula to live with a local family until graduation. Based upon this representation, the father indicated he would provide monetary assistance to the family that Paula resided with, so long as he deemed that family appropriate.

When Paula and her mother were unable to secure a temporary living arrangement with a family in Allentown near the school, they unilaterally and without any notice or discussion with the father, entered into a lease for an apartment for Paula. Paula's apartment was a one-bedroom apartment in a three-apartment building in Allentown with a monthly rental of $335.00 per month. Thereafter, Paula's mother sought reimbursement of expenses incurred by Paula, from the father.

During the hearing, testimony was given by the parties and their daughter. All parties agreed that the father was willing to have Paula reside with him at his expense to enable her to complete her final year of high school at Allen High School. The mother testified that in good conscience she could not or would not force her daughter Paula to live with her father. To do so, the mother felt it would effectively be taking advantage of her daughter because by making this forced living arrangement, the mother would then be free to pursue her own goals or opportunities and that being her desire to receive an internship at Yale University Art Gallery. Paula testified that she did not want to live with her father because she and her stepmother did not get along. Specifically, her stepmother was "too neat" for her, which meant everything had to be "picked up and put away" which was contrary to her style of living. Although she also indicated that she wanted to live closer to her friends, she admitted that her father's house was only ten to fifteen minutes from her school by car.

Based upon this record, the trial court concluded that the father had made his home available to his daughter and that she had no justifiable reason for refusing to live with him. Furthermore, the court noted that the mother and daughter unilaterally made alternative living arrangements without any consultation with the father. * * * [T]he trial court concluded that Paula's action in refusing her father's offer prevented her from reaping any financial gains.

On appeal, in a memorandum opinion, Superior Court reversed the trial court concluding that the duty of a parent to support his/her minor child is absolute which cannot be waived by actions of that minor child. * * *

Because the trial court did not abuse its discretion in terminating the father's obligation to support Paula in her apartment, we must reverse the Superior Court order and reinstate the order of the trial court.

* * *

At common law, the duty of a parent to support his child was conditioned upon a parent receiving love, affection and assistance from that child. Contrary to the common law, today, the duty to support a minor child is absolute. However, in awarding child support, we must be cognizant of its purpose which is to promote the best interests of the child.

It is quite clear from reviewing this record that the father is not refusing to support his daughter. Rather, he is refusing to allow his daughter to dictate the proper allocation of support monies. In other words, the father is willing to provide housing, food, clothing and an education for his daughter. The disagreement arises because Paula wants to reside under her own roof at her father's expense. In granting the father's termination of support request, the trial court believed that Paula offered no justifiable reason for not living with her father. We agree. In essence, the best interest of Paula would not be served by permitting her to reside alone.

* * *

The decision of the trial court is reasonable and in complete accord with traditional values of child rearing. What the Supreme Court of Massachusetts cogently stated over a century and a half ago is still applicable today.

> Where a child leaves his parents' house, voluntarily . . . to avoid the discipline and restraint so necessary for the due regulations of families, he carries with him no credit; and the parent is under no obligation to pay for his support . . .

That Supreme Court further commented that to permit the minor, at his election, to depart from his parents' house, with power to charge that parent with his support, would tend to the destruction of all parental authority, and invert the order of family government.

* * *

Notes and Questions

1. *Emancipation.* Is the result in *Oeler* the same as emancipation? *Oeler* is typical of decisions that allow a parent to terminate support for a child who is nearing the age of majority and is employed or employable. See, e.g., Roe v. Doe, 272 N.E.2d 567 (N.Y. 1971) (at a time when the age of majority was twenty-one, court upheld father's right to terminate support of his twenty year-old daughter who refused his "reasonable demands" to live on-campus, rather than off-campus, at a college in a distant state). Disobedience cases sometimes lead courts to speak of a doctrine of constructive emancipation. Where a minor of employable age in full possession of his or her faculties voluntarily and without cause abandons the parental home in an effort to

evade parental control, the child may lose the right to receive further parental support. Courts have also applied the doctrine to terminate a noncustodial parent's future support obligations where the child unreasonably refuses all contact and visitation with the parent. See, e.g., Comm'r of Soc. Servs. v. Jones–Gamble, 643 N.Y.S.2d 182 (App.Div.1996). The doctrine terminates the support obligation only where the court finds termination appropriate in the light of the child's age and ability to fend for himself. Parents sometimes seek to emancipate an ungovernable child who appears beyond their ability to discipline. The reports are replete with decisions that deny emancipation where the unruly or disobedient child would be left with inadequate means of support. See, e.g., In re Thomas C., supra at 195.

2. *Separation agreements.* Should a child of divorced parents be able to enforce a separation agreement's child support provisions as a third party beneficiary? Generally no, because the support is owed to the custodial parent who has discretion about how the money will be spent. The child can enforce provisions that directly benefit the child, such as a promise to establish a trust fund or make the child the beneficiary of a life insurance policy, however. In special circumstances, such as the death of the custodial parent, the child may have standing to enforce the support provisions. See, e.g., Morelli v. Morelli, 720 P.2d 704 (Nev.1986); Drake v. Drake, 455 N.Y.S.2d 420 (App.Div.1982).

3. *Parental control.* Withholding money is one way parents can discipline disobedient children, but many parents today must provide support for children who are in the custody and control of someone else, such as a former spouse after a divorce or in state custody following a delinquency proceeding. Sometimes child support disputes are about control—over the child or the other parent. In *Haxton v. Haxton* (in the first section of this Chapter), for example, control was an important part of the dispute:

> Though not apparent from the appellate opinions, the real dispute, in significant part, was whether the Haxton's son had the ability to be self-supporting and whether he was trying hard enough to find and maintain work. At trial the mother testified at length about her unsuccessful efforts to help her son, who was learning disabled and emotionally disturbed. She considered him unable to work without close supervision and unable to understand simple obligations of employees, such as having to come to work every day. The father, who resisted having to support his son, believed that the son was able to work but lacked motivation. From the parents' perspective (and perhaps from the son's) this case was about who should decide whether the son was able to be self-supporting, and the extent to which the parents' power of the purse could be used as motivator.

Leslie J. Harris et al., Making and Breaking Connections Between Parents' Duty to Support and Right To Control Their Children, 69 Oregon L. Rev. 689 (1990).

4. *Governmental control.* When a government is providing welfare benefits to a low-income family, it may try to regulate family behavior and enforce regulations by reducing or eliminating the welfare grant. A parent's TANF grant may be reduced if a child does not attend school regularly, for example.

D. *Amount*

LINDA HENRY ELROD, THE FEDERALIZATION OF CHILD SUPPORT GUIDELINES

6 J. Am. Acad. Matrim. Law. 103, 109–15 (1990).

Within the short span of fifteen years the federal government has systematically revolutionized the process for establishing and enforcing child support throughout the United States. Within the past six years, the federal government has effectively usurped traditional state supremacy over such family law issues as the setting and enforcing of child support and establishment of paternity. For years, the establishment and enforcement of child support obligations in one state were "of no special interest to other states." Each state had its own procedures for setting the amount of child support. Most states allowed the trial judge broad discretion in setting the amount of child support in divorce or paternity actions as equity required because each family's circumstances were considered unique.

The creation of the Office of Child Support Enforcement (OCSE) in 1975 created a mechanism for intra and interstate enforcement of support obligations in every state and set the stage for later federal intervention into areas previously viewed as the domain of the states. The major revolution came in August 1984 when Congress unanimously passed the Child Support Enforcement Amendments which radically changed the way states viewed child support orders. The 1984 Amendments required each state to adopt statewide advisory child support guidelines by October 1, 1987. Federal regulations added the requirement that the guidelines be numerical. The Family Support Act of 1988 not only affirmed the use of mathematical child support guidelines but also mandated that those setting child support in all states use the guidelines as a rebuttable presumption of the proper child support award by October 13, 1989.

* * *

B. Federal Child Support Enforcement

The federalization of child support guidelines probably would not have been accomplished without some of the "New Deal" legislation of the 1930's. In 1935 the Social Security Act established a public assistance program called Aid to Families with Dependent Children (AFDC). The AFDC program was designed to provide support for "dependent" children who were not being properly supported by their parents. At the time the program was created, 42% of the children were eligible for benefits because of death of a parent. By 1949, however, the cost of benefits was estimated to be $205 million to aid families where the father was alive but not in the family and not paying support.

Congress began to look for ways to collect support from the absent parents of these children as a way to reduce the welfare roles by enacting the first federal child support legislation in 1950. During the 1960's the child support enforcement program expanded by allowing use of Social Security records to obtain addresses and information on absent parents. In 1967 each state was required to establish a single unit whose task was to collect child support and establish paternity.

In 1975, Congress passed Title IV–D of the Social Security Act. Title IV–D represented a national attempt to find a solution to enforce parental support obligations by tying federal welfare benefits to state attempts to recoup costs from parents. It came after a congressional committee concluded that "[t]he problem of welfare in the United States is, to a considerable extent, a problem of the nonsupport of children by their absent parents."

Title IV–D created the Office of Child Support Enforcement (OCSE) as a cooperative federal agency to work with state governments and the United States Department of Health and Human Services to provide four basic child support services: location of absent parents, establishment of paternity, establishment of support and enforcement of support. The child support program is often called the "IV–D program" and it originally focused on those receiving AFDC benefits. The significant provisions of the 1975 legislation are:

* IV–D plan requirements for federal approval of state assistance plans;

* creation of the federal parent locator service;

* creation of penalties for states which failed to implement effective IV–D services;

* requirement that support in AFDC cases be paid to the state for distribution;

* federal incentive payments of 12% of collection in interstate AFDC cases;

* federal funding for 75% of states' administrative costs; and

* support services were made available for those not receiving welfare.

Applicants for IV–D services must assign their rights to uncollected child support to the state; agree to cooperate in getting a support order established, including obtaining a paternity determination, if necessary; and agree to help find the absent parent. Failure to cooperate will deny the parent benefits but not the child. The trend since 1975 has been to expand both the scope and purpose of the child support enforcement program. Additional federal legislation authorized garnishment of federal employee wages for support orders. In 1980 federal funding was made permanent for non-AFDC cases and incentives were expanded to include all AFDC cases, not just interstate cases. In 1982 the Federal Parent Locator Service was created.

The creation of OCSE to monitor, assist and supervise state collection efforts coupled with the provisions for federal monetary incentives, such as ninety percent funding for development and use of automated systems, set the stage for the federal government to play a larger role in the child support area should it need (or desire) to do so. If the federal government now wanted states to cooperate in establishment and enforcement endeavors, it could threaten the loss of valuable federal funding for failure to comply.

III. The Need for Guidelines

The Congressional desire to decrease the federal costs of the welfare system by shifting more of the economic burden for children to their parents, in particular the "absent" parent, provided the major impetus for guidelines. Two major problems existed nationally when the 1984 Amendments were enacted. First, child support awards were inadequate to cover the actual costs of raising a child, and second, child support orders varied drastically for no apparent reason.

A. Adequacy of Child Support Awards

Female-headed households have increased due to the number of unmarried women having and keeping their babies and the rising divorce rate of the 1960's and 70's. Out of wedlock births rose dramatically from 4% of total births in 1950 to 23.4% in 1985. Many women did not seek to establish paternity so no judicial support order was entered. When paternity was established, often the judge set a token payment of $10.00.

In the divorce context, mothers have traditionally been awarded custody of minor children. In many cases women either did not have a support order, fathers did not pay the amounts ordered, or the amounts ordered were far too low to maintain a child at subsistence level even when noncustodial parents could afford to pay more. A Census report found that only 46% of all women who were potentially eligible to receive support had support orders entered. Only half of the women received the full amount of support ordered, with 26% receiving partial payment and 24% receiving no payment.

Rarely did child support orders have any relationship to the actual costs of maintaining a child. The average support award in 1983 was $191 a month for one and seven-tenths children which was only 25% of the average expenditures for children at a middle income level. It was only 80% of the poverty level.

In the post divorce situation, one researcher found that the standard of living for the custodial parent and minor children declined 73% while the noncustodial parent's standard of living rose 42%. One professor's study found that the mother with custody of two children needs 76% to 80% of the intact family's former income to maintain the family's predivorce standard of living, but child support awards equaled only 33% of that amount.

The lack of spousal support, the custodial mother's reduced earning capacity (either due to increased child care responsibilities or lack of skills), combined with nonexistent or unrealistically low child support awards resulted in an increase in women and children receiving government assistance. During the 1970's, increasing numbers of female-headed households fell below the poverty level, until one half of all families in poverty were headed by women. Close to 90% of the beneficiaries of AFDC are mother-headed single parent households with minor children. The burgeoning numbers of female-headed households seeking government assistance led Congress to consider ways to get noncustodial parents to pay adequately for their children. The Senate Report accompanying the 1984 Amendments indicated that part of the motivation for the requirement for guidelines was to meet "[the] problem that the amounts of support ordered are in many cases unrealistic. This frequently results in awards which are lower than what is needed to provide reasonable funds for the needs of the child in light of the absent parent's ability to pay."

The Office of Child Support Enforcement (OCSE) reported that $10.9 billion dollars was due in child support in 1985. A 1985 study done for OCSE found that if a normative child support guideline had been used that tied child support to the absent parent's income, instead of relying on judicial discretion, the amount of child support owed would have been $26.6 billion. Therefore, increasing the amount of child support owed by absent parents was seen as one means of alleviating some of the problems associated with the growing impoverishment of women and children.

B. *Consistency in Support Orders*

Because judges traditionally set child support on a case by case basis, the amounts ordered varied considerably between similarly situated parents. The vague use of factors such as a "just and proper" amount of support or the "financial resources of the parents and standard of living of the family" led to wide disparities in awards. For example, a father with a monthly income of $900 paid $50 for two children while another father with $450 monthly income paid $60 for two children.

Sometimes judges used other factors not mentioned specifically in the statutes, such as the existence of other children or a new spouse, the earnings of a new spouse, expenses of visitation, custodial arrangements, child care expenses, tax exemption, medical expenses and the like. Inconsistencies in the amount of support ordered between persons similarly situated created negative perceptions of the judicial system.

Predicting what a child support award would be varied depending on the judge, the attorneys and numerous other factors. Several studies demonstrated the wide range of support awards depending on the judge or variations based on geographical locations. Most jurisdictions that had developed schedules prior to 1984 based them on custom rather than economic data. Objective guidelines based on schedules or charts for all child support orders would provide greater consistency and greater predictability which, in turn, would reduce litigable issues and encourage settlement as well as create the perception of "fairness" in the judicial system.

* * *

Questions

What was the major impetus behind requiring the states to establish child support guidelines? Why do you think child support awards historically had been inadequate and inconsistent?

E. Collection

In addition to the problem of low or nonexistent child support awards, rates of collection have also been very low. The following materials explain some of the federal initiatives that have made major, substantive changes in state, intrastate and federal enforcement of child support orders.

PAUL K. LEGLER, THE COMING REVOLUTION IN CHILD SUPPORT POLICY: IMPLICATIONS OF THE 1996 WELFARE ACT

30 Family Law Quarterly 519, 538–57 (1996).

* * *

IV. Collecting Support

A. The Vision

The vision for child support enforcement that guided much of the development of the legislation [the Personal Responsibility and Work Opportunity Reconciliation Act of 1996 or PRWORA] is that the payment of child support should be automatic and inescapable—"like death or taxes." This vision is reflected in three key elements: (1) Access to Information—the ability to locate individuals and assets; (2) Mass Case Processing—the capacity to work cases in volume using computers, automation, and information technology; and (3) Pro–Active Enforcement—the ability to take enforcement action automatically, preferably administratively, without reliance on a complaint-driven process. Each of these elements interacts and supports the other.

B. Access to Information

There has been a growing recognition that access to information is a prerequisite to effective child support enforcement. Unless child support is paid voluntarily, unpaid child support obligations can only be collected from one of two sources: a current income stream or accumulated assets. In order to tap into either of these, information regarding the obligor is essential: Where is the obligor located? Is the obligor working? If so, where is he or she working? What is the obligor's income? What other sources of income does he or she have? Does the obligor have bank accounts or other liquid assets? What other assets does he or she have that are subject to seizure?

Marilyn Ray Smith, a key proponent of the child support enforcement legislation, made the case for increased access to information at a Senate hearing: "If you can't find the noncustodial parent, you can't make him support his family. A child support enforcement program is only as good as the information available to locate the noncustodial parent, and income and assets."

This viewpoint was incorporated throughout the PRWORA, and the ability of child support agencies to access information is greatly enhanced. Foremost, the Act sets up a national system to track the employment of delinquent obligors. This national system was established so that child support collections could more closely mimic tax collection. Just as withholding of taxes from wages has proven to be the most efficient method to collect taxes, withholding of child support directly from wages is the most efficient method to collect child support. Automatic withholding changes the system from one that relies primarily on voluntary compliance to one that is automatic and mandatory.

Withholding child support directly from wages in cases where the obligor is delinquent in payments has been a state requirement since 1984. The Family Support Act of 1988 expanded wage withholding to all new child support orders as of 1994 (exceptions are made in cases of good cause or if the parties mutually agree to an alternate agreement). Fifty-five percent of all collections, over $5 billion dollars in 1994, now comes through wage withholding. * * *

The major obstacle preventing a higher use of wage withholding for collections has been job turnover. * * *

* * *

* * * In this new national system, all employers in the country will be required to report new hires within twenty days of hire to a designated state agency. * * * This national new hire program will revolutionize interstate enforcement because it dramatically improves the capacity to trace delinquent parents across state lines. About 30 percent of child support cases are currently interstate cases, so the potential for increased collections is enormous. Moreover, the PRWORA mandates that all states adopt the Uniform Interstate Family Support Act (UIFSA). Under UIFSA, state agencies can send income withholding orders directly across state lines to employers. Thus, within days of starting work in another state, the noncustodial parent could have his or her income attached and the children could begin receiving child support. It has been estimated that a national program of reporting of new hires could result in additional child support collections of $6.4 billion, and additional savings in reduced welfare costs to the federal government of $1.1 billion over a ten-year period.

* * *

Besides the new hire program, the PRWORA also significantly expands access to information in other areas. Section 325 provides that the state child support agency must have access to two important categories of records. The first category is records of state and local government agencies, including vital statistics; state and local tax and revenue records; records concerning real and titled personal property; records of occupational and professional licenses; records concerning the ownership and control of corporations, partnerships, and other business entities; employment security records; records of agencies administering public assistance programs; records of motor vehicle departments; and correction records. In addition, a U.S. military locate system will allow persons in the military to be located instantly. Finally certain motor vehicle and law enforcement records also can be accessed.

The second category of records that the child support agency will have access to is certain records held by private entities, including customer records of public utilities and cable television companies and information (including assets and liabilities) on individuals who owe support held by financial institutions. In addition, information from credit histories can be used to establish and modify child support orders, as well as to enforce orders.

* * *

With the broad access to information authorized under the Act it ought to be possible to find a delinquent obligor anywhere in the country with only a few exceptions. The vast majority of obligors will have some record which will allow the child support agency to find them, e.g., a driver's license, bank account, automobile, utilities, or cable television. So delinquent obligors may be able to run, but they will no longer be able to hide.

Such broad access to information may raise privacy concerns for some people, but it need not. The Act requires numerous and comprehensive safeguards to protect privacy rights. It specifically requires numerous protections against disclosure for unauthorized purposes. In addition, the uses of information are very narrowly specified to protect the privacy of individuals beyond the needs of the program.

C. Mass Case Processing

Mass case processing, the handling of cases in volume using advanced technology, is another key element of the future collection system. "Child support enforcement needs to be run like modern businesses that use computers, automation, and information technology. With 17 million cases and a growing caseload, we cannot simply improve collections simply by adding more caseworkers. Routine cases have to be handled in volume."

A major problem with the child support system historically is that cases are usually processed individually, one case at a time. This process is an outgrowth of the fact that initiation of action on a case in the traditional judicial model for child support enforcement is dependent on a complainant who individually takes the necessary legal steps to bring the case to the attention of the court. Thus, generally, either a prosecutor or an individual's attorney must raise the issue in court. * * *

Mass case processing requires that case information and payment records be computerized. These records are then matched against other databases, such as the state unemployment compensation records, workers compensation records, or bank account records.

Once a hit [match] is made, the computer does the walking. It automatically spits out a wage assignment if it is income, or a levy notice if it is a bank account, puts it in the envelope, affixes the stamp, and mails the notice—all without human intervention.

* * *

2. CENTRAL REGISTRIES AND CENTRALIZED COLLECTIONS

The PRWORA imposes two state requirements that will vastly facilitate mass case processing: (1) central state registries of child support orders, and (2) centralized collection and disbursement units.

Central state registries of child support orders are registries that maintain current records of all child support orders. They are required to contain all new and modified orders and must maintain and update payment records. The registry must also be capable of extracting data for matching with other databases. This state registry requirement is designed to end the current system of fragmented state records which often makes it virtually impossible to determine what action has been taken by multiple caseworkers or courts within a state. * * *

* * *

D.   Pro–Active Enforcement

One of the goals for child support enforcement reform was to make enforcement much more "pro-active," that is, taking enforcement action automatically whenever a payment is missed.

Child support cases are too often handled on a complaint-driven basis in which the IV–D agency only takes action when the custodial parent pressures the agency to do so. This puts a heavy burden on the custodial parent (usually the mother). Because she is sometimes threatened with intimidation or abuse if she asserts her right to support, she may be reluctant to take such action. Also, little attention is paid to difficult cases unless the mother acts as the enforcer, seeking new information and leads about the noncustodial parent (sometimes even tracking him down in other states) and constantly pressuring her caseworker to do more. When custodial parents do not see results or when the system is too slow to respond to requests or to new information, they are left frustrated and disillusioned. Ideally, if the custodial parent has an award in place, then any disruption in regular payments should trigger automatic enforcement mechanisms.

One only has to look at the roots of child support enforcement to see why it is such a complaint-driven process. Child support enforcement evolved out of a view that it was a private matter, except where welfare dollars were involved, and best left to state court discretion. The result of that legacy is the adversarial, judicial nature of support proceedings, broad court discretion and involvement, and the lack of self-starting payment mechanisms.

The PRWORA child support provisions provide that states must have certain "expedited procedures" for handling the routine cases.* * * These expedited procedures grant authority to the state child support agency to take certain routine enforcement steps "without the necessity of obtaining an order from any other judicial or administrative tribunal." This distinction is an important one: child support agencies will have sufficient administrative authority to process the vast majority of cases without requiring prior court intervention, yet states can maintain limited court-based processes for the collection of support to the extent that they are necessary for the exceptional cases.

The required expedited procedures under the Act include ordering a genetic test; subpoenaing information or requiring entities in the state to provide employment information (and imposing penalties or sanctions for failure to respond to subpoenas); accessing certain records; changing payees in cases of assignment; ordering income withholding; intercepting or seizing periodic or lump-sum payments (including unemployment compensation, workers' compensation, other state benefits, judgments, settlements, and lotteries); attaching and seizing assets of the obligor held in financial institutions; attaching public and private retirement funds; imposing liens (and, in appropriate cases, forcing the sale of property and the distribution of proceeds); and increasing the amount of the monthly payment to cover amounts for arrearages.

These expedited processes work in conjunction with the central registries and centralized collection and disbursement. For IV–D cases, any delay or failure to make payment should automatically trigger these enforcement actions. This is broad, new authority for child support agencies in many states, and when fully implemented, should revolutionize the collection process.

* * *

There can be little doubt that these changes toward greater child support agency authority, expedited procedures, mass-case processing, and pro-active enforcement will send repercussions throughout the judicial system. When all the changes are implemented, the child support enforcement system will have moved from one that was primarily self-initiated, adversarial, judicial-based, and discretionary to one that is pro-active, less adversarial, highly administrative, and based on rule. Fewer cases will be enforced through the traditional court system. Yet, few will mourn the passing of the old regime. Its legacy, no matter how well intended many of its defenders, is a record of enforcement that let the "deadbeats" off, and left most children with only a fraction of the child support they deserved.

E. Interstate and Other Enforcement Issues

As the U.S. Commission on Interstate Child Support reported, some of the states' most difficult cases involve families who reside in different states, largely because states do not have similar laws governing essential functions—such as the enforcement of support, service of process, and jurisdiction. According to a recent GAO report, even though interstate cases are just as likely to have awards in place, the chance of them receiving a payment is much less. This discrepancy raises a significant problem given that interstate cases represent almost 30 percent of all child support awards, yet only yield 7 percent of all public collections.

In developing the reform proposals, there was a strong consensus that with an increasingly mobile society, the need for a stronger federal role in interstate location and enforcement had grown. One key part of the expanded federal role is the new hire program and expanded Federal Parent Locator Service. The second key is having some mandated national uniform procedures for interstate cases. Under the Act, all states are required to adopt the Uniform Interstate Family Support Act (UIFSA), a uniform state law approved by the National Conference of Commissioners on Uniform State Laws (NCCUSL) in 1992. The Act requires that the 1992 version of UIFSA be enacted "as approved by the American Bar Association on February 9, 1993, together with any amendments officially adopted before January 1, 1998," by NCCUSL. UIFSA replaces a previous uniform act, the Uniform Reciprocal Enforcement of Support Act (URESA). UIFSA is a significant departure from URESA, and should dramatically improve the ability of parents to obtain child support across state lines. Under UIFSA, all states will have long-arm statutes; there will be only one controlling order; states can modify orders only if they have jurisdiction under the Act; choice of law is specified; there is direct income withholding between states; and other procedures and evidentiary rules will be uniform.

Another prominent enforcement remedy required under the Act is the authority to revoke drivers, professional, occupational, and recreational licenses. This remedy is especially useful in forcing these obligors who are self-employed to comply. States are given broad authority to determine the due process for doing so, but all states must have and use such authority. Preliminary reports from a number of states indicate that license revocation can significantly boost collections.

Numerous other changes will also improve enforcement, including rights to notifications of hearings, requirements for a presumed address of the obligor, improving enforcement of child support obligations in international cases by providing authority for the U.S. State Department to enter reciprocal agreements with foreign nations, authority for courts to impose work requirements, expanded and simplified wage withholding, denial of passports by the Secretary of State for nonpayment, requirements for laws voiding fraudulent transfers, improvements to full faith and credit for child support orders, expanded reporting to credit bureaus, child support enforcement for Indian Tribes, enforcement of orders for health care coverage, and enhanced enforcement against government employees. Finally, the Act opens up more room for privatization, an ongoing trend in child support enforcement that is likely to accelerate in the coming years as states continue to try to find ways to deliver services with fewer state employees.

* * *

Notes

1. *Federal Full Faith and Credit for Child Support Orders Act.* Another important aid to intrastate enforcement is the Federal Full Faith and Credit For Child Support Orders Act, effective on October 20, 1994. It requires the states to give full faith and credit to other states' child support orders. Child support orders are to be enforced without modification in most cases.

2. *More work needed.* According to the Office of Child Support Enforcement's Twentieth Annual Report to Congress (for the 1995 fiscal year):

> [O]nly half of all families with one custodial parent and with a child support award received the full amount of child support due to them.
> * * *

> The Census Bureau reports that 11.5 million families are potentially eligible for child support because one parent lives elsewhere. Slightly more than half, 54% or 6.2 million families, had a child support order in place. Of those with orders, 5.3 million were due payment and 4 million received all or some payment. The total amount families received was $11.9 billion in child support leaving $5.8 billion uncollected of the $17.7 billion due in 1991. These numbers reflect only the amount of child support owed for custodial parents who had child support orders.

For a discussion of the advantages of non-discretionary rules for child support, see Jane C. Murphy, Eroding the Myth of Discretionary Justice in Family Law: The Child Support Experiment, 70 N.C.L. Rev. 209 (1991).

3. *Lack of compliance.* Unfortunately not all states fully comply with the requirements of Title IV–D of the Social Security Act. In Blessing v. Freestone, 520 U.S. 329 (1997), five Arizona mothers whose children were eligible to receive IV–D services sued under 42 U.S.C. § 1983, claiming that they had "an enforceable individual right to have the State's program achieve 'substantial compliance' with the requirements of Title IV–D." The Court held that Title IV–D does not give individuals such a general right, but did not foreclose the possibility that some Title IV–D provisions could give rise to specific individual rights. The Court remanded the case to determine "what rights, considered in their most concrete, specific form, respondents are asserting." The Court noted that:

> Arizona's record of enforcing child support obligations is less than stellar, particularly compared with those of other States. In a 1992 report, Arizona's Auditor General chronicled many of the State's problems. In the 1989–1990 fiscal year, Arizona failed to collect enough child

support payments and federal incentives to cover the administrative costs of its Title IV–D program—1 of only 10 States to fall below that target. The Auditor General also pointed out that the cost-effectiveness of Arizona's support enforcement efforts had been "minimal." For every dollar spent on enforcement, the State collected barely two dollars—almost half the nationwide average. In 1992, nearly three-quarters of Arizona's 275,000 child support cases were still in the earliest stages of the enforcement process. In 42 percent of all cases, paternity had yet to be established. In a further 29 percent, the absent parent had been identified but his or her whereabouts were unknown. Overall, the Auditor General found that Arizona "obtains regular child support payments for fewer than five percent of the parents it serves."

Federal audits by OCSE have also identified shortcomings in Arizona's child support system. In several reviews of the State's performance from 1984 to 1989, the Secretary found that Arizona had not substantially complied with significant program requirements, and she repeatedly penalized the State one percent of its AFDC grant. The State developed a corrective action plan after each failed audit, which prompted the Secretary to suspend and—in every instance but one—waive the one-percent reduction in Arizona's AFDC funding.

4. *Bankruptcy and social security*. Child support orders have had a favored status in some areas. Child support is exempt from discharge under the Bankruptcy Code (11 U.S.C. § 523(a)(5)) and an obligor's social security benefits can be garnished for child support, (42 U.S.C. § 659).

5. *Jailing for contempt*. Courts can use their contempt power to jail a parent who is in arrears on child support, if the failure to pay is wilful. For a comprehensive study of the use of jailing for contempt to enforce child support orders, see David Chambers, Making Fathers Pay (1979). Contempt has even been used for arrearages that have been reduced to a money judgment. See, e.g., Pettit v. Pettit, 626 N.E.2d 444 (Ind.1993). In a civil proceeding a state may presume that a parent is able to pay, placing the burden on the obligor to rebut the presumption. Hicks v. Feiock, 485 U.S. 624 (1988).

6. *Criminal proceedings*. In addition to civil proceedings, states can bring criminal actions for non-support against a parent. If more than one state is involved, a failure to provide support is now a federal crime under the Child Support Recovery Act of 1992 (18 U.S.C. § 228). The Act has been challenged unsuccessfully as an unconstitutional exercise of Congress's regulatory power under the commerce clause. See, e.g., United States v. Crawford, 115 F.3d 1397 (8th Cir.1997)(Dr. Crawford had been ordered to pay over $91,000 in restitution.)

The Department of Justice has selected some high profile cases to publicize the Child Support Recovery Act. According to the OCSE's 20th Annual Report to Congress, the 1995 cases included "the highly publicized case of Dr. Frank Bongiorno who was convicted in Massachusetts and sentenced to five years in probation, ordered to pay $5,000 per month until his $220,000 obligation is paid, and required to spend 12 hours a day for 12 months in a correctional facility."

7. *Lawyers in arrears.* Should an attorney be suspended from the practice of law for wilfully refusing to pay child support? See In re Petition for Disciplinary Action Against Giberson, 581 N.W.2d 351, 354 (Minn.1998) (The attorney's "willful failure to obey court orders was prejudicial to the administration of justice and caused substantial injury to [his] wife and children"; the attorney was suspended indefinitely and was required to show that he was in compliance before reinstatement.)

8. *Additional references*: The OCSE website is <http:/www.acf.dhhs.gov/gov/programs/CSE/index.html>. For a succinct comparison of the Uniform Reciprocal Enforcement of Support Act (URESA) and the Uniform Interstate Family Support Act (UIFSA), see Marygold S. Melli , The United States: Child Support Enforcement For The 21st Century, 32 U. of Louisville J. of Fam. L. 475 (1993–94).

SECTION 2. CAPACITY TO CONTRACT

MITCHELL v. MIZERSKI

Court of Appeals of Nebraska.
1995 WL 118429

Sievers, C.J., and Hannon and Mues, JJ.

Mark Mizerski, owner of M & M Precision Body and Paint, appeals the judgment of the district court which affirmed the county court's determination that Travis Mitchell, a minor, and not his father, Ted Mitchell, entered into contracts for repairs to a vehicle with Mizerski and was entitled to disaffirm the contracts and have all amounts paid under those contracts returned. For the following reasons, we affirm.

FACTS

In December 1989, 16–year-old Travis Mitchell, born October 31, 1973, brought a 1970 Pontiac GTO into M & M Precision Body and Paint to obtain an estimate on repairs to the vehicle from Mark Mizerski. After examining the vehicle, Mizerski provided Travis with an estimate for repairs in the amount of $1,550.35 and informed him that a $1,000 deposit to cover the cost of parts and materials would be required before the work was begun.

Travis delivered the vehicle to Mizerski's body shop in April 1990 to have the vehicle repaired and presented the required deposit in the form of a $1,000 cashier's check. In late April or early May, Travis and his father, Ted Mitchell, went to the body shop to check on the vehicle and to discuss and authorize additional repairs which were estimated to cost another $300 to $400. The estimate for these additional repairs was added to the total of the original estimate. In the middle of July, Travis and Ted again returned to the body shop, and Ted became involved in a "heated" argument with Mizerski concerning the balance due for all the repairs. Mizerski and Ted subsequently compromised on a balance due of $850. This amount was paid to Mizerski in the form of a cashier's check drawn on Travis' parents' account when Travis picked up the vehicle at the end of July.

The car was returned to the body shop on two separate occasions soon thereafter to have the body shop fix a crack in the paint on the hood and repaint the front bumper covering which had cracked and peeled. In July 1991, Travis brought the vehicle to the body shop to have several chips in the paint repaired for the agreed amount of $50, said amount being paid by Travis.

On August 4, 1991, Mizerski received a letter from Ted and Travis complaining about Mizerski's poor workmanship on the vehicle and asking how Mizerski intended to resolve the problems. Mizerski did not reply, and this lawsuit followed.

Ted filed suit as next friend of Travis, a minor, and in the second amended petition, Travis sought to disaffirm the contracts which were the basis for the repair work performed by Mizerski and to have all amounts paid under those contracts returned to Travis. Travis was still a minor when he elected to disaffirm the contracts. The two causes of action asserted were based upon the alleged existence of two separate contracts between Mizerski and Travis. The first action involved the contract for the original major body work and sought the return of the $1,850 paid under that contract. The second action concerned the contract for the repair of the chipped paint and sought the return of the $50 paid under the contract. In his answer, Mizerski admitted that he performed the work on the vehicle, but denied that the work constituted a contract with a minor and instead alleged that all of the work was performed at the request of both Travis and Ted.

* * *

ANALYSIS

Parties to Contracts.

* * * Viewing the evidence in the light most favorable to Travis, as we must, we cannot say that the county court was clearly erroneous in its finding that Travis, not Ted, was the party entering into the contracts with Mizerski.

In regard to the first cause of action, dealing with the major body repairs, Travis testified at trial that he received the estimate from Mizerski in his own name; he brought the car into the shop for repairs; he picked up the car when repairs were completed; and that, although the checks for payment were written from his mother's account, he paid for the repairs with funds deposited by him into his mother's account because he did not have a checking account. Travis acknowledges that his father, Ted, went to the body shop with him on two occasions to observe the progression of the repairs and that on one of those occasions Ted argued with Mizerski about the remaining balance for the repairs. The individual who replaced the car's vinyl top during the time Mizerski was repairing the car testified that in a conversation he had with

Mizerski, Mizerski stated that he was dealing directly with Travis and not with Ted for the repairs on the car. Mizerski could not recall that conversation.

Mizerski argues that although he initially dealt with Travis, the contract was actually between him and Ted as evidenced by these facts: Ted was the title owner of the vehicle, the initial deposit and balance were paid with checks from Travis' parents' bank account, Ted requested the additional repairs, Ted argued with Mizerski and compromised on the payment of $850 as the balance due, and the complaint letter was written by both Travis and Ted. Mizerski essentially argues that Travis was merely acting as Ted's agent in these dealings. * * *

The original agreement was formed after Travis accepted Mizerski's estimate by returning the vehicle to the body shop and paying the $1,000 deposit. As of that time, Mizerski had had no contact with Travis' father and no reason to believe that Mizerski was entering into a contract with anyone other than Travis. Mizerski offered no evidence that he relied on the name printed on the $1,000 cashier's check or on the title to the car to ensure payment for the repairs. It is entirely reasonable for the trial court to conclude that Mizerski began working on the vehicle based solely upon Travis' promise to pay. * * *

Travis also contends that he alone entered the contract with Mizerski regarding the repair of the chips in the paint for $50. Mizerski himself testified that one of the stipulations to his doing the repair was that he would deal directly with Travis and not with Ted. Ted played no role in this contract and had no contract with Mizerski. Based on Travis' testimony and Mizerski's admission, it was not clearly erroneous for the county court to conclude that the contract in dispute in the second cause of action was exclusively between Travis and Mizerski.

Disaffirmance of Contract by Minor.

* * * Travis may be permitted to disaffirm the contracts and have all payments made pursuant to that contract returned.

As a general rule, an infant does not have the capacity to bind himself absolutely by contract.... The right of the infant to avoid his contract is one conferred by law for his protection against his own improvidence and the designs of others.... The policy of the law is to discourage adults from contracting with an infant; they cannot complain if, as a consequence of violating that rule, they are unable to enforce their contracts. * * * "The result seems hardly just to the [adult], but persons dealing with infants do so at their peril. The law is plain as to their disability to contract, and safety lies in refusing to transact business with them."

The privilege of infancy does not enable an infant to escape liability in all cases and under all circumstances and a well-established exception to the general rule is that an infant remains liable for "necessaries" furnished to him or her. Mizerski does not contend that the repairs performed on the car were "necessaries." * * * [A]ll contracts of an infant, except those for necessaries, are voidable by the infant, at his or her election made within a reasonable time after he or she becomes of age. This rule has been held to generally apply to all contracts, whether executory or executed.

* * *

* * * [B]ecause the repairs to the car were not necessaries, Travis is entitled to disaffirm the contracts while he is a minor or within a reasonable time after reaching the age of majority and to have all amounts he paid under the contract returned to him.

Nebraska law is clear that to disaffirm a contract because of infancy, the infant must return so much of the consideration received as remains in his or her possession at the time of the election, but he or she is not required to return an equivalent for such part as may have been disposed of during minority. * * *

Although Mizerski would normally be entitled to have whatever was received by the minor returned to him, the county court found that there was nothing of value that could be returned. That finding is not challenged on appeal and is further supported by the evidence. Due to the nature of the consideration furnished by Mizerski, i.e., paint and body work on the vehicle, and the ownership of the vehicle, there was nothing that could be returned by Travis. Although this result may appear unjust to Mizerski, Nebraska law imposes such consequence upon adults who enter into contracts with minors, as a means to discourage such contracts. * * *

Notes and Questions

1. *Questions about* Mizerski. Assume Mr. Mizerski, the adult party in the principal case, did not wish to take unfair advantage of minors such as Travis Mitchell. If you were Mizerski's counsel, what advice would you offer the client that would enable him to deal with minors yet protect his financial interests?

2. *The identity of the contracting parties. Mitchell* demonstrates that a threshold question may arise concerning whether the contracting party is the child or the child's parent. Under quite different circumstances, the question arose in North Carolina Baptist Hosps., Inc. v. Franklin, 405 S.E.2d 814 (N.C.App.1991). The plaintiff hospital provided emergency medical care for the nine-year-old patient following an automobile accident. The child's parents agreed in writing to pay for the care (which ultimately amounted to more than $16,000), but then failed to pay because they could not afford payment and did not apply for Medicaid.

Franklin held that the medical care was "admittedly necessary" but rejected the hospital's effort to invoke the necessaries doctrine and impose liability on the child, who had received a settlement from the insurer of the other driver involved in the accident. The court held that the hospital's contract was with the parents and not with the child: "[The hospital] having expressly contracted with the parents for payment, a contract between the hospital and the child for payment cannot be implied. * * * To hold otherwise * * * would make children the guarantors of their parents' debts for clothes, lodging, schooling, medical care and other necessaries." 405 S.E.2d at 817.

3. *Adult co-obligors*. Parents or other competent adults frequently co-sign notes and other instruments for obligations incurred by children. The adult co-obligor has responsibility for the obligation even if the child seeks to disaffirm the contract or otherwise does not fulfill its obligations. 2 Williston on Contracts § 327. Adult co-obligors act at their own peril, however, because the child's default may adversely affect the co-obligor's credit rating. Where the co-obligor pays on the child's default, the co-obligor may not deduct the payment from federal income tax as a bad debt.

4. *Age of general contractual capacity*. At common law, persons achieved general contractual capacity at the age of twenty-one. In the early 1970s, virtually all states lowered the general age of contractual capacity to eighteen. The nationwide trend coincided with the lowering to the general age of majority to eighteen. Statutes in forty-seven states now fix eighteen as the general age of contractual capacity. The general age is higher in only Alabama (19), Mississippi (21) and Nebraska (19). See Restatement (Second) Contracts § 14 (Reporter's Note). Section 14 of the Restatement recognizes that a statute may deprive a minor of the common law right to disaffirm a particular class of contracts covered by the statute.

5. *Disaffirmance*. In the absence of contrary statutory directive, a minor's contract is voidable by the minor, provided the minor "disaffirms" the contract during minority or within a reasonable time after reaching majority. Disaffirmance occurs where the minor expresses any desire to void the contract, whether by a lawsuit to void, by interposing minority as a defense to an enforcement action, or by stating orally or in writing a desire to void the contract. The minor must disaffirm either the entire contract or none of it. Once the minor disaffirms the contract, the action is irrevocable.

Because the operative policy is to protect children from overreaching by adult parties, the power to disaffirm is usually held only by the minor or, in the event of his death, by his heirs or personal representatives. Occasional decisions also permit parents to disaffirm a contract on behalf of their unemancipated child. In any event, an adult party may not disaffirm the contract on the ground of the other party's minority. See, e.g., Calamari and Perillo, Contracts § 8.2 (3d ed. 1987).

What constitutes a "reasonable time" for disaffirmance depends on the circumstances. Under some statutes a minor's contract ripens into a binding obligation unless the minor disaffirms not later than a particular period after reaching majority. See, e.g., Okla. Stat. tit. 15 § 19 (allowing a minor to disaffirm either before his majority or within (one) year's time afterwards.)

Despite the general power of disaffirmance, the common law deprives minors of the power to disaffirm in limited circumstances. For example, minors may not disaffirm agreements to perform obligations that the law otherwise commands that they perform, such as agreements to support their children born in or out of wedlock. A number of states have enacted statutes codifying this rule. See, e.g., Idaho Code 32–105. Insurance and banking legislation frequently deprives children of the power to disaffirm. See, e.g., N.Y. Ins. L. § 3207; Ohio Rev. Code Ann. § 3911.08.

6. *Children as commodities.* In 1975, ten-year-old Brooke Shields posed nude in a bathtub in a series of photographs financed by Playboy Press. On the child's behalf, her mother executed two unrestricted consents in the photographer's favor. In the next few years, the photographs were used, with the knowledge of Brooke and her mother, in various publications and in a display of larger-than-life photo enlargements in the windows of a store on Fifth Avenue in New York City. After her mother received authorization from the photographer, Brooke also used the photos in a book she published about herself.

In 1980, the child actress became concerned that the photographer planned further publications of the photos. After failing in her attempt to purchase the negatives, she sued for compensatory and punitive damages and an injunction permanently enjoining the defendant from any further use of the photographs. Without alleging that the photographs were obscene or pornographic, she alleged violation of the state's civil rights law, which creates a right to privacy. That law permits the use of a living person's name, portrait or picture where the user "first obtained the written consent of such person, or if a minor of his or her parent or guardian * * *." The court denied the plaintiff relief on the ground that her mother had executed a valid, enforceable consent:

> Concededly, at common law an infant could disaffirm his written consent or, for that matter, a consent executed by another on his or her behalf. Notwithstanding these rules, it is clear that the Legislature may abrogate an infant's common-law right to disaffirm or, conversely, it may confer upon infants the right to make binding contracts. Where a statute expressly permits a certain class of agreements to be made by infants, that settles the question and makes the agreement valid and enforceable. * * * Construing the statute strictly, as we must since it is in derogation of the common law, the parent's consent is binding on the infant and no words prohibiting disaffirmance are necessary to effectuate the legislative intent. Inasmuch as the consents in this case complied with the statutory requirements, they were valid and may not be disaffirmed. * * *

Shields v. Gross, 448 N.E.2d 108, 111 (N.Y.1983).

Should court approval have been required for the *Shields* contract? Should a portion of the contract proceeds have been set aside for Brooke? A New York statute required court approval for contracts with minors who were performing artists, such as actors, and professional athletes, but *Shields* held that child models were not covered under the statute. Further, the court noted that the statute "was not designed to expand the rights of infants to disaffirm their contracts, but to provide assurance to those required to deal with infants that the infants would not later disaffirm executory contracts to the adult contracting party's disadvantage." The court reasoned that the statutory requirements for prior court approval, "while entirely appropriate and necessary for performing artists and professional athletes, are impractical for a child model who, whether employed regularly or sporadically, works from session to session, sometimes for many different photographers. Moreover, they work for fees which are relatively modest when compared to those received by actors or professional athletes who may be employed by one employer at considerably greater remuneration for a statutorily permissible three-year term. Indeed, the fee in this case was $450, hardly sufficient to warrant the elaborate court proceedings required by [the statute] to necessitate a court's determination of what part should be set aside and preserved for the infant's future needs. Given the nature of the employment, it is entirely reasonable for the Legislature to substitute the parents' judgment and approval of what is best for their child for that of a court." Id. at 112. (For information on child labor laws, see Chapter 10.)

For an unsuccessful argument that "skin" magazines not be allowed to use photographs of nude children without court approval, see Faloona v. Hustler Magazine, Inc., 607 F.Supp. 1341 (N.D.Tex.1985). The court stated that it would not substitute its judgment for that of the mother, who gave an unrestricted consent for the use of the photos. The court agreed with plaintiffs that Hustler magazine was tasteless, offensive and filled with "unmitigated raunch," but held that the publication was protected by the First Amendment because the photos were not obscenity or child pornography.

7. *Ratification.* The minor loses the right to disaffirm a contract when, after reaching majority, he "ratifies" it before disaffirming. The minor party may ratify only after reaching majority because any purported ratification during minority would be the product of the same incapacity that attended the contract.

Ratification occurs when the minor party agrees, after reaching majority, to perform all or part of his obligations under the contract. See Restatement, Second of Contracts § 85. The minor may ratify by express statement (which may be oral unless a statute requires a writing), or by conduct (such as by using property received under the contract without disaffirming within a reasonable time). See Calamari and Perillo, supra § 8–4. Statutes frequently prescribe acts that constitute ratification as a matter of law. See, e.g., Mo. Rev. Stat. 431.060, which prescribes these acts: "(1) An acknowledgement of, or promise to pay such debt, made in writing; (2) A partial payment upon such debt; (3) A disposal of part or all of the property for which such debt was contracted; (4) A refusal to deliver property in his possession or under his control, for which such debt was contracted, to the person to whom the debt is due, on demand therefor made in writing."

8. *Restitution.* When the minor disaffirms the contract, the other party may be left in an unenviable position akin to Mr. Mizerski's. The common law rule is that when the minor disaffirms, the minor must return any property he received under the contract and still possesses or controls. If the minor party has dissipated or negligently destroyed the consideration in the interim, however, he may disaffirm without returning the property. As *Mitchell* indicates, the common law concludes that to condition disaffirmance on return of the property would penalize the minor for the very improvidence that underlies the capacity doctrine.

By statute or judicial decision, some states have tempered the harshness of disaffirmance by requiring the minor to pay the fair value the minor received from use of the property, or to pay depreciation on the property returned. Notice that *Mitchell* did not embrace this view, and thus left Mr. Mizerski empty-handed.

9. *What if the minor misrepresents his age?* Assume that when Mr. Mizerski questioned sixteen year-old Travis Mitchell about his age, the boy presented an artfully altered driver's license indicating that he was twenty-two. If Travis looked older than he was, would Mizerski have any legal recourse when Travis sued to disaffirm the contract? Could Mizerski sue in tort for misrepresentation? See Calamari and Perillo, Contracts § 8.7 (3d ed. 1987) (children are generally not liable for contracts but are liable for their torts); Doenges–Long Motors, Inc. v. Gillen, 328 P.2d 1077, 1081–82 (Colo. 1958). In some states, statutes prohibit disaffirmance in some circumstances. See, e.g., Iowa Code § 599.3 ("No contract can be thus disaffirmed in cases where, on account of the minor's own misrepresentations as to the minor's majority, or from the minor's having engaged in business as an adult, the other party had good reason to believe the minor capable of contracting.")

10. *Does the capacity doctrine necessarily protect minors?* Now that Mr. Mizerski has learned his lesson, what is likely to happen when the next sixteen-year-old seeking auto body work enters the shop unaccompanied by a parent? What if the next sixteen-year-old needs the automobile to drive to and from vocational school but cannot drive it at all without repairs?

The capacity doctrine may sometimes dissuade adults from contracting with a minor about matters important to the minor's welfare. In Rivera v. Reading Housing Authority, 819 F.Supp. 1323 (E.D.Pa.1993), for example, the local public housing authority required public housing applicants under eighteen to submit a judicial decree of emancipation as a condition of eligibility. Ms. Rivera, a teenage, single mother living with her infant daughter in a rat-infested one-bedroom apartment she could not afford challenged the requirement. The court upheld the housing authority's requirement: "Unless a minor is adjudicated as emancipated, a contract for housing may not be enforced, unless it is for a 'necessary.' In the absence of an emancipation decree and determination, [the public housing authority] would not be certain whether a lease agreement will be enforceable and would run the risk of entering into unenforceable contracts with minors. * * * To assume the risks of entering into unenforceable contracts would be to jeopardize sound fiscal policy as well as a fair allocation of scarce housing resources * * *." Id. at 1333–34.

11. *Necessaries doctrine.* The necessaries doctrine, which is a major exception to the capacity doctrine. When a person provides a minor with a necessity of life under circumstances indicating that the person expected payment pursuant to an agreement, the minor is not liable for the contract price, but is liable for the reasonable value of what was provided under the contract. When the child is unemancipated, the common law permits a party to invoke the doctrine only if the child's parents or guardians have refused to provide the goods or services in question. In some states, the common law doctrine is now codified by statute. See, e.g., Ga. Code Ann. § 13-3-20(b).

A layperson might expect that courts would find food, clothing and shelter to be quintessential necessaries. No such bright line rule exists, however. *Rivera* rejected the teenage single mother's contention that shelter is a necessary as a matter of law: "What constitutes a necessary is not fixed, but depends upon such factors as the minor's standard of living and particular circumstances, as well as the ability and willingness of the minor's parent or guardian, if one exists, to supply the needed services or articles. Thus, what constitutes a necessary for a particular minor is not determined by a fixed rule, but is a question of fact." *Rivera,* 819 F. Supp. at 1332.

Rivera stated the law this way: " '[W]here the parent has the ability and is willing to support his minor child, board, lodging, etc., furnished to such infant by another without the parent's consent are not necessaries for which the infant is liable.' Therefore, it follows that if a minor is living with a parent or guardian who is able and willing to furnish the minor with housing, housing is not a necessary and a contract entered into by the minor for housing will not be binding. Accordingly, while a court can find housing to be a 'necessary,' thereby withdrawing from the minor the right to disaffirm the lease, housing is not per se a necessary. A broader rule would unnecessarily extend the liability of minors for their contracts and would be contrary to the underlying purpose of the rule." Id. at 1332.

Courts must frequently determine whether the automobile or motorcycle a disaffirming minor purchased qualifies as a necessary. In accordance with the flexible approach *Rivera* discusses, the answer depends on the circumstances. Most decisions, however, do not find the vehicle to be a necessary, even when the minor assertedly "needs" it to travel to school or employment.

What policy ends does the necessaries doctrine seek to serve? Does the exception truly protect scrupulous adult parties that seek to serve the interests of minors? Does the exception protect minors by enabling them to contract with adults on particularly important matters?

12. *Marriage.* Marriage is "a civil contract, to which the consent of parties capable in law of making a contract is essential." N.Y. Dom. Rel. L. § 10. In virtually all states, a person eighteen or older may marry without the need for parental or judicial consent. Higher ages of consent prevail in only Nebraska and Mississippi. See Neb. Rev. Stat. §§ 42–105, 43–2101; Miss. Code Ann. § 93–1–5.

Where a party seeking to marry is under this age of individual consent, states typically require older minors to secure the consent of a parent or guardian, and younger minors to secure both parental and judicial consent. See, e.g., Alaska Stat. § 25.05.171 (sixteen or seventeen year-old must secure consent of parent or guardian; fifteen year-old must also secure judicial approval). States do not clearly articulate a minimum age of capacity, the lowest age at which a person may marry under any circumstances. See generally Lynn D. Wardle, Rethinking Marital Age Restrictions, 22 J. Fam. L. 1, 17–18 (1983–84).

13. *Pawnbrokers.* Most states prohibit pawnbrokers from accepting pledges or purchasing property from children under eighteen. See, e.g., Fla. Stat. Ann. § 539.001(12)(d). A few states, however, permit pawnbrokers to contract with a child whose parent consents. See, e.g., Vt. Stat. Ann. Ch. 97 § 3870.

14. *Student loans.* Children under eighteen may need to finance their higher education with loans from institutions of higher learning, private lending institutions or government agencies. They may be unable to secure their parent's guaranty, perhaps because they are estranged from their

parents or because they seek independence from them. Case law does not provide a bright-line rule that contracts to provide funding for higher education are contracts for "necessaries" binding on minor signatories.

In 1969, the Uniform Law Commissioners proposed the Uniform Minor Student Capacity to Borrow Act. The Act provides that where a minor signs a contract with any person (including a college, bank or other financial institution) for a loan to further the minor's higher education, the minor may not disaffirm. Six states have enacted the uniform law, all in 1970 or 1971 (Arizona, Mississippi, New Mexico, North Dakota, Oklahoma and Washington). See 9B U.L.A. 3–5 (1987 & Supp. 1996).

Legislative action on the uniform act has been dormant for more than a quarter-century, largely because states lowered the general age of contractual capacity from twenty-one to eighteen shortly after the act was proposed. Relatively few children under eighteen need to contract for higher education funding. Without enacting the uniform act, however, a handful of other states have nonetheless conferred capacity on minors to contract for such funding. See, e.g., Or. Rev. Stat. § 348.105.

15. *Some proposals for change.* Standard 6.1 of the ILA–ABA Juvenile Justice Standards Relating to Rights of Minors recommends that in any of three circumstances, a contract of a child at least twelve years old should be enforceable if the contract would be enforceable against an adult: (a) Where the parent or guardian gave written consent to the contract; (b) where the minor represented that he or she was at least eighteen and the other party reasonably believed the minor; or (3) where the minor was a purchaser "unable to return the goods to the seller in substantially the condition they were in when purchased because the minor has lost or caused them to be damaged, the minor consumed them, or the minor gave them away." The Standards would void any contract of a minor under age twelve. In what ways are these recommendations consistent with prevailing law, and what do they change? Would you favor legislation effectuating the recommended changes?

In 1974, before she ascended to the District of Columbia Circuit bench, Patricia M. Wald made the following recommendation: "Age should no longer be a bar to retaining and using one's own money, making valid purchases and contracts. This * * * does not and should not mean that children are presumed to be no less vulnerable and gullible than adults, and that adults therefore have no greater obligation to them. To the contrary, those who deal with children—manufacturers, merchants, advertisers, etc.— ought to be held to a higher standard of care to prevent fraud, duress, or exploitation based on the age of their clients." Patricia M. Wald, Making Sense Out of the Rights of Youth, 4 Hum. Rts. 13, 18–19 (1974). Do you agree?

PROBLEM 9–3

Ms. Statler was engaged to Mr. Ware and was pregnant with their child, but Mr. Ware died before they were married. Ms. Statler employed you to represent her and the unborn child in a claim against Mr. Ware's estate. You were to be paid on a contingency basis, with your fee coming from the infant's share of the estate if you were successful. After the child was born, you arranged for blood testing. You established that Mr. Ware was the father and that the child would have a claim to the estate.

Ms. Statler then terminated your services and settled with the estate on her child's behalf. She has refused to pay you for your services. The trial court denied your motion for attorneys' fees from the child's share of the estate, finding that the unborn child could not enter into a contract, even through a next friend.

What other arguments could you make to collect your fee?

PROBLEM 9–4

Sixteen-year-old Eugene purchased a used pick-up truck for $4,900 from Mr. and Mrs. Smith, owners of Smith's Auto Sales. Nine months after the purchase, the truck developed mechanical problems. A mechanic thought the problem was a burnt valve. Eugene did not want to pay for repairs and continued to drive the truck. About one month later the truck's engine "blew up," making the truck inoperable and reducing its fair market value to $500.

Eugene parked the truck in his parents' front yard and asked to rescind the purchase. The Smiths refuse to take the truck back and refund Eugene's money without compensation for depreciation.

What result?

SECTION 3.   THE CHILD'S PROPERTY

Minors may own real and personal property. In general, however, they cannot manage property effectively because their minority allows them to disaffirm their contracts, deeds, agreements to purchase, leases and other arrangements related to the property. Because of their right to disaffirm, parties are reluctant to deal with them. Hence guardians or conservators who can make binding arrangements are needed to manage the minor's property. Unless there has been a determination to the contrary, parents are naturally the guardians of the person of the child, and hence are a logical choice to be guardians of the child's property as well. Guardianships can be cumbersome, however, particularly if court approval is needed for property transfers. Hence trusts and the Uniform Transfers to Minors Act or its predecessor, the Uniform Gifts to Minors Act, are frequently used to give property to a minor. These transfers allow the minor's property to be managed for the benefit of minor privately, without court supervision.

A.   *Uniform Transfers to Minors Act*

The Uniform Gifts to Minors Act (UGMA) was promulgated by the National Conference of Commissioners on Uniform State Laws in 1956. The Act went through several revisions and is now called the Uniform Transfer to Minors Act (UTMA). Every state has some version of the UGMA or the UTMA.

The definition of "custodial property" that can transferred under the UMTA is very broad and is intended to include legal and equitable interests in all types of property, including real property, without regard to its location. A "minor" under the Act is a person who has not attained the age of 21. Twenty-one was chosen rather than age 18 because the drafters believed that most donors preferred that property be managed for the donee for the longer period and because the Internal Revenue Code permitted "minority trusts" under § 2503 (c) to continue until age 21.

The procedure for transferring property under the Act is very simple. To create custodial property in money or securities, for example, "money is paid or delivered, or a security held in the name of a broker, financial institution, or its nominee is transferred, to a broker or financial institution for credit to an account in the name of the transferor, an adult other than the transferor, or a trust company, followed in substance by the words: 'as custodian for [name of minor] under the [Name of Enacting State] Uniform Transfers to Minors Act.' " § 9(2). To create custodial real property, "an interest in real property is recorded in the name of the transferor, an adult other than the transferor, or a trust company, followed in substance by the words: 'as custodian for [name of minor] under the [Name of Enacting State] Uniform Transfers to Minors Act.' " § 9(5).

Once a transfer is made, it is irrevocable and the property is indefeasibly vested in the minor (§ 11). The Act enumerates the custodian's responsibilities. The standard of care the custodian must follow is one that "would be observed by a prudent person dealing with property of another and is not limited by any other statute restricting investments by fiduciaries. If a custodian has a special skill or expertise or is named custodian on the basis of representations of a special skill or expertise, the custodian shall use that skill or expertise. However, a custodian, in the custodian's discretion and without liability to the minor or the minor's estate, may retain any custodial property received from a transferor." § 12 (3)(b). When dealing with custodial property, however, the custodian must keep the minor's property separate from other property so that it can be clearly identified. § 12 (3)(d).

The Act also specifies the possible uses of custodial property (§ 14):

(a) A custodian may deliver or pay to the minor or expend for the minor's benefit so much of the custodial property as the custodian considers advisable for the use and benefit of the minor, without court order and without regard to (i) the duty or ability of the custodian personally or of any other person to support the minor, or (ii) any other income or property of the minor which may be applicable or available for that purpose.

(b) On petition of an interested person or the minor if the minor has attained the age of 14 years, the court may order the custodian to deliver or pay to the minor or expend for the minor's benefit so much of the custodial property as the court considers advisable for the use and benefit of the minor.

(c) A delivery, payment, or expenditure under this section is in addition to, not in substitution for, and does not affect any obligation of a person to support the minor.

A minor who has attained the age of 14 may petition the court for an accounting by the custodian. The guardian of the person of the minor or an adult member of the minor's family may petition at any time. § 19.

B. Use of The Child's Assets

SUTLIFF v. SUTLIFF

Supreme Court of Pennsylvania,1987.
528 A.2d 1318.

HUTCHINSON, JUSTICE.

* * *

The issues presented for our review concern the use of property given under the Pennsylvania Uniform Gifts to Minors Act (UGMA), 20 Pa.C.S. SS 5301–10, specifically, whether such funds should be considered by the court in fashioning a support order and whether they may be used to fulfill a parent's support obligation. * * * On the merits, we hold that a parent's obligation to support minor children is independent of the minor's assets. UGMA funds may not be used to fulfill the parent's support obligation where the parent has sufficient means to discharge it himself. Upon determining that the parent has sufficient funds to reasonably support the minor without seriously depriving himself or other persons to whom he has a similar obligation, the court should not thereafter consider the minor's funds in setting the support obligation. This is not to say that a custodian cannot, as a fiduciary, exercise his statutory discretion in certain circumstances to distribute custodial funds for a minor's support in addition to those due from the parent. However, where the parent is also custodian, his dual obligation comes into conflict. In such case, he may not credit his custodial distribution against his support obligation. In the event of a dispute over the extent of his parental obligation, the parent custodian is removable at Common Pleas' discretion on petition by or on behalf of the child.

Gregory L. Sutliff (father) and Carlene S. Sutliff (mother) were married in 1960; they had four children. At the time of the couple's separation in 1981 only the three youngest, Kimberly, Julia and Laura, were minors. The father owns and operates a successful car dealership in the Harrisburg area. His net worth is approximately $3,000,000 and he earns in excess of $130,000 per year. The mother is an emergency room physician. She works part time and earns $26,000 per year. She claims that she cannot work full time because that would prevent her from properly raising the children.

The father and his parents gave substantial assets to the children under the UGMA. The children's aggregate accounts contained cash, stocks and bonds worth over $466,000. These assets were divided equally among the children. Father is the custodian of those assets given by his parents; Fred K. Collins, the father's business associate, is custodian of those assets given by the father.

In November, 1981 the mother filed a petition for support for herself and the three minor children. An interim support order providing $400.00 per week exclusively for the support of the minor children was entered against the father. Collins and he used the UGMA funds to fulfill up to 75% of the support obligation.

The mother then filed a suit alleging misuse of the children's custodial funds by the father and Collins. She sought a full accounting and their removal as custodians. She also sought to surcharge the custodians for any UGMA funds spent to discharge the father's support obligation. Cumberland County Common Pleas, Orphans' Court Division, held that the custodians could use the children's UGMA funds to fulfill the father's support obligation to the children. The court relied on statutory language which gives the custodian broad discretion in expending UGMA funds.

§ 5305. Duties and powers of custodian

* * *

(b) The custodian shall pay over to the minor for expenditure by him or expend for the minor's benefit so much of or all the custodial property as the custodian deems advisable for the support, maintenance, education and benefit of the minor, in the manner, at the time or times, and to the extent that the custodian, in his discretion, deems suitable and proper, with or without court order, with or without regard to the duty of himself or of any other person to support the minor, or his ability to do so, and with or without regard to any other income or property of the minor, which may be applicable or available for any such purpose.

The court did not limit the amount of custodial funds that the father and Collins could use to discharge the father's support obligation. Mother appealed this order.

Subsequently, Common Pleas entered a final support order which required the father to pay $600.00 per week for support of the minor children. In reaching its decision on support, the court considered, among other factors, the assets and income of the father and the mother, housing expense and prior standard of living. The court stated that it had previously resolved the issue of the availability of the children's UGMA assets to fulfill the father's child support obligation. It stated that "[t]here is no doubt that [father] can reasonably pay this support order," but did not restrict or limit the father's use of UGMA funds to fulfill his support obligation.

Both parties appealed the final support order to Superior Court. The mother claimed that Common Pleas improperly permitted father to satisfy his support obligations from custodial funds. In addition, she argued that the father and Collins, his business associate, should be removed as custodians and surcharged for their improper use of the UGMA funds. The father appealed the support order, claiming that he should not be required to support children who have substantial assets of their own.

* * *

The purpose of child support is to promote the best interest of the child; the associated legal obligation of parents is to provide for the reasonable expenses of raising the child. Indeed, parents have a duty to support their minor children even if it causes them some hardship. The cost of raising children is a function of several factors including custom, the children's needs and the parents' financial status. It is intended to provide for more than bare necessities. * * *.

* * *

The purpose of the UGMA is to provide an inexpensive, easy mechanism for giving property to minors. Before passage of the UGMA, a trust or guardianship was required. These methods were unwieldy, raised federal tax problems and were often prohibitively expensive for all but large gifts. The UGMA seeks to solve the problem of administrative expense and complexity while preserving certain federal tax benefits for the donor. Property transferred under UGMA is owned by the donee-minor; the minor is vested with full and indefeasible title. A custodian holds, manages, invests and dispenses the property during the child's minority, but must deliver the property and proceeds, plus accumulated interest and profit, to the minor when he reaches the age of twenty-one.[5] Unlike a trust for support or education, the proceeds of which must be used for the stated purpose, the UGMA property and proceeds may generally be used by custodians for the child's support. It is, however, the custodian's duty to use the property for the child's benefit. We have stated that a custodian may not use UGMA property to benefit himself, and suggested that a custodian may not use it to fulfill an existing support obligation.

The minor-custodian relationship under UGMA involves at a minimum the fiduciary obligation of an agent. The custodian is expected to use the property for the minor's benefit and act in the minor's interest. An agency relationship is a fiduciary one, and the agent is subject to a duty of loyalty to act only for the principal's benefit. A custodian under UGMA should be held to a no less rigorous standard. Indeed, a custodian's duties may be more properly analogous to those of a trustee with

---

5. This also distinguishes a minor given assets under UGMA from a trust beneficiary. Though a beneficiary of a trust enjoys the fruits of the corpus, he may or may not eventually own it; a beneficiary does not have title to the corpus. The minor actually owns the property.

the broadest possible discretionary powers. A trustee owes a fiduciary duty to the beneficiary. He violates that duty when he has a personal interest in trust dealings that might affect his judgment.

Were we to permit unrestrained credit against child support for these custodians' distributions, the father's action as custodian would be self-serving and Collins's would benefit the father, not the children. When he can "reasonably" do so, the father is obliged to provide support for his minor children regardless of the UGMA property. Whether it is reasonable to require a father to supply all or part of the support his children require without regard to their own means is a threshold question. It involves balancing the parent's income, assets, earning power and needs against the children's needs. If the court determines that the parent can reasonably provide for their needs at an appropriate level, that obligation is paramount and the children's means should not be considered. The inquiry should thereafter deal only with the children's reasonable requirements, with a possible exception for children seeking higher education If, however, the parent's assets are not adequate, the court should state, on the record, both the children's total needs and the parent's reasonable contribution. Common Pleas' failure to separate the issue of father's reasonable obligation from the children's needs has led to much of the confusion in this case.

On this record, it is plain that father and his business associate exercised their powers as custodians of the children's UGMA property to fulfill some part of the father's support obligation out of the children's assets. To the extent that this expenditure of the children's assets relieved the father from his "reasonable" support obligation, it is, we believe, a breach of duty of loyalty by the father, discussed supra, and brings into question Collins's good faith in exercising his custodial discretion. We also believe that these facts present a conflict of interest which would require the custodians' removal. A support order must state the amount for which the father is personally responsible and must pay from his own funds. * * *

Even if a parent lacks the resources to fully provide for his children's needs, no court should grant him or her the unbridled right to pay as much of the children's support from UGMA funds as he or she sees fit. This would be akin to removing the parent's support obligation to the extent the children have assets and is contrary to law. Child support is a parent's personal obligation and must be paid by him. * * *

Under this analysis, UGMA property, like other assets, can be used for the children's needs if the father could not or would not fulfill his support obligation. The parent's obligation remains paramount.

As discussed earlier, Superior Court has held in similar contexts that a judge fashioning a support order may consider a child's assets and income if the parent's resources are lacking. UGMA funds should also be considered in those circumstances. Such an expenditure would save the child from need or destitution and clearly would be in the child's interest. However, that is not the case here. * * * If a parent did refuse to fulfill his support obligation, a custodian acting in good faith could make interim expenditures for the children's necessary support. Thereafter, he could seek to recover any distributions he made on behalf of the children from the responsible parent and in doing so should be protected against any other personal responsibility.

Although a parent has an absolute duty to support his or her minor children, this support obligation does not always extend to financing a college education. * * * [A] court may more freely consider UGMA assets when apportioning financial responsibility for a child's education. However, there was no finding here that husband's assets are lacking or that provision of a college education would impose any hardship on him. Indeed, the present record belies any such problem.

A parent-custodian who uses custodial funds to satisfy his own support obligation violates his duty of loyalty and hereafter is subject to surcharge and removal for such violation. It seems to us, however, that automatic removal and surcharge for past acts of the custodians which violate this fiduciary duty of loyalty are inappropriate because it has not heretofore been considered in the context of UGMA. Any custodian, however, who uses UGMA funds to satisfy a parent's support obligation is subject to surcharge and removal if his acts were in bad faith.

In this case, the question of bad faith was not considered by the lower courts. For that reason, the record is inadequate for a decision on that issue.

Accordingly, the record is remanded to the Court of Common Pleas of Cumberland County for such further proceedings as may be necessary to determine the custodians' good faith as well as the question of whether this father has sufficient means to meet his children's needs without using their own property. Otherwise, the order of Superior Court is affirmed.

* * *

GUARDIANSHIP OF NELSON

Court of Appeals of Minnesota, 1996.
547 N.W.2d 105.

WILLIS, JUDGE.

Guardian appeals from the district court's order denying his petition for allocation of the social security income of his son.

FACTS

Blake Evert Nelson (Blake) receives approximately $786 monthly in social security survivor benefits due to his mother's death. The Social Security Administration disburses the benefits to William G. Nelson (Nelson), Blake's father and legal guardian, as Blake's representative payee. Nelson petitioned the district court to allow him, as Blake's guardian and representative payee, to use Blake's social security benefits to pay for Blake's food, shelter, and clothing.[1]

The district court denied Nelson's petition, concluding that Nelson could use Blake's social security benefits only to pay for "a computer, recreational equipment and fees, personal allowances, appropriate legal fees, and other purchases which may not be considered necessities." The district court relied on the following Minnesota statute regarding the duties of guardians:

The duties and powers of a guardian * * * include, but are not limited to:

(1) The duty to pay the reasonable charges for the support, maintenance, and education of the ward or conservatee in a manner suitable to the ward's or conservatee's station in life and the value of estate. Nothing herein contained shall release parents from obligations imposed by law for the support, maintenance, and education of their children. The guardian * * * has no duty to pay for these requirements out of personal funds. Wherever possible and appropriate, the guardian * * * should meet these requirements through governmental benefits or services to which the ward * * * is entitled, rather than from the ward's * * * estate.

Minn.Stat. § 525.56, subd. 4(1) (1994). The district court interpreted the statute to require Nelson to pay for Blake's necessities without using Blake's social security benefits. The court reasoned that because Nelson is Blake's father, he is obligated to provide for Blake.

ISSUE

Do federal social security regulations preempt state law that requires a representative payee parent to provide personally for the support, maintenance, and education of his or her child?

ANALYSIS

Nelson argues that federal regulations preempt Minn.Stat. § 525.56, subd. 4(1) (1994), to the extent that the statute prevents Nelson from using Blake's social security survivor benefits for Blake's current maintenance needs. * * *

* * *

If a representative payee does not use payments in accordance with Social Security Administration regulations, the administration will select a new payee. A representative payee commits a felony if he or she "knowingly and willfully converts * * * a payment * * * to a use other than for the use and benefit of [the beneficiary]." The Social Security Administration considers payments to "have been used for the use and benefit of the beneficiary if they are used for the beneficiary's current

---

1. Nelson also petitioned the district court for allocation of Blake's monthly income of $1641 from his mother's Teacher's Retirement Association annuity. The district court also denied Nelson's petition regarding Blake's annuity income. Nelson does not appeal that portion of the district court's order.

maintenance," which includes (1) costs of food, shelter, clothing, medical care, and personal comfort items and (2) costs of institutional care. 20 C.F.R. §§ 404.2040(a)(1), (b) (1994). If payments exceed the costs of the beneficiary's current maintenance needs, a payee may use a beneficiary's payments for (1) support of the beneficiary's legal dependents or (2) debts of the beneficiary that arose before payments began (d). After the representative payee has used the payments to satisfy the requirements of 20 C.F.R. § 404.2040, "any remaining amount shall be conserved or invested on behalf of the beneficiary." Federal regulations do not authorize a representative payee to use survivor benefits for any other purpose.

The district court's order prohibiting Nelson from applying Blake's social security benefits to Blake's current maintenance needs directly conflicts with federal law; compliance with both the court's order and federal law is impossible. Further, the district court's order prevents accomplishment of Congress's goal in establishing social security disability and survivor benefits: to replace income that would otherwise be available from a disabled or deceased parent for the beneficiary's current maintenance. Because social security survivor benefits replace a deceased parent's income, they "are not a windfall" to the beneficiary. The availability of such benefits to pay a child's current maintenance costs also is not a windfall to a surviving parent, because the benefits replace a deceased parent's income that would otherwise be available for that purpose. We hold that federal law preempts Minn.Stat. § 525.56, subd. 4(1), to the extent that the statute prevents representative payee parents from using their children's social security survivor benefits for the children's current maintenance.

Our conclusion comports with decisions of other jurisdictions.* * *

* * *

* * * Federal regulations provide that social security survivor payments are for a beneficiary's current maintenance, not for a beneficiary's future use, unless the payments exceed the costs of current maintenance. See 20 C.F.R. § 404.2040. We recognize that parents have a duty to provide for their children's needs. See Minn.Stat. § 260.221, subd. 1(b)(2) (stating that failure to provide for a child's needs may be a ground to terminate parental rights). Preemption principles, however, lead us to conclude that a representative payee parent can use his or her child's social security survivor benefits for the child's current maintenance regardless of the parent's financial ability to meet those needs.

* * *

Notes and Questions

1. *Tort awards and child support.* If a child of divorced parents receives a large personal injury award because of an accident, some states allow the award to be a basis for reducing the child support obligation. In Rainwater v. Williams, 930 S.W.2d 405 (Ky.App.1996), the child was to receive the

cumulative sum of $13,381,000.00 over sixty years. Under Kentucky law a court could deviate from the child support guidelines if application of the guidelines would be unjust or inappropriate, based on consideration of criteria specified in the statute. Because these criteria allowed consideration of "the independent financial resources of the child, if any," the court could consider the tort award, and reduce the child support obligation.

2. *The child's wages.* At common law and in some states by statute (e.g., Mo. Rev. Stat. §§ 452.150, 452.220), a child's wages belonged to the parent and could be used to support the child. Should this common law rule be amended and if so, how? As note 6 on page 894 mentions, some states require court approval of contracts with minors in certain professions, such as acting. Typically the court would require that the money the child earns be used for the child's benefit rather than belonging to the parent. Court approval also would mean that the child could not disaffirm the contract.

3. *Trusts.* Trusts can also be used for gifts to children and have some advantages over custodianships created under the UTMA, particularly for large amounts of property. A trust can have all the donor's children or grandchildren as beneficiaries, with the trustee authorized to postpone distribution until all the children have attained the age of majority or to make unequal distributions among the children, depending on their needs. The custodianship ends when the child reaches age 21, but a trust can specify that the distribution will not occur until the child is older. In addition, a trust that accumulates income can be taxed separately, whereas the custodianship is not a separate tax entity. The major advantage of the UTMA is that it allows the transfer of property to the child without requiring the donor to spend time and money on the preparation of a trust instrument. For additional information, see William M. McGovern, Jr., Trusts, Custodianships, and Durable Powers of Attorney, 27 Real Prop. Probate and Trusts J. 1 (1992).

PROBLEM 9–5

After a bitter divorce Dr. Cahn received custody of her four-year-old daughter. Three years after the divorce Dr. Cahn gave her daughter $50,000 under the UTMA, naming herself as custodian. She spent money from the custodial fund on summer camps and lessons for her daughter, on clothes and medical expenses for her daughter, and also reimbursed herself $15,000 for attorneys' fees incurred during subsequent custody litigation with her former husband.

When her daughter turned 16, she sued her mother for an accounting and for reimbursement of the monies expended. Should Dr. Cahn be required to reimburse the custodial account for all monies expended?

PROBLEM 9–6

A father is the UTMA custodian of a grandparent's gift of money to his son. He spends $10,000 of custodial property for services that, upon an accounting, were found to be inappropriate, but not made in bad faith. The custodian is required to reimburse the fund for $10,000.

Should he also pay interest on the $10,000 from the time he removed it from the fund?

SECTION 4.   TORTS AND FAMILY RELATIONS

In general, minors have the same rights and responsibilities as adults in tort matters, but some special rules apply. As noted in Chapter 3, although children can sue and be sued for their torts, but usually cannot bring or defend a legal action in their own name, but must have a court-appointed representative. In addition, the child's age may be relevant to the issue of intent in suits alleging intentional torts. Some jurisdictions have a conclusive presumption that a child under the age of seven is incapable of negligence.

The parent-child relationship also may set up special tort rules concerning liability and compensable interests. In many jurisdictions, parents may be held partially responsible for some of their children's torts. Immunity doctrines may bar intrafamily tort suits. Wrongful death and loss of consortium actions may depend on family relationships. The following decisions illustrate some of these issues. While reading them, consider whether children have more or less control over financial matters relating to torts than contracts or property. Consider also how these decisions view children's competence and the parent-child relationship.

A. *Liability*

STANDARD v. SHINE

Supreme Court of South Carolina, 1982.
295 S.E.2d 786.

HARWELL, JUSTICE:

* * *

Appellant Larry Shine, Jr., lived with his parents in an apartment operated by the respondent. He was six years old at the time this action arose. Respondent's complaint alleged that the appellant minor negligently set fire to the leased premises resulting in actual damages which respondent sought to recover from him. In a separate cause of action, respondent proceeded against the parents of the minor under Section 20–7–340, Code of Laws of South Carolina, 1976 (Cum.Supp.1981).

The appellants' demurrers asserted that the minor defendant was as a matter of law incapable of either negligence or an intentional and malicious tort. Essentially these demurrers rested upon the conclusive presumption of incapacity that has shielded minors of tender years (that is, below age seven) from allegations of contributory negligence in South Carolina.

Heretofore, we have held, by analogy to the criminal law, that a child under seven years of age was conclusively presumed to be incapable of contributory negligence; a rebuttable presumption existed that a child between the ages of seven and fourteen was incapable of contributory negligence; and a child of fourteen years and over was presumed capable of contributory negligence. However, we have never addressed the primary negligence of minors, the issue before us today. Despite our previous holdings, the prevailing view in cases of both primary and contributory negligence of minors is that no arbitrary limits as to a minimum age should be set. The capacities of children vary greatly, not only with age, but also with individuals of the same age. Therefore, no very definite statement can be made as to just what standard is to be applied to them. Of course, a child of tender years is not required to conform to an adult standard of care. The Restatement (Second) of Torts § 283A suggests that a minor's conduct should be judged by the standard of behavior to be expected of a child of like age, intelligence, and experience under like circumstances.

Today we adopt that standard of care for minors in both primary and contributory negligence cases. Insofar as today's decision differs from our previous cases dealing with the contributory negligence of minors, those cases are overruled. * * *

Respondent also stated a cause of action against the alleged tort feasor's parents pursuant to the South Carolina Parental Responsibility Act.

> When any unmarried minor under the age of seventeen years and living with his parent shall maliciously and intentionally destroy, damage or steal property, real, personal or mixed, the owner of such property shall be entitled to recover from such parent of such minor actual damages in a civil action court of competent jurisdiction in an amount not exceeding one thousand dollars.... S.C.Code Ann. § 20–7–340.

Although our statute has never been construed, North Carolina's similar statute was considered * * * and found to be constitutionally within the state's police power. The North Carolina court stated that parental responsibility acts were adopted as an aid in the control of juvenile delinquency. The limitation of amount of liability fails to serve any of the general compensatory objectives of tort law. Instead, their rationale is that parental indifference and failure to supervise the activities of children are the major causes of juvenile delinquency; that parental liability for harm done by children will stimulate attention and supervision; and that the total effect will be a reduction in the anti-social behavior of children.

Because parental responsibility statutes create liability in derogation of the common law, they are strictly construed. Where no conflict with common law exists, however, this Court will not substitute its view of public policy for that of the legislature. The General Assembly has made clear its choice; no presumptions will be indulged; minors of any age can commit intentional and malicious torts, specifically the tortious destruction of property. Hence, the appellants' demurrer to respondent's action * * * was properly overruled.

* * *

Notes and Questions

1. *Children's liability for their torts.* In sharp contrast to the doctrine that minors are generally not liable on their contracts, minors are generally liable for their intentional and negligent torts. Two qualifications to this general rule, however, frequently enable children to avoid tort liability in circumstances that would leave adults subject to liability. W. Page Keeton et al., Prosser and Keeton on the Law of Torts § 134 (5th ed. 1984). These are (a) mental capacity and (b) negligent performance of contractual obligations.

(a) Mental capacity

A child's mental capacity may be determined by standards different from the standards that help determine adults' mental capacity. Where a particularly young child is charged with an intentional tort, for example, the child may be effectively immune from liability under the common law because of inability to hold the requisite intent. The child must have some awareness of the natural consequences of the intentional acts. See, e.g., Farm Bureau Mutual Ins. Co. v. Henley, 628 S.W.2d 301, 303 (Ark.1982) (whether six-year-old can commit trespass is a jury question); DeLuca v. Bowden, 329 N.E.2d 109, 110–13 (Ohio 1975) (as a matter of law, child under seven incapable of committing intentional tort). A statute, however, may limit or abrogate common law immunity. See, e.g., Mont. Code Ann. § 41–1–201 ("A minor is civilly liable for a wrong done by him but is not liable in exemplary damages unless at the time of the act he was capable of knowing that it was wrongful.")

Similarly, courts generally hold that as a matter of law, particularly young children are presumptively or absolutely incapable of negligence. The question has arisen most frequently on affirmative defenses that the child plaintiff bears responsibility for contributory or comparative negligence. Courts might be more sympathetic to child plaintiffs, and hence unwilling to let adults profit by these defenses, than would be the case if the child were the defendant.

By statute or case law in many states, children under seven are incapable of negligence as a matter of law, children between seven and fourteen are presumptively incapable, and children over fourteen are presumptively capable. See, e.g., Lemond Construction Co. v. Wheeler, 669 So.2d 855, 860, 860–61 (Ala.1995). Whether a presumption has been rebutted is normally a fact question for the jury. See, e.g., Cates v. Kinnard, 626 N.E.2d 770, 774 (Ill.1994). Some decisions, however, reject such arbitrary classifications and hold that even children below seven are capable of some negligence.

What if the allegedly negligent child is fifteen years old but the parties concede that the child functions at the psychological and physical level of a three- to six-year-old? Is the child incapable of negligence as a matter of law, or is the child presumptively capable? See Burch v. American Family Mut. Ins. Co., 492 N.W.2d 338, 340 (Wis.Ct.App.1992) (child presumptively capable; applicable statute referred to the child's chronological age, not the child's functional age in terms of intellectual and physical ability).

Where a child is not incapable of negligence as a matter of law, courts ordinarily instruct juries that the child must meet only the standard of care that would be expected of a "reasonable person of like age, intelligence, and experience under the circumstances." Restatement (Second) of Torts § 283A. The law departs from the reasonable-person standard ordinarily imposed on adults because "A child is a person of such immature years as to be incapable of exercising the judgment, intelligence, knowledge, experience, and prudence demanded by" the adult standard. Id. comment a. "The special standard to be applied in the case of children arises out of the public interest in their welfare and protection, together with the fact that there is a wide basis of community experience upon which it is possible, as a practical matter, to determine what is to be expected of them." Id. comment b.

The law generally recognizes a limited exception to the doctrines stated in the previous paragraph. The adult reasonable-person standard applies when the negligence suit arises from a child's engagement in an activity normally undertaken only by adults, and for which adult qualifications are required. Such activities include operating a motor vehicle or airplane, but what constitutes an "adult activity" is not always clear. Should golf, for example, be considered an "adult activity"? See, e.g., Restatement (Second) of Torts § 283A, comment c. Riding a bicycle is generally held not to be an adult activity. See, e.g., Chu v. Bowers, 656 N.E.2d 436, 440 (Ill.App.1995) (citing decisions). The adult-activity exception applies even if at the time of the incident in question, it was obvious to the other party that he or she was involved with a child. See, e.g., Baumgartner v. Ziessow, 523 N.E.2d 1010, 1014 (Ill.App.1988).

(b) Negligent performance of contractual obligations

The second qualification concerns the interrelationship between contract law and tort law. What if a child contracts to perform a task and proceeds to perform negligently? If the child disaffirms the contract, may the adult party nonetheless recover in tort? Most courts do not permit tort recovery unless the child breached an obligation imposed by law independent of the contractual obligations. See Keeton et al., supra § 134, at 1071–72.

What policy considerations account for the general rule that minors, generally not liable for their contracts, are generally liable for their torts?

2. *Parental liability arising from children's torts.* The great weight of authority holds that in the absence of a statute, parents are not vicariously liable for their children's torts merely because of the parent-child relationship. Because the common law does not impose general vicarious liability on parents, many tort judgments against children go unrecovered unless insurance covers the child. In an effort to protect victims and decrease delinquency, however, most states now have statutes imposing parental liability for some intentional, and generally malicious, conduct by their children. The evident aim is to give parents a financial incentive to control their children. These statutes normally cap parental liability at an amount between a few hundred and a few thousand dollars. A tort lawyer working on a contingency fee probably would not be interested in a case with such limited recovery, however. See, e.g., Ga. Code Ann. § 51–2–3 ($10,000 cap). Florida is typical

of states that have recently repealed their caps. See Fla. Stat. Ann. § 741.24, amended by Laws 1988, c. 88–381, § 36. Is it good policy to impose liability on parents? What can parents do to avoid liability?

Where a statute imposes liability on the "parents" of a minor tortfeasor, may liability be imposed on foster parents? Do you think imposition of liability on foster parents would be sound as a policy matter? See Kerins v. Lima, 680 N.E.2d 32 (Mass.1997) (holding that the term "parent" in the liability statute does not include foster parents; the court noted that amid a chronic shortage of foster parents, imposing liability on them for their foster children's torts would "have a chilling effect on the willingness of families to open their homes to children in need of care").

In the absence of statute, plaintiffs in three general circumstances may prevail against the parents of a child who commits an intentional or negligent tort. First, parents may be found negligent if they unreasonably allow the child to use a dangerous instrument such as a firearm or an automobile, or if they carelessly leave such an instrument in a place where the child may gain access to it; the issue is whether the facts are sufficient to impose on the parent a duty to anticipate injury to another through the child's use of the instrument. Second, parents have been held liable for the child's tort where they have aided, abetted, encouraged or facilitated the act or where they have accepted benefits resulting from the act. Finally, where the parent has notice of the child's propensity for dangerous or violent conduct that might injure third parties, the parent has a duty to warn others of the potential danger or otherwise take reasonable measures to protect their safety. See Keeton et al., supra, § 124, at 914–15.

A frequently more fruitful avenue is to sue the parents for negligently failing to supervise or control the child. Suppose, for example, that parents are told that their six year-old child has a rifle and is shooting at a target on a public street. The target shooting endangers other users of the street. The parents fail to take the rifle away from the child or to take any other action. The child unintentionally shoots a pedestrian in the leg. Section 316 of the Restatement (Second) of Torts is worthy of the pedestrian's attention:

> A parent is under a duty to exercise reasonable care so to control his minor child as to prevent it from intentionally harming others or from so conducting itself as to create an unreasonable risk of bodily harm to them, if the parent
>
> > (a) knows or has reason to know that he has the ability to control his child, and
> >
> > (b) knows or should know of the necessity and opportunity for exercising such control.

3. *Loss of consortium.* Should parents be able to sue for the loss of a child's companionship? A majority of states do not allow loss of consortium actions by parents. Courts that reject the action express concern about the difficulty in measuring damages, the increase in litigation, multiple claims and the rise in insurance costs. See Siciliano v. Capitol City Shows, Inc., 475 A.2d 19 (N.H.1984).

Should children be able to sue for injury to a parent that causes a loss of parental care and society? States are split on this issue. For a review of the arguments for and against allowing recovery, see Klaus v. Fox Valley Sys., Inc., 912 P.2d 703 (Kan.1996). (The court noted that 22 states had rejected a cause of action for loss of parental consortium.)

4. *The priceless child.* What value does the life of a child have in a wrongful death action? Nineteenth century courts priced a child by estimating the value of the child's services from the time of death to the age of majority, less the expense of maintaining the child. As the economic value of children decreased, however, this formula resulted in some nominal awards. In one case, for example, the trial court awarded six cents for the wrongful death of a child of a wealthy man who had testified that his son had never earned any money and that the child had been a source of expense to him. Although a larger award was given on appeal, this case strikingly illustrated the problem of assigning an economic value to a child. The problem was exacerbated by child labor laws that restricted the child's employment. Gradually the emotional value of the child was established by considering noneconomic factors, such as the quality of the parent-child relationship, the extent of the parent's grief, and the characteristics of the child. Ironically, the value of a modern child in a wrongful death action has increased, even though most children today are a major financial expense to their parents rather than sources of additional family income. Some wrongful death awards have exceeded two million dollars for the death of a child.

In her fascinating account of the development of the law relating to the value of children, Viviana Zelizer notes that "the child death trial hinges on determining the subjective emotional value of a *particular* child." She notes that:

> Lawyers are urged to bring the child "back to life," dramatizing their brief with home movies and photographs showing the deceased child, "playing baseball, riding a merry-go-round, building sand castles at the beach * * *. To convey the uniqueness of the life lost, lawyers are also advised to visit the child's home 'take some time to see the room where the child slept and carefully catalog every detail' * * *." The irony, of course, is that the irreplaceability of the child's personal qualities must be established with the purpose of converting them into their cash equivalent.

Viviana Zelizer, Pricing the Priceless Child 159 (1985).

5. *Wrongful death of parent.* Wrongful death statutes usually make children beneficiaries, entitled to compensation for their parent's wrongful death. The wrongful death statutes, however, may define "child" and "parent" narrowly so that not all children who were dependent upon the decedent are included. For example, a dependent stepchild often is not considered a "child" under wrongful death statutes. The Social Security Act and workers' compensation statutes typically are less restrictive and allow children, such as stepchildren and grandchildren, who are actually dependent to receive benefits upon the death or injury of the wage-earner who supported them. See Margaret M. Mahoney, Stepfamilies and the Law 101–22 (1997).

6. *Wrongful birth and wrongful life.* Should parents be able to recover for expenses of caring for a "defective" child (wrongful birth) or an unwanted child (sometimes called wrongful conception)? Should a "defective" child be able to recover for general damages for having been permitted to be born (wrongful life)? A number of courts have allowed recovery for wrongful birth, although fewer allow an action for the birth of an unwanted, but healthy child. E.g., Boone v. Mullendore, 416 So.2d 718 (Ala.1982). Very few courts have allowed recovery for wrongful life, however, and some states have prohibited wrongful life claims by statute. When recovery is allowed, it may be very limited. E.g., Harbeson v. Parke–Davis, Inc., 656 P.2d 483 (Wash. 1983). For comprehensive discussions of wrongful life actions, see Donald T. Kramer, Legal Rights of Children, § 9.13 (2d ed. 1994), and Philip G. Peters, Jr., Rethinking Wrongful Life: Bridging the Boundary Between Tort and Family Law, 67 Tul. L.Rev. 397 (1992).

PROBLEM 9–7

Your state conclusively presumes that children under seven are incapable of negligence. The legislator you work for just got a call from an irate, and very important constituent, Mr. Burns. Mr. Burns had seen his neighbor's five-year-old child in his yard playing with and removing the grate over his sewer line. He had reprimanded the child and told the parents that the child should not be allowed to enter his yard without supervision.

While Mr. Burns was away, the child removed the grate, threw rocks and pop bottles into the line, blocked the line and caused Mr. Burns' basement to flood with raw sewage. Under state law "a person shall be entitled to recover damages from parents of any minor under age 18 who unlawfully or maliciously destroys property." Mr. Burns sued for the damage to his property, emotional distress and humiliation but lost because the court ruled that the child was not negligent because of his age. Before he talks to Mr. Burns again, the legislator wants to know the policy reasons for the presumption and whether he should work to get it changed to some other rule. What do you tell him? Does Mr. Burns have another basis for recovery?

PROBLEM 9–8

Harold, age 12, hit Jay, also age 12, at a track meet, breaking his nose and a tooth. Jay wants his medical expenses and punitive damages. The general rule in this jurisdiction is that minors are liable for their own torts, but the courts have never decided whether a minor is capable of the malicious intent necessary for a punitive damage award. What arguments would you make that Harold should be liable? Could you use a parental liability statute such as that in Standard v. Shine to help your argument?

B. Immunity

HARTMAN v. HARTMAN
Supreme Court of Missouri 1991.
821 S.W.2d 852.

COVINGTON, JUDGE.

The Court has consolidated for opinion two cases in which the appellants request re-examination of the parental immunity doctrine articulated in Baker v. Baker (Mo.1953). * * *

I.

In the Hartman case, Christine and Todd Hartman, by their mother and next friend, Sheila Hartman, filed an action in the Circuit Court of Jefferson County against their father, William E. Hartman, and their grandfather, William R. Hartman, for personal injuries suffered while on vacation near Climax Springs, Missouri. The minor children allege in their petition that their father and grandfather negligently maintained and operated a propane gas stove and propane tank causing them to explode, thereby injuring the children.

* * *

In the Armstrong case, plaintiffs' second amended petition alleges that Mary Armstrong's vehicle stalled while she was crossing the Missouri River on the I-435 bridge in Kansas City. Mary Armstrong's unemancipated minor children, Tracy and Michael, Jr., attempted to push the car off the bridge. According to the averments, the children were struck by a van operated by Jeffrey Tiller. As a result of the collision, Tracy sustained severe injuries and Michael, Jr., died.

Tracy, by her next friend and father Michael Armstrong, filed suit in the Circuit Court of Clay County against Mary Armstrong, Jeffrey Tiller, and American Family Insurance. Michael Armstrong on his own behalf filed suit against the same defendants for the wrongful death of Michael, Jr. Appellants claim that the negligence of Mary Armstrong and Tiller combined to cause the death of Michael, Jr., and injuries to Tracy. They further claim that Tiller's van was an uninsured motor vehicle within the coverage afforded by American Family to the Armstrongs on their vehicle.

* * *

II.

The first issue for decision in each case is the efficacy of the parental immunity doctrine in Missouri. Prior to 1891 no reported cases in the United States applied the doctrine. The first recorded application of the doctrine, a product of judicial policy making without common law basis, was in Mississippi in Hewellette v. George (Miss.1891). The Hewellette court grounded its decision in the need to preserve family harmony.

A Missouri court first recognized and applied the doctrine of parental immunity in [1939] * * *.

* * *

Determining whether to abrogate, retain, further modify, or carve yet additional exceptions to the doctrine requires reconsideration of the policy underpinning the immunity, which is an exception to the general rule of tort liability. In Missouri the adoption of the immunity rested primarily upon the need to "preserve and maintain the security, peace and tranquility of the home.... " Once adopted, it was feared that abrogation of the doctrine would "either disrupt the tranquility of the domestic establishment or subvert parental control or discipline." * * *

Re-examination of the significant interest in avoiding disruption of family harmony reveals that the interest exists in tension with the consequences of the sometimes brutal application of the doctrine, which bars an injured party's right to recover for injuries. In certain circumstances family harmony may be jeopardized by disallowing compensation for a child injured by the negligent act of a parent. * * * Taken to its logical conclusion, the doctrine has the effect of causing the parent to owe a greater duty to the general public than to his or her own child.

* * *

In retrospect, the interest in avoiding disruption of family harmony, while not insignificant, appears in the weighing to be less significant than the interest in the right of an injured child to recover for injuries, particularly when Missouri recognizes all other forms of intra-family liability and applies the immunity only to actions in negligence involving unemancipated minors. It is also apparent that the ever-increasing number of exceptions, which reflect the fault of the doctrine, will eventually engulf the rule. The preferred course is to abrogate the doctrine in its entirety.

III.

What remains of concern, however, is the interest in avoiding subversion of parental care, control, and discipline. In view of this interest, the question becomes whether the need to preserve parental prerogatives regarding child rearing justifies barring all suits for negligence between child and parent. This Court believes not. Parents should not be permitted to exercise parental prerogatives completely without concern for liability. It is uncontrovertible, however, that parents must be able to exercise a great degree of discretion in control over the relationship with their child.

In acknowledging that the doctrine of parental immunity, perhaps too hastily adopted, is difficult to justify, other jurisdictions have retained various exceptions to tort liability as a means of protecting the integrity of the parent's right and ability to exercise independent judgment in raising a child. While the majority of courts that have recently reevaluated the parental immunity doctrine have decided that some form of abrogation is warranted, courts have not reached a clear consensus regarding whether there is a standard of care required of parents or whether a limited immunity should be retained. * * *

A review of other jurisdictions' efforts is instructive. One approach to parental immunity attempts to ensure that suits between parent and child will never engender familial discord by retaining immunity except to the extent of the parent's insurance. An approach that takes into account the presence of liability insurance furthers the public policy enunciated by the Missouri legislature in requiring motor vehicle liability insurance, the purpose of which is to afford a means of redress for damages. Formulation of different rules for the insured and uninsured, however, is not justified. Furthermore, such a limited approach in Missouri would constitute an addition to the ever-lengthening list of exceptions to the immunity, thereby advancing the undesirable effects of piecemeal abrogation.

Other jurisdictions have abrogated parental immunity and substituted approaches that they believe adequately protect the family unit without unduly denying unemancipated minors a tort remedy. The first attempt at reform was undertaken by the Supreme Court of Wisconsin in 1963, which held that parental immunity was abrogated except: "(1) where the alleged negligent act involves an exercise of parental authority over the child; and (2) where the alleged negligent act involves an exercise of ordinary parental discretion with respect to the provision of food, clothing, housing, medical and dental services, and other care." Goller v. White (Wis.1963).

There has been sufficient time since *Goller* for its standards to have been tested and critiqued. The principal difficulty with the *Goller* approach has been found to be that the exceptions are vague; courts are forced to make arbitrary distinctions regarding whether the parental conduct at issue fits within one of the exceptions. Arbitrary line-drawing in determining which parental activities involve exercise of discretion or authority has resulted in inconsistent verdicts among courts applying *Goller* or a derivative of the *Goller* exceptions.

Perhaps even more troubling than the interpretative difficulties associated with the *Goller* approach is that the exceptions appear to give parents "carte blanche" to act negligently with respect to their children so long as the parents' conduct falls within one of the exceptions. There is no sound reason to distinguish among the various parental duties so as to permit unfettered parental discretion with respect to provision of necessities or the administration of discipline.

In order to ameliorate the problems caused by the abrogation with exceptions approach, the Supreme Court of California adopted a "reasonable parent" standard. [Gibson v. Gibson (Cal.1971)] The reasoning of *Gibson* gives deference to a parent's exercise of broad discretion in performing parental functions yet recognizes that parental prerogatives must be exercised within reasonable limits.

* * *

The *Gibson* alternative is sufficiently flexible to accommodate disparate child-rearing practices yet protects children from negligent parental excesses. The reasonable parent standard permits an injured child, or a third party plaintiff, to recover only if the parent fails to meet the standard of care required of parents. This Court, in the spousal immunity context, has recognized that courts are capable of examining and adjusting the duty of care required between family members according to the facts of the case.

The Restatement (Second) of Torts (1979) also addresses the issues. Section 895(G) provides: "(1) A parent or child is not immune from tort liability to the other solely by reason of that relationship; (2) repudiation of general tort immunity does not establish liability for an act or omission that, because of the parent-child relationship, is otherwise privileged or not tortious." The Restatement recognizes that the reasonable prudent parent is the applicable standard to be applied in suits involving negligent exercises of parental discretion.

* * *

This Court concludes that a reasonable parent standard should be adopted. The primary criticism of the reasonableness standard is the belief that parental judgment regarding the required degree of discipline and supervision of a particular child cannot be subjected to a judicial determination of reasonableness. Use of the reasonable parent standard, however, provides a single test for all aspects of the parent-child relationship. The standard can be managed to ensure that clearly unacceptable conduct giving rise to tort liability may be subjected to scrutiny. Courts will take into account, as they do in the context of the marital relationship, the relevant facts and circumstances of each parent and child so as to examine and adjust the duty of care required between family members, according to the facts of the case. Adoption of a reasonable parent standard is particularly appropriate in Missouri in view of the fact that the legislature has adopted the standard in relation to a parent's duty in the context of the juvenile code. A parent is expected "to exercise reasonable parental discipline or authority" and may be subject to a judgment of restitution, along with the child, to a victim, a governmental entity, or a third party payor, when the child has inflicted property damage or caused damages resulting in personal injury or death.

IV.

* * *

In summary, this Court abrogates the parental immunity doctrine of Baker v. Baker. Minor unemancipated children are authorized to bring actions sounding in negligence against their parents. The actions of parents are to be measured by a reasonable parent standard. * * *

Notes and Questions

1. *Erosion of the immunity doctrine.* Preservation of family harmony, fear of fraud, collusion, support for parental authority, and protection of family assets were reasons for protecting parents from tort suits by their unemancipated children. Beginning in the 1930's the courts began to limit the parental immunity doctrine, although most have not abolished it entirely:

> Collusion and fraud are no longer feared in these cases. They are considered to be no more likely in these cases than in actions brought by emancipated minors against their parents. Courts have noted that protection against fraud falls within the normal province of the trial judge and jury. As one court professed, it "would be a sad commentary on the law if 'the judicial processes are so ineffective that we must deny relief to a person otherwise entitled because in some future case a litigant may be guilty of fraud or collusion.'" The family harmony argument has also been rejected, especially since children have always been allowed to bring actions against their parents based on contract and property rights. The *coup de grace* for the immunity doctrine has been the growth of liability insurance, viewed as sparing the family purse.

Donald T. Kramer, Legal Rights of Children § 9.07 (2nd ed. 1994).

> For examples from jurisdictions that retain immunity in some circumstances, see Squeglia v. Squeglia, 661 A.2d 1007 (Conn.1995) (parental immunity doctrine barred child's strict liability action against father for dogbite); Hoffmeyer v. Hoffmeyer, 869 S.W.2d 667 (Tex.App.1994)(father's actions, which included leaving a loaded gun with his son and another child, failing to tell them it was loaded, and failing to supervise them, are the type of discretionary acts protected by the parental immunity doctrine). Parental immunity can be an issue also when a defendant wrongdoer seeks contribution from a parent or when a defendant seeks to show that parent's negligent supervision was the supervening cause of the child's injuries. Sears, Roebuck & Co. v. Huang, 652 A.2d 568 (Del.1995)(if "a parent's negligence was a proximate cause but not a supervening cause, the parent's negligence does not provide a basis for reducing full payment to the minor child or the basis for a claim of contribution by any defendant determined to be a tortfeasor, since by definition the parent cannot be a joint tortfeasor").

C. Release, Waiver and Settlement

Seven-year-old Sammy Smith's parents enrolled him in the local youth soccer league. As part of the application, the parents signed the required release discharging the league from liability to them or the child for any injury the child might suffer. In the team's first practice, Sammy suffered a broken leg, which did not heal properly and left him with a slight, though noticeable, limp. May the parents overcome the release and sue the league for damages? May the child, with his parents as guardians ad litem or next friends, overcome the release and sue the league? If the child does not sue now, may he sue the league a few months after he turns eighteen?

These questions may surface whenever a child has a potential or actual tort claim against a third party. As a condition of participation, schools, athletic leagues and other non-profit youth activities frequently require parents to sign releases waiving not only their own right to sue, but also the child's right. These releases frequently are also required by private businesses such as ski slopes. The releases are not nearly as ironclad as they may appear.

Waiver and Release. Consistent with the doctrine that competent adults generally may execute binding contracts, parents may waive their future right to sue on claims they themselves might have arising from their child's injury, such as claims for medical expenses and loss of the child's services and companionship. The common law rule, however, is that a parent, guardian ad litem or next friend may not waive the child's future right to sue. The common law prevails except in the relatively rare circumstances in which a statute speaks to the question.

What if the youth soccer league's required release was signed not only by Sammy Smith's parents, but also by seven-year-old Sammy himself? Could the child nonetheless sue for damages a few months after he turns eighteen? See, e.g., Simmons v. Parkette National Gymnastic Training Center, Inc., 670 F. Supp. 140 (E.D. Pa. 1987) (a release is a voidable contract that the child may disaffirm).

What if Sammy Smith's parents signed an agreement to indemnify the youth soccer league against any litigation expenses and damages the league might have to pay in a damage suit by Sammy? Should the parents' indemnification agreement be enforceable? See, e.g., Valdimer v. Mount Vernon Hebrew Camps, Inc., 172 N.E.2d 283, 210 (N.Y. 1961)(holding that indemnity agreement was against public policy because it would motivate the parent to discourage child's claim and would disturb family harmony if child sued); Childress v. Madison County, 777 S.W.2d 1, 7 (Tenn. Ct. App. 1989) (indemnity agreement invalid because it would place the parents' interests against the child's).

Settlement. Now suppose Sammy's parents signed no release when they enrolled him in the league. After Sammy breaks his leg, may the parents settle any claims they and the child have against the league? Is Sammy bound by the settlement now or after he turns eighteen?

Because competent adults generally may settle their existing civil claims, parents may settle their own claims arising from the child's injury. But they may not settle the child's existing claims without court approval that the settlement is in the child's best interests. Where a parent's effort to settle the child's claim precedes the filing of a lawsuit, an action may be filed to secure judicial approval. Some states permit court approval of a parent's settlement of the child's claim only after the court has appointed the parent as guardian ad litem or next friend.

Because waivers and unapproved settlements of the child's claims are void agreements contrary to public policy, they do not preclude the child from suing during minority or within the applicable limitations period after reaching majority. See, e.g., Scott v. Pacific West Mountain

Resort, 834 P.2d 6, 10–12 (Wash. 1992); Meyer v. Naperville Manner, Inc., 634 N.E.2d 411, 414–15 (Ill. App.1994). See also, e.g., International Union, UAW v. Johnson Controls, Inc. 499 U.S. 187, 213 & n.3 (1991) (White, J., concurring in part and concurring in the judgment) ("The general rule is that parents cannot waive causes of action on behalf of their children.")

Notes and Questions

1. If the law permits the parent, guardian ad litem or next friend to sue on the child's behalf, resulting in a final judgment after trial, why should a waiver or unapproved settlement agreement executed by one of these adults not bind the child? Should the child be able to upset an unapproved settlement after he receives some benefit from it during minority? What if the child knowingly continues to receive some benefit from the unapproved settlement after reaching majority? See Simmons, supra, 670 F. Supp. 140. (suggesting that the child cannot disaffirm a release that is part of a claim settlement when the child has received a benefit from it). What practical difficulties might the child face if he sues to overturn the release or unapproved settlement shortly after he reaches majority?

What policies does each of the general waiver and settlement rules seek to advance? By refusing to enforce parental releases or unapproved settlements of their child's claims, does the law unduly interfere with the parents' right to direct their child's upbringing? Do the general rules deter some groups and organizations from providing youth sports and other activities for children? Do the rules encourage organizations providing children's activities to adopt safe practices? With parental releases generally unenforceable, how can businesses, athletic leagues and other youth activities protect themselves against the prospect of children's lawsuits and the attendant liability?

One final question. Given the dubious enforceability of parental releases that purport to waive the child's right to sue, why do so many businesses, youth leagues and other activities nonetheless persist in requiring parents to sign them?

2. *School districts.* Should school districts be able to require exculpatory clauses as a condition for participation in athletic programs? See Note, Negligence–Exculpatory Clauses—School Districts Cannot Contract Out of Negligence Liability in Interscholastic Athletics—Wagenblast v. Odessa School District, 102 Harv. L.Rev. 729 (1989).

3. *Volunteers.* Should volunteers and non-profit organizations be able to enforce exculpatory agreements? See Zivich v. Mentor Soccer Club, Inc., 696 N.E. 2d 201, 207 (Ohio 1998) ("parents have the authority to bind their minor children to exculpatory agreements in favor of volunteers and sponsors of nonprofit sports activities where the cause of action sounds in negligence"). The Federal Volunteer Protection Act of 1997, 42 U.S.C. § 14503, protects volunteers of nonprofit organizations or governmental entities for liability for harm they caused if "the harm was not caused by willful or criminal misconduct, gross negligence, reckless misconduct, or a conscious, flagrant indifference to the rights or safety of the individual harmed by the volunteer." The liability limitations explicitly do not apply to

certain misconduct, including violations of civil rights laws, sexual offenses, hate crimes and "where the defendant was under the influence * * * of intoxicating alcohol or any drug at the time of the misconduct." Id. Would you be in favor of extending liability protection to the non-profit organizations as well?

4. *Statutes of limitation.* When a person has a civil cause of action, the statute of limitations defines the time within which suit may be filed. If the person fails to sue within the limitations period, the person loses the right to sue on the claim. In the absence of special legislation relating to children's claims, statutes of limitations apply to adult and child claimants alike. Children, however, generally receive special protection. The general approach is to enact tolling statutes, which provide that where a civil cause of action accrues to a child, the limitations period begins to run only when the child reaches majority. The child then has the full limitations period within which to sue. Some statutes operate differently, providing that the limitations period on the child's claim begins to run as it would if the claimant were an adult. If the period expires before the child reaches majority, the child upon reaching majority may sue within a specified period, which may be shorter than the ordinary limitations period. Some statutes also have specific repose provisions stating that regardless of the child's age when the cause of action accrued, suit may not be maintained more than a specified number of years after the date of accrual.

A child holding a claim may sue immediately by a guardian ad litem or next friend. But tolling statutes give the child the option to wait until some period after he or she turns eighteen. What policies do these protective statutes seek to effectuate? If the child may sue by an adult representative within the ordinary limitations period, why should the child have the option to wait until some period after turning eighteen? Statutes of limitations intend in part to protect against open-ended exposure to litigation and liability, and allowing minors this option may seem unfair to potential defendants. On the other hand, the absence of a tolling provision may result in hardship to a child plaintiff. See e.g., Gasparro v. Horner, 245 So.2d 901 (Fla. Dist. Ct. App. 1971) (Tort claim of four year old who was orphaned and severely injured in a car crash was barred by 4 year statute of limitations.) Why might counsel for a child plaintiff wish to sue within the ordinary period, rather than wait until the child turns eighteen?

Recall the injured seven year-old soccer player Sammy Smith and his parents. If Sammy wishes to sue the soccer league for his own pain and suffering, the applicable protective statute would permit him to wait until sometime after he turns eighteen. If his parents wish to sue the league for their medical expenses and loss of the child's services during minority, may the parents wait if Sammy waits, or must they sue within the considerably shorter limitations period ordinarily applicable to adults? The question may turn on close interpretation of the applicable statutes. See, e.g., Perez v. Espinola, 749 F. Supp. 732, 733–36 (E.D. Va. 1990) (parents must sue within ordinary limitations period); Korth v. American Family Ins.Co., 340 N.W.2d 494, 495–97 (Wis. 1983) (parents may wait and sue with child).

5. *References.* Richard B. Malamuc and John E. Karayan, Contractual Waivers for Minors in Sports–Related Activities, 2 Marq. Sports L.J. 151, 172 (1992); Joseph H. King, Jr., Exculpatory Agreements for Volunteers in

Youth Activities—The Alternative to "Nerf(R)" Tiddlywinks, 53 Ohio St. L. J. 683 (1992).

PROBLEM 9–9

An 11-year-old was caught shoplifting in a supermarket and was detained by the store. The child and her parent signed a release, agreeing not to bring a civil action against the store in consideration for the store's not prosecuting the child. Is the child bound by the release?

CHAPTER 10

REGULATION OF CHILDREN'S CONDUCT

Throughout this book, we have seen that the parens patriae doctrine is grounded in the proposition that children sometimes need protection against their improvidence or immaturity, and sometimes even against the conduct of their parents. The result is a panoply of protective legislation that began in earnest with enactment of the child labor laws during the latter part of the nineteenth century and has spread to other areas of our national life.

SECTION 1.   CHILD LABOR LAWS

A.   *The Historical Background and the Present Situation*

BARBARA BENNETT WOODHOUSE, "WHO OWNS THE CHILD?": *MEYER* AND *PIERCE* AND THE CHILD AS PROPERTY

33 Wm. & Mary L. Rev. 995, 1059–68 (1992).

* * *

Children have always worked. In colonial times, children had jobs on family farms and as apprentices. The Industrial Revolution, however, with urban factories and textile mills ushering in a new mechanized age, altered the context and rhythm of child labor. In 1900, one out of every six children between the ages of ten and fifteen worked for wages. One-third of the workforce in southern textile mills was children aged ten to thirteen. Stories of sixty-hour workweeks in the deafening roar of the mill, the perpetual gloom of the coal mine, or the blazing sun of industrialized farms supplanted cultural images of children learning a skill in apprenticeship to a local craftsman or tending farm animals at mother's or father's side. At the same time, a cultural uncertainty grew over the proper role of children in the economic scheme. Whereas children's work in the eighteenth and early nineteenth centuries had been an integral part of both the child's education and the family's economy, by the twentieth century, child labor was increasingly condemned as "commercialization" of the "sacred" child. Moreover, the emergence in family theory of a new model challenging the patriarchal family model—that of a family composed of individuals—undercut the established family hierarchy and the presumed unity of interests between parent and child that had served as a theoretical justification for paternal authority freely to exploit the child as a family asset. Also challenging the patriarchal tradition * * * was the reformers' image of the child as a public and societal asset, not to be exploited for private ends, but to be nurtured and educated for long-term economic productivity and responsible citizenship.

States responded to these pressures by enacting various child labor laws. The economics of price competition, however, placed those states that enacted stricter reforms at a disadvantage. Nationwide uniformity was essential. During the first two decades of the century, reform-minded Progressives, in coalition with child-savers, trade unionists, and religious leaders, made enormous strides on a state-by-state basis toward raising the ages and reducing the hours of child workers. Yet their goal of enacting uniform protective laws in every state was frustrated by opposition from the South, where low wages were deemed essential to the revitalization of the textile industry and, in the conservative business community of the North, where distrust of any federal economic regulation was widespread.

The movement to enact federal laws regulating child labor suffered a heavy blow in 1918 when the Supreme Court, in *Hammer v. Dagenhart*, invalidated the immensely popular Keating–Owens child labor bill as exceeding Congress's Commerce Clause powers. Reformers soon made another attempt, this time under the taxing power. In the 1923 *Child Labor Tax Case*, however, the Court held again that Congress lacked the power to regulate this area of "local" concern. The reformers' only recourse was an amendment to the United States Constitution that would explicitly empower Congress to regulate the employment of children under eighteen. * * *

Predictably, the political alliances for and against education and labor laws tended to be similar. The progressive "child-savers" viewed child labor legislation and compulsory education laws as integral parts in a unified campaign to improve the lot of children. Likewise, organized labor strongly supported both child labor laws and compulsory school laws as keys to an increased living wage for working-class parents and equal opportunity for working-class children. Among the most active opponents of the Child Labor Amendment, and of expansion of compulsory education in general, were many leading Catholic organizations, churchmen, and laymen. Mainstream Catholics viewed the Amendment with alarm, believing it posed a danger to parochial education and transferred to the state powers that ought to belong to parents. Business also had cause to oppose both compulsory education and child labor regulation. Although business promoted education, and especially vocational training, as necessary to create competent workers, businessmen were often arrayed against reformers when it came to passing the taxes to support expanded common schooling. Likewise, employers benefitted from using children as workers. Not only were they cheap labor, but their contributions to family income meant adults would accept less than a living wage. Moreover, children who went to work at an early age provided a future docile workforce. Parents were divided between the two camps. Many middle class parents embraced the new notions of childhood, but conservative or traditional parents, particularly immigrant parents who depended on children's wages for survival, felt that compulsory education and labor laws infringed upon their rights in their children.

Functionally and historically, child labor regulation and compulsory education laws were intimately related. Though some disputed whether the eventual decline in child labor was the cause or the effect of government intervention, obviously the amount of time children could spend at school closely correlated with the time spent at work. * * *

Children's labor in early twentieth-century America was still, quite literally, parental property. Under the "family labor system," the employer would contract with the head of a family to pay to him a given sum in exchange for the labor of all or some family members. Children who received pay envelopes were expected to turn them over to the parent unopened. * * *

Given this legacy, it is not surprising that public debates on child labor analogized the family to a kingdom and parental rights to property rights. Proponents descended to the enemy's turf and argued that even horses were protected by law from their owner's abuse, and children should receive at least the protection given to a chattel. Detractors minimized the furor over parents' abuse of their children, comparing it to the antebellum furor over the slaveholder's abuse of his human property. In a letter to Congress, one former senator suggested that the evil of child labor, like the evil of slavery, was exaggerated because "men do not in general treat their property" with brutality.

Echoing arguments raised against the school laws, opponents of child labor regulation predicted that it would undermine parental authority and ultimately result in the downfall of the Republic, if not a revolution. The Child Labor Amendment, critics said, "would dethrone parents and subvert family government."[365] President [Nicholas Murray] Butler of Columbia University added that "[n]o American mother would favor the adoption of an amendment that would empower Congress to invade the rights of parents and to shape family life to its liking." It is doubtful, however, that America's mothers were those who felt most threatened by the Amendment. One Nevada assemblyman spoke for

---

365. *See, e.g.,* 65 CONG.REC. 10,007 (1924) [statement of Sen. King] (stating that "under the guise of the amendment they will take charge of the children same as the Bolsheviks are doing in Russia.").

multitudes when he complained, "They have taken our women away from us by constitutional amendments; they have taken our liquor away from us; and now they want to take our children."

* * * Like universal common schooling, the Child Labor Amendment was condemned as "a communistic effort to nationalize children." Commenting on the Amendment, Senator Ransdell of Louisiana said:

> Parents will remain in the background after being permitted to bring children into the world and nurture them during their tender years of toddling infancy. Just as soon as the children are large enough to be of some assistance to their real parents they must be delivered to their statutory father in Washington.

Faced with such passionate opposition, the Child Labor Amendment languished. By 1934, New York had become the critical state in the ratification process. The Catholic community and the New York State Committee Opposing Ratification chose William Dameron Guthrie, a key champion of parental rights in *Meyer* and *Pierce*, to speak for their organizations. He appeared at hearings, spoke on radio, and authored arguments presented to the New York Legislature's Judiciary Committee in 1934 when it considered and ultimately refused to report the Amendment. Guthrie painted a picture of moral decay, with idle children devoid of individualist values failing to milk the cows or gas the family Ford or help their widowed mothers with the dishes. Parents who had been deprived of their children's services would be forced to turn to the taxpayer for support. On February 25, 1934, Guthrie addressed the citizens of New York on WOR radio. He condemned the Child Labor Amendment as a "menace to the family to the home and to our local self-government.... [Under its language, Congress] could regulate the help children might give their parents in the home, or on the farm," and thereby control the education of children under the guise of limiting or regulating their mental labor. The Amendment was defeated. Again on January 23, 1935, Guthrie debated the Amendment with Mayor Fiorello La Guardia before a crowd that overflowed the Albany Senate Chamber. He charged that it would bring the federal government into the home and reach "the boy on the farm [picking] blueberries on the mountain, the schoolboy [carrying] newspapers out of school hours, or the boy of 16 to 17 [earning] money to pay his way through college." The Amendment was again defeated. It was to die unratified.

* * *

AMERICAN ACADEMY OF PEDIATRICS, THE HAZARDS OF CHILD LABOR
95 Pediatrics 311 (Feb. 1995).

Child labor is the paid employment of children under 18 years of age. Today, more than 4 million children and adolescents in the United States are legally employed.

Illegal child labor is also widespread and apparently has increased in frequency over the past decade. An estimated 1 to 2 million American children and adolescents are employed under unlawful, often exploitative conditions—working under age, for long hours, at less than minimum wage, on dangerous, prohibited machinery. Widespread employment of children in sweatshops—establishments that repeatedly violate fair labor as well as occupational health and safety standards—has been documented. Tens of thousands of children are employed in illegal farm labor. Detected violations of child labor laws increased fourfold from 1983 to 1989.

* * *

CURRENT SITUATION

Until the 1980s, as a result of strong enforcement of FLSA [Fair Labor Standards Act] and generally favorable economic conditions, child labor outside of agriculture was not a widespread problem in the United States. In the past decade, however, a combination of economic and social factors have been responsible for a resurgence of child labor:

Increased child poverty. More American children live below the poverty level today than 20 years ago.

Immigration. Unstable world conditions, particularly war and poverty, have led to increasing numbers of immigrants, both documented and undocumented, into the United States. In the past decade there has been more immigration to the United States than in any other 10–year period since 1900 through 1910. Immigrants, particularly undocumented immigrants and their children, are highly vulnerable to exploitation in the workplace.

Relaxation in federal enforcement. Since 1980, the federal government has substantially relaxed administration of the FLSA. Fewer inspectors are in the field. Regulations limiting the maximum number of hours of work and prohibitions against use of dangerous machinery by children have not been adequately enforced. The previous federal administration's repeal of the federal ban on industrial piece-work undertaken at home (a practice termed "industrial homework"), a prohibition specifically intended to protect women and children from exploitation in the piece-work industry, has further undermined enforcement of child labor laws. The recently enacted federal School to Work Act of 1993 contains no mandated provisions for occupational health and safety training of adolescents; such provisions can, however, be added on a state-by-state basis.

HAZARDS OF CHILD LABOR

Although work can encourage the development of discipline, teach a child the meaning of money, and provide valuable role models, employment during childhood and adolescence carries significant risks. These risks are magnified greatly when employment is illegal or exploitative.

Health Risks

* * * Work is a major, although until recently, an insufficiently appreciated contributor to the ongoing epidemic of childhood injury in the United States. Recent reports have documented that each year among children and adolescents, the work place accounts for more than 30 000 injuries, 20 000 compensation claims, thousands of cases of permanent disability, and more than 100 deaths. Injuries to working children include amputations, burns, scalds, scalpings, fractures, eye loss, and electrocutions. Although precise data are lacking, the portion of all adolescent injuries that are work-related appears to be substantial. The estimated number of 15–to 19–year olds killed each year at work (110) is comparable to the number who die in falls (103), in fires (126), on bicycles (129), and by poisoning (191). A population-based survey of emergency department visits and hospitalizations in eastern Massachusetts found that 24% of all adolescent injuries had occurred at work. * * *

Toxic Hazards and Chronic Illness

Working children can be exposed occupationally to toxins such as benzene (from pumping gasoline), pesticides (from lawn care and agriculture), and asbestos (from construction and maintenance work). Exposures in childhood and adolescence may result in serious diseases in adulthood. Given the wide range of exposure to toxins, some cases of adolescent asthma might be related to occupational exposures to solvents and pesticides, and some leukemias or lymphomas may result from occupational exposure to benzene.

Risks of Agricultural Child Labor

Agriculture is the least regulated sector of American industry. Children on farms are permitted under the FLSA to operate heavy equipment at younger ages than in other sectors of American industry. In rural areas, farm labor is a major cause of morbidity and mortality among children. Serious injuries occur on family farms as well as in commercial agriculture. Fatal injury rates among farm children have been calculated to be 13.7/100 000 among 10–to 14–year-olds and 16.8/100 000 among 15–to 19–year-olds. For every death there are an estimated 102 injuries among 10–to 14–year-olds and 154 injuries among 15–to 19–year-olds. Agriculture has surpassed mining as the most dangerous occupation, accounting for 61 fatalities per 100 000 workers in 1981.

Hazards to Education and Development

Another serious consequence of child labor is interference with school attendance and performance. Employed children risk not having enough time for homework and being tired on school days. Teachers of children in areas where preholiday employment is common or industrial homework is escalating have reported declines in the academic performances of previously good students. Child labor also interferes with the normal, necessary play of children. Child labor can expose children to undesirable role models and to adverse habits such as smoking, drinking, and drug abuse.

Notes and Questions

1. *The framework of regulation.* Child labor is regulated by both federal and state legislation, each refined by administrative rules and regulations. The Fair Labor Standards Act of 1938 creates federal regulation, and every state has a child labor law. The various state laws tend to follow a common pattern because many are modeled on the Uniform Child Labor Law, which the Uniform Law Commissioners first proposed in 1911.

Section 18 of the FLSA specifies that "no provision of this Act relating to the employment of child labor shall justify noncompliance with any Federal or State law or municipal ordinance establishing a higher standard than the standard established under this Act." 29 U.S.C. § 218. A covered person is thus subject to the stricter of the federal or state standard in the particular case.

Child labor acts challenge employers and their counsel because inelegant drafting sometimes leaves meaning unclear. Broad statutory and administrative provisions also sometimes hold open the prospect of enforcement in circumstances arguably "acceptable" in our contemporary society. Before providing advice concerning state law, lawyers must also scrutinize applicable statutes elsewhere in the state code. Alcohol beverage control laws, for example, may prohibit or regulate employment of children in establishments where beer or liquor is sold or consumed. Other statutes may restrict or prohibit employers from hiring children to work in such places as gambling establishments or pool halls, or to manufacture or sell such products as explosives, fireworks or firearms.

The constitutionality of federal and state child labor legislation is now assured. The Child Labor Amendment became unnecessary when the Supreme Court decided United States v. Darby, 312 U.S. 100 (1941), which unanimously upheld the Fair Labor Standards Act and overruled the 5–4 decision in Hammer v. Dagenhart. Three years later, Prince v. Massachusetts [supra p. 27] upheld general state authority to enact child labor legislation under the police power. See generally Walter I. Trattner, Crusade for the Children: A History of the National Child Labor Committee and Child Labor Reform in America (1970); Stephen B. Wood, Constitutional Politics in the Progressive Era: Child Labor and the Law (1968).

2. *Age discrimination.* Challengers sometimes mount equal protection challenges to protective legislation discussed in this chapter, contending that the legislation constitutes age discrimination. These challenges regularly fail because age classifications are not suspect and need satisfy only rational basis scrutiny. See Massachusetts Bd. of Retirement v. Murgia, 427 U.S. 307, 312–13 (1976). Indeed the Court has long upheld legislative authority to set the minimum age at which a person may perform a particular act or begin enjoying a particular right; the age may be the general age of majority, or it may be higher or lower. See, e.g., Morrissey v. Perry, 137 U.S. 157, 159 (1890). As you proceed through this chapter, you should formulate the rational bases for the various statutes discussed.

3. *Agricultural employment.* The American Academy of Pediatrics article summarizes studies demonstrating the hazards to children posed by modern agricultural employment. The Fair Labor Standards Act and typical state child labor legislation provide broad exemptions allowing employment of young children in agriculture. Strong farm lobbies in Congress and the states may help explain the favorable position enjoyed by agricultural employers. Professor Wendy Anton Fitzgerald also writes that "[t]he exemption of agricultural work from prohibitions against child labor may in part reflect American nostalgia (however accurate) for the bucolic 'family farm.'" She also notes, however that "[o]n their face, * * * the exemptions apply not only to family farmers, but also to corporate agribusiness typically employing families of migrant workers." Maturity, Difference, and Mystery: Children's Perspectives and the Law, 36 Ariz. L. Rev. 11, 89 n.512 (1994). Federal and state agricultural exemptions persist even as the number of family farms decreases in favor of mechanized conglomerates with greater rates of serious injuries among child workers.

Should federal and state child labor laws be amended to provide closer regulation, particularly where employment exposes children to pesticides and heavy machinery such as tractors? "[T]ractors are involved in most farming accidents," and pose particular dangers to child operators. See, e.g., Phyllis R. Cotten, Improving Child Safety Amid the Farm Culture, 42 Prof. Safety 18 (Dec. 1997). The American Academy of Pediatrics recommends that "[t]he exemptions in the FLSA that allow young children in agriculture to work with pesticides and heavy machinery need to be stricken from the law." American Acad. of Pediatrics, The Hazards of Child Labor, 95 Pediatrics 311 (Feb. 1995).

4. *Children of migrant farm workers.* Agricultural employment is particularly harsh on children of migrant workers. A leading business magazine reported that in California, Texas and south Florida, "young children still work beside their parents for up to 12 hours a day as migrant farmers." Brian Dumaine, Illegal Child Labor Comes Back, Fortune, Apr. 5, 1993, at 86. The magazine told of a 13–year-old Mexican–American boy who "started picking olives and strawberries in California. He missed months of school that year, working from 6:30 a.m. until 8 p.m., with a 20–minute lunch break, six days a week, at less than the minimum wage." Id.

The United States has about six million migrant farmworkers, most of whom are young married Hispanic men with families who travel to find seasonal farm work and who take up temporary residence at the work sites. After 30 Years, America's Continuing Harvest of Shame: Hearing Before the House Select Comm. on Aging, 101st Cong., 2d Sess. 14 (1990). The migrants are generally among the working poor, with average annual earnings considerably below the poverty level, even with two-wage-earner families. Most migrant families qualify for public assistance, but only about 18% actually receive it. See American Acad. of Pediatrics, Health Care for Children of Farmworker Families, 95 Pediatrics 952 (1995).

Because most farm workers are manual laborers paid by the bucket or bushel or basket, young children frequently supplement the family income, even when employment means working long hours alongside their parents in hot fields exposed to pesticides, either from direct spray or from working with recently sprayed crops. Without access to day care, migrant workers may have little alternative but to bring their children into the fields to work or play amid the pesticides and dangerous farm machinery. The parents may not know the identities and dangers of the specific chemicals to which they are exposed, the children's access to quality health care may be limited or nonexistent, and the children may be encouraged or permitted to operate the machinery and perform other hazardous farm work without adequate training. The federal Environmental Protection Agency, which regulates pesticides and their uses, has estimated that hired farm workers suffer up to 300,000 acute illnesses and injuries from pesticide exposure each year. See, e.g., Harvesting Heartache: Child Labor in the Agricultural Sector, 57 Occupational Hazards 25 (Nov. 1995); U.S. Gen'l Accounting Office, Hired Farmworkers: Health and Well–Being at Risk 2, 3, 8 (1992). The General Accounting Office provided this summary of the difficult circumstances faced by hired farmworkers and their families: "Many of the nation's hired farmworkers face the hardships of substandard living and working conditions: Pesticides poison hired farmworkers every year, and fields without sanitation facilities expose these workers to many health hazards. Some families have no homes or live in overcrowded and unsanitary housing. * * * Their children, who often work in the fields, are exposed to the same poor conditions and may be more susceptible to health risks." Id. at 27. The children and their families normally go without adequate medical care because they move from place to place so often, because employers do not provide health insurance, and because the families cannot afford to purchase health insurance.

Migrant farmworkers' children typically are deprived of appropriate formal education. "When always on the move, there can be no stable school life for children. Migrants live in many different places during the school year; their children are constantly in and out of different schools. * * * [The children] have no assistance at home because their parents are away all day and often are without means and abilities to be helpful when they return." Ronald Goldfarb, Migrant Farm Workers: A Caste of Despair 46 (1981). Parental involvement is critical to children's educational progress, but 80% of adult migrant farmworkers function at a fifth-grade reading level or below. See 2 U.S. Dep't of Educ., The Education of Adult Migrant Farmworkers (Jan. 1991).

A generation ago, two Senators provided this somber assessment of the FLSA provisions relating to child labor in agriculture: "[W]hat we condemned with indignation over a generation ago in the textile mills and agricultural plants of this Nation we continue to accept in an often equally oppressive form–agricultural child labor. There are the same long hours, the same negligible pay, the same back breaking work, the same exposure to the elements, the same lack of educational opportunity despite nominal restrictions on working 'during school hours'–all the same practices which deprive the child of a real childhood." S. Rep. No. 89–1487, at 20 (1966), reprinted in 1966 U.S.C.C.A.N. 3002, 3039 (statement of Sens. Javits and Williams). See generally Ronald B. Taylor, Sweatshops in the Sun: Child Labor on the Farm (1973).

Lawyers and other advocates seeking to improve the lot of migrant farm children and their families may face imposing obstacles from growers who invoke private property rights, criminal trespass law and other theories in an effort to keep the advocates away from the migrants and to keep the migrants "rootless and isolated." State v. Shack, 277 A.2d 369, 372 (N.J. 1971).

5. *The parental right to the child's earnings.* Parents had a common law right to their children's wages, which demonstrated the law's willingness to permit parents to put their children to work at an early age, and indeed the law's expectation that many parents would do so. When the child labor debate raged early in the twentieth century, the parental right to children's wages was meaningful for many parents because poor families often depended on their children's earnings. See, e.g., Viviana Zelizer, Pricing the Priceless Child: The Changing Social Value of Children 59 (1985). Indeed, the father in Hammer v. Dagenhart prevailed on the contention that federal law deprived him of his vested right in his two boys' earnings for working under bitter conditions in a North Carolina cotton mill. Nowadays few children help support their families, and most working children use their earnings as discretionary income to save for higher education or to purchase clothes, automobiles or other consumer goods. See, e.g., David Stern et al., How Children Used to Work, 39 Law & Contemp. Probs. 93 (Summer 1975). Child labor is more prevalent among children of households earning more than $60,000 per year than among children of households earning less than $20,000 per year. See U.S. Gen'l Accounting Office, Child Labor: Characteristics of Working Children 4 (June 1991).

The parents' right to the earnings of their unemancipated children nonetheless survives in most states. See, e.g., Mo. Rev. Stat. §§ 452.150, 452.220. Some states, however, have abolished the parental right. See, e.g., Cal. Civ. Code § 202. Where the parent employs the child, the child is generally not entitled to wages unless the parent and child have expressly agreed otherwise. See, e.g., N.Y. Gen'l Oblig. Law § 3–109.

B. *The Sources of Regulation*

INTRODUCTORY PROBLEM

A few months ago, your client opened a Busy Burger fast food restaurant in a small Michigan town. The client's ten-year-old daughter sometimes helps out during the dinner rush and the restaurant has a few adult shift workers, but more hands are needed. With adult help hard to find, your client hires three high school students who appear industrious and hard working during their brief interviews. Your client does not require employment applications or any other paperwork, except for tax reporting forms required by federal and state authorities. All three students are paid in excess of the minimum wage.

Sixteen-year-old Alan is hired to make deliveries in town because he just got his license after passing the high school's driver education course and likes to drive. Fifteen year-old Beth helps load orders into the car for Alan and also works in the kitchen, cooking burgers on the grill and cutting meat in the electric meat slicer. Sixteen-year old Charlie serves sit-down customers, clears the tables and sometimes stacks the automatic dishwasher. Because the dinner rush continues past 8:30 each evening, Charlie usually stays until around 10:30 or 11:00 cleaning up and serving a few remaining customers. Charlie's classmate Dan sometimes comes by around 10:00 and ends up sweeping the floors and doing other assorted tasks, though he has never applied for employment and the restaurant has never hired or paid him.

After a few weeks, Alan, Beth and Charlie are doing such a good job that your client allows them to set their own schedules. All three choose to work after school each day and for full days on many Saturdays and Sundays. To maximize their take-home pay, Beth and Charlie find they have the energy to work continuously without taking a lunch or dinner break. The adult shift workers sometimes go home at about 9:00 at night and leave Charlie alone to serve the occasional customers until security personnel come by at 11:00 to close up.

Your client is thrilled with the performance of these industrious adolescents, who in turn are thrilled to be working for such a considerate employer. The youngsters like the spending money and are also saving for clothes, other personal items and college tuition. Is Busy Burger in compliance with Michigan's child labor act excerpted below and with the Fair Labor Standards Act beginning on page 941? If the answer is no but child labor authorities do not cite the restaurant, would your client have anything else to worry about if he continues to employ the minors in the manner described?

    1. State Regulation

MICHIGAN COMPILED LAWS

409.102. Definitions

    As used in this act:

    (a) "Employ" means engage, permit, or allow to work.

    (b) "Employer" means a person, firm, or corporation that employs a minor * * *

* * *

    (d) "Minor" means a person under 18 years of age. * * *

409.103. Hazardous or injurious occupations; minimum age

    (1) A minor shall not be employed in, about, or in connection with an occupation that is hazardous or injurious to the minor's health or personal well-being or that is contrary to standards established under this act, unless a deviation is granted [by the state department of labor].

    (2) The minimum age for employment of minors is 14 years, subject to the following exceptions and limitations:

    (a) A minor at least 11 years of age and less than 14 years of age may be employed as a youth athletic program referee or umpire for an age bracket younger than his or her own age if an adult representing the athletic program is on the premises at which the athletic program event is occurring and a person responsible for the athletic program possesses a written acknowledgment of the minor's parent or guardian consenting to the minor's employment as a referee or umpire.

(b) A minor 11 years of age or older may be employed as a golf caddy.

(c) A minor 13 years of age or older may be employed in farming operations * * *.

* * *

409.110. Minors under 16 years; hours of employment

A minor under 16 years shall not be employed in an occupation subject to this act for more than 6 days in 1 week, nor for a period longer than a weekly average of 8 hours per day or 48 hours in 1 week, nor more than 10 hours in 1 day. The minor shall not be employed between the hours of 9 p.m. and 7 a.m. A minor who is a student in school shall not be employed more than a combined school and work week of 48 hours during the period when school is in session.

409.111. Minors 16 years and over; hours of employment

(1) Except as provided in subsection (3), a minor 16 years of age or older shall not be employed in an occupation subject to this act for more than any of the following periods:

(a) Six days in 1 week.

(b) A period longer than a weekly average of 8 hours per day or 48 hours in 1 week.

(c) Ten hours in 1 day.

(d) For a minor 16 years of age or older who is a student in school, a combined school and work week of 48 hours during the period school is in session.

(2) Except as provided in subsection (3), a minor 16 years of age or older shall not be employed between 10:30 p.m. and 6 a.m. However, except as provided in subsection (3), a minor 16 years of age or older who is a student in school may be employed until 11:30 p.m. during school vacation periods or when the minor is not regularly enrolled in school.

(3) A minor 16 years of age or older may be employed in farming operations involved in the production of seed or in agricultural processing for a period greater than the periods described in subsections (1) and (2) if all of the following conditions are met:

(a) If the minor is a student in school, the period greater than the periods described in subsections (1) and (2) occurs when school is not in session.

(b) The minor is employed for not more than 11 hours in 1 day.

(c) The minor is employed for not more than 62 hours in any week, for not more than 6 weeks, and for the remaining weeks not more than 48 hours per week in a calendar year.

(d) The minor is not employed between 2 a.m. and 5:30 a.m.

(e) The agricultural processing employer maintains on file a written acknowledgment of the minor's parent or guardian consenting to the period of employment authorized under this subsection.

* * *

409.119. Exemptions; work outside school hours

(1) This act shall not apply to or prohibit a minor from engaging in:

(a) Domestic work or chores in connection with private residences.

(b) Soliciting, distributing, selling, or offering for sale newspapers, magazines, periodicals, political or advertising matter.

(c) Shoe shining.

(d) Services performed as members of recognized youth oriented organizations that are engaged in citizenship training and character building, if the services are not intended to replace employees in occupations for which workers are ordinarily paid.

(e) Employment in a business owned and operated by the parent or guardian of the minor. * * *

(f) Farm work if the employment is not in violation of a standard established by the department of labor. * * * Farm work includes any practices performed on a farm as an incident to or in conjunction with such farming operations including preparation for market delivery to storage or market or to carriers for transportation to market.

(g) Employment by a school, academy, or college in which the student minor 14 years of age or older is enrolled.

(2) If a minor is required by law to attend school, the work may only be performed outside of school hours, unless the minor enrolled and employed under a work-related educational program.

* * *

Notes and Questions

1. *Coverage.* Like the Michigan act, many child labor acts impose general regulations on employment of children under eighteen. Some states, however, end general regulation at a lower age. See, e.g., Colo. Rev. Stat. § 8–12–109 (sixteen); Fla. Stat. § 450.012(3) (seventeen).

Some child labor statutes exempt children who are or have been married, who are parents, or who have graduated from high school or vocational or technical school. See, e.g, Mich. Comp. Laws § 409.116. Despite the fact that teenage parenthood, teenage marriage and early high school graduation are familiar in modern America, however, many child labor acts do not expressly exempt minors in these circumstances. Some child labor statutes authorize administrative exemption on a case-by-case basis. See, e.g., Fla. Stat. Ann. § 450.095. Michigan and some other state child labor laws exempt children who have been emancipated by operation of law or by court order. See Mich. Comp. Laws § 409.117. Otherwise the emancipation statute may specify a partial or total exemption.

2. *Hazardous occupations.* Even where general regulation ends before majority, state child labor laws typically prohibit employment of children in enumerated hazardous occupations until the age of eighteen. Frequently these occupations are enumerated in the child labor act itself. Prohibitions may also be found in other state acts, such as those relating to the sale and use of fireworks, explosives or firearms. The legislature may delegate authority to an administrative agency to promulgate rules and regulations defining additional hazardous occupations. See, e.g., Ky. Rev. Stat. § 339.230(3). Michigan and several other states leave definition entirely to the administrative authorities. See, e.g., Mich. Comp. Laws § 409.120.

Mich. R. 408.6208, for example, prohibits employment of minors in a variety of occupations, including construction work such as roofing, excavation and demolition; manufacturing or storing of explosives; occupations involving exposure to hazardous substances; occupations involving use of power-driven bakery machines or power-driven meat-processing machines; and occupations requiring "operation of a motor vehicle on any public road or highway, except when such operation is occasional and incidental to the minor's primary work activities * * *."

3. *"Work" and "employment."* The Michigan act is typical of child labor acts that pervasively regulate "work" or "employment" without defining these critical terms. The two terms do not necessarily have the same reach. See, e.g., Gabin v. Skyline Cabana Club, 258 A.2d 6, 9 (N.J.1969) ("labor" includes more than compensatory employment, and "work" has broader meaning than "employment"). Could you draft definitions that would provide meaningful guidance? See, e.g., Colo. Rev. Stat. § 8–12–103(4); Ky. Rev. Stat. § 339.210.

As the Michigan act indicates, the formulations of "work" or "employment" frequently carry exemptions for such activities as agricultural work, work for parents or guardians, or work in family-owned or family-operated businesses. Work as a child actor, performer or model may also be exempted.

4. *Volunteer activity.* Do child labor laws permit children to perform as "volunteers," or otherwise without promise, expectation or receipt of remuneration? The answer is important to scouting, youth sports, and similar groups whose fundraising projects require children to sell cookies, raffle tickets, candy or similar products as a condition of participation. Only a handful of states have provisions such as section 409.119(d) of the Michigan act, which reaches the question.

In 1978, questions were raised in Pennsylvania about whether volunteer clean-up activities performed by children as part of civic conservation projects in state parks and forests constituted "work" in violation of the state child labor act. The act had no provision relating to volunteer activity. After concluding that the proposed activities did not violate the Fair Labor Standards Act because the children's efforts would introduce no product into interstate commerce, the attorney general concluded that the activities did not offend the state act either: "Child labor laws are highly remedial in character, being intended to protect children, in their healthful development to adult age, from exploitation by business and industry, and to ensure to them, in the interests of the public welfare, that condition of freedom from debilitating spiritual and physical labor in which alone they can develop into fully efficient economic and social units of the State. * * * [The laws'] penal provisions cannot be extended by interpretation to include those activities of children which are not essentially 'work' in its ordinarily accepted meaning, or which cannot fairly be said to tend to the exploitation of the labor of children for commercial or other remunerative purposes." 1978 Op. Atty. Gen. No. 22 (Pa.).

Where the minor receives no remuneration, should the definition of "work" or "employment" turn on whether the person engaging a minor receives a benefit similar to what it would receive if it paid someone to perform the activity? For example, if a person allows children to enter on land to remove kindling wood and take it home, has the person "employed" the children? See, e.g., Devine v. Armour & Co., 159 Ill.App. 74 (1910) (no).

5. *Regulation of hours and working conditions.* The Michigan act is typical of child labor legislation that closely regulates the maximum hours children may work weekly and the late hours they may work on school nights during the school term.

Several state acts also regulate children's working conditions, frequently providing greater protections than adults would receive in the same workplace under generally applicable federal and state workplace safety legislation. See, e.g., Mich. Comp. Laws § 409.112: "A minor shall not be employed for more than 5 hours continuously without an interval of at least 30 minutes for a meal and rest period. An interval of less than 30 minutes shall not be considered to interrupt a continuous period of work." Child labor acts also typically authorize a state agency to conduct periodic inspections of places where children are employed. See, e.g., Mich. Comp. Laws § 409.121. Mich. R. 408.6207 provides that a minor may not be employed "unless the employer or an employee who is 18 years of age or older provides supervision."

6. *Work permits.* Most state child labor acts require children to secure work permits or certificates, usually from a school official. The applicant must present proof of age and a description of the prospective employment. In most states, a physician must sign the permit to indicate the child is fit for the anticipated employment. Frequently the prospective employer must sign the description. The school official may also be required to certify that the applicant regularly attends school and is performing satisfactorily in the classroom, though school officials generally do not exercise their discretion to withhold or revoke permits for poor academic performance. The child's parent or guardian frequently must provide written consent to the prospective employment.

An employer who employs a child without receiving the required permit or certificate commits a criminal offense. The employer must retain the permit or certificate on file throughout the employment. See, e.g., Mich. Comp. Laws § 409.104. Several states specify that in actions alleging child labor act violations, the work permit or certificate is conclusive proof of the child's age. This specification protects employers against proceedings under the act for employing children who misrepresent their age to secure employment. See, e.g., Mich. Comp. Laws § 409.109. Where the statute does not contain this specification, should courts nonetheless accord employers this protection in proceedings under the act? See, e.g., Shipp v. Farrens Tree Surgeons, 72 So.2d 387 (Fla.1954) (yes); Gorczynski v. Nugent, 83 N.E.2d 495 (Ill.1948) (no).

The Fair Labor Standards Act does not require that children secure a work permit or certificate. When federal authorities question the lawfulness of a child's employment, however, the Act requires the employer to prove the child is employed in accordance with the Act and Department of Labor regulations. The Department accepts state-issued work permits and certificates as proof of age. Where the state does not issue permits or certificates meeting standards established in federal regulations, the Department issues age certificates on request. See U.S. Gen'l Accounting Office, Work Permit and Death and Injury Reporting Systems in Selected States 2 (1992).

7. *Criminal and civil penalties.* Child labor acts impose criminal or civil penalties on employers. See, e.g., Mich. Comp. Laws § 409.122. Several states also impose criminal or civil penalties on parents or guardians who permit their child to work in violation of the act. See, e.g., Wis. Stat. §§ 103.29, 103.31. Because budget cutbacks have reduced the number of enforcement agents, enforcement by state authorities is generally lax. See, Gina Kolata, More Children Are Employed, Often Perilously, N.Y. Times, June 21, 1992, at 1.

Where the child labor act does not sanction parents, a parent may nonetheless face sanction under compulsory school attendance laws where unlawful employment leads the child to miss school. Where unlawful employment harms the child physically or emotionally, the parent might also face sanction under criminal endangerment or civil neglect statutes.

The employer normally may not defend by asserting that the minor or parent consented to the otherwise unlawful employment, that the child or the family needed the child's salary or wages to avoid hardship or maintain their lifestyle, or that the child was saving for a worthy cause such as college tuition. Should consent or family hardship be a defense, particularly when public welfare budgets are shrinking and some children or families may be in difficult straits? Does the absence of such a defense invite hardship where the child or family needs the child's income, or some part of it? Consider whether S.D. Cod. L. § 60–12–5 provides a sound approach: "If it appears upon investigation that the labor of a minor who would otherwise be barred from employment by law is necessary for the minor's support or that of the family to which the minor belongs, the department of labor may issue a permit authorizing employment within certain hours to be fixed therein."

Virtually no child labor acts impose criminal punishment on the child for working in violation of the act. Should a child face delinquency proceedings (based on violation of criminal fraud statutes) if the child knowingly misrepresents his age? Would the prospect of delinquency deter children from participating in child labor violations? What policy considerations might underlie the nearly universal determination to punish the employer, parent or guardian, but not the child?

8. *Regulation of employment agencies.* Some states prohibit employment agencies from placing minors in employment that violates the child labor act. See, e.g., 225 Ill. Comp. Stat. 515/10.

9. *Professional and occupational licensing.* State licensing statutes establish the minimum ages at which persons may practice specified professions and occupations. The age is usually eighteen, but some licensing statutes establish a higher or lower minimum age. The statutes effectively prohibit employment in the covered professions and occupations by most children.

Statutes and court rules, for example, typically regulate the minimum age at which a person may be admitted to the state bar and licensed to practice law. The minimum age is generally eighteen. See, e.g., Cal. Bus. & Prof. Code § 6060(a); Mich. R. Bd. of Law Examiners 1(A). A few states set higher minimum ages. See, e.g., Ala. R. Governing Admission to the Bar IV(A) (nineteen); Ohio S. Ct. R., Gov't of the Bar 1(A) (twenty-one).

Other covered professions and occupations vary from state to state, but frequently include the following: acupuncturist, auctioneer, barber, certified public accountant, chiropractor, collection agency operator, cosmetologist and beautician, dental hygienist, dentist, embalmer and funeral director or funeral home administrator, emergency medical technician, hearing aid dealer or fitter, insurance agent or broker or adjuster, marriage or family or child counselor, physician, nursing home administrator, optometrist, pharmacist, physical therapist, podiatrist, polygraph examiner, private investigator or detective, psychologist, real estate agent or broker or appraiser, social worker, and veterinarian.

2. Federal Regulation

FAIR LABOR STANDARDS ACT
29 U.S.C. § 201 et seq.

* * *

§ 203. Definitions

As used in this chapter—

* * *

(g) "Employ" includes to suffer or permit to work.

* * *

(*l*) "Oppressive child labor" means a condition of employment under which (1) any employee under the age of sixteen years is employed by an employer (other than a parent or a person standing in place of a parent employing his own child or a child in his custody under the age of sixteen years in an occupation other than manufacturing or mining or an occupation found by the Secretary of Labor to be particularly hazardous for the employment of children between the ages of sixteen and eighteen years or detrimental to their health or well-being) in any occupation, or (2) any employee between the ages of sixteen and eighteen years is employed by an employer in any occupation which the Secretary of Labor shall find and by order declare to be particularly hazardous for the employment of children between such ages or detrimental to their health or well-being; but oppressive child labor shall not be deemed to exist by virtue of the employment in any occupation of any person with respect to whom the employer shall have on file an unexpired certificate issued and held pursuant to regulations of the Secretary of Labor certifying that such person is above the oppressive child-labor age. The Secretary of Labor shall provide by regulation or by order that the employment of employees between the ages of fourteen and sixteen years in occupations other than manufacturing and mining shall not be deemed to constitute oppressive child labor if and to the extent that the Secretary of Labor determines that such employment is confined to periods which will not interfere with their schooling and to conditions which will not interfere with their health and well-being.

* * *

§ 212. Child labor provisions

(a) No producer, manufacturer, or dealer shall ship or deliver for shipment in commerce any goods produced in an establishment situated in the United States in or about which within thirty days prior to the removal of such goods therefrom any oppressive child labor has been employed * * *.

(b) The Secretary of Labor or any of his authorized representatives, shall make all investigations and inspections * * * with respect to the employment of minors, and, subject to the direction and control of the Attorney General, shall bring all actions * * * to enjoin any act or practice which is unlawful by reason of the existence of oppressive child labor, and shall administer all other provisions of this chapter relating to oppressive child labor.

(c) No employer shall employ any oppressive child labor in commerce or in the production of goods for commerce or in any enterprise engaged in commerce or in the production of goods for commerce.

* * *

§ 213. Exemptions

* * *

(c)(1) Except as provided in paragraph (2) or (4), the provisions of section 212 of this title relating to child labor shall not apply to any employee employed in agriculture outside of school hours for the school district where such employee is living while he is so employed, if such employee—

(A) is less than twelve years of age and (i) is employed by his parent, or by a person standing in the place of his parent, on a farm owned or operated by such parent or person, or (ii) is employed, with the consent of his parent or person standing in the place of his parent, on a farm, none of the employees of which are * * * required to be paid at the [minimum] wage rate * * *,

(B) is twelve years or thirteen years of age and (i) such employment is with the consent of his parent or person standing in the place of his parent, or (ii) his parent or such person is employed on the same farm as such employee, or

(C) is fourteen years of age or older.

(2) The provisions of section 212 of this title relating to child labor shall apply to an employee below the age of sixteen employed in agriculture in an occupation that the Secretary of Labor finds and declares to be particularly hazardous for the employment of children below the age of sixteen, except where such employee is employed by his parent or by a person standing in the place of his parent on a farm owned or operated by such parent or person.

(3) The provisions of section 212 of this title relating to child labor shall not apply to any child employed as an actor or performer in motion pictures or theatrical productions, or in radio or television productions.

(4)(A) An employer or group of employers may apply to the Secretary for a waiver of the application of section 212 of this title to the employment for not more than eight weeks in any calendar year of individuals who are less than twelve years of age, but not less than ten years of age, as hand harvest laborers in an agricultural operation which has been, and is customarily and generally recognized as being, paid on a piece rate basis in the region in which such individuals would be employed. The Secretary may not grant such a waiver unless he finds, based on objective data submitted by the applicant, that—

(i) the crop to be harvested is one with a particularly short harvesting season and the application of section 212 of this title would cause severe economic disruption in the industry of the employer or group of employers applying for the waiver;

(ii) the employment of the individuals to whom the waiver would apply would not be deleterious to their health or well-being;

(iii) the level and type of pesticides and other chemicals used would not have an adverse effect on the health or well-being of the individuals to whom the waiver would apply;

(iv) individuals age twelve and above are not available for such employment; and

(v) the industry of such employer or group of employers has traditionally and substantially employed individuals under twelve years of age without displacing substantial job opportunities for individuals over sixteen years of age.

(B) Any waiver granted by the Secretary under subparagraph (A) shall require that—

(i) the individuals employed under such waiver be employed outside of school hours for the school district where they are living while so employed;

(ii) such individuals while so employed commute daily from their permanent residence to the farm on which they are so employed; and

(iii) such individuals be employed under such waiver (I) for not more than eight weeks between June 1 and October 15 of any calendar year, and (II) in accordance with such other terms and conditions as the Secretary shall prescribe for such individuals' protection.

* * *

(f) The provisions of section[] * * * 212 of this title shall not apply with respect to any employee whose services during the workweek are performed with a workplace within a foreign country * * * .

* * *

Notes and Questions

1. *Hazardous occupations.* The Secretary of Labor has found these occupations "particularly hazardous or detrimental to the health or well-being of minors 16 and 17 years of age":

No. 1. Occupations in or about plants manufacturing explosives or articles containing explosive components.

No. 2. Occupations of motor-vehicle driver and helper.

No. 3. Coal-mine occupations.

No. 4. Logging occupations and occupations in the operation of any sawmill, lath mill, shingle mill, or cooperage-stock mill.

No. 5. Occupations involved in the operation of power-driven woodworking machines.

No. 6. Occupations involving exposure to radioactive substances.

No. 7. Occupations involved in the operation of power-driven hoisting apparatus.

No. 8. Occupations involved in the operation of power-driven metal forming, punching, and shearing machines.

No. 9. Occupations in connection with mining, other than coal.

No. 10. Occupations in or about slaughtering and meat packing establishments and rendering plants.

No. 11. Occupations involved in the operation of bakery machines.

No. 12. Occupations involved in the operations of paper products machines.

No. 13. Occupations involved in the manufacture of brick, tile, and kindred products.

No. 14. Occupations involved in the operation of circular saws, bandsaws, and guillotine shears.

No. 15. Occupations in wrecking, demolition, and shipbreaking operations.

No. 16. Occupations in roofing operations.

No. 17. Occupations in excavation operations.

29 C.F.R. § 570.120. The effect of this enumeration is "to raise the minimum age of employment to 18 years in the occupations covered." Id.

2. *Retail and food service establishments.* The Secretary of Labor has promulgated regulations concerning employment of minors 14-to-16-years-old in retail and food service establishments. Such employment does not constitute oppressive child labor if it involves specified permitted activities, and if it "does not interfere with their schooling or with their health and well-being." 29 C.F.R. § 570.31.

Permitted activities include "[b]agging and carrying out customers' orders"; "[e]rrand and delivery work by foot, bicycle, and public transportation"; "[c]leanup work, including the use of vacuum cleaners and floor waxers"; and "[k]itchen work and other work involved in preparing and serving food and beverages." 29 C.F.R. § 570.34(a). Permission, however, does not extend to "[c]ooking (except at soda fountains, lunch counters, snack bars, or cafeteria serving counters) and baking"; "[o]ccupations which involve operating, setting up, adjusting, cleaning, oiling, or repairing power-driven food slicers and grinders, food choppers, and cutters"; and "[w]ork in freezers and meat coolers and all work in the preparation of meats for sale." 29 C.F.R. § 570.34(b).

Such employment must be confined to these periods:

(1) Outside school hours;

(2) Not more than 40 hours in any 1 week when school is not in session;

(3) Not more than 18 hours in any 1 week when school is in session;

(4) Not more than 8 hours in any 1 day when school is not in session;

(5) Not more than 3 hours in any 1 day when school is in session;

(6) Between 7 a.m. and 7 p.m. in any 1 day, except during the summer (June 1 through Labor Day) when the evening hour will be 9 p.m.

29 C.F.R. § 570.35(a).

3. *Federal enforcement.* General federal employment safety standards, such as those promulgated by the U.S. Occupational Safety and Health Administration (OSHA), govern establishments employing children and adults alike. The Fair Labor Standards Act provides children enhanced federal protection.

Federal child labor enforcement has generally been spotty in recent years. In 1992, the U.S. Fish and Wildlife Service had about twelve thousand inspectors. Detecting federal child labor violations was the responsibility of only about two thousand OSHA inspectors and about one thousand Department of Labor wage-and-hour compliance officers. And such detection was not the only responsibility of these inspectors and officers. OSHA inspectors also monitor workplace violations relating to adult workers; Labor Department officers also enforce several other regulations, including the minimum wage laws. Because of budget cutbacks, these agencies normally can only respond to child labor complaints, without seeking out violations. See Gina Kolata, More Children Are Employed, Often Perilously, N.Y. Times, June 21, 1992, at 1.

From time to time, federal authorities conduct well publicized enforcement initiatives in a particular industry or a particular region. Nevertheless, in 1989, the Department of Labor inspected only 1.5% of all workplaces covered by the Fair Labor Standards Act. See U.S. Gen. Accounting Office, Hired Farmworkers: Health and Well–Being at Risk 22 (Feb. 1992). The National Safe Workplace Institute, a nonprofit group funded by foundations and corporations, has estimated that a business can expect a visit from a federal labor inspector once every fifty years. Brian Dumaine, Illegal Child Labor Comes Back, Fortune, Apr. 5, 1993, at 86.

4. *Remedies for violation.* The FLSA's child labor provisions create criminal and civil remedies on behalf of the Secretary of Labor. An employer that willfully violates the provisions may be fined not more than $10,000 or (after a prior conviction for violation of the provisions) imprisoned for not more than six months, or both. See 29 U.S.C. § 216(a). The employer is also subject to a civil penalty of not more than $10,000 for each employee who was the subject of a violation. See id. at § 216(e). Given the infrequency of federal enforcement efforts, these remedies have been criticized as inadequate to deter violations by employers, particularly large employers. See, e.g., Tom Lantos, The Silence of the Kids: Children at Risk in the Workplace, 43 Lab. L.J. 67, 68–70 (1992). In 1991, for example, a nationwide fast food chain was fined $94,000 for FLSA child labor violations; the chain's president candidly told Congress that with an annual business volume of $700 million, the company did not view the fines as a "severe financial deterrent." Id. at 69.

5. *Child deaths on the job.* Studies indicate that throughout the 1980s, between 30% and 86% of work-related deaths among children were associated with activities prohibited by the federal child labor laws. See Work–Related Injuries and Illnesses Associated With Child Labor—United States, 1993, 45 Morbidity and Mortality Weekly Rep. 464 (June 7, 1996).

6. *International child labor.* Dissenting in Hammer v. Dagenhart, 247 U.S. 251, 280 (1918), Justice Holmes wrote that "if there is any matter upon which civilized countries have agreed * * * it is the evil of premature and excessive child labor." Nearly eighty years later, however, the International Labor Organization has called child labor "the single most important source of exploitation and child abuse in the world today." ILO, Child Labour: Targeting the Intolerable 4 (1996). The ILO estimates that in developing countries alone, at least 120 million children between five and fourteen work full-time; the estimate of workers in this age group is 250 million if part-time workers are counted. Id. at 7. Working conditions are frequently deplorable. The organization describes "many millions of children * * * working throughout the world, trapped in forced labor, debt bondage, prostitution, pornography, and other kinds of work which cause lasting damage and

immediate dangers." Id. at 8–9. See also 1–5 U.S. Dep't of Labor, By the Sweat and Toil of Children (1994–98).

American companies directly or indirectly employ many of these children, and Americans purchase many of the goods manufactured by child labor abroad, frequently at prices that would be considerably higher without such labor. Many voices have urged boycotts of such goods in an effort to improve the lot of children worldwide. Ralph Nader, for example, has argued that "[m]anufacturers in the United States cannot legally exploit child labor in our country; they should not be able to profit from brutalized child labor abroad." No Child Should Work, USA Today, June 12, 1996, at 14A. Nader has urged Americans to boycott goods made overseas with child labor, American manufacturers and retailers to pledge not to use child labor in their overseas subcontracts, and celebrities not to endorse products made with child labor. He argues that "[c]hildren do not work because economic conditions demand it but rather because societies permit it." "In every developing country where child labor is widespread," he concludes, "there is widespread adult unemployment. Putting children in schools would put more adults to work." Id.

Boycotts, however, have been challenged as counter-productive. Calling boycott proponents "sentimental do-gooders and hard-headed interest groups," for example, one commentator says that "[c]hild labor in the Third World is not a cause of poverty and suffering but a result of it. People put their kids to work because they need the money to survive." Stephen Chapman, Do Third–World Kids a Favor: Buy the Goods They're Producing, Chicago Tribune, Dec. 19, 1996, at 31. "Abolishing child labor in exporting industries will stop kids from working in factories," Chapman argues, "but it won't prevent them from working as beggars, thieves or prostitutes. Nor will it prevent them from starving." His advice to concerned Americans? "Buy what [the children] make, buy more of it, and tell friends to buy it too. That will boost the manufacturer's profits, which will induce it to produce more, which will require hiring more workers, which will push up wages, which will make workers' families better off, which will speed the day that they can send their kids to school instead of the factory."

Without success, Senator Tom Harkin (D–Iowa) has introduced the Child Labor Deterrence Act for several years. Similar bills have also been introduced in the House and Senate. Senator Harkin calls international child labor "a major form of child abuse," and argues that "[c]hildren in developing countries, for the sake of their future and that of their economies, should be in schools and not in factories working long hours for little or no pay under hazardous conditions." Tom Harkin, Put an End to the Exploitation of Child Labor, USA Today (magazine), Jan. 1, 1996, at 73. Among other things, the proposed Act (1) would urge the President to seek an agreement with the government of each nation that trades with the United States to secure an international ban on trade in products of child labor (commercial exploitation of children under 15), (2) would require the Secretary of Labor to identify foreign nations that do not comply with applicable national laws that prohibit child labor in the workplace, that use child labor in the export of products, and that have exported such products to the United States on a continuing basis, and (3) would prohibit importation into the United States of products produced by child labor. See Child Labor Deterrence Act of 1997, S. 332, 105th Congress, 1st Sess. (1997).

* * *

3. *Private Enforcement*

HENDERSON v. BEAR

Colorado Court of Appeals, 1998.
968 P.2d 144.

Opinion by JUDGE MARQUEZ.

Mark and Toni Henderson (parents), individually and as the parents of Joshua Henderson (child), appeal the trial court's dismissal of their action for the death of their child which they filed against William Bear, Susan Bear, and David Cordes, all individually and doing business as Bears Car Wash & Detail, and BCD, Ltd., doing business as Bears Car Wash (collectively employer).* * *

When he was 15 years old, the child died from electrocution while working for employer. His parents received a $4000 funeral benefit and reimbursement for medical expenses under the Workers' Compensation Act. The parents specifically raised the issue of their entitlement to dependency benefits at the administrative proceedings, but those benefits were not awarded.

The parents then filed an action against employer for wrongful death, violation of the Colorado Youth Employment Opportunity Act (Youth Act), violation of the Fair Labor Standards Act, and extreme and outrageous conduct. Employer filed a combined motion to dismiss and motion for summary judgment, arguing that the Workers' Compensation Act was the parents' exclusive remedy for claims based on the death of their child and that the statutes under which the claims are brought do not support private causes of action.

The trial court granted the motion to dismiss under C.R.C.P. 12(b)(5) [failure to state a claim upon which relief can be granted]. It declined to imply a private civil remedy under either the Youth Act or the FLSA, and noted that the parties agreed to dismissal of the wrongful death claims. Attorney fees in the amount of $4000 were assessed against the parents' counsel under * * * § 13–17–102(2) (award of fees for maintaining action that lacks substantial justification).

I.

The parents contend that the trial court erred in dismissing the complaint because the FLSA and Youth Act create implied private causes of action that supersede the exclusivity provisions of the Workers' Compensation Act. We disagree.

For work-related injuries, an employee surrenders his "rights to any method, form, or amount of compensation or determination thereof or to any cause of action, action at law, suit in equity, or statutory or common-law right, remedy, or proceeding ... other than is provided in [the Workers' Compensation Act]." This broad language articulates a legislative decision to establish exclusive as well as comprehensive remedies for injuries that are covered by the Act.

When an employer-employee relationship exists under this Act, the immunity from common-law suits should be broadly construed. Therefore, if an injury comes within the coverage of the Act, an action for damages is barred even though compensation is not provided for a particular element of damages.

A wrongful death action brought against an employer by an employee's nondependent parents, based upon the death of the employee which occurred in the course and scope of the employee's employment, is strictly derivative and barred by the exclusivity provisions of the act, even though the parents suffer their own distinct injuries.

Accordingly, the dispositive issues become whether private civil remedies are implied under the Youth Act and FLSA, and if so, whether those remedies supersede the exclusivity principles of the Workers' Compensation Act.

A.

The parents argue that the child labor provisions of the FLSA were violated because their child performed prohibited labor. Therefore, they claim entitlement to remedies under an implied private cause of action. We are not persuaded.

* * *

* * * [T]he Workers' Compensation Act here provides the parents a remedy. * * * Questions as to the inadequacy of that remedy do not justify the creation of a new federal remedy in addition to the criminal penalties provided by the FLSA.

For this reason, we decline to infer a private civil remedy for violation of the FLSA.

B.

Similarly, we decline to infer the existence of a private remedy under the Youth Act.

* * *

The purpose of the Youth Act, as set forth in the legislative declaration, is "to foster the economic, social and educational development of young people through employment." Our refusal to infer a private cause of action for violations of the Act does not frustrate this purpose.

The stated purpose of the Youth Act indicates that it benefits children, not their parents. Accordingly, a private cause of action for parents is not contemplated by the Youth Act. * * *

* * *

II.

* * *

* * * Employer * * * is entitled to reasonable attorney fees for defending the appeal.

The judgment of dismissal is affirmed, the appeal of the award of attorney fees against parents' attorney is dismissed, and the cause is remanded for consideration of an award of reasonable attorney fees to employer for defending the appeal.

Notes and Questions

1. *Private federal remedies.* The FLSA does not provide an express private right of action for violation of the child labor provisions, and *Henderson* is typical of decisions that have refused to imply such a right. Should Congress amend the FLSA to provide an express private damage remedy against the employer on behalf of a child injured or killed while engaging in labor that violates the Act? Would such a "private attorney general" remedy assist federal enforcement efforts?

2. *Private state remedies.* Without a private federal remedy, children and parents seeking private relief against employers arising from child labor violations are left to state law remedies. Private tort suits are usually barred under the "exclusive remedy" provisions of workers' compensation acts, which prohibit employees from suing employers outside the acts.

Most state workers' compensation acts bar private tort suits against employers because the acts cover minors lawfully and unlawfully employed. If the minor was employed in violation of the child labor act, many acts award an enhanced remedy, ranging from 150% of the ordinary rate to double or even triple the ordinary rate. See, e.g., Ohio Rev. Code § 4123.89 (double); R.I. Gen. Laws § 28–33–22(a) (triple). Enhancement is ordinarily awarded even if the minor secured the employment by misrepresenting his age. But see Cal. Lab. Code § 4557 (no enhancement where employer reasonably relied on written documentation of age). Several states expressly prohibit insurers from insuring employers against payment of the enhanced portion of the award. See, e.g., Cal. Ins. Code § 11661.5. The constitutionality of workers' compensation enhancement provisions has been upheld as rationally related to the state purpose of protecting children by encouraging employers to heed child labor mandates. See, e.g., Ligonier Tavern, Inc. v. Workmen's Comp. Appeal Bd., 714 A.2d 1008, 1011–12 (Pa.1998).

Even with enhancement, workers' compensation acts have been said to provide only "shockingly meager" recovery for death or serious injury suffered by unlawfully employed children. B. Nathaniel Richter and Lois G. Forer, Federal Employers' Liability Act–A Real Compensatory Law for Railroad Workers, 36 Cornell L.Q. 203, 209 (1951). Would the Hendersons have been adequately compensated for their fifteen-year-old son's death if their $4000 award had been doubled or even tripled?

Where the workers' compensation act is silent about child employees, the exclusive-remedies provision may not bar private tort suits against employers. If a minor is killed or injured by employment that violates the child labor act, a handful of states permit the minor or the estate to choose between workers' compensation and other common law and statutory remedies. See, e.g., 820 Ill. Comp. Stat. 305/5(a).

Even in states where a private tort suit may be maintained against the employer, private enforcement may still not assume a serious role in enforcing the child labor laws. Can you think of any reasons why authorities cannot reasonably expect much private help in child labor enforcement?

Could the Hendersons have sued a non-employer allegedly responsible for their son's death, such as a manufacturer of the car wash equipment? See Arthur Larson and Lex K. Larson, Larson's Workers' Compensation, ch. 14 (desk ed. 1999).

3. *Defenses.* Where a private tort suit is permitted, the defendant employer may not defeat liability by asserting that the child was contributorily negligent or that the child's parents consented to the unlawful employment. See, e.g., Restatement (Second) of Torts § 483 cmts. c, e, f; Strain v. Christians, 483 N.W.2d 783 (S.D.1992). In jurisdictions that have replaced contributory negligence with comparative negligence, courts have similarly refused to permit employers to introduce evidence of the child's comparative negligence. See, e.g., D.L. v. Huebner, 329 N.W.2d 890, 918–19 (Wis. 1983). What policy considerations underlie these holdings?

In a damage action brought on behalf of a child injured while working in violation of the child labor act, should the employer have the defense that the child assumed the risk of the employment? Most decisions answer in the negative. See, e.g., Boyer v. Johnson, 360 So.2d 1164 (La.1978), on remand, 366 So.2d 192 (La.Ct.App.1978). That the child or family needed the money?

If a child misrepresents his or her age to secure employment that violates the child labor act, should the child be able to sue the employer for injuries sustained in the employment? In jurisdictions that permit private tort suits, most decisions answer in the affirmative, despite the doctrine that children are generally liable for their torts though not for their contracts. What policy considerations might justify the answer? See, e.g., Shelpman v. Evans Prods. Co., 258 N.E.2d 868 (Ind.Ct.App.1970).

4. *Injury to third persons. Henderson* dismissed the parents' damage suit for their son's death. Workers' compensation statutes, however, do not preclude suits against the employer by third persons injured by an unlawfully employed child.

See, e.g., Beard v. Lee Enterprises, Inc., 591 N.W.2d 156 (Wis.1999).

5. *Final thoughts about societal commitment.* Federal and state authorities are generally lax in their public enforcement of child labor laws. The Fair Labor Standards Act does not carry a private right of action, and state workers' compensation laws generally limit killed or injured child workers and their parents to minuscule recovery. Does this state of affairs provide a commentary on society's commitment to regulate child labor?

SECTION 2. ALCOHOL REGULATION

A. *The Minimum Drinking Age*

MICHAEL P. ROSENTHAL, THE MINIMUM DRINKING AGE FOR YOUNG PEOPLE: AN OBSERVATION

92 Dick. L. Rev. 649, 649–55 (1988).

* * *

A.   The Colonial Period

* * *

No matter how one labels the drinking habits of Colonial America, colonists considered alcohol as an "essential" part of life. It was used daily in homes, inns, and taverns. The tavern itself was "a focal point of community life, a place for political decisions, recreation, and entertainment, and the tavernkeeper was a respected community leader."

Children, as well as adults, drank in Colonial America. According to one study, parents taught their children to drink when they were young, sometimes even when they were babies. Adults also encouraged adolescents to openly experiment with adult drinking behaviors. For example, twelve-year old boys often entered taverns to drink, and "fathers would even escort their sons, proud that their offspring could participate in this manly activity."

In addition, students drank heavily at colleges, and colleges encouraged drinking by supplying alcohol to students. One commentator noted that the laws of this period reflected a "general acceptance or even encouragement of youthful drinking." Many regulations of the liquor trade were passed during this period, but very few of them dealt with drinking by the young. Those that did addressed special problems and did not deal with general prohibitions on youthful drinking.

B.   The Immediate Post–Revolutionary Period to Prohibition

The use of alcohol changed after the Revolutionary War and during the nineteenth century. The pattern of the colonial period included drinking daily, but not to drunkenness. As time went on, however, this pattern became less common. It was replaced by regular heavy drinking bouts that included frequent drunkenness. In the last years of the eighteenth century and the first two decades of the nineteenth century, drunkenness became the norm. Heavy drinkers who drank to drunkenness generally were members of the lower and middle classes. Before the Revolution, the strict standards of the colonial aristocracy controlled their drinking. After the war, however, the power of the aristocracy weakened and it could no longer enforce the old norm. Nevertheless, the aristocracy attacked the new drinking habits (including drunkenness) and began the temperance movement in an attempt to maintain some of its power, leadership, and prestige. Although the aristocracy began the temperance movement, this movement became important in American life only as it became dominated by the lower and middle classes.

There is not a great deal of evidence on the drinking patterns of young people after the Revolutionary war, but it appears that at least some minors changed their drinking habits. "[The] post-Revolutionary generation of students indulged in unprecedented lusty drinking;" and there was very heavy drinking along the frontier where men worked as trappers, miners, cowboys, and soldiers—all trades begun at early ages.

As young people began to drink heavily, pressure on them to moderate or cease drinking arose. Colleges tried to restrict student drinking, and legislation was enacted later that prohibited sellers of alcohol from selling or giving it to minors. No state, however, made it a crime for minors to drink. Society viewed the minors as innocent victims, not persons at fault.

There was probably a special reason why states enacted legislation banning sales to minors. One commentator * * * believes that stricter controls against children's drinking "coincided with a major shift in societal attitudes toward adolescence."

    * * * [T]he state increasingly dictated the fates of the family and young people after 1870. Child-labor laws, compulsory-education laws, and juvenile courts, which had the power to restrict or terminate parental rights if neglect or abuse was established, became common throughout the country. These had the effect of extending childhood to a later age and of restricting the rights of children and parents to determine the child's destiny . * * *

Thus, the change in youthful-drinking laws, which became pronounced during the 1880's, can be viewed as one aspect of the state's intervention into the parent-child relationship. Young adults' participation in the state's economy became restricted * * * and adolescence became synonymous with "incompetency." * * * The state began treating sixteen-to twenty-year olds with the same legal constraints as those imposed on preadolescents.

C. Prohibition and Immediate Post–Prohibition

During state and national prohibition, bans on sales to minors were, of course, unnecessary, but regulations again became necessary after prohibition was repealed in 1933. The twenty-first amendment left the control of alcohol to the states. Almost all states that legalized beverage alcohol prescribed a minimum drinking age of twenty-one. New York, then the most populous state, was an exception; it chose a minimum drinking age of eighteen.

D. The Vietnam Period to the Present

There was no significant quarrel with the twenty-one-year minimum drinking age until the early 1970's. At that time, a large number of states switched to minimum drinking ages below twenty-one and also lowered their ages of majority. While a number of factors were involved, the primary cause for this switch was the Vietnam War and the youth culture that developed largely as a result of the war. Young men under the age of twenty-one were drafted and killed in Vietnam, but they were legally minors and did not have the rights and privileges of adults. They could not vote; they could not drink; but they could serve and fall in battle.

To the extent the Vietnam War was responsible for lowering the age of majority in general and the minimum drinking age in particular in a large number of states, it should be realized that the changes were for reasons somewhat different than the reasons an age of majority is usually lowered or raised. Normally, a change is based on society's view of the age that should be considered the age of responsible decision-making or competency. When states lowered the age of majority and the minimum drinking age because boys were serving and dying in the War, however, they did so because society felt it was *unfair* to have them serve and die and yet not have the rights and privileges of adults. The states did not inquire whether the boys were mature enough to vote or to handle liquor; they just deemed the treatment to be unfair.

Another factor may have contributed to legislation reducing the minimum drinking age. In the late 1960's and early 1970's, American attitudes toward adolescence became less paternalistic and moved toward increased autonomy.* * *

As a result of these factors, twenty-nine states lowered their minimum legal drinking age, generally from twenty-one to eighteen, during the early 1970's. Studies showed that lowering the minimum drinking age brought with it an increase in *fatal* accidents, although the validity of the data is controversial. Regretfully, however, the studies "leave some question as to the amount of the increase."

An increasing number of states reacted to these statistics and once again *raised* their minimum drinking ages (in the great majority of cases to twenty-one) in the late 1970's and early 1980's. More studies followed, and again there was controversy about the validity of the data. This time the great majority of the soundly designed studies found that raising the drinking age decreased fatal accidents. A major evaluative study recently prepared by the General Accounting Office concluded * * * that it could not "estimate the size of the traffic accident reduction that individual States might expect to see after enacting a minimum drinking age law." It stated: "[w]hat we do know is that, in general, States can expect reductions, but the magnitude of the reduction will depend on the particular outcome measured and on the characteristics—geographic or demographic or cultural—of the individual State."

With public concern about drunken driving mounting, President Reagan created the Presidential Commission on Drunken Driving, which recommended that the states raise their minimum drinking ages to twenty-one. One year after this recommendation was made, however, only four of the twenty-three states that still had minimum drinking ages below twenty-one had raised their minimum ages. It appeared that the Commission's recommendation was not enough. * * *

* * *

Notes and Questions

1. *National minimum drinking age.* In response to foot-dragging by the states, Congress in 1984 enacted the National Minimum Drinking Age Act, 23 U.S.C. § 158. The Act sought to encourage a uniform nationwide minimum drinking age by directing the Secretary of Transportation to withhold percentages of otherwise allocable federal highway funds from any state "in which the purchase or public possession * * * of any alcoholic beverage by a person who is less that twenty-one years of age is lawful." In South Dakota v. Dole, 483 U.S. 203 (1987), the Supreme Court upheld section 158 as a proper exercise of Congress' spending power. Statutes now set the minimum drinking age at twenty-one in all states and virtually all territories and possessions. The sole holdout is Puerto Rico, where the minimum age remains eighteen.

2. *Closing "blood borders."* Was Congress right to conclude that the minimum drinking age is a matter for national uniformity rather than state-by-state choice? In early 1996, a short-lived Louisiana Supreme Court decision provided an opportunity to examine this question. The court held, 4–3, that by departing from the general age of majority, the Louisiana statute creating the minimum age of twenty-one violated the state constitution's protection against arbitrary age discrimination. See Manuel v. State, 95–2189 (La. Mar. 8, 1996).

Reaction to the decision by bar owners and teenage drinkers in New Orleans was described as "the judicial equivalent of a keg party," and Louisiana bar owners began beaming radio advertisements into adjoining states encouraging 18–21–year-olds to drive into Louisiana to drink lawfully. See Rick Bragg, Louisiana Stands Alone on Drinking at 18, N.Y. Times, March 23, 1996, at 1, 7. A Louisiana newspaper editorialized that the 1984 congressional mandate amounted to "financial blackmail." See Federal "Financial Blackmail," Times–Picayune (New Orleans), June 13, 1996, at B6.

Safety advocates and many Louisiana state legislators, however, sternly condemned the court decision for inviting a return of the "blood borders" that plagued many states by the early 1980s. Where adjoining states had different minimum drinking ages, juveniles from a state with a higher age would drive into a state with a lower age to drink lawfully, then attempt to drive home intoxicated. Four months after *Manuel*, the state supreme court reversed itself on rehearing. The court now held that the drinking-age statutes were not arbitrary because they "substantially further the appropriate governmental purpose of improving highway safety." Manuel v. State, 692 So.2d 320, 338 (La.1996). The court reasoned that "[t]he eighteen-to-twenty-year-old age group, who are barely experienced at driving legally, are totally inexperienced at drinking legally." Id. at 341. With the state now in line with the rest of the nation, the executive director of the Beer Industry League of Louisiana called the decision on rehearing "totally political." Joe Gyan, Jr. and Doug Myers, Drinking Age Revived, Baton Rouge Morning Advoc., July 3, 1996, at A1.

3. *Some dangers of underage drinking.* The American Academy of Pediatrics reports that the leading cause of death among 15-to-24-year-olds is alcohol-related motor vehicle crashes, that thousands survive these crashes with serious and sometimes permanent injuries each year, that alcohol is implicated in the majority of other unintentional deaths of children such as drownings and fatal falls, that many child suicide and homicide victims have elevated blood alcohol levels, and that a history of suicide attempts is more prevalent among adolescents in alcohol and drug treatment facilities. See American Acad. of Pediatrics, Alcohol Use and Abuse: A Pediatric Concern, 95 Pediatrics 439 (1995). "The negative consequences of alcohol use include impaired relationships with family, peers, or teachers; problems with school performance; problems with authorities; and high-risk behavior, such as driving or swimming while drinking. Alcohol use or abuse also increases the likelihood of other risk-taking behaviors such as unprotected or unplanned intercourse that may lead to adolescent pregnancy. Additional associated risks include acquiring a sexually transmitted disease and increased risk of physical or sexual abuse, often by an acquaintance of the same age." Id.

In a 1991 study, the U.S. Department of Health and Human Services reported that almost a third of seventh-to-twelfth-grade students surveyed had accepted a ride in an automobile operated by a driver they knew had been drinking. Youth and Alcohol: A National Survey 12 (1991). About 67% of teenage passengers who die in automobile crashes were in vehicles driven by another teen, and alcohol figures in a significant percentage of these crashes. See Ins. Inst. for Highway Safety, Teenagers, Fatality Facts (1995).

B. Do Criminal and Civil Enforcement Work?

MICHAEL KLITZNER ET AL., REDUCING UNDERAGE DRINKING AND ITS CONSEQUENCES
17 Alcohol Health & Research World 12, 13 (Jan. 1993).

* * *

Several national epidemiologic studies * * * indicate that underage drinking is common and that a significant minority of underage youths are heavy, episodic drinkers.

According to these surveys, of American 12–to 18–year-olds (1) between 50 and 80 percent have experimented with alcohol; (2) by high school graduation, the percentage of students who have used alcohol at least once approaches 90 percent; (3) about one-half of those surveyed had at least one drink in the past year; and (4) about one-third are heavy, episodic drinkers. Among high school seniors from the class of 1990 who were surveyed, about 10 percent reported drinking at grade 6 or earlier, and about 4 percent reported getting drunk at grade 6 or earlier. After high school, alcohol use tends to increase, peaking at ages 21–22 and then leveling off or declining over the next 10 years.[a]

---

a. [ed.] In a 1993 study, the U.S. General Accounting Office called alcohol "the drug of choice among adolescents, "with more than 57% of high school seniors re- porting current use. See Drug Use Among Youth: No Simple Answers to Guide Prevention 4 (U.S. GAO Dec. 1993).

American young people report little trouble in obtaining alcohol. * * * About 64 percent of 8th-graders and 83 percent of 10th-graders report that it is "fairly" or "very" easy for them to obtain alcohol.

Although some young people obtain alcohol from older friends or by persuading adult strangers to purchase it for them, almost two-thirds of 7th-to 12th-graders report buying it themselves. A study by the Insurance Institute for Highway Safety found that underage decoys sent into alcohol outlets to buy a six-pack of beer were able to purchase the beer up to 97 percent of time without lying about their age or producing any identification. * * *

* * *

To summarize the current situation in the United States, most young people drink, a significant minority drink heavily, and few young people have difficulty obtaining alcohol. The MLDA [minimum legal drinking age] laws in many States are not well enforced, and those same laws are often filled with loopholes. Despite widespread and well-justified concern on the part of both government and the public, there is considerable room for improvement in our national response to underage drinking.

* * *

MARK WOLFSON, LAW OFFICERS' VIEWS ON ENFORCEMENT OF THE MINIMUM DRINKING AGE: A FOUR–STATE STUDY

110 Pub. Health Reps. 428 (1995).

* * *

Recently, considerable attention has been focused on enforcing the minimum drinking age. A number of sources suggest that such enforcement is not given high priority by many law enforcement agencies. * * *

In general, rates of enforcement are extremely low relative to the incidence of underage drinking. An estimated 2 of every 1,000 occasions of illegal drinking by youth under 21 result in an arrest. When enforcement actions are taken, they are typically focused on individual young drinkers, rather than commercial outlets or private persons who may supply alcoholic beverages to youth. For every 1,000 arrests of a 16–20–year-old for underage possession of alcohol, only 130 outlets have any action taken against them, and only 88 adults 21 or older are arrested for furnishing alcohol to youth. * * * *

Background on Enforcement

All 50 States and the District of Columbia now have a minimum drinking age of 21. However, statutory language and procedures for enforcing the law vary considerably from State to State. States have laws that prohibit some or all of the following: possession by a minor, possession with intent to consume by a minor, consumption by a minor, misrepresentation of age by a minor, purchase by a minor, sale to a minor, and furnishing to a minor.

Complicating enforcement efforts is the fact that many States allow underage persons to obtain and possess alcohol in certain circumstances. Five States allow underage youth to possess alcohol if they do not intend to consume, and six States have no laws against minors attempting to or purchasing alcohol. Many States allow persons younger than 21 to possess and consume alcohol in private residences, private establishments, or when accompanied by a legal guardian 21 or older.

There are also significant differences across States in the definition of consumption by minors. Twenty-one States have no specific statutory-language which prohibits the consumption of alcohol by minors, although possession of alcohol may be prohibited. Sixteen States have no statutory language explicitly prohibiting the deliberate misrepresentation of age by youth to obtain alcohol, and 19 States do not explicitly prohibit youth from using false identification to obtain alcohol.

Minimum drinking age laws are enforced by State administrative agencies (usually referred to as Alcoholic Beverage Control or ABC agencies), police departments, and county sheriffs' departments. Given that ABC agencies have many liquor laws to enforce, limited enforcement staff, and no jurisdiction or authority to cite or arrest minors, the burden of enforcing the age–21 policy frequently falls to county or local law enforcement officers, and in this paper we focus on their efforts.

* * *

Enforcement constraints

Personnel. Officers in virtually every agency cited personnel shortages as an obstacle to enforcement of the legal drinking age. Officers in both rural and urban agencies reported that insufficient staffing often forced officers to give priority to other areas of law enforcement, resulting in relatively few citations and arrests for underage drinking.

* * *

Juvenile detention facilities. A lack of juvenile detention facilities in some communities was reported to influence the level of enforcement of the minimum drinking age. In most jurisdictions represented in this study, it was reported that any juvenile detained by a police agency must be held in an area separate from adult detainees. In the absence of a separate juvenile detention facility, a juvenile detainee must be constantly supervised by a police officer until he or she is released to a parent or guardian. The process of locating and waiting for the arrival of a guardian can occupy an officer for hours.

* * *

Identifying the source of confiscated alcohol. Usually at least one officer per agency knew of one or more alcohol merchants or other adults who regularly provided alcohol to youth. However, most officers reported that identifying the source of confiscated alcohol is usually impossible. * * *

Little monitoring of bars, liquor stores, or other establishments selling alcoholic beverages was reported. Aside from a few reports of sting operations, most agencies were not able to provide the investigative effort necessary to catch offenders in the act. Consequently, citations for providing alcohol to minors were rare in many of the agencies surveyed.

* * *

Perceived ineffectiveness of the court system. Most officers were extremely skeptical of the court system's ability to mete out what they considered to be appropriate punishment to young alcohol offenders. Many officers reported that the penalties for drinking offenses are light and unevenly applied, resulting (in their view) in negligible deterrent effects.

* * *

For many officers, the perception that punishment is insufficiently certain and severe appears to lead to a sense that their enforcement efforts in this area amount to a waste of time. Several reported that repeat offenders become more defiant with each citation or arrest. A number of officers said they deliberately avoid making underage drinking citations or arrests because they are convinced that it will result in little or no punishment.

Processing and paperwork. Some officers complained of the large volume of paperwork sometimes associated with juvenile offenses, which is especially frustrating to them when combined with the perceived ineffectiveness of the court system. One supervisory officer said that his officers " ... dislike dealing with juveniles altogether. There's tons of paperwork. They have to treat them with kid gloves. And then [the courts] pat them on the hand and they go out the next night and do the same thing."

The processing of drinking age violations, especially possession violations, often is considered a mundane task for arresting officers. This, combined with the aforementioned perception of ineffective court-administered punishment, seems to discourage some officers from issuing citations or making arrests, particularly in cases of possession or borderline intoxication.

On the other hand, procedural requirements do not seem to impede citations or arrests in DUI [driving under the influence of alcohol] cases, despite the fact that the arrest process for DUI typically consists of several field sobriety tests and many hours of supervision and processing. Several officers stated that, in contrast to drinking age violations, DUI involving a minor presents a clear danger to the minor and others. Most officers expressed a strong desire to keep DUI offenders of all ages off the road.

Low status of enforcement of the drinking age. Citations or arrests for providing to minors or possession or consumption by minors do not seem to bring much favorable publicity to the law enforcement agencies surveyed. Police actions targeting illicit drugs seem to garner much more attention and acclaim from community groups and persons, including the local press. * * *

Dissatisfaction with existing law. In some agencies surveyed, State law allows officers to treat consumption of alcohol as possession, meaning that if an officer can smell alcohol on a minor's breath, he can cite him or her for possessing alcohol. Officers in jurisdictions where that is not the case must see actual physical evidence of alcohol possession before a minor can be cited. Officers reported that this is especially problematic at large parties where underage drinkers drop their alcoholic beverages as police arrive on the scene. Officers who were able to cite minors for "possession by consumption" were very enthusiastic about this law and reported it was much easier to process a citation this way.

Many officers reported frustration with existing case and statutory law concerning possession of alcohol. A number of officers felt that the courts place an unreasonable burden of proof upon an arresting officer to provide physical evidence of alcohol consumption. For example, one officer reported that underage drinkers in his jurisdiction will often transfer alcoholic beverages from their original containers into plain, plastic containers or "squeeze bottles." Despite his suspicion that these containers are used to conceal alcohol, he is reluctant to inspect the bottles because that suspicion may not meet the court's standard for probable cause.

Another officer reported that defense attorneys in alcohol-related arrests of underage persons sometimes demand laboratory tests on samples of confiscated beverages with the knowledge that these tests are costly, and lack of such tests will often result in dismissal of the case.

Discretionary enforcement. Officers commonly reported that they are forced to make judgement calls at the scene of underage drinking violations. For the reasons cited previously (personnel shortages, lack of a holding facility), officers feel they cannot issue citations or make arrests every time they witness a violation of underage drinking laws. Officers must decide on a case-by-case basis whether a violator will be arrested or not. In cases involving large parties or gatherings of underage drinkers, few youth, if any, are typically cited for underage drinking. Respondents offered a number of examples of situations in which officers would often decide not to cite underage drinkers.

1. The officer is satisfied that the offender's parents or guardian, once notified, will handle the matter more effectively than the court system.

2. The offender shows enough fear or remorse at the time of being caught or questioned that the officer feels an appropriate lesson was learned and further punishment is unnecessary.

3. The officer does not have the time to complete a citation or arrest because of other calls away from the scene that are assigned higher priority.

4. The officer performs other tasks at the scene that take priority over citations. For example, several officers reported that the most important thing to do at a keg party is to confiscate or dispose of the alcohol before any more can be consumed. Officers arriving at the scene of such a party will often move first to find and confiscate the alcohol, during which time most underage drinkers flee the scene or discard their drinks.

Most officers reported that party "busts" are considered routine and are not threatening to underage drinkers or adult providers at the scene. Officers believe that underage drinkers are aware that citations are rarely issued at a "busted" party, and that youth are not deterred by the potential consequences of taking part in such a party.

* * *

Notes and Questions

1. *Teenage alcoholism.* In 1990, the California Medical Association estimated that at least 3.5 million American teenagers were alcoholics. Calif. Med. Ass'n, Teenage Alcoholism, Health Tips 5 (Feb. 1990). The American Academy of Pediatrics reports that "[a]ddiction to alcohol is underdiagnosed in the young," and recommends that "[a]lcoholism should be suspected in youths who are frequently intoxicated or experience withdrawal symptoms from chronic or recurrent alcohol use; tolerate large quantities of alcohol; attempt unsuccessfully at cutting down or stopping alcohol use; experience blackouts due to drinking; or continue drinking despite adverse social, occupational (educational), physical, or psychological consequences and/or alcohol-related injuries." American Acad. of Pediatrics, Alcohol Use and Abuse: A Pediatric Concern, 95 Pediatrics 439 (1995).

2. *Exemptions.* Debate continues about whether "youths should postpone the use of alcohol until the legal drinking age or be encouraged to develop safe, responsible drinking patterns through progressive, controlled exposure in family or religious settings." American Acad. of Pediatrics, Alcohol Use and Abuse: A Pediatric Concern, 95 Pediatrics 439 (1995). Many state alcohol laws exempt parents who provide alcohol to their underage children, clergy who provide alcohol to underage children as part of a religious service or ceremony, or physicians and pharmacists who prescribe alcohol in their professional practices. See, e.g., Ala. Code § 28–3–15 (physicians and clergy); Mo. Rev. Stat. §§ 311.310, 312.400 (parent or guardian), 311.470 (physicians and pharmacists).

What policy grounds support each of these exemptions? Should the law permit, or even encourage, parents to introduce their underage children to alcohol in their own homes? What if a parent provides so much alcohol that the child becomes intoxicated and causes injury to himself or personal or property damage to someone else? Does the parent, even if immunized from prosecution under the alcohol control laws, nonetheless face any potential legal consequences? See, e.g., People v. Garbarino, 549 N.Y.S.2d 527 (App. Div.1989).

3. *Proximity to schools.* Legislation frequently prohibits the state licensing authority from granting licenses to furnish or sell alcoholic beverages near schools. See, e.g., Ariz. Rev. Stat. § 4–207(A) (300 feet).

4. *"Zero tolerance" laws.* In 1995, Congress enacted a nationwide "zero tolerance" statute. To combat underage drinking, the lawmakers encouraged states to enact and enforce legislation that "considers an individual under the age of 21 who has a blood alcohol concentration of 0.02 percent or greater while operating a motor vehicle in the State to be driving while intoxicated or driving under the influence of alcohol." 23 U.S.C. § 161(a)(3). States failing to comply with the congressional mandate face loss of a portion of their federal highway funds. More than thirty-five states had already enacted "zero tolerance" legislation, providing for suspension or revocation of licenses of persons under twenty-one convicted of driving with even a minuscule blood-alcohol level. See, e.g., Fla. Stat. § 322.2616. This legislation has been upheld against equal protection challenges as rationally related to a legitimate state purposes of reducing the number of teenage driving fatalities and of protecting the public. See, e.g., Barnett v. State, 510 S.E.2d 527, 528 & n. 1 (Ga. 1999) (citing decisions).

The congressionally mandated 0.02% cap is roughly equivalent to one glass of beer or wine. (A true zero-tolerance measure was deemed unworkable because some prescription and over-the-counter drugs, and some foods, contain alcohol or other substances that might register on a drug test.). The cap is considerably higher for persons over twenty-one. In most states, adult drivers are not legally drunk unless they test more than .10% blood alcohol content; in some states, the adult level is .08%.

5. *Identification.* Statutes frequently specify the identification young people must show to establish that they have reached the minimum drinking age. Generally acceptable identification are drivers' licenses, military identification cards, and passports. See, e.g., Ariz. Rev. Stat. § 4–241. To help prevent use of false or altered drivers' licenses, a number of states issue minors special color-coded licenses, or licenses with distinctive photographs or special wording or characters.

Most states have statutes that provide sanctions for possessing or using a false or altered drivers' license. The statutes frequently apply regardless of the driver's age, and any person might present such a license when stopped by a police officer on the highway. A prime purpose of these statutes, however, is to regulate persons under twenty-one who display them as "proof" when they seek to purchase or be served alcohol. The statutes generally provide for criminal penalties, suspension or revocation of the offender's license, or postponement of the right to apply for a license. See, e.g., Kan. Stat. § 8–260.

PROBLEM 10–1

Your client, Easy Al's Place, holds a liquor license in a college town and does not always check identification of would-be patrons who appear young. The client tells you that "the liquor laws are hardly ever enforced anyway, so I'll take my chances. Besides, a dollar is a dollar, even if it comes from a nineteen-year-old.'' What legal advice would you provide? After you provide your advice, Easy Al's seeks further advice about what steps to take to avoid liability for serving underage patrons. What would you suggest to the client?

A NOTE ABOUT DRAM–SHOP AND SOCIAL–HOST LIABILITY

Persons who provide or serve alcoholic beverages to underage drinkers may face tort liability in private suits alleging injury or death caused by the drinker's ensuing conduct. Typically the young drinker consumes liquor provided on the defendant's premises, then drives off in an automobile and has an accident causing death or serious injury to himself or others. Providers often make alluring defendants because they may be better able to pay a judgment than the young drinker, who may be without significant resources and either uninsured or underinsured. Providers have been hit with a number of sizeable verdicts recently, perhaps reflecting growing social disapproval of drunken driving and other alcohol-related misconduct.

At early common law, a person who provided alcohol to an able-bodied individual did not risk tort liability in a suit by the individual or a person the individual injured; the proximate cause of any damage was the consumption of the alcohol and not the providing of it. The law was the same whether the alcohol was sold to the individual or provided socially. Today, however, a growing number of decisions permit negligence suits against defendants who provide alcoholic beverages to underage consumers. And provider liability is no longer limited to bars, convenience stores and other businesses holding liquor licenses. Increasingly, ''social hosts and such noncommercial providers of liquor as churches, colleges and hospitals are being held liable for the torts or injuries of intoxicated guests and employees. And the costs [of settlements and judgments] are staggering.'' James M. Goldberg, One for the Road: Liquor Liability Broadens, 73 A.B.A.J. 84 (June 1987).

In Schooley v. Pinch's Deli Market, Inc., 951 P.2d 749 (Wash.1998), the defendant sold four cases of beer to three underage customers without requesting identification. The purchasers brought the beer to a party with other underage guests. After considerable drinking, the partygoers decided to throw a girl into the backyard pool. Not knowing the pool was only two feet deep, she dove in first, fracturing her spinal cord, and became a quadriplegic. The state supreme court held that the nonpurchaser victim could sue the market for negligence: ''The recognized purpose of legislation prohibiting the sale of alcohol to minors is to protect minors' health and safety interests from their 'own inability to drink responsibly' and to protect against the particular hazard of 'alcohol in the hands of minors.' Because minors who drink commonly do so with other minors, protecting all those injured as a result of the illegal sale of alcohol to minors is the best way to serve the purpose for which the legislation was created, to prevent minors from drinking." Id. at 753.

Common law decisions disagree about the defenses the provider may assert. Where the underage consumer or the consumer's estate sues the provider, some courts deny recovery based on the underage consumer's contributory negligence, assumption of risk, or wilful misconduct. Other courts, however, refuse to recognize these defenses on the ground that the alcohol laws seek to protect underage persons from their own improvidence. In any event, these defenses would not defeat a third party's suit. See Richard J. Leighton, Beyond the Dram Shop Act: Imposition of Common Law Liability on Purveyors of Liquor, 63 Iowa L. Rev. 1282 (1978). Where the defendant provided alcoholic beverages to an underage consumer over eighteen, may the defendant avoid liability on the ground that the consumer was an adult responsible for his or her own conduct? See Schooley, supra, 951 P.2d at 756–57 (no).

More than thirty-five states have enacted "dram shop" acts or social host acts. These acts may preclude imposition of common law liability on licensees, and sometimes on non-licensees such as social hosts, that provide alcohol outside the circumstances defined in the acts. See, e.g., Charles v. Seigfried, 651 N.E.2d 154, 156 (Ill.1995) (social hosts). Other decisions, however, do not find legislative intent to displace the common law.

Dram shop acts define circumstances in which providers incur strict liability, without regard to contributory or comparative negligence or assumption of risk, for death or injury proximately caused by an under-age or visibly intoxicated drinker. Some dram shop acts specifically limit liability to providers that hold liquor licenses, while other acts have sufficiently broad language to reach social hosts and other providers as well. Dram shop acts began to appear during the temperance movement in the mid–1850s. Many states repealed their acts after the repeal of Prohibition in 1933, only to reenact them in the 1970s. The various acts are not uniform in their coverage or operation. Suit may ordinarily be maintained only by third parties, and not by the consumer or his estate, or by members of the consumer's family seeking derivative damages. See, e.g., N.Y. Gen. Oblig. Law § 11–101.

A few states disallow dram shop liability, except where the commercial provider knew or should have known the consumer was underage or intoxicated at the time of provision. See, e.g., Idaho Code § 23–808(3)(a). A few states prohibit dram shop liability altogether. See, e.g., S.D. Cod. L. § 35–4–78.

For their part, social host acts generally permit recovery by family members and injured third-persons against persons who provide alcohol gratuitously to an underage or intoxicated drinker. See, e.g., N.Y. Gen. Oblig. Law § 11–100(1). These acts seek to encourage hosts to "take greater care in serving alcoholic beverages at social gatherings so as avoid not only the moral responsibility but the economic liability that would occur if the guest were to injure someone as a result of his drunken driving." Kelly v. Gwinnell, 476 A.2d 1219, 1226 (N.J.1984). A few states have rejected or strictly limited social host liability. See, e.g., N.M. Stat. § 41–11–1(E).

PROBLEM 10–2

You represent a schoolteacher who suffered a broken neck when her car was sideswiped by a speeding car driven by an intoxicated sixteen-year-old, who was on his way home from four hours of drinking at a party at a seventeen-year-old friend's house. The youngsters had partied unsupervised because the friend's parents were not at home that night. Could you successfully argue that the parents are liable under a social host statute which provides that "[a]ny person injured by reason of the intoxication or impairment of any person under 21 may recover actual damages against anyone who knowingly causes such intoxication or impairment by unlawfully furnishing to or unlawfully assisting in procuring alcoholic beverages for such person with knowledge or reasonable cause to believe the person was under 21." What if the absent parents neither knew nor should have known that their child had previously served alcohol to underage friends when the parents were not home, if the parents left no alcohol in the home, and forbade use of alcohol during their absence? How might the outcome be affected if the absent parents had financed the party, knew it was taking place, and knew alcohol would be served?

PROBLEM 10–3

You represent a 16–year-old high school football star who furnished alcoholic beverages at a pep rally to an underage friend, who was injured when his car hit a tree on the way home later that night. The friend has now sued your client for damages under the state's social host statute, which is identical to the one quoted in Problem 10–2. Could you argue that your client is not within the statute's defendant class? What arguments would you expect your opponents to make?

SECTION 3.   TOBACCO REGULATION

1. "Cigarette smoking causes over 420,000 deaths annually in the United States, roughly twenty percent of all U.S. deaths, making cigarettes the single greatest preventable cause of death in this country. Indeed, tobacco kills more people every year than alcohol, illicit drugs, automobile accidents, violent crime, and AIDS combined. And not only are cigarettes deadly to smokers; they kill nonsmokers as well. According to a recent report from the Environmental Protection Agency (EPA), the 'sidestream' or 'passive' smoke from cigarettes—so-called environmental tobacco smoke (ETS)—is responsible annually for approximately 3000 lung cancer deaths, between 150,000 and 300,000 lower respiratory ailments in children, and approximately 37,000 heart disease deaths."

Jon D. Hanson & Kyle D. Logue, The Costs of Cigarettes: The Economic Case for Incentive–Based Regulation, 107 Yale L.J. 1163, 1167 (1998).

2. *Children and smoking.* Former Food and Drug Administration Commissioner David A. Kessler has called teenage smoking a "pediatric disease." Dr. David Kessler Talks About the Anti–Tobacco Crusade, Meet the Press (NBC), June 22, 1997. Some studies have found that as many as 90% of adult smokers begin smoking as children. See, e.g., American College of Chest Physicians, Smoking and Health: Physician Responsibility: A Statement of the Joint Committee on Smoking and Health, 108 Chest 1118 (Oct. 1995); U.S. Dep't of Health and Human Services, Centers for Disease Control and Prevention, Smoking and Health in the Americas: A 1992 Report of the Surgeon General 105 (1992). Studies have also shown that if people do not begin smoking as children, they are unlikely ever to begin. David A. Kessler, The Food and Drug Administration's Rule on Tobacco: Blending Science and Law, 99 Pediatrics 884 (1997).

In 1998, 9% of eighth graders, 16% of tenth graders and 22% of twelfth graders reported that they were currently smoking cigarettes on a regular basis. See Howard N. Snyder and Melissa Sickmund, Juvenile Offenders and Victims: 1999 National Report 65 (OJJDP 1999). A 1992 Gallup poll found that about two-thirds of adolescent smokers wanted to quit smoking, and that 70% indicated they would not have started smoking if they could make the decision again. See George H. Gallup Int'l Institute, Teen-age Attitudes and Behavior Concerning Tobacco: Report of the Findings (1992).

Adolescents face particular health risks from smoking. The younger a person is when he or she begins smoking, the more difficult it is to quit. Early adolescent smokers are more likely to smoke for the rest of their lives, to smoke heavily, to suffer smoking-related disease, and to die prematurely from such disease. See U.S. Dep't of HHS, Preventing Tobacco Use Among Young People: A Report of the Surgeon General 6 (1994). Teenagers who smoke regularly experience a general decrease in physical fitness, increased coughing and phlegm, greater risk and severity of respiratory illness, earlier development of artery disease (a forerunner of heart disease), and slower lung growth which can reduce the level of lung function by adulthood. Id. at 6–9.

3. *Advertising.* "The evidence showing that the tobacco companies have deliberately aimed their advertising at minors is compelling. Corroborating the evidence based on leaked memos and insiders' anecdotes, the Liggett Group has dramatically and publicly confessed that it, and its competitors, aim their advertising at teenagers as young as 14 years of age. * * * Whether other tobacco corporations will admit that they aim their ads at children or not, it is primarily children who are hit by the advertising message. Numerous studies have shown that not only do children see and retain tobacco advertising messages, but that a strong correlation exists between the youth-oriented ads and the rate of consumption of those brands among minors." Donald W. Garner & Richard

J. Whitney, Protecting Children From Joe Camel and His Friends: A New First Amendment and Federal Preemption Analysis of Tobacco Billboard Regulation, 46 Emory L.J. 479, 535 (1997).

"In 1996, the cigarette industry spent $5.1 billion on advertising and promoting its products to virtually all segments of society. Special target populations include women, racial and ethnic populations, and bluecollar workers. Adolescents are especially susceptible to cigarette marketing. Brands that are popular among adolescents are more likely than adult brands to be advertised in magazines with high youth readership." Phyllis A. Wingo et al., Annual Report to the Nation on the Status of Cancer, 1973–1996, With a Special Section on Lung Cancer and Tobacco Smoking, 91 J. Nat'l Cancer Inst. 675–90 (1999).

"Children and adolescents are responsive to the visual images and messages of cigarette advertisements. Advertisers present images of smoking that downplay health concerns and instead associate smoking with positive attributes, such as beauty and youth. The majority of advertisements portray healthy, enthusiastic, young people engaged in outdoor or social activities, sports, or feats of personal achievement. Since experimentation with new social behaviors often begins with the imitation of attractive models, who appear to be rewarded for their behavior, carefully crafted advertisements using attractive models are likely to increase the possibility that children and adolescents will try cigarettes." Gilbert J. Botvin et al., Smoking Behavior of Adolescents Exposed to Cigarette Advertising, 108 Public Health Reps. 217 (1993).

In a 1994 study, the U.S. Centers for Disease Control found that the three most heavily advertised cigarette brands (the ones associated with Joe Camel, the Marlboro Man and the young Newport couples) accounted for 86% of the unlawful teenage market but only 36% of overall tobacco sales, indicating significantly less interest in these brands among adults. See Changes in the Cigarette Brand Preferences of Adolescent Smokers–United States, 1989–1993, 43 Morbidity and Mortality Weekly Rep. (Aug. 19, 1994).

4. *The minimum age.* In the 1992 Synar Amendment, 42 U.S.C. § 300x–26, Congress required states to enact legislation restricting sale and distribution of tobacco products to minors as a condition of receiving federal substance abuse prevention and treatment block grant funds. The mandate also requires states to enforce these laws "in a manner that can reasonably be expected to reduce the extent to which tobacco products are available to individuals under the age of 18." Id. § 300x–26(b)(1).

In the wake of the Synar Amendment, all states now prohibit the sale of tobacco products to persons under eighteen. Regulation reaches not only cigarettes and other conventional tobacco products, but also chewing tobacco; in virtually all states, regulation also reaches snuff. In at least three states, nineteen is the minimum age for the sale of tobacco products (Alabama, Alaska and Utah). Pennsylvania prohibits the sale of cigarettes to persons under twenty-one, and of other tobacco products to persons under eighteen. See U.S. Centers for Disease Control and Prevention, State Laws on Tobacco Control—United States, 1995, 44 Morbidity and Mortality Weekly Rep. 7, 16 tabl. 3A (Nov. 3, 1995).

Despite minimum-age legislation, however, children can frequently purchase cigarettes. In 1994, the Surgeon General summarized thirteen studies of over-the-counter sales; the studies reported that the weighted average percentage of minors able to purchase tobacco was sixty-seven percent, ranging from thirty-two percent to eighty-seven percent. In studies that included vending machine sales, the weighted average of successful purchases was eighty-eight percent, ranging from eighty-two percent to one hundred percent. See U.S. Dep't of HHS, Preventing Tobacco Use Among Young People: A Report of the Surgeon General 6 (1994). Children's most prevalent sources of cigarettes are small convenience stores and gas stations, followed by larger stores such as supermarkets. See K. Michael Cummings et al., Where Teenagers Get Their Cigarettes: A Survey of the Purchasing Habits of 13–16 Year–Olds in 12 U.S. Communities, 1 Tobacco Control 264 (1992).

5. *Sanctions.* In some states, sanctions for unlawfully providing alcohol to minors are greater than sanctions for unlawfully providing tobacco. The tobacco statutes usually provide for only a small fine for first violations. Dr. C. Everett Koop, former U.S. Surgeon General, has criticized these disparities in regulation: "There is no logical reason why we should have a double standard for controlling the sale of tobacco and alcohol, the two major legal addicting drugs used in our society." Koop, A Parting Shot at Tobacco, 262 JAMA 2894 (1989).

6. *Licensing.* More than half the states license retailers that sell tobacco products and provide penalties for licensees that sell to children. At least fourteen of the states provide for license suspension or revocation, but only a handful of the states have designated an agency to enforce the delicensing provisions. See U.S. Centers for Disease Control and Prevention, State Laws on Tobacco Control—United States, 1995, 44 Morbidity and Mortality Weekly Rep. 7, 11, Table 3C (Nov. 3, 1995) (presenting state-by-state summary). The rationale for licensing is that the specter of suspension or revocation may have a greater deterrent effect than modest fines because many retailers receive substantial revenue from tobacco sales to adults. A record of lax enforcement, however, sometimes compromises deterrent effect.

7. *Vending machines.* Effective August 27, 1997, the U.S. Food and Drug Administration has outlawed the sale of cigarettes and smokeless tobacco in vending machines, except where the vending machine is located in "facilities where the retailer ensures that no person younger than 18 years of age is present, or permitted to enter, at any time." 21 C.F.R. § 897.16.

Even before the FDA promulgated its regulation, most states sought to restrict youth access by regulating vending machines that dispense tobacco products. A number of states, for example, ban these machines from areas accessible to children while allowing placement in bars, liquor stores, adult clubs and other adult-only establishments. A few states require supervision of cigarette vending machines even though they are banned from areas accessible to minors. A number of states ban place-ment in areas accessible to children unless the machines have locking devices, are supervised, or both. U.S. Centers for Disease Control and Prevention, State Laws on Tobacco Control—United States, 1995, 44 Morbidity and Mortality Weekly Rep. 7 (Nov. 3, 1995).

Restricted-access vending machine measures seemingly have not reduced child access to these machines. Despite restrictions, a number of studies report that children have successfully purchased cigarettes from vending machines between 70% and 100% of the time. See, e.g., U.S. Dep't of Health and Human Services, Preventing Tobacco Use Among Young People: A Report of the Surgeon General 252 (1994) (summariz-ing published studies).

Studies indicate that vending machines are most often abused by children under fifteen, who would feel most reluctant to try to purchase cigarettes in face-to-face transactions from clerks in retail stores. See, e.g., U.S. Dep't of Health and Human Servs., Accessibility of Tobacco Products to Youth Ages 12–17 Years—United States, 1989 and 1993, 45 Morbidity and Mortality Weekly Rep. 125 (Feb. 16, 1996).

Courts have upheld the constitutionality of local statutes and ordi-nances banning cigarette vending machines. See, e.g., C.I.C. Corp. v. Township of E. Brunswick, 638 A.2d 812 (N.J.1994), aff'g 266 N.J.Super. 1, 628 A.2d 753 (App.Div.1993) (equal protection, due process); Take Five Vending, Ltd. v. Town of Provincetown, 615 N.E.2d 576, 580–82 (Mass.1993) (due process, equal protection).

8. *Smokeless tobacco.* Two major types of smokeless tobacco are preva-lent in the United States–moist oral snuff and chewing tobacco. Snuff is finely shredded tobacco containing sweeteners and flavorings. Chewing tobacco is coarser than snuff and comes in small strips of loosely packaged "looseleaf," compressed "bricks" or "plugs," or twisted rope-like strands. See Mario A. Orlandi and Gayle M. Boyd, Smokeless Tobacco Use Among Adolescents: A Theoretical Overview, 8 NCI Mon-ogr. 1, 5 (1989).

Studies have demonstrated the health risks of smokeless tobacco, particularly the substantially increased risk of oral cancer and cancer of the cheek and gums. See, e.g., National Institutes of Health, Health Implications of Smokeless Tobacco Use, 101 Pub. Health Reps. 349 (1986); U.S. Public Health Serv., The Health Consequences of Using Smokeless Tobacco: A Report of the Advisory Committee to the Surgeon General (1986). Indeed levels of carcinogens in smokeless tobacco far exceed the levels in other tobacco products, apparently because of curing and fermentation. See American Acad. of Pediatrics, Smokeless Tobacco–A Carcinogenic Hazard to Children, 76 Pediatrics 1009 (1985). Perhaps partly because of the persisting belief that smokeless tobacco is harm-less, however, smokeless-tobacco use has increased dramatically in re-cent years, particularly among children and adolescents. Use by children as young as ten or eleven has been documented. See, e.g, Ross C. Brownson, et al., Smokeless Tobacco Use Among Missouri Youth, 87 Missouri Medicine 351 (1990). The Missouri study found that 27% of the state's twelfth-grade males were current users of smokeless tobacco. Id. A number of other studies have found almost identical rates of adolescent use. See American Acad. of Pediatrics, supra.

9. *The national tobacco settlement.* On June 20, 1997, the tobacco industry reached a tentative $368.5 billion settlement of damage suits brought by the attorneys general of more than forty states seeking reimbursement for medical costs of treating sick smokers. Calling children's use of tobacco products "a 'pediatric disease' of epic and worsening proportions," the settlement contained numerous provisions designed to reduce children's access to these products. The parties recited that "[p]reventing youth access [was] a major objective" of the settlement. The settlement, which would have imposed unprecedented restrictions on the production and marketing of tobacco products in return for a measure of immunity from future damage liability, never took effect because Congress failed to enact the necessary enabling legislation. The full text of the proposed settlement appeared at <www.usatoday.com/news/smoke/smoke01.htm.> (visited July 8, 1999).

In November, 1998, the tobacco industry and the suing states reached a settlement that did not require congressional action. The settlement produced a smaller monetary recovery for the states and imposed fewer restrictions on the industry than the proposed 1997 settlement. Among other things, the 1998 settlement reaches a number of matters related to children. The settlement:

- requires the industry each year for ten years to pay $25 million to fund a charitable foundation that will support the study of programs to reduce teen smoking and substance abuse and the prevention of diseases associated with tobacco use;

- bans use of cartoons in the advertising, promotion, packaging or labeling of tobacco products;

- prohibits the industry from targeting youth in advertising, promotions, or marketing;

- bans industry actions aimed at initiating, maintaining or increasing youth smoking;

- regulates specified advertising practices (it bans all outdoor advertising of tobacco products, including advertising on billboards, signs and placards in arenas, stadiums, shopping malls, and video game arcades; limits advertising outside retail establishments to 14 square feet; bans transit advertising of tobacco products; and allows states to substitute, for the duration of billboard lease periods, alternative advertising that discourages youth smoking);

- beginning July 1, 1999, bans tobacco companies' distribution and sale of apparel and merchandise with brand-name logos (caps, T-shirts, backpacks, etc.);

- bans payments to promote tobacco products in movies, television shows, theater productions or live performances, live or recorded music performances, videos and video games;

- regulates sponsorships (it prohibits brand name sponsorship of events with a significant youth audience or team sports (football, basketball, baseball, hockey or soccer)); prohibits sponsorship of events whose paid participants or contestants are underage; limits tobacco companies to one brand name sponsorship per year (after current contracts expire or after three years—whichever comes first); and bans tobacco brand names for stadiums and arenas;

- bans distribution of free samples except in facilities or enclosed areas where the operator ensures no underage person is present;

- bans gifts based on purchases of tobacco products without proof of age; and

- prohibits tobacco companies from opposing proposed state or local laws or administrative rules that are intended to limit youth access to and consumption of tobacco products.

See <http://www.wa.gov/ago/tobaccosettlement/summary.html> (visited Nov. 15, 1999). Unlike the proposed 1997 settlement, the 1998 settlement does not ban sales of tobacco products from vending machines, or mandate minimum federal standards for licensing retailers that sell tobacco products directly to consumers, or for suspending or revoking the license for selling to minors.

10. *Foreign export of U.S. tobacco products.* In the United States during the past three decades, the overall consumption of tobacco products has fallen significantly while the rate of teen smoking has increased. Major American tobacco companies have moved to establish markets overseas, first in Africa, Latin America and western Europe and more recently in Asia and eastern Europe. Speaking of these moves Dr. Koop has called it "reprehensible that this country allows exportation of disease, disability and death to the Third World, putting a burden on them they'll never be able to handle." Nancy Shute, The Cutting Edge, St. Louis Post–Dispatch, July 2, 1989, at 1C. United States tobacco companies have been accused of targeting children overseas with government assistance:

> The United States has contributed to [the worldwide] increase in cancer deaths by changing consumption patterns within developing countries through private industry and official government action. U.S. tobacco manufacturers have contributed by (1) targeting the Asia–Pacific region (particularly China), Eastern Europe, and Russia as growth areas suited for significant investment; (2) using sophisticated marketing and advertising techniques to sell their tobacco products; and (3) petitioning the U.S. government to open markets on their behalf. * * * The U.S. government has contributed to the increase in cancer deaths by (1) threatening trade sanctions if markets are not opened to U.S. tobacco products and advertising bans are not lifted; (2) attempting to increase the sale of U.S.

tobacco products abroad through the lobbying efforts of members of Congress and congressional committee staff members, the creation of federally funded foreign market development programs for tobacco, and the former inclusion of tobacco within the list of surplus crops to be distributed "to less developed or famine stricken regions of the world" through the Food For Peace program; and (3) exempting U.S. cigarette exports from major federal controls on the export of potentially harmful products or substances. * * *

* * *

The impact of smoking has significantly increased in two segments of the world's population: children and women. Globally, of all the children under the age of twenty alive in 1990, a quarter of a billion will die prematurely from tobacco consumption; seventy percent of these deaths will occur in the third world. * * *

* * *

U.S. manufacturers' marketing efforts that target children * * * are of particular concern. Free cigarette samples are distributed in video parlors, discos, and bars. The sponsorship of rock concerts of groups popular with teens is particularly effective. In Taiwan, R. J. Reynolds sponsored a local concert featuring a popular teen idol, charging five empty packets of Winston cigarettes for admission. Firms also create demand by selling paraphernalia targeted at children: children's notebooks, school supplies, shirts, jeans, jackets, and kites with cigarette logos such as Marlboro Gear and Winston House. Finally, they advertise in comic books popular with elementary school pupils, heavily push vending machines, which permit young people to buy cigarettes, and attract first-time smokers through menthol filters and blends that are easier to smoke. * * *

* * *

Heidi S. Gruner, The Export of U.S. Tobacco Products to Developing Countries and Previously Closed Markets, 28 Law and Pol'y in Int'l Bus. 217, 217–18, 221, 229–31 (1996).

PROBLEM 10–4

In at least seventeen states, the law does not punish children who purchase, possess or use tobacco products. See U.S. Centers for Disease Control and Prevention, State Tobacco Control Highlights, 1996, at 10–11. The business owner, manager or clerk who provides the product is subject to sanction (and may suffer suspension or revocation of the tobacco license in states that require licensure), but the child suffers no sanction. If you were a state legislator, would you vote to criminalize purchase, possession or use by the children themselves? What policy considerations would weigh in favor of punishing the children, and what policy considerations would weigh against it?

SECTION 4.   DRIVING PRIVILEGES

AMERICAN ACADEMY OF PEDIATRICS, THE TEENAGE DRIVER

98 Pediatrics 987 (Nov. 1996).

MAGNITUDE OF THE PROBLEM

Motor vehicle-related crashes remain the leading cause of death in youth from 16 through 20 years of age, resulting in more than 5000 such deaths annually. This age group constitutes only 7% of the US population yet accounts for 14% of all motor vehicle-related deaths. Youth 16 through 19 years of age constitute 5% of all licensed drivers and 3% of all vehicle miles traveled, yet teenage drivers are involved in 15% of the crashes in which they or other occupants are killed. The motor vehicle fatality rate of teenagers is higher than that of any other age group; on a per-mile-driven basis, 16–year-old drivers are more than 20 times as likely to have a crash as is the general population of drivers, and 17–year-old drivers are more than 6 times as likely. Young men are at especially high risk, having nearly twice the risk of fatality as young women. For every adolescent killed in a motor vehicle crash, about 100 nonfatal injuries occur. Crashes are a leading cause of disability related to head and spinal cord injuries in this age group.

ADOLESCENT RISK FACTORS

Two main factors, the lack of driving experience and the risk-taking behavior of adolescents, account for their increased risk of crashing. Five principal reasons are commonly cited:

1.   The adolescent, as a novice driver, lacks the experience and ability to perform many of the complex tasks of ordinary driving. Compared with experienced drivers, the adolescent is less proficient in detecting and responding to hazards, controlling the vehicle, and integrating speed. The adolescent's overall judgment and decision-making ability may not yet be fully developed. Although such deficiencies disappear gradually with driving experience and age, years of behind-the-wheel experience are required. * * *

2.   The adolescent's driving habits and propensity to take risks may be particularly influenced by emotions, peer group pressure, and other stresses.

3.   Nighttime driving is inherently more difficult and challenging for novice drivers. As a group, teenagers drive fewer hours than adults overall, but they drive disproportionately more at night and have a much higher nighttime crash fatality rate. A teenager is more than four times as likely to be killed while driving at night than during the day.

4.   The use of alcohol and other drugs by adolescents puts them at particularly great risk. Alcohol use is implicated in about one

third of all fatal crashes involving teenagers. Small amounts of alcohol impair the driving abilities of adolescents more than those of older drivers. Drunk and drugged driving remains a major problem for American teenagers. In one study, an estimated 6% to 14% of drivers younger than 21 years who were stopped at roadside sobriety checkpoints had been drinking. Drugs other than alcohol are involved in 10% to 15% of teenage fatalities. The combination of alcohol and marijuana is particularly popular and deadly.

5. The low rate of safety belt use by teenagers increases their risk of injury in a crash. Youth 10 to 20 years old use safety belts only about 35% of the time, the lowest observed use rate of any group. Less than one fourth of high school students report always wearing a safety belt when another person is driving. Without restraints, the risk of injury to the teenage occupant involved in a severe crash more than triples. Air bags alone are insufficient. They may not adequately restrain and therefore may not protect the occupant, particularly in side-impact, rear-impact, or rollover crashes. In rare cases, an occupant may be hurt or killed by the rapidly deploying air bag used without a seat belt. The seat belt holds the occupant in place while the air bag deploys and then deflates.

* * *

Notes and Questions

1. *Age restrictions.* All states establish a minimum age at which persons may secure licenses to drive various types of motor vehicles on public roads. Of greatest interest to most youngsters, of course, are the statutes that establish the minimum age for securing a standard operator's license. The minimum age is usually between fifteen and seventeen. Statutes typically establish higher minimum ages for securing licenses to drive such specialized vehicles as school buses, other buses, commercial vehicles, taxis, and chauffeured vehicles.

2. *Graduated licensing.* In recent years, a growing number of states have instituted graduated licensing, which enables children to secure a standard operator's license only after proceeding through stages designed to help encourage them to develop the experience, ability and maturity to drive safely. See generally Allan F. Williams, Earning a Driver's License, 112 Pub. Health Reps. 453, 455–60 (1997).

Pennsylvania's formula demonstrates the typical three stages. First, a person seeking to obtain a driver's license may apply for a 120–day learner's permit, which authorizes the holder to drive an automobile while accompanied in the front seat by a licensed driver who is at least eighteen. 75 Pa. Cons. Stat. § 1505. Second, a sixteen- or seventeen-year-old may obtain a "junior driver's license," which (with limited exceptions) does not permit the holder to drive between midnight and 5:00 A.M. unless accompanied by a spouse eighteen or older, a parent, or a person in loco parentis. Id. § 1503(c). A junior driver's license automatically becomes a regular driver's license when the holder becomes eighteen. Id. Third, persons seventeen or older may obtain a full driver's license after completing an approved driver training course, provided they have not been involved in an accident for which they were partially or fully responsible. Id. § 1503(b). Without such a course, the minimum age for securing a driver's license is eighteen. Id. § 1503(a)(7). (In some states, a full license is available during minority only if the child stays in school.).

3. *Parental permission and parental liability*. In a number of states, statutes permit minors to secure drivers' licenses only where a parent, custodian or other adult signs the license application as a sponsor. The purpose is to protect the public by "insur[ing] financial responsibility by individuals who may exercise some control over a minor's actions." Johnson v. Schlitt, 565 N.W.2d 305, 307 (Wis.Ct.App.1997). The adult assumes liability for damages caused by the minor's negligent or intentional conduct behind the wheel; the liability is generally joint and several with the minor. See, e.g., Fla. Stat. § 322.09. Some statutes impose liability on the adult only where proof of financial responsibility is not deposited by the minor or by someone on his or her behalf. See, e.g., Tenn. Code § 55–50–312(c). In most states, parents may avoid liability by requesting the motor vehicle department to revoke their children's licenses. See, e.g., Wis. Stat. § 343.15. Where the parent fails to make this request, the parent remains liable even where the state has revoked the child's license. See, e.g., Johnson, supra, 565 N.W.2d at 306–07.

In the absence of statute, the mere existence of a parent-child relationship does not make a parent liable for the child's negligent operation of a motor vehicle, even if the parent owns the vehicle or otherwise provided it to the child. Parents may be liable for damages, however, where they entrust a vehicle to a child they know is an incompetent, inexperienced or reckless driver. The young driver's condition is normally a question of fact for the jury. See, e.g., Dortman v. Lester, 155 N.W.2d 846 (Mich.1968). Parents and other adults have also been held liable where they provided the motor vehicle to a minor who is below the minimum licensing age or is otherwise unlicensed. See, e.g., Carter v. Montgomery, 296 S.W.2d 442 (Ark.1956). The parent may also be liable if the parent and child were engaged in a joint venture or if they held a principal-agent or master-servant relationship.

A number of states apply the common law "family purpose" doctrine. Where a motor vehicle owner maintains the vehicle for the family's pleasure use, the owner is liable for damages arising from negligent operation by any family member who uses the vehicle with the owner's express or implied consent for that purpose, including the owner's children. The doctrine treats the operator as the owner's agent or servant. W. Page Keeton et al., Prosser and Keeton on Torts § 73, at 524 (5th ed. 1984). A number of states have rejected the doctrine, though many achieve similar results with statutes imposing liability on the owner for damages caused by anyone operating the vehicle with the owner's express or implied consent.

4. *Discrimination by automobile rental companies*. Several major automobile rental companies refuse to rent to drivers under twenty-five on the ground that such drivers have accidents with greater frequency and severity than older drivers. No state prohibits discrimination against drivers under eighteen, the age of general contractual capacity. New York appears to be

the only state with a statute that specifically regulates refusal to rent to drivers who are at least eighteen. Section 391–g of the General Business Law makes it unlawful for auto rental companies to refuse to rent motor vehicles to persons eighteen or older based solely on age, "provided that insurance coverage for persons of such age is available." Recognizing the statistically higher risk of accidents among drivers under twenty-five, the statute also provides that "[a]ny actual extra cost for insurance related to the age of the person renting such motor vehicle may be passed on to such person."

New York also prohibits automobile rental companies from refusing to rent solely on the ground that the would-be renter does not hold a credit card. See N.Y. Gen'l Bus. Law § 391–l. In other states, credit card requirements have enabled companies to screen out many younger customers. To help assure that these customers will not pass through the screen, the major companies generally do not accept debit cards, which banks now issue to almost anyone who maintains a bank account. See, e.g., Saul Hansell, Not All Plastic Is Created Equal When It Comes to Renting a Car, N.Y. Times, April 2, 1997, at A1.

5. *Regulating children's use of other motor vehicles.* A number of states restrict children's operation of snowmobiles or all-terrain vehicles on public roads. See, e.g., Iowa Code, ch. 321G.

6. *The expansion of "abuse and lose" laws.* In recent years, a growing number of states have enacted so-called "abuse and lose" laws that seek to influence minors' behavior not occurring behind the wheel. Recognizing the importance most teenagers attach to drivers' licenses, these laws provide for denial, suspension or revocation of drivers' licenses of minors who commit specified crimes or other acts not directly related to driving. If the minor does not yet have a license, abuse-and-lose laws typically provide for postponement of the minor's right to apply for one. Courts have generally upheld the constitutionality of these laws. See, e.g., State v. Shawn P., 859 P.2d 1220 (Wash.1993).

In at least fifteen states, children subject to the compulsory school attendance act may secure or hold a driver's license only if they show satisfactory educational attendance and performance. Some states specifically target habitual truants, students who have been expelled from school, or students who have quit school without graduating for reasons other than financial hardship. See, e.g., Ind. Code § 9–24–2–1. More than half the states suspend or revoke licenses of persons under twenty-one convicted of possessing or using drugs or alcohol, even if the possession or use does not occur while driving. See, e.g., N.J. Stat. § 33:1–81. A few states suspend or revoke the licenses of minors convicted of purchasing or attempting to purchase tobacco products. See, e.g., Minn. Stat. § 171.171. A few states target graffiti. See, e.g., Mass. Gen. Laws ch. 266 § 126B.

California has enacted a wider array of abuse-and-lose laws than any other state. The laws reach, among others, (1) minors convicted of committing a public offense with a concealable firearm, Cal. Veh. Code § 13202.4(a)(1); (2) persons under twenty-one convicted of specified offenses relating to drug or alcohol possession, id. § 13202.5; (3) persons thirteen or older convicted of vandalism (including graffiti) by destroying or defacing property, id. § 13202.6; (4) minors who are habitual truants or wards of the juvenile court, id. § 13202.7; and (5) minors convicted of driving while intoxicated, id. § 13352.3.

PROBLEM 10–5

You are a lawyer in a state whose legislature is considering whether to enact "abuse and lose" legislation for the first time. The legislation would suspend or revoke the drivers' licenses of minors who drive drunk and also of minors who engage in a variety of other acts not directly related to driving safety, such as dropping out of school and possessing alcohol or drugs. A local newspaper has asked you to write an editorial-page article concerning the pending bill. What policy arguments might be made in support of the abuse-and-lose legislation and what arguments might be made in opposition? Which side's arguments would you find more persuasive?

SECTION 5.   HEALTH, SAFETY AND WELFARE REGULATION

A. *Child Highway Safety*

1. *Child passenger restraint systems and safety belts.* All states require that particularly young children be restrained in a child-restraint system (a "car seat") when riding on public roadways. See, e.g, N.C. Gen. Stat. § 20–137.1(a) (children under four). Coverage, however, does not necessarily extend to all vehicles. See, e.g., Colo. Rev. Stat. § 42–4–236(2)(a) (only privately owned noncommercial passenger vehicles and vehicles operated by child care centers).

Congress has mandated that federal highway funds may be withheld from states that do not have "a law which makes unlawful throughout the state the operation of a passenger vehicle whenever an individual in a front seat of the vehicle (other than a child who is secured in a child restraint system) does not have a safety belt properly fastened about the individual's body." 23 U.S.C. § 153. The congressional mandate, however, does not reach some aspects of child safety:

a. *Primary vs. secondary enforcement.* Most states permit only secondary enforcement of child restraint and child safety belt laws. Secondary enforcement permits a police officer to stop a vehicle only if the officer sees a violation other than the unprotected child; primary enforcement permits the officer to stop the vehicle solely because the officer sees a violation of restraint or seat belt requirements.

Primary enforcement laws appear to produce higher compliance rates. In 1993, for example, four of the five states with the highest rates of safety belt usage had primary enforcement laws; of the ten states with the lowest rates of usage, two had no safety belt law and seven had secondary enforcement laws. See National Safety Council, Perspectives on Safety: Safety Belt Facts: Primary Enforcement: A Key Factor in Making Belt Laws Work 1 (1995).

b. *Rear-seat passengers.* Some states do not require rear-seat passengers to wear safety belts, even though children disproportionately occupy the rear seat of motor vehicles. One study found that 44% of 5–9 year-olds and 34% of 10–14-year-olds are rear seat passengers at the time of crash, compared with 10% of all occupants in motor vehicle crashes. See Frederick P. Rivara and David C. Grossman, Prevention of Traumatic Deaths to Children in the United States: How Far Have We Come and Where Do We Need to Go?, 97 Pediatrics 791, 792 (1996). The study also found that when children wear lap/shoulder safety belts in the rear seat, child fatalities decrease 27%. Id.

Safety professionals recommend that children ride in rear seats to avoid dangers associated with front-seat air bags. See, e.g., Air–Bag–Associated Fatal Injuries to Infants and Children Riding in Front Passenger Seats—United States, 274 JAMA 1752 (Dec. 13, 1995). Air bags have saved many adult lives, but have caused the deaths of some infants and young children in front seats.

c. *Truck exemption.* In a few states, safety belt legislation creates a blanket exemption for trucks. This exemption removes any requirement that passengers, including children over the four-year-old age for child restraint systems, be restrained by a safety belt while riding in the front seat or any other seat of a truck.

d. *Cargo areas.* Only a few states have legislation prohibiting children from riding unrestrained in the open cargo areas of pickup trucks. Most cargo area passengers are children, and passengers thrown from a vehicle in a crash usually die or suffer serious physical injury, even if the vehicle is traveling at a relatively moderate speed. See e.g., Kenneth W. Kizer, Safety Belts and Public Health: The Role of Medical Practitioners, 154 Western J. Med. 303 (Mar. 1991); Phyllis F. Agran et al., Injuries to Occupants in Cargo Areas of Pickup Trucks, 161Western J. Med. 479 (Nov. 1994).

With children comprising the bulk of cargo area passengers, it is not surprising that most fatalities among such passengers are children. In a 1981 study, for example, more than half of cargo area fatalities were between ten and nineteen. See A.F. Williams et al., Fatal Falls and Jumps From Motor Vehicles, 71 Am. J. Public Health 275 (1981); A.F. Williams et al., Children Killed in Falls From Motor Vehicles, 68 Pediatrics 576 (1981). In 1991, 238 occupants of pickup truck cargo areas were killed in crashes throughout the nation; 50% of these fatalities were children under eighteen. Agran et al., supra.

Amid the death and serious injury suffered by children thrown from cargo areas, carbon monoxide risks are sometimes overlooked. One researcher reported that when he treated children suffering nausea and related symptoms after riding in cargo areas, "many of the parents initially believed their children to be sleeping in the back of the pickup truck when they in fact were unconscious due to carbon monoxide intoxication." See Neil B. Hampson et al., Carbon Monoxide Poisoning in

Children Riding in the Back of Pickup Trucks, 267 JAMA 538, 939 (Jan. 22, 1992).

2. *Bicycle helmets.* At least fifteen states have enacted legislation requiring children to wear approved helmets when they ride bicycles as operators or passengers on public roadways. See Cal. Veh. Code § 21212 (under eighteen); Ga. Code § 40–6–296(e)(under sixteen); Mass. Laws ch. 85 § 11(B)(2)(iii) (under twelve).

A 1989 study found that the use of bicycle helmets reduced the risk of head injury by 85% and brain injury by 88%. See R.S. Thompson et al., A Case–Control Study of the Effectiveness of Bicycle Safety Helmets, 320 New Eng. J. Med. 1361–1367 (1989). Unhelmeted child bicyclists suffer death and head injuries in numbers that far exceed their percentage of the general population. From 1984 through 1988, children under fifteen were more than 75% of persons treated in hospital emergency departments for bicycle-related head injuries, and more than 40% of persons killed from bicycle-related head injury. See Jeffrey L. Sacks et al., Bicycle–Associated Head Injuries and Deaths in the United States from 1984 Through 1988: How Many Are Preventable?, 266 JAMA 3016 (1991). Data from 1987, 1989 and 1990 show that nearly 67% of bicyclists treated in hospital emergency departments were under fifteen. Susan P. Baker et al., Injuries to Bicyclists: A National Perspective 51–62 (Johns Hopkins Injury Prevention Center 1993).

The Consumer Products Safety Commission found that 71% of bicyclists treated in hospital emergency departments in 1990 were under fifteen. The Commission's findings also suggested that children are particularly susceptible to head injury—about half the injuries to children under ten involved the head or face, while only 20% of the injuries to older bicyclists (including adults) involved the head or face. See Deborah Tinsworth et al., Bicycle–Related Injuries: Injury, Hazards and Risk Patterns, 1 Int'l J. Consumer Safety 207, 220 (1994). The unusually high rates of juvenile death and serious head injury may not be due entirely to the fact that bicycles are ridden by a greater percentage of children than of adults. Researchers at the Johns Hopkins Injury Prevention Center concluded that these rates may also reflect children's "inexperience as well as developmental limitations in coordination and in their ability to participate in the traffic environment." See Baker et al., supra, at 51–62.

In the absence of legislation requiring bicycle helmet usage, the rate of usage appears lowest among children under fifteen, the group that suffers the greatest rate of bicycle-related deaths and serious head injuries. Most studies indicate that in the absence of legislation, only about 2–5% of child bicyclists under fifteen wear helmets. See, e.g., Safety–Belt and Helmet Use Among High School Students—United States, 1990, 268 JAMA 314 (1992). These percentages appear lower than the overall percentages of American bicyclists who wear helmets in the absence of legislation. See, e.g., Sacks et al., supra (in the absence of legislation, fewer than 10% of all bicyclists wear helmets).

3. *Watercraft safety*. Drowning causes 90% of boating deaths, and victims in 80% of drownings do not wear an approved personal flotation device (PFD). See, e.g., U.S. Newswire, AMA: Millions Injured in Summer Recreation Each Year (May 23, 1996). On the rationale that most preteens are inexperienced in collisions and other sudden boating mishaps, several states require that PFDs be worn by particularly young children on public waterways. See, e.g., Ariz. Rev. Stat. § 5–331(C) (children under twelve); Kan. Stat. § 32–1129(a) (1996) (same).

A NOTE ABOUT PERSONAL AND FAMILY AUTONOMY

Child safety regulations spark heated debate between safety advocates and persons who argue that parents should determine the extent of protection their children should receive. A debate over public enforcement of safety regulations versus parents' autonomy recently took place in Missouri.

In 1997, Missouri strengthened its child safety belt statutes and enacted a new statute prohibiting children from riding unrestrained in open cargo areas of pickup trucks in most circumstances. Shortly before the legislation took effect, a newspaper article quoted supporters and opponents. Holding his young son, one father expressed support for the legislation because "[t]hey only made one of him, and I don't want to lose him." An opponent accused the government of "intruding on our privacy rights." "I feel like if I want to put the kids, the grandkids, whoever, in the back of my truck, they're my responsibility." Ron Davis, Pickup–Bed Law Effective This Week, Springfield News–Leader, Aug. 24, 1997, at 1B.

In determining the proper balance between safety regulations and parental autonomy, consider the arguments advanced in this editorial-page article written in support of the safety belt and cargo area measures shortly before the Missouri legislature began debate:

> * * * In 1995, one motor vehicle occupant under 16 was killed or injured every hour in Missouri. The vast bulk of these young victims were not wearing safety belts. About every three days, a person riding unrestrained in a pickup truck's open cargo area was killed or injured. Most of the victims were thrown from the cargo area, and most were under 21. * * *

> Past legislative efforts [to enact stronger safety laws] have been thwarted by assertions that safety belt and cargo area bills intrude on personal liberty. Each of us, the argument goes, should be allowed to decide what precautions we and our families will take on the roads, free from government mandate.

> This argument has already been rejected because the Missouri statute books are replete with motor vehicle regulations that "intrude" on personal liberty. You may not drive without insurance, for example, even if you want to. You may not drive 90 miles per hour, drive through red lights, or drive while intoxicated. When we choose

to take a multi-ton vehicle onto public roads at speeds up to 70 miles per hour, our personal liberty is subject to reasonable regulation because each of us is affected by the conduct of other drivers.

Safety belt and cargo area legislation profoundly affect everyone on the roads. People do not wish to kill or maim someone else's child in a crash when buckling a safety belt would have prevented injury. Taxpayers build, maintain and pay for the public road system, and they have every right to protect their consciences with safety legislation.

* * *

Douglas E. Abrams, A Better Safety Belt Law Would Save Lives, St. Louis Post–Dispatch, Mar. 3, 1997, at 15B. The public pays much of the costs of preventable motor vehicle injuries suffered by children, including the costs of emergency services, uninsured medical care, tax-supported rehabilitation programs, higher insurance premiums, and survivor payments. The National Safety Council estimates that each serious injury prevented by safety belt usage saves $35,000 in health care costs, and that every $40 child safety seat saves $80 in direct health care costs and $1200 in indirect care costs and costs to society. See National Safety Council, Safeguarding the Motoring Public 30 (1996); National Safety Council, Motor Vehicle Crashes: Enormous Economic Costs to Individuals and Society (1996).

The National Highway Traffic Safety Administration has pointed out that it "is very expensive to treat children with bicycle-related head injuries because these injuries may endure throughout a child's lifetime. * * * Bicycle helmets significantly reduce the total medical costs for such injuries. For children ages 4–15, it has been estimated that every dollar spent on bicycle helmets saves $2 in health care costs. If 85% of all child bicyclists wore helmets in one year, the lifetime medical costs savings would total $109 million to $142 million." Nat'l Highway Traffic Safety Admin., State Legislative Fact Sheet, Sept. 1995, at 2.

PROBLEM 10–6

You represent a parent stopped by a highway patrol officer and cited for allowing her eight-year-old child to ride unrestrained in the front seat in violation of state law while the family car was proceeding at 65 miles per hour on a public highway. Deciding to fight the citation, the parent pleads not guilty and asserts that the state safety belt law violates her due process right to direct her children's upbringing. How should the court decide the case under the Supreme Court decisions presented in Chapter 1?

PROBLEM 10–7

Fred Jones, father of 12–year-old Allen, thinks bicycle helmets are silly. He never wore one when he was a kid, and he never got hurt. Allen has a bicycle helmet, but he never wears it because he thinks it does not look cool. His father has never told him to wear the helmet. State law requires unemancipated child bicyclists under 16 to wear helmets; a violation is punishable by a fine of up to $25. The parent or legal guardian having control or custody of a minor whose conduct violates the helmet law is jointly and severally liable with the minor for the amount of the fine. Allen is cited for not wearing a helmet. If you were the judge imposing the fine, would you require Fred, Allen, or both to pay?

One day Allen receives a severe head injury because he collided with a parked car while biking without a helmet on a public street. Would you charge his parents with neglect?

B. Gambling

Teenage compulsive gambling appears to be a growing problem. According to a 1999 study, approximately 2–5% of adults in the United States are compulsive and problem gamblers. By contrast, the study found that 6–12% of 13–17-year-olds have serious gambling problems. See Adolescent Compulsive and Problem Gamblers, 6 Prevention Researcher (Winter 1999), available at <http//:www.integres.org/prevres.> (visited Dec. 10, 1999).

1. *Gambling generally.* A number of states have criminal statutes proscribing gambling by or with minors generally. See, e.g., N.M. Stat. § 44–5–6 (parent may recover minor's gambling losses).

2. *State lotteries.* Most states prohibit the offer or sale of state lottery tickets or shares to persons under eighteen. See, e.g., Cal. Gov't Code § 8880.52. Most of the state acts, however, permit adults to make gifts of lottery tickets to persons under eighteen. See, e.g., Mich. Comp. Laws § 432.29. If a child wins a lottery prize, the prize ordinarily must be paid to the child's parent or guardian, or to another adult member of the child's family for the child's benefit. See, e.g., N.J. Stat. § 5:9–20.

Several state lottery acts provide that persons under eighteen may not be licensed to sell lottery tickets at retail, and some provide that children may not be employed by a licensee to sell tickets at retail. See, e.g., Minn. Stat. § 349A.06(2)(a)(1).

3. *Riverboat gambling.* Statutes regulating riverboat gambling generally prohibit persons under twenty-one from placing a wager or otherwise gambling. See, e.g., Ind. Code §§ 4–33–9–13, 4–33–10–1. The statutes also generally establish the minimum age at which persons may work in the riverboat's gambling operations. See, e.g., 230 Ill. Comp. Stat. 10/9(a)(1), 10/11(a)(10) (twenty-one).

4. *Racing and jai alai.* Several states establish a minimum age at which a person may place a wager at a horse racing track. See, e.g., Iowa Code § 99D.11(7) (twenty-one); 4 Pa. Cons. Stat. § 325.228 (eighteen). A handful of states go a step further, prohibiting persons under eighteen from placing bets at off-track betting facilities. See, e.g., Conn. Gen. Stat. § 12–576.

Some states similarly establish a minimum age for wagering at (1) dog racing tracks, see, e.g., Wis. Stat. § 562.06(4), (5) (eighteen); or (2) jai alai frontons, see, e.g., Conn. Gen. Stat. § 12–576(b) (eighteen).

5. *Bingo*. Several states prohibit children from playing bingo, or from being in the vicinity where bingo is played. The minimum age varies. See, e.g., Fla. Stat. § 849.0931(10)(a) (eighteen); Me. Rev. Stat. tit. 17 § 319 (sixteen). A few states allow children under the general minimum age to play or be in the vicinity of a bingo game when accompanied by a parent or guardian, or sometimes by another adult. See, e.g., N.Y. Gen. Mun. Law § 486. A few states prohibit minors from conducting a bingo game. See, e.g., Ohio Rev. Code § 2915.11(A).

6. *Raffles*. By constitution or statute, some states regulate raffles, a favorite fundraising method of youth groups. Generally children may sell raffle tickets. See, e.g., Ind. Code § 4–32–9–34(b). But see Conn. Gen. Stat. § 7–172 (children under sixteen may not sell or promote the sale of raffle tickets). In some states, raffles are not regulated by name, but fall within general regulation of "games of chance" or some similar designation.

C. Firearms

1. *General prohibitions and restrictions*. The Violent Crime Control and Law Enforcement Act of 1994, Pub. L. No. 103–322, 108 Stat. 2010, seeks to restrict juveniles' access to firearms. The Act prohibits persons under eighteen (with enumerated exceptions relating to farming, hunting and other specified uses) from knowingly possessing handguns or ammunition suitable for use only in handguns. The Act also prohibits persons from selling or otherwise transferring these weapons or ammunition to someone they know or have reasonable cause to believe is under eighteen. 18 U.S.C. § 922(x). The Act further prohibits licensed importers, licensed manufacturers, licensed dealers or licensed collectors from selling or delivering a firearm or ammunition to an individual the licensee knows or has reason to believe is under eighteen (or, if the firearm or ammunition is other than a shotgun or rifle, to an individual the licensee knows or has reason to believe is under twenty-one). Id. § 922(b)(1). The Act also permits states to detain in secure facilities juveniles arrested or convicted for possessing handguns in violation of section 922(x) or of any similar state statute. 42 U.S.C.§ 5633(a)(12)(A).

All states prohibit or restrict juveniles' possession and use of firearms or handguns. Possession of firearms in violation of these prohibitions or restrictions may expose the juvenile to criminal liability or delinquency. Nearly half the states prohibit firearms possession for some period of time by adjudicated delinquents, at least ones adjudicated for acts that would be felonies if committed by an adult. See, e.g., Ariz. Rev. Stat. § 13–904(H).

Legislation typically also prohibits persons from selling or otherwise providing firearms to juveniles. See, e.g., Colo. Rev. Stat. § 18–12–108.7. Some states permit sale, provision or possession where the juvenile's parent or guardian consents, or where the seller or provider is the parent or guardian. See, e.g., Vt. Stat. tit. 13 §§ 4007, 4008. States typically also set the minimum age at which a person may secure a license or permit to carry a firearm. See, e.g., Ga. Code § 16–11–129 (twenty-one; pistol or revolver). Possession statutes normally do not operate against juveniles who use the firearm to hunt with a valid hunting license.

In a 1993 Louis Harris poll of students in grades six through twelve, 59% said they could "get a handgun if they wanted," 35% maintained it would take less than an hour to acquire a firearm, and 15% reported carrying a handgun in the prior month. See Reducing Youth Gun Violence: An Overview of Programs and Initiatives (OJJDP 1996).

2. *"Gun-free schools" and "safety zones" acts.* The federal Gun–Free Schools Act, which took effect March 31, 1994, provides that local educational agencies receiving federal funds must have a policy requiring expulsion for not less than a year of any student who brings a firearm to school; the local agency, however, may modify the expulsion requirement on a case-by-case basis. See 20 U.S.C. § 8921(b)(1). A second federal Gun–Free Schools Act, enacted in October 1994, requires local agencies to implement a policy of "referral to the criminal justice or juvenile delinquency system of any student who brings a firearm or weapon to a school served by such agency." 20 U.S.C. § 8922(a).

More than forty states prohibit possession of firearms by students and others on or near school grounds. See United States v. Lopez, 514 U.S. 549, 581 (1995) (Kennedy, J., concurring). In many of these states, the prohibition extends to school grounds, school owned vehicles, and school sponsored activities. Students who violate these provisions are typically subject to expulsion and delinquency proceedings or criminal prosecution.

The federal Gun–Free School Zones Act of 1990 forbade "any individual knowingly to possess a firearm at a place that the individual knows, or has reasonable cause to believe, is a school zone." *Lopez* held that the 1990 Act exceeded Congress' Commerce Clause authority because it neither regulated a commercial activity nor required that possession be connected in any way to interstate commerce.

3. *"Safe storage" and "child access prevention" statutes.* Several states prohibit persons from leaving firearms unattended in places where children may gain access to them. Most of the statutes permit prosecution only where the child uses the firearm to cause death or serious physical injury to himself or someone else. Minnesota's statute, however, is typical of those that permit prosecution regardless of the use the child makes of the weapon. Minn. Stat. § 609.666. Some statutes specify that reasonable preventive action includes keeping the firearm in a securely locked box or container or securely locking the firearm with a trigger lock. See, e.g., Cal. Penal Code § 12035(c).

4. *Alternative education.* The federal Gun–Free Schools Act allows states to make alternative arrangements for educating students expelled for firearms possession in school. Where a child is expelled from public

school for firearms possession, or for other criminal or noncriminal misconduct, the state's obligation to provide alternative education at public expense may turn on the compulsory education statute or the state constitution's guarantee of a free public education. See, e.g., Cathe A. v. Doddridge County Bd. of Educ., 490 S.E.2d 340, 349–51 (W.Va. 1997) (holding that the state constitution creates a fundamental right to public education and thus requires the state to provide alternative education); Doe v. Superintendent, 653 N.E.2d 1088, 1095 (Mass.1995) (holding that the state constitution does not create a fundamental right to a free public education and thus does not require the state to provide alternative education).

D. *Other Harmful Conduct*

1. *Fireworks.* Several thousand persons each year suffer fireworks-related injuries requiring hospital treatment. Children suffer more than half these injuries, most commonly to their head, hands, eyes or legs. About a third of the eye injuries result in permanent blindness, and hand and finger injuries frequently require amputation. See American Acad. of Pediatrics, Children and Fireworks, 88 Pediatrics 652 (1991). A number of states have outlawed private possession of fireworks entirely. Even in states in which sale or distribution of fireworks is lawful, sale or distribution to children is frequently regulated. Some states prohibit sale or distribution to children below a minimum age, frequently lower than the age of majority. See, e.g., Cal. Health and Safety Code § 12689(b) (sixteen). A few states establish a minimum age but permit sale or distribution to younger children accompanied by a parent. See, e.g., Okla. Stat. tit. 68 § 1627(b) (twelve).

A few states establish a minimum age below which a person may not secure a license to sell or distribute fireworks, or may not be employed in an establishment that sells or distributes fireworks. See, e.g., Okla. Stat. tit. 68 § 1623(d) (sixteen).

2. *Explosives.* Several states prohibit persons from selling, giving or otherwise providing explosives to minors. See, e.g., Cal. Health and Safety Code § 12082. Some states seek to keep explosives away from minors by prohibiting transfer or possession of explosives without a license, and by limiting licensure to adults. See, e.g., Minn. Stat. §§ 299F.77(a), 299F.78.

3. *Tattooing and body piercing.* At least twenty states prohibit or regulate tattooing of minors. Some of these states have enacted flat prohibitions. See, e.g., Iowa Code § 135.37(2). Some states exempt tattooing performed on minors by licensed medical personnel in the performance of their medical practice. See, e.g., Cal. Penal Code § 653. Some states permit persons to tattoo minors with the consent of one or both parents. See, e.g., Mich. Comp. Laws § 333.13102(1). Other states require that a parent be present while the tattoo procedure is performed. See, e.g., Ariz. Rev. Stat. § 13–3721(A). A few states also regulate body-piercing of minors. See, e.g., Mich. Comp. Laws § 333.13102(1).

In one study of tattooed adolescents, the mean age at which they received their first tattoo was fourteen. See Myrna L. Armstrong and Kathleen Pace Murphy, Adolescent Tattooing, 5 Prevention Researcher, No. 3 (1998), available at <www.tpronline.org/articles/5398article.htm> (visited Aug. 12, 1999). In late 1997, an Iowa mother reportedly tattooed a cross on the ankle of her 14–year-old daughter, who had been requesting a tattoo for some time. On the ex-husband's complaint, Iowa authorities charged the mother with violating the state's flat-prohibition statute. If you were the local prosecutor, would you have charged the mother? What would your arguments be at trial if you were (a) counsel for the mother?, (b) the prosecutor? (The case was discussed on CNN Burden of Proof, Oct. 3, 1997, 12:30 a.m. ET.).

4. *Pool and billiards.* Several states establish a minimum age below which a person may not play in a pool hall or billiards room, and may not remain on the premises. See, e.g., 53 Pa. Cons. Stat. § 15404 (eighteen). Under a few of the statutes, the age restriction is inapplicable to children who are accompanied by, or who hold the consent of, their parent or guardian. See, e.g., Mass. Gen. Laws ch. 20 ch. 140 § 179.

5. *Boxing and wrestling.* Several states prohibit persons under eighteen from participating in professional boxing matches. See, e.g., Kan. Stat. § 12–5113 (governing body may grant special permission to person under eighteen). A few statutes extend the prohibition to participation in professional wrestling matches. See, e.g., Colo. Rev. Stat. § 12–10–119. The statutory prohibitions do not normally extend to amateur matches. See, e.g., Wis. Stat. § 444.09 (persons between fourteen and eighteen may participate in amateur boxing exhibitions with parent's or guardian's consent).

A few states have established a minimum age below which a person may not attend professional boxing or wrestling matches as a spectator. See, e.g., Conn. Gen. Stat. § 21a–209 (eighteen for boxing, but child fourteen or older may attend when accompanied by parent or guardian).

6. *May adults be excluded from premises open to children?* Several notes in this section concern enactments that restrict children's entry into places of public accommodation frequented by adults. These statutes are generally upheld against constitutional challenge. See, e.g., St. John's Melkite Catholic Church v. Commissioner of Revenue, 242 S.E.2d 108, 114 (Ga.1978).

In City of Dallas v. Stanglin, 490 U.S. 19 (1989), the Court upheld a city ordinance that restricted admission to some dance halls to 14–18–year-olds, thus excluding adults and younger children. The purpose was to provide places where teenagers could socialize with each other, without the potentially detrimental influences of older teenagers or adults. The Court held that the ordinance did not infringe on any First Amendment right of association. Nor did the ordinance violate equal protection: "The city could reasonably conclude * * * that teenagers might be susceptible to corrupting influences if permitted, unaccompanied by their parents to frequent a dance hall with older persons. The city could reasonably conclude that limiting dance-hall contacts between juveniles and adults would make less likely illicit or undesirable juvenile involvement with alcohol, illegal drugs, or promiscuous sex." 490 U.S. at 27.

SECTION 6. JUVENILE CURFEWS

HUTCHINS v. DISTRICT OF COLUMBIA

United States Court of Appeals, D.C. Cir. (en banc), 1999.
188 F.3d 531.

Before: EDWARDS, CHIEF JUDGE, WALD, SILBERMAN, WILLIAMS, GINSBURG, SENTELLE, HENDERSON, RANDOLPH, ROGERS, TATEL, and GARLAND, CIRCUIT JUDGES.

Opinion for the Court filed by CIRCUIT JUDGE SILBERMAN.

SILBERMAN, CIRCUIT JUDGE:

The District of Columbia appeals the district court's grant of summary judgment to plaintiffs/appellees, a group of minors, parents, and a private business, enjoining enforcement of the District's Juvenile Curfew, and holding that it violates the fundamental rights of minors and their parents and is unconstitutionally vague. A divided panel of our circuit affirmed the district court, and rehearing *en banc* was granted. A plurality believes that the curfew implicates no fundamental rights of minors or their parents. Even assuming the curfew does implicate such rights, we hold that it survives heightened scrutiny. And, it does not violate the First or Fourth Amendment rights of minors.

I.

The District of Columbia Council, determining that juvenile crime and victimization in the District was a serious problem—and growing worse—unanimously adopted the Juvenile Curfew Act of 1995, which bars juveniles 16 and under from being in a public place unaccompanied by a parent or without equivalent adult supervision from 11:00 p.m. on Sunday through Thursday to 6:00 a.m. on the following day and from midnight to 6:00 a.m. on Saturday and Sunday, subject to certain enumerated defenses. The curfew provides that a minor (defined as "any person under the age of 17 years," but not "a judicially emancipated minor or a married minor") cannot remain in a public place or on the premises of any establishment within the District of Columbia during curfew hours. A parent or guardian commits an offense by knowingly permitting, or through insufficient control allowing, the minor to violate the curfew. Owners, operators, or employees of public establishments also violate the curfew by knowingly allowing the minor to remain on the premises, unless the minor has refused to leave and the owner or operator has so notified the police. The curfew contains eight "defenses": it is not violated if the minor is (1) accompanied by the minor's parent or guardian or any other person 21 years or older authorized by a parent to be a caretaker for the minor; (2) on an errand at the direction of the minor's parent, guardian, or caretaker, without any detour or stop; (3) in a vehicle involved in interstate travel; (4) engaged in certain employment activity, or going to or from employment, without any detour or stop; (5) involved in an emergency; (6) on the sidewalk that abuts the minor's or the next-door neighbor's residence, if the neighbor has not complained to the police; (7) in attendance at an official school, religious, or other recreational activity sponsored by the District of Columbia, a civic organization, or another similar entity that takes responsibility for the minor, or going to or from, without any detour or stop, such an activity supervised by adults; or (8) exercising First Amendment rights, including free exercise of religion, freedom of speech, and the right of assembly. If, after questioning an apparent offender to determine his age and reason for being in a public place, a police officer reasonably believes that an offense has occurred under the curfew law and that no defense exists, the minor will be detained by the police and then released into the custody of the minor's parent, guardian, or an adult acting *in loco parentis*. If no one claims responsibility for the minor, the minor may be taken either to his residence or placed into the custody of the Family Services Administration until 6:00 a.m. the following morning. Minors found in violation of the curfew may be ordered to perform up to 25 hours of community service for each violation, while parents violating the curfew may be fined up to $500 or required to perform community service, and may be required to attend parenting classes.

* * *

II.
A.

Appellees contend (and the district court determined) that the curfew infringes on a *substantive* fundamental right–the right to free movement * * *. * * * [A]ny government impingement on a *substantive* fundamental right to free movement would be measured under a strict scrutiny standard and would be justified only if the infringement is narrowly tailored to serve a compelling state interest. * * * But does such a substantive right exist?

* * *

We think that juveniles do not have a fundamental right to be on the streets at night without adult supervision. The Supreme Court has already rejected the idea that juveniles have a right to "come and go at will" because "juveniles, unlike adults, are always in some form of custody" [*Schall v. Martin* (1984), infra p. 1110], and we see no reason why the asserted right here would fare any better. That the rights of juveniles are not necessarily coextensive with those of adults is undisputed, and "unemancipated minors lack some of the most fundamental rights of self-determination—including even the right of liberty in its narrow sense, *i.e.*, the right to come and go at will." *Vernonia Sch. Dist. 47J v. Acton* (1995). While appellees claim that this reasoning obscures the differences between parental custody and governmental custody, appellees necessarily concede that juveniles are always in *some* form of custody. Not only is it anomalous to say that juveniles have a right to be unsupervised when they are always in some form of custody, but the recognition of such a right would fly in the face of the state's well-established powers of *parens patriae* in preserving and promoting the welfare of children. The state's authority over children's activities is unquestionably broader than that over like actions of adults. *See Prince v. Massachusetts* (1944). And it would be inconsistent to find a fundamental right here, when the Court has concluded that the state may intrude upon the "freedom" of juveniles in a variety of similar circumstances without implicating fundamental rights, *see id.* (citing compulsory school attendance and child labor laws), and can do so in far more intrusive ways than is contemplated here, *see, e.g., Schall* (upholding pretrial detention of juvenile delinquents after a finding of "serious risk" on the ground that it served a legitimate, nonpunitive regulatory purpose); *Prince* (upholding law prohibiting children from selling magazines on the street, even when accompanied by parent or guardian, against claim that the law violated child's freedom of religion); *Ginsberg v. New York* (1968) [supra p. 625] (upholding on rational basis review a ban on sale of material to minors that would not be considered "obscene" for adults).

* * *

B.

Even if juveniles themselves lack a fundamental right of movement, appellees claim that parents have a fundamental, substantive due process right to direct and control their children's upbringing and that such a right is abridged by the curfew. Whether children under the age of 17 are to be free to be abroad at night is presumptively a matter for their parents to determine, as part and parcel of that upbringing. (Appellees suggest that this concept extends to permitting a child of any age—even four—to be on the street in the middle of the night.) This parental fundamental right alone, it is argued, obliges us to judge the D.C. curfew by heightened scrutiny. We disagree, not because we think that no such fundamental right exists in any dimension, but rather because we think it not implicated by the curfew.

* * * Although [*Meyer v. Nebraska* (1923) and *Pierce v. Society of Sisters* (1925)] could be thought to rest on the Court's perception that the statutes had an irrational basis, in *Pierce* the Court did observe that "[t]he child is not the mere creature of the state; those who nurture him and direct his destiny have the right, coupled with the high duty, to recognize and prepare him for additional obligations." And by 1944 in *Prince*, the Court said that "[i]t is cardinal with us that the *custody, care* and *nurture* of the child reside first in the parents, whose primary function and freedom include preparation for obligations the state can neither supply nor hinder." (emphasis added). * * * But [*Prince*] emphasized that the state's interest in guarding the welfare of children—even against the wishes of a parent—was particularly powerful to ward off the "evils . . . [of] public places" and the "possible harms arising from other activities subject to all the diverse influences of the street." By so reasoning, the Court distinguished between the "private realm of family life," and those activities subject to the evils of public places, applying something very close to rational basis review for laws restricting the latter.

We glean from these cases, then, that insofar as a parent can be thought to have a fundamental right, as against the state, in the upbringing of his or her children, that right is focused on the parents' control of the home and the parents' interest in controlling, if he or she wishes, the formal education of children. It does not extend to a parent's right to unilaterally determine when and if children will be on the streets—certainly at night. That is not among the "intimate family decisions" encompassed by such a right.

III.

A.

Even if the curfew implicated fundamental rights of children or their parents, it would survive heightened scrutiny. Assuming such rights are implicated, we must first decide whether * * * strict scrutiny applies or whether * * * intermediate scrutiny is called for. We think the latter. Considering children's rights first, we agree that constitutional rights do not instantaneously appear only when juveniles reach the age of majority. Still, children's rights are not coextensive with those of adults. *See Prince; see also Bellotti v. Baird* (1979) (plurality opinion). So "although children generally are protected by the same constitutional guarantees . . . as are adults, the State is entitled to adjust its legal system to account for children's vulnerability" by exercising broader authority over their activities. *Bellotti*. This means, at minimum, that a lesser degree of scrutiny is appropriate when evaluating restrictions on minors' activities where their unique vulnerability, immaturity, and need for parental guidance warrant increased state oversight. *See Bellotti*. The reasoning of *Bellotti* [and] *Prince* * * * necessarily suggests that something less than strict scrutiny—intermediate scrutiny—would be appropriate here. Not only can juveniles be thought to be more vulnerable to harm during curfew hours than adults, but they are less able to make mature decisions in the face of peer pressure, and are more in need of parental supervision during curfew hours.

To withstand intermediate scrutiny, the curfew must be "substantially related" (rather than narrowly tailored) to the achievement of "important" (rather than compelling) government interests. The asserted government interest here is to protect the welfare of minors by reducing the likelihood that minors will perpetrate or become victims of crime and by promoting parental responsibility. The District presented reams of evidence depicting the devastating impact of juvenile crime and victimization in the District * * *. Given this picture of juvenile crime and victimization, there can be no serious dispute that protecting the welfare of minors by reducing juvenile crime and victimization is an important government interest.

Whether the curfew is "substantially related" to the achievement of that interest is the more difficult question here. * * * That test obviously calls for a more searching inquiry than rational basis (the minimum standard for judging equal protection claims), yet a more deferential one than strict scrutiny's narrow tailoring component. In judging the closeness of the relationship between the means chosen (the curfew), and the government's interest, we see three interrelated concepts: the factual premises upon which the legislature based its decision, the logical connection the remedy has to those premises, and the scope of the remedy employed.

* * *

* * * [T]he District is not obliged to prove a precise fit between the nature of the problem and the legislative remedy—just a substantial relation. * * *

Appellees also claim that the District's data is flawed because it failed to establish that the District had a problem with juvenile crime and victimization *during curfew hours*. * * * The bottom line is that the District's statistics indicate that more than 50% of juvenile arrests took place during curfew hours. * * * That serious crimes such as murder, rape, and aggravated assault, *committed by groups of all ages*, were more likely to occur during curfew hours was sufficient to demonstrate a "fit" between the curfew ordinance and the compelling state interest. Similarly, that the District did not produce data showing *where* juvenile crime and victimization occurred (*i.e.*, that it occurred primarily outside of the home) is not problematic. That a substantial percentage of *violent* juvenile victimizations (approximately 33%) occurred on the streets adequately supports the relationship between the government's interest and the imposition of the curfew.

Nevertheless, appellees argue that the District was obliged to confine the curfew to high-crime areas of the city. We flatly disagree. To have done so would have opened the Council to charges of racial discrimination. * * *

Appellees' claim that the District was not entitled to rely on curfew experiences in other cities strikes us as particularly weak. Of course no city is exactly comparable to any other, but it would be folly for any city not to look at experiences of other cities. And in drawing conclusions from those experiences, legislatures are not obliged to insist on scientific methodology. * * * In any event, the District had its own indications that the curfew was effective in the District of Columbia—the Deputy Chief of the Metropolitan Police Department testified before the D.C. Council that in its first three months the curfew had resulted in fewer juveniles on the streets during curfew hours, and thus a "reduction of the number of juvenile late night arrests," noting a 34% decrease in arrests of juveniles under 17 years old. Appellees question the relevance of this testimony because the District did not demonstrate that this drop in juvenile arrests was attributable to the curfew as opposed to some other factor. We think that objection calls for an absurd preciseness in legislative decisionmaking which would make it virtually impossible for any city to adopt any curfew.

Finally, we note that the eight defenses to the curfew strengthen the relationship between the curfew and its goal of reducing juvenile crime and victimization by narrowing the scope of the curfew. That is, the defenses (the constitutionality of which we take up below) help ensure that the ordinance does not sweep all of a minor's activities into its ambit but instead focuses on those nocturnal activities most likely to result in crime or victimization.

B.

Assuming, as we do in this section of the opinion, that the fundamental rights of parents are implicated by curfews, we also conclude that this curfew passes intermediate scrutiny because it is carefully fashioned much more to enhance parental authority than to challenge it. If the parents' interests were in conflict with the state's interests, we would be faced with a more difficult balancing of sharply competing claims. * * * The curfew's defenses allow the parents *almost* total discretion over their children's activities during curfew hours. There are no restrictions whatsoever on a juvenile's activities if the juvenile is accompanied by a parent, guardian, or an adult over the age of 21 authorized by the parent to supervise the juvenile. Parents can allow their children to run errands, which gives the parents great flexibility in exercising their authority. Contrary to appellees' view, we do not see how the curfew would preclude parents from allowing their children to walk the dog or go to the store. Juveniles may attend any "official school, religious, or other recreational activity sponsored by the District of Columbia, a civic organization, or another similar entity that takes responsibility for the minor" as well as to travel to and from such activities. * * * Together with the defenses provided for employment and emergencies, parents retain ample authority to exercise parental control. * * *

IV.

Appellees' remaining attacks on the curfew fall away. [The plurality held that the curfew (1) is not unconstitutionally vague, but rather marked by flexibility that "enhances parental control," (2) does not violate the First Amendment because it does not itself regulate or proscribe expression, and (3) does not allow police officers to arrest a person without probable cause in violation of the Fourth Amendment.].

* * *

HARRY T. EDWARDS, CHIEF JUDGE, concurring in part and concurring in the result, with whom CIRCUIT JUDGES WALD and GARLAND join in Part II:

In my view, the disputed curfew law implicates significant rights of both minors and parents and, accordingly, is subject to no less than so-called "intermediate scrutiny." * * * However * * * I agree that the law survives intermediate scrutiny with respect to the rights of minors. I also agree that, in the final analysis, the law survives intermediate scrutiny with respect to parents' rights as well. * * * In my view, parental rights are implicated in this case and they are truly significant—indeed, these rights are at the core of our society's moral and constitutional fiber. I have more than a little difficulty in finding that the curfew law passes constitutional muster as against the claim of parents.

I.

* * *

Certainly it should be clear that parents' rights cannot be limited to only those activities that are within the home or involve the formal education of one's child—such a formulation is *much too narrow*. * * *

* * *

To be sure, there are circumstances, as I discuss below, under which the state's interests may trump the rights of parents. To say, however, as Part II.B of the opinion for the court suggests, that a curfew law that regulates and restricts minors' activities outside the home during the nighttime hours does not even *implicate* the broad fundamental rights of parents is to disregard the teachings of decades of Supreme Court case law. The Court has *never* limited its definition of parental rights to include only the right to supervise activities that take place literally inside the home or literally inside the classroom. Indeed, such a limitation is implausible.

Surely a nighttime curfew law implicates parents' rights to control the "care," "nurture," "upbringing," "management," and "rearing" of their children, even if the law—by definition—regulates activity that takes place outside the home and school. The fact that some of the aforecited Supreme Court cases involve parents' rights to control the education of their children is not surprising, but neither is it evidence that the Court meant to imply that parents have no rights to control *other* aspects of their children's lives. Thus, when the Court explained in *Ginsberg v. New York* (1968), that "constitutional interpretation has consistently recognized that the parents' claim to authority in their own household to direct the rearing of their children is basic in the structure of our society," no one could reasonably believe that the Court meant to limit parents' authority to only child-rearing that takes place literally within the physical confines of "their own household." Such a view would come as a stunning surprise to countless parents throughout our history who have imposed restrictions on their children's dating habits, driving, movie selections, part-time jobs, and places to visit, and who have permitted, paid for, and supported their children's activities in sports programs, summer camps, tutorial counseling, college selection, and scores of other such activities, all arising outside of the family residence and school classroom. To ignore this reality is to ignore the

Supreme Court's admonition in *Yoder* that the "primary role of the parents in the upbringing of their children is now established beyond debate as an enduring American tradition."

There is no doubt that, in certain instances, the state may lawfully regulate the activity of children without regard to parental preferences. Indeed, the Supreme Court has noted that "the state has a wide range of power for limiting parental freedom and authority in things affecting the child's welfare," *Prince*, and has permitted parental rights to be circumscribed to accommodate the Government's legitimate interest in the "moral, emotional, mental, and physical welfare of the minor." However, when the Government does intervene in the rearing of children without regard to parents' preferences, "it is usually in response to some significant breakdown within the family unit or in the complete absence of parental caretaking," or to enforce a norm that is critical to the health, safety, or welfare of minors. The difficult question, then, is how to accommodate both the state's interests and parents' rights where there has been no specific finding of a breakdown within an identified family unit and there is no indisputable threat to the health, safety, or welfare of minors.

* * *

* * * [T]he case law suggests that if there is a significant and important goal to be achieved that generally enhances the health, safety, or welfare of unemancipated minors, the state may pass legislation to achieve that goal, so long as the legislation does not unduly tread on parents' rights to raise their children.

There are three obvious categories of cases in which the state may pass legislation that is aimed at protecting children: (1) laws in which parents' rights are not accommodated, because accommodating parents' interests would defeat the entire purpose of the legislation, *e.g.*, preventing parents from retaining custody of children they have abused; (2) laws in which parents' rights are not implicated at all, *e.g.*, preventing convicted sex offenders from working in places where they would have substantial contact with children; and (3) laws in which parents' rights are implicated, but are accommodated.

This case involves the third category, *i.e.*, accommodation. A good example of the "accommodation" category is found in the area of education. It is by now well-established that a state may enact compulsory education requirements; however, it is equally clear that the state must accommodate parents' rights to raise their children by allowing a child to attend private, rather than public school, *see Pierce*, or by allowing parents to teach their children at home, *see Yoder*. In other words, as long as certain standards are met, parents may educate their children as they see fit.

II.

* * * In my view, *Prince* and other such cases indicate that there must be a substantial relationship between the objectives of a law that limits parents' rights and the protection of children. Such a law must also reasonably accommodate parents' rights to raise their children as they see fit.

In this case, I have no real doubt that, as the opinion for the court shows, the curfew law is substantially related to the protection of minors from the dangers of juvenile crime. The difficult question here is whether the curfew law, in seeking to protect children, adequately accommodates parents' rights to determine what activities are necessary to their children's upbringing and growth. In my view, the D.C. law adequately accommodates parents' rights, because, although parents' decision making is not unfettered, the law allows parents great discretion in how to manage the activities of their children.

* * *

* * * [I]n my view, this case involves a situation in which the Government's interests are clear, as is the connection between the objectives of the law and the protection of minors. In fact, this is one of those unique cases in which the governmental regulations both serve to protect minors and, also, to facilitate parents' control over the activities of their children. No responsible parent would willingly send a child into danger. A law designed to curb the possibility of danger, while at the same time affording parents wide freedom to direct their children's activities, is one that passes constitutional muster. Although parental rights have been implicated by the curfew law, they have not been impermissibly infringed.

I therefore concur in the conclusion that the curfew is constitutional, but only because I find that the curfew law is substantially related to the protection of children and that the rights of parents have been adequately accommodated.

WALD and GARLAND, Circuit Judges, concurring in part and concurring in the result [omitted].

ROGERS, Circuit Judge, with whom Circuit Judge TATEL, joins, concurring in part and dissenting in part, and with whom Circuit Judge WALD joins in Parts II and III, and Circuit Judge GARLAND joins in Part III:

All members of the court agree that a test at least as rigorous as intermediate scrutiny would be proper for evaluating burdens on minors' fundamental right to freedom of movement. To the extent that the court hedges on the breadth of the right to free movement, however, the court mistakenly concludes that the right, if it exists at all, does not protect minors here. Were the plurality to define the right without regard to age, inasmuch as the Constitution applies to people of all ages, and consider age only in determining that minors can less successfully resist the interests of the government in their welfare, then it could avoid departing from traditional analysis of fundamental rights and suggesting that adults may lack a right to freedom of movement.

* * * When properly applied, intermediate scrutiny reveals that key elements of the curfew—age and time—are insufficiently tailored to address the problem of juvenile crime and victimization that confronted the legislature. By ignoring evidence that almost half of juvenile crime is committed by persons not covered by the curfew, and that most of that crime occurs at hours not within the curfew, the legislature has failed to demonstrate, on this record, the requisite fit between the problem and the chosen solution.

* * *

Accordingly, because the court accords less respect to minors than is constitutionally required, and more deference to the D.C. Council than is constitutionally warranted, I respectfully dissent from its holding that the curfew survives intermediate scrutiny.

I.

* * *

B.

* * *

The plurality defines a right that is coherent only in cases involving minors, as the age of the claimant is an element of the definition. Apparently, the plurality views freedom of movement as a privilege earned—if at all—by ritual passage into adulthood. Yet "[c]onstitutional rights do not mature and come into being magically only when one attains the state-defined age of majority. Minors, as well as adults, are protected by the Constitution and possess constitutional rights." The question here is whether "fundamental" rights, like "constitutional" rights more generally, apply to minors.

* * *

* * * [M]inors and adults share many fundamental rights, but * * * the protective force of some of these rights is contracted or diluted when applied to minors. To the extent that a right defines a boundary to state authority, age is generally not a meaningful credential for access to the protected zone, "magically" conferring admission on a given birthday. There may be good reasons for making the boundaries of a right more malleable for minors than adults—states have stronger countervailing interests and minority status renders minors less competent to resist state intervention—but not for denying the existence of the right altogether, at least not where minors are capable of exercising the right. * * *

In a relative sense, a right that is "fundamental" for adults in their relationship with the state is equally fundamental, if not equally forceful, for minors because it defines the few areas of activity warranting especially careful tailoring of intrusive state means to worthy state ends. Minors, like adults, are able to enjoy the fruits of free movement and to chafe under its restriction, and thus there is little reason to link the fundamentality of the right to the age of the claimant. The cases on which the court relies to contract the scope of minors' rights are inapposite to curfews because they arise in unique contexts, such as challenges to school regulations and disciplinary procedures, involving state interests associated with the educational environment warranting enhanced control over minors' behavior. *See, e.g., Vernonia School Dist. 47J v. Acton* (1995); *Hazelwood School Dist. v. Kuhlmeier* (1988); *Bethel School Dist. No. 403 v. Fraser* (1986); *Ingraham v. Wright* (1977). Just as adults may have more freedom as civilians than as prison inmates or members of the armed forces, minors' rights vary depending on whether they are at home, on the streets, or in school.

The plurality assumes that minors cannot claim a right to be "unsupervised" because they are always in "some form of custody." This characterization misses the point. Minors subject to the curfew are by definition unaccompanied by a responsible adult. To say that they are in some metaphysical bond of "custody" begs the question of whose custody they are in, and the extent to which certain personal prerogatives are immune from custodial restraint, at least by a government custodian. At a minimum, unaccompanied minors are not under direct government control, and thus theories of custody announced in a case dealing with incarcerated juvenile delinquents are unhelpful in assessing the burdens imposed by a curfew. *Schall v. Martin* (1984). The Supreme Court appeared to recognize as much in *Prince*, which relied on a balancing of state and parental interests rather than an undifferentiated notion of custody to regulate the activities of minors in public streets.

C.

For the reasons discussed, the conduct at issue should be more generally defined to encompass the activity of movement rather than how particular minors engage in it. The plurality's limited definition of the contested right appears to flow from an unarticulated perception of what minors might be doing while "freely wander[ing] ... at night." How minors exercise, and whether they abuse, their right to movement is relevant in weighing the constitutionality of a contrary state burden, but should not be part of the definition of the right itself. * * * Therefore, the question before the court should be defined as whether there is a fundamental right to walk in public without thereby subjecting oneself to police custody; in short, a right to free movement.

* * *

III.

Having concluded in Part II that the curfew burdens a fundamental right, I join the court in holding * * * that the appropriate standard of review is intermediate scrutiny.

* * *

IV.

Some juvenile curfews may survive intermediate scrutiny, but the present curfew does not. The curfew has legitimate ends, but the D.C. Council inadequately tailored its means to these ends in light of the severe burdens that the curfew imposes on minors' fundamental rights.

* * *

The curfew clearly satisfies the "important interest" requirement of intermediate scrutiny. The curfew seeks to reduce crime by and against minors, and to assist parents and guardians "in carrying out their responsibility to exercise reasonable supervision of minors." Each is a laudable goal. As the court notes, the D.C. Council was presented with a wealth of evidence of the seriousness of the juvenile crime problem in the District of Columbia. The difficulty, however, lies in the D.C. Council's conclusion that these ends warrant the particular burdens that the curfew imposes on minors. There are many ways to reduce juvenile crime and victimization and to strengthen family units, some of which are more extreme than others. The question here is whether the curfew is too extreme given the evidence considered by the D.C. Council before adopting it.

* * *

[Judge Rogers criticized the evidence on which the Council acted, and then stated:]

The weakness of the evidence that the D.C. Council did consider is particularly troubling in light of evidence it did not consider. As the district court noted, the D.C. Council ignored evidence showing that more than 90% of all juveniles do not commit any crimes, at night or otherwise. The curfew thus burdens a far larger class of minors than are responsible for crime or at risk because of it. * * *

* * *

Given the inadequacy of the District's statistics, all that remains to justify the curfew are bare assumptions about the demographics of crime and conventional political wisdom. Neither is sufficient to justify a sweeping restriction of minors' fundamental right to movement. If the legislature wants to solve pressing problems by carving exceptions to fundamental rights, intermediate scrutiny requires that it use a restrained and delicate blade; here, the D.C. Council sliced broadly with too little regard for available evidence.

Nor can the evidentiary deficiencies be overcome by looking to the experiences of other cities, as the court and the District of Columbia urge. The experience of other cities with law enforcement tools may be relevant and may provide useful information to inform the D.C. Council's decisions. But this is not the same as saying that the tools used by other cities can be imported without consideration of the characteristics of the two communities. * * *

Finally, efficacy can be no substitute for constitutional scrutiny. Assuming that the decline in arrests of juveniles during curfew hours demonstrates the curfew's effectiveness during its brief three-month period of operation, the efficacy of the curfew cannot alone save it from constitutional infirmity. The fact that well-enforced nocturnal juvenile curfews reduce crime is hardly surprising; minors cannot readily injure the public when not permitted to mingle with it. But it is equally clear that a nocturnal adult curfew would also reduce crime, as would extending the present juvenile curfew to cover the entire day. Yet both options would be extreme, and raise the same question as the instant case: whether the severity of the District of Columbia's remedy is warranted by a substantial relation to an important interest. A court reviewing an adult curfew could not substitute effectiveness as a proxy for constitutional propriety, and this court likewise must look beyond any apparent attractiveness of the curfew to determine if it is a constitutionally acceptable exercise of legislative authority.

In a time too-often punctuated by reports of senseless youth violence and untimely death, and of promising lives lost to the sadly familiar vices of the streets, minors are easy targets of ambitious law enforcement measures, as well as well-intentioned government paternalism, and cannot readily defend their rights in political fora. When challenges to legislative reforms are presented, it falls to the courts to ensure that the political branches respect minors' rights even as they exercise their considerable discretion to assess and promote minors' best interests in the face of pervasive threats. * * *

TATEL, CIRCUIT JUDGE, dissenting:

I agree with Judge Rogers that the District of Columbia juvenile curfew implicates a fundamental right to free movement and that the right should be defined without regard to the age of the right-holder. Although I still believe that the curfew should be subject to strict scrutiny and that the compelling interest prong of the analysis can adequately account for "the government's legitimate need to regulate minors," I join Judge Rogers's conclusion that this curfew fails to survive even intermediate scrutiny. * * * * I write separately to express my view that quite apart from the question of its constitutionality with respect to the rights of minors, the D.C. curfew fails to survive the strict scrutiny triggered by the restriction it imposes on parents' fundamental right to control the upbringing of their children.

* * *

State interference with th[e] long-recognized parental right to raise children demands strict judicial scrutiny. It is in the context of family, in addition to school and other societal institutions, that children of this diverse and democratic nation begin to develop habits of responsibility necessary for self-governance and to observe not only the formal rules established by government but also the informal rules and understandings that undergird civil society. Through parents, children first learn to relate conduct to consequences, to exercise freedom with responsibility, and to respect the views of others. * * * The parenting process * * *—the very process that the curfew curtails for these plaintiffs—is likewise essential, in my view, to equipping young people with the confidence they need to resist the many destructive influences of society. Schools and other governmental institutions, to be sure, are indispensable to this learning process. Parents, however, retain a critical role because "[w]e have believed in this country that this process, in large part, is beyond the competence of impersonal political institutions."

Heightened constitutional protection for parental autonomy is required for another reason. In *Yoder*, the Supreme Court's unqualified characterization of parents' "primary role" in child-rearing as "an enduring American tradition" reflected its recognition that " '[t]he fundamental theory of liberty upon which all governments in this Union repose excludes any general power of the State to standardize its children. . . .' " (quoting *Pierce*). Indeed, we refuse to regard "[t]he child [as] the mere creature of the state," *Pierce*, because insistence on a particular theory of parenting, like "affirmative sponsorship of particular ethical, religious, or political beliefs[,] is something we expect the State not to attempt in a society constitutionally committed to the ideal of individual liberty and freedom of choice," *Bellotti* (opinion of Powell, J.). Of course, this does not mean that [parents'] authority to raise their children is impervious to state regulation. It does mean that to be valid, limitations on parental rights not only must seek to achieve compelling objectives (which the D.C. juvenile curfew does), but also must demonstrate a close fit—substantiated by record evidence–between means and ends (which the curfew does not).

* * *

Notes and Questions

1. *Historical background.* Curfews have had a long, and not always noble, history. Before the Civil War, many localities imposed curfews prohibiting slaves or free blacks from being on the streets during specified hours. Toward the end of the nineteenth century, states and localities began enacting curfew statutes and ordinances directed solely at juveniles. The juvenile curfews received their first substantial boost when President Benjamin Harrison called them "the most important municipal regulation for the protection of children of American homes, from the vices of the street." A number of localities enacted curfews after Colonel Alexander Hogeland, "the Father of the curfew law," expressed strong support for juvenile curfews at the 1884 National Convention of the Boys and Girls Home Employment Association. By the turn of the century, about 3000 villages and municipalities had enacted such ordinances, which were frequently seen as measures to help control wayward immigrant children. See Note, Curfew Ordinances and the Control of Nocturnal Juvenile Crime, 107 U. Pa. L. Rev. 66, 66 n.5 (1958).

In 1896, for example, one writer voiced strong support for juvenile curfews because children's "free and untrammeled life in this country is appalling." The new immigrants were her target. "We have a foreign population who apparently believe that unlimited license is the definition of freedom. Where there are thirty-one nationalities in one school, * * * and other schools where hundreds of children hear English only during their hours of attendance, * * * with such a large class unable to comprehend American conditions, is it wonderful that we are confronted with crime, in every form, among the youth of the country?" Mrs. John D. Townsend, Curfew for City Children, 163 N. Am. Rev. 725, 725 (1896). Mrs. Townsend did not stop with support for curfews: "We should stop promiscuous immigration for thirty years, and allow for a generation of American children." Id.

The first decision to determine a juvenile curfew's validity was Ex parte McCarver, 46 S.W. 936, 937 (Tex. Ct. Crim. App. 1898), which struck down the curfew as an improper exercise of the city's general power to preserve the peace and protect order and morals. The court found the curfew an "undue invasion" of children's personal liberties, and "an attempt to usurp the parental functions": "It may be that there are some bad boys in our cities and towns whose parents do not properly control them at home, and who prowl about the streets and alleys during the nighttime and commit offenses. Of course, whenever they do, they are amenable to the law. But does it therefore follow that it is a legitimate function of government to restrain them and keep them off the streets when they are committing no offense, and when they may be on not only legitimate errands, but engaged in some necessary business." Id.

Interest in juvenile curfews diminished until World War II, when they were seen as helpful to control children while their parents were in the armed forces or employed in war industries, frequently on night shifts. In an episode now viewed with embarrassment, a Presidential executive order also imposed a curfew against Japanese–Americans of all ages in military zones. The Supreme Court upheld the executive order as a valid exercise of the federal war power in an emergency. See, e.g., Hirabayashi v. United States, 320 U.S. 81 (1943).

With the end of the War, the focus once again shifted away from juvenile curfews, which remained on the books in many jurisdictions but were rarely enforced. Indeed, curfews went unmentioned in the recommendations made in the final report of the Katzenbach Commission's Juvenile Delinquency Task Force in 1967. See President's Commission on Law Enforcement and Administration of Justice, Task Force Report: Juvenile Delinquency and Youth Crime x (1967).

Throughout the 1990s, juvenile curfews have proliferated as never before in reaction to increased violent juvenile crime and growing gang activity. Only a few states (including Florida, Hawaii, Illinois, Indiana, Michigan, New Hampshire and Oregon) have enacted statewide curfew laws, sometimes authorizing localities to fashion their own curfew ordinances in place of the statewide measure. Most juvenile curfews are enacted by local governments pursuant to their general police powers. According to a 1997 survey of 347 cities with a population over thirty thousand persons, 276 of the cities has a nighttime youth curfew. Fifty-six percent of the cities had a youth curfew in effect for ten years or less. See U.S. Conference of Mayors, A Status Report on Youth Curfews in America's Cities 2 (Dec. 1997).

2. *The scorecard in the courts.* As the number of juvenile curfew statutes and ordinances has increased nationwide, litigation challenging their constitutionality has also increased. In the absence of Supreme Court resolution, no discernible trend has yet appeared. Decisions upholding juvenile curfews include Schleifer v. City of Charlottesville, 159 F.3d 843 (4th Cir. 1998); Qutb v. Strauss, 11 F.3d 488 (5th Cir.1993). Decisions striking down juvenile curfews include Nunez v. City of San Diego, 114 F.3d 935 (9th Cir.1997); Gaffney v. City of Allentown, 1997 WL 597989 (E.D.Pa.1997). *Hutchins* was not the District of Columbia's first effort to enact a juvenile curfew ordinance. An earlier D.C. ordinance was struck down in Waters v. Barry, 711 F.Supp. 1125 (D.D.C.1989).

3.   Should the law recognize a four-year-old's right to roam the city streets alone at 2 a.m., or the parents' right to permit the child to do so? If parents permit their four-year-old to roam the city streets alone at 2 a.m., why does the state have an interest in enforcing a curfew?

4. *Defenses or exemptions.* *Hutchins* and other recent decisions indicate that a juvenile curfew is unlikely to pass constitutional muster without defenses or exemptions that permit children to be on the streets with their parents, in emergencies, and so forth. Do the exemptions weaken the curfew and perhaps make it counterproductive? Or do the exemptions empower parents while protecting children?

More than a century ago, a curfew opponent wrote that such defenses or exemptions "would simply put a premium on lying": "[E]very boy on the street who hadn't just been sent to get medicine for his sick father would be on his way to some highly improving society, and those who could tell a lie with the straightest faces, and could best simulate an expression of real piety or sympathy for the sick parent would be allowed to go on their way unmolested." Winifred Buck, Objections to a Children's Curfew, 164 N. Am. Rev. 381, 384 (1897). And what if the lie were discovered? "Arrest a boy and call him a lawbreaker, and he is just one step nearer to becoming one in fact." Id.

5. *Public safety.* In communities where juvenile drug dealing and violent crime are rampant, a juvenile curfew may be a public safety measure. This letter-to-the-editor appeared shortly after district judge Emmet G. Sullivan struck down the District of Columbia curfew ordinance ultimately upheld by the en banc court of appeals. "If [Judge] Sullivan really needs credible evidence that youths commit more crimes late at night * * *, I invite him to live in my home for two weeks. * * * Let him monitor the calls that my neighbors and I place to '911' and to the Metropolitan Police Department's non-emergency number. Let him peer out my window to see the drug-dealing that occurs late into the evening and to observe youths hiding handguns in their waistbands after firing off several rounds. I'm quite sure Judge Sullivan doesn't live near my community, because if he did he would understand his expressed point of view is entirely counterintuitive and at odds with the experiences of a majority of the District's residents." Wash. Post, Nov. 9, 1996, at A26.

6. *Policy questions.* Quite apart from the simmering constitutional controversy evident in *Hutchins*, juvenile curfews remain controversial as a policy matter. Curfew proponents generally stress the need to assist parents in

controlling their children during curfew hours, the need to compel parents to supervise their children, the need to protect juveniles from criminal violence perpetrated by other juveniles, the need to regulate criminal gang activity, the need to protect society from the violence of juveniles on the streets in the middle of the night, and the need to relieve juveniles from peer pressures that produce criminality in children not otherwise disposed to crime. Proponents assert that where a juvenile appears prone to criminality, the curfew's relatively minor sanctions may send a message that helps the juvenile avoid acts that produce considerably stiffer sanctions.

Curfew opponents generally argue that curfews are an undesirable crutch for parents unable or unwilling to discipline and control their children, that curfews violate parents' prerogatives to control their children's upbringing, that curfews have the greatest effect on the law-abiding juveniles most likely to obey them and not on violent teens likely to ignore them, that curfews unnecessarily involve otherwise law-abiding juveniles in the criminal justice system, and that curfews unfairly punish innocent youths for the acts of the criminal few. Opponents argue that understaffed police departments should devote their resources to apprehending violent juvenile and adult offenders rather than children whose only offense is being out in public after hours. Opponents often argue that curfew statutes are popular because children do not vote and because the statutes do not treat poverty, inadequate public schools, insufficient employment opportunities, and similar core problems.

Opponents also sometimes assert that curfews are likely to have disparate impact on urban youth whose homes are less likely to have yards where children may congregate free from the curfew's reach. Some opponents fear that by requiring children to remain indoors on the pain of criminal punishment, curfews may leave some children vulnerable to domestic violence or other abuse they could escape, at least temporarily, by leaving the home during difficult hours.

Opponents also frequently assert that juvenile curfews invite discriminatory enforcement. In a 1971 policy statement urging repeal of curfews, the National Council on Crime and Delinquency found a "great" potential for discrimination because police "cannot thoroughly enforce a juvenile curfew ordinance": "The police tend to mete out more severe dispositions to Negroes and to boys who look 'tough' because from both prejudice and, to some extent, departmental statistics they assume that these juveniles commit crimes more frequently than do other types of youths. * * *. Police make different dispositions of lower-class and middle-class juvenile offenders, the reason for this difference being that police 'expect' to have trouble with young people from homes described as 'broken, on welfare, etc.'" National Council on Crime and Delinquency, Juvenile Curfews: A Policy Statement, 18 Crime and Delinq. 132 (Apr. 1972).

7. *Curfew-like measures.* Localities have experimented with a variety of curfew-like ordinances designed to regulate children's public activities. In Rothner v. City of Chicago, 929 F.2d 297 (7th Cir.1991), for example, the Seventh Circuit upheld a Chicago ordinance that prohibits children under seventeen from playing video games during school hours on days when school is in session. The ordinance's purpose was "to encourage all minors to

complete at least a high school education and to discourage truancy." Id. at 303. The plaintiff, a distributor and operator of video games, alleged that the ordinance violated his young customers' First Amendment rights. The court of appeals held that even if the ordinance regulates expression protected by the First Amendment, the ordinance is a legitimate time, place and manner restriction on that expression narrowly tailored to an important governmental interest: "in insuring that children receive an adequate education."

In Lutz v. City of York, 899 F.2d 255 (3d Cir.1990), the court of appeals upheld a city ordinance that prohibited "cruising," driving repeatedly around a loop of major roads through the heart of the city. Cruising was reportedly a favorite activity of local youth. The ordinance prohibited persons from driving on designated streets more than twice in any two-hour period between 7:00 p.m. and 3:30 a.m. The court recognized a federal constitutional right to intrastate travel, but held that the challenged ordinance was a reasonable, time, place and manner restriction narrowly tailored to combat the safety and traffic congestion problems identified by the city. Id. at 258–70.

Chicago's Gang Congregation Ordinance, on the other hand, did not survive a court challenge. The ordinance provided that "[w]henever a police officer observes a person whom he reasonably believes to be a criminal street gang member loitering in any public place with one or more other persons, he shall order all such persons to disperse and remove themselves from the area." The Supreme Court held that the ordinance was void for vagueness. City of Chicago v. Morales, 119 S.Ct. 1849, 1856 (1999) (plurality opinion).

8. *Adult curfews.* Courts generally agree that in the absence of an emergency, the state may not constitutionally impose a general curfew on adults. See, e.g., Bykofsky v. Middletown, 401 F.Supp. 1242 (M.D.Pa.1975), aff'd without opinion, 535 F.2d 1245 (3d Cir.), cert. denied, 429 U.S. 964 (1976) (Marshall and Brennan, J.J., dissenting from denial of certiorari); Ruff v. Marshall, 438 F.Supp. 303 (M.D.Ga.1977) (striking down general curfew and loitering statute that applied to all persons). Curfews reaching adults and children alike, however, have almost always been upheld where they are limited in duration and narrowly tailored to help insure public safety during specific emergencies such as natural disasters or riots. See, e.g., Ervin v. State, 163 N.W.2d 207, 210–11 (Wis.1968) (upholding challenge to curfew imposed after a riot).

9. *Shopping mall curfews.* In 1996, Minneapolis' Mall of America, the nation's largest shopping mall with 4.2 million square feet of gross building area, imposed a curfew that denies entry on Friday and Saturday nights to children under sixteen who are unaccompanied by a parent or other adult over twenty-one. The Mall saw the curfew as a way of controlling teenage rowdyism. A Mall spokesman explained that before imposition of the curfew, a few thousand teenagers would swarm the four-million square-foot mall on wintery weekend evenings, disturbing other shoppers with chases, foul language, practical jokes, fistfights and frequent gang-related violence. The Mall expressed fear of damage suits by innocent shoppers injured by such conduct.

An American Civil Liberties Union staff counsel responded that "parents, not the mall or the government" should decide whether unchaperoned children may enter the Mall. The president of the Minneapolis chapter of the Urban Coalition charged that the curfew was "drawn up in reaction to and in large part because of the large number of young people of color who congregate in the mall in the evening." See Robyn Meredith, Big Mall's Curfew Raises Questions Of Rights and Bias, N.Y. Times, Sept. 4, 1996, at A1.

The threshold legal issue is whether shopping malls are deemed private or public property. In the absence of unlawful behavior, identifiable groups of persons may be excluded from private property but not from public areas. Federal courts applying federal constitutional guarantees have held that malls are private property, see, e.g., Hudgens v. NLRB, 424 U.S. 507, 520–21 (1976), but state courts throughout the nation remain divided on the issue in decisions applying state constitutional guarantees. Minnesota courts have not viewed shopping malls as public property. See Meredith, supra. Reportedly only a few other malls have imposed similar curfews. See Amanda Vogt, Hang Out? You Like to But Do Malls Want You?, Chicago Tribune, Apr. 8, 1997, at 3.

10. *Curfews on adjudicated juveniles.* Appellate courts ordinarily uphold the authority of juvenile and criminal courts to impose particularized curfews on juveniles adjudicated as delinquents or sentenced as adults. Also ordinarily upheld are particularized curfews imposed on juveniles as part of informal, negotiated dispositions or plea bargains. Curfews imposed on juveniles as a sanction for committing a particular offense do not implicate the constitutional questions raised by blanket curfews that operate against juveniles generally regardless of prior individual behavior. See, e.g., A.B.C. v. State, 682 So.2d 553, 554 (Fla.1996).

11. *Daytime curfews.* Several localities have enacted daytime curfews as anti-truancy measures. Subject to enumerated exceptions, these curfews require school-age children to be off the streets during the hours when schools are in session during the academic year. A 1997 survey of 347 cities by the U.S. Conference of Mayors found that 26% had daytime curfews. See U.S. Conference of Mayors, A Status Report on Youth Curfews in America's Cities 2 (Dec. 1997). Status offense statutes enable authorities to move against truancy, and compulsory school attendance laws punish parents for keeping their children out of school. On top of these existing statutes, why does a locality need a daytime curfew to combat truancy?

12. *Do juvenile curfews work?* A 1999 report by the U.S. Office of Juvenile Justice and Delinquency Prevention concluded that "[a]fterschool programs have more crime reduction potential than juvenile curfews." See Howard N. Snyder and Melissa Sickmund, Juvenile Offenders and Victims: 1999 National Report 65 (OJJDP 1999). The report compared the number of reported violent crimes committed by juveniles during the standard curfew hours (between 10 p.m. and 6 a.m.) with the number of reported violent crimes committed by juveniles during the afterschool hours (3:00 to 7:00 p.m.). The report found that the number committed during the afterschool hours is four times the number committed during the curfew hours. In particular, sexual assaults by juveniles peak during the afterschool hours. Id. The report also found that juveniles are at the highest risk of being victims of violence between noon and 6:00 p.m. Id. at 34–35.

PROBLEM 10–8

You are the city attorney, and the mayor has just asked you to draft a curfew ordinance for the city council's consideration. The mayor knows that courts disagree about the constitutionality of juvenile curfew statutes, and he expects a court challenge to any ordinance the council might enact. Based on *Hutchins*, what can you do to maximize the chances that the curfew ordinance will survive constitutional challenge? What would you anticipate would be the strongest arguments against constitutionality made by a minor? By his or her parents?

If you were a city council member, would you vote to enact a juvenile curfew ordinance you believed would pass constitutional muster?

SECTION 7. STATUS OFFENSES

A. *The Nature of Status–Offense Jurisdiction*

1. *Overview*

This last section is a prelude to Chapter 11's study of delinquency. A delinquency proceeding alleges that the juvenile has committed an act that would be a crime if committed by an adult. A status offense proceeding, on the other hand, alleges conduct sanctionable only where the person committing it is a juvenile.

This section treats the quintessential status offenses—ungovernability (which alleges that the juvenile is beyond the control of his or her parents or guardian), truancy, and runaway behavior. Also sometimes considered status offenses are various other acts sanctionable only when committed by a juvenile, such as underage purchase, possession or consumption of tobacco or alcohol, curfew violations, and other acts deemed harmful to the juveniles themselves or the public. See, e.g., D.P. v. State, 705 So.2d 593, 594–95 (Fla.Dist.Ct.App.1997) (upholding ordinance that prohibited minors from possessing spray paint or jumbo markers on public property, except when the minor is in the company of a supervising adult).

OHIO REVISED CODE ANNOTATED

§ 2151.23

(A) The juvenile court has exclusive original jurisdiction under the Revised Code as follows:

(1) Concerning any child who * * * is alleged to be a juvenile traffic offender or a delinquent, unruly, abused, neglected, or dependent child; * * *

§ 2151.022

As used in this chapter, "unruly child" includes any of the following:

(A) Any child who does not subject himself or herself to the reasonable control of his or her parents, teachers, guardian, or custodian, by reason of being wayward or habitually disobedient;

(B) Any child who is an habitual truant from home or school;

(C) Any child who so deports himself or herself as to injure or endanger his or her health or morals or the health or morals of others; * * *

(E) Any child who is found in a disreputable place, visits or patronizes a place prohibited by law, or associates with vagrant, vicious, criminal, notorious, or immoral persons; * * *

(G) Any child who violates a law * * * that is applicable only to a child.

Notes and Questions

1. *Referral.* Alleged status offenders may be referred to the juvenile court by law enforcement agents, parents, school authorities, social service agencies or other adults. Law enforcement agencies made 48% of status offense referrals in 1996, but a significant percentage of referrals are made each year by the child's parents. See Anne L. Stahl et al., Juvenile Court Statistics 1996, at 34 (1999). The nomenclature varies from state to state, but a status offender is typically known as a PINS (person in need of supervision), a CHINS (child in need of supervision), a MINS (minor in need of supervision), or an unruly child.

2. *The volume and nature of status offense cases.* Status offense cases remain a relatively small, but nonetheless significant, part of the juvenile court docket. About 80% of status offenders are diverted from the system without filing a court petition, usually to community services programs or similar providers. See David J. Steinhart, Status Offenses, in 6 The Future of Children 86, 87–88 (Winter 1996). Truancy cases, for example, are frequently diverted to the public school district.

The remaining 20% of status offense cases are petitioned, that is, filed in juvenile court after arrest or citation of the juvenile. In 1996, juvenile courts petitioned and formally disposed of about 162,000 status offense cases, 101% more than the number of petitioned status offense cases handled in 1987. Between 1987 and 1996, petitioned truancy cases increased 92%, petitioned runaway cases increased 83%, petitioned status liquor offense cases increased 77%, and petitioned ungovernability cases increased 42%. See Anne L. Stahl et al., Juvenile Court Statistics 1996, at 33 (1999).

In 1996, 52% of petitioned status offense cases resulted in formal adjudication by the juvenile court. Most of the adjudicated cases (59%) resulted in probation as the most restrictive sanction. Fourteen percent of the adjudicated cases resulted in placement of the youth outside the home in a residential facility, and 24% resulted in such dispositions as restitution or fines, community service, or enrollment in nonresidential treatment or counseling programs. About 3% resulted in dismissal or release without sanction. See id. at 35–36.

One group of researchers reports that processing of status offense cases "varies from virtually no intervention in some locales to highly developed intervention programs in others." Carol S. Stevenson et al., The Juvenile Court: Analysis and Recommendations, in 6 The Future of Children 4,13 (Winter 1996).

3. *Constitutional challenges.* Broad frontal attacks on the constitutionality of status offense jurisdiction have generally failed. Among other things, challengers have unsuccessfully asserted that the jurisdiction is void for vagueness, constitutes cruel and unusual punishment, and violates equal protection and substantive due process. See Irene Merker Rosenberg, Juvenile Status Offender Statutes–New Perspectives on an Old Problem, 16 U.C. Davis L. Rev. 283, 294–99 (1983).

   2. *Ungovernability*

IN THE MATTER OF LEIF Z.

Family Court, Richmond County, 1980.
431 N.Y.S.2d 290.

DANIEL D. LEDDY, JR., JUDGE.

* * * The present petition, filed by the boy's natural father, alleges that the respondent is a person in need of supervision in that he

"... threatened petitioner's wife with a knife on June 16, 1980 at about 8:30 P.M. Respondent refuses to obey the just and reasonable commands of his step-mother at times."

After listening to the testimony adduced at the hearing, the Court finds that the following facts have been established beyond a reasonable doubt.

(1) The respondent was born on November 26, 1966 and resided with his parents until their divorce. Thereafter, custody was given to the natural mother with the father obtaining visitation rights which he exercised regularly. When the father remarried, his new wife was thoroughly antagonistic to Leif, making it clear to the boy that he was not welcome in her home, even for brief visitation periods with his father. This attitude on her part was unprovoked.

Unfortunately, the boy's natural mother became increasingly ill and was eventually unable to care for him any longer. Leif was sent to live with his father and stepmother during the Columbus day weekend of 1979. Tragically, Leif's mother passed away in December of that year.

When the boy's initial stay at his father's home proved difficult, he was sent to live with a sister and then an aunt. Eventually, however, he returned to his father in June of this year.

During her testimony, the stepmother admitted that she had no love for Leif and had told him so. She further made it clear to the boy that he was not welcome in the home but was living there only as an accommodation to his father. She made remarks such as "Get this fucking kid out of the house", and even taunted her husband to choose between his son and her.

For his part, the boy was given a 9 P.M. curfew which he obeyed regularly. He liked to sing and play his guitar but his stepmother made him stop, telling him that he sounded like a dead cow.

The stepmother repeatedly faulted the boy for failing to put away his personal belongings, and keep his room in order. On one occasion, following an argument, she jumped on his back, knocking the youngster to the ground. Leif weighs only seventy-seven pounds while his stepmother weighs at least twice that amount.

On June 16, 1980, when Leif returned home from a friend's house, his stepmother warned him to stop making certain noises with his mouth. A shouting match ensued during which she called his dead mother a "whore". The youngster broke down in tears, grabbing a knife. He did not, however, make any overt move toward his stepmother and was willingly disarmed by his father. After the police were called and the situation calmed, Leif spoke quietly of his behavior, indicating that he had been upset at the cruel charge made against his deceased mother. Incredibly, his stepmother once again repeated her assertion that the boy's mother was a "whore" and when Leif protested, she commented that the boy wasn't old enough to know the difference.

The boy's father severely reprimanded his wife for her remarks and accompanied his son to a motel to spend the night. His father acknowledged that Leif had been hurt many times by his stepmother's actions. He noted that the boy rarely cries but that he was brought to tears by the vicious attack on his dead mother.

Based on the foregoing, any suggestion that Leif is "incorrigible, ungovernable or habitually disobedient" shocks the conscience. It is crystal clear that this vulnerable little child has himself been subjected to an unabated course of cruel, emotional torment. Indeed, the record of this proceeding fully supports a finding that Leif is a neglected child * * *.

Both PINS proceedings and neglect proceedings purport to deal with the realities of a child in trouble. It is often difficult to delineate clearly whether the source of that trouble is properly within the PINS statute or the neglect statute. For where there is a crisis in the life of a child requiring court intervention, the indicia of both statutes are often present and may, indeed, overlap. The ultimate determination may depend more upon the social mores of the time than upon the dictates of clearly defined criteria. * * *

Where a parent files a PINS petition, he chooses to air the problems of the child and the home in a judicial forum. He further consents to court jurisdiction over the parent-child relationship, the exercise of which could ultimately result in placement. If, during the course of the fact-finding hearing, it develops that the problem is properly one of neglect, there is no reason for the court to close its eyes to that fact or to avoid labeling it as such. * * *

The Court is aware that a certain stigma may attach to a parent whose child has been neglected by him. However, the thrust of an Article 10 [neglect] proceeding is to assess the status of the child and not to label the parent. Thus, Sec. 1012 of the Family Court Act defines a "neglected child" and not a "neglectful parent".

* * *

By way of comparison, a child adjudged to be in need of supervision not only suffers the stigma of being branded "incorrigible, ungovernable or habitually disobedient" but also faces the prospect of placement. * * *

(3) In this case, the respondent's father and stepmother voluntarily sought Court intervention, thereby subjecting the problems of their home to judicial scrutiny. Although the petitioner is the boy's natural father, it is clear that the prime mover is the stepmother. * * * [T]he Court has identified the problem in the home as being the fact that Leif is a neglected child. * * *

Consistent with its parens patriae function, this Court will act decisively to assist the child, the first step of which is the recognition of his status. It is difficult enough to discover the plight of a suffering child without suggesting that the Family Court turn away when confronted with overt neglect. The present PINS petition is a transparent sham, the final act of cruelty directed against a defenseless little boy.

* * * A neglect finding is substituted and Leif is adjudged to be a neglected child in that his physical, mental and emotional condition has been impaired as a result of the failure of his stepmother to exercise a minimum degree of care in providing him with proper supervision and guardianship.

Notes and Questions

1. *Assessing ungovernability jurisdiction.* Judge Leddy was perceptive in identifying the father and stepmother as the true wrongdoers in *Leif Z.* Ungovernability jurisdiction, however, has been criticized for enabling authorities and courts to blame children for their parents' failings. Two commentators found that "[i]n a substantial number of reported cases, children designated as PINS appear to be either neglected or the victims of parental inadequacies." Irene Merker Rosenberg and Yale L. Rosenberg, The Legacy of the Stubborn and Rebellious Son, 74 Mich. L. Rev. 1097, 1111 (1976). These commentators find that "tactical and psychological factors may influence juvenile court personnel to proceed against a child as a PINS, rather than against a parent for neglect":

> There is less hesitancy in prosecuting a neglect case if the child is young and the parent's misconduct overt, because no one in the juvenile court system is apt to attach blame to a small child or to identify with a

parent who has evidenced aberrant behavior. Moreover, proving neglect under these circumstances presents minimal difficulty.

However, when older children are involved, judges and other court personnel are more likely to favor PINS proceedings. One possible explanation for this preference is that the individuals who comprise juvenile court systems tend to identify with a parent who has charged a teen-ager with misbehavior, since these individuals may also be struggling with adolescent rebelliousness in their own families. Another factor is the comparative difficulty of proving parental neglect of older adolescents, which is often more subtle and passive than neglect of younger children. If the parents secure attorneys who vigorously defend against the neglect charges, the proceedings will certainly be protracted, and the petition may eventually be dismissed. Juvenile court personnel will thus prefer PINS proceedings, which in all likelihood will be speedily concluded by admissions of "guilt" from the children. * * *

Id. at 1113. Where family dysfunction is a root cause of a child's distress, does a status offense petition permit the court to provide treatment as effectively as a neglect petition would?

Without necessarily questioning the soundness of the views expressed above, what are parents supposed to do when the child is truly beyond their control, endangering himself and perhaps others, and threatening violent behavior? Should the parents be able to invoke ungovernability jurisdiction as a preventive measure, or should they have to postpone court intervention until the child commits a crime (perhaps one that would produce a hefty prison term)?

2. *Financial considerations.* Where an ungovernable child is removed from the home (for example, to a shelter or a foster placement), the parents may effectively be relieved of the obligation to support the child during the period of removal. Does this circumstance suggest a reason for abolishing ungovernability jurisdiction, or at least for invoking it only sparingly? A number of states now require parents to reimburse the state for part or all of the cost of out-of-home care provided for their children found ungovernable. See, e.g., Mo. Rev. Stat. § 211.241.

3. What is the proper role of ungovernability jurisdiction? When, if at all, should the juvenile court intervene, and when should it decline to intervene?

3. *Truancy*

The Ohio act defines "unruly child" to include "[a]ny child who is an habitual truant from * * * school." The fault for missing school must lie with the child and not with the parents. See, e.g., In re C.S., 382 N.W.2d 381, 383–84 (N.D.1986) (holding that because their parents removed them from public school, the children were not truants). In 1996, juvenile courts formally processed 39,300 status offense cases with truancy as the most serious offense, a 53% increase since 1992 and a 92% increase since 1987. See Anne L. Stahl et al., Juvenile Court Statistics 1996, at 33 (1999).

Where a student is habitually absent from school, truancy might be a harbinger of future distress, such as gang membership, drug and alcohol abuse, dropping out of school, and delinquency. A report compiled by the Los Angeles County Office of Education, for example, concluded that chronic absenteeism is "the most powerful predictor of delinquent behavior." Beth Shuster, School Truancy Exacts a Growing Social Price, L.A. Times, June 28, 1995, at 1A.

Much truancy, however, may stem from problems beyond the child's effective control. Many child welfare workers believe, for example, that a substantial number of truants have undiagnosed learning disabilities and attention deficit disorders but are labeled as discipline problems without receiving needed special education. See, e.g., Robin Russel et al., Status Offenders: Attitudes of Child Welfare Practitioners Toward Practice and Policy Issues, 72 Child Welfare 13, 19 (1993 No. 1). Perceptive courts are alert for latent disabilities. See, e.g., Simon v. Doe, 629 N.Y.S.2d 681, 683 (Fam. Ct. 1995) (holding that because child suffered from school phobia, her failure to attend school was not intentional and she was not a truant).

A 1979 study found that truancy was "commonly associated with difficulties at home, at school and with peers." Arthur Neilsen and Dan Gerbner, Psychosocial Aspects of Truancy in Early Adolescence, 14 Adolescence 313 (1979). The truants' families were subject to multiple serious stresses: 40% of the sample families had experienced a divorce or separation, 27% were single-parent families, and 40% had moved in the past two years; underemployment was present in 38% of the families, serious illness in 41%, parental discord in 41%, and alcoholism in 19%. Three or more of these stresses were present in 76% of the families. Id. at 316.

A significant number of the truants in the Neilson–Gerbner sample reported that their aversion to school stemmed from anxiety and embarrassment in interactions with other students. Some of the truants were teased in the hallways, ridiculed in gym class, or otherwise harassed for their shyness or peculiar behavior. Id. at 323. The researchers found that many of the truants were depressed or angry, or both, and that a few had attempted suicide or had expressed homicidal thoughts. Id. at 316. The study concluded that truancy is "a useful marker for identifying adolescents with significant problems in all areas of social functioning. * * * [E]ven students truant only once were likely to be experiencing substantial psychological and social difficulties." Id. at 323. The researchers concluded that "[a] student's being truant should precipitate a thorough assessment of the surrounding circumstances at home, at school, and in the peer group." Id. Can the juvenile court make this sort of assessment on a status offense petition? If not, does the court nonetheless have a role to play in assuring that the assessment is made?

A significant number of truants apparently stay away from school because they fear for their personal safety on the campus. A 1993 survey of over 16,000 high school students, for example, found that "[n]ationwide, 4.4% of students had missed at least 1 day of school during the 30 days preceding the survey because they felt unsafe at school or felt unsafe traveling to or from school." U.S. Centers for Disease Control and Prevention, Youth Risk Behavior Surveillance—United States, 1993, 44 Morbidity and Mortality Weekly Rep. 6 (Mar. 24, 1995). A 1995 Louis Harris survey of seventh through twelfth graders found that 11% had stayed home from school or cut class because they were concerned about crime and violence in their communities. See June L. Arnette and Marjorie C. Walsleben, Combatting Fear and Restoring Safety in Schools 11 (Apr. 1998). Fearful truants may receive their parents' tacit or overt approval. A 1994 survey found that 40% of high schoolers' parents were "very or somewhat worried" about their child's safety in school or traveling to and from school. See id. at 2. Well-publicized school shootings late in the 1990s have done little too calm fears.

4. Runaways

a. The Scope of the Problem

By creating jurisdiction over "[a]ny child who is an habitual truant from home," the Ohio act enumerates runway behavior as a distinct category of status offense. Some juvenile codes instead reach runaways with provisions relating more generally to children who are "beyond parental control."

More than a million children each year run away from home and live on the streets, frequently to escape persistent physical, emotional or sexual abuse, alcoholic or drug addicted parents, divorce, sickness, poverty or school problems. The cause is more typically ongoing family dysfunction rather than a single precipitating event. Precise accountings of runaway children are unavailable because children who leave their families, foster homes or group homes frequently do not get reported.

Runaways are of both genders and represent all ethnic groups, geographic areas, sexual identities and socioeconomic backgrounds. According to a 1992 U.S. Conference of Mayors study, most street kids are black (52%), while 33% are white, 11% are Hispanic, 4% are Native American, and 1% are Asian. U.S. Conference of Mayors, A Status Report on Hunger and Homelessness in America's Cities (1992). Gay and lesbian youth appear to be overrepresented in street youth populations. See G. Kruks, Gay and Lesbian Homeless/Street Youth: Special Issues and Concerns, 12 J. Adolesc. Health 515 (1991).

A 1991 nationwide survey by the National Association of Social Workers (NASW) indicated that more than 60% of runaway and homeless youth reported physical or sexual abuse by their parents before they left home, while 20% reported violence by other family members. See Testimony of Peter LaVallee (Director, Youth Service Bureau, Redwood Community Action Agency, Eureka, Cal.) Before the Subcommittee on Early Childhood, Youth and Families Committee on Education and the Workforce, U.S. House of Representatives, 1997 WL 271597 (F.D.C.H.) (May 21, 1997). "[M]ost youth who run away from home do so for very legitimate reasons," the director said. "We may not agree with this behavior, but it is a reasonable and logical response to want to escape from a family environment that not only provides inadequate care and protection, but is so often abusive." Id.

Many runaways (more than a fifth and as many as 46%, depending on the study) are more aptly labeled "throwaways" because they are directly told to leave the household, because they have been away from home and a caretaker refused to allow them back, because they have run away but the caretaker makes no effort to recover them or does not care whether they return, or because they are abandoned or deserted. See U.S. Justice Dep't, Office of Juvenile Justice and Delinquency Prevention, Missing, Abducted, Runaway, and Thrownaway Children in America, First Report: Numbers and Characteristics National Incidence Studies, Executive Summary 14 (1990) (estimating that there were 127,000 throwaways in the United States). Throwaways come from all social classes, generally come from households without both natural parents present, and are generally left destitute by their families. See Ilse Nehring, "Throwaway Rights": Empowering a Forgotten Minority, 18 Whittier L. Rev. 767, 771 (1997).

Some runaway children receive help in shelters funded by the federal or state governments or by private caregivers. Many others find shelter with friends or relatives. Many, however, live on the streets, frequently turning to prostitution, pornography, panhandling and crimes against persons or property for survival. Some street children land in jail before encountering a shelter.

Many runaways and throwaways return home after a brief period. For many, however, family dysfunction makes returning home impossible or undesirable. See, e.g., J.N. Penbridge et al., Runaway and Homeless Youth in Los Angeles County, California, 11 J. Adolesc. Health Care 159 (1990) (concluding that only 20% of youth in L.A. shelters were candidates for family reunification). Some are repeat runaways because they try to return home, only to encounter the same domestic circumstances that led them to leave in the first place. Many runaways and throwaways report they do not even know their parents' whereabouts. See Patricia Hersch, Coming of Age on the City Streets, 22 Psychology Today 28 (1988) (stating that 35% of interviewed street children did not know where their parents could be contacted). A San Francisco youth shelter director reported that when he contacted runaways' parents, 68% of the parents told him flatly, "You keep the kid." Pete Axthelm, Somebody Else's Kids, Newsweek, Apr. 25, 1988, at 64.

Without family support, runaways and throwaways on the streets are much more likely than other children to suffer malnutrition, inadequate hygiene, respiratory infections, mental illness, suicidal ideation, drug and alcohol abuse, unwanted pregnancies, and HIV and other sexually transmitted diseases resulting from prostitution and other high-risk sexual conduct and drug abuse with shared needles. The NASW estimates that nearly a quarter of runaways suffer from mental health problems and that 20% have attempted suicide. See Deborah S. Bass, Helping Vulnerable Youths: Runaway and Homeless Adolescents in the

United States (1992). The 1992 U.S. Conference of Mayors study estimated that 9% of street children had AIDS or were infected with HIV. It has been estimated that four of every five runaways suffer from depression.

Even if runaways and throwaways overcome fear or ignorance to seek medical treatment, they may face legal barriers. Ordinarily they cannot consent to treatment because they have not reached majority. They also lack documentation to qualify for entitlement programs and cannot use private insurance without parental consent. See Paul Chance, No Place Like Home; Study of Runaway Teenagers, 20 Psychology Today 12 (1986); Deborah J. Sherman, The Neglected Health Care Needs of Street Youth, 107 Pub. Health Rep. 433 (1992). Most employment remains unavailable to them because of child labor legislation and their lack of skills. Some of these barriers may be overcome with a judicial order of emancipation, but such orders are unlikely at best because runaways normally lack counsel and could not qualify as economically and emotionally self-sufficient.

One writer has painted a grim picture of the circumstances faced by runaway and throwaway children: "[M]ost of them run away not because they want to but because they have to; because even the streets are safer than where they're running from, where many of them have been physically and sexually abused by their families. Even so, they are not running to anything but death. Nationwide, more than 5,000 children a year are buried in unmarked graves" because their bodies are unidentified or unclaimed. David Levi Strauss, A Threnody for Street Kids: The Youngest Homeless, The Nation, June 1, 1992, at 752.

b. *Federal and State Legislation*

The Supreme Court has evidently put to rest any sustained argument that runaway and throwaway children have a constitutional right to government-provided care and treatment. See, e.g., DeShaney v. Winnebago County Dep't of Soc. Servs., 489 U.S. 189, 196 (1989) (holding that an abused or neglected child has "no affirmative right to governmental aid, even where such aid may be necessary to secure life, liberty, or property interests of which the government itself may not deprive the individual"); Jefferson v. Hackney, 406 U.S. 535, 548–49 (1972) (holding that state's formula for dividing fixed pool of welfare funds did not violate Fourteenth Amendment); Lindsey v. Normet, 405 U.S. 56, 73 (1972) (holding that "the need for decent shelter" is not a "fundamental interest" under the Constitution); Dandridge v. Williams, 397 U.S. 471, 487 (1970) (the Constitution does not "empower the Supreme Court to second-guess" state officials' allocation of welfare funds).

Despite the evident absence of a federal constitutional imperative, the federal government and a few states have forged initiatives to assist runaway, throwaway and unaccompanied homeless children. The major federal initiative designed to assist state and local efforts is the Runaway and Homeless Youth Act, as amended (RYHA), 42 U.S.C. § 5700 et seq. The Act authorizes grants to states, localities and community-based agencies that operate existing or proposed local shelters for runaway and homeless youth outside the law enforcement system, the child welfare system, the mental health system and the juvenile justice system. Id. § 5711(a). Some children seek shelter on their own initiative; most, however, are referred to shelters by child welfare and protective services agencies, juvenile law enforcement officers, or school personnel. U.S. Gen. Accounting Office, Homelessness: Homeless and Runaway Youth Receiving Services at Federally Funded Shelters 30–31 (1990).

Depending on the amount of annual appropriations, the RYHA also authorizes grants for "street-based services" and "home-based services." Street-based services include crisis intervention and counseling, and provision of information about housing, health services, and prevention services for alcohol and drug abuse, sexually transmitted diseases, and physical and sexual assault. "Home-based services" relate to counseling programs for children and parents designed to prevent children from running away or to cause runaways to return home. 42 U.S.C. §§ 5711(c), (d), 5712(c), (d).

To qualify for RYHA grant assistance, an applicant must, among other things, develop plans (1) for contacting the children's parents or other relatives and ensuring the child's safe return "according to the best interests of the youth" and for contacting local government officials, and (2) for providing the children counseling and aftercare services, and for encouraging involvement of their parents or guardians in counseling. Id. § 5712(b) (3), (5).

Is status offense jurisdiction a sound way to protect runaway and throwaway children? Is it the best way? In what other ways may the state seek to protect these children? See, e.g., Gregory A. Loken, "Thrownaway" Children and Throwaway Parenthood, 68 Temp. L. Rev. 1715 (1995).

B. *The Deinstitutionalization Mandate*

The Juvenile Justice and Delinquency Prevention Act of 1974, as amended, 42 U.S.C. § 5601 et seq., enables state and local governments to secure federal formula grant funds for projects and programs related to juvenile justice and delinquency. To secure these funds, a state must satisfy several mandates. The "deinstitutionalization" mandate requires states to prohibit detention of status offenders (and also of such nonoffenders as dependent or neglected children) in secure detention facilities or secure correctional facilities. A secure facility is one the juvenile may not leave without permission, such as a jail, police lockup, juvenile detention center, or training school.

Under a 1980 amendment to the 1974 Act, however, a state may authorize its courts to order secure detention of status offenders who violate valid court orders. See 42 U.S.C. § 5633 (a)(12)(A). Where a status offender violates a court order mandating treatment, such authorization permits the court to hold the status offender in criminal contempt and confine him in secure detention for a limited period. The amendment was enacted on the recommendation of the National Council of Juvenile and Family Court Judges, which testified that the deinstitutionalization mandate had compromised their ability to protect some at-risk juveniles, particularly chronic runaways or chronic truants. Many states, however, have not exercised the authority granted by the 1980 amendment. See, e.g., Commonwealth v. Florence F., 709 N.E.2d 418, 419 (Mass.1999).

The next decision expresses a judge's frustrations in a state that has not expressly authorized juvenile courts to hold status offenders in contempt for violating an order prescribing non-secure treatment. The ensuing notes explore the continuing controversy surrounding the deinstitutionalization mandate.

MATTER OF JENNIFER G.

Family Court, Queens County, N.Y.
N.Y.L.J., July 29, 1999, at 26.

JUDGE DePHILLIPS

On April 21, 1998, petitioner L.G. the father of the respondent Jennifer G. filed a petition under Article 7 of the Family Court Act seeking to have her adjudged a person in need of supervision [PINS]. Among his allegations are the following: "Respondent absconded one month ago and is still away. Petitioner saw respondent about one week ago, grabbed respondent, and respondent was placed with her mother. Respondent left the mother's house and whereabouts are presently unknown." Respondent * * * was twelve years old at the time of filing of the Article 7 petition. A warrant issued to secure the appearance of respondent. * * * On April 22, 1998, respondent was brought to court on the warrant which was then vacated. Respondent was appointed counsel and remanded to the custody of the Commissioner of Social Services. * * * The matter was set down for possible factfinding hearing on May 29, 1998.

On May 22, 1998, a judicial application was filed, alerting the court to respondent's absconding from custody of the Commissioner of Social Services. A second warrant issued for the arrest of respondent. On May 29, 1998, this warrant was vacated and respondent was again remanded to the Commissioner of Social Services with a directive that a diagnostic evaluation be conducted. The new adjourned date was July 30, 1998. On June 8, 1998, a judicial application was filed alerting the court to the fact that respondent had absconded from the Commissioner for the second time. A third warrant issued for the respondent's arrest. On June 22, 1998, respondent was returned to court on the warrant. The warrant was vacated and respondent again returned to the custody of the Commissioner of Social Services. The court renewed its direction that a diagnostic evaluation of respondent be conducted while respondent was in the custody of the Commissioner pursuant to the remand order.

Respondent was instructed to comply with the remand and not to abscond again. * * *

On July 1, 1998, pursuant to a judicial application, a fourth warrant issued for the arrest of respondent who had again absconded from the Commissioner's care. On July 30, 1998, the scheduled date for fact-finding hearing, the petitioner father accompanied by the stepmother appeared. Respondent not appearing, the warrant was continued. On September 2, 1998, respondent appeared in court with her court appointed counsel. The warrant was vacated and the matter set down for hearing on October 21, 1998. Respondent was again remanded to the Commissioner of Social Services.

On September 22, 1998, a further judicial application was filed, advising the court that respondent had again absconded. A fifth warrant issued for her arrest. The matter was adjourned to October 21, 1998 for control. On September 29, 1998, respondent appeared. The warrant was vacated. Respondent was again remanded to the Commissioner of Social Services for diagnostic evaluation.

On October 1, 1998, a further judicial application advised the court that respondent had absconded again. A sixth warrant issued for respondent's arrest. On December 16, 1998, respondent who had turned thirteen years old on October 18, 1998, was produced in court. The warrant was vacated. Again respondent was remanded to the Commissioner for completion of a diagnostic evaluation. The court continued to plead with respondent to be respectful of the court's authority, parental authority and her own self interest. The Article 7 proceeding was adjourned to January 11, 1999. * * *

On December 17, 1998, * * * another judicial application informed the court that respondent, despite the pleas of the court and her law guardian and in violation of the admonition and mandate of the court, had again absconded. A seventh warrant issued for the arrest of respondent. On December 30, 1998, respondent was returned on this warrant. Respondent was again remanded to the Commissioner of Social Services. On January 26, 1999, on judicial application of the petitioner father an eighth warrant issued for respondent's arrest, respondent having again absconded.

On March 26, 1999, respondent was returned on the warrant. * * * In view of the respondent's young age, thirteen, and of her inveterate history of absconding, and aware of the lack of power to remand respondent to a secure setting, the court on its own authority, remanded respondent to the Health and Hospitals Corporation (Elmhurst Hospital) for full psychological evaluation. The setting at Elmhurst permitted requisite security to give reasonable assurance that respondent would not easily abscond. The Article 7 proceeding was adjourned to March 31, 1999, with privilege to advance the case on the calendar and with a direction that respondent be released to court only. * * *

On March 31, 1999, petitioner father appeared with the stepmother. * * * Respondent was advised by the Court that in view of her lengthy history of running away, any further violation of the court's remand directive would be deemed criminal contempt. The proceeding was adjourned to April 7, 1999.

On April 7, 1999, the matter was further adjourned to April 28, 1999 and the remand of respondent to Health and Hospital Corporation continued. On April 14, 1999 the court was advised that respondent had absconded from Elmhurst Hospital. A forthwith warrant, the ninth warrant, issued for the arrest of respondent. On April 28, 1999, respondent was produced. * * * The court was advised that during the period of the numerous abscondings by respondent, she was victimized (raped) * * *.

The Court again importuned respondent to co-operate with the court's direction and with the rehabilitative public policy underlying Article 7. As respondent was already aware of the court's lack of effective power to enforce its directive, the court stated: "Now, I can't hold you in any sort of *secure* facility in this PINS litigation. You are already aware of that. That is because every time I remand you to the Commissioner of Social Services, you run away. You see what happens is that I issue a warrant, you come back on the warrant. I vacate the warrant and you run away." * * * The court also admonished respondent in clear and unequivocal terms that if she absconded one more time, her contempt for parental authority in the person of the court would be viewed as criminal contempt with an Article 3 delinquency proceeding being instituted against her. The matter was adjourned to May 20, 1999. On April 29, 1999, the court was advised that * * * at approximately 1:10 A.M. on April 29, 1999 [respondent] absconded from the Bronx Teen Center maintained by ACS [Administration for Children's Services]. A missing person report was filed by ACS.

The court issued a forthwith warrant (the tenth warrant) for the arrest of the respondent. At the request of the court and, in its own discretion, the Corporation Counsel of the City of New York filed an Article 3 Juvenile Delinquency petition on April 30, 1999 against the respondent alleging an act which if committed by an adult would constitute Criminal Contempt in the Second Degree. * * * A warrant was issued for respondent's arrest on the delinquency petition in addition to the outstanding warrant on the PINS proceeding.

On May 5, 1999, respondent was returned on these warrants. The warrants were vacated. However, respondent, in view of the fact that an Article 3 juvenile delinquency proceeding was now pending, was for the first time remanded to secure detention. On May 10, 1999, at fact-finding, * * * the court found that respondent had committed an act which if committed by an adult constitutes the crime of Criminal Contempt in the Second Degree, a Class A Misdemeanor. * * * On June 3, 1999, the court received for the first time reports of respondent's receiving certificates of achievement in educational studies and social participation. On all of these recent adjournments respondent appeared, her appearance being reasonably assured by the secure detention remand in the Article 3 proceeding.

* * *

Family Court Act § 720(2) provides: "The detention of a child in a secure facility shall not be directed under any of the provisions of this article [7]." This legislative policy is grounded on pecuniary considerations. "* * * [T]he purpose of this section is to insure continued federal funding to the state under the provisions of the Juvenile Justice and Delinquency Prevention Act of 1974, which requires that all alleged or adjudicated PINS be phased out of secure detention facilities by 1980. * * *. The JJDPA conditions receipt of federal funding, inter alia, upon demonstration by a state or territory that it prohibits secure detention of status offenders * * *."

* * *

The court noted that in a PINS proceeding, Article 7 does not expressly authorize the court to substitute a petition charging delinquency or to substitute a finding that the child is delinquent. The court concluded that absence of this authority has "in effect, rendered the efficacy of Article 7 illusory."]

A respondent in an Article 7 proceeding who has a history of absconding from home already has rebelled against and shown disrespect for parental authority. Common sense and right reason dictate that the fractured parental authority should be supported by the court's authority as the third branch of government. Instead the respondent with a history of absconding from home soon perceives that the court in enforcing its authority, which in a real sense is another form of parental authority, is incapable of enforcing its authority. The history of this instant PINS proceeding is a classic example of this charade. * * * The lesson taught the respondent is that the law may be disobeyed and evaded without legal consequence as long as the respondent is charged only with PINS conduct. Yet, the respondents in PINS proceedings have been, in this court's experience, among the most needy of children even taking into consideration those children who come before the court in the context of delinquency or child protective proceedings. * * *

* * *

The inability of the Family Court to enforce its remand or dispositional order of placement in a PINS proceeding due to the abrogation of secure detention as a preventive remedy, where appropriate and warranted, has reduced Article 7 to a proceeding of form over substance. * * * Appropriate treatment is inextricably intertwined with adequate supervision. The inability of Family Court to maintain and enforce that supervision by remand or the threat of remand to a secure PINS facility when warranted and for non-punitive purposes, is a serious jurisprudential and sociological flaw in implementing the public policy concerns envisioned in the creation of Family Court and the enactment of PINS jurisdiction.

If it is posited that a PINS child is needy and has a right to treatment to meet those needs, and if it is posited that society through its courts may exercise parens patriae controls to implement such treatment, then common sense, human nature, life experience and sound jurisprudential teaching instructs that the power to insure necessary supervision to the PINS child is essential. * * *

The truth of the matter is that there are no clear dividing lines between delinquent and PINS children. Their truancy rates are equally and extremely high.

PINS children frequently commit criminal acts which either do or do not come to the attention of the authorities. They both often have a long history of contacts with the court and social agencies. According to one study, nearly half of them have experimented with drugs.

Both delinquent and PINS children often come from similar, one-parent, multi-problem families with a history of poverty and strong evidence of neglectful or at least rejecting parents. In fact, juvenile justice professionals see some categories of PINS children as more disturbed and more difficult to treat than all but the most severe delinquents. * * *

* * *

[After discussing "[t]he inanity of weakening the concept and efficacy of supervision for PINS children by depriving the court of the power to remand to an appropriate secure setting when necessary to accomplish the rehabilitative and non-punitive policy underlying PINS proceedings," the court continued:]

* * * [T]he court and through the court, his parents, his family, society, the state, cannot do anything to [a PINS] and therefore cannot do anything for him. To state the obvious, this is ludicrous. The undermining of the ability to mandate compliance by respondent when appropriate in PINS litigation teaches the respondent the wrong lesson, to wit the law, justice, is ineffectual and may be viewed with contempt, derision, and mockery. * * * Apart from sophistry, there is no response, only an acknowledgment—that for monetary consideration alone, New York through its legislative branch abandoned PINS children to their self will even if self destructive and paid obeisance to a pejorative social concept that a status offense, PINS, never under any circumstances whatsoever, no matter how inimical or dangerous for the child, warrants secure detention. If the State were called to task by way of analogy in a child protective proceeding for this act, it must be deemed an act of improper supervision and therefore neglect.

* * *

[After discussing the "pernicious consequences visited upon PINS children because of the nonsensical social concept that secure detention may never be utilized," the court continued:] Without equivocation, it must be declared and recognized that * * * instances of harm befalling PINS children and supreme contempt for the court's directives in PINS proceedings because of the inability of the court to hold respondent in a secure setting when appropriate to meet the needs of and to advance the best interest of the respondent, are not isolated; are not the exception! * * *

* * *

* * * In depriving society through its Family Court of the power to utilize secure detention when appropriate to protect and advance the welfare and to meet the needs of the PINS child, the legislature insofar as PINS children are concerned, has amputated the right hand of the Lady of Justice. * * *

* * *

* * * The absence of the power to remand to secure detention in PINS litigation to meet the needs and the best interest of and to protect the respondent is a cancer that enfeebles the public policy envisioned by the creation of Family Court. In many instances, parents have already exhausted all reasonable means to secure compliance with appropriate household rules and regulation by their absconding child. They come to Family Court as a last resort. Remand to the Commissioner of Social Services merely substitutes an agency and its employees for the parent. Unless there is an expectation that parental authority may be enforced and re-enforced, the PINS child will ignore or treat that authority with contempt. * * * It is remarkable that New York in abrogating secure detention for PINS children did so to obtain federal funds pursuant to [the JJDPA], which itself did not demand such abrogation in order for the state to obtain the federal funding. * * * New York, in conformance with the federal dictate regarding preventive detention and dispositional orders in PINS proceedings, could have provided that the detention of a child in a secure detention facility under Article 7 shall not be directed unless it is found that the child violated a valid order of the court. * * *

[The court cited and discussed Matter of D.L.D., 327 N.W.2d 682 (Wis.1983), which held that "all courts have an inherent power to hold in contempt those who disobey the court's lawful orders," and that "the power exists independently of statute because 'it is a necessary incident to the exercise of judicial power and is reasonably to be implied from the grant of such power'."). The court intimated that the Family Court has such inherent power in PINS proceedings under New York law.]

There is nothing inherently suspect or wrong with the concept of secure detention in the context of juvenile justice. Of course, sound principles of reason, social common sense and intelligent jurisprudence require that PINS children not be housed with delinquent children or with adult criminals. Meeting the needs of such children does carry fiscal implication.

The dictum "penny wise, pound foolish" echoes the value our society places on its children. This court earnestly and urgently requests that the other branches of government, the executive and the legislative revisit the issue of secure detention for PINS children for all of the reasons delineated above. To that end, it is requested that if the power is not restored, the legislature remove Article 7 from the Family Court act so that the Lady Justice is not mocked. To that end, this court because its conscience wills it so, pledges that it will endeavor at all times to meet the needs of PINS children even if the endeavor requires, to the extent permitted by existing power and law, the invocation of Article 3 as a means to accomplish justice for the PINS child.

Notes and Questions

1. *Questions about* Jennifer G. Does *Jennifer G.* indicate whether the court ever investigated the possibility that the child may have kept running away because of persistent abuse or neglect at home? As the social services agency and the court focused on the child's status offense, should they have also examined the conduct of the parents and stepmother?

2. *The deinstitutionalization controversy.* Without necessarily arguing for a return to widespread secure detention of status offenders, several commentators argue that the deinstitutionalization mandate has had unintended effects inconsistent with its benign purpose. The U.S. Attorney General's Advisory Board on Missing Children, for example, charged that because of the mandate, "police in many states have lost all authority to deal with runaway and homeless children," who are now "simply ignored–permitted to walk out of police stations or runaway shelters and resume their flight," despite the evident dangers of life on the streets. The Advisory Board recommended that Congress amend the 1974 Act "to ensure that each State juvenile justice system has the legal authority, where necessary and appropriate, to take into custody and safely control runaway and homeless children," without placing such children in detention facilities with delinquents or adult offenders. See America's Missing and Exploited Children: Their Safety and Their Future 19–20 (OJJDP 1986). Another commentator has similarly stated that while deinstitutionalization is best for most status offenders, it has released others "into the grasp of hustlers, pimps, pornographers, gangsters, rapists, and murderers who are ready to exploit the youthfulness of their victims." William G. Kearon, Deinstitutionalization, Street Children, and the Coming AIDS Epidemic in the Adolescent Population, 41 Juv. & Fam. Ct. J. 9, 9–10 (No. 1 1990).

Critics also charge that the deinstitutionalization mandate sometimes encourages subterfuge. For one thing, the mandate has led to commitment of greater numbers of youth to secure mental health and drug treatment facilities. One commentator, for example, writes that "rising rates of psychiatric admission of children and adolescents reflect an increasing use of hospitalization to manage 'troublesome' youth who do not suffer from severe mental disorders." "[R]ecent legal reforms in the juvenile justice system have made that system relatively inaccessible to families desperate for an intensive intervention from outside of the family. Many children now hospitalized in mental health facilities probably would have been admitted to juvenile justice facilities prior to recent efforts to deinstitutionalize the juvenile justice system." Lois K. Weithorn, Mental Hospitalization of Troublesome Youth: An Analysis of Skyrocketing Admission Rates, 40 Stan. L. Rev. 773, 773–74 (1988). Another commentator concludes that "[h]ospitals are rapidly becoming the new jails for middle-class and upper-middle-class kids * * * usually committed for medical problems that do not require hospitalization and for which there is little evidence that psychiatric intervention is appropriate or effective." Payment for the private treatment comes from parents, frequently through health insurance. Ira M. Schwartz, (In)justice for Children: Rethinking the Best Interests of the Child 137, 143 (1989).

Authorities seeking to impose secure detention on a juvenile may also avoid the deinstitutionalization mandate by charging minor criminal offenses rather than status offenses, even when the facts would reasonably support only a status offense petition. The juvenile may then be processed as a delinquent, free from the mandate. See Barry C. Feld, The Transformation of the Juvenile Court, 75 Minn. L. Rev. 691, 699 (1991). In addition, a youth charged with both a status offense and a crime may be detained in a secure facility because of the crime. See, e.g., People v. Juvenile Ct., 893 P.2d 81, 91 (Colo.1995).

3. *Punishing criminal behavior with status offense jurisdiction.* The overlap between status offense and delinquency jurisdiction, noted by Professor Feld above, may also work in reverse. The breadth of status offense jurisdiction, illustrated by Ohio's formulation on page ___, may permit authorities to petition juveniles suspected of criminal behavior that might be difficult or impossible to prove in a delinquency or criminal proceeding. Where a juvenile is suspected of breaking and entering a retail establishment with some friends, for example, authorities may forego delinquency and instead charge the status offense of ungovernability. Proof of the status offense need not meet the beyond-a-reasonable-doubt standard that In re Winship, 397 U.S. 358, 90 S.Ct. 1068, 25 L.Ed.2d 368 (1970), mandates in delinquency proceedings, and the juvenile is not constitutionally entitled to other protections mandated by *Gault* and later decisions. The state might not provide some of these protections by state constitution, statute or court rule. Because more than half of adjudicated delinquency petitions result in probation as the most restrictive sanction, a status offense petition may produce the same sanction as a delinquency petition would, even though the sanction might be based on proof insufficient to sustain a delinquency petition.

Accused status offenders have fewer constitutional procedural rights than alleged delinquents, and are less likely to be represented by counsel. See Barry C. Feld, *In re Gault* Revisited: A Cross–State Comparison of the Right to Counsel in Juvenile Court, 34 Crime & Delinq. 393, 404 (1988). When juveniles plead to the alleged status offense, they are unlikely to be informed of any future ramifications of the plea. The status offender may be pressured into pleading so necessary treatment may be made available.

4. *Treatment.* The 1974 Act encourages states to refer deinstitutionalized status offenders to counseling, treatment, and other non-secure programs. Some commentators have complained, however, that states have been slow to provide adequate funding for treatment programs: "Only a handful of

states appropriated funds for new programs to meet the needs of the deinstitutionalized status offender population. In most states, policymakers sought to achieve minimum compliance with the [deinstitutionalization] mandate by reducing nonoffender detention levels without spending state dollars for new programs." David J. Steinhart, Status Offenses, 6 The Future of Children 86 (Winter 1996).

5. *Escape.* Contempt is not the only way to "bootstrap" a status offense into a delinquent offense, thus permitting secure detention without running afoul of the deinstitutionalization mandate. Some states have enacted the crime of "escape," which authorities sometimes seek to invoke against a status offender who leaves a foster home, group home or other nonsecure placement without permission. Most decisions however, hold that escape statutes do not reach such nonsecure placements, State v. Puckett, 259 S.E.2d 310, 312 (N.C.Ct.App.1979), or do not reach delinquents, In re J.B., 474 S.E.2d 111, 111 (Ga.Ct.App.1996).

6. *Further provisions.* By rule, the U.S. Office of Juvenile Justice and Delinquency Prevention has created an exception to the deinstitutionaliza- tion mandate to permit secure placement of accused status offenders for a maximum of twenty-four hours, excluding weekends and holidays, to permit identification, investigation, release to parents, or transfer to a nonsecure facility or to court. A second 24–hour period may follow a initial court contact. In 1992, Congress specified that a status offender who violates a court order may be held in secure detention only if before entry of the violated order, (1) the offender was brought before a judge and given full due process rights, and (2) it was determined that all dispositions (including treatment), other than placement in a secure detention or correctional facility were exhausted or clearly inappropriate. 42 U.S.C. § 5603 (16).

The 1974 congressional Act's other mandates are discussed in Chapter 11, Delinquency.

7. When, if at all, should courts be authorized to order secure detention of status offenders? What safeguards should be imposed on such authority?

C. *The Future of Status–Offense Jurisdiction*

The appropriateness of status offense jurisdiction has been hotly debated for the past generation, and the debate continues. In 1967, the Katzenbach Commission recommended that "[s]erious consideration, at the least, should be given to complete elimination of the [juvenile] court's power over children for noncriminal conduct." In the meantime, the Commission urged that status offense jurisdiction "should be sub- stantially circumscribed so that it * * * comprehends only acts that entail a real risk of long-range harm to the child." President's Commis- sion on Law Enforcement and Administration of Justice: The Challenge of Crime in a Free Society 85 (1967). Seven years later, the National Council of Crime and Delinquency advocated outright repeal of status offense jurisdiction. The Council concluded that "[a]lthough a matter for community concern, noncriminal [juvenile] conduct should be referred to social agencies, not to courts of law." National Council of Crime and

Delinquency, Jurisdiction Over Status Offenses Should Be Removed from the Juvenile Court, 21 Crime and Delinq. 97, 99 (Apr. 1975).

In 1976, the tentative draft of the IJA–ABA Standards Relating to Noncriminal Misbehavior recommended repeal of general juvenile court jurisdiction over status offenses, with retention of only limited jurisdiction to determine emergency non-criminal matters concerning juveniles. The ABA House of Delegates tabled the Standards as "too controversial," however, and the Standards were never approved by that body. See Robert E. Shepherd, Jr. (ed.), IJA–ABA Juvenile Justice Standards Annotated xviii (1996). Before the tabling, two leading juvenile court judges staked out divergent positions on the merits of the draft Standards. Judge Lindsay G. Arthur noted that juvenile courts divert most status offense cases to schools and other community service agencies, but argued that courts must retain authority "to handle the residuum of juveniles who cannot or will not accept diversion; those children who need help but will not get it voluntarily." In these remaining cases, children "need protection, unequal protection, from themselves and their own immaturity." "In the very few undivertible cases," Judge Arthur concluded, "there is no one else but the juvenile court that stands between helping the child and abandoning her. * * * [C]ourts are able to resolve many family problems that would not be resolved without a court's involuntary intercession." Lindsay G. Arthur, Status Offenders Need a Court of Last Resort, 57 B.U. L. Rev. 631, 632–34, 636–37, 641–43 (1977).

Judge Orman W. Ketcham disagreed. He argued that "status offense jurisdiction is so inherently discretionary in principle that it is subject to manipulation by police, parents and social workers." Orman W. Ketcham, Why Jurisdiction Over Status Offenders Should Be Eliminated from Juvenile Courts, 57 B.U. L. Rev. 645, 661 (1977).

Judge Ketcham also argued that status offenders "are more likely to become criminal offenders than youths who are not so labeled. Many observers attribute this to the self-fulfilling prophecy theory; a juvenile who is officially designated a nonconforming offender is thus alienated and tends to justify such classification by more serious antisocial acts. Others believe that the underlying problems causing a youth to engage in noncriminal misbehavior eventually will escalate into more serious antisocial behavior constituting criminal offenses. Whatever the theory, there is no certainty that treatment of such youths by the juvenile court prevents or deters subsequent criminal acts." Id. at 652.

In 1976, the National Council of Juvenile and Family Court Judges announced firm opposition to repeal of status offense jurisdiction. Calling status offenses "anti-social and self-destructive adolescent conduct," the Council resolved that "such conduct is contrary to the welfare of the child, hinders his development to responsible adulthood, impairs the parent's ability to guide and regulate the child's behavior, and may also violate the rights of the community." NCJFCJ, Resolution #10 (1976).

In 1980, the National Advisory Committee for Juvenile Justice and Delinquency Prevention concluded that "there must be some means available to provide services to families in conflict and children who run away from home, stay away from school, or abuse alcoholic beverages." The Committee recommended that court intervention in such status offense cases "be limited to the provision of services on a voluntary basis unless such services have been offered and unreasonably refused or have proven ineffective after a reasonable period of utilization." See Standards for the Administration of Criminal Justice 175 (1980).

A recent article urges that "[t]he first line of response to status offenders should be community and public services designed to help children and their families, with court intervention only after services have been offered but have not been successful, or if the child's behavior continues to pose a threat to his or her own safety or well-being. Court-ordered incarceration of a status offender is appropriate only in exceptional cases when an adjudicated status offender repeatedly refuses to cooperate with the court or service providers, or when a status offender's behavior is proven to be of significant risk of harm." Carol S. Stevenson et al., The Juvenile Court: Analysis and Recommendations, in 6 The Future of Children 4,15 (Winter 1996).

Some observers believe that status offense jurisdiction should play a significant role in crime and delinquency prevention efforts. Edward Humes, for example, argues that this jurisdiction is an "effective crime prevention tool" that "makes perfect sense, because the experts knew in 1905, as they do now, that this sort of misbehavior is in virtually every case the precursor of more serious crimes * * *. It is almost impossible to find a juvenile who committed a serious crime today who did not first commit a passel of status offenses." Humes laments the decriminalization of status offenses, which he attributes to *Gault's* "giving kids the same rights as adults," and to the desire to "save money by cutting back services, particularly by gutting the ranks of probation officers who previously supervised status offenders." Edward Humes, No Matter How Loud I Shout: A Year in the Life of Juvenile Court 51 (1996).

The Coalition for Juvenile Justice believes that juvenile courts "should be involved with status offenders, mainly runaways, truants, and alcohol abusers, primarily in order to facilitate efficient provision of services to these youth, especially if their behaviors present a substantial risk to their well-being, safety, or health." See Coalition for Juvenile Justice, A Celebration or a Wake?: The Juvenile Court After 100 Years 48 (1998). "Generally, other agencies, such as social services or mental health, should have the principal responsibility for developing and providing services for these young people," and "[c]ourt intervention should be reserved for those cases where services have been offered but not utilized or where a youth's behaviors pose a significant threat to his or her own safety." Id.

NATIONAL COUNCIL OF JUVENILE AND FAMILY COURT JUDGES, A NEW APPROACH TO RUNAWAY, TRUANT, SUBSTANCE ABUSING, AND BEYOND CONTROL CHILDREN

41 Juv. & Fam. Ct. J. iii, 5–6 (1990).

* * *

Back in what perhaps were simpler times, our society dealt with [status offenders] through the heavy hand of law enforcement and the juvenile justice system, including locking many of them up in training schools and detention centers. The idea, of course, was that society (1) has an obligation to guide and control the behavior of its youth and (2) has the right to use the means necessary to carry out its responsibility.

Fortunately we have learned in recent years a great deal about these children and a great deal about what works for them and what doesn't work. Indeed, one can also make a strong case for the proposition that the children themselves are not the same as twenty or thirty years ago. At least they are facing entirely new sets of problems and are exposed to a wide array of new and more serious risks.

In any event, we know that many who are on the streets are there as a result of sound rational choices they have made for their own safety and welfare, such as avoiding physical abuse, or extreme self destructive behaviors. Some simply do not have a home. The causes are many and varied.

We also know that treating these children as "offenders" and locking them up with delinquent youth is no longer an acceptable answer if indeed it ever was.

What has happened, however, is equally unacceptable. Society in general, and the juvenile justice system in particular, has thrown up its hands and decided that there is nothing it can do. So it does nothing.

We have on our streets a growing number of children who are essentially homeless, powerless, exposed to drugs, AIDS and exploitation; who are lacking in education, job skills and the basic tools to cope with life; who are tomorrow's homeless adults, parents of drug or AIDS infected babies; who are permanently placed on the bottom rung of society's ladder.

The social service system for runaways consists primarily of woefully under-funded and understaffed drop-in shelters operating for the most part on a voluntary and charitable basis. All too often these agencies exist as islands of care, scrabbling for funds, for resources, for housing, for programs and stretching their dollars to the snapping point.

If adequate resources were in place, and a system to coordinate them, these voluntary service agencies would be the answer for all but a few of these children. Even as they are, these agencies provide an essential resource on which a more adequate system can be based. They can and do provide food, shelter, health care, individual and family counseling, independent living programs and other skill development for some of the children whose problems this report addresses.

* * *

A refocusing of the attention of the schools, the juvenile court, and the community upon truancy and other minor misbehavior by children of late elementary and middle school age as precursors for more serious problems in later adolescence is necessary. As a generation, because their numbers are small and the needs of society for well educated and skilled workers are great, we can ill afford to lose or abandon any of them. Timely prevention and intervention at the middle school level can help forestall the lost potential and misspent lives of many of our nation's youth.

Alcohol and substance abuse run as a constant thread through the lives of these children. The abuse may be their abuse, their adult caretakers' abuse, or both. However it occurs, recognition of the dimensions of substance abuse both by children and their families must be part of any intervention in their behalf.

There are a few children, however, who simply will not or cannot seek help on a voluntary basis, or who will continue a course of self destructive behavior unless and until forceful intervention occurs.

Society does have an obligation to these youth. It simply is not acceptable to allow any of them to destroy their lives and the lives of others with whom they may interact solely because we can't figure out how to help them if they don't ask for it, don't want help or cannot find it. There is a vital role for the juvenile court where these children are concerned.

The court is the one institution society has charged with the duty of holding itself and its institutions accountable. That role should not be abandoned just because this segment of our population presents problems that are difficult. * * *

It is time for a sensible alternative to the extreme positions and the very old and outworn argument between those who would compel through incarceration and those would default on society's responsibility to care for, protect, and "raise" its most difficult children.

Notes and Questions

1. *Gender bias.* Debate continues about whether status offense jurisdiction produces gender bias. Critics assert that "girls are disproportionately represented among those charged with status offenses, even though they represent only a modest percentage of juvenile offenders overall and are not disproportionately involved in the behaviors constituting status offenses." Anne Bowen Poulin, Female Delinquents: Defining Their Place in the Justice System, 1996 Wis. L. Rev. 541, 546. Critics charge that status offense jurisdiction is "the traditional vehicle for asserting jurisdiction over girls," id., noting that in 1996, 41% of petitioned status offenses cases involved girls

while only 23% of delinquency cases involved females. See Anne L. Stahl et al., Juvenile Court Statistics 1996, at 22, 42 (1999).

In a 1995 report, the U.S. General Accounting Office analyzed six years of national data (1986–91) and found "only relatively small differences in the percentages of female and male status offenders detained, adjudicated, and placed." From a survey of county probation officers and visits to selected facilities, the GAO report found no significant differences in the facilities and services available to female and male status offenders. Minimal Gender Bias Occurred In Processing Noncriminal Juveniles 9–10, 15 (GAO Feb. 1995).

By 1996 the numbers found by the GAO analysis had changed little. Fifty-nine percent of petitioned status offense cases nationwide that year involved boys. Boys were named in 53% of truancy cases, 57% of ungovernability cases, 69% of status liquor cases, but only 40% of runaway cases. Between 1986 and 1995, the number of status offense cases involving girls increased 75% and the number involving boys increased 79%. See Anne L. Stahl et al., supra, at 42.

In 1995, status offense dispositions also differed little by gender. The percentages of formally handled cases that were adjudicated were almost the same (51% for boys and 49% for girls). The figures were quite close in all categories: runaways (44% for boys, 41% for girls), truancy (53% for boys, 52% for girls), ungovernability (54% for each), and liquor (55% for boys, 49% for girls). Id. at 43–44. Detention was imposed on 7% of boys and 7% of girls. The likelihood of out-of-home placement for adjudicated status offenders was 16% for both boys and girls. Probation was imposed on 55% of boys and 59% of girls. Id. at 43, 45.

2. *Race.* Critics of status offense jurisdiction have often cited racial disparities in processing. Judge Orman W. Ketcham, for example, charged that "[s]tatus offenders are usually the children of poor or minority parents" and "many of the actions of children from poor, black, or Chicano families are more likely to trigger police arrest or parental referral to juvenile court than the same actions of children from white or affluent homes." Orman W. Ketcham, Why Jurisdiction Over Status Offenders Should Be Eliminated from Juvenile Courts, 57 B.U. L. Rev. 645, 647–52, 656–68, 661 (1977).

Professor John DeWitt Gregory, however, argues that abolition of status offense jurisdiction "would have the most severe ramifications upon poor and minority group parents who lack alternatives for dealing with the child and who use the juvenile court as a last resort." John DeWitt Gregory, Juvenile Court Jurisdiction Over Noncriminal Misbehavior: The Argument Against Abolition, 39 Ohio St. L.J. 242, 267 (1978).

In recent years, "[o]verall status offense case rates were more similar across racial groups than were delinquency case rates." Howard N. Snyder and Melissa Sickmund, Juvenile Offenders and Victims: A National Report 138 (1995). In 1996, 78% of formally processed status offense cases involved white juveniles, "a proportion comparable to their representation in the general population"; 17% involved black juveniles, and 5% involved juveniles of other races. White juveniles were involved in 90% of status liquor law violation cases, 75% of runaway cases, 74% of incorrigibility cases, and 72% of truancy cases. Detention was used at some point between referral and disposition in 5% of petitioned status offense cases involving white juveniles,

8% of those involving black juveniles, and 5% of those involving juveniles of other races. Probation was the most restrictive disposition ordered in 65% of adjudicated status offense cases involving black juveniles and 58% of cases involving whites or juveniles of other races. See Stahl et al., supra, at 46, 50.

3. *State actions.* A few states have repealed status offense jurisdiction, though dependency or neglect jurisdiction may now reach such conduct in some of these states. See, e.g., 42 Pa. Cons. Stat. § 6302 ("dependent child" includes child who is truant, without proper parental care or control, or ungovernable). The move from status offense jurisdiction to dependency or neglect jurisdiction is significant, however. Repeal of status offense jurisdiction ends the juvenile court's quasi-criminal control over juvenile conduct that would not expose adults to criminal sanction, and eliminates the possibility that the juvenile court adjudication will be used against the juvenile in a later delinquency or criminal proceeding. Where family dysfunction appears as a root cause, reliance on dependency or neglect also places the "blame" on parents rather than on the child. By making child protective agencies primarily responsible for wayward juveniles not processed as delinquents or tried as adults, dependency jurisdiction identifies such juveniles as needing treatment and not as quasi-criminals.

Concluding that status offense jurisdiction does not effectively address children's needs, the Massachusetts Supreme Judicial Court Commission on Juvenile Justice recommended repeal in 1994. The Commission urged creation of community boards and panels to resolve cases presently within the juvenile court's jurisdiction. "In CHINS cases, the courts are asked to play the role of disciplinarian without the sanctions available in delinquency cases. The provision of discipline and the development of functional behavior within the family by both parents and children is the responsibility of the family and/or school with assistance as necessary from child welfare organizations." See Supreme Judicial Court Commission on Juvenile Justice, Final Report 12 (June 1994).

4. *Non-judicial alternatives to status offense jurisdiction.* If status offense jurisdiction were repealed, would schools and other community service providers be suitable alternatives to court intervention? Professor Gregory concludes that calls to rely on these providers rest on "highly questionable assumptions": (1) that "voluntary agencies, in those communities where they exist, either have the resources to take on the task or the necessary resources will in some way be made available to them," (2) that "where such agencies exist, they would be willing to offer a full range of services to children who would otherwise be subject to" status offense jurisdiction, (3) that "children will be willing to make use of the services of voluntary agencies." Professor Gregory cautions that "in the absence of PINS jurisdiction, there is reason to believe that significant numbers of children will be abandoned to their own devices." John DeWitt Gregory, Juvenile Court Jurisdiction Over Noncriminal Misbehavior: The Argument Against Abolition, 39 Ohio St. L.J. 242, 268–69 (1978).

5. *Parting questions.* Should states repeal the juvenile court's status offense jurisdiction? If you believe the answer is yes, what social institutions or controls, if any, should replace it? If you believe the answer is no, would you retain the jurisdiction as-is, or would you propose structural reforms? If you

support reducing the reach of that jurisdiction rather than outright repeal, what aspects of that jurisdiction would you retain?

6. *References.* Joel F. Handler & Julie Zatz, Neither Angels Nor Thieves: Studies in Deinstitutionalization of Status Offenders (1982); Beyond Control: Status Offenders in the Juvenile Court (Lee E. Teitelbaum and Aidan R. Gough eds., 1977); R. Hale Andrews, Jr., & Andrew H. Cohn, Ungovernability: The Unjustifiable Jurisdiction, 83 Yale L.J. 1383 (1974); Meda Chesney–Lind, Judicial Paternalism and the Female Status Offender, 23 Crime & Delinq. 121 (1977); Jan C. Costello & Nancy L. Worthington, Incarcerating Status Offenders: Attempts to Circumvent the Juvenile Justice and Delinquency Prevention Act, 16 Harv. C.R.-C.L. L. Rev. 41 (1981); Cheryl Dalby, Gender Bias Toward Status Offenders: A Paternalistic Agenda Carried Out Through the JJDPA, 12 Law & Ineq. 429 (1994); Peter D. Garlock, "Wayward" Children and the Law, 1820–1900: The Genesis of the Status Offense Jurisdiction of the Juvenile Court, 13 Ga. L. Rev. 341 (1979); Al Katz & Lee E. Teitelbaum, PINS Jurisdiction, the Vagueness Doctrine, and the Rule of Law, 53 Ind. L.J. 1 (1978); Robert W. Sweet, Deinstitutionalization of Status Offenders: In Perspective, 18 Pepp. L. Rev. 389 (1991).

CHAPTER 11

DELINQUENCY

SECTION 1. JUVENILE CRIME IN AMERICA

Juvenile crime has held the national attention in recent years. The lion's share of the attention has focused on violent crime (murder and nonnegligent manslaughter, forcible rape, robbery, and aggravated assault). In 1989, the juvenile violent crime arrest rate reached its highest level since the 1960s, the earliest period for which comparable data are available. The rate continued to climb each year until it reached a peak in 1994. The rate rose 62% between 1988 and 1994, a period when the violent crime arrest rate increased for all age groups, including adults. A decline in the juvenile violent crime arrest rate followed. By 1997 the juvenile violent crime arrest rate had fallen to its lowest level in the 1990s, just 7% above the 1989 rate, though still 25% above the 1988 rate. See Howard N. Snyder and Melissa Sickmund, Juvenile Offenders and Victims: 1999 National Report 120, 130 (1999) ("1999 National Report").

The proportion of violent crimes cleared by juvenile arrest shows similar patterns. In 1980 and 1990, 11% of all violent crimes cleared by law enforcement were cleared by juvenile arrest. In the early 1990s, the proportion grew to new levels, reaching a peak of 14% in 1994. By 1997, however, the proportion had dropped back to 12%. Id. at 120.

Examining increases in violent juvenile crime for much of the prior decade, a researcher warned in 1996 that the nation was "in the lull before the crime storm" because the number of males in the crime-prone 14–to–17–year-old cohort will grow by 23 percent by 2005. Fox Butterfield, Experts on Crime Warn Of a "Ticking Time Bomb," N.Y. Times, Jan. 6, 1996, at 6 (quoting John J. DiIulio, Jr.). Some juvenile justice experts predicted that this growth would produce even greater numbers of violent juvenile offenders, dubbed "superpredators" by DiIulio and popularized in the media. John J. DiIulio, Jr., How to Stop the Coming Crime Wave (1996).

Even before the recent declines in the violent juvenile crime rate, a number of observers challenged the empirical basis for such dire predictions. "In 1994, less than one-half of 1% of all juveniles (ages 10–17) in the United States were arrested for a violent offense," criminologist James C. Howell noted. "Only 6% of all juveniles were arrested for any offense. Among all juvenile arrests in 1994, only about 7% were for an FBI Violent Crime Index offense." Juvenile Justice & Youth Violence 48 (1997). "Even these small numbers likely exaggerate the actual number of guilty juveniles represented in arrest statistics," he continues, "because juveniles often are arrested in groups." Id. Noting that in 1994, adults accounted for 86% of the clearances for violent crimes, and for 9 out of 10 clearances for murder, Howell argues that "[v]iolence and murder are overwhelmingly adult crimes." Id. at 49. He also suggests that the adult share of the violent crime rate would likely be even higher except substantial "hidden adult crime," such as spousal and child abuse, goes unreported. Id. at 52–57.

Notes and Questions

1. *The scope of delinquency jurisdiction.* The juvenile court has exclusive original jurisdiction over claims that a child has committed a "delinquent" act, that is, an act that would be a crime if committed by an adult. Delinquency jurisdiction reaches most acts that would be felonies or misdemeanors, though states frequently exclude from that jurisdiction some relatively minor errant behavior, such as traffic violations not involving driving while intoxicated.

To be distinguished from delinquency jurisdiction is the juvenile court's status offense jurisdiction, which Chapter 10 treats. A status offense concerns conduct such as ungovernability, truancy and runaway behavior, which is sanctionable only when committed by a juvenile.

All states also have so-called "transfer" statutes, which define the circumstances in which a juvenile may or must be tried in criminal court as an adult.

2. *The geographical concentration of juvenile homicide.* According to FBI data, 85% of United States counties had no juvenile murderers in 1997. Another 8% of the counties had only one homicide committed by a juvenile. Thus, only 7% of all counties experienced two or more homicides committed by juveniles. Nearly 24% of all homicides committed by juveniles were reported in just five counties, the counties that contain Los Angeles, Chicago, New York City, Philadelphia and Detroit. See 1999 National Report 21.

3. *Juvenile recidivism.* It appears that most juveniles who come in contact with the juvenile justice system do so only once. A study of Philadelphia males who turned 18 in 1976, for example, found that 42% of those with police contacts had only one contact by their eighteenth birthday. A 1988 study of the juvenile court careers of 60,000 youth in Arizona and Utah found that 59% of all youth referred once to juvenile court intake did not return to juvenile court again. See Howard N. Snyder and Melissa Sickmund, Juvenile Offenders and Victims: A National Report 158 (1995) ("1995 National Report").

Recidivism is not necessarily a foolproof measure of persistent criminality because absence of rearrest may simply mean that the offender has learned how to reoffend without being caught, and because rearrest may be a factor of heightened surveillance by police or probation officers arising from the prior arrest. Nevertheless, several studies have found that a relatively small number of chronic offenders commit the bulk of juvenile crime. The 1988 Arizona–Utah study, for example, found that 16% of youth referred to juvenile court had four or more referrals, accounting for 51% of all juvenile court referrals, including a disproportionate share of serious referrals: 70% of motor vehicle thefts, 67% of robberies, 67% of burglaries, 66% of forcible rapes, 64% of murders and 61% of aggravated assaults. Id. at 50.

4. *Defining "juvenile crime."* When juvenile arrest rates rise, the rise might partly reflect changed law enforcement policy, and not merely deteriorating juvenile behavior. Drug arrests provide an example. "Juvenile drug abuse arrest rates nearly doubled between 1992 and 1996. Self-report studies do not indicate a large change in drug use among youth during this period. Since most of the increase in drug abuse arrests was attributable to arrests for marijuana possession, it seems clear that communities became more concerned about marijuana use among youth and that law enforcement, responding to this concern, arrested more juveniles for this offense." 1999 National Report 132.

5. *Females.* Most juvenile offenders are males, but the percentage of females arrested has been steadily increasing. In 1996, males were involved in 77% of the delinquency cases handled by juvenile courts. The delinquency case rate for males was more than three times greater than the rate for females, but the male rate had been four times greater in 1987. (The case rate is the number of cases disposed per 1,000 juveniles in the population.). See Anne L. Stahl et al., Juvenile Court Statistics 1996, at 22–23, 59 (1999).

In 1981, the female juvenile Violent Crime Index arrest rate was 12% of the male rate; by 1997, it was 20% of the male rate. During the same period, the female proportion of juvenile property crime arrests increased from 24% of the male rate to 40%. See 1999 National Report 121, 127. According to one veteran juvenile justice professional, "[t]he system had not anticipated this change in the offending patterns of youth, and is still trying to cope with the influx by developing program specializations and modifying staffing patterns to be more responsive to female offenders." E. Hunter Hurst, III, The Juvenile Court at 100 Years of Age: The Death of Optimism, 49 Juv. & Fam. Ct. J. 39, 51 (1998 No. 4).

6. *Minorities.* Minorities appear overrepresented in the juvenile justice system from arrest forward. See generally Minority Youth in the Juvenile Justice System: A Judicial Response, 41 Juv. & Fam. Ct. J. (No. 3A 1990). In 1997, for example, 15% of the nation's juvenile population was black, but black youth were involved in 26% of juvenile arrests, including 44% of juvenile violent crime arrests and 27% of property crime arrests. See 1999 National Report 115.

The reasons for minority overrepresentation in the juvenile justice system have been a matter of serious study. One group of researchers concludes that while overrepresentation may be partly related to differences in the rates of offenses by black and white youths, these differences alone "cannot explain the level of disparity." The researchers reported that "approximately two-thirds of [existing] studies showed that racial and/or ethnic status did influence decisionmaking within the juvenile justice system." Discriminatory effects occurred at every stage of the judicial process, but they were most pronounced at the earlier stages, at the time of arrests and referrals to juvenile court. See 1995 National Report at 92.

Professor Michael Tonry argues that while "[r]acial bias and stereotyping no doubt play some role" in minority overrepresentation, the principal cause is "the War on Drugs and the movement toward increased use of incarceration." Racial Politics, Racial Disparities, and the War on Crime, 40 Crime and Delinq. 475, 480 (1994). Professor Tonry presents data indicating that blacks are no more likely than whites to use illicit drugs, but concludes that blacks are overrepresented among drug arrestees because "[d]rug arrests are easier to make in socially disorganized inner-city minority areas than in working- or middle-class urban or suburban areas. * * * Because arrests are fungible for purposes of both the individual officer's personnel file and the department's year-to-year statistical comparisons, more easy arrests look better than fewer hard ones." Id. at 485, 487.

7. *Native Americans.* Reservation-based Native American juveniles alleged to have committed delinquent acts are processed in tribal courts for misdemeanors, but in federal courts for enumerated serious felonies defined by Congress as "major crimes." 18 U.S.C. § 1153. If the alleged offense occurs off-reservation, the juvenile is processed in state juvenile courts. Native American youths who live off-reservation are also processed in state juvenile courts. See H. Ted Rubin, The Nature of the Court Today, in 6 The Future of Children 40, 45 (Winter 1996).

8. *Poverty.* A generation ago, the Katzenbach Commission found it "inescapable that juvenile delinquency is directly related to conditions bred by poverty." The Commission concluded that "the most promising and so the most important method of dealing with crime is by preventing it–by ameliorating the conditions of life that drive people to commit crimes and that undermine the restraining rules and institutions erected by society against antisocial conduct." President's Commission on Law Enforcement and Administration of Justice: The Challenge of Crime in a Free Society 57, 58 (1967).

In 1966, a commentator advanced an institutional reason why poor children appear overrepresented on delinquency dockets: "The upper and middle classes show surprising agility in keeping their delinquent children out of the court. In some cases we can be sure that a petition has not been filed against an offending middle-class youngster because restitution has been supplied to the victim of the child's misconduct. In other cases, the upper and middle-class youths have been shielded against juvenile court adjudications by their parents' ability to provide privately arranged corrective treatment. After an adjudication, a person of means can often arrange for the use of private facilities not available to the poor." Monrad G. Paulsen, Juvenile Courts, Family Courts, and the Poor Man, 54 Calif. L. Rev. 694, 696 (1966).

9. *The media's role.* Recent public alarm at violent juvenile crime has produced much legislation designed to "crack down" on juvenile offenders.

Professor Franklin E. Zimring argues that "talk of a 'coming storm' creates a riskless environment for getting tough in advance of the future threat. If the crime rate rises, the prediction has been validated. If the crime rate does not rise, the policies that the alarmists put in place can be credited with avoiding the bloodbath. The predication cannot be falsified, currently or ever." Franklin E. Zimring, American Youth Violence 63 (1988).

Some observers argue that when comparing increases in juvenile crime and adult crime, the media often exaggerate the former. Consider, for example, the "tyranny of small numbers":

> * * * Of the 100 violent crimes committed in 1988 in a small town, assume that juveniles were responsible for 10, and adults for 90. If the number of juvenile crimes increased 50%, juveniles would be committing 15 (or 5 more) violent crimes in 1992. A 20% increase in adult violent crimes would mean that adults were committing 108 (or 18 more) violent crimes in 1992. If each crime resulted in an arrest, the percentage increase in juvenile arrests would be more than double the adult increase (50% versus 20%). However, nearly 80% of the increase in violent crime (18 of the 23 additional violent crimes) would have been committed by adults. Large percentage increases can yield relatively small overall changes. Juvenile arrests represent a relatively small fraction of the total; consequently, a large percentage increase in juvenile arrests does not necessarily translate into a large contribution to overall crime growth.

1995 National Report at 110. Howell argues that the "tyranny of small numbers" contributes to public misperceptions and enables the media to make juveniles "the scapegoat for extremely high levels of violence in this country." Howell, supra at 50.

10. *Gangs*. The nation's youth gang problem affects communities of all sizes. According to a 1996 survey, 31,000 gangs were operating in more than 4800 cities. The gangs had more than 846,000 members, half of whom were under eighteen. The survey data showed that "[t]he youth gang problem in this country is substantial and affects communities of all sizes." National Youth Gang Center, 1996 Nat'l Youth Gang Survey 45 (OJJDP 1999). "[S]elf-report studies indicate that youth gang members are responsible for a disproportionate share of all offenses, violent and nonviolent." 1999 National Report at 79.

11. *Public opinion*. The debate about juvenile crime reflects widely divergent opinions about its causes and effects. Consider these four contributions to the public discourse:

(a) "The victim of violence is just as ravaged by a victimizer who is 13 as one who is 30." Rita Kramer, New York's Juvenile–Thug Mill, N.Y. Times, July 10, 1989, at A17.

(b) "I am fed up with my tax dollars being used to send these little hoodlums through rehabilitation programs that seldom work. Juveniles are coddled by the legal system. They know right from wrong even as toddlers, and should be punished the same as adults if they commit adult crimes. * * * I am tired of hearing that I should be doing my part in cleaning up society to protect children that aren't even mine. * * * Force these little criminals to take responsibility for their own actions, and get this monkey of a juvenile system off the taxpayers' backs! The bleeding-heart socialists will insist that we should protect our children. Excuse me! It should be the parents that protect the children—not society!" Ariz. Republic, Mar. 3, 1996, at H5 (letter to the editor).

(c) "Juvenile crime is closely tied to youth poverty and the growing opportunity gap between wealthier, older people and destitute, younger people. Of California's fifty-eight counties, thirty-one with a total of 2.5 million people recorded zero teenage murders in 1993. Central Los Angeles, which has roughly the same number of people, reported more than 200 teen murders. In the thirty-one counties free of teenage killers, the same blood-soaked media and rock and rap music are readily available (more, since white suburban families over-subscribe to cable TV), and guns are easy to obtain." Mike Males and Faye Docuyanan, Giving Up on the Young, The Progressive, Feb. 1996, at 24.

(d) "Most Americans * * * grow up in settings where they are taught right from wrong * * *. Most of us were blessed to be born to loving and responsible parents or guardians * * *. And most of us were lucky enough to have other adults in our lives (teachers, coaches, clergy) who reinforced the moral lessons that we learned at home * * *. But some Americans grow up in moral poverty * * * in the virtual absence of people who teach morality by their own everyday example and who insist that you follow suit. * * * Most predatory street criminals–black and white, adult and juvenile, past and present–have grown up in abject moral poverty." John J. DiIulio, Jr., Moral Poverty, Chicago Tribune, Dec. 15, 1995, at 31.

SECTION 2. THE JUVENILE COURT AS AN INSTITUTION

A. The Juvenile Court's Original Conception

Illinois enacted the first statewide juvenile court act in 1899. The act culminated years of reform efforts, and the ideal of a special court for children spread swiftly throughout the nation. Juvenile courts had been created in twenty-two other states by 1911, and in forty-five other states by 1925. Today every state has a specialized juvenile or family court with exclusive original delinquency jurisdiction.

The 1899 Illinois legislation and its swift nationwide embrace are a matter of historical record, but the impulses that produced the juvenile court remain a source of spirited debate. The prevailing view is that juvenile court legislation climaxed an essentially humanitarian movement that sought to extricate children from the harshness of the adult criminal process and adult punishment. "At common law, * * * [a]ll offenders were processed through the same criminal court system, were bound by the same substantive law, and, absent the greater likelihood of pardon for children, were punished in similar fashion." Andrew Walkover, The Infancy Defense in the New Juvenile Court, 31 UCLA L. Rev. 503, 509 (1984). Children were subject to incarceration with hardened criminals, and to harsh sentences, sometimes including hanging during the colonial period. Reformers sought to substitute rehabilitative treatment for criminal sanction because contemporary scientific thought no longer viewed children as miniature adults, but rather as persons with undeveloped moral and cognitive faculties. The reformers perceived children both as less responsible than adults for antisocial behavior and as more amenable than adults to rehabilitation.

Judge Julian W. Mack, a prominent leader of the juvenile court movement, wrote that the new court's ultimate purpose was "to treat these juvenile offenders, as we deal with the neglected children, as a wise and merciful father handles his own child whose errors are not discovered by the authorities." Julian W. Mack, The Juvenile Court, 23 Harv. L. Rev. 104, 107 (1909). Another early leader wrote that the juvenile court "tear[s] down primitive prejudice, hatred, and hostility toward the lawbreaker in that most hide-bound of all human institutions, the court of law, and * * * attempt[s], as far as possible, to administer justice in the name of truth, love, and understanding." Herbert H. Lou, Juvenile Courts in the United States 2 (1927). Juvenile courts "serve as a fountain of mercy, truth, and justice to our handicapped children." Id. at 220. Sixty years later, the Supreme Court embraced the prevailing view, concluding that the juvenile court movement was driven by "the highest motives and most enlightened impulses." In re Gault, 387 U.S. 1 (1967).

Revisionists, however, have asserted that while many reformers undeniably perceived the juvenile court as a moral imperative, altruism was sometimes tempered by motives that appear less noble today. The revisionists argue that many reformers also perceived the court as a vehicle for imposing traditional agrarian values on an increasingly urban industrialized nation, and particularly for imposing mainstream values on wayward children of the immigrant poor. Early juvenile court acts did not distinguish between delinquency (children's acts that would be punishable as crimes if committed by adults) and other antisocial behavior that today would be status offenses (such as ungovernability and truancy). "The juvenile court movement went beyond a humanitarian concern for the special treatment of adolescents," Professor Anthony M. Platt states. "It was not by accident that the behavior selected for penalizing by the child savers–drinking, begging, roaming the streets, frequenting dance-halls and movies, fighting, sexuality, staying out late at night, and incorrigibility–was primarily attributable to the children of lower-class migrant and immigrant families." Platt concludes that "[t]he child-saving movement had its most direct consequences on the children of the urban poor [and] consolidated the inferior social status and dependency of lower-class youth." Anthony M. Platt, The Child Savers: The Invention of Delinquency 3, 139 (2d ed. 1977).

Historian Lawrence M. Friedman, in turn, has criticized Platt for exaggerating the reformers' class-based impulses and minimizing their child-protective goals. Lawrence M. Friedman, Crime and Punishment in American History 413–17 (1993). Judge Justine Wise Polier similarly lauded the reformers as part of "a comparatively small group who opposed exploitation of adults and children by the robber barons of their day. They supported the rights of workers to organize and were among the first to support legislation to protect women and children in industry." Justice Wise Polier, Prescriptions for Reform: Doing What We Set Out to Do?, in Juvenile Justice: The Progressive Legacy and Current Reforms 216 (LaMar T. Empey ed., 1979).

Regardless of the motives that energized the juvenile court movement throughout the nineteenth century, the court's delinquency jurisdiction was marked by four characteristics that distinguished it from the criminal justice system–individualized rehabilitation and treatment, informal procedure, confidentiality, and separate incapacitation.

1. *Individualized rehabilitation and treatment*

Without necessarily overlooking rehabilitation and treatment of prisoners who will someday be released into the general population, the criminal law imposes sanctions defined primarily by the nature of the act committed. Each crime carries a sanction or sanction range (usually imprisonment, fine or both) prescribed by statute or sentencing guidelines. The court may have discretion to impose a sentence calibrated after considering the defendant's particular condition, but the sentence must remain within the range prescribed according to the nature of the defendant's act.

By contrast, delinquency sanctions were based not on the nature of the act committed, but on the juvenile's condition. Acting in effect as a quasi-welfare agency, the juvenile court held broad discretion to fashion a disposition after examining not only such factors as the juvenile's attitude, school performance, standing in the community, and mental health but also the family's stability and supportiveness.

The aim of such individualized treatment was to rehabilitate the juvenile, much as a benevolent social services provider would. "[I]nstead of asking merely whether a boy or girl has committed a specific offense," Judge Mack wrote in 1909, the juvenile court seeks "to find out what he is, physically, mentally, morally, and then if it learns that he is treading the path that leads to criminality, to take him in charge, not so much to punish as to reform, not to degrade but to uplift, not to crush but to develop, not to make him a criminal but a worthy citizen." 23 Harv. L. Rev. at 107. Another early juvenile court proponent wrote that the court "points away from the slow and dreary processes in criminal jurisprudence to the dawn of a more enlightened day when the state will have for its chief object the reclamation and reform, if possible, of its erring child citizen rather than the exhibition of revenge." Herbert H. Lou, Juvenile Courts in the United States 31 (1927).

A sanction grounded in the delinquent's condition could be more or less severe than the sanction a court could impose on an adult convicted of the same act. In *Gault*, for example, the juvenile court found that that the fifteen-year-old delinquent had made lewd telephone calls to a neighbor. The court sent the boy to a reform school for as long as six years (until he reached majority, unless released earlier); an adult committing the same offense could have received no more than two months' imprisonment or a fine of five to fifty dollars. If young Gault had committed first-degree murder, the juvenile court could have institutionalized him for no more than the same six years, though the criminal court could have sentenced an adult to life imprisonment or worse.

2. *Informal procedure*

Because the aim of delinquency jurisdiction was to rehabilitate rather than punish, informal procedure became the court's hallmark. The 1899 Illinois Juvenile Court Act, for example, provided that on the return of the summons or other process, "or as soon thereafter as may be, the court shall proceed to hear and dispose of the case in a summary manner." 1899 Ill. L. 133. Due process was perceived as a formality impeding rehabilitation because the juvenile court acted "not as an enemy but as a protector, as the ultimate guardian" of the child. "The child who must be brought into court should, of course, be made to know that he is face to face with the power of the state, but he should at the same time, and more emphatically, be made to feel that he is the object of its care and solicitude. The ordinary trappings of the court-room are out of place in such hearings. The judge on a bench, looking down upon the boy standing at the bar, can never evoke a proper sympathetic spirit. Seated at a desk, with the child at his side, where he can on occasion put his arm around his shoulder and draw the lad to him, the judge, while losing none of his judicial dignity, will gain immensely in the effectiveness of his work." Mack, supra, 23 Harv. L. Rev. at 107, 120.

Courts quickly upheld the relaxed procedures that marked delinquency adjudication. The Pennsylvania Supreme Court, for example, held that "[t]o save a child from becoming a criminal, or from continuing in a career of crime, to end in maturer years in public punishment and disgrace, the Legislature surely may provide for the salvation of such a child * * * by bringing it into one of the courts of the state without any process at all." Commonwealth v. Fisher, 62 A. 198, 200 (Pa.1905).

Informal procedure produced a vocabulary laden with euphemisms. The juvenile offender was an alleged "delinquent" who had committed an "act of delinquency," not an accused criminal who had committed a crime. The juvenile was "taken into custody," not arrested; juvenile court proceedings began with a "petition of delinquency," not a complaint, indictment or charge, and with a "summons," not a warrant; the juvenile proceeded to an "initial hearing," not to arraignment; the juvenile might be "held in detention," but was not jailed; if matters proceeded further, the court would conduct a "hearing," not a trial; an "adjudication," a "finding of involvement" or a "finding of delinquency" might follow, not a conviction; the court would enter a "disposition," not an order of conviction or acquittal; the juvenile might be "placed" in a "training school," "reformatory," or "group home," not convicted and sent to a prison; "aftercare," not parole, might follow. The sanitized vocabulary persisted despite criticism that it diminished the general deterrence effect of delinquency determinations. See, e.g., John H. Wigmore, Juvenile Court vs. Criminal Court, 21 U. Ill. L. Rev. 375, 377 (1927).

The juvenile court's procedural informality left little place for lawyers, and created a role for non-lawyer judges. "Lawyers were unnecessary–adversary tactics were out of place, for the mutual aim of all was not to contest or object but to determine the treatment plan best for the child. That plan was to be devised by the increasingly popular psychologists and psychiatrists; delinquency was thought of almost as a disease, to be diagnosed by specialists and the patient kindly but firmly dosed. Even the judicial role began to attract extralegal specialists, men and women aware of and interested in the social and scientific developments of the day * * *." President's Commission on Law Enforcement and Administration of Justice, Task Force Report: Juvenile Delinquency and Youth Crime 3 (1967). In 1967, *Gault* reported that a quarter of all juvenile court judges had no law school training. 387 U.S. at 14 n.14.

3. *Confidentiality*

To enhance prospects for treatment and rehabilitation, juvenile court proceedings were closed to the public except in rare circumstances. Juvenile court records and dispositions were sealed or expunged to protect the juvenile's privacy, and juvenile court adjudications did not leave the juvenile with a criminal record. Delinquency jurisdiction sought "[t]o get away from the notion that the child is to be dealt with as a criminal; to save it from the brand of criminality, the brand that sticks to it for life; to take it in hand and * * * to protect it from the stigma." Mack, supra, 23 Harv. L. Rev. at 109.

4. *Separate incapacitation*

Juvenile court reformers sought to segregate confined delinquents from hardened adult criminals. The institutions to which juvenile courts sent delinquents before or after adjudication were frequently as harsh as adult prisons, but the reformers believed the ultimate success of treatment and rehabilitation depended on protecting children from adult criminal influences and from assaults by adult convicts. When children and adults were incarcerated together, "instead of the state's training its bad boys so as to make of them decent citizens, it permitted them to become the outlaws and outcasts of society; it criminalized them by the very methods that it used in dealing with them." Mack, supra, 23 Harv. L. Rev. at 107.

Notes and Questions

1. *The juvenile court's purposes today.* The four characteristics that marked the juvenile court's traditional rehabilitative model have undergone strain in the past few decades as the public has grown increasingly impatient with juvenile crime, particularly violent juvenile crime. Public pressure has led state legislatures to depart from these characteristics and to move toward a model that increasingly resembles the adult criminal process.

The federal Office of Juvenile Justice and Delinquency Prevention now identifies three objectives of an effective juvenile justice system: to "(1) hold the juvenile offender accountable; (2) enable the juvenile to become a capable, productive, and responsible citizen; and (3) ensure the safety of the community." Shay Bilchik, A Juvenile Justice System for the 21st Century, 44 Crime and Delinq. 89, 89–90 (1998). The National Council of Juvenile and Family Court Judges states that "the principal purpose of the juvenile justice court system is to protect the public," and that "[t]o the extent public safety will permit, the primary goal of the juvenile court should be rehabilitation." According to the National Council, "[r]ehabilitation has been remarkably successful for most juvenile offenders. It has not been successful for the small number of chronic and serious offenders. For them, strict accountability appears necessary." The Juvenile Court and Serious Offenders: 38 Recommendations, Juv. & Fam. Ct. J. 1, 9 (Summer 1984).

Personal accountability and public safety concerns now coexist uneasily with (and sometimes eclipse) the juvenile court's traditional rehabilitative model. The uneasy coexistence is evident in both legislation and decisional law. In recent years, several states have amended their juvenile codes' general purpose provisions to stress juvenile accountability and community protection. As amended in 1997, for example, New Hampshire's code recites the need "to protect and improve the public safety by creating a system of juvenile justice that will appropriately sanction juveniles who violate the law. * * * [W]hile holding paramount the public safety, the juvenile justice system shall take into consideration the best interests of the juvenile in providing appropriate treatment to reduce the rate of recidivism in the juvenile justice system and to assist the juvenile in becoming a productive member of society." N.H. Rev. Stat. Ann. § 19–2–102.

Several state legislatures have also either renamed their juvenile justice agencies or removed juvenile justice authority from the state social welfare agency. Wisconsin, for example, has shifted delinquency programs from the Department of Health and Social Services to the Department of Corrections. Courts also struggle to balance public safety concerns and rehabilitation. See, e.g., State ex rel. D.D.H. v. Dostert, 269 S.E.2d 401, 415–16 (W.Va.1980) ("We acknowledge [that] our treatment looks a lot like punishment * * * [and] treatment is often disguised punishment.").

2. *A relic?* Critics perceive the juvenile court's rehabilitative model as a relic of a bygone era unsuited for contemporary circumstances. As one writer put it, the juvenile court "was developed with truants, vandals and petty thieves in mind. But this model is not appropriate for the violent juvenile offender of today. Detaining a rapist or murderer in a juvenile facility until the age of 18 or 21 isn't even a slap on the hand. If a juvenile is accused of murdering, raping or assaulting someone with a deadly weapon, the suspect should automatically be sent to adult criminal court." Linda J. Collier, Adult Crime, Adult Time, Wash. Post, Mar. 29, 1998, at C1.

3. *References.* James C. Howell, Juvenile Justice & Youth Violence 3–23 (1997); Robert M. Mennel, Thorns & Thistles: Juvenile Delinquency in the United States, 1825–1940 (1973); Ellen Ryerson, The Best–Laid Plans: America's Juvenile Court Experiment (1978); Steven L. Schlossman, Love and the American Delinquent: The Theory and Practice of "Progressive" Juvenile Justice, 1825–1920 (1977); Merril Sobie, The Creation of Juvenile Justice: A History of New York's Children's Laws (1987); John R. Sutton, Stubborn Children: Controlling Delinquency in the United States, 1640–1981

(1988); Sanford J. Fox, The Early History of the Court, 6 The Future of Children 29 (Winter 1996); Sanford J. Fox, Juvenile Justice Reform: An Historical Perspective, 22 Stan. L. Rev. 1187 (1970); Barry Krisberg and James F. Austin, Reinventing Juvenile Justice 8–52 (1993).

B. *The Juvenile Court's Contemporary Operation*

"Fragmented and lacking resources, [juvenile and family courts] are places in which only relatively few, exceptionally dedicated, legal professionals wish to spend their careers." Catherine J. Ross, The Failure of Fragmentation: The Promise of a System of Unified Family Courts, 32 Fam. L.Q. 3, 3 (1998). "On a scale of one to ten the United States Supreme Court would undoubtedly be scored ten in prestige and importance by lawyers and judges. Family courts would barely rate one. * * * Prosecutors and public defenders usually consider assignment to family court an exile in purgatory, as do many judges." Lois G. Forer, Money and Justice: Who Owns the Courts? 132–33 (1984).

"Less time is allocated to the trial of children than any American legal proceeding except perhaps traffic court." Id. at 132. In 1967, the Katzenbach Commission found that juvenile court hearings "often turn out to be little more than attenuated interviews of 10 to 15 minutes' duration." President's Commission on Law Enforcement and Administration of Justice: The Challenge of Crime in a Free Society 80 (1967). Little had changed fifteen years later, when a study of one northern city found that the median delinquency hearing lasted only fifteen minutes. See James D. Walter and Susan A. Ostrander, An Observational Study of a Juvenile Court, 33 Juv. & Fam. Ct. J. 53, 57 (1982).

In many jurisdictions, the situation is not much different today. In 1998, the President of the American Bar Association reported that "[i]n many cities an overworked juvenile court judge's average disposal rate for a case is less than 10 minutes. Sometimes the juvenile and family members have not even met their lawyer before they appear in court." Jerome J. Shestack, What About Juvenile Justice?, A.B.A.J. 8 (May 1998). In 1992, it was reported that the Baltimore (Md.) City Juvenile Court conducted more than a thousand hearings a week, and that "[m]oving cases through the gridlocked court is often more important than dispensing justice." Michael Riley, Corridors of Agony, Time, Jan. 27, 1992, at 51. In Chicago, home of the nation's first juvenile court, juvenile court judges in 1996 heard an average of sixty cases a day, reportedly spending an average of only six minutes on each case. See Fox Butterfield, With Juvenile Courts in Chaos, Critics Propose Scrapping Them, N.Y. Times, July 21, 1997, at A1. A 1997 study found that in the New York City Family Court, forty-one judges heard more than 225,000 cases a year, resulting in "assembly-line justice" with each judge hearing approximately 5,500 cases. Fund For Modern Courts, The Good, the Bad and the Ugly of the New York City Family Court 6, 9 (Sept. 1997). In Los Angeles, the juvenile court docket is "swollen by a workload many times greater than judges in adult court deign to tolerate–fifty or sixty cases a day is not unusual," with each child getting only a four- to five-minute hearing. Edward Humes, No Matter How Loud I Shout: A Year in the Life of Juvenile Court 36, 78–79 (1996).

SECTION 3. THE CONTOURS OF DELINQUENCY

INTRODUCTORY PROBLEM

Fourth-grader Jeremy Richards has had significant difficulty adjusting to his new school and the teasing of his new classmates. One afternoon, his teacher reprimands him for disruptive behavior in the hallway during recess. In a fit of anger, Jeremy hits the teacher and begins wrestling with her. The teacher, who had a preexisting heart condition, collapses and dies of cardiac arrest shortly after the scuffle.[a] May nine-year-old Jeremy be adjudicated a delinquent in juvenile court for conduct that would constitute manslaughter if committed by an adult? May Jeremy be charged as an adult and tried for manslaughter in criminal court?

A. The Infancy Defense

GAMMONS v. BERLAT

Supreme Court of Arizona, 1985.
696 P.2d 700.

HOLOHAN, CHIEF JUSTICE.

The petitioner, a thirteen year old, was arrested on February 17, 1984 for sexual abuse and sexual conduct with a minor. He was charged by a petition filed in juvenile court with delinquency for his alleged act in the sexual abuse and sexual conduct incident. During trial review, petitioner denied the allegations of the petition and, through counsel, requested a hearing to determine his legal capacity to understand the wrongfulness of his conduct pursuant to A.R.S. § 13–501.[1] * * *

The issue presented is whether the provisions of A.R.S. § 13–501 in the criminal code are applicable to delinquency proceedings in juvenile court. The State urges us to restrict the operation of A.R.S. § 13–501 to those instances where children are tried in adult criminal proceedings following transfer from juvenile court. The State's contention is that the delinquency adjudication provisions of the juvenile code create an independent procedure for the disposition of juvenile offenders which is separate from adult criminal prosecution and which thereby renders A.R.S. § 13–501 inapplicable. The petitioner argues that the presumption of incapacity for children under fourteen years of age is a safeguard

---

a. See Teacher's Death is Ruled a Homicide: Hearing Set For Boy, 9, Who Tussled With Her, St. Louis Post–Dispatch, Oct. 18, 1995, at 1A.

1. A.R.S. § 13–501 provides:

A person less than fourteen years old at the time of the conduct charged is not criminally responsible in the absence of clear proof that at the time of committing the conduct charged the person knew it was wrong.

for all children accused of criminal behavior whether charged in an adult criminal proceeding or in juvenile court.

A.R.S. § 13–501 codifies a variant of the common law infancy defense to criminal prosecution. * * * The common law infancy defense precluded criminal prosecution for children under the age of seven, and created a rebuttable presumption of incapacity for children seven to fourteen on the ground that "[c]ommon law criminal culpability was based on both an assumption of capacity to know wrongfulness and proof of the specific *mens rea* required to commit a crime . . . [and] children are less capable than adults of understanding wrongfulness or of possessing the intent required to legitimately impose punishment." Arizona's codified incapacity provision modifies the common law in that it does not bar criminal adjudication of children under seven; rather it extends the rebuttable presumption to all youth under fourteen.

The juvenile code defines a "delinquent act" as "an act by a child, which if committed by an adult would be a criminal offense. . . . " * * * The definition of "delinquent act" refers to criminal provisions to establish which acts constitute delinquent conduct. Capacity to understand the wrongfulness of one's behavior is a prerequisite to criminal liability under the criminal code when the age of the offender is less than fourteen years. A.R.S. § 13–501. Does the definition of delinquent act in the juvenile code include the capacity limitation of the criminal code?

* * *

Those jurisdictions rejecting a capacity requirement in juvenile delinquency proceedings have * * * relied on the rationale that a delinquency adjudication does not result in the imposition of criminal sanctions; rather the purpose of a delinquency proceeding is rehabilitative. The approach of the Supreme Court of Rhode Island is representative of those jurisdictions rejecting a capacity requirement:

> Once one accepts the principle that a finding of delinquency or waywardness in a juvenile proceeding is not the equivalent of a finding that the juvenile has committed a crime, there is no necessity of a finding that the juvenile had such maturity that he or she knew what he or she was doing was wrong. A juvenile is delinquent or wayward, not because the juvenile has committed a crime, but because the juvenile has committed an act that would be a crime if committed by a person not a juvenile and because the juvenile requires "such care, guidance and control * * * as will serve the child's welfare and the best interests of the state * * *."

* * *

We believe that the authorities rejecting application of criminal code capacity requirements to juvenile proceedings are more persuasive than those which take the opposite view. Ultimately the decision of this court rests on the determination of the legislative intent in enacting the juvenile code and the statute at issue.

* * *

The legislature has provided in the juvenile code a specific method of dealing with children who have committed crimes. We note that the juvenile code has its own capacity provision. A child under the age of eight years who is found to have committed an act that would result in adjudication as a delinquent is a "dependent child," not a delinquent. The juvenile code also makes special provisions for the developmentally disabled when such children have been adjudicated delinquent. The juvenile code has its own separate and distinct provisions for dealing with mentally ill children in the custody of the juvenile court. These various provisions in the juvenile code indicate that the legislature intended to provide a different standard to be applied in juvenile cases, and we conclude that the legislature did not intend for the provisions of A.R.S. § 13–501 to apply to juvenile proceedings. The relief sought by petitioner is denied.

GORDON, V.C.J., and HAYS and CAMERON, JJ., concur.

FELDMAN, JUSTICE, concurring in part and dissenting in part.

I agree that a juvenile may be subjected to the jurisdiction of the juvenile court for treatment or rehabilitation upon a showing that he has committed an act which, if committed by an adult, would be a public offense. The problem with the majority opinion, however, is that it assumes that the delinquency adjudication sought in this case "does not result in the imposition of criminal sanctions ..." This view is quite incorrect. A.R.S. § 8–241 provides that if the court finds a child "delinquent," it may make any one of a variety of placements, all of them "subject to the supervision of a probation department," or may "award" the child "to the department of corrections without further directions as to placement by that department." If "awarded" to the department of corrections, the child remains under its control until discharge or until the child's eighteenth birthday.

It is true that * * * the "delinquent" child may not be kept in an institution "used primarily for the execution of sentences of persons convicted of a crime." Thus, the institution is not called a prison, and may have a more palatable label—such as industrial school, juvenile institution, receiving home, or the like. Nevertheless, commitment to the department of corrections results in a type of confinement and is a criminal sanction. In *Gault*, the United States Supreme Court held that the possible imposition of criminal sanctions, however euphemistically titled, requires the observance of certain procedural safeguards necessary to preserve due process. "Under our Constitution, the condition of being a boy does not justify a kangaroo court." Nor should the condition of being a child justify the imposition of criminal sanctions absent proof that a crime was committed.

The facts of the case at bench well illustrate the situation. The juvenile who is to receive "the benefit" of "treatment" and "rehabilitation" is a 13 year old boy with a mental age of 9 or 10. He will be required to stand trial and possibly receive criminal punishment for having consensual sexual relations with a 15 year old girl. No adult could be convicted of such a public offense without proof of the requisite mental capacity—that he knew the nature and quality of his act, and knew that it was wrong. The legislature has provided that where a person is less than 14 years of age at the time of the criminal conduct charged, the State must submit "clear proof that at the time of committing the conduct charged the person knew it was wrong." A.R.S. § 13–501. To try, convict, and punish this retarded 13 year old for "sexual conduct with a minor" absent proof of his capacity to know and understand the wrongfulness of that conduct, is to invoke and apply the criminal aspects of the juvenile justice system without due process of law. If the State were to seek prosecution of this minor in adult court, it would have to meet the burden of proof imposed by § 13–501.[1] Why should it be able to evade that requirement by "prosecution" in juvenile court? I believe that it cannot.

This is not to say that the State is without power or that it must turn such children loose without supervision or control. The State may differentiate between delinquent, dependent, and incorrigible children and may, where necessary, require that a dependent child undergo custodial treatment. If the present statutes are insufficient for that purpose, they can be amended. What the State cannot do is impose criminal sanctions upon a juvenile under the guise of treatment or rehabilitation, when confinement and incarceration is the likely or possible result. Allowing criminal prosecution and punishment without proof of *mens rea* by the simple expedient of calling such prosecution "civil" or "rehabilitative" confers too much dignity on juvenile court euphemisms. It is only to the love-struck poet that stone walls do not a prison make, nor iron bars a cage. To the rest of mankind, to be "awarded" to the department of corrections and put behind stone walls or iron bars is to be in prison, even if it is called "juvenile rehabilitation."

> So wide a gulf between the State's treatment of the adult and of the child requires a bridge sturdier than mere verbiage, and reasons more persuasive than cliche can provide.

I dissent.

Notes and Questions

1. How did the majority's view of juvenile court sanctions differ from the dissenter's view? Which side had the better argument?

---

1. The maximum sentence possible for this class 6 felony would be 18 months. Confined as a juvenile, however, this 13 year old may be incarcerated for up to 5 years at the discretion of the department of corrections.

2. *Later amendment.* In 1996, the Arizona legislature enacted Article 8 of the Children's Code. Ariz. Rev. Stat. § 8–291.01 provides that "[a] juvenile shall not participate in a delinquency, incorrigibility or criminal proceeding if the court determines that the juvenile is incompetent to proceed." "Incompetent" means "a juvenile who does not have sufficient present ability to consult with the juvenile's lawyer with a reasonable degree of rational understanding or who does not have a rational and factual understanding of the proceedings against the juvenile." Id. § 8–291. A "juvenile" is a person under eighteen at the time the competency issue is raised. Section 13–501 of the Criminal Code now contains special provisions concerning 15–17-year-old felony defendants in criminal court.

3. *The minimum age of delinquency jurisdiction.* As *Gammons* indicates, a young child's infancy defense may depend on the juvenile court's perception of the child's criminal intent and mens rea. About fifteen states, however, have also legislated a minimum age of delinquency jurisdiction. The age is ten in most of these states. See, e.g., Colo. Rev. Stat. § 19–2–104(1)(a).

In a state where children under, say, ten are beyond the court's delinquency jurisdiction, does the court have any way to treat a six-year-old who commits an act that would be a crime if committed by an adult? In a state where such children remain within delinquency jurisdiction but are likely to assert the infancy defense, does the court have any alternative to contorting that defense to retain jurisdiction?

In 1999, an Illinois commission recommended enactment of a ten-year-old minimum age for delinquency jurisdiction. The Commission also recommended enactment of a "civil prosecution" process for children younger than ten (and for older children shown on a case-by-case basis to be incompetent to stand trial in the juvenile justice or criminal justice systems). Operating within the juvenile justice system, the proposed civil process would focus on obtaining court-ordered and monitored treatment for the child and the family. The Commission concluded that the proposed process would "fill the existing void in the law that leaves the State with no means by which it can obtain court ordered and monitored treatment and services for a particularly vulnerable group of children." The child's incompetency would not thwart jurisdiction because the process would be civil rather than criminal. See Interim Report, State's Attorney's Commission on Juvenile Competency (Cook County, Ill. 1999).

4. *The maximum age of delinquency jurisdiction.* All states have enacted statutes defining the maximum age of delinquency jurisdiction. In most states the juvenile court has such jurisdiction over persons who were under eighteen at the time of the offense, arrest, or referral to court. The maximum age is sixteen in ten states and fifteen in three states (Connecticut, New York and North Carolina). See Howard N. Snyder and Melissa Sickmund, Juvenile Offenders and Victims: 1999 National Report 93 (1999).

Many states have statutory exceptions to the maximum age, which accelerate the criminal court's exclusive original jurisdiction. The exceptions are related to the minor's age, alleged offense, and court history. In some states, a combination of the youth's age, offense and court history place the minor under the original jurisdiction of both the juvenile court and the criminal court; the prosecutor has authority to determine which court initially handles the case. Id.

5. *Determining capacity*. How does the court determine whether the juvenile knew the wrongfulness of the conduct? In State v. J.P.S., 954 P.2d 894, 896–97 (Wash.1997), the court found these factors relevant: "(1) the nature of the crime; (2) the child's age and maturity; (3) whether the child showed a desire for secrecy; (4) whether the child admonished the victim not to tell; (5) prior conduct similar to that charged; (6) any consequences that attached to the conduct; and (7) acknowledgment that the behavior was wrong and could lead to detention."

Do factors such as these make sense with particularly young children? "[M]any psychiatric professionals say no young child can truly understand an adversarial proceeding, or appreciate the consequences of a criminal act. Children will say they know what they did was wrong, * * * [b]ut when an evaluator asks a child, 'How do you think the other person felt?' the child will respond with, 'What do you mean?' * * * 'They can't make that leap * * *. They do not have deductive or inductive reasoning skills.' " See Janan Hanna, Kids' "Competence" a Tender Issue For Courts, Chicago Tribune, Aug. 30, 1998, at 1C (quoting Dr. Carl Bell, professor of psychiatry at the University of Illinois at Chicago).

6. *Strategic considerations*. Some defense counsel report that they rarely place the juvenile's competency in question because an incompetency finding may make things worse, rather than better, for the client. According to one legal aid counsel, "If a young person is found incompetent, he will be put in state custody and will lose significant control over his life," perhaps through foster placement, psychiatric commitment or court monitoring. See Janan Hanna, supra, at 1C. Delinquency sanctions normally do not include removal from the home.

B. The Insanity Defense

CHATMAN v. COMMONWEALTH

Court of Appeals of Virginia, 1999.
518 S.E.2d 847.

COLE, SENIOR JUDGE.

* * *

Appellant and Lamont Waller were students in a public school special education program in Greensville County. Both appellant and Waller were transported to their homes after school in the same school station wagon.

On January 22, 1997, appellant and Waller exchanged angry words at school. After school, both appellant and Waller rode home in the school station wagon. The vehicle stopped at appellant's home. Appellant got out of the vehicle. Although he had been warned not to do so, Waller got out of the station wagon to fight appellant. Appellant pulled out a knife and cut Waller in the shoulder. The two exchanged more blows with their fists. Eventually, Waller got back into the station wagon, which left the scene. Waller later received medical treatment for his injury. Appellant was thirteen years old at the time of the incident.

* * * [A]ppellant filed a motion for a psychiatric evaluation to determine his sanity at the time of the offense. In his brief in support of his motion, appellant asserted that, on the day of the offense, Dr. C.R. Amara found appellant to have homicidal ideations requiring inpatient psychiatric treatment. Appellant was diagnosed with a schizophrenic disorder two days after the incident involving Waller. The evaluator also concluded that appellant exhibited inappropriately aggressive and violent behavior which appeared to be a function of serious psychiatric difficulties. The circuit court denied appellant's motion, citing the opportunities for mental health treatment provided under Virginia law in the event appellant was found to be delinquent. [Appellant was found delinquent and was committed to the Department of Juvenile Justice.].

ANALYSIS

* * *

The Juvenile and Domestic Relations District Court Law does not expressly provide for or prohibit an insanity defense * * *.

* * * To establish an insanity defense in Virginia, the accused must show that "he did not know the difference between right and wrong or that he did not understand the nature and consequences of his acts." "The defendant must prove to the satisfaction of the [trier of fact] that he was insane at the time of the offense. He has the burden of affirmatively raising the issue of insanity and proving his mental disease or defect by a preponderance of the evidence."

* * *

A defendant found not guilty by reason of insanity is acquitted of the charged offense but is subject to the disposition defined by Virginia statutes. [ed—The acquittee is placed in the temporary custody of the appropriate state agency for determination whether he or she may be released with or without conditions or requires commitment in a mental health facility. The statutes further provide for periodic hearings to determine whether the acquittee's future condition warrants release or continued commitment.]

Courts charged with the duty of adjudicating juveniles "are to provide measures of guidance and rehabilitation for the child and protection for society, not to fix criminal responsibility, guilt and punishment. The State is parens patriae rather than prosecuting attorney and judge." Kent v. United States, 383 U.S. 541, 555–56 (1966).

Despite this noble objective, an adjudication of delinquency has wide and serious ramifications. For instance, an adjudication of delinquency may be considered in the preparation of the accused's future adult sentencing guideline reports. Furthermore,

[i]rrespective of what we call the juvenile procedure, and no matter how benign and well intended the judge who administers the system, the juvenile procedures, to some degree at least, smack of "crime and punishment." ... Despite all protestations to the contrary, the adjudication of delinquency carries with it a social stigma.

The Supreme Court of Virginia has recognized that an adjudication of delinquency

is a serious reflection upon [a juvenile's] ... character and habits. The stain against him is not removed merely because the statute says no judgment in this particular proceeding shall be deemed a conviction for crime or so considered. The stigma of conviction will reflect upon him for life. It hurts his self-respect. It may, at some inopportune, unfortunate moment, rear its ugly head to destroy his opportunity for advancement, and blast his ambition to build up a character and reputation entitling him to the esteem and respect of his fellow man.

In *In re Gault* (1967), the United States Supreme Court * * * found that [delinquency] proceedings "must measure up to the essentials of due process and fair treatment" as required by the Due Process Clause of the Fourteenth Amendment. * * *

A number of states have found the right to assert an insanity defense to be an essential of "due process and fair treatment" that must be provided to a juvenile at the adjudicatory stage of the proceeding. * * *

We find no reasonable basis for concluding that an insanity defense is unavailable to a juvenile at a proceeding to adjudicate him or her delinquent as it would be to an adult defendant in a criminal trial. We agree that the right to assert an insanity defense is an essential of "due process and fair treatment" which is required at a juvenile delinquency adjudication.

* * *

Notes and Questions

1. *Questions about* Chatman. (a) How did the court of appeals' view of juvenile court sanctions differ from the lower court's view? Which court had the better argument?,

(b) What will happen to Chatman if he prevails on his insanity defense?,

(c) What should defense counsel do if they believe that needed psychiatric care will be available in a mental health facility if the juvenile is found insane, but will not necessarily be available in a secure correctional facility if the juvenile is found delinquent?,

(d) Might defense counsel have reasons to choose not to interpose an insanity defense on behalf of an alleged delinquent whose mental condition at the time of the offense might qualify for the defense?

2. Some state juvenile codes or rules permit invocation of the insanity defense in delinquency proceedings. See, e.g., Fla. R. Juv. Proc. R. 8.095. Where the code and rules are silent (as in Virginia), the matter turns on constitutional entitlement. The decisions are not unanimous on the constitutional question. Contrast *Chatman*, for example, with In re C.W.M., 407 A.2d 617 (D.C.1979), which rejected the contention that the alleged delinquent had a due process right to raise an insanity defense at the adjudicatory hearing: "[U]nlike a criminal trial a juvenile factfinding hearing does not result in a determination of criminal responsibility. Nor is the succeeding dispositional hearing intended to result in the imposition of any penal sanction on the child." Id. at 622. *C.W.M.* concluded that because the court at the dispositional hearing must consider the delinquent's mental condition and must order the necessary mental health treatment, the insanity defense was not an essential of fairness required by due process at the adjudicatory hearing.

C. Transfer: The "Adultification" of Juvenile Crime

Amid rising juvenile crime rates in recent years, public pressure has produced legislation enabling more and more juveniles to be sent to criminal court for trial as adults. Transfer decisions have been called "juvenile justice's hardest 'hard cases.' " Franklin E. Zimring, The Treatment of Hard Cases in American Juvenile Justice: In Defense of Discretionary Waiver, 5 Notre Dame J. L. Ethics & Pub. Pol'y 267, 268 (1991). After Professor Redding's article surveys state transfer laws, *Mitchell* illustrates the high stakes involved when deciding whether to proceed by delinquency adjudication or to prosecute a juvenile as an adult. Where the juvenile is processed as a delinquent, the juvenile justice system may impose confinement or other sanction for a few years, usually until majority or shortly thereafter. Transfer exposed Eric Mitchell to sanctions far graver and a future far different than what he would have faced if the case had remained in juvenile court.

As you read *Mitchell*, you should prepare for Problem 11–1 (page 1063), which will ask how you would have decided if you were the trial judge hearing the prosecutor's transfer motion, or if you were a member of the panel hearing the appeal from the order referring the 15-year-old juvenile to criminal court.

RICHARD E. REDDING, JUVENILES TRANSFERRED TO CRIMINAL COURT: LEGAL REFORM PROPOSALS BASED ON SOCIAL SCIENCE RESEARCH

1997 Utah L. Rev. 709, 711–21.

* * *

The public is demanding a "get tough" approach to the increase in juvenile crime, with seventy-three percent of respondents in a 1993 Gallup poll in favor of trying violent juveniles as adults. Some agree with Los Angeles County District Attorney Gil Garcetti that " '[w]e need to throw out our entire juvenile justice system.' " There is a growing consensus that: (1) juvenile offenders are responsible for their actions and should be punished; (2) many juvenile offenders are beyond rehabilitation; (3) rehabilitation does not work, (4) greater deterrence is needed, and (5) that violent juveniles must be incarcerated into adulthood. The juvenile codes of twenty-eight states now emphasize punishment. The new consensus has returned the juvenile justice system to its original purpose of providing rehabilitation for minor offenders while punishing serious offenders in the criminal justice system. Only minor offenses were handled in the first juvenile court, established in 1899. Over time, the juvenile courts became courts of original jurisdiction for all juveniles below the age of majority, regardless of the offense. The presumption was that the child should be tried in juvenile court, and only after a full due process hearing could the judge order that the child be transferred for prosecution in adult court.

Politicians and legislatures are responding to public sentiment about the juvenile crime problem. * * * Most states have revised their transfer statutes to make it easier to transfer, waive, refer, remand, or certify (collectively hereafter "transfer") juveniles for trial and sentencing in adult court. States have reduced the minimum age for transfer, expanded the list of transferable offenses, or made transfer easier by eliminating some of the factors that must be considered before transferring. For example, many states no longer require that to be transferred, the juvenile must first be found "unamenable to treatment" (i.e., not rehabilitatable) in the juvenile system. Virtually all states have lowered the minimum age for transfer to fourteen or younger, and at least five states now allow children of any age to be transferred for any crime. Many states now require transfer for juveniles who commit violent felonies such as murder, rape, or armed robbery. * * *

* * *

Every state, and the District of Columbia, has a transfer statute. There are three types of transfer laws: automatic (also called legislative), judicial-discretionary, and prosecutorial-discretionary. "Automatic" transfer laws require transfer for enumerated offenses if certain statutory requirements are met. The offenses generally include violent felonies such as murder, manslaughter, kidnaping, rape, aggravated assault, arson, and crimes committed with a firearm. Some states also require transfer for certain serious drug offenses, and other states for felonies committed in furtherance of gang activities. Typically, juveniles above a certain age who commit specified crimes are automatically transferred. Sometimes different age cutoffs are specified, with younger children automatically transferred only for the most serious felonies. For instance, in Maryland sixteen-year-olds are automatically transferred for a variety of felonies, whereas fourteen-and fifteen-year-olds are automatically transferred only for crimes punishable by death or life imprisonment.

Most statutes give prosecutors the discretion to transfer certain cases, thus combining automatic with discretionary transfer: transfer is mandatory for specified crimes while discretionary for others. The prosecutor files a transfer petition or motion with the juvenile court, and the judge decides whether to transfer. Some states vest discretion in prosecutors, who decide whether to file a case in juvenile or adult court. This prosecutorial discretion is absolute and non-reviewable except in states with "reverse certification procedures," and has been criticized by legal scholars and some judges.

The age at which juveniles may be transferred varies across states. State laws can be sorted into groups according to the four broad categories of offenses for which juveniles of a certain age *may* be transferred: (1) any crime; (2) capital crimes and murder; (3) certain violent felonies; and (4) certain crimes committed by a juvenile with a prior record.

Statutory factors indicate what judges must consider before ordering transfer. These factors vary from state to state, as does whether the judge must make certain findings or simply consider the factors in making a decision. In *Kent v. United States* [1966], the United States Supreme Court defined the due process requirements for transfer hearings. The Court included in the appendix the eight criteria that District of Columbia judges considered in making the transfer decision.[60] These criteria have since been adopted by many states with little or no modification, and relate generally to the nature of the offense, the characteristics of the child, and the system's rehabilitative capacities. Three criteria are especially significant: (1) the seriousness of the offense and the need to protect the community; (2) the maturity of the juvenile; and (3) the juvenile's amenability to treatment and rehabilitation through available services. All states require consideration of the seriousness of the offense and the need to protect the community.

60. Kent was prosecuted in the District of Columbia. The transfer criteria were presented in an appendix containing the transfer policy statement of the District of Columbia's juvenile court. Those eight criteria are:

1. The seriousness of the alleged offense to the community and whether the protection of the community requires waiver.

2. Whether the alleged offense was committed in an aggressive, violent, premeditated or willful manner.

3. Whether the alleged offense was against persons or against property, greater weight being given to offenses against persons especially if personal injury resulted.

4. The prosecutive merit of the complaint, i.e., whether there is evidence upon which a Grand Jury may be expected to return an indictment....

5. The desirability of trial and disposition of the entire offense in one court when the juvenile's associates in the alleged offense are adults who will be charged with a crime....

6. The sophistication and maturity of the juvenile as determined by a consideration of his home, environmental situation, emotional attitude and pattern of living;

7. The record and previous history of the juvenile, including previous contacts with the Youth Aid Division, other law enforcement agencies, juvenile courts and other jurisdictions, prior periods of probation to this Court, or prior commitments to juvenile institutions.

8. The prospects for adequate protection of the public and the likelihood of reasonable rehabilitation of the juvenile (if he is found to have committed the alleged offense) by the use of procedures, services and facilities currently available to the Juvenile Court.

Not all states, however, explicitly require a consideration of the juvenile's amenability to treatment in the juvenile system. State laws generally provide either that: (1) the juvenile cannot be transferred unless he or she is unamenable to treatment; (2) amenability is a key or controlling factor; (3) amenability is one of several or many factors; or that (4) amenability is not a factor. While Washington's statute does not mention amenability to treatment or rehabilitation, it appears to allow for the consideration of amenability by stating that the court must consider "relevant reports, facts, opinions, and arguments presented by the parties and their counsel." The wording in some statutes is similarly vague or ambiguous, but in most states amenability to treatment apparently is just one of many factors to be considered.

Nor do all states require that the juvenile's "competence" or "maturity" be considered. While the exact meaning of competence is unclear in many statutes, it probably means competence to stand trial in adult court. "Maturity," on the other hand, usually refers to judgment, psychosocial development, and/or general cognitive abilities. State laws provide either that: (1) the juvenile cannot be transferred unless found competent or mature; (2) competence or maturity apparently must be considered as a factor in the decision; (3) competence or maturity are implicitly included as factors; or that (4) competence or maturity are not factors that need to be considered. Apparently, about half the states require that competency or maturity be considered.

Three states (Alaska, Oklahoma, and Rhode Island) allow children of any age to be transferred without requiring the judge to consider competence or maturity. North Carolina allows transfer for children as young as thirteen for any felony, with no specific findings necessary (the judge need only state the reasons). In these states, very young children may be transferred without any consideration of their competence or maturity. In some states, the judge need not consider *any* factors at all.

* * *

STATE v. MITCHELL
Supreme Court of Minnesota, 1998.
577 N.W.2d 481.

ANDERSON, JUSTICE.

In November 1994, 15–year-old Eric William Mitchell participated in a convenience store robbery in Hutchinson, Minnesota during which he shot and killed the 19–year-old store clerk. Mitchell was charged with the murder and was certified to stand trial as an adult. A jury found him guilty of intentional first-degree murder during an aggravated robbery. The district court sentenced Mitchell to the mandatory adult sentence— life imprisonment with no possibility of parole for a minimum of 30 years. * * *. We affirm Mitchell's conviction and sentence.

School let out early in Hutchinson on November 17, 1994, and several high school students and other young people "hung out" and listened to music at Jeffrey Meidl's apartment. Early that evening, 19–year-old Meidl, 20–year-old Jason Walters, 17–year-old Harley Hildenbrand, and 15–year-old Mitchell gathered in the back bedroom of Meidl's apartment. Mitchell was the youngest boy and the newest member to the group. Hildenbrand testified that although he was "not really good friends" with Mitchell, he had known him for about a year prior to the murder; Walters testified that he had known Mitchell for only a few weeks.

Walters told the other members of the group that he needed money, showed them his gun, an Intertech .22 semi-automatic, and asked if they knew of anyone who would buy it from him. When they could not find a buyer, they formulated another plan. Hildenbrand and Mitchell, the two minors of the group, would rob a convenience store. Meidl would provide them with a car, and Walters would let them use his gun. Walters, the oldest member of the group, made a list telling the two younger boys what to do during the robbery. Walters then loaded the gun and handed it to Mitchell.

Hildenbrand and Mitchell took Meidl's car, drove around Hutchinson for a while, and then drove to George's Food and Fuel at 600 Adams Street. They parked the car and separately entered and exited the store at least two times. They returned to the store, where surveillance cameras recorded on videotape aspects of the shooting that followed. The videotape shows that Mitchell entered the store at 9:37:39 p.m. and confronted the cashier, Mickey Wilfert. Although Wilfert appeared to offer no resistance to the robbery, within 12 seconds, he was shot in the face. The force of the bullet pushed Wilfert back, and he fell to the floor. Mitchell then came around the counter and pointed the gun at Wilfert again. Unknown to Mitchell at the time, his wallet fell out of his pocket and onto the floor below the cash register. Mitchell then kicked at Wilfert with his right leg. He kicked so hard that his hand, which was on the open drawer of the cash register, caused the register to rock back and forth. The videotape showed that Hildenbrand was also in the store about this time. However, Hildenbrand testified at trial that he was not in the store when Wilfert was shot, but instead was outside operating as the lookout. Hildenbrand stated that he ran into the store after hearing a gunshot. After the shooting, Mitchell took the money from the cash register, Hildenbrand grabbed several packs of cigarettes, and the two boys ran from the store.

After they left the store, the videotape shows that Wilfert struggled to pull himself up. He pushed the burglar alarm button and then fell back to the floor. Minutes later, the police arrived and provided medical assistance. Wilfert was rushed to the hospital where the doctors tried to resuscitate him, but, at 10:30 p.m., Wilfert died from the gunshot wound to his head. At about the time Wilfert died, three police officers were at his parents' home to notify them of the shooting of their son.

At the Food and Fuel, the police recovered Mitchell's wallet from behind the counter and the videotape of the robbery from the store's surveillance cameras. The police soon ascertained that Hildenbrand and Mitchell were their prime suspects. The police obtained a description of the car that Hildenbrand and Mitchell were driving, and soon thereafter arrested the boys traveling west on Highway 19 in Sibley County between Gaylord and Winthrop. Mitchell and Hildenbrand were arrested at around 1:00 a.m., less than four hours after the murder. When arrested, Mitchell had blood stains on his tennis shoes and his right pants leg.

The police took Hildenbrand and Mitchell to the Sibley County Sheriff's Office. Shortly thereafter, the police concluded that Meidl and Walters were also involved in the crime. In the early morning hours of the next day, the police went to Meidl's apartment, and Meidl gave his consent for the police to search his apartment. In the apartment, the police found a jacket similar to the one Mitchell was wearing on the videotape. The police then went to Walters' home, and Walters led them to his pickup truck where the Intertech .22 was in a plastic case inside a nylon bag.

[The juvenile court referred the case to criminal court for trial and sentencing.].

* * *

[The jury found Mitchell guilty.] The Department of Corrections compiled a presentence investigation report, and a psychologist prepared an evaluation of Mitchell. These reports contained information about Mitchell's childhood and past behaviors and revealed that Mitchell had already led a very difficult and troubled life.

Mitchell was born in Willmar, Minnesota on April 3, 1979. His parents were married at the time, but divorced when Mitchell was about one year old. After the divorce, Mitchell lived with his mother, who physically and emotionally abused him. Mitchell told the psychologist that his mother often hit him with objects including knives, wooden spoons, spatulas, and a broomstick. In recounting incidents of physical abuse, Mitchell said,

> I would give her the satisfaction of falling to the ground, although I learned not to whimper when she was doing it. Then she would say if I whimpered that she would give me something to cry about. Then one time I smiled when she was beating me and then she said "so smiling about it" and then beat me even harder.

Mitchell also recounted incidents of emotional abuse:

> Sometimes I have little flashbacks about her standing there telling me that I am a worthless loser, "stupid worthless son of a bitch, you're nothing, you'll never be anything, you're just a loser like your father. I wish I had a girl instead" and sometimes she would launch into that and say that's what she thought she had because I whined or something when she hit me.

Mitchell's aunt, his mother's sister, corroborated Mitchell's statements, saying she had seen welts on Mitchell and that she would not leave her own daughter in the care of Mitchell's mother because Mitchell's mother had once "slugged [the aunt's daughter] in the mouth without provocation."

While in the fourth grade, a bus knocked Mitchell off his bicycle. When he came home upset and hurt, his mother told him "if [he] kept crying she would really give [him] something to cry about." Mitchell said, "I wasn't going to die by her hands, I was going to kill myself and just get it over with." This incident led Mitchell to make his first suicide attempt. He described the suicide attempt and his mother's reaction:

> About the bus, she told me I deserved to be hit by the bus. I tried to hang myself and every time I passed out. I just kept coming back. That kind of sucked. Mom found me once in the house after I tried to hang myself in fourth grade and she dragged me into the bathroom and handed me a knife and said if you're going to do it, do it right and let's get it over with and don't waste my time. I started crying then and she said "I'll give you something to cry about."

In his report, the psychologist noted that this incident was one of Mitchell's earliest memories and expressed his opinion that Mitchell began to suffer from post-traumatic stress disorder at that time.

Mitchell made numerous other suicide attempts, repeatedly inflicted wounds on himself, and ran away from home on several occasions. At the time of the murder, he had dropped out of school, having completed the ninth grade and part of tenth grade. Before quitting school, he was doing poorly academically and had truancy problems. He was arrested twice for theft, but was not adjudicated either time. He was no longer living with his mother, but was staying at an apartment with friends. The psychologist described Mitchell as a "lost soul," basically a "street child," "seeking to find ways to belong somewhere after he had fallen out with his mother and gone on his own." The psychologist described Mitchell's participation in the crime as "no doubt an effort to prove himself and to find someplace to be included."

Mitchell stated that he had little or no contact with his father after his parents' divorce. On the rare occasions when his father did visit, he introduced Mitchell to alcohol. Mitchell started using alcohol in the fourth grade and started using marijuana in the fifth or sixth grade. At the time of the presentence investigation, Mitchell still did not know his father's address or where his mother was living.

Mitchell stated that he does not remember the night of the murder and continues to have nightmares about what happened. The psychologist stated that Mitchell "feels haunted by the victim, [and is] terrified to go to sleep for fear of having more nightmares and [demonstrates] frequent vigilance in that he hears the victim's voice whispering to him. There should be no mistaking that Mr. Mitchell experiences guilt." In a letter Mitchell prepared for the presentence investigation, he expressed remorse for what happened. He stated:

Many of you wish I were dead for what happened that night. And personally, I could not agree with you more. If I could switch places with Mickey Wilfert I would do it and not think twice about it. If there was a death sentence I'd personally ask for it, and I'd never appeal once. No body should have been shot that night, and if someone should have been shot that night, it should have been me not Mickey Wilfert. I have never had a chance, never had any hopes or dreams, never had much to live for, so I've never cared much for living. Not many people have ever cared either way either, just because no one's ever cared.

The psychologist found that Mitchell has an above average IQ— 109—which places him at the 73rd percentile of intellectual ability. As such, he "shows the capacity to develop strong occupational skills and to function at an upper level vocational or entry-level professional/managerial level of occupational functioning." Further, his intelligence is evidence that he could benefit from and be able to actively participate in psychotherapy. The psychologist stated that Mitchell could receive successful treatment, but that it would need to be "extensive and long term," and concluded that "we might find quite a different individual in ten to fifteen years given appropriate treatment and education."

* * *

At the sentencing hearing, * * * the judge said that he had been practicing law for 35 years, and there was "no question in [his] mind that this is the darkest day [he has] ever had." The judge went on to state that he had "searched [his] soul really to determine what is the mitigating factor here. The only mitigating factor I can find is his age." Because age is not a basis to reduce a mandatory sentence, the judge observed "that the law should have a middle ground," but that he has a "responsibility beyond what I personally feel. * * * I have to determine [the sentence] from the law." The judge sentenced Mitchell to life imprisonment for the first-degree murder and 48 months for the aggravated robbery, the sentences to run concurrently. The judge then said that he believed it was his legal duty to impose the mandatory sentence and stated that "[w]hether it's cruel and inhuman punishment is something that the appellate courts are going to have to make a determination."

* * *

I.

Mitchell first argues that sentencing a 15–year-old child to life imprisonment without the possibility of parole for a minimum of 30 years is a cruel or unusual punishment in violation of the Minnesota Constitution. The Minnesota Constitution differs from the United States Constitution in that it provides that no "cruel *or* unusual punishments be inflicted" (emphasis added), while the United States Constitution provides that no "cruel *and* unusual punishments" be inflicted (emphasis added). This difference is not trivial. The United States Supreme Court has upheld punishments that, although they may be cruel, are not unusual.

* * *

Generally, when determining whether a punishment is cruel or unusual, this court focuses on the proportionality of the crime to the punishment. The [U.S.] Supreme Court, in deciding whether punishment is cruel and unusual, asks if the punishment comports with the "evolving standards of decency that mark the progress of a maturing society." * * *

Mitchell committed one of the most heinous crimes, murder in the first degree. As such, he was given a harsh penalty—life imprisonment for a minimum of 30 years. Therefore, we cannot say that his punishment was out of proportion to his crime. But, given that Mitchell was only 15 years old at the time of his crime, we also look to the evolving standard of decency at the time that Mitchell committed his crime to determine whether the punishment was cruel as applied to him.

* * *

Given that the public, the legislature, and the courts were growing increasingly intolerant of child crime and more tolerant of harsher penalties for child criminals, we cannot say that the life imprisonment of a 15–year-old child convicted of first-degree murder offended evolving standards of decency in 1994 or was generally abhorrent to the community.[3] Accordingly, we hold that such a punishment is not cruel under the Minnesota Constitution.

The conclusion that Mitchell's sentence is not cruel does not end our discussion because the Minnesota Constitution forbids punishments that are either cruel *or* unusual. Therefore, we must analyze whether such a sentence as applied to a 15–year-old child is unusual. * * * [T]here are two states with statutes that explicitly preclude mandatory adult sentences for children below the age of 16, two states where the high courts have prohibited mandatory life sentences for children, 26 states which do not punish anyone with mandatory life sentences without the possibility of parole, and at least 21 states that do sentence 15–year-old children to life imprisonment without the possibility of parole. * * *

The fact that states are split on this issue provides some evidence that sentencing a 15–year-old child to life imprisonment is not unusual. * * * As the state pointed out at oral argument, if this sentence is unusual in any way, it is only because it is unusual for a 15–year-old

---

3. It is often difficult to ascertain the community's evolving standard of decency regarding children, especially because the attitudes towards children are often ambivalent. On the one hand, the legislature has moved towards more punitive sanctions for child criminals whom they believe should be held as accountable for their crimes as adults. On the other hand, the legislature continues to pass statutes that it considers to be protective of children, assuming that children are not as accountable as adults.

child to commit such a heinous crime. Therefore, we hold that Mitchell's punishment is not unusual.

* * *

II.

Mitchell argues that the wide disparity in punishment for first-degree murder for adults versus children violates his right to substantive due process. Mitchell points out that first-degree murder is the only offense for which a court cannot consider mitigating factors, and he argues that the fact that he was certified to be tried as an adult is separate from whether he should be sentenced as an adult. The state responds that the legislature has the power to determine appropriate punishment and that a life sentence for first-degree murder serves the legitimate state goal of protecting society.

* * *

* * * [W]e find no constitutional violation in the child's sentence, but we are sympathetic to the concern expressed by the district court judge who sentenced Mitchell when he stated that there should have been a "middle ground." Had Mitchell remained under the jurisdiction of the juvenile court, that court would have only had jurisdiction over him until he turned 19. His sentence would have been four years at most. * * * Because he was certified as an adult, Mitchell must serve a mandatory minimum of 30 years, and may serve up to a life term in prison. A strong argument can be made that a four-year sentence is insufficient for a crime of this magnitude. After all, Mitchell shot Wilfert in the face while committing a robbery. But an equally strong argument can be made that 30 years in prison is excessive when applied to a 15–year-old child such as Mitchell who has never had a network of family and friends to provide him emotional support and was offered very little guidance from either his parents or his community.

Mitchell's background does not excuse or justify his crime—he is guilty of murder. But his background does speak to culpability and it adds to the tragedy of what occurred on the night of November 17, 1994. Just as Wilfert's life would have been spared had Mitchell not pulled the trigger, perhaps Mitchell would not have pulled the trigger had he had the support needed to grow up emotionally healthy. The greatest tragedy of this crime is that it was potentially preventable. It is a further tragedy that a 15–year-old will spend a minimum of 30 years in prison, especially given that his psychologist concluded that Mitchell could be "quite a different individual in ten to fifteen years given appropriate treatment and education."

We would prefer that the legislature had provided a sentencing alternative, such as indeterminate sentencing, for someone like Mitchell—someone still a child, yet certified to stand trial as an adult. But the legislature did not choose to provide such an alternative. Moreover, the legislature did not choose to grant the district court the authority to consider factors such as age when sentencing a 15–year-old child such as Mitchell who has been certified to stand trial as an adult and convicted of first-degree murder. * * *

* * *

IV.

* * *

* * * [T]he fact that children who are tried as adults receive harsher punishments than those retained in the juvenile system does not violate equal protection. After the court has determined that a child should be tried as an adult, the legislature then has a legitimate interest in public safety that is rationally related to the sentences it prescribes.

* * *

Mitchell's sentence does not violate his right to equal protection because he is not similarly situated to 15–year-olds who remain in the juvenile system. Mitchell is treated the same as all persons convicted of first-degree murder in adult court.

* * *

PROBLEM 11–1

(a) The trial court was permitted to refer 15-year-old Eric Mitchell to criminal court only if it found, by clear and convincing evidence, that he was not suitable for treatment or that the public safety would not be served by juvenile court processing. The court was required to weigh the totality of the circumstances, including the following factors: (a) the seriousness of the offense in terms of community protection, (b) the circumstances surrounding the offense, (c) whether the offense was committed in an aggressive, violent, premeditated or willful manner, (d) whether the offense was directed against persons or property, the greater weight being given to an offense against persons, especially if personal injury resulted, (e) the reasonably foreseeable consequences of the act, (f) the absence of adequate protective and security facilities available to the juvenile treatment system, (g) the sophistication and maturity of the child as determined by consideration of the child's home, environmental situation, emotional attitude and pattern of living, (h) the record and previous history of the child, (i) whether the child acted with particular cruelty or disregard for the life or safety of another, (j) whether the offense involved a high degree of sophistication or planning by the child, and (k) whether there is sufficient time available before the child reaches age nineteen to provide appropriate treatment and control. Minn. R. Juv. P. 32.05, since amended.

If you were the juvenile court judge in *Mitchell*, would you have transferred Eric Mitchell to criminal court for trial and sentencing?

(b) Because of the perception that juvenile court dispositions were often too lenient but criminal court sentences imposed on children were often too harsh, the Minnesota legislature created "extended jurisdiction juvenile prosecutions" (EJJ) in 1994. EJJ authorizes the juvenile court to retain jurisdiction and impose both a juvenile and an adult sanction on older juveniles. The adult sanction is stayed pending satisfaction of the juvenile sanction, and the adult sanction becomes operative only where the juvenile fails to satisfy the juvenile sanction or commits a new offense. At the same time, the legislature amended the certification statute to provide that an alleged felon between 14 and 17 may be certified to criminal court if the prosecutor proves by clear and convincing evidence that retaining the child in juvenile court would not serve public safety; the prosecutor no longer has the burden of proving that the child was not suitable for treatment or that the public safety would not be served by juvenile court processing. See Minn. Stat. Ann. §§ 260B.125, 260B.130 (1999). (Eric Mitchell was not eligible for EJJ treatment because he committed the murder a month before the new statute's effective date.)

Does EJJ treatment provide an appropriate middle ground between a juvenile court sanction and life imprisonment? If Mitchell had been eligible for EJJ treatment, should the juvenile court have retained jurisdiction with an eye toward imposing a dual sentence, or should the court have transferred Mitchell to criminal court where he ultimately received life imprisonment without possibility of parole for thirty years?

Notes and Questions

1. *Questions about transfer.* (a) Should children below the age of majority be subject to trial and sentencing in criminal court? If so, for what sorts of crimes should transfer be authorized?,

(b) Who should make the transfer decision, the judge or the prosecutor?,

(c) Should transfer be mandatory for some serious crimes, or should all transfer be discretionary based on the court's analysis of factors defined by statute?,

(d) Should states lower, or repeal, their minimum transfer ages for the most serious crimes?

2. *Rationales for transfer.* Children have no federal or state constitutional right to be processed as delinquents in juvenile court. A juvenile's right to delinquency proceedings emanates solely from statute, which may provide instead for criminal court trial and sentencing under a discretionary or mandatory formula. See, e.g., State v. Angel C., 715 A.2d 652, 660 (Conn. 1998).

Professor Zimring would reserve transfer for "hard cases": "[T]he modern juvenile court is preferable to the criminal justice system for the vast majority of young offenders under seventeen or eighteen years old. [But] it is inevitable, where the juvenile court retains jurisdiction to ages seventeen or eighteen, that cases will arise where the minimum punitive response believed necessary by the court and the community exceeds that available to the juvenile court. * * * [S]trong measures must be taken in cases where police officers are killed, elderly widows raped, and eight-year-old girls molested and strangled by offenders under the normal age of the adult courts' jurisdiction. These are not typical cases; they occur infrequently. But one cannot evade the responsibility for dealing with such cases simply by documenting their rarity. They happen." Franklin E. Zimring, The Treatment of Hard Cases in American Juvenile Justice: In Defense of Discretionary Waiver, 5 Notre Dame J. L. Ethics & Pub. Pol'y 267, 268 (1991).

Professor Katherine Hunt Federle takes a contrary position: "[W]e need to insure that the juvenile court retains jurisdiction over the most serious cases and the most serious offenders. If we are to maintain a separate system for youthful offenders, then that system should not, as a matter of policy, seek to exclude those who most challenge the system's rehabilitative and beneficial aspects. If we are to say that the juvenile court provides an alternative to the harsh realities of the criminal justice system, then we cannot simply claim that the most difficult cases are beyond its reach." Katherine Hunt Federle, Emancipation and Execution: Transferring Children to Criminal Court in Capital Cases, 1996 Wis. L. Rev. 447, 447–48.

3. *The volume of transferred cases.* In 1996, 1.0% of petitioned delinquency cases were judicially transferred to criminal court. See Anne L. Stahl et al., Juvenile Court Statistics 1996, at 13 (1999). Forty-three percent of judicially transferred cases involved crimes against persons, 37% involved crimes against property, 14% involved drug cases, and 6% involved public order cases. Ninety-five percent of judicially transferred cases involved male offenders, and 88% involved offenders 16 or older. Fifty-one percent involved white offenders, and 46% involved black offenders. (Three percent involved offenders of other races.). See Howard N. Snyder and Melissa Sickmund, Juvenile Offenders and Victims: 1999 National Report 170–71 (1999).

4. *Breadth.* Transfer is generally seen as a response to violent juvenile crime, but some transfer statutes reach well beyond such offenses. In a number of states, juveniles may be transferred for any crime or for any felony. Some states require or permit adult prosecution of juveniles for misdemeanors, ordinance violations, and summary statute violations such as fish and game violations. See Patrick Griffin et al., Trying Juveniles as Adults in Criminal Court: An Analysis of State Transfer Provisions 13 (1998). Courts, however, evidently do not transfer nonviolent offenders in large numbers. Of the juveniles transferred nationwide from 1990 to 1994, (1) two-thirds were charged with a violent felony, including murder (11%), robbery (34%), assault (15%), and rape (3%); (2) 17% were charged with property offenses, primarily burglary (6%) and theft (8%); (3) 14% were charged with drug offenses; and (4) 3% were charged with public order offenses such as weapons charges and driving-related charges. See Bureau of Justice Statistics, Juvenile Felony Defendants in Criminal Courts 1, 2 (1998).

5. *The transfer hearing and its trappings.* Kent v. United States, 383 U.S. 541, 554 (1966), held that a juvenile may not be transferred to criminal court pursuant to a discretionary transfer statute "without ceremony—without

hearing, without effective assistance of counsel, without a statement of reasons."

Kent held that the transfer hearing "must measure up to the essentials of due process and fair treatment," but that the court is not bound by the rules of evidence or procedure. 383 U.S. at 562. States are free to take a stricter approach, but most states do not bind courts to the rules of evidence or procedure in transfer hearings. Courts generally may admit hearsay such as reports by psychologists, psychiatrists, child welfare personnel or law enforcement officers. See, e.g., Commonwealth v. Spencer, 695 N.E.2d 677, 680 (Mass.App.Ct.1998); contra, In re Darcy S., 936 P.2d 888, 892 (N.M. 1997). Courts disagree about whether the Sixth Amendment right to confrontation applies in transfer hearings. See, e.g., In re P.W.N., 301 N.W.2d 636, 640 (1981) (right applicable); State v. Wright, 456 N.W.2d 661, 664 (Iowa 1990) (right not applicable because it applies only in criminal prosecutions).

In the transfer hearing, the state need not prove the juvenile's guilt of the conduct charged; the court need determine only that the statutory requirements for discretionary transfer have been met. See, e.g., In re B.N.E., 927 S.W.2d 271, 274 (Tex. Ct. App. 1996). The juvenile's counsel must have access to the social records and probation or similar reports that are before the court. Some states require the court to consider a prehearing investigative report on the juvenile, prepared by the juvenile probation office or other agency.

6. *The factors to consider.* In more than half the states, the juvenile court may grant the prosecutor's discretionary transfer motion only if it finds probable cause to believe that the juvenile committed the offense charged. The court generally must also consider enumerated factors similar to the eight *Kent* factors reproduced in note 60 of the Redding article. A few states add other factors. Arizona courts, for example, must also consider the victim's views and whether the juvenile was involved in a gang. See Ariz. Rev. Stat. § 8–327. Missouri courts must also consider "racial disparity in certification" of juveniles for criminal trial. See Mo. Rev. Stat. § 211.071. The court generally may order transfer only where its propriety is established by the ordinary civil "preponderance of the evidence" standard; a handful of states impose the higher "clear and convincing evidence" standard in some or all cases. Most states impose the burden of proof on the prosecutor, though a few states require some older juveniles to demonstrate that transfer should be denied. See, e.g., N.J. Stat. § 2A–4A–26(a)(3).

A serious violent offense, without more, may be a sufficient basis for trying a juvenile as an adult. See, e.g., Carroll v. State, 932 S.W.2d 339, 341 (Ark.1996). Transfer may also be appropriate even when one or more of the statutory factors point in the juvenile's favor. See, e.g., State v. Stephens, 975 P.2d 801, 806 (Kan.1999).

Examine the factors enumerated in note 60 of the Redding article. Does the court have virtually unfettered discretion to order transfer in any case alleging a serious act of violence or any case which receives widespread press coverage? See, e.g., Jeffrey Fagan and Elizabeth Piper Deschenes, Determinants of Judicial Waiver Decisions for Violent Juvenile Offenders, 81 J. Crim. L. & Criminology 314, 345–46 (1990) ("[I]nformal criteria and the statutory language that seem to guide the transfer decision are subjective and may invite disparity, if not capriciousness by prosecutors and judges.''). Are disparity and caprice acceptable when transfer can mean the difference between a few years' confinement in a juvenile facility and life imprisonment without the possibility of parole, or even exposure to capital punishment?

7. *Mandatory waiver.* In many states, transfer to criminal court is mandatory without any judicial weighing of statutory factors once the prosecutor charges an enumerated serious crime such as murder, rape or armed robbery. Proceedings begin in juvenile court, but the court's only role is to conduct a preliminary hearing to determine whether mandatory-waiver requirements are satisfied. If the answer is yes, the juvenile is transferred to criminal court. In a 1994 National Law Journal poll, 69% of juvenile court judges opposed mandatory waiver statutes. See Rorie Sherman, Juvenile Judges Say: Time to Get Tough, Nat'l L.J., Aug. 8, 1994, at A1.

Mandatory waiver must be distinguished from "statutory exclusion" provisions, which prevail in more than half the states for particularly serious crimes by older juveniles. Where the legislature has excluded a particular crime from juvenile court jurisdiction, juvenile court jurisdiction never attaches and the juvenile charged with that crime is processed directly in criminal court.

8. *Lesser included offenses.* Where transfer to criminal court is mandatory for a serious crime, the court may also try and sentence the youth for any lesser non-mandatory crimes arising from the same incident. See, e.g., State v. Behl, 564 N.W.2d 560, 565 (Minn.1997). The decisions appear motivated by the prospect that double jeopardy would prohibit prosecutors from trying the youth in criminal court for the mandated crime and in juvenile court for the less serious crime. Id.

Where the juvenile is later acquitted of the serious crime that mandated transfer, but convicted of only a lesser crime that would not have mandated transfer, may the criminal court retain jurisdiction and sentence him? States have not reached consensus on this question. Oregon, for example, specifies that in this circumstance, "the trial court shall not sentence the defendant therein, but * * * shall order a presentence report to be made in the case, shall set forth in a memorandum such observations as the court may make regarding the case and shall return the case to the juvenile court in order that the juvenile court make disposition in the case based upon the guilty finding." Or. Rev. Stat. § 419C.361. In the absence of such a statute, however, the criminal court retains jurisdiction to impose an adult sentence on the juvenile for the lesser crime, without any further juvenile court proceedings. See, e.g., State v. Morales, 694 A.2d 758, 761–65 (Conn.1997).

9. *Reverse transfer.* About half the states have provisions authorizing the criminal court to transfer back to the juvenile court some categories of cases involving alleged juvenile offenders. See Patrick Griffin et al., Trying Juveniles as Adults in Criminal Court: An Analysis of State Transfer Provisions 9–10 (1998).

10. *Loss of juvenile protections.* A juvenile transferred to criminal court receives only the rights and protections afforded adult defendants. The juvenile court act's protections no longer apply. See, e.g., State v. Loukaitis, 918 P.2d 535 (Wash.Ct.App.1996). Nor do the rules of juvenile procedure

apply in the criminal court trial. See, e.g., State v. Pillow, 1998 WL 351219 *3 (Tenn. Ct. Crim. App.1998). The transferred juvenile loses such rights as the right to a finding of delinquency rather than criminality, the right to confidentiality rather than a public proceeding and disposition, the right to a juvenile disposition rather than adult sentencing, and the right to isolation from adult inmates during the proceedings and after conviction.

In 14 states, persons convicted in criminal court of felonies committed while a juvenile are among the persons barred for life from voting. See See Human Rights Watch, No Minor Matter: Children in Maryland's Jails (1999), available at <http://www.hrw.org/reports/1999/maryland> (visited Dec. 6, 1999).

11. *Petition by the juvenile.* Some states authorize older juveniles to petition to be tried as adults in criminal court. See, e.g., N.H. Rev. Stat. § 169–B:26 (juveniles who committed alleged act after sixteenth birthday). If you were representing an older juvenile, why might you petition to have your client tried as an adult?

12. *Interlocutory appeals.* May the juvenile take an immediate appeal from the trial court's transfer decision? The answer depends on application of the state's final judgment rule. This rule provides that with narrow exceptions specified by statute or case law, a party may appeal only from the trial court's final order.

States disagree about whether a transfer order is final, and if not, whether an interlocutory appeal may be taken. See, e.g., State v. T.D.R., 495 S.E.2d 700, 703 (N.C.1998) (holding that an order transferring a juvenile for adult court prosecution is immediately appealable because it is a final order in the juvenile matter); Robinson v. State, 704 A.2d 269, 271 (Del.1998) (holding that a transfer order is neither an adjudication on the merits nor a final resolution of the case, which continues as a criminal prosecution; defendant may not appeal transfer decision until after the conclusion of the criminal proceeding).

13. *Racial disparities in transfer?* In 1995, 1.6% of formal delinquency cases involving black juveniles were waived to criminal court, compared with 0.8% for whites. See Bureau of Justice Statistics, Sourcebook of Criminal Justice Statistics 1997, Table 2.12, at 104 (1998). From 1990 to 1994, 63% of juveniles transferred to criminal courts were black males, 29% were white males, 3% were black females and 2% were white females. See Bureau of Justice Stats., Juvenile Felony Defendants in Criminal Courts 1 (1998).

Several studies have found that disproportionate numbers of minorities are transferred to criminal court. A 1995 report found that 73% of Maryland cases in which the juvenile court waived jurisdiction involved black youths while 27% of the state's population is black. In Ohio in 1994, 62.6% of waived cases involved black youths, while blacks make up just over 11% of the state's population. In Minnesota, "minority juveniles comprised nearly nine out of ten (88 percent) of the youths whom prosecutors sought to waive" in 1992, although minorities represent less than 7% of the state's population. In 1990 and 1991, 34.3% of California juvenile cases waived involved African–Americans and 60.2% involved other minorities; 60.1% of Florida waived cases involved black juvenile offenders; 70.5% percent of Missouri youths waived were black; 55.6% of Pennsylvania waived cases involved black youth; and 85.7% of South Carolina youth waived were black.

See Human Rights Watch, No Minor Matter: Children in Maryland's Jails (1999), available at http://www.hrw.org/reports/1999/maryland.

The National Coalition for Juvenile Justice argues that despite enumerated statutory factors the court must consider, discrimination may infect the discretionary transfer process. When called on to decide whether the youth is "amenable to treatment in the juvenile system," for example, the court may be influenced if the prosecutor charges a more serious rather than a less serious crime, or may order transfer more readily if the juvenile lives in a depressed area distant from available treatment facilities. See Coalition for Juvenile Justice, No Easy Answers: Juvenile Justice in a Climate of Fear 21 (1994). A recent study of urban Hennepin County, Minnesota (Minneapolis and its suburbs) found prosecutorial discretion to be central: "Prosecutors charge most minority juveniles with violent crimes and more white offenders with property offenses; most differences in waiver administration result from the way the juvenile court processes violent and property offenses, regardless of race." Marcy Rasmussen Podkopacz and Barry C. Feld, Judicial Waiver Policy and Practice: Persistence, Seriousness and Race, 14 Law and Ineq. 73, 177 (1995).

14. *Is transfer effective?* Transfer statutes reflect the public's belief that criminal courts are harsher than juvenile courts on children who commit crimes. In the main case, Eric Mitchell certainly received a stern sentence. Some transferred juveniles have been sentenced to life imprisonment without any possibility of parole, e.g., Harris v. Wright, 93 F.3d 581 (9th Cir. 1996) (fifteen-year-old defendant convicted of murder), or even to death, e.g., Stanford v. Kentucky, 492 U.S. 361 (1989) (on appeal by transferred juvenile, holding that executing a defendant who was sixteen or seventeen at the time of the crime does not constitute cruel and unusual punishment in violation of the Eighth Amendment). In a case that held the national attention in 1998, for example, 15-year-old Kipland Kinkel murdered his parents and two classmates, and wounded several other students, in Springfield, Oregon. He was sentenced to 112 years in prison without the possible of parole. See Sam Howe Verhovek, Teenager To Spend Life in Prison For Shootings, N.Y. Times, Nov. 11, 1999.

Research casts some doubt, however, on the accuracy of the belief that criminal courts necessarily impose sentences harsher than juvenile court dispositions. The doubt appears greatest in cases involving property offenses and other less serious crimes. In the late 1970s and early 1980s, some studies found that transferred juveniles often received more lenient sentences in criminal court than they would have in received in juvenile court, probably because they were appearing in adult court for the first time. A 1978 study, for example, found that a majority of transferred juveniles sentenced in criminal court received probation, fines or other nonconfinement sentences. See Donna M. Hamparian et al., Youth in Adult Courts: Between Two Worlds (1982). A 1982 study found that nearly two-thirds of transferred juveniles received probation. See M.A. Bortner, Traditional Rhetoric, Organizational Realities: Remand of Juveniles to Adult Court, 32 Crime and Delinq. 53 (1986).

On the other hand, a 1982 study of four New York–New Jersey counties found that 46% of the 15- and 16-year-old felony offenders in adult court were incarcerated, while only 18% of similar offenders were sanctioned in New Jersey juvenile courts. See Cary Rudman et al., Violent Youth in Adult Court: Process and Punishment, 32 Crime and Delinq. 75 (1986). A 1987 followup study of the same counties, however, yielded the opposite results: 57% of 15- to 16-year-old robbers were incarcerated by juvenile courts but only 27% by adult courts. See Jeffrey Fagan, Comparative Impacts of Juvenile and Criminal Court Sanctions on Adolescent Felony Offenders (1991).

Some early studies found that when adult courts incarcerated transferred juveniles, their sentences generally were not longer than the confinement similar juvenile offenders received after adjudication in juvenile court. One study found no difference in the minimum and maximum sentences imposed on burglary and robbery offenders in juvenile and adult courts. See Fagan, supra. One group of researchers cites anecdotal evidence suggesting that transferred juveniles are often released early, particularly in states subject to court orders to reduce adult prison populations. The researchers speculate that juvenile offenders usually have records shorter and less serious than adult offenders sentenced for similar crimes, making the juveniles candidates for early release. See Dale Parent et al., Transferring Serious Juvenile Offenders to Adult Courts 2 (OJJDP Jan. 1997).

Data gathered by the Georgia Indigent Defense Council show that from 1994 to 1998, about 2700 juveniles were charged as adults statewide. Only 20% were convicted, and only 14% were sentenced to more than five years, the maximum juvenile period of confinement. R. Robin McDonald, Punishing Choices: How to Try Teens Charged With Major Crimes?, Atlanta J. & Const., Aug. 8, 1999, at 1F.

A 1996 study found no correlation between rates of transfer and rates of juvenile homicide. The researchers reported that "[s]ome states have high transfer and high juvenile homicide, some have low transfer and low juvenile homicide; still others have high transfer and low juvenile homicide or low transfer and high juvenile homicide." Eric Lotke and Vincent Schiraldi, An Analysis of Juvenile Homicides: Where They Occur and The Effectiveness of Adult Court Intervention (1996).

15. *Recidivism.* Several studies have shown that recidivism rates are considerably higher for youth tried in criminal court than for youth processed as delinquents in juvenile court. One recent study of juveniles transferred to criminal court in Florida, for example, found that transfer "actually aggravated short-term recidivism" of juveniles accused of felonies and misdemeanors alike. Donna M. Bishop et al., The Transfer of Juveniles to Criminal Court: Does It Make a Difference?, 42 Crime and Delinq. 171, 183 (1996). A followup Florida study by the same researchers yielded the same general conclusion: "Transfer was more likely to aggravate recidivism than to stem it." Lawrence Winner et al., Transfer of Juveniles to Criminal Court: Reexamining Recidivism Over the Long Term, 43 Crime & Delinq. 548, 558–59 (1997). What reasons might help explain these general findings?

16. *Confining juveniles in adult prisons.* Pursuant to the mandate enacted in the federal Juvenile Justice and Delinquency Prevention Act of 1974, states may not incarcerate delinquents in adult prisons. The Act imposes no such mandate, however, when a juvenile is tried and sentenced as an adult.

See, e.g., Hunter v. State, 676 N.E.2d 14, 17 (Ind.1996). Some states indeed incarcerate transferred juveniles in adult prisons pending criminal court trial and immediately after conviction. In other states, juveniles sentenced as adults are placed in separate facilities for younger adult convicts. Some states provide that such juveniles begin their sentences in juvenile facilities and are moved to adult correctional facilities for the remainder of their sentence when they reach a particular age.

The Coalition for Juvenile Justice strenuously opposes placement of children in adult prisons because "[t]he risks of suicidal and assaultive behaviors are just too great, especially since there may be lengthy delays between the time of the transfer decision and the trial in the adult court." See Coalition for Juvenile Justice, A Celebration or a Wake?: The Juvenile Court After 100 Years 54 (1998). One study found that juveniles in adult prisons are five times more likely to be sexually attacked, twice as likely to be beaten by staff, and 50% more likely to be attacked with a weapon than juveniles in youth facilities. See Martin Forst et al., Youth in Prisons and Training Schools: Perceptions and Consequences of the Treatment–Custody Dichotomy, 40 Juv. & Fam. Ct. J. 1, 10 (1989 No. 1).

Incarceration of juveniles with adult prisoners presents housing problems for the states. In 1994, 36 states placed juveniles in housing with adult inmates. (Half did so as a general practice, and half did so only in some circumstances.). Nine states housed juveniles with 18- to 21-year-old inmates but not with older ones. Only six states never housed juveniles with adult inmates; these states either house juveniles in state juvenile training schools until they turn eighteen, or house them in segregated living units in adult prisons. See Dale Parent et al., Transferring Serious Juvenile Offenders to Adult Courts 5 (OJJDP Jan. 1997).

17. *"Once an adult, always an adult."* Where a transferred juvenile is tried in criminal court, more than half the states require that any future proceedings alleging an offense by the juvenile must be heard in criminal court. See, e.g., N.H. Rev. Stat. § 169–B:27. The requirement generally applies only where the juvenile was convicted on the earlier transfer. See Howard N. Snyder and Melissa Sickmund, Juvenile Offenders and Victims: 1999 National Report 103 (1999).

18. *A jury of one's peers?* In the federal system and in forty-six states, the minimum age for jury service in civil and criminal cases is eighteen. No state permits younger persons to sit on a jury. See Bureau of Justice Statistics, State Court Organization 1993, at 256–63 (Jan. 1995).

Federal and state courts have rejected juveniles' claims that the Sixth Amendment or due process guarantees them the right to trial by a jury that includes juveniles. See, e.g., United States v. McVean, 436 F.2d 1120, 1122 (5th Cir.1971); In re Welfare of J.K.B., 552 N.W.2d 732, 733–34 (Minn.Ct. App.1996). Rejection is normally grounded in the Supreme Court's pronouncement that "the Constitution does not forbid the States to prescribe relevant qualifications for their jurors. The States remain free to confine the selection to * * * persons meeting specified qualifications of age * * *." Carter v. Jury Comm'n, 396 U.S. 320, 332 (1970).

19. *Transfer to juvenile drug courts.* In 1994, Congress authorized the Attorney General to make grants to states, state and local courts, local

government units and Indian tribal governments to create "drug courts." Violent Crime Control and Law Enforcement Act of 1994, 42 U.S.C. §§ 3796ii–3796ii–8. These courts hear cases against non-violent adults and juveniles, who are often first-time offenders and who are usually charged with possessing drugs or with committing minor drug-related crimes. In 1995, the U.S. Justice Department promulgated a rule prohibiting grantee courts from adjudicating cases involving violent offenders. 60 Fed. Reg. 32104, 32105, 28 CFR § 93.3(d) (June 20, 1995).

Drug courts focus on treatment rather than incarceration. Some courts use a deferred prosecution approach, under which an offender agrees before trial to enter a treatment and counseling program mandated and monitored by the court. The charges are dismissed if the offender completes the program, but failure to complete the program returns the offender to court for criminal processing. Other courts use a post-adjudication approach. The offender may enter the treatment program only after conviction and sentencing, but sentence is suspended during treatment and reinstated only if the offender fails to complete the treatment program.

Juvenile drug courts operate as distinct parts of existing trial courts, especially busy juvenile courts that might otherwise be unable to provide the specialized ongoing individualized treatment often needed by juvenile drug abusers and their families. "Local teams of judges, prosecutors, attorneys, treatment providers, law enforcement officials, and others are using the coercive power of the court to force abstinence and alter behavior with a combination of intensive judicial supervision, escalating sanctions, mandatory drug testing, treatment, and strong aftercare programs." See Marilyn Roberts et al., The Juvenile Drug Court Movement (OJJDP 1997). Most existing juvenile drug courts operate post-adjudication programs, which begin after establishment of the juvenile's guilt by plea or court determination. Adult drug courts do not hear cases against juvenile offenders, but their dockets nonetheless concern child advocates because adult drug offenders are responsible for much reported and unreported child abuse and neglect.

20. *Alternatives to delinquency proceedings.* Where a child has committed a delinquent act or status offense, the act might signal abuse or neglect in the family. For example, a child victimized by abuse at home might begin skipping school, or might fall in with peers who commit a robbery. Where a juvenile has evidently committed a delinquent act, what factors might lead authorities to proceed under abuse or neglect jurisdiction rather than, or in addition to, delinquency?

21. *Reflections on children's rights and responsibilities.* One criminal justice professional links the trend toward adult punishment of juveniles with the enhancement of children's rights chronicled in Chapter 1. "[T]he major force driving the juvenile justice system's response to serious offenders has been the continued emphasis on legal enfranchisement of youth. In our society, rights are balanced by corresponding responsibilities. Reformers' zealous pursuit of a full panoply of constitutional rights for juveniles has finally confronted criminal responsibility. It is not clear * * * that juveniles are now, have been, or will be able in the future to fully benefit from their new-found rights, but it is painfully apparent that we have concluded that they must be held criminally responsible, diminished capacity for crime

and/or freedom notwithstanding." E. Hunter Hurst, III, The Juvenile Court at 100 Years of Age: The Death of Optimism, 49 Juv. & Fam. Ct. J. 39, 51 (1998 No. 4).

Chapter 6 presented sex crimes that afford children special protection because of their immaturity. Chapter 10 presented protective legislation grounded in the perception that children lack adult maturity and judgment and thus must be protected from their own improvidence. In light of this vast array of protective legislation that treats children as immature, should the criminal law turn around and prosecute children as adults in criminal court?

SECTION 4. DELINQUENCY PROCEDURE

A. *Overview*

PRESIDENT'S COMMISSION ON LAW ENFORCEMENT AND ADMINISTRATION OF JUSTICE, TASK FORCE REPORT: JUVENILE DELINQUENCY AND YOUTH CRIME 4–6 (1967)

* * * Most juveniles who appear in juvenile court are sent there by the police. Extensive screening and informal adjustment by the police on the street and in the police station significantly reduce the number of apprehended juveniles referred to court * * *. Parents, social agencies, and others may also have direct recourse to the court.

Juvenile court statutes frequently provide that when a complaint is received, the court shall make a preliminary inquiry to determine whether the interest of the child or the public require court action. * * * In many juvenile courts, especially the larger metropolitan ones, the preliminary screening function, known as intake, is performed by a special division of the probation department. Depending upon his judgment as to basis for court jurisdiction, sufficiency of evidence, and desirability of court action, the intake officer may dismiss the case, authorize the filing of a petition, or in many courts dispose of the case by "informal adjustment." In many juvenile courts approximately half the cases referred there are informally adjusted at intake—by referral to another agency, by continuation on "informal probation," or in some other way.

The intake officer also determines whether a juvenile should be detained pending court action. In about one-fifth of the jurisdictions the right to bail is extended by statute to juveniles. In most jurisdictions a juvenile taken into custody by the police has no right to bail but is to be released to his parents or other suitable person unless no such individual can be found or the juvenile is believed to present a serious threat of immediate danger to himself or the community. * * *

Where a petition is filed, the juvenile then appears before the judge for an initial hearing (arraignment). If the juvenile denies involvement, there may be, immediately or subsequently, an adjudication hearing. In most jurisdictions, * * * there is no right to jury trial in juvenile court.

The disposition hearing is conducted separately from the adjudication proceeding in some courts. In many, however, it is held at the same time or is separate only in the minority of cases in which the allegations of the petition are at issue. In determining disposition, the court places great reliance on the social and clinical report (similar to the presentence investigation report in adult criminal court) prepared by the probation officer to whom the case has been assigned for social study (an assignment made in some courts before and in others not until after a hearing has been held on contested allegations in the petition). The social study embodies the juvenile court's emphasis on inquiring into the child's background and its attempt to apply the social and behavior sciences to diagnosing and dealing with the problems behind his errant conduct. * * * [I]n many jurisdictions the social reports, in theory a guide to disposition, in practice are given to the judge before the adjudication hearing. * * *

Most juvenile court judges have broad discretion in disposing of cases, being empowered to dismiss the case, warn the juvenile, fine him, place him on probation, arrange for restitution, refer him to an agency or treatment facility, or commit him to an institution.

* * *

The juvenile court judge's right-hand man is the probation officer. Probation * * * embodies the ideal of individualized, rehabilitative diagnosis and treatment. Probation officers serve as investigators into the juvenile's all-important social history, establish a link between the legally trained or lay judge and the social scientists who guide him, and provide a vehicle for disposition with supervision but without institutionalization. Probation, therefore, was and still is central to the juvenile court's special functions, and its limitations are inseparable from the juvenile court's own shortcomings. * * *

[J]uvenile court probation officers serve two major functions: making social studies of cases referred to the court and supervising juveniles placed on probation. Their duties may in addition entail intake functions such as screening cases referred to the court and determining the necessity for detention, administering the juvenile detention facility, and managing the court's probation department and court-attached diagnostic and treatment services (clinics, camps, halfway houses, community residential facilities).

* * *

B. Arrest and Custody

1. Arrest

The delinquency process begins when a juvenile is referred to the juvenile court. In 1996, 86% of delinquency cases were referred by law enforcement authorities, with the remainder referred by other sources such as social service agencies, schools, parents, probation officers or victims. See Anne L. Stahl et al., Juvenile Court Statistics 1996, 7 (1999).

MAINE REVISED STATUTES, TITLE 15

§ 3201

1. Arrests without warrants of juveniles for juvenile crimes * * * by law enforcement officers or private persons shall be made pursuant to the provisions [relating to arrests without warrants under the criminal code]. * * *

* * *

§ 3202.

An arrest warrant for a juvenile shall be issued in the manner provided by [the] Maine District Court Criminal Rules, provided that affidavits alone shall be presented and a petition shall not be necessary. Following arrest, the juvenile shall be subject to the procedures [relating to intake and diversion].

§ 3203–A.

1. A juvenile caseworker shall receive notification under the following circumstances.

A. When, in the judgment of a law enforcement officer, Juvenile Court proceedings should be commenced against a juvenile, but detention is not necessary, the law enforcement officer shall notify a juvenile caseworker as soon as possible after such a determination is made; but if the juvenile has been arrested, the law enforcement officer shall notify the juvenile caseworker within 12 hours following the arrest.

A–1. If the law enforcement officer determines that detention is not necessary but the officer is unable to immediately return the juvenile to the custody of his legal custodian or another suitable person, the officer, with the juvenile's consent, may deliver the juvenile to any public or private agency which provides nonsecure services to juveniles, including an agency which provides attendant care.

B. When, in the judgment of a law enforcement officer, a juvenile should be detained prior to his initial appearance in juvenile court, the law enforcement officer shall immediately notify a juvenile caseworker. [Provisions relating to preventive detention are omitted. Preventive detention is discussed below in Schall v. Martin and the notes following the decision.]

* * *

2. A legal custodian shall receive notification under the following circumstances.

A. When a juvenile is arrested, the law enforcement officer or the juvenile caseworker shall notify the legal custodian of the juvenile without unnecessary delay and inform the legal custodian of the juvenile's whereabouts, the name and telephone number of the juvenile caseworker who has been contacted and, if a juvenile has been placed in a secure detention facility, that a detention hearing will be held within 24 hours following this placement, excluding Saturday, Sunday and legal holidays.

B. Notification required by paragraph A may be made to a person of sufficient maturity with whom the juvenile is residing if the juvenile's legal custodian cannot be located.

* * *

4. The release or detention of a juvenile may be ordered by a juvenile caseworker * * *. [Provisions relating to intake and diversion are omitted. This subject is discussed below.]

Notes and Questions

1. *"Arraignment."* A juvenile taken into custody must be brought before the court within a short time, normally about twenty-four hours. The court informs the juvenile of the charges, explains applicable constitutional rights, appoints counsel where necessary, determines the conditions for release or orders preventive detention pending the adjudicatory hearing, and sets a hearing date. See, e.g., N.H. Rev. Stat. § 169–B:13.

2. *Fingerprints and photographs.* Consistent with the juvenile court's rehabilitative focus, many states traditionally prohibited police or juvenile authorities from taking fingerprints or photographs ("mug shots") of juvenile suspects, at least unless such taking was necessary to the investigation or was otherwise approved by the court. Juvenile codes also typically required law enforcement to turn over this evidence to the juvenile court, which would treat it in accordance with general confidentiality statutes and statutes providing for sealing or expunging the record.

The recent juvenile justice trend toward punishment and accountability has changed the landscape considerably. For juveniles charged only with less serious offenses or for particularly young juveniles, some states still prohibit fingerprinting or photographing without court approval. See, e.g., La. Stat. Ch. Code Art. 818 (misdemeanors not involving use of a weapon); Neb. Rev. Stat. § 43–252(1) (juveniles under fourteen). Most states, however, permit authorities to fingerprint or photograph juvenile suspects without application to the court, at least where the child has reached a specific age or is charged with a serious felony. See, e.g., Conn. Gen. Stat. § 46b–133(a). Indeed many states now mandate fingerprinting and photographing of juvenile suspects in some or all circumstances. See, e.g., Fla. Stat. § 985.212 (juveniles charged with felonies and other enumerated serious offenses); N.C. Gen. Stat. § 7B–2102(a) (juveniles 10 or older).

Several states still provide for destruction of fingerprints or photographs where no charge is filed or where the juvenile court determines the juvenile did not commit the offense charged. See, e.g., Ind. Code § 31–39–5–4. Otherwise fingerprints and photographs normally become part of the juvenile court record, and thus remain subject to statutes providing for expungement or sealing of the record. See, e.g., Ky. Rev. Stat. Ann. § 610.300(2). Where a juvenile is transferred to criminal court, the juvenile may be fingerprinted and photographed in accordance with the statutes and rules governing adult suspects. See, e.g., Kan. Stat. Ann. § 38–1611(a)(3)(A).

What policy considerations should the legislature weigh in determining whether to permit or mandate fingerprinting or photographing of juveniles in custody? In what circumstances, if any, should court approval be required?

3. *Lineups.* Only a few state juvenile codes have statutes relating to lineups. The statutes normally require a court order before authorities may place an alleged delinquent in a lineup. See, e.g., Mich. Comp. Laws § 712A.32(1).

2. *Search and Seizure*

NEW JERSEY v. T.L.O.

Supreme Court of the United States, 1985.
469 U.S. 325.

JUSTICE WHITE delivered the opinion of the Court.

* * *

I

On March 7, 1980, a teacher at Piscataway High School in Middlesex County, N.J., discovered two girls smoking in a lavatory. One of the two girls was the respondent T.L.O., who at that time was a 14–year-old high school freshman. Because smoking in the lavatory was a violation of a school rule, the teacher took the two girls to the Principal's office, where they met with Assistant Vice Principal Theodore Choplick. In response to questioning by Mr. Choplick, T.L.O.'s companion admitted that she had violated the rule. T.L.O., however, denied that she had been smoking in the lavatory and claimed that she did not smoke at all.

Mr. Choplick asked T.L.O. to come into his private office and demanded to see her purse. Opening the purse, he found a pack of cigarettes, which he removed from the purse and held before T.L.O. as he accused her of having lied to him. As he reached into the purse for the cigarettes, Mr. Choplick also noticed a package of cigarette rolling papers. In his experience, possession of rolling papers by high school students was closely associated with the use of marihuana. Suspecting that a closer examination of the purse might yield further evidence of drug use, Mr. Choplick proceeded to search the purse thoroughly. The search revealed a small amount of marihuana, a pipe, a number of empty plastic bags, a substantial quantity of money in one-dollar bills, an index card that appeared to be a list of students who owed T.L.O. money, and two letters that implicated T.L.O. in marihuana dealing.

Mr. Choplick notified T.L.O.'s mother and the police, and turned the evidence of drug dealing over to the police. At the request of the police, T.L.O.'s mother took her daughter to police headquarters, where T.L.O. confessed that she had been selling marihuana at the high school. On the basis of the confession and the evidence seized by Mr. Choplick, the State brought delinquency charges against T.L.O. in the Juvenile and Domestic Relations Court of Middlesex County. Contending that Mr. Choplick's search of her purse violated the Fourth Amendment, T.L.O. moved to suppress the evidence found in her purse as well as her confession, which, she argued, was tainted by the allegedly unlawful search. The Juvenile Court denied the motion to suppress. * * * [The court found T.L.O. delinquent and sentenced her to a year's probation. The state supreme court ordered suppression of the evidence found in her purse.].

* * *

* * * Having heard argument on the legality of the search of T.L.O.'s purse, we are satisfied that the search did not violate the Fourth Amendment.[4]

II

In determining whether the search at issue in this case violated the Fourth Amendment, we are faced initially with the question whether that Amendment's prohibition on unreasonable searches and seizures applies to searches conducted by public school officials. We hold that it does.

* * *

[T]his Court has never limited the Amendment's prohibition on unreasonable searches and seizures to operations conducted by the police. Rather, the Court has long spoken of the Fourth Amendment's strictures as restraints imposed upon "governmental action"—that is, "upon the activities of sovereign authority." * * *

Notwithstanding the general applicability of the Fourth Amendment to the activities of civil authorities, a few courts have concluded that school officials are exempt from the dictates of the Fourth Amendment by virtue of the special nature of their authority over schoolchildren. Teachers and school administrators, it is said, act *in loco parentis* in their dealings with students: their authority is that of the parent, not the State, and is therefore not subject to the limits of the Fourth Amendment.

4. * * * [O]ur determination that the search at issue in this case did not violate the Fourth Amendment implies no particu- lar resolution of the question of the applicability of the exclusionary rule.

Such reasoning is in tension with contemporary reality and the teachings of this Court. We have held school officials subject to the commands of the First Amendment, see *Tinker* v. *Des Moines Independent Community School District* (1969), and the Due Process Clause of the Fourteenth Amendment, see *Goss* v. *Lopez* (1975). If school authorities are state actors for purposes of the constitutional guarantees of freedom of expression and due process, it is difficult to understand why they should be deemed to be exercising parental rather than public authority when conducting searches of their students. More generally, the Court has recognized that "the concept of parental delegation" as a source of school authority is not entirely "consonant with compulsory education laws." Today's public school officials do not merely exercise authority voluntarily conferred on them by individual parents; rather, they act in furtherance of publicly mandated educational and disciplinary policies. In carrying out searches and other disciplinary functions pursuant to such policies, school officials act as representatives of the State, not merely as surrogates for the parents, and they cannot claim the parents' immunity from the strictures of the Fourth Amendment.

III

To hold that the Fourth Amendment applies to searches conducted by school authorities is only to begin the inquiry into the standards governing such searches. Although the underlying command of the Fourth Amendment is always that searches and seizures be reasonable, what is reasonable depends on the context within which a search takes place. The determination of the standard of reasonableness governing any specific class of searches requires "balancing the need to search against the invasion which the search entails." On one side of the balance are arrayed the individual's legitimate expectations of privacy and personal security; on the other, the government's need for effective methods to deal with breaches of public order.

We have recognized that even a limited search of the person is a substantial invasion of privacy. * * * A search of a child's person or of a closed purse or other bag carried on her person,[5] no less than a similar search carried out on an adult, is undoubtedly a severe violation of subjective expectations of privacy.

* * *

Although this Court may take notice of the difficulty of maintaining discipline in the public schools today, the situation is not so dire that students in the schools may claim no legitimate expectations of privacy. * * *

---

5. We do not address the question, not presented by this case, whether a schoolchild has a legitimate expectation of privacy in lockers, desks, or other school property provided for the storage of school supplies. Nor do we express any opinion on the standards (if any) governing searches of such areas by school officials or by other public authorities acting at the request of school officials.

Nor does the State's suggestion that children have no legitimate need to bring personal property into the schools seem well anchored in reality. Students at a minimum must bring to school not only the supplies needed for their studies, but also keys, money, and the necessaries of personal hygiene and grooming. In addition, students may carry on their persons or in purses or wallets such nondisruptive yet highly personal items as photographs, letters, and diaries. Finally, students may have perfectly legitimate reasons to carry with them articles of property needed in connection with extracurricular or recreational activities. In short, schoolchildren may find it necessary to carry with them a variety of legitimate, noncontraband items, and there is no reason to conclude that they have necessarily waived all rights to privacy in such items merely by bringing them onto school grounds.

Against the child's interest in privacy must be set the substantial interest of teachers and administrators in maintaining discipline in the classroom and on school grounds. Maintaining order in the classroom has never been easy, but in recent years, school disorder has often taken particularly ugly forms: drug use and violent crime in the schools have become major social problems. Even in schools that have been spared the most severe disciplinary problems, the preservation of order and a proper educational environment requires close supervision of schoolchildren, as well as the enforcement of rules against conduct that would be perfectly permissible if undertaken by an adult. "Events calling for discipline are frequent occurrences and sometimes require immediate, effective action." Accordingly, we have recognized that maintaining security and order in the schools requires a certain degree of flexibility in school disciplinary procedures, and we have respected the value of preserving the informality of the student-teacher relationship.

How, then, should we strike the balance between the schoolchild's legitimate expectations of privacy and the school's equally legitimate need to maintain an environment in which learning can take place? It is evident that the school setting requires some easing of the restrictions to which searches by public authorities are ordinarily subject. The warrant requirement, in particular, is unsuited to the school environment: requiring a teacher to obtain a warrant before searching a child suspected of an infraction of school rules (or of the criminal law) would unduly interfere with the maintenance of the swift and informal disciplinary procedures needed in the schools. Just as we have in other cases dispensed with the warrant requirement when "the burden of obtaining a warrant is likely to frustrate the governmental purpose behind the search," we hold today that school officials need not obtain a warrant before searching a student who is under their authority.

The school setting also requires some modification of the level of suspicion of illicit activity needed to justify a search. Ordinarily, a search—even one that may permissibly be carried out without a warrant—must be based upon "probable cause" to believe that a violation of the law has occurred. However, "probable cause" is not an irreducible requirement of a valid search. The fundamental command of the Fourth

Amendment is that searches and seizures be reasonable, and although "both the concept of probable cause and the requirement of a warrant bear on the reasonableness of a search, . . . in certain limited circumstances neither is required." * * * Where a careful balancing of governmental and private interests suggests that the public interest is best served by a Fourth Amendment standard of reasonableness that stops short of probable cause, we have not hesitated to adopt such a standard.

We join the majority of courts that have examined this issue in concluding that the accommodation of the privacy interests of schoolchildren with the substantial need of teachers and administrators for freedom to maintain order in the schools does not require strict adherence to the requirement that searches be based on probable cause to believe that the subject of the search has violated or is violating the law. Rather, the legality of a search of a student should depend simply on the reasonableness, under all the circumstances, of the search. Determining the reasonableness of any search involves a twofold inquiry: first, one must consider "whether the . . . action was justified at its inception"; second, one must determine whether the search as actually conducted "was reasonably related in scope to the circumstances which justified the interference in the first place." Under ordinary circumstances, a search of a student by a teacher or other school official[7] will be "justified at its inception" when there are reasonable grounds for suspecting that the search will turn up evidence that the student has violated or is violating either the law or the rules of the school.[8] Such a search will be permissible in its scope when the measures adopted are reasonably related to the objectives of the search and not excessively intrusive in light of the age and sex of the student and the nature of the infraction.

This standard will, we trust, neither unduly burden the efforts of school authorities to maintain order in their schools nor authorize unrestrained intrusions upon the privacy of schoolchildren. By focusing attention on the question of reasonableness, the standard will spare teachers and school administrators the necessity of schooling themselves in the niceties of probable cause and permit them to regulate their conduct according to the dictates of reason and common sense. At the same time, the reasonableness standard should ensure that the interests

---

7. We here consider only searches carried out by school authorities acting alone and on their own authority. This case does not present the question of the appropriate standard for assessing the legality of searches conducted by school officials in conjunction with or at the behest of law enforcement agencies, and we express no opinion on that question.

8. We do not decide whether individualized suspicion is an essential element of the reasonableness standard we adopt for searches by school authorities. In other contexts, however, we have held that although "some quantum of individualized suspicion is usually a prerequisite to a constitutional search or seizure[,] . . . the Fourth Amend-

ment imposes no irreducible requirement of such suspicion." Exceptions to the requirement of individualized suspicion are generally appropriate only where the privacy interests implicated by a search are minimal and where "other safeguards" are available "to assure that the individual's reasonable expectation of privacy is not 'subject to the discretion of the official in the field.' " Because the search of T.L.O.'s purse was based upon an individualized suspicion that she had violated school rules, we need not consider the circumstances that might justify school authorities in conducting searches unsupported by individualized suspicion.

of students will be invaded no more than is necessary to achieve the legitimate end of preserving order in the schools.

IV

[The Court upheld the reasonableness, and hence the lawfulness, of the search in this case.].

Reversed.

[Concurring and dissenting opinions are omitted.].

Notes and Questions

1. *Questions about* T.L.O. *T.L.O.* was a "compromise between the privacy interests of a schoolchild and the school's responsibility for maintaining discipline." Homer H. Clark, Jr., Children and the Constitution, 1992 U. Ill. L. Rev. 1, 7.

(a) What must the state show to sustain the constitutionality of a public school official's search of a student?,

(b) *T.L.O.* held that the constitutionality of a public school official's search of a student is determined by the reasonableness of the search itself, rather than by probable cause. How does the Court justify this departure from general Fourth Amendment jurisprudence?,

(c) A few months before *T.L.O.*, the Court held that because of the need to maintain prison security and discipline, the Fourth Amendment does not apply to searches of prison inmates. Hudson v. Palmer, 468 U.S. 517 (1984). Why, then, did *T.L.O.* reject lower court holdings that "school officials are exempt from the dictates of the Fourth Amendment by virtue of the special nature of their authority over schoolchildren"?

2. *Acting in concert with police. T.L.O.* left open the question whether the reasonable suspicion test applies to searches conducted by school officials "in conjunction with or at the behest of law enforcement agencies." 469 U.S. at 341 n.7. Whether a principal or other school official conducted the search as a police agent depends on the circumstances. See, e.g., People In re P.E.A., 754 P.2d 382, 385 (Colo.1988).

Lower courts generally apply *T.L.O.'s* reasonableness standard to searches and seizures done by school officials, even when they later turn over the fruits of the search to law enforcement authorities. Courts recognize that law enforcement officers might try to avoid Fourth Amendment strictures by having school officials conduct searches or make seizures that would be unlawful if done by the police themselves. School officials, however, have a duty to take reasonable measures, including searches and seizures, to detect and prevent crime that might compromise a safe and secure learning environment. See, e.g., id. at 385–86.

The probable cause test has been applied where police conduct the search at the school, e.g., In re Thomas B.D., 486 S.E.2d 498, 501 (S.C.Ct. App.1997), or where school officials call police before conducting the search, Picha v. Wielgos, 410 F.Supp. 1214, 1219–21 (N.D.Ill.1976).

Throughout the 1990s, many states have enacted safe-schools acts that require school officials to report to police crimes occurring on school premises. In light of these acts, should the Fourth Amendment any longer set a lower threshold for searches by school officials than for searches by police officers?

3. *Age and sex.* T.L.O. says that a search's constitutionality depends in part on "the age and sex of the student." Did the Court weigh T.L.O.'s age or sex or otherwise offer guidance helpful to lower courts that must apply these factors?

Should the burden on a school official seeking to justify a search increase or decrease the older the student? An argument can be made that a search would be more traumatic to elementary students than high school students; an argument can also be made that high school students are more sensitive about their personal privacy than elementary school students. Speaking of strip searches, the Seventh Circuit has made the latter argument: "Perhaps counterintuitively, a very young child would suffer a lesser degree of trauma from a nude search than an older child. As children go through puberty, they become more conscious of their bodies and self-conscious about them. Consequently, the potential for a search to cause embarrassment and humiliation increases as children grow older." Cornfield v. Consolidated High Sch. Dist., 991 F.2d 1316, 1321 n. 1 (7th Cir. 1993).

As long as a search does not involve examination of the body, should searches of boys' property be judged by different standards than searches of girls' property? As long as a strip search or search of the body is done by an officer of the same sex as the student (as it inevitably must if it is to be found reasonable), should searches of boys and girls be judged by different standards?

4. *The degree of intrusion.* "The search of a person always involves a greater degree of intrusion upon one's privacy interest than the search of a thing." In re F.B., 726 A.2d 361, 365 (Pa.1999). Did *T.L.O.* concern a search of the student's person or her things? This note surveys various types of searches occurring in public schools, from the relatively less intrusive to the more intrusive:

(a) *Lockers.* T.L.O. did not decide whether public school students have a legitimate expectation of privacy with respect to their lockers, which may hold intimate personal effects but which may also hide weapons, drugs and other contraband.

Most courts have held that students have a legitimate expectation of privacy in their lockers and their contents. See, e.g., In re Patrick Y., 723 A.2d 523, 528 (Md.Ct.Spec.App.1999) (citing decisions). Some courts, however, have specified that the students' legitimate expectation is only minimal, at least where written school policy states that the student's possession of the locker is not exclusive as against the school, or that lockers may be searched without warning on reasonable suspicion that the contents threaten student health, welfare and safety. See, e.g., Commonwealth v. Cass, 709 A.2d 350, 356–57 (Pa.1998).

Some courts have held that students have no legitimate expectation of privacy because the locker is school property under school authorities' control. See, e.g., Shoemaker v. State, 971 S.W.2d 178, 182 (Tex. Ct. App. 1998). Other courts find no legitimate expectation where the school district's written policy states that lockers are not private property. See, e.g., In re Isiah B., 500 N.W.2d 637, 639 n. 1 (Wis.1993).

Even where a legitimate privacy expectation is recognized, courts ordinarily uphold the reasonableness of locker searches, including blanket searches of school lockers without individualized suspicion, by weighing the students' privacy interest against school officials' duty to maintain safety and discipline. See, e.g., In re Patrick Y., supra (upholding blanket locker search).

In a 1997 poll conducted by Columbia University's National Center on Addiction and Substance Abuse, 32% of teenagers "strongly favored" random locker searches at their schools for drugs and drug paraphernalia, and 23% "somewhat favored" such searches. Searches were "strongly favored" by 56% of parents and "somewhat favored" by 21%. See Bureau of Justice Statistics, Sourcebook of Criminal Justice Statistics 1997, tbl. 2.12 at 104 (1998).

(b) *Metal detectors.* Metal detectors (magnetometers) have become common fixtures in airports, courthouses, and some other public buildings. These devices have also appeared in many schools concerned about students who bring drugs or concealed guns, knives and other weapons to the campus. Hand-held or walk-through metal detectors may screen all persons who enter the school, or these devices may be directed only at particular persons at entrances or other places within the building. See National Inst. of Justice, The Appropriate and Effective Use of Security Technologies in U.S. Schools: A Guide for Schools and Law Enforcement Agencies (1999).

Use of the metal detector constitutes a Fourth Amendment search. See, e.g., McMorris v. Alioto, 567 F.2d 897, 900 (9th Cir. 1978). Where a metal detector screens all persons entering a public building as part of a general practice not associated with a criminal investigation to secure evidence, however, courts balance the government's interest in safety with "the absolutely minimal invasion of privacy" occasioned by the screen. Day v. Chicago Bd. of Educ., 1998 WL 60770 * 5 (N.D.Ill.). The Seventh Circuit has explained that the metal detector's use, "being unintrusive, is constitutionally unproblematic where * * * there is some reason—there needn't be much—to expect that armed and dangerous people might otherwise enter." Justice v. Elrod, 832 F.2d 1048, 1050 (7th Cir.1987). Courts have consistently upheld the constitutionality of general metal detector screening in public schools because "[t]he prevalence and general acceptance of metal scanners in today's society underscores the minimal nature of the intrusion." In re F.B., 726 A.2d 361, 366 (Pa.1999). Where school officials use a hand-held detector, the search's validity is not upset by the fact that a walk-through detector might be deemed less intrusive. Id.

Even in the absence of individualized suspicion, courts have upheld the constitutionality of metal detector scans against particular students, which may lead to a pat-down or further search if the detector is activated. See, e.g., In re Latasha W., 70 Cal.Rptr.2d 886, 886–87 (Ct.App.1998).

Courts have rejected contentions that school screening is unreasonable under the Fourth Amendment on the ground that students, unlike citizens entering most other public buildings, cannot withhold consent to search because they must attend school. See, e.g., People v. Pruitt, 662 N.E.2d 540, 545 (Ill.App.Ct.1996).

(c) *Sniff searches.* School officials sometimes use trained drug-sniffing dogs to search student lockers or students themselves. The reported decisions generally involve use of Doberman pinschers or German shepherds, large breeds designed to intimidate the target.

Sniff searches of students' persons have generally been upheld only on individualized suspicion relating to the particular students sniffed because "society recognizes the interest in the integrity of one's person, and the fourth amendment applies with its fullest vigor against any intrusion on the human body." Horton v. Goose Creek Indep. Sch. Dist., 690 F.2d 470, 478, 481–82 (5th Cir.1982). In Doe v. Renfrow, 631 F.2d 91 (7th Cir.1980), however, the court held that a dog-sniff of a student is not a search because of the diminished expectation of privacy in public schools, the school's in loco parentis duty to supervise students, and the minimal intrusion involved. Do *T.L.O.* and *Acton,* the next principal decision, implicitly overrule *Doe's* holding that a dog sniff of a student's person is not a Fourth Amendment search? But does *Acton* also implicitly overrule *Horton,* which held that a generalized dog-sniff search of all students' bodies may be done only on individualized suspicion?

Justice Brennan, dissenting from the Court's denial of certiorari in *Doe,* described the events that gave rise to the thirteen-year-old plaintiff's suit after a one-day general exploratory dog-sniffing of 2,780 junior and senior high school students:

> On the morning of March 23, 1979, petitioner went to her first-period class as usual. Shortly before 9:15, when the class was scheduled to adjourn, petitioner's teacher ordered everyone to remain seated until further notice. An assistant principal, accompanied by a police-trained German shepherd, a dog handler, and a uniformed police officer, then entered the classroom as one of six teams conducting simultaneous raids at the Highland schools. For the next 2 1/2 hours, petitioner and her classmates were required to sit quietly in their seats with their belongings in view and their hands upon their desks. They were forbidden to use the washroom unless accompanied by an escort. Uniformed police officers and school administrators were stationed in the halls. Guards were posted at the schoolhouse doors. While no student was allowed to leave the schoolhouse, representatives of the press and other news media, on invitation of the school authorities, were permitted to enter the classrooms to observe the proceedings.

> The dogs were led up and down each aisle of the classroom, from desk to desk, and from student to student. Each student was probed, sniffed, and inspected by at least 1 of the 14 German shepherds detailed to the school. When the search team assigned to petitioner's classroom reached petitioner, the police dog pressed forward, sniffed at her body, and repeatedly pushed its nose and muzzle into her legs. The uniformed officer then ordered petitioner to stand and empty her pockets, apparently because the dog "alerted" to the presence of drugs. However, no drugs were found. After petitioner emptied her pockets, the dog again

sniffed her body and again it apparently "alerted." Petitioner was then escorted to the nurse's office for a more thorough physical inspection.

Petitioner was met at the nurse's office by two adult women, one a uniformed police officer. After denying that she had ever used marihuana, petitioner was ordered to strip. She did so, removing her clothing in the presence of the two women. The women then looked over petitioner's body, inspected her clothing, and touched and examined the hair on her head. Again, no drugs were found. [Justice Brennan's footnote— Apparently the police dogs alerted to petitioner because she had been playing with her own dog, which was in heat, on the morning of the raid.] Petitioner was subsequently allowed to dress and was escorted back to her classroom.

Doe v. Renfrow, 451 U.S. 1022, 1022–24 (1981) (Brennan, J., dissenting from denial of certiorari).

The Supreme Court has held that dog sniffs of personal property are not Fourth Amendment searches, United States v. Place, 462 U.S. 696, 707 (1983), thus seemingly disposing of the constitutional question when a dog sniffs only student lockers.

(d) *Strip searches.* A strip search requires a person to remove all or most clothes to reveal areas of his or her body, including areas normally covered by underclothes. Strip searches, sometimes called nude searches, have been termed "the greatest personal indignity" the state can impose on a person, Bell v. Wolfish, 441 U.S. 520, 594 (1979) (Stevens, J., dissenting), and "a violation of every known principle of human decency." Doe v. Renfrow, 631 F.2d 91, 93 (7th Cir.1980).

T.L.O. did not address public school strip searches, but left the door open to their use by stating that a search's "intrusiveness" was only one factor to weigh in determining its reasonableness. Americans, however, evidently show little enthusiasm for them. In a 1999 USA WEEKEND scientific poll of adults, 71% of respondents rejected strip searches of students by school officials. See Gregg Easterbrook, USA WEEKEND's Third Annual America's Poll, USA Weekend, July 4, 1999. Perusal of press reports nevertheless suggests that strip searches periodically occur in the public schools, producing damage actions that frequently result in out-of-court settlements, sometimes with sizeable payments to the searched students.

The reported decisions involve strip searches conducted by school officials seeking drugs, stolen money (sometimes in quite minuscule amounts), or other contraband. At least in the reported decisions, strip searches have usually turned up empty, not yielding the contraband the school officials were seeking. The reported strip searches have been done by school officials of the same sex as the student because "[a] nude search of a student by an administrator or teacher of the opposite sex would obviously violate [*T.L.O's*] standard." Cornfield v. Consolidated High Sch. Dist., 991 F.2d 1316, 1320 (7th Cir. 1993).

Most decisions have found strip searches of students unreasonable under the Fourth Amendment. In Konop v. Northwestern Sch. Dist., 26 F. Supp. 2d 1189 (D.S.D.1998), for example, the court held that strip searches of two eighth grade students were unreasonable because school officials did not have a reasonable basis for believing that either student had stolen the $200 the officials sought. *Konop's* survey of strip search precedent yielded three "clear" rules: "(1) a strip search is not justified absent individualized suspicion unless there is a legitimate safety concern (e.g. weapons); (2) school officials must be investigating allegations of violations of the law or school rules and only individual accusations justify a strip search; and (3) strip searches must be designed to be minimally intrusive, taking into account the item for which the search is conducted." Id. at 1201. See also, e.g., Sostarecz v. Misko, 1999 WL 239401 *6 (E.D.Pa.) (holding that once tests of suspected junior high school student's pupils and vital signs produced normal results, school officials did not act reasonably by requiring student to remove her pants so her legs could be checked for drug use); Oliver v. McClung, 919 F.Supp. 1206 (N.D.Ind.1995) (holding that strip searching several seventh grade girls after $4.50 was reported stolen was unreasonable); Bellnier v. Lund, 438 F.Supp. 47, 53–54 (N.D.N.Y.1977) (holding that strip search of entire fifth grade class for stolen three dollars was unreasonable for lack of particularized suspicion and because of the "relatively slight danger of the conduct involved").

Courts have sometimes held strip searches reasonable under the Fourth Amendment, however, where school officials had reasonable suspicion that the particular student possessed the material sought. In Cornfield v. Consolidated High School District, supra, 991 F.2d 1316, for example, the court of appeals held that the school officials acted reasonably because they had information that the searched sixteen-year-old high school student had smoked marijuana on a school bus, "crotched" marijuana, dealt drugs, tested positive for marijuana, and failed to complete a drug rehabilitation program. The panel emphasized, however, that "as the intrusiveness of the search of a student intensifies, so too does the standard of Fourth Amendment reasonableness. What may constitute reasonable suspicion for a search of a locker or even a pocket or pocketbook may fall well short of reasonableness for a nude search." Id. at 1321. See also, e.g., Williams ex rel. Williams v. Ellington, 936 F.2d 881 (6th Cir. 1991) (holding that strip search of two high school students was reasonable because an informant had twice told the principal that the students possessed drugs in school).

If the principal suspected that a teacher or other adult employee possessed drugs on school premises or had stolen money, would the Fourth Amendment permit a strip search of the teacher or employee based only on reasonable suspicion in the absence of probable cause? Do you think the principal would conduct or order the strip search?

Children may be strip searched when they are in custody for a crime or delinquent act, when they visit prisoners in penal institutions, or when they are a victim of suspected abuse. See Steven F. Shatz et al., The Strip Search of Children and the Fourth Amendment, 26 U. S.F. L. Rev. 1, 18–39 (1991).

5. *The exclusionary rule.* T.L.O. declined to decide whether the Fourth Amendment exclusionary rule applies in delinquency proceedings arising from unlawful searches by school authorities. 469 U.S. at 333 n.3. At the very least, application of the rule to school disciplinary proceedings would now seem to be foreclosed by Pennsylvania Bd. of Probation and Parole v.

Scott, 524 U.S. 357, 363 (1998), which refused to "extend the exclusionary rule to proceedings other than criminal trials."

The Court, however, has not determined whether the rule applies in delinquency proceedings, which hold a hybrid status as civil proceedings on which the Court has engrafted some significant constitutional protections applicable in criminal trials. One commentator finds it "unlikely" that the Supreme Court would apply the rule in delinquency proceedings "especially for school searches, with the possible exception of gross governmental incursions that sink to the level of shock-the-conscience due process violations." See Irene Merker Rosenberg, A Door Left Open: Applicability of the Fourth Amendment Exclusionary Rule to Juvenile Court Delinquency Hearings, 24 Am. J. Crim. L. 29, 33 (1996).

6. *Rights under state law.* T.L.O. determined only the student's Fourth Amendment rights. A search that passes muster under the federal Constitution might nonetheless violate state constitutional guarantees. See, e.g., In re F.B., 726 A.2d 361, 365 (Pa.1999). Most state education acts remain silent about strip searches, but a handful prohibit them. See, e.g., Okla. Stat. tit. 70, § 24–102.

7. *Judicial deference to school authorities.* Several commentators have criticized *T.L.O.* for applying a reasonable suspicion standard that would ordinarily result in judicial deference to school authorities at the expense of student privacy. See, e.g., Martin R. Gardner, Student Privacy in the Wake of *T.L.O.*: An Appeal for an Individualized Suspicion Requirement For Valid Searches and Seizures in the Schools, 22 Ga. L. Rev. 897 (1988); Irene Merker Rosenberg, *New Jersey v. T.L.O.*: Of Children and Smokescreens, 19 Fam. L.Q. 311 (1985). One researcher found thirty-six student-search decisions where reasonable suspicion was a disputed question between 1985 (when *T.L.O.* was decided) and November, 1993. (Cases arising from random or mass searches were not included). Courts upheld the search in 31 of the 36 decisions. From January 1, 1990 to November 1993, courts held that school authorities lacked reasonable suspicion in only two of twenty-one decisions. See Joseph R. McKinney, The Fourth Amendment and the Public Schools: Reasonable Suspicion in the 1990s, 91 Ed. Law Rep. 455 (1994).

8. *Consent to search.* May a juvenile give valid consent to a search of his or her person or property? May a parent give valid consent to search the home for evidence concerning suspected criminality of a child living in the home? See Wayne R. LaFave and Jerold H. Israel, Criminal Procedure § 3.10(b), (e), at 235–36, 242 (2d ed. 1992); In re Tariq A–R–Y, 701 A.2d 691, 692 (Md.1997).

PROBLEM 11–2

You are counsel to a public school district in a state without a statute addressing the permissibility of student strip searches. Should the district adopt a written policy permitting school authorities to strip search students, or should the policy deny such permission? If permission is granted, what guidelines should be established for determining when a strip search may be done? Should strip searches be permissible only on reasonable suspicion that the particular student possesses contraband, or should strip searches of groups of students or entire classes be permissible without individualized suspicion? If the need to strip search a particular student is so great, should the police be summoned instead?

VERNONIA SCHOOL DISTRICT 47J v. ACTON

Supreme Court of the United States, 1995.
515 U.S. 646.

[The majority and concurring opinions appear in Chapter 1, p. 52]

JUSTICE O'CONNOR, with whom JUSTICE STEVENS and JUSTICE SOUTER join, dissenting.

The population of our Nation's public schools, grades 7 through 12, numbers around 18 million. By the reasoning of today's decision, the millions of these students who participate in interscholastic sports, an overwhelming majority of whom have given school officials no reason whatsoever to suspect they use drugs at school, are open to an intrusive bodily search.

* * *

* * * For most of our constitutional history, mass, suspicionless searches have been generally considered *per se* unreasonable within the meaning of the Fourth Amendment. And we have allowed exceptions in recent years only where it has been clear that a suspicion-based regime would be ineffectual. Because that is not the case here, I dissent.

I

A

* * * The view that mass, suspicionless searches, however even-handed, are generally unreasonable remains inviolate in the criminal law enforcement context, at least where the search is more than minimally intrusive. * * *

* * * Outside the criminal context, however, in response to the exigencies of modern life, our cases have upheld several evenhanded blanket searches, including some that are more than minimally intrusive, after balancing the invasion of privacy against the government's strong need. Most of these cases, of course, are distinguishable insofar as they involved searches either not of a personally intrusive nature, such as searches of closely regulated businesses, or arising in unique contexts such as prisons. * * *

In any event, in many of the cases that can be distinguished on the grounds suggested above and, more important, in *all* of the cases that cannot, we upheld the suspicionless search only after first recognizing the Fourth Amendment's longstanding preference for a suspicion-based search regime, and then pointing to sound reasons why such a regime would likely be ineffectual under the unusual circumstances presented. * * * "In limited circumstances, where the privacy interests implicated by the search are minimal, and where an important governmental interest furthered by the intrusion *would be placed in jeopardy by a requirement of individualized suspicion*, a search may be reasonable despite the absence of such suspicion." (emphasis added). The obvious negative implication of this reasoning is that, if such an individualized suspicion requirement would not place the government's objectives in jeopardy, the requirement should not be forsaken.

* * *

B

* * *

* * * The great irony of this case is that most (though not all) of the evidence the District introduced to justify its suspicionless drug testing program consisted of first-or second-hand stories of particular, identifiable students acting in ways that plainly gave rise to reasonable suspicion of in-school drug use—and thus that would have justified a drug-related search under our *T.L.O.* decision. * * *

In light of all this evidence of drug use by particular students, there is a substantial basis for concluding that a vigorous regime of suspicion-based testing * * * would have gone a long way toward solving Vernonia's school drug problem while preserving the Fourth Amendment rights of James Acton and others like him. And were there any doubt about such a conclusion, it is removed by indications in the record that suspicion-based testing could have been supplemented by an equally vigorous campaign to have Vernonia's parents encourage their children to submit to the District's *voluntary* drug testing program. In these circumstances, the Fourth Amendment dictates that a mass, suspicionless search regime is categorically unreasonable.

* * *

The principal counterargument to all this, central to the Court's opinion, is that the Fourth Amendment is more lenient with respect to school searches. That is no doubt correct, for, as the Court explains, schools have traditionally had special guardian-like responsibilities for children that necessitate a degree of constitutional leeway. This principle explains the considerable Fourth Amendment leeway we gave school officials in *T.L.O.* * * *

The instant case, however, asks whether the Fourth Amendment is even more lenient than that, *i.e.*, whether it is *so* lenient that students may be deprived of the Fourth Amendment's only remaining, and most basic, categorical protection: its strong preference for an individualized suspicion requirement, with its accompanying antipathy toward personally intrusive, blanket searches of mostly innocent people. It is not at all clear that people in *prison* lack this categorical protection, and we have said "[w]e are not yet ready to hold that the schools and the prisons need be equated for purposes of the Fourth Amendment." Thus, if we are to mean what we often proclaim—that students do not "shed their constitutional rights ... at the schoolhouse gate," *Tinker* v. *Des Moines Independent Community School Dist.*—the answer must plainly be no. * * *

* * *

II

* * *

On this record, then, it seems to me that the far more reasonable choice would have been to focus on the class of students found to have violated published school rules against severe disruption in class and around campus—disruption that had a strong nexus to drug use, as the District established at trial. Such a choice would share two of the virtues of a suspicion-based regime: testing dramatically fewer students, tens as against hundreds, and giving students control, through their behavior, over the likelihood that they would be tested. Moreover, there would be a reduced concern for the accusatory nature of the search, because the Court's feared "badge of shame" would already exist, due to the antecedent accusation and finding of severe disruption. * * *

III

It cannot be too often stated that the greatest threats to our constitutional freedoms come in times of crisis. But we must also stay mindful that not all government responses to such times are hysterical overreactions; some crises are quite real, and when they are, they serve precisely as the compelling state interest that we have said may justify a measured intrusion on constitutional rights. The only way for judges to mediate these conflicting impulses is to do what they should do anyway: stay close to the record in each case that appears before them, and make their judgments based on that alone. Having reviewed the record here, I cannot avoid the conclusion that the District's suspicionless policy of testing all student athletes sweeps too broadly, and too imprecisely, to be reasonable under the Fourth Amendment.

Notes and Questions

1. Notes exploring *Acton's* reach appear in Chapter 1. (a) Does *Acton* take a different view than *T.L.O.* of the in loco parentis doctrine's role in public elementary and secondary education?,

(b) The dissenters asserted that *Acton* "dispenses with a requirement of individualized suspicion" in circumstances not fitting within one of the traditional, limited exceptions. If the assertion is true, what explains the Court's action?,

(c) Would *Acton* necessarily permit school authorities, seeking evidence of drugs, to do strip searches of student-athletes in the absence of individualized suspicion?,

(d) *T.L.O.* did not decide whether individualized suspicion is an essential element of the reasonableness standard applicable to searches of students by public school authorities. Does *Acton* provide an answer for some or all searches?,

(e) Because of the peculiar intrusiveness of student strip searches, should the Supreme Court interpret the Fourth Amendment to permit such searches based only on probable cause or a warrant? Does *Acton* offer any basis for believing the Court might do this in an appropriate case?,

(f) Under what circumstances, if any, would the *Acton* dissenters approve drug tests of student-athletes in the absence of individualized suspicion?

2.   In Smith v. McGlothlin, 119 F.3d 786 (9th Cir. 1997), the high school vice principal and a school security guard responded to neighbors' complaints that congregating students were smoking in a nearby cul-de-sac. As the vice principal approached a group of about twenty students, he noticed a cloud of smoke over their heads and furtive motions he associated with the discarding of smoking materials. Because he could not see which students had been smoking, he brought them all to school and ordered them to remain in the suspension room. He then had each student searched individually, which took about two hours. The sixteen-year-old student plaintiff was found to be carrying three knives: a double-edged dagger with a 4–inch blade, a folding knife with a 3–inch blade, and a smaller folding knife. School authorities turned her over to the police, but the juvenile court suppressed the evidence and dismissed the charges.

   The student then filed a 42 U.S.C. § 1983 action alleging that the vice principal had violated her civil rights by searching her without individualized suspicion that she had been smoking, and that he conducted the search unreasonably. The Ninth Circuit indicated that the juvenile court erred because *Acton* does not require individualized suspicion, but did not decide the question because it affirmed dismissal of the action on other grounds. Concurring for himself and Judge Betty B. Fletcher, Judge Alex Kozinski delivered this tongue-lashing:

> * * * A teenager who gets into trouble because she is caught bringing knives to school might, for lack of mature judgment, feel that she is the one who has been wronged. But she can't turn such wishful thinking into a lawsuit without support from her parents and the services of a lawyer-adults who do not have youth and inexperience as excuses. Before bringing suit, Smith's parents might profitably have pondered their own culpability and considered what they might have done to prevent their child's misconduct. Smith's lawyer might have thought about whether it was right to impose the cost, risk and pain of a lawsuit on a civil servant who acted responsibly under difficult circumstances. And Smith herself might have thanked her lucky stars when she got off easy because her juvenile court judge misread the law and suppressed the evidence. Smith and the adults who abetted her might all have taken a lesson in common sense from the other students who were subjected to the same search—and thus suffered the same "harm"—but did not make a federal case out of it.

119 F.3d at 788–89.

PROBLEM 11–3

You are counsel to a public school district that is considering whether to institute a random metal detector search policy. Walkthrough detectors may be used at all entrances without notice, or individual students may be subjected to hand-held detectors without prior notice. What advice would you provide to the school board?

PROBLEM 11–4

By the late 1990s, public school safety became a transcendent national issue when students shot and killed classmates in Pearl, Mississippi, West Paducah, Kentucky, Jonesboro, Arkansas, Springfield, Oregon, Conyers, Georgia, Edinboro, Pennsylvania, and Littleton, Colorado. In response to these tragedies, school authorities in your town have begun periodically searching student lockers, book bags and purses, sometimes with the help of drug sniffing dogs. The aims are to confiscate weapons and to crack down on drug use (which authorities believe sometimes leads to weapons possession and other violent behavior not conducive to a safe and secure learning environment). So far, some searches have yielded weapons or drugs, but many have not.

Assisted by their irate parents, a group of students has filed suit challenging the constitutionality of the search policy. As legal commentary editor of the leading local daily newspaper, you wish to write an article stating the law underlying the plaintiffs' claims and providing your views about the extent of disciplinary authority the school should hold.

Your article will treat several questions, including these: With the passage of time, does *T.L.O.'s* reasonableness standard appear as a prescient response to life in contemporary public schools? Or does the decision unwisely sacrifice students' constitutional rights in the face of perceived threat? Should the Fourth Amendment balancing test lean in favor of school authorities, even in the absence of individualized suspicion? Does *T.L.O.'s* reasonableness standard reflect the state's obligation to provide a safe and secure learning environment to children required by law to attend school? Do your answers depend on whether a generalized search is directed at property such as school lockers and their contents rather than the students' persons? After *T.L.O.* and *Acton*, what is the law regarding searches in the public schools?

PROBLEM 11–5

John Smith, principal of Central High School in southern Illinois, chaperoned a group of students on the school sponsored senior trip to Disney World in Florida. Before leaving on the voluntary trip, school officials provided students a brochure notifying them that their hotel rooms would be subjected to "room checks" throughout the trip. The brochure also stated that "[a]ny behavior discrepancies, either direct or by close association, will be dealt with through standard School Disciplinary Codes and Procedures." Permission slips, signed by each participant and his or her parent, stated in part: "We understand the absolute forbidden use of any alcohol or drugs by our son/daughter, and that partaking in such substances would subject him/her to early departure and school discipline policies upon return." In addition, each student and a parent signed a "Drug, Alcohol and Incident Free Pledge."

Returning to their hotel room on the second day of the trip, principal Smith and his wife walked past several student rooms, where they saw a large group of students together in the hallway and smelled a strong odor of marijuana. Shortly thereafter, the principal and hotel security officers searched a majority of the twenty student rooms, generally searching only areas in plain view without opening suitcases or other containers. Using a pass key provided by hotel security officers, the principal also searched the rooms' safes, where he found alcohol and significant quantities of marijuana belonging to several of the students. The offending students were sent home early from the trip and ultimately suspended from school for three days. The students sued the principal and the school district under 42 U.S.C. § 1983, claiming a violation of their Fourth Amendment right to be free from unreasonable searches and seizures. How should the court decide the case under *T.L.O.* and *Acton*?

3. *Interrogation and Confession*

In Miranda v. Arizona, 384 U.S. 436, 444 (1966), an adult criminal proceeding, the Court held that "the prosecution may not use statements, whether exculpatory or inculpatory, stemming from custodial interrogation of the defendant unless it demonstrates the use of procedural safeguards effective to secure the [Fifth Amendment] privilege against self-incrimination." Writing for the Court, Chief Justice Warren stated the rule this way:

> By custodial interrogation, we mean questioning initiated by law enforcement officers after a person has been taken into custody or otherwise deprived of his freedom of action in any significant way. As for the procedural safeguards to be employed, unless other fully effective means are devised to inform accused persons of their right of silence and to assure a continuous opportunity to exercise it, the following measures are required. Prior to any questioning, the person must be warned that he has a right to remain silent, that any statement he does make may be used as evidence against him, and that he has a right to the presence of an attorney, either retained or appointed. The defendant may waive effectuation of these rights, provided the waiver is made voluntarily, knowingly and intelligently. If, however, he indicates in any manner and at any stage of the process that he wishes to consult with an attorney before speaking there can be no questioning. Likewise, if the individual is alone and indicates in any manner that he does not wish to be interrogated, the police may not question him. The mere fact that he may have

answered some questions or volunteered some statements on his own does not deprive him of the right to refrain from answering any further inquiries until he has consulted with an attorney and thereafter consents to be questioned.

Id. A waiver of the right to remain silent is voluntary when it is the "product of a free and deliberate choice rather than intimidation, coercion, or deception." Moran v. Burbine, 475 U.S. 412, 421 (1986). The waiver is knowing and intelligent when the suspect was aware "both of the nature of the right being abandoned and the consequences of the decision to abandon it." Colorado v. Spring, 479 U.S. 564, 573 (1987).

The following decision was the Court's first effort to apply *Miranda* when the suspect is a juvenile who might later be the subject of a delinquency proceeding or a criminal trial after transfer.

FARE v. MICHAEL C.

Supreme Court of the United States, 1979.
442 U.S. 707.

MR. JUSTICE BLACKMUN delivered the opinion of the Court.

* * *

I

Respondent Michael C. was implicated in the murder of Robert Yeager. The murder occurred during a robbery of the victim's home on January 19, 1976. A small truck registered in the name of respondent's mother was identified as having been near the Yeager home at the time of the killing, and a young man answering respondent's description was seen by witnesses near the truck and near the home shortly before Yeager was murdered.

On the basis of this information, Van Nuys, Cal., police took respondent into custody at approximately 6:30 p. m. on February 4. Respondent then was 16 1/2 years old and on probation to the Juvenile Court. He had been on probation since the age of 12. Approximately one year earlier he had served a term in a youth corrections camp under the supervision of the Juvenile Court. He had a record of several previous offenses, including burglary of guns and purse snatching, stretching back over several years.

Upon respondent's arrival at the Van Nuys station house two police officers began to interrogate him. The officers and respondent were the only persons in the room during the interrogation. The conversation was tape-recorded. One of the officers initiated the interview by informing respondent that he had been brought in for questioning in relation to a murder. The officer fully advised respondent of his *Miranda* rights. The following exchange then occurred * * *

"Q. . . . Do you understand all of these rights as I have explained them to you?

"A. Yeah.

"Q. Okay, do you wish to give up your right to remain silent and talk to us about this murder?

"A. What murder? I don't know about no murder.

"Q. I'll explain to you which one it is if you want to talk to us about it.

"A. Yeah, I might talk to you.

"Q. Do you want to give up your right to have an attorney present here while we talk about it?

"A. *Can I have my probation officer here?*

"Q. Well I can't get a hold of your probation officer right now. You have the right to an attorney.

"A. How I know you guys won't pull no police officer in and tell me he's an attorney?

"Q. Huh?

"A. [How I know you guys won't pull no police officer in and tell me he's an attorney?]

"Q. Your probation officer is Mr. Christiansen.

"A. Yeah.

"Q. Well I'm not going to call Mr. Christiansen tonight. There's a good chance we can talk to him later, but I'm not going to call him right now. If you want to talk to us without an attorney present, you can. If you don't want to, you don't have to. But if you want to say something, you can, and if you don't want to say something you don't have to. That's your right. You understand that right?

"A. Yeah.

"Q. Okay, will you talk to us without an attorney present?

"A. Yeah I want to talk to you."

Respondent thereupon proceeded to answer questions put to him by the officers. He made statements and drew sketches that incriminated him in the Yeager murder. [He was charged in juvenile court with the murder. He moved to suppress the statements and sketches on the ground that they were made in violation of *Miranda* because his request to see his probation officer was per se an invocation of his Fifth Amendment right to remain silent, just as if he had requested an attorney. The juvenile court denied the suppression motion, the court of appeals affirmed, but the state supreme court reversed. The Supreme Court granted the state's motion for a writ of certiorari and now reverses.].

II

* * *

The California court in this case * * * significantly has extended [*Miranda's*] rule by providing that a request by a juvenile for his probation officer has the same effect as a request for an attorney. Based on the court's belief that the probation officer occupies a position as a trusted guardian figure in the minor's life that would make it normal for the minor to turn to the officer when apprehended by the police, and based as well on the state-law requirement that the officer represent the interest of the juvenile, the California decision found that consultation with a probation officer fulfilled the role for the juvenile that consultation with an attorney does in general, acting as a " 'protective [device] . . . to dispel the compulsion inherent in custodial surroundings.' "

The rule in *Miranda*, however, was based on this Court's perception that the lawyer occupies a critical position in our legal system because of his unique ability to protect the Fifth Amendment rights of a client undergoing custodial interrogation. Because of this special ability of the lawyer to help the client preserve his Fifth Amendment rights once the client becomes enmeshed in the adversary process, the Court found that "the right to have counsel present at the interrogation is indispensable to the protection of the Fifth Amendment privilege under the system" established by the Court. Moreover, the lawyer's presence helps guard against overreaching by the police and ensures that any statements actually obtained are accurately transcribed for presentation into evidence.

The *per se* aspect of *Miranda* was thus based on the unique role the lawyer plays in the adversary system of criminal justice in this country. Whether it is a minor or an adult who stands accused, the lawyer is the one person to whom society as a whole looks as the protector of the legal rights of that person in his dealings with the police and the courts. For this reason, the Court fashioned in *Miranda* the rigid rule that an accused's request for an attorney is *per se* an invocation of his Fifth Amendment rights, requiring that all interrogation cease.

A probation officer is not in the same posture with regard to either the accused or the system of justice as a whole. Often he is not trained in the law, and so is not in a position to advise the accused as to his legal rights. Neither is he a trained advocate, skilled in the representation of the interests of his client before both police and courts. He does not assume the power to act on behalf of his client by virtue of his status as adviser, nor are the communications of the accused to the probation officer shielded by the lawyer-client privilege.

Moreover, the probation officer is the employee of the State which seeks to prosecute the alleged offender. He is a peace officer, and as such is allied, to a greater or lesser extent, with his fellow peace officers. He owes an obligation to the State, notwithstanding the obligation he may also owe the juvenile under his supervision. In most cases, the probation officer is duty bound to report wrongdoing by the juvenile when it comes to his attention, even if by communication from the juvenile himself. * * *

In these circumstances, it cannot be said that the probation officer is able to offer the type of independent advice that an accused would expect from a lawyer retained or assigned to assist him during questioning. Indeed, the probation officer's duty to his employer in many, if not most, cases would conflict sharply with the interests of the juvenile. For where an attorney might well advise his client to remain silent in the face of interrogation by the police, and in doing so would be "exercising [his] good professional judgment . . . to protect to the extent of his ability the rights of his client," a probation officer would be bound to advise his charge to cooperate with the police. * * * It thus is doubtful that a general rule can be established that a juvenile, in every case, looks to his probation officer as a "trusted guardian figure" rather than as an officer of the court system that imposes punishment.

By the same token, a lawyer is able to protect his client's rights by learning the extent, if any, of the client's involvement in the crime under investigation, and advising his client accordingly. To facilitate this, the law rightly protects the communications between client and attorney from discovery. We doubt, however, that similar protection will be afforded the communications between the probation officer and the minor. Indeed, we doubt that a probation officer, consistent with his responsibilities to the public and his profession, could withhold from the police or the courts facts made known to him by the juvenile implicating the juvenile in the crime under investigation.

We thus believe it clear that the probation officer is not in a position to offer the type of legal assistance necessary to protect the Fifth Amendment rights of an accused undergoing custodial interrogation that a lawyer can offer. The Court in *Miranda* recognized that "the attorney plays a vital role in the administration of criminal justice under our Constitution." It is this pivotal role of legal counsel that justifies the *per se* rule established in *Miranda*, and that distinguishes the request for counsel from the request for a probation officer, a clergyman, or a close friend. A probation officer simply is not necessary, in the way an attorney is, for the protection of the legal rights of the accused, juvenile or adult. He is significantly handicapped by the position he occupies in the juvenile system from serving as an effective protector of the rights of a juvenile suspected of a crime.

* * *

Nor do we believe that a request by a juvenile to speak with his probation officer constitutes a *per se* request to remain silent. As indicated, since a probation officer does not fulfill the important role in protecting the rights of the accused juvenile that an attorney plays, we decline to find that the request for the probation officer is tantamount to the request for an attorney. And there is nothing inherent in the request for a probation officer that requires us to find that a juvenile's request to see one necessarily constitutes an expression of the juvenile's right to remain silent. As discussed below, courts may take into account such a request in evaluating whether a juvenile in fact had waived his Fifth

Amendment rights before confessing. But in other circumstances such a request might well be consistent with a desire to speak with the police. In the absence of further evidence that the minor intended in the circumstances to invoke his Fifth Amendment rights by such a request, we decline to attach such overwhelming significance to this request.

* * *

III

Miranda further recognized that after the required warnings are given the accused, "[i]f the interrogation continues without the presence of an attorney and a statement is taken, a heavy burden rests on the government to demonstrate that the defendant knowingly and intelligently waived his privilege against self-incrimination and his right to retained or appointed counsel." * * * [T]he question whether the accused waived his rights "is not one of form, but rather whether the defendant in fact knowingly and voluntarily waived the rights delineated in the *Miranda* case." Thus, the determination whether statements obtained during custodial interrogation are admissible against the accused is to be made upon an inquiry into the totality of the circumstances surrounding the interrogation, to ascertain whether the accused in fact knowingly and voluntarily decided to forgo his rights to remain silent and to have the assistance of counsel.

This totality-of-the-circumstances approach is adequate to determine whether there has been a waiver even where interrogation of juveniles is involved. We discern no persuasive reasons why any other approach is required where the question is whether a juvenile has waived his rights, as opposed to whether an adult has done so. The totality approach permits—indeed, it mandates—inquiry into all the circumstances surrounding the interrogation. This includes evaluation of the juvenile's age, experience, education, background, and intelligence, and into whether he has the capacity to understand the warnings given him, the nature of his Fifth Amendment rights, and the consequences of waiving those rights.

Courts repeatedly must deal with these issues of waiver with regard to a broad variety of constitutional rights. There is no reason to assume that such courts—especially juvenile courts, with their special expertise in this area—will be unable to apply the totality-of-the-circumstances analysis so as to take into account those special concerns that are present when young persons, often with limited experience and education and with immature judgment, are involved. Where the age and experience of a juvenile indicate that his request for his probation officer or his parents is, in fact, an invocation of his right to remain silent, the totality approach will allow the court the necessary flexibility to take this into account in making a waiver determination. At the same time, that approach refrains from imposing rigid restraints on police and courts in dealing with an experienced older juvenile with an extensive prior record who knowingly and intelligently waives his Fifth Amendment rights and voluntarily consents to interrogation.

* * *

* * * The transcript of the interrogation reveals that the police officers conducting the interrogation took care to ensure that respondent understood his rights. They fully explained to respondent that he was being questioned in connection with a murder. They then informed him of all the rights delineated in *Miranda*, and ascertained that respondent understood those rights. There is no indication in the record that respondent failed to understand what the officers told him. Moreover, after his request to see his probation officer had been denied, and after the police officer once more had explained his rights to him, respondent clearly expressed his willingness to waive his rights and continue the interrogation.

Further, no special factors indicate that respondent was unable to understand the nature of his actions. He was a 16 1/2-year-old juvenile with considerable experience with the police. He had a record of several arrests. He had served time in a youth camp, and he had been on probation for several years. He was under the full-time supervision of probation authorities. There is no indication that he was of insufficient intelligence to understand the rights he was waiving, or what the consequences of that waiver would be. He was not worn down by improper interrogation tactics or lengthy questioning or by trickery or deceit.

On these facts, we think it clear that respondent voluntarily and knowingly waived his Fifth Amendment rights. * * *

* * *

Mr. Justice Marshall, with whom Mr. Justice Brennan and Mr. Justice Stevens join, dissenting.

* * *

* * * I believe *Miranda* requires that interrogation cease whenever a juvenile requests an adult who is obligated to represent his interests. Such a request, in my judgment, constitutes both an attempt to obtain advice and a general invocation of the right to silence. For * * * * " '[i]t is fatuous to assume that a minor in custody will be in a position to call an attorney for assistance,' "or that he will trust the police to obtain a lawyer for him. A juvenile in these circumstances will likely turn to his parents, or another adult responsible for his welfare, as the only means of securing legal counsel. Moreover, a request for such adult assistance is surely inconsistent with a present desire to speak freely. Requiring a strict verbal formula to invoke the protections of *Miranda* would "protect the knowledgeable accused from stationhouse coercion while abandoning the young person who knows no more than to ask for the . . . person he trusts."

[A] juvenile's request for a probation officer may frequently be an attempt to secure protection from the coercive aspects of custodial questioning.[2]

* * *

MR. JUSTICE POWELL, dissenting.

* * * This Court repeatedly has recognized that "the greatest care" must be taken to assure that an alleged confession of a juvenile was voluntary. Respondent was a young person, 16 years old at the time of his arrest and the subsequent prolonged interrogation at the stationhouse. Although respondent had had prior brushes with the law, and was under supervision by a probation officer, the taped transcript of his interrogation—as well as his testimony at the suppression hearing—demonstrates that he was immature, emotional, and uneducated, and therefore was likely to be vulnerable to the skillful, two-on-one, repetitive style of interrogation to which he was subjected.

* * *

Although I view the case as close, I am not satisfied that this particular 16–year-old boy, in this particular situation, was subjected to a fair interrogation free from inherently coercive circumstances. For these reasons, I would affirm the judgment of the Supreme Court of California.

Notes and Questions

1. *Juvenile waiver of* Miranda *rights. Fare* held that the totality-of-the-circumstances approach is "adequate" under the Fifth Amendment to determine whether a juvenile knowingly and voluntarily waived the rights to remain silent and to have counsel. States, however, are free to provide greater protection by constitutional directive, statute, or court rule. Some states have enacted per se "juvenile Miranda" statutes or rules, which typically permit waiver only where the juvenile is informed of the right to communicate with a parent, relative, lawyer or other adult interested in the juvenile's welfare, or to have such a person present during questioning. See, e.g., Colo. Rev. Stat. § 19–2–511. A few statutes mandate heightened protection only for younger juveniles. See, e.g., Wash. Rev. Code § 13.40.140(10) (stating that where the juvenile is under twelve, waiver of Miranda rights may be made only by the parent or guardian). The enhanced protections apply even when the juvenile is suspected of a crime that might result in transfer to criminal court. See, e.g., Anderson v. State, 729 So.2d 900, 903 (Ala. Ct. Crim. App. 1998).

What policies underlie a state's decision whether to apply *Fare's* totality standard or else to mandate per se protection for juveniles by statute or rule?

2. * * *

Although I agree with my Brother POWELL that, on the facts here, respondent was not "subjected to a fair interrogation free from inherently coercive circumstances," I do not believe a case-by-case approach provides police sufficient guidance, or affords juveniles adequate protection.

In the absence of statute or rule, most decisions have not extended juveniles protections beyond those that *Fare* held satisfy the Fifth Amendment. The absence of an interested adult may be a factor to consider but is not dispositive. See, e.g., Quick v. State, 599 P.2d 712, 719 (Alaska 1979) (finding it "unquestionably a better practice to see to it that a juvenile consults with an adult before he waives his Miranda rights," but declining to mandate consultation).

Some decisions, however, have held that juveniles lack capacity, as a matter of law, to waive the right to remain silent without the concurrence of a parent, guardian or other fully informed adult. In In re E.T.C., 449 A.2d 937, 939, 940 (Vt.1982), for example, the court was persuaded by children's general "subordinate and protected status": "It would indeed be inconsistent and unjust to hold that one whom the State deems incapable of being able to marry, purchase alcoholic beverages, or even donate their own blood, should be compelled to stand on the same footing as an adult when asked to waive important * * * rights at a time most critical to him and in an atmosphere most foreign and unfamiliar." In Commonwealth v. A Juvenile, 449 N.E.2d 654, 657 (Mass.1983), the court distinguished between younger and older juveniles: (1) a juvenile under fourteen cannot waive Miranda rights unless a parent or interested adult is present, understands the warnings, and has the opportunity to explain these rights to the juvenile, but (2) where the juvenile is fourteen or older, "there should ordinarily be a meaningful consultation" with the parent or other adult, but waiver is valid without such a consultation where the juvenile has "a high degree of intelligence, experience, knowledge, or sophistication."

2. *Status offense proceedings.* Miranda warnings are required where the juvenile is processed as a delinquent or transferred to criminal court, but not when the juvenile is processed as a status offender. See, e.g., In re Thomas J.W., 570 N.W.2d 586, 586 (Wis.Ct.App.1997). Does this distinction help explain why authorities sometimes invoke only status offense jurisdiction when the juvenile's alleged conduct would constitute a crime if committed by an adult?

3. *Judicial discretion.* Professor Thomas Grisso has criticized *Fare's* totality-of-the-circumstances standard for conferring "almost unlimited judicial discretion." Juveniles' Capacities to Waive *Miranda* Rights: An Empirical Analysis, 68 Cal. L. Rev. 1134, 1139, 1141–42 (1980). He argues that "[w]hile a majority of the Supreme Court in *Fare* professed confidence in the ability of juvenile courts to balance all the variables in a manner that would consistently identify juveniles capable of making a meaningful waiver, this confidence seems misplaced given the Court's own split over the validity of the waiver at bar." Id.

Judicial discretion may loom large even in states with a per se juvenile Miranda standard. For example, the court may have to decide whether the adult was truly concerned with the juvenile's welfare, whether the adult was informed of the juvenile's rights and understood them, or whether the juvenile and adult had adequate opportunity to confer in private.

If judicial discretion dominates decisionmaking under totality-of-the circumstances and per se regimes alike, do you think courts generally exercise this discretion in favor of finding juvenile confessions admissible or in favor of finding them inadmissible? What if the juvenile court judge believes a sanction would be "for the juvenile's own good"? In answering these questions, you might wish to reconsider the facts of In re W.C., presented in Chapter 3, Representing Children.

4. *Can children's waiver of Miranda rights be voluntary, knowing and intelligent?* It appears that the vast majority of unrepresented children waive their right to remain silent, and that children waive much more often than adult suspects. In one study, for example, the juvenile waiver rate was 90%. See A. Bruce Ferguson and Alan Charles Douglas, A Study of Juvenile Waiver, 7 San Diego L. Rev. 39, 53 (1970). Another study found that unrepresented children under fifteen virtually never refuse to talk, and that only 12–14% of 15- to 16-year-olds refuse. Another study found that the adult refusal rate was more than 40%. See Thomas Grisso and Carolyn Pomicter, Interrogation of Juveniles: An Empirical Study of Procedures, Safeguards, and Rights Waiver, 1 Law and Hum. Behav. 321, 337, 339 (1977).

Empirical studies have produced strong evidence that the vast majority of children under fifteen cannot understand the nature and significance of the rights to remain silent and to have counsel. Professor Grisso's study of 10- to 16-year-olds also found that older juveniles "generally understand their rights as well as adults do," though the study did not test the capacity of these juveniles to waive their rights under the stress of actual police questioning. 68 Cal. L. Rev. at 1160–66. One study suggested that high juvenile waiver rates stem at least in part from the beliefs of many juveniles that police may try to dissuade a person from a decision to remain silent, or that a judge may later revoke a person's right to remain silent. See Thomas Grisso, Juveniles' Waiver of Rights: Legal and Psychological Competence 129 (1981).

Do these findings cause concern when juveniles who give statements are later transferred to criminal court for trial and sentencing? Does *Fare* sufficiently protect juvenile suspects?

In 1998, nationwide headlines corroborated empirical findings that interrogation of unrepresented children (particularly younger children) by experienced law enforcement officers holds risks of unreliability that exceed any such risks that attend questioning of adult suspects. An eleven-year-old girl was brutally assaulted, sexually abused and murdered while riding her bicycle in one of Chicago's most depressed neighborhoods. Less than two weeks later, the police charged two local boys (a seven-year-old and an eight-year-old) with first-degree murder after police said they confessed to the crime after lengthy interrogation in the absence of their parents or a lawyer. Nearly a month later, however, Cook County prosecutors dropped the charges when laboratory tests on the victim's underclothing revealed traces of semen, which almost certainly could not have been produced by boys so young. DNA tests later revealed that the semen came from a neighborhood adult ex-convict. Peter Annin and John McCormick, Who Killed Ryan Harris?, Newsweek, Oct. 5, 1998, at 42.

Reflecting on the Chicago case, one expert on confession evidence said that for veteran police interrogators, questioning a seven-year-old "would be child's play. If you're willing to threaten him, even mildly, he'll say anything you want." Jonathan Eig, Making Them Talk, Chicago, Jan. 1, 1999, at 50 (quoting Dr. Richard Ofshe). One veteran juvenile defense attorney observed that in jurisdictions that permit waiver by the child without an adult present, "[p]olice officers who cut parents out of the process risk losing the ability to use the child's statements at trial. But many officers are willing to take that risk because they know they can get away with it. In courtrooms, detectives, who are professional witnesses, have a built-in credibility advantage over children–who often make lousy witnesses. * * * Furthermore, police don't have to read kids their Miranda if the child 'spontaneously confesses'–a situation that police regularly claim occurs. When police do read Miranda to children, it might as well be a foreign language." Steven Andrew Drizin, When Little Tykes Give "Full Confessions," Chicago Tribune, Aug. 26, 1998, at 19.

Would many doubts about the voluntariness of juvenile confessions be removed if the entire interrogation were videotaped? See, e.g., Lawrence Schlam, Police Interrogation of Children and State Constitutions: Why Not Videotape the MTV Generation?, 26 U. Tol. L. Rev. 901 (1995); Welsh S. White, False Confessions and the Constitution: Safeguards Against Untrustworthy Confessions, 32 Harv. C.R.-C.L. L. Rev. 105, 153–55 (1997). Maintenance of a videotape may be prudent even where it is not required. In In re Doe, 948 P.2d 166, 170 (Idaho Ct.App.1997), for example, the court held that when the trial judge evaluates a police officer's credibility at a juvenile suppression hearing, the judge may draw a negative inference from the absence of a recording when the officer conveniently could have made one.

5. *Questions about the parent's role.* The parent's presence before and during interrogation may not help, and may indeed hurt, a child who has no attorney present. Pressure to confess may be exerted by a parent who is angry or resentful if the child has offended in the past, or who is inconvenienced or embarrassed by the present charge. One juvenile court judge reported that parents frequently would say, "Just take him, get him out of here." See Thomas Grisso, Juveniles' Waiver of Rights: Legal and Psychological Competence 167 (1981).

Professor Grisso says children feel stress even with a parent in the room. The parents are "almost as scared as the child is, and in some cases the parents are actually adding to the coercive effect." Moreover he has found that only about 2% of parents tell their children not to talk without an attorney present, about 16% of parents encourage their children to talk, and 71% of parents say nothing and thus allow the child to talk. When parents encourage or permit their children to waive their right to remain silent, they "think they're teaching their children to respect authority or take responsibility. Those are good principles, but under the circumstances they present a great risk to the child because it does cause some kids to admit to things they have not done or to admit a greater role than they actually played." Jonathan Eig, Making Them Talk, Chicago, Jan. 1, 1999, at 50.

6. *Questions about counsel's role.* Notice that Michael C., who was no stranger to the station house, distrusted the police officers' willingness to provide him with an attorney he did not know. If a "repeat player" like Michael C. did not know enough to say yes to a free lawyer, what can we expect from less savvy juveniles with no prior experience with custodial

interrogation (including, presumably, innocent juveniles)? Research indicates that many juveniles do not understand defense counsel's role, are afraid to confide in their lawyer because they believe the lawyer must assist the court rather than maintain the client's confidences, or feel they have more in common with their probation officers than with their unfamiliar defense counsel. By rejecting per se Fifth Amendment protection for juveniles who seek to communicate with a non-lawyer adult, does *Fare* significantly diminish children's Miranda rights? If *Fare* had announced a per se rule, would juveniles' consultations with the adult frequently lead them to request retained or appointed counsel, whose presence *Gault* had found essential only twelve years earlier?

7. *Who are "law enforcement officers"?* Miranda applies to custodial interrogation by law enforcement officers. Where a juvenile is suspected of criminal behavior, interrogation is frequently conducted by persons not employed by the police department. The interrogator may be a principal or other school administrator, a juvenile officer, or an employee of a juvenile treatment facility. Where the custodial interrogation is not conducted by a police officer, *Miranda* nonetheless applies where the interrogator acts as an agent or instrument of the police. See, e.g, Commonwealth v. A Juvenile, 521 N.E.2d 1368, 1369–70 (Mass.1988) (suppressing juvenile's confession to assistant director of home for troubled adolescents, who had a duty to report crime to police).

Principals and other school administrators are generally not required to give Miranda warnings before questioning students about infractions on school grounds during school hours. Courts generally find that these officials do not act as police agents because they can fulfill their duty to protect the student body's welfare only if they "have leeway to question students regarding activities that constitute either a violation of the law or a violation of school rules." State v. Biancamano, 666 A.2d 199, 202 (N.J.App.Div.1995). This rule prevails even where the school official intends to report any evidence of crime to the police. See, e.g., Commonwealth v. Snyder, 597 N.E.2d 1363, 1369 (Mass.1992).

8. *When is a juvenile "in custody"?* Miranda applies where the person interrogated has been "taken into custody or otherwise deprived of his freedom of action in any significant way." The suspect is in custody if under all the circumstances, a reasonable person in the defendant's position would have understood himself to be in custody or under restraints comparable to those associated with a formal arrest. Berkemer v. McCarty, 468 U.S. 420, 441–42 (1984). Some courts have applied a "reasonable juvenile" test, which considers "whether a reasonable person in child's position—that is, a child of similar age, knowledge and experience, placed in a similar environment— would have felt required to stay and answer all of [the officer's] questions." State ex rel. Juvenile Dep't v. Loredo, 865 P.2d 1312, 1315 (Or.Ct.App.1993).

Questioning of juveniles frequently does not occur in police headquarters. The facts of the case determine whether the interrogation was custodial. See, e.g, Loredo, supra, 865 P.2d at 1315 (police officer not required to give *Miranda* warnings to thirteen-year-old junior high school student he questioned for twenty minutes in school principal's office about an alleged rape; the officer identified himself as a police officer but told the juvenile that he was not under arrest, did not have to speak and could leave if he wished; the juvenile was in familiar surroundings, was not subject to punishment for refusing to answer, the officer was not in uniform and displayed no firearm); State ex rel. Juvenile Dep't v. Killitz, 651 P.2d 1382, 1384 (Or.App.1982) (granting suppression motion by junior high school student questioned in the principal's office by an armed, uniformed police officer who did not tell the student he was free to leave, and who said and did nothing "to dispel the clear impression communicated to defendant that he was not free to leave").

9. *When does "interrogation" occur?* The Supreme Court has held that interrogation takes place "whenever a person in custody is subjected either to express questioning or to its functional equivalent." For *Miranda* purposes, the term "interrogation" refers to any words or action by the police, other than those normally attendant on arrest and custody, that the police should know are reasonably likely to elicit an incriminating response from the suspect. See Rhode Island v. Innis, 446 U.S. 291, 298–302 (1980).

10. *Must police inform the juvenile that a statement may be used in a criminal proceeding?* In State v. Callahan, 979 S.W.2d 577, 582 (Tenn.1998), the court upheld the conviction of a juvenile defendant who had not been warned that he might be tried as an adult. The decision distinguished between interrogation and prosecution: "Whether a juvenile shall be prosecuted as an adult is a method of prosecution. Methods of prosecution are simply not within the purview of law enforcement officials. Decisions concerning methods of prosecution and modes of punishment are legal decisions within the authority of the district attorneys and the courts. An officer's representation as to either the mode of punishment or the method of prosecution is prophetic and potentially misleading."

Callahan's approach is not the unanimous view. Some decisions hold that where a juvenile is questioned about an act that could produce transfer to criminal court, any purported waiver of Miranda rights is per se invalid unless the juvenile has been advised of that possibility. See, e.g., State v. Benoit, 490 A.2d 295, 303 (N.H.1985).

11. *"Terry stops."* A police officer may briefly detain a person and make reasonable inquiries when the officer observes unusual conduct that leads him to reasonably suspect in light of experience that the person is engaged or about to engage in criminal activity. The officer may frisk the person if the officer reasonably believes the person may be armed and presently dangerous to the officer or others. See Terry v. Ohio, 392 U.S. 1, 19–22, 30 (1968). Whether the detainee is a juvenile or an adult, "Terry stops" are generally limited investigative stops not subject to *Miranda* because the detainee is not "in custody."

Juveniles driving automobiles may find themselves subjects of Terry stops. In In re Welfare of M.A., 310 N.W.2d 699, 700 (Minn.1981), for example, the police found the juvenile near a stopped car on the side of a highway, apparently out of gas. The juvenile told the police he had stolen the car. The state supreme court held that *Miranda* warnings were not required because the juvenile was not in custody.

Not all traffic stops, however, are outside *Miranda's* mandate. "A valid stop can ripen into an illegal detention for Miranda purposes if events transpire sufficient for a reasonable person in the defendant's position to consider himself or herself to be in custody." In re Eric J.D., 1998 WL 149486 *1 (Wis.Ct.App. Apr.2, 1998).

12. Miranda *in criminal prosecutions*. *Fare* assumed without deciding that *Miranda* principles were "fully applicable" to delinquency proceedings. Because lower courts have applied *Miranda* to these proceedings, counsel representing alleged delinquents must remain abreast of Miranda decisions in adult criminal prosecutions, including the Supreme Court's frequent refinements of the seminal decision. Criminal decisions may shape the contours of the juvenile privilege.

4. Intake and Diversion

In the criminal justice system, the prosecutor determines whether to charge a person with a crime and thus invoke the judicial process. "[T]he capacity of prosecutorial discretion to provide individualized justice is 'firmly entrenched in American law.'" McCleskey v. Kemp, 481 U.S. 279, 311–12 (1987). Under the traditional juvenile court rehabilitative model, however, the court staff itself normally decided during intake whether to proceed to formal adjudication. The intake decision focused largely or entirely on the juvenile's needs and circumstances, and not on legal doctrine. The traditional model has undergone considerable strain in recent years.

HOWARD N. SNYDER AND MELISSA SICKMUND, JUVENILE OFFENDERS AND VICTIMS: 1999 NATIONAL REPORT 97

* * *

At arrest, a decision is made either to send the matter further into the justice system or to divert the case out of the system, often into alternative programs. Usually, law enforcement makes this decision, after talking to the victim, the juvenile, and the parents, and after reviewing the juvenile's prior contacts with the juvenile justice system. Approximately one-quarter of all juveniles arrested in 1996 were handled within the police department and then released; nearly 7 in 10 arrested juveniles were referred to juvenile court.

* * *

The court intake function is generally the responsibility of the juvenile probation department and/or the prosecutor's office. Intake decides whether to dismiss the case, to handle the matter informally, or to request formal intervention by the juvenile court.

To make this decision, an intake officer first reviews the facts of the case to determine whether there is sufficient evidence to prove the allegation. If there is sufficient evidence, intake then determines whether formal intervention is necessary.

About half of all cases referred to juvenile court intake are handled informally. Most informally processed cases are dismissed. In the other informally processed cases, the juvenile voluntarily agrees to specific conditions for a specific time period. These conditions often are outlined in a written agreement, generally called a "consent decree." Conditions may include such things as victim restitution, school attendance, drug counseling, or a curfew. In most jurisdictions a juvenile may be offered an informal disposition only if he or she admits to committing the act. The juvenile's compliance with the informal agreement often is monitored by a probation officer. Consequently, this process is sometimes labeled "informal probation."

If the juvenile successfully complies with the informal disposition, the case is dismissed. If, however, the juvenile fails to meet the conditions, the intake decision may be revised to prosecute the case formally, and the case then proceeds just as it would have if the initial decision had been to refer the case for an adjudicatory hearing.

* * *

Notes and Questions

1. *Disposition.* In 1996, 56% of delinquency cases disposed of by the juvenile courts were processed formally, that is, by filing a petition requesting an adjudicatory or waiver hearing. Of the 44% of the cases handled informally (that is, without filing a petition), nearly half were dismissed by the court; most of the rest resulted in voluntary probation or other dispositions, but some involved voluntary out-of-home placements. See Anne L. Stahl, Delinquency Cases in Juvenile Courts, 1996, at 2 (1999).

2. *Restraining discretion.* Virginia is typical of states that limit intake officers' discretion, at least in some cases. Officers may not divert the case, and a petition must be filed, where a violent felony is charged or where the juvenile was previously diverted or adjudicated a delinquent or status offender. See Va. Code Ann. § 16.1–260.

3. *The prosecutor's growing role.* Probation officers and other juvenile court personnel traditionally remained at the forefront during intake. Amid growing public concern that juvenile courts are "soft" on juvenile offenders, however, prosecutors now play a central role through statutory authorization, informal practice, or both. "The clear trend is toward the inclusion of the prosecutor in either the first- or second-level screening functions or, at the least, toward agreements with intake officers that prosecution must be consulted regarding recommendations for informal disposition of certain more serious or repetitive offenders." H. Ted Rubin, The Emerging Prosecutor Dominance of the Juvenile Court Intake Process, 26 Crime & Delinq. 299, 310 (1980).

At one extreme, a prosecutor may review court petitions filed by the intake officer merely to determine their accuracy and legal sufficiency. At the other extreme, the prosecutor may receive all law enforcement referrals, with authority to determine whether to charge the case without consulting the intake officer. Between the extremes, the intake officer may consult the prosecutor on felony cases and dismiss or divert the case only with the prosecutor's approval; all decisions of the intake officer may be subject to the prosecutor's approval; or the prosecutor may receive all felony cases, with the intake officer handling only other cases. See Minority Youth in the Juvenile Justice System: A Judicial Response, 41 Juv. & Fam. Ct. J. 19 (No. 3A 1990).

4. *Teen courts.* In more than half the states, some local jurisdictions have provided for diversion to so-called "teen courts" or "youth courts." Juveniles who have acknowledged their guilt or responsibility, usually first-time misdemeanor offenders, consent to appear before a "jury" of their peers for disposition within a fixed range, generally community service, counseling or restitution. A volunteer attorney typically serves as judge, and a juvenile officer serves as bailiff. The American Bar Association encourages creation of these courts, which are seen as ways to discourage criminal behavior by offenders and jurors alike through positive peer pressure and reinforcement. See, e.g., Barbara Gilleran Johnson and Daniel Rosman, Recent Developments in Nontraditional Alternatives in Juvenile Justice, 28 Loy. U. Chi. L.J. 718, 723–30 & n.36 (1997).

5. *Discrimination in police encounters and intake.* Some research indicates that police are more likely to detain and arrest minority youth than white youth, even when the research controls for offense seriousness and prior offenses. Madeline Wordes and Timothy S. Bynum, Policing Juveniles: Is There Bias Against Youths of Color?, in Minorities in Juvenile Justice 47, 62 (Kimberly Kempf Leonard et al. eds., 1995).

Some commentators also allege that the broad discretion permeating intake and diversion may result in discriminatory treatment: "[S]chool performance, demeanor, family situation, prior record, degree of contrition, and other factors will come into play, with many of these reflecting race, ethnicity, or social status." Robert E. Shepherd, Jr., Juvenile Justice, 9 Crim. Just. 42, 43 (Summer 1994). In 1996, 46% of delinquency cases involving white juveniles and 38% of cases involving black juveniles were diverted informally; 54% of delinquency cases involving female juveniles and 41% involving male juveniles were diverted informally. Howard N. Snyder and Melissa Sickmund, Juvenile Offenders and Victims: 1999 National Report 156 (1999).

Budget constraints may also adversely affect minority juveniles. "The juvenile justice system lacks the resources needed to respond effectively to delinquency in general and to minority youth problems in particular. Diversion and alternative disposition programs that used to be available have disappeared, leaving juvenile justice decision makers with fewer options and contributing to higher incarceration rates for some minority groups." Barry Krisberg and James F. Austin, Reinventing Juvenile Justice 131 (1993).

6. *A darker side of diversion?* Professor Barry C. Feld argues that diversion, theoretically a means to diminish juvenile court control over children, may actually have the opposite effect. Diversion may enable police, prosecutors or juvenile court personnel to retain control over juveniles the court could not adjudicate delinquent, and to exercise this control largely free of due process strictures that would apply if the case proceeded to court. Barry C. Feld, Violent Youth and Public Policy: A Case Study of Juvenile Justice Law Reform, 79 Minn. L. Rev. 965, 1095–96 (1995).

7. *Plea bargaining.* In cases not diverted, prosecutors and alleged delinquents frequently engage in plea bargaining.

The interests at stake resemble the interests that drive criminal plea bargaining. The juvenile may seek adjudication to reduced charges or a disposition with less restrictive restraints (for example, probation rather than institutionalization, or the shortest possible probationary period). The prosecutor may seek to assure a result for the state (much as prosecutors may seek to create the highest possible conviction record), may seek to spare witnesses the ordeal of unpleasant testimony, may seek to conserve the office's resources by clearing backlog, and may even seek to spare the juvenile an adjudication on serious charges. Plea bargaining may serve the court's interest in moving the clogged docket, assuring that the juvenile will receive necessary treatment not available after acquittal or dismissal, and assuring that the juvenile will receive treatment quickly. Some courts also believe a juvenile's plea bargain may be tantamount to an acknowledgment of responsibility that enhances prospects for rehabilitation. See Joseph B. Sanborn, Jr., Philosophical, Legal, and Systemic Aspects of Juvenile Court Plea Bargaining, 39 Crime & Delinq. 509, 514–17 (1993).

Analogies between juvenile plea bargaining and criminal plea bargaining may break down. See, e.g., In re Jimmy P., 58 Cal.Rptr.2d 632, 633–34 (Ct.App.1996) (holding that criminal court rule which precludes sentencing court from considering charges dismissed as part of plea bargain is inapplicable when the juvenile court determines the proper placement for a juvenile after a plea bargain; the court must consider all available social and behavioral evidence bearing on the juvenile's fitness).

5. *Preventive Detention*

SCHALL v. MARTIN

Supreme Court of the United States, 1984.
467 U.S. 253.

JUSTICE REHNQUIST delivered the opinion of the Court.

Section 320.5(3)(B) of the New York Family Court Act authorizes pretrial detention of an accused juvenile delinquent based on a finding that there is a "serious risk" that the child "may before the return date commit an act which if committed by an adult would constitute a crime." Appellees brought suit on behalf of a class of all juveniles detained pursuant to that provision. * * * We conclude that preventive detention under the FCA serves a legitimate state objective, and that the procedural protections afforded pretrial detainees by the New York Statute satisfy the requirements of the due process clause of the Fourteenth Amendment to the United States Constitution.

I

Appellee Gregory Martin was arrested on December 13, 1977, and charged with first-degree robbery, second-degree assault, and criminal possession of a weapon based on an incident in which he, with two others, allegedly hit a youth on the head with a loaded gun and stole his jacket and sneakers. Martin had possession of the gun when he was arrested. He was 14 years old at the time and, therefore, came within the jurisdiction of New York's Family Court. The incident occurred at 11:30 at night, and Martin lied to the police about where and with whom he lived. He was consequently detained overnight.[5]

A petition of delinquency was filed,[6] and Martin made his "initial appearance" in Family Court on December 14th, accompanied by his grandmother. The Family Court Judge, citing the possession of the loaded weapon, the false address given to the police, and the lateness of the hour, as evidencing a lack of supervision, ordered Martin detained under § 320.5(3)(b). A probable cause hearing was held five days later, on December 19th, and probable cause was found to exist for all the crimes charged. At the factfinding hearing held December 27–29, Martin was found guilty on the robbery and criminal possession charges. He was adjudicated a delinquent and placed on two years' probation.[8] He had been detained pursuant to § 320.5(3)(b), between the initial appearance and the completion of the factfinding hearing, for a total of 15 days.

* * *

5. When a juvenile is arrested, the arresting officer must immediately notify the parent or other person legally responsible for the child's care. Ordinarily, the child will be released into the custody of his parent or guardian after being issued an "appearance ticket" requiring him to meet with the probation service on a specified day. If, however, he is charged with a serious crime, one of several designated felonies, or if his parent or guardian cannot be reached, the juvenile may be taken directly before the Family Court. The Family Court judge will make a preliminary determination as to the jurisdiction of the court, appoint a law guardian for the child, and advise the child of his or her rights, including the right to counsel and the right to remain silent.

Only if, as in Martin's case, the Family Court is not in session and special circumstances exist, such as an inability to notify the parents, will the child be taken directly by the arresting officer to a juvenile detention facility. If the juvenile is so detained, he must be brought before the Family Court within 72 hours or the next day the court is in session, whichever is sooner. * * *

6. A delinquency petition, prepared by the "presentment agency," originates delinquency proceedings. The petition must contain, *inter alia*, a precise statement of each crime charged and factual allegations which "clearly apprise" the juvenile of the conduct which is the subject of the accusation. A petition is not deemed sufficient unless the allegations of the factual part of the petition, together with those of any supporting depositions which may accompany it, provide reasonable cause to believe that the juvenile committed the crime or crimes charged. Also, nonhearsay allegations in the petition and supporting deposition must establish, if true, every element of each crime charged and the juvenile's commission thereof. The sufficiency of a petition may be tested by filing a motion to dismiss * * *.

8. The "factfinding" is the juvenile's analogue of a trial. As in the earlier proceedings, the juvenile has a right to counsel at this hearing. Evidence may be suppressed on the same grounds as in criminal cases, and proof of guilt, based on the record evidence, must be beyond a reasonable doubt. If guilt is established, the court enters an appropriate order and schedules a dispositional hearing. The dispositional hearing is the final and most important proceeding in the Family Court. If the juvenile has committed a designated felony, the court must order a probation investigation and a diagnostic assessment. Any other material and relevant evidence may be offered by the probation agency or the juvenile. Both sides may call and cross-examine witnesses and recommend specific dispositional alternatives. The court must find, based on a preponderance of the evidence, that the juvenile is delinquent and requires supervision, treatment, or confinement. Otherwise, the petition is dismissed.

If the juvenile is found to be delinquent, then the court enters an order of disposition. * * *

II

There is no doubt that the Due Process Clause is applicable in juvenile proceedings. "The problem," we have stressed, "is to ascertain the precise impact of the due process requirement upon such proceedings." *In re Gault* (1967). We have held that certain basic constitutional protections enjoyed by adults accused of crimes also apply to juveniles. But the Constitution does not mandate elimination of all differences in the treatment of juveniles. The State has "a *parens patriae* interest in preserving and promoting the welfare of the child," *Santosky* v. *Kramer* (1982), which makes a juvenile proceeding fundamentally different from an adult criminal trial. We have tried, therefore, to strike a balance—to respect the "informality" and "flexibility" that characterize juvenile proceedings, and yet to ensure that such proceedings comport with the "fundamental fairness" demanded by the Due Process Clause.

The statutory provision at issue in these cases, § 320.5(3)(b), permits a brief pretrial detention based on a finding of a "serious risk" that an arrested juvenile may commit a crime before his return date. The question before us is whether preventive detention of juveniles pursuant to § 320.5(3)(b) is compatible with the "fundamental fairness" required by due process. Two separate inquiries are necessary to answer this question. First, does preventive detention under the New York statute serve a legitimate state objective? And, second, are the procedural safeguards contained in the FCA adequate to authorize the pretrial detention of at least some juveniles charged with crimes?

A.

Preventive detention under the FCA is purportedly designed to protect the child and society from the potential consequences of his criminal acts. When making any detention decision, the Family Court judge is specifically directed to consider the needs and best interests of the juvenile as well as the need for the protection of the community. * * * As an initial matter, therefore, we must decide whether, in the context of the juvenile system, the combined interest in protecting both the community and the juvenile himself from the consequences of future criminal conduct is sufficient to justify such detention.

The "legitimate and compelling state interest" in protecting the community from crime cannot be doubted. We have stressed before that crime prevention is "a weighty social objective," and this interest persists undiluted in the juvenile context. The harm suffered by the victim of a crime is not dependent upon the age of the perpetrator. And the harm to society generally may even be greater in this context given the high rate of recidivism among juveniles.

The juvenile's countervailing interest in freedom from institutional restraints, even for the brief time involved here, is undoubtedly substantial as well. But that interest must be qualified by the recognition that juveniles, unlike adults, are always in some form of custody. Children, by definition, are not assumed to have the capacity to take care of themselves. They are assumed to be subject to the control of their parents, and if parental control falters, the State must play its part as *parens patriae*. In this respect, the juvenile's liberty interest may, in appropriate circumstances, be subordinated to the State's "*parens patriae* interest in preserving and promoting the welfare of the child."

* * * Society has a legitimate interest in protecting a juvenile from the consequences of his criminal activity—both from potential physical injury which may be suffered when a victim fights back or a policeman attempts to make an arrest and from the downward spiral of criminal activity into which peer pressure may lead the child.

The substantiality and legitimacy of the state interests underlying this statute are confirmed by the widespread use and judicial acceptance of preventive detention for juveniles. Every State, as well as the United States in the District of Columbia, permits preventive detention of juveniles accused of crime. A number of model juvenile justice Acts also contain provisions permitting preventive detention. And the courts of eight States * * * have upheld their statutes with specific reference to protecting the juvenile and the community from harmful pretrial conduct, including pretrial crime.

* * * In light of the uniform legislative judgment that pretrial detention of juveniles properly promotes the interests both of society and the juvenile, we conclude that the practice serves a legitimate regulatory purpose compatible with the "fundamental fairness" demanded by the Due Process Clause in juvenile proceedings.

Of course, the mere invocation of a legitimate purpose will not justify particular restrictions and conditions of confinement amounting to punishment. It is axiomatic that "[d]ue process requires that a pretrial detainee not be punished." * * *

There is no indication in the statute itself that preventive detention is used or intended as a punishment. First of all, the detention is strictly limited in time. If a juvenile is detained at his initial appearance and has denied the charges against him, he is entitled to a probable-cause hearing to be held not more than three days after the conclusion of the initial appearance or four days after the filing of the petition, whichever is sooner.[19] If the Family Court judge finds probable cause, he must also determine whether continued detention is necessary pursuant to § 320.5(3)(b).

Detained juveniles are also entitled to an expedited factfinding hearing. If the juvenile is charged with one of a limited number of designated felonies, the factfinding hearing must be scheduled to commence not more than 14 days after the conclusion of the initial appearance. If the juvenile is charged with a lesser offense, then the factfinding hearing must be held not more than three days after the initial appear-

---

19. For good cause shown, the court may adjourn the hearing, but for no more than three additional court days.

ance.[20] In the latter case, since the times for the probable-cause hearing and the factfinding hearing coincide, the two hearings are merged.

Thus, the maximum possible detention under § 320.5(3)(b) of a youth accused of a serious crime, assuming a 3–day extension of the factfinding hearing for good cause shown, is 17 days. The maximum detention for less serious crimes, again assuming a 3–day extension for good cause shown, is six days. These time frames seem suited to the limited purpose of providing the youth with a controlled environment and separating him from improper influences pending the speedy disposition of his case.

The conditions of confinement also appear to reflect the regulatory purposes relied upon by the State. When a juvenile is remanded after his initial appearance, he cannot, absent exceptional circumstances, be sent to a prison or lockup where he would be exposed to adult criminals. Instead, the child is screened by an "assessment unit" of the Department of Juvenile Justice. The assessment unit places the child in either nonsecure or secure detention. Nonsecure detention involves an open facility in the community, a sort of "halfway house," without locks, bars, or security officers where the child receives schooling and counseling and has access to recreational facilities.

Secure detention is more restrictive, but it is still consistent with the regulatory and *parens patriae* objectives relied upon by the State. Children are assigned to separate dorms based on age, size, and behavior. They wear street clothes provided by the institution and partake in educational and recreational programs and counseling sessions run by trained social workers. Misbehavior is punished by confinement to one's room. We cannot conclude from this record that the controlled environment briefly imposed by the State on juveniles in secure pretrial detention "is imposed for the purpose of punishment" rather than as "an incident of some other legitimate governmental purpose."

* * *

* * * [E]ven assuming it to be the case that "by far the greater number of juveniles incarcerated under [§ 320.5(3)(b)] will never be confined as a consequence of a disposition imposed after an adjudication of delinquency," we find that to be an insufficient ground for upsetting the widely shared legislative judgment that preventive detention serves an important and legitimate function in the juvenile justice system. * * *

Pretrial detention need not be considered punitive merely because a juvenile is subsequently discharged subject to conditions or put on probation. In fact, such actions reinforce the original finding that close supervision of the juvenile is required. Lenient but supervised disposition is in keeping with the Act's purpose to promote the welfare and development of the child. * * *

20. In either case, the court may adjourn the hearing for not more than three days for good cause shown. The court must state on the record the reason for any adjournment.

Even when a case is terminated prior to fact finding, it does not follow that the decision to detain the juvenile pursuant to § 320.5(3)(b) amounted to a due process violation. A delinquency petition may be dismissed for any number of reasons collateral to its merits, such as the failure of a witness to testify. The Family Court judge cannot be expected to anticipate such developments at the initial hearing. * * *

It may be, of course, that in some circumstances detention of a juvenile would not pass constitutional muster. But the validity of those detentions must be determined on a case-by-case basis. Section 320.5(3)(b) is not invalid "on its face" by reason of the ambiguous statistics and case histories relied upon by the court below. We find no justification for the conclusion that, contrary to the express language of the statute and the judgment of the highest state court, § 320.5(3)(b) is a punitive rather than a regulatory measure. Preventive detention under the FCA serves the legitimate state objective, held in common with every State in the country, of protecting both the juvenile and society from the hazards of pretrial crime.

B

Given the legitimacy of the State's interest in preventive detention, and the nonpunitive nature of that detention, the remaining question is whether the procedures afforded juveniles detained prior to factfinding provide sufficient protection against erroneous and unnecessary deprivations of liberty. * * *

* * *

* * *[N]otice, a hearing, and a statement of facts and reasons are given prior to any detention under § 320.5(3)(b). A formal probable-cause hearing is then held within a short while thereafter, if the factfinding hearing is not itself scheduled within three days. These flexible procedures have been found constitutionally adequate under the Fourth Amendment. * * *

[The Court rejected the contention that the standard for detention is "fatally vague" because it is based on a finding only that there is a "serious risk" that the juvenile, if released, would commit a crime prior to his next court appearance. The Court concluded that "there is nothing inherently unattainable about a prediction of future criminal conduct," and that "a prediction of future criminal conduct is 'an experienced prediction based on a host of variables' which cannot be readily codified. * * * Given the right to a hearing, to counsel, and to a statement of reasons, there is no reason that the specific factors upon which the Family Court judge might rely must be specified in the statute."].

Justice Marshall, with whom Justice Brennan and Justice Stevens join, dissenting.

* * *

There are few limitations on § 320.5(3)(b). Detention need not be predicated on a finding that there is probable cause to believe the child committed the offense for which he was arrested. The provision applies to all juveniles, regardless of their prior records or the severity of the offenses of which they are accused. The provision is not limited to the prevention of dangerous crimes; a prediction that a juvenile if released may commit a minor misdemeanor is sufficient to justify his detention. Aside from the reference to "serious risk," the requisite likelihood that the juvenile will misbehave before his trial is not specified by the statute.

* * *

II

A

* * *

To comport with "fundamental fairness," § 320.5(3)(b) must satisfy two requirements. First, it must advance goals commensurate with the burdens it imposes on constitutionally protected interests. Second, it must not punish the juveniles to whom it applies.

* * *

The majority's * * * characterization of preventive detention as merely a transfer of custody from a parent or guardian to the State is difficult to take seriously. Surely there is a qualitative difference between imprisonment and the condition of being subject to the supervision and control of an adult who has one's best interests at heart. * * * [S]ecure detention entails incarceration in a facility closely resembling a jail and that pretrial detainees are sometimes mixed with juveniles who have been found to be delinquent. * * *

In short, fairly viewed, pretrial detention of a juvenile pursuant to § 320.5(3)(b) gives rise to injuries comparable to those associated with imprisonment of an adult. In both situations, the detainee suffers stigmatization and severe limitation of his freedom of movement. Indeed, the impressionability of juveniles may make the experience of incarceration more injurious to them than to adults; all too quickly juveniles subjected to preventive detention come to see society at large as hostile and oppressive and to regard themselves as irremediably "delinquent." Such serious injuries to presumptively innocent persons—encompassing the curtailment of their constitutional rights to liberty—can be justified only by a weighty public interest that is substantially advanced by the statute.

* * *

B

Appellants and the majority contend that § 320.5(3)(b) advances a pair of intertwined government objectives: "protecting the community from crime," and "protecting a juvenile from the consequences of his criminal activity." More specifically, the majority argues that detaining a juvenile for a period of up to 17 days prior to his trial has two desirable effects: it protects society at large from the crimes he might have committed during that period if released; and it protects the juvenile himself "both from potential physical injury which may be suffered when a victim fights back or a policeman attempts to make an arrest and from the downward spiral of criminal activity into which peer pressure may lead the child."

* * * [E]ven if the purposes identified by the majority are conceded to be compelling, they are not sufficiently promoted by detention pursuant to § 320.5(3)(b) to justify the concomitant impairment of the juveniles' liberty interests. To state the case more precisely, two circumstances in combination render § 320.5(3)(b) invalid *in toto*: in the large majority of cases in which the provision is invoked, its asserted objectives are either not advanced at all or are only minimally promoted; and, as the provision is written and administered by the state courts, the cases in which its asserted ends are significantly advanced cannot practicably be distinguished from the cases in which they are not.

1

Both of the courts below concluded that only occasionally and accidentally does pretrial detention of a juvenile under § 320.5(3)(b) prevent the commission of a crime. Three subsidiary findings undergird that conclusion. First, Family Court judges are incapable of determining which of the juveniles who appear before them would commit offenses before their trials if left at large and which would not. In part, this incapacity derives from the limitations of current knowledge concerning the dynamics of human behavior. * * *

Second, § 320.5(3)(b) is not limited to classes of juveniles whose past conduct suggests that they are substantially more likely than average juveniles to misbehave in the immediate future. The provision authorizes the detention of persons arrested for trivial offenses and persons without any prior contacts with juvenile court. Even a finding that there is probable cause to believe a juvenile committed the offense with which he was charged is not a prerequisite to his detention.

Third, the courts below concluded that circumstances surrounding most of the cases in which § 320.5(3)(b) has been invoked strongly suggest that the detainee would not have committed a crime during the period before his trial if he had been released. In a significant proportion of the cases, the juvenile had been released after his arrest and had not committed any reported crimes while at large; it is not apparent why a juvenile would be more likely to misbehave between his initial appearance and his trial than between his arrest and initial appearance. Even more telling is the fact that "the vast majority" of persons detained under § 320.5(3)(b) are released either before or immediately after their trials. The inference is powerful that most detainees, when examined more carefully than at their initial appearances, are deemed insufficiently dangerous to warrant further incarceration.

The argument that § 320.5(3)(b) protects the welfare of the community fares little better. Certainly the public reaps no benefit from incarceration of the majority of the detainees who would not have committed any crimes had they been released. Prevention of the minor offenses that would have been committed by a small proportion of the persons detained confers only a slight benefit on the community. Only in occasional cases does incarceration of a juvenile pending his trial serve to prevent a crime of violence and thereby significantly promote the public interest. Such an infrequent and haphazard gain is insufficient to justify curtailment of the liberty interests of all the presumptively innocent juveniles who would have obeyed the law pending their trials had they been given the chance.

* * *

C

The findings reviewed in the preceding section lend credence to the conclusion reached by the courts below: § 320.5(3)(b) "is utilized principally, not for preventive purposes, but to impose punishment for unadjudicated criminal acts."

* * * § 320.5(3)(b) frequently is invoked under circumstances in which it is extremely unlikely that the juvenile in question would commit a crime while awaiting trial. The most striking of these cases involve juveniles who have been at large without mishap for a substantial period of time prior to their initial appearances, and detainees who are adjudged delinquent and are nevertheless released into the community. * * *

The inference that § 320.5(3)(b) is punitive in nature is supported by additional materials in the record. * * * [O]ne of the reasons juveniles detained pursuant to § 320.5(3)(b) usually are released after the determination of their guilt is that the judge decides that their pretrial detention constitutes sufficient punishment. * * *

* * *

III

* * *

* * * § 320.5(3)(b) lacks two crucial procedural constraints. First, a New York Family Court judge is given no guidance regarding what kinds of evidence he should consider or what weight he should accord different sorts of material in deciding whether to detain a juvenile. For example, there is no requirement in the statute that the judge take into account the juvenile's background or current living situation. Nor is a judge obliged to attach significance to the nature of a juvenile's criminal record or the severity of the crime for which he was arrested. Second, § 320.5(3)(b) does not specify how likely it must be that a juvenile will commit a crime before his trial to warrant his detention. The provision indicates only that there must be a "serious risk" that he will commit an offense and does not prescribe the standard of proof that should govern the judge's determination of that issue.

Not surprisingly, in view of the lack of directions provided by the statute, different judges have adopted different ways of estimating the chances whether a juvenile will misbehave in the near future. "Each judge follows his own individual approach to [the detention] determination." This discretion exercised by Family Court judges in making detention decisions gives rise to two related constitutional problems. First, it creates an excessive risk that juveniles will be detained "erroneously"—*i.e.*, under circumstances in which no public interest would be served by their incarceration. Second, it fosters arbitrariness and inequality in a decisionmaking process that impinges upon fundamental rights.

* * *

Notes and Questions

1. *Questions about* Schall. (a) What guidelines does the New York statute provide to trial judges who must determine whether a juvenile should be held in preventive detention? How does the statute restrain the court's discretion? Does *Schall* require states to provide such guidelines or restraints by statute or rule? According to *Schall*, what are the permissible purposes of juvenile preventive detention?,

(b) After *Schall*, what minimum procedures must a juvenile preventive detention statute provide to pass constitutional muster? How protective are these procedures when the trial court need apply only a "serious risk" test in the end? Is *Schall's* standard for ordering preventive detention as strict as the beyond-a-reasonable-doubt standard later necessary to adjudicate the juvenile a delinquent? Can it be? In the preventive detention context, does the parens patriae doctrine, the basis for child protective legislation, protect children?,

(c) In *Schall*, Justice Rehnquist stated that juveniles are "always in some form of custody" so that "if parental control falters, the State must play its part as parens patriae." Is this approach consistent with DeShaney v. Winnebago County Department of Social Services, written by Justice Rehnquist five years later, which held that a child's due process rights are not violated when state welfare officials know or have reason to know the child is a victim of parental abuse but fail to take steps to remove him from parental custody? (*DeShaney* appears in Chapter 4.),

(d) By authorizing the state to step in "if parental control falters," does *Schall* authorize trial courts to punish children for the sins of their parents? After all, an alleged delinquent might be released into his parents' custody if they are willing and able to supervise him but might suffer preventive detention if they are not. It has been suggested that many alleged delinquents are detained not because they pose any danger to themselves or the community, but because they cannot be released to parents: "[Y]outh who have no home or whose parents refuse to accept them run the highest risk of detention regardless of what they have or have not done." Rosemary Sarri, Service Technologies: Diversion, Probation, and Detention, in Brought to Justice? Juveniles, the Courts, and the Law 151, 167 (Rosemary Sarri et al. eds., 1976),

(e) *Schall* says that "[c]hildren, by definition, are not assumed to have the capacity to take care of themselves." Should a child's right to prehearing liberty depend on capacity?,

(f) Even if the applicable statute recites only regulatory motives for preventive detention, is such detention nonetheless also inherently punitive? If the detained juvenile is later found not to have committed the charged offense, has the juvenile nonetheless suffered "punishment"?

2. Schall *in context.* When *Schall* held that due process did not forbid preventive detention of alleged delinquents, the Court had not yet decided the constitutionality of such detention of adult suspects. The Bail Reform Act of 1984 authorizes federal courts to hold criminal suspects without bail solely because they are found to present a danger to any other person or the community. 18 U.S.C. § 3142. In United States v. Salerno, 481 U.S. 739 (1987), the Court relied heavily on *Schall* to hold that the Act's preventive detention provisions did not violate Fifth Amendment substantive or procedural due process or the Eighth Amendment excessive bail clause.

3. *The growth of juvenile preventive detention.* Most juvenile codes authorize preventive detention where the juvenile is a fugitive from another jurisdiction, would be a danger of himself or others if released, would be likely to flee the jurisdiction if released, has no parent or other adult to assume supervision, or has been charged with a serious crime such as murder.

In 1996, juveniles were held in preventive detention at some time between intake and disposition in 18% of delinquency cases nationwide. Twenty percent of male delinquency cases and 14% of female cases involved detention. See Anne L. Stahl et al., Juvenile Court Statistics 1996, at 7, 23 (1999). The percentages may appear relatively low, but the rate of preventive detention has increased to the point that detention facilities in many jurisdictions are filled beyond capacity. The U.S. Office of Juvenile Justice and Delinquency Prevention recommends that "[t]o control the large increase of juveniles admitted to juvenile detention programs and facilities, objective criteria need to be developed to assist courts in ensuring that only dangerous youth and those most likely to flee are detained. Alternatives to traditional detention, such as home detention, electronic monitoring, and group homes, must be developed." Shay Bilchik, A Juvenile Justice System for the 21st Century, 44 Crime and Delinq. 89, 92 (1998).

4. *Counsel's role in the detention hearing.* As *Schall* indicates, the juvenile court must swiftly hold a hearing to determine whether the juvenile should be continued in detention. Inadequate preparation by defense counsel, however, may diminish the protections afforded to the child. See, e.g., In re J.E., 668 N.E.2d 1052, 1055 (Ill.App.Ct.1996) ("In this case, as in most detention hearings, defense counsel filed his appearance moments before the hearing

began. He first saw the police report as his cross-examination began. Obviously, time for investigation was limited, if it existed at all."). The rules of evidence are applied loosely if at all, and hearsay is generally admissible. See, e.g., Id. at 1056.

5. *Preventive detention's effect on disposition.* In a study published in 1989, Professor Barry C. Feld found that juvenile preventive detention has a "substantial impact" on disposition because the fact of detention fuels a perception that the detainee is dangerous to himself or the community. "Detention constitutes a highly arbitrary and capricious process of short-term confinement with no tenable or objective rationale. Once it occurs, however, it then increases the likelihood of additional post-adjudication sanctions as well. In operation, detention almost randomly imposes punishment on some juveniles for no obvious reason and then punishes them again for having been punished before." Barry C. Feld, The Right to Counsel in Juvenile Court: An Empirical Study of When Lawyers Appear and the Difference They Make, 79 J. Crim. L. & Criminology 1185, 1337–38 (1989).

In a 1995 study, the U.S. General Accounting Office stated that the positive association between preventive detention and later placement was "not surprising" because "detention prior to adjudication was viewed as an indication of the severity of the offense, and juveniles who were part of more severe cases were more likely to be placed." See GAO, Juvenile Justice: Representation Rates Varied As Did Counsel's Impact On Court Outcomes 25 (June 1995).

6. *Race and preventive detention.* Some researchers conclude that preventive detention is a major cause of racial discrimination in the juvenile justice system. Their studies indicate that black youths are much more likely to be detained than white youths, and that (as Professor Feld found above) detained youths receive more severe dispositions than other youths. See, e.g., Carl E. Pope and William H. Feyerherm, Minority Status and Juvenile Justice Processing: An Assessment of the Research Literature (Part I), 22 Crim. Just. Abstracts 327, 331 (1990) (discussing studies). Racial disparities have grown in recent years largely because of detention policies in drug cases. See, e.g., National Coalition of State Juvenile Justice Advisory Groups, Myths and Realities: Meeting the Challenge of Serious, Violent, and Chronic Juvenile Offenders 23 (1993).

In 1996, 14% of white alleged delinquents and 27% of black alleged delinquents were detained at some point between referral and disposition. See Anne L. Stahl, Delinquency Cases in Juvenile Courts, 1996, 28 (1999).

7. *Bail.* The Eighth Amendment provides that "[e]xcessive bail shall not be required." The Amendment "says nothing about whether bail shall be available at all," United States v. Salerno, 481 U.S. 739, 752 (1987), and "fails to say all arrests must be bailable." Carlson v. Landon, 342 U.S. 524, 546 (1952). The Supreme Court has not determined whether juveniles have an Eighth Amendment right to bail in delinquency cases, but lower courts have held that they do not. See, e.g., State v. M.L.C., 933 P.2d 380, 385 (Utah 1997).

In the absence of a federal constitutional right, states disagree about whether a detained juvenile is entitled to release on bail pending the adjudicatory hearing or an appeal. Some juvenile court acts authorize bail and others preclude it. See, e.g., Conn. Gen. Stat. § 46b–133(b) (authorizing bail); N.J. Stat. § 2A:4A–40 (stating that there is no right to bail). In the absence of a statute authorizing bail in delinquency cases, state constitutional provisions guaranteeing the right to bail in criminal cases provide little help to juveniles because delinquency proceedings are civil in nature. See, e.g., M.L.C., supra, 933 P.2d at 384–85.

Where the juvenile code is silent about entitlement to bail, courts reason that the code's express safeguards obviate the need for bail. In L.O.W. v. District Ct., 623 P.2d 1253, 1258 (Colo.1981), for example, the court warned that "were it recognized, a right to bail would become a substitute for other, more appropriate forms of release." A generation ago, the Katzenbach Commission concurred, stating that "[r]elease as of right plainly may interfere with the protection or care required in some cases, and availability of freedom should not turn on the ability of the child or his family to purchase it." President's Commission on Law Enforcement and Administration of Justice, Juvenile Delinquency and Youth Crime 36 (1967).

A juvenile transferred to criminal court thereafter enjoys the same right to bail held by adult defendants. Courts, however, have rejected claims that a constitutional right to bail attaches where an alleged delinquent is confined in juvenile detention under conditions that assertedly resemble the conditions that mark preventive detention of adults. See, e.g., People v. Juvenile Ct., 893 P.2d 81, 92 (Colo.1995).

8. *The Juvenile Justice and Delinquency Prevention Act of 1974.* The 1974 federal Act, as amended, establishes four mandates relating to juvenile detention and confinement. States must comply with the mandates as a condition for receiving formula grant funds under the Act. Chapter 10 discussed one mandate, deinstitutionalization of status offenders and nonoffenders.

The second mandate—"sight and sound separation"—provides that juveniles may not have regular contact with adults who have been convicted of a crime or who are awaiting trial on criminal charges. 42 U.S.C. § 5633(a)(13). States must assure that juveniles and adult inmates may not see each other and that no conversation between them is possible. The major aims are to prevent adult prisoners from committing assault (including sexual assault) on juveniles, and to prevent juveniles from being infected with the criminal culture of adult prisons. (The Violent Crime Control and Law Enforcement Act of 1994 permits secure detention of juveniles charged with or convicted of possessing handguns or ammunition in violation of federal law or state statute.).

The "jail and lockup removal" mandate, the product of a 1980 amendment, requires states to provide that juveniles charged with delinquency "shall not be detained or confined in any institution in which they have contact with adult [inmates]." The mandate has a few exceptions. An arrested juvenile, for example, may be held in a lockup for only a short period (usually up to six hours). Juveniles charged in criminal court with a felony may be detained in a secure adult facility. 42 U.S.C. § 5633(14).

A 1992 amendment creates the "disproportionate confinement of minority youth" mandate, which requires states to determine whether such disproportion exists and, if so, to demonstrate efforts to reduce it.

The "sight and sound separation" and "jail and lockup removal" mandates seek to protect children from physical and sexual assault in adult prisons and to keep children from the influence of hardened adult criminals. The two mandates sometimes stir passions. Consider this letter-to-the-editor written by a retired police officer who reported that he had "dealt with the scum of society" for 22 years: "A criminal is a criminal, no matter what the race, age or sex. We need to do away with the better-than-home-like environments that baby-sit our juvenile criminals. Let's incarcerate them with the adult prison population that they so idolize. It's time to fit the punishment to the crime, for juveniles and adults equally. How young a person is should never be the determining factor to prevent a judge and/or jury from imposing a stiff prison sentence, or even the death penalty." " 'Kid Glove' Justice System Won't Halt Juvenile Crime," Wash. Times, Nov. 3, 1993, at C2.

In 1996, a number of Republican Senators and House members introduced legislation to repeal the "sight and sound separation" and "jail and lockup removal" mandates. The lawmakers said they were seeking both to reduce the costs the mandates impose on state and local governments (which must provide separate facilities), and to end what they perceived as leniency toward violent young offenders. "We've got to quit coddling these violent kids like nothing is going on," said Senator Orrin G. Hatch, one of the sponsors. "Getting some of these do-gooder liberals to do what is right is real tough." Fox Butterfield, Republicans Challenge Notion Of Separate Jails for Juveniles, N.Y. Times, June 24, 1996, at A1.

9. *Should a child be "scared straight"?* The 1974 Act recognizes that adult jails and lockups leave children easy prey for physical and sexual assault by hardened inmates. Because of lack of space or separate juvenile facilities, however, children are sometimes placed briefly in adult institutions despite the state's general adherence to the 1974 Act's mandates. First-time juvenile offenders may also be placed in juvenile detention facilities with hardened, violent or mentally ill delinquents. See, e.g., Madeline Wordes and Sharon M. Jones, Trends in Juvenile Detention and Steps Toward Reform, 44 Crime & Delinq. 544, 546 (1998). Detained girls may face particular threats of physical, sexual and emotional abuse, especially in detention facilities not well equipped for female detainees. See, e.g., Meda Chesney–Lind, Girls in Jail, 34 Crime and Delinq. 150, 161–64 (1988).

Children sometimes remain in detention awaiting adjudication or trial because their parents, seeking to "teach them a lesson," make no effort to secure their release. What advice would you give parents who contemplate this "tough-love" approach with their child? Consider the tragic story of seventeen-year-old Christopher Peterman who, detained in 1982 for $73 in unpaid parking tickets, was tortured for fourteen hours and beaten to death in his cell by five other juveniles who had histories of violent offenses. The boy's parents reportedly hoped a taste of confinement would cause him to be "scared straight." "We had no idea it would turn out like this," the parents said later. See Aric Press, When Children Go to Jail, Newsweek, May 27, 1985, at 87.

10. *References.* See, e.g., Albert W. Alschuler, Preventive Pretrial Detention and the Failure of Interest–Balancing Approaches to Due Process, 85 Mich.

L. Rev. 510 (1986); Jean Koh Peters, *Schall v. Martin* and the Transformation of Judicial Precedent, 31 B.C. L. Rev. 641 (1990); Irene Merker Rosenberg, *Schall v. Martin*: A Child is a Child is a Child, 12 Am. J. Crim. L. 253 (1984).

C. The Adjudicatory Hearing

1. Gault *and the "Constitutional Domestication"* [a] *of Delinquency*

If the intake staff decides to process the case formally, a petition alleging delinquency is filed and the case is placed on the calendar for an adjudicatory hearing. The overwhelming majority of juvenile court petitions are resolved when the juvenile admits the alleged facts; less than 10% of filed petitions require a full hearing. See H. Ted Rubin, Juvenile Justice Policy, Practice and Law 195 (1985).

If the petition proceeds to an adjudicatory hearing and the state fails to prove delinquency beyond a reasonable doubt, the court enters judgment for the juvenile. If the juvenile admits delinquency or if delinquency is proved, the case normally proceeds to the dispositional hearing. Sometimes, however, the case may be dismissed or continued in contemplation of dismissal if the juvenile takes some action the court recommends, such as paying restitution or entering a substance abuse treatment program. In 1995, juveniles were adjudicated delinquent in 58% of all formally processed delinquency cases. See Anne L. Stahl, Delinquency Cases in Juvenile Courts, 1996, at 2 (1999).

The Supreme Court first wrestled with delinquency procedure in Kent v. United States, 383 U.S. 541 (1966). *Kent* invalidated the District of Columbia juvenile court order that waived jurisdiction over a teenager charged with housebreaking, robbery and rape, and transferred him for trial as an adult in criminal court. The Supreme Court found that the juvenile court had deprived the teenager Kent of a hearing, had denied his counsel access to the social and probation reports prepared about him, and had failed to enter a statement of reasons for waiver. Writing for the five-member majority, however, Justice Fortas left it somewhat unclear whether the decision was grounded thoroughly in constitutional mandate. The Court held that the rights in question were "required by the [D.C. Juvenile Court Act] read in the context of constitutional principles relating to due process and the assistance of counsel." Id. at 557.

Less than fourteen months after *Kent*, the Supreme Court removed doubt about the Constitution's role as the ultimate source of procedural rights in delinquency cases. With Justice Fortas again writing for the majority, the Court handed down In re Gault, which Chief Justice Warren predicted would become known as "the Magna Carta for juveniles." Laura Kalman, Abe Fortas: A Biography 254 (1990). Shortly after Justice Fortas' death in 1982, the Solicitor General called *Gault* "the

a. In re Gault, 387 U.S. 1, 22 (1967).

charter of juvenile justice." In Memoriam Honorable Abe Fortas, 102 S.Ct. 17, 45 (1982).

Gault was not the first Supreme Court decision to confer constitutional protections on juveniles charged with criminal conduct. See, e.g., Haley v. Ohio, 332 U.S. 596 (1948) (due process prohibited introduction of 15-year-old boy's coerced confession in criminal case). It was, however, "the first juvenile court case in history to be decided on constitutional grounds." Monrad G. Paulsen, The Constitutional Domestication of the Juvenile Court, 1967 S. Ct. Rev. 233, 234. "Juvenile justice was a latecomer to the area of constitutional rights accepted for Supreme Court scrutiny." Justine Wise Polier, Prescriptions for Reform: Doing What We Set Out to Do?, in Juvenile Justice: The Progressive Legacy and Current Reforms 216 (LaMar T. Empey ed., 1979).

IN RE GAULT

Supreme Court of the United States, 1967.
387 U.S. 1.

MR. JUSTICE FORTAS delivered the opinion of the Court.

This is an appeal under 28 U.S.C. § 1257(2) from a judgment of the Supreme Court of Arizona affirming the dismissal of a petition for a writ of habeas corpus. The petition sought the release of Gerald Francis Gault, appellants' 15–year-old son, who had been committed as a juvenile delinquent to the State Industrial School by the Juvenile Court of Gila County, Arizona. The Supreme Court of Arizona * * * proceeded to identify and describe "the particular elements which constitute due process in a juvenile hearing." It concluded that the proceedings ending in commitment of Gerald Gault did not offend those requirements. We do not agree, and we reverse. We begin with a statement of the facts.

I.

On Monday, June 8, 1964, at about 10 a.m., Gerald Francis Gault and a friend, Ronald Lewis, were taken into custody by the Sheriff of Gila County. Gerald was then still subject to a six months' probation order which had been entered on February 25, 1964, as a result of his having been in the company of another boy who had stolen a wallet from a lady's purse. The police action on June 8 was taken as the result of a verbal complaint by a neighbor of the boys, Mrs. Cook, about a telephone call made to her in which the caller or callers made lewd or indecent remarks. It will suffice for purposes of this opinion to say that the remarks or questions put to her were of the irritatingly offensive, adolescent, sex variety.

At the time Gerald was picked up, his mother and father were both at work. No notice that Gerald was being taken into custody was left at the home. No other steps were taken to advise them that their son had, in effect, been arrested. Gerald was taken to the Children's Detention Home. When his mother arrived home at about 6 o'clock, Gerald was not there. Gerald's older brother was sent to look for him at the trailer home of the Lewis family. He apparently learned then that Gerald was in custody. He so informed his mother. The two of them went to the Detention Home. The deputy probation officer, Flagg, who was also superintendent of the Detention Home, told Mrs. Gault "why Jerry was there" and said that a hearing would be held in Juvenile Court at 3 o'clock the following day, June 9.

Officer Flagg filed a petition with the court on the hearing day, June 9, 1964. It was not served on the Gaults. Indeed, none of them saw this petition until the habeas corpus hearing on August 17, 1964. The petition was entirely formal. It made no reference to any factual basis for the judicial action which it initiated. It recited only that "said minor is under the age of eighteen years, and is in need of the protection of this Honorable Court; [and that] said minor is a delinquent minor." It prayed for a hearing and an order regarding "the care and custody of said minor." Officer Flagg executed a formal affidavit in support of the petition.

On June 9, Gerald, his mother, his older brother, and Probation Officers Flagg and Henderson appeared before the Juvenile Judge in chambers. Gerald's father was not there. He was at work out of the city. Mrs. Cook, the complainant, was not there. No one was sworn at this hearing. No transcript or recording was made. No memorandum or record of the substance of the proceedings was prepared. Our information about the proceedings and the subsequent hearing on June 15, derives entirely from the testimony of the Juvenile Court Judge, Mr. and Mrs. Gault and Officer Flagg at the habeas corpus proceeding conducted two months later. From this, it appears that at the June 9 hearing Gerald was questioned by the judge about the telephone call. There was conflict as to what he said. His mother recalled that Gerald said he only dialed Mrs. Cook's number and handed the telephone to his friend, Ronald. Officer Flagg recalled that Gerald had admitted making the lewd remarks. Judge McGhee testified that Gerald "admitted making one of these [lewd] statements." At the conclusion of the hearing, the judge said he would "think about it." Gerald was taken back to the Detention Home. He was not sent to his own home with his parents. On June 11 or 12, after having been detained since June 8, Gerald was released and driven home. There is no explanation in the record as to why he was kept in the Detention Home or why he was released. At 5 p.m. on the day of Gerald's release, Mrs. Gault received a note signed by Officer Flagg. It was on plain paper, not letterhead. Its entire text was as follows:

"Mrs. Gault:

"Judge McGHEE has set Monday June 15, 1964 at 11:00 A.M. as the date and time for further Hearings on Gerald's delinquency

"/s/ Flagg"

At the appointed time on Monday, June 15, Gerald, his father and mother, Ronald Lewis and his father, and Officers Flagg and Henderson were present before Judge McGhee. Witnesses at the habeas corpus proceeding differed in their recollections of Gerald's testimony at the June 15 hearing. Mr. and Mrs. Gault recalled that Gerald again testified that he had only dialed the number and that the other boy had made the remarks. Officer Flagg agreed that at this hearing Gerald did not admit making the lewd remarks. But Judge McGhee recalled that "there was some admission again of some of the lewd statements. He—he didn't admit any of the more serious lewd statements." Again, the complainant, Mrs. Cook, was not present. Mrs. Gault asked that Mrs. Cook be present "so she could see which boy that done the talking, the dirty talking over the phone." The Juvenile Judge said "she didn't have to be present at that hearing." The judge did not speak to Mrs. Cook or communicate with her at any time. Probation Officer Flagg had talked to her once—over the telephone on June 9.

At this June 15 hearing a "referral report" made by the probation officers was filed with the court, although not disclosed to Gerald or his parents. This listed the charge as "Lewd Phone Calls." At the conclusion of the hearing, the judge committed Gerald as a juvenile delinquent to the State Industrial School "for the period of his minority [that is, until 21], unless sooner discharged by due process of law." An order to that effect was entered. It recites that "after a full hearing and due deliberation the Court finds that said minor is a delinquent child, and that said minor is of the age of 15 years."

No appeal is permitted by Arizona law in juvenile cases. On August 3, 1964, a petition for a writ of habeas corpus was filed with the Supreme Court of Arizona and referred by it to the Superior Court for hearing.

At the habeas corpus hearing on August 17, Judge McGhee was vigorously cross-examined as to the basis for his actions. He testified that he had taken into account the fact that Gerald was on probation. He was asked "under what section of * * * the code you found the boy delinquent?"

His answer is set forth in the margin.[5] In substance, he concluded that Gerald came within ARS § 8–201, subsec. 6(a), which specifies that a "delinquent child" includes one "who has violated a law of the state or an ordinance or regulation of a political subdivision thereof." The law which Gerald was found to have violated is ARS § 13–377. This section of the Arizona Criminal Code provides that a person who "in the presence or hearing of any woman or child * * * uses vulgar, abusive or

---

5. "Q. All right. Now, Judge, would you tell me under what section of the law or tell me under what section of—of the code you found the boy delinquent?

"A. Well, there is a—I think it amounts to disturbing the peace. I can't give you the section, but I can tell you the law, that when one person uses lewd language in the presence of another person, that it can amount to—and I consider that when a person makes it over the phone, that it is considered in the presence, I might be wrong, that is one section. The other section upon which I consider the boy delinquent is Section 8—201, Subsection (d), habitually involved in immoral matters."

obscene language, is guilty of a misdemeanor * * *." The penalty specified in the Criminal Code, which would apply to an adult, is $5 to $50, or imprisonment for not more than two months. The judge also testified that he acted under ARS § 8–201–6(d) which includes in the definition of a "delinquent child" one who, as the judge phrased it, is "habitually involved in immoral matters."[6]

Asked about the basis for his conclusion that Gerald was "habitually involved in immoral matters," the judge testified, somewhat vaguely, that two years earlier, on July 2, 1962, a "referral" was made concerning Gerald, "where the boy had stolen a baseball glove from another boy and lied to the Police Department about it." The judge said there was "no hearing," and "no accusation" relating to this incident, "because of lack of material foundation." But it seems to have remained in his mind as a relevant factor. The judge also testified that Gerald had admitted making other nuisance phone calls in the past which, as the judge recalled the boy's testimony, were "silly calls, or funny calls, or something like that."

[The Superior Court dismissed the writ of habeas corpus, and the state supreme court affirmed.].

II.

* * *

This Court has not heretofore decided the precise question. In *Kent* v. *United States*, we considered the requirements for a valid waiver of the "exclusive" jurisdiction of the Juvenile Court of the District of Columbia so that a juvenile could be tried in the adult criminal court of the District. Although our decision turned upon the language of the statute, we emphasized the necessity that "the basic requirements of due process and fairness" be satisfied in such proceedings. *Haley* v. *State of Ohio* (1948), involved the admissibility, in a state criminal court of general jurisdiction, of a confession by a 15–year-old boy. The Court held that the Fourteenth Amendment applied to prohibit the use of the coerced confession. * * * Accordingly, while these cases relate only to restricted aspects of the subject, they unmistakably indicate that, whatever may be their precise impact, neither the Fourteenth Amendment nor the Bill of Rights is for adults alone.

We do not in this opinion consider the impact of these constitutional provisions upon the totality of the relationship of the juvenile and the state. We do not even consider the entire process relating to juvenile

---

6. ARS § 8—201, subsec. 6, the section of the Arizona Juvenile Code which defines a delinquent child, reads:

" 'Delinquent child' includes:

"(a) A child who has violated a law of the state or an ordinance or regulation of a political subdivision thereof.

"(b) A child who, by reason of being incorrigible, wayward or habitually disobe-

dient, is uncontrolled by his parent, guardian or custodian.

"(c) A child who is habitually truant from school or home.

"(d) A child who habitually so deports himself as to injure or endanger the morals or health of himself or others."

"delinquents." For example, we are not here concerned with the procedures or constitutional rights applicable to the pre-judicial stages of the juvenile process, nor do we direct our attention to the post-adjudicative or dispositional process. We consider only the problems presented to us by this case. These relate to the proceedings by which a determination is made as to whether a juvenile is a "delinquent" as a result of alleged misconduct on his part, with the consequence that he may be committed to a state institution. As to these proceedings, there appears to be little current dissent from the proposition that the Due Process Clause has a role to play. The problem is to ascertain the precise impact of the due process requirement upon such proceedings.

From the inception of the juvenile court system, wide differences have been tolerated—indeed insisted upon—between the procedural rights accorded to adults and those of juveniles. In practically all jurisdictions, there are rights granted to adults which are withheld from juveniles. In addition to the specific problems involved in the present case, for example, it has been held that the juvenile is not entitled to bail, to indictment by grand jury, to a public trial or to trial by jury. It is frequent practice that rules governing the arrest and interrogation of adults by the police are not observed in the case of juveniles.

The history and theory underlying this development are well-known, but a recapitulation is necessary for purposes of this opinion. The Juvenile Court movement began in this country at the end of the last century. From the juvenile court statute adopted in Illinois in 1899, the system has spread to every State in the Union, the District of Columbia, and Puerto Rico.[14] The constitutionality of Juvenile Court laws has been sustained in over 40 jurisdictions against a variety of attacks.

The early reformers were appalled by adult procedures and penalties, and by the fact that children could be given long prison sentences and mixed in jails with hardened criminals. They were profoundly convinced that society's duty to the child could not be confined by the concept of justice alone. They believed that society's role was not to ascertain whether the child was "guilty" or "innocent," but "What is he, how has he become what he is, and what had best be done in his interest and in the interest of the state to save him from a downward career." The child—essentially good, as they saw it—was to be made "to feel that he is the object of [the state's] care and solicitude," not that he was under arrest or on trial. The rules of criminal procedure were therefore altogether inapplicable. The apparent rigidities, technicalities, and

14. The number of Juvenile Judges as of 1964 is listed as 2,987, of whom 213 are full-time Juvenile Court Judges. The Nat'l Crime Comm'n Report indicates that half of these judges have no undergraduate degree, a fifth have no college education at all, a fifth are not members of the bar, and three-quarters devote less than one-quarter of their time to juvenile matters. * * * [A]bout a quarter of these judges have no law school training at all. About one-third of all judges have no probation and social work staff available to them; between eighty and ninety percent have no available psychologist or psychiatrist. It has been observed that while "good will, compassion, and similar virtues are * * * admirably prevalent throughout the system * * * expertise, the keystone of the whole venture, is lacking." * * *

harshness which they observed in both substantive and procedural criminal law were therefore to be discarded. The idea of crime and punishment was to be abandoned. The child was to be "treated" and "rehabilitated" and the procedures, from apprehension through institutionalization, were to be "clinical" rather than punitive.

These results were to be achieved, without coming to conceptual and constitutional grief, by insisting that the proceedings were not adversary, but that the state was proceeding as *parens patriae*. The Latin phrase proved to be a great help to those who sought to rationalize the exclusion of juveniles from the constitutional scheme; but its meaning is murky and its historic credentials are of dubious relevance. The phrase was taken from chancery practice, where, however, it was used to describe the power of the state to act *in loco parentis* for the purpose of protecting the property interests and the person of the child. But there is no trace of the doctrine in the history of criminal jurisprudence. At common law, children under seven were considered incapable of possessing criminal intent. Beyond that age, they were subjected to arrest, trial, and in theory to punishment like adult offenders. In these old days, the state was not deemed to have authority to accord them fewer procedural rights than adults.

The right of the state, as *parens patriae*, to deny to the child procedural rights available to his elders was elaborated by the assertion that a child, unlike an adult, has a right "not to liberty but to custody." He can be made to attorn to his parents, to go to school, etc. If his parents default in effectively performing their custodial functions—that is, if the child is "delinquent"—the state may intervene. In doing so, it does not deprive the child of any rights, because he has none. It merely provides the "custody" to which the child is entitled. On this basis, proceedings involving juveniles were described as "civil" not "criminal" and therefore not subject to the requirements which restrict the state when it seeks to deprive a person of his liberty.

Accordingly, the highest motives and most enlightened impulses led to a peculiar system for juveniles, unknown to our law in any comparable context. The constitutional and theoretical basis for this peculiar system is—to say the least—debatable. And in practice, * * * the results have not been entirely satisfactory. Juvenile Court history has again demonstrated that unbridled discretion, however benevolently motivated, is frequently a poor substitute for principle and procedure. In 1937, Dean Pound wrote: "The powers of the Star Chamber were a trifle in comparison with those of our juvenile courts * * *." The absence of substantive standards has not necessarily meant that children receive careful, compassionate, individualized treatment. The absence of procedural rules based upon constitutional principle has not always produced fair, efficient, and effective procedures. Departures from established principles of due process have frequently resulted not in enlightened procedure, but in arbitrariness. * * *

Failure to observe the fundamental requirements of due process has resulted in instances, which might have been avoided, of unfairness to individuals and inadequate or inaccurate findings of fact and unfortunate prescriptions of remedy. Due process of law is the primary and indispensable foundation of individual freedom. It is the basic and essential term in the social compact which defines the rights of the individual and delimits the powers which the state may exercise. As Mr. Justice Frankfurter has said: "The history of American freedom is, in no small measure, the history of procedure." But, in addition, the procedural rules which have been fashioned from the generality of due process are our best instruments for the distillation and evaluation of essential facts from the conflicting welter of data that life and our adversary methods present. It is these instruments of due process which enhance the possibility that truth will emerge from the confrontation of opposing versions and conflicting data. "Procedure is to law what 'scientific method' is to science."

It is claimed that juveniles obtain benefits from the special procedures applicable to them which more than offset the disadvantages of denial of the substance of normal due process. As we shall discuss, the observance of due process standards, intelligently and not ruthlessly administered, will not compel the States to abandon or displace any of the substantive benefits of the juvenile process. But it is important, we think, that the claimed benefits of the juvenile process should be candidly appraised. * * *

Certainly, * * * the high crime rates among juveniles * * * could not lead us to conclude that the absence of constitutional protections reduces crime, or that the juvenile system, functioning free of constitutional inhibitions as it has largely done, is effective to reduce crime or rehabilitate offenders. We do not mean by this to denigrate the juvenile court process or to suggest that there are not aspects of the juvenile system relating to offenders which are valuable. But the features of the juvenile system which its proponents have asserted are of unique benefit will not be impaired by constitutional domestication. For example, the commendable principles relating to the processing and treatment of juveniles separately from adults are in no way involved or affected by the procedural issues under discussion. Further, we are told that one of the important benefits of the special juvenile court procedures is that they avoid classifying the juvenile as a "criminal." The juvenile offender is now classed as a "delinquent." There is, of course, no reason why this should not continue. It is disconcerting, however, that this term has come to involve only slightly less stigma than the term "criminal" applied to adults. It is also emphasized that in practically all jurisdictions, statutes provide that an adjudication of the child as a delinquent shall not operate as a civil disability or disqualify him for civil service appointment. There is no reason why the application of due process requirements should interfere with such provisions.

Beyond this, it is frequently said that juveniles are protected by the process from disclosure of their deviational behavior * * *

* * * [T]here is no reason why, consistently with due process, a State cannot continue if it deems it appropriate, to provide and to improve provision for the confidentiality of records of police contacts and court action relating to juveniles. * * *

Further, it is urged that the juvenile benefits from informal proceedings in the court. The early conception of the Juvenile Court proceeding was one in which a fatherly judge touched the heart and conscience of the erring youth by talking over his problems, by paternal advice and admonition, and in which, in extreme situations, benevolent and wise institutions of the State provided guidance and help "to save him from downward career." Then, as now, goodwill and compassion were admirably prevalent. But recent studies have, with surprising unanimity, entered sharp dissent as to the validity of this gentle conception. They suggest that the appearance as well as the actuality of fairness, impartiality and orderliness—in short, the essentials of due process—may be a more impressive and more therapeutic attitude so far as the juvenile is concerned. For example, [a recent study observed] that when the procedural laxness of the *"parens patriae"* attitude is followed by stern disciplining, the contrast may have an adverse effect upon the child, who feels that he has been deceived or enticed. * * * "Unless appropriate due process of law is followed, even the juvenile who has violated the law may not feel that he is being fairly treated and may therefore resist the rehabilitative efforts of court personnel." * * * Of course, it is not suggested that juvenile court judges should fail appropriately to take account, in their demeanor and conduct, of the emotional and psychological attitude of the juveniles with whom they are confronted. While due process requirements will, in some instances, introduce a degree of order and regularity to Juvenile Court proceedings to determine delinquency, and in contested cases will introduce some elements of the adversary system, nothing will require that the conception of the kindly juvenile judge be replaced by its opposite, nor do we here rule upon the question whether ordinary due process requirements must be observed with respect to hearings to determine the disposition of the delinquent child.

Ultimately, however, we confront the reality of that portion of the Juvenile Court process with which we deal in this case. A boy is charged with misconduct. The boy is committed to an institution where he may be restrained of liberty for years. It is of no constitutional consequence— and of limited practical meaning—that the institution to which he is committed is called an Industrial School. The fact of the matter is that, however euphemistic the title, a "receiving home" or an "industrial school" for juveniles is an institution of confinement in which the child is incarcerated for a greater or lesser time. His world becomes "a building with whitewashed walls, regimented routine and institutional hours * * *." Instead of mother and father and sisters and brothers and friends and classmates, his world is peopled by guards, custodians, state employees, and "delinquents" confined with him for anything from waywardness to rape and homicide.

In view of this, it would be extraordinary if our Constitution did not require the procedural regularity and the exercise of care implied in the phrase "due process." Under our Constitution, the condition of being a boy does not justify a kangaroo court. The traditional ideas of Juvenile Court procedure, indeed, contemplated that time would be available and care would be used to establish precisely what the juvenile did and why he did it—was it a prank of adolescence or a brutal act threatening serious consequences to himself or society unless corrected? Under traditional notions, one would assume that in a case like that of Gerald Gault, where the juvenile appears to have a home, a working mother and father, and an older brother, the Juvenile Judge would have made a careful inquiry and judgment as to the possibility that the boy could be disciplined and dealt with at home, despite his previous transgressions. Indeed, so far as appears in the record before us, except for some conversation with Gerald about his school work and his "wanting to go to * * * Grand Canyon with his father," the points to which the judge directed his attention were little different from those that would be involved in determining any charge of violation of a penal statute. The essential difference between Gerald's case and a normal criminal case is that safeguards available to adults were discarded in Gerald's case. The summary procedure as well as the long commitment was possible because Gerald was 15 years of age instead of over 18.

If Gerald had been over 18, he would not have been subject to Juvenile Court proceedings. For the particular offense immediately involved, the maximum punishment would have been a fine of $5 to $50, or imprisonment in jail for not more than two months. Instead, he was committed to custody for a maximum of six years. If he had been over 18 and had committed an offense to which such a sentence might apply, he would have been entitled to substantial rights under the Constitution of the United States as well as under Arizona's laws and constitution. The United States Constitution would guarantee him rights and protections with respect to arrest, search, and seizure, and pretrial interrogation. It would assure him of specific notice of the charges and adequate time to decide his course of action and to prepare his defense. He would be entitled to clear advice that he could be represented by counsel, and, at least if a felony were involved, the State would be required to provide counsel if his parents were unable to afford it. If the court acted on the basis of his confession, careful procedures would be required to assure its voluntariness. If the case went to trial, confrontation and opportunity for cross-examination would be guaranteed. So wide a gulf between the State's treatment of the adult and of the child requires a bridge sturdier than mere verbiage, and reasons more persuasive than cliche can provide. * * * "The rhetoric of the juvenile court movement has developed without any necessarily close correspondence to the realities of court and institutional routines."

In *Kent* v. *United States*, we stated that the Juvenile Court Judge's exercise of the power of the state as *parens patriae* was not unlimited. We said that " 'the admonition to function in a 'parental' relationship is not an invitation to procedural arbitrariness." With respect to the waiver by the Juvenile Court to the adult court of jurisdiction over an offense committed by a youth, we said that "there is no place in our system of law for reaching a result of such tremendous consequences without ceremony—without hearing, without effective assistance of counsel, without a statement of reasons." We announced with respect to such waiver proceedings that while "We do not mean * * * to indicate that the hearing to be held must conform with all of the requirements of a criminal trial or even of the usual administrative hearing; but we do hold that the hearing must measure up to the essentials of due process and fair treatment." We reiterate this view, here in connection with a juvenile court adjudication of "delinquency," as a requirement which is part of the Due Process Clause of the Fourteenth Amendment of our Constitution.

We now turn to the specific issues which are presented to us in the present case.

III.

Notice of Charges.

* * *

* * * Notice, to comply with due process requirements, must be given sufficiently in advance of scheduled court proceedings so that reasonable opportunity to prepare will be afforded, and it must "set forth the alleged misconduct with particularity." It is obvious, as we have discussed above, that no purpose of shielding the child from the public stigma of knowledge of his having been taken into custody and scheduled for hearing is served by the procedure approved by the court below. The "initial hearing" in the present case was a hearing on the merits. Notice at that time is not timely; and even if there were a conceivable purpose served by the deferral proposed by the court below, it would have to yield to the requirements that the child and his parents or guardian be notified, in writing, of the specific charge or factual allegations to be considered at the hearing, and that such written notice be given at the earliest practicable time, and in any event sufficiently in advance of the hearing to permit preparation. Due process of law requires notice of the sort we have described—that is, notice which would be deemed constitutionally adequate in a civil or criminal proceeding. It does not allow a hearing to be held in which a youth's freedom and his parents' right to his custody are at stake without giving them timely notice, in advance of the hearing, of the specific issues that they must meet. Nor, in the circumstances of this case, can it reasonably be said that the requirement of notice was waived.[54]

---

54. Mrs. Gault's "knowledge" of the charge against Gerald, and/or the asserted failure to object, does not excuse the lack of adequate notice. Indeed, one of the purposes of notice is to clarify the issues to be considered * * *.

IV.

Right to Counsel.

* * * [The Supreme Court of Arizona] argued that "The parent and the probation officer may be relied upon to protect the infant's interests." Accordingly it rejected the proposition that "due process requires that an infant have a right to counsel." It said that juvenile courts have the discretion, but not the duty, to allow such representation; it referred specifically to the situation in which the Juvenile Court discerns conflict between the child and his parents as an instance in which this discretion might be exercised. We do not agree. Probation officers, in the Arizona scheme, are also arresting officers. They initiate proceedings and file petitions which they verify, as here, alleging the delinquency of the child; and they testify, as here, against the child. And here the probation officer was also the superintendent of the Detention Home. The probation officer cannot act as counsel for the child. His role in the adjudicatory hearing, by statute and in fact, is as arresting officer and witness against the child. Nor can the judge represent the child. There is no material difference in this respect between adult and juvenile proceedings of the sort here involved. In adult proceedings, this contention has been foreclosed by decisions of this Court. A proceeding where the issue is whether the child will be found to be "delinquent" and subjected to the loss of his liberty for years is comparable in seriousness to a felony prosecution. The juvenile needs the assistance of counsel to cope with problems of law, to make skilled inquiry into the facts, to insist upon regularity of the proceedings, and to ascertain whether he has a defense and to prepare and submit it. The child "requires the guiding hand of counsel at every step in the proceedings against him." Just as in *Kent* v. *United States*, we indicated our agreement with the United States Court of Appeals for the District of Columbia Circuit that the assistance of counsel is essential for purposes of waiver proceedings, so we hold now that it is equally essential for the determination of delinquency, carrying with it the awesome prospect of incarceration in a state institution until the juvenile reaches the age of 21.

* * *

We conclude that the Due Process Clause of the Fourteenth Amendment requires that in respect of proceedings to determine delinquency which may result in commitment to an institution in which the juvenile's freedom is curtailed, the child and his parents must be notified of the child's right to be represented by counsel retained by them, or if they are unable to afford counsel, that counsel will be appointed to represent the child.

At the habeas corpus proceeding, Mrs. Gault testified that she knew that she could have appeared with counsel at the juvenile hearing. This knowledge is not a waiver of the right to counsel which she and her juvenile son had, as we have defined it. They had a right expressly to be advised that they might retain counsel and to be confronted with the need for specific consideration of whether they did or did not choose to waive the right. If they were unable to afford to employ counsel, they were entitled in view of the seriousness of the charge and the potential commitment, to appointed counsel, unless they chose waiver. Mrs. Gault's knowledge that she could employ counsel was not an "intentional relinquishment or abandonment" of a fully known right.

V.

Confrontation, Self–incrimination, Cross–examination.

* * *

This Court has emphasized that admissions and confessions of juveniles require special caution. * * *

* * *

The privilege against self-incrimination is, of course, related to the question of the safeguards necessary to assure that admissions or confessions are reasonably trustworthy, that they are not the mere fruits of fear or coercion, but are reliable expressions of the truth. The roots of the privilege are, however, far deeper. They tap the basic stream of religious and political principle because the privilege reflects the limits of the individual's attornment to the state and—in a philosophical sense—insists upon the equality of the individual and the state. In other words, the privilege has a broader and deeper thrust than the rule which prevents the use of confessions which are the product of coercion because coercion is thought to carry with it the danger of unreliability. One of its purposes is to prevent the state, whether by force or by psychological domination, from overcoming the mind and will of the person under investigation and depriving him of the freedom to decide whether to assist the state in securing his conviction.

It would indeed be surprising if the privilege against self-incrimination were available to hardened criminals but not to children. The language of the Fifth Amendment, applicable to the States by operation of the Fourteenth Amendment, is unequivocal and without exception. And the scope of the privilege is comprehensive. * * *

With respect to juveniles, both common observation and expert opinion emphasize that the "distrust of confessions made in certain situations" to which Dean Wigmore referred * * * is imperative in the case of children from an early age through adolescence. * * *

* * *

Against the application to juveniles of the right to silence, it is argued that juvenile proceedings are "civil" and not "criminal," and therefore the privilege should not apply. It is true that the statement of the privilege in the Fifth Amendment, which is applicable to the States by reason of the Fourteenth Amendment, is that no person "shall be compelled in any *criminal case* to be a witness against himself." However, it is also clear that the availability of the privilege does not turn upon the type of proceeding in which its protection is invoked, but upon the nature of the statement or admission and the exposure which it invites. The privilege may, for example, be claimed in a civil or administrative proceeding, if the statement is or may be inculpatory.

It would be entirely unrealistic to carve out of the Fifth Amendment all statements by juveniles on the ground that these cannot lead to "criminal" involvement. In the first place, juvenile proceedings to determine "delinquency," which may lead to commitment to a state institution, must be regarded as "criminal" for purposes of the privilege against self-incrimination. To hold otherwise would be to disregard substance because of the feeble enticement of the "civil" label-of-convenience which has been attached to juvenile proceedings. * * * And our Constitution guarantees that no person shall be "compelled" to be a witness against himself when he is threatened with deprivation of his liberty—a command which this Court has broadly applied and generously implemented in accordance with the teaching of the history of the privilege and its great office in mankind's battle for freedom.

In addition, apart from the equivalence for this purpose of exposure to commitment as a juvenile delinquent and exposure to imprisonment as an adult offender, the fact of the matter is that there is little or no assurance in Arizona, as in most if not all of the States, that a juvenile apprehended and interrogated by the police or even by the Juvenile Court itself will remain outside of the reach of adult courts as a consequence of the offense for which he has been taken into custody. In Arizona, as in other States, provision is made for Juvenile Courts to relinquish or waive jurisdiction to the ordinary criminal courts. * * *

It is also urged, as the Supreme Court of Arizona here asserted, that the juvenile and presumably his parents should not be advised of the juvenile's right to silence because confession is good for the child as the commencement of the assumed therapy of the juvenile court process, and he should be encouraged to assume an attitude of trust and confidence toward the officials of the juvenile process. This proposition has been subjected to widespread challenge on the basis of current reappraisals of the rhetoric and realities of the handling of juvenile offenders.

In fact, evidence is accumulating that confessions by juveniles do not aid in "individualized treatment," as the court below put it, and that compelling the child to answer questions, without warning or advice as to his right to remain silent, does not serve this or any other good purpose. * * * [I]t seems probable that where children are induced to confess by "paternal'" urgings on the part of officials and the confession is then followed by disciplinary action, the child's reaction is likely to be hostile and adverse—the child may well feel that he has been led or tricked into confession and that despite his confession, he is being punished.

Further, authoritative opinion has cast formidable doubt upon the reliability and trustworthiness of "confessions" by children. * * *

* * *

We conclude that the constitutional privilege against self-incrimination is applicable in the case of juveniles as it is with respect to adults. We appreciate that special problems may arise with respect to waiver of the privilege by or on behalf of children, and that there may well be some differences in technique—but not in principle—depending upon the age of the child and the presence and competence of parents. The participation of counsel will, of course, assist the police, Juvenile Courts and appellate tribunals in administering the privilege. If counsel was not present for some permissible reason when an admission was obtained, the greatest care must be taken to assure that the admission was voluntary, in the sense not only that it was not coerced or suggested, but also that it was not the product of ignorance of rights or of adolescent fantasy, fright or despair.

* * *

* * * We now hold that, absent a valid confession, a determination of delinquency and an order of commitment to a state institution cannot be sustained in the absence of sworn testimony subjected to the opportunity for cross-examination in accordance with our law and constitutional requirements.

VI.

Appellate Review and Transcript of Proceedings.

Appellants urge that the Arizona statute is unconstitutional under the Due Process Clause because, as construed by its Supreme Court, "there is no right of appeal from a juvenile court order * * *." The court held that there is no right to a transcript because there is no right to appeal and because the proceedings are confidential and any record must be destroyed after a prescribed period of time. Whether a transcript or other recording is made, it held, is a matter for the discretion of the juvenile court.

This Court has not held that a State is required by the Federal Constitution "to provide appellate courts or a right to appellate review at all." In view of the fact that we must reverse the Supreme Court of Arizona's affirmance of the dismissal of the writ of habeas corpus for other reasons, we need not rule on this question in the present case or upon the failure to provide a transcript or recording of the hearings—or, indeed, the failure of the Juvenile Judge to state the grounds for his conclusion. * * *

* * *

Mr. Justice Black, concurring.

* * *

Where a person, infant or adult, can be seized by the State, charged, and convicted for violating a state criminal law, and then ordered by the State to be confined for six years, I think the Constitution requires that he be tried in accordance with the guarantees of all the provisions of the

Bill of Rights made applicable to the States by the Fourteenth Amendment. Undoubtedly this would be true of an adult defendant, and it would be a plain denial of equal protection of the laws—an invidious discrimination—to hold that others subject to heavier punishments could, because they are children, be denied these same constitutional safeguards. I consequently agree with the Court that the Arizona law as applied here denied to the parents and their son the right of notice, right to counsel, right against self-incrimination, and right to confront the witnesses against young Gault. Appellants are entitled to these rights, not because "fairness, impartiality and orderliness—in short, the essentials of due process"—require them and not because they are "the procedural rules which have been fashioned from the generality of due process," but because they are specifically and unequivocally granted by provisions of the Fifth and Sixth Amendments which the Fourteenth Amendment makes applicable to the States.

* * *

[Mr. Justice White's concurrence is omitted.].

Mr. Justice Harlan, concurring in part and dissenting in part.

* * *

I.

* * *

The proper issue here is * * * whether the proceedings in Arizona's juvenile courts include procedural guarantees which satisfy the requirements of the Fourteenth Amendment. * * *

The central issue here, and the principal one upon which I am divided from the Court, is the method by which the procedural requirements of due process should be measured. It must at the outset be emphasized that the protections necessary here cannot be determined by resort to any classification of juvenile proceedings either as criminal or as civil, whether made by the State or by this Court. Both formulae are simply too imprecise to permit reasoned analysis of these difficult constitutional issues. The Court should instead measure the requirements of due process by reference both to the problems which confront the State and to the actual character of the procedural system which the State has created. * * *

* * *

* * * [T]he rate of juvenile crime is steadily rising. All this, as the Court suggests, indicates the importance of these due process issues, but it mirrors no less vividly that state authorities are confronted by formidable and immediate problems involving the most fundamental social values. The state legislatures have determined that the most hopeful solution for these problems is to be found in specialized courts, organized under their own rules and imposing distinctive consequences. The terms and limitations of these systems are not identical, nor are the procedural arrangements which they include, but the States are uniform in their insistence that the ordinary processes of criminal justice are inappropriate, and that relatively informal proceedings, dedicated to premises and purposes only imperfectly reflected in the criminal law, are instead necessary.

* * *

II.

[O]nly three procedural requirements should, in my opinion, now be deemed required of state juvenile courts by the Due Process Clause of the Fourteenth Amendment: first, timely notice must be provided to parents and children of the nature and terms of any juvenile court proceeding in which a determination affecting their rights or interests may be made; second, unequivocal and timely notice must be given that counsel may appear in any such proceeding in behalf of the child and its parents, and that in cases in which the child may be confined in an institution, counsel may, in circumstances of indigency, be appointed for them; and third, the court must maintain a written record, or its equivalent, adequate to permit effective review on appeal or in collateral proceedings. These requirements would guarantee to juveniles the tools with which their rights could be fully vindicated, and yet permit the States to pursue without unnecessary hindrance the purposes which they believe imperative in this field. Further, their imposition now would later permit more intelligent assessment of the necessity under the Fourteenth Amendment of additional requirements, by creating suitable records from which the character and deficiencies of juvenile proceedings could be accurately judged. * * *

* * *

Mr. Justice Stewart, dissenting.

* * *

Juvenile proceedings are not criminal trials. They are not civil trials. They are simply not adversary proceedings. Whether treating with a delinquent child, a neglected child, a defective child, or a dependent child, a juvenile proceeding's whole purpose and mission is the very opposite of the mission and purpose of a prosecution in a criminal court. The object of the one is correction of a condition. The object of the other is conviction and punishment for a criminal act.

* * *

The inflexible restrictions that the Constitution so wisely made applicable to adversary criminal trials have no inevitable place in the proceedings of those public social agencies known as juvenile or family courts. And to impose the Court's long catalog of requirements upon juvenile proceedings in every area of the country is to invite a long step backwards into the nineteenth century. In that era there were no juvenile proceedings, and a child was tried in a conventional criminal court will all the trappings of a conventional criminal trial. So it was that a 12–year-old boy named James Guild was tried in New Jersey for killing Catharine Beakes. A jury found him guilty of murder, and he was sentenced to death by hanging. The sentence was executed. It was all very constitutional.

* * *

Notes and Questions

1. *Questions about* Gault. (a) What did *Gault* hold?,

(b) Why did *Gault* rely on Fourteenth Amendment due process rather than on specific Bill of Rights provisions applicable to the states?,

(c) The majority says that "neither the Fourteenth Amendment nor the Bill of Rights is for adults alone." Does this statement suggest that alleged delinquents should receive all the guarantees of these provisions, such as the right to a jury trial, a public trial, a grand jury indictment, and sanction only after conviction on proof beyond a reasonable doubt? If not, does the statement offer guidance for distinguishing between rights alleged delinquents must receive and rights the state may withhold?,

(d) If the Court had accepted Justice Black's invitation to invoke all Bill of Rights provisions applicable to the states, would juvenile court delinquency jurisdiction serve any further purpose?,

(e) By imposing due process constraints on the exercise of delinquency jurisdiction, did *Gault* invite imposition of more serious sanctions on juvenile offenders, particularly violent offenders? By stating that delinquency treatment was indeed punitive, did *Gault* encourage states to move away from treatment toward punishment?

2. *Justice Fortas*. Children's rights were of particular concern of Justice Fortas during his three and a half years on the Court. According to one of his law clerks, the concern stemmed from his "determination to reduce the number of 'non-persons' in our society–people who are left out of due process and equal protection because of some exclusionary formula." Laura Kalman, Abe Fortas: A Biography 250 (1990).

Justice Fortas wrote the majority opinions in *Kent, Gault* and Tinker v. Des Moines Independent Community School District [supra p. 36]. One historian intimates that these decisions still left his work undone: "Even more important than [*Gault's*] new set of guarantees was Fortas's flowing language in the opinion and his vast body of citations of supporting psychological, historical, and sociological data. It was clear that given time he would be willing to write into law a still greater set of protections for juvenile defendants. * * * Based on his performance in *Gault,* the rest of the court seemed sure to follow." Bruce Allen Murphy, Fortas: The Rise and Ruin of a Supreme Court Justice 532–33 (1988).

Time ran out on Justice Fortas, however, before he could carry any further plans to fruition. In June of 1968, a lame-duck President Johnson nominated him to succeed Earl Warren as Chief Justice, but the nomination quickly ran into trouble and was withdrawn in October, a month before

Tinker's oral argument. In April of 1969, two months after the Court handed down *Tinker*, Justice Fortas resigned following disclosure that while he was on the Court he had accepted a fee from a foundation controlled by a former client who was under federal investigation for securities fraud. By 1971, new Justices had replaced a number of the Warren Court members who had produced the Fortas trilogy.

3. *Aftermath.* In 1985, the Seattle Times reported that Gerald Gault "turned out just fine. Today he's an Army sergeant stationed in Germany, living with his wife and two children. [His lawyer Amelia Dietrich] Lewis gets a card from him every Christmas." Peyton Whitely, The Boy Who Made Legal History, Seattle Times, June 18, 1985, at H3. In 1994, when Ms. Lewis died in Arizona at the age of 91, the chief justice of the state supreme court said, "She made history for the law in many ways. Her life and career epitomized the practice of law as it should be." The Law and Amelia Lewis, Phoenix Gazette, Nov. 19, 1994, at B8 (editorial).

4. *A hybrid jurisdiction. Gault* highlights delinquency's uneasy status as a hybrid jurisdiction. A delinquency proceeding is in the nature of a civil proceeding, and general civil procedure rules may apply with respect to matters not governed by the juvenile code. *Gault* and later federal and state decisions, however, apply many constitutional criminal law guarantees and thus establish delinquency as at least a quasi-criminal proceeding.

5. *Pre-*Gault *realities.* The juvenile court's procedural shortcuts in *Gault* were not uncommon before the Supreme Court decision. Juvenile authorities were seen as protectors rather than prosecutors of the child, and due process was widely seen as an impediment to rehabilitation and treatment. Some observers reported that adjudicatory and dispositional hearings were frequently hollow formalities because the outcome was a forgone conclusion even before the juvenile court heard evidence. Juveniles and their families ordinarily stood alone because only a minuscule percentage of alleged delinquents were represented by counsel. A 1962 study found that in New York, for example, 92% of alleged delinquents went unrepresented. See Charles Schinitsky, The Role of the Lawyer in Children's Court, 17 Record 10, 15 (1962). From a nationwide survey of juvenile court judges, researchers determined that "in most courts lawyers represent children in less than 5% of the cases which go to hearing." Daniel L. Skoler and Charles W. Tenney, Attorney Representation in Juvenile Court, 4 J. Fam. L. 77, 97 (1964).

6. *Post-*Gault *realities.* "[M]any juvenile courts have failed to implement [*Gault's*] mandate fully [and] neglect the due process rights basic to an adversary system." Gary B. Melton, Taking *Gault* Seriously: Toward a New Juvenile Court, 68 Neb. L. Rev. 146, 149 (1989). The failure and neglect are particularly apparent with respect to the right to counsel. "Although there is a scarcity of data, surveys of representation by counsel in several jurisdictions suggest that lawyers actually appear much less frequently than the law on the book might lead one to expect. In many states, * * * less than half of the juveniles adjudicated delinquent receive the assistance of counsel to which they are constitutionally entitled. The most comprehensive study available reports that in three of the six states surveyed, nearly half or more of juveniles were unrepresented." Barry C. Feld, Justice For Children: The Right to Counsel and the Juvenile Courts 4 (1993). Several explanations are

offered for low representation rates—parents may be unwilling to retain counsel for the juvenile, public defenders may be scarce outside urban centers, and juvenile courts may pressure juveniles and their parents to waive the right to counsel.

7. *Juvenile waiver of the right to counsel.* A few states prohibit juvenile waiver of the right to counsel. See, e.g., Iowa Code § 232.11(2); Tex. Fam. Code § 51.10(b). Most states, however, permit juveniles to waive the right voluntarily and intelligently, though many states require particular formalities. See, e.g., Minn. R. Juv. Proc. 3.04(1): "Any waiver shall be in writing and on the record. The child must be fully and effectively informed of the child's right to counsel and the disadvantages of self-representation by an in-person consultation with an attorney, and counsel shall appear with the child in court and inform the court that such consultation has occurred. In determining whether a child has knowingly, voluntarily, and intelligently waived the right to counsel, the court shall look to the totality of the circumstances including, but not limited to: the child's age, maturity, intelligence, education, experience, ability to comprehend, and the presence of the child's parents, legal guardian, legal custodian or guardian ad litem. The court shall inquire to determine if the child has met privately with the attorney, and if the child understands the charges and proceedings, including the possible disposition, any collateral consequences, and any additional facts essential to a broad understanding of the case." If the court accepts the waiver, the court must appoint standby counsel for the child. Id. R. 3.04(2).

Despite prescribed formalities, a former American Bar Association president reports that "[t]housands of juveniles are urged or cajoled into waiving their rights without adequate representation, without a full vetting of their charges and without a complete and detailed understanding of their rights." N. Lee Cooper, Conveyor Belt Justice, 83 A.B.A. J. 6 (July 1997). An ABA Juvenile Justice Center report states that "[w]aivers of counsel by young people are sometimes induced by suggestions that lawyers are not needed because no serious dispositional consequences are anticipated–or by parental concerns that they will have to pay for any counsel that is appointed. These circumstances raise the possibility–perhaps the likelihood–that a substantial number of juvenile waivers are not 'knowing and intelligent.'" A Call For Justice: An Assessment of Access to Counsel and Quality of Representation in Delinquency Proceedings 7–8 (1995). Waiver of delinquency counsel is further discussed in Chapter 3.

8. *Discovery.* Discovery is generally available in delinquency cases. In several states, the criminal discovery rules apply in delinquency cases. See, e.g., Fla. R. Juv. P. 8.060. In other states, disclosure obligations in delinquency cases are defined in special juvenile court discovery rules, generally in considerable detail. See, e.g., Calif. Juv. Ct. R. 1420. In the absence of express authority, juvenile courts may hold inherent authority to order discovery. See, e.g., Robert S. v. Superior Ct., 12 Cal.Rptr.2d 489, 492–95 (Ct.App.1992).

Some delinquency decisions have applied Brady v. Maryland, 373 U.S. 83, 87 (1963), which held that "suppression by the prosecution of evidence favorable to an accused upon request violates due process where the evidence is material either to guilt or to punishment, irrespective of the good faith or bad faith of the prosecution." See, e.g., In re C.J., 652 N.E.2d 315, 319 (Ill.1995).

9. *Admitting the delinquency petition's allegations.* In Boykin v. Alabama, 395 U.S. 238 (1969), the Court held that before accepting a criminal defendant's guilty plea, due process requires the trial judge to address the defendant personally in open court; the judge must inform the defendant of, and determine that the defendant understands, the nature and consequences of the plea and the rights the plea waives. The court must also determine that the plea is voluntary and not the result of force or threats or promises apart from a plea agreement.

Boykin arose in a criminal prosecution, and the Supreme Court has not decided whether the decision applies in delinquency proceedings. State statutes, rules or decisions, however, generally require juvenile courts to adhere to the decision's mandate and to determine after a colloquy in open court that the juvenile's admission to the petition's allegations are knowing and voluntary. See, e.g., In re Arisha K.S., 501 S.E.2d 128, 131 (S.C.1998). Some states require only substantial adherence to *Boykin* in delinquency proceedings. See, e.g., In re John D., 479 A.2d 1173, 1177–78 (R.I.1984). Even where no statute or rule requires adherence to *Boykin*, juvenile courts tend to mandate adherence anyway. See, e.g., In re C.K.G., 685 N.E.2d 1032, 1035 (Ill.App.Ct.1997).

Criminal defendants sometimes seek to withdraw their guilty plea and proceed to trial. Courts have held that alleged delinquents may withdraw their plea and proceed to adjudication for reasons analogous to those that would support criminal withdrawal. Juvenile withdrawal is permitted, for example, (1) where the state does not comply with the terms of the plea bargain that produced the plea, e.g., In re Jermaine B., 81 Cal.Rptr.2d 734, 737–38 (Ct.App.1999); (2) where the plea colloquy did not comply with statutory or rule requirements, for example because the juvenile court did not inform the alleged delinquent of the right to counsel, e.g., A.P. v. State, 730 So.2d 425, 426 (Fla.Dist.Ct.App.1999); or (3) where the record raises doubt that the juvenile knowingly and voluntarily waived the right to counsel, e.g., D.L. v. State, 719 So.2d 931, 933 (Fla.Dist.Ct.App.1998). The alleged delinquent may not withdraw the plea merely because the court refuses to accept the prosecutor's sentencing recommendation. See, e.g., In re S.L.L., 906 S.W.2d 190, 194 (Tex. Crim. App. 1995). Courts disagree about whether an alleged delinquent may withdraw a plea where withdrawal would be in the best interests of the child. See, e.g., In re Bradford, 705 A.2d 443, 447 (Pa. Super. Ct. 1997) (yes); In re J.E.H., 689 A.2d 528, 529–30 (D.C.Ct. App.1996) (no).

10. *Rules of evidence.* In the juvenile court's early years, the rules of evidence did not apply or were relaxed because they, like formal procedure, were seen as an impediment to a process perceived to protect rather than punish the child. The court was able to "scrap once and for all the old legal trial of children with its absurd and obsolete limitations of testimony and to inquire into the causes of the children's neglect or delinquency untrammeled by narrow rules of evidence." Children's Court of the City of New York, Annual Report 16 (1925).

In the years since *Gault*, however, states have applied the criminal rules of evidence in the adjudicatory phase of delinquency proceedings. See, e.g., Tex. Fam. Code § 51.17; In re R.G., 669 N.E.2d 1225 (Ill.App.Ct.1996). Subject to due process constraints, however, statutes or rules generally permit the court at the dispositional phase to consider all information relevant to the circumstances of the delinquent and his or her family. See, e.g., 42 Pa. Cons. Stat. § 6341(d).

11. *The parents' role.* Juvenile codes typically make the alleged delinquent's parent, guardian or custodian a party to the proceedings, thus conferring an absolute right to attend. See, e.g., Ind. Code § 31–37–10–7. Indeed many states require attendance of these adults. See, e.g., N.Y. Fam. Ct. Act § 341.2. The juvenile and his or her parent, guardian or custodian are entitled to be heard, to present material evidence, and to cross-examine witnesses.

Where the adult will testify, may the trial judge exclude the adult from a portion of the hearing pursuant to an order excluding prospective witnesses until their testimony? In In re J.E., 675 N.E.2d 156, 167 (Ill.App.1996), the court upheld the parents' exclusion because "there is nothing in the record that suggests that the presence of [the] parents could have been of any particular benefit during the course of the trial nor were there any incidents cited where they might have counseled their son," and because the juvenile was "adequately represented by able counsel." On the other hand, in In re L.B., 675 N.E.2d 1104, 1108 (Ind.Ct.App.1996), the court reversed the delinquency adjudication because the parents were excluded: "Without the careful guidance of an adult who would be mindful of the child's best interest, there can be no meaningful due process for those from whom society does not expect the sophistication to understand judicial proceedings. * * *." What interests of the state and the juvenile are at issue when appellate courts consider whether parents may be excluded, and which outcome do you prefer?

12. *Race and delinquency adjudication.* In 1990, an advisory committee of the National Council of Juvenile and Family Court Judges found that "differences in the adjudication rates for minority v. non-minority groups do not appear significant, and one may conclude that the judiciary relies on the evidence in making an adjudicatory judgment." See Minority Youth in the Juvenile Justice System: A Judicial Response, 41 Juv. & Fam. Ct. J. 25 (No. 3A 1990). In 1995, 57.6% of white alleged delinquents and 53.4% of black alleged delinquents were adjudicated. See Bureau of Justice Statistics, Sourcebook of Criminal Justice Statistics 1997, Table 5.76, at 441 (1998). Some researchers have found, however, that once the adjudication decision is made, minority youth may receive harsher sanctions than white youth for similar offenses. See, e.g., Charles E. Frazier and Donna M. Bishop, Reflections on Race Effects in Juvenile Justice, in Minorities in Juvenile Justice 16, 23–25 (Kimberly Kempf Leonard et al. eds., 1995); Alan J. Tomkins et al., Subtle Discrimination in Juvenile Justice Decisionmaking: Social Science Perspectives and Explanations, 29 Creighton L. Rev. 1619, 1631–45 (1996).

13. *Juvenile court confidentiality and its relaxation.* To advance the juvenile court's rehabilitative mission, delinquency proceedings and records were traditionally closed to the public. "This insistence on confidentiality is born

of a tender concern for the welfare of the child, to hide his youthful errors and 'bury them in the graveyard of the forgotten past.' " Smith v. Daily Mail Publ'g Co., 443 U.S. 97, 107 (1979) (Rehnquist, J., concurring). The public could not attend delinquency proceedings; delinquency records, including the disposition, were sealed or expunged immediately or after a period of time, and could be released only on court order.

Juvenile court confidentiality stands in contrast to the openness that prevails in general criminal and civil courts by constitutional and statutory mandate. Throughout the 1990s, most states modified or removed traditional juvenile court confidentiality provisions to make proceedings and records more open.

a. *Proceedings.* Some states have replaced closed juvenile court proceedings with a presumption of open proceedings, at least in cases involving older juveniles or specified serious crimes. See, e.g., Colo. Rev. Stat. § 19–1–106(2).

Many observers advocate open adjudicatory proceedings as necessary to generate greater public confidence in the juvenile court and to foster reform. "[W]e cannot begin to reform the system when the public does not know what goes on inside it." Patrick T. Murphy, Crime and Punishment, Juvenile Division, N.Y. Times, Mar. 26, 1998, at A15. Two juvenile court judges argue that "the juvenile justice system is far more successful than the public and law enforcement authorities believe. But the successes, because of the confidentiality laws, are private, so the public generally hears only about the failures." See R. Robin McDonald, Punishing Choices: How to Try Teens Charged With Major Crimes?, Atlanta J. & Const., Aug. 8, 1999, at 1F. According to another juvenile court judge, "[a] good court system does not need to operate behind closed doors, and a bad one does not deserve to hide its proceedings." Hal Gaither, Juvenile Courts Shouldn't Be Closed to the Public, Dallas Morning News, Apr. 26, 1997, at 31A.

Other writers, however, have criticized calls for public adjudicatory proceedings, arguing that openness would help guarantee that "a schoolyard assault committed at age 16 becomes a lifetime barrier to future opportunity." "[G]ainful employment is the most effective form of rehabilitation. * * * [T]he greatest obstacle to gainful employment for adult parolees is the presence of a criminal record." Dan Macallair and Tom Gitchoff, Washington Politics and Juvenile Crime, San Diego Union–Tribune, Aug. 28, 1997, at B7.

The National Council of Juvenile and Family Court Judges would distinguish between adjudicatory hearings and disposition hearings, ordinarily opening the former but closing the latter: "[W]hen a child is involved in a serious crime, the public, the victims and the police have a right to know how the juvenile court manages the trial where guilt or innocence is determined unless, in a rare case, the publicity will demonstrably cause more harm than good. Public safety overrides the reasons for confidentiality. Except in a rare case, however, public safety does not require the public to be present at the disposition hearing where all of the intimate details of the family will be discussed in order to determine the best means of helping the child and protecting the public." The Juvenile Court and Serious Offenders: 38 Recommendations, Juv. & Fam. Ct. J. 1, 14 (Spec. Issue Summer 1984).

The public-trial issue raises interesting questions. What factors would you consider in determining whether to open some or all juvenile court proceedings to the public? Does confidentiality serve any real purpose where the juvenile has committed a particularly serious crime so that the perpetrator and the event are likely to be well known in the community? Does confidentiality diminish the general deterrent effect of delinquency decisions? Should victims and their families have the right to attend juvenile court proceedings involving their alleged assailants, and to be informed of the court's disposition? Should courts weigh heavily the desires of victims and their families to close a trial that would likely prove particularly embarrassing, such as sex crime trials?

b. *Records.* By the end of the 1997 legislative session, juvenile codes in forty-seven states had provided for release of information contained in juvenile court records to at least one of the following: the prosecutor, law enforcement, social agencies, schools, the victim or the public. Howard N. Snyder and Melissa Sickmund, Juvenile Offenders and Victims: 1999 National Report 101 (1999).

The National Council of Juvenile and Family Court Judges would distinguish between the "legal record" and the social histories prepared to guide the court's disposition: "Legal records of juveniles adjudicated for criminal law violations should be open to the child, the child's attorney, the guardian ad litem, the prosecutor and, at the discretion of the judge, to any other person having a legitimate interest. 'Legal' records would not include social histories, medical and psychological reports, educational records or a transcript of the dispositional hearings." The National Council explained that disclosure of legal records helps assure public safety and inform the public about the court's workings, but that social histories concern only the problems of the family and the juvenile and thus should be open only to immediate participants unless the court orders otherwise for good cause. The Juvenile Court and Serious Offenders: 38 Recommendations, Juv. & Fam. Ct. J. 1, 14–15 (Spec. Issue Summer 1984).

14. *Confidentiality and the media.* As a matter of self-restraint based on cooperation with juvenile court personnel, the media normally does not reveal the identities of accused juveniles, at least unless the crime is serious or unless the juvenile is transferred to criminal court. In more than forty states, the names of juveniles involved in delinquency proceedings may be released to the media in some or all cases. Even where total or partial confidentiality is mandated, however, neither the court nor the legislature may restrain or prohibit the press from reporting an alleged delinquent's name that the media learns through a leak, community disclosure or otherwise. A media report naming the offender in effect becomes a permanent record, regardless of statutes providing for confidentiality or for sealing or expunging the record after a period of years.

In Oklahoma Publishing Co. v. District Ct., 430 U.S. 308 (1977), the Court struck down an injunction that prohibited the news media from publishing the name or photograph of an eleven-year-old alleged delinquent. The juvenile court had permitted reporters and other members of the public to attend a hearing in the case, and then had attempted to halt publication of information obtained from that hearing. The Court held that once truthful information was "publicly revealed" or "in the public domain," the

First Amendment prohibited the juvenile court from restraining its dissemination. Id. at 311.

In Smith v. Daily Mail Publishing Co., 443 U.S. 97 (1979), the Court struck down a state statute that made it a crime for a newspaper to publish, without the juvenile court's written approval, the name of a youth charged as a juvenile offender. The Court held that where a newspaper lawfully obtains truthful information about a matter of public significance, the state may not constitutionally punish publication of the information, absent a need to further "a state interest of the highest order." Id at 103. The Court rejected the state's contention that the challenged statute, which concededly imposed a prior restraint on speech, nonetheless passed constitutional muster because the state held an interest in protecting the identity of juveniles to aid their rehabilitation.

If you were counsel to a newspaper publisher, what advice would you offer about when the newspaper should reveal a juvenile suspect's name and when the newspaper should exercise restraint and not reveal the name?

15. *Lawyer's access to records.* Regardless of confidentiality guidelines, counsel for the child or the parents may have access to the court record, including social service agency files, and reports that form the basis for any recommendation made to the court. See, e.g., Colo. Rev. Stat. § 19–1–304.

16. *"Infants".* Notice that in *Gault*, the Arizona Supreme Court and Justice Black each referred to alleged delinquents as "infants." Because today we normally associate the term "infant" with toddlers, use of the term may appear odd in a proceeding like *Gault*, whose subject was fifteen years old when he was taken into custody. Particularly in older decisions and statutes, however, the term "infant" referred to all minors (including ones barely under twenty-one, when that was the age of majority). Use of the term underscores the framework implicit in *Meyer* and *Pierce* and the accompanying discussion in Chapter 1, that the law deemed children of any age voiceless in matters concerning their status, rights and obligations. The word "infant" is derived from Latin, meaning "unable to speak." See Oxford Desk Dictionary 289 (Am. ed. 1995).

17. *Standard of proof.* The Court's first post-*Gault* foray into the juvenile justice process was In re Winship, 397 U.S. 358 (1970), which held that the criminal beyond-a-reasonable-doubt standard applies in delinquency proceedings. *Winship* concluded that "civil labels and good intentions do not themselves obviate the need for criminal due process safeguards in juvenile courts, for '[a] proceeding where the issue is whether the child will be found to be "delinquent" and subjected to the loss of his liberty for years is comparable in seriousness to a felony prosecution.'" Id. at 365–66.

Some question remains about *Winship's* practical impact. Some studies suggest that juvenile court judges sometimes find juveniles delinquent on less evidence than would satisfy the beyond-a-reasonable-doubt standard in criminal cases, presumably because the judge believes disposition would be for the juvenile's own good. See, e.g., Joseph B. Sanborn, Jr., Remnants of *Parens Patriae* in the Adjudicatory Hearing: Is a Fair Trial Possible in Juvenile Court?, 40 Crime & Delinq. 599, 604 (1994).

2. Competency to Participate in the Proceeding

MATTER OF WELFARE OF D.D.N.

Court of Appeals of Minnesota, 1998.
582 N.W.2d 278.

CRIPPEN, JUDGE.

* * *

Facts

In June 1997, appellant D.D.N., then 15 years old, was charged by petition with first-degree attempted burglary. Because of competency concerns, the juvenile court ordered that appellant undergo a 35–day evaluation at a residential treatment center.

A representative from the treatment center and experts for both appellant and the prosecution testified at the competency hearing. Following the hearing, the juvenile court concluded that appellant was competent to proceed to trial. The court subsequently adjudicated appellant a delinquent and placed him in a juvenile treatment facility. Appellant now appeals the court's pretrial competency ruling.

* * *

Analysis

1. Juvenile Competency Standard

The briefs of the parties allude to an expanding body of research and reporting on the diminished capacity of adolescents to assist their own interests at various stages in the prosecution of their alleged offenses. The prosecuting attorney points to the scholarly opinion in this literature that, notwithstanding evidence of the diminished capacity of adolescent offenders to participate in court proceedings, a relaxed standard of competency might be justified in proceedings where the court will make a rehabilitative disposition. But in Minnesota, a lower standard for juvenile competency is precluded both by the supreme court's juvenile justice rules and by that court's earlier decision.

Minnesota rules of court relating to juvenile and adult competency hold children and adults to the same competency standard. Minn. R. Juv. P. 20.01, subd. 1(B), which sets the standard for juvenile competency, states:

A child shall not be permitted to enter a plea or be tried or sentenced for any offense if the child lacks sufficient ability to:

(1) consult with a reasonable degree of rational understanding with defense counsel; or

(2) understand the proceedings or participate in the defense due to mental illness or mental deficiency.

The adult competency standard similarly defines competency as the ability to consult with counsel and to understand the nature of the proceeding.[2] * * *

Here, the prosecuting attorney argues that the availability of shorter-term sanctions and the rehabilitative nature of those dispositions may justify a lower level of competency. But this argument overlooks the reality that rehabilitative sanctions can and do involve a major loss of a child's liberties.

* * *

The prosecutor's argument also overlooks the fact that, although rehabilitation eliminates retribution and deterrence of others, it does not always eliminate punishment. The juvenile court's dispositions must be rehabilitative and tied to the needs of and opportunities for the child, but these laws do not prohibit "a rational, punitive disposition, one where the record shows that correction or rehabilitation of the child reasonably cannot be achieved without a penalty."

A determination of competency, even in the context of juvenile adjudicatory proceedings, is a fundamental right. Because of this and because dispositions in juvenile proceedings, including rehabilitative dispositions, may involve both punishment and a substantial loss of liberty, the level of competence required to permit a child's participation in juvenile court proceedings can be no less than the competence demanded for trial or sentencing of an adult. Children, like adults, must be able "to understand the nature of the proceedings against [them] and to participate in [their] own defense." * * * *

3. Competency of D.D.N.

* * *

Testing at the treatment center indicated that appellant's performance IQ was "Low Average," but his verbal IQ fell within the "Intellectually Deficient" range.[4] Testing also showed that appellant had "very limited verbal memory, poor verbal abstraction abilities, minimal verbal reasoning and a marginal vocabulary." Each of the experts who examined appellant found him to be limited in his communication and slow to respond to questions.

At the competency hearing, Dr. Hoberman [a licensed psychologist named by the court] testified that appellant was competent to stand

---

2. The adult competency standard is

[a] defendant shall not be permitted to enter a plea or be tried or sentenced for any offense if the defendant:

    (1) lacks sufficient ability to consult with a reasonable degree of rational understanding with defense counsel; or

    (2) is mentally ill or mentally deficient so as to be incapable of understanding the proceedings or participating in the defense.

Minn. R.Crim. P. 20.01, subd. 1.

4. Appellant's verbal IQ was in the 0.4th percentile (or in the lowest 4/10th of 1%) when compared with others his own age. To put this into context, for every 2,500 15-year-olds, only 10 would have the same score or lower.

trial. Hoberman felt that, despite the low verbal IQ score, appellant was able to respond to questions and understood what was asked of him. Dr. Hoberman testified that when appellant was asked questions about the roles of various persons involved in the judicial process, about his relationship with his attorney, about whether he understood what his attorney was telling him, and about the nature of the trial process, he was able to respond "to almost all of the questions." Hoberman also testified that he believed appellant understood the charges against him and the possible outcomes. Further, appellant recalled the reading of his *Miranda* rights and his decision not to speak to police without counsel. Dr. Hoberman further testified that appellant discussed a previous court experience and that "he had been part of making the decision" to plea bargain in that case. But the witness cautioned that, due to appellant's deficiencies in processing verbal information, appellant's understanding of the events at trial should be continually scrutinized.

Eric Beuning, the treatment center case manager, testified that appellant seemed to understand fully what was going on while at the center. He also testified that appellant was "very outgoing, very friendly" with his peers and had no apparent difficulty expressing himself. On one occasion, Beuning reported that appellant said he would "call his lawyer" when told that food spilled on the table would not be replaced.

Dr. Nelson [a clinical psychologist whose testimony the defense requested] testified that appellant "has some very significant cognitive limitations that accordingly limit to a great degree his ability to understand the proceedings and to participate in his defense." He also testified that he did not believe that appellant understood the judicial process. But Nelson admitted that appellant had "a basic awareness of what's right and wrong," a "limited" understanding of who did what in the criminal justice system, and the cognitive capability of participating in his defense.[5]

To be competent to proceed to trial or sentencing, the accused person must be able to consult with counsel and understand the nature of the proceedings in which he or she is involved. Our review of the record indicates that, notwithstanding appellant's limited intellectual abilities, the trial court properly inferred from the evidence presented that appellant was competent to proceed. In our collective view, the evidence identifies narrow areas of difficulty, principally in communicating with counsel during interrogation of witnesses. These difficulties do not compel reversal of the juvenile court's finding that appellant had the ability to understand and participate in proceedings and to consult with counsel.

5. We are troubled by Dr. Nelson's testimony that "in terms of that part of the [trial] process that is fluid and ongoing, I can't think of anything that would in my opinion render [appellant] competent." But in light of appellant's previous experience with the juvenile court process, his understanding about the work of an attorney, his recollection of the reading of the *Miranda* rights, and his decision not to speak to police without counsel, we believe that appellant has a less sweeping kind of disability than what appears to be indicated by Dr. Nelson's generalized opinion.

Affirmed.

Notes and Questions

1. *Questions about* D.D.N. (a) How high should the competency threshold be in delinquency proceedings? Are you comfortable with the finding that D.D.N. was competent?,

(b) If the court found D.D.N. incompetent to participate in the proceedings and thus dismissed the delinquency petition, would the court necessarily have lost jurisdiction to order treatment?,

(c) Under Minnesota law, a 15-year-old is incompetent to sign a binding contract or get a driver's license. Particularly in light of 15–year-old D.D.N.'s diminished mental condition, why should he be competent to participate in a delinquency proceeding which could result in a substantial period of confinement? In State v. Mitchell [supra p. 1056], why was 15-year-old Eric Mitchell, similarly incompetent to sign a contract or get a driver's license, nonetheless competent to participate in a criminal proceeding that left him imprisoned for life with no possibility of parole for at least 30 years?

2. *Children's competency in juvenile court.* The issue of alleged delinquents' competency does not have a long pedigree because the issue did not normally arise before *Gault* imposed due process constraints on the juvenile court. The issue has arisen with increased frequency in recent years as juvenile court sanctions have grown more punitive, conditions of juvenile confinement have remained harsh in many places, and juveniles have faced greater likelihood of transfer to criminal court. Minnesota is typical of states with statutes or rules that define competency in delinquency proceedings. In other states, courts may hold that due process requires application of the criminal law competency standard and prohibits adjudication of juveniles who fail to satisfy the standard. See, e.g, In re S.H., 469 S.E.2d 810, 811 (Ga.Ct.App.1996).

The stakes can also be high when competency is contested in a transfer hearing before adjudication. For Eric Mitchell, for example [supra p. 1056], transfer meant the difference between a potential few years confinement after a delinquency adjudication and potential life imprisonment after a criminal conviction.

3. *Children's competency in criminal court.* D.D.N. was subject to Minnesota's juvenile competency rule because the delinquency proceeding remained in juvenile court. With states transferring more and more juveniles to criminal court at ever younger ages, however, the competency issue may also arise once the juvenile lands in that court. Even 12- or 13-year-olds may be transferred in some states, and some states no longer have a minimum transfer age for juveniles charged with the most serious crimes. In criminal court, a defendant's competency to stand trial depends on "whether he has sufficient present ability to consult with his lawyer with a reasonable degree of rational understanding—and whether he has a rational as well as factual understanding of the proceedings against him." Dusky v. United States, 362 U.S. 402, 402 (1960).

4. *Are children different?* Adults' competency has generally focused on mental illness or retardation. See, e.g., Drope v. Missouri, 420 U.S. 162, 171

(1975). In juvenile or criminal court, however, a juvenile's competency might also be questioned based on developmental immaturity. See Thomas Grisso, The Competence of Adolescents as Trial Defendants, 3 Psychol. Pub. Pol'y & L. 3 (1997). Behavioral research has begun to indicate that children below fourteen are considerably less able than older children or adults to understand the meaning of a trial, to assist counsel, and to make decisions. See id. at 7–9. Courts have found particularly young children incompetent even when they do not suffer from any mental illness or retardation. See, e.g., In re Charles B., 978 P.2d 659 (Ariz.Ct.App.1998) (11–year-old boy charged with aggravated assault).

3. Jury trial

Gault held that due process guaranteed alleged delinquents a number of valuable rights designed to elevate juvenile courts from, as Justice Fortas put it, "kangaroo courts." The Court, however, declined Justice Black's invitation to hold the Bill of Rights directly applicable to delinquency proceedings. *McKeiver* demonstrated the practical differences between the two approaches.

McKEIVER v. PENNSYLVANIA

Supreme Court of the United States, 1971.
403 U.S. 528.

MR. JUSTICE BLACKMUN announced the judgments of the Court and an opinion in which THE CHIEF JUSTICE, MR. JUSTICE STEWART, and MR. JUSTICE WHITE join.

These cases present the narrow but precise issue whether the Due Process Clause of the Fourteenth Amendment assures the right to trial by jury in the adjudicative phase of a state juvenile court delinquency proceeding.

II

[In the Pennsylvania delinquency cases, (1) Joseph McKeiver was charged with committing robbery, larceny, and receipt of stolen goods (felonies under state law) when he was sixteen, and (2) Edward Terry was charged with assault and battery on a police officer and conspiracy (misdemeanors under state law) when he was fifteen. In the North Carolina delinquency cases, Barbara Burrus and approximately 45 other black children, ranging in age from 11 to 15 years, were charged with various misdemeanors arising from their participation in a series of demonstrations by black adults and children protesting school assignments and a school consolidation plan.

The respective state courts of appeals and state supreme courts affirmed the delinquency adjudications and rejected contentions that the juveniles had a constitutional right to a jury trial.].

* * *

IV

The right to an impartial jury "[i]n all criminal prosecutions" under federal law is guaranteed by the Sixth Amendment. Through the Fourteenth Amendment that requirement has now been imposed upon the States "in all criminal cases which—were they to be tried in a federal court—would come within the Sixth Amendment's guarantee." This is because the Court has said it believes "that trial by jury in criminal cases is fundamental to the American scheme of justice."

This, of course, does not automatically provide the answer to the present jury trial issue, if for no other reason than that the juvenile court proceeding has not yet been held to be a "criminal prosecution," within the meaning and reach of the Sixth Amendment, and also has not yet been regarded as devoid of criminal aspects merely because it usually has been given the civil label.

Little, indeed, is to be gained by any attempt simplistically to call the juvenile court proceeding either "civil" or "criminal." The Court carefully has avoided this wooden approach. Before *Gault* was decided in 1967, the Fifth Amendment's guarantee against self-incrimination had been imposed upon the state criminal trial. So, too, had the Sixth Amendment's rights of confrontation and cross-examination. Yet the Court did not automatically and peremptorily apply those rights to the juvenile proceeding. A reading of *Gault* reveals the opposite. And the same separate approach to the standard-of-proof issue is evident from the carefully separated application of the standard, first to the criminal trial, and then to the juvenile proceeding, displayed in *Winship*.

Thus, accepting "the proposition that the Due Process Clause has a role to play," *Gault*, our task here with respect to trial by jury, as it was in *Gault* with respect to other claimed rights, "is to ascertain the precise impact of the due process requirement."

V

The Pennsylvania juveniles' basic argument is that they were tried in proceedings "substantially similar to a criminal trial." * * * *

The North Carolina juveniles particularly urge that the requirement of a jury trial would not operate to deny the supposed benefits of the juvenile court system; that the system's primary benefits are its discretionary intake procedure permitting disposition short of adjudication, and its flexible sentencing permitting emphasis on rehabilitation; that realization of these benefits does not depend upon dispensing with the jury; that adjudication of factual issues on the one hand and disposition of the case on the other are very different matters with very different purposes; that the purpose of the former is indistinguishable from that of the criminal trial; that the jury trial provides an independent protective factor; that experience has shown that jury trials in juvenile courts are manageable; that no reason exists why protection traditionally accorded in criminal proceedings should be denied young people subject to involuntary incarceration for lengthy periods; and that the juvenile courts deserve healthy public scrutiny.

VI

All the litigants here agree that the applicable due process standard in juvenile proceedings, as developed by *Gault* and *Winship*, is fundamental fairness. As that standard was applied in those two cases, we have an emphasis on factfinding procedures. The requirements of notice, counsel, confrontation, cross-examination, and standard of proof naturally flowed from this emphasis. But one cannot say that in our legal system the jury is a necessary component of accurate factfinding. There is much to be said for it, to be sure, but we have been content to pursue other ways for determining facts. Juries are not required, and have not been, for example, in equity cases, in workmen's compensation, in probate, or in deportation cases. Neither have they been generally used in military trials. * * *

We must recognize, as the Court has recognized before, that the fond and idealistic hopes of the juvenile court proponents and early reformers of three generations ago have not been realized. * * * Too often the juvenile court judge falls far short of that stalwart, protective, and communicating figure the system envisaged. The community's unwillingness to provide people and facilities and to be concerned, the insufficiency of time devoted, the scarcity of professional help, the inadequacy of dispositional alternatives, and our general lack of knowledge all contribute to dissatisfaction with the experiment.

* * *

Despite all these disappointments, all these failures, and all these shortcomings, we conclude that trial by jury in the juvenile court's adjudicative stage is not a constitutional requirement. We so conclude for a number of reasons:

1. The Court has refrained, in the cases heretofore decided, from taking the easy way with a flat holding that all rights constitutionally assured for the adult accused are to be imposed upon the state juvenile proceeding [citing *Gault* and *Winship*].

2. There is a possibility, at least, that the jury trial, if required as a matter of constitutional precept, will remake the juvenile proceeding into a fully adversary process and will put an effective end to what has been the idealistic prospect of an intimate, informal protective proceeding.

* * *

5. The imposition of the jury trial on the juvenile court system would not strengthen greatly, if at all, the factfinding function, and would, contrarily, provide an attrition of the juvenile court's assumed ability to function in a unique manner. It would not remedy the defects of the system. Meager as has been the hoped-for advance in the juvenile field, the alternative would be regressive, would lose what has been

gained, and would tend once again to place the juvenile squarely in the routine of the criminal process.

6. The juvenile concept held high promise. We are reluctant to say that, despite disappointments of grave dimensions, it still does not hold promise, and we are particularly reluctant to say * * * that the system cannot accomplish its rehabilitative goals. So much depends on the availability of resources, on the interest and commitment of the public, on willingness to learn, and on understanding as to cause and effect and cure. In this field, as in so many others, one perhaps learns best by doing. We are reluctant to disallow the States to experiment further and to seek in new and different ways the elusive answers to the problems of the young, and we feel that we would be impeding that experimentation by imposing the jury trial. The States, indeed, must go forward. If, in its wisdom, any State feels the jury trial is desirable in all cases, or in certain kinds, there appears to be no impediment to its installing a system embracing that feature. That, however, is the State's privilege and not its obligation.

7. Of course there have been abuses. * * * We refrain from saying at this point that those abuses are of constitutional dimension. They relate to the lack of resources and of dedication rather than to inherent unfairness.

8. There is, of course, nothing to prevent a juvenile court judge, in a particular case where he feels the need, or when the need is demonstrated, from using an advisory jury.

9. "The fact that a practice is followed by a large number of states is not conclusive in a decision as to whether that practice accords with due process, but it is plainly worth considering in determining whether the practice 'offends some principle of justice so rooted in the traditions and conscience of our people as to be ranked as fundamental.'" It therefore is of more than passing interest that at least 28 States and the District of Columbia by statute deny the juvenile a right to a jury trial in cases such as these. The same result is achieved in other States by judicial decision. In 10 States statutes provide for a jury trial under certain circumstances.

10. Since *Gault* and since *Duncan* [v. *Louisiana*, 391 U.S. 145 (1968), which applied the Sixth Amendment jury trial right to the states] the great majority of States, in addition to Pennsylvania and North Carolina, that have faced the issue have concluded that the considerations that led to the result in those two cases do not compel trial by jury in the juvenile court.

* * *

12. If the jury trial were to be injected into the juvenile court system as a matter of right, it would bring with it into that system the traditional delay, the formality, and the clamor of the adversary system and, possibly, the public trial. * * *

13.   Finally, the arguments advanced by the juveniles here are, of course, the identical arguments that underlie the demand for the jury trial for criminal proceedings. The arguments necessarily equate the juvenile proceeding—or at least the adjudicative phase of it—with the criminal trial. Whether they should be so equated is our issue. Concern about the inapplicability of exclusionary and other rules of evidence, about the juvenile court judge's possible awareness of the juvenile's prior record and of the contents of the social file; about repeated appearances of the same familiar witnesses in the persons of juvenile and probation officers and social workers—all to the effect that this will create the likelihood of pre-judgment—chooses to ignore it seems to us, every aspect of fairness, of concern, of sympathy, and of paternal attention that the juvenile court system contemplates.

If the formalities of the criminal adjudicative process are to be superimposed upon the juvenile court system, there is little need for its separate existence. Perhaps that ultimate disillusionment will come one day, but for the moment we are disinclined to give impetus to it.

Affirmed.

MR. JUSTICE WHITE, concurring.

Although the function of the jury is to find facts, that body is not necessarily or even probably better at the job than the conscientious judge. Nevertheless, the consequences of criminal guilt are so severe that the Constitution mandates a jury to prevent abuses of official power by insuring, where demanded, community participation in imposing serious deprivations of liberty and to provide a hedge against corrupt, biased, or political justice. * * *

The criminal law proceeds on the theory that defendants have a will and are responsible for their actions. A finding of guilt establishes that they have chosen to engage in conduct so reprehensible and injurious to others that they must be punished to deter them and others from crime. Guilty defendants are considered blameworthy; they are branded and treated as such, however much the State also pursues rehabilitative ends in the criminal justice system.

For the most part, the juvenile justice system rests on more deterministic assumptions. Reprehensible acts by juveniles are not deemed the consequence of mature and malevolent choice but of environmental pressures (or lack of them) or of other forces beyond their control. * * *

* * * To the extent that the jury is a buffer to the corrupt or overzealous prosecutor in the criminal law system, the distinctive intake policies and procedures of the juvenile court system to a great extent obviate this important function of the jury. As for the necessity to guard against judicial bias, a system eschewing blameworthiness and punishment for evil choice is itself an operative force against prejudice and short-tempered justice. Nor where juveniles are involved is there the same opportunity for corruption to the juvenile's detriment or the same temptation to use the courts for political ends.

Not only are those risks that mandate juries in criminal cases of lesser magnitude in juvenile court adjudications, but the consequences of adjudication are less severe than those flowing from verdicts of criminal guilt. * * *

* * *

[Concurring opinions of Justices Brennan and Harlan are omitted.]

MR. JUSTICE DOUGLAS, with whom MR. JUSTICE BLACK and MR. JUSTICE MARSHALL concur, dissenting.

* * * I believe the guarantees of the Bill of Rights, made applicable to the States by the Fourteenth Amendment, require a jury trial.

* * *

[W]here a State uses its juvenile court proceedings to prosecute a juvenile for a criminal act and to order "confinement" until the child reaches 21 years of age or where the child at the threshold of the proceedings faces that prospect, then he is entitled to the same procedural protection as an adult. * * *

* * *

In the present cases imprisonment or confinement up to 10 years was possible for one child and each faced at least a possible five-year incarceration. No adult could be denied a jury trial in those circumstances. The Fourteenth Amendment, which makes trial by jury provided in the Sixth Amendment applicable to the States, speaks of denial of rights to "any person," not denial of rights to "any adult person" * * *.

* * *

Notes and Questions

1. *Questions about* McKeiver. (a) Only four years after *Gault*, what explains *McKeiver's* decidedly more pessimistic assessment of the juvenile court's capacity to rehabilitate delinquents outside the adult criminal process?,

(b) Under *Gault's* fundamental fairness test, how does the Court decide what procedures due process requires in delinquency proceedings?,

(c) Are you convinced by the distinction *McKeiver* draws between the constitutional rights at issue in *Gault* and the right to a jury trial?,

(d) *McKeiver* says *Gault* emphasized "accurate factfinding." Was that all *Gault* emphasized, or did it also emphasize other virtues?

(e) Justice White says "the consequences of [delinquency] adjudication are less severe than those flowing from verdicts of criminal guilt." Is this statement consistent with *Gault*? Is it necessarily true?,

(f) If alleged delinquents had a federal constitutional right to a jury trial, would states be more likely to agree to divert larger numbers of juveniles out of the system short of trial? Would increased reliance on diversion be a good idea?,

(g) While passing harsh judgment on the efficacy of the juvenile justice system, does *McKeiver* nonetheless seek to resurrect images of the benevolent, paternalistic juvenile court judge rejected in *Gault* only four years earlier?

2. *The early years.* When juvenile courts were perceived purely as agents of rehabilitation, most courts gave short shrift to assertions of a right to a jury trial in delinquency cases. "Whether the child deserves to be saved by the state is no more a question for a jury than whether the father, if able to save it, ought to save it." Commonwealth v. Fisher, 62 A. 198, 200 (Pa.1905).

An early juvenile court proponent wrote that a jury trial right was "injurious and * * * entirely inconsistent with both the law and the theory upon which juvenile courts rest": "[T]he employment of a jury increases the cost of administration; it invites publicity; it involves a formal criminal procedure; and it seriously interferes with the moral and educational influence of the judge and other officers of the court. By retaining his control over the disposition of the case, the judge can more effectively facilitate constructive treatment." Herbert H. Lou, Juvenile Courts in the United States 137 (1927).

3. *State right to a jury trial.* As *McKeiver* notes, only a few states have granted the right under the state constitution or by statute or court rule. See, e.g., Peyton v. Nord, 437 P.2d 716 (N.M.1968) (state constitution); W. Va. Code § 49–5–6.

4. *Accurate factfinding.* *McKeiver's* plurality states that "one cannot say that in our legal system the jury is a necessary component of accurate factfinding." What support did *McKeiver* provide for this conclusion? Only two years earlier, the Court had called the criminal jury a "fundamental right, essential for preventing miscarriages of justice and for assuring that fair trials are provided for all defendants." Duncan v. Louisiana, 391 U.S. 145, 158 (1968). Are the two statements consistent? If they are not, what might account for the inconsistency?

It has been persuasively argued that the difference between bench trials and jury trials may be significant and even outcome determinative in juvenile court and criminal court alike. Observers have noted that juries acquit more often than do judges, apply a higher standard for finding guilt beyond a reasonable doubt, and apply community values to decisionmaking. See, e.g., Harry Kalven, Jr. and Hans Zeisel, The American Jury (1966); Martin Guggenheim and Randy Hertz, Reflections on Judges, Juries, and Justice: Ensuring the Fairness of Juvenile Delinquency Trials, 33 Wake Forest L. Rev. 553, 562–82 (1998).

Professor Janet E. Ainsworth has argued that a juvenile court judge who hears hundreds, or even a few thousand, cases a year "may become less careful in weighing the evidence and more cynical in evaluating the credibility of the juveniles who appear," particularly when (as is often the case) the judge knows the juvenile's prior record before the hearing. Janet E. Ainsworth, The Court's Effectiveness in Protecting the Rights of Juveniles in Delinquency Cases, 6 The Future of Children 64, 68 (Winter 1996). Another commentator raised a similar concern. "In many juvenile courts the same individual conducts both preliminary/detention hearings as well as the adjudicatory hearing. This exposes the fact finder to prejudicial information (like prior record) that is inadmissible at the trial stage. Often, juvenile court judges also are familiar with defendants from previous prosecutions or from their siblings who preceded them into the juvenile justice system. Many other sources can literally scream to a judge that the defendant has a record or a problem that can add momentum to adjudicating the youth. That there is no jury to neutralize this contamination only serves to highlight the frail justice that can result from a juvenile court proceeding." Joseph B. Sanborn, Jr., Second–Class Justice, First–Class Punishment: The Use of Juvenile Records in Sentencing Adults, 81 Judicature 206, 212 (1998).

According to one court, the benefits of a jury trial "appear to have as much meaning for juvenile delinquency proceedings as for adult criminal court. We have been given no reason to believe the juvenile court bench is immune from the assignment of weak or biased judges. Indeed some juvenile judges may be subject to a subtle form of bias seldom found in adult court— the bias of good intentions." In re Javier A., 206 Cal.Rptr. 386, 426 (Ct.App.1984).

5. *Efforts to overcome* McKeiver. In the years since *McKeiver*, alleged delinquents have usually failed in efforts to establish a right to a jury trial under general federal or state constitutional guarantees. In State v. J.H., 978 P.2d 1121 (Wash.Ct.App.1999), for example, the court rejected the contention that recent juvenile justice code amendments had made delinquency proceedings so much less rehabilitative and more punitive as to require a jury trial right under the federal and state constitutions. In In re G.O., 710 N.E.2d 140, 144 (Ill.App.Ct.1999), however, the court held that the federal and state constitutions' equal protection clauses were offended by trying the 16-year-old in juvenile court for first degree murder without that right. The delinquent was committed to the Department of Corrections' Juvenile Division until his 21st birthday without possibility of parole or furlough or good-time credit. The court found the sentence "punitive" and observed that "[t]he passage of time has weakened the underpinnings of *McKeiver*" because "[t]oday's juvenile justice system is a far cry from" the juvenile court's traditional rehabilitative model.

6. *Effect of potential incarceration in adult prison.* Absence of the jury trial right may limit the juvenile court's authority to impose incarceration in an adult facility. In In re C.B., 708 So.2d 391, 399–400 (La.1998), for example, the court invalidated under the state constitution's due process clause a statute that, without affording the right to a jury trial in juvenile court, required the transfer of juveniles at age seventeen to an adult penal institution, where they would be confined at hard labor like adult felons for as much as four years. The court had earlier held that the state constitution did not afford the right to a jury trial in delinquency proceedings; now the court specified that the earlier holding "was predicated upon the non-criminal treatment of the adjudicated juvenile delinquent. * * * [I]f the civil trappings of the juvenile adjudication are sufficiently subverted, then a proceeding without [a jury trial] is fundamentally unfair."

In Monroe v. Soliz, 939 P.2d 205, 208 (Wash.1997), however, the court rejected state and federal constitutional challenges to a statute that authorized transfer to an adult facility of a juvenile who "presents a continuing and serious threat to the safety of others in the [juvenile] institution." The state supreme court held that the statute did not deprive the juvenile of his right to a jury trial because "he has none in a juvenile proceeding. The nature of incarceration remains juvenile regardless of the custody venue. This state statute merely changes that venue."

7. *The effect of jury trials on public perceptions of the juvenile court.* Many Americans never enter a courtroom except to serve jury duty. By denying a federal constitutional right to a jury trial, did *McKeiver* further weaken the juvenile court by diminishing public access to, and public participation in, the court's operations? Consider In re Javier A., 206 Cal.Rptr. 386, 426 (Ct.App.1984), which stated that "meaningful reform and adequate resources will not come without public support. Meantime we have closed the general public's main window into [juvenile] courts—serving on a jury personally or hearing from someone who has."

8. *Double jeopardy.* In Breed v. Jones, 421 U.S. 519 (1975), the juvenile was convicted in criminal court after a juvenile court adjudicatory proceeding found that he had violated a criminal statute and that he was unfit for treatment as a juvenile. *Breed* unanimously held that jeopardy attached when the juvenile court began hearing evidence, and thus that the later criminal prosecution violated the Fifth Amendment Double Jeopardy Clause, as applied to the states through the Fourteenth Amendment.

Before *Gault* imposed due process constraints on the juvenile court, the conceptual basis for a double jeopardy claim was not at all clear because noncriminal delinquency proceedings created no jeopardy. Like *Gault* and *Winship,* however, *Breed* refused to treat delinquency proceedings as purely civil because the Court noted "a gap between the originally benign conception of [the juvenile court] system and its realities." Id. at 528. "[I]t is simply too late in the day," Chief Justice Burger wrote in *Breed,* "to conclude * * * that a juvenile is not put in jeopardy at a proceeding whose object is to determine whether he has committed acts that violate a criminal law and whose potential consequences include both the stigma inherent in such a determination and the deprivation of liberty for many years." Id. at 529. The Court declined to follow *McKeiver,* which concerned merely "the formalities of the criminal adjudicative process." Id. at 531.

Double jeopardy concerns may also arise where successive proceedings are held in juvenile court, as in Swisher v. Brady, 438 U.S. 204 (1978), which distinguished *Breed. Swisher* challenged Maryland procedures which, designed to meet heavy juvenile court caseloads, provided that delinquency petitions would often be heard by masters, who would make proposed findings and recommendations to the juvenile court judge. The judge was empowered to accept, modify or reject the findings and recommendations and had sole authority to enter a final order. Where the state filed objections to the master's recommendation of nondelinquency, the court could rule on the objections based only on the record made before the master and on any additional relevant evidence to which the parties did not object. The juvenile contended that the state thus had the opportunity to convince two factfinders of his guilt, and that the state had the functional equivalent of appealing an incipient acquittal (the recommendation of nondelinquency). *Swisher* held that the state's right to file objections did not violate the Double Jeopardy Clause because "the juvenile is subjected to a single proceeding which begins with a master's hearing and culminates with an adjudication by a judge." Id. at 215.

At least twenty-five states allow juvenile court masters or referees to conduct adjudicatory hearings, with only a judge authorized to enter final judgments. Some states do not require masters or referees to be lawyers or do not require the juvenile's consent before a master or referee may sit. Is the final judgment fundamentally fair to the delinquent when it is entered by a judge who relies on a cold record without hearing the evidence or observing the witnesses? Should trial-by-referee be permitted in juvenile court when no such device exists in criminal court? See Joseph B. Sanborn, Jr., Constitutional Problems of Juvenile Delinquency Trials, 78 Judicature 81, 82–83, 88 (1994).

A juvenile expelled or otherwise disciplined by school authorities may thereafter be the subject of a delinquency proceeding (or a criminal trial) arising from the conduct that gave rise to the disciplinary action. Double jeopardy is not implicated because the disciplinary action is a civil administrative action and not a judicially imposed criminal punishment. See, e.g., Ex Parte K.H., 700 So.2d 1201, 1203 (Ala. Ct. Crim. App. 1997) (citing decisions).

9. *The constitutionalizing of delinquency practice.* *Gault* revolutionized delinquency practice by importing several constitutional criminal rights into delinquency proceedings under due process. *Winship* and *Breed* imported yet more rights. By statute and court rule, states have applied other criminal guarantees and procedures until delinquency practice has come to resemble criminal practice in important respects.

Gault and its progeny affect lawyers who represent children in delinquency proceedings. These lawyers must remain alert for decisions that interpret constitutional requirements held applicable in delinquency proceedings. Where the Supreme Court or a lower court interprets the Fifth Amendment privilege against compulsory self-incrimination in a criminal case, for example, the interpretation is relevant to the privilege's scope in delinquency proceedings.

4. Speedy Trial

IN THE MATTER OF BENJAMIN L.

Court of Appeals of New York, 1999.
708 N.E.2d 156.

WESLEY, J.

In this case we are asked to consider whether the constitutional right to a speedy trial, which is afforded to every defendant in criminal prosecutions in New York State, should be extended to juveniles in delinquency proceedings.

On July 7, 1994 Benjamin L., a 15 year old, was arrested and detained overnight after he allegedly menaced a delivery person and attempted to steal Chinese food from him in Yonkers. The following day the director of the Woodfield Detention Cottage submitted a pre-petition detention application to Family Court pursuant to sections 307.3 and 307.4 of the Family Court Act. At a hearing held on the same day Family Court denied the application, remanded appellant to his mother's care and ordered him to observe a 10:00 P.M. curfew.

Over one year later, on August 2, 1995, the Westchester County Attorney's office, acting in its capacity as presentment agency, filed a petition relating to the July 7, 1994 incident. The petition alleged that Benjamin, along with other youths, committed acts which, if committed by an adult, would constitute the crimes of attempted robbery in the second degree and menacing in the third degree. Appellant made an initial appearance with counsel on August 8, 1995 and entered a denial. The matter was adjourned to September 13, 1995 for a fact-finding hearing. On August 30, 1995, appellant moved to dismiss the petition, challenging its sufficiency and alleging that the delay in filing the petition violated his statutory right to a speedy hearing as codified in Family Court Act §§ 310.2, 320.2 and 340.1, or, in the alternative, his constitutional right to due process * * *.

[Without a hearing, Family Court denied Benjamin's motion to dismiss. After the factfinding and dispositional hearings, the court adjudicated him a delinquent and placed him on probation for one year. The Appellate Division affirmed.] We granted Benjamin leave to appeal and now reverse and remit the matter to Family Court for further proceedings in accordance with this opinion.

* * *

In keeping with the focus established by *Gault*, the Legislature amended the Family Court Act to add specific procedural rights for juveniles. The revised procedural rules include specific time limitations in the Family Court Act to govern each stage of the proceeding from arrest through final disposition. The express purpose of these provisions is to assure swift and certain adjudication at all phases of the delinquency proceeding. * * *

Benjamin argues that the Family Court Act prohibits specified delays between the filing of the pre-petition detention application and the commencement of a fact-finding hearing. He contends that a pre-petition detention application should be equated with a petition for the purpose of commencing the statutory speedy hearing clock. Contrary to Benjamin's contention, it cannot be inferred from the language of article 3 [of the Family Court Act] or the procedural structure of juvenile proceedings that a pre-petition detention application can be equated with a petition to bring into play the time limits set forth in article 3.

Family Court Act § 310.1(1) states that a proceeding to adjudicate a person a juvenile delinquent is originated by the filing of a petition. A pre-petition detention application differs in form, substance and purpose from a petition. A pre-petition detention application is filed by the detention facility, whereas a petition is filed by the presentment agency. Under a pre-petition detention application, a youth is subject to a quick yet careful determination by Family Court on the detention issue. The statute does provide for the *release* of a juvenile, held in custody following the detention hearing, when a petition is not filed within four days of completion of the detention hearing. The statute thus explicitly prescribes a procedural difference between pre-petition detention and commencement of the proceeding.

Moreover, while the purpose of a pre-petition detention application is primarily to determine whether a youth should be detained prior to the filing of a petition, a petition is "a written accusation by an authorized presentment agency" that formally commences the juvenile proceeding. Sections 310.2, 320.2 and 340.1 apply to time periods *after the initial petition is filed*.[2] Thus, the statute clearly mandates that the filing of the petition by the presentment agency signals the commencement of a juvenile proceeding.

* * *

Although article 3 of the Family Court Act establishes specific time limitations at each stage of the proceeding, there is no statutory time limitation for the period between filing a pre-petition detention application and filing a petition itself when the juvenile is not at a detention facility. The statute simply does not offer a remedy for Benjamin.

Benjamin also contends that the delay in question violated his State constitutional right to due process. Although New York does not have a constitutional speedy trial provision, we have long held that in criminal prosecutions an unreasonable delay in prosecuting a defendant following an arrest can constitute a violation of the Due Process Clause of our Constitution.

The right to a speedy trial is derived from an overarching interest in ensuring that all defendants are treated according to fair and reasonable procedures. Moreover, there are societal interests in providing a speedy trial that exist separate from the interests of the accused. These interests include preventing extensive backlogs of cases that diminish the legitimacy of the proceedings in the eyes of accuseds and their accusers while creating additional pressure on prosecutors to negotiate plea bargains premised on length of delay, not merit. Additionally, long delays

---

2. Family Court Act § 310.2, the "speedy trial" provision of the Family Court Act, states, "After a petition has been filed, or upon the signing of an order of removal pursuant to section 725.05 of the criminal procedure law, the respondent is entitled to a speedy fact-finding hearing." Family Court Act § 320.2(1) states in relevant part that "[i]f the respondent is detained, the initial appearance shall be held no later than seventy-two hours after a petition is filed or the next day the court is in session, whichever is sooner. If the respondent is not detained, the initial appearance shall be held as soon as practicable and, absent good cause shown, within ten days after a petition is filed." Family Court Act § 340.1, which addresses the time of the fact-finding hearing, sets different time periods within which the fact-finding hearing shall be commenced, contingent upon the type of crime committed and whether the juvenile is in detention. The commencement mechanism of these timing provisions is the "conclusion of the initial appearance," which is defined as "the proceeding on the date the respondent first appears before the court after a petition has been filed".

may harm the case of the prosecution or the defense because a witness's memory may fade.

These same concerns are even more compelling in the juvenile context. Minimizing the time between arrest and disposition in juvenile delinquency cases may be especially desirable because of the nature of adolescence. Indeed, a delay in the proceedings may undermine a court's ability to act in its adjudicative and rehabilitative capacities. Legal sanctions in the juvenile setting are designed to teach offenders that unlawful behavior has consequences. * * *

In sum, many of the same policies that warrant the articulation and enforcement of a criminal defendant's right to a speedy trial are applicable as a matter of fundamental fairness to juveniles in delinquency proceedings. The deterrence afforded by prompt disposition, the potential prejudice to a defense and the personal disruption created by a criminal charge are present whether the accused is a juvenile or an adult. In light of the need for swift and certain adjudication at all phases of a delinquency proceeding, we conclude that the speedy trial protections afforded under the Due Process Clause are not for criminal proceedings alone and are not at odds with the goals of juvenile proceedings.

Almost 25 years ago, in *People v. Taranovich* [1975], this Court articulated the factors to be examined in balancing the merits of an assertion of a denial of a defendant's right to a speedy trial in a criminal prosecution. Although *Taranovich* specifically addressed a defendant's right to a speedy trial in a Sixth Amendment context, we have previously acknowledged that the "due process right to prompt prosecution must be tested on a balancing analysis". Accepting these factors as an appropriate template, we conclude that the *Taranovich* test should be adopted to the juvenile delinquency context.

Benjamin * * * posits that the *Taranovich* weighing procedure is inapplicable in light of the 13–month delay here. In *Taranovich* we reaffirmed our prior case law in this area stating that where the "delay is great enough there need be neither proof nor fact of prejudice to the defendant". [The Court held that the delay was not sufficiently great here.].

In *Taranovich*, we held that several factors should be examined in determining the merits of a speedy trial claim: (1) the extent of the delay; (2) the reason for the delay; (3) the nature of the underlying charge; (4) whether or not there has been an extended period of pretrial incarceration; and (5) whether or not there is any indication that the defense has been impaired by reason of the delay. A *Taranovich*-like test is appropriate for determining whether a juvenile has been denied the right to a speedy adjudication following an arrest for both Sixth Amendment and State due process analyses.

In applying this test, however, courts must remain acutely cognizant of the goals, character and unique nature of juvenile proceedings. Indeed, given the differences between juvenile and criminal proceedings, a court's analysis cannot merely mimic that undertaken in criminal cases. For example, there would likely not be an extended period of pretrial incarceration in the juvenile context, given the strict time limitations promulgated in the Family Court Act for filing a petition when a juvenile is detained. Moreover, two of the *Taranovich* factors—prejudice and length of delay—may carry different connotations in the context of juvenile proceedings when compared to adult criminal prosecutions.

In criminal cases, establishing actual prejudice may be a particularly difficult factor to prove in a speedy trial analysis due to the fact that time's erosion of exculpatory evidence and testimony " 'can rarely be shown' ". Determining whether the juvenile's defense is impaired due to a delay may be even more arduous. Typically, a juvenile released by a court with no direction to reappear is unlikely to appreciate the importance of taking affirmative steps toward the ultimate resolution of the case, and is just as unlikely to possess the means and sophistication to do so. Moreover, many youths in juvenile proceedings suffer from educational handicaps and mental health problems, which undermine their capacity to anticipate a future presentment and to appreciate the need to take self-protective measures. Courts will have to be particularly mindful of these unique circumstances when assessing whether a speedy trial violation occurred.

In a criminal prosecution the sheer length of a delay is important because it is likely that "all other factors being equal, the greater the delay the more probable it is that the accused will be harmed thereby". The effects of that kind of delay in the juvenile context may be even more profound. A juvenile, experiencing the vicissitudes of childhood and adolescence, is more likely to suffer from a lack of memory than an adult. A juvenile is less likely than an adult to preserve his or her memory concerning the incident in question, his or her whereabouts on relevant dates, the identity of potential witnesses, and various other crucial details. Thus, there is an even greater potential for impairment of a juvenile's defense.

Undue delay especially disrupts the rehabilitative process, a key feature of the juvenile system. While in a criminal prosecution the accepted goals of punishment and deterrence are still served even when a defendant is prosecuted long after the crime was committed, the central goal of any juvenile proceeding—rehabilitation of the juvenile through prompt intervention and treatment—can seem trivialized when a presentment agency delays the filing of a petition. A child who is subjected to a long delay before a proceeding is commenced only to have it dismissed after a court determines at a dispositional hearing that supervision, treatment or confinement are not required is poorly served by our justice system. However, a child in need of rehabilitative efforts should not be denied that ameliorative attention merely because of some delay. To cut off the rehabilitation opportunity for a juvenile in the name of due process might defeat or contradict the express goals of article 3— to "consider the needs and best interests of the respondent as well as the need for protection of the community". Thus, when evaluating the length of delay a court must carefully consider the complex and varied realities of juveniles and their problems.

In concluding that juveniles have a right to speedy adjudication, we do not endorse a per se rule regarding speedy trial violations. The factors must be collectively evaluated on a case-by-case basis since "no rigid precepts may be formulated which apply to each and every instance in which it is averred that there has been a deprivation of the speedy trial right".

* * *

Notes and Questions

1. *The juvenile speedy trial right.* The Sixth Amendment guarantees that "[i]n all criminal prosecutions, the accused shall enjoy the right to a speedy * * * trial." In Barker v. Wingo, 407 U.S. 514, 530 (1972), the Court established a four-factor test for implementing the Sixth Amendment right. On a motion to dismiss for lack of a speedy trial, the trial judge must weigh the length of the delay, the reason the government assigns for the delay, whether and how the defendant asserted the right, and whether the delay prejudiced the defendant.

The speedy trial issue did not surface in juvenile courts before *Gault* established the core proposition that juveniles hold constitutional rights in delinquency cases. *Gault*, of course, conferred federal due process rights but also established that a delinquency proceeding is not a "criminal prosecution." Neither *Gault* nor any later Supreme Court decision has held that an alleged delinquent holds a federal due process right to a speedy trial. State courts disagree about whether delinquents hold a federal or state constitutional right to a speedy trial. In more than half the states, however, statutes or court rules create a speedy trial right by imposing time standards for processing and determining delinquency petitions. In other states, delay may be considerable, raising the question whether the policy goals discussed in *Benjamin L.* have been compromised. See generally Jeffrey A. Butts, Speedy Trial in the Juvenile Court, 23 Am. J. Crim. L. 515 (1996).

2. *The record in the courts.* The National District Attorneys Association recommends that no more than sixty days pass between police referral and disposition for juveniles held in secure detention, and no more than ninety days for juveniles not detained. Other professional associations recommend even shorter maximum time periods. The IJA–ABA Juvenile Justice Standards, for example, recommend maximum periods of thirty days and sixty days respectively. A significant percentage of delinquency cases nationwide do not reach disposition within ninety days, including nearly half the cases pending in large jurisdictions. See Jeffrey A. Butts, Delays in Juvenile Court Processing of Delinquency Cases 2 (OJJDP Mar. 1997).

3. *The effects of delay on victims of juvenile crime.* Delays in juvenile court case processing and adjudication may adversely affect victims, a matter of attention in light of victims' rights provisions now in many states' juvenile codes. Continuances and postponements may discourage victims and their families from exercising their rights to observe and participate in the proceedings, may lead them to question whether the offender will ever be

brought to justice, and may diminish the offender's willingness to participate in restorative justice programs. Undue delay may be especially harsh on child victims, who experience the passage of time differently than adults. With victims' interests in mind, juvenile court judges are reportedly "quicker to deny unnecessary continuances to avoid delay." See Robert E. Shepherd, Jr., Juvenile Justice, 13 Crim. Just. 27, 28 (Fall 1998).

D. Disposition

1. General Standards

At the dispositional hearing after delinquency is admitted or proved, the court considers what sanction or sanctions to impose on the juvenile. The juvenile court disposition has been described as "not simply a sentencing," but rather a delicate balancing of needs. The disposition "should be in the best interests of the child, which in this context means effectively to provide the help necessary to resolve or meet the individual's definable needs, while, at the same time, meeting society's need for protection." National Bench Book For Juvenile Courts 43 (Lindsay G. Arthur ed., rev. ed. 1979).

From the least severe to the most severe, the range of delinquency sanctions normally includes reprimanding or warning the juvenile; placing the juvenile on probation; ordering that the juvenile or parent, or both, attend counseling or mental health treatment; ordering that the juvenile pay a fine, make restitution or perform community service; placing the juvenile in a group home, foster home or similar residential facility; committing the juvenile to a secure institution (that is, one the juvenile may not leave without permission); or committing the juvenile to an outside agency or mental health program. As discussed above at page–, federal and state law precludes incarcerating adjudicated delinquents in adult jails.

In more than thirty states, the juvenile court may impose a term of probation or confinement that extends beyond the maximum age of the court's original exclusive delinquency jurisdiction. In most states, that age is eighteen, though a few states have enacted maximum ages between fifteen and seventeen. The maximum dispositional age, for example, is twenty-four in California, Montana, Oregon and Wisconsin. See Howard N. Snyder and Melissa Sickmund, Juvenile Offenders and Victims: 1999 National Report 93 (1999). In some states, the extended dispositional ages apply only to particular offenses or particular juveniles, such as violent crimes or habitual offenders. Id. Where the juvenile has committed a serious crime such as murder, the swiftly approaching maximum dispositional age may lead the court to transfer the juvenile to criminal court for trial and sentencing as an adult.

In recent years, delinquency dispositions have aroused strident criticism from many quarters. Juvenile courts have been criticized for enabling many juvenile offenders to develop lengthy "rap sheets" before ever holding them truly accountable for their conduct. Juvenile courts have been criticized for imposing unduly lenient sanctions that amount to little more than a "slap on the wrist," "coddle" persistent offenders, and compromise public safety. On the other hand, juvenile courts have also been criticized for imposing unduly harsh sanctions that place punishment ahead of rehabilitation, frequently without affording constitutional rights available in criminal court, such as the right to a jury trial. Juvenile courts have also been criticized for allowing racial and gender bias to infect the disposition process.

The following article describes "graduated sanctions," a blueprint provided by the U.S. Office of Juvenile Justice and Delinquency Prevention (OJJDP) to guide juvenile court judges in the exercise of their broad discretion to fashion dispositions.

JOHN J. WILSON AND JAMES C. HOWELL, SERIOUS AND VIOLENT JUVENILE CRIME: A COMPREHENSIVE STRATEGY

45 Juv. & Fam. Ct. J. 3, 9–11 (No. 2 1994).

* * *

An effective juvenile justice system program model for the treatment and rehabilitation of delinquent offenders is one that combines accountability and sanctions with increasingly intensive treatment and rehabilitation services. These graduated sanctions must be wide-ranging to fit the offense and include both intervention and secure corrections components. The intervention component includes the use of immediate intervention and intermediate sanctions, and the secure corrections component includes the use of community confinement and incarceration in training schools, camps, and ranches.

Each of these graduated sanctions components should consist of sublevels, or gradations, that together with appropriate services constitute an integrated approach. The purpose of this approach is to stop the juvenile's further penetration into the system by inducing law-abiding behavior as early as possible through the combination of appropriate intervention and treatment sanctions. The juvenile justice system must work with law enforcement, courts, and corrections to develop reasonable, fair, and humane sanctions.

At each level in the continuum, the family must continue to be integrally involved in treatment and rehabilitation efforts. Aftercare must be a formal component of all residential placements, actively involving the family and the community in supporting and reintegrating the juvenile into the community.

Programs will need to use Risk and Needs Assessments to determine the appropriate placement for the offender. Risk assessments should be based on clearly defined objective criteria that focus on: (1) the seriousness of the delinquent act; (2) the potential risk for re-offending, based on the presence of risk factors; and (3) the risk to the public safety. Effective risk assessment at intake, for example, can be used to identify those juveniles who require the use of detention as well as those who can be released to parental custody or diverted to nonsecure community-based programs. Needs assessments will help ensure that: (1) different types of problems are taken into account when formulating a case plan; (2) a baseline for monitoring a juvenile's progress is established; (3) periodic reassessments of treatment effectiveness are conducted; and (4) a system-wide data base of treatment needs can be used for the planning and evaluation of programs, policies, and procedures. Together, risk and needs assessments will help to allocate scarce resources more efficiently and effectively. A system of graduated sanctions requires a broad continuum of options.

For intervention efforts to be most effective, they must be swift, certain, consistent, and incorporate increasing sanctions, including the possible loss of freedom. As the severity of sanctions increases, so must the intensity of treatment. At each level, offenders must be aware that, should they continue to violate the law, they will be subject to more severe sanctions and could ultimately be confined in a secure setting, ranging from a secure community-based juvenile facility to a training school, camp, or ranch.

The juvenile court plays an important role in the provision of treatment and sanctions. Probation has traditionally been viewed as the court's main vehicle for delivery of treatment services and community supervision. However, traditional probation services and sanctions have not had the resources to effectively target delinquent offenders, particularly serious, violent, and chronic offenders.

The following graduated sanctions are proposed within the intervention component:

Immediate Intervention. First-time delinquent offenders (misdemeanors and nonviolent felonies) and nonserious repeat offenders (generally misdemeanor repeat offenses) must be targeted for system intervention based on their probability of becoming more serious or chronic in their delinquent activities. Nonresidential community-based programs, including prevention programs for at-risk youth, may be appropriate for many of these offenders. Such programs are small and open, located in or near the juvenile's home, and maintain community participation in program planning, operation, and evaluation. Community police officers, working as part of Neighborhood Resource Teams, can help monitor the juvenile's progress. Other offenders may require sanctions tailored to their offense(s) and their needs to deter them from committing additional crimes.

The following programs apply to these offenders: Neighborhood Resource Teams, diversion, informal probation, school counselors serving as probation officers, home on probation, mediation (victims), community service, restitution, day-treatment programs, alcohol and drug abuse treatment (outpatient), and peer juries.

Intermediate sanctions. Offenders who are inappropriate for immediate intervention (first-time serious or violent offenders) or who fail to respond successfully to immediate intervention as evidenced by re-offending (such as repeat property offenders or drug-involved juveniles) would begin with or be subject to intermediate sanctions. These sanctions may be nonresidential or residential.

Many of the serious and violent offenders at this stage may be appropriate for placement in an intensive supervision program as an alternative to secure incarceration. OJJDP's Intensive Supervision of Probationers Program Model is a highly structured, continuously monitored individualized plan that consists of five phases with decreasing levels of restrictiveness: (1)Short–Term Placement in Community Confinement; (2) Day Treatment; (3) Outreach and Tracking; (4) Routine Supervision; and (5) Discharge and Follow-up.

Other appropriate programs include: drug testing, weekend detention, alcohol and drug abuse treatment (inpatient), challenge outdoor, community-based residential, electronic monitoring, and boot camp facilities and programs.

Secure Corrections. Large congregate-care juvenile facilities (training schools, camps, and ranches) have not proven to be particularly effective in rehabilitating juvenile offenders. Although some continued use of these types of facilities will remain a necessary alternative for those juveniles who require enhanced security to protect the public, the establishment of small community-based facilities to provide intensive services in a secure environment offers the best hope for successful treatment of those juveniles who require a structured setting. Secure sanctions are most effective in changing future conduct when they are coupled with comprehensive treatment and rehabilitation services.

Standard parole practices, particularly those that have a primary focus on social control, have not been effective in normalizing the behavior of high-risk juvenile parolees over the long term, and consequently, growing interest has developed in intensive aftercare programs that provide high levels of social control and treatment services. OJJDP's Intensive Community–Based Aftercare for High–Risk Juvenile Parolees Program provides an effective aftercare model.

The following graduated sanctions strategies are proposed within the Secure Corrections component:

Community confinement. Offenders whose presenting offense is sufficiently serious (such as a violent felony) or who fail to respond to intermediate sanctions as evidenced by continued re-offending may be appropriate for community confinement. Offenders at this level represent the more serious (such as repeat felony drug trafficking or property offenders) and violent offenders among the juvenile justice system correctional population.

The concept of community confinement provides secure confinement in small community-based facilities that offer intensive treatment and rehabilitation services. These services include individual and group counseling, educational programs, medical services, and intensive staff supervision. Proximity to the community enables direct and regular family involvement with the treatment process as well as a phased re-entry into the community that draws upon community resources and services.

Incarceration in training schools, camps, and ranches. Juveniles whose confinement in the community would constitute an ongoing threat to community safety or who have failed to respond to community-based corrections may require an extended correctional placement in training schools, camps, ranches, or other secure options that are not community-based. These facilities should offer comprehensive treatment programs for these youth with a focus on education, skills development, and vocational or employment training and experience. These juveniles may include those convicted in the criminal justice system prior to their reaching the age at which they are no longer subject to the original or extended jurisdiction of the juvenile justice system.

Transfer to the criminal justice system. Public safety concerns are resulting in increasing demands for transfer of the most violent juvenile offenders to the criminal justice system. These demands will grow as long as American society perceives juveniles to present a disproportionate threat to the public safety. Although state legislatures are increasingly excluding certain categories of juvenile offenders from the jurisdiction of the juvenile court, judicial waiver holds the most promise as the mechanism for determining that a particular juvenile cannot be rehabilitated in the juvenile justice system. This consideration should be paramount, consistent with the original aims of the juvenile justice system and the juvenile court.

* * *

Notes and Questions

1. *Graduated sanctions.* The Coalition for Juvenile Justice reports "growing sentiment that a youth before the juvenile court should receive some sanction at his or her first appearance before a judge, and that progressively more severe sanctions should be utilized for every subsequent entry into the system." A system of graduated sanctions works best, however, when the court can provide a range of services at the various gradations, rather than merely probation at one extreme and institutional commitment or transfer to adult court on the other, with little in between. See Coalition for Juvenile Justice, A Celebration or a Wake?: The Juvenile Court After 100 Years 38–39 (1998). In 1995, Texas enacted legislation requiring localities to establish first-offender programs and a seven-step system of graduated sanctions. See Tex. Family Code Ann. §§ 52.031, 59.003.

2. *Securing information necessary for disposition.* If the court adjudicates the juvenile a delinquent, the probation staff prepares a social history (or predisposition report) describing the condition and circumstances of the child and family, and recommending an appropriate disposition, including recommended treatment and support services. To aid in preparation, the court may order that mental health and medical professionals examine the juvenile. The prosecutor and the juvenile may also make recommendations to the court. After reviewing the various recommendations, the court enters its disposition. The social history is persuasive because the juvenile court

follows the probation staff's recommendations more than 90% of the time. See Minority Youth in the Juvenile Justice System: A Judicial Response, 41 Juv. & Fam. Ct. J. 27 (No. 3A 1990).

3. *Probation.* Probation is the sanction most frequently imposed on delinquents. In 1996, 54% of adjudicated delinquents nationwide received probation as the most severe disposition; by contrast, only 28% of adjudicated delinquents were placed in some type of out-of-home residential facility, 13% received some other disposition (such as an order to pay a fine, make restitution or perform community service), and 4% were dismissed with no further sanctions. See Anne L. Stahl et al., Juvenile Court Statistics 1996, 15 (1999). In 1995, 54.6% of adjudicated white delinquents and 52.0% of adjudicated black delinquents received probation. See U.S. Dep't of Justice, Bureau of Justice Statistics, Sourcebook of Criminal Justice Statistics 1997, Table 5.76, at 441 (1998).

Probation may be voluntary (where the juvenile agrees to comply rather than proceed to adjudication), though probation is more often imposed by the court after adjudication. A probation order, which might last for a specified period or might be open-ended, may include such requirements as participation in drug counseling, community service or payment of restitution to the the victim. See, e.g., Dennis Maloney et al., Juvenile Probation: The Balanced Approach, 39 Juv. & Fam. Ct. J. (No. 3 1988).

Many appellate courts hold that probation conditions must be reasonably related to the juvenile's rehabilitation or to the offense committed. In In re J.G., 692 N.E.2d 1226, 1227, 1229 (Ill.App.Ct.1998), for example, the court held that after the juvenile's adjudication for shooting two people with a pellet gun, the juvenile court abused its discretion by ordering the juvenile during the probation period not to enter the village where his girl friend lived. The girl's parents did not want the juvenile to associate with their daughter, but the girl was not one of the two victims and neither victim lived in the village. The appellate court did not upset the order requiring the juvenile to have no contact with either victim.

Courts, however, may take a generous view of reasonableness. In In re McDonald, 515 S.E.2d 719, 721–22 (N.C.Ct.App.1999), for example, the court upheld a probation order that prohibited the juvenile from watching television for one year. The order was based on a determination that television contributed to her delinquency because she had watched television program on Charles Manson and then spray painted "Charles Manson rules" on a private boathouse.

The court may hold periodic hearings to review the juvenile's compliance with the terms of probation, and to consider probation staff reports. The court terminates the case when the juvenile has fully complied. If the juvenile does not fully comply, the court may revoke probation and consider stricter sanctions.

The court may revoke probation where the juvenile violates its terms. The petition for revocation must reasonably describe the time, place and manner in which the violation occurred. See, e.g., In re Jessica N., 695 N.Y.S.2d 379 (App. Div. 1999). The juvenile is entitled to notice and a revocation hearing with the right to counsel. See, e.g., Ohio Juv. R. 35(B).

4. *Parental responsibility.* In a growing number of states, the juvenile court may require the delinquent's parents to participate in the disposition, for example by attending parenting classes or by contributing to restitution paid to the victim. Courts have upheld these statutes as rationally related to the legitimate state purposes of casting the burden of loss on delinquents' parents rather than on innocent victims, and of encouraging parents to "exercise their 'guiding role' in the upbringing of their children." See, e.g., In re B.D., 720 So.2d 476, 478 (Miss.1998). A number of states have enacted statutes requiring parents to pay reasonable costs of maintaining their child in a state institution following a delinquency adjudication. See, e.g., N.H. Rev. Stat. § 169–B:40.

In 1995, a South Carolina family court judge made national headlines when he ordered a mother shackled to her 15–year-old daughter with a two-foot chain for two months while the daughter awaited sentencing for truancy, shoplifting, burglary and grand larceny. Saying that he knew of no other way to keep the girl out of trouble, the judge threatened the mother with a 30–day jail sentence if the girl went outdoors alone. The mother died a year later in a head-on highway collision on the way home from visiting the girl in juvenile prison. See Woman Once Shackled to Teen Daughter Dies in Car Accident, Chicago Tribune, Sept. 23, 1996, at 2.

5. *Race and disposition.* In 1995, 32% of the United States population were classified as minorities, but minorities comprised 68% of the juvenile detention center population. This proportion had risen from 53% in 1983 and 65% in 1991. The minority proportion of the custody population in public long-term facilities with institutional environments (such as training schools) had similarly risen from 56% in 1983 to 69% in 1991 before dropping slightly to 68% in 1995. See Melissa Sickmund et al., Juvenile Offenders and Victims: 1997 Update on Violence 42 (1997).

One study found that black delinquents were underrepresented in community treatment programs such as inpatient drug and psychiatric facilities and in out-of-home placements such as foster home placements. The author raised the question whether juvenile courts are more likely to commit black youths to institutions without exhausting less restrictive community treatment alternatives. See Donna B. Towberman, Racial Bias in the Criminal Justice System: Shifting the Focus from Outcome to Underlying Causes, 45 Juv. & Fam. Ct. J. 15, 24 (1994 No. 1).

6. *Victims' rights measures.* Every state juvenile code now has a provision granting rights to victims in the juvenile justice disposition process. In recent years, about half the states have enacted legislation significantly increasing these rights. The new legislation grants victims most or all of the rights of crime victims generally.

Victims of juvenile crime may now have such rights as the right to receive notice of the various court proceedings involving the alleged offender, to attend juvenile proceedings otherwise closed to the public, to be heard throughout the proceedings and to make a statement the court must consider in determining the appropriate sanctions, to participate in compensation programs available to crime victims generally, to learn the names and addresses of the offender and his or her parents, and to receive notice of the offender's release from custody. See, e.g., N.H. Rev. Stat. § 169–B:35–a.

Legislation may permit child victims to have a parent or other adult present during the victim's testimony, and may mandate increased sanctions if the juvenile's victim is elderly or disabled. See Patricia Torbet et al., State Responses to Serious and Violent Juvenile Crime (OJJDP 1996).

7. *Aftercare.* When a juvenile is released from an out-of-home placement, the court may place the juvenile on supervised aftercare, which is similar to adult parole. The juvenile must report periodically to the court or the juvenile office, which monitors the juvenile's compliance. If the juvenile fails to comply with the conditions of aftercare, he or she may be subject to further sanction.

The U.S. Office of Juvenile Justice and Delinquency Prevention has stated that aftercare should be seen as "an essential part of the continuum of services and sanctions that form an effective juvenile justice system," combining appropriate levels of social control with ongoing treatment services: "Properly implemented, aftercare can serve to protect public safety by monitoring the juvenile's reintegration into the community while developing his or her capacity to overcome negative influences (risk factors for delinquency) by enhancing the skills needed to become a productive and law-abiding member of society." Shay Bilchik, A Juvenile Justice System for the 21st Century 5 (OJJDP May 1998).

8. *Serious and habitual juvenile offender statutes.* Criminal sentences, grounded primarily in the nature of the act rather than the offender's condition, are generally determinate, that is defined by a minimum and maximum number of years. Juvenile sanctions, grounded in the offender's condition, have traditionally been indeterminate, that is, lasting until the age at which the juvenile court's dispositional authority ends but terminable sooner if the court finds that the offender has been rehabilitated.

A number of state juvenile codes now provide for determinate sanctions in at least some circumstances. Several codes have serious and habitual offender provisions, which seek to achieve their goals in a variety of ways, such as by (1) imposing mandatory minimum sentences or sentencing ranges for listed offenses, (2) authorizing the juvenile court to impose a determinate sentence for specified offenses, rather than the traditional indeterminate period used for most delinquent acts; (3) authorizing the juvenile court to impose a longer period of incarceration, up to a statutory maximum, for some serious offenses; (4) authorizing the juvenile court to impose harsher sentences, at the juvenile court's discretion, on youths who commit specified crimes; (5) extending juvenile court jurisdiction over serious juvenile offenders to a later age than is permitted for delinquents generally, and (6) authorizing the juvenile court to place serious or habitual offenders in adult facilities or in juvenile boot camps. In some states, serious and habitual offender statutes seek to combine punishment and rehabilitation in a single, comprehensive plan. See Julianne P. Sheffer, Serious and Habitual Juvenile Offender Statutes: Reconciling Punishment and Rehabilitation Within the Juvenile Justice System, 48 Vand. L. Rev. 479, 491–99 (1995).

9. *Expungement or sealing of the record.* Juvenile codes have traditionally provided that juvenile court records, including the transcript and exhibits, may be expunged or sealed at a future time, for example when the juvenile reaches majority. Expungement or sealing normally occurs on the juvenile's

motion after he reaches the appropriate age. As a practical matter, the right to file the motion may ripen only years after the adjudication, when the juvenile is unrepresented and may not even know of the right. Where the record is expunged or sealed, it is "deemed never to have existed" and the juvenile, agency and court "may properly indicate that no record exists." Colo. Rev. Stat. §§ 19–1–103(48), 19–1–306. Confidentiality prevails over state open records and open meetings laws because such laws do not operate against courts engaged in decisionmaking. Expunged records may later be inspected only on court order.

Most expungement and sealing statutes are no longer unconditional. For example, Colorado specifies that expunged records are nonetheless available to any court or probation department for use in sentencing the youth in future juvenile or criminal proceedings. Id. § 19–1–306(5)(a). The state also permits expungement only where (1) the juvenile has not been convicted of a further crime and has not been adjudicated a delinquent for a further offense, (2) no criminal or delinquency proceeding is pending or being instituted against the juvenile, (3) the juvenile's rehabilitation has been attained, and (4) expungement is in the best interests of the juvenile and the community. Id. § 19–1–306(5)(c). Some states have increased the number of years the juvenile must wait before the record is expunged. In some states, delinquency records may not be expunged where the underlying offense was a violent or other serious felony.

Are the rehabilitative purposes of expungement and sealing statutes sufficiently strong to outweigh the need of courts, law enforcement, prosecutors, future employers and other members of the public for information concerning the delinquent's identity and offense? What limits, if any, would you place on a person's ability to have the juvenile record expunged or sealed?

10. *Collateral use of juvenile dispositions.* Until recently, expungement or sealing often left judges and prosecutors unaware of many offenders' juvenile records. Criminal courts were sometimes inclined to "go easy" on defendants they thought were first-time offenders, not knowing that the defendants had a long record of juvenile offending.

Most states, however, have now enacted "three-strikes" laws, other legislation or sentencing guidelines that permit criminal courts to consider some earlier delinquency adjudications when determining pretrial release or when sentencing an adult or transferred juvenile. In forty-five states, for example, limitations on the use or disclosure of juvenile court records do not apply to sentencing proceedings following adult convictions, at least where the adjudication or conviction was for a designated felony or where the record is relatively recent. Thirty-five jurisdictions specify that juvenile courts may consider records at sentencing, and such consideration probably occurs in other jurisdictions as well. Case law in forty-five jurisdictions has upheld factoring juvenile adjudications into adult sentencing. In a number of states, juvenile adjudications may even be considered in determining whether to impose the death penalty in criminal court. See Joseph B. Sanborn, Jr., Second–Class Justice, First–Class Punishment: The Use of Juvenile Records in Sentencing Adults, 81 Judicature 206, 209–11 (1998). A growing number of states have also enacted provisions permitting use of delinquency adjudications for impeachment in later civil or criminal proceedings. See, e.g., Mo. Rev. Stat. § 491.078 (delinquency adjudications for acts that would be specified serious felonies if committed by an adult may be used to affect the credibility of a witness or a defendant in a criminal case, if the acts occurred within three years of the date of any sworn testimony by the witness or defendant).

The effect of juvenile adjudications on criminal sentences may be significant. In McCullough v. Singletary, 967 F.2d 530, 531 (11th Cir.1992), for example, the defendant was tried as an adult for first-degree burglary and sexual assault committed when he was seventeen. Pursuant to state sentencing guidelines that authorized the court to consider delinquency adjudications that were no more than three years old, his sentence was enhanced by four prior delinquency adjudications. Without the enhancement, the sentence would have been about seventeen years, or about seven years with actual time served. With the enhancement, the defendant was sentenced to life imprisonment without possibility of parole. The federal courts denied the defendant's habeas corpus petition.

Broad collateral use of delinquency adjudications may raise fairness questions grounded in juvenile court procedure. For example, juveniles often appear unrepresented, or represented by counsel who seek to accommodate the court; are often cajoled into admitting responsibility "for their own good" (and without notice that the adjudication may be used against them in the future); are often found responsible on less proof than would satisfy the beyond-a-reasonable-doubt standard in criminal court; and do not enjoy the right to a jury trial in most states. Juvenile courts may take liberties with the hearsay rule and other rules of evidence, and may use masters or referees rather than judges to preside at the hearing, affording the state a second opportunity to convince a decisionmaker when the judge must decide whether to confirm the initial report. Courts, however, have generally rejected claims of constitutional deprivation arising from collateral use of delinquency adjudications. See, e.g., State v. Little, 423 N.W.2d 722, 724 (Minn.Ct.App.1988) (holding that due process was not violated by enhancing adult criminal history scores with delinquency adjudications secured without right to a jury trial).

Should juvenile adjudications be treated years later as the equivalent of adult convictions to enhance punishment for adult crimes or to provide basis for impeachment? Should the juvenile court be required to inform alleged delinquents and their parents of the potential future use of any juvenile adjudication? If delinquency adjudications count for sentencing and impeachment, should alleged delinquents in juvenile court have all the constitutional rights that adult criminal defendants have? If juveniles and their parents and counsel understand the potential for future use of the adjudication, will juvenile court dockets become even more crowded as juveniles insist on full procedure rather than agreeing to a plea?

11. *Interagency sharing of information.* Juvenile court confidentiality statutes have sometimes led juvenile justice and child welfare agencies to practice "informational territorialism," failing to share information about a troubled juvenile. The failure may stem from such reasons as ignorance about which other agencies are serving the child, interagency mistrust, or

fear that information may be misused, altered or released. See Tamryn J. Etten and Robert F. Petrone, Sharing Data and Information in Juvenile Justice: Legal, Ethical, and Practice Considerations, 45 Juv. & Fam. Ct. J. 65, 76–79 (1994 No. 3). A consensus has emerged that courts, school officials, law enforcement and child welfare agencies need to share information about troubled and delinquent youth under their care. For one thing, lack of information sharing frequently causes wasteful duplication of effort by agencies with limited budgets. Information sharing also enhances prospects for successful treatment because, as one law enforcement officer put it, "If you don't know the history, your intervention is worthless." See Christina Nifong, Search for Answers To Juvenile Crime, Christian Science Monitor, June 17, 1996, at 3. Without shared information, criminal courts sometimes sentence violent juveniles as first-time offenders without knowing their extensive delinquency record. See Peter Reinharz, Juvenile Injustice in New York, Wall St. J., July 20, 1994, at A13.

A growing number of states now specify that where a delinquency adjudication is for an offense committed on school property, a serious violent offense, or a drug offense, the disposition shall be transmitted to the delinquent's school. The evident purpose is to provide schools information needed to protect students against violent classmates.

12. *The Interstate Compact on Juveniles.* "Delinquency is commonly thought of as a local problem. But we live in an era when state boundaries may be crossed with ease by even the very young, and when, because of their frequent movement, families may take children away from the area of their early supervision." Gordon A. Martin, Jr., Interstate Compact on Juveniles, 7 Crime and Delinq. 121, 122 (1961). Interstate relations may become an issue at the disposition stage and afterwards. States have responded with the Interstate Compact on Juveniles, which authorizes, among other things, (1) supervision of a juvenile on probation by a state other than the state that adjudicated the juvenile, (2) return to the home state of escaped delinquents, and (3) pooling of funds by states to create cooperative facilities to treat juveniles.

13. *The role of prevention programs.* In 1995, the average yearly cost for confining a juvenile in a public juvenile correctional facility was $32,488, and in a private facility (such as ranches, forestry camps, farms, halfway houses and group homes) was $45,710. See Bradford Smith, Children in Custody: 20–Year Trends in Juvenile Detention, Correctional, and Shelter Facilities, 44 Crime & Delinq. 526, 537–39 (1998). In light of such figures, many juvenile justice professionals stress that prevention programs are "the most cost-effective approach to dealing with juvenile delinquency." John J. Wilson and James C. Howell, Serious and Violent Juvenile Crime: A Comprehensive Strategy, 45 Juv. & Fam. Ct. J. 3, 4–5 (1994 No. 2). "[M]aximum impact on future delinquent conduct can be achieved by seeking to identify and involve in prevention programs youth at greatest risk of involvement in delinquent activity," including status offenders such as runaways, truants, alcohol offenders, and ungovernable children. Id.

In Alexander S. v. Boyd, 876 F.Supp. 773 (D.S.C.1995) [infra p. 1183], a four-year class action suit challenging conditions in South Carolina's juvenile detention facilities, the court questioned each expert witness about the causes underlying violent juvenile crime. The causes most commonly advanced were "a significant increase in the number of single-parent families, involvement with alcohol and other drugs, involvement in gangs and other anti-social groups, exposure to violence in entertainment and in the mass media, and access to firearms." The court concluded that "[m]ost juveniles who are at greatest risk of becoming extremely aggressive and violent tend to share some of these common experiences or characteristics that appear to place them on what one organization has termed a 'trajectory toward violence.' " Id. at 782–83.

To neutralize the sort of underlying causes *Alexander S.* found, Marian Wright Edelman advocates prevention grounded in "positive youth development":

> A variety of negative influences in a child's life, particularly in the absence of compensating positive factors, increases the risk of involvement in violence. For example, exposure to violence, poor educational opportunities and employment prospects, childhood abuse and neglect, living in a single-parent family, delinquent peer groups, drugs and alcohol, and media violence all put children at risk of becoming involved in violence. Many of these factors, such as poverty, also increase a child's risk of becoming a victim of violence.

> * * *

> Common sense also tells us that the reason not all children who experience these risk factors get involved in crime and violence is that for many children, other countervailing positive factors exist. In fact, research documents that a nurturing family, positive role models, a strong and lasting bond to an adult who provides unconditional love, and a family that has a degree of orderliness and clear expectations, all decrease the likelihood of a child's becoming involved in violence. For example, caring adults can help instill in young people important community-building values such as respect for oneself and others, personal responsibility, a sense of purpose, and achievement through commitment and work. These are vital parts of the moral armor that can help young people reject the lure of the streets in favor of healthy and productive lives.

> * * *

> Positive youth development programs, both recreational and educational (such as mentoring, tutoring, job training, "midnight basketball" leagues, and community service), can provide young people with positive supports, particularly connections to committed, caring adults. These initiatives do not necessarily try to educate children directly about the problem of violence. Rather, they seek to provide the life-skills and supports that enable children to deal with the source—and not the symptom—of the problem. In other words, such community-or school-based programs help children to cope with the risk factors, and to emphasize the protective factors, in their lives. And these programs help young people build personal resilience through enhanced social compe-

tence, problem-solving skills, autonomy, a sense of purpose, and a belief in their future.

* * *

At the same time that dwindling funds for such youth development programs leave many children without access to any recreational or educational supports during non-school hours, our public policies allocate increasingly vast sums to children once they have gotten into trouble. That simply is not rational public policy, being neither humane nor cost-effective. And it ignores a growing body of research documenting the net positive effect of structured after-school, summer, and even purely recreational programs for children.* * *

Marian Wright Edelman and Hattie Ruttenberg, Legislating for Other People's Children: Failing to Protect America's Youth, 7 Stan. L. & Pol'y Rev. 11, 14–15 (1995–96).

One writer provides this explanation, however, for why calls to fund prevention programs frequently meet stiff resistance: "[P]rograms that punish are far more popular than those that prevent. Changing the system's course now would cost money, lots of it, without any immediate results. Ten years down the line, juvenile crime may recede * * *, but it would call for political and economic commitments no one wants to make. On the other hand, if you build a prison cell today, then fill it, the results appear immediate, even if crime continues unabated." Edward Humes, No Matter How Loud I Shout: A Year in the Life of Juvenile Court 178 (1996).

14. *Juveniles with special needs.* The Coalition for Juvenile Justice has called on juvenile courts and their supporting agencies to provide racially and culturally sensitive programs and services for minority youth, greater gender-specific services for girls, and essential services for children with learning disabilities, attention deficit disorders and other disabilities. The Coalition perceives a pressing need at all stages of the juvenile justice process because minorities remain overrepresented, girls are entering the system in increasing numbers, and the system "increasingly is becoming the repository of last resort for children with mental health and mental retardation needs." See Coalition for Juvenile Justice, A Celebration or a Wake?: The Juvenile Court After 100 Years 58–59 (1998).

A NOTE ABOUT INNOVATIVE DISPOSITIONS

(a) *"Restorative justice."* In a number of states, juvenile courts may order "restorative justice," that is, sanctions that focus on "restoring the health of the community, repairing the harm done, meeting victims' needs, and emphasizing that the offender can–and must–contribute to those repairs." Thomas Quinn, Restorative Justice: An Interview With Visiting Fellow Thomas Quinn, 235 Nat'l Inst. Just. J. 10 (Mar. 1998). Restorative-justice sanctions seek a "balanced approach" that produces the least restrictive disposition for the juvenile while enhancing the juvenile's accountability for the offense, providing the victim relief and protecting the community. See, e.g., Mark S. Umbreit, Holding Juvenile Offenders Accountable: A Restorative Justice Perspective, 46 Juv. & Fam. Ct. J. 31 (Spring 1995).

The juvenile offender may be ordered to make restitution to the victim in money or services, to perform community service, to participate in mediation with the victim, or some similar disposition. In some states, one or more of these remedies are preconditions to probation.

Juvenile restitution imposes punishment at less cost than incarceration or extended probation, provides some compensation to the victim, and may be more likely than incarceration to encourage rehabilitation and discourage recidivism. The court may order the juvenile to perform services or pay full or partial restitution, depending on the juvenile's age, physical and mental condition, and earning capacity. To avoid reprisals by an angry juvenile, payment of money is usually made to a court officer rather than directly to the victim.

Juvenile restitution statutes generally specify that the court may order restitution only in an amount the juvenile can reasonably pay, either from presently available funds or from employment reasonably available. See, e.g., State v. M.D.J., 289 S.E.2d 191, 196 (W.Va.1982) (reversing monetary restitution order because it was unreasonable to expect the juvenile offender, a 17-year-old high school junior, to secure even part-time employment when the community's youth unemployment rate was 31.5%). In any event, a monetary restitution order may be unlikely to serve the intended purposes when the amount is beyond the juvenile's realistic earning capacity.

Statutes sometimes authorize courts to order a delinquent's parents to pay an amount the parent is reasonably able to pay, at least where the offense was intentional or malicious. Courts have rejected contentions that such orders impose liability without fault, holding instead that the orders reasonably encourage parental supervision while compensating victims. See, e.g., In re John H., 433 A.2d 1239 (Md.Ct.Spec.App.1981), aff'd, 443 A.2d 594 (Md.1982).

Community service may be attractive as a means of rehabilitating the delinquent, particularly where the service is somehow related to the wrongdoing. Courts have upheld community service orders against contentions that they violate the Thirteenth Amendment, which prohibits "slavery [or] involuntary servitude, except as a punishment for crime whereof the party shall have been duly convicted." See, e.g., In re Erickson, 604 P.2d 513, 514 (Wash.Ct.App.1979) (holding that community service order constituted "punishment for crime" because the state juvenile justice act defines a juvenile offense as "an act which would constitute a crime if it was committed by an adult").

In *juvenile victim-offender mediation*, victims of property crimes and minor assaults meet with a mediator to describe to the offender how the offense affected them and how the offender may assume responsibility and provide restitution. "Victim-offender mediation is different from other types of mediation [because] the involved parties are not 'disputants.' One has clearly committed a criminal offense and has admitted doing so. The other clearly has been victimized. * * * While many other types of mediation are largely 'settlement driven,' victim-offender mediation is primarily 'dialogue driven,' with the emphasis upon victim healing, offender accountability, and restoration of losses." Mark S. Umbreit and William Bradshaw, Victim Experience of Meeting Adult vs. Juvenile Offenders: A Cross–National Comparison, 61 Fed. Probation 33, 33–34 (Dec. 1997). Most victim-offender mediation sessions result in signed restitution agreements, though most victims find the agreements less important than the opportunity to discuss the offense with the offender and reach an accommodation. Id. at 34. Some juvenile courts have also used other alternative dispute resolution mechanisms such as arbitration and conferencing.

(b) *"Blended sentences."* More than a third of the states have enacted statutes authorizing imposition on juveniles of "blended sentences," which involve some combination of delinquency sanctions and criminal court sanctions. A blended sentencing scheme permits efforts at rehabilitation while also introducing punishment into the formula. For example, Minnesota's recent "extended jurisdiction juvenile prosecution" legislation is discussed above in Problem 11–1 [page 1063].

(c) *Boot camps.* In a growing number of jurisdictions, older juvenile offenders may be sent to "boot camps," also known as "shock incarceration programs." These specialized programs generally serve non-violent first-time male offenders between seventeen and twenty-five. The aim is to instill discipline and self-respect through military drill and ceremony, physical training, manual labor, academic education, vocational assessment, drug abuse education and life skills training. In recent years, boot camps have won public support because they appear "tough on crime," but their efficacy has been called "questionable at best." National Criminal Justice Ass'n, Juvenile Justice Reform Initiatives in the States: 1994–1996, at 29 (1997). One review article concluded that "boot camps have proven ineffective in reducing recidivism and controlling drug use." Developments in the Law: Alternatives to Incarceration, 111 Harv. L. Rev. 1863, 1909 (1998).

2. The Right to Treatment

Chapters 4 and 5 treated the states' constitutional obligation to provide a minimal level of care to foster children and other abuse and neglect victims in state custody. Shortly after *Gault,* lawsuits began challenging conditions in secure juvenile correctional facilities in several states. A number of federal courts mandated minimum standards of care and treatment, sometimes after finding conditions so harsh as to violate the Eighth Amendment ban on cruel and unusual punishment. See, e.g., Morales v. Turman, 383 F.Supp. 53, 77 (E.D.Tex.1974), rev'd on other grounds, 535 F.2d 864 (5th Cir.1976), rev'd on other grounds, 430 U.S. 322 (1977) (describing "the widespread practice of beating, slapping, kicking and otherwise physically abusing juveniles in the absence of any exigent circumstances; the use of tear gas and other chemical crowd-control devices in situations not posing an imminent threat to human life or an imminent and substantial threat to property; the placing of juveniles in solitary confinement or other secured facilities, in the absence of any legislative or administrative limitation on the duration and intensity of the confinement and subject only to the unfettered discretion of corrections officers"); Nelson v. Heyne, 355 F.Supp. 451 (N.D.Ind.1972), aff'd, 491 F.2d 352 (7th Cir. 1974) (describing supervised beatings of juvenile inmates with a thick board for violating institutional rules; the use of major tranquilizing drugs to control inmates' excited behavior, without medically competent staff members to evaluate the inmates before or after administration, despite the potential for serious medical side effects; and the use of solitary confinement for prolonged periods on any staff member's request); Inmates of Boys' Training School v. Affleck, 346 F.Supp. 1354, 1358–62 (D.R.I.1972) (describing dark, cold solitary confinement room where boys would be kept for as long as a week, wearing only their underwear, without being provided toilet paper, sheets, blanket, or change of clothes).

"Conditions in many American juvenile detention centers are awful, and they have been for years." Michael J. Dale, Lawsuits and Public Policy: The Role of Litigation in Correcting Conditions in Juvenile Detention Centers, 32 U.S.F.L. Rev. 675, 675 (1998). Speaking in 1998 about nationwide conditions in such facilities, the president of the National Juvenile Detention Association (which represents the heads of the nation's juvenile jails) said, "The issues of violence against offenders, lack of adequate education and mental health, of crowding and of poorly paid and poorly trained staff are the norm rather than the exception." See Fox Butterfield, Profits at a Juvenile Prison Come With a Chilling Cost, N.Y. Times, July 15, 1998, at A1.

ALEXANDER S. v. BOYD

United States District Court, D.S.C., 1995.
876 F.Supp. 773.

JOSEPH F. ANDERSON, JR., DISTRICT JUDGE.

[Youths incarcerated in South Carolina's public juvenile correctional institutions brought suit, alleging that conditions in these institutions violated the federal Constitution and various federal statutes. During the four-year litigation, the court held hearings and status conferences, appointed expert witnesses, inspected juvenile detention facilities and conducted a two-month trial that generated several thousand pages of exhibits. The court found several violations, including these: (1) Authorities used a potent form of tear gas "on a fairly regular basis * * * for purposes other than the protection of staff or others" and "as a form of punishment," (2) cell doors used individual padlocks, creating unreasonable danger in the event of fire, (3) "frequently cockroaches and other foreign matter [were] present in the food served to the juveniles," (4) the institutions did not provide adequate medical care to incarcerated juveniles, and (5) the institutions compromised safety by holding considerably more youths than permitted by design capacity. The court provided these conclusions of law:]

* * *

A. The Constitutional Standard

Courts around the country are not in agreement as to the appropriate federal standard by which to judge state juvenile detention facility conditions. The Seventh Circuit has applied the cruel and unusual punishment test of the Eighth Amendment. The First, Ninth, Tenth, and Eleventh Circuits have applied the Due Process Clause of the Fourteenth Amendment. The United States Supreme Court has not decided the issue.

After reviewing these authorities, the court has determined that the Due Process Clause of the Fourteenth Amendment, which implicitly encompasses the protections of the Eighth Amendment, is the appropriate standard for reviewing the conditions at the DJJ facilities. Adoption of the more stringent Due Process Clause is appropriate in this case because the juveniles incarcerated at DJJ facilities have, with few exceptions, not been convicted of a crime; rather, they have merely been adjudicated to be juvenile delinquents.

* * *

Numerous district courts have [held] that where, as in South Carolina, the purpose of incarcerating juveniles in a state training school is treatment and rehabilitation, the Due Process Clause "requires that the conditions and programs at the school must be reasonably related to that purpose."[43]

In addition, the Due Process Clause guarantees to juveniles who are incarcerated the right to reasonably safe conditions of confinement, freedom from unreasonable bodily restraint, and minimally adequate

---

43. Traditionally, courts that have recognized a constitutional right to rehabilitative treatment for incarcerated juveniles have generally employed two basic theories to divine such a right. These theories were initially developed in the context of mentally ill or retarded persons committed to state mental institutions or hospitals. Courts extended these theories to the context of juvenile delinquents incarcerated in training schools, because juveniles, like mentally incompetent or retarded individuals, generally fall within the same *parens patriae* authority of the state.

The first theory, which is adopted by this court, finds support in the Supreme Court's pronouncement in *Jackson v. Indiana* (1972), that "due process requires that the nature and duration of commitment bear some reasonable relation to the purpose for which the individual is committed." * * * [W]hen a state incarcerates juveniles for the purpose of treatment or rehabilitation, as does South Carolina, due process requires that the conditions of confinement be reasonably related to that purpose.

The second theory is known as the *quid pro quo*, or mutual compact, theory. Under this approach, courts have held that states are required to rehabilitate incarcerated juveniles as consideration for affording juveniles fewer procedural safeguards than those afforded to adult criminal defendants. In other words, the *quid pro quo* theory provides that because juvenile delinquency proceedings generally do not involve the full range of procedural due process protections of a criminal trial, the state must provide rehabilitation to incarcerated juveniles to make up for the difference. [The court rejected this theory as "quite suspect" under prevailing law.].

* * *

Accordingly, because South Carolina's policy behind incarcerating juvenile delinquents is to provide them with rehabilitation, the court has determined that the juveniles at DJJ are entitled under the Constitution to rehabilitative treatment.

training to protect those interests. *Youngberg v. Romeo*, 457 U.S. 307 (1982).[44]

Safety, in the context of this case, encompasses the Plaintiffs' right to reasonable protection from the aggression of others, whether "others" be juveniles or staff.

The interest in freedom from unreasonable bodily restraint includes freedom from unnecessary bodily restraint through mechanical devices as well as unreasonably restrictive conditions of confinement. Unreasonably restrictive conditions of confinement are those which unduly restrict the juveniles' freedom of action and are not reasonably related to legitimate security or safety needs of the institution.

The right to minimally adequate training is more difficult to define. As noted by the Supreme Court in *Youngberg*:

It is not feasible ... to define or identify the type of training that may be required in every case. A court properly may start with the generalization that there is a right to minimally adequate training. The basic requirement of adequacy, in terms more familiar to courts, may be stated as that training which is reasonable in light of identifiable liberty interests and the circumstances of the case.

Additionally, as noted by the *Youngberg* court, when a court is called upon to decide what is reasonable under the circumstances presented, the court

must show deference to the judgment exercised by a qualified professional.... [T]he decision, if made by a professional, is presumptively valid; liability may be imposed only when the decision by the professional is such a substantial departure from accepted professional judgment, practice, or standards as to demonstrate that the person responsible actually did not base the decision on such a judgment.

* * * The test in this case is whether the state is providing minimally adequate or reasonable services and training necessary to ensure the protected interests of the Plaintiffs. It is not appropriate that the state be held to a standard which imposes an affirmative duty to succeed in the purpose of correcting the juveniles' behavior. Although such a standard may be desirable, it is not constitutionally mandated. All that is required is that the juveniles be housed under conditions that provide them with a reasonable opportunity to correct their behavior. Obviously, this standard incorporates the security, program, and service functions that are basic to juvenile corrections. These basic services include

---

44. *Youngberg* * * * involved a challenge by a mental retardate to the conditions of his confinement. Although *Youngberg* is not squarely applicable to juveniles, this court has determined that the *Youngberg* analysis is appropriate in a juvenile correctional setting because juvenile delinquents, like mental retardates, have been deprived of their liberty because of their status. Additionally, the three parts of the *Youngberg* test are all based upon a determination of what is reasonable under the circumstances—an elastic concept that allows for appropriate adjustments in view of the fact that some juvenile delinquents have demonstrated a propensity toward violence.

sufficient numbers of adequately trained staff so that the purpose of the confinement may be advanced, minimal levels of programming reasonably geared toward aiding juveniles to correct their behavior, and other services that are minimally necessary to give the Plaintiffs a reasonable opportunity to accomplish the purpose of the confinement while protecting the other recognized interests in safety and reasonable restraint.

* * *

B.   The Statutory Standards

Juveniles attending the training schools operated by DJJ are potentially covered by three federal education statutes: the Individuals with Disabilities Education Act ("IDEA"); Section 504 of the Rehabilitation Act of 1973 ("Section 504"); and the Americans with Disabilities Act [ADA].

* * *

The centerpiece of the IDEA and Section 504 is the "Individualized Education Program" or IEP. * * *

Because DJJ is an independent school district, the reassignment of a juvenile from his or her home school district to DJJ facilities triggers the obligation by DJJ to screen the juvenile for special education needs and, if necessary, develop a new IEP for the juvenile. * * *

* * *

The more familiar provisions of the ADA relate to barrier-free architectural design requirements. DJJ is subject to the physical and programmatic accessibility requirements applicable to governmental entities * * *. Indeed, the Defendants have conceded that the ADA barrier-free requirements apply to DJJ facilities.

* * *

Note and Questions

1.   During the *Alexander S*. litigation, a newspaper reported that "[v]iolence is a way of life at the state Department of Youth Services facilities, where officials say severe overcrowding prompts brawls that stifle recreation and positive treatment for youth. Juveniles, warehoused in facilities holding up to twice the number for which they were built, say guards ignore the daily brawls and scuffles among teen-agers. Instead, guards rely on 'tough guy' juveniles to keep control." S.C. Youth Facilities Plagued by Violence, Herald (Rock Hill, S.C.), Mar. 22, 1992, at 7A. The DYS Commissioner defended the agency: "We treat the kids as nice as they let us or as tough as they make us. We're the dumping ground. The kids come here after society has given up on them." Id.

2.   *Questions about* Alexander S. (a) What constitutional rights does *Alexander S*. guarantee to juveniles detained or confined in juvenile correctional facilities? Has the Supreme Court determined that the juveniles hold these rights?,

(b) What level of financial commitment should states and localities make to help assure adequate treatment of confined delinquents?

3. *Recent legislation. Alexander S.* was unusual because the decision resulted from final judgment after trial. Most private suits challenging conditions of juvenile detention have resulted in settlements or consent decrees without full trial. Consent decrees will be much more difficult to secure after enactment of the Prison Litigation Reform Act of 1995, 18 U.S.C. § 3626. The Act applies to accused or adjudicated delinquents, and to federal, state or local facilities that incarcerate or detain them. Id. § 3626(g)(3), (5).

The Act provides that "[p]rospective relief in any civil action with respect to prison conditions shall extend no further than necessary to correct the violation of the Federal right of a particular plaintiff or plaintiffs. The court shall not grant or approve any prospective relief unless the court finds that such relief is narrowly drawn, extends no further than necessary to correct the violation of the Federal right, and is the least intrusive means necessary to correct the violation of the Federal right." Id. § 3626(a)(1)(A). A court may not enter a consent decree unless the decree complies with these three conditions. Id. § 3626(c). A consent decree is thus possible only where corrections authorities admit violations of federal rights. Such an admission is unlikely because it would expose prison authorities to private civil damage suits.

A NOTE ABOUT FEDERAL ENFORCEMENT

In 1980, Congress enacted the Civil Rights of Incarcerated Persons Act, 42 U.S.C. §§ 1997–1997j (CRIPA), which authorizes the U.S. Department of Justice to sue state and local governments to remedy "egregious or flagrant" conditions that deny constitutional rights to persons residing or confined in public institutions. The covered institutions include ones for juveniles awaiting trial, receiving care or treatment, or residing for any other state purpose (except solely for educational purposes). Id. § 1997(1)(B)(iv). The court may order equitable remedies that "insure the minimum corrective measures necessary to insure the full enjoyment" of these rights. Id. § 1997a(a). The Justice Department may also sue under a provision of the Violent Crime Control and Law Enforcement Act of 1994 prohibiting a "pattern or practice" of civil rights abuses by law enforcement officers. 42 U.S.C. § 14141.

CRIPA authorizes the Justice Department to sue only to remedy systemic problems and not to represent individuals. The Act does not create constitutional rights, but provides a cause of action to enforce and effectuate rights otherwise created by constitution or statute. The Department may secure voluntary compliance from investigated facilities, or it may commence litigation seeking minimum corrective measures after exhausting the Act's notice and conciliation provisions designed to permit states to voluntarily remedy deficiencies found by the Department. The Act does not preclude private litigants from filing suit alleging unconstitutional conditions.

As of November 1997, the Justice Department had investigated 73 juvenile detention and correctional facilities. The investigations have led to consent decrees relating to more than thirty such facilities, including ones in Kentucky, New Jersey and Puerto Rico. Patricia Puritz et al., Beyond the Walls, Improving Conditions of Confinement for Youth in Custody 1–7 (1998). As of December 1999, the Department had ongoing investigations concerning facilities in Mississippi, Michigan, Virginia and Ohio.

The Justice Department sued Georgia in 1998. Because of the rapid growth in the juvenile prison population, Georgia's juvenile corrections budget had risen from $80 million to $220 million in just four years; most of the increase, however, financed new prison construction rather than improvement in existing conditions. The chairman of the state Department of Juvenile Justice (DJJ) explained that it was "much easier to get new facilities from the Legislature than to get more programs." See Fox Butterfield, U.S. and Georgia in Deal To Improve Juvenile Prisons, N.Y. Times, Mar. 22, 1998, at § 1, p. 16.

The Justice Department charged that Georgia's juvenile detention facilities, including the twenty-two regional youth detention centers (RYDCs), were marked by a pattern, among other things, of severe overcrowding, physical abuse by staff, use of pepper spray to restrain mentally ill juveniles, inadequate education, inadequate medical care, and guards who pitted inmates against one another for sport and who routinely stripped young inmates and locked them in their cells for days at a time. The Department's report stated the following:

> * * * [T]he population of most of the RYDCs in the system ranged from 150 percent to almost 300 percent of design capacity, with more than half the facilities operating at or above double their capacity. As a result, between two and five youths share the eight-by-ten-foot cells designed for one youth, with several youths having to sleep shoulder-to-shoulder on thin mattresses on the floor (often with their heads inches away from the cell toilet). The facilities lack adequate space for functional classrooms and little room to accommodate youths' spending time outside of their cells. Prolonged periods of lock-down are especially common on weekends when there are no classes and the facilities lack sufficient staff to supervise activities out of the cells. * * *

> Conditions during lock-down are especially punitive. Many of the facilities take the youths' mattresses away during the day, leaving the youths with no choice but to lie on the cold, hard metal bed frames and concrete floors. And, * * * the prolonged unsupervised idleness leads to fights and sexual assaults, resulting in numerous injuries and hospitalizations in all the facilities.

> * * *

> Youths [at the Fulton County Detention Center] often live doubled up in decaying, ill-ventilated rooms built for one. They spend inordinate amounts of time in their rooms, in part because the school lacks sufficient space for all youths to attend * * * . Even

though the facility has a large, enclosed outdoor recreation area, youths never go outdoors because of insufficient staffing. While locked in their rooms, youths must rely on staff to take them from their cells to the bathroom, since the cells have no toilets. The severe understaffing at the facility—sometimes one staff must supervise an entire wing, consisting of twenty or more youths housed n a long, twisting hallway—often means that staff are unavailable to respond to requests to use the bathroom (or simply refuse to respond). As a result, youths urinate in cups or out the window—the smell of urine was present throughout the facility (even though substantial efforts had been undertaken to clean the facility prior to our visit). Moreover, the bathrooms themselves are in disrepair, many with broken fixtures, mold and mildew.

* * *

The lack of space in the RYDCs prevents implementation of an adequate classification system to separate younger, more vulnerable youths from older, potentially predatory detainees. * * * For example, in one incident, a youth held for violation of probation * * * was housed with three youths accused of armed robbery and aggravated assault and was beaten and sexually assaulted without intervention by staff. * * *

* * *

RYDC residents have significant mental health care needs. A 1996 study conducted by Emory University for DJJ found that sixty-one percent of RYDC residents had psychiatric disorders and that thirty percent had substance abuse problems. These youths are systematically denied access to adequate mental health care in the RYDCs.

* * *

The RYDCs and the Fulton County facility do not have access to sufficient resources to meet the serious mental health needs of their most troubled residents. The State's medical contractor provides a very limited amount of psychiatric consultation. These psychiatric subcontractors are paid $75 per hour to provide up to two hours of services per week at some of the RYDCs. However, we found little evidence that these services were being used even to that limited extent at the facilities we toured. Recently, the contractor has begun paying psychologist consultants $300 per month to provide services "as needed." Again, we saw little evidence of their use in these facilities.

We found that the quality of mental health care provided in the RYDCs we visited was also deficient. * * * [Y]ouths are generally monitored and counseled by overworked, bachelor-degree-level counselors at the facility unless the youth's level of distress reaches a point where hospitalization is required. Even then, the State has almost no capacity to provide hospital treatment to youths who need it. DJJ contracts with the State psychiatric hospitals to provide only *five* long-term treatment beds for youths throughout the DJJ system * * *. Thus, hospitalization is limited to a short period of evaluation, medication and stabilization, after which youths are returned to the facility. We frequently encountered severely troubled youths in the RYDCs who had long histories of self-mutilation, psychotic episodes, or suicide attempts followed by hospitalization, mediation, and return to the RYDC where the cycle repeated. * * * *

* * *

At most RYDCs, once a youth has been identified as being at immediate risk for suicidal behavior, staff lock the youth alone in a cell, removing the youth's sheets, clothing and personal effects, leaving the depressed youth alone in a paper gown, sometimes for days. Suicidal youth are then monitored more closely, but they are not permitted to leave their rooms to eat with the other youths, attend school or (often) even to obtain exercise or recreation. This practice of isolating depressed youths in demeaning conditions for hours (and sometimes days) usually exacerbates the youth's depression.

* * *

Moreover, even the attempts to prevent actual self-harm are inadequate. On more than one occasion, we observed suicidal youths locked in their rooms, alone on the living unit hall without any supervision while the only available staff supervised the other detainees in school or at recreation. These staff admitted that they were unable to conduct even fifteen-minute checks on the suicidal youths back in their rooms. In November, a youth on suicide watch at the Augusta YDC [youth development campus] hanged himself after staff failed to conduct fifteen-minute checks.

* * *

Staff in some of the facilities routinely use mechanical restraints as a form of punishment for behavior that does not represent a threat to the safety of the youth or others. * * * Most commonly, we found that staff used the restraint chair—a plastic chair into which a youth can be shackled and strapped—to punish youths for making noise, kicking their doors or flooding their toilets.

* * * [S]taff sometimes strip detainees who are kicking their doors or being disruptive and remove the youths' mattress from the cell, forcing them to sit in their underwear on the cold concrete floor or metal bed.

In Fulton County, staff routinely place youths on high level suicide watch as punishment, stripping them of their clothes (sometimes providing paper gowns, sometimes leaving the youths naked), removing their mattresses and confining them alone in their rooms for days without access to education or exercise. Youths who refuse to remove their clothes are forcibly stripped, and male staff are sometimes involved in stripping female residents. * * *

* * *

[S]taff persistently used excessive physical force against youths, in the form of hitting or slamming youths onto the ground and into walls, or otherwise injuring the youths. * * * Staff at the DeKalb RYDC have used OC spray (pepper spray) to punish youths for non-compliant or otherwise annoying, but non-dangerous, behavior.

U.S. Dep't of Justice, Findings of Investigation of [Georgia] State Juvenile Justice Facilities (Feb. 13, 1998). To avoid federal takeover of the juvenile correctional system, Georgia swiftly reached an agreement with the Justice Department to appoint an independent monitor and to spend $10 million to hire more teachers, guards and medical personnel. The president of the National Mental Health Association criticized the agreement for lacking an enforcement mechanism and for allowing the state to monitor its own compliance. See Fox Butterfield, U.S. and Georgia in Deal to Improve Juvenile Prisons, N.Y. Times, Mar. 22, 1998 at § 1, p. 16.

In late 1998, the Justice Department sued Louisiana over conditions at the state's four secure juvenile correctional facilities—Bridge City, Jetson, Swanson and Tallulah. In response to the Department's early concerns, the state had sought to eliminate violence from these facilities by instituting Project Zero Tolerance. The suit followed a two-year Department investigation and unsuccessful negotiations with the state. The Department's report stated the following:

> Serious physical injuries to youth from officer assault or from attacks by other youth have occurred at all four facilities. Literally dozens of juveniles are being seriously injured on a monthly basis across the four facilities. Especially at Tallulah and Swanson, the incidence of fractures to jaws, noses, cheeks, and eye sockets, as well as serious lacerations requiring sutures (usually also to faces) is disturbing. At all four training institutes, correctional staff abuse the juveniles. The abuse ranges from officers physically hitting, punching or kicking youth (sometimes when they are handcuffed), to officers negotiating "contracts" with juveniles to beat up other juveniles to officers compelling juveniles to sit, stand, or lay in positions that are clearly painful and constitute corporal punishment. We also found evidence of sexual abuse and assault at each of the four facilities. The violence at the facilities is * * * pervasive.
>
> * * * [A]t all facilities, little attention has been paid to sexual activity between juveniles and between officers and juveniles.

* * *

[S]ince the inception of Project Zero Tolerance, the following examples of staff abuse have occurred:

- a lieutenant at Bridge City punched a child in the eye and threw him through a screen door, while the teacher watched;

- videotapes at Swanson have recorded separate incidents of a guard karate kicking a juvenile in the head and a guard punching a juvenile;

- at Jetson, juveniles alleged that guards beat them with broken brooms hidden in the attic above their dorm, and when facility investigators found the brooms, the guards refused to be finger-printed;

- at Jetson, a guard repeatedly whipped two females with a belt— one girl was whipped allegedly because it was her birthday and the guard had a practice of whipping juveniles on their birthdays, and the other girl was whipped allegedly because she was going to be discharged shortly;

- at Tallulah, a captain discovered guards beating up juveniles, including one child whose hands were cuffed behind his back who was bleeding heavily from the mouth, and guards macing youth while they were being held by other guards; and

- at Tallulah, a guard told a juvenile that he wanted to "drive his dick" in the juvenile's mother's mouth during visitation, leading to a verbal argument that resulted in the guard repeatedly punch-ing the child in the jaw with both his left and right fists, even after the child fell to the floor and attempted to block the guard's blows, and the guard throwing and hitting the child in the head with a radio.

* * *

The abusive use of mace at all facilities except Bridge City also violates juveniles' constitutional rights. Many juveniles at Swanson and Tallulah reported that guards sometimes mace juveniles in restraints, which clearly constitutes use of excessive force. At all facilities except Bridge City, juveniles also continue to be sprayed inappropriately with mace in situations where there is no present danger to the juvenile or to others. * * * In none of these incidents did the juvenile engage in dangerous behavior prior to being sprayed. * * *

* * * Staff who are poorly trained and supervised have resorted to unapproved methods of disciplining youth that have become institution-alized. Examples include: unit "initiations" (whipping and beating juve-niles) and forcing offenders into "the cut" (out of camera range) to fight other youth or be punished physically by guards.

* * *

[A]t all facilities except Bridge City, segregated isolation continues to be used frequently, often in non-dangerous situations, often not as a last resort, and often as a punitive measure. * * * In addition, at Tallulah, youth with suicidal tendencies and youth engaging in self-mutilation are disciplined with segregated isolation for their mental health problems. This response to such dangerous behaviors is contrary to accepted medical standards.

* * *

* * * Infirmary logs at all four facilities still document daily fights among juveniles, some of which result in severe injuries. Furthermore, because these altercations are often halted with use of force by the officers, juveniles continue to get hurt in situations where less restrictive interventions than physical force would have been appropriate. * * *

* * *

* * * [A]t Bridge City, which is supposed to provide protective custody for the system's most vulnerable children, older, stronger juveniles are often housed with younger, smaller boys. * * * Almost all of the younger children at Bridge City voiced fears about their safety not only to us but to counselors and medical staff. We heard repeated accounts of physical and sexual assault by other children. At Swanson, some juveniles, through no fault of their own, are forced to live in restrictive conditions with aggressive peers in order that the facility fill all of its beds. Finally, youth with mental health problems that result in disruptive and/or self-destructive behaviors are transferred routinely to Swanson's and Tallulah's restrictive units where they experience prolonged periods of isolation and deprivation of a number of services without needed treatment for their underlying mental health problems. For many of these youth, such a transfer is counterproductive to treatment needs. Many of these youth increased their self-mutilation and disruptive behaviors as a result of increased isolation.

* * *

Louisiana fails to provide adequate medical and mental health care to a substantial number of juveniles confined in its secure correctional system. None of the four facilities have adequate physician and psychiatrist coverage to ensure adequate medical and mental health services. * * *

* * *

U.S. Dep't of Justice, Findings of Investigation of Secure Correctional Facilities for Juveniles in Louisiana (June 18, 1997).

Notes and Questions

1. *Overcrowding.* Some juvenile correctional facilities operate at 200% to 300% of design capacity. See Mark Soler, Juvenile Justice in the Next Century: Programs or Politics?, 10 Crim. Just. 27, 27 (Winter 1996). As the Georgia and Louisiana reports suggest, overcrowding is associated with higher rates of institutional violence and suicidal behavior, and with greater reliance by authorities on short-term isolation. See John J. Wilson and James C. Howell, Serious and Violent Juvenile Crime: A Comprehensive Strategy, 45 Juv. & Fam. Ct. J. 3, 4 (1994 No. 2).

Amid nationwide overcrowding, some observers argue that many children placed in secure detention do not belong there. For example, the Justice Department alleged that Louisiana was "failing to protect a substantial number of the children confined in its secure facilities from harm by placing them in these facilities in the first place. The State's own post-adjudication screenings identified a number of juveniles, many of whom have special needs, including mental or physical disabilities, who were appropriate for nonsecure placements upon commitment." The Department alleged that these youth were nonetheless placed in secure facilities because the state had an insufficient number of appropriate nonsecure placements for them. U.S. Dep't of Justice, Findings of Investigation of Secure Correctional Facilities for Juveniles in Louisiana (June 18, 1997).

2. *Mental disabilities.* A sizeable number of delinquents confined in secure facilities nationwide suffer from mental disabilities, including mental retardation. In a 1979 survey, juvenile corrections administrators reported that more than 42% of confined delinquents had mental disabilities, including emotional disturbance (16%), specific learning disability (10%) and mental retardation (10%). D.J. Morgan, Prevalence and Types of Handicapping Conditions Found in Juvenile Correctional Institutions: A National Survey, 13 J. Spec. Educ. 283, 285, 291–92 (1979). A 1990 study found that an estimated 35.6% of confined juveniles were learning disabled and that 12.6% were mentally retarded. See Pamela Casey and Ingo Keilitz, Estimating the Prevalence of Learning Disabled and Mentally Retarded Juvenile Offenders: A Meta–Analysis, in Understanding Troubled and Troubling Youth 82, 96 (Peter E. Leone ed., 1990). In 1998, mental health authorities estimated that 20% of juveniles incarcerated nationwide have serious mental illnesses, including juveniles who cannot get mental health treatment outside the prison system because of budget cuts. See Fox Butterfield, Profits at a Juvenile Prison Come With a Chilling Cost, N.Y. Times, July 15, 1998, at A1.

The Individuals With Disabilities Education Act (IDEA) provides potential relief to confined delinquents with mental disabilities. Since 1975, more than twenty class actions concerning special education services have been filed. Most have resulted in settlements or consent decrees without trial. See Patricia Puritz et al., Beyond the Walls, Improving Conditions of Confinement for Youth in Custody 17 (1998).

3. Schall v. Martin [supra p. 1110] stated that "[i]t is axiomatic that '[d]ue process requires that a pretrial detainee not be punished.' " In light of conditions in some detention facilities, can an argument be made that preventive detention is inherently punitive?

4. *Criminal prosecution.* Federal prosecution of juvenile corrections officers for conduct against inmates remains possible under 18 U.S.C. §§ 241 and 242. Section 241 permits prosecution of persons who conspire to "injure, oppress, threaten, or intimidate" a person in the "free exercise or enjoyment" of a federal constitutional or statutory right. Section 242 permits prosecution of a person who, under color of law, willfully deprives any person of a federal constitutional or statutory right. Convicting an officer under either provision, however, would be difficult because the Justice Department would need to prove that the defendant acted with specific intent to interfere with the federal right and knowingly and willfully participated in the

violation. See, e.g., Screws v. United States, 325 U.S. 91, 101–03 (1945); United States v. Guest, 383 U.S. 745, 760 (1966).

5. *Reform efforts.* Some states have taken decisive steps to reform their juvenile correctional systems. The national leaders are Massachusetts and Missouri. Massachusetts closed its training schools beginning in the early 1970s. Based on their current crime and their prior record, about 15% of committed youths receive secure detention. The remaining youths are referred to a wide range of community-based programs, including group homes, forestry programs, day treatment programs, outreach and tracking programs, and foster care. "The hallmark of Massachusetts programs is their small size. No residential program houses more than 30 youths. Community programs and supervision caseloads likewise are kept very small to facilitate * * * individualization of care * * *." See Barry Krisberg and James F. Austin, Reinventing Juvenile Justice 146–47 (1993).

The Massachusetts reforms influenced other states, including Missouri, which closed its training schools in the early 1980s. Missouri reserves secure confinement for violent offenders and chronic repeaters, and places other youth in the less restrictive programs. The state stresses small decentralized facilities, regional management, and expansion of a full range of community based alternative placements. "Today the residential programs in Missouri have units housing 10 or fewer youths. The remaining secure units hold a maximum of 70 youths. Most youngsters are placed in wilderness programs, community group homes, proctor homes in which youths live with college students, day treatment programs, or individual supervision programs." Id. at 166–67. See also Center for the Study of Youth Policy, Incarcerating Youth: The Minnesota and Missouri Experiences (1996); Center for the Study of Youth Policy, Missouri and Hawaii: Leaders in Youth Correction Policy (1992).

6. *Other reports.* In the 1990s, Human Rights Watch (HRW) has investigated conditions in secure juvenile detention facilities in Louisiana, Georgia, Colorado and Maryland. See United States Children in Confinement in Louisiana (1995); Modern Capital of Human Rights? Abuses in the State of Georgia (1996); High Country Lockup: Children in Confinement in Colorado (1997); No Minor Matter: Children in Maryland's Jails (1999), available at <www.hrw.org/reports/1999/maryland> (visited Dec. 6, 1999).

In the Colorado juvenile corrections system, HRW found, among other things, (1) overcrowding at almost every secure institution, with some occupied at two and a half times their planned capacity, (2) secure commitment of children who posed no threat to public safety and who could learn and be supervised in the community, (3) misuse of restraints and punitive segregation, (4) lack of education and psychological treatment for many children, (5) complaints about chronic hunger, (6) unsafe conditions ranging from staff failure to protect children from assaults by other children, to health code violations, (7) unreported incidents of physical and verbal abuse of children by staff, and (8) "[s]tate abdication of its responsibilities and surrender of its powers to protect children committed to its care, by sending children to private facilities, * * * where the state has little control over day-to-day operations or the quality and training of staff." High Country Lockup, supra at 12–13.

This last criticism implicates the "privatizing" of juvenile corrections, which has seen a number of states assign children to secure juvenile prisons built and maintained by for-profit corporations. The nation has more than twice as many privately operated juvenile correctional facilities as public facilities, though the public facilities hold more than twice as many juveniles as the private facilities. See Howard N. Snyder and Melissa Sickmund, Juvenile Offenders and Victims: 1999 National Report 185 (1999). Critics charge that "some of the worst conditions in juvenile prisons" exist in many of these private facilities. See Fox Butterfield, Profits at a Juvenile Prison Come With a Chilling Cost, N.Y. Times, July 15, 1998, at A1. The next article explores the growth of privatized juvenile justice.

DAVID JACKSON AND CORNELIA GRUMMAN, STATES PUT KIDS' LIVES ON THE BLOCK: HOW TROUBLED YOUTH BECOME BIG BUSINESS

Chicago Tribune, September 26, 1999, at 1.

In what amounts to a vast social experiment, government is retreating from its historic role of caring for orphaned and delinquent children and is parceling them out to an expanding private industry of youth jails and foster programs.

The reliance on private entrepreneurs has quietly created one of the most fundamental shifts in the way America handles troubled youth since the introduction of juvenile courts a century ago.

But the lucrative private programs, which were touted as an antidote to the wretched conditions found in state institutions, are rife with corruption and abuse, and are scantly monitored, a Tribune investigation has found.

At a for-profit Florida prison that reaped $9 million a year, guards staged gladiator matches called "The Main Event" in which 13–and 14–year-olds pummeled each other as fellow inmates watched. The prison held some juveniles beyond their release dates to increase the company's state income.

In a violence-plagued South Carolina youth prison that garnered $8.6 million in one year, a 14–year-old inmate was hogtied, doused with Mace or pepper spray and beaten by guards, according to court records.

* * *

Once the exclusive province of local charities, small churches and child advocates, the youth services industry of the 1990s ranges from a handful of multistate corporations that dominate the market to smaller start-ups that win million-dollar contracts with little more than a shabby bungalow and a few empty cots.

The seven largest publicly traded companies saw their income from government youth contracts soar to $645 million from $75 million six years ago. Four of those seven companies did not exist or did not handle youth before 1990.

The burgeoning market attracted corporate executives whose careers were checkered by accusations of swindling and fraud. Using public funds, some administrators treated themselves to luxury car allowances, country club memberships and million dollar management fees, records and interviews show.

Some non-profits were every bit as avaricious as their profit-making counterparts. As the stakes rose, many were bought up or squeezed out by the new competition, and some collapsed under their growing responsibilities, with devastating results for their young wards.

Children's case files examined by the Tribune point to a fundamental collision between the traditional mission of child work–to normalize youth and move them out of the system—and the profit motive, which seeks to keep them in. Even in the non-profit sector, many fee-per-child contracts give private companies no incentive to discharge children or reduce their level of care or confinement as functioning improves, because doing so would cut revenues, government studies found.

Once states subcontracted these children to the private sector, they left the new caretakers largely to their own devices. State officials gave fledgling companies some of government's most far-reaching responsibilities, putting them in charge of licensing and policing other firms and making crucial choices about young wards.

* * *

In the best of circumstances, private detention and foster care programs offer a host of potential benefits. The free market has produced innovators who pioneered influential treatment methods and the competition for contracts spurs some providers to maintain their highest standards.

But while some children unquestionably have fared better in private hands, there is no conclusive evidence that those sent to private programs are as a whole better off, or that taxpayers saved money, as the companies promised. Audits and independent studies present a mixed and murky picture.

* * *

To garner the wards, some companies funnel campaign contributions to public officials while others deploy elaborate marketing schemes, enticing social workers and judges with lavish dinners and compelling promises.

* * *

Thumbing cellular phones and stacks of bright brochures, marketers from Century HealthCare Corp. trolled the corridors of Cook County Juvenile Court. They sought violent and abused children who came with lucrative government funding.

The children "were seen as bodies that we got $300 a day for," said Florence Simcoe, who served as clinical director of Century's Westbridge

Treatment Center in Phoenix until 1996 and marketed that facility to Illinois officials.

On the promise that Westbridge's intensive treatment programs would salvage violent and disturbed wards who had failed in every other setting, Illinois paid the company $15 million during the 1990s.

* * *

On visits to Century's Westbridge facility in sun-soaked Phoenix, beleaguered Cook County child workers were treated to sumptuous meals in the petunia-laced courtyard of Lon's restaurant, then offered after-dinner drinks and cigars.

"We took them out to a lovely dinner. The next day, breakfast at their hotel," Simcoe said.

Simcoe said she resigned when she realized her marketing promises were hollow.

"Instead of two kids to a room, we had three," she said. "Violent kids were mixed with psychiatric patients. And Westbridge made a lot of money."

Illinois withdrew its children from Westbridge in 1996 after a series of state inspections revealed unsanitary conditions and a pattern of aggressive and sexual acting out by the young residents. A 13–year-old sexual predator had been placed in the children's unit, where he bullied smaller youth into a sex ring, Phoenix police records show. A 10–year-old told Phoenix police he was molested repeatedly.

Unknown to the Illinois bureaucrats who placed more than 40 children there, a $25 million bank debt was threatening Century Health-Care, Westbridge's parent company, and driving down the conditions of care.

* * *

A barren industrial park behind an interstate truck stop some 90 miles northeast of Denver was the setting for one of the emerging juvenile detention industry's bellwether dramas.

Built in 1987, Rebound Corp.'s High Plains Youth Center stood as a bright emblem of private industry's promise to rehabilitate delinquent wards more cheaply and effectively than government bureaucrats ever could.

Well-trained and caring staff members were equipped with radios linking them to a 24–hour communications control center, the company said, and rigorous work and exercise schedules would occupy more than 99 percent of the boys waking hours.

Today, a sagging, 14–foot-high chain-link fence guards the empty campus of sleet-gray bungalows.

Rebound's owners and staff didn't deliver on their promise to protect and rehabilitate children, who instead suffered abuses. State juvenile corrections officials never really knew who they were dealing with: a set of entrepreneurs whose previous business dealings had come under law enforcement scrutiny. In the end, the problem spilled beyond the borders of Colorado.

* * *

The Colorado Department of Human Services, which licensed High Plains, never tried to sort out the facility's intricate finances, spokesman Dwight Eisnach said.

"In terms of tracing where the money goes, we're not very good at that, frankly," Eisnach said. "We're not sure we fully understand what they were doing."

The oversight of conditions for children seemed little more stringent. Despite high numbers of abuse allegations and other violent incidents, the state renewed Rebound's contract every year, adding no provisions to improve performance.

A December 1995 review by Illinois inspectors found a pattern of violence and clinical malpractice at the facility, and contained this note: "One frightened resident, pounding on the door for help, was reportedly told by staff to just get back in bed . . . There is substantive evidence that this youth had been serially raped for months on this unit while staff deliberately ignored his plight."

* * *

Note

The Civil Rights of Incarcerated Persons Act (CRIPA) would likely authorize the Justice Department to sue to rectify conditions in privately operated juvenile detention facilities operating under contract with a state or locality, even where the contractor retains full control of the facility. The Act reaches a facility which "is owned, operated or managed by, or provides services on behalf of any State or political subdivision of a State." 42 U.S.C. § 1997(1)(A).

A NOTE ABOUT THE JUVENILE DEATH PENALTY

The federal government and thirty-eight states authorize the death penalty for some forms of murder. In fifteen of these jurisdictions, capital punishment may be imposed only on persons who were at least eighteen at the time of the crime. In four, however, the minimum age is seventeen. In the other twenty, the minimum age is sixteen. See Victor L. Streib, The Juvenile Death Penalty Today: Death Sentences and Executions for Juvenile Crimes, January 1973–June 1999, available at <http://www.law.onu.edu/faculty/streib/juvdeath.htm> (visited Dec. 7, 1999); Victor L. Streib, Moratorium on the Death Penalty for Juveniles, 61 Law & Contemp. Probs. 55, 63 (1998). The United States is one of only a handful of nations that permit executions of persons for crimes committed while a juvenile. Since 1985, the only other nations that have executed persons for such crimes are Bangladesh, Iran, Iraq, Nigeria,

Pakistan, Saudi Arabia and Yemen. Id. at 65. The United States had nine such executions between 1990 and 1998, half the known worldwide total for the period. See Human Rights Watch, World Report 1999, available at www:hrw.org/hrw/worldreport99/usa/index.html. As discussed in Chapter 1, the U.N. Convention on the Rights of the Child, which the United States has not ratified, prohibits capital punishment for offenses committed before the age of eighteen.

In fact, the death penalty in the United States is invoked only relatively rarely against defendants for crimes committed before the age of eighteen. From January 1, 1973 to October 31, 1998, 177 death sentences were imposed on 164 persons who were under 18 at the time of the crime. (These sentences represent about 3% of the persons sentenced to death during this period.). Fifty per cent of these juvenile death sentences have been reversed, 7% have resulted in executions, and 43% were still in force in early 1999. See Howard N. Snyder and Melissa Sickmund, Juvenile Offenders and Victims: 1999 National Report 211 (1999).

In Thompson v. Oklahoma, 487 U.S. 815 (1988), the Court set aside a death sentence imposed on a defendant who was fifteen when he committed the crime. Justice Stevens' plurality opinion (for himself and Justices Brennan, Marshall and Blackmun) concluded that executing a defendant who was under sixteen at the time of the crime would be contrary to "evolving standards of decency that mark the progress of a maturing society," and thus would constitute cruel and unusual punishment in violation of the Eighth Amendment. From several sources, the plurality found that imposition of the death penalty on a 15–year-old is "now generally abhorrent to the conscience of the community" and would "offend civilized standards of decency." Among other things, the plurality examined the behavior of juries—between eighteen and twenty persons under sixteen were executed during the first half of the twentieth century, but no such execution has taken place since 1948, and only five of the 1,393 persons sentenced to death for willful homicide between 1982 and 1986 were less than sixteen at the time of the crime. Id. at 823–33. The plurality declined, however, to establish a firm constitutional rule prohibiting execution of persons under eighteen at the time of the crime. (In 1997, the ABA reaffirmed its opposition to capital punishment of any person for an offense committed before the age of eighteen; see James Podgers, Time Out for Executions, 83 A.B.A.J. 26 (Apr. 1997)).

Justice O'Connor concluded that "a national consensus forbidding the execution of any person for a crime committed before the age of 16 very likely does exist," Id. at 848–49, but she concurred on the ground that Oklahoma's statute did not express a minimum age, creating "a considerable risk" that the legislature "either did not realize that its actions would have the effect of rendering 15–year-old defendants death eligible or did not give the question the serious consideration that would have been reflected in the explicit choice of some minimum age for death eligibility." Id. at 857.

Dissenting for himself and the Chief Justice and Justice White, Justice Scalia found no "evolving standards of decency" that prohibited imposition of the death penalty on a defendant who committed the crime when he was fifteen. Justice Scalia cited (1) a trend in federal and state legislation to lower the age of juvenile criminal responsibility, and (2) the nineteen state death penalty statutes that express no minimum age, "leaving that to be governed by their general rules for the age at which juveniles can be criminally responsible." Id. at 868.

Justice Scalia also concluded that "the statistics of executions demonstrate nothing except the fact that our society has always agreed that executions of 15–year-old criminals should be rare, and in more modern times has agreed that they (like all other executions) should be even rarer still. There is no rational basis for discerning in that a societal judgment that no one as much as a day under 16 can *ever* be mature and morally responsible enough to deserve that penalty; and there is no justification except our own predilection for converting a statistical rarity of occurrence into an absolute constitutional ban." Id. at 870–71.

In light of *Thompson*, does the Eighth Amendment prohibit a state from imposing the death penalty on a defendant who was fifteen when he committed the crime, provided the statute expresses the minimum age for execution?

In Stanford v. Kentucky, 492 U.S. 361 (1989), the Court held that executing a defendant who was sixteen or seventeen at the time of the crime does not constitute cruel and unusual punishment. The majority stressed that most states that permitted capital punishment authorized it for crimes committed at age sixteen or above. Id. at 371. In Eddings v. Oklahoma, 455 U.S. 104, 115–16 (1982), the Court held that in a capital case, a juvenile's age, mental condition and maturity must be considered as important mitigating factors in determining whether to invoke the death penalty.

Even where a death sentence is within the constitutional boundaries established by *Thompson* and *Stanford*, the sentence remains open to challenge under the state constitution. See, e.g., Brennan v. State, 1999 WL 506966 *5 (Fla.) (holding that imposition of death penalty for crime committed when the defendant was sixteen violates the state constitution's cruel or unusual punishment clause).

Writings about the juvenile death penalty include Robert L. Hale, A Review of Juvenile Executions in America (1997); Victor L. Streib, Death Penalty for Juveniles (1987); Amnesty Int'l, U.S.A., The Death Penalty and Juvenile Offenders (Oct. 1991); Elisabeth Gasparini, Juvenile Capital Punishment: A Spectacle of a Child's Injustice, 49 S.C. L. Rev. 1073 (1998); Suzanne D. Strater, The Juvenile Death Penalty: In the Best Interests of the Child?, 26 Loy. U. Chi. L.J. 147 (1995); Victor L. Streib and Lynn Sametz, Executing Female Juveniles, 22 Conn. L. Rev. 3 (1989).

E. Appeal

Notes and Questions

1. *The right to an appeal. Gault* declined to decide whether due process requires states to provide transcripts or recordings of juvenile court proceedings, or to provide an appeal from juvenile court judgments. States provide a statutory right of appeal from such judgments, but a 1995 survey demonstrates "the infrequency with which appeals are taken":

> * * * Public defenders rarely take appeals in juvenile cases. Among public defender offices responding to the survey, 32% are not even authorized to handle appeals. Of the offices that do handle appeals, 46% took no appeals in juvenile cases during the year prior to the survey.
>
> Appointed lawyers also take appeals rarely. Among the appointed lawyers surveyed, three-quarters were authorized to handle appeals but four out of five took none during the prior year.

A Call For Justice: An Assessment of Access to Counsel and Quality of Representation in Delinquency Proceedings 10 (1995).

2. *The trial transcript.* Statutes or court rules provide for a transcript of contested and uncontested juvenile court proceedings. The major purpose is to preserve a meaningful basis for appellate review. See, e.g., N.J. Sup. Ct. Comm. on Court Reporting (Stenographic and Electronic), Final Rep. 13 (1991). When most observers think of the trial transcript, they think of a stenographic transcript made by a court reporter at the parties' expense. Because of budgetary constraints, however, juvenile statutes or rules now frequently permit audiotaped or videotaped transcripts instead. The primary aims of audio and video technology are to make the juvenile court accessible to litigants of lesser means and to spare the state the expense of providing transcripts to indigents. In sometimes frenetic courtrooms, however, parties may be left without a thoroughly trustworthy transcript. See, e.g., T.T.J. v. State, 716 So.2d 258 (Ala. Ct. Crim. App. 1998) (tape recorder was turned off during a break in the proceedings and was inadvertently left off during a portion of testimony).

> The transcript and exhibits, if any, remain confidential and subject to statutes requiring sealing or expunging of the record. Where a statute or rule requires a transcript or recording to be made only on the juvenile's timely request, failure to make a request operates as a waiver. See, e.g., In re Hannah, 667 N.E.2d 76, 77 (Ohio Ct.App.1995).

3. *Appellate practice.* A number of familiar appellate practice doctrines apply in delinquency cases:

(a) *The record.* Appellate courts are bound by the record on appeal. See, e.g., *T.T.J.* supra. Does this doctrine disadvantage delinquents who appear in juvenile court without counsel, or with counsel who has little time to prepare?

(b) *Aggrievement.* An appeal may be taken only by an aggrieved party. For example, in T.T.J. v. State, supra, a 15–year-old murder suspect appealed the order transferring him to criminal court. The transfer order meant the difference between being processed in juvenile court (where he would have faced no more than a few years' confinement) or in adult court (where he faced an adult sentence for capital murder).

(c) *Preserving claims of error.* Appellate courts normally hear only claims or objections raised below, at least unless failure to hear an unpreserved claim or objection would work a fundamental injustice. Is this rule entirely fair in juvenile court, where the juvenile may be unrepresented, represented by counsel unfamiliar with the working of the court, or represented by counsel who have little time to prepare or who may be encouraged to "get along and go along" by not making objections?

(d) *The final judgment rule.* In most states, the general rule is that appellate courts exercise jurisdiction over final trial court judgments. Review of interlocutory, or nonfinal, rulings is severely limited or nonexistent. *T.T.J.* demonstrated that Alabama considers juvenile court transfer orders final, though some states treat them as nonfinal, and thus not appealable by the juvenile until after criminal court conviction.

Under the final judgment rule's ordinary operation, an aggrieved party may seek review of the court's interlocutory decisions as well as the final judgment. The delinquent could assert error arising at any point in the process leading to adjudication and disposition.

(e) *Standard of review.* The standard of review on juvenile court decisions generally depends on the nature of the question raised. See, e.g., Commonwealth v. Jackson, 722 A.2d 1030, 1032 (Pa. 1999) (holding that juvenile court decision to certify juvenile to adult court is reversible only for gross abuse of discretion); In re Cory P., 584 N.W.2d 820, 823 (Neb. Ct. App. 1998) (holding that appellate court reviews delinquency proceedings de novo on the record and must reach a conclusion independent of the juvenile court's findings).

(f) *Harmless error.* Appellate courts do not reverse for harmless error, but only for error that "results in a miscarriage of justice or constitutes a substantial violation of a constitutional or statutory right." In re D.T.C., 487 S.E.2d 21, 24 (Ga. Ct. App. 1997).

PROBLEM 11–6

After 15-year-old Billy Barnes was adjudicated a delinquent in juvenile court, his public defender filed a notice of appeal. The trial court refused to appoint the public defender as appellate counsel, however, because it learned Billy's parents were not indigent and thus did not qualify for appointed counsel. The boy's father then decided not to proceed with the appeal.

Before dismissing the appeal, the court of appeals must determine whether to compel the father to fund the appeal. The relevant statute provides: "A nonindigent parent or legal guardian of a person under eighteen shall furnish such person with the necessary legal services and costs incident to a delinquency proceeding." Should the court compel Bill's father to fund the appeal? What if the parents have a conflict of interest, for example if they were the victims of the offense?

A NOTE ABOUT FEDERAL DELINQUENCY JURISDICTION

This chapter has concerned juvenile court delinquency proceedings, which adjudicate acts that would be state crimes if committed by an adult. In 1996, state courts with juvenile jurisdiction handled approximately 1,757,600 delinquency cases. See Anne L. Stahl et al., Juvenile Court Statistics 1996, at 5 (1999).

Federal delinquency law also merits attention. In 1995, federal courts adjudicated delinquency proceedings involving 122 juveniles charged with acts committed before their eighteenth birthday that would violate federal law if committed by an adult. See Bureau of Justice Statistics, Sourcebook of Criminal Justice Statistics 1997, Table 5.78, at 442 (1998). These acts typically implicate federal law because they are committed on military bases, other federal lands or Indian reservations, or because they violate federal drug laws or other federal criminal statutes. Federal delinquency cases are subject to the Juvenile Delinquency Act, 18 U.S.C. § 5031 et seq., which was enacted in 1938 and has undergone periodic amendments.

The Act sharply limits the scope of federal delinquency jurisdiction because Congress recognized that delinquency is "essentially a local concern[,] * * * at bottom a responsibility of the community." District of Columbia v. P.L.M., 325 A.2d 600, 601 (D.Ct.App.1974). Section 5032 creates blanket federal authority to prosecute misdemeanors committed by juveniles within the "special maritime and territorial jurisdiction of the United States," such as national parks. Outside this narrow category of minor offenses, however, a juvenile alleged to have violated federal law is not processed in federal court unless the Attorney General certifies to the court (1) that the juvenile court or other appropriate state court does not have jurisdiction or refuses to assume jurisdiction, (2) that the state does not have available programs and services adequate for the needs of juveniles, or (3) that the offense charged is a crime of violence that is a felony or an offense under specified federal drug or firearms possession laws, and that "there is a substantial Federal interest in the case or the offense to warrant the exercise of Federal jurisdiction." Id.

Where the Attorney General does not make the required certification, federal authorities must surrender the juvenile to state authorities. See, e.g., United States v. Wellington, 102 F.3d 499, 503 (11th Cir.1996). Professor Abraham Abramovsky has noted, however, that "[t]he burden faced by federal prosecutors in obtaining jurisdiction over a juvenile is not, in practice, a difficult one." Abraham Abramovsky, Trying Juveniles as Adults, N.Y.L.J., June 8, 1998, at 3. Where a juvenile is charged with a serious crime in a state that would not permit transfer for trial as an adult, for example, state prosecutors might refuse to prosecute if the underlying acts would also constitute a federal crime for which adult prosecution would be possible in federal court; the Attorney General could then certify that the state court has refused to assume jurisdiction. Professor Abramovsky challenges such exercise of prosecutorial discretion: "[T]he history of federal juvenile law indicates that it was not intended to be used as a backup system of justice where state laws are less advantageous to prosecutors. * * * [W]here state law is inadequate to provide for the effective prosecution of juvenile offenders, the remedy should be created by state legislatures." Id. Nevertheless courts have held that in the absence of bad faith or facial noncompliance with the statute, the Attorney General's decision whether to certify a juvenile case under any of the three prongs of § 5032 is a matter of prosecutorial discretion not subject to judicial review. See United States v. I.D.P., 102 F.3d 507, 510–13 (11th Cir.1996) (citing decisions).

Unlike state systems, the federal system does not have a separate "juvenile court"; federal delinquency hearings are heard by a district judge or magistrate judge. Where the case remains in federal court, § 5032 provides that the government may proceed in a delinquency proceeding or may seek to "transfer" the juvenile to adult status for trial in the district court. Juveniles have no constitutional right to be processed as delinquents under the federal Act. See, e.g., United States v. Rombom, 421 F.Supp. 1295, 1300 (S.D.N.Y.1976). For most offenses, a delinquency proceeding ensues unless the juvenile requests in writing on advice of counsel to be processed as an adult. The Attorney General may move to prosecute as an adult, however, where a juvenile fifteen or older is charged with committing specified acts of violence, specified offenses involving sale or importation of drugs or firearms, or handgun possession. The minimum transfer age is thirteen for a few specified serious offenses such as murder, robbery or bank robbery or if the juvenile possessed a firearm while committing a violent crime.

When seeking to transfer a juvenile to adult status in federal court, the government must rebut the statutory presumption of juvenile treatment by a preponderance of the evidence. See, e.g., United States v. Juvenile Male No. 1, 86 F.3d 1314, 1323 (4th Cir. 1996). The court after a hearing may grant the motion to prosecute as an adult if it finds that "transfer would be in the interest of justice" according to factors enumerated in § 5032. The court must make written findings concerning each factor, which (like the factors recited in most state transfer statutes) relate generally to the nature of the alleged offense and the juvenile's circumstances, condition and prior record. "A court may weigh the statutory factors as it deems appropriate and 'is free to determine how much weight to give each factor.' " Wellington, supra, 102 F.3d at 506 (citing decisions). As courts must do in state transfer proceedings, the federal court balances the need to "remove juveniles from the ordinary criminal process in order to avoid the stigma of a prior criminal conviction and to encourage treatment and rehabilitation," with the need to "protect the public from 'violent and dangerous individuals and provid[e] sanctions for antisocial acts * * *.' " United States v. Doe, 94 F.3d 532, 536 (9th Cir. 1996). "[A] motion to transfer is properly granted where a court determines that the risk of harm to society posed by affording the defendant more lenient treatment within the juvenile justice system outweighs the defendant's chance for rehabilitation." United States v. One Juvenile Male, 40 F.3d 841, 844 (6th Cir. 1994).

Transfer to adult status is automatic for some repeat offenders sixteen or older charged with specified crimes of violence, or drug or firearms possession crimes. An order transferring a juvenile to adult status is immediately appealable under the collateral order exception to the final judgment rule, but the § 5032 interests-of-justice analysis ordinarily "gives the district court broad discretion," which the court of appeals reviews only for abuse of discretion. See, e.g., Wellington, supra, 102 F.3d at 503, 506 (citing decisions).

Where the federal case is tried as a delinquency proceeding, the proceeding resembles state delinquency proceedings. The beyond-a-reasonable-doubt standard of proof applies and the juvenile has a right to counsel, but the hearing is closed to the public and carries no right to a jury trial. See, e.g., United States v. C.L.O., 77 F.3d 1075, 1076, 1077 (8th Cir. 1996). The proceeding is civil rather than criminal, and a delinquency adjudication does not constitute a criminal conviction. See United States v. Gonzalez–Cervantes, 668 F.2d 1073, 1076 (9th Cir. 1981).

Where an alleged delinquent is taken into custody, the arresting officer must immediately advise the juvenile of his legal rights "in language comprehensive [sic?] to a juvenile," and must immediately notify the juvenile's parents, guardian or custodian of the custody, the alleged offense and these rights. 18 U.S.C. § 5033. Where the government makes a good faith, though unsuccessful, effort to locate and notify the adult, the government satisfies the latter requirement and may introduce the juvenile's otherwise admissible statements. See, e.g., United States v. Burrous, 147 F.3d 111, 116 (2d Cir.1998).

Where an alleged delinquent is held in preventive detention under § 5035, § 5036 grants the right to a speedy trial. If the detainee "is not brought to trial within thirty days from the date upon which such detention was begun, the information shall be dismissed on motion of the alleged delinquent or at the direction of the court, unless the Attorney General shows that additional delay was caused by the juvenile or his counsel, or consented to by the juvenile and his counsel, or would be in the interest of justice in the particular case. Delays attributable solely to court calendar congestion may not be considered in the interest of justice. Except in extraordinary circumstances, an information dismissed * * * may not be reinstituted."

If the district court adjudicates the juvenile a delinquent, the court must hold a dispositional hearing and may suspend the delinquency findings, order the juvenile to pay restitution, place the juvenile on probation, or commit the juvenile to official detention. 18 U.S.C. § 5037. Section 5039 prohibits incarceration of delinquents in "an adult jail or correctional institution in which he has regular contact with adults incarcerated because they have been convicted of a crime or are awaiting trial on criminal charges."

SECTION 5.   THE JUVENILE COURT'S FUTURE

In 1997 a leading newspaper wrote that "[t]he worst-kept secret in the American criminal justice system is the nearly complete failure of juvenile justice." The editorial, however, acknowledged that "[a]lmost 60 percent of juveniles never commit another crime after one trip to juvenile courts," and concluded that "[f]orcing these children into the unforgiving adult court and penal system is unlikely to improve on that percentage." See Keep Kids in Their Own Court, Plain Dealer (Cleveland), July 27, 1997, at 2E. The editorial's ambivalence highlights the debate between persons who would maintain and reform the juvenile court and those who would abolish it.

The juvenile court has its unabashed supporters. Professor Stephen A. Drizin, for example, calls the court "one of the most important and enduring contributions the United States has made to the world": "The simple fact is that juvenile court success stories greatly outnumber its failures. Most children who get in trouble with the law never reoffend, and most whose crimes are so serious that they are referred to the court never come back after court intervention. The juvenile court is also more likely to impose sanctions on violent offenders than the adult court, although adult sanctions are more severe. * * * [J]uveniles who are kept in juvenile court rather than transferred to adult court are less likely to recidivate." The Juvenile Court at 100, 83 Judicature 9, 14–15 (July–Aug. 1999).

This chapter has already explored much of the criticism leveled at the juvenile court. Some critics ridicule the court for "coddling" violent juveniles at the expense of public safety, while other critics assail the court for imposing punishment in the guise of rehabilitation without many of the procedural safeguards available in the criminal court. Charges of racial and gender bias also punctuate the public discussion. The Supreme Court itself has been harsh on the juvenile court, most notably in *McKeiver*. The next two entries demonstrate the tenor of the ongoing debate about the court's future.

BARRY C. FELD, ABOLISH THE JUVENILE COURT: YOUTHFULNESS, CRIMINAL RESPONSIBILITY, AND SENTENCING POLICY

88 J. Crim. L. & Criminology 68, 68–69, 74, 87, 91–97, 133–34 (1997).

Within the past three decades, judicial decisions, legislative amendments, and administrative changes have transformed the juvenile court from a nominally rehabilitative social welfare agency into a scaled-down, second-class criminal court for young people. These reforms have converted the historical ideal of the juvenile court as a social welfare institution into a penal system that provides young offenders with neither therapy nor justice. The substantive and procedural convergence between juvenile and criminal courts eliminates virtually all of the conceptual and operational differences in strategies of criminal social control for youths and adults. No compelling reasons exist to maintain separate from an adult criminal court, a punitive juvenile court whose only remaining distinctions are its persisting procedural deficiencies. Rather, states should abolish juvenile courts' delinquency jurisdiction and formally recognize youthfulness as a mitigating factor in the sentencing of younger criminal offenders. Such a policy would provide younger offenders with substantive protections comparable to those afforded by juvenile courts, assure greater procedural regularity in the determination of guilt, and avoid the disjunctions in social control caused by maintaining two duplicative and inconsistent criminal justice systems.

* * *

In the decades since *Gault*, legislative, judicial, and administrative changes have modified juvenile courts' jurisdiction, purpose, and procedures and fostered their convergence with criminal courts. These interrelated developments—increased procedural formality, removal of status offenders from juvenile court jurisdiction, waiver of serious offenders to the adult system, and an increased emphasis on punishment in sentencing delinquents—constitute a form of criminological "triage," crucial components of the criminalizing of the juvenile court, and elements of the erosion of the theoretical and practical differences between the two systems. This "triage" strategy removes many middle-class, white, and female non-criminal status offenders from the juvenile court, simultaneously transfers persistent, violent, and disproportionally minority youths to criminal court for prosecution as adults, and imposes increasingly punitive sanctions on those middle-range delinquent criminal offenders who remain under the jurisdiction of the juvenile court. As a result of these implicit triage policies, juvenile courts increasingly function similarly to adult criminal courts.

* * *

Although the formal procedures of juvenile and criminal courts have converged under *Gault's* impetus, a substantial gulf remains between theory and reality, between the "law on the books" and the "law in action." Theoretically, the Constitution and state juvenile statutes entitle delinquents to formal trials and assistance of counsel. But, the actual quality of procedural justice differs considerably from theory; a gap persists between "rhetoric" and "reality." Despite the criminalizing of juvenile courts, most states provide neither special procedures to protect youths from their own immaturity nor the full panoply of adult procedural safeguards. Instead, states treat juveniles just like adult criminal defendants when treating them equally places youths at a practical disadvantage, and use less effective juvenile court safeguards when those deficient procedures provide an advantage to the state.

* * *

The juvenile court treatment model constitutes an inappropriate policy response to young offenders. If we formulated a child welfare policy *ab initio*, would we choose a juvenile court as the most appropriate agency through which to deliver social services, and make criminality a condition precedent to the receipt of services? If we would not create a court to deliver social services, then does the fact of a youth's criminality confer upon a court any special competency as a welfare agency? Many young people who do not commit crimes desperately need social services and many youths who commit crimes do not require or will not respond to social services. In short, criminality represents an inaccurate and haphazard criterion upon which to allocate social services. Because our society denies adequate help and assistance to meet the social welfare needs of all young people, the juvenile court's treatment ideology serves primarily to legitimate the exercise of judicial coercion of some *because of their criminality*.

Quite apart from its unsuitability as a social welfare agency, the individualized justice of a rehabilitative juvenile court fosters lawlessness and thus detracts from its utility as a court of law as well. Despite statutes and rules, juvenile court judges make discretionary decisions effectively unconstrained by the rule of law. If judges intervene to meet each child's "real needs," then every case is unique and decisional rules or objective criteria cannot constrain clinical intuitions. The *idea* of treatment necessarily entails individual differentiation, indeterminacy, a rejection of proportionality, and a disregard of normative valuations of the seriousness of behavior. But, if judges possess neither practical scientific bases by which to classify youths for treatment nor demonstrably effective programs to prescribe for them, then the exercise of "sound discretion" simply constitutes a euphemism for idiosyncratic judicial subjectivity. Racial, gender, geographic, and socio-economic disparities constitute almost inevitable corollaries of a treatment ideology that lacks a scientific foundation. At the least, judges will sentence youths differently based on extraneous personal characteristics for which they bear no responsibility. At the worst, judges will impose haphazard, unequal, and discriminatory punishment on similarly situated offenders without effective procedural or appellate checks.

* * *

The juvenile court predicates its procedural informality on the assumptions that it provides benign and effective treatment. The continuing absence or co-optation of defense counsel in many jurisdictions reduces the likelihood that juvenile courts will adhere to existing legal mandates. The closed, informal, and confidential nature of delinquency proceedings reduces the visibility and accountability of the justice process and precludes external checks on coercive interventions. So long as the mythology prevails that juvenile court intervention constitutes only benign coercion and that, in any event, children should not expect more, youths will continue to receive the "worst of both worlds."

* * *

The fundamental shortcoming of the juvenile court's welfare *idea* reflects a failure of conception rather than *simply* a failure of implementation. The juvenile court's creators envisioned a social service agency in a judicial setting, and attempted to fuse its welfare mission with the power of state coercion. The juvenile court *idea* that judicial-clinicians successfully can combine social welfare and penal social control in one agency represents an inherent conceptual flaw and an innate contradiction. Combining social welfare and penal social control functions in one agency assures that the court does both badly. Providing for child welfare is a societal responsibility rather than a judicial one. Juvenile courts lack control over the resources necessary to meet child welfare needs exactly because of the social class and racial characteristics of their clients. In practice, juvenile courts subordinate welfare concerns to crime control considerations.

* * *

* * * [J]uvenile court law does not define eligibility for services or create an enforceable right or entitlement based upon young peoples' lack of access to decent education, lack of adequate housing or nutrition, unmet health needs, or impoverished families—*none of which are their fault*. In all of these instances, children bear the social burdens of their parents' circumstances literally as innocent bystanders. If states defined juvenile courts' jurisdiction on the basis of young people's needs for social welfare, then they would declare a broad category of at-risk children who are eligible for public assistance. Such a policy would require a substantial commitment of social resources and public will to children's welfare.

Instead, states' juvenile codes define juvenile courts' jurisdiction based on a youth committing a crime, a prerequisite that detracts from a compassionate response. Unlike disadvantaged social conditions that are not their fault, criminal behavior represents the one characteristic for which adolescent offenders do bear at least partial responsibility. As long as juvenile courts define eligibility for "services" on the basis of criminality, they highlight that aspect of youths which rationally elicits the least sympathy, and ignore personal circumstances or social conditions that evoke a desire to help. Thus, the juvenile courts' defining characteristic simply reinforces the public's antipathy to young people by emphasizing that they are law violators. Recent changes in juvenile court waiver and sentencing policies to emphasize punishment, "accountability," and personal responsibility further re-enforce juvenile courts' penal foundations and reduce the legitimacy of youths' claims to compassion or humanitarian assistance.

* * *

* * * Society collectively bears responsibility to provide for the welfare of its children, and does so by supporting families, communities, schools, and social institutions that nurture all young people—not by cynically incarcerating its most disadvantaged children "for their own good." Neither juvenile court judges nor any other criminal justice agencies realistically can ameliorate the social ills that afflict young people or significantly reduce youth crime.

* * *

Once we uncouple social welfare from penal social control, then no need remains for a separate juvenile court for young offenders. We can try all offenders in criminal court with certain modifications of substantive and procedural criminal law to accommodate younger defendants. Some proponents of juvenile courts properly object that criminal courts suffer from profound deficiencies: crushing caseloads; ineffective attorneys; insufficient sentencing alternatives; coercive plea bargains; and assembly-line justice. Unfortunately, these shortcomings equally characterize juvenile courts as well. * * *

* * *

If the child is a criminal and the "real" reason for formal intervention is criminal social control, then states should abolish juvenile courts' delinquency jurisdiction and try young offenders in criminal courts alongside their adult counterparts. But, if the criminal is a child, then states must modify their criminal justice system to accommodate the youthfulness of some defendants. Before prosecuting a child as a criminal in an integrated court, a legislature must address issues of substance and procedure. Substantive justice requires a rationale to sentence younger offenders differently, and more *leniently*, than older defendants, a formal recognition of *youthfulness as a mitigating factor in sentencing*. Procedural justice requires providing youths with full procedural parity with adult defendants and additional safeguards to account for the disadvantages of youth in the justice system. Taken in combination, these substantive and procedural modifications can avoid the "worst of both worlds," provide youths with protections functionally equivalent to those accorded adults, and do justice in sentencing.

* * *

I propose to abolish the juvenile court with trepidation. On the one hand, combining enhanced procedural safeguards with a "youth discount" in an integrated criminal court can provide young offenders with greater protections and justice than they currently receive in the juvenile system, and more proportional and humane consequences than judges presently inflict on them in the criminal justice system. Integration may foster a more consistent crime control response than the present dual systems permit to violent and chronic young offenders at various stages of the developmental and criminal career continuum. On the other hand, politicians may ignore the significance of youthfulness as a mitigating factor and use these proposals to escalate the punishment of young people. Although abolition of the juvenile court, enhanced procedural protections, and a "youth discount" constitute essential components of a youth sentencing policy package, nothing can prevent legislators from selectively choosing only those elements that serve their "get tough" agenda, even though doing so unravels the threads that make coherent a proposal for an integrated court. * * *

* * * My proposal to abolish the juvenile court does not entail an abandonment of its welfare ideal. Rather, uncoupling policies of social welfare from penal social control enables us to expand a societal commitment to the welfare of all children regardless of their criminality. If we frame child welfare policy reforms in terms of child welfare rather than crime control, then we may expand the possibilities for positive intervention for all young people. For example, a public health approach to youth crime that identified the social, environmental, community structural, and ecological correlates of youth violence, such as poverty, the proliferation of handguns, and the commercialization of violence, would suggest wholly different intervention strategies than simply incarcerating minority youths. Youth violence occurs as part of a social ecological structure; high rates of violent youth crime arise in areas of concentrated poverty, high teenage pregnancy, and AFDC dependency. Such social indicators could identify census tracts or even zip-codes for community organizing, economic development, and preventive and remedial intervention.

* * *

IRENE MERKER ROSENBERG, LEAVING BAD ENOUGH ALONE: A RESPONSE TO THE JUVENILE COURT ABOLITIONISTS

1993 Wis. L. Rev. 163, 163, 165–69, 171–75, 178–79, 182–85.

* * * I do not believe that it would be wise to abolish the delinquency jurisdiction and try children as criminals in the adult court * * *.

* * * I am aware of the various ways in which the states do not fulfill their promises to provide care, treatment, and rehabilitation, and to assure adequate procedural protection. And yet, as much as I agree with Barry Feld that the juvenile courts impose punishment in the name of treatment and give reduced constitutional and procedural protection to children, I do not share his belief in the abolitionist solution, even though it is prompted by a despair that I do share. The proposed alternative of trial in the adult criminal courts * * * is even worse than what we now have.

* * *

First, the abolitionists claim that there is a significant disparity between the constitutional and procedural rights afforded adults charged with crime and children charged with delinquency. In my opinion, these differences are not as substantial as they appear to be, or at least not substantial enough to be a basis for giving up on the juvenile justice system. The conceded inequality in safeguards should not blind us to the incremental changes over the years that have benefitted children. The *Gault* line of cases does give alleged delinquents significant constitutional protection. Indeed, in cases such as *In re Winship* and *Breed v. Jones*, applying the reasonable doubt standard and the double jeopardy requirement to delinquency adjudicatory proceedings, the Supreme Court treated delinquency and adult criminal trials as functionally equivalent for purposes of the implicated constitutional guarantees.

Moreover, even where the Court has given juveniles less, as in *New Jersey v. T.L.O.*, the disparity is often more apparent than real. In *T.L.O.*, the majority concluded that school officials could conduct warrantless searches of students without adhering to the probable cause requirement; school searches need only be reasonable under all the circumstances. By virtue of this decision, public school students seem to be accorded less Fourth Amendment protection than adults. School searches, however, come within the category of so-called administrative inspections, and searches of adults in such contexts are also upheld without adherence to either the warrant or probable cause requirements.* * *

To be sure, in *Schall v. Martin*, which upheld a vague preventive detention law for alleged delinquents, the Court made much of the differences between children and adults, and used these distinctions as a basis for giving children less constitutional protection. * * * Yet, in the end *Schall* was simply a prelude to the Court's decision in *United States v. Salerno*, rejecting substantive due process and Eighth Amendment challenges to the federal preventive detention statute governing adults. Thus, notwithstanding *Schall*'s emphatic pronouncement that children are entitled to custody rather than liberty, *Salerno*, which relies on *Schall*, puts adults in roughly the same position as far as preventive detention is concerned.

The major setback for juveniles was denial of the right to a jury trial in *McKeiver v. Pennsylvania*. * * * I do not, however, view the loss of even this right as catastrophic. After all, there are relatively few jury trials in the adult criminal court. Instead, the right to trial by jury is primarily a chip to be used in the poker game of plea bargaining—a game of far greater seriousness in the adult courts, where the sentencing stakes, at least for serious offenses, are much higher. * * *

More broadly, I think we have not sufficiently appreciated that in a substantial number of jurisdictions state law gives children many of the same rights as adult defendants, and sometimes more.[39] * * * It is questionable whether such increased protection would be preserved if the juvenile courts were abolished and children were instead tried as adults in the criminal courts.

In determining whether to abandon the juvenile courts because of the disparity in protection, it is also necessary to make a realistic assessment of the constitutional safeguards available in the criminal courts. The Burger and Rehnquist Courts have, after all, taken their toll. Much of *Miranda* has been eviscerated, and the Fourth Amendment and the exclusionary rule are being severely constricted. If children are tried

---

39. In several states, for example, a child cannot waive *Miranda* rights unless he or she has first consulted with an interested adult.

in the criminal courts, they will receive only this diluted constitutional protection, and since minors are less likely to invoke their rights and more likely to waive them, effectively they will still receive less protection than adults. While it is true that the latest Supreme Court decisions give juveniles little more than the right to fundamental fairness, that also is just about all the Justices are now affording to adult defendants. * * *

In addition, this low level of constitutional protection granted to adults is available only theoretically. Nationwide, approximately 90% of defendants plead guilty. A series of Supreme Court decisions establishes that if a defendant does plead guilty, almost all antecedent constitutional violations are waived. So even if children were tried in the criminal courts where they would be entitled to the same guarantees as adults, it is just as likely, if not more so, that they would join the vast majority of their older counterparts who waive such protection to secure the purported benefit of a reduced sentence.[58] In any event, do we really want the child's fate to be determined on an ad hoc basis by individual prosecutors and defense attorneys pursuant to plea bargaining, rather than by a juvenile court judge who has at least some obligation to act in the youth's best interest?

It seems to me that underlying the views of the abolitionists, at least unconsciously, is a somewhat idealized or romanticized vision of adult courts in which the criminal guarantees of the Bill of Rights are meaningfully enforced. Yes, there is a right to trial by jury that is missing in the juvenile court unless supplied by state law. Yes, there is a right to counsel that * * * is too often denied in practice in juvenile court. And I surely would not denigrate either of these important safeguards. At the same time, however, the reality of adult criminal proceedings is crowded courtrooms in which justice is dispensed through waivers and pleas negotiated by defense attorneys who are often less than zealous and well-prepared advocates, and in which racism is at least as much a fact of life as in juvenile court. For the most part, the typical criminal court in urban areas is a harsh, tough, mean institution cranking out pleas, with few pauses for individualized attention. It is no place for an adult defendant to be, much less a child. * * *

Initially, perhaps there would be a burst of concern for the kiddie defendants. But once the glow wore off, and that would not take long, it would be back to business as usual: treadmill processing for adults both over and under the age of eighteen. Let us face it: As bad as the juvenile courts are, the adult criminal courts are worse. Adding a new class of defendants to an already overburdened system can only exacerbate the situation, all to the detriment of children.

* * * Professor Feld and other abolitionists believe that if children are tried in criminal court, rationales will be developed to give them special protection in ascertaining guilt and punishment. While I agree

---

58. Since children are more apt to waive their rights and confess, and since they generally make poor witnesses, the likelihood of a guilty plea is enhanced.

that is what children should get, am not so sure that is what they will get. This looks a lot like having your cake and eating it too, a difficult request to be making in these hard-nosed, law-and-order times. On the one hand, the abolitionists are asking that children be treated as adults in order to secure equal constitutional guarantees, and on the other, they are asking that children be treated as children in order to protect their unique disabilities. * * *

If states are unwilling to give minors enhanced constitutional and procedural protection when they are within the supposedly benevolent confines of the juvenile court, why would they do so in the criminal court? Bringing children within the criminal jurisdiction is an assertion by the state that minors do not deserve specialized treatment. While it is true that the state will no longer have the bogus rehabilitation argument as a basis for diminishing constitutional protection, the state may argue that because it has elected to treat children and adults the same, there is no reason to give youngsters enhanced safeguards.

Moreover, it is unclear whether the common law infancy defense * * *is constitutionally mandated as a matter of federal law. * * *

Even assuming, however, that the infancy defense were either constitutionally mandated or afforded as a matter of state law, it might still be insufficiently protective of children tried in adult criminal courts. The irrebuttable presumption for children under seven would be invoked in very few cases because there are few crimes committed by children so young, and when they are, the state generally chooses not to prosecute them even in the juvenile courts. At the other end of the spectrum, children over fourteen are presumed to be criminally responsible, and many of the juveniles accused of serious crimes fall within that age bracket, making the infancy defense irrelevant in such cases. Thus, the defense generally would be applicable only to children between seven and fourteen, who are entitled to the rebuttable presumption of incapacity, and a large number of juveniles accused of crime do fall within that age bracket. Many of those within this intermediate category are approaching fourteen, however, and unfortunately the rebuttable presumption decreases in strength as the child gets older. Therefore, the closer a child is to fourteen, the less evidence the state needs to prove capacity. Moreover, the prosecutor can establish capacity simply by showing consciousness of wrongdoing, not an onerous burden, especially since many jurisdictions allow that burden to be met by inferences from the very circumstances of the crime. Finally, since it is based on chronological rather than mental age, and is concerned with cognitive rather than volitional capacity, the infancy defense would not, in my view, give children parity in the criminal courts.

* * *

At bottom, Professor Feld seems to believe that, even if the nation's highest court shows no mercy, state legislatures will be less Draconian. I think his position is problematic. If states are willing to deprive children of constitutional protection and keep them in appalling facilities that provide neither care nor rehabilitation, why should we assume that they will do any better if juveniles are treated as adults? * * *

If the legislature is willing to authorize forty-year sentences for ten-year-olds within the juvenile court system, what will it do to them if they are tried at the outset in the criminal court? At least within the present framework, there is the possibility the child will remain within the jurisdiction of the juvenile authorities and perhaps be released on parole. If the original proceeding were held in criminal court, however, there would be no such option. Barry Feld sees [laws] which impose punishment based on the nature of the particular offense committed rather than the needs of the child, as evidence that the juvenile courts are virtually as punitive as criminal courts and therefore should be abandoned. I see such laws as an omen that there is surely worse to come if children are thrown into the adult jurisdiction.

If children are tried as adults, and convicted, they presumably will be subject to the jurisdiction of adult correctional authorities rather than youth services agencies, which are at least to some extent child-oriented. Sometimes I think we forget how terrible the prison facilities for adult criminals in this country are. * * *

Abandoning the juvenile court is an admission that its humane purposes were misguided or unattainable. I do not believe that. We should stay and fight—fight for a reordering of societal resources, one that will protect and nourish children. * * * We can and should seek both procedural and dispositional reform in the juvenile courts.

Despite all their failings, of which there are many, the juvenile courts do afford benefits that are unlikely to be replicated in the criminal courts, such as the institutionalized intake diversionary system, anonymity, diminished stigma, shorter sentences, and recognition of rehabilitation as a viable goal. We should build on these strengths rather than abandon ship.

It is important to take into account both the chimerical quality of enhanced constitutional safeguards in the criminal courts and the significant benefits afforded to minors even by the existing juvenile justice system, before relegating children to criminal courts and prisons with no guarantee that their immaturity will be adequately considered or their vulnerability meaningfully protected.

Notes and Questions

1. *Through the law school lens?* Hunter Hurst, Director of the National Center for Criminal Justice, believes some juvenile court abolitionists may be influenced by legal education, which he argues distorts the realities of the juvenile justice system. "Schools of law generally do an excellent job of teaching the theory or criminal law and procedure but a poor job of teaching the reality of criminal justice in the United States. As a consequence, law graduates * * * tend to romanticize our criminal justice system. Conversely, when schools of law do offer a course in juvenile law, it * * * invariably compares juvenile law and procedure with criminal law and procedure. In

such a comparison, juvenile law and procedure is forever destined to be the loser because the theory of criminal justice is used as the standard for measurement. If the reality of criminal law and procedure were used as the standard, the outcome would be reversed." Hunter Hurst, Imagining Legal Scholarship: The Case for the Juvenile Court and for Teaching Juvenile Law and Procedure, in Child, Parent, & State: Law and Policy Reader 611, 620–21 (S. Randall Humm et al. eds., 1994).

2. *The courts' viewpoint.* In a 1994 National Law Journal poll, a third of juvenile court judges believed the juvenile justice system is too lenient. Among the major findings, (a) 41% of the judges said juveniles should face the death penalty under some circumstances, (b) two out of five judges said courts should be able to try as adults murder suspects as young as 14–15, while 17% said the minimum age should be as low as 12–13, (c) a quarter of the judges said parents should be held liable for their children's criminal acts, (d) 17% of the judges said they would like to be able to order the caning (corporal punishment) of children, and (e) 91% favored granting juvenile courts authority to incarcerate and supervise juveniles past the age of majority, provided greater resources and options were made available. Ninety-three percent of the judges favored fingerprinting juveniles, 85% said juvenile criminal records should be available to adult law enforcement (though 71% said such records should not be open to the public), and 68% favored open court hearings for accused juvenile felons. See Rorie Sherman, Juvenile Judges Say: Time to Get Tough, Nat'l L.J., Aug. 8, 1994, at 1.

3. *Resources.* Many observers argue that any failures of the juvenile justice system's rehabilitation efforts stem largely from public refusal to fund courts and treatment programs sufficiently. In 1998, for example, the President of the American Bar Association reported that "[i]n most American cities, the scene in juvenile courts is jarring and oppressive, the results of badly overburdened and grossly underfunded conditions." Jerome J. Shestack, What About Juvenile Justice?, A.B.A.J. 8 (May 1998). After four years of hearings and investigation, *Alexander S.*, [supra p. 1183] found that "unsuccessful efforts at rehabilitation stem primarily, if not exclusively, from the lack of adequate funding to devise and implement programs that will allow juveniles to correct their behavior" while in state custody. Alexander S. v. Boyd, 876 F.Supp. 773, 780–81 & n. 15, 782–83 (D.S.C.1995).

Two commentators point to the "repeated failure of governments to allocate resources to effective rehabilitation programs" amid the "clamor of contemporary politicians battling furiously to prove themselves the toughest on children who have broken the law." Paul Holland and Wallace J. Mlyniec, Whatever Happened to the Right to Treatment?: The Modern Quest for a Historical Promise, 68 Temp. L. Rev. 1791, 1791, 1794, 1829 (1995). One Georgia district attorney pointedly concluded that "[j]uvenile court is not going to work where there are thousands of kids and not enough resources. Our state system is popping at the seams. * * * Nobody wants to invest in troubled kids." R. Robin McDonald, Punishing Choices: How to Try Teens Charged With Major Crimes?, Atlanta J. & Const., Aug. 8, 1999, at 1F.

In the National Law Journal poll discussed in note 2, 48% of the juvenile court judges flatly admitted that the juvenile justice system was failing. Three-quarters of the judges, however, said that if well-financed rehabilitation programs were available, most youths could be saved from criminality. Nearly half the judges said that only 10% or less of the youth that come before them could not be rehabilitated under any circumstances. Id.

4. *Public attitudes about the juvenile justice system.* Public impatience with juvenile courts can be overstated. In a 1988 California poll, 71% of respondents endorsed rehabilitation as the juvenile court's primary goal and 92% believed that incarcerated juveniles should have access to job training, education and counseling before their release. See Barry Krisberg and James F. Austin, Reinventing Juvenile Justice 2–3 (1993). In a 1997 poll of American adults, respondents "overwhelmingly opposed housing juveniles in adult jails, jailing status offenders with adults, * * * and granting prosecutors exclusive discretion over whether juveniles should be tried as adults." Respondents also "strongly supported setting aside funds * * * specifically for juvenile crime prevention programs." Vincent Schiraldi and Mark Soler, The Will of the People: The Public's Opinion of the Violent and Repeat Juvenile Offender Act of 1997, 44 Crime & Delinq. 590, 599–600 (1998).

5. *References.* Barry C. Feld, Bad Kids: Race and the Transformation of the Juvenile Court (1999); Janet E. Ainsworth, Re–Imagining Childhood and Reconstructing the Legal Order: The Case for Abolishing the Juvenile Court, 69 N.C. L. Rev. 1083 (1991); Mark I. Soler, Re–Imagining the Juvenile Court, in Child, Parent, & State 596 (S. Randall Humm et al. eds., 1994); Various authors, Will the Juvenile Court Survive?, 564 Annals Am. Acad. Polit. & Soc. Sci. (1999); David Yellen, What Juvenile Court Abolitionists Can Learn From the Failures of Sentencing Reform, 1996 Wis. L. Rev. 577.

PROBLEM 11–7

You are a real estate lawyer and a productive member of the state bar association's Juvenile Justice committee, which you joined because you believe committees devoted to children's welfare profit from the perspectives of concerned lawyers who practice other specialties. You have agreed to participate in a panel discussion on "The Juvenile Court: The Uneasy Coexistence Between Rehabilitation and Punishment," which will be televised live on C–Span. The panel will wrestle with two main subjects: (1) Should states retain delinquency jurisdiction in a separate trial-level juvenile court, or should criminal courts have exclusive original jurisdiction over charges that juveniles have violated the criminal law?, and (2) If delinquency jurisdiction remains vested in the juvenile court, should alleged delinquents enjoy all the constitutional rights (including the right to a jury trial) that criminal defendants enjoy? To explore the second question, the panel will review the juvenile court's original conception, trace its development over the decades, and assess its contemporary operation. The panel will also examine *McKeiver* and discuss whether its reasoning remains persuasive today. What will you say on the panel?

INDEX

References are to pages